Московский Метро

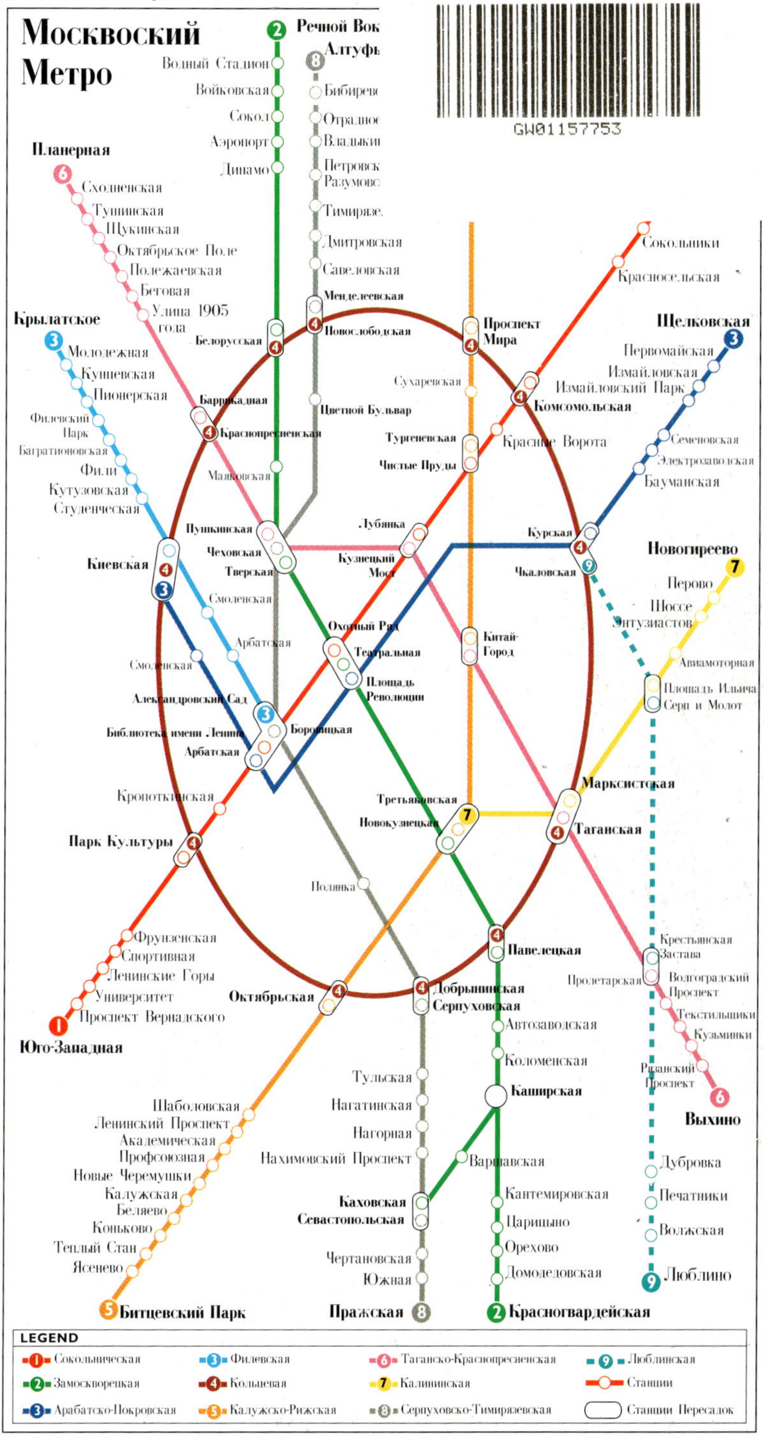

Moscow

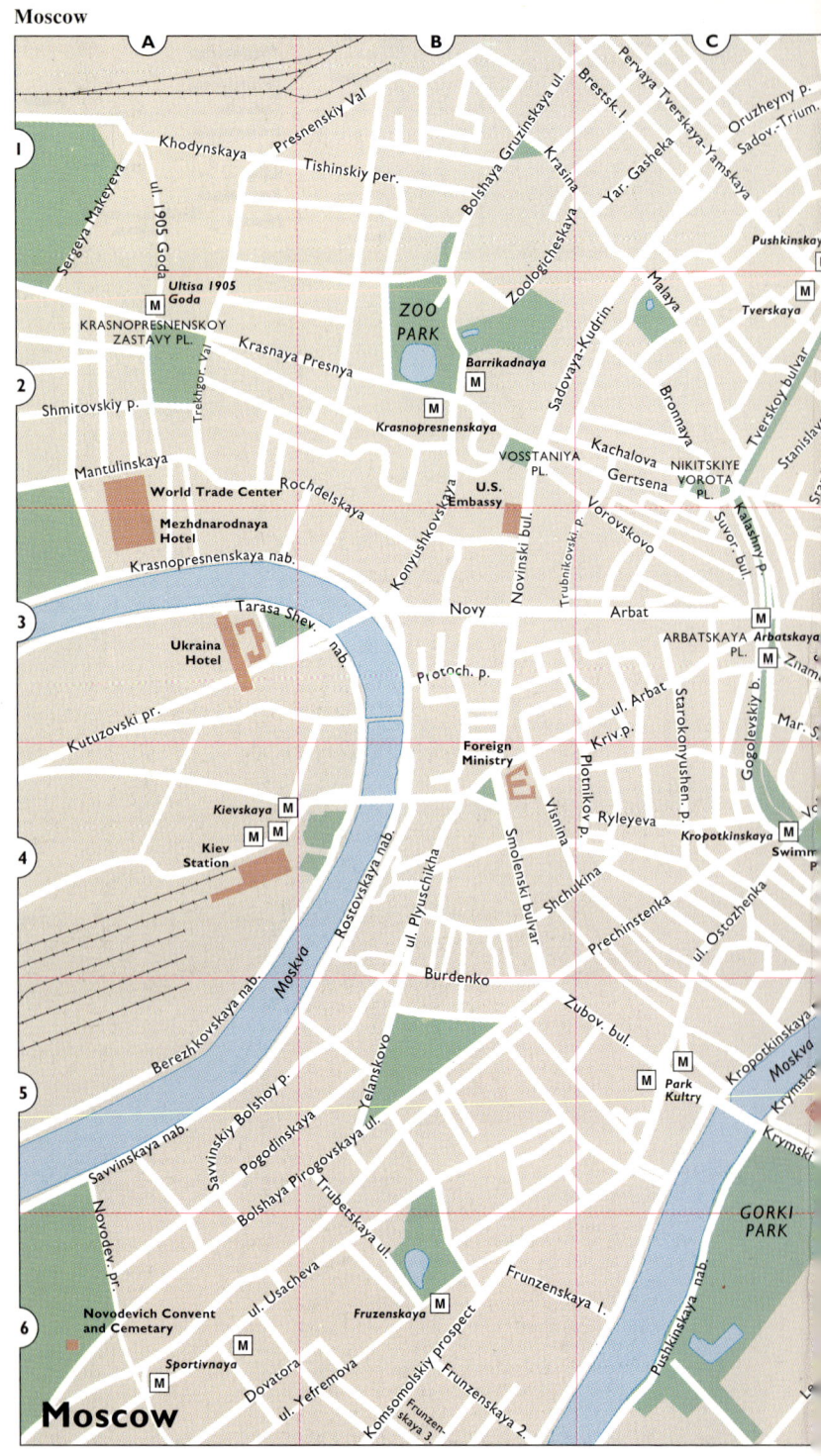

Moscow

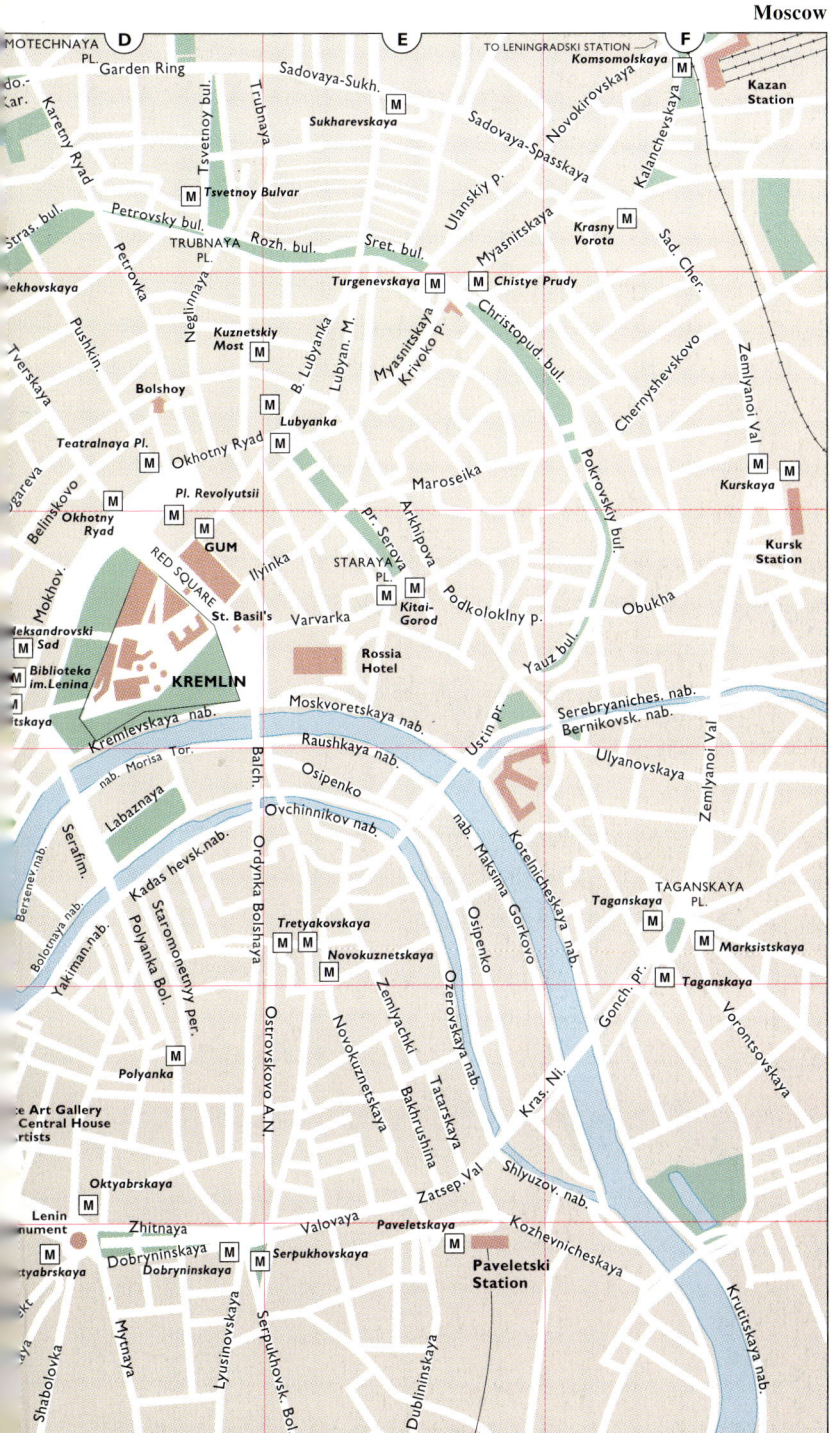

Let's Go:
Eastern Europe

"Its yearly revision by a new crop of Harvard students makes it as valuable as ever." —**The New York Times**

"Value-packed, unbeatable, accurate, and comprehensive." —**The Los Angeles Times**

"A world-wise traveling companion—always ready with friendly advice and helpful hints, all sprinkled with a bit of wit." —**The Philadelphia Inquirer**

"Lighthearted and sophisticated, informative and fun to read. [Let's Go] helps the novice traveler navigate like a knowledgeable old hand." —*Atlanta Journal-Constitution*

"All the essential information you need, from making a phone call to exchanging money to contacting your embassy. [Let's Go] provides maps to help you find your way from every train station to a full range of youth hostels and hotels." —**Minneapolis Star Tribune**

"Unbeatable: good sight-seeing advice; up-to-date info on restaurants, hotels, and inns; a commitment to money-saving travel; and a wry style that brightens nearly every page." —**The Washington Post**

■ Let's Go researchers have to make it on their own.

"The writers seem to have experienced every rooster-packed bus and lunar-surfaced mattress about which they write." —**The New York Times**

"Retains the spirit of the student-written publication it is: candid, opinionated, resourceful, amusing info for the traveler of limited means but broad curiosity." —*Mademoiselle*

■ No other guidebook is as comprehensive.

"Whether you're touring the United States, Europe, Southeast Asia, or Central America, a Let's Go guide will clue you in to the cheapest, yet safe, hotels and hostels, food and transportation. Going beyond the call of duty, the guides reveal a country's latest news, cultural hints, and off-beat information that any tourist is likely to miss." —**Tulsa World**

■ Let's Go is completely revised each year.

"Up-to-date travel tips for touring four continents on skimpy budgets." —*Time*

"Inimitable.... Let's Go's 24 guides are updated yearly (as opposed to the general guidebook standard of every two to three years), and in a marvelously spunky way." —**The New York Times**

Let's Go Publications

Let's Go: Alaska & The Pacific Northwest
Let's Go: Britain & Ireland
Let's Go: California
Let's Go: Central America
Let's Go: Eastern Europe
Let's Go: Ecuador & The Galápagos Islands
Let's Go: Europe
Let's Go: France
Let's Go: Germany
Let's Go: Greece & Turkey
Let's Go: India & Nepal
Let's Go: Ireland
Let's Go: Israel & Egypt
Let's Go: Italy
Let's Go: London
Let's Go: Mexico
Let's Go: New York City
Let's Go: Paris
Let's Go: Rome
Let's Go: Southeast Asia
Let's Go: Spain & Portugal
Let's Go: Switzerland & Austria
Let's Go: USA
Let's Go: Washington, D.C.

Let's Go **Map Guide:** Boston
Let's Go **Map Guide:** London
Let's Go **Map Guide:** New York City
Let's Go **Map Guide:** Paris
Let's Go **Map Guide:** San Francisco
Let's Go **Map Guide:** Washington, D.C.

LET'S GO

The Budget Guide to
Eastern Europe
1997

Anne I. Eelkema
Editor

Megan Brenn-White
Associate Editor

Dan Hruschka
Associate Editor

St. Martin's Press ⚜ New York

HELPING LET'S GO

If you want to share your discoveries, suggestions, or corrections, please drop us a line. We read every piece of correspondence, whether a postcard, a 10-page e-mail, or a coconut. All suggestions are passed along to our researcher-writers. Please note that mail received after May 1997 may be too late for the 1998 book, but will be retained for the following edition. **Address mail to:**

> **Let's Go: Eastern Europe**
> 67 Mt. Auburn Street
> Cambridge, MA 02138
> USA

Visit Let's Go at **http://www.letsgo.com**, or send e-mail to:

> **Fanmail@letsgo.com**
> **Subject: "Let's Go: Eastern Europe"**

In addition to the invaluable travel advice our readers share with us, many are kind enough to offer their services as researchers or editors. Unfortunately, the charter of Let's Go, Inc. enables us to employ only currently enrolled Harvard-Radcliffe students.

Maps by David Lindroth copyright © 1997, 1996, 1995, 1994, 1993, 1992, 1991, 1990, 1989, 1988 by St. Martin's Press, Inc.

Map revisions pp. 2-3, 40-41, 51, 63, 73, 81, 101, 111, 139, 153, 179, 181, 221, 229, 249, 258-259, 261, 293, 337, 343, 363, 377, 381, 385, 394-395, 413, 441, 473, 483, 519, 573, 575, 585, 594-595, 597, 619, 629, 635, 671, 681, 694-695, 697, 717, 727, 738-739 by Let's Go, Inc.

Distributed outside the USA and Canada by Macmillan.

Let's Go: Eastern Europe. Copyright © 1997 by Let's Go, Inc. All rights reserved. Printed in the United States of America. No part of this book may be used or reproduced in any manner whatsoever without written permission except in the case of brief quotations embodied in critical articles or reviews. For information, address St. Martin's Press, 175 Fifth Avenue, New York, NY 10010, USA.

ISBN: 0-312-14649-3

First edition
10 9 8 7 6 5 4 3 2 1

Let's Go: Eastern Europe is written by Let's Go Publications, 67 Mt. Auburn Street, Cambridge, MA 02138, USA.

Let's Go® and the thumb logo are trademarks of Let's Go, Inc. Printed in the USA on recycled paper with biodegradable soy ink.

Contents

Maps .... vii-viii
Acknowledgements ix
Researcher-writers .... x-xi
About Let's Go xii
Use Me—But Do It Right. xiii

ESSENTIALS 1
Getting There 34
Once There 39
Let's Go Picks 54

ALBANIA (SHQIPËRIA) 55
Tirana (Tiranë) 62
Southwestern Albania 67
Lake Ohrid 71

BELARUS (БЕЛАРУСЬ) 73
Minsk (Мінск) 78

BOSNIA-HERZEGOVINA 87
Sarajevo 93

BULGARIA (БЪЛГАРИЯ) 101
Sofia (София) 108
Southern Mountains 117
Valley of Roses (Розова Долина) 123
Northern Bulgaria 127
Black Sea Coast 136

CROATIA (HRVATSKA) 147
Zagreb 152
Istria 157
The Dalmatian Coast 162

CZECH REPUBLIC (ČECHY) 167
Prague (Praha) 173
West Bohemia 199
South Bohemia 208
Moravia 212

ESTONIA (EESTI) 221
Tallinn 227

HUNGARY (MAGYARORSZÁG) 249
Budapest 256
The Danube Bend 275
Northern Hungary 278
Nagyalföld (The Great Plain) 284
Transdanubia 292
Lake Balaton 308

LATVIA (LATVIJA) 315
Rīga 320
Kurzeme 328
Latgale 330
Vidzeme 334

LITHUANIA (LIETUVA) 337
Vilnius 342
The Baltic Coast 356

F. Y. R. MACEDONIA (МАКЕДОНИЈА) 363
Skopje (Скопје) 368
Lake Ohrid 372
Central Macedonia 375

MOLDOVA 377
Chişinău (Kishinev) 380

POLAND (POLSKA) 385
Warsaw (Warszawa) 392
Pomorze 406
Trójmiasto (Tri-City Area) 412
Mazury 424
Podlasie 426
Wielkopolska (Greater Poland) 429
Małopolska (Lesser Poland) 439
Karpaty (The Carpathians) 458
Dolny Śląsk (Lower Silesia) 466

ROMANIA (ROMÂNIA) 473
Bucharest (Bucureşti) 480
Transylvania 489
Carpathian Mountains 498
Romanian Moldova and Bucovina 506
Black Sea Coast 514
Dobrogea 517

RUSSIA (РОССИЯ) 519
Moscow (Москва) 530
Golden Ring (Золотое Кольцо) 557
The Trans-Siberian Railroad 565
The Volga-Don Region (Волго-донская Область) 572
The Caucasus (Кавказ) 589
The Northwest (Северо-запад) 592
Karelia (Карелия) 621
The Kaliningrad Region (Калининградская Область) 624

SLOVAKIA (SLOVENSKO) 629
Bratislava 635
Central Slovakia 640
Vysoké Tatry (The High Tatras) 645
Spiš 652
Šariš 658

SLOVENIA (SLOVENIJA) 665
Ljubljana 670
Julijske Alpe (The Julian Alps) 674
The Slovenian Coast 679

UKRAINE (УКРАЇНА) 681
Kiev (Київ) 692
Eastern Ukraine (Схід України) 706
The Crimea (Крим) 708
Odeshchina (ОдеЩина) 716
Western Ukraine (Західн України) 722
Transcarpathia (Закарпаття) 734

GATEWAY CITIES 737
Berlin, Germany 737
Helsinki, Finland 747
Vienna (Wien), Austria 753

APPENDICES 763
INDEX 790

Maps

Eastern Europe 2-3
Railways of Eastern Europe 40-41
Castles and Monasteries 51
Albania 55
Tirana 63
Belarus 73
Central Minsk 81
Bosnia-Herzegovina 87
Central Sarajevo 95
Bulgaria 101
Central Sofia 111
Central Varna 137
The Black Sea Coast 139
Croatia 147
Zagreb 153
Czech Republic 167
Prague 176-177
Central Prague 179
Prague Metro 181
Prague Castle 191
Central Brno 213
Estonia 221
Tallinn 229
Estonian Islands 243
Hungary 249
Budapest 258-259
Budapest Public Transport 261
Pécs 293
Lake Balaton 309
Latvia 315
Central Rīga 321
Lithuania 337
Central Vilnius 343
Kaunas 351
Macedonia 363
Skopje 369
Moldova 377
Central Chişinău 381
Poland 385
Central Warsaw 394-395
Baltic Coast of Poland 407
Central Gdańsk 413
Central Poznań 431
Central Kraków 441
Romania 473
Bucharest 481
Bucharest Metro 483
Iaşi 507
Western Russia 519
Kremlin 541
Trans-Siberian Rail Routes 567
Volga-Don Region 573
Central Nizhny Novgorod 575
Central Volgograd 581
Central Rostov-na-Donu 585

St. Petersburg 594-595
St. Petersburg Metro 597
Novgorod 619
Slovakia 629
Bratislava 635
Polish and Slovak Tatras 650-651
Slovenia 665
Central Ljubljana 671
Ukraine 681
Central Kiev 694-695
Kiev Metro 697
Crimean Peninsula 711
Central Yalta 713
Central Odesa 717
Central Lviv 727
Berlin Overview 738-739
Helsinki 749
Vienna 754-755

Color Maps

Московский Метро .... color insert
Moscow .... color insert
Moscow Metro .... color insert

Acknowledgements

Team EEUR thanks: Our "fourth editor" Nance-bo for smoky treats, juicy gossip, and the fastest typing in the West. You're all the best, girl! The Cold Room for being so damn chill: Jeremy for Cure-ative serenades, Ali for keeping the beat, jumpin' Gene for believing in us, Kitty for keeping her cool, and D.J. Jazzy Fagunge for keeping us all in line. SoRelle for grayboxes and being there. Mike "Sick-Boy" and "Beat box" Dan-O, founts of font fun. Mapping maniacs Amanda, Mark, and Jonathan, and Tom le French masseur—*ooh là là!* Guest MEs Jake and Liz. Michelle for letting us do Sarajevo and captaining the hippest ship this side of the Baltic. Our R-Ws. Also Krzys Owerkowicz, Kate Galbraith, Steven Caron, the Beagle Brigade, Anne Chisholm.

Thanks to: Dan for sticking it out to the very end—from dorm crew to deadline, Megan for being a fellow format freak, and Nancy, our better fourth. Kate for volunteering. Krzys for ideas. Ian—a belated thanks from '95 plus one of my own. Hanna, Pai, Leah, David, Catherine, Derek, Michaela, Jen, Sarah, and SoRelle. Rachel for too much wine. Hillary, Liz, and Roland for aural inspiration. Peter for light and letters… And to my family: Mum, Dad, Raye (for housing me), Gretchen, and Grace.—**AIE**

Thanks to: Anne, our esteemed leader, Meg for making me crack (up), and Nance (what can I say in one line?). Murph-dog for Stratego time, and Leah for midnight runs. The Guys in Playland—Heidmaster, Dave "Sandra-slayer" Fagundes, the Dan-o-saur, and GI Jake. Pogio HackNeilage and Chuck "guru" Kapelke for four fun and weird and weird and fun years. Swedish Cookie and Monsters for fulfilling a dream. The soda jerk for vanilla Cokes. Mom, Poppa, the Tom-inater, and family—**DJH**

Thanks to: Anne, the baddest pink pen around, Danimal for witty (stupid?) banter and bittersweet-and-marzipan moments, and Nance, the coolest val-girl. The four of us opened up a serious can… Leah, for being there and crazy. 94-A Cedar Crew—Kayla, Jen, Sarah—what a summah! My parents and Maris, Dabby and Grampy, the Whites, and all the fam. Toomas for driving safe. Also Madhu, Sasha, Julie, Charlie, Wendy, Sal, Claire, Adele, Hana, our R-Ws, and *Let's Go*ers everywhere —**MBW**

Editor	Anne I. Eelkema
Associate Editor	Daniel J. Hruschka
Associate Editor	Megan Brenn-White
Managing Editor	SoRelle B. Braun
Publishing Director	Michelle C. Sullivan
Production Manager	Daniel O. Williams
Associate Production Manager	Michael S. Campbell
Cartography Manager	Amanda K. Bean
Editorial Manager	John R. Brooks
Editorial Manager	Allison Crapo
Financial Manager	Stephen P. Janiak
Personnel Manager	Alexander H. Travelli
Publicity Manager	SoRelle B. Braun
Associate Publicity Manager	David Fagundes
Associate Publicity Manager	Elisabeth Mayer
Assistant Cartographer	Jonathan D. Kibera
Assistant Cartographer	Mark C. Staloff
Office Coordinator	Jennifer L. Schuberth
Director of Advertising and Sales	Amit Tiwari
Senior Sales Executives	Andrew T. Rourke
	Nicholas A. Valtz, Charles E. Varner
General Manager	Richard Olken
Assistant General Manager	Anne E. Chisholm

Researcher-Writers

Dina Dudkin *Central Russia, Trans-Siberian Railroad*
Dina dares. Due to legal considerations, we can't tell you the extent of Dina's deeds, but just trust us—Dina dares. Our veteran researcher began her itinerary in Moscow, scoping out the cheapest sleeps, seeking Moscow's bomb-est burritos, and ducking into shady mafia-ridden watering holes. When all of Capital City's joints had been seen and conquered, Agent Dudkin, armed with fake Russian papers, hit the road—the Trans-Siberian Railroad. Weathering the cold and packing heat, Dudkin crossed eight time zones and ventured where no *Let's Go* itinerant had researched before, sending back three new cities (and a lake). Our very own lady luck loved them, especially the lake, and she's sure you will too.

Kate Galbraith *Sarejevo, Bosnia*
Last summer, this former *Let's Go* editor and researcher-writer took the high road to Bosnia to volunteer in post-war relief efforts. When she wasn't volunteering and making *sooo* many Bosnian friends, Kate busied herself researching peaceful riverside cafés and writing up Sarajevo for *Let's Go* for the first time since 1991. Newspaper reporters took a liking to her, but our media darling remained characteristically modest, found the latest digs in fast-changing Sarajevo, and sent back prose to make our hearts flip and our editors' pens drop. We felt useless; her batches were perfect. Kate thanks the folks at ONASA.

Alexis Goodman *Northern Russia, Estonia*
This former tour guide at the Hermitage returned to St. Petersburg for *Let's Go* to be on the receiving end of that and every other museum tour in town. Affable Alexis found a friend in every hostel, a pal in every town; travelers wrote us about how cool *she* was. Her amiability paid off as charmed locals showed her the quietest mime performances and cheapest founts of *Saku* in Estonia. She even shook hands with Hillary Clinton. Witty and cutting, Lady Lex taught us to ask, "How much does it cost?"—the Goodman way, and then trotted to Ukraine to intern for a symphony.

Kevin Groszkowski *Poland*
In search of his blond roots, Kevin traipsed through Poland, brandishing a smidgeon o' pidgin Polish. Singing throughout Poland's "summer of rain," this mild-mannered trooper scaled Socialist skyscrapers, leapt off moving trains, and tamed sprawling Warsaw with the cool of a secret agent. Kevin logged in to Poland's Internet café scene, suckled at Warsaw's cheapest milk bars, and proved the truth of at least one saying—you can take a Pole out of Poland, but you can't take Poland out of a Pole.

Catharine Hornby *Eastern Hungary, Slovakia, Southern Poland*
Although this gentle Jersey girl didn't have the *chutzpa* (or rather, macho stupidity) to kick down the door of the ribald Polish *chata* party, she managed to run wild with the big dogs in Hungary and stomp through every bit of Slovakia's wilderness. She did what everyone does in the Valley of the Beautiful Women. Unfettered by kielbasa poisoning in the Polish Tatras, Catharine the Great pulled through her itinerary like a true tsarina, sending us neatly written, thoroughly researched batches.

Cuong Hoang *Eastern Ukraine*
Equipped with freshly dyed hair and a knack for the incredible, Cuong discovered out-of-the-way pubs in the strangest of places—Grendel's was our fave. Flying through his itinerary, the King braved police inquisitions, dehydration on the sunny shores of the Crimea, and the nefarious pickpockets of Odesa's mafia, only to hand-deliver pristine copy which both stunned and overwhelmed.

Jason Morton *Belarus, Kaliningrad, Latvia, Lithuania, Southern Russia*
As the Belarusian gymnastics team was whooping it up in Atlanta this summer, Dr. J. was doing some body-bending of his own. Mr. Cool bopped and twirled to techno tunes wherever he found them (and he found them everywhere). When the heavy beats became a heavy pain, he danced on down to southern Russia and yearned to play the *balalaika*. Our budding poet realized his literary potential, sending back verbally adventurous prose and writing the best graybox ever. Jason recommends fried dough balls, for substance, taste, and color.

Krzysztof Owerkowicz *Czech Republic, Western Ukraine*
Armed with a knowledge of more languages than most people have fingers, last year's *Let's Go: Eastern Europe* editor hit the road aiming to relive his glory days as researcher-writer for *Let's Go: France*. Krzysiu sailed through the spired cities of Ukraine, lightening our lives with pounds of insightful prose and tons of humor. In Prague, this Czech and Russian literature major used his language skills to find the city's craziest nightspots, discovering his inner frat-boy in the process. Two words describe his marginalia—simply stimulating. He thanks Marcin Szefler, Gene Mazo, Taras Koznarsky, Marta Baziuk, Pai Yang, and, of course, fam, friends, and editors.

Javor Pishev *Albania, Bulgaria, Macedonia*
A beautiful human in every respect. Caring, considerate, funny, sexy, friendly, and gorgeous, Javor "da' Man" Pishev took time out of his exhausting itinerary to console distressed souls, help old ladies across the street, and make friends with almost every hotelier and restaurant owner in Albania. Javor rewrote the book on his native Bulgaria, making our mouths water over descriptions of organ-based dishes and our eyes yearn for views of the Black Sea's beaches. This poet's marginalia touched our hearts, and his flowing script matched his prose in beauty. We only wish that for every one of his pages, we had a frame and a place to hang it.

Joel Pulliam *Croatia, Western Hungary, Slovenia*
Before embarking on his voyage, this incorrigible scholar leafed through every book on 13th-century Croatian flora ever published, and with this knowledge, somehow pinpointed each and every late-night club in Hungary. The Honcho of Haus then boom-chicka-boomed his way to the Adriatic coast, reminisced about the days he had spent there as a missionary, and added the best of former Yugoslavia's resorts to the book. In the land of postcards, this medieval history and literature major is indubitably king. From Budapest to Dubrovnik, Joel sent us some of Europe's most beautiful cities, and posted well-researched copybatches to match.

Cristina Vatulescu *Moldova, Romania*
Hailing from Cluj-Napoca, this native of Romania instructed us on the intricacies of Romanian culture, the delicacies of Romanian cuisine, and the art of Romanian handwriting. In her vivid copybatches, meticulous Chef Cristina brought every flavor of *clatite* to our table, and threw in a description of the table to boot. She bathed in the Black Sea waters, hiked the majestic peaks of the Apuseni mountains, and described her experiences in prose so ornate, that there should be some 18th-century style named after it.

Ruth Halikman	*Berlin*
Alex Speier	*Berlin*
Christina Svendsen	*Vienna*
Alex Zakaras	*Helsinki*

About Let's Go

THIRTY-SIX YEARS OF WISDOM

Back in 1960, a few students at Harvard University banded together to produce a 20-page pamphlet offering a collection of tips on budget travel in Europe. This modest, mimeographed packet, offered as an extra to passengers on student charter flights to Europe, met with instant popularity. The following year, students traveling to Europe researched the first, full-fledged edition of *Let's Go: Europe*, a pocket-sized book featuring honest, irreverent writing and a decidedly youthful outlook on the world. Throughout the 60s, our guides reflected the times; the 1969 guide to America led off by inviting travelers to "dig the scene" at San Francisco's Haight-Ashbury. During the 70s and 80s, we gradually added regional guides and expanded coverage into the Middle East and Central America. With the addition of our in-depth city guides, handy map guides, and extensive coverage of Asia, the 90s are also proving to be a time of explosive growth for Let's Go, and there's certainly no end in sight. The first editions of *Let's Go: India & Nepal* and *Let's Go: Ecuador & The Galápagos Islands* hit the shelves this year, and research for next year's series has already begun.

We've seen a lot in 37 years. *Let's Go: Europe* is now the world's best-selling international guide, translated into seven languages. And our new guides bring Let's Go's total number of titles, with their spirit of adventure and their reputation for honesty, accuracy, and editorial integrity, to 30. But some things never change: our guides are still researched, written, and produced entirely by students who know first-hand how to see the world on the cheap.

HOW WE DO IT

Each guide is completely revised and thoroughly updated every year by a well-traveled set of 200 students. Every winter, we recruit over 120 researchers and 60 editors to write the books anew. After several months of training, Researcher-Writers hit the road for seven weeks of exploration, from Anchorage to Ankara, Estonia to El Salvador, Iceland to Indonesia. Hired for their rare combination of budget travel sense, writing ability, stamina, and courage, these adventurous travelers know that train strikes, stolen luggage, food poisoning, and marriage proposals are all part of a day's work. Back at our offices, editors work from spring to fall, massaging copy written on Himalayan bus rides into witty yet informative prose. A student staff of typesetters, cartographers, publicists, and managers keeps our lively team together. In September, the collected efforts of the summer are delivered to our printer, who turns them into books in record time, so that you have the most up-to-date information available for *your* vacation. And even as you read this, work on next year's editions is well underway.

WHY WE DO IT

At Let's Go, our goal is to give you a great vacation. We don't think of budget travel as the last recourse of the destitute; we believe that it's the only way to travel. Living cheaply and simply brings you closer to the people and places you've been saving up to visit. Our books will ease your anxieties and answer your questions about the basics—so you can get off the beaten track and explore. Once you learn the ropes, we encourage you to put Let's Go away now and then to strike out on your own. As any seasoned traveler will tell you, the best discoveries are often those you make yourself. When you find something worth sharing, drop us a line. We're Let's Go Publications, 67 Mt. Auburn St., Cambridge, MA 02138, USA (e-mail: fanmail@letsgo.com).

HAPPY TRAVELS!

Use me—but do it right.

Contrary to popular belief, this book is not a Bible. Though the 3rd edition of *Let's Go: Eastern Europe* comes pretty darn close to divine information, it remains a guide—only a guide. It is meant to lead modern-day voyagers to the doorway of Europe's budget-est and wildest regions—places most travelers couldn't even visit before 1990. Our researchers have risked run-ins with police, the Russian mafia, and crazed hostel-owners to find some of the cheapest, freshest digs in Eastern Europe. Armed with this book and their picks, take a step over the threshold and choose your own adventure—preferably one that doesn't include Prague in August.

Wherever you are going with the book, take time to peruse **Essentials** *before* heading for the airport. Chock-a-block with info on how to obtain passports and visas, where to find the cheapest flights, and which credit cards will be worth more than just the plastic they're made of, the Essentials section cuts through the bureaucracy. It also addresses specific travelers' concerns, such as those of women, older travelers, bisexuals, gays, lesbians, vegetarians, and travelers with disabilities.

The meat of the book lies in its eighteen alphabetically arranged country chapters and the "Gateway Cities" section, which includes Berlin, Helsinki, and Vienna. Each chapter gets more specific with an **Essentials** section of its own, and a dose of history, literature, and current events in **Life and Times**. After the fact-filled intro, the capital city comes first, followed by other towns grouped into historical regions. In each town's **Orientation and Practical Information** section, we give you the nitty-gritty of how to cruise the streets and where to find valuable services—bike rentals, exchange bureaus, or ferries to Istanbul. The **Accommodations** section doles the scoop on finding a bed and ranks hotels, hostels, and pensions according to our estimate of their value and quality. **Food** follows with outdoor bazaars, old-style socialist hypermarkets, and a list of restaurants also ordered according to what we think are the best deals. **Sights, Near,** and **Around** sections are grouped in orderly geographical packages. In small towns all this gets crunched into three paragraphs: Sights, Practical Info, and Accommodations and Food.

This year we've added to the language guides and consolidated them into easy-access **language glossaries** in the **Appendices**. Check the Appendices for the **climate chart, train travel time graph,** and list of **holidays and festivals**.

Also new this year are sections on the **Trans-Siberian Railway** and some of the paradisical cities which the war in Bosnia had, for a while, placed off limits to travelers—**Dubrovnik** and **Split** in Croatia and **Sarajevo** in Bosnia.

Eastern Europe is busy re-inventing itself every day. By the time you get there, hotels, restaurants, and more than anything, nightclubs will have shut down, moved, or transformed into holiday camps for colonies of rich tourists. When in doubt, visit the tourist office—hopefully, it'll be where it was a year ago. Take this guide, choose any of the many unbeaten paths that still run through Eastern Europe, and when you find something new, drop us a line.

A NOTE TO OUR READERS

The information for this book is gathered by *Let's Go*'s researchers during the late spring and summer months. Each listing is derived from the assigned researcher's opinion based upon his or her visit at a particular time. The opinions are expressed in a candid and forthright manner. Other travelers might disagree. Those traveling at a different time may have different experiences since prices, dates, hours, and conditions are always subject to change. You are urged to check beforehand to avoid inconvenience and surprises. Travel always involves a certain degree of risk, especially in low-cost areas. When traveling, especially on a budget, always take particular care to ensure your safety.

JUST TELL YOUR PARENTS YOU'LL BE EXPLORING POLISH CULTURE

And when you're not busy checking out the local bands, you can even live up to your promise. Because Poland has hundreds of medieval castles, palaces, cathedrals and museums. Not to mention the homes of Madame Curie, Copernicus and Chopin, and the places where Pope John Paul II and Lech Walesa grew up. Or take a break from culture and hike through mountain villages, go canoeing, and roam the largest primeval forest in Europe. Whatever you do, you won't go broke. Because Poland has one of the best exchange rates in Europe. Just hop on one of LOT Polish Airlines' roomy new 767s. We fly the only non-stops from the U.S. to Poland, so you'll save time on your trip. And with our low fares, you'll also save money on your ticket. Visit our Web site at http://www.poland.net/LOT/ or call your travel agent or LOT at 1-800-223-0593. And while you're at it, don't forget to call your parents.

T H E   P O L I S H   A I R L I N E

ESSENTIALS

PLANNING YOUR TRIP

Sometimes bureaucratic and Kafka-esque, sometimes utterly lawless, travel in Eastern Europe is never predictable. Start your travel planning well in advance: begin stalking consulates for visas the moment you decide to go, attempt to contact the useful organizations we list, faithfully follow the news, plan out every detail of your itinerary—and be prepared to scrap the whole thing once you arrive. Things change quickly in Eastern Europe: exchange rates, telephone numbers, borders. The most important thing to bring along is flexibility.

What we have called "Eastern Europe" is not a single monolithic region but an area containing several sub-regions and 18 very different countries. *Let's Go: Eastern Europe* can take you as far east as Irkutsk in the middle of Siberia; farther north than Anchorage, Alaska; as far south as the Greek border; and west into the very heart of Europe. We urge you to unleash your curiosity and to follow your own spirit; whether you put it to work in historic cultural centers such as Prague, Budapest, or St. Petersburg, on an alpine hike in Slovenia, along a wilderness trip through the Carpathian mountains, or in beach towns along the Black Sea, Baltic, or Adriatic.

■ Useful Information

NATIONAL TOURIST OFFICES

Balkan Holidays (Bulgaria): U.S.: 317 Madison Ave., Suite 508, New York, NY 10017 (tel. (212) 573-5530; fax 573-5538). **U.K.:** Sofia House, 19 Conduit St., London W1R 9TD (tel. (0171) 491 4499; fax 491 7068).

Croatia: U.K.: 2 The Lanchesters 162-164 Fulham Palace Road, London W6 9ER (tel. (0181) 563 7979; fax 563 2616).

Hungarian Tourist Board: U.S.: 150 E. 58th St., 33rd Fl., New York, NY 10155 (tel. (212) 355-0240; fax 207-4103). **U.K.:** P.O. Box 4336, London, SW18 4XE (tel. (0891) 171 200; fax 669 970).

Polish National Tourist Office: U.S.: 275 Madison Ave., Suite 1711, New York, NY 10016 (tel. (212) 338-9412; fax 338-9283).

Romanian National Tourist Office: U.S.: 342 Madison Ave., Suite 210, New York, NY 10173 (tel. (212) 697-6971; fax 697-6972). **U.K.:** 17 Nottingham St., London W1M 3RD (tel. (0171) 224 3692).

Russian Travel Information Office: U.S.: 8 Third Ave., Suite 3101, New York, NY 10002 (tel. (212) 758-1162; fax 758-0933). **Canada:** 1801 McGill College Ave., Suite 930, Montréal, Qué. H3A 2N4 (tel. (514) 849-6394; fax 849-6742). **U.K.:** 219 Marsh Wall, London E14 9PD (tel. (0171) 538 8600; fax 538 5967; e-mail info@intourus.demm.co.uk).

Slovenian Tourist Office: U.S.: 122 E. 42nd St., New York, NY 10168-0072 (tel. (212) 682-5896; fax 661-2469). **U.K.:** 2 Canfield Pl., London NW6 3BT (tel. (0171) 372 3767; fax 372 3763).

TRAVEL ORGANIZATIONS

Council on International Educational Exchange (Council), 205 E. 42nd St., New York, NY 10017-5706 (tel. (888) COUNCIL (268-6245); fax (212) 822-2699; e-mail info@ciee.org; http://www.ciee.org). A private, nonprofit organization, Council administers work, volunteer, academic, and professional programs around the world. They also offer identity cards, including the ISIC and the GO25, and a range

TRAVEL ORGANIZATIONS 3

of publications, among them the magazine *Student Travels* (free). Call or write for further information.

Federation of International Youth Travel Organizations (FIYTO), Bredgade 25H, DK-1260 Copenhagen K, Denmark (tel. (45) 33 33 96 00; fax 33 93 96 76; e-mail mailbox@fiyto.org). An international organization promoting educational, cultural, and social travel for young people. Member organizations include language schools, educational travel companies, national tourist boards, accommodations centers, and other suppliers of travel services. FIYTO sponsors the GO25 card. For more information on the card, see Youth and Student Identification, p. 15.

International Student Travel Confederation, Herengracht 479, 1017 BS Amsterdam, the Netherlands (tel. (31) 204 21 28 00; fax 204 21 28 10; e-mail istcinfo@istc.org; http://www.istc.org). The ISTC is a nonprofit confederation of student travel organizations whose focus is to develop, promote, and facilitate travel among young people and students. Member organizations include the International Student Rail Association (ISRA), Student Air Travel Association (SATA), ISIS Travel Insurance, and the International Association for Educational and Work Exchange Programs (IAEWEP).

USEFUL PUBLICATIONS

Although *Let's Go* tries to cover all aspects of budget travel, we can't put *everything* in our guides. You might supplement your *Let's Go* library with publications that serve more specific purposes. Hard-to-find **maps** are stocked by **Wide World Books and Maps,** 1911 N. 45th St., Seattle, WA 98103 (tel. (206) 634-3453; fax 634-0558; e-mail travelbk@mail.nwlink.com; http://nwlink.com/travelbk). Maps, guidebooks, railpasses, train and ferry schedules, and youth hostel memberships can be purchased from the **Forsyth Travel Library,** P.O. Box 480800, Kansas City, MO 64148 (tel. (800) 367-7984; fax (816) 942-6969; http://www.forsyth.com). Write for their free catalog and newsletter. The **College Connection, Inc.,** 1295 Prospect St. A, La Jolla, CA 92037 (tel. (619) 551-9487; fax 551-9987; e-mail eurailnow@aol.com; http://www.eurail-pass.com), publishes *The Passport,* a booklet listing hints about traveling and studying abroad. **Transitions Abroad** is an invaluable magazine that lists publications and resources for overseas study, work, and volunteering. They also publish *The Alternative Travel Directory,* a comprehensive guide to living, leaving, and working overseas (US$20; postage US$4). Contact Transitions Abroad at 18 Hulst Rd., P.O. Box 1300, Amherst, MA 01004-1300 (tel. (413) 256-3414; fax 256-0375; e-mail trabroad@aol.com).

GETTIN' IT ON-LINE ;)

Keeping up-to-date with events in Eastern Europe is an art. Though events in the former Yugoslavia and in Russia are energetically covered by the mainstream press, other areas receive scant coverage unless Madonna happens to be filming in town. Luckily, the international computer network known as the **Internet** offers a vast amount of information to travelers, from daily news digests to ferry schedules. There are a number of ways to access the **Internet.** Most popular are commercial Internet providers, such as **America On-Line** (U.S. tel. (800) 827-6394) and **Compuserve** (U.S. tel. (800) 433-0389). Many employers and schools also offer gateways to the Internet, often at no cost.

The World Wide Web Increasingly the Internet forum of choice, the **World Wide Web (WWW)** provides its users with graphics and sound, as well as textual information. This and the huge proliferation of "web pages" (individual sites within the World Wide Web) have made the Web the most active and exciting of the Internet's destinations, though the Web's success has also made it the newest path of corporate advertisers to impressionable consumer minds; be sure to distinguish between good information and feckless marketing. The introduction of **search engines** (services that search for web pages under specific subjects) has aided the search process. **Lycos** (http://a2z.lycos.com) and **Infoseek** (http://guide.infoseek.com) are the two of

DOCUMENTS & FORMALITIES

the most popular. **Yahoo!** is a more organized search engine; check out its travel links at http://www.yahoo.com/Recreation/Travel. However, it is often better to know a good site and start "surfing" from there.

One of the best resources for up-to-date information on central and eastern Europe is the web page of the **Open Media Research Institute** (OMRI; http://www.omri.cz), where news and analysis are updated daily for the entire region. They also publish three different daily news and economic digests. The following are some of our favorite sites of departure for budget travel information. **Dr. Memory's Favorite Travel Pages** (http://www.access.digex.net/~drmemory/cyber_travel.html) links to hundreds of web pages pertaining to the globe and its trotters. **Rent-A-Wreck's Travel Links** (http://www.rent-a-wreck.com/raw/travlist.html) are surprisingly good and complete. **Big World Magazine** (http://boss.cpcnet.com/personal/bigworld/bigworld.htm), a budget travel 'zine, has a web page and a great collection of links to travel pages. **The CIA World Factbook** (http://www.odci.gov/cia/publications/95fact) has vital statistics on any country you want to visit. **Shoestring Travel** (http://www.stratpub.com), a budget travel e-zine, offers feature articles, links, user exchange, and accommodations information. **The Student and Budget Travel Guide** (http://asa.ugl.lib.umich.edu/chdocs/travel/travel-guide.html) is just what it sounds like. **Foreign Language for Travelers** (http://www.travelang.com) can help you brush up on your Czech. In addition to the above sites, we list relevant web sites throughout other sections of the **Essentials** chapter.

■ Documents & Formalities

Travel to most of Eastern Europe has become less bureaucratic than it once was. However, procuring appropriate travel documents, especially from Russia, Belarus, Ukraine, and Moldova can be time-consuming and expensive. Be sure to file all applications several weeks or months in advance of your planned departure date.

When you travel, always carry two or more forms of identification; a passport combined with a driver's license or birth certificate usually serves as adequate proof of identity and citizenship. Many establishments require several IDs to cash traveler's checks. Never carry all your IDs together, as you risk being left entirely without ID or funds in case of theft or loss. If you plan an extended stay, register your passport with the nearest embassy or consulate. U.S. citizens seeking info about documents and travel abroad should request the booklet *Your Trip Abroad* (US$1.25) from the **Superintendent of Documents,** U.S. Government Printing Office, P.O. Box 371954, Pittsburgh, PA 15250-7954 (tel. (202) 512-1800; fax 512-2250).

EMBASSIES AND CONSULATES

Albania: U.S. (Embassy): 1511 K St. NW, Suite 1000, Washington, D.C. 20005 (tel. (202) 223-4942; fax 628-7342).
Belarus: U.S. (Embassy): 1619 New Hampshire Ave. NW, Washington, D.C. 20009 (tel. (202) 986-1604 or 986-1606; fax 986-1805). **(Consulate):** 708 Third Ave., 24th Fl., New York, NY 10017 (tel. (212) 682-5392; fax 682-5491). **U.K. (Embassy):** 6 Kensington Court, London, W8 5DL (tel. (0171) 937 3288; fax 361 0005).
Bulgaria: U.S. (Embassy): 1621 22nd St. NW, Washington, D.C. 20008 (tel. (202) 387-7969; fax 234-7973). **Canada (Consulate):** 65 Overlea Blvd., Suite 406, Toronto, Ont. M4H 1P1 (tel. (416) 696-2420 or 696-2778; fax 696-8019). **U.K. (Embassy):** Sofia House, 19 Conduit St., London W1R 9TD (tel. (0171) 491 4499; fax 491 7068). **Ireland (Trade Representative):** 22 Burlington Rd., Dublin (tel. (01) 684010). **Australia (Consulate):** 1/4 Carlotta Rd., Double Bay, Sydney, NSW 2028 (tel. (02) 327 75 92 or 327 44 40; fax 327 80 67).
Croatia: U.S. (Embassy): 2343 Massachusetts Ave. NW, Washington, D.C. 20008 (tel. (202) 588-8936; fax 588-8938). **Canada (Embassy):** 130 Albert St., Suite 1700, Ottawa, Ont. K1P 5G4 (tel. (613) 230-7351; fax 230-7388). **(Office):** 918 Dundas St. E., Suite 302, Mississauga, Ont. L4Y 2B8 (tel. (905) 277-9051; fax 277-5432). **U.K. (Embassy):** 21 Conway St., London W1P 5HL. **Australia (Embassy):** O'Malley,

6 ■ DOCUMENTS & FORMALITIES

ESSENTIALS

Start Speaking a Foreign Language Today!

With the LANGUAGE/30 Courses
Learn while biking, driving, exercising... anytime, anywhere!
The perfect course for travelers. Only $16.95

Enhance your travels by communicating in the language of the country you're visiting! Recommended for beginners, business travelers, vacationers or as a refresher course. Based on the widely acclaimed method developed for U.S. Government personnel, these **revised and expanded** courses feature:

- Two Audio cassettes and Phrase Book
- Basic conversational phrases include Greetings, Personal Needs, Transportation, Business, Health and Emergency Terms, and more.
- Native Voices with authentic pronunciation
- Phrases spoken in English & target language, so tapes may be used without Book
- Introduction by world-famous linguist Charles Berlitz
- Basic Grammar Section, Pronunciation Hints, **updated** Social Customs, Vocabulary Index, Phonetic Pronunciation and Foreign Scripts
- Phrase Book can be used separately as a handy, pocket-size reference guide.

33 Languages Available

Arabic	Hebrew	Norwegian	Swedish
Chinese (Mandarin)	Hindi	Persian (Farsi)	Tagalog (Pilipino)
Czech	Hungarian	Polish	Thai
Danish	Indonesian	Portuguese	Turkish
Dutch	Irish	Romanian	Vietnamese
Finnish	Italian	Russian	Yiddish
French	Japanese	Serbo-Croatian*	
German	Korean	Spanish	
Greek	Latin	Swahili	*Serbo-Croatian not revised.

To order: Send Check or Money Order for $20.95 ($16.95+$4.00 S&H), payable to LET'S GO/EDUCATIONAL SERVICES. Please specify shipping address and language(s).
SAVE... order additional courses at $16.95 each, and still pay only $4.00 shipping!

CD-ROM COMPUTER PROGRAMS also available. Call or write for catalog.
LET'S GO/EDUCATIONAL SERVICES, 1725 K Street, N.W., #408, Washington, D.C. 20006
TELE: (202) 298-8424, Ext. 130

EMBASSIES AND CONSULATES ■ 7

Canberra ACT 2606 (tel. (06) 286 69 88; fax 186 35 44). **(Consulate):** 9/24 Albert Rd., South Melbourne, Victoria 3205 (tel (03) 699 26 33; fax 696 82 71).

Czech Republic: U.S. (Embassy): 3900 Spring of Freedom St. NW, Washington, D.C. 20008 (tel. (202) 363-6315; fax 966-8540). **(Consulate):** 10990 Wilshire Blvd., Suite 1100, Los Angeles, CA 90024 (tel. (310) 473-0889; fax 473-9813). **Canada (Embassy):** 541 Sussex Dr., Ottawa, Ont. K1N 6Z6 (tel. (613) 562-3875; fax 562-3878). **(Consulate):** 1305 Av. des Peins Ouest, Montréal, Qué. H3G 1B2 (tel. (514) 849-4495; fax 849-4117). **U.K. (Embassy):** 26 Kensington Palace Gardens, London W8 4QY (tel. (0171) 243 1115 or 243 7901; fax 727 9654). **Australia (Embassy):** 38 Culgoa Circuit, O'Malley, Canberra, ACT 2606 (tel. (06) 290 13 86; fax 290 00 06). **South Africa (Embassy):** 936 Pretorius St., Arcadia, Pretoria 0083, or P.O. Box 3326, Pretoria 0001 (tel. (12) 342 34 77; fax 43 20 33).

Estonia: U.S. (Embassy): 2131 Massachusetts Ave. NW, Washington, D.C. 20008 (tel. (202) 588-0101; fax 588-0108). **(Consulate):** 630 Fifth Ave., Suite 2415, New York, NY 10111 (tel. (212) 247-7634; fax 262-0893). **Canada (Honorary Consulate):** 958 Broadview Ave., Toronto, Ont. M4K 2R6 (tel. (416) 461-0764; fax 461-0448). **U.K. (Consulate):** 16 Hyde Park Gate, London SW7 5DG (tel. (0171) 589 3428; fax 589 3430). **Australia (Honorary Consul):** 86 Louisa Rd., Birchgrove 2041, NSW (tel. (612) 810 74 68; fax 818 17 79).

Hungary: U.S. (Embassy): 3910 Shoemaker St. NW, Washington, D.C. 20008 (tel. (202) 362-6730; fax 966-8135). **(Consulate):** 223 East 52nd St., New York, NY 10022 (tel. (212) 752-0661; fax 755-5986). **(Consulate):** 11766 Wilshire Blvd., Suite 410, Los Angeles, CA 90025 (tel. (310) 473-9344; fax 479-6443). **Canada (Embassy):** 299 Waverley St., Ottawa, Ont. K2P 0Z9 (tel. (613) 230-2717; fax 230-7560). **(Consulate):** 1212 Bloor St. E., Suite 1110, Toronto, Ont. M4W 3M5 (tel. (416) 923-3596; fax 923-2097). **(Consulate):** 1200 McGill College Ave., Apt. 2040, Montréal, Qué. H3B 4G7 (tel. (514) 393-1555; fax 393-3528). **U.K. (Embassy):** 35 Eaton Place, London SW 1X 8BY (tel. (0171) 235 7191; fax 823 1348). **Ireland (Embassy):** 2 Fitzwilliam Pl., Dublin 2 (tel. (01) 661 2903; fax 661 2880). **Australia:** Edgecliff Centre 203-233, Suite 405, New South Head Road Edgecliff, NSW 2027 Sydney (tel. (02) 328 78 59; fax 327 18 29). **South Africa (Consulate):** P.O. Box 27077, Sunnyside 0132, 959 Arcadia St., Arcadia (tel. (012) 43 30 30; fax 43 30 29).

Latvia: U.S. (Embassy): 4325 17th St. NW, Washington, D.C. 20011 (tel. (202) 726-8213; fax 726-6785). **(Consulate):** 420 Fifth Ave., New York, NY 10018 (tel. (212) 354–7849; fax 354-7911). **Canada (Embassy):** 112 Kent St., Suite 208, Place de Ville, Tower B, Ottawa, Ont. K1P 5P2 (tel. (613) 238-6868; fax 238-7044). **U.K. (Embassy):** 45 Nottingham Pl., London W1M 3FE (tel. (0171) 312 0040; fax 312 0042).

Lithuania: U.S. (Embassy): 2622 16th St. NW, Washington, D.C. 20009 (tel. (202) 234-5860; fax 328-0466). **(Consulate):** 420 Fifth Ave., New York, NY 10018 (tel. (212) 354-7849; fax 354-7911). **Canada (Embassy):** 130 Albert St., Suite 204, Ottawa, Ont. K1P 5G4 (tel. (613) 567-5458; fax 567-5315). **U.K. (Embassy):** 84 Gloucester Pl., London W1 H3H (tel. (0171) 486 6401; fax 486 6403). **Australia (Consulate):** 40B Fiddens Wharf Rd., Killara NSW 2071 (tel. (612) 498 25 71; fax 498 25 71).

F.Y.R. of Macedonia: U.S. (Embassy): 3050 K St. NW, Suite 210, Washington, D.C. 20007 (tel. (202) 337-3063; fax 337-3093). **(Consulate):** 866 United Nations Plaza, Suite 4018, New York, NY 10017 (tel. (212) 317-1727). **U.K. (Embassy):** 10 Harcourt House, 19A Cavendish Sq., London W1M 9AD.

Moldova: U.S. (Embassy): 1511 K St. NW, Suite 329, Washington, D.C. 20005 (tel. (202) 783-3012; fax 783-3342).

Poland: U.S. (Embassy): 2224 Wyoming Ave. NW, Washington, D.C. 20008 (tel. (202) 232-2501; fax 328-2152). **(Consulate):** 233 Madison Ave., New York, NY 10016 (tel. (212) 889-8360; fax 779-3062). **(Consulate):** 12400 Wilshire Blvd., Suite 555, Los Angeles, CA 90025 (tel. (310) 442-8500; fax 442-8515). **Canada: (Embassy):** 443 Daly St., Ottawa, Ont., K1N 6H3 (tel. (613) 789-0468; fax 789-1218). **(Consulate):** 1500 Pine Ave. West, Montréal, Qué. H3G 1B4 (tel. (514) 937-9481; fax 937-7271). **(Consulate):** 2603 Lakeshore Blvd. W., Toronto, Ont. M8Z 1G5 (tel (416) 252-8171; fax 252-0509). **U.K. (Embassy):** 47 Portland Place, London W1N 3AG (tel. (171) 580 4324; fax 323 4018). **(Consulate):** 73 New Cavendish St., London W1M 8LS (tel. (0171) 580 0476; fax 323 2320). **(Consulate):** 2 Kinnear Rd., Edinburgh EH3 5PE (tel. (0131) 552 0301; fax 552 1086). **Ireland**

8 ■ DOCUMENTS & FORMALITIES

(Embassy): 5 Ailesbury Rd., Dublin 4 (tel. (01) 269 1370; fax 269 8309). **Australia (Embassy):** 7 Turrana St., Yarralumla ACT 2600 Canberra (tel. (06) 273 12 08 or 273 12 11; fax 273 31 84). **New Zealand (Embassy):** 17 Upland Rd., Kelburn, Wellington (tel. (04) 71 24 56; fax 71 24 55). **South Africa (Embassy):** 14 Arnos St., Colbyn, Pretoria 0083 (tel. (012) 43 26 21; fax 346 13 66).

Romania: U.S. (Embassy): 1607 23rd St. NW, Washington, D.C. 20008 (tel. (202) 332-4846; fax 232-4748). **Canada (Embassy):** 655 Rideau St., Ottawa, Ont. K1N 6A3 (tel. (613) 789-3709; fax 789-4365). **U.K. (Embassy):** 4 Palace Green, Kensington Palace Gardens, London W84 QD (tel. (0171) 937 9666; fax 937 8069). **Australia (Consulate):** 333 Old South Head Rd., Bondi, Sydney (tel. (02) 36 50 15; fax 30 57 14). **South Africa (Consulate):** 16 Breda St. Gardens, Capetown (tel. (021) 461 48 60; fax 461 24 85).

Russia: U.S. (Embassy): Consular Division, 1825 Phelps Place NW, Washington, D.C. 20008 (tel. (202) 939-8907, info 232-6020; fax 483-7579). **(Consulate):** 9 East 91st St., New York, NY 10128 (tel. (212) 348-0926; fax 831-9162). **(Consulate):** 2790 Green St., San Francisco, CA 94123 (tel. (415) 202-9800; fax 929-0306). **Canada (Embassy):** 285 Charlotte St., Ottawa, Ont. K1N 8L5 (tel. (613) 235-4341; fax 236-6342). **(Consulate)** 52 Range Rd., Ottawa, Ont. K1N 8J5 (tel. (613) 236-6215; fax 238-6158). **U.K. (Embassy):** Consular Division, 5 Kensington Palace Gardens, London W84 QX (tel. (0171) 229 8027; fax 229 3215). **Ireland (Embassy):** 186 Orwell Rd., Dublin 14 (tel. (01) 492 3525). **Australia (Embassy):** 78 Canberra Ave., Griffith ACT 2603 Canberra (tel. (06) 295 90 33; fax 295 18 47). **New Zealand (Embassy):** 57 Messines Rd., KAR 0RI Wellington (tel. (04) 476 61 13; fax 476 38 43).

Slovakia: U.S. (Embassy): 2201 Wisconsin Ave. NW, Suite 250, Washington, D.C. 20007 (tel. (202) 965-5161; fax 965-5166). **Canada (Embassy):** 50 Rideau Terrace, Ottawa, Ont. K1M 2A1 (tel. (613) 749-4442; fax 749-4989). **U.K. (Embassy):** 25 Kensington Palace Gardens, London W8T 4QY (tel. (0171) 243 0803; fax 727 5824). **Australia (Embassy):** 47 Culgoa Circuit, O'Malley, Canberra ACT 2606 (tel. (616) 290 15 16; fax 290 17 55). **South Africa (Embassy):** 930 Arcadia St., Arcadia 0083, Pretoria (tel. (2712) 342 20 51; fax 342 36 88).

Slovenia: U.S. (Embassy): 1525 New Hampshire Ave. NW, Washington, D.C. 20036 (tel. (202) 667-5363; fax 667-4563). **(Consulate):** 600 Third Ave., 24th Fl., New York, NY 10016 (tel. (212) 370-3006; fax 370-3581). **Canada (Embassy):** 150 Metcalfe St., Suite 2101, Ottawa, Ont. K2P 1P1 (tel. (613) 565-5781; fax 565-5783). **U.K. (Embassy):** Suite One, Cavendish Court 11-15, Wigmore St., London W1H 9LA (tel. (0171) 495 7775; fax 495 7776). **Australia (Embassy):** P.O. Box 284-60, Marcus Clarke St., Canberra ACT 2601 (tel. (616) 243 48 30). **(Honorary Consulate):** P.O. Box 118, Coogee, Sydney NSW 2034 (tel. (612) 314 51 16; fax 399 62 46). **New Zealand (Consulate):** Eastern Hutt Rd., Pomare, Lower Hutt, Wellington (tel. (04) 567 00 27; fax 567 00 24).

Ukraine: U.S. (Embassy and Consulate): 3350 M St. NW, Washington, D.C. 20007 (embassy tel. (202) 333-0606; consulate tel. 333-7507; fax 333-5547). **(Consulate):** 240 East 49th St., New York, NY 10017 (tel. (212) 371-5690; fax 371-7510). **Canada (Embassy):** 331 Metcalfe St., Ottawa, Ont. K2P 1S3 (tel. (613) 230-2961; fax 230-2400). **U.K. (Embassy):** 78 Kensington Park Rd., London W1 12PL (tel. (0171) 727 6312; fax 792 1708). **Australia (Embassy):** 4 Bloom St., Moonee Pons, 3039, Melbourne (tel. (613) 326 01 35; fax 326 01 39).

PASSPORTS

Before you leave, photocopy the page of your passport that contains your photograph and identifying information. Carry this photocopy in a safe place apart from your passport, and leave another copy at home. These measures will help prove your citizenship and facilitate the issuing of a new passport if you lose the original document. Consulates recommend that you carry an expired passport or an official copy of your birth certificate separate from other documents. You can request a duplicate birth certificate from the Bureau of Vital Records and Statistics in your state or province of birth.

If you do lose your passport, it may take weeks to process a replacement, and your new one may be valid only for a limited time. In addition, any visas stamped in your old passport will be irretrievably lost. If this happens, immediately notify the local police and the nearest embassy or consulate of your home government. To expedite its replacement, you will need to know all information previously recorded and show identification and proof of citizenship. Some consulates can issue new passports within two days if you give them proof of citizenship. In an emergency, ask for immediate temporary traveling papers that will permit you to reenter your home country. Your passport is a public document belonging to your nation's government. You may have to surrender it to a foreign government official; but, if you don't get it back in a reasonable amount of time, inform the nearest mission of your home country.

United States Citizens may apply for a passport, valid for 10 years (5 years if under 18) at any federal or state courthouse or post office authorized to accept passport applications, or at one of 12 regional U.S. Passport Agencies. Refer to the "U.S. Government, State Department" section of the telephone directory, or call your local post office for addresses. Parents must apply in person for children under age 13. You must apply in person if this is your first passport, if you're under age 18, or if your current passport is more than 12 years old or was issued before your 18th birthday. It costs US$65 (under 18 US$40). You can renew your passport by mail or in person for US$55. Processing takes two to four weeks. Passport agencies offer rush service for a surcharge of US$30 if you have proof that you're departing within ten working days (e.g., an airplane ticket or itinerary). Abroad, a U.S. embassy or consulate can usually issue a new passport, given proof of citizenship. If your passport is lost or stolen in the U.S., report it in writing to Passport Services, U.S. Department of State, 111 19th St. NW, Washington, D.C., 20522-1705 or to the nearest passport agency. For more information, contact the U.S. Passport Information's 24-hour recorded message (tel. (202) 647-0518).

Canada Application forms in English and French are available at all passport offices, post offices, and most travel agencies. Citizens may apply in person at any one of 28 regional Passport Offices across Canada. Travel agents can direct the applicant to the nearest location. The fee is CDN$60. The application and one of the photographs must be signed by an eligible guarantor (someone who has known the applicant for two years and whose profession falls into one of the categories listed on the application). Processing takes approximately five business days for in-person applications and three weeks for mailed ones. Children under 16 may be included on a parent's passport, though some countries require children to carry their own passports. A passport is valid for five years and is not renewable. If a passport is lost abroad, Canadians must be able to prove citizenship with another document. For additional information, call (800) 567-6868 (24hr.; from Canada only), or call one of the passport offices: in Québec City (819) 994-3500, in metro Toronto (416) 973-3251, in Montréal (514) 283-2152. Refer to the booklet *Bon Voyage, But...* for further help and a list of Canadian embassies and consulates abroad. It is available free of charge from any passport office.

United Kingdom British citizens, British Dependent Territories citizens, British Nationals (overseas), and British Overseas citizens may apply for a full passport. For a full passport, valid for 10 years (five years if under 16), apply in person or by mail to a passport office, located in London, Liverpool, Newport, Peterborough, Glasgow, or Belfast. The fee is UK£18. Children under 16 may be included on a parent's passport though some countries require that they have their own for entry. Processing by mail usually takes four to six weeks. The London office offers same-day, walk-in rush service; arrive early.

Ireland Citizens can apply for a passport by mail to either the Department of Foreign Affairs, Passport Office, Setanta Centre, Molesworth St., Dublin 2 (tel. (01) 671

1633), or the Passport Office, 1A South Mall, Cork (tel. (021) 627 2525). Obtain an application at a local Garda station or request one from a passport office. The new Passport Express Service offers a two-week turn-around and is available through post offices for an extra IR£3. Passports cost IR£45 and are valid for 10 years. Citizens under 18 or over 65 can request a three-year passport that costs IR£10.

Australia Citizens must apply for a passport in person at a post office, a passport office, or an Australian diplomatic mission overseas. An appointment may be necessary. Passport offices are located in Adelaide, Brisbane, Canberra City, Darwin, Hobart, Melbourne, Newcastle, Perth, and Sydney. A parent may file an application for a child who is under 18 and unmarried. Application fees are adjusted frequently. For more information, call toll-free (in Australia) 13 12 32.

New Zealand Application forms for passports are available in New Zealand from travel agents and Department of Internal Affairs Link Centres, and overseas from New Zealand embassies, high commissions, and consulates. Completed applications may be lodged at Link Centres and at overseas posts, or forwarded to the Passport Office, P.O. Box 10-526, Wellington, New Zealand. Processing time is 10 working days from receipt of a correctly completed application. An urgent passport service is also available. The application fee for an adult passport is NZ$80 in New Zealand, and NZ$130 overseas for applications lodged under the standard service.

South Africa Citizens can apply for a passport at any Home Affairs Office. Two photos, either a birth certificate or an identity book, and a SAR80 fee must accompany a completed application. South African passports remain valid for 10 years. For further information, contact the nearest Department of Home Affairs Office.

ENTRANCE REQUIREMENTS AND VISAS

Citizens of the U.S., Canada, the U.K., Ireland, Australia, New Zealand, and South Africa all need valid **passports** to enter any Eastern European country and to re-enter their own country. Some countries do not allow entrance if the holder's passport expires in under six months, and returning to the U.S. with an expired passport may result in a fine. Many countries in Eastern Europe also require a **visa;** Ukraine, Belarus, Russia, and Moldova require an **invitation** from a sponsoring individual or organization. Moldova does not require an invitation for American travelers.

Upon entering a country, you must declare certain items from abroad and must pay a duty on the value of those articles that exceed the allowance established by that country's **customs** service. Holding onto receipts for purchases made abroad will help establish values when you return. It is wise to make a list, including serial numbers, of any valuables that you carry with you from home; if you register this list with customs before your departure and have an official stamp it, you will avoid import duty charges and facilitate an easy passage upon your return. Be especially careful to document items manufactured abroad; no-one wants to be mistaken for a used Walkman smuggler.

When you enter a country, dress neatly and carry **proof of your financial independence,** such as a visa to the next country on your itinerary, an airplane ticket to depart, enough money to cover the cost of your living expenses, etc. Admission as a visitor does not include the right to work, which is authorized only by a work permit. Entering certain countries to study requires a special visa, and immigration officers may also want to see proof of acceptance from a school, proof that the course of study will take up most of your time in the country, and as always, proof that you can support yourself.

A **visa** is an endorsement that a foreign government stamps into a passport; it allows the bearer to stay in that country for a specified purpose and period of time. Prices for visas to Eastern Europe vary greatly, depending upon the country as well as the applicant's nationality. We list prices in the **Getting There** section of each country's Essentials section; check the countries you are planning to visit. Requirements are always subject to change. For more info, send for *Foreign Entry Requirements* (US$0.50) from the **Consumer Information Center,** Pueblo, CO 81009 (tel. (719) 948-3334), or contact the **Center for International Business and Travel (CIBT),** 25 W. 43rd St. Suite 1420, New York, NY 10036 (tel. (800) 925-2428, or from NYC (212) 575-2811). This organization charges a fee to secure visas for any country.

Certain countries in Eastern Europe might require travelers to register with the local police or a special office upon arrival. Other countries require travelers to keep a statistical card on which they must keep track of where they spend each and every night while in the country. Again, this info is listed in each country's general introduction. To stay longer, apply for a visa extension at the country's embassy or consulate in your home country well before your departure. Unless you are a student, extending your stay is difficult. You must contact the country's immigration officials or local police well before your time is up, and show proof of financial resources.

Russia, Belarus, Ukraine, and Moldova will only issue visas to travelers possessing invitations from friends, relatives, or a sponsoring organization in the country. The one exception is Moldova, which grants visas to Americans without an invitation. If you don't have someone to invite you, there are several organizations in the West that can arrange the appropriate paperwork for a fee. Visas to Russia and Ukraine also require a list of all the cities and towns on the itinerary. Although this rule is inconsistently enforced, local police and hotel managers can be nasty when the mood strikes them. Failing to produce the required documents when asked has ruined, and even ended, many trips.

CUSTOMS

Upon returning home, you must declare all articles you acquired abroad and must pay a duty on their value exceeding the allowance established by your country's customs service. Holding onto receipts for purchases made abroad will help establish values when you return. In some Eastern European countries, it is illegal to take anything out of the country that was manufactured there before 1945. And, despite the name, goods and gifts purchased at duty-free shops abroad are not exempt from duty or sales tax at your point of return; you must declare these items, as well.

United States Citizens returning home may bring US$400 worth of accompanying goods duty-free and must pay a 10% tax on the next US$1000. You must declare all purchases, so have sales slips ready. Goods are considered duty-free if they are for personal or household use (this includes gifts) and cannot include more than 100 cigars, 200 cigarettes (1 carton), and 1L wine or liquor. You must be over 21 to bring liquor into the U.S. If you mail home personal goods of U.S. origin, you can avoid duty charges by marking the package "American goods returned." For more information, consult the brochure *Know Before You Go,* available from the U.S. Customs Service, Box 7407, Washington, D.C. 20044 (tel. (202) 927-6524).

Canada Citizens who remain abroad for at least one week may bring back up to CDN$500 worth of goods duty-free once per calendar year. Canadian citizens or residents who travel for a period between 48 hours and six days may bring back up to CDN$200 with the exception of tobacco and alcohol. You are permitted to ship goods—except tobacco and alcohol—home under this exemption as long as you declare them when you arrive. Citizens of legal age (which varies by province) may import in person up to 200 cigarettes, 50 cigars, 400g loose tobacco, 400 tobacco sticks, 1.14L wine or alcohol, and twenty-four 355mL cans/bottles of beer; the value of these products is included in the CDN$500. For more information, write to Canadian Customs, 2265 St. Laurent Blvd., Ottawa, Ont. K1G 4K3 (tel. (613) 993-0534).

United Kingdom Citizens or visitors arriving in the U.K. from outside the EU must declare any goods in excess of the following allowances: 200 cigarettes, 100 cigarillos, 50 cigars, or 250g tobacco; 2L still table wine; 1L strong liqueurs over 22% volume; 2L fortified or sparkling wine or other liqueurs; 60cc/mL perfume; 250 cc/

mL toilet water; and UK£145 worth of all other goods including gifts and souvenirs. You must be over 17 to import liquor or tobacco. These allowances also apply to duty-free purchases within the EU, except for the last category which then has an allowance of UK£75. Goods obtained duty- and tax-paid for personal use within the EU do not require any further customs duty. For more information, contact Her Majesty's Customs and Excise, Customs House, Nettleton Rd., Heathrow Airport, Hounslow, Middlesex TW6 2LA (tel. (0181) 910 3744; fax 910 3765).

Ireland Citizens must declare everything in excess of IR£34 (IR£17 per traveler under 15 years of age) obtained outside the EU or duty- and tax-free in the EU above the following allowances: 200 cigarettes, 100 cigarillos, 50 cigars, or 250g tobacco; 1L liquor or 2L wine; 50g perfume; and 250mL toilet water. Goods obtained—duty and tax paid—in another EU country up to a value of IR£460 (IR£115 per traveler under 15) are not subject to additional customs duties. Travelers under 17 are not entitled to any allowance for tobacco or alcohol products. For more information, contact The Revenue Commissioners, Dublin Castle (tel. (01) 679 2777; fax 671 2021; e-mail taxes@ior.ie; http://www.revenue.ie) or The Collector of Customs and Excise, The Customs House, Dublin 1.

Australia Citizens may import AUS$400 (under 18 AUS$200) of goods duty-free, in addition to the allowance of 1.125L alcohol and 250 cigarettes or 250g tobacco. You must be over 18 to import either of these. There is no limit to the amount of Australian and/or foreign cash that may be brought into or taken out of the country. However, amounts of AUS$5000 or more, or the equivalent in foreign currency, must be reported. All foodstuffs and animal products must be declared on arrival. For information, contact the Regional Director, Australian Customs Service, GPO Box 8, Sydney NSW 2001 (tel. (02) 213 20 00; fax 213 40 00).

New Zealand Citizens may bring home up to NZ$700 worth of goods duty-free if they are intended for personal use or are unsolicited gifts. The concession is 200 cigarettes (1 carton), 250g tobacco, 50 cigars, or a combination of all three not to exceed 250g. You may also bring in 4.5L beer or wine and 1.125L liquor. Only travelers over 17 may bring tobacco or alcoholic beverages into the country. For more information, consult the *New Zealand Customs Guide for Travelers*, available from customs offices, or contact New Zealand Customs, 50 Anzac Ave., Box 29, Auckland (tel. (09) 377 35 20; fax 309 29 78).

South Africa Citizens may import duty-free: 400 cigarettes, 50 cigars, 250g tobacco; 2L wine, 1L of spirits; 250mL toilet water, 50mL perfume; and other items up to a value of SAR500. Amounts exceeding this limit but not SAR10,000 are dutiable at 20%. Certain items such as golf clubs and firearms require a duty higher than the standard 20%. Goods acquired abroad and sent to the Republic as unaccompanied baggage do not qualify for any allowances. You may not export or import South African bank notes in excess of SAR500. For more information, write to the Commissioner for Customs and Excise, Private Bag X47, Pretoria 0001. This agency distributes the pamphlet *South African Customs Information* for visitors and residents who travel abroad. South Africans residing in the U.S. should contact the Embassy of South Africa, 3051 Massachusetts Ave. NW, Washington, D.C. 20008 (tel. (202) 232-4400; fax 244-9417), or the South African Home Annex, 3201 New Mexico Ave. Suite 380 NW, Washington, D.C. 20016 (tel. (202) 966-1650).

YOUTH, STUDENT, & TEACHER IDENTIFICATION

The **International Student Identity Card (ISIC)** is the most widely accepted form of student identification. Flashing this card can procure you discounts for sights, entertainment, travel, and other services. Present the card everywhere, and ask about discounts even when none are advertised. It also provides accident insurance of up to US$3000 with no daily limit. In addition, cardholders have access to a toll-free Trav-

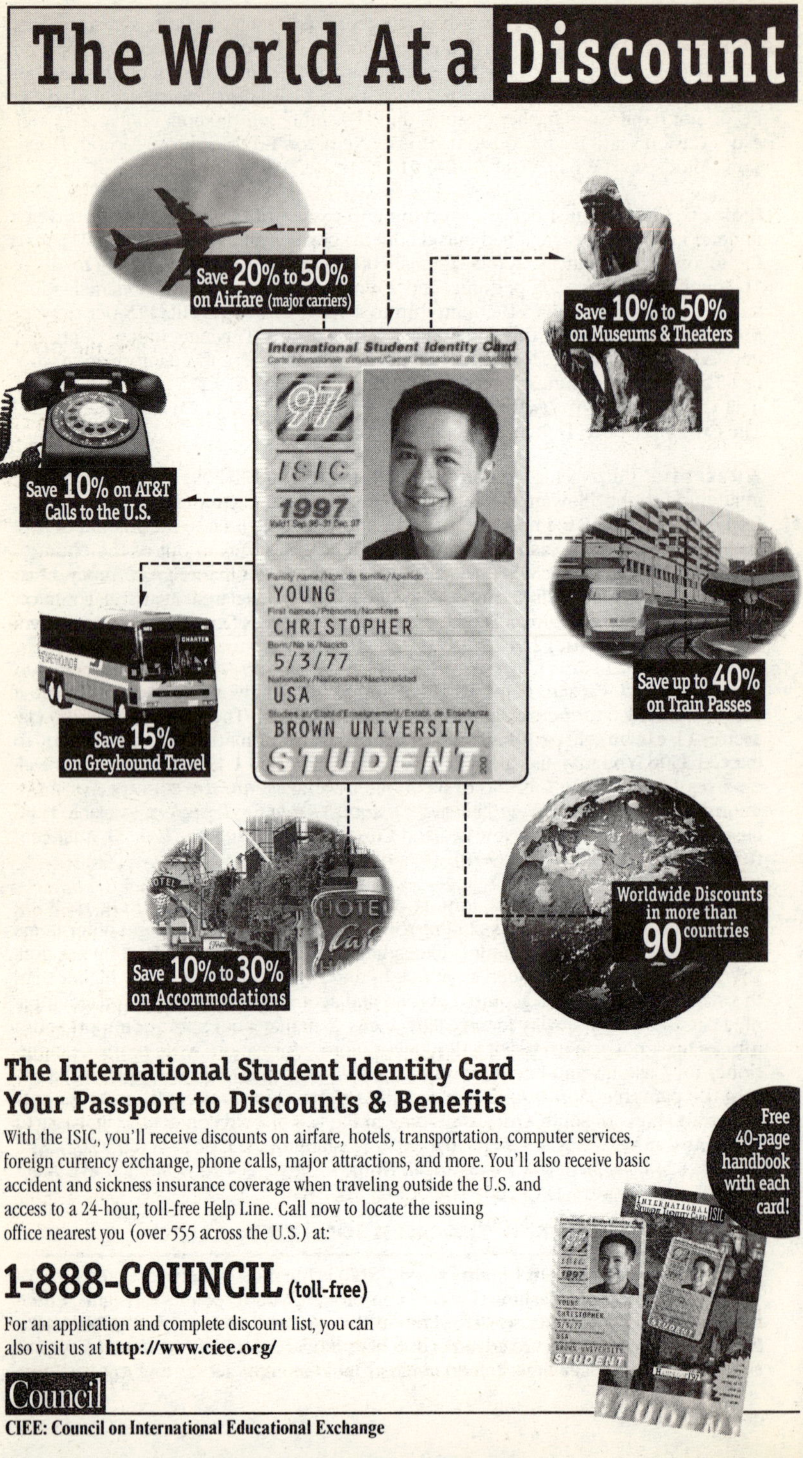

The World At a Discount

Save 20% to 50% on Airfare (major carriers)

Save 10% to 50% on Museums & Theaters

Save 10% on AT&T Calls to the U.S.

Save up to 40% on Train Passes

Save 15% on Greyhound Travel

Save 10% to 30% on Accommodations

Worldwide Discounts in more than 90 countries

The International Student Identity Card
Your Passport to Discounts & Benefits

With the ISIC, you'll receive discounts on airfare, hotels, transportation, computer services, foreign currency exchange, phone calls, major attractions, and more. You'll also receive basic accident and sickness insurance coverage when traveling outside the U.S. and access to a 24-hour, toll-free Help Line. Call now to locate the issuing office nearest you (over 555 across the U.S.) at:

Free 40-page handbook with each card!

1-888-COUNCIL (toll-free)

For an application and complete discount list, you can also visit us at **http://www.ciee.org/**

CIEE: Council on International Educational Exchange

eler's Assistance hotline whose multilingual staff can provide help in medical, legal, and financial emergencies overseas. Many student travel offices and any of the organizations under the auspices of the International Student Travel Confederation (ISTC) around the world issue ISICs. When applying, request a copy of the *International Student Identity Card Handbook,* which lists by country some of the available discounts. You can also write to Council for a copy (see Travel Organizations, p. 1). The fee is US$18. Applicants must be at least 12 years old and degree-seeking students of a secondary or post-secondary school. Because of the proliferation of phony ISICs, many airlines and some other services require other proof of student identity. The **International Teacher Identity Card (ITIC;** US$19) offers similar but limited discounts, as well as medical insurance coverage. For more information on the cards consult the organization's web site (http://www.istc.org).

The Federation of International Youth Travel Organizations (FIYTO) issues a discount card to travelers who are under 26 but not students. Known as the **GO25 Card,** this one-year card offers many of the same benefits as the ISIC, and most organizations that sell the ISIC also sell the GO25 Card. A brochure that lists discounts is free when you purchase the card. To apply, you will need a passport, valid driver's license, or copy of your certified birth certificate; and a passport-sized photo with your name printed on the back. The fee is US$16, CDN$15, or UK£5. For information, contact Council or FIYTO (see Travel Organizations, p. 1).

INTERNATIONAL DRIVER'S PERMIT

If you plan to drive a car while abroad, you must have an **International Driving Permit (IDP),** though certain countries allow travelers to drive with a valid American or Canadian license for a limited number of months. The card is essentially a transliteration of your license into a variety of languages. Most car-rental agencies don't require the permit. A valid driver's license from your home country must always accompany the IDP. Call an automobile association to find out if your destination country requires the IDP. It may still be a good idea, in case you're in an accident or stranded in a smaller town where the police don't know English.

Your IDP must be issued in your own country before you depart. Contact your local automobile association or a travel agency for information on how to apply. U.S. license holders can obtain an IDP (US$10), valid for one year, at any **American Automobile Association (AAA)** office or by writing to the main office, AAA Florida, Travel Agency Services Department, 1000 AAA Drive (mail stop 28), Heathrow, FL 32746-5080 (tel. (407) 444-4245; fax 444-4247). For further information, contact a local AAA office. Canadian license holders can obtain an IDP (CDN$10) through any **Canadian Automobile Association (CAA)** branch office in Canada, or by writing to CAA Central Ontario, 60 Commerce Valley Drive E., Thornhill, Ont. L3T 7P9 (tel. (416) 221-4300).

Most credit cards cover standard auto insurance. If you rent, lease, or borrow a car, you will need a **green card,** or **International Insurance Certificate,** to prove that you have liability insurance. Obtain it through the car rental agency; most of them include coverage in their prices. If you lease a car, you can obtain a green card from the dealer. Some travel agents also offer the card, and it may be available at the border. Verify whether your auto insurance applies abroad. If you have a collision abroad, the accident will show up on your domestic records if you report it to your insurance company. Rental agencies may require you to purchase theft insurance in some countries that they consider to have a high risk of auto theft. Ask your rental agency about each of your destination countries.

■ Money

If you stay in hostels and prepare your own food, expect to spend approximately US$40 per day plus transportation (this is much higher in Slovenia and Croatia). Don't sacrifice health or safety for a cheaper tab. Also remember to check the financial pages of a large newspaper for up-to-the-minute exchange rates before embarking on your journey. Certain countries in Central and Eastern Europe are experiencing high levels of inflation and currency depreciation. Many prices are given in **Deutschmarks:** see Gateway Cities: Berlin, p. 737, for the exchange rates.

CURRENCY AND EXCHANGE

It is more expensive to buy foreign currency than domestic; i.e., Hungarian forints will be less costly in Hungary than in the U.S. However, converting some money before you go will allow you to breeze through the airport while others languish in exchange lines. This is a good practice in case you find yourself stuck with no money after banking hours or on a holiday. Also, check commission rates closely, and scan newspapers to get the standard rate of exchange. Bank rates are generally the best, but at times (we have indicated this in the appropriate sections) tourist offices or exchange kiosks have better rates.

Always save **transaction receipts,** as some countries require them to reconvert unused local currency. Exchanging some of your old currency before moving on to a new country, although more costly, is good insurance against arriving after hours or in a bankless town. **American Express** offices usually charge no commission, but they often have slightly worse rates than other exchanges. In general, carry a range of denominations since charges may be levied per check cashed. Australian and New Zealand dollars are impossible to exchange in many Eastern European countries. U.S. dollars are generally preferred, though certain establishments will only accept Deutschmarks. Western currency will sometimes be the preferred payment in Eastern European hotels; find out which hotels and restaurants require hard currency, and don't use Western money when you don't need to. Don't throw dollars around to gain preferential treatment; it's offensive and you'll be an instant target for theft.

TRAVELER'S CHECKS

Traveler's checks are the safest way to hold money: if they get lost or stolen, travelers get reimbursed by the checks' issuers. Though many establishments in Eastern Europe do not yet accept traveler's checks, there is usually a place in town that will exchange them into local currency; this is infinitely safer than carrying large amounts of Western currency. Checks should be ordered well in advance, especially if large sums are being requested. Keep check receipts and a record of which checks you've cashed in a separate place from the checks themselves. Leave a photocopy of check serial numbers with someone at home as back-up in case you lose your copy. Never countersign checks until you're prepared to cash them. Be sure to keep cash on hand, particularly in less touristy regions: many establishments may not accept or cash traveler's checks. Finally, be sure to bring your passport with you any time you plan to use the checks.

> **American Express:** Call (800) 221-7282 in the U.S. and Canada; in the U.K. (0800) 521 313; in New Zealand (0800) 44 10 68; in Australia (008) 25 19 02. Elsewhere, call U.S. collect (801) 964-6665 (http://www.americanexpress.com). American Express traveler's checks are now available in British, Canadian, German, and other currencies. They are the most widely recognized worldwide and the easiest to replace if lost or stolen. Checks can be purchased for a small fee at American Express Travel Service Offices, banks, and AAA offices (AAA members can buy the checks commission-free). Cardmembers can also purchase checks at American Express Dispensers at Travel Service Offices, at airports, via phone (U.S. and Canada tel. (800) 673-3782), or via the Internet on America On-line. AmEx offices cash their checks commission-free (except where prohibited by national governments), although they often offer slightly worse rates than banks. They also sell checks for Two which can be signed by either of two people. Request AmEx's *Traveler's Companion,* which lists travel office addresses and stolen check hotlines for each European country.

CREDIT CARDS AND CASH CARDS ■ 17

Citicorp: Call (800) 645-6556 in the U.S. and Canada; in the U.K. (0171) 297 4781; from elsewhere, call U.S. collect (813) 623-1709. Sells both Citicorp and Citicorp Visa traveler's checks in U.S., Australian, British, Canadian, German, Swiss, and Japanese currencies. Commission is 1-2% on check purchases. Checkholders are automatically enrolled for 45 days in the Travel Assist Program which provides travelers with English-speaking doctor, lawyer, and interpreter referrals as well as check refund assistance. Citicorp's World Courier Service guarantees worldwide hand-delivery of replacement traveler's checks.

Thomas Cook MasterCard: Call (800) 223-9920 in the U.S. and Canada; in the U.K. call (0800) 622 101; elsewhere call the U.S. collect (609) 987-7300. Offers checks in U.S., Canadian, Australian, British, French, Swiss, and German currencies as well as the still semi-unreal ECUs. Commission 1-2% for purchases. Buying the checks at a Thomas Cook office may get you lower commissions.

Visa: Call (800) 227-6811 in the U.S.; in the U.K. (0800) 895 492; from elsewhere call (733) 318 949 which is a toll call, but the charge can be reversed. They will let you know where the nearest office is or help you with lost checks.

CREDIT CARDS AND CASH CARDS

Credit cards can be either invaluable or a frustrating nuisance. For the most part, only expensive, Western-oriented establishments in Eastern Europe take them, but some banks will allow you to withdraw money from ATM machines or give you a cash advance. Major credit cards like **MasterCard (MC)** and **Visa** are the most likely to be recognized. Cash advances can be a great bargain because credit-card companies get the wholesale exchange rate, which is generally 5% better than the retail rate used by banks and even better than that used by other currency-exchange establishments. **American Express (AmEx)** cards work in some ATMs, as well as at AmEx offices and major airports. All such machines require a **Personal Identification Number (PIN),** which credit cards in the United States do not usually carry. You must ask your credit card company to assign you one before you leave; without this PIN, *you will be unable to withdraw cash.* Keep in mind that MasterCard and Visa have different names elsewhere ("EuroCard" or "Access" for MasterCard and "Carte Bleue" or "Barclaycard" for Visa), which some cashiers may not know. Credit cards are also invaluable in an emergency—an unexpected hospital bill or ticket home or the loss of traveler's checks—which may leave you temporarily without other resources. Credit cards also offer an array of other services, from car insurance to emergency assistance; these depend completely, however, on the issuer.

American Express (tel. U.S. (800) CASH-NOW (528-4800)) offers several services that might be of use to travelers, including a 24-hour hotline offering medical and legal assistance in emergencies (from abroad call U.S. collect (310) 214-8228). At AmEx offices abroad members can pick up mail, find assistance in changing airline, hotel, and car-rental reservations, and cash personal checks. **MasterCard** (U.S. tel. (800) 999-0454) and **Visa** (U.S. tel. (800) 336-8472) are issued in cooperation with individual banks and some other organizations.

Cash cards, popularly called **ATM** (Automated Teller Machine) cards are rare in Eastern Europe, but some banks in larger cities are connected to an international money network, usually **CIRRUS** (U.S. tel. (800) 4-CIRRUS (424-7787)) or **PLUS** (U.S. tel. (800) 843-7587). Cirrus has cash machines in 80 countries and territories. It charges US$1-2 to withdraw, depending on your bank. PLUS is not quite as extensive, but is still fairly widespread. ATM machines also dispense the money at the same wholesale rate that you can get with credit cards, so using a cash card can pay off in the long run. An important note: European ATMs may not have letters on their keypads, so be sure you memorize your PIN by its numbers before you take off (it must be 4 digits).

MONEY FROM HOME

American Express allows cardholders to draw cash from their checking accounts at any of its major offices and many of its representatives' offices with no service charge and no interest. There is also an Express Cash service which tranforms your card into a debit card that makes withdrawals from a bank account instead of a line of credit. For information on how to contact AmEx, see Traveler's Checks, p. 16. Unless using this service, avoid cashing checks in foreign currencies: they may take weeks and a US$30 fee to clear.

Money can also be **wired** abroad through international money transfer services operated by **Western Union** (U.S. tel. (800) 325-6000). The money is usually available in the country to which you're sending it within an hour, although this may vary.

In emergencies, U.S. citizens can have money sent via the State Department's **Citizens Emergency Center, American Citizens Services,** Consular Affairs, Public Affairs Staff, Room 4831, U.S. Department of State, Washington, D.C. 20520 (tel. (202) 647-5225, at night and on Sundays and holidays 647-4000; fax 647-300; http://travel.state.gov). For a fee of US$15, the State Department forwards money within hours to the nearest consular office.

■ Safety and Security

Safe travel in Eastern Europe calls for some special effort. Laws are minimally observed of late and con-artists abound, in official positions as well as unofficial ones. Should an emergency arise, contact your local embassy, as the police in Eastern Europe usually don't speak English, To avoid unwanted attention, try to blend in as much as possible. Respecting local customs can often placate would-be hecklers. The gawking camera-toter is a more obvious target than the low-profile local look-alike. Walking into a café or shop to check your map beats checking it on a street corner. Better yet, look over your map carefully before leaving your hotel room. Muggings are more often impromptu than planned; walking with nervous, over-the-shoulder glances can be a tip that you have something valuable to protect. Look like you know where you're going at all times—whether you do or not.

Carry all your valuables (including your passport, railpass, traveler's checks, and airline ticket) either in a **money belt** or **neckpouch** stashed securely *inside* your clothing; this will protect you from skilled thieves who use razors to slash open backpacks and fanny packs (particular favorites of bag-snatchers). You should keep these valuables on your person at all times, including trips to the shower—try hanging the pouch from the showerhead. Making photocopies of important documents will allow you to recover them if they are lost or stolen. Carry one copy separately from the documents and leave another copy at home. A simple but effective deterrent is a small padlock, available in luggage stores, which can ensure that your pack stays shut (though not unslashed). If you must carry a shoulder bag, make sure that the strap passes over your head and runs diagonally across your torso.

When exploring a new **city**, extra vigilance is wise, but avoid turning precautions into panic. Carry a small whistle to scare off attackers or attract attention. When walking at night, keep to crowded, well lit places and don't attempt to cross parks, parking lots, or other deserted areas. **Con artists** are on the prowl in many cities; be aware of classic ploys: sob stories requiring money or a spill on your shoulder distracting you while your bag is snatched. Hustlers often work in groups, and children are among the most effective. A firm "no" should communicate that you are no dupe. Contact the authorities if a hustler acts particularly insistent or aggressive.

Trains are notoriously easy spots for thieving. Professional thieves wait for tourists to fall asleep and then carry off everything they can. If you're traveling in pairs, sleep in alternating shifts. When alone, use good judgment in selecting a train compartment; never stay in an empty one, and try to get a top bunk. Wrap the straps of your luggage securely around you or tie them to the overhead luggage racks. Travelers taking the Moscow-St.Petersburg train route in Russia should be especially vigilant. The U.S. Embassy confirms that "a powerful odorless gas, derived from ether, has been used by criminals to drug passengers to prevent their waking during a robbery." Trains from major Western cities like Vienna and Berlin are generally considered to be more dangerous than intra-country trains, and there have been rumors of the gas being used on these lines also (e.g., Berlin-Warsaw, Vienna-Budapest, etc.). Travelers are advised to secure their door with heavy wire while they sleep. Sleeping in your **automobile** is one of the more dangerous ways to get your rest. If you must, park in a well lit area as close to a police station or 24-hour service station as possible. **Sleeping outside** is often illegal and exposes you to even more hazards—camping is recommended only in official, supervised campsites. *Let's Go* does not recommend hitchhiking, particularly for women; see Getting There, p. 34, for more.

A good self-defense course will give you more concrete ways to react to different types of aggression, though it might cost you more money than your trip. **Model Mugging,** an organization with offices in several major U.S. cities, teaches a comprehensive course on self-defense for men or women. Contact Lynn S. Auerbach on the East Coast (tel. (617) 232-7900); Alice Tibits in the Midwest (tel. (612) 645-6189); and Cori Couture on the West Coast (tel. (415) 592-7300). Prices vary from US$400-500. Community colleges and YWCAs frequently offer courses at more affordable prices.

For official **United States Department of State** travel advisories, including crime and security, call their 24-hour hotline at (202) 647-5225. To order publications, including a pamphlet entitled *A Safe Trip Abroad,* write them at Superintendent of Documents, U.S. Government Printing Office, Washington, D.C. 20402, or call (202) 783-3238. Another useful, although expensive, service to look into is **Travel Assistance International** by Worldwide Assistance Services, Inc., which provides its members with a 24-hour hotline for emergencies and referrals. Their year-long Frequent Traveler package (US$226) includes medical and travel insurance, financial assistance, and help in replacing lost documents. In the U.S., call (800) 821-2828, fax (202) 828-5896, or write them at 1133 15th St. NW, Suite 400, Washington, D.C. 20005-2710. More complete information on safety while traveling can be found in *Americans Traveling Abroad: What You Should Know Before You Go,* by Gladson Nwanna (World Travel Institute: US$40), available at *Barnes and Noble* booksellers across the United States.

■ Health

Common sense is the simplest prescription for good health while you travel: eat well, drink and sleep enough, and don't overexert yourself. Travelers complain most often about their feet and their gut, so take precautionary measures. Drinking lots of fluids can help prevent dehydration and constipation, and wearing sturdy shoes and clean socks and using talcum powder can help keep your feet dry. To minimize the effects of jet lag, "reset" your body's clock by adopting the schedule of your destination immediately upon arrival.

BEFORE YOU GO

Though no amount of planning can guarantee an accident-free trip, preparation can help minimize the likelihood of contracting a disease and maximize the chances of receiving effective health care in the event of an emergency. For minor health problems, bring a compact **first-aid kit,** including bandages, aspirin or other pain killer, antibiotic cream, a thermometer, a Swiss Army knife with tweezers, moleskin, a decongestant for colds, motion sickness remedy, medicine for diarrhea or stomach problems, sunscreen, insect repellent, and burn ointment.

In your passport, write the names of any people you wish to be contacted in case of a medical emergency, and also list any allergies or medical conditions. If you wear glasses or **contact lenses,** carry an extra prescription, a pair of glasses, and cleaning solution, or arrange to have your doctor or a family member send a replacement pair in an emergency. **Allergy** sufferers should find out if their conditions are likely to be aggravated in the regions they plan to visit, and obtain a full supply of any necessary medication before the trip, since matching a prescription to a foreign equivalent is not always easy, safe, or possible. Carry up-to-date, legible prescriptions or a statement from your doctor, especially if you use insulin, a syringe, or a narcotic. While traveling, be sure to keep all medication with you in carry-on luggage.

Take a look at your **immunization** records before you go. Some countries require visitors to carry vaccination certificates. Travelers over two years old should be sure that the following vaccines are up to date: Measles, Mumps, and Rubella (MMR); Diphtheria, Tetanus, and Pertussis (DTP or DTap); Polio (OPV); Haemophilus Influenza B (HbCV); and Hepatitis B (HBV). A booster of Tetanus-diphtheria (Td) is recommended once every ten years, and adults traveling to most of the New Independent States of the former Soviet Union should consider an additional dose of **Polio vaccine** if they have not had one during their adult years. **Hepatitis A** vaccine and/or **Immune Globulin** (IG) is recommended for travelers to Eastern Europe. Have a doctor guide you through this maze of injections, and try to remember that no matter how bad the needles are, they're better than the diseases they prevent.

For up-to-date information about which vaccinations are recommended for your destination and region-specific health data, try these resources: the **United States Center for Disease Control and Prevention** (based in Atlanta, Georgia), an excellent source of information for travelers around the world, maintains an international travelers' hotline (tel. (404) 332-4559; fax 332-4565; http://www.cdc.gov). Or write directly to the Centers for Disease Control and Prevention, Travelers' Health, 1600 Clifton Rd. NE, Atlanta, GA 30333. The CDC publishes the booklet *Health Information for International Travelers* (US$14), an annual global rundown of disease, immunization, and general health advice, including risks in particular countries.

Those with medical conditions (i.e. diabetes, allergies to antibiotics, epilepsy, heart conditions) may want to obtain a **Medic Alert** identification tag (US$35 the first year, and US$15 annually thereafter), which identifies their diseases and gives a 24-hour collect-call info number. Contact Medic Alert in the U.S. at (800) 825-3785, or write to Medic Alert Foundation, 2323 Colorado Ave., Turlock, CA 95382. Diabetics can contact the **American Diabetes Association,** 1660 Duke St., Alexandria, VA 22314 (tel. (800) 232-3472), to receive copies of the article *Travel and Diabetes* and an ID card, which carries messages in 18 languages explaining the carrier's diabetic status.

ON-THE-ROAD AILMENTS

Hot and Cold Common sense goes a long way toward preventing **heat exhaustion:** relax in hot weather, drink lots of non-alcoholic fluids, and lie down inside if you feel awful. Continuous heat stress can eventually lead to **heatstroke,** characterized by rising body temperature, severe headache, and cessation of sweating. Wear a hat, sunglasses, and a lightweight longsleeve shirt to avoid heatstroke. Victims must be cooled off with wet towels and taken to a doctor as soon as possible.

Always drink enough liquids to keep your urine clear. Alcoholic beverages are dehydrating, as are coffee, strong tea, and caffeinated sodas. Also, be sure to eat enough salty food to prevent electrolyte depletion, which causes severe headaches. Less debilitating, but still dangerous, is **sunburn.** If you're prone to sunburn, bring sunscreen with you (it's often more expensive and hard to find when traveling), and apply liberally and often to avoid burns and risk of skin cancer. If you do get sunburned, drink more fluids than usual.

Extreme cold is just as dangerous as heat—overexposure to cold brings the risk of **hypothermia.** Warning signs are easy to detect: body temperature drops rapidly, resulting in the failure to produce body heat. You may shiver, have poor coordination, feel exhausted, have slurred speech, hallucinate, or even suffer amnesia. *Do not let hypothermia victims fall asleep* if they are in the advanced stages—their body temperature will drop more, and if they lose consciousness they may die. Seek medical help as soon as possible. To avoid hypothermia, keep dry and stay out of the wind. In wet weather, wool and most synthetics, such as pile, will keep you warm but most other fabric, especially cotton, will make you colder. Dress in layers, and watch for **frostbite** in cold weather and strong winds. Look for skin that has turned white, waxy, and cold, and if you find frostbite do not rub the skin. Drink warm beverages, get dry, and slowly warm the area with dry fabric or steady body contact. Take serious cases to a doctor as soon as possible.

Travelers to **high altitudes** must allow their bodies a couple of days to adjust to lower oxygen levels in the air before exerting themselves. Also be careful about alcohol, especially if you're used to U.S. standards for beer—many foreign brews and liquors pack more punch, and at high altitudes where the air has less oxygen, any alcohol will do you in quickly.

Diseases Transmitted by Insects When hiking, camping, or working in or around forest regions, you should remain in well screened areas, use mosquito nets, tuck long pants into socks, and wear clothes that cover most of the body. Always use insect repellent; the ingredient to look for is DEET, which is the strongest and most effective repellent. **Ticks**—responsible for Lyme and other diseases—can be particularly dangerous in rural and forested regions all over Europe. Brush off ticks periodically when walking, using a fine-toothed comb on your neck and scalp. Do not try to remove ticks by burning them or coating them with nail polish remover or petroleum jelly. Topical cortisones may help quell the itching.

Tick-borne Encephalitis is a viral infection of the central nervous system transmitted by tick bites or by ingestion of unpasteurized dairy products. Symptoms range from none at all to the abrupt onset of headache, fever, and flu-like symptoms to actual swelling of the brain (encephalitis). A vaccine is available in Europe, but the immunization schedule is impractical for most tourists, and the risk of contracting the disease is relatively low, especially if you take precautions against tick bites. There is particular risk in Hungary, Poland, the Czech Republic, Slovakia, the former USSR, and Yugoslavia, and some risk in Bulgaria and Romania.

Ticks also carry the infamous **Lyme disease,** a bacterial infection marked by a circular bull's-eye rash of two inches or more that appears around the bite. Other symptoms include fever, headache, tiredness, and aches and pains. Antibiotics are effective if administered early. Left untreated, Lyme can cause problems in the joints, the heart, and the nervous system. Again, avoiding tick bites in the first place is the best way to prevent the disease. If you do find a tick attached to your skin, grasp the tick's head parts with tweezers as close to your skin as possible and apply slow, steady traction in a counter-clockwise direction. However, the ticks that carry Lyme disease are mostly Deer ticks that are about the size of a pin head and cannot be removed. If you are able to remove a tick before it has been attached for more than 24 hours, you greatly reduce your risk of infection. You are at risk for Lyme disease when hiking, camping, or visiting rural areas in Eastern Europe.

Diseases Transmitted by Food and Water Food- and water-borne diseases are the number-one cause of illness to travelers in Eastern Europe. Viruses and bacte-

---

On the Run in Eastern Europe

Traveler's diarrhea, the most commonly reported illness for travelers in Eastern Europe, is the dastardly consequence of ignoring our warnings against drinking untreated water. The illness can last from three to seven days, and symptoms include diarrhea, nausea, bloating, and malaise. If the nasties hit you, eat quick-energy, non-sugary foods—like salted crackers—with protein and carbohydrates to keep your strength up. Over-the-counter remedies (such as Pepto-Bismol© or Immodium©) may counteract the problems, but they can complicate serious infections. Avoid anti-diarrheals if you suspect you've been exposed to contaminated food or water, which puts you at risk for other diseases. The most dangerous effect of diarrhea is dehydration; the simplest and most effective anti-dehydration formula is eight oz. of water with a ½ tsp. of sugar or honey and a pinch of salt. Down several of these remedies a day, rest, and wait for the disease to run its course. If you develop a fever or your symptoms don't go away after four or five days, consult a doctor. Also, consult a doctor if children develop traveler's diarrhea, since treatment is different.

HEALTH

ria can cause diarrhea and vomiting (typhoid fever, cholera, and parasites), liver damage (hepatitis), and muscle paralysis (polio).

Hepatitis A, a viral infection of the liver that is most frequently transmitted through contaminated water, ice, shellfish, unpeeled fruits, or uncooked vegetables, is an immediate risk in Eastern Europe. It can also be transmitted through direct contact with an infected person. Symptoms include fatigue, fever, loss of appetite, nausea, dark urine, jaundice, vomiting, aches and pains, and light stools. There is no specific treatment and no vaccine, but an injection of Havrix or immune globulin (IG) is highly recommended by the CDC before travel to Eastern Europe.

Cholera is an intestinal infection caused by a bacterium that lives in contaminated water or food; it causes voluminous diarrhea, dehydration, vomiting, and muscle cramps. The CDC reports that risk of infection for Westerners is low if they follow the usual tourist itineraries and stay in standard accommodations. Otherwise, eat only thoroughly cooked food, peel your own fruit, and drink either boiled water, bottled carbonated water, or bottled carbonated soft drinks. A vaccine is only recommended if you have stomach ulcers, use anti-acid therapy, or will be living in unsanitary conditions in areas of high cholera activity. Cholera may be treated by simple fluid and electrolyte-replacement therapy, but treatment must be immediate.

Parasitic infections result from eating or drinking contaminated food or water, from direct contact with soil or water containing parasites or their larvae, or from insect bites. Symptoms include swollen lymph nodes, rashes or itchy skin, digestive problems such as abdominal pain or diarrhea, eye problems, and anemia. Again, travelers should eat only thoroughly cooked food, drink safe water, wear shoes, and avoid contact with insects, particularly mosquitoes, biting flies, gnats, and midges. Giardia, for example, is one serious parasitic disease you can get by drinking untreated water from streams or lakes all over the world. Many backpackers and campers not scrupulous about their water get giardia, and it sometimes stays with them for years. St. Petersburg has particularly dangerous water. Have a doctor pre-

AVE
a.s. Travel agency
YOUR PARTNER FOR PRAGUE

- accommodation for groups and individuals in Prague and other cities in Czech Republic in hotels, pensions, hostels and private apartments
- congress and incentive programes
- transport services
- guide services
- sightseeing tours and excursions
- ticket reservation
- exchange services

Information and reservation:
AVE, a.s., Křížová 59, 150 00 Praha 5
Tel.: +42 2 24617133, 24617132
Fax: +42 2 542239, 24617113
E-mail: avetours @ avetours. anet. cz
http: \\ www. ave. anet. CZ

scribe the cure—*flagyll*—before you leave. Water purification tablets and boiling water (at least 10min.) will kill giardia before it enters your system.

Diseases Transmitted by Intimate Contact Travelers should take precautions to protect themselves against infection by **sexually transmitted diseases (STDs)** by using latex condoms. All condoms are not equal, however; purchase well known brands and bring them with you. Check the Essentials sections for each country to see where buying reliable condoms—a must for preventing any **STD**—is problematic. Even "safe sex" isn't with some non-Western brands.

Hepatitis B is a viral infection of the liver transmitted by sharing needles, having unprotected sex, or coming into direct contact with an infected person's lesioned skin. If you think you may be sexually active while traveling, if you will be a health worker overseas, or if you are working or living in rural areas, you are typically advised to get the vaccination for Hepatitis B. Ideally, the vaccination series begins six months before travel, but it should be started even if it will not be finished before you leave. Risk is moderate in Eastern Europe.

Other Diseases in Eastern Europe Except for Bulgaria, where the animals are apparently all happy and healthy, there is a risk of **rabies,** a viral infection that affects the central nervous system and is transmitted by all warm-blooded animal bites, especially by dogs and foxes. Do not handle any animals. Any animal bite should be promptly cleaned with large amounts of soap and (clean) water and should receive medical attention. Vaccination is recommended for those visiting for more than 30 days, visiting areas where rabies is known to exist, and spelunking. The CDC also warns travelers that since 1990 outbreaks of **diphtheria,** an acute contagious bacterial disease marked by fever and by the coating of the air passages with a membrane that interferes with breathing, have been reported in **Moscow** and **St. Petersburg,** Russia, and **Kiev,** Ukraine. Proof of immunity is not required, but the Advisory Committee on Immunization Practices recommends diphtheria immunization for anyone traveling to these cities.

HIV AND AIDS

Human Immunodeficiency Virus (HIV), which causes acquired immunodeficiency syndrome or **AIDS,** is found in Eastern Europe, but its magnitude and modes of transmission in the region are not well defined. HIV is transmitted through the exchange of body fluids with an infected individual or through the transfusion of infected blood. Remember that there is no assurance that someone is not infected: HIV tests only show antibodies after a six-month lapse. Some new strands of HIV are not testable. Never have sex without using a condom, and never share intravenous needles. The U.S. Center for Disease Control's 24-hr. **AIDS Hotline** can refer you to organizations with information on European countries (U.S. tel. (800) 342-2437).

BIRTH CONTROL AND ABORTION

Reliable contraceptive devices may be difficult to find while traveling. Women on the pill should bring enough to allow for possible loss or extended stays and should bring a prescription, since forms of the pill vary. The sponge is probably too bulky to be worthwhile on the road. If you use a diaphragm, be sure that you have enough contraceptive jelly on hand. Though condoms are increasingly available, you might want to bring your favorite national brand with you, as availability and quality vary.

For information on abortion, contact the **United States abortion hotline** (U.S. tel. (800) 772-9100; Mon.-Fri. 9:30am-12:30pm, 1:30-5:30pm). The hotline can direct you to organizations which provide information on the availability of and techniques for abortion in other countries. Or contact your embassy to receive a list of ob/gyn doctors who perform abortions. For general information on contraception, condoms, and abortion worldwide, contact the **International Planned Parenthood Federa-**

tion, European Regional Office, Regent's College Inner Circle, Regent's Park, London NW1 4NS (tel. (0171 486 0741; fax 487 7950).

WOMEN'S HEALTH

Women traveling in unsanitary conditions are vulnerable to urinary tract and bladder infections, common and severely uncomfortable bacterial diseases which cause a burning sensation, and painful and sometimes frequent urination. Drink tons of vitamin C-rich juice, plenty of clean water, and urinate frequently, especially right after intercourse. Untreated, these infections can lead to kidney infections, sterility, and even death. If symptoms persist, see a doctor. If you often develop vaginal yeast infections, take along an over-the-counter medicine, as treatments may not be readily available in Eastern Europe. Women may also be more susceptible to vaginal thrush and cystitis, two treatable but uncomfortable illnesses. Tampons and pads can be hard to find when travelling; your preferred brands may not be available, so it may be advisable to take supplies. Some women also use diaphragms or cervical caps to temporarily trap menstrual flow. Refer to the *Handbook for Women Travellers* by Maggie and Gemma Moss (published by Piatkus Books) or to the women's health guide *Our Bodies, Our Selves* (published by the Boston Women's Health Collective) for more information specific to women's health on the road.

HEALTH ADVISORIES

The Center for Disease Control and Prevention (CDC) warns that travelers to Eastern Europe must (1) protect themselves from insects, (2) ensure the quality of their food and drinking water, (3) have Immune Globulin (IG) or the Hepatitis A vaccine, (4) consider booster shorts of tetanus (Td) and polio vaccines and (5) be knowledgeable about potential diseases in the region. Pregnant travelers or travelers with children

---

Speak the Language When You Get There!

You *can*...with Audio-Forum's famous self-study audio-cassette courses. Choose your own time, pace, and place to learn the language, and save hundreds of dollars compared with the cost of a private language school. All our courses feature native speakers.

You'll learn naturally by listening to the cassettes (while driving, jogging, or whatever) and repeating during the pauses on the tape. By the end of the course, you'll be speaking naturally and comfortably in your new language.

- ☐ **Basic Bulgarian:** 23 cassettes and 487-page text, $245.
- ☐ **Fast-Track Czech:** 6 cassettes and 300-page text, $125.
- ☐ **Basic Estonian:** 32 cassettes and 393-page text, $295.
- ☐ **Basic Hungarian:** 12 cassettes and 266-page text, $195.
- ☐ **Easy Way to Latvian:** 12 cassettes and 283-page text, $185.
- ☐ **Easy Way to Lithuanian:** 6 cassettes and 292-page text, $135.
- ☐ **Conversational Polish:** 8 cassettes and 327-page text, $185.
- ☐ **Spoken Romanian:** 6 cassettes and 342-page text, $115.
- ☐ **Modern Russian:** 24 cassettes and 480-page text, $255.
- ☐ **Serbo-Croatian, Vol. I:** 12 cassettes and 633-page text, $195.
- ☐ **Beginning Slovak:** 8 cassettes and 522-page text, $185.
- ☐ **Everyday Ukrainian:** 10 cassettes and 342-page text, $195.

There is no risk. We offer a full 3-week money-back guarantee. Our free 56-page *Whole World Language Catalog* offers courses in 96 languages. Our 25th year. Call toll-free **1-800-243-1234**, Fax (203) 453-9774, e-mail: 74537.550@compuserve.com, or write:

AUDIO·FORUM
THE LANGUAGE SOURCE

Audio-Forum Room K100, 96 Broad Street, Guilford, CT 06437 U.S.A. • (203) 453-9794

should contact the CDC for additional information; call the **CDC International Traveler's Hotline** in the U.S. at (404) 332-4559.

■ Insurance

Don't buy unnecessary travel coverage—your regular policies may well extend to many travel-related accidents. **Medical insurance** (especially university policies) often cover costs incurred abroad; check with your provider. **Canadians** are protected by their home province's health insurance plan for up to 90 days after leaving the country; check with the provincial Ministry of Health or Health Plan Headquarters for details. **Australia** has Reciprocal Health Care Agreements (RHCAs) with certain countries, where traveling Australians are entitled to many of the services they receive at home. The Commonwealth Department of Human Services and Health can provide more information. **Homeowners' insurance** often covers theft during travel and loss of travel documents (passport, plane ticket, etc.) up to US$500.

    ISIC and **ITIC** provide US$3000 worth of accident and illness insurance and US$100 per day for up to 60 days of hospitalization. The cards also give access to a toll-free Traveler's Assistance hotline whose multilingual staff can provide help in emergencies overseas. To supplement ISIC's insurance plan, **Council** (see Travel Organizations, p. 1) offers the inexpensive Trip-Safe plan, with options covering medical treatment and hospitalization, accidents, baggage loss, and charter flights missed due to illness; **Council Travel** and **STA** offer more expensive and comprehensive policies. **American Express** cardholders receive automatic car rental and travel accident insurance on flight purchases made with their card.

    Insurance companies usually require a copy of police reports for thefts or evidence of having paid medical expenses (doctor's statements, receipts) before they will honor a claim, and they may have time limits on filing for reimbursement. Always carry policy numbers and proof of insurance. Check with each insurance carrier for specific policies. Most of the carriers listed below have 24-hour hotlines.

    Globalcare Travel Insurance, 220 Broadway, Lynnfield MA, 01940 (U.S. tel. (800) 821-2488; fax (617) 592-7720; e-mail global@nebc.mv.com; http://nebc.mv.com/globalcare). Complete medical, legal, emergency, and travel-related services. On-the-spot payments and special student programs, including benefits for trip cancellation and interruption.

    Travel Assistance International (TAI), by Worldwide Assistance Services, Inc., 1133 15th St. NW, Suite 400, Washington, D.C. 20005-2710 (U.S. tel. (800) 821-2828; fax 828-5896; e-mail wassis@aol.com). 24-hr. hotline for emergencies and referrals. Per-Trip (from US$52) and Frequent Traveler (from US$226) plans include medical, travel, and financial insurance, translation, and lost document/item assistance.

    Travel Guard International, 1145 Clark St., Stevens Point, WI 54481 (tel. (800) 826-1300 or (715) 345-0505; fax (715) 345-0505). Comprehensive insurance programs starting at US$44. Programs cover trip cancellation and interruption, bankruptcy, financial default, lost luggage, medical coverage abroad, emergency assistance, accidental death. 24-hr. hotline.

    Travel Insured International, Inc., 52-S Oakland Ave., P.O. Box 280568, East Hartford, CT 06128-0568 (tel. (800) 243-3174; fax (203) 528-8005). Insurance for accident; baggage loss; sickness; and trip cancellation, interruption, delay, and default. Covers emergency medical evacuation. Automatic flight insurance.

■ Alternatives to Tourism

STUDY

Since the Cold War ceased, foreign study programs have multiplied rapidly in Eastern Europe. Most American undergraduates enroll in programs sponsored by U.S. universities, and many colleges staff offices that provide advice and information on study abroad. Local libraries and bookstores are also helpful sources for current information on study abroad, and the Internet has a study abroad website—http://www.study-abroad.com/liteimage.html. Take advantage of these counselors and put in some hours at their libraries, or request the names of recent program participants and get in touch. Depending on your interests and language skills, though, you may wish to enroll directly in an Eastern European university. This can be much less expensive and a more intense cultural experience. Contact the nearest consulate for a list of institutions in your country of choice. The largest official programs offer study mostly in Russia and the Czech Republic, but you can find the occasional Latvian university exchange. There are also several international and national fellowships available (i.e. Fulbright, Rotary) to fund adventures abroad.

American Field Service (AFS), 220 E. 42nd St., 3rd floor, New York, NY 10017 (U.S. tel. (800) 237-4636 or (212) 876-2376; fax (212) 949-9379; http//www.afs.org/usa). AFS offers summer-, semester-, and year-long homestay international exchange programs for high school students and graduating high-school seniors, and short-term service projects for adults. Financial aid available. Exchanges in Prague and St. Petersburg, as well as in cities around the world.

College Semester Abroad, School for International Training, Admissions, Kipling Rd., P.O. Box 676, Brattleboro, VT 05302 (tel. (800) 336-1616 or 258-3279; fax 258-3500). Runs semester- and year-long programs featuring cultural orientation, intensive language study, homestay, and field and independent study. Programs cost US$8200-10,300, all expenses included. Financial aid available and U.S. university financial aid is transferable. Most U.S. colleges will transfer credit for semester work done abroad. There are programs in the Czech Republic and Russia.

Institute of International Education (IIE), 809 United Nations Plaza, New York, NY 10017-3580 (tel. (212) 984-5413; fax 984-5358). For book orders: IIE Books, Institute of International Education, P.O. Box 371, Annapolis Junction, MD 20701 (tel. (800) 445-0443; fax (301) 953-2838; e-mail iiebooks@iie.org). A nonprofit interna-

PREPARE FOR TAKEOFF!

Launch your overseas English teaching career with certificate training at *The School of Teaching English as a Second Language* in Seattle, Washington.

- Year-round intensive 4-week certificate programs in **Teaching English as a Second or Foreign Language**
- Graduates teaching in more than 30 countries
- Employment information and counseling
- Credits from Seattle University
- Can be applied to master's programs in education at Seattle University
- Bachelor's degree required

write, call, fax, or e-mail the Director of Admissions at

The School of Teaching English as a Second Language

2601 N.W. 56th Street; Seattle, Washington 98107
phone: (206) 781-8607; fax: (206) 781-8922
email: tulare@seattleu.edu

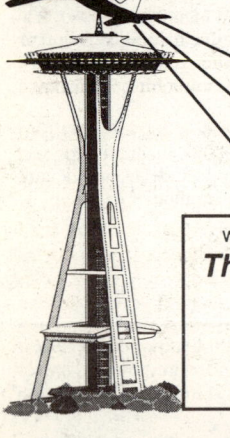

tional and cultural exchange agency. IIE's library of study-abroad resources is open to the public Tues.-Thurs. 11am-3:45pm. Publishes *Academic Year Abroad* (US$43 plus US$4 shipping) detailing over 2300 semester- and year-long programs worldwide and *Vacation Study Abroad* (US$37 plus US$4 shipping), which lists over 1800 short-term, summer, and language programs. Write for a list of publications.

Language Immersion Institute, 75 South Manheim Blvd., The College at New Paltz, New Paltz, NY 12561 (tel. (914) 257-3500; fax 257-3569; e-mail Lii@Newpaltz.edu), provides language instruction at all levels in Yiddish, Czech, Hungarian, Polish, Russian, Ukrainian, and many other languages. Weekend courses offered at New Paltz and in NYC. They also conduct 2-week summer courses and some overseas courses. Program fees are about US$275 for a weekend or US$625 per week for the longer courses.

Youth For Understanding (YFU) International Exchange, 3501 Newark St. NW, Washington, D.C. 20016 (tel. (800) 833-6243) or (202) 966-6800; fax (202) 895-1104; http://www.yfu.org). One of the oldest and largest exchange organizations, YFU has placed over 175,000 high school students between the ages of 14 and 18 with families worldwide for year, semester, summer, and sport homestays.

WORK AND VOLUNTEER

The good news is that there's no better way to immerse yourself in a foreign culture than to become part of its economy. The bad news is that in many Eastern European countries it's difficult to find a temporary unskilled job: even the most menial labor may be taking needed employment away from local citizens. There are opportunities to work in agriculture, as an *au pair,* in summer camps, as an English teacher, or at tourist sites. Be warned: these jobs will rarely be glamorous and may not even pay for your plane ticket over.

On the flip side, many foreign companies are infiltrating Eastern Europe and often require office workers who speak English and are familiar with Western business practices. Before leaving, find out which companies in your country have offices in Eastern Europe and get the name of a contact person in the country that interests you. Once abroad, your best bet is to be brazen and contact the local offices of any foreign company that you come across, and to look for ads in local newspapers. If you speak an Eastern European language, translation jobs are easy to find. Another possibility is to try your luck with the local English-language newspaper.

Teaching English has long been the traditional job for foreign visitors to Eastern Europe. These days, so many foreigners are descending on Prague, Budapest, and Warsaw that finding a position is difficult, but not impossible. Teacher of English as a Foreign Language (TEFL) certification is becoming an increasingly necessary credential. Work in rural areas is easier to find. Students can check with their universities' foreign language departments, which may have official or unofficial connections to job openings abroad. Post a sign in markets or learning centers stating that you are a native speaker, and scan the classifieds of local newspapers, where residents often advertise for language instruction. Various organizations in the U.S. will place you in a (low-paying) teaching job. Professional English-teaching positions are harder to get: many schools require at least a bachelor's degree and training in teaching English as a foreign language.

Like paid jobs, **volunteer** jobs are not necessarily as readily available in Eastern Europe as in the West; nevertheless, they do exist. You may receive room and board in exchange for labor, and the work can be fascinating. Opportunities include community service, workcamp projects, and office work for international organizations. You can sometimes avoid extra fees by contacting workcamps directly; check with the organization. English-language newspapers and some international aid agencies also love unpaid interns. In the war-torn Balkans, you can often simply arrive in an area and find volunteering opportunities on the spot—particularly if you are able to house yourself. Bosnia and Croatia abound with relief organizations that can always use an extra hand; just bring a resumé, and a letter of recommendation. Listed below are some sources providing more detailed information:

28 ■ ALTERNATIVES TO TOURISM

ESSENTIALS

teach English overseas

TEFL teaching course
100+ hours, 4 weeks
international TEFL certificate

no second language required

practical training with foreign students

BA/BS preferred, but not essential

worldwide opportunities

housing available

job guarantee

Prague
a fantastic first step
train and teach in the heart of Europe

ITC

INTERNATIONAL TEFL CERTIFICATE

ITC Prague
Spanielova 1292
163 00 Prague 6
Czech Republic
tel (42 2) 96 14 10 14
fax (42 2) 301 9784
E-mail: praginfo@mbox.vol.cz

ITC Information
655 Powell Street
Suite 505
San Francisco, CA 94108
tel (415) 544-0447
fax (415) 433-4833

call the ITC hotline, a recorded newsletter, 415-789-8336
ITC is an American-owned European school
member Prague American Chamber of Commerce
sessions also in U.S., Mexico, and S.E. Asia

WOMEN TRAVELERS ■ 29

Council (see Travel Organizations, p. 1). Offers 2- to 4-week environmental or community-service projects in the Czech Republic, Lithuania, Poland, Slovenia, and Ukraine through its Voluntary Services Department (US$250-750 placement fee). Participants must be at least 18 years of age.

InterExchange, 161 Sixth Avenue, New York, NY 10013 (tel. (212) 924-0446; fax 924-0575). Provides information in pamphlet form on international work programs and *au pair* positions.

Now Hiring! Jobs in Eastern Europe by Clarke Canfield, is an excellent and comprehensive source of information about all aspects of finding work and accommodations in the Czech Republic, Hungary, Poland, and Slovakia; it can be found in most bookstores (Perpetual Press; US$15; U.S. tel. (800) 807-3030).

Peterson's, Princeton, NJ 08543 (U.S. tel. (800) 338-3282 or elsewhere (609) 243-9111). The *ISS Directory of Overseas Schools* (US$35) is published by International School Services but distributed by Peterson's. The useful annual *Directory of Overseas Summer Jobs* (US$15) and *Work Your Way Around the World* (US$18), are published by Vacation Work Publications but distributed by Peterson's. These books can be requested from a good bookstore or ordered directly from Peterson's (postage US$5.75 for the first book and US$1 for additional ones).

Volunteers for Peace, 43 Tiffany Rd., Belmont, VT 05730 (tel. (802) 259-2759; fax 259-2922; e-mail vfp@vermontel.com; http://www.vfp.org). A non-profit organization that arranges for speedy placement in over 800 workcamps in more than 60 countries worldwide. Many camps last for 2 to 3 weeks, and are for 10 to 15 people. Complete and up-to-date listings are in the annual *International Workcamp Directory* (US$12). Registration fee US$175. Some workcamps are open to 16- and 17-year-olds (US$200 fee). Free newsletter. Programs in Croatia, Czech Republic, Hungary, Lithuania, Poland, Romania, Russia, Slovakia, Slovenia, and Ukraine.

■ Specific Concerns

WOMEN TRAVELERS

Women exploring on their own face additional safety concerns. Always trust your instincts; if you'd feel better somewhere else, move on. Always carry extra money for a phone call, bus, or taxi. Consider staying in hostels which offer single rooms that lock from the inside or in religious organizations that offer rooms for women only; avoid any hostel with "communal" showers. Stick to centrally located accommodations, and avoid late-night treks or metro rides. Hitching is never safe, even for two women traveling together. Choose train compartments occupied by other women or couples, or ask the conductor to put together a women-only compartment.

Single women in Eastern Europe almost never go to restaurants and may be significantly harassed if they do, even at midday. Small cafés and cafeterias are much safer options; even hotel restaurants may be dangerous. In crowds, you may be pinched or squeezed by oversexed slimeballs; wearing a wedding band may help prevent such incidents. The look on your face is the key to avoiding unwanted attention. Feigned deafness, sitting motionless and staring at the ground will do a world of good that no indignant reaction will ever achieve. If need be, turn to an older woman for help in an uncomfortable situation; her stern rebukes will usually be enough to embarrass the most persistent jerks. It's a good idea to observe the way local women dress and to invest in the newest "in" thing, even if you wouldn't dream of wearing it at home. The best way to repulse amorous Eastern European men is to don a *babushka*-style kerchief, tied under the chin.

Don't hesitate to seek out a police officer or a passerby if you are being harassed. Memorize or keep note of the emergency numbers in the countries you visit. Carry a whistle or an airhorn on your keychain, and don't hesitate to use it in an emergency. A **Model Mugging** course will not only prepare you for a potential mugging, but will also raise your level of awareness of your surroundings as well as your confidence (see Safety and Security, p. 18). Women also face additional health concerns when traveling (see Health, p. 19). All of these warnings and suggestions should not discourage women from traveling alone. Be adventurous in your travels, but avoid unnecessary risks

A Journey of One's Own by Thalia Zepatos, (Eighth Mountain Press US$17), The latest thing on the market, interesting and full of good advice, plus a specific and manageable bibliography of books and resources.

Women Travel: Adventures, Advice & Experience by Miranda Davies and Natania Jansz (Penguin, US$13). Info on specific foreign countries plus a decent bibliography and resource index. The sequel, *More Women Travel,* is US$15.

Women Going Places, a women's travel and resource guide emphasizing women-owned enterprises. Geared towards lesbians, but offers advice appropriate for all women. US$14 from Inland Book Company, 1436 W. Randolph St. Chicago, IL 60607 (U.S. tel. (800) 243-0138), or order from a local bookstore.

OLDER TRAVELERS

Seniors are rarely given discounts in Eastern Europe, but it doesn't hurt to ask. Proof of senior citizen status is required for many of the services and discounts below.

Elderhostel, 75 Federal St., 3rd Fl., Boston, MA 02110-1941 (tel. (617) 426-7788; fax 426-8351; http://www.elderhostel.org). For those 55 or over (spouse of any age). Programs at colleges and universities in over 50 countries on varied subjects lasting 1 to 4 weeks.

National Council of Senior Citizens, 1331 F St. NW, Washington, D.C. 20004 (tel. (202) 347-8800). Memberships are US$12 a year, US$30 for three years, or US$150 for a lifetime. Individuals or couples can receive hotel and auto rental discounts, a senior citizen newspaper, use of a discount travel agency, supplemental Medicare insurance (if you're over 65), and a mail-order prescription drug service.

Pilot Books, 103 Cooper St., Babylon, NY 11702 (tel. (516) 422-2225). Publishes a large number of helpful guides including *The International Health Guide for Senior Citizens* (US$5, postage US$2) and *The Senior Citizens' Guide to Budget Travel in Europe* (US$6, postage US$2). Call or write for a complete list of titles.

Unbelievably Good Deals and Great Adventures That You Absolutely Can't Get Unless You're Over 50 by Joan Heilman. After reading the title page, check inside for some great tips on senior discounts, etc. Contemporary Books, US$10.

BISEXUAL, GAY, AND LESBIAN TRAVELERS

Attitudes toward bisexual, gay, and lesbian travelers are, naturally, particular to each country and to the cities within it. Listed below are contact organizations and publishers which offer materials addressing those concerns.

Are You Two...Together? A Gay and Lesbian Travel Guide to Europe. A travel guide with anecdotes and tips for gays and lesbians traveling in Europe. Includes overviews of regional laws relating to gays and lesbians, lists of gay/lesbian organizations, and establishments catering to, friendly to, or indifferent to gays and lesbians. Available in bookstores. Random House, US$18.

Ferrari Publications, Inc., P.O. Box 37887, Phoenix, AZ 85069 (tel. (602) 863-2408; fax 439-3952; e-mail ferrari@q-net.com). Gay and lesbian travel guides: *Ferrari Guides' Gay Travel A to Z* (US $16), *Ferrari Guides' Men's Travel in Your Pocket* (US $14), and *Ferrari Guides' Women's Travel in Your Pocket* (US $14). Available in bookstores or by mail order. Postage/handling US$4.50 for the first item, US$1 for each additional item. Overseas, call or write for shipping cost.

Gay Europe (Perigee Books, US$14). A gay guide providing a quick look at gay life in countries throughout Europe, including restaurants, clubs, and beaches. Intros to each country cover laws and gay-friendliness. Available in bookstores.

Gay's the Word, 66 Marchmont St., London WC1N 1AB (tel. (0171) 278 7654). The largest gay and lesbian bookshop in the U.K. Mail-order service available. No catalog of listings, but they will provide a list of titles on a given subject.

Giovanni's Room, 345 S. 12th St. Philadelphia, PA 19107 (tel. (215) 923-2960; fax 923-0813; e-mail gilphilp@netaxs.com). International feminist, lesbian, and gay bookstore with many of the books listed here. Call or write for a free catalogue.

International Gay Travel Association, Box 4974, Key West, FL 33041 (U.S. tel. (800) 448-8550; fax (305) 296-6633; e-mail IGTA@aol.com; http://www.rainbow-mall.com/igta). An organization of over 1100 companies serving gay and lesbian travelers worldwide. Call for lists of travel agents, accommodations, and events.

International Lesbian and Gay Association, 81 rue Marché-au-Charbon, B-1000 Bruxelles, Belgium (tel./fax (02) 502 24 71). Not a travel service. Provides cultural information, such as homosexuality laws of individual countries.

Spartacus International Gay Guides (US$33), published by Bruno Gmünder, Postfach 110729, D-10837 Berlin, Germany (tel. (30) 615 00 30; fax 615 91 34). Lists bars, restaurants, hotels, and bookstores around the world catering to gays. Also lists hotlines for gays in various countries and homosexuality laws for each country. Available in bookstores and by mail from Giovanni's Room (see above).

DISABLED TRAVELERS

Countries vary in their general accessibility to travelers with disabilities—Eastern Europe tends to be relatively inaccessible. Contact your destination's consulate or tourist office in advance for information. Call ahead to restaurants, hotels, parks, and other facilities to find out about the existence of ramps, the width of doors, etc.

Arrange transportation well in advance to ensure a smooth trip. If you give sufficient notice, some major car rental agencies offer hand-controlled vehicles at select locations. Guide-dog owners should inquire as to the specific quarantine policies of each destination country. At the very least, they will need to provide a certificate of immunization against rabies. The following organizations provide information or publications that might be of assistance:

Graphic Language Press, P.O. Box 270, Cardiff by the Sea, CA 92007 (tel. (619) 944-9594). Publishers of *Wheelchair Through Europe* (US$13). Comprehensive advice for the wheelchair-bound traveler. Specifics on wheelchair-related resources and accessible sites in various cities throughout Europe.

The Guided Tour Inc., Elkins Park House, Suite 114B, 7900 Old York Road, Elkins Park, PA 19027-2339 (U.S. tel. (800) 783-5841 or (215) 782-1370; (215) fax 635-2637). Organizes travel programs for persons with developmental and physical challenges and those requiring renal dialysis. Call, fax, or write for a free brochure.

Mobility International, USA (MIUSA), P.O. Box 10767, Eugene, OR 97440 (tel. (503) 343-1284 voice and TDD; fax 343-6812). International headquarters in Brussels, rue de Manchester 25, Brussels, Belgium, B-1070 (tel (322) 41 06 297; fax 41 06 874). Contacts in 30 countries. Information on travel programs, international workcamps, accommodations, access guides, and organized tours for those with physical disabilities. Membership US$25 per year. Newsletter US$15. Sells the periodically updated and expanded *A World of Options: A Guide to International Educational Exchange, Community Service, and Travel for Persons with Disabilities* (US$14, nonmembers US$16). In addition, MIUSA offers a series of courses that teach on-the-road strategies helpful for travelers with disabilities.

Moss Rehabilitation Hospital Travel Information Service (tel. (215) 456-9600; TDD 456-9602). A telephone information resource center on international travel accessibility and other travel-related concerns for those with disabilities. If Moss Rehab cannot provide information, it refers callers to other agencies.

Society for the Advancement of Travel for the Handicapped (SATH), 347 Fifth Ave. #610, New York, NY 10016 (tel. (212) 447-7284; fax 725-8253). Publishes quarterly travel newsletter *SATH News* and information booklets (free for members; US$3 each for nonmembers) with advice on trip planning for people with disabilities. Annual membership US$45, students and seniors US$25.

Twin Peaks Press, P.O. Box 129, Vancouver, WA 98666-0129 (tel. (360) 694-2462; orders only with MC or Visa (800) 637-2256; fax (360) 696-3210). Publishers of *Travel for the Disabled,* which provides travel tips, lists of accessible tourist attractions, and advice on other resources for disabled travelers (US$20). Also publishes the *Directory for Travel Agencies of the Disabled* (US$20), *Wheelchair Vagabond* (US$15), and *Directory of Accessible Van Rentals* (US$10). Postage US$3 for first book, US$1.50 for each additional book.

KOSHER AND VEGETARIAN TRAVELERS

Vegetarian and kosher travelers will have their work cut out for them in Eastern Europe. Most of the national cuisines tend to be meat- and especially pork-heavy. Markets are always a safe bet for fresh vegetables, fruit, cheese, and bread (one word of warning: *watch for veggies grown near the Chernobyl region*—ask the sellers where they are from).

Travelers who keep **kosher** should contact synagogues in larger cities for information on kosher restaurants; your own synagogue or college Hillel should have access to lists of Jewish institutions across Eastern Europe. If you are strict in your observance, consider preparing your own food on the road.

- **The European Vegetarian Guide to Restaurants and Hotels** (US$13.95, plus US$1.75 shipping) is available from the Vegetarian Times Bookshelf (U.S. tel. (800) 435-9610, orders only).
- **The International Vegetarian Travel Guide** (UK£2) was last published in 1991. Order back copies from the Vegetarian Society of the UK (VSUK), Parkdale, Dunham Rd., Altrincham, Cheshire WA14 4QG (tel. (0161) 928 0793). VSUK also publishes other titles, including *The European Vegetarian Guide to Hotels and Restaurants*. Call or write for information.
- **The Jewish Travel Guide** (US$12, postage US$1.75), lists synagogues, kosher restaurants, and Jewish institutions in over 80 countries. Available from Ballantine-Mitchell Publishers, Newbury House 890-900, Eastern Ave., Newbury Park, Ilford, Essex, U.K. IG2 7HH (tel. (0181) 599 8866; fax 599 0984). It is available in the U.S. from Sepher-Hermon Press, 1265 46th St., Brooklyn, NY 11219 (tel. (718) 972-9010; US$13.95 plus US$2.50 shipping).

MINORITY TRAVELERS

The most ill-regarded minority in Eastern Europe are Gypsies *(Romany)*. Travelers with darker skin of any nationality might be mistaken for Gypsies and face some of the same unpleasant consequences. Other minority travelers, especially those of African or Asian descent, will usually meet more curiosity than hostility, especially outside of big cities. Travelers of Arab ethnicity may be treated more suspiciously. Skinheads are on the rise in Eastern Europe, and minority travelers should regard them with caution. This is one of the few occasions where it might be useful to play up your Westernness.

■ Packing

If you want to get away from it all, don't take it all with you.

PACK LIGHT! The more you know, the less you need, so plan your packing according to the type of travel and the high and low temperatures in the area you will be visiting. The more you have, the more you have to carry and the more you have to lose. Eschew colorful luggage that screams "rich-Western-tourist" for boring brown or drab grey to keep muggers away. The larger your pack, the more cumbersome it is to store safely. Before you leave, pack your bag, strap it on, and imagine walking uphill on hot asphalt for hours. At the least sign of heaviness, unpack something. A general rule is to pack only what you think you absolutely need, then take half the clothes and twice the money.

LUGGAGE

Backpack: If you plan to cover most ground by foot, a sturdy backpack is unbeatable. Some convert into suitcases, which can be useful on planes or trains. In general, **internal-frame** packs are easier to carry and more efficient for general traveling purposes. If you'll be doing extensive camping or hiking, you may want to consider an **external-frame** pack, which offers added support, distributes weight better, and allows a sleeping bag to be strapped on. If you are checking any backpack, tie down loose parts to minimize risk. When carried correctly, a pack's weight should rest entirely on your hips. Always avoid excessively low-end prices—you get what you pay for. Quality packs cost from US$125-420.

Suitcase/trunk/other large or heavy luggage: Fine if you plan to live in one or two cities and explore from there, but a bad idea if you're going to be moving around a lot. Features to look for: wheels on suitcases, PVC frame for soft luggage, and the 3 main characteristics of any good piece of luggage: weight, durability, and maneuverability. Remember: you bring it, you carry it.

Shoulder bag: If you aren't backpacking, an empty, lightweight duffel bag packed inside your luggage will be useful: once abroad you can fill your luggage with purchases and keep your dirty clothes in the duffel.

Daypack or courier bag: An essential. Bringing a smaller bag in addition to your pack or suitcase allows you to leave your big bag in the hostel while you go sightseeing and keep your valuables with you. More importantly, it can be used as an airplane carry-on; keep the absolute bare essentials with you to avoid the lost-luggage blues. Try a handbag instead of the "yes, I am a foreigner" school backpack.

Moneybelt or neck pouch: Guard your money, passport, railpass, and other important articles in either one of these, and keep it with you *at all times*. Moneybelts and neck pouches are available at any good camping store. See Safety and Security, p. 18 for more information on protecting you and your valuables.

CLOTHING AND FOOTWEAR

Comfortable **shoes** are crucial. Do not bring flashy Nikes or Reeboks to Eastern Europe, especially to the former Soviet Union. They will brand you a tourist and a target for theft (and will make it difficult for you to pass as a local in hotels and museums that charge higher rates for foreigners). In hot, summer weather **sandals** or other light shoes serve well. It might be worth the extra bulk to carry two pairs of shoes: you might not want to go out in the same shoes you've been trekking in all day. For heavy-duty hiking, sturdy lace-up **walking boots** are necessary. Make sure they have good ventilation. A double pair of **socks**—light absorbent cotton inside and thick wool outside—will cushion feet, keep them dry, and help prevent blisters. Bring a pair of light **flip-flops** for protection against the fungal floors of hostel and hotel showers. In wet regions, **raingear** is essential. A waterproof jacket plus a backpack rain cover will take care of you and your pack at a moment's notice.

MISCELLANEOUS

Carry extra toiletries—especially aspirin, razor blades, and tampons—and either buy or bring toilet paper. Eastern European trains are grimier than those in the West and the toilet facilities are unreliable. Trains are not air-conditioned, and on-board soft drinks are overpriced. Bring a full, sturdy plastic **water-bottle**. Also consider taking the following items: pocketknife, needle and thread, safety pins, masking tape, umbrella, garbage bags, **contact lens supplies,** a rubber squash ball to stop up the sink, flashlight, cutlery (for use in hostels), cold-water soap, an alarm clock, a bath towel, bags that seal shut (for damp clothing, soaps, or messy foods), sunglasses, earplugs, sunscreen, and a padlock. It is always a good idea to bring along a **first-aid kit.** Pack extra rolls of **film:** it can be quite expensive in well touristed areas. And don't forget your travel journal! You might not believe it at the moment, but the day will come when you'll want to remember that 1000th church or castle you visited or that horrifying face rash you picked up in Budapest.

Across Eastern Europe, **electricity** is 220 volts AC, enough to fry any 110V North American appliance. Visit a hardware store for an adaptor (which changes the shape of the plug) and a converter (which changes the voltage). Do not make the mistake of using only an adaptor, or you'll melt your radio.

GETTING THERE

Finding a cheap airfare to Eastern Europe in the airline industry's computerized jungle will be easier if you understand the airlines' systems better than they think you do. Call every toll-free number you find and ask about discounts. Have a knowledgeable travel agent guide you. Better yet, have several knowledgeable travel agents guide you. Remember that travel agents may not want to do the legwork to find the cheapest fares (for which they receive the lowest commissions). Students and people under 26 should never pay full price for a ticket. Seniors can also get great deals; many airlines offer senior traveler clubs or airline passes and discounts for their companions as well. Major Sunday newspapers have travel sections that list bargain fares from the local airport. Outsmart airline reps with the phonebook-sized *Official Airline Guide* (check your local library), a monthly guide listing nearly every scheduled flight in the world (with prices) and toll-free numbers for all the airlines that allow you to call in reservations directly. On the web, try the **Air Traveler's Handbook** (http://www.cis.ohio-state.edu/hypertext/faq/usenet/travel/air/handbook/top.html) for complete information on air travel.

Most airfares peak between mid-June and early September. Mid-week (Mon.-Thurs. morning) flights run about US$40-50 cheaper each way than on weekends. Traveling from larger cities or travel hubs will almost always win a more competitive fare than from smaller cities. Return-date flexibility is usually not an option for the budget traveler; except on youth fares purchased through the airlines, traveling with an "open return" ticket can be pricier than fixing a return date and paying to change it. Be wary of one-way tickets, too: the flight to Europe may be economical, but the return fares are outrageous. Whenever flying internationally, pick up your ticket well in advance of the departure date, have the flight confirmed within 72 hours of departure, and arrive at the airport at least two hours before your flight.

PETRS - TRAVEL AGENCY

Legerova 48, Praha 2

(Corner of the streets Legerova and Rumunská, two stations from main railway station)

OPEN DAILY 9 am. - 8 pm.

Tel./Fax: ++ 42 / 2 / 29 10 57, Fax:: 25 85 96

Travel agency with five years tradition offers accommodation in privat rooms and pensions from **300,- Kč (CZK) pro person.** We also offer **10% discount for all cultural performances** (theatres, concerts, galeries, cinemas, etc.) and in some selected restaurants in Prague.

■ Budget Travel Agencies

Students and people under 26 ("youth") with proper ID qualify for enticing reduced airfares. These are rarely available from airlines or travel agents, but instead from student travel agencies like **Council Travel, Let's Go Travel, STA, Travel CUTS,** and **USTN**. These agencies negotiate special, reduced-rate bulk purchases with the airlines, then resell them to the youth market; in 1996, peak-season round-trip rates from the East Coast of North America to even the offbeat corners of Europe rarely topped US$800 and off-season fares were considerably lower. Return-date change fees also tend to be low (around US$25 per segment). Most flights are on major airlines, though in peak season some agencies may sell seats on less reliable chartered aircraft. Student travel agencies can also help non-students and people over 26, but probably won't get them the same low fares.

Council Travel (http://www.ciee.org/cts/ctshome/htm), the travel division of Council, is a full-service travel agency specializing in youth and budget travel. They offer railpasses, discount airfares, hosteling cards, guidebooks, budget tours, travel gear, and student (ISIC), youth (GO 25), and teacher (ITIC) identity cards. U.S. offices include Emory Village, 1561 N. Decatur Rd., **Atlanta**, GA 30307 (tel. (404) 377-9997); 2000 Guadalupe, **Austin**, TX 78705 (tel. (512) 472-4931); 273 Boylston St., **Boston**, MA 02116 (tel. (617) 266-1926); 1138 13th St., **Boulder**, CO 80302 (tel. (303) 447-8101); 1153 N. Dearborn, **Chicago**, IL 60610 (tel. (312) 951-0585); 10904 Linbrook Dr., **Los Angeles**, CA 90024 (tel. (310) 208-3551); 1501 University Ave. SE, **Minneapolis**, MN 55414 (tel. (612) 379-2323); 205 E. 42nd St., **New York**, NY 10017 (tel. (212) 822-2700); 3606A Chestnut St., **San Diego**, CA 92109 (tel. (619) 270-6401); 530 Bush St., **San Francisco**, CA 94108 (tel. (415) 421-3473); 1314 N.E. 43rd St., **Seattle**, WA 98105 (tel. (206) 632-2448); 3300 M St. NW, **Washington, D.C.** 20007 (tel. (202) 337-65464). For **U.S. cities not listed**, call 800-2-COUNCIL (226-8624). Overseas offices include: 28A Poland St. (Oxford Circus), **London**, W1V 3DB (tel. (0171) 437 7767); 22, Rue des Pyramides 75001 **Paris** (01 44 55 55 65); **Munich** (tel. (089) 39 50 22); **Tokyo** (3 35 81 55 17); **Singapore** (65 738 70 66).

Council Charter, 205 E. 42nd St., New York, NY 10017 (tel. (212) 661-0311; fax 972-0194). Offers a combination of inexpensive charter and scheduled airfares from a variety of U.S. gateways to most major European destinations. One-way fares and open jaws (fly into one city and out of another) are available.

Let's Go Travel, Harvard Student Agencies, 67 Mount Auburn St., Cambridge, MA 02138 (U.S. tel. 800-5-LETS GO/553-8746) or (617) 495-9649). Railpasses, HI-AYH memberships, ISICs, ITICs, GO25 cards, guidebooks (including *Let's Go*), maps, bargain flights, and a complete line of budget travel gear. All items available by mail; call or write for a catalog (or see the catalog in center of this publication).

Rail Europe Inc., 226 Westchester Ave., White Plains, NY 10604 (U.S. tel. (800) 438-7245; fax 432-1329; http://www.raileurope.com). Sells all Eurail products and passes, national railpasses, and point-to-point tickets. Up-to-date information on all rail travel in Europe, including Eurostar, the English Channel train.

STA Travel, 6560 Scottsdale Rd. #F100, Scottsdale, AZ 85253 (U.S. tel. (800) 777-0112; fax (602) 922-0793). A student and youth travel organization with over 100 offices worldwide offering discount airfares for young travelers, railpasses, accommodations, tours, insurance, and ISICs. 16 offices in the U.S. including: 297 Newbury Street, **Boston**, MA 02115 (tel. (617) 266-6014); 429 S. Dearborn St., **Chicago**, IL 60605 (tel. (312) 786-9050; 7202 Melrose Ave., **Los Angeles**, CA 90046 (tel. (213) 934-8722); 10 Downing St., Ste. G, **New York**, NY 10003 (tel. (212) 627-3111); 4341 University Way NE, Seattle, WA 98105 (tel. (206) 633-5000); 2401 Pennsylvania Ave., **Washington, D.C.** 20037 (tel. (202) 887-0912); 51 Grant Ave., **San Francisco**, CA 94108 (tel. (415) 391-8407), **Miami**, FL 33133 (tel. (305) 461-3444). In the U.K., 6 Wrights Ln., **London** W8 6TA (tel. (0171) 938 4711 for North American travel). In New Zealand, 10 High St., **Auckland** (tel. (09) 309 97 23). In Australia, 222 Faraday St., **Melbourne** VIC 3050 (tel. (03) 349 69 11).

Travel CUTS (Canadian Universities Travel Services Limited): 187 College St., **Toronto,** Ont. M5T 1P7 (tel. (416) 979-2406; fax 979-8167). Canada's national student travel bureau and equivalent of Council, with 40 offices across Canada. Also in the U.K., 295-A Regent St., **London** W1R 7YA (tel. (0171) 637 3161). Discounted domestic and international airfares open to all; special student fares to all destinations with valid ISIC. Issues ISIC, GO25, and HI hostel cards, as well as railpasses. Offers free *Student Traveller* magazine, as well as information on the Student Work Abroad Program (SWAP).

Usit Youth and Student Travel, 19-21 Aston Quay, O'Connell Bridge, **Dublin** 2 (tel. (01) 677 8117; fax 679 8833). In the U.S.: New York Student Center, 895 Amsterdam Ave., **New York,** NY 10025 (tel. (212) 663-5435). **Additional offices** in Cork, Galway, Limerick, Waterford, Maynooth, Coleraine, Derry, Athlone, Jordanstown, Belfast, and Greece. Specializes in youth and student travel. Low-cost tickets and flexible travel arrangements all over the world. Sells ISIC and GO25 cards.

■ By Plane

COMMERCIAL AIRLINES

Even if you pay the airline's lowest published fare, you may waste hundreds of dollars. For the adventurous or the bargain-hungry, there are other, perhaps more inconvenient or time-consuming, options. Before shopping around, it's a good idea to find out the average commercial price in order to measure just how great a "bargain" you are being offered.

The commercial airlines' lowest regular offer is the **APEX** (Advance Purchase Excursion Fare); specials advertised in newspapers may be cheaper, but have more restrictions and fewer available seats. APEX fares provide you with confirmed reservations and allow "open-jaw" tickets (landing in and returning from different cities). Generally, reservations must be made 7-21 days in advance, with 7- to 14-day mini-

---

EUROCENTRES

Live & Learn Russian Overseas

● Moscow ● Moscow ● Moscow

Whether beginning or advanced, our 2-12 week language & culture immersion programs will give you the opportunity to explore Russia as a local.

Students of all ages from around the world study 20 hours per week.

Optional excursions, and afternoon electives in history, art or business language.

Host Families & College Credit available

(703)-684-1494 or **(800) 648-4809** in the USA
(41) 1 485 50 40 in Europe

www.clark.net/pub/eurocent/home.htm

mum and up to 90-day maximum stay limits, as well as hefty cancellation and change penalties. For summer travel, book APEX fares early; by May you will have a hard time getting the departure date you want.

Look into flights to less-popular destinations or on smaller carriers. **Icelandair** (U.S. tel. (800) 223-5500) has last-minute offers and a stand-by fare from New York to Luxembourg (April-June 15 and Sept.-Oct. US$398; June 15-Aug. US$598). Reservations must be made within three days of departure.

EASTERN EUROPEAN AIRLINES

The safety and service of airlines in Eastern Europe varies wildly. Some airlines have completely modernized since 1989 and operate according to Western standards; others have seen safety and service deteriorate. Be careful when choosing a carrier. In April 1994 the International Airline Passenger Association advised travelers to avoid air travel in the former Soviet Union because of declining safety standards. Check with your travel agent to insure that you are traveling on a safe airline. For information on individual national airlines, see the "Getting There" sections of each country.

CHARTER FLIGHTS AND CONSOLIDATORS

Ticket consolidators resell unsold tickets on commercial and charter airlines. Look for their tiny ads in weekend papers (the *Sunday Times* in New York or London is best), and start calling them all. In London, the real "bucket shop" center, the Air Travel Advisory Bureau (tel. (0171) 636 5000) provides a list of consolidators. There is rarely a maximum age or stay limit; tickets are also heavily discounted, and may offer extra flexibility or bypass advance purchase requirements, since you aren't tangled in airline bureaucracy. But unlike tickets bought through an airline, you won't be able to use your tickets on another flight if you miss yours, and you will have to go back to the consolidator, rather than the airline, to get a refund.

Be a smart and careful shopper. Contact the local Better Business Bureau to find out how long the company has been in business and its track record. Ask to receive your tickets as quickly as possible so you have time to fix any problems. Get the company's policy in writing: insist on a **receipt** that gives full details about the tickets, refunds, and restrictions, and record the full name of who you talked to and when. It may be worth paying with a credit card (despite the 2-5% fee) so you can stop payment if you never receive your tickets. Ask also about accommodations and car rental discounts; some consolidators have fingers in many pies. Consult Kelly Monaghan's *Consolidators: Air Travel's Bargain Basement* (US$7, plus US$2 shipping) from the Intrepid Traveler, P.O. Box 438, New York, NY 10034 (e-mail intreptrav@aol.com), a valuable source for more information and lists of consolidators by location and destination. Cyber-resources Edward Hasbrouck's incredibly informative web site (http://www.gnn.com/gnn/wic/wics/trav.97.html).

For destinations worldwide, try **Airfare Busters** in Washington, D.C. (tel. (800) 776-0481), Boca Raton, FL (tel. (800) 881-3273), and Houston, TX (tel. (232-8783); **Pennsylvania Travel,** Paoli, PA (tel. (800) 331-0947); **Cheap Tickets** in Los Angeles, CA, San Francisco, CA, Honolulu, HI, Overland Park, KS, and New York, NY (tel. (800) 377-1000); **Moment's Notice,** New York, NY (tel. (718) 234-6295; fax 234-6450). For a processing fee, depending on the number of travelers and the itinerary, **Travel Avenue,** Chicago, IL (tel. (800) 333-3335), searches for the lowest international airfare available and even gives you a rebate on fares over US$300.

The theory behind a **charter** is that a tour operator contracts with an airline to fly extra loads of passengers to peak-season destinations. Charter flights fly less frequently than major airlines and have more restrictions, particularly on refunds. They are also almost always fully booked, and schedules and itineraries may change or be cancelled at the last moment (as late as 48 hours before the flight, and without a full refund); you'll be much better off purchasing a ticket on a regularly scheduled airline. Consider travelers' insurance against trip interruption. As always, pay with a credit card. It's best to buy from an organization that has experience with charter flights.

Try **Travac** (U.S. tel. (800) 872-8800, **Interworld** (tel. (305) 443-4929), or **Rebel** (U.S. tel. (800) 227-3235). Don't be afraid to call every number to find the best deal.

STAND-BY FLIGHTS

Airhitch, 2641 Broadway, 3rd Floor, New York, NY 10025 (tel. (800) 326-2009 or (212) 864-2000) and Los Angeles, CA (tel. (310) 726-5000), will add a certain thrill to the prospects of when you leave and where exactly you will end up. Complete flexibility on both sides of the Atlantic is necessary. Flights cost US$169 each way when departing from the Northeast, US$269 from the West Coast or Northwest, and US$229 from the Southeast or Midwest. The snag is that you don't buy a ticket, but the promise that you will get to a destination near where you're intending to go within a window of time (usually 5 days) from a location in a region you've specified. You call in before your date-range to hear all of your flight options for the next seven days and your probability of boarding. You then decide which flights you want to try to make and present a voucher at the airport which grants you the right to board a flight on a space-available basis. This procedure must be followed again for the return trip. You may only receive a refund if all available flights which departed within your date and destination-range were full. There are several offices in Europe, so you can wait to register for your return; the main one is in Paris (tel. 01 47 00 16 30).

Air-Tech, Ltd., 584 Broadway #1007, New York, NY 10012 (tel. (212) 219-7000; fax 219-0066), offers a similar service. Their Travel Window is one to four days; rates to and from Europe (continually updated; call and verify) are: Northeast US$169; West Coast US$249; Midwest/Southeast US$199. Upon registration and payment, Air-Tech sends you a FlightPass with a contact date falling soon before your Travel Window, when you are to call them for flight instructions. This service is one-way—you must go through the same procedure to return—and *no refunds* are granted unless the company fails to get you a seat before your Travel Window expires. Air-Tech also arranges courier flights and regular confirmed-reserved flights at discount rates. Be sure to read all the fine print in your agreements with either company—a call to The Better Business Bureau of New York City may be worthwhile. Be warned that it is difficult to receive refunds, and that clients' vouchers will not be honored if an airline fails to receive payment in time.

Eleventh-hour **discount clubs** and **fare brokers** offer members savings on travel, including charter flights and tour packages. Research your options carefully. **Last Minute Travel Club**, 1249 Boylston St., Boston, MA 02215 (U.S. tel. (800) 527-8646 or (617) 267-9800), and **Discount Travel International**, New York, NY (tel. (212) 362-3636; fax 362-3236), are among the few travel clubs that don't charge a membership fee. For a fee, you can join **Moment's Notice**, New York, NY (tel. (718) 234-6295; fax 234 6450; US$25 annual fee), **Travelers Advantage**, Stanford, CT, (U.S. tel. (800) 835-8747; US$49 annual fee), and **Travel Avenue** (U.S. tel. (800) 333-3335; see Ticket Consolidators, above). Study your contracts closely; you don't want to end up with an unwanted overnight layover—or worse.

COURIER COMPANIES

Those who travel light should consider flying as a **courier**. The company hiring you will use your checked luggage space for freight; you're only allowed to bring carry-ons. You must be over 18, procure your own visa (if necessary) and have a valid passport. Most flights are roundtrip only with short fixed-length stays and are from New York. Roundtrip fares to Western Europe from the U.S. range from US$250-400 (off-season) to US$400-550 (summer). **NOW Voyager**, 74 Varick St. #307, New York, NY 10013 (tel. (212) 431-1616), acts as an agent for courier flights worldwide, and offers last-minute deals to such cities as London, Paris, and Frankfurt for as little as US$200 roundtrip plus a US$50 registration fee. Other agents to try are **Halbart Express**, 147-05 176th St., Jamaica, NY 11434 (tel. (718) 656-5000), and **Courier Travel Service**, 530 Central Ave., Cedarhurst, NY 11516 (tel. (516) 763-6898).

You can also go directly through courier companies in New York, or check your bookstore or library for handbooks such as *Air Courier Bargains* (US$15, plus US$3.50 shipping) from the Intrepid Traveler, P.O. Box 438, New York, NY 10034. *The Courier Air Travel Handbook* (US$10, plus US$3.50 shipping) explains traveling as an air courier and contains names, phone numbers, and contact points of courier companies. It can be ordered from Bookmasters, Inc., P.O. Box 2039, Mansfield, OH 44905 (U.S. tel. (800) 507-2665).

ONCE THERE

■ Travel in the Region

BY PLANE

Unless you're under 26, flying across Eastern Europe on regularly scheduled flights will eat your budget. If you are 25 or under, special fares on most European airlines requiring ticket purchase either the day before or the day of departure will merely gnaw at your funds. These are often cheaper than the corresponding regular train fares, though not always as cheap as student rail tickets or railpasses. Student travel agencies also sell cheap tickets. Consult budget travel agents and local newspapers and magazines. London's **Air Travel Advisory Bureau** (tel. (0171) 636 5000) can put you in touch with discount flights for free. In addition, many European airlines offer visitor ticket packages, which give intercontinental passengers discount rates on flights within Europe after arrival. Check with a travel agent for details.

BY TRAIN

Many train stations have different counters for domestic and international tickets, seat reservations, and information; check before lining up. On major routes, reservations are always advisable, and often required, even with a railpass; make them at least a few hours in advance at the train station (usually less than US$3). In the former Soviet Union, you may need to purchase tickets days in advance.

Railpasses You may find it tough to make your railpass pay for itself in Eastern Europe, where train fares are rising quickly, but still reasonable. Ideally conceived, a railpass allows you to jump on any train in Europe, go wherever you want whenever you want, and change your plans at will. The handbook that comes with your railpass tells you everything you need to know and includes a timetable for major routes, a map, and details on ferry discounts. In practice, of course, it's not so simple. You still must stand in line to pay for seat reservations, supplements, and couchette reservations, as well as to have your pass validated when you first use it. More importantly, railpasses don't always pay off. Find a travel agent with a copy of the **Eurail tariff manual** to weigh the wisdom of purchasing them. Add up the second-class fares for your planned routes and deduct 5% (listed prices automatically include commission) for comparison.

Eurailpass covers only Hungary in Eastern Europe, while the **European East Pass** covers Poland, the Czech Republic, Slovakia, and Hungary. You'll almost certainly find it easiest to buy a pass before you arrive in Europe. Contact Council Travel, Travel CUTS, or Let's Go Travel (see Useful Publications, p. 4), or other travel agents. **Rail Europe,** 226-300 Westchester Ave., White Plains, NY 10604 (tel. (800) 432-1329 and (800) 361-7245; Canada fax (905) 602-4298) provides extensive information on pass options and publishes the *Europe on Track* booklet. Rail Europe also offers several passes that are good for one or a combination of Eastern European countries for various durations and prices.

NORWAY
Oslo
FINLAND
Helsinki
Aland Island
Lake Ladoga
Vyborg
St. Petersburg
SWEDEN
Stockholm
Tallinn
ESTONIA
Tartu
Pärnu
Novgorod
Pskov
Skagerrak
Kattegat
Alborg
Göteborg
Gotland Island
Ventspils
Gulf of Riga
Riga
Öland
Liepaja
Jelgava
LATVIA
Copenhagen
DENMARK
Malmö
LITHUANIA
Polatsk
Kaunas
Kaliningrad
(RUS.)
Vilnius
Minsk
Mahileu
Sopot
Gdańsk
Olsztyn
Hrodna
BELARUS
Hamburg
Szczecin
Białystok
Zhlobin
Baranavichy
Berlin
Toruń
Luninets
Poznań
Warsaw
Frankfurt
POLAND
Brest
Łodź
Leipzig
Dresden
Kovel
Sarny
Wrocław
Lublin
Korosten
GERMANY
Rovno
Prague
Kraków
Przemyśl
Lviv
CZECH REP.
Brno
Plezň
SLOVAKIA
Vienna
Bratislava
Mukacheve
Munich
Salzburg
Satu Mare
Budapest
AUSTRIA
MOLDOVA
Chişinău
Vaduz
HUNGARY
Graz
Oradea
Cluj-Napoca
Bacău
ROMANIA
SLOVENIA
Ljubljana
Szeged
Sighişoara
Venice
Pécs
Trieste
Zagreb
Braşov
Tulcea
Po R.
Timişoara
Buzău
Pula
Rijeka
Belgrade
Tîrgu Jiu
SAN MARINO
CROATIA
BOSNIA-HERZEGOVINA
Bucharest
Zenica
Zadar
Sarajevo
Craiova
Constanta
Split
Ruse
YUGOSLAVIA
Mostar
Varna
Nis
Pec
BULGARIA
Sofia
Burgas
Dubrovnik
Stara Zagora
Malko Turnovo
Shkodër
Skopje
Plovdiv
Rome
VATICAN CITY
ITALY
Tirana
F.Y.R. MACEDONIA
Durrës
ALBANIA
Korcë
Thessaloniki
Naples
N
0
200 miles
0
200 kilometers
Gjirokastër
GREECE
AEGEAN SEA

BY TRAIN ■ 41

Railways of Eastern Europe

ESSENTIALS

42 ■ TRAVEL IN THE REGION

WITH OUR RAIL PASSES YOU'LL HAVE UP TO 70% MORE MONEY TO WASTE.

With savings of up to 70% off the price of point to point tickets, you'll be laughing all the way to the souvenir stand. Rail passes are available for travel throughout Europe or the country of your choice and we'll even help you fly there. So all you'll have to do is leave some extra room in your suitcase. To learn more call **1-800-4-EURAIL (1-800-438-7245).**

Rail Europe

Discount rail tickets For travelers under 26, **BIJ** tickets (Billets Internationals de Jeunesse; sold under the names **Wasteels, Eurotrain,** and **Route 26**) are a great alternative to railpasses. Available for international trips within Europe as well as most ferry services, they knock 25-40% off regular second-class fares. Tickets are good for 60 days after purchase and allow a number of stopovers (no longer unlimited) along the normal direct route of the train journey. Issued for a specific international route between two points, they must be used in the direction and order of the designated route without side- or back-tracking. You must buy BIJ tickets in Europe. They are available from European travel agents, at Wasteels or Eurotrain offices (usually in or near train stations), or occasionally at ticket counters. Contact Wasteels in London's Victoria Station for more information (tel. (0171) 834 7066; fax 630 7628).

Useful Resources The ultimate reference for planning rail trips is the **Thomas Cook European Timetable** (US$28; US$39 includes a map of Europe highlighting all train and ferry routes; plus US$4.50 shipping). This timetable, updated seasonally, covers all major and most minor train routes in Europe. In the U.S., order it from the Forsyth Travel Library (see Useful Publications, p. 4). Available in most bookstores or from Houghton Mifflin Co., 222 Berkeley St., Boston, MA 02116 (tel. (617) 351-5974; fax 351-1113) is the annual **Eurail Guide to Train Travel in the New Europe** (US$15), giving timetables, instructions, and prices for international train trips, day-trips, and excursions in Europe. The annual railpass special edition of Rick Steves' free **Europe Through the Back Door** travel newsletter and catalog (tel. (206) 771-8303; fax 771-0833; e-mail ricksteves@aol.com; http://www.halcyon.com) provides a comprehensive comparative analysis of railpasses with national or regional passes and point-to-point tickets sold in Europe. Contact 120 Fourth Ave. N., P.O. Box 2009, Edmonds, WA 98020. **Hunter Publishing,** 300 Raritan Center Parkway, Edison, NJ 08818 (tel. (908) 225-1900; fax 417-0482), offers a catalog of rail atlases and travel guides including Eastern Europe by Rail, and country-specific materials.

BY BUS

Though trains are extremely popular, long-distance bus networks may be more extensive, efficient, and often more comfortable than train services. All over Eastern Europe, short-haul buses reach rural areas inaccessible by train. In the Balkans, air-conditioned buses run by private companies are a godsend. **Eurolines,** 4 Cardiff Road, Luton LU1 1PP (tel. (01582) 404 511, in London (0171) 730 8235), Europe's largest operator of coach services offers passes for unlimited 30- or 60- day travel between 18 major tourist destinations, including spots in Eastern Europe and Russia.

BY CAR

Cars offer speed, freedom, access to the countryside, and an escape from the town-to-town mentality of trains. Unfortunately, they also insulate you from the *esprit de corps* rail travelers enjoy and subject to the dangers of road travel in Eastern Europe. Rail Europe and other railpass vendors also offer economical **rail-and-drive** packages for both individual countries and all of Europe. The availability of **rental cars** varies across Eastern Europe, and rates there are the most expensive in Europe—and we do mean *expensive.* One option is to rent a car in a Western European country and drive it eastward if the rental agreement allows. However, a loss/damage waiver then becomes mandatory. Car-rental agencies in the Balkans often require you to rent a driver along with the car. The former Soviet Union is generally off-limits to cars rented in the West.

You can rent a car from either a U.S.-based firm (Avis, Budget, or Hertz) with its own European offices or from a local agency. Rates vary considerably by company, season, and pick-up point; expect to pay over US$100 per day, plus tax, for a teensy car. Check if prices include tax and collision insurance; some credit card companies cover this automatically. Ask about student and other discounts, and ask your airline about special packages. Sometimes you can get up to a week of free rental. Minimum age restrictions vary by country; often you must be at least 25.

Before setting off, be sure you know the laws of the countries in which you'll be driving. Be careful, road conditions in Eastern Europe are rarely driver- or pedestrian-friendly. The **Association for Safe International Road Travel (ASIRT)** can provide more information about conditions in specific countries. They are located at 5413 West Cedar Lane, Suite 103C, Bethesda, MD 20814 (tel. (301) 983-5252; fax 983-3663). Unleaded gas is almost nonexistent in Eastern Europe.

Moto-Europa, by Eric Bredesen (US$16; shipping US$3, overseas US$7), available from Seren Publishing, 2935 Saint Anne Drive, Dubuque, IA 52001 (U.S. tel. (800) 387-6728; fax (319) 583-7853), is a comprehensive guide to all these moto-options. From itinerary suggestions to a motorists' phrasebook, it provides loads of tips, whatever the mode of transport, and chapters on leasing and buying vehicles.

BY BOAT

Sometimes, yes, boats go to Yalta...but not today.
—ferry ticket clerk in Odesa

Ferries serving Eastern Europe divide into two major groups. **Riverboats** acquaint you with many towns and enclaves that trains can only wink at. The legendary waterways of Eastern Europe—the Danube, the Volga, the Dnieper—offer a bewitching alternative to land travel. However, the farther east you go, the more often your travel plans may be interrupted by fuel shortages. Most riverboats are palatial and well equipped; the cheapest fare still gives you full use of the boat—including reclining chairs and couchettes that allow you to sleep the trip away in the sun or shade. Schedule information is scarce; inquire in the area of your trip.

Ferries in the **North Sea** and **Baltic Sea** are prized by Scandinavians for their duty-free candy and alcohol shops; they also offer student and youth discounts, are universally reliable, and go everywhere (in summer, you can go from St. Petersburg to Iceland or Scotland without once using land transport). Those content with deck passage rarely need to book ahead. You should check in at least two hours early for a prime spot and allow plenty of time for late trains and getting to the port. It's a good idea to bring your own food and avoid the astronomically priced cafeteria cuisine. Fares jump sharply in July and August. Always ask for discounts; ISIC holders can often get student fares, and Eurail passholders get many reductions and free trips (check the brochure that comes with your railpass). You'll occasionally have to pay a small port tax (under US$10). Advance planning and reserved ticket purchases through a travel agency can spare you several tedious days of waiting in dreary ports for the next sailing. The best American source for information on Scandinavian ferries and visa-free cruises to Russia is **EuroCruises,** 303 W. 13th St., New York, NY 10014 (U.S. tel. (800) 688-3876 or (212) 691-2099).

BY BICYCLE

Biking is one of the key elements of the classic budget Eurovoyage. Everyone else in the youth hostel is doing it, and with the proliferation of mountain bikes, you can do some serious natural sight-seeing. Be aware that touring involves pedaling both yourself and whatever you store in the panniers (those odd-looking bags balanced precariously on each side of the true bike traveler's steed). Take some reasonably challenging day-long rides at home to prepare yourself before you leave. Have your bike tuned up by a reputable shop. Wear highly visible clothing, drink plenty of water (even if you're not thirsty), and ride on the same side as the traffic. Learn the international signals for turns and use them. Learn how to fix a modern derailleur-equipped mount and change a tire, and practice on your own bike before you have to do it overseas. A few simple tools and a good bike manual will be invaluable. For information about touring routes, consult national tourist offices or any of the numerous books available.

Most airlines will count your bike as your second free piece of luggage (you're usually allowed 2 pieces of checked baggage and a carry-on). As an extra piece, it will cost about US$50 each way. Policies on charters and budget flights vary; check with the airline. The safest way to send your bike is in a box, with the handlebars, pedals, and front wheel detached. Within Europe, most ferries let you take your bike for free. You can always ship your bike on trains; when it's not free, the cost varies from a small fixed fee to a substantial fraction of the ticket price.

Riding a bike with a frame pack strapped on it or on your back is about as safe as pedaling blindfolded over a sheet of ice; panniers are essential. The first thing to buy, however, is a suitable **bike helmet.** At about US$25-50, they're a much better buy than head injury or death. To lessen the odds of theft, buy a U-shaped **Citadel** or **Kryptonite lock.** These are expensive (about US$20-55), but the companies insure their locks against theft of your bike for one to two years. **Bike Nashbar,** 4111 Simon Rd., Youngstown, OH 44512 (U.S. tel. (800) 627-4227; fax 456-1223), has excellent prices on equipment and beats all competitors' printed offers by US$5.

BY THUMB

> *Let's Go* strongly urges you to seriously consider the risks before you choose to hitch. We do not recommend hitching as a safe means of transportation and none of the information presented here is intended to do so.

No one should hitch without careful consideration of the risks involved. Not everyone can be an airplane pilot, but almost any bozo can drive a car. Hitching means entrusting your life to a random person who happens to stop beside you on the road and risking theft, assault, sexual harassment, and unsafe driving. In spite of this, many who live by the thumb see benefits to hitching. Favorable hitching experiences allow hitchers to meet local people and get where they're going where public transportation is sketchy. If you decide to hitch, consider where you are. Hitching remains common in Eastern Europe, though Westerners are a definite target for theft. In Russia, the Baltics, and some other Eastern European countries, there is no clear difference between hitchhiking and hailing a taxi. The choice, however, remains yours.

BY FOOT

Eastern Europe's grandest scenery can often be seen only on foot. *Let's Go* describes many daytrips for those who want to hoof it, but native inhabitants (Europeans are fervent, almost obsessive hikers), hostel proprietors, and fellow travelers are the best source of tips. There are also numerous books with tales of the Great Outdoors that can give you ideas and practical advice on hiking in Eastern Europe. Check your local wilderness- or bookstore for regional or country-specific guides.

■ Accommodations

If you arrive in a town without a reservation, your first stop should be the local tourist office. These offices often distribute extensive accommodations listings free of charge and will also reserve a room for a small fee (though some favor their friends' establishments). As a rule, expect all prices to rise each January.

ROOMS IN PRIVATE HOMES

Throughout Eastern Europe, it is commonplace for locals with rooms to rent to approach tourists in ports or train stations. This may seem dangerous, but it is an accepted custom and is often a more attractive option for individual travelers than a night in an overpriced 1970s-revival hotel. Some parts of Eastern Europe, the former Soviet Union especially, are not prepared for solo travelers; the tourism industry in many places is still recovering from an era when all travel was done by organized groups. In small villages in the Balkans, travelers find a roof for the night simply by walking the streets and knocking on doors, or by asking locals for tips. The conditions are sometimes far superior to those at local hotels. However, there is no guarantee of these hawkers' trustworthiness or of the quality of their establishments. Carry your own baggage, ask for their identification, check the bathroom facilities, have them write down the offered price, and make sure the place is located conveniently or near a bus or tram stop.

HOSTELS

Especially in summer, much of Eastern Europe is overrun by young, budget-conscious travelers. Hostels are the hub of this gigantic subculture, providing innumerable opportunities to meet students from all over the world, find new traveling partners, trade stories, and learn about places to visit. At US$3-20 per night, prices are extraordinarily low; only camping is cheaper. Guests tend to be in their teens and twenties, but most hostels welcome travelers of all ages. They are also much less likely to require an international hostel membership (see below). In the average hostel, you and anywhere from one to fifty roommates will sleep in a gender-segregated room full of bunkbeds, with common bathrooms and a lounge down the hall. The hostel warden may be a laid-back student, a hippie dropout, or a crotchety disciplinarian. Most hostels have well equipped kitchens; some serve hot meals.

The basic disadvantage of hostels is their regimentation. In Eastern Europe, however, most hostel owners seem to be less concerned with creating rules than with filling beds. There can be a lockout from morning to mid-afternoon, which necessitates some good planning and a heavier daypack than usual. Conditions are generally spartan and cramped, with little privacy, and you may run into more screaming pre-teen tour groups than you care to remember. Hostel quality also varies dramatically. Some are set in strikingly beautiful castles, others in run-down barracks far from the town

---

Auberge Internationale des Jeunes

Open 24 hours
Rooms from
2 to 6 beds
Breakfast included
Free showers
New building

Credit cards accepted
(Visa, Mastercard,
American Express)
Traveller's cheques
Change of foreign
currencies

Hostel in the city centre of Paris

81 FRF
from November to February

91 FRF
from March to October

An ideal location for young people, a lively area with many
CAFES, PUBS, RESTAURANTS, DISCOS.
INTERNATIONAL ATMOSPHERE

Other Hostels might be less comfortable, and more expensive...!!

10, rue Trousseau - 75011 PARIS - FRANCE
Tél.: 01 47 00 62 00 - Fax: 01 47 00 33 16
Métro: LEDRU ROLLIN - Line 8 (Next to Bastille)

center. Rural hostels are generally more appealing than those in large cities. Hostels usually prohibit sleeping bags for sanitary reasons and provide blankets and sheets instead. Some require **sleepsacks;** make your own by folding a sheet and sewing it shut on two sides. If you're lazy or less domestic, you can usually buy one at a youth hostel federation. Large hostels are reluctant to take advance telephone reservations because of the high no-show rate; citing an exact train arrival time or promising to call again and confirm can sometimes help.

Hosteling Membership

Several groups offer memberships that will give you discounts and special privileges in hostels around the world. The largest of these is **Hostelling International (HI)**, although there are others such as the American Association of Independent Hostels, Backpackers Resorts International, Budget Backpackers Hostels, or Federation of International Youth Hostels. HI-affiliated hostels can be recognized by their blue triangular logo; a complete multilingual listing of their hostels in Europe (including many countries in Eastern Europe) can be bought for US$10.95 through national hostel offices. Access the Internet Guide to Hosteling at http://www.hostels.com. You need not be a youth; travelers over 26 will only sometimes have to pay a slight surcharge for a bed. If you did not get a membership at home, it is often possible to join on the fly. In much of Eastern Europe, HI-affiliated hostels are few and far between, and a card will be less helpful here than in Western European countries.

A one-year HI membership permits you to stay at hostels all over Europe at great prices. **Reservations** for HI hostels may be made via the International Booking Network (IBN), a computerized system which allows you to book to and from HI hostels (more than 300 centers worldwide) months in advance for a nominal fee. Credit-card bookings may be made over the phone—contact your local hosteling organization for details. Most student travel agencies (see Budget Travel Agencies, p. 35) sell HI cards; otherwise, contact one of the national hostel organizations listed below.

Hostelling International-American Youth Hostels (HI-AYH), 733 15th St. NW, Suite 840, Washington, D.C. 20005 (tel. (202) 783-6161; fax 783-6171; http://www.taponline.com/tap/travel/hostels/pages/hosthp.html). HI-AYH maintains 34 offices in the U.S. Twelve-month HI memberships: US$25, under 18 US$10, over 54 US$15, and family US$35. These can be purchased at many travel agencies, local council offices, and the national office in D.C. Reservations may be made by letter, phone, fax, or through the IBN.

Hostelling International-Canada (HI-C), 400-205 Catherine St., Ottawa, Ont. K2P 1C3 (tel. (613) 237-7884; fax 237-7868). Canada-wide customer service line (800) 663-5777). CDN$9-22.50 per night. One-year membership CDN$25, under 18 CDN$12; over 18 2-year CDN$35; lifetime membership CDN$175.

Youth Hostels Association of England and Wales (YHA), Trevelyan House, 8 St. Stephen's Hill, St. Albans, Hertfordshire AL1 2DY (tel. (01727) 855215; fax 844126). Enrollment fees are: UK£9.30; under 18 UK£3.20; UK£18.60 for both parents with children under 18 enrolled free, UK£9.30 for one parent with children under 18 enrolled free; UK£125.00 for lifetime membership.

An Óige (Irish Youth Hostel Association), 61 Mountjoy St., Dublin 7 (tel. (01) 830 4555; fax 830 5808; http://www.touchtel.ie). One-year membership is IR£7.50; under 18 IR£4; family IR£7.50 for each adult with children under 16 free.

Youth Hostels Association of Northern Ireland (YHANI), 22 Donegall Rd., Belfast BT12 5JN (tel. (01232) 315435; fax 439699). Prices range from UK£6.50-10.

Scottish Youth Hostels Association (SYHA), 7 Glebe Crescent, Stirling FK8 2JA (tel. (01786) 451181; fax 450198). Membership UK£6, under 18 UK£2.50.

Australian Youth Hostels Association (AYHA), Level 3, 10 Mallett St., Camperdown NSW 2050 (tel. (02) 565 1699; fax 565 1325; e-mail YHA@zeta.org.au). AUS$42, renewal AUS$26; under 18 AUS$12.

Youth Hostels Association of New Zealand (YHANZ), P.O. Box 436, 173 Gloucester St., Christchurch 1 (tel. (643) 379 99 70; fax 365 44 76; e-mail hostel.operations@yha.org.nz; http://yha.org.nz/yha). Annual membership fee NZ$24.

Hostel Association of South Africa, P.O. Box 4402, Cape Town 8000 (tel. (21) 419 18 53; fax 21 69 37). Between SAR25-1100 a night, with 14 IBN-linked (36 total) hostels in South Africa. Membership SAR45; students SAR30; family SAR90; lifetime SAR225.

HOTELS

In hotels, couples can usually get by fairly well (rooms with a double bed are generally cheaper than those with two twin beds), as can groups of three or four. Always specify that you want the cheapest room available; some managers assume that Westerners expect rooms with phone, fridge, and TV—and that they're willing to pay for the privilege. Inexpensive East European hotels may come as a rude shock to pampered North American travelers. You'll share a bathroom down the hall; one of your own is a rarity and costs extra when provided. Hot showers may also cost more, *if* they're available. Also check to make sure that toilets flush. Some hotels offer "full pension" (all meals) and "half pension" (breakfast and lunch). Unmarried couples will generally have no trouble getting a room together, although couples under age 21 may occasionally encounter resistance.

ALTERNATIVE ACCOMMODATIONS

In university and college towns, **student dormitories** may be open to travelers when school is not in session. Prices are usually comparable to those of youth hostels, and you probably won't have to share a room with strangers or endure stringent curfew and eviction regulations. Also, some **monasteries** and **convents** will open their doors for weary backpackers. A letter on stationary from a clergy member at home could facilitate matters. Sleeping in European train stations is a time-honored tradition. It's free and often tolerated by authorities, but it's neither comfortable nor safe. Don't spend the night in an urban park unless you place a low value on your life.

■ Camping & the Outdoors

The wilds of Eastern Europe can be truly experienced only at one of the sometimes beautiful and sometimes simply enormous **organized campgrounds** that exist in many of the cities and rural areas. Most are accessible by foot, car, or public transportation. Showers, bathrooms, and a small restaurant or store are common; some sites have more elaborate facilities. Prices range from US$1-10 per person with an additional charge for a tent. Money and time expended in getting to the campsite may eat away at your budget and your patience, but camping will bring you into the vacation subculture of young Eastern Europeans since it is often the only affordable accommodation for locals. For travelers who opted for the lighter, tent-free backpack, many campgrounds also offer cabins or bungalows for a slightly higher fee.

CAMPING EQUIPMENT

Prospective campers will need to invest a lot of money in good camping equipment and a lot of energy in carrying it on their shoulders. Many of the better **sleeping bags** are rated according to the lowest outdoor temperature at which they will still keep you warm. Sleeping bags are made either of down (warmer and lighter) or synthetic material (cheaper, heavier, more durable, and warmer when wet). **Sleeping-bag pads** run from US$13 and up for closed-cell foam and US$25 and up for open-cell foam, while **air mattresses** go for about US$25-50 (do not get the kind designed for swimming pools. If you plan on doing a lot of camping, the amount of comfort a pad or mattress provides makes up for its bulk; they also come in handy for sitting on hard train station floors. The best **tents** are free-standing—they set up quickly and require no staking. If you intend to do a lot of hiking, you should have a **frame backpack.** Although the costs of all this might seem daunting, you can often find last year's version for half the price. See Packing, p. 32, for hints on backpacks and a continuation of the eternal internal/external frame debate.

Other camping basics include a battery-operated **lantern** (gas is inconvenient and dangerous) and a simple plastic **groundcloth** to protect the tent floor. Don't go anywhere without a **canteen** or water bottle. **Campstoves** come in all sizes, weights, and fuel types, but none are truly cheap (US$30-120) or light. Consider GAZ-powered stoves, which come with bottled propane gas that is easy to use and widely available in Europe. The lower-tech camper should bring a small **metal grate** or a grill to take advantage of the campfire. A **canteen, waterproof matches, Swiss army knife,** and **insect repellent** are essential items. Finally, for any season, make sure you bring a **hat** to protect your ears from the biting frost or burning sun. For more information about camping concerns, contact the **Wilderness Press,** 2440 Bancroft Way, Berkeley, CA 94704 (tel. (800) 443-7227 or (510) 843-8080; fax (510) 548-1355), which publishes books such as *Backpacking Basics* (US$11, including U.S. postage). Also, check out the colorful, comprehensive **Backpacker's Handbook** by Hugh McManners, in bookstores (US$15).

WILDERNESS AND SAFETY CONCERNS

The three most important things to remember when hiking or camping: stay warm, stay dry, stay hydrated. The vast majority of life-threatening wilderness problems stem from a failure to follow this advice. If you are going on any hike that will take you more than one mile from civilization, you should pack enough equipment to keep you alive should disaster befall. This includes raingear, warm layers (not cotton!)—especially **hat** and **mittens, a first-aid kit, high energy food,** and **water.** *There are no exceptions to this list.* Always check weather forecasts and pay attention to the skies when hiking. If possible, you should let someone know that you are going hiking, either a friend, your hostel, a park ranger, the police or a local hiking organization. Do not attempt a hike beyond your ability—you'll be endangering your life.

Use caution when encountering any untamed animal, and cultivate a respect for the environment while remembering that the environment will not always return the favor. Weather patterns can change instantly. A bright blue sky can turn to rain—or even snow—before you can say "hypothermia." If you're on a day hike, and the weather turns nasty, turn back. If on an overnight, start looking immediately for shelter. You should never rely on cotton for warmth. This "death cloth" will be absolutely useless should it get wet. Instead wear wool or synthetic materials designed for the outdoors. Pile fleece jackets and Gore-Tex© raingear are excellent choices.

Be sure to wear **hiking boots** appropriate for the terrain you are hiking. Two watchwords sum up the essentials of good footwear: ankle support. Twisted or sprained ankles can be serious, and could keep you from walking for hours or days. Your boots should be sized so they fit snugly and comfortably over one or two wool socks and a thin liner sock. Be sure that the boots are broken in. A bad blister will ruin your hike. If you feel a "hot-spot" coming, cover it with moleskin immediately.

The most important thing to remember while camping is to protect yourself from the environment. This means having a proper tent with rain-fly, warm sleeping bag, and proper clothing. Another major concern is safe water. Many rivers and lakes are contaminated with **giardia,** a bacterium which causes gas, painful cramps, loss of appetite, and violent diarrhea. If caught, it can stay in your system for weeks. To protect yourself from this invisible trip-wrecker, bring your water to a rolling boil for at least five minutes, purifying it with iodine tablets, or using a portable water purification system. A good guide to outdoor survival is *How to Stay Alive in the Woods,* by Bradford Angier (Macmillan, US$8). For more information, see Health, p. 19.

Be concerned with the safety of the environment. Don't unnecessarily trample vegetation by walking off established paths. Because firewood is scarce in popular areas, campers are asked to make fires using only dead branches or brush; using a campstove is a more cautious (and efficient) way to cook. Don't cut vegetation, and don't clear new campsites. Make sure your campsite is at least 150 feet from water supplies or bodies of water. If there are no toilet facilities, bury human waste at least four inches deep and 150 feet or more from any water supply or campsite. Pack your trash in a plastic bag and carry it with you until you reach the next trash can.

Keeping in Touch

MAIL

Sending Mail to Eastern Europe Mail can be sent internationally through **Poste Restante** (the international phrase for General Delivery) to most cities or towns; it's well worth using and much more reliable than you might think. Mark the envelope "HOLD" and address it, for example, "Ruth <u>BRENN</u>, Poste Restante, City, Country." The last name should be capitalized and underlined. The mail will go to a special desk in the central post office, unless you specify a post office by street address or postal code. For towns in the Czech Republic and Slovakia, you should put a "1" after the city name to ensure mail goes to the central post office. In Hungary, the last name is written first (i.e. BRENN, Ruth). As a rule, it is best to use the largest post office in the area. Letters are often opened by criminals in search of valuables; *never* send cash. The cheapest letters you can send are aerograms (available at the post office), which provide a limited amount of writing space and fold into envelopes (no enclosures). It helps to mark air mail in the appropriate language if possible, though *par avion* is universally understood.

When picking up your mail, bring your passport or other ID. If the clerk insists there is nothing for you, check under your first name. In a few countries you have to pay a minimal fee (perhaps US$0.50) per item. *Let's Go* lists post offices in the Practical Information section for each city and most towns.

American Express offices worldwide will act as a mail service for cardholders if contacted in advance. Under this free **"Client Letter Service"**, they hold mail for 30 days, forward upon request, and accept telegrams. Just like *Poste Restante,* the last name of the person to whom the mail is addressed should be capitalized and underlined. Some offices offer these services to non-cardholders (especially those who have purchased AmEx Traveler's checks), but you should call ahead to make sure.

ISRAEL
COME SEE FOR YOURSELF!!

- Accredited Programs in English or Hebrew, undergrad or grad
- Touring
- Internships
- Intensive Hebrew Study
- Kibbutz
- Archaeology

Odyssey '97: E. Europe & Israel!

University Student Department
World Zionist Organization
The Israel Action Center

USD

1-800-27-ISRAEL OR USD@NETCOM.COM
OR AT 110 E. 59TH ST., 4TH FL., NY, NY 10022
OR BY FAX AT 212-755 4781

EL AL אל על

Castles and Monasteries

(Map showing Eastern Europe with locations of Castles, Fortresses, Citadels, and Palaces, and Monasteries)

W Castles, Fortresses, Citadels, and Palaces
† Monasteries

Check the Practical Information sections of the countries you plan to visit; *Let's Go* lists AmEx office locations for most large cities. A complete list is available free from AmEx (U.S. tel. (800) 528-4800) in the booklet *Traveller's Companion* (see p. 16).

Sending Mail from Eastern Europe Allow at least one week for **airmail** from Eastern Europe to reach the U.S. or U.K., and more for Australia, New Zealand, and South Africa. Mail from parts of Eastern Europe can require up to four to six weeks. From Russia to anywhere has been known to take a year. It is far from guaranteed that the letter will actually reach its final destination, though chances are better in Central Europe and the Baltic States.

Surface mail is by far the cheapest and slowest way to send mail. It takes one to three months to cross the Atlantic, appropriate for sending large quantities of items you won't need to see for a while. It is vital, therefore, to distinguish your airmail from surface mail by explicitly labeling airmail in the appropriate language or writing "par avion". When ordering books and materials from another country, include one or two **International Reply Coupons (IRC)**, available at the post office, with your request. IRCs provide the recipient of your order with postage to cover delivery.

TELEPHONES

> In Essentials and country listings, the **country code** is not included with phone numbers; please consult the beginning of each country's chapter, where the country code is listed with exchange rates, or the Appendices. In the Practical Information section for large cities and towns, city **phone codes** are listed under Telephones. For smaller towns, look for the local code at the end of a paragraph.

Some countries in Eastern Europe do not have an international dialing code; you must go through the operator. In some others, you must wait for a tone after the international dialing code. For more information, see each country's Essentials.

You can sometimes make **direct international calls** from a pay phone, but you may need to feed money in as you speak. In some countries, pay phones are card-operated; some even accept credit cards. Try to call from phone booths and post offices since phones in cafés, hotels, and restaurants tend to carry surcharges of 30% or more. English-speaking operators are often available for assistance. Operators in most European countries will place **collect (reverse charge) calls** for you. It's cheaper to find a pay phone and deposit just enough money to be able to say "Call me" and give your number (though some pay phones can't receive calls).

Some companies, seizing upon this "call-me-back" concept, have created **callback phone services.** Under these plans, you call a specified number, ring once, and hang up. The company's computer calls back and gives you a dial tone. You can then make all the calls as you want, at rates about 20-60% lower than you'd pay using credit cards or pay phones. This option is most economical for loquacious travelers, as services may include a US$10-25 minimum billing per month. For information, call **America Tele-Fone** (U.S. tel. (800) 321-5817), **Globaltel** (tel. (770) 449-1295), **International Telephone** (U.S. tel. (800) 638-5558), and **Telegroup** (U.S. tel. (800) 338-0225).

A **calling card** is another alternative; your local long-distance phone company will have a number for you to dial while in Europe (either toll-free or charged as a local call) to connect instantly to an operator in your home country. The calls (plus a small surcharge) are then billed either collect or to a calling card. Some companies will be able to connect you to numbers only in your home country; others will be able to provide other European or worldwide connections. For more information in the U.S., call **AT&T Direct** services at (tel. (800) 331-1140, from abroad (412) 553-7458), **Sprint** (tel. (800) 877-4646), or **MCI WorldPhone** and **World Reach** (tel. (800) 996-7535). MCI's WorldPhone also provides access to MCI's Traveler's Assist, which gives legal and medical advice, exchange rate information, and translation services. For similar services for countries outside the U.S., contact your local phone company. In Canada, contact Bell Canada **Canada Direct** (tel. (800) 565-4708); in the U.K., British Telecom **BT Direct** (tel. (800) 345144); in Ireland, Telecom Eireann **Ireland Direct** (tel. (800) 250250); in Australia, Telsta **Australia Direct** (tel. 13 22 00); in New Zealand, **Telecom New Zealand** (tel. 123); and in South Africa, **Telkom South Africa** (tel. 09 03).

Remember **time differences** when you call. Estonia, Latvia, Lithuania, western Russia, Romania, and Bulgaria are two hours ahead of Greenwich Mean Time (GMT)—seven hours ahead of Eastern Standard Time. Moscow is three hours ahead; Irkutsk is 13. Everywhere else in this book is one hour ahead of GMT. Some countries ignore daylight savings time, and fall and spring switchover times vary between those countries that do use it.

FAXES, E-MAIL, AND MORE

Major cities have bureaus where you can pay to send and receive **faxes.** If you're spending a year abroad and want to keep in touch with friends or colleagues, **electronic mail** ("e-mail") is an attractive option. It takes a minimum of computer knowledge, a little prearranged planning, and it beams messages anywhere for no per-message charges. Befriend college students as you go and ask if you can use their e-mail accounts. If you're not the finagling type, look for bureaus that offer access to e-mail for sending individual messages. Search through http://www.easynet.co.uk/pages/cafe/ccafe.htm to find a list of cybercafés around the world from which you can drink a cup of joe, and e-mail him, too.

Let's Go Picks

Of all the beds we slept in, of all the clubs we crashed, of all the views that made us wish we had a 3-D camera with smell-scope and sound, these picks are the sleeps, sights, and attractions that EEUR '97 loved the most. Check 'em out or discover your own; either way, post us some mail—"e" or snail—and tell us what you thought.

Spots to Crash Feel like a turn-of-the-century diplomat in the spacious rooms of Lviv's beautifully restored, **Hotel George**—without cashing all your T-checks. UKR (p. 728). **U Vodníka** and **Moldau Hilton** in Česky Krumlov (p. 210), Bohemian riverside sleeps in the Czech Republic's most idyllic town. The **youth hostel**—new, friendly, cheap, *and* near the nightlife—in Dubrovnik, CRO (p. 162). In Prague, CZE, thumbs up to hip **Hostel Sokol** smack dab in the center of town, and **The Boathouse**, a relaxing crash-pad away from the thick of Prague's action (p. 181).

Views for Which to Kill Of Hradcany and Malá Strana from the Charles Bridge in Prague, CZE (p. 188). From **St. Mary's Cathedral** in Gdańsk, POL (p. 415). Anywhere in the **Slovak Tatras** (p. 645-652). The **white dunes** overlooking the unruffled sea of Nida, LIT (p. 361). The fantastical clear-blue **Lake Baikal**, RUS (p. 571). Forbidden to outsiders for 50 years, the island of **Hiiumaa**, EST, emerges from its time capsule with a wealth of untouched natural wonders—ideal for a bit of bucolic biking (p. 245). Our R-W Joel assures us that **Bled**, SLN (p. 674), and **Split** (p. 162) and **Dubrovnik** (p. 165), CRO, are as gorgeous as the postcards he sent us to drool over!

The Most Smashing of the Smashed Olsztyn—a 12th-century castle sacked by Swedes, now only two towers and ghosts remain—on the Trail of Eagles' Nests near Częstochowa, POL (p. 451). Central Europe's largest castle, **Spišský hrad**, sprawls in magnificent decay after a 1780 fire, in Spišské Podhradie, SLK (p. 655). **Shlisselburg**, an island fortress whose crumbled remains once protected Peter the Great and later imprisoned Lenin's brother, near St. Petersburg, RUS (p. 617). The ruins of the **Madara** fortress guard Stone and Copper Age caves and the inspiration for the back of all *leva* coins, the famous Madara Horseman, in Madara, BUL (p. 136).

Adrenaline Rush **Kievo-Pecherska Lavra**, Kiev's oldest and holiest religious site, complete with candles, catacombs, and mummies in Kiev, UKR (p. 703). The **Trans-Siberian Railroad** to Irkutsk (p. 565-572). The 1 to 3m-wide peninsula of **Sääretirp** extending 3km from Hiiuma, EST (p. 248)—surrounded by water, you feel as if you should sink, but looking down, all you see is strawberries.

Best of the Bizarre Statue: Bust of Frank Zappa in Vilnius, LIT (p. 347). **Jurassic Park II:** The Amber Museum in Kaliningrad, RUS, provides magnifying glasses so you can spy the little amber-encased buggers that started this nasty, modern-day dinosaur mess (p. 357). **Cross-covered hill:** Kryžių Kalnas (Hill of Crosses) in Šiauliai, LIT (p. 356). **Communist architecture:** SNP Bridge—yeah, the rein-holding flying saucer—in Bratislava, SLK (p. 639). **Devil museum:** The Devil Museum in Kaunus, LIT, has created a merry little hell populated by nearly 2000 traditional devil icons gathered from all around the world (p. 353).

Watering Holes Diesel, jazz bar/club in a centuries-old cellar with intimate tables and dim lighting in Cluj-Napoca, ROM (p. 492). **Paddy Whelan's** in Rīga, LAT (p. 326), where they tap the *Guinness* to form a clover imprint in the head. The perfect ambience for coffee sipping in Ukraine coalesces at **Italisky Dvorik** in Lviv (p. 729). For smokin' grooves, check out **Pod lampou** in Plzeň, CZE (p. 207). **Stará Sladovňa** rules as a mammoth malthouse—one of Europe's largest—in Bratislava, SLK (p. 639). Then there was Cuong's favored haunt, good ol' **Grendel's** (p. x).

ALBANIA (SHQIPËRIA)

US$1 = 109 lekë	100 lekë =	US$0.91
CDN$1 = 80 lekë	100 lekë =	CDN$1.25
UK£1 = 171 lekë	100 lekë =	UK£0.59
IR£1 = 178 lekë	100 lekë =	IR£0.56
AUS$1 = 86 lekë	100 lekë =	AUS$1.16
NZ$1 = 76 lekë	100 lekë =	NZ$1.31

SAR1 = 25 lekë	100 lekë = SAR4.06
DM1 = 74 lekë	100 lekë = DM1.35
Country Phone Code: 355	International Dialing Prefix: 00

Proud, fierce, and defiant, Albania has played a part in every upsurge of the struggle between East and West. Over the centuries, the nation has had barely a moment's rest between attacks from its neighbors, yet every time it has resisted with a fury that frightened far stronger powers. "Albanians have always had a taste for killing or getting themselves killed," snorts a frustrated enemy general in Albanian author Ismail Kadarë's novel *The General of the Dead Army*, p. 1. Yet in spite of their historical belligerence, Albanians are friendly and considerate, working peacefully to keep up with neighbors while preserving their ancient society in a shrinking world.

ALBANIA ESSENTIALS

A visa is not required of citizens of the U.S., Canada, Ireland, or the U.K. Australians, New Zealanders and South Africans need a visa valid for three months. The application must include a letter of invitation—or, on some cases, a letter explicating the reason for the trip, costs US$15, and takes over three weeks to process. See Essentials: Embassies and Consulates, p. 1. Travelers of all nationalities may or may not need to pay an unofficial US$20 "entrance fee" (a.k.a. bribe) at the door, depending on whether the border guards feel like demanding it. You may obtain a visa extension at the Ministry of Foreign Affairs in Tirana. A similarly unofficial "exit fee" of US$10 may be necessary. Some rules: 1) Only Americans must pay, 2) Only Americans needn't pay, 3) You only have to pay if you're German, Italian, or Greek, 4) You pay if you're female, 5) You pay if you're male, 6) You don't pay if you bribe the guard, 7) You don't pay if you proposition the guard. Welcome to Albania.

GETTING THERE AND GETTING AROUND

The most convenient way to reach Albania is by **plane**. Tirana can be accessed from Athens, Bari, Budapest, Ljubljana, Rome, Skopje, Sofia, Warsaw, or Zürich. **Hemus Air,** a private Bulgarian airline, offers an especially appealing option from Sofia (one-way US$200, under 25 US$96). **Ferries** link Durrës and Vlorë with Italian ports, and Sarandë with Corfu. International **buses,** of a higher quality than domestic ones, but still not 100% reliable, run to a few locations outside Albania, mostly Sofia and Istanbul. Purchase tickets at the kiosks on Blvd. Dëshmorët e Kombit, to the north of Skanderbeg Sq. in Tirana. When crossing to Macedonia, head for the southern pass at Lake Ohrid; choose the cheap bus (around US$2) over the costly taxis (US$20).

Albanian roads cling to steep mountains, while giant, old vehicles compete like road-warriors on the narrow paths. There are no traffic lights outside the capital, nor are there road rules. Drivers, however, are surprisingly considerate. Even honking, an outburst of anger in the West, is used as a warning near low visibility turns.

Between cities, **buses** are the least offensive choice. The driver usually owns his bus; few are air-conditioned (although many falsely advertise as such). Radios blasting Greek tunes from the 70s compensate for the discomfort. There are a few main routes: the north one runs to Shkodër; the southeast to Elbasan, Pogradec, and Korçë; the southwest to Gjirokastër and Sarandë. Buses also run between Lushnjë and Berat. Buses go almost anywhere in the country for less than 500 lekë; the conductor (the driver's friend, cousin, or brother) will come around to collect fares and sometimes give you a ticket, which you must keep until the end of the ride (police do check). During longer trips, the bus may pull into a rest stop, and the driver will announce *"Pushim!"* There's time to grab lunch or a beer, as the driver probably will. There are no precise schedules, although most buses leave between 5 to 8am.

A fleet of **"Taksi"** or **"Taxi" microbuses** plough through the countryside in all directions for a bit more than larger buses. They leave when they're full and offer more flexible schedules. Particularly useful for daytrips, they cost around US$1.50 per 100km, but they're usually packed, and a longer trip is bound to be exhausting.

Trains are slower and less comfortable, but cheaper. Substantial sections of track were destroyed during the anti-Communist upheaval in 1991. All rails lead to Durrës, and trains run to Tirana, Vlorë, Fier, Pogradec, and Ballsh, but no foreign cities.

Car rental is one way to see the countryside without restricting yourself to train or bus "schedules." A driver often comes with the deal. Either through an agency in Tirana or Durrës or simply by approaching a taxi in the street, one may argue the price down to a third of the first quoted price. A good way to get a low price is to ask if anyone knows a friend willing to drive. Renting a car is possible with an international driver's license. Driving in Albania without insurance is not recommended.

Hitchhiking is legal, and those who do it hold out one hand and wave. Riders are expected to pay. Accidents on Albania's narrow mountain roads are usually head-on collision or cliff dives. In light of this, entrusting a motoring yahoo with one's life may not be such a great idea, and *Let's Go* does not recommend it.

TOURIST SERVICES

Travel agencies are usually open from 9am-7pm, with a long afternoon break (typically 1-4pm). **Skanderbeg Travel** is the closest thing to a tourist office in the country. Most travel bureaus that sell international bus tickets (Albes-Turist, Agencja Turistike "Arta," Travel Agency Memedheu) speak English. **American Express** in Tirana performs all the tasks of a tourist agency.

MONEY

The **monetary unit** is the lek, the plural of which—lekë—is pronounced the same way. A massive influx of foreign currency from Albanians living abroad has kept the currency stable. The U.S. dollar enjoys limited usage, but people will feel more comfortable being paid in lekë. **Traveler's checks** are virtually unknown outside of Tirana. **Exchange** is legal pretty much anywhere and with whomever is willing. **Moneychangers** offer the highest rates and are especially trustworthy in smaller towns, but be sure you know what the lek looks like. In larger towns, **exchange bureaus** offer good rates and safety. **Credit cards** are slowly coming into use. Mastercard and Diner's Club are commonly honored. The lek was devalued by a factor of 10 in 1965, and surprisingly, many still insist on quoting prices in old lekë.

COMMUNICATION

Postal service within Albania is reliable but slow. The **telephone** is probably faster, although only occasionally capable of international calls. International calls can be made via a local operator, or direct from certain locations. The prices for a minute to the U.S. run from 230 lekë to 600 lekë. Most Albania towns have no direct telephone code. Public telephones can be found at all post offices.

LANGUAGE

Years of Italian television account for the popularity of the language in Tirana, although younger Tiranans are liable to speak some English too. Learned Albanians may know French, Russian, or German. Greek is common in the south, along with some Turkish. Beware if you are attempting to communicate non-verbally that Albanians nod to mean "no" and shake their heads to indicate "yes." "No" is also indicated by a wagging of the index finger. This can be very confusing when you're trying to ascertain where a bus is headed or whether a hotel is in a particular direction. Remember to reinforce your own responses with *"po"* (yes) and *"jo"* (no).

Albanian (called *Shqip* by Albanians) is the only surviving descendant of Illyrian. During centuries of foreign rule, it adopted many words from Latin, Greek, Turkish, Italian, and Slavic languages. Two main dialects can be distinguished: *Geg* (or *Gheg*) in the North and *Tosk* in the South. **Pronunciation** is phonetic. There are seven **vow-**

els: *i* (ee), *e* (eh), *a* (ah), *o* (oh), *u* (oo), *ë* (e as in "chooses"), and *y* (ü as in German "über"). The final *ë* is silent. **Consonants** are as in English, except for: *ç* (ch as in "chimichanga"), *dh* (th as in "this"), *gj* (j as in "jinx"), *j* (y as in "yen"), *q* (ch as in "cheesy"), *x* (dz as in "adze"), and *xh* (j as in "judge"). See the Glossary, p. 772.

HEALTH AND SAFETY

Little official **legislation** is enforced. Yet the mere presence of police officers—easily spotted at most strategic locations—keeps Albania relatively crime-free. Armed with anything from pistols to AK-47s, policemen play at directing the chaotic traffic.

Single **women** travelers may feel uncomfortable, since foreign women are still sometimes seen as "easy." Although Albanian men are fairly polite, they are prone to catcalls in the afternoon and early evening. Later in the day, there are many more men than women on the streets, and women almost never go into a café or restaurant alone. However, even there you will likely encounter surprise, not hostility. Avoid loud cafés; the crowd there has probably had more *raki* (the local firewater) and less *kakao* (hot chocolate). Going out alone at night is not advised.

Electrical grids cover only a block or two, so even if you have no power, your neighbor might. Power outages are worst in winter. Currently, tap **water** is not always available. The shortage is most dire from mid-July to mid-August. Tap water is generally safe to drink as it usually comes from mountain springs. Bottled water is easily available for about 70 lekë per 1.5 liters. Although there are **pharmacies** in many cities, they are not very well stocked. Foreign brands of shampoo, razors, and tampons are common in Tirana, but less so elsewhere. Condoms are nowhere.

ACCOMMODATIONS AND CAMPING

Tourist agencies outside the country will still sometimes try to fool you: "Hotels are of a modest standard" or "Suitable for a brief visit." Let's face it: many Albanian **state-owned hotels** define the expression "big dump." Albturist constructed a large hotel in each town specially for tour groups. These are now open to independent travelers but often lack running water, modern toilets, or even heat. Carpets are usually faded and tattered, beds sagging and uncomfortable. Fortunately, **private hotels** are springing up with encouraging frequency. These range from gorgeous and friendly to cramped but still friendly, and the facilities are generally better than those of their state-run counterparts. Many larger hotels may be refurbished in the next few years. Rooms run 1000 to 3000 lekë (US$10-30) per person. As of yet, there are no **hostels** in Albania except those directly connected with missionary groups. A few travel agencies in Tirana now find **private rooms** for those who inquire. Although hot water, or water at all, is usually not guaranteed, the stay is much more pleasant than in a large hotel. Many people you meet will offer a night in their home for US$5-15. Whether you find your lodging through an agency or through luck, you will probably be given the largest bed in the house, possibly in a room with a few other people, and be fed dinner, coffee, and *raki*. There are no **camping** facilities in Albania. Free camping is legal—but consider the safety risks. You might see tents in the countryside, but they are likely the homes of impoverished Albanians.

FOOD AND DRINK

Albanian **cuisine** revolves around *mish* (meat) and *patate* (potatoes), which usually can be ordered *me garniturë* (with vegetables), probably salted and oiled, for an additional 50-100 lekë. The predominance of *djathë* (feta cheese) recalls Greek cuisine. *Kos*, Albanian yogurt, is served at most meals. Salads are a popular prelude to a meal and are often accompanied by *raki*, made of fruit juice and drunk in small sips. In the north mountains, try *oriz më tamel*, a sheep's-milk rice pudding, or *byrek*, meat or cheese dumplings. Poverty has shortened the menu for most Albanians. Bread frequently constitutes more than 50% of one's diet. The remaining portion consists mainly of milk products, most notably feta and yellow cheese *(kaçkaval)*.

CUSTOMS AND ETIQUETTE

Albanian **hospitality** is influenced by the *Kanun*—the legendary code of the medieval lawgiver Lek Dukagjini, who succeeded Skanderbeg as leader of the Krujë fortress. It will even override revenge, so that a house will shelter and feed a man who has killed one of its members. (The *Kanun* is available in English, with prescriptions on all aspects of life from vendetta etiquette to the ritual of the first haircut.) Assuming things don't get so dramatic, you will be served coffee and *raki* and offered a smoke whenever you enter a home. It is polite to accept it, but no offense will be taken if a cigarette is refused. It is customary to take off your shoes upon crossing the threshold of a house. In the north, it is considered a sign of satisfaction if you wipe your plate with bread at the end of your meal.

In restaurants, **tipping** is not expected, yet it is greatly appreciated. To get rid of the uncertainty around "to tip or not to tip," many restaurants now have a *kuver* or cover charge of 20-30 lekë, which, in part, functions as a tip.

For women, **dress** is more conservative in Albania than elsewhere in Europe, although shorts and jeans are becoming more common, especially in larger cities. Men rarely wear shorts, even under the hottest sun. Long hair and beards, forbidden under the Communist regime, are increasingly popular, especially among young'ns.

Public physical **affection** between members of the opposite sex is scandalous. A man and a woman will usually just shake hands. This rule breaks down most frequently in urban areas where young iconoclasts are more abundant. A two-sided kiss is the normal greeting and farewell between women. Men greet each other with several kisses on the cheek and often walk around arm in arm.

Homosexuality was legalized in Albania on 19 January, 1995, thanks to international pressures. However, there are still no bars or discos specifically for gay men; this way of life hasn't made its way to Albania. Contact "Shoquata Gay Albania" (P.O. Box 104, Tiranë, Albania) for a free copy of their English-language paper *Enigma*.

A harmful by-product of Albanian nationalism is **racial prejudice**—directed mainly against gypsies, but fortunately, as far as foreigners are concerned, racism is overridden by the rules of hospitality.

LIFE AND TIMES

HISTORY

Archaeological and anthropological studies indicate that Albanians are the direct descendants of the ancient **Illyrian tribes** who inhabited the west part of the Balkans in the 12th and 11th centuries BCE. In the 8th century BCE, the **Greeks** started founding colonies—most notably, Epidamnus (modern Durrës) and Apollonia (near modern Vlorë). Illyrian tribes began to create alliances, thus forming the basis for future kingdoms. In 229BCE, the **Roman Empire** defeated Illyria—recreating it as Illyricum. **Apollonia** soon became the province's cultural center. Throughout this period, the Illyrians managed to maintain their own culture, although Latin came into use and the Illyrian religion was increasingly replaced by Christianity after it was introduced in the 1st century CE. A bishopric was established in **Dyrrachium**.

In 395CE, the Roman Empire was divided, the lands of the Illyrians were partitioned, and the territory of modern Albania became part of the **Byzantine Empire**. The most prominent ruler of the time, **Justinian I**, was himself Illyrian. The Illyrian lands were invaded year after year by tribes of Visigoths, Huns, and Ostrogots; not to be outdone, the Slavs arrived in the 6th to 8th centuries. The southern tribes of modern Albania resisted assimilation, and succeeded in preserving their unique tongue. The name Illyria over time became **Albanoi**, then **Arbëri**, and, finally Albania. Later, around the 17th century, Albanians started calling themselves *shqiptarë*, meaning "sons of eagles," and their country *Shqipëri*, "the land of the eagle."

The Albanian Church was controlled from Rome until 732 when it began to fall under Constantinople's jurisdiction. Albania experienced its first religious fragmentation in 1054 when the Christian church split between the East and Rome. Northern Albania reverted to the control of the Roman pope and Greek and Latin were officially the languages for literary and cultural pursuits. Albanian was recognized neither by church nor state as an official language. The Byzantine Empire proved too weak to protect Albania from successive invasions by Bulgarians, Normans, Serbs, and Venetians, and in 1347, the country was occupied by the **Serbs.**

Under later **Ottoman** rule, Albania was built on a feudal system of landed estates *(timars).* As the empire began to decline, the power of the *timar*-holding military lords, or *pashas,* increased. Some tried to create separate states within the empire, but were overthrown by the sultan. Turkey eventually abolished the *timar* system in 1831, and power passed from feudal lords to tribal chieftains. To escape persecution, two-thirds of the population had converted to Islam by the 17th century.

In response to the oppressive Ottoman rule, the **Albanian League** was founded in 1878 with the goal of unifying all Albanian territories (Kosovo, Shkodër, Monastir, and Janina), and stimulating the growth of Albanian language, literature, and education. By the time the Turks suppressed the League in 1881, and its leaders went into exile, it had become a symbol of national feeling and desire for independence. When the Balkan states declared war on Turkey in October 1912, the Albanians issued the **Vlorë Proclamation** of independence to protect Albania from Slavic invaders. After the defeat of Turkey, the **conference of the Great Powers**—Britain, Germany, Russia, Austria-Hungary, France, and Italy—convened, and agreed to recognize independent Albania. However, ethnic divisions were ignored: Kosovo was given to Serbia—still an object of Balkan ethnic strife—and other regions to Greece.

During WWI, Albania's neighbors threatened to partition the country; U.S. President Wilson vetoed this at the **Paris Peace Conference of 1918,** and Albania was free again. In the early 1920s, Albania experienced internal conflict between conservatives *(bajraktars)* led by the chieftain **Ahmet Zog,** and liberals led by **Bishop Fan Noli.** Noli was elected prime minister in 1924 and began democratization. The process lasted only a few months before Zog overthrew the government. He crowned himself king in 1928, but his reign collapsed under occupations in WWII. Albania was unified under the Nazis from 1941-45, but after the war, the territories of Kosovo and Camëria were lost and Albania once again fell under the heavy yoke of dictatorship. This time the yoke was the self-aggrandizing Communist **Enver Hoxha,** who had led the wartime resistance. Until his death in 1985, he formed and then rejected ties with Yugoslavia, the Soviet Union, and China, finally closing Albania's doors to foreigners entirely. Travel abroad was severely restricted and religion banned, while Hoxha's portrait was found in every home.

Hoxha's successor, **Ramiz Alia,** faced growing opposition after the fall of Communism throughout Eastern Europe in 1989. Seeking to preserve the regime, Alia granted the right to travel abroad, restored religious freedom, and endorsed the creation of independent political parties. Finally, after numerous concessions to the opposition (largely intellectuals, the working class, and youth), the regime collapsed

---

The Great Skanderbeg Mystery Solved

Skanderbeg Square, Skanderbeg Street, Skanderbeg Boulevard—see a pattern? Although not yet a figure enshrined in global pop culture, Skanderbeg is Albania's greatest national hero. Born **Gjergj Kastrioti,** he began his career as a singer in Vienna's world-famous boy's choir...Wait, no. From 1388, the Ottoman Turks tried to occupy Albania, but Skanderbeg united the Albanian opposition, recaptured his homeland in the 15th century, and, with the strength of Mel Gibson, repelled over 25 Turkish attacks. Unfortunately, his death led to a breakdown in Albanian resistance that allowed the Turks to re-occupy Albania and cut it off from West European civilization for more than four centuries. Skanderbeg's movement, while ultimately unsuccessful, created an Albanian national identity and continues to inspire Albanian nationalists—and street-namers—to this day.

when it lost the March 1992 elections. Alia was succeeded by **Sali Berisha,** the first democratic president of Albania since Bishop Noli.

LITERATURE

For centuries, politics and power have controlled the tongues in which Albanian authors could express themselves. Albanians have not taken this cultural subservience lying down, however, and have protested with counter-attacks of their own. Writers have struggled to maintain the mother tongue and preserve traditional sources like medieval folk tales, and the many legends of Skanderbeg.

Latin dominated the vernacular and written language until medieval times. The earliest known Albanian work was the 1462 "Baptizing Formula," by **Archbishop Paul Angelus.** During the period of Turkish occupation, Albania was subject to the cultural constraints, and isolated from the rest of Europe. Many Albanians, rejecting Ottoman cultural dominance, migrated to Southern Italy, forming a group now known as the **Arbëresh.** These ex-pats remained fiercely loyal to Albania, and created a literature of patriotic pieces on exile and the homeland. A school of writers arose from those who remained. Turkish, Arabic, and Persian literature impressed its spirit upon them, and their work became known as "the literature of the Oriental-style poets." This work became increasingly secular, and its major proponents included **Nezim Frakulla,** lyric poet **Sulejman Naibi,** social critic **Hasan Zylo Kamberi,** and **Muhamet Kyçyky.** Peruse Arshi Pipa's *Albanian Folk Verse: Structure and Genre* for more information on these poets and Albanian poetry.

Later nationalists criticized the "Oriental poets" for diluting and corrupting the Albanian language. Their rebellion against the Ottoman Empire became a linguistic as well as a physical struggle. In the early 1800s, Albania underwent a **National Renaissance,** which accompanied the political attempt to emerge from under the thumb of the Turks. Still unable to express overt nationalism within Albania, Albanian expatriates established "The Association of Printing Letters in Albanian" in Istanbul, and similar organizations in the U.S. Arbëresh journalist and poet **Jeronim de Rada** (1814-1903) essentially fathered the movement, compiling fragments of folklore in his *Këngët e Milosaos (The Songs of Milosao),* a romantic ballad set in the 15th century. The poem "The Lament of the Nightingale," by another participant in the Renaissance, **Ndrë Mjeda,** is a patriotic allegory. Mjeda, his brothers, and other contemporary Albanian authors also considered new alternatives for the alphabet, and a revised, standard orthography in Roman letters was constructed by the poet **Gjerj Fishta,** and adopted by the **Monastir Congress** in 1908.

When the **"Albanian Cultural Renaissance"** (1966-69) occurred, the Party deemed it important that a "unified" Albanian language be formulated from the Gheg and Tosk variants. The results of this concoction was a Tosk-oriented language, from which numerous words employed in literary Gheg were eliminated. **Naim Frashëri** (1846-1900), one of the most famous Albanian poets, and his Tosk philologist brother Sami, had already enriched the literary language of that dialect enough to allow such a change. The "Cultural Renaissance" in reality occasioned "cultural suppression," and the most independent of the post-war authors were imperiously suppressed. Poet and novelist **Ismaïl Kadarë** did, however, manage to continue his creations unscathed, and, although he finally went into exile in 1990, composed numerous fictional works. These include *The General of the Dead Army* (Quartet Encounters), about an Italian army general who enters Albania after the war, and *Doruntine,* a mythic tale set in the medieval period.

ALBANIA TODAY

Things are looking up—sort of. Albania was admitted to the Council of Europe on June 29, 1995, and its relationship with Greece, long contentious on account of minority issues, has steadily improved. In a major step forward, the Greek defence minister visited Tirana on July 3, 1995. On May 26, 1996, the Democratic Party of President Sali Berisha won the latest elections for Parliament, but the results and procedures of the election were contested by the opposition—mostly notably the former Communists, now called the Socialist Party. Tension escalated to such an extent that police were used to dissipate protesters from Tirana's main square on May 28. In addition to political problems, economic ones also persist. Albania remains the poorest country in Europe. The closing of many state-run factories has driven unemployment rates higher, especially in the north. The country's inadequate infrastructure makes large-scale tourism only a hope for the future. Thus the gorgeous landscapes and rugged stone cities of Albania remain largely unspoiled.

Tirana (Tiranë)

Appearing from nowhere among the Albanian hills, Tirana is one of those places where horses and carts still jostle in traffic with the latest European and Japanese cars. In some ways the entire city looks like a construction zone, with open manholes, crumbling exteriors, broken glass, and banana peels scattered over the streets. The unprepared little village heroically withstood a series of grandiose Communist designs to become what it is now—a somewhat awkward, but still endearing city. Made the capital in 1920 when it was only a few huts divided by a cobbled path, Tirana could never be accused of being glamorous, yet it is anything but dull.

ORIENTATION AND PRACTICAL INFORMATION

With the advent of the copy machine (in Albania, that is), **maps** of Tirana are becoming easier to find. In general, however, Albanians are not big on grids, street names, or street numbers. A street may not be marked, and if it is, the name may not correspond to that on the map; building numbers present an equally baffling prospect. In attempting to identify with the locals' sense of landmarks, position yourself in **Sheshi Skanderbeg** (Skanderbeg Sq.) facing south. Through the square runs **Bulevardi Dëshmorët e Kombit,** the town's main thoroughfare, which extends towards Tirana University in the south, and the **train station** to the north.

Tourist Office: Skanderbeg Travel, Rr. Durrësit 5/11 (tel./fax 239 46). English spoken. Arranges private (US$20-30 per person) and hotel rooms. Car and driver rental. Guided excursions to Berat, Shkodër, Vlorë Pogradec (US$60), and Krujë (US$20). Sells ferry tickets. Open Mon.-Sat. 8am-1pm and 4:30-7:30pm.

Embassies: U.S., Rr. Elbasanit (tel. 328 75 or 335 20; fax 322 22). Walk towards the university on Blvd. Dëshmorët e Kombit, turn left after the Prime Minister's office, right at the TV station, then immediately left. The street ends when it hits Rr. Elbasanit and the yellow embassy is ahead towards the right. Open Mon.-Fri 1-4pm for American citizens. Most of the other embassies are on Rr. Karvajës.

Currency Exchange: Private dealers stationed in front banks usually boast the best rates, but if careless you may end up with a wad of useless paper. The safer exchange counter inside the **Hotel Dajti** and the receptionists at **Tirana International Hotel** will gladly exchange US$ at a usurious rate. Many exchange offices have opened around the city. They offer both safety and higher rates. One is **JOARD,** Rr. Ded Gjo Luli, right next to the DHL office (open daily 8am-3pm).

American Express: 65 Rr. Durrësit (tel. 279 08). Provides cash advances and emergency cash, cashes traveler's checks in lekë and US$ for a 1-4% commission (depending on the sum), stocks **maps** (150 lekë), holds mail for members (others are not officially refused), sells ferry tickets, rents cars and drivers, arranges private accommodations (US$10 and up), and organizes group and individual tours. Open Mon.-Fri. 8am-2pm and 5-8pm, Sat.8am-1pm, Sun. 9am-1pm.

Flights: Rinas Airport, 26km from town. A small blue bus shuttles to Skanderbeg Sq. (50 lekë). In Tirana, the bus leaves from in front of the airline agency, to the right of the Restorant Hambo (5-6 per day). For schedule info ask inside the last office in the building 30m to the left of the airline agency. If taking a taxi, negotiate a price first, and don't pay above US$10.

Trains: north end of Blvd. Dëshmorët e Kombit. Domestic trains only to Vlorë (2 per day), Pogradec (2 per day), Durrës (6 per day), Shkodër (2 per day), Elbasan (3 per

Tirana

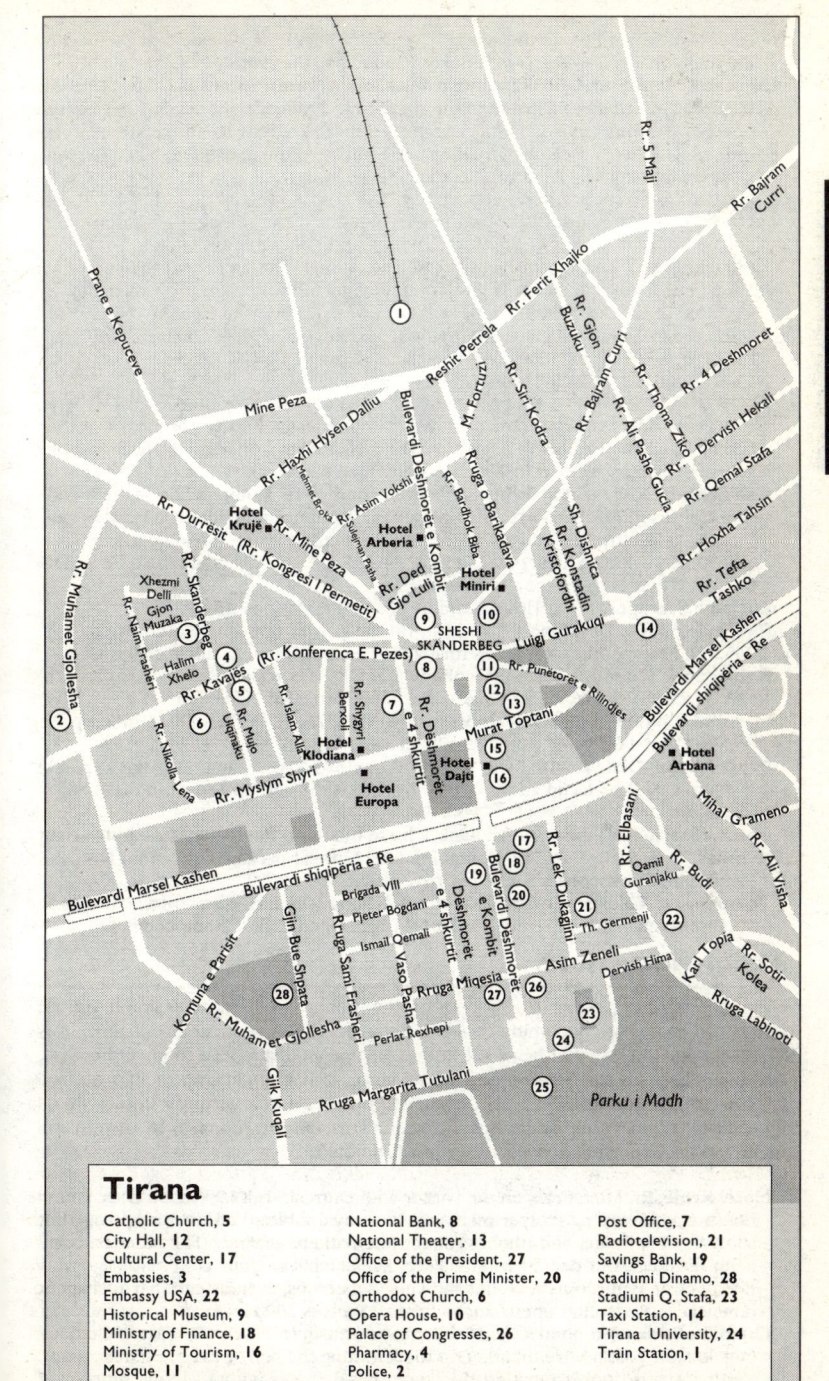

Catholic Church, 5
City Hall, 12
Cultural Center, 17
Embassies, 3
Embassy USA, 22
Historical Museum, 9
Ministry of Finance, 18
Ministry of Tourism, 16
Mosque, 11
National Art Gallery, 15
National Bank, 8
National Theater, 13
Office of the President, 27
Office of the Prime Minister, 20
Orthodox Church, 6
Opera House, 10
Palace of Congresses, 26
Pharmacy, 4
Police, 2
Polytechnic University, 25
Post Office, 7
Radiotelevision, 21
Savings Bank, 19
Stadiumi Dinamo, 28
Stadiumi Q. Stafa, 23
Taxi Station, 14
Tirana University, 24
Train Station, 1

day). One way rates vary between 7-76 lekë. Schedules are posted on the wall by the track on a yellow sign, with ticket windows to the right.

Buses: Kavajë-Fier-Gjirokastër-Sarandë and **Elbasan-Pogradec-Korçë** routes begin behind Stadium Dinamo in the southwest. From Skanderbeg Sq., walk south on Blvd. Dëshmorët e Kombit, and turn right at the "river" (a trickle of water through concrete). Follow it, then turn left and cross the footbridge when the long white building with one central entrance is on your right. Ask for *stacioni i autobuzit*. Microbuses are more convenient. The cost is almost equal (US$1-1.50 per 100km), and they are faster and more frequent. Elbasan-Pogradec microbuses depart from the corner of Rr. Murat Toptani and Punëtoret e Rilindjes. To: Durrës (50 lekë, 1hr.). Vans to Fush Krujë (40 lekë, 40min.) congregate at the end of Rr. Mine Peza. Turn right at the train station, then look for the vans on your right after a couple of blocks. **Albes-Turist** (tel. 421 66) sends buses to Istanbul (US$40) and Sofia (US$25). **Travel Agency Memedheu** operates out of a kiosk on the left of Tirana International Hotel and runs buses to Istanbul (2 per week, US$40), Sofia (2 per week, US$25), and Skopje (daily, DM30).

Taxis: In Skanderbeg Sq., near the train station, and in front of hotels Dajti, Arberia, and Tirana International. Low cost makes trips outside Tirana not inconceivable; US$10 should be enough to get you to Kruje. Negotiate a price first. Dollars happily accepted. Almost any car in Tirana is a potential taxi.

Car Rental: Most car rentals include a driver and often require additional expenditures for his room and board; it's a reasonable option mainly for groups of 2-4 people. Go to Skanderbeg Travel or AmEx (see above). It is only possible to rent a car individually without insurance, an atrocious idea. Taxi drivers may also be willing to "rent" their services for a few days.

Luggage Storage: Free at Hotels Dajti or Tirana International Hotel.

Pharmacy: Blvd. Dëshmorët e Kombit, on the corner opposite Hotel Arberia (tel. 245 42). Among other things, German-made tampons. Open daily 8am-9pm.

Bookstores: Quendra Stefan (Stephen's Center) sells recent U.S., British, French, and German newspapers and magazines. Open Mon.-Sat. 8am-8pm.

Hospital: Qendra Spitalore Universitare (tel. 326 31 or 321 21), a hike up Rr. Bajram Curri. Better yet, don't get sick in Albania.

Express Mail: DHL, Rr. Ded Gjo Luli 6 (tel./fax 276 67). Separate document/parcel rates: to U.S. (US$46/63 and up); to U.K. (US$40/58 and up); to Australia (US$52/69 and up).

Post Office: Behind the National Bank, a bit to the right. **Poste Restante** in the right corner. Open daily 7am-7pm; outgoing international packages accepted Mon.-Fri. 7am-11am. **Photocopies** 8 lekë per page.

Telephones: Telekomi office near Hotel Arberia. Open 6:30am-2pm, 2:30-10pm, 10:30pm-6am. Thrice the price at **Hotel Dajti.** Open 24hr. **Phone code:** 42.

ACCOMMODATIONS

Older hotels' offerings are usually poor for the money, while more desirable private hotels and rooms are becoming easier to find. Any time you meet an Albanian, it is worth finding out whether he or she knows anyone willing to let a room. Otherwise, **American Express** and **Skanderbeg Travel** make such arrangements in an organized fashion (private rooms US$10 per person and up). It's worth getting a hotel with its own supply of water and water-heating facilities, as, despite promises by the government, tap water is often unavailable or just plain cold.

Hotel Krujë, Rr. Mine Peza, on the corner with Durrësit. Fall 1996 should see 6 new floors, each featuring an apartment and 3 roomy doubles (US$50) with private hot showers, TV, fridge, and phones (direct international dialing). The older part will keep its small, but decent rooms. Feels like staying in your aunt's house. Functional, clean bathrooms with hot showers. Boisterous, friendly café/bar/restaurant downstairs. Reception open 9am-midnight. Doubles 2000 lekë.

Quendra Stefan (Stephen's Center), 1 Hoxha Tahsin (tel. 347 48), east of Skanderbeg Sq., just past the fruit market on the left. Ring the bell or ask in the restaurant. Run by American missionaries, the center has 3 rooms with a varying number of beds (up to 6). The US$20 per person price goes down to US$15 with groups larger than 4. A/C in one room. Clean, shared bathrooms and hot showers. Laundry. Breakfast included. Closed Sun. Reserve in advance, especially in summer or if you plan to arrive on a Sunday.

Hotel Klodiana, 1 Rr. Shyqyri Bërxolli (tel./fax 274 03 shared with Hotel Europa). From the post office follow the street until it ends. Take a left on Shyqiri Bërxoli. The hotel is marked with a sign 25m ahead. Two spotless doubles with modern bathrooms, TV, fan, and heater 4000 lekë. Breakfast included.

Hotel Dajti, Blvd. Dëshmorët e Kombit (tel. 333 26, 278 60, or 278 26; fax 320 12), on the left as you walk towards the university, behind a verdant pine grove. Reservoir and water heater in most rooms, currency exchange, duty-free shop, telephones, TVs. Perfect English spoken. Singles 3500 lekë, larger ones with bath 4000 lekë. 11 doubles go for 3000 lekë and have fans, but share clean showers. Doubles with bath 6000 lekë. Breakfast included.

Hotel Europa, (tel./fax 274 03), near Hotel Klodiana. Turn right on Myslym Shyri just before Hotel Dajti, then turn right again at the Hotel Europa sign and look for the tall white building. To reach its majestic, 3-star carpeted entrance with potted plants (watch out for the cactus as you go in), come around from the right. All rooms equipped with hot shower/bath, TV, telephone (direct international calls), and a fan. Marble-floored bar-lounge entices with comfy furniture and satellite TV. Singles 6000 lekë. Doubles 7000 lekë. Matrimonial suite 10,000 lekë. Non-guests can negotiate a price for their **laundry** to be done. English spoken.

Hotel Arbana, Blvd. Shqipëria e Re (tel. 30 781), a 1½-km hike until the spot where the "river" is freed from its concrete bed. One wing has recently been renovated with a fresh coat of paint, new carpets, and private bathrooms. Phones available. Singles 2500 lekë. Doubles 5000 lekë. The old wing has clean but sagging beds. There might have been running water here. The stand-up toilets may have worked. There probably never was a shower or sink. Check-out 10am. Reception open 5am-midnight. Pay only in lekë.

Miniri Hotel, 3 Rr. e Dibres (tel. 309 30; fax 330 96), between Tirana International Hotel and the Opera House. This brand new hotel seems to deserve all of its 4 stars. Medium-sized rooms have satellite TV, hot showers, mini-bar, and phone (direct international calls). Singles US$60. Doubles US$100. Triples US$120. Copies 20 lekë per page. English spoken. Free map of Tirana.

FOOD

As part of the inexplicable building boom, restaurants and cafés seem to pop up as mushrooms after the rain. A few bottles of *raki*, some music, and a jolly crowd of Tiranans discussing the world and patting each other on the back make the day go by in a flash. Summer street vendors sell fruits and vegetables; these are usually safe to eat, but be sure to wash and peel them. An especially lively and well stocked **frutaperime** (fruit-and-vegetable market) can be found at the roundabout on Rr. Luigj Gurakuqi, right next to Stephen's Center. **Bakeries,** identifiable by "Bukë" signs, are more common on quiet streets off the main thoroughfares. Read the posted prices, hand your money through the window, and your bread will be handed back. **Kiosks,** selling chocolate bars and soft drinks, are like the police force—numerous and strategically placed. There are also plentiful cafés—one of the best is the **Bar Pergola** on Rr. Lek Dukagjini, which serves java under the shade of an apricot grove and a sprawling grapevine (coffee 20 lekë, beer 100-200 lekë, assorted ice-creams 100-250 lekë; open daily 7am-10pm).

Taverna Tafaj, 86 Rr. Mine Peza (tel./fax 275 81). The first private restaurant in Tirana. A grapevine shields two marble-floored terraces from the sun. The *fergjes*, a local dish of meat, feta cheese, and flour, is wonderful. Soup 100 lekë. Entrées 200-500 lekë. Fish 500-1000 lekë. English spoken. Open daily 10am-11pm.

Restaurant Bujtina e Gjelit, Rr. Pranë e Kepucëve (tel. 276 58). Take Rr. Mine Peza and continue along Pranë until the bus stop. A stone-fenced courtyard shelters a cool gallery of tables. Artwork shines through a prism of cascading water. Worth the hike. Salad (100-150 lekë) is a good choice with the meat-laden entrées. Entrées 400-600 lekë. Fish 800 lekë. Open daily 8am-11pm. Diners Club accepted.

Restaurant Don Kishoti, Rr. Murat Toptani. Third restaurant from the corner of Dëshmorët e Kombit. Not much in the way of atmosphere, but the prices are unbeatable. *Fergjes* 80 lekë. *Biftek me garniturë* 250 lekë. Beer 90 lekë. Some English spoken. Open daily 6am-11pm.

La Perla, 84 Rr. K. Kristoforidhi (tel./fax 309 51). Turn left from the Tirana International Hotel, pass Hotel Miniri, and turn right into a cul-de-sac after the first intersection. An oasis for businesspeople from across the Adriatic: Italian food, owner, and chef. A Karaoke machine lurks in the piano bar. Pizza 400-700 lekë. Spaghetti 700 lekë. *Antipasti* 300-400 lekë. Beer 200 lekë. Open daily noon-midnight.

China Restaurant Hong Kong, 1 Rr. Komuna e Parisit (tel. 221 42), west along the river, hidden behind a few kiosks and a heavy metal grill. On the way to Stadium Dinamo. English menus. Soups 190 lekë. Smallish entrées 250-780 lekë. Seafood 850-1200 lekë. Open daily noon-3pm and 7-11pm. Diner's Club accepted.

Restorant Dajti, in Hotel Dajti. A unique view from the terrace: the flying-saucer-like Cultural Center to the right, a gorgeous garden in front, and Mt. Dajti in the distance. The famous menu includes some vegetarian fare. Entrées 330-1060 lekë. Desserts under 100 lekë. Open daily 6-9:30am, 12:30-3:30pm, and 6:30-10:30pm.

Hambo, Rr. Durrësit and Mine Peza. Have a Happy Hambo Day at this Greek-owned Albanian McDonald's. Fries 100 lekë. Beer 110 lekë. Cheeseburger 130 lekë. English spoken. Open daily 7am-midnight.

SIGHTS AND ENTERTAINMENT

Communism has not been entirely eradicated from Skanderbeg Sq. Stark architecture stares from blank façades, and a Socialist **mural "Albania"** adorns the front of the **National Historic Museum,** which offers a crash course in Albanian history on three floors (open Tues.-Sat. 9am-noon and 4-7pm; 300 lekë, students 50 lekë). The once ominous site now serves as a playground with bumper cars and swirly rides. **Skanderbeg's statue** stands near an **18th-century mosque** (a small donation is expected; don't forget to take off your shoes). Down Blvd. Dëshmorët e Kombit on the left, the **National Art Gallery** exhibits contemporary paintings, some definitive works of Albanian Communist Realism, anonymous Renaissance works, and, of course, several large busts and paintings featuring the omnipresent Skanderbeg (open Tues.-Sun. 9am-noon and 5-8pm, closed Thurs. 9am-noon; 100 lekë, students free). Further along, the immense pyramidal **Cultural Center**—a must in all Eastern Bloc capitals—houses temporary displays arranged by various industrial or political groups, but is worth entering just to glimpse the structure's genius (open Mon.-Sat. 11am-2pm, 3-8pm). **Tirana University** fills the adjacent area. Behind it **Parku i Madh** (Big Park) provides a welcome rush of untamed greenery, as it fuels the local makeout scene. Beyond the top of the hill, local kids have turned a **lake** into an impromptu beach. Along the "river" and in the park that begins at the corner of Dëshmorë e Kombit and Myslym Shyri you can find the biggest concentration of **cafés**—enough to accommodate all of Tirana's citizens. The **Opera House** holds evening performances. Its ticket window (tel. 274 95) is on the left of the façade (open Mon.-Fri. 9am-noon and 5-6pm, Sat.-Sun. 9am-noon). **Soccer** games are popular weekend entertainment.

■ Near Tirana: Krujë

Skanderbeg's **Krujë fortress** stands an hour away from Tirana. A **microbus** from Tirana takes you to **Fush Krujë** (Krujë Field; 40 lekë, 40 min.). If you hike up to the castle via the serpentine road, be ready for a 16km trip (imagine what the poor Turks must have suffered in their four attempts to capture the fort, or read Ismail Kadarë's version in his novel, *The Castle*). Alternatively, riding up in one of the omnipresent minivans takes only 15 minutes (30 lekë). Between the closer bus stop and the **citadel,** a dozen or so shops form the **bazaar** (look for the miniature Albanian bunkers), a feeding-ground for souvenir-finders, and all that's left of the Old Town. Younger vendors who speak English may act as guides. Buying some of their wares will serve as payment. The restored castle embodies nationalism and hero-worship in its most exalted state. A **museum,** built by Enver Hoxha's daughter in 1982, provides a peculiar combination of Communist fervor and epic fantasy. An enormous statue of Skanderbeg greets the visitor on entering the museum, where huge murals depict bloody battle scenes, and the hero, over and over again, bludgeons his way through a thick Turkish army. The museum sends you even further back in time with depictions of Ilyrian soldiers routing the Roman army. Belligerent busts—including one of Skanderbeg's warrior sister Donika Kastrioti—line the halls of the second floor, and at one end, as though in a shrine, sit replicas of Skanderbeg's sword and helmet. On the third floor you can find a **library** which houses more than 1000 books about the hero. English subtitles complement the visual effects, telling us, among other things, of the origin of the name Skanderbeg. The curator, who speaks good English, will be glad to clarify all details lost in the translation (open Tues.-Wed. and Fri.-Sun. 9am-1pm and 4-7pm, Thurs. 9am-1pm; 100 lekë). One traditional Albanian house within the citadel has been converted into an **Ethnographic Museum,** including Turkish baths, a working mill, a spinning wheel, and a *raki* still (open Mon. and Wed.-Sat. 9am-1pm and 3-6pm, Sun. 9am-3pm; 100 lekë). Amid the ruins of the fortress lie the remains of a **Turkish bath,** and a **Roman Church.** Its **mosque** still functions, and features a combination of Christian, Muslim, and Baroque artwork inside. The fourth generation dervish caretaker proudly points to the graves of his ancestors in the garden outside.

SOUTHWESTERN ALBANIA

■ Durrës

Albania's second largest city combines history under Greek and Roman rule with 20th-century importance as political center, port, and focal point of the country's skeletal railroad system. The tourist heading for the radiant blue of the beach will observe scattered Roman ruins and bunkers stationed side-by-side, the bunkers slowly turning into ruins themselves.

Orientation and Practical Information All points of interest cling close to the train station and Sheshi Lirisë (Lirisë Sq; turn left at the end of the main street from the train station). **Buses** to various cities (Tirana: 1hr., 50 lekë) leave three blocks from the **train station** from a square on the main street. Frequent orange **city buses** leave here to the **beach** (5 lekë; pay on the bus and get off at the 4th stop). Train tickets are available at the windows in the ground floor of the apartment building immediately to the right of the train station—look for the easy-to-miss cardboard signs *("Biletari Treni").* Trains run to Pogradec (2 per day, 120 lekë), and Tirana (6 per day, 30 lekë). **Ferries** leave for Ancona (2 per week, 18hr., US$80-170), Bari (3 per week, 9hr., US$60-135), and Trieste (2 per week, 25hr., US$90-195). **Shqip Agencies,** Rr. Skanderbeg 934 (tel. 222 36; first left after train station), arranges ferries. The **post office** owns a **fax** machine. Take a left on the second street after the train station and look to the right after 100m (open Mon.-Sat. 8am-8pm). The adjacent **telephone office** is open 24 hours. Outside await money changers, but for an official **currency exchange,** try Hotel Adriatik. **Phone code:** 52.

Accommodations and Food **Hotel Luli,** Lagjia 12, Rr. Vasil Kuqi (tel./fax 242 16), on the first street to the right after the Alenti Supermarket, offers doubles for 3000 lekë and triples for 4000 lekë. Two communal, though immaculate, floor bathrooms; 24-hr. hot water; laundry. MC accepted. **Hotel Pameba,** Lagjia 1, Rr. Kalase (tel. 242 70; fax 241 49), near Sheshi Lirise, just beyond the amphitheater, has very comfortable singles (5000 lekë) and doubles (7000 lekë) with breakfast. A fleet of state-run hotels lies on both sides of a palm-flanked alley along the beach. Its aging flagship **Hotel Adriatik,** (tel. 230 01 or 236 12; fax 250 51), offers doubles with TV, shower, direct international phone and water on a tight schedule for US$46. Breakfast included. English spoken (reception open 7-8am, 1-3pm, and 8-10pm). **Apolonia Hotel** is a lesser state-run operation on the beach. In-room bathrooms enjoy sporadic water. Those who manage to communicate with the staff may get singles for 1500 lekë or doubles for 2500 lekë. Breakfast costs 250 lekë.

To get to the **Alenti Supermarket,** continue along the main street from the train station and turn right after Palati Sportit Ramazan Kjala (the big white building). "*Pesht*" means fish. On the way to King Zog's palace, **Restaurant Red House** serves meals on a covered wooden deck overhanging the evergreen hill. Albanian or Italian entrées 300-800 lekë. Soups 250 lekë. English spoken (open daily 8am until the last client leaves). **Restaurant Luli** inside Hotel Luli offers cheap entrées (100-350 lekë), and fish (350-900 lekë; open daily 8am-11pm; MC accepted).

Sights and Entertainment Roman ruins pepper the landscape of ancient Durrës. The best classical relics appear in the **Roman Amphitheater** excavations and the **Archaeological Museum.** Among the amphitheater's fallen rocks, an English guide lurks and waits to give tours for 100 lekë. The museum, down the street from Hotel Pamelea, across the street from the beach, opposite the **monument to the Albanian partisan,** holds an impressive but disorganized collection of artifacts (open Wed.-Sun. 9am-1pm; 100 lekë). The **Palace of King Zog** stands on a hill, a 10-minute hike up Rr. Kalase (a.k.a. Rr. Anastas Durrsaku). Built in 1937, it protected the king and his family until Zog fled to England at the outbreak of WWII. The palace, off-limits to most, is used for visiting dignitaries. The winding road reveals mind-boggling views of the Adriatic amidst the fresh smell of evergreen.

■ Gjirokastër

Cobbled streets, breathtaking mountains, and an ominous stone citadel have inspired legends, mysteries, and fine literature in the town of Gjirokastër. The birthplace of two of Albania's most famous sons—writer Ismail Kadarë and dictator Enver Hoxha, the city has preserved an ancient feel in its older hillside half.

Orientation and Practical Information High above the valley, the Old Town center is by the **Greek consulate** and **mosque.** The new town thrives around the **market.** Street names exist, but no inhabitants know them, and roads themselves thwart the traveler by twisting into bizarre contortions. To make it worse, no one sells maps. **Buses** drop passengers 20 minutes away from the town, but for 200 lekë a **taxi** will expedite the trip uphill. Departing buses are caught higher up, a few minutes from **Hotel Çajupi.** Buses travel to Tirana (3 per day, 7hr., 250 lekë) and Sarandë (2 per day, 1¾hr., 100 lekë). It is also possible to intercept buses to and from Sarandë on the main road near the valley (see Sarandë, p. 70, and add 1½hrs. to the departure times). The **bank** down the street from the Greek consulate **exchanges currency** in cash (open Mon.-Fri. 7am-2pm). In the morning, Greek drachma and dollars can be changed at the bottom of the hill, next to the central market. The fledgling agency **Ghino Tours** (tel./fax 30 75, home tel. 24 66), next to the bank, arranges private accommodations (800-1200 lekë), speaks French and German, finds **translators** (1000 lekë per day), and can supply **bikes** (700 lekë per day) and **horses** (400 lekë per hour). The **post office** is down the street from the bank (open daily 8am-2pm). **Telephones** there boast occasional international capability (open Mon.-Sat. 6am-10pma). **Phone code:** 726.

Accommodations and Food Haxhi Kotoni and his family, Lagjia Pazorto 8, Rr. Bashkim Kokona, provide six firm beds and breakfast for 1500 lekë per person. The three doubles now have private showers with 24-hour hot water and satellite TV. Half board is an extra 500 lekë, full board 1000 lekë—homemade and served in the garden. The family's English improves daily—all the better to kill you with kindness that includes **laundry** and **ironing.** Walk up the hill past the consulate and turn right;

it's up the stairs on the left. **Drago Kalemi** (tel. 37 24), a former English teacher, provides two simple doubles in his house, a few houses past the Kotoni's on Rr. Bashkim Kokona. The bathroom is equipped with a stand-up toilet and lukewarm shower (US$10; breakfast included). The big, state-owned **Hotel Çajupi** (tel. 23 67 or 24 07), below the citadel, has probably seen better days (doubles 1200 lekë, with modern toilet and hot water 2500 lekë).

Food can be bought cheaply from any number of little stores lining the cobbled streets. The **market** in the new part of town has a reasonable variety of fruits and vegetables. Establishments bearing *"Pasticeri"* signs yield desserts. **Stadium,** on the left-hand side of the stadium next to the university as you go downhill, fills up with university students and serves an impressive selection of salads (150-250 lekë), omelettes (110-180 lekë), sandwiches (up to 100 lekë), and various entrées (250-700 lekë), complemented by a bow-tied *maitre d'* (English menu; open daily 8pm until the last customer leaves). **Kandella Manxios,** at the bottom of the hill past the stadium on the left, offers Albanian cuisine—mostly veal and lamb—for 250-420 lekë and salads for 50-120 lekë. The delicacy here is lamb's head for 250 lekë (A/C, modern toilets; open daily 6am-11pm or later).

Sights From the base of the hill, buildings crawl up towards the castle; at the apex emerges a spectacular scene centered on **Mt. Lunxhri.** The **Ethnographic Museum,** sits upon the foundation of Enver Hoxha's former domicile. Go down from the Greek consulate and take the first left at the bank. Bear left at the fork in the street and knock on the heavy doors. The curator will let you in and give you an English tour (call her home at 37 63 if no one is there). Local craftsmen created all the artwork inside in hopes of preserving the town's ancient traditions. At the top of the hill, the 6th-century **castle** is a "choose your own adventure" story with one central entrance. The portal leads to a menacing arcade, flanked by enormous WWII guns. Bring a friend and hold his/her hand. The scary procession ends in brown double-doors, closed with a cartoon-sized padlock. This is the **Museum of Arms.** The caretaker, who speaks some English, occupies the office to the left. Unfortunately some time ago brazen "art collectors" dug through the castle's 3m-wide wall and made off with its collection of swords and stone-age weapons. All that remains are guns from the various wars in Albanian history. The caretaker will willingly tell you about them, about the true story behind Ismail Kadarë's novel *The General of the Dead Army,* and about the castle's years as a prison. For like all old castles worth their salt, part of the edifice was employed as such until 1968 (open daily 8am-noon and 4-7pm; 100 lekë). In town, the 1pm **call for Muslim prayer** carries majestically over the hills. Fresh springs replenish the waters of **Viroi Lake,** 2km away from town. Surrounded by cool forests, the area makes a perfect picnic spot.

Sarandë

Warmed by Ionian breezes, the beach resort of Sarandë enjoys mild weather year-round. A substantial Greek minority, and the town's proximity to the Greek island of Corfu, give Sarandë a Hellenic atmosphere unseen elsewhere in Albania. Empty beaches and mellow seaside cafés are its biggest assets—still undiscovered by tourist hordes whose arrival is anticipated by the newly built private hotels and restaurants. Relaxation and warmth await; just don't expect to rock the night away.

Orientation and Practical Information Most amenities cluster near the beach, easily accessible from the bus stop. **Buses** head to Tirana (4 per day, 9hr., 450

No, It's Not a Sandwich.

Every evening when the sun sets on Albania, families don their best suits and dresses and make their rounds of the village. The nightly event, not to be confused with the eponymous middle eastern sandwich, is called a **gyro.**

lekë), Fier (7:30am, 4-5hr., 300 lekë), Vlorë (7am, 4hr., 350 lekë), Gjirokastër (4 per day, 2hr., 100 lekë). English is spoken more widely here than elsewhere in Albania, as is Greek. **Ferries** to Corfu (1½hr.) leave 10 minutes from the bus station. **Shkëndia Travel,** Rr. Skanderbeg 40 (tel. 33 80), provides one-day cruises and guided tours to Butrint in English, German, French, Italian, and Spanish (US$20). It also finds accommodations and exchanges currency. Ask for student discounts. **Banka e Kursimeve** (tel. 23 06), accepts traveler's checks, gives Mastercard cash advances, and changes even Japanese yen. Take the seashore road left from the bus stop; the bank is on the left (open Mon.-Fri. 8am-4pm). A **post office** (open Mon.-Fri. 7:30am-2:30pm, Sat. 8am-1pm, Sun. 10am-2:30pm), two to three minutes to the left of the bus stop, houses telephones. Calls are routed through Tirana as Sarandë has no code; international calls can sometimes be made (open daily 6:30am-10:30pm).

Accommodations and Food Private hotels are springing up all over Sarandë. The quality is generally high; even state-owned hotels are more comfortable here than in other parts of Albania. Private accommodations can also be arranged (about US$10 per night); talk to anyone. Once Enver Hoxha's pad, **Caonia B&B** (Greek cellular tel. 30 94 34 89 21), to the left of Restaurant Palmat and Hotel Butrini at the fork in the road, has bedded such greats as Nikita Kruschev. Spotless communal bathrooms with 24-hr. hot water (doubles US$50, triples US$60, quad US$72; breakfast included). The owners also arrange trekking tours.

Four minutes straight ahead from the bus stop, **Hotel Korali** (tel. 29 35) rents brand-new rooms with private showers and 24-hr. hot water (in summer, doubles 3000 lekë, triples 4000 lekë; off-season doubles 1500 lekë, triples 2000 lekë). **Hotel Gjika** (tel. 24 13), boasts a great view of Corfu, but visitors may feel uncomfortable walking to the hotel after dark. Continue straight ahead from the bus stop and turn left up the dirt road just before Taverna Korali; bear left, then turn right on the next "street" near the last row of houses on the hill (singles, doubles and triples with private American-style bathrooms and 24-hr. hot water 1000 lekë per person, depending on how rich you appear to the owner).

There seem to be more **cafés** than people in Sarandë. Several of these serve low-cost staples like rice or fish soup, and meat or fish with vegetables. Somewhat more elegant but still eminently affordable restaurants are arising along the beachfront. **Restaurant Palmat** (tel. 36 31 and 36 32), left of Hotel Butrinti, offers a slightly more grounded location for the seasick (salads 80-150 lekë, fish soup 120 lekë, meat entrées 300-360 lekë). MC accepted for bills over 1000 lekë (open daily 7am-11pm). Opposite Hotel Butrinti, the chic **Paradise** (tel. 32 92), attracts local beautiful people and visiting foreigners. An outdoor terrace juts out over the sea. The English menu offers salads for under 100 lekë, soups for 110-160 lekë, and omelettes for 110-160 lekë (open daily 7am-4:30pm and 6pm-midnight; MC accepted).

Sights Sarandë's emptier and more unspoiled **beaches** lie beyond the ferry port. They seem even cleaner after you have made your way there through the debris of nearby apartment buildings. One caveat: pebbles, not sand. The series of rock layers leading directly into the water will disappoint those longing for endless strips of sand. Steer clear of the water by the town itself—the walk will be worth it, and you won't be competing for seaspace with garbage. **Bar Ardi** is a perfect lookout point at evening, when the population begins its **gyro.** For a party, head to Corfu in the afternoon, drink and dance the night away, then catch the morning boat back.

■ Near Sarandë: Butrint

The Greek settlement of Butrint, 19km and 45 minutes from Sarandë, is one of archaeology's better-kept secrets. Layers of civilization, from the 6th century BCE to the 19th CE, arise from the soil. Little effort has been made to maintain Butrint, now overgrown, deserted, and ripe for exploration. In Butrint, no one will tell you to climb out of that 2nd-century well when you feel like playing Indiana Jones.

As of 1996 there were no English signs, so here's a key to the rocky playground. A makeshift path takes you around the site in more or less methodical fashion. Start by passing through the columns. On the right **public baths** from the first through 2nd century stand before a 17th-century **watchtower.** Proceeding up the path, steps lead up to the 13th- to 14th-century **fortress.** The museum inside has no plans to open soon. The pathway to the fortress steps also turns right. Follow it to a complex of Roman buildings. The 1st- to 2nd-century **Temple of Asclepius** is adjacent to the 4th-century **theater.** Try standing in the center of the dry part and talking softly while someone else sits in the seats. On the other side of the theater lie more **public baths** from the 1st to 2nd century. The path proceeds towards the 6th-century **baptistry**, its columns still intact. A surprisingly brilliant **mosaic** covers the floor. Just beyond the baptistry stands a **church** of the same era, for now missing only its roof. Behind rises a 4th-century BCE **gateway,** leading to a massive wall. Follow it around to another gateway, over which presides the **relief** of a bull and a lion in combat. The pathway leads around the perimeter wall and stops at the other side of the medieval fortress (open daily 8am-sunset; 150 lekë). For a tour, contact Spiro Angjeli at Shkëndia Travel (see p. 70) or Ani Tare at Caonia B&B (see p. 70).

The best way to reach Butrint is by **taxi.** It costs around US$10 roundtrip from Sarandë, including the wait while you tour around the site; bargain down higher prices. There may also be a morning bus. A one-minute ride in the **ferry** stationed across from the entrance to the ruins takes you to an **island** dominated by a 19th-century Turkish **fortress.** A minute's walk down the road from the ruins, a **hotel-restaurant** offers snacks, meals, and ice cream (entrées around 300 lekë), and four doubles (2500 lekë) with communal bathrooms and hot water.

LAKE OHRID

■ Pogradec

The proximity of mountains, Lake Ohrid, and sheer altitude (600m) have blessed Pogradec with unusually—for Albania—cool weather, while its typically warm and hospitable people have made the town a favorite vacation spot for years. Once threatened by rising industry, Pogradec is now working to save its lake and poppy-strewn hills thanks to recent international initiatives

Orientation and Practical Information The two main streets in the town are **Blvd. Reshit Çollaku,** which runs along the lake, and its inland parallel **Rr. Kajo Karafili.** Traveling to Pogradec by **train** misses the mountainous view. Plus, the train stops 4km from town. A **microbus** service goes to Tirana (3hr., 240 lekë) and Durrës (3hr., 250 lekë). From the south, frequent buses arrive via Korçë (1¾hr., 80 lekë). The bus station is on Rr. Kajo Karafili, next to the market. **Hotel Enkellana,** the town's only tall building, makes a good landmark on Reshit Çollaku. The road forks 100m later. **Exchange currency,** cash Thomas Cook traveler's checks, or obtain an MC cash advance (up to US$100) at **Dega e Bankes,** on the corner of Blvd. Çollaku and Rr. Rinia (open Mon.-Fri. 9am-1:30pm). **Moneychangers** crowd Rr. Kajo Karafili, across from the market. The **post and telephone office** lies across from the hotel, to the left (open daily 7am-2pm; telephones open daily 6am-10pm). Pogradec has no **phone code;** calls are routed through Korçë (phone code: 3558244002).

Accommodations and Food Nuçi Gegprifti (tel. 414 at Enkellana, home tel. 309), will arrange **private rooms** for 1000 lekë or less. He also offers his services as an English guide or interpreter for 2000 lekë per day. Ask him for student discounts at **Hotel Llakmani,** upstairs from Bar-Restaurant Llakmani, to the right of Hotel Enkellana. The hotel has two triples and a double equipped with wall-to-wall carpets and eight firm beds. Two communal showers guarantee at least one hot shower per day

(US$7 per person with discount). **Hotel Enkellana** (tel. 414), a serviceable state-run operation, provides in-room showers with hot water (singles 1725 lekë, doubles 2300 lekë; apartment 2530 lekë).

Found only in Lake Ohrid, *koran* fish pops up in most local eateries. **Restorant Borana,** on the left fork of the main street, serves it for 550-1000 lekë. The owner gave jobs to two of Hoxha's former chefs, who have attracted many dignitaries with their rich menu—most notably Albanian President Sali Berisha and…James Belushi, whose family tree stems from nearby Korçë (open daily 8am-midnight). Accepts MC. English spoken. Less glamorous but also less expensive, **Restorant Pogradeci,** the town's first private eatery, concentrates on local dishes and clientele. *Koran* costs 600-700 lekë, lighter meals 120-160 lekë, and desserts 40-70 lekë. To get there, turn right at Enkellana and left after the Palace of Culture on Rr. Naim Frasheri. Locals hang out at **Restorant Majami,** Rr. Naim Frasheri (tel. 231), which serves hamburgers for 100 lekë and *koran* for 650 lekë (open daily 8am-noon).

Sights and Entertainment On a hot summer day, the fresh mountain air and the smooth lake are invitingly refreshing; but under cloudy skies, Pogradec's closed metal refinery looms larger than it should. The undeveloped **beach,** open right up to the Macedonian border 7km away, gets sandier and less pebbly as you walk east, yet is never wider than 5m. Five km from Pogradec is **Drilonë** (formerly known as Voloreka), a popular park and picnic spot, closed to the common Albanians in the past. Amidst the soothing shade of trees, streams teem with fish. A bit farther the small village of **Tushëmisht** runs a genuine **fish farm.** From June through August, up to 50 **rowboats** line the shore, and their owners are often willing to rent them (100 lekë per hour). In bad weather, the lake can be dangerously windy; remember it's 310m to the bottom. The first **art colony** in the town uses the two floors of the Borana Restaurant as an art gallery. Temporary displays and a big annual exhibition fuel Pogradec's artistic life. Behind the restaurant, the **Nearo Public Library,** shelters 300,000 English books and some oldish American magazines and newspapers (open Mon.-Tues. and Thurs.-Fri. noon-3pm, Wed. and Sat. 9am-noon).

At night, you can visit the **Diamond Disco Club** in the Palace of Culture on the main Blvd. Reshit Çollaku. It plays anything from reggae to techno. Run by an Australian of Albanian descent, it's probably the only place in the country where you'll find *Foster's* (100 lekë). Be prepared for male-bonding of the beer-swilling, leather-jacketed variety (cover 50 lekë, women free on slower nights; open nightly 7:30pm until everyone is tired, and Sat. 11am-3pm). If you're feeling restless at 3am, **Nonstop Café,** off Rr. Rinia to the right past the Coca-Cola sign as you walk away from the lake, sells coffee (20 lekë), beer (60 lekë), and spirits (100-250 lekë).

BELARUS
(БЕЛАРУСЬ)

US$1 = 14,400BR (Belarusian Rubles)	10,000BR = US$0.70
CDN$1 = 10,490BR	10,000BR = CDN$1.00
UK£1 = 22,440BR	10,000BR = UK£0.42
IR£1 = 23,330BR	10,000BR = IR£0.40
AUS$1 = 11,350BR	10,000BR = AUS$0.90
NZ$1 = 10,010BR	10,000BR = NZ$1.00
SAR1 = 3240BR	10,000BR = SAR3.10
DM1 = 9730BR	10,000BR = DM1.04
Country Phone Code: 7	International Dialing Prefix: 00

> Inflation is rampant in Belarus, meaning that the Belarusian Ruble is likely to lose much of its value and probably throw off many of the prices *Let's Go* lists.

The fall of the USSR left Belarus directionless, grasping for a national identity. While other republics were toppling their statues of Lenin, Belarusians polished theirs. Predominantly Russian-speaking, the identity Belarus has chosen seems intimately linked to Russia and its former empire. Soviet bureaucracy persists needlessly in much of the nation: businesses lack effective management and services; border and travel regulations discourage tourism and unnecessarily restrict natives; taxes and regulations make living devastatingly difficult. Where old structures have completely burned out, little has been built to fill the gap.

Capitalism is seeping into Belarus, but its action on the house that Lenin built is more like that of a nest of termites than the Big Bad Wolf. Most Belarusians live in a gray area. From the old women dodging *militsya* to peddle cigarettes and sunflower seeds, to the routine mafia "protection" money that businesses must write off, everyone is involved. Burdened by low wages, rising prices, crippling inflation, and a nightmare of a legal system, the Belarusian people take care of themselves.

BELARUS ESSENTIALS

To visit Belarus' lowlands, you must secure an invitation and a visa—an expensive and head-spinning process. If you have an acquaintance in Belarus who can provide you with an official invitation, you may obtain a single-entry (5-day service US$50, next-day US$100) or a multiple-entry (US$250) visa at an embassy or consulate (see Embassies And Consulates, p. 5). The document will allow you up to 90 days of travel in the country. Together with the visa application and fee (by check or money order), you must submit your passport and one photograph. Prospective tourists without any Belarusian friends may turn to Chris Poor of **Russia House** (see Russia Essentials, p. 520), who will get you a Belarusian invitation and visa in five days for US$100 (rush service US$200), and an extra US$15 for a FedEx return. **Host Families Association (HOFA)** provides invitations for HOFA guests (see Russia Essentials, p. 521). You may also obtain an invitation by planning your trip through a **Belintourist** office. They will provide you with documentation after you have pre-paid all your hotel nights. Transit visas (US$20-30), valid for 48 hours, are issued at a consulate or at the border, but if your train leaves while you're still outside getting your visa, that's your problem; at some Belarusian embassies and consulates, such as the ones in Daugavpils, Latvia and Kiev, Ukraine, transit visas may be cheaper. At the border, expect to be carefully watched, documented, interrogated, and escorted as scads of soldiers do the old-school evil-empire thing. Don't worry, it's harmless.

GETTING THERE AND GETTING AROUND

Three words: don't fly in. **Buses** and **trains** connect Brest to Warsaw, Prague, Kiev, and Lviv and Hrodna to Warsaw and Vilnius. Brest and Hrodna are massive railway junctions, so you'll see more trains headed there than you'll see Lenin statues in Minsk. Tickets for same-day **trains** within Belarus can be purchased at the station. Belintourist has ended its reign, so foreigners can travel as they please. There are information booths in the stations which charge 2000BR per inquiry; better to ask a cashier or just walk away from the info booth like the confused foreigner you are. For **city buses**, buy tickets at a kiosk and punch them on board. **Hitchhiking** is popular, and locals do not consider it dangerous. *Let's Go* does not recommend hitchhiking.

TOURIST SERVICES

Belintourist, a different sort of fossil in each city, is the organizational remnant of the once-omnipotent Intourist. It varies from mostly helpful to merely rubble, but it is often the only resource available. The staff hands out cool Soviet-era brochures and sometimes offers pricey excursions, but seems to cater to businessmen, locals, or often nobody. **Private travel agencies** are springing up. In Minsk is the very helpful Belarusian Society for Friendship and Cultural Relations with Foreign Countries.

MONEY

Be sure to carry a supply of hard **cash**. U.S. dollars, Deutschmarks, and Russian rubles are the preferred media of exchange; you will have a great deal of trouble changing "minor" currencies such as the British pound, to say nothing of Canadian or Australian dollars and other currencies. In addition, bills over US$20 may be difficult to exchange—the same is true of bills that are worn or pre-1990. A black currency market still exists, and its kings will easily fool naive foreigners. There are, of course, no ATM machines, and bank clerks leaf through their English dictionaries at the mention of "traveler's checks." Some hotels accept **credit cards**, mostly AmEx, Eurocard, and Visa. Cash advances for Visa and sometimes MC are available at Priorbank (Приорбанк) offices in most cities, and at the occasional hotel lobby.

COMMUNICATION

Avoid the unreliable **mail** system for important messages; there is an off chance that something sent will reach you by *Poste Restante*—if the postal clerk knows what that is. Public **telephones** have poor sound quality. Pay for **local calls** with tokens, BR, or magnetic cards available at the post office. For **international calls**, you'll have to go to the post office, where you pay exorbitant rates in advance, in cash, to contact foreign lands. To call the U.S. (31,000BR per min.), say *"Yah kha-choo poz-vah-neet seh shah ah,"* and hand the clerk the phone number and your life savings. Blue magnetic **cardphones** in the post office, train station, and some hotels also do the trick; buy cards at the post office. To reach the **BT Direct operator (U.K.)**, dial 88 00 44.

LANGUAGE

Belarusians speak mostly **Russian** and only rarely Belarusian (see the Cyrillic Alphabet, p. 771, and the Russian Glossary, p. 787). In western cities such as Hrodna and Brest, **Polish** is fairly common. Many people also speak **German** and **English**—at least enough to sing along to an utterly random collection of American tunes. Many young people will speak some English. Don't worry too much about learning Belarusian phrases if you'll just be staying in big cities such as Minsk and Brest—most townies won't know them either. Some street names have been converted into Belarusian, although locals still use the old Russian versions. If you can handle substituting the Belarusian "i" for the Russian "и" and other minor spelling changes, you'll be fine.

HEALTH AND SAFETY

> **Emergency Numbers: Fire:** tel. 01. **Police:** tel. 02. **Ambulance:** tel. 03.

Belarus was more affected by the **Chernobyl** accident than any other country, including Ukraine. With the faulty reactor situated just 12km south of the Belarusian border, and winds blowing north for the first six days after the explosion, much of the radioactive material was blown into Belarus and deposited into the soil of the southeast quarter of the nation. An area of approximately 1200 sq. km just north of Chernobyl has been totally evacuated on account of the extremely high concentrations of Strontium-90, Plutonium-239/240, and Cesium-137. Don't panic—the radiation danger to visitors is practically nil, and none of the Belarusian cities covered in *Let's Go* are in affected regions. Nonetheless, stay cautious. Avoid inexpensive Belarusian dairy products (opt for something German or Dutch, with no Cyrillic on it), which are likely to come from the region, and mushrooms, which tend to collect radioactivity.

Belarusian **crime** seems as underdeveloped and inefficient as the rest of its economy, but economic hardship has brought many opportunists. The police number for the country is listed above, but your embassy is probably a better bet in an emergency. High-heeled Belarusian women can be seen walking and riding public transportation alone even after dark, but they may face catcalls or harassment and probably do so out of financial necessity rather than real security. Expect to be approached by poor young and old 'uns asking if you need your bottle once your drink is empty; give it to them—they need the return-money more than you do.

Toilet paper is touch-and-go, generally absent in public restrooms (1000BR). It's available in most supermarkets. Western **condoms** are rare, but feminine hygiene supplies from the other side of the former Iron Curtain are beginning to turn up.

ACCOMMODATIONS AND CAMPING

There are no **hostels** in Belarus, apart from *turbazy* ("tour-bases"), which only leading Stalinist pioneers with very cold upbringings will be able to bear. Keep all those little slips of paper from your hotels, because you just might have to show them to avoid paying fines on your way out of the country. In another example of warped Belarusian/Soviet logic, **hotels** in Belarus have three sets of rates—one very cheap for Belarusians, one often outrageous for foreigners, and one in between for citizens of the CIS. The desk clerks will probably immediately ask you where you are from and request your passport, making it easier to get nookie in a nunnery than to pass as a native. Some **private hotels** don't accept foreigners at all for some arcane reason, but those that do are usually much cheaper and friendlier than the Soviet dinosaurs. **Private rooms** are worth a shot; get a day in the life of a Belarusian, a couple of meals, and coddled by the resident *babushka* for US$10 or less.

FOOD AND DRINK

Belarusian cuisine consists purely of what the farmers can grow or fatten: potatoes, bread, chicken, and pork. However, thanks to Stalinist repatriations, enough Georgian and Uzbek chefs made Belarus their home to allow you to sprinkle distant spices on your cholesterol. Brest basks in the glory of having the best restaurant south of Tallinn, while each town's market (рынак; *rynak*) displays a spectrum of veggies and fruits. Bread, sausage, and a thinly sliced vegetable are what you should expect to receive in homes or if you guess at a menu. Fried entities like meat-filled, crispy *cheburiki* (чебурики; 2800BR) or puffy divine *panchiki* (панчики) will fill you up for a dollar and hospitalize you for two. The favorite Belarusian drink is a bread-based alcohol, *kvas* (квас), which you can buy at any store—just look for the long line.

CUSTOMS AND ETIQUETTE

If you want to simulate the threads of a hip, wealthy, or semi-criminal young male Belarusian, just stop by the sporting goods store. Pick out the brightest, tackiest two-piece track suit you can find, preferably with Adidas, Nike or—the-end-all—Mercedes Benz plastered on the back. Subtlety is just as dominant in women's fashions: see-through white blouses (and even dresses) aren't necessarily the least modest garb on the street. Sunglasses are everywhere, so if you've shelved your shades for fear of looking like a hood, fear no more: you will, but so will everyone else. With the rapidly inflating 20,000BR note the highest bill you'll probably carry, you're going to be walking around with wads of cash anyway. Nearly all shops and restaurants close an hour for lunch, dinner, and occasionally breakfast. **Discrimination** exists in Belarus, and there are almost no ethnic minorities. If you want to fit in, don't smile too much. **Homosexuality** is definitely frowned upon, and a gay man is bound to be beaten if he winks at a local skinhead; but no one will assume you are gay unless you openly announce your sexual preferences.

LIFE AND TIMES

HISTORY

The area known today as Belarus has survived centuries of invasion and subdivision in a shifting mosaic of political boundaries. Modern Belarus is therefore a unique political and cultural hybrid, bearing the traces of long-dead and recent empires. Russian influence remains strong as Belarusians try to construct a national identity in the post-Soviet world. While often invaded, Belarus has also witnessed many historic triumphs; the Belarusians succeeded in barring the Mongols from Western Europe after the **Battle of Koydanovo,** and defeated Napoleon along the Berezina.

Modern Belarus has its origin in the province of **Polatsk,** which grew as a result of the extensive trading along the Dnieper River initiated by the Vikings (Varangians) in the 9th century. Belarus prospered under Viking rule, and Smolensk, which lies along the Dnieper, was reputedly a significant trade and industrial center by the end of the 9th century. The ties this trade created between what would become Russia, Ukraine, and Belarus foreshadowed future union, particularly as 9th-century Belarusian principalities were subject to the first East Slavic state, **Kievan Rus** (modern-day Ukraine). By the late 12th century, many towns in present-day Belarus, such as Minsk and Brest, had already been established.

In the 13th century, Polatsk managed to avoid the Mongol yoke, and escaped the isolation which Russia and parts of modern Ukraine endured for 250 years. Instead, Belarus knew Western masters. Beginning in the 13th century, the **Grand Duchy of Lithuania** gradually swelled to include a large portion of Belarus; after Lithuania united with Poland in 1386, Polish cultural and political influences were added to the melting pot of Belarusian identity. The Belarusian aristocracy was mainly Polish-speaking and Roman Catholic, and a codified feudal system stripped Eastern Orthodox Belarusian peasants of their liberties

Unhappy with Polish rule, Belarus peasants staged rebellions, led by Cossacks, in the period from 1648-54. At the same time Poland and Russia struggled over Belarusian territory. Under the three **Partitions of Poland,** Russia succeeded in taking over Belarus, gaining Eastern Belarus after the first partition (1772), central Belarus after the second (1793), and the rest after the third and final partition (1795) that wiped Poland from the map of Europe. Small timber and glass industries grew up in Belarusian towns, but many areas—especially the remote Pripet Marshes—remained economically stagnant. The emancipation of the serfs in the 1860s gave Belarusian industry a shot in the arm. But the regional economy was still so impoverished that between 1896 and 1915, over 600,000 people left Belarus—for Siberia. The area witnessed heavy fighting between German and Russian troops during WWI; in early 1918, Russia ceded part of Belarus to Germany, only to get it back a few months later at the end of the war.

Meanwhile, Belarus was stumbling toward statehood. The **Russian Revolution of 1905** triggered peasant revolts in the region, and in 1918 Belarus declared itself a democratic republic. As soon as Germany left Belarus, however, the Bolsheviks muscled in, while Polish troops marched in from the west. In 1919, Russia and Poland divided the region among themselves, and the Russian portion metamorphosed into the **Belarusian Soviet Socialist Republic.** Moscow tacked on bits and pieces of nearby regions to the Belarusian SSR., meanwhile establishing new industries in Belarusian cities and purging the republic of dissidents and intellectuals.

World War I brought more turmoil to Belarus and shifted its political boundaries once again. Soviet troops invaded Poland from the east, occupying the region up to the Bug River and taking back some of the Belarusian land ceded to Poland in 1921. German armies quickly occupied the Belarusian SSR in 1941, despite the brave resistance of a Belarusian garrison at Brest. When the Soviets retook Belarus after the war, they deported the region's Polish population to Poland. Wartime damage was rapidly repaired, and major cities were further industrialized, sapping rural areas of their population. By 1973, Minsk's population had reached the one million mark.

In 1986, the explosion of the nuclear plant at **Chernobyl** spewed radioactive material across the southernmost part of the republic; the Belarusian zone nearest Chernobyl was immediately evacuated, but other dangerously contaminated regions in the republic were not evacuated until 1990.

While nearby Baltic republics struggled to break away from Moscow in the late 1980s, Belarus moved sluggishly. Separatism grew slowly under *glasnost* and *perestroika,* and Belarus finally declared **sovereignty** on July 27, 1990 and independence on August 25, 1991 amid political turmoil in Moscow. The fledgling republic joined the **Commonwealth of Independent States**—a weak amalgam of former Soviet Republics—but faces a tough path to capitalism and true independence.

LITERATURE

From the 11th- to 14th-century, Belarusian literature suckled at the same literary teat as Ukrainian and Russian. Their mother was Old Church Slavonic. But as early as the 1400s, chroniclers were writing in a distinctive Belarusian tongue. Literary aristocrats like **Fiodor Jeŭlaševski** wrote in Belarusian as they participated in the memoir publishing fad of the 16th century. Another 16th-century fashion—strictly 13-syllable panegyrics—attracted a mass of dabblers. As Poland gained increasing control over Belarus in the 18th century, and a Polish ruling class began banning and confiscating Belarusian literature, the home literary movement slowed to a halt. During this period, **Kaeten Maraševski** published the only major Belarusian work—*Kameidyja* (Comedy). A century later, **Dunin-Marcinkievič** revived Belarusian poetry with his humorous verse. In the late 1800s a circle of poets including the "parent of modern Belarusian literature," **Bahuševič,** fought for literary freedom and gained it in 1905. A year later, the Belarusian newspaper, *Naša niva,* hit newsstands. In its first three years, the journal included over a thousand contributions from nearly 500 villages. With its egalitarian approach, *Naša* served as a springboard for many Belarusian writers, including **Kupała, Kołas,** and **Bahdanovič.** The Russian Revolution in 1917 inspired the Belarusian National Republic in 1918, and although the state had the lifespan of a mayfly, the spirit of nationalism continued with an official policy of Belarusification. A slew of literary groups spawned a generation of poets who attacked both the aristocratic past and communist repression. Many writers disappeared during Stalin's purges (1936-39), and not until the 1950s did a new generation appear to focus on the preservation of Belarusian as a language. With the reconsideration of Stalin, prose flourished and diversified. A few big names include **Bykaŭ**, famous for war novels, **Karatkievič,** known for historical works, and **Barys Sačanka,** a leader in psychological realism. Currently, **Ales' Razanau** crafts in free verse.

BELARUS TODAY

It was Belarus, of all the former Soviet republics, that had the weakest national identity, Belarus where the clamor for independence was quietest. On April 2, 1996, the country took a step back toward the fold, signing an integration treaty with Russia. The treaty created the "Community of Sovereign Republics", the closest political and economic relationship of any former Soviet republics, which calls for a coordinated foreign and military policy; unification of taxation, transport, and energy legislation; and a common currency by 1997. The last is unlikely.

Chernobyl's tragic legacy still haunts Belarus; as much as 40% of the country was contaminated with radioactive cesium that has triggered a rash of thyroid cancers among children. Minsk marked the 10th anniversary of the 1986 disaster with a violent demonstration of 50,000—200 were arrested. And in a country with the most oppressive political climate in Europe, complete with purges in education and the press, the repression only worsens as Lukashenka tightens his grip on the economy which was only 27% privatized in 1996. Taxes on profits are so high (80%) that they discourage private enterprise, and inflation ran an estimated 90% in 1996. Belarus's future seems shaky; only time will heal the wounds of this scarred nation.

Minsk (Мінск)

The fall of Communism in Minsk has been more a reluctant shuffle than a wanton gallop to the West. Lenin's statue still stands in Independence Square. Red Army and Communism streets still intersect, and statues of Felix Dzerzhinski—the Belarusian founder of the KGB—line the avenues bearing his name. Flattened in World War I, the entire city was redesigned as a showpiece of Soviet style. Yet recently a capitalist breeze has begun to tease centrally planned Minsk. Young western entrepreneurs willing to brave the rapid inflation and political and legal chaos that have begun to take root, Minsk flaunts a new cosmopolitan air in outdoor cafés buzzing with multilingual, pricey new restaurants, and wild nightclubs.

ORIENTATION AND PRACTICAL INFORMATION

Minsk appears to have been built for the super-sized youths of Soviet statues. The main area is contained in the 3km between northeast **pl. Peramohi** (Перамогі), and southwest **pl. Nezalezhnastsi** (Незалежнасці). **Pr. Frantsishka Skaryny** (Францішка Скарыны) runs between the two squares. Halfway up pr. F. Skaryny and perpendicular to it runs **pr. Masherava** (Машэрава). **Nyamiha** (Няміга) and **Ulyanaiskaya** (Ульянаўская) complete the fencing of the city center. The rail station sits behind **Privakzalnaya pl.** (Прывакзальная)—a walk up vul. Kirava (Кірава) and a left on Svyardlova (Свярдлова) to pl. Nezalezhnastsi.

Make the necessary effort to find a copy of the up-to-the-minute **Minsk in Your Pocket,** a brilliant city-guide whose city and metro maps are well worth the price (US$1 in BR). By the way, **jaywalking** carries a fine, so use the underpasses.

- **Tourist Office: Belintourist,** pr. Masherava 19 (tel. 26 95 01), next to Gastsinitsa Yubileyni. Lacking good maps, they attempt to make up for it with dated brochures on *"Sovietska Belarussia".* Open Mon.-Fri. 9am-6pm. **Belarusian Society for Friendship and Cultural Relations with Foreign Countries,** vul. Zakharava 28 (Захарава; tel. 33 15 02). English speakers ask for Dmitry Khoolakov. Lives up to its name with the most effusively friendly and helpful treatment of any government agency. Open Mon.-Fri. 9am-6pm.
- **Passport Office:** To extend your visa, you must plead with whomever provided your original visa invitation to apply to for the extension with the **Ministry of Foreign Affairs.** The central office, which may or may not be helpful depending on its mood, can be reached at 32 64 29. Otherwise, contact your embassy.
- **Currency Exchange:** Follow the "Абмен Валюты" *(Abmen Valyuty)* signs, but do not be deceived by the posted hours or services—they're completely random. The exchange office on the 2nd floor of the **GUM** store, on pr. F. Skaryny and vul. Lenina, offers decent rates. The exchange office in **Gastinitsa Yubileyni** lobby provides US$ advances on your MC or Visa at a 4% commission. It also cashes Thomas Cook traveler's checks (open 24hr., off-hours at 6:30am, 1, and 7pm).
- **Embassies: Russia,** vul. Staravilenskaya 48 (Старавіленскай; tel. 50 36 65; fax 50 36 64); **Ukraine,** vul. Kirava 17-306 (tel. 27 27 96; fax 27 28 61); **U.S.,** vul. Staravilenskaya 46 (tel. 34 77 61 or 31 50 00; fax 34 78 53); **U.K.,** vul. Karla Marxa 37 (Карла Маркса; tel. 29 23 03, 29 23 04, or 29 23 05; fax 29 23 06).
- **Trains: Advance-Booking Office,** pr. F. Skaryny 18 (tel. 96 30 67). Open Mon.-Sat. 9am-1pm and 2-6pm. Same-day tickets for destinations in Belarus on station's 2nd floor (open 24hr.). To: Kiev (3 per day, 11hr.); Moscow (23 per day, 12hr.); Rīga (1 per day, 12½hr.); Vilnius (2 per day, 4hr.); Warsaw (4 per day, 8hr.).
- **Buses:** There are 2 stations. The **Central Station,** vul. Babruskaya 12 (Бабруйская; tel. 36 32 14 or 27 04 73; for info, dial 004), just east of the train station, handles buses to all points west of Minsk. To: Vilnius (3 per day, 4-5½hr., 53,700BR); Warsaw (1 per day, 11hr., 210,000BR). The **East Station** is almost 9km out of town at vul. Vaneyeva 34 (Ванэева; tel. 48 08 82). Take trolleybus #20 from Kirava, near the Central Station, about 9 stops to the "Автовакзал". It's the concrete-and-glass monstrosity on the opposite side of the traffic circle. Most connections are within Belarus. Buses to Rīga (1 per day, 12hr., 130,000BR) and Warsaw.
- **Public Transportation:** The **Metro,** with several useful stops, runs round the clock under pr. F. Skaryny. It's worth it just to see all the "CCCP" logos. Also buses, trolleybuses, and trams (daily 5:35am-12:55am). All are 1500BR per ride; monthly passes 45,000BR. Pick up a pass and **map** at any kiosk around the city.
- **Car Rental:** Avis (tel. 34 79 90; fax 39 16 13), in Gastinitsa Belarus, offers Toyotas, Volvos, and Fords. The cheapest class is US$41 per day, plus US$0.41 per km. For unlimited kilometrage, pay US$114 or less per day. Open daily 8am-6pm.

Taxis: Free-enterprise "competition" in Minsk is one company driving Volvos and Ladas for different rates (tel. 061 or 70 90 11), and the occasional independent driver. Fares are negotiable—pay no more than US$2 between the 2 main squares.
Pharmacy: Skaryny 16 (tel. 27 83 40). Open Mon.-Fri. 8am-8pm, Sat. 10am-5pm.
Post Office: pr. F. Skaryny 10 (tel. 27 77 71), opposite Gastsinitsa Minsk. To send or receive packages, enter on vul. Svyardlova (Свярдлова) and go up to the second floor. Open Mon.-Fri. 8am-8pm, Sat.-Sun. 10am-5pm. **Postal code:** 220050.
Telephones and Telegraph: In the same building as the central post office, in the hall to the left immediately upon entering. Book a call to the U.S. on a numbered booth for 31,000BR per min. All numbers in Minsk are 7 digits and start with a "2", so if you happen across a 6-digit number, simply add an initial "2". Open daily 7:30am-11pm. **Faxes** at booth #6 (tel. 26 02 22; fax 26 05 30). Open Mon.-Fri. 8am-8pm. **Phone code:** 0172.

ACCOMMODATIONS

Hostels as such don't exist here, despite a long list of hostels in the phonebook (e.g., the poetic "October Revolution Tractor Plant no. 9 Tool-Makers' Association Hostel of Comrades"). *Minsk in Your Pocket* lists some cheaper hotels. **Private rooms** are another option; people invite you or taxi drivers may know. For US$10 or less per night, you get a room, and probably meals too—just don't expect hot water.

Gastsinitsa Svisloch (Гасцініца Свіслочь), vul. Kirava 13 (tel. 20 97 83), across from the Dynamo ticket office. Singles *sans* bathroom but with hot water and even a small TV 153,400BR. Doubles 248,000BR, with bath 261,800BR.

Gastsinitsa Minsk (Мінск), pr. F. Skaryny 11 (tel. 20 01 32), in the center of town, 1km from the train station. Renovated rooms with TV, phone, fridge, toilet paper, and showers. The usual Intourist security features. Singles US$46, doubles US$62.

Gastsinitsa Belarus (Беларусь), vul. Starazoskaya 15 (Старазоўская; tel. 39 17 05), on the north side of the river 3km out of town opposite the Gastinitsa Yubileyni. Rooms on floors 4-5 of this 23-story monster have been "renovated" to higher prices. Private bath, TV, sauna. Singles US$50. Doubles US$60. AmEx and Visa accepted. Roll the rest of your cash away at the casino (open nightly 5pm-5am).

Gastsinitsa Yubileyni (Юбілейны), pr. Masherava 19 (tel. 26 90 24). Great for a glimpse of the local "businessmen." Singles with TV, phone, and shower US$53. Doubles US$63. MC and Visa accepted. Casino downstairs open nightly 4pm-4am.

FOOD

Universam (Універсам), vul. F. Skaryny. Only counter service, but the delicious pastries, meats, and matchless *morozhenoe* (мороженое; 5,200BR) make it clear why this place is always packed. Open daily 9am-11pm.

Sem Pyatnid (Сем Пятніц), pr. F. Skaryny 19 (tel. 27 69 01). Popular among the local Mercedes-and-cellular-phone crowd, this Polish restaurant is crowded in the evenings, so go for lunch. Start your meal with a *solyanka* (солянка) full of raisins, peanuts, and green onions (23,000BR); add *zharkoe s chernochlivom* (жаркое с черносливом), a rich dish of pork with prunes (31,500BR); and finish with coffee (7600BR). Open daily noon-5pm and 7pm-4am.

Restaran Uzbekistan (Рэстаран Узбекистан), vul. F. Skaryny 30 (tel. 27 75 51). Recently upgraded from a closet café to shiny new quarters, the hot-spot retains its drawing power. Uzbek dishes chock-full of *cardamom*, a welcome change from boiled potatoes and pork, in a tiny co-op restaurant. Spicy *shurpa* (шурпа; "soup") warms you on cold and rainy days (69,000BR). *Plov no uzbeski* (плов но узбески) is a rice dish with lamb morsels (90,000BR). Open Mon.-Sat. noon-midnight.

Café Berezka (Кафе Бярозка), pr. F. Skaryny 40 (tel. 33 15 89). Beloved by the locals for reasonable prices and the café's specialty—stuffed fish filet *Berezka* (40,200BR). Various salads average 8900BR. Outside seating available in Victory Square. Open daily 11am-11:30pm.

Restaran Novolunie (Рэстаран Новолуне), vul. Zakharava 31 (Захарава; tel. 36 74 55), 500m east of pl. Peramohi. A cozy semi-underground place just past the British Embassy. Main courses around 50,000-200,000BR. Open daily 11am-11pm.

Central Minsk

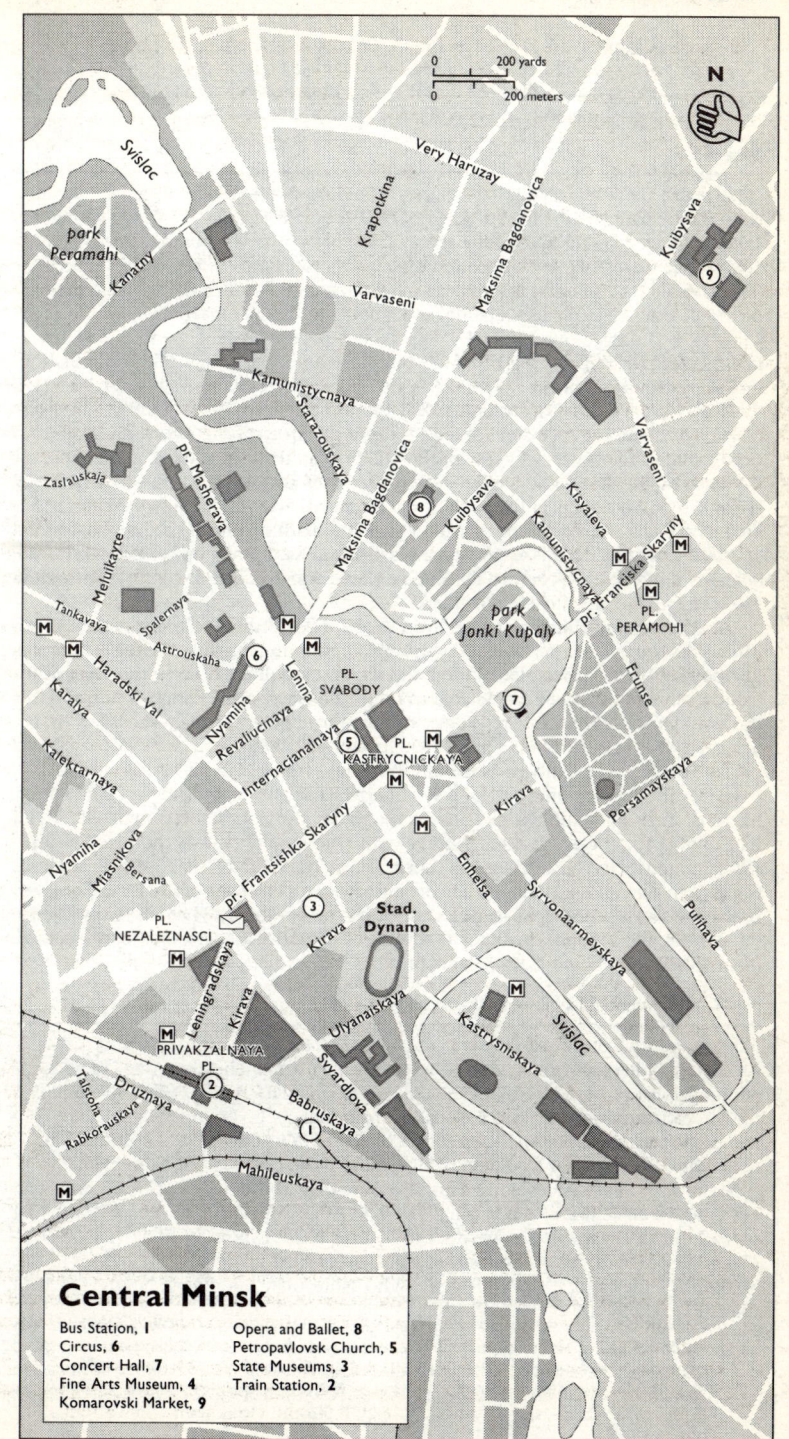

Bus Station, **1**
Circus, **6**
Concert Hall, **7**
Fine Arts Museum, **4**
Komarovski Market, **9**
Opera and Ballet, **8**
Petropavlovsk Church, **5**
State Museums, **3**
Train Station, **2**

El Rincon Español, vul. F. Skaryny (tel. 27 23 31). A little out of the budget traveler's reach, but considered the best restaurant in Minsk. Some items are easy on the wallet—warm vegetable salad (34,000BR)—but most entrées aren't. The house speciality, *Paella Marinera,* runs 323,000BR. Visa and MC accepted.

SIGHTS

A journalist once suggested that Belarus should be developed as a sort of "Communism theme park," with Minsk as its hub *à la* Cinderella's castle. If arguing with Belintourist and standing in lines at the train station hasn't left you feeling like you're in a Soviet time warp, take a walk around the city. Minsk is most noteworthy for its utter Sovietness, a state of mind that exudes from the architecture, emanates from the people, radiates from every street name, and culminates in the museums.

Minsk was named one of the 13 "Hero Cities" of the Soviet Union because it was decimated in WWII. Over 80% of the buildings and nearly 60% of the population, including almost all of the 300,000 Jews who lived here, were obliterated between 1941 and 1944. The reconstructed **Old Town** on the north bank of the Svislac, west of vul. Nyamiha, is a nice area for a mid-afternoon stroll through souvenir shops and beer gardens. However, very few of the buildings in these blocks are authentic. Past the Planeta, the vast flatness is broken by the painfully pointy Soviet **war memorial** spike. Go down the hill at the back of the memorial and you'll find yourself in a rare area of pre-war Minsk complete with a park and bathing beach (paddle boat rental 20,000BR per hr.). In the square east of the Nyamiha metro stop (pl. Svobody; Свободы), a dazzling 18th-century **Orthodox Cathedral** and a 17th-century **Bernadine Monastery** have recently been restored.

The **Museum of the Great Patriotic War** (Музей Великой Отечественной Войны; *Muzey Velikoy Otechestvennoy Voyny*), pr. F. Skaryny 25a (tel. 27 56 11), features 28 rooms of maps, guns, tanks, documents, and a hall devoted to the Nazi death camps. More than 20% of the Belarusian population was killed during WWII, and this museum gives a grim, detailed picture of the war in Belarus (open Tues.-Sun. 10am-5pm; 5000BR; call ahead for a tour in English for 45,000BR).

The **History and Culture National Museum,** vul. K. Marxa 12 (tel. 27 56 12), explores the history of everything Belarusian. Discover arrowheads, 19th-century folk costumes, and whole halls consecrated to the glory of the Belarusian SSR. If you had doubts that Belarus was a country with true culture, this is the place to visit. Exhibits are labeled only in Russian (open Thurs.-Tues. 11am-7pm; 5000BR, students 800BR). In a green house on the banks of the Svisilac, **Museum of the First Congress of the Russian Social-Democratic Labor Party,** pr. F. Skaryny 31-a (tel. 36 68 47), the table is set and the bed made for the founder of tsarist Russia's first Marxist party, circa 1898 (open Thurs.-Tues. 10am-6pm).

ENTERTAINMENT AND NIGHTLIFE

A major philharmonic **orchestra,** an impressive **opera** company, and a world-renowned **ballet,** provide a wide array of cultural events. Theater groups of all kinds add to the list of performances. The ticket offices are at pl. Parizhskoy Kommuny 1 (Парижской Коммуны; opera tel. 39 10 41, ballet tel. 34 06 66; open daily 11am-1pm and 1:30-7pm; opera 10,000BR, ballet 1000-15,000BR). To watch folks just hanging—over a hushed crowd or a column of air—there is the **circus,** pr. F. Skaryny 32.

Nightlife in Minsk is developing at least as quickly as the rest of its nearly free market. The **Paradise disco,** vul. Masherava 13, in Kino "Moskva," has plenty of dancing spread out over two floors, with a mildly erotic floor-show to boot. (Disco Sun.-Thurs. 11pm-4am; 50,000BR before 1pm, afterward it doubles for men; Fri.-Sat. 50,000BR ladies and 100,000BR gents who were busy boogeying before the 11th hour, 130,000BR and 200,000BR after).

Hrodna (Гродна)

On the road between Warsaw and Vilnius, Hrodna offers a rarity in Belarus—the towers to God overpower the towers to Lenin. Catholic cathedrals, the sole reason to stop here, loom over twisting streets of Baroque buildings. Unfortunately, the Soviets did have some say in the city, plotting the train and bus stations and hotels in an inconveniently wide ring around the center.

Orientation and Practical Information Trains are the only realistic way to reach Hrodna. A vast blank wall rising from a park full of vendors, the station (tel. 005; open 24hr.) marks the end of vul. Azheshka (Ажешка), just northeast of the city. Trains run to Minsk (4 per day, 9hr., 50,000BR), Rīga (1 per day, 13½hr., 285,000BR), Vilnius (2 per day, 3½hr., 135,000BR), and Warsaw (4 per day, 6hr.). **Store luggage** in lockers in the station's basement (7000BR). The **bus** station (tel. 004) sits 1.5km south of the train station on pr. Kasmanaitai (Касманаўтаў) over the railroad bridge from the end of vul. Kirava (Кірава). Buses run to Minsk (12 per day, 5½hr., 83,700BR). A crash course in Hrodna's layout: the main north-south streets are, from east to west, **vul. Satsiyalistychnaya** (Сацыялістычная), **vul. Krupskay** (Крупскай), and **vul. Savetskaya** (Савецкая). Running perpendicular to these, the important roads are **vul. K. Marxa** (К. Маркса) and **vul. Kirava**. The **tourist office**, vul. Azheshka 49 (tel. 45 26 27), offers assistance in Russian (open Mon.-Fri. 8:30am-5pm). To **exchange currency**, look for the "Абмен Валюты" signs, or stop by Prior Bank (Приор Банк), vul. Savetskaya 10, for cash courtesy of MC or Visa (open Mon.-Fri. 9am-4pm). The **post and telephone office** stamps and dials from vul. K. Marxa 35. (Post open Mon.-Fri. 8am-8pm, Sat. 10am-4pm; tel. 47 36 81. Telephones open 7:30am-10:30pm; tel. 45 35 12.) **Postal code:** 230025. **Phone code:** 0152.

Accommodations and Food With all the trains streaming past Hrodna, there's not much reason to stay the night. If you're stuck, take bus #15 four stops from the train station to **Gastsinitsa Belarus** (Гасцініца Беларусь), vul. M. Gorkovo (М. Горького), where rooms will run you 201,000BR for a single or 314,000BR for a double. Lotsa hot water, and they take MC and Visa.

The city's cleanest and busiest (which bodes well for the food) is probably the Kafé-Bar (Кафэ-Бар), opposite the train station. Try the *cheburiki* (чебурики; beef fried in a flaky shell; 2800BR) accompanied by a *Guinness* (26,300BR; open daily 10am-10pm). Lounge at the outdoor tables of the popular café **Magazin Grodsop** (Магазин Гродсоуп), at the south end of vul. Savetskaya (coffee 3300BR; open daily 10am-10pm). **Grocery stores** pepper the city.

Sights and Entertainment Leaving the train station, make a right to the **Hrodna Zoo**, vul. Timiryazeva (Тимирязева; tel. 47 28 38; open May-Sept. daily 10am-6pm; Oct.-April 10am-5pm). For 5000BR, you can get within two feet of a lion, tigers, dingoes, and jackals—crammed into tiny and not particularly clean cages.

Once in town, take in the awe-inspiring **Farnoy Cathedral** (Фарной), at the corner of vul. K. Marxa and vul. Krupskay. The dingy exterior conceals the golden, halo-like chandeliers that bathe the paintings and intricately carved altarpiece with light. Also on vul. K. Marxa lies the Polish **Najswiętsze Serce Jezusa** (Holy Church of Jesus). The 16th-century **Bernadine giant**, being restored in 1996, near the end of Krupskay, and the obligatory, blue-domed **Russian Orthodox gem** on vul. Azheshka round out the collection. Mmm… Packed with churches—Hrodna really satisfies.

Where vul. Azheshka cuts vul. Satsiyalistychnaya, indulge in a detour to the **Lenin statue** in the eponymous square just to the north. From here, take a right on vul. Uritskaha which transforms into vul. Krupskay. The 1970s **drama theater** is complemented by a spectacularly tasteless statue. The cashier's office is at the rear (open Tues. 4-7:15pm, Wed.-Sat. 2-7:15pm, Sun. 11am-7:15pm).

Vul. Savetskaya flows with cheap beer; try **Disco Club Adam**, on the corner of vul. Savetskaya and vul. Azheshka at #30 (open Fri-Sat. 6pm-midnight). The **central mar-**

ket, just beyond the post office, also entertains a daily mob seeking socks, dirt-covered vegetables, and raw capitalism sold from blankets on the street. Say "hi".

■ Brest (Брэст)

Made famous by the 1918 Treaty of Brest-Litovsk, whereby Lenin and Co. ceded Poland, the Baltics, Belarus, and most of Ukraine to the Germans to get out of World War I, Brest remained a Polish city between the wars. World War II thrust Brest into the spotlight again, as Brest Fortress held for over a month against the Germans. Blessed by its Soviet planners, the city is dotted with monuments and shady avenues.

ORIENTATION AND PRACTICAL INFORMATION

Maps of the small city are available in the kiosk at the train station. The **Mukhavets** and **Bug** rivers mark off the south and west boundaries. At their confluence lies the **Brest Fortress.** The Bug also marks the Polish border. From the rail station, cross the overpass to **vul. Lenina** (Леніна). At the open square—**pl. Lenina, vul. Pushkinskaya** (Пушкінская) is to the left. Farther down runs **vul. Gogalya** (Гогаля), the main east-west thoroughfare. **Vul. Maskaiskaya** (Маскаўская) parallels the Mukhavets at the end of vul. Lenina leading from the Gastsinitsa Intourist to the Fortress.

- **Tourist Office: Belintourist,** vul. Maskaiskaya 15 (tel. 25 10 71), in Gastsinitsa Intourist. The only show in town. Not a lot of maps or brochures, but they try. English spoken. **Tours** of the Brest Fortress can be arranged in English if you call a week in advance. Price varies. Open Mon.-Fri. 8am-5pm.
- **Currency Exchange: Five Stars** (tel. 23 86 85), a private currency-change operation at vul. Pushkinskaya 10, offers possibly the best of the awful rates in town. Open Mon.-Sat. 9am-9pm, Sun. 9am-7pm. **Prior Bank** (Приор Банк), vul. Pushkinskaya 16/1 (tel. 23 99 18), cash advances on Visa. Open Mon.-Fri. 9am-4pm.
- **Trains:** (tel. 005, open 24hr.), just north of vul. Ardzhanikidze (Арджанікідзе). Busy, busy, busy. This consumer-dwarfing Soviet monument is a sight in itself. To: Kiev (1 per day, 16½hr., 128,700BR); Minsk (6 per day, 7hr., 57,400BR); Moscow (4 per day, 16hr., 204,400BR); Prague (2 per day, 18hr.); Warsaw (6 per day). **Luggage storage** off the main hall. Locker 3500BR, backpack size space 7000BR.
- **Buses:** (tel. 25 51 36) at the corner of vul. Kuibyshava (Куйбышава) and vul. Mitskevicha (Мішкевіча) near the central market. Tickets sold daily 6am-11pm. To: Hrodna (6 per day, 7½hr., 20,800BR) and Warsaw (4 per day, 6hr., 110,800BR).
- **Post Office:** vul. Pushkinskaya (tel. 26 26 12), on pl. Lenina. Open Mon.-Fri. 8:30am-8pm, Sat. 8:30am-5pm, Sun. 8:30am-3pm. **Postal code:** 224005.
- **Telephones and Telegraph:** In the post office. Open daily 7:30am-9:30pm. **Phone code:** from Belarus 8-016-2, from the former USSR 888-2, from beyond 37516-2. The last "2" is the first digit of all listed numbers in Brest.

ACCOMMODATIONS

- **Gastsinitsa Instituta** (Гасьцініна Иніптитута), vul. Pushkinskaya 16/1 (tel. 23 93 72), entrance from the driveway on the building's left. A budget oasis in the Belarusian accommodations desert. Basic rooms with some hot water. Singles 80,000BR, with shower 110,000BR.
- **Gastsinitsa Vesta** (Веста), vul. Krupskay 16 (Крупская; tel. 23 71 69), 2km from the train station, in the left back corner of the green, park-like plaza west of pl. Lenina. The best hotel in Brest for the money, the Vesta's marble floors echo with the occasional English conversation. Rooms boast fridges, TVs, and closets big enough to start your own business. Singles 300,000BR. Doubles 500,000BR.
- **Gastsinitsa Intourist** (Інтуріст), vul. Maskaiskaya 15 (tel. 25 20 83). The place seems to get most of the German and Polish businesspeople that swarm around Brest. The 70s Preservation Society would feel right at home in the rooms. TV and hot water for the private baths. Singles US$40. Doubles US$62.

FOOD

Brest is rightly famed among foreigners living in Belarus for having the single **best restaurant** in the country. Diplomats in Minsk drive to Brest on weekends just to dine there. **Restaurant India,** vul. Gogalya 29, at vul. K. Marxa (tel. 26 63 25), revives your deadened palate with authentic, spicy Indian food. It may be the best restaurant west of Moscow; a businessman who missed Indian food hired the chefs from Delhi. Feast on sumptuous *yakhni sherba* (15,400BR), creamy *gosht korma* (lamb in sauce; 31,000BR), or hot Indian bread (8700BR; open daily noon-10:30pm). A faded establishment of the Soviet era, **Restaran Brest** (Рестаран Брэст) sits at vul. Pushkinskaya 20, a block west of the market. This elaborate two-story dining and dancing hall is still a popular place for a night out on the town (pork with mushrooms 47,900BR, Belarusian beer 7200BR; open Wed.-Mon. noon-5pm and 6pm-midnight, Tues. noon-5pm and 6-9pm). Or you can do-it-yourself from the **grocery store** just past the post office (open Mon.-Fri. 7:30am-9pm, Sat. 8am-8pm, Sun. 8am-3pm).

SIGHTS

Brest Fortress (Крэпасць Брэст-Літоўск; *Krepasts Brest-Litoisk*) dominates three sq. km of area around the Bug and Mukhavets rivers. What are now grassy hills and tree-strewn streets used to be the best-equipped fortress in Tsarist Russia. After Napoleon's 1812 attack on Russia, several cities in Poland, Lithuania, and Belarus were heavily fortified, with this massive fortress intended to be the central defensive point against future aggression. From 1838 to 1841 the entire city was moved east to open up the site for the fort. Brick walls 15m-thick, moats, rivers, and encasements made this a formidable battlement.

In the 1918 **Treaty of Brest-Litovsk,** however, Lenin ceded Brest to the Germans. The Poles held it between the wars, but another Russian-German agreement, this time the 1939 **Molotrov-Ribbentrop Pact,** brought Brest-Litovsk back into the Russian fold. Embarrassed by the associations of the old name, Stalin dropped the Litovsk, just in time for Hitler's armies to attack the Soviet Union on June 22, 1941. While the Germans swept forward to Minsk and beyond, the garrison of Brest stood firm for six weeks. Nearly the entire fortress was reduced to rubble before the Russian Alamo finally surrendered. The defenders' courage earned Brest the honor "Hero City," one of 13 in the USSR. What remains of the always-open fortress has been turned into a sometimes dramatic, sometimes dogmatic testimonial to those heroes.

Patriotic Red Army songs and the sounds of gunfire emanate eerily from openings above your head at the **Principal Entrance** (Галоўны уваход; *Galoiny ivakhod*), at the end of vul. Maskaiskaya. To the right lies the **Eastern Fort** (Усходні Форт; *Uskhodni Fort*), a football-field-sized complex where tenacious Russians completely cut off from their comrades held their ground for three weeks. To the north lies the **Northern Gate** (Паўночная Брама; *Painochnaya Brama*), the only remaining fully intact gate. To gain a sense of the fortress's former magnitude, remember the whole place used to look like this.

To the right of the main gate, an immense **boulder** towers over the central island of the fortress. Around the base of the soldier-in-the-boulder monolith are **memorials**

The Wild, Wild East

Belavezhskaya Pushcha (Белавежская Пушча), the only virgin forest left in Europe, spreads over 200 acres 70km north of Brest. Home to the continent's largest animal—the East European bison (зубр; *zubr*), the ocean of centuries-old dark-coniferous and broad-leaved trees gained the status of a natural reserve as early as the 13th century, and began attracting research scientists in the 17th century. The untouched expanse protects species which are threatened by extinction elsewhere in Europe, such as the European deer, otter, golden eagle, red eagle, black stork, and black grouse. Ask the Brest Belintourist office for information on visiting this eco-labyrinth.

to the defenders, and an eternal flame dedicated to all 13 of the "Hero Cities". Ethereal, mournful music rises from under the slabs. In front of the sculpture are the foundations of the **White Palace** (Белы Палац; *Bely Palats*), where the 1918 treaty was signed. To the right, the **Museum of the Defense of the Brest Hero-Fortress** (Музей Абароны Брэсцкай Крэпасці-Героя; *Muzey Abarony Brestskay Krepastsi-Geroya*) is in the reconstructed barracks. A 10-room, detailed history of the fort, it recounts the siege during WWII and the perfection of Communism as demonstrated by this heroic defense (never mind they ultimately lost). A display on the Molotrov-Ribbentrop Pact has been added to explain why Soviet soldiers happened to be here when WWII started. Through the ruined gate to the left of the boulder is the **Brest Archaeology Museum** (Музей Археалагічны Брэсце; *Muzey Arkhealagichny Brestse*), a glass-enclosed fieldhouse full of coins and combs, and the wooden foundations of 13th-century Brest exposed in a giant pit.

Elsewhere in this one-sight city, the blue onion domes of **St. Nicholas' Church,** vul. Savetskaya 4, can be spotted when approaching the town center along the bridge from the train station. Inside, gold carvings adorn 18 red-and-blue paintings. On the left, carved-wood stairs lead to the pulpit (open daily 8:30-11:30am and 6-9:30pm).

BOSNIA-HERZEGOVINA

US$1 = 148BHD (dinars, or BAD)	100BHD = US$0.68
CDN$1= 114BHD	100BHD = CDN$0.83
UK£1 = 231BHD	100BHD = UK£0.43
IR£ = 240BHD	100BHD = IR£0.42
AUS$1 = 117BHD	100BHD = AUS$0.86
NZ$1 = 103BHD	100BHD = NZ$0.97
SAR1 = 33BHD	100BHD = SAR3.01
DM1 = 100BHD	100BHD = DM1.00
Country Phone Code: 387	International Dialing Prefix: 00

Defying the odds of centuries, the nation of Bosnia-Herzegovina persists, the physical centerpiece of the former Yugoslavia. Bosnia's distinction, and its troubles, spring from its self-regard as a mixing ground for Muslims, Croats, and Serbs. In Sarajevo, Bosnia's cosmopolitan capital, that ideal is at least verbally maintained, but in the countryside and smaller towns, ethnic problems persist. Physically, Bosnia is a beautiful country of rolling green hills and valleys. But the past years, as the world knows, have been deadly. The road to Sarajevo passes through endless fields guarded by roofless, abandoned houses. A large part of the population has become refugees, displaced and scattered. The future of Bosnia is uncertain, but its people are resilient. In this period of post-Dayton peace, the process of rebuilding is underway.

> In 1996, the U.S. Department of State issued the following warning. "The Department of State warns U.S. citizens not to travel to the Republic of Bosnia-Herzegovina. The three-year civil war has left landmines and unexploded ordinances throughout the country; roads, airports and railways have been bombed and are not functional. Law enforcement and civil authority is nonexistent in many regions which are still controlled by Serb militia. A peace agreement has been signed which calls for withdrawal of forces to barracks and introduction of a new constitution, but it has not yet been fully implemented." Be aware that the situation in Bosnia will likely have changed dramatically by 1997. If the 60,000-strong peace implementation force (IFOR) pulls out, it may be quite unstable.

BOSNIA ESSENTIALS

The Bosnian border, with its accumulation of trucks and army vehicles, is sufficiently intimidating. However, entrance is a fairly smooth procedure—if the prevailing political climate allows. U.S. citizens should check the State Department web page at http://www.stolaf.edu/network/travel-advisories.html before leaving home; other citizens should ask their government or their country's embassy in Bosnia for updates. As of summer 1996, only a passport was required, and the border was a five-minute procedure for most foreigners. There are also occasional police checkpoints within Bosnia. Register with your embassy upon arrival, and keep your papers with you at all times.

GETTING THERE AND GETTING AROUND

Buses run daily between Sarajevo and Split, Dubrovnik, and Zagreb. They are reliable, but brace yourself for Balkan driving—there is a certain specialty here of passing other cars as often and as narrowly as possible. Commercial **plane** service into Sarajevo was reinstated in mid-August 1996. **Croatia Airlines** (tel. in Zagrab (41) 42 77 52, in Split (21) 362 202) has scheduled regular service to Zagreb. Air service was also planned to Ljubljana and Istanbul (see Sarajevo: Flights, p. 94). There are travel agencies in Sarajevo to arrange and change flights, but to buy a ticket, you must pay in cash. **Train** service was nominally operational as of July 1996; however, the regularity of service is questionable.

STAYING SAFE

> **Emergencies: Police:** tel. 664 211. **Fire:** tel. 93. **Emergency:** tel. 94.

Outside Sarajevo, **do NOT set foot off the pavement** under any circumstances. Even in Sarajevo, use caution—do not venture onto dirt without first watching the locals. Millions of **landmines** and **unexploded ordinances (UXOs)** lace the country. Mine injuries occur daily. Fifteen percent of landmine injuries occur on **road shoulders**—partly because farmers who find unexploded ordinances in their fields occasionally bring them to the sides of the roads for the troops to pick up. If you must take pictures, do so from your car, while the car remains firmly on pavement. If you must go to the bathroom during a road trip, stop at a gas station. **Abandoned houses** are unsafe as well; often they have been laced with booby traps by a retreating army. Absolute caution at all times is essential. The de-mining process is underway, but estimates are that 30 years of intensive, full-time effort would be necessary to declare

TOURIST SERVICES ■ 89

Bosnia "mine-free"—and even de-mining is not 100% foolproof. See Sarajevo: Security Information, p. 94, for details on the Mine Action Center and other points regarding safety.

News coverage of Bosnia has reported numerous incidents of ethnic violence. However, foreigners are rarely implicated in these incidents. Moreover, the violence has taken place in the countryside, not in Sarajevo itself. For that reason, *Let's Go* has confined its coverage of Bosnia to Sarajevo. As of summer 1996, Sarajevo itself was entirely peaceful, with petty crime virtually non-existent.

TOURIST SERVICES

Few residents of Bosnia-Herzegovina are anticipating a tourist influx in the near future. Tourist services are correspondingly limited. Residents of smaller towns may regard foreigners with suspicion, but much depends on the town's political and ethnic affiliation. In Sarajevo, however, travelers (and their money) are welcomed. Many Bosnians speak **English** and **German,** making the visitor's task easier.

In Sarajevo, a fledgling **tourist office** provides guidance to the city. The **U.S. Embassy,** equipped with full-time consul, is also a source of useful information. Hopefully, the number of independent tourist agencies will have increased by summer 1997. Despair not: the Bosnian people, with their love of the city, can replace the softer functions of a tourist bureau.

MONEY

The Bosnia's currency is the **dinar,** which comes in paper only in divisions of 10, 20, 50, 100, and 500. It is firmly attached to the **Deutschmark** at an exchange rate of 100 dinars per DM1. Transactions take place in either, or both, currencies. There is nothing unusual or suspicious about paying DM and receiving dinars in change. The Croatian **kuna** was also named an official currency of Bosnia in late summer 1996, but given awkward exchange rates, it is unlikely that the kuna will catch on quickly.

The system of **banks** is quickly improving; within Sarajevo, their number is mushrooming. However, **ATMs** are non-existent. **Traveler's checks** can be exchanged at some Sarajevo banks. **American Express** has an emergency cash service at Central Banka in Sarajevo, and a **wire service** is available through the same bank. If your itinerary lies outside of Sarajevo, the best advice is BYOD—Bring Your Own Deutschmarks. **Cash** is almost exclusively the method of payment.

Bringing many small Deutschmark bills rather than large ones will save time and hassle; Bosnia's economy operates on a small scale, and even DM10 bills are often not accepted in the marketplace or cafés. Occasionally, smaller stores will provide sticks of chewing gum or additional produce as a substitute for change.

COMMUNICATIONS

Bosnia's **postal** system, operative since early 1996, is re-collecting itself. With a central post office and a few others scattered through town, Sarajevo can accommodate outgoing mail. It is not a wise idea to rely on mail reaching Bosnia. The only way to receive mail is to befriend a U.S. government employee and borrow their address, as **Poste Restante** is unavailable. Look for the small yellow sign with diagonal lines through it; these mark the post offices. Few towns outside of the capital are equipped with reasonable mail service. Mail to the U.S. usually takes three weeks, somewhat less within Europe. **Postcards** cost DM1 to mail.

Telephones have the opposite difficulty: dialing into Bosnia is feasible, but dialing out is problematic. As of summer 1996, a caller from Bosnia could reach Croatia and other parts of Bosnia, but not elsewhere. **Satellite** telephones, for making international calls beyond Croatia, are found in post offices; go early or late, as the midday lines are long. To call **AT&T Direct,** dial tel. 008 00 00 10. Calling the U.S. is DM5 per minute, U.K. roughly DM3.50. Calls *from* abroad can come over non-satellite phones but are blocked at unpredictable times. Prepare for relative isolation. For those who bring notebook computers, **Compuserv** has a reliable server in Zagreb. Compuserv accounts can be established before you leave home. Remember to bring a power adapter. **Faxes** can be sent from the post office; the price to the U.S. is DM5 per page.

LANGUAGE

When in Bosnia, speak **Bosnian.** When in Croatia, Croatian. When in Serbia, Serbian. The distinction is more in name than in substance, but never underestimate its importance. Languages in the former Yugoslavia have been co-opted by the governments as tools of nationalism. If you say you are speaking "Croatian" or "Serbian" in Bosnia, and vice-versa, people will immediately correct you. The languages do have certain distinctions. Take, for example, the translation of coffee. *Kava* is the Croatian term, *kafa* the Bosnian. The difference exists for bread also: in Croatian *kruh,* in Bosnia *hljeb.* So in the former Yugoslavia, mind your Ps and Qs—and Zs, Ks, Us, and Js. The standard greeting, *"Šta ima?"* means "What's up?", and the appropriate response is either *"Nema ništa"* or *"Mane štani,"* both of which mean "Not much." For learning the language in depth, *Colloquial Serbo-Croat* by Celia Hawkesworth is widely recommended. The book, available with listening tapes available, is an excellent guide to a difficult language. For more words, see the Croatian Glossary, p. 774. Note that **English** and **German** are also widely spoken.

FOOD AND DRINK

Sorry, vegetarians, almost every *Bosanski specijalitet* includes meat—beef, lamb, or to a rarer degree, fish. *Bosanki Lonac* is a stew-like dish which spices up vegetables and beef with plenty of paprika. Cabbage rolls stuffed with meat and rice are *japrak. Slatki* is the same but with sugar. *Pite* resembles pie, with the usual meat, cheese, and potatoes. A shepherd's pie-like concoction, *musaka* features (once again) meat and potatoes, this time with eggplant. Look for *čevabdžinica* or *aščinica* shops; both serve Bosnian national dishes and are abundant, particularly in Sarajevo. Vegetarians with kitchens can subsist on *hljeb* (bread), dairy products, and vegetables fresh from the daily summer **markets.** Or request a sandwich *bez meso* (without meat) from a lunch stand. Pasta and rice were daily staples of the three-year war; now a bare mention of the words will be met with a grimace. For dessert, baklava and *tufahija* (apple stuffed with walnuts and topped with whipped cream) are the regional preference, with *hurmasica* (a glazed cake) a popular third.

It will quickly become apparent that cultural life revolves around a cup—or several—of *kafa.* More daring and uniquely Bosnian selections include varieties of gullet-stinging *rakija* (brandy). *Loza* is the grape variety, *šlijivoca,* plum.

CUSTOMS AND ETIQUETTE

Tipping is not customary except in more expensive settings—but is always welcomed. Some places may anticipate that foreigners will tip; the option is yours. Ten percent is generous; 5% is "tip"-ical. At restaurants and cafés, the bill is never split. Instead, one person pays—always the man the first time, and the woman should offer the second or third time. The man, or the waiter, will also open and pour the

Terminology

Croat, Serb, and Bosnian refer to people with that nation-based, or "ethnic," affiliation. Croatian, Serbian, and Bosnian are terms indicating the country. Thus, to say a Bosnian Serb denotes a Serb living in Bosnia. These distinctions are important particularly for Bosnians, who envision Bosnia as a residence for Bosnians, Croats, and serbs. A "Serb" can be a neighbor in Bosnia; but a Serbian Serb is a resident of Serbia. Bosnians often refer to their Bosnian Serb enemies as "Četnik," or "Chetnik," a revived WWII ethnic slur. In other words, a Serb is different from a Chetnik—do not make this mistake. Another lingual caveat: the Bosnian Army is precisely that; it is not the "Muslim army."

woman's drink. In **Muslim homes,** it is customary to remove one's shoes at the door. **Smoking** is practically a national pastime; cigarettes have gone from a wartime black-market price of DM15 per pack to a reasonable DM1.

Bargaining is possible, particularly in the outdoor clothing markets. Ask a Bosnian to accompany you; the price will be miraculously cheaper. **Fashion** was important during the war, when there was little else to focus on, leaving Sarajevo on par with the rest of Europe. Tourists in grubby t-shirts are easily identified.

Foreigners are welcomed and regarded with great interest in Sarajevo. Even the taxi driver or the man in the kiosk will ask you friendly questions. America, particularly, is beloved among Sarajevans who amused themselves during the war with pirated American TV such as the bastion of 90s pop culture, *Beverly Hills 90210*. And however paradoxically, Sarajevans look to America as an ideal of the diversity they seek to achieve.

LIFE AND TIMES

HISTORY

The history of Bosnia-Herzegovina depends to an extreme extent on the informant. Historical events, particularly of WWII and the Tito era, have become nationalistic property.

Bosnia originated as a state in 960CE, when this small enclave in the center of the Balkan peninsula broke away from the Kingdom of Serbia. Independence proved turbulent: Bosnia was then, as today, the subject of a wrestling match between Serbia and Croatia. In the 11th century, Bosnia further carved out its independence by adopting the ways of the **Bogamils**, a fringe religious group with beliefs similar to Manichaeism. From 1386 to 1463, the country found its freedom trespassed upon when the Turks of the **Ottoman Empire** overtook Bosnia. In 1463, Bosnia became officially a Turkish province, and Sarajevo was its capital. Unlike other parts of the Balkan peninsula that were similarly occupied, the Bosnians converted to Islam with relative speed. Bosnia is thus distinguished from its neighbors by the mark of Islam, both religious and cultural—in the mosques and Turkish architecture of Sarajevo.

Yet, as with any state, the Ottoman Empire was destined to melt away. Its decline was facilitated by the increasing power of the Christian empires that surrounded it—Orthodox Serbia to the east and Catholic Croatia to the north. A series of **peasant revolts** in the late 19th century helped topple the empire. In 1862, Christian peasants, resentful of higher taxes demanded by their Ottoman overloads, revolted. Christian powers eventually intervened. The situation was uneasily settled in 1878, when the **Congress of Berlin** declared Bosnia an Austrian protectorate.

The nationalistic unrest spreading through Europe in the late 19th century proved infectious. In the Balkans, it increased with the exodus of intellectuals to Germany who returned with new Bismarckian ideals of potential nationhood.

The early 20th century converted Austria-Hungary, a tottering empire herself, to a deeper and almost hysterical suspicion of South Slav nationalism. A desire to damage South Slav morale (as well as to embarrass the nominal South Slav "protector," Russia) motivated Austria-Hungary's **annexation** of Bosnia-Herzegovina in 1908. This and subsequent antagonistic moves by Austria backfired, inflaming pan-Slavic sentiments and focusing them against Austria. The notorious anti-Austrian Black Hand was one of several terrorist groups that emerged in the new nationalistic context. **Gavrilo Princip,** a member of the Young Bosnians (another Serb-nationalist group), assassinated Austrian Archduke Franz Ferdinand in Sarajevo on June 28, 1914. Many consider this to be the act which sparked **World War I.**

Following WWI, the Kingdom of Serbs, Croats, and Slovenes was born, to be renamed Yugoslavia in 1929. Power fell to the Serb dynasty named Karadjordjević, to which Bosnia was annexed. While the situation was a realization of the long cherished ideal of South Slav unity, Croats quickly began to chafe under what they perceived as a Serb dictatorship. During **WWII,** Yugoslavia was divided between the German-aligned Croat Ustashas, and the Partisan (Russian-aligned) Serb Chetniks, whose strong-hold was in Bosnia. Concentration camps set up in the region brought the massacre of hundreds of thousands of Serbs; the exact number is a political issue today. Enter Joseph Broz, a.k.a. **Tito,** a half-Slovene, half-Croat Partisan during WWII, whose independence from mainstream Communism earned Moscow's disfavor and sanctions. Tito sought to hold Yugoslavia together through decentralizing power, striving for rough equality among republics. In his fairness, he purged members from all three ethnic groups. Yugoslavia, under Tito's strong hand, experienced an economic revival. His death in 1980 was met with sorrow throughout Yugoslavia and occasioned the disintegration of the Yugoslav nation. Communism's strength declined in the late 1980s as Serbian Communist Slobodan Milošević rose to power spewing forth nationalistic rhetoric.

The Federal Republic of Yugoslavia began to come apart in 1990. Within a year, two of the country's provinces, Slovenia and Croatia, had declared independence. Their **secession** was opposed both by the increasingly Serb-dominated federal government and, in the case of Croats at least, by ethnic Serbs living in the self-declared independent states. In April 1992, events came to a head in Bosnia-Herzegovina, the most ethnically mixed of the former Yugoslav republics. The Bosnian government, unwilling to see the republic remain in a Serb-dominated Yugoslavia, opted for independence and was soon recognized by the international community (as were Croatia and Slovenia). The referendum for independence, endorsed by 99% of voters, was largely boycotted by Serbs in Bosnia. Violence broke out as the federal army and Serb militias quickly took control of 70% of Bosnian territory. The capital city, Sarajevo, was placed under a brutal siege that lasted from May 2, 1992, to February 26, 1996. A United Nations force sent to deliver humanitarian assistance **(UNPROFOR)** had little success in stopping the process of ethnic cleansing undertaken principally, though not exclusively, by Serb forces.

READING LIST

A wealth of excellent literature is available on Bosnia and its Balkan neighbors. The long-standing classic is *Black Lamb, Grey Falcon* by Rebecca West, a lively volume of over 1000 pages detailing her impressions during a 1937 journey through Yugoslavia. Facts and opinions are interspersed with spirited (if random) commentary on the male-female dynamic. A more modern, and less physically massive, travel narrative is Brian Hall's *Impossible Country.* Hall, an American, traveled through Yugoslavia in summer 1991, just as the "Impossible Country" began to disintegrate. He presents human portraits and political events perceptively and fluidly.

For a history of the recent war, turn to *The Death of Yugoslavia,* a work co-authored by Laura Silber and Alan Little. Theirs is a scintillating, blow-by-blow account of the rise of Slobodan Milošević of Serbia and the tragic events of 1991 through 1994. Misha Glenny's *The Fall of Yugoslavia* recounts 1991 through 1993, with an eye closely attuned to the region's history. Both books should come out in updated editions next year. Another option is the narrative *Love Thy Neighbor* by Peter Maas. The book that reportedly stalled U.S. President Clinton's intervention in the region is *Balkan Ghosts,* a 1993 work by Robert D. Kaplan. Kaplan reaches even more deeply into history, broadly characterizing the region as prone to dark conflict.

The scope of Bosnian history, however, is best given by a Bosnian himself—Ivo Andrič, who earned the Nobel Prize for *Bridge on the Drina.* This dense book relates Bosnian history through the lens of a border town and its Turkish-built bridge.

BOSNIA TODAY

Fighting in Bosnia, between Serb, Bosnian, and Croatian forces, continued until October 1995, when a peace agreement was brokered on November 21 at Dayton, Ohio, and signed in Paris later that month. The area under dispute was divided into the Federation of Bosnia-Herzegovina and the Republika Srpska. The destruction caused by the war has been severe in many areas, and town and villages are now largely divided along ethnic lines. The Bosnian elections of September 14, 1996, gave victory to Alija Izetbegovic of the dominant Muslim Party of Democratic Actions (SDA), meaning that he will chair the tri-partite presidency which also includes an ethnic Croat and and ethnic Serb. While election day saw little violence, it is widely feared that the election results gave an official sanction to ethnic division.

CALENDAR OF EVENTS

National holidays are: March 1, Independence Day; May 1, Labor Day; April 15, Day of the Army; May 4, Victory Day; and November 25, Day of the Republic.

Sarajevo

Tall, Communist-era buildings tower silently, abandoned, their windows jagged black holes. The city streets, thronged 13 years ago with Olympic fervor, bear the marks of grenades and shrapnel. The arches of the beautiful old library ring a pile of rubble. Sarajevans speak of the pre-war beauty of their city; now it evinces a different, strange sort of beauty. Sarajevo possesses an incredible spirit—a spirit determined to restore what was lost in the four-year siege. The downtown buzzes with life. People crowd the streets, euphoric with restored freedom, and shops beckon with expensive European clothing. But nobody has forgotten, and for a foreigner, the greatest reward of Sarajevo comes when a local tells about his or her city.

In 1914, Sarajevo struck the alleged spark to WWI, when Serb nationalist, Gavrilo Princip shot Austrian Archduke Franz Ferdinand. Pilgrims of history can still mull the commemorative plaque, but most other classic tourist features of Sarajevo are largely destroyed or non-functional. It is the city itself that must be seen. Internationals crowd Sarajevo, using the peacetime advantage to promote reconstruction efforts. IFOR troops were omnipresent in summer 1996, rolling by in armored vehicles or haunting the cafés during off-hours. Sarajevo is stepping slowly toward normalcy—with some tensions, invisible to the tourist, created by the recent influx of refugees from the country. Keep a cautious eye on the political situation, but in the end, you may share with the Sarajevans a total love for this city.

> The following outlying areas of Sarajevo have served as confrontation lines and are thus at particular risk for **mines:** Grbavica, Lukavica, Illidža, and Dobrinja.

ORIENTATION AND PRACTICAL INFORMATION

Sarajevo lies in the heart of Bosnia. Its downtown is easily navigable. **Maršala Titova** (a.k.a. Maršala Tita) is the main street *(ulica)*, running east to west through town. At the **eternal flame,** a 1945 marker to the Bosnian state, Maršala Titova branches into **Ferhadija,** a pedestrian-only thoroughfare, and **Mula Mustafe Bašekija,** a street that holds a large market slightly farther down. Most of the cafés, particularly the loudest ones, are arranged along Ferhadija and its intersecting streets. The cobbled streets of the "Turkish Quarter", or **Baščaršija,** straddle the east end of Ferhadija. Both Ferhadija and Maršala Titova run roughly parallel to the river **Miljacka,** which borders the downtown area to the south. The road alongside the river is **Obala Kulina Bana;** heading west, it merges with Maršala Titova to become **Zmaj od Bosne** (Dragon of Bosnia), the erstwhile **"Sniper's Alley"** (so-called because its proximity to the front lines made it a constant target of Serb snipers). The yellow **Holiday Inn** building, a well known landmark, lies along Zmaj od Bosne. Further out from town, the road enters **Novo Sarajevo,** the residential area with heavy Socialist influence. **Skenkerija** lies to the south of the Presidency building (itself on the west end of Maršala Titova) and extends across the river. East of downtown lie the important government buildings; the U.S. Embassy is next to the IFOR headquarters on **Alipašina,** which intersects Maršala Titova just east of downtown. The main **market** in town lies beneath the road-bridge between Alipašina and Koševo streets. Don't get confused—in the hills above the downtown area, streets become maze-like. It is easy to get lost, but by going downhill, you will eventually reach downtown. Streets have acquired new names since the war—patriotic titles such as Branilada Grada (Defense of the City) or Putživota (Street of Life). Kiosks and bookstores should stock 1996 city **maps**.

Embassies and Consulates: Australians should contact their embassy in Vienna at Mattielstr. 2/1 A-1010 Vienna, Austria (tel. (1) 512 85 80; fax 504 11 78). **Canada,** Logavina 3b (tel. 447 900; fax 447 901). Citizens of **New Zealand** should contact their embassy in Rome at Via Zara 28,00 198 Rome, Italy (tel. (6) 440 29 28, 440 29 29, or 440 29 30; fax 440 29 84). **U.K.,** Tina Ujevića 8 (tel. 663 922 or 664 085; fax 444 429). **U.S.,** Alipašina 43 (tel. 659 969, 659 743, or 445 700; fax 659 722).

Security Information: Incoming citizens should register immediately with their embassy; at the U.S. embassy, a security briefing is held every few days for government officials—if you ask nicely, you may be included. The **Mine Action Center** (tel. 667 610; fax 667 611) is located in the Tito Barracks on Zmaj od Bosne. The entrance is 200m past the Holiday Inn. The MAC provides important pamphlets on the location and nature of landmines; a 1-hr. **mine awareness briefing** is held daily or every 2 days, depending on demand. Call or fax for the schedule.

Tourist Information: A **tourist bureau,** Zelenih Beretki 50 (tel. 532 281), is staffed by friendly, chatty old men who sell maps, provide information about hotels, and answer general questions. The **Consular Department** of the U.S. Embassy (see above) is also a fine source of tourist info.

Travel Agencies: Kompas Tours, Maršala Titova 8 (tel./fax 667 573), past the Presidency building going toward the Holiday Inn. A Slovenian tour agency. Flights from Ljubljana, Zagreb, and other destinations can be arranged. Helps with car rentals and can also arrange hotel stays for a visit to the coast (a week of staying at a hotel, breakfast and sometimes dinner included, is DM200-300). Knows the bus schedule. Open Mon.-Fri. 9am-4pm, Sat. 9am-9pm. **Air Bosna,** 15 Ferhadija (tel. 610 000 or 667 954; fax 667 955). For flight arrangements on all airlines. Service charge of DM10 per reservation. Open Mon.-Fri. 9am-4pm, Sat. 9am-2pm.

Currency Exchange: Among the largest of Sarajevo's many banks is **Central Banka,** Zelenih Beretki 54 (tel. 536 688; fax 532 406 or 663 855). Changes AmEx, Thomas Cook, and Visa traveler's checks to Bosnian dinars at a 3% commission. DM may be available. Personal checks up to US$200 cashed immediately; 15-day wait for higher. An **emergency check-cashing service,** up to US$500 at a time is available to those with personal checks, a passport photocopy, and an AmEx card. With a 2% commission plus DM10, money can be **wired** here. Open Mon.-Sat. 8:30am-3pm; cash counter closes daily at 2pm. Leftover Croatian kuna might be changed at **Gospodarska Banka,** near the eternal flame on Maršala Titova, at a painful rate. Open Mon.-Fri. 9am-4pm, Sat. 9am-1pm.

Flights: Flights from Sarajevo are planned to: Istanbul (TOP Air), Ljubljana (Adria Air; US$225-246), and Zagreb (Croatia Airlines; US$215). The airport began sporadic commercial service in mid-August 1996; check before assuming there are flights.

Trains: The train station had its first ceremonial run on July 30 (tel. 652 800; fax 647 401). The opened route was to the Croatian port town of Ploce and went through Mostar; however the regularity of service is doubtful. **BiH Railways Company** runs the one railway line currently open (tel. 663 719; fax 652 396).

Buses: Bus station, Kranjćevića 9 (tel. 670 180 or 445 442), near the old railway station behind the Holiday Inn. **Centrotrans** (tel. 532 874, 670 807, and 466 388; fax 670 699) services Sarajevo. To: Dubrovnik (7:15am; 8hr.; one-way DM40, roundtrip DM60); Frankfurt (Tues., Wed., and Sun.; 15hr.; one-way DM180, roundtrip DM245); Split (8am; 8hr.; one-way DM35, roundtrip DM50); Zagreb (6:30am and 7pm; 10hr.; one-way DM60, roundtrip DM100). DM5 per bag.

Public Transportation: An excellent **tram** network serves downtown; it runs west along Maršala Titova and east along Obala Kulina Bana. Regular service from around 6am to 6:15pm or 10pm, depending on the route (70BHD, buy tickets at a kiosk). Your ticket will probably not be checked (particularly in view of the disorganized state of the Bosnian government), but hold onto one to show possible inspectors. **Buses** cover more area but for fewer hours (6:45am-6pm or 7pm). Pur-

ORIENTATION AND PRACTICAL INFORMATION ■ 95

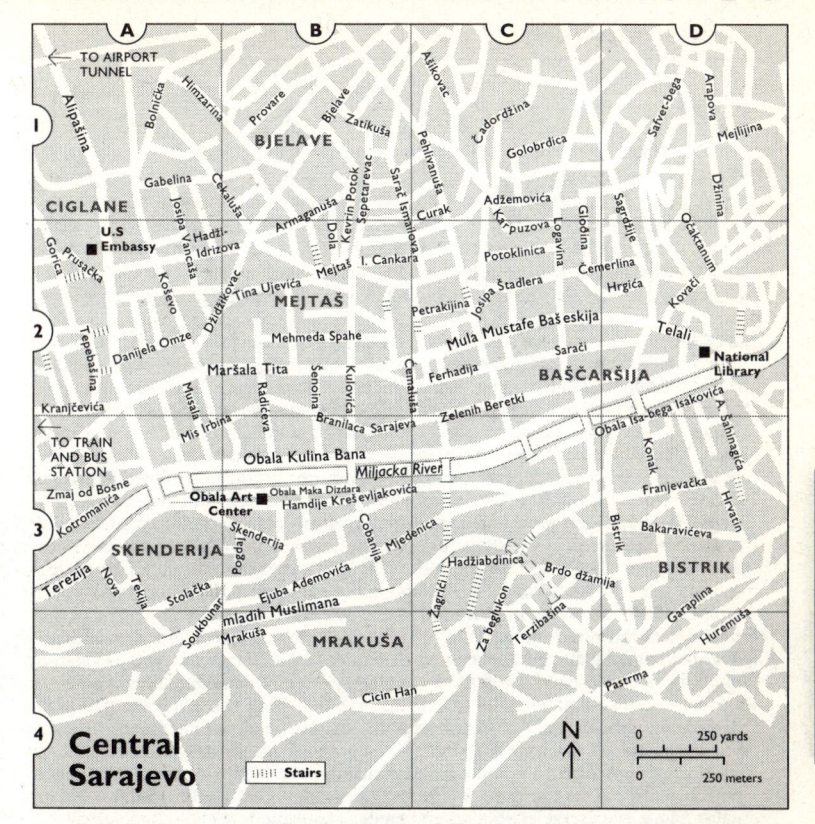

Central Sarajevo

chase DM1 tickets on bus. A full-month bus pass is available for under DM10. **Oslobodjenje,** the daily paper (50BHD), lists a complete schedule of trams and buses.
Taxis: Radio Taxi (tel. 970). DM2 initial fare plus DM1 per km. Taxi stands are plentiful; don't call—they charge for getting to you. Make sure the meter's on.
Car Rental: Bosnia Tours, 54 Maršala Titova (tel. 470 913), rents cars for DM132 and up per day; DM300 deposit required. Open Mon.-Sat. 8am-7pm.
English-Language Publications: Available at "Svjetlost" bookshop near the eternal flame on Maršala Titova. *International Herald-Tribune* DM4. *Time Out,* a weekly magazine at newsstands, includes info in English on cultural activities in Sarajevo. EuroClub (see Accommodations, below) has international magazines.
Jewish Community Center: La Benevolencija, Hanidije Krevavjakovica 83 (tel. 663 472; fax 663 473; e-mail LA_BENE@ZAMIR-TZ.ZNT.APC.ORG), across the river from town, just west of the massive green and yellow building. A cultural and educational organization with about 1000 members. Visitors are welcomed and well cared for. As well as religious services, the center can arrange housing with host family, and organize excursions and volunteer opportunities. Contact in advance.
Hospital: Koševo, 25 Bolnicka (tel. 663 611). Also a **City Hospital,** 12 Kranjćevića (tel. 664 724).
Post Office: Corner of Ferhadija and Cemaluša (tel. 663 617; fax 473 103), just behind the eternal flame. No *Poste Restante.* Satellite telephones, faxes. Open Mon.-Sat. 7:30am-8pm. **Postal code:** 71000.
Telephones: At the post office. **Directory information:** tel. 988. **Phone code:** 071.

ACCOMMODATIONS

As the old saying has it, friends are like gold. In Sarajevo, friends *are* gold—plus a few hundred Deutschmarks. Due to the influx of business travelers and a dearth of accommodations, housing is absurdly expensive. Private rooms and *pansions* are the realistic options (although, as competition regenerates, prices may go down). The **Jewish Community Center** (see Practical information, above) can arrange housing with a family for visitors wishing a cultural experience, given a week's advance notice. **Oglasi,** available for DM1 at newsstands, advertises apartments under the heading "*Iznajmljivanje*"—pronounce this word at your own risk. Typically, the apartment owners will want to rent for a month or more, but wheedle (or get a Bosnian speaker to wheedle for you) and you may be able to negotiate a shorter stay.

   EuroClub, 20 Valtera Perica (tel./fax 670 695), in Skenderija. This funky, blue- and orange-pillared place arranges stays in apartments for DM20-50 per might. Contact them a week in advance. Open Mon.-Fri. 10am-7:30pm, Sat. 10am-2pm.
   Bosnia Tours (see Car Rental, above) runs a **private accommodations** service. Eighty modest but neat, clean rooms with bath are available in family apartments along Maršala Titova. Clean sheets provided. 1-2 day stays preferred, as the landlord gets paid on a per-traveler basis. Longer stays can be arranged, independently with the landlord, for DM500-700 per month. Call in advance. One bed DM60. Two beds DM100. Open Mon.-Sat. 8am-7pm, so those planning to stay Sun. should reserve in advance.
   Internet Cafe, Pruščakova 3 (tel. 668 447), on a street off Maršala Titova. A tiny, spartan but cool 4-bed youth hostel above the cafe, just getting underway in September 1996. Expected price around DM20 per bed.
   Private Accommodations (tel. 472 013) are available through an office on Ferhadija near the eternal flame in town center. In summer 1996, the facility was just starting up, but prices were estimated to be DM60-80 per night, including breakfast.
   Pansion Hondo, Zaima Šarca 23 (tel. 469 375 or 666 564), above a restaurant in the Bjelave neighborhood. Call for directions; or just head uphill (north) from the Cathedral and ask for help. A 25-min. hike up, but that's the only direction. Eleven spacious rooms with TVs. Some singles with double beds. One large family room with balcony on the top floor. DM50 per person, plus DM10 for breakfast. A journalist haunt, so reserve at least several weeks in advance.
   Hotel Park, (tel. 461 329 or 460 997; fax 461 312) in Vogošća, about 9km from Sarajevo. A bus (70 BHD) runs from Sutjeska, which intersects Alipašina near the U.S. Embassy; the bus stop is in front of an abandoned school building. The bus also stops at the Ciglane market beneath the bridge. Buses run daily 6am-8pm, every 15min. The lowest-priced hotel around, it's really a *pansion* with more facilities, including conference rooms, restaurant (service until midnight), and physical therapy facilities (20min. massage DM30; sauna DM25). Frequented by international businessmen. Plain, functional rooms; request TV and balcony (the view is bucolic). Singles DM105, doubles DM160, suites DM180 plus DM5 per person. Breakfast included (served 6:30-10am). Prices expected to drop significantly by 1997; call and check. Reserve at least one week in advance.

FOOD

Though one might not think it given the preponderance of cafés, yes, Bosnians do eat. Scour the Turkish quarter for **Čevabdžinića** shops; DM3 buys a *čevapčići* (or simply, *čevaps*), small, oblong lamb sausages encased in *somun*, Bosnia's tasty elastic flat bread. The same quick service is found in the numerous **Buregdžinica** shops; the namesake dish is a meat and potato pie, but vegetarians can usually find *sirnica* (cheese pie) or *zeljanica* (spinach pie). The general poverty among Bosnians means that restaurants are the domain of internationals; in summer 1996, one could rarely eat out without an adjacent table of relaxing IFOR troops, journalists, or businessmen. Usual dining hours are 8-10pm. Two main **markets** bring vegetables to the table during the summer. The larger one on Alipašina, under the Ciglane bridge, is a five-minute walk from the U.S. embassy. Another more convenient market lies on Mula

Mustafe Bašekija a few blocks east from where Maršala Titova diverges to Ferhadija and Mula Mustafe Bašekija (open Mon.-Sat. 8am-5pm, Sun. 8am-noon).

Klub Preporod, 30 Branilaca Sarajeva (tel. 670 750), near the National Theater on the street behind Ferhadija. A dining experience, in this restaurant named after a famed Muslim newspaper. Sit indoors in cavernous armchairs around a low table, or outdoors in the back of the Klub. The music is relatively soft, the food excellent (if a bit greasy) and fairly inexpensive. Entrées, classic Bosnian meat and fish, DM7-12. Bread accompanies the meal. Delicious *Lignje* (squid) DM7. No alcohol served—it's dining the Muslim way. Open daily 9am-9pm.

Ragusa, Ferhadija 10b (tel. 442 541). Expensive but all the best. A favorite among internationals. More crowded than most places; divine dining on cobbled outdoor patio in back. *Lignje* is swimmingly delicious at DM11; but DM20 is a more standard entrée price. Splurging-only territory. Open daily 9am-11pm.

Restoran-Klub Novinara, Pruščakova 8 (tel. 470 850), on a small street intersecting Maršala Titova to the north, about 200m from the eternal flame in the other direction than downtown. A.k.a. "the journalist's club", the reputed wartime hangout of reporters, now with less exclusive clientele. A comfortable, casual place. There's definite atmosphere in the putrid green tablecloths and 1970s-era chairs. Food-wise, it's among the few spots in Sarajevo with tastes from home. Entrées offer the usual barrage of meat, but vegetarians can make excellent meals of potato, egg, salad, and rice appetizers. Open daily 9am-11pm.

Aeroplan, Sarci bb (tel. 535 690), at Ferhadija in the Turkish quarter. A local favorite which now lures the international after-work crowd. Waiters in traditional attire serve excellent food (*Lonac* DM3). No alcohol. Tomato soup DM2, excellent cheese pie DM3. Entrées DM8-10. English menu. Open daily 10am-10pm.

Galija, Chobanija 20 (tel. 443 350), across the river from the center. In locals' eyes, the superior Sarajevo pizza spot for atmosphere and food. Open daily 9am-10pm.

Ćevabdžinica Hodžic, Bravadžiluk 34 (tel. 532 866), near the library in the old quarter. Among the best *ćevap* places for taste and variety, in a pristine white-arched building. All kinds of meat on display, vegetarians can eat too—try *Raymak*, a melted cheese sandwich on *somun* (DM2). Open daily 8am-10pm.

Dom Pisaca, Kranjčevićeva 24 (tel. 471 158; fax 443 514), directly behind the Holiday Inn on the street parallel to Zmaje od Bosne; look for a glass-fronted building. Sketches of literary lights peer down from the walls in the renowned "Writer's Club" of Sarajevo. Two levels of dining: below with glass walls, above in a peaceful outdoor garden. Rumors of snobbery come perhaps from the prices: steak entrées DM12-15. Spaghetti *milanese* DM10. Open Mon.-Sat. 10am-10pm.

Bazeni, Bentbasa bb (tel. 537 877), on the river a few hundred meters past the burned library heading east out of town. Relaxing open-air atmosphere overlooking the river. Eat below on the green mini-golf surface, or eat above on the wood balcony. Small bands tune up at night. Excellent lamb, beefsteak, and fish available. Entrées range DM8-20. Open daily for food 2-11pm; earlier for drinks.

New Concept Club, 61 Hazima Sabanovica (tel. 668 526), near the park-like area along Titova (near the Internet Café). Take a right on Koševo, go about 300m to where Kosevo branches, take a gentle right on Bolnicka, and then take the first right off Bolnicka and go up the hill about 50m. The restaurant's name suits its ambiance. A lovely, if kitsch, indoor, greenhouse setting, with food cooked over old wood stoves. Prices to match (entrées DM15-20). Trout DM15, *ranstek* and its cousin, beefsteak, DM20. Famed appetizer plate (cheese, olives, mushrooms, meat) DM5 each, DM20 altogether. Vegetarians are accommodated. Internationals throng the place, so reservations are wise. Open Mon.-Sat. 12:30-10pm.

SIGHTS

The **eternal flame,** on Maršala Titova in the center of town where Ferhadija branches off, actually does not specifically commemorate the recent war. Rather, it is a 1945 marker to all Sarajevans who died in WWII. Documentation of the more recent, four-year siege is all around. At least half of Sarajevo's buildings sustained damage, to varying degrees, as a result of the war. The **National Library,** at the east end of town on

Obala Kulina Bana, the road running alongside the river, exemplifies the tragedy. Dating from the late 19th century, the building was once regarded as the most beautiful in Sarajevo. It functioned as the City Hall until 1945, when it was declared a library. It is now an open-air structure housing piles of rubble, its pillars still standing as testimony to the lost beauty of the Austro-Hungarian structure. The besieging Serbs, attempting to demoralize the city, targeted civilian institutions early on in the war; the library was an early victim, firebombed on August 25, 1992—exactly 100 years after construction was begun. Most of the books and, more tragically, the archives of old periodicals, were burned.

Up in the hills, a **treeline** is sharply evident, demarcating the front lines. The Bosnians trapped in Sarajevo cut down all available wood for winter warmth; the Serbs had no need to do so. Climb the hilly streets of Bistrik, the neighborhood on the other side of town from the river. An old **road** with a beautiful view of the city snakes along, past an old railway station. Do NOT, however, leave the pavement at any time. Though mines are not thought to be in this area, it's good practice.

Back in town, note the four different religious structures—their proximity is symbolic of Sarajevo itself: a Catholic church, an Orthodox church, a mosque, and a synagogue, all in the downtown area. As of summer '96, only the Catholic site was open for visiting (see Upcoming Sights, below for the others). Activity swirls around this Catholic **cathedral** (named Katedrala Srce Isusovo, Cathedral of Jesus's Heart) along Ferhadija. It was built in 1889 and designed by Josipa Vancasa, a prolific Sarajevan architect whose mark appears on numerous other city buildings.

The cobbled **Baščaršija** (known as the "Turkish quarter") lies on the east end of town, further east on Ferhadija. Jewelry and brassworks shops proliferate; sometimes the bronze-makers can be seen at work. If you wish to make a purchase, borrow the services of a Bosnian friend; tell him/her what you want, and do the vanishing act—prices double in a funny way in a foreigner's presence. The charming 17th-century **Morića Han,** now a café/restaurant slightly set off from Ferhadija in Baščaršija, served as an inn for passing merchants for many centuries while Sarajevo was a station between East and West. Diners and *kafa* drinkers now occupy the former horse's stables; the rooms of the former inn are above.

The 1888-vintage **Regional Museum,** Zmaj od Bosne 3 (tel./fax 440-197), across from the Holiday Inn, is among the most famous on the Balkan peninsula, with botanical gardens and a superb ethnographic collection. The museum was on the front lines and was severely damaged during the war. Many exhibits were saved, but the

---

Fired-Up News

Some days the only newsprint was green, some days lavender, and all days in limited supply. But *Oslobodjenje,* Sarajevo's oldest and best independent newspaper, continued to print daily during the war. The *Oslobodjenje* offices were fifty meters from the front lines; by June 1992, they were destroyed. Bosnian Serb shells had little affinity for Sarajevo's independent media. The printers, cloistered in a bunker below, were saved. The bunker gained some beds and became *Oslobodjenje*'s lightless wartime offices. Electricity to run the printers was totally cut off, so the paper turned to oil-operated generators. Oil also was in short supply, occasionally provided by the UN Protection Force (UNPROFOR), and occasionally sneaked in via the makeshift airport tunnel that was then the only, albeit high-risk, route to Sarajevo. Generator power lasted about two hours each day, a window during which the newspaper was madly compiled. Editors and reporters spent the rest of the day surviving. Wartime circulation reached about 200, or as many copies as possible, and 4-8 pages was the norm.

Today, *Oslobodjenje*'s circulation within Sarajevo approaches 10,000, and its page count is high in the 20s. Internationally, around 25,000 copies circulate to Slovenia, Austria, Italy, and Germany, where they are available to Bosnian refugees. So at least once, heed the call: "*Oslobodjenje, Oslobodjenje*".

museum remains closed to visitors, officially. Unofficially, visitors are welcomed, you will never be turned away. As of summer 1996, only two rooms and the botanical gardens, a lovely oasis within a city largely devoid of arboreal nature, could be viewed. A visit is worthwhile, to see the gardens and to see the reconstruction process of one of Sarajevo's greatest cultural sites. Visits are best Mon-Fri. 9am-5pm, Sat. 9am-2pm. A donation is welcomed and appropriate.

And finally, the act that made Sarajevo famous: on the corner of Obala Kulina Bana (by the river) and Zelenih Beretki, near a white-railinged bridge about 200m before the library, is a plaque commemorating the birthplace, debatably, of **WWI**. It was here that Gavrilo Princip shot Austrian Archduke Franz Ferdinand on June 28, 1914, leading to Austria's declaration of war on Serbia and the subsequent, dramatic spiraling of events that have become world history. Princip fired his shots and then leapt down into the river; he was captured, and ended his short days in prison.

Aspirants to culture can consult *Time Out*, a bi-weekly newsprint leaflet tucked inside the Sarajevo papers *Oslobodjenje* (50 BHD) and *Slobodna Bosna*. *Time Out* is written half in English, and gives information on the art, festival, and museum scene. Sarajevo has several art galleries; the most general is the **National Art Gallery of Bosnia-Herzegovina,** Branilaca Sarajeva bb (tel. 64 162), which also has occasional exhibitions of war-time art (open Mon.-Sat. 10am-4pm). For contemporary art, the **Obala Art Center,** Obala Maka Dizdara 3 (tel. 524 127; fax 665 304), in the large yellow mosque-type building across the river, showcases rotating month-long exhibitions (open Tues.-Sun. 11am-8pm). As of summer 1996, all gallery visits were free.

Upcoming Sights

Many of Sarajevo's traditional tourist sites were damaged during the war; inquire at the U.S. Embassy or at the tourist agency for an update. In Baščaršija, the **Gazi Husref-Gebova Mosque** has towered over Ferhadija since its 1530 construction by the Ottoman Turks. Renovations should be completed by 1997. The **Jewish Museum** (tel. 535 688), on Mula Mustafe Bašekija, near the old quarter of town, was built as a synogogue in 1580, when Jews fleeing the Spanish Inquisition arrived in Bosnia. Now it has exhibits which trace the history of Jewish settlement in Bosnia. It is expected to re-open by summer 1997; check with the Jewish Community Center (see Orientation and Practical Information, p. 93). The yellowish-brown **Orthodox church** (tel. 472 672), on Zmaj od Bosne, is also not open regularly due to wartime shelling damage. But try anyway; the beautiful interior is worth seeing. Renovations of the **airport tunnel** for tourist purposes are being discussed. The tunnel was built during the seige, the only wartime route in and out of Sarajevo.

ENTERTAINMENT

Sarajevo bops and hops with **cafés,** their style cramped only by the 11pm "police hour" which will likely be history by 1997. In the summer, everyone is outside, relaxing with *kafa* (remember, only the Croatians say *"kava"* or *"pivo"* (beer). American pop music-lovers will dig the cafés along **Ferhadija,** the pedestrian street. Equipped with outdoor speakers, the cafés seem to compete for airwaves. The international crowd plugs in at the **Internet Café,** Pruščakova 3 (tel. 668 447), on a street off Maršala Titova near Restaurant Klub Novinara (see Food, above). It's got one Internet terminal with plans to connect two more. The evenings are lively, helped out by Czech *Budweiser,* the self-proclaimed best beer in town, on tap (large DM4; open daily 8am-10:30pm; after curfew is lifted, the café plans to be open nightly til 2am).

Alternatives to the café scene are limited, and generally more popular during winter when it's too cold to be outdoors. A mixed-age crowd of 18- to 30-year-olds jams until well past police hour at **Б.B,** the only **disco** in town, in a basement adjacent to the Hotel Bosna, on Kulovića just off Maršala Titova. Smoking and scoping to loud techno music is the name of this game; dancing doesn't get hot until late (cover DM5). **Club Kuk,** on the small street Čekaluša off Bolnička, near Koševo Hospital, acts like flypaper for the younger, alternative crowd. Look for posters around town advertising concerts, mostly of hard-core Croatian bands (cover DM1); the place packs and spills into the streets on concert nights. Kuk, operated by the wacky NGO Serious Road Trip, planned to introduce Internet terminals in fall '96, so net-surfers could be right at home (open daily 9am-2pm and 7-10:30pm, or a ½hr. before curfew). The **S.B.C. Bock** (a self-styled "Billiard Club"), 10 Mis-Irbina, occupies a basement room in the sports complex behind the Presidency building. A journalists' wartime hangout, its attraction now is a pool table, occasional live blues at 8pm, and a strange, mixed, but usually sparse crowd. Less hopping in summer, when locals prefer to be outside (open daily 4-11pm).

Shoppers will find clothing and tourist items, like the Turkish coffee sets sold in the Turkish quarter, to be rather expensive. But there are tricks to the trade. Ask a Bosnian acquaintance to accompany you. He or she can bargain a bit, especially at open-air stalls or in the Turkish quarter, where a tourist might simply pay the tag price. Those searching for clothing should avoid the numerous shops along Titova. Instead, duck through a small archway near Maršala Titova 60 (the sign says "Kamie-aeion" 100M) to the open-air clothing stalls, where the same clothes appear for cheaper prices. An underground mall in Skenderija across the river can also outfit shoppers in European styles.

It's lights, camera, action time in mid-September when the third annual **Sarajevo Film Festival** starts rolling: the city turns out for eight days of movies, many of them contemporary European productions. Last year's festival recruited the likes of Ingmar Bergman, Susan Sarandon, and Richard Gere for its "Honorary Board." The festival is organized by the Obala Art Center, 10 Obala Kulina Bana (tel. 524 127; fax 664 547). Movie tickets in '96, were to be a token DM1; in 1997, perhaps capitalism will raise the prices. Since 1984 (read: Olympic nostalgia), Sarajevo has annually held a **Winter Festival,** a celebration of culture and art, which carried on even through the seige. The 13th annual event will take place Feb. 7-March 21, 1997 (for more details tel./fax 663 626). The bi-weekly **Time Out** (see Sights, above) details concerts and upcoming cultural events.

BULGARIA
(БЪЛГАРИЯ)

US$1	= 187 lv (leva, or BGL)	100 lv=	US$0.53
CDN$1	= 136 lv	100 lv=	CDN$0.73
UK£1	= 291 lv	100 lv=	UK£0.34
IR£1	= 303 lv	100 lv=	IR£0.33
AUS$1	= 147 lv	100 lv=	AUS$0.68
NZ$1	= 1305 lv	100 lv=	NZ$0.78
SAR1	= 42 lv	100 lv=	SAR2.39
DM1	= 126 lv	100 lv=	DM0.80

Country Phone Code: 359   **International Dialing Prefix: 00**

Pristine Black Sea beaches, resplendent monasteries, and stunning ski slopes have made Bulgaria Eastern Europe's coveted vacation spot for years. Nearly half the country is covered in mountains. The Stara Planina range bisects Bulgaria horizontally from Sofia to Varna, sloping down to the Danube in the north. The Rila and Pirin mountains are south of Sofia, and the Rhodopi mountains rise south of Plovdiv. Between Sredna Gora and Stara Planina hides the famous Valley of Roses. While the West groggily awakens to Bulgaria's possibilities, visitors can still lose themselves in its natural and artistic grandeur for a pittance.

BULGARIA ESSENTIALS

U.S. citizens can visit Bulgaria visa-free for up to 30 days, or get a three-month visa for US$50. Australian, British, Canadian, Irish, South African, and New Zealand citizens must obtain a visa (single-entry US$50, multiple-entry US$120, transit US$40) from their local consulate. See Essentials: Embassies and Consulates, p. 5. Visas take at least a week to process, unless you opt for US$80 rush service. The application requires a passport, a photograph, and payment by cash or money order. A stay of more than 30 days requires a visit to a Bureau for Foreigners, located in every major Bulgarian city. The visa price includes a US$20 border tax which those who do not need visas are required to pay upon entering the country.

GETTING THERE

For info, contact **Balkan Holidays,** 317 Madison Ave., Suite 508, New York, NY 10017 (tel. (212) 573-5530; fax 573-5538). The war in the former Yugoslavia cut Bulgarian **train** links to Western Europe. Competition between Bulgarian **Balkan Air,** Lufthansa, and British Airways has made **air travel** the best option. Balkan Air flies direct to Sofia from New York and other cities. There are also train lines through Romania (enter through Ruse), Greece, and Turkey. **Rila** is the main international train ticket company. **Group Travel** and **Adress buses** run to Romania, Greece, and Turkey. There are ferries from coastal cities to Istanbul.

GETTING AROUND

Public transportation in Bulgaria costs about 100lv per km. The **train** system is comprehensive, though slow, crowded, and aged. Direct trains run from Sofia to major towns. There are three train types: express (експрес), fast (бърз; *burz*), and slow (пътнически; *putnicheski*). Avoid the "slow"—they stop at anything that looks inhabited. Purchase couchettes in advance. To buy an international ticket, go to the appropriate office, usually in the town center (look for **Rila Travel;** Рила), or go to the international ticket counter at Sofia Central Railway Station (Централна Гара-София). Rila gives under-26 discounts. The only direct trains to central Europe are to Budapest. Once there, switch trains for other destinations. Domestic tickets are sold at stations. Buying a ticket on the train entails an unregulated fine. Stations are poorly marked, often only in Cyrillic. Know when you should reach your destination, bring along a map of the route, or ask a friendly person on the train for help.

Express trains usually have cafés with snacks and alcohol. Be prepared for smoke-filled corridors, unaesthetic bathrooms, breathtaking views, and friendly travelers. Some useful words: влак (*vlak*—train); автобус (*avtobus*—bus); гара (*gara*—station); перон (*peron*—platform); коловоз (*kolovoz*—track); билет (*bilet*—ticket); заминаваши (*zaminavashti*—departure); пристигаши (*pristigashti*—arrival); не/пушачи (*ne/pushachi*—non-/smoking); спален вагон (*spalen vagon*—sleeping car); първа класа (*purva klasa*—first class); втора класа (*vtora klasa*—second class).

Rising train ticket prices make **bus** travel an attractive option. You'll save up to three hours traveling from Sofia to the Black Sea coast. For long distances, **Group Travel** and **Etap** offer modern buses with A/C, bathrooms, and VCRs at around 1½ times the price of trains. Buy a seat in advance from the agency office or pay when boarding. Buses stop in many towns *en route* and let passengers off for snacks. Some buses have set departures; others leave only when full. Private companies have great package deals on international travel, and representatives speak English.

Balkan Air fares have swollen enormously (Sofia to Varna or Burgas: US$65 one-way), and there are no youth discounts on domestic flights. Major companies such as **Hertz** and **EuroDollar** are in most cities. The cheapest prices, usually for a *Seat,* average about US$70-80 per day. Be prepared for high speeds, questionable maneuvers, and unfamiliar signs. **Taxis** are usually a good deal in cities and larger towns. Eschew private taxis; cab cars are all the same make, and have the company name and number on the side. Refuse to pay in dollars and insist on a metered ride *("sus apparata").* Ask the distance and price per km to do your own calculations. From Sofia airport, don't pay more than US$10 to reach the center. In Sofia, fares are 35-45lv per kilometer (and rising with gas prices), with a 10% increase after 10pm. **Hitchhiking** is a growing risk, and drivers are more reluctant to pick up hitchers.

TOURIST SERVICES

Balkantourist, the former national tourist bureau, maintains offices, though many have been privatized. They change money and book hotel and private rooms. Hotels often maintain tourist offices. It may be difficult to get information unless you're booking an expensive excursion or hotel room. If not, try the reception at a hotel.

MONEY

One **lev** (lv; plural: leva), the standard monetary unit, used to be divided into 100 stotinki (st). One, 2, 5, and 10 leva coins have been introduced to save money on printing bills. We list most prices in U.S. dollars (US$) due to the ever-changing value of the lev. In May-July 1996, the exchange rate rocketed from around 70lv per US$1, to 200lv per US$1. This had yet to have its repercussions on the economy and prices, as of August, 1996. The official rate coincides with rates offered by private banks and **exchange bureaus.** The latter tend to have extended hours (24-hr. ones have a "Change Non-Stop" sign in English) and better rates, but may not be able to buy all currencies (especially NZ$). Private exchange bureaus sometimes take American Express **traveler's checks** and many banks accept major credit cards for **cash advances** (Visa is most widely accepted). Banks have a fixed commission or percentage, while exchange bureaus have a lower (3-4lv) rate for checks than cash. Hotels have less favorable rates. Any Bulgarian bill from before 1974 is worthless—check carefully. Well-worn or ripped foreign bills will not be accepted. Cash AmEx traveler's checks in dollars or leva at major banks such as **TSBank** or **Balkan Bank.** A banking crisis and the lack of enough hard currency caused many banks to stop cashing traveler's checks in the currency in which they are issued. Credit card cash advances are most often done in leva as well. **Credit cards** are not widely accepted, except in larger hotels and more expensive resorts. Do not be misled by credit card advertisements in store windows; many are for show. In most hotels, U.S. dollars and leva are both accepted. In all other transactions use leva.

COMMUNICATION

Making international **telephone** calls from Bulgaria requires tremendous patience. **AT&T Direct** (tel. 00 18 00 00 10), **Sprint** (tel. 008 00 1010) and **MCI** (tel. 008 00 00 01) provide direct calling card connections. To call collect, dial 01 23 for an international operator or have the phone office or hotel receptionist order the call. The operator won't speak English, the post office may claim they can't make the call, and hotel receptionists are protective of phones. In Sofia or Varna, try the AmEx office. The Bulgarian word for a collect call is *za tyahna smetka* (за Тяхна Сметка). You can make international calls at most post offices, but connections are poor outside large cities and often break down during a call. Calls to the U.S. average US$2 per minute, but expect to pay as much as US$4 per minute at hotels. **Betkom** or **Bulfon** direct dial phones with digital display screens are at major hotels and resorts. They service only Europe and the Middle East, and require a special calling card sold from a kiosk near the phone (450lv and up). **Faxes** are widely used; send and receive them from post offices. Many hotels have business centers with faxes, typewriters, and phones, for a steep fee. **E-mail** can be sent from the Sofia Sheraton business center at the Sheraton in Sofia, pl. Sveta Nedelya (US$5 per min.). Some universities also have access to the Internet—beg or befriend a student or two. **Foreign papers** can be found in large hotels; the *International Herald Tribune* and *USA Today* at the Sheraton and at the Central Department Store (TSUM) in Sofia. Catch **CNN** in the lobbies of major hotels. The **BBC** and **VOA Europe** (103.5 FM for Sofia) play all day on Bulgarian radio.

LANGUAGE

Bulgarian is a South-Slavic language of the Indo-European family. A few words in Bulgarian are borrowed from Turkish and Greek, but by and large Bulgarian is most similar to **Russian. English** is spoken in travel agencies and tourist areas. In the countryside, you're on your own. Bulgarian-English phrasebooks are sold at bookstands and bookstores (30lv). Many older Bulgarians speak **French; German** is understood in Black Sea resorts. Street names are in the process of changing; use both the old and new names. Bulgarian transliteration is much the same as Russian (see p. 771) except that "х" is *h*, "щ" is *sht*, and "ъ" is transliterated as *â* or *u* (pronounced as in the English b*u*g). Key phrases include "поща" (*poshta*—post office"), "частна квартира" (*chastna kvarteera*—private room), "говорите-ли английски?" (*govorite lih anliiski?*—do you speak English?), "тоалетна" (*toaletna*—toilet; Ж for women, М for men), "Отворено/затворено" (*otvoreno/zatvoreno*—open/closed), and the all-purpose "добре" (*dobreh*—OK, used in almost every sentence). See Glossary, p. 773.

HEALTH AND SAFETY

> **Emergency Numbers: Ambulance:** tel. 150. **Fire:** tel. 160. **Police:** tel. 166.

Public **bathrooms** often are holes in the ground; pack a small bar of soap and toilet paper, and have a 5 or 10lv note ready. Look for **pharmacy** signs: аптека (*apteka*). There is always a "night-duty" pharmacy in larger towns whose address will be posted on the doors of the others. Pharmacists should be able to recommend medications and direct you to a doctor or hospital. *Analgin* is headache medicine; *analgin chinin* is cold/flu medicine; band-aids are *sitoplast;* cotton wool is *pamuk*. Imported medications are popping up in larger cities. Condoms (*prezervatif*) can be bought in pharmacies. Foreign brands are safer. **Contact lens** wearers should bring supplies, if traveling in the country; in cities, just look for an Оптика (optician).

After 40 years of Communist misuse, Sofia and other large cities in Bulgaria are **polluted,** though the air is usually brisk and fresh. While Sofia is as safe as most European capitals, there is a certain sense of lawlessness. Locals generally don't trust the police, and stories circulate of people being terrorized by local mafias. Contact your embassy in an emergency. The end of central government control has left consumers vulnerable to scams. Don't buy bottles of **alcohol** from street vendors and be careful with homemade liquor—there have been cases of poisoning and contamination. Anything you buy on the street is likely to be counterfeit and/or contraband. Sofia **streets** can be deadly; pedestrians do not have the right of way, and Bulgarians park on sidewalks. If you take a taxi, ones driving for established companies are generally safer and more honest. Avoid walking alone after dark, under any circumstances. There is a general lack of tolerance towards **homosexuals.** Discretion makes life easier.

ACCOMMODATIONS AND CAMPING

Upon crossing the border, most people are given a yellow **statistical card** to document where they stay at night; without it, you may have difficulty getting a hotel room. If you don't get a card at all (which could be the case if you don't need a visa to enter), don't worry. If you are staying with friends, you'll have to register with the **Bulgarian Registration Office.** See the consular section of your embassy for details.

Private rooms are arranged through Balkantourist or other tourist offices for US$3-11 a night. Be sure to ask for a central location. Look for signs: стаи за нощувка (room for rent). It is also common for people to come to train and bus stations and offer private accommodations. In crowded locations, such as the Black Sea resorts in the summer, this may be your only chance to get a room; don't do it if you are by yourself (just in case). Bulgarian **hotels** are classed by a star-system and licensed by the Government Committee on Tourism; rooms in one-star hotels are almost identical to those in two- and three-star hotels, but have no private bathrooms; they average about US$8 for singles and US$17 for doubles. Foreigners are always charged higher prices. The majority of Bulgarian **youth hostels** are in the countryside and are popular with student groups; in Sofia, make reservations through **ORBITA,** Hristo Botev 48 (Христо Ботев; tel. (02) 80 01 02; fax 88 58 14), or **Pirin Tourist,** Poszitano 12 (Позитано; tel. (02) 87 33 80; fax 65 00 52). Many give **HI** discounts and almost all provide bedding. In many cities hostels don't exist, but ORBITA and Pirin Tours may be able to arrange university housing. Outside major towns, **campgrounds** provide a chance to meet backpackers. Spartan bungalows await at nearly every site but are often full. Freelance camping is popular, but you risk a fine (and your safety); watch for signs.

FOOD AND DRINK

Food from **kiosks** is cheap (meal 100-150lv); **restaurants** average 400lv per meal. Kiosks sell *kebabcheta* (кебабчета; small sausage-shaped hamburgers), sandwiches, pizzas, *banitsa sus sirene* (баница със сирене; cheese-filled pastries) and filled rolls. Fruit and vegetables are sold in a *plod-zelenchuk* (плод-зеленчук), *pazar* (пазар), and on the street. Find 24-hour snacks at mini-markets. **Vegetarians** won't starve. In summer, Bulgaria is blessed with delicious fruits and vegetables, especially tomatoes and peaches. Try *shopska salata* (шопска салата), an addictive salad of tomatoes, peppers, cucumbers, and onions with feta cheese. *Kyopoolu* (кьопоолу) and *imam bayaldu* (имам баялдъ) are eggplant dishes. *Tikvichki s mlyako* (тиквички с мляко) is fried zucchini in milk and garlic sauce. *Gyuvech* (гювеч) is stew with meat, onion, peppers, potatoes, and other veggies. Also try *tarator* (таратор)—a cold soup made with yogurt, cucumber, and garlic, ideally also with walnuts.

There is a heavy emphasis on **meat** in the Bulgarian menu. Try *kavarma* (каварма)—a meat dish with lots of onions and sometimes an egg on top. There are many organ-based dishes such as *mozik* (мозик; brain) or *ezik* (език; tongue). Bulgarians are known for cheese and yogurt—the bacterium that makes yogurt from milk bears the scientific names *bacilicus bulgaricus*. *Sirene* (сирене) is a feta cheese, and *kashkaval*, a hard yellow cheese. Baklava and *sladoled* (сладолед; ice cream) are in shops marked сладкарница *(sladkarnitsa)*.

Well-stirred *airan* (айран; yogurt with water and ice cubes) and *boza* (боза; beer, but sweet and thicker) are popular drinks, excellent with breakfast. Bulgaria exports mineral water; locals swear by its healing qualities (good brands are Gorna Banya and Hissaria). Delicious red and white wines are produced in various regions; the most expensive bottles are US$1-2. Melnik is famous for its red wine, and the area around the old capitals in the north-northeast make excellent white wines. Bulgarians begin meals with *rakiya*—a grape brandy. Be careful; it's got a kick. The traditional toast is *"Na Zdrave"* (to your health). Good Bulgarian beers are *Astika* and *Zagorka*.

Tipping is not obligatory, but 10% doesn't hurt. A 7-10% service charge will occasionally be added automatically. The word for bill is сметка *(smetka)*. Remember—restaurants and *mehani* (taverns) usually charge a small fee to use restrooms. Don't drink unpasteurized milk unless it's been well heated. *Dobur appetit!*

CUSTOMS AND ETIQUETTE

Businesses open around 8-9am and take an hour lunch break some time between 11 and 2pm. Banks' hours are usually 8:30am-4pm, but some close at 2pm. Tourist bureaus, post offices, and shops remain open until 6 or 8pm; in tourist areas and big cities shops may close as late as 10pm, but are often shut Sundays. "Every day" (Всеки ден; *Vseki den*) usually means Monday through Friday. Bulgarians shake their heads to indicate "yes" and "no" in the opposite directions from Brits and Yanks. It is easier to just hold your head still while saying yes (да; *da*) or no (не; *neh*). Bring an odd numbers of **flowers** when visiting Bulgarian families; even numbers of flowers are brought only to funerals. It is customary to share tables in restaurants and taverns. In churches, it is respectful to buy a candle or two from the souvenir stand out front. Candles placed high are in honor of the living and low in remembrance of the dead.

LIFE AND TIMES

HISTORY

Ancient **Thracian** tribes occupied Bulgaria from at least 3500BCE. Skilled warriors and artisans, they left behind over 1000 ruins as well as vast collections of gold and silver artifacts. Influenced and colonized by the **Greeks** from the 8th century BCE, Southern and Eastern Thrace served as a crossroads for Greek-Persian trade and warfare until the Macedonian conquest of 343-342BCE. The death of Lysimachus of Thrace (323-281BCE), a general of Alexander the Great, ushered in two centuries of chaos punctuated by Celtic invasions. By 46CE, Thrace had fallen to the **Romans.** The crumbling of the Roman empire led to invasion in the 370s, as Visigoths, Huns, and bad Samaritans swept in, followed by Slav tribes. The **Huns** retreated to the steppes of what is now Eastern Ukraine and established the original Bulgar state. Acting in alliance with resident Slavs, the proto-Bulgarian tribes of the Danube began raiding the Byzantine Empire; the Byzantines surrendered in 681 and the tribes united under one king, thus creating the first Slavic state—Bulgaria.

Bulgaria prospered in the 8th and 9th centuries. Brothers Cyril and Methodius created the first Bulgarian alphabet, *glagolitsa*, in the 8th century; their disciple Kliment Ohridski was the author of the **Cyrillic** alphabet. Tsar Boris I (852-889) accepted **Orthodox Christianity** in 865 to overcome Bulgaria's barbaric reputation, and established the Bulgarian Church. The adoption of a common religion brought the people closer together, and an independent church helped ward off the ambitions of the Constantinople Patriarchate and the *Curia Romana*. The powerful **First Greater Bulgarian Empire,** created under Tsar Simeon, united Southern Slavs under Bulgarian rule and overthew the Byzantines in the Balkans. After his death in 927, Bulgaria's fortunes declined; East Bulgaria was taken during the Russian Wars of 969-976, and West Bulgaria (modern Serbia and Macedonia) was taken in 1014 by **Basil II.** To ensure submission, Basil blinded 99 out of every 100 captured soldiers. After 100 years as a Byzantine province, the **Second Greater Bulgarian Empire** (1187-1242) arose, its borders extending from the Black Sea to the Aegean and the Adriatic after the 1204 sack of Constantinople. Towns, roads, fortresses, royal palaces, churches and monasteries were erected. Among these were the monasteries of Rila and Bachkovo and the churches in Nesebur. Wars with the Serbian and Hungarian Kingdoms soon weakened the new nation, and **Mongols** arrived in 1242 taking advantage of the state's faltering condition. In 1352, the **Ottoman Turks** swarmed the Balkan Peninsula, destroying the Bulgarian capital in 1393; Bulgaria became a nation of oppressed peasants for the next five centuries.

Over time, a **haidouk resistance** movement emerged. As churches were turned into mosques, monasteries became repositories of Bulgarian culture. Liturgical books were transcribed into Bulgarian, thus ensuring the continuation of national language and literature. A liberation ideology was born in 1762 with the publishing of the Slav-Bulgarian History by Paissi of Hilendar. Meanwhile, Bulgarian towns grew and an urban bourgeoisie developed trade. At the beginning of the 19th century, many Bulgarians took part in the liberation struggle which first broke out in Serbia, and then in Greece. Though this was also the time of the Bulgarian National Revival, Bulgarians' main goal remained liberation from foreign occupation. Leaders such as Georgi Rakovski, Vasil Levski, and Hristo Botev provided the arms, organization, and common ideology the people lacked. The April Uprising triggered revolts across Bulgaria in 1875-76, each viciously snuffed by the Turks.

Bulgarians then pinned hopes for liberation on **Russia.** In 1877, Russo-Bulgarian troops under Tsar Aleksandr II defeated Turkey against great odds, at the battle of the **Shipka Pass.** A truce signed January 31, 1878 granted Bulgaria large territories in the

Balkans; however, in an effort to preserve a Turkish bulwark against Russia, the **Berlin Congress** of 1878 decided that South Bulgaria would remain within the sphere of the Ottoman Empire. Problems soon erupted in the form of the First and Second Balkan Wars. The result was a loss of territory for Bulgaria, which, frustrated, sided with the Central Powers (Germany, Austria-Hungary, and Turkey) in **WWI**. However, troops mutinied, leading to an early armistice and further losses of territory. Bulgarian claims on Macedonia led it to support Germany in **WWII;** still, Bulgaria resisted German pressure to declare war on the USSR and protected its Jewish population. An anti-German movement emerged in 1942, as Agrarian and Social Democrats, leftist intellectuals, military reserve officers called *Zveno* (Link), and the underground Communist Party joined in the **Fatherland Front.** Bulgaria quickly declared neutrality, disarmed resident Nazi troops, then fought alongside the Soviets until war's end. On September 9, 1944, Fatherland Front partisans took Sofia; Bulgaria was declared a republic two years later.

The late 1940s saw the collectivization of agriculture and the beginnings of industrialization. Under Communist leader **Georgi Dimitrov,** good economic and political relations with the Soviet Union allowed Bulgaria to specialize in light manufacturing and serve as the breadbasket of the Eastern Bloc. **Todor Zhivkov** led Bulgaria from 1954-89; his regime brought stability, restraint and fanatical alignment with the Soviet Union. Under Zhivkov, Bulgaria's international image was epitomized by world-champion female shot-putters, rumored ties to the attempted assassination of the Pope, and a security service that used poisoned umbrella tips to assassinate its dissidents.

On November 10, 1989, the Bulgarian Communist Party retired Todor Zhivkov, by then unpopular and much-ridiculed, and held elections after changing its name to the **Bulgarian Socialist Party** (BSP). Despite initial socialist victories, Bulgaria succeeded in establishing a non-Communist government in November, 1991. The country's first open presidential elections, held in January 1992, re-elected philosopher **Zhelu Zhelev** as president and poet **Blaga Dimitrova** as vice-president. The following year, however, Dimitrova resigned in protest of economic and social policies supported by the government. In the most recent elections, the Turks, who make up approximately 10% of the Bulgarian population, have exercised a disproportionate influence on the country's politics through their party, the Movement for Rights and Freedoms. Meanwhile, Bulgaria's other major ethnic group, the Gypsies, remain politically unconsolidated and on the fringes of mainstream society.

LITERATURE

Modern Bulgarian literature dates back only to the late 19th century. It has not gradually evolved from the first texts written in the language, but rather is separated from them by the Turks' centuries-long suppression of Bulgarian culture.

Old Bulgarian literature developed in the 10th century, Bulgaria's Golden Age. Its beginnings are closely related to Tsar Boris I's adoption of Christianity in 865, and the subsequent efforts to spread the new religion. The Preslav literary school was established in 893 by the pupils of Cyril and Methodius, the inventors of the Cyrillic alphabet. From here stemmed translations of liturgical texts and religious dogma, which tied the country culturally to Constantinople and the Greek Orthodox tradition. However, while monks and tsars tried to convert the people, the scriptural invention of the devout also boosted secular literature, mostly legends about chivalrous warriors, princesses, and innkeepers.

Bulgaria's religious and literary links to the Byzantine Empire did not ensure peace between the two states. Constantinople's capture of Bulgaria in the early 11th century subjugated the country to Byzantine rule and hindered all literary developments until the 13th century—the **Middle Bulgarian,** or Silver, Age. The Turnovo School's attempts to revive Old Church Slavonic literature brought about stylistic cleansing and standardization. Despite political tensions, the period's scribes still felt a thematic affinity to Byzantium, penning mystical and religious works.

A second lull in forging a nation through literature occurred after Mongols overrode Bulgaria in 1242, followed by the Turks in 1352. The hush lasted until 1762, the date on **Paissi of Hilendar's** *Slav-Bulgarian History.* The *History,* together with the publication of Bishop Sofrony's *Sunday-Book,* the first book in modern Bulgarian, sparked off the **National Revival** movement *(Vuzrazhdane).* Romanticism flourished, reminding the people of its independent past and roots in national folklore. **Ivan Vazov's** epics, novellas, short stories, and plays earned him the title of a "national poet," while his *Under the Yoke* (1894), gained the status of a "national novel." Vazov based the novel on Victor Hugo's *Les Misérables.* The hero, Boycho Ognyanov, starts off as a scoundrel but transforms himself into a symbol of Bulgarian patriotism, arriving at the lofty level of existence by way of labor and love.

Nineteenth-century Romanticism's national and social awareness was rejected by the early 20th century's **Missul** (Thought) group. The school glorified the frustrated intellectual and encouraged individual freedom over societal good.

An author who incorporated elements of both the Romantic and the post-Romantic ages was **Pencho Slaveykov.** While drawing many elements for his poems and ballads from folk songs, he refused to confine his writing to the national context. Slaveykov based his song of Bulgaria's centuries-long suffering, *Simfonya na beznadezhnosta* (Symphony of Hopelessness), on the tale of Prometheus, while more poems in the cycle *Epicheski pesni* (Epic Songs) depicted other non-Bulgarian heroes. Unlike the Romantics', Slaveykov's works describe personal philosophies of life rather than adopting a moralizing tone.

The shifting of writers' interests away from national problems continued during the inter-war years. **Elizaveta Bagryana** gained inspiration from technological progress for her love poems, while **Emilian Stanev** in *Prez zimata* (During the Winter) followed the saga of a partridge family in his search for knowledge of human reality. The simultaneous popularization of Marxistideas re-directed the literary focus onto the society. This ideology came to dominate Bulgarian literature after the 1944 Communist coup, when **Socialist Realism** became the publicly enforced current.

BULGARIA TODAY

Personal freedoms in Bulgaria have bounded ahead, yet many Bulgarians are starting to feel the stranglehold of financial limitations and skyrocketing inflation, brought about by the difficult transition to a market economy. The transformation to capitalism has also resulted in the creation of social classes in a formerly classless society. Crime is on the rise, and travelers are increasingly at risk. Premier Jean Videnov of the Bulgarian Socialist Party (BSP) is commonly perceived as lacking direction and authority. The opposition union of Democratic Forces is foretelling a quick end in total disgrace for his cabinet. In June 1996, president Zhelyu Zhelev lost the opposition primaries, preventing him from competing for another term. Instead, Peur Stoyanov, a rising political star, was slated to run in October 1996 against the contested figure of socialist Georgi Pirinski—born in the US and likely to be disqualified if elected. Projected inflation for 1996 is over 700 percent. Despite all hardships, the country has remained peaceful and unrest is not expected.

Sofia (София)

Affordable and undiscovered, feeding on cool jazz and cheap wine, Sofia offers a great night on the town for pocket change. The city's motto is "It grows, but never ages". Since the overthrow of Communism, youth has dominated the tempo of life. Sofia's aspirations to join the West are mercilessly checked by its aging infrastructure and confusion created by the new free market. In the downtown area, BMWs maneuver around pot-holes and vie for space on narrow alleys. The desire to be modern falls short just outside the city, in an aesthetic nightmare of run-down neighborhoods and shoddy high-rises. Most Sofians don't seem worried and advance at their own pace, enjoying new-found freedom and endless espressos at one of Sofia's many cafés.

ORIENTATION AND PRACTICAL INFORMATION

Sofia's 1.2 million inhabitants occupy the center of the Balkan peninsula, 500km southeast of Belgrade. International trains run to Athens, Belgrade, Bucharest, Istanbul, and Thessaloniki. Street names remain the most damning legacy of Communism. After the arrival of democracy in 1989, successive magistrates summarily changed names such as "Heavy Tank" street to more democratic ones, rendering most city maps useless. **Patriarh Evtimii blvd.** (Патриарх Евтимий), **Hristo Botev blvd.** (Христо Ботев), **Alexksandr Stamboliiski blvd.** (Александър Стамболийски), **Kniaz Aleksandr Dondukov blvd.** (Княз Александър Дондуков), and **Vasil Levski blvd.** (Васил Левски) surround the most important administrative and tourist sites. **Sveta Nedelya pl.** (Света Неделя; formerly pl. Lenin), is the center of Sofia, recognizable by St. Nedelya Church and the enormous **Sheraton Hotel.** The **train station,** (централна гар; *tsentralna gara*), is connected to pl. Sveta Nedelya by **Knyaginya Maria Luiza blvd.** (Княгиня Мария Луиза). Young people often meet at **Popa,** the slightly irreverent nickname for **Patriarch Evtimii's monument.** Two good "post-name-change" publications with useful phone numbers, site guides, and maps are the **Sofia City Guide** (free at the airport, hotels, and travel agencies) and the **Sofia Guide** (130lv).

Tourist Offices: BalkanTour Ltd., Stamboliiski blvd. 37 (tel./fax 88 07 95). From pl. Sveta Nedelya, walk 3 blocks up Stamboliiski. Books accommodations in hotels and private houses, exchanges currency, and sells current maps. Arranges for bus travel to Istanbul, Prague, Budapest, Warsaw and other cities. Cashes traveler's checks. Open daily 9am-6pm. The office at Vitosha 1 (tel. 97 51 92; fax 80 01 34), provides hotel reservations, rental cars, bus tickets, and excursions (Rila Monastery with English-speaking guide US$30 per person), though is reluctant to supply tourist info. Open Mon.-Fri. 8am-7pm, Sat. 8:30am-1:30pm.

Budget Travel: Walking about Vitosha from NDK, make a left turn on Pozitano (Позитано) right before pl. Sv. Nedelya, to find **Pirin Tourist,** Pozitano 12, 3rd floor (tel. 981 49 54; fax 981 90 36). Worn out carpets and the stale smell of cigarettes give away the true budget travel establishment. Arranges private rooms and ISIC discounts. Open Mon.-Fri. 9am-5:30pm. **ORBITA Travel,** Hristo Botev 48 (tel. 80 15 03; fax 80 15 06). From pl. Sveta Nedelya, walk up Stamboliiski, and take a left on Hristo Botev. University, dorm rooms, private rooms, and hotel rooms. Issues and renews ISICs. *Sofia Guide* found here (130lv). Open Mon.-Fri. 9am-5:30pm.

American Express: Megatours, Levski 1 (tel. 88 04 19 or 981 42 01; fax 981 21 67). Take Tsar Osvoboditel to left of Mausoleum. Cashes traveler's checks at 4% commission, replaces cards, and issues plane and bus tickets. Office in Hotel Rila, Lege ul. (Леге), holds mail. Open Mon.-Fri. 9am-6:30pm, Sat. 9am-noon.

Embassies and Cultural Centers: U.K., Vasil Levski bul. 65 (*not* Vasil Levski ul.; tel. 981 53 61 or 981 57 22) three blocks northwest of the Palace of Culture. Open Mon.-Thurs. 8:30am-12:30pm and 1:30-5pm, Fri. 8:30am-1pm. Citizens of **Canada, Australia,** and **New Zealand** should contact the British embassy. **U.S.,** ul. Suborna 1a (Съборна; tel. 88 48 01 through 05), three blocks from pl. Sv. Nedelya behind the Sheraton. Consular section, Kapitan Andreev 1 (Капитан Андреев; tel. 65 94 59), behind Economic Tehnikum near Hotel Hemus. Americans are advised to register with the consular section upon arriving in Bulgaria. Open Mon.-Fri. 9am-4:30pm for American citizens. United States Information Service's **American Center,** Vitosha 18 (tel. 980 48 85 or 980 48 38; fax 980 36 46; http:\\www.usis.b), has a library and exhibits. Open Mon.-Fri. 8:30am-5pm, library 1-5pm. **South Africa,** Vasil Aprilov ul. 3 (Васил Априлов; tel. 44 29 16).

Currency Exchange: The largest concentrations of exchange bureaus are along bul. Vitosha, Stamboliiski, and Graf Ignatiev. **Bulgarian Foreign Trade Bank** (Българска Бъншнютърговска Банка), pl. Sv. Nedelya 7 (tel. 84 95 82) across from the Sheraton. Cashes traveler's checks to leva (2% commission). Open Mon.-Fri. 8:30am-12:30pm and 1-4:30pm. **7M** has many branches and gives Visa, MC, and Diner's Club cash advances at 7% commission. Open Mon.-Fri. 9am-5pm, Sat. 10am-1pm. **TSBank,** pl. Sv. Nedelya 4 (tel. 88 831), gives Visa cash advances (4% commission), cashes travelers' checks (2% commission in leva; 3% for US$) and has a Visa/Plus **ATM.** Open Mon.-Thurs. 9am-3pm, Fri. 9am-1pm.

Flights: Airport Sofia (tel. 793 21, international departures tel. 72 06 72, international arrivals tel. 79 32 11, domestic flights tel. 72 24 14). To get to city center, take bus #84 (15lv). The bus stop will be on left from international arrivals; ask for *tsentur* (център). Most airlines offer **youth fares** for travellers under 26. **Bulgarian Balkan Airlines,** pl. Narodno Subranie 12 (tel. 68 41 48 or 68 93 61; fax 68 94 18), offers flights to Burgas, Moscow, Warsaw, Prague, London, Athens, Istanbul. Open Mon.-Fri. 7:30am-7pm, Sat. 8am-2pm; **Lufthansa,** Suborna 9 (tel. 980 41 41; fax 981 29 11), offers student discounts to Frankfurt and Munich; **Air France,** Suborna 2 (tel. 981 78 30); **Czech Airlines (ČSA),** Suborna 9 (tel. 88 56 68). Open Mon.-Fri. 8:30am-12:30pm and 1:30-5pm.

Trains: Sofia's **central train station** is north of the center on Knyaginya Maria Luiza bul. Trams #1 and 7 travel to pl. Sv. Nedelya. Buses #305, 313, and 213 can get you there from different points in town. Tickets for Northern Bulgaria sold on ground floor; Southern Bulgaria and international tickets in the basement. International tickets sold daily 7am-11pm. Info, international or domestic tickets, and reservations also at the all-purpose **ticket office** (tel. 65 71 86), under the NDK. Descend the stairs in front of the main entry. To: Athens; Budapest; Istanbul; Thessaloniki.

> There have been reports of travelers being drugged with sleep-inducing gas and robbed on the Sofia-Istanbul line. Never travel on this line alone.

Open Mon.-Fri. 7am-3pm, Sat. 7am-2pm. No ISIC discounts.

Buses: Matri (Матри), ul. Damyan Gruev 23 (Дамян Груев; tel. 52 50 04), services all Balkan Peninsula connections. Student discounts on trips to Athens (1 per day, US$37; $30 with discount). To: Belgrade (2 per day, US$10); Istanbul (2 per week, US$20); Skopje (2 per day, US$10); Tirana (2 per week, US$26). Pay in leva at central bank exchange rate. Private **buses** leave from the parking lot across from the Central Train Station. The private bus company, **Group Travel,** Rakovski 85 (tel. 83 14 54; fax 83 24 26) goes everywhere in and around Bulgaria. Their fast and comfortable buses are a rich Bulgarian's Greyhound. From the Sheraton, walk up Knyaz Dondukov Blvd., and take a left on Rakovski. To: Budapest (US$40); Prague (DM70); Warsaw (US$36). Same-day tickets at Novotel parking kiosk; up to 7 days in advance from central office. **ETAP,** Rakovski 91 (tel. 88 33 76 and 83 24 69), has equally modern buses and nearly identical prices. Bargains await in the multiple kiosks of lesser companies. The bus station at **Ovcha Kupel** (Овча Купел), along Tsar Boris III Blvd., handles Sofia-region buses with some of the oldest vehicles. The station can be reached by tram #5 from the National History Museum near Sveta Nedelya. For info and international and domestic tickets, try the office under the NDK (tel. 65 71 87). No ISIC discounts.

Public Transportation: The system of trams, trolley buses, and buses is gleefully cheap (15lv per ride, day-pass 55lv). Buy tickets at kiosks or from the driver; punch 'em in the machines between the bus windows. Operating hours officially 4am-1am, but most lines don't run later than 11pm or earlier than 6am. If caught without a ticket, you'll be fined and mercilessly thrown off the vehicle.

Taxis: Everywhere. A green light in the front window means that the taxi is available, and you can flag it down. **Softaxi** (tel. 12 84) or **New Chance** (tel. 73 53).

Car Rental: Hertz and **Europcar** all over. **Eurodollar,** bul. Vitosha 25 (tel. 87 57 79), offers everything from a Fiat 500 (US$68 per day) to an Opel Omega Sedan (US$173 per day). Open Mon.-Fri. 9am-6pm. Airport office open daily 9am-9pm.

Hitchhiking: Hitching in the Sofia area is said to be getting increasingly dangerous and drivers rarely stop. Those hitching to Rila Monastery take tram #5 to highway E79. Those headed to Koprivshtitsa take tram #3 from Sofia.

Luggage Storage: Downstairs at the central train station. Look for "гардероб" (*garderob*) signs. 10lv per piece. Open 24hr. with lunch break 11:30-noon.

Laundromats: None per se, and larger hotels are often unwilling to wash non-guests' dirty underwear. Hosts of private rooms may do it for a minimal charge. A good dry cleaner is **Svezhest** (Свежест), Vasil Kolarov 19. From pl. Sveta Nedelya, walk up Vitosha and make a left on Vasil Kolarov. Open Mon.-Fri. 7am-7pm.

Film and Photo Developing: Agfa and **Kodak** centers on nearly every major street. Most labs have separate developing and per-picture prices. **Bulgarian Photogra-**

ORIENTATION AND PRACTICAL INFORMATION

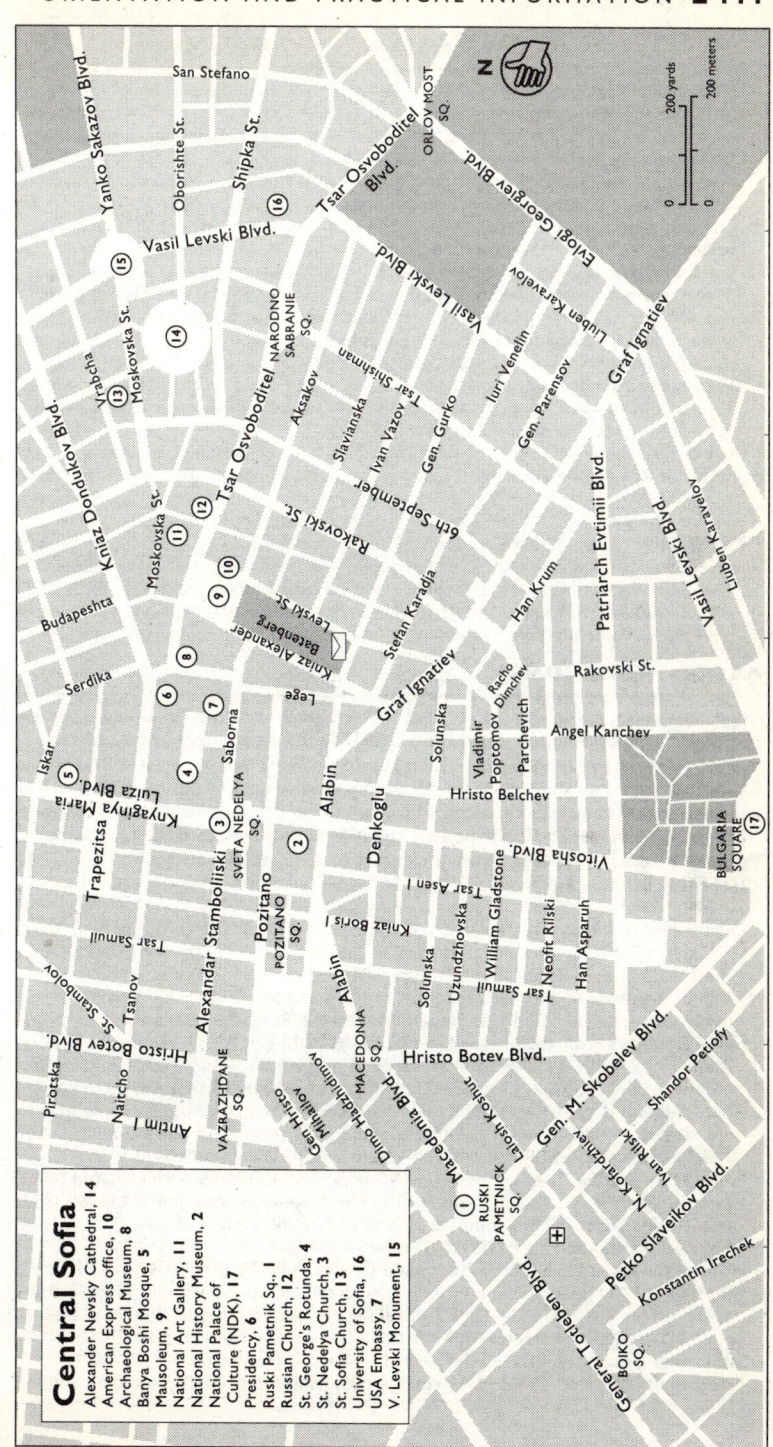

Central Sofia

- Alexander Nevsky Cathedral, 14
- American Express office, 10
- Archaeological Museum, 8
- Banya Boshi Mosque, 5
- Mausoleum, 9
- National Art Gallery, 11
- National History Museum, 2
- National Palace of Culture (NDK), 17
- Presidency, 6
- Ruski Pametnik Sq., 1
- Russian Church, 12
- St. George's Rotunda, 4
- St. Nedelya Church, 3
- St. Sofia Church, 13
- University of Sofia, 16
- USA Embassy, 7
- V. Levski Monument, 15

BULGARIA

phy (Българска фотография), Graf Ignatiev 2 (tel. 87 30 07), charges 75lv for developing and 20lv per picture. Open Mon.-Sat. 8:30am-1pm.

Photocopies: Look for "кѕерокѕ" signs. 8lv per page at the post office. Open Mon.-Fri. 8am-noon and 12:30-4:30pm. **Rank Xerox Copy Center,** across from the Sheraton, charges 6.5lv per page. Open Mon.-Fri. 8am-8pm, Sat 8am-4pm.

Pharmacies: (info tel. 178). **First Private Pharmacy** (Първа Частна Аптека), Tsar Asen 42, at the intersection of Neofit Rilski is well stocked with **condoms** and feminine hygiene products. Open 24hr. **Megapharma,** Vitosha 69 (tel. 80 97 76), on the corner of Patriarch Evtimii across from the NDK. Open daily 8am-11pm.

Medical Assistance: In an emergency, contact a hotel receptionist. Emergency aid for foreigners, offered by state-owned hospitals, is free of charge. If mobile, go to **Pirogov emergency hospital,** Totleben bul. 21 (tel. 53 31), across from Hotel Rodina. Open 24hr. An English-speaking **dentist** with modern equipment is Dr. Anton Filchev (tel. 66 29 84 or 516 92 34). For more info about medical care in Bulgaria, ask for a handout when you register at your embassy.

Express Mail: DHL, Tsar Osvoboditel bul. 8 (tel. 87 79 27), accepts AmEx, Diners Club, MC, and Visa. Next day delivery to New York and Washington. Otherwise 2-3 business days. Open Mon.-Fri. 9am-5:30pm.

Post Office: General Gurko 2 (Гурко). Walk down Suborna behind Sv. Nedelya, turn right on Knyaz Battenberg and left on Gurko. **Poste Restante** with 10lv charge. Mon.-Fri. 8am-8pm. Many hotels provide postal services. **Bulpost** express mail service is open Mon.-Fri. 8-11:30am and 1-3:30pm. **Postal code:** 1000.

Telephones: On ul. Stefan Karadzhna (Стефан Караджа), near the post office. Dial directly as far as Singapore. A minute costs: U.S. 240lv, U.K. 95lv, Australia 295lv. Use 2lv coins for local calls. For **collect** or **card calls,** dial 00-1-800-0010 for **AT&T,** 00-800-000 for **MCI,** and 00-800-1010 for **Sprint. Bulfon** and **Betkom** phone cards sold here. **Faxes** available 8am-9:30pm. Open 24hr. **Phone code:** 02.

ACCOMMODATIONS

Hotels are rarely worth their price, and the cheapest ones can be unsafe—**private rooms** are a logical solution. Apart from **ORBITA,** which arranges private accommodations (US$7-8 per person) and dorm rooms (US$3-4 per person), try **Markella,** Knyaginya Maria Luiza 17 (tel. 81 52 99), across from Central Department Store. They will stamp your statistical card and give you keys and directions (three-star rooms with hot showers US$8-10 per person; open Mon.-Sat. 8:30am-8:30pm). **Camping Vrana** (tel. 78 12 13) is 10km from the center on E-80, and **Cherniya Kos** (tel. 57 11 29) is 11km from the center on E-79; ask at tourist office for details.

Orbita Hotel, James Baucher bul. 76 (Джеймс Баучер; tel. 639 39), behind Hotel Vitosha. Take tram #9 south past NDK to Anton Ivanov. A 2-star behemoth, larger than Stalin's ego. Clean, plain rooms with private bath, phone, fridge. Singles US$35. Doubles US$46. ISIC discount reduces rates to US$16 and US$20 respectively. Breakfast included with non-discount rates. Rocking disco awaits.

Hotel Baldjieva (Балдиева), Tsar Asen 23 (tel. 87 29 14 or 87 37 84). A private hotel in the city center. Walking from Sv. Nedelya to the NDK, Tsar Asen is on the right, parallel to bul. Vitosha. Clean, small rooms, with direct-dial phones, fridges, minibar, and laundry. The complimentary bathrobe makes you forget the bathrooms are shared. Potted plants surround the lounge for peace and photosynthesis. Singles US$30. Doubles US$40. Add US$3 for breakfast. Pay in dollars or leva.

Hotel Niky, Neofit Rilski 16 (tel. 51 19 15 or 951 51 04), off Vitosha. Shared toilet, private showers, phone, and satellite TV. The wood panelling smells like it's fresh out of the forest. Billiard room, café, and restaurant. Pay in dollars, DM, or leva. Check-out at noon. Singles US$20. Doubles US$40.

Hotel Tsar Asen (Цар Асен), Tsar Asen 68 (tel. 54 78 01 or 70 59 20). Walking toward the ND on Tsar Asen, cross Patr. Evtimii and continue 40m. Ring doorbell at the gate and the friendly English-speaking receptionist will let you in. 4 doubles (US$34) used also as singles (US$27). Cable TV, private shower, phone.

Slavianska Beseda (Славянска Беседа), Slavianska 3 (tel. 88 04 41; fax 981 25 23), near the post office. From pl. Slaveikov, take Rakovski towards Tsar Osvoboditel.

Depressing halls lead to clean rooms with showers and tubs, TVs, phones, and fridges. Pay in dollars or leva. Singles US$30. Doubles US$40. Ask about the availability of hot water before taking a room.

Instead of staying in the expensive, sometimes unpleasant hotels in central Sofia, many choose a suburb. The small town **Dragalevtzi** (Драгалевци) offers many private, clean, and cheap hotels. Take tram #9 to the last stop, then pick up bus #64. Get off in the main square of Dragalevtzi.

Hotel Orhidea (Орхидея), Angel Bukoreshtliev 9 (Ангел Букорешлиев; tel. 67 27 39). Leaving the square on Yabulkova Gradina (Ябълкова Градина), take left on Angel Bukoreshtliev. 3 doubles with shared bathroom (DM10 per person).

Hotel Darling (Дарлинг), Yabulkova Gradina 14 (tel. 67 19 86), the unvarnished house next to Hotel Orhidea. Doubles DM20.

FOOD

From fast food to Bulgarian specialties, inexpensive meals are easy to find in Sofia. Supermarket **Zornitsa** (Зорница), Denkogli 34 (Денкогли), off bul. Vitosha, is particularly well stocked. Open Mon.-Sat. 8am-8pm. 24-hr. markets lie along Vitosha. An **open market,** known as the women's market (женски пазар; *zhenski pazar*), extends for several blocks. Take Knyaginya Maria Luiza from Pl. Sveta Nedelya, then make a left on Ekzarh Yosif (Екзарх Йосиф); bring plastic bags for fresh fruit and vegetables (open daily, but especially busy on weekends). Take any tram from Pl. Slaveikov away from the center, and you'll get to the **Roman Wall** outdoor market, bul. Hristo Smirnenski (Христо Смирненски).

Restaurants

The House (Къщата, *Kushtata*), Verila 4 (Верила; tel. 52 08 30), off bul. Vitosha near the NDK. Two floors with private tables inside a beautiful old house. Thick-necked Bulgarian youths enjoy *Pasta Mafiosa* (meat, tomato sauce, zucchini; 175lv) amidst delicate paintings and flowers. Other favorites are *mish-mash* (veggies and feta cheese; 135lv) and *mousaka* (195lv). Entrées cost 300-400lv, salads 90-110lv, soups 80lv and up. English menu. Open daily noon-midnight.

Borsalino (Борсалино), Chervena Stena 10 (Червен Стена; tel. 66 71 53), behind Hotel Orbita. Heavy wooden tables, fireplace, cozy outdoor area. Tasty Bulgarian specialties like *sarmi lozov list* (meat-stuffed vine leaves served with Bulgarian sour cream, 185lv), or *svinsko sus zele* (stewed pork with cabbage, 220lv). Filled mushrooms *(pulneni guby)* is the secret home recipe (195lv). English menu. Open 24hr. At night, take a taxi (about 200lv from central Sofia).

Eddy's Tex-Mex Diner, Vitosha 4 (tel. 981 85 58). Break through the saloon doors into one of Sofia's hippest eateries. Buffalo wings (US$2), nachos (US$1.50), and fajitas (US$3) grace the imaginative English menu. Add a cold margarita to feel a bit more south-of-the-border. Live music nightly from 9:30pm (cover 120lv). Poduene Blues Band with Vasko Krupkata (Vasko the "Patch") appear every Thurs. MC, Visa. 10% service charge. Open daily 12:30pm til the last customer leaves.

Ramayana, Hristo Belchev 32 (Христо Белчев; tel. 80 49 89), one street over from Vitosha between the NDK and the Sheraton. Sofia's first Indian restaurant. Outdoor seating area and A/C to cool you down while gulping the extra-hot curry. The chefs offer real *samosa*, spicy shrimp, chicken, and lamb dishes, and lots of veggie specials. Entrées 175-400lv. English menu. The lunch menu gives you a choice of soup, appetizer and main course for 600lv. Open daily noon-midnight.

Chinese Restaurant Chen, Rakovski 86 (tel. 87 34 99), across from the Opera House. Genuine Chinese staff serves genuine Chinese dishes. Entrées 160-360lv, vegetarian 130-270lv, beef in oyster sauce 310lv. Chinese/English/Bulgarian menu. English spoken. Open daily noon-3pm and 6-11pm.

Mexicano, Krakra 11 (Кракра; tel. 44 65 98). From the bus stop on ul. Shipka at Sofia University, walk down the street and take a right on Krakra. Offers a variety of Mexican specialties, drinks, and friendly service. Chili con carne 330lv, fajitas for two 940lv, vegetarian dish "San Lucas" 320lv, tequila shots 95-130lv. The atmosphere is spiced up nightly by the Latin music of the duo "Los Gemelos" (after 9pm). US$, DM, and French francs accepted. Open daily noon-midnight.

Korona (Корона; the Crown), Rakovski 163 (tel. 81 33 40). Go up Rakovski from pl. Slaveikov. In Bulgaria eat as the Bulgarians. Vegetarians may like *tikvichki s mlyako* (zucchini with milk sauce, 120lv) or the specialty "cheeses on grill Bella" (300lv). Carnivore entrées and grills 200-400lv. Lamb rolls *(agneshki rultsa,* 400lv) are the meat specialty. As the name suggests, monarchists love this place. A/C; English menu and English spoken. Open daily noon-midnight.

Savoy, Milin Kamuk 1 (Милин Камък; tel. 65 74 20). From the NDK, walk down Evlogi Georgiev Blvd. (Евлоги Георгев) and make a right on Milim Kamuk. A French/Bulgarian mix makes for hot *cuisine.* Soups 50-120lv. Entrées 300-400lv. The specialty "Savoy for two" *(Savoy za dvama;* 998lv) is a generous concoction of veal, pork, chick fillet, mushrooms, some animal's tongue, yellow cheese, sauce and garnishes. Sautéed veggies for 350lv. For dessert, try blueberries with cream (135lv). A/C; English spoken. Open daily 11am-midnight.

Miss Kaprize, Stamboliiski 72 (tel. 920 12 14). Bulgaria's answer to Pizza Hut. Pasta 96-185lv, small/large pizzas 105-209/125-277lv *(vegetariana* 105/125lv). Open daily 11am-12:30am (last phone order midnight). For delivery, call 43 53 74.

Cafés

Markrit, Patriarch Evtimii bul. 66 (tel. 54 92 41). A heaven for sweets-lovers, the café offers excellent fresh pastries, fruit cakes, fruit salads, and ice cream. Close to the NDK, Markrit also has a new coffee-bar in Hotel Hemus. Coffee, cake and a soda for less than US$1. Open daily 8am-9pm.

Café Luciano (Лучано), Rakovski, two blocks from Hotel Sevastopol. A chain of pastry cafés worth visiting each time you pass a new one. Low prices and excellent, jet-black caffeine. Coffee and cake for less than 50 U.S. cents. Open Mon.-Fri. 7:30am-9pm, Sat.-Sun. 9am-9pm.

SIGHTS

One of Sofia's two most venerable churches, the 4th-century **St. George's Rotunda** church, hides behind padlocked doors in the courtyard of the Sheraton Hotel, accompanied by a complex of ruins that used to be an ancient canal system. The Rotunda itself is a brick structure, with 14th- to 16th-century murals, and a long, complicated history. The other church, the 6th-century **St. Sofia**—the city's namesake from the 14th century—stands several blocks behind the Party house. Its 5th-century floor mosaic have been preserved intact. Used as the city's main mosque during the 19th century, a series of earthquakes repeatedly destroyed the mosque's minarets; the Ottoman rulers interpreted the catastrophe as a warning sign, and the Turks gave up St. Sophia as their house of prayer.

Across the square from St. Sofia looms the gold-domed **St. Aleksandr Nevsky Cathedral** (Свети Александър Невски), erected between 1904-1912 in memory of the 200,000 Russians who died in the 1877-78 Russo-Turkish War, and named after the patron saint of the tsar-liberator. During the first couple years of frail democracy after 1989, politicians of all colors used the cathedrals's steps as a podium to speak to their supporters gathered by the thousands on the cathedral square. The **crypt** houses a monstrous collection of painted icons and religious artifacts from the past 1000 years—undoubtedly the richest collection of its kind in Bulgaria (cathedral open Sun.-Fri. 8am-6pm, Sat. 8-10am and 4-8pm; crypt open Wed.-Mon. 10:30am-12:30pm and 2-6:30pm; 150lv). The **Church of St. Nedelya** (Катедрален Храм Света Неделя), the focal point of Pl. Sveta Nedelya, is a reconstruction from 1925, when a bomb destroyed the 14th-century medieval original in an attempt on the life of King Boris III. The king escaped, but the cupola buried 190 generals and politicians. The current frescos were made in 1975 (open daily 8am-7pm). In the underpass between Pl. Sveta Nedelya and TSUM, the tiny 14th-century **Church of St. Petka Samardzhiiska** contains some eye-grabbing frescos. The bones of Vasil Levski, Bulgaria's national hero, are rumored to have been found inside. A museum during Communist times, Sv. Petka is again an active church (open daily 8am-7pm).

Along the way to the central train station from Pl. Sveta Nedelya, on bul. Maria Luiza, sits the **Banya Bashi Mosque.** Built in the 16th century and named after the nearby mineral baths and is again a place of worship (open daily 1-10pm; long pants required). Across the street, and behind what used to be the covered market (Централни Хали; *Tsentralny Hali*), the **Central Synagogue,** Exarh Yosif 16 (Екзарх Йосиф), opened for services in 1909. The building's foundations were built with stones from Sofia's old Jewish cemetery. Designed by the Austrian architect Grunanger, it took four years to build, ultimately becoming one of Europe's three largest. Its six towers, six domes, and twelve stars point towards Jerusalem. Down Tsar Osvoboditel from Sv. Nedelya, the beautiful 1913 **Russian church** named for St. Nicholas the miracle-maker, with five onion domes built in accordance with Moscow architectural style. A chandelier reminiscent of Foucault's pendulum fills the empty space underneath the central dome (open daily 8am-6pm, Sunday until 3pm). As you stroll down the spacious boulevard, keep in mind that your boots are soiling the first paved street in Sofia. This enormous boulevard once performed a central function for the capital; at its ends lie the House of Parliament and the royal palace. The **National Assembly,** built in 1884 and finished with materials from Vienna, used to be the pride of every patriotic Sofian, but political mishaps have recently made the parliament square a favorite spot for the indignant to pour their gall.

Between the Central Department Store and the Sheraton, you'll see the old **Communist Party Headquarters.** There used to be a red star atop the metal pole on the roof—some believed it was made of rubies. You can still see the blackened exterior from the orgy of looting and arson that shook the building in the 1989-90 transition.

The former **Georgi Dimitrov Mausoleum,** pl. Aleksandr Batenberg (Александър Батенберг), is a memorial to Stalin's former right-hand man, long-hated and now officially vilified and buried. While debate still rages over the fate of the building, Bulgarians have put it to practical use as a public bathroom. Practice your Bulgarian by reading the graffiti or help the tag artists with their English. Continuing up the yellow brick road and making a left on Rakovski leads to the **National Opera House,** Rakovski 59 (the main entrance is at Vrabcha 1; врабча), built in 1950 to seat 1270. The box-office is to the right of the main entrance (call 87 13 66 for tickets or info; open daily 8:30am-7:30pm; prices vary between 50-1000lv). **Rakovski** is Bulgaria's Broadway, with half a dozen theaters in a half-mile stretch. The Neoclassical **Ivan Vazov National Theatre,** Levski 5, was built in 1907, destroyed by fire in 1923, and restored in 1927. Unlike the theater, which is on vacation in summer, 100lv chess and backgammon games never stop in the park outside.

The **University of Sofia,** Tsar Osvoboditel 15, on the corner of Vasil Levski, was designed by the French architect Breancon and built between 1920-31. The sculptures at the main entrance represent Evolgi and Hristo Gheorghiev, who funded the University's construction. You can see students as late as the end of July when candidates for admission visit the "wall of Tears"—the spot where acceptance results are posted after a series of rigorous exams. Nearby, on Vasil Levski, is the **National Library Sts. Cyril and Methodius** (Кародка Библиотекаuв св. Кирил и Методий), Bulgaria's largest depository of knowledge. The **Bulgarian Artists' Union** (Съюз на Българските Художниuи) has a four floor gallery on Shipka (Шипка; tel. 433 51, ext. 214), behind the University. Bi-weekly literary exhibits grace the marble halls (open Mon.-Sat. 10am-6pm; free). See posters ahead of entrance for schedules.

The **National Palace of Culture (NDK)** is located at the end of Vitosha. Opened in 1981 in connection with the 13th-century anniversary of Bulgaria's creation, contains restaurants, theaters, and movie halls. The best cinema in the country, and one of the only two air-conditioned establishments, shows mostly subtitled American movies. Buy tickets (150lv) from the ticket office to the left of the main entrance.

The labels in the **National Museum of History,** Vitosha Blvd. 2 (tel. 88 41 60), off Pl. Sveta Nedelya, are in Bulgarian only, but a guided tour in English can be arranged (800lv per group). Arranged in chronological order in two floors and 33 halls, the exposition goes from as far back as 200,000BCE to 1908 CE. From Thracian treasures to medieval war glory, it has it all. A perfect place to ask what the National Revival really is (open in summer Mon.-Fri. 9:30am-5:15pm, off-season Tues.-Sun. 10:30am-6:15pm; box office closes 45min. earlier; 250lv, students 150lv). The **Archeological Museum,** Suborna 2, houses items from the Thracian, Greek, Roman, and Turkish settlements. It was closed for renovations in the summer of 1996. Traditional Bulgaria is preserved at the **National Ethnographic Museum,** Moskovska 6a (tel. 87 41 91), in the Royal Palace building (enter from the back, not from the Tsar Osvoboditel side). Founded immediately after the 1878 liberation, the museum contains over 50,000 items from the past four centuries. The second floor is devoted to the Bulgarian Woman (open Wed.-Sun. 10:30am-5pm; 50lv). The **National Museum of Fine Arts** is also located in the Royal Palace, but on the side across from the Mausoleum. Its pride is a permanent exhibit of Bulgarian classic masters (open Tues.-Sun. 10:30am-12:30pm and 2-7pm; 150lv, students 20lv).

Down the street, on Tsar Osvoboditel 1, is the **National Museum of Natural History** (Национален Приподонаучен Музей; tel. 88 51 15, ext. 706), the last home of a Mississippi alligator (now stuffed) who once lived in the Sofia zoo from 1905-1942. Live animals and insects—from singing and flying cockroaches to an albino python—the museum's permanent collection is a thrill (open daily 10am-7pm; 120lv, students 30lv). Bulgarian impressionist and modern art can be found at the **Sofia Municipal Art Gallery,** ul. General Gurko 1 (tel. 87 21 81), near the post office, at the edge of National Theater park (open Wed.-Sun. 10:30am-6:30pm; free).

There are two **artist parks** in Sofia. In front of **Nevsky Cathedral,** you can find antiques, Soviet paraphernalia, and handmade crafts. If you walk diagonally to the other side of the square, the market continues with lots of Bulgarian grannies offering handmade lace and embroidery. In the second park, in the underpass between the Sheraton and the Central Department Store, artists of varying talent display their works. Jewelry, paintings, icons, and some genuine finds float in this sea of kitsch.

A great escape from the metropolis is **Vitosha** mountain, not alive with the songs of the von Trapp family, but certainly invigorating. On a clear day, the panorama extends to the southern Rila mountains. There are several chalets, lodges and campsites. In winter, Vitosha becomes a popular **skiing area.** It can be reached by **bus** from Hladiknika (Хладилника; last stop of trams #9 and 12; dir. "Vitosha"). Bus #66 takes you to the **Aleko Hut** (Хижа Алеко) in the middle of the skiing area (45min.). A **gondola** also goes there from the suburb of Simeonovo (Симеоново). To get to the lift, take bus #122 from Hladilnika; it may work summer weekends (30min. to Aleko). Vitosha is also home to **monasteries** and **churches,** including the 14th-century **Dragalevtsi Monastery** and the 10th-century **Boyans Church.**

ENTERTAINMENT

The nightlife in the center of Bulgarian civilization gets wilder every year. Outdoor cafés and bars share **Vitosha Bul.** with musicians and dancing bears. **Frankie's Jazz Club/Piano Bar,** right off Vitosha Bul. across from the American Center, invites some of Bulgaria's best jazz-people (cover 100-400lv; no music in summer until Sept. 15; open 10am-2am). Vasil Petrov, a locally famous jazzman makes frequent appearances. Smartly-dressed Sofians fill up the cafés around the park outside the **NDK** to scam and be scammed. A religious crowd of regulars congregate 10pm-4am at **Yalta** (Ялта; tel. 981 01 43), one of Sofia's most experienced discos (200lv cover, women free). Euro-techno pop brings down the house at the **Orbilux** disco at Hotel Orbita, Anton Ivanov 76 (tel. 66 89 97). Music starts around 10pm (men pay 200lv). The **disco Neron** (Нерон) underneath the NDK, rocks until 4am (200lv) and is rocked itself by members of Sofia's thick-necked criminal elite. Don't pick fights. There is a **gay café** at Septemvri 6, near Pl. Narodno Subrane.

The **opera** and **theater** seasons run September to June. Good seats at the **Opera** can be found for under US$1 (tel. 87 70 11; box office open daily 9:30am-7pm; no performances Mon.). You can get tickets for the **Ivan Vazov National Theatre** at Levski 5 (tel. 88 28 84). Cinemas most often run subtitled Hollywood films. Two good ones are at Vitosha Blvd. 62 (tel. 88 58 78) and Pl. Vasil Levski 1 (tel. 43 17 97).

SOUTHERN MOUNTAINS

▓ Rila Monastery

Holy Ivan of Rila built **Rila Monastery** (Рилски Манастир) in the 10th century as a refuge from the lascivious outer world. The monastery sheltered the arts of icon painting and manuscript copying during Byzantine and Ottoman occupations, and remained an oasis of Bulgarian history and culture in their hardest hours (well, more like five centuries). The easiest way to reach the monastery is to travel to Rila by **bus** from Sofia's Ovcha Kupel station (2 per day, 2½hr., 160lv), and then take a bus from there (7 per day, ½hr., 40lv). You can also make the Sofia-Blagoevgrad-Rila-Rila Monastery journey by **train** (5 per day, 3hr., 160lv) or bus (15 per day, 2hr., 150lv). **Balkantourist** and **Group Travel** have guided **excursions** in English to the monastery (US$30 per person). Bring a sweater—Rila is always chilly. **Exchange money** in Rila town at **Hebros Bank** (open Mon.-Fri. 8am-noon and 1-3:45pm).

Inquire in room 170—or with any monk—for a heated **monastery cell,** with toilet and cold mountain water (tel. 22 08; reception open 9am-noon, 2-4pm, and 6-8pm; lockout midnight). **Turisticheska Spalnya Turist** (Туристическа Спалня Турист) next door, offers rooms packed with up to 14 people (360lv). The three-star **Hotel Rilets** (Рилец; tel. 21 06), a 15-minute walk from the monastery, rents fairly clean singles for US$24, doubles for US$36, and accepts Visa, MC, Eurocard, and Diner's Club. The culinary options are limited at this solemn place of hermits. **Restaurant Rila** (tel. 22 90), outside the monastery, sells phone cards, and serves up a beautiful view and delicious trout (Балканска Пастърва; *Balkanska Pasturva*; 250lv). The few vegetarian options revolve around eggs (90-140lv; open daily 7:30am-11:30pm). Although there have been bread shortages when they didn't sell to tourists. The **monastery bakery** tops the list of breakfast options. When you can get it, they bake delicious *mekitsi* (мекици; fried dough with sugar; 8lv) and bread (28lv a loaf; open daily 8am-7pm).

The monastery's vibrant **murals** were created by National Revival artists of the Samokov and Bansko schools of painting, most notably the brothers Dimitar and Zahari Zograf. Not only are these two famous for their other work at the Troyan and Bachkovo monasteries, but their surname actually means "one who paints murals." The 1200 **frescos** on the central **chapel** and surrounding walls form an outdoor art **gallery.** Inside you can find the grave of Bulgaria's last Tsar Boris III (no cameras, no shorts). A 23m tower looms nearby in the courtyard, once used for protection of the monastery and of a little chapel on top, containing more 14th-century frescos. The monastery also houses **museums** with religious objects, coins, weapons, jewelry, and embroidery. The exhibit includes a carved wooden cross, which took 12 years to finish and left its master, the monk Rafail, without his eyesight (50lv, English tours 200lv per person; monastery open 6am-dusk; services 6:30am or 4:30pm).

You can find maps and suggested **hiking** routes (2-9hr.) outside the monastery. Hiking trails in Bulgaria are marked by colored lines on white background, painted on rocks, trees or anything that doesn't look like it'll walk away. Infrequent signs with directions and time left pop up along the way. Try to see **Sedemte Ezera** (Седемте Езера) or climb a peak near **Malyovitsa** (Мальвица). Breathtaking views, dozens of mountain lakes, and welcoming huts await. Follow the yellow markings to the 7th lake hut (хижа седемте езера; Sedemte Ezera hut; 6½-hr. trek). Blue leads to Malyovitsa hut (хижа мальовица; 7hr.). Red leads to the highest hut on the Balkans: Ivan Vazov hut (хижа Иван Вазов). Expect to pay around 350lv for a spot (not necessarily a bed) to sleep. Be prepared—weather in high mountains changes quickly.

▓ Bansko (Банско)

At the base of the Pirin mountains, Bansko is a gateway to over 100 steep peaks and 180 lakes scattered across a sea of forget-me-nots and alpine poppies. The highest peak, Vihren, is at 2914m. The Pirin range around Bansko offers summer hiking and winter skiing, while a collection of wonderfully-preserved stone houses, taverns, and hotels line the narrow cobbled streets of the town itself.

Orientation and Practical Information Take a **bus** from Sofia's Ovcha Kupel station (5 per day, 3½hr., 260lv), Blagoevgrad (9 per day, 1½hr., 100lv), or Plovdiv (1 per day, 3hr., 250lv). Alternately, take a **train** from Sofia to Blagoevgrad (5 per day, 3hr., 78lv) or a **bus** from Novotel Europa (across from Sofia's train station) to Blagoevgrad (every ½hr., 2hr., 160lv) and make a bus connection there. From Bansko's **bus station,** Patriarh Evtimij, cross the street, walk straight to Todor Aleksandrov, and take a right to **Pl. Demokratsia,** the town center. Take a left on Tsar Simeon (Цар Симеон) to get to **Hotel Pirin,** which sells a comprehensive English brochure about the area with a useful map (75lv). You will also see **Tourist and Change Bureau Bansko** (tel. 2486) which sells **maps** (10lv and up), **exchanges currency,** and finds **private rooms** (US$8 per person) and **hotel** rooms (US$11-13 per person; open daily 9am-8pm). **TS Bank** (tel. 50 91; fax 50 90), on the corner of Pl. Demokratsia and Todor Aleksandrov, gives Visa cash advances and accepts traveler's checks (open Mon.-Fri. 8:30am-4:30pm). The **post office** is across from Hotel Pirin (see above; open Mon.-Fri. 7:30am-4:30pm). **Telephones** in the post office are open daily 7am to 10pm. **Postal code:** 2770. **Phone code:** 07443.

Accommodations and Food Shelters dotting the mountains protect hikers for around US$2 a night. **Private rooms** can be arranged informally with locals for US$3-5 a head. Book in advance for winter. An exemplary private hotel is **Mir** (tel. 2500 or 2160), Neofit Rilski 28 (Неофит Рилски). Marble and wood floors, spotless American-style bathrooms with 24-hr. hot water and firm beds. Singles, doubles, and triples with breakfast cost US$10 per person. **Edelweis HI** (Еделвайс), Nikola Vaptsarov 12 (Вапцаров; tel. 22 71), offers bedding and sinks with the room, but the shared showers long for Lysol. Doubles, triples, and quads cost 450lv per person, 580lv for nonmembers. **Hotel Strazhite** (Стражите; tel. 40 92 or 40 93), bul. Pirin, has clean but tired rooms with bath (hot water after 6pm) for US$18 per person.

A **mehana** (tavern) hides in almost every house or courtyard, and Bansko is a dining heaven—at least for carnivores. **Sirleshtova Kushta** (Цирешова Къща; tel. 4668), Yane Sandanski 12 (Яне Сандански) is open 24hr. and occupies the oldest preserved house in town. The wooden menu offers main courses for 150-250lv, beer 60-80lv and salads for 50-95lv. Vegetarians will appreciate the shepherd's salad (овчарска салата; *ovcharska salata;* 95lv) made of cucumbers, tomatoes, onions, baked peppers, mushrooms, parsley, cheese, and a boiled egg. Live old Bansko songs after 8pm on Friday to Sunday for 10% more. **Dedo Pene** (Дедо Пене), off Vuzrazhdane pl. (tel. 5071), can sate the heaviest appetite around its heavy wooden tables. One of the specialties is *shish po haidushki* (шиш по хайдушки, shish kebob with garnish, 230lv), salads (52-100lv), and wines 300lv. Veggie options hover at 120lv. Live folk music in the evening (open daily 10am-whenever).

Sights and Hiking The 20th century has not destroyed Bansko's established way of life, although the increase in tourism in the past 10 years is pushing the town towards modernity. Still, the highlanders send their cattle and sheep to pasture in the morning and the herds stroll back around 7pm. Surprisingly well kept museums and century-old houses make Bansko a living memory of the National Revival. **Nikola Vaptsarov** (Никола Вапцаров; tel. 3038) house-museum, corner of pl. Demokratsia and Vaptsarov, may well be Bulgaria's most modern museum. Its older part recalls the life and works of the 20th-century poet who gave his life in the struggle against the Bulgarian brand of Fascism in the 1940s. The new wing shows images of the epoch which shaped the young poet's thoughts and actions. Colorful characters from National Revival and the liberation struggles of Southern Bulgaria at the outset of the century influenced Vaptsarov's poetry, now translated into 35 languages. Also called the **House of Poetry and the Arts,** the new wing houses temporary exhibits of paintings and typical Bulgarian clothing and fabrics. Laser disc video shows of poetry, music, and stories are a welcome break (taped tours in English, French, German, and Russian; open Tues.-Sun. 8am-noon and 2-6pm; 90lv, tape tours 50lv). **Velianova House** (Велянова Къща; 4181), Velian Ognev off pl. Vuzrazhdane, is named after the painter from Debur (formerly in Bulgaria, now in Macedonia) responsible for the interior decoration of the Sv. Troitsa church. A typical Revival house, its thick walls once protected the inhabitants from *kurdzhali* brigands (taped multilingual tours; open Mon.-Fri. 9am-noon and 2-5pm). **Neofit Rilski Museum,** corner of Pirin and Rilski (Музей Неофит Рилски; tel. 2540), was the house of one of the National Revival's initiators. A man of letters, a collector of folk songs and sayings, and one of the founders of the Rila school of church singing, Neofit Rilski also once taught the muralist Zahari Zograf (taped tours; open Tues.-Sun. 9am-noon and 2-5pm). Subdued church music accompanies the stroll through the **Icon Exhibit** (Иконна изложба) off Pl. Vuzrazhdene (taped tours; open Tues.-Sat. 9am-noon and 2-5pm). Pl. Vuzrazhdene's 1835 **Holy Trinity Church** (Света Троица) was once surrounded by a wall, and served as shelter during many attacks of the city. Most wealthy houses in town were connected to the church yard by a network of tunnels, and older people may even remember playing in them as kids. The church itself is Bulgaria's second largest (open daily 7:30am-noon and 1-6pm). The older, icon-filled **Church of the Holy Virgin** sits near the bus station on ul. Bulgaria. It opens for funerals and holidays and townsfolk often refer to it as the "cemetery church" (гробишна църква; *grobishtna tsurkva*).

For hikers and skiers, Bansko offers Pirin trails and five ski lifts. **Hiking** routes are marked with different colored signs. If you are in the mood for climbing and descending 2000m in three days or less, then Bansko is the perfect base camp. Hike (6hr.) or drive to the **Vihren Hut** (хижа вихрен) through **Bunderitsa Hut** (хижа бъндерица), and **Baikushevata Mura** (байкушевата мура), a 13-century-old tree that's as old as the Bulgarian state. On day two, climb **Vihren peak** (бръх вихрен, 2914m) and reach **Javor's Hut** (хижа яворов; 1740m) walking on the edge of the mountain (not everyone can handle the beauty or excitement of **Koncheto** (Кончето), a narrow path, flanked by a precipice on either side). Get to **Razlog** (Разлог) in the valley below where buses await. Another hike takes you around **Todorin peak** (Тодорин Връх) to **Demyanitsa Hut** (хижа деняница) in about six hours. **Bezbog Hut** (хижа безбог) is another eight hours away. It is becoming increasingly popular as a ski resort. A **lift** connects it to **Gotse Delchev Hut** (хижа гоце делчев), which is two hours away by foot from the village of **Dobrinishte** (Добринище). Buses to Bansko or Razlog can be caught there. Expect to pay around US$2 for a place to sleep (not necessarily a bed) in mountain huts and bring your own food. **Hotel Alpin**, Neofit Rilski 6, **rents skis** (walk down bul. Pirin past pl. Vuzrazhdane and make a left on Neofit Rilski).

■ Melnik (Мелник)

Deep in a sandstone gorge, tiny Melnik quietly produces delicious wine in exquisitely preserved National Revival houses. Although its population has been waning throughout this century, neither the town's beauty nor its ability to greet its guests has diminished. A few rich houses, churches, and ruins remain to shed light on its past. **Kordopulova Kashta** (Кордопулова Къща; tel. 399) was built in 1754 by the Greek Manolous Kordopolous family, who settled here to make and trade wine (open 8am-6pm; 50lv). Formerly a national museum, it has recently been returned to the heirs of its last owner. Recognized as the biggest National Revival house in Bulgaria, it also contains the largest wine cellar in Melnik. Its caves inside the sandstone hill took a full 12 years to carve. This natural fridge can store up to 300 tons of wine, but also shelters a few bats. Mitko Manolev's **Izba za Degustatsiyana** (Вино изба за Дегустация на Вино; wine-tasting cellar; tel. 234) is a 200-year-old establishment which offers the freshness of its naturally air-conditioned caverns and some of the best Melnik wine (glass 30-40lv, bottle 120lv). A brochure in English and German reveals some of the trade's secrets (open daily 10am-dusk). Turn right at the fork and climb the hillside on the left at the end of town, through the ruins of the 10th-century

Boyar's House. Take the path behind Sv. Nikola, where a 15-minute walk leads to the plateau from where all of Melnik and the surrounding hills can be seen. Take a right to reach the ruins of the **ancient fortress** that protected and served as refuge for the town in the Middle Ages. Two rings of walls surround a central **church** whose altar remains. The 13th-century **Rozhenski Manastir** (Роженски Манастир), 6km away, can be reached by foot (expect amazing views). Check out the 16th-century murals, 17th-century stained glass, icon collection, and carved lecterns. Ask someone about the miraculous icon of Bogoroditsa Iverska.

Buses arrive here via Sandanski (Sofia-Sandanski 3 per day, 250lv, 2½hr.; Sandanski-Melnik 3 per day, 40min., 55lv) or Blagoevgrad (7 per day from Blagoevgrad, 1hr., 100lv). Melnik's main street, running along a dry river bed, is its only one. There are no tourist bureaus in town—the last two were closed. Fortunately, **maps** are sold at hotels and restaurants (60lv). **Private rooms** cost around 300-400lv and can be arranged with almost anyone you meet in town. **Hotel-Winery MNO** (МНО; tel. 249) is on the left, 50m past the post office. Its 30 beds are split among large doubles and triples with private showers (600lv or US$4 per person). On your way, you'll pass by **Uzunova Keshta** (Узунова Къща; tel. 270), with pleasant rooms and home cooking (doubles with bath US$15 per person, quads US$13 per person). When it comes to culinary offerings, Melnik is a tiny giant. **Mehana Loznitsite** (tel. 362) is on the right side of the river bed, just over the second bridge into town. A *svinska purzhola s gubi* (pork chip with mushrooms and sauce; 180lv) can be had under the grapevine of this lesser National Revival house, complemented with *chorba* (soup, 40lv), and local wine (180-250lv; open noon-11pm). The **mini-market** near the beginning of the main street presents a do-it-yourself option with a variety of sandwich materials and drinks (open 7am-9pm). Up the main street is the **post office** with **telephones** (open Mon.-Fri. 7:30m-noon and 1-7pm). **Postal code:** 2820. **Phone code:** 0997437.

■ Plovdiv (Пловдив)

Condemned to the fate of remaining Bulgaria's "second city", Plovdiv is tops for those seeking immersion in Bulgarian history and culture. Pass by socialist neighborhoods of gray apartment buildings, and stroll into the Old Town, where National Revival houses hang beamed and protruding upper stories over the cobblestones below, windows stare into alleys at impossible angles, and churches and mosques hide in secluded corners. Founded around 600BCE, Plovdiv achieved prominence under Philip of Macedonia as a center of trade and culture—a distinction which has survived from antiquity to today. Its two annual trade fairs are the focus of the Bulgarian business world, and Plovdiv now rivals Sofia as a tourist and cultural center.

ORIENTATION AND PRACTICAL INFORMATION

Plovdiv's central point is **pl. Tsentralen** (Централен), marked by **Hotel Trimondium** (Тримондиум). From the train station, take bus #2, 20, or 26 (buy 15lv tickets on the bus). Or walk: cross **Hristo Botev** (Христо Ботев) via an underground pass, and take **Ivan Vazov** (Иван Вазов) to the square. Street names are changing, but most maps still show the old names. One of Plovdiv's most important boulevards, currently **Tsar Boris III Obedinitel** (Цар Борис III Обединител), recently got rid of the name **Vuzdrezhdane** (Възраждане), while older people still remember it as **Georgi Dimitrov.** Whatever its name, it connects Hristo Botev and **bul. Bulgaria** (България; old Moskva, Москва) on the north side of the **Maritsa River.** The main street is a pedestrian walkway **Knyaz Aleksandr** (Княз Александър; old Vasil Kolarov, Васил Лоларов), running from **pl. Tsentralen** to **pl. Dzhumayata** (Джумаята; old pl. 19 Novemvri). It continues as **Rayko Daskalov** (Райко Даскалов). To get to the **Old Town,** make any right off Knyaz Aleksandr while walking away from pl. Tsentralen.

> **Tourist Offices: Puldin Tours '91,** bul. Bulgaria 106 (old Moskva; tel. 55 38 48), might have copies of a good map in English. Arranges excursions, changes money, and provides info. Private rooms also arranged (singles US$13, doubles US$16, 1-

bedroom apartments US$20). From train station, ride trolley #102 or 2 (15lv) nine stops to bul. Bulgaria and backtrack a block. By foot, cross the river via Tsar Boris III Obedinitel, pass Hotel Maritsa, and look for Puldin on the corner with bul. Bulgaria. Open Mon.-Fri. 9am-5:30pm (until 9pm during fairs).

Currency Exchange: Exchange bureaus await on Knyaz Aleksandr. **TSBank,** Patriarch Evtimii 13 (Патриарх Евтимий; tel. 22 30 11), off Knyaz Aleksandr, cashes traveler's checks (1% commission) and gives Visa cash advances (4% commission). Open Mon.-Thurs. 9am-3pm, Fri. 9am-1pm.

ATMs: Located in the post office on pl. Tsentralen; accepts Visa and Plus cards.

Trains: Most trains from Sofia to Istanbul or Burgas stop in Plovdiv. To Sofia (approx. hourly, 2½hr., 116lv). Good local train connections. Only **Rila,** bul. Hristo Botev 31a (tel. 44 61 20), sells international tickets. Open Mon.-Fri. 8am-7pm, Sat. 8am-4pm. **Luggage storage** open daily 7am-6:25pm and 6:50pm-6:30am (10lv).

Buses: There are three stations serving the areas indicated by their names. **Yug** (Юг), Hristo Botev, sends buses south; **Rodopi** (Родопи), behind the trains, serves the Rodopi mountains; and **Sever** (Север), across the river past Novotel down Vasil Levski, goes north—take bus #2 from pl. Tsentralen. Buses from Sofia leave from Sofia's Novotel Europa (every 40min., 1hr., US$1.50). Return buses depart from the Yug station. **Traffic Express** (Трафик Експрес), bul. Hristo Botev 45 (tel. 26 57 87; fax 26 51 51), at the Yug station, sells tickets for the Black Sea Coast. **Matri** (Матри; tel. 22 26 33; tel./fax 22 24 42), in the underpass below Tsar Boris III Obedinitel next to Hotel Trimontium, deals with all Balkan connections: directly to Istanbul (US$20), Athens (US$43; US$35 for those under 26), Thesaloniki (US$28/22). The buses to Greece on Wed. and Fri. have connections with ferries to Italy (open daily 8am-7pm). **Agency Suzana** (Сузана; tel./fax 55 91 74) runs direct buses to Istanbul, Munich, and Frankfurt. Open Mon.-Fri. 9am-9pm.

Taxis: Call 56 60 60.

Film and Photo Developing: Bulgarian Photography (Българска Фотография; tel. 22 22 21), on the edge of Dzhumayata Square. Open Mon.-Fri. 8am-7pm.

24-Hour Pharmacy: Pharmacy #47 "The Tunnel" (Аптека 47 Тунела; tel. 27 07 93), Tsar Boris III Obedinitel 64, on the opposite side of the tunnel from Pl. Tsentralen. **Fleming** (Флеминг), Knyaz Aleksandr 22 (tel. 26 00 57). Open daily 8:30am-8pm. Both well stocked with western **condoms** and feminine products.

Express Mail: DHL, bul. Svoboda 19 (Свобода; old Malchika; tel. 44 21 11).

Post Office: pl. Tsentralen. **Poste Restante** in the room to the left of the entrance. Open Mon.-Sat. 7am-7pm, Sun. 7-11am. **Postal code:** 4000.

Telephones: In post office. Direct international calling. Open daily 6:30am-11pm. Send or receive **faxes** (fax 493 00 44). Open daily 6:30am-9pm. **Phone code:** 032.

ACCOMMODATIONS

Prices can rise 500% during trade fairs beginning the first Monday of May and the last Monday of September. **Private rooms** may be the only salvation. **Puldin Tours** (see above) and **Prima Vista Agency,** ul. General Gurko 6 (tel. 27 27 78; fax 27 20 54; open daily 10am-6pm), find private lodgings. **Bureau Esperansa** (tel. 26 06 53; open daily 10am-6pm), Ivan Vazov 14, offers rooms downtown (US$8 per person).

Hostel Turisticheski Dom (Туристически Дом; tel. 23 32 11), P.R. Slaveykov 5 (П.Р. Славейков), in the Old Town. From Knyaz Aleksandr, take Patriarch Evtimii into the Old Town and take a left on Slaveykov. Clean 2- to 4-bed rooms with sinks in a spacious National Revival building listed among Plovdiv's monuments. Students have always slept in these (class)rooms—the building was once a school. Shared bathrooms. Lockout midnight. 1400lv per person. Café/restaurant.

Hotel Feniks (Феникс), Kapitan Raicho 79 (Капитан Райчо; tel. 22 47 29). From pl. Tsentralen, walk across Vuzrazhdane to Kapitan Raicho. Reception on 3rd floor of the first entry off Kapitan Raicho. Satellite TV and laundry access. The unintentionally antique but functional furniture may still have a few years left in it. Shared bathrooms. Singles US$20, doubles US$30.

Trakia Camping, (tel. 55 13 60), on the E-80 highway to Sofia. Take the hourly #23 bus from the train station. Orange mini-van taxis drop you off 100m away (30lv);

buses #4 and 44 stop ½km away. Bungalows have 2 rooms and showers each; a bed in a single, double, or triple costs 1000lv. Tents cost 500lv per person. Every June, Bulgaria's Hell's Angels hold their annual "festival" here...and the place looks it—the beds, showers, and carpets show signs of extreme wear. Open year-round.

FOOD

Plovdiv can offer a generous culinary programme for less than US$5. On the way to the hostel on Patriarch Evtimii, an **outdoor market** sells fresh fruit and veggies.

Kambanata (Камбаната), Suborna 20 (tel. 26 06 65), will surprise vegetarians with its large selection of traditional dishes—*kyopoolu* (eggplant), *pecheni chushki* (baked peppers), *tikvichki* (zucchini with milk sauce)—for under US$0.50. Main courses hover at US$1-2. The chef's specialty, "Kambanata", is a concoction of filet, cream, mushrooms, smoked cheese and spaghetti (US$2). English menu. A/C. Open daily 10:30am-midnight.

Union Club (Юниън Клуб), Hayne 6 (Хайне; tel. 27 05 51), is run by a master chef. Take Suborna from Pl. Dzhumayata, then turn right up the steep alley before the church, to the beautiful outdoor garden. Frequented by local *intelligentsia*. Try the specialty, the *Union Club* (baked pork covered with *kavarma*, bananas and cheese) with fries, fresh cabbage, and veggies (280lv). The 230-item menu contains some vegetarian fare, too. Open daily 9am-late.

Alafrangite (Алафрангите), Kiril Nektariev 17 (Кирил Нектариев; tel. 26 95 95), in an Old Town National Revival house, cooks up a mean *vreteno* (pork or veal fillet with cheese and mushrooms, 452lv). Classic national dishes run 185-382lv. From behind the Dzhumayata Mosque, follow Suborna (old Gorky) and make the third right. Open daily 11:30am-midnight.

Cocktail Restaurant Maniika (Манийка, tel. 22 52 41), P.R. Slaveykov 4, serves up a number of organ-based dishes and main courses around US$1. Shady National Revival courtyard. English menu. Open daily 11am-midnight.

SIGHTS

With over 150 houses designated as cultural monuments, **Stari Plovdiv** (Стари Пловдив; Old Town) is a giant historical museum. Its narrow cobblestone alleys are irresistible, but be careful at night: it gets dark and desolate, and local hoodlums find tourists particularly tasty. The Old Town's location on three hills (the **Trimontium**), makes the tiny streets steep as they wind up and down between tightly-built rows of houses. The area's most ancient treasure is the **Roman Marble Amphitheater,** dating from the 2nd century. Take a right off Knyaz Aleksandr to Stanislav Dospevski (Станислав Доспевски) and walk ahead to the theater. Today, the amphitheater hosts the **Festival of the Arts** in summer and early fall (contact Puldin Tours '91 for details; see p.120) and opera-singers cross their voices in noble competition during the annual **Opera Festival** in June. In the middle of pl. Dzhumayata lies **Philipopolis Stadium.** Contemplation of its ancient stones becomes almost impossible at night, when parading Plovdiv youths steal the show and fill up the nearby cafés. The building that gave its name to pl. Dzhumayata is the **Dzhumayata Mosque** (Джумаята), whose colorful minaret peers around the other buildings.

At the end of Suborna, the **Ethnographic Museum** (Етнографски Музей; tel. 22 56 56), exhibits ancient Bulgarian crafts, including an interesting exhibition on the production of precious rose oil (open in summer Mon.-Fri. 9am-noon and 2-5pm; off-season closed Fri. morning and Mon.; 150lv, English guide 300lv). Colorful **Baroque houses** are found down the hill, through the Roman gate. For more Bulgarian history (and to finally discover what "National Revival" is all about), try the **National Revival and National Liberation Museum**, Tsanko Lavrenov 1 (Цанко Лавренов; tel. 22 59 23). Make a right at the end of Suborna and go through the Turkish gate (open Mon.-Sat. 9am-noon, 2-5pm; 150lv). Ancient history is also preserved in the **Archeological Museum** at pl. Suedinene, but unfortunately the museum itself is not holding up as well as its artifacts—when last visited, it was being renovated. To check if it's open again, walk down Rayko Daskalov and take a left on 6 Septemvri. Its pride is one heavy collection of golden vessels from the 4th century BCE. For an out-of-museum experience, wander down little Strumna (Стръмна) alley and watch the few remaining Plovdiv craftsmen pound and polish their lives away in workshops, just as their ancestors did. Just be careful: those hoodlums also love the narrow streets of Old Town. The **park** in the west side of the town, beyond the train tracks and near the stadium, comes as a welcome break from the steep cobblestone streets and the antiquity of touristed areas. There you will find the Plovdiv **zoo**, outdoor **swimming pools**, and the biggest man-made **rowing canal** in Bulgaria. The **State Gallery of Art** (Държавна Художествена Галерия; tel. 22 37 90) has a permanent collection of Bulgarian masters on Suborna 14a and also holds bi-weekly temporary exhibits of contemporary graphics, sculptures, and watercolors at its other location on Knyaz Aleksandr 15. On a cool evening, head to the fountainside café in the **Public Garden**, near pl. Tsentralen, where multicolored strobes illuminate the spring. One of the many **movie theaters** on Knyaz Aleksandr is bound to be showing a film in English, always a good last resort.

■ Near Plovdiv: Bachkovo Monastery

28km south of Plovdiv lies Bulgaria's second largest monastery, the 11th-century **Bachkovo Monastery** (Бачковски Манастир; *Bachkovski Manastir*) built by Georgian brothers Grigorii and Abazii Bakuriani. Mostly destroyed by the Turks in the early 16th century, it was rebuilt a century later. Always an oasis of Bulgarian culture, history, and literature, the holy place maintained and even strengthened its spirit during five centuries of Ottoman rule. The monastery's treasure is the miracle-working **icon of the Virgin Mary and Child**, kept in the Holy Trinity Church (open daily 6am-10pm). The **Chapel of Saint Nikola** (Храм Свети Никола; *Hram Sveti Nikola*) is blessed with the work of **Zahari Zograf** (1840) and cursed with the work of some modern fans who have etched their mark next to his on the outside murals. To get to Bachkovo, take a **train** from Plovdiv to Asenovgrad (every ½hr., 25min., 22lv); once there, catch a bus to the monastery (10min., 25lv). Buses to Smolyan from the Rodopi bus station also get you there (40min., 70lv). Inquire about the spartan **accommodations** at the administrative office on the monastery's second floor; ask for Brother German (tel. (03327) 277). 10 to 20 person dorms share bathrooms (200lv per bed; cold water only). The monks allow visitors to pitch **tents** on the monastery lawn for free. Every August 15th, believers flock to the monastery to celebrate the holiday of the Virgin Mary. Everyone crashes in the courtyard (free) "for good health," after the **Kurban** (Курбан; feast). The monastery is booked around traditional holidays. Several gift shops, cafés, and food stands flank the street leading to the monks' haven. **Gradina** (Градина), by the road near the monastery, has stuffed rabbit (пълнен заяк; *pulnen zayak*; 310lv), trout (250lv), and great wine—try *magareshko mlyako* (магарешко мляко; donkey's milk; 210lv).

VALLEY OF ROSES (РОЗОВА ДОЛИНА)

■ Koprivshtitsa (Копривщица)

Wood and stone cottages and a proud history of revolution make Koprivshtitsa one of Bulgaria's most enchanting villages. Todor Kableshkov's 1876 "letter of blood," announcing an uprising against Ottoman rule, started its tour of the country here. Quelled in the most bloody manner, the uprising nevertheless succeeded in turning Europe's eye toward the small nation; the Russo-Turkish war of 1877-78 ensued and brought Bulgarian freedom after five centuries. Every five years, tranquility is shaken by the thousands who come to enjoy the **Koprivshtitsa International Folk Festival.** Book rooms early (the next one takes place in August 2000).

Orientation and Practical Information Trains from Sofia (10 per day, 1½-2hr., 50lv) stop at the Koprivshtitsa train station (the stop after Anton), 8km from town. Other trains arrive from Plovdiv via Karlovo (change trains at Karlovo; total time 3½hr.; 72lv). Fear not, a bus awaits to take you into town (10min.; 30lv), but it doesn't wait for dawdlers, so go quickly. Get off at the Koprivshtitsa **bus station** (a dark wooden building), which posts the bus and train schedules. To reach the **main square**, backtrack a bit along the river that bisects the town. The few streets have no names. **Biochim Commercial Bank** (tel. 21 86), across the river, next to the school, **exchanges money** (open Mon.-Fri. 9am-12:15pm and 1:15-4:15pm). The alley to the right of the monument on the main square leads to a private **pharmacy** (open daily 9am-noon, 3-6pm). The **post office** sits behind the bus station, on the other town square (open Mon.-Fri. 7:30am-noon and 1-4pm; **telephones** Mon.-Fri. 7:30am-8pm; Sat. 8am-7pm; Sun. 8am-6pm; closed noon-1). **Phone code: 997184**.

Accommodations and Food Hotel Byaloto Konche (Бялото Конче; tel. 22 50), up the steep street from the main square, has five doubles in a classic *koprivshtitsa* house, shared shower and toilet (US$8 per person; breakfast included). Go to the bar-mehana 20m down the street to ask for a room. **Hotel Dalmatinets** (Далматинец, tel. 29 04), Georgi Benkovski 62 (Георги Бенковски), is near the end of town on the left bank of the river. Five doubles with private showers and 24-hour hot water go for US$12 per person. Arrange **private rooms** through the English-speaking owner of the souvenir shop (tel. 21 64) advertising *chastni kvartiri* (частни квартири; US$10 per person with breakfast), in the square (open daily 10am-6pm). Seize the opportunity to buy all kinds of **tourist maps** of Bulgaria—the owner is a geographer by education. In the main square, Tsonka Tormanova deals in private rooms (US$6 with breakfast) out of her **Kvatirno Byuro** (Квартирно Бюро; tel. 25 16; open daily 8:30am-6pm).

Byaloto Konche has a separate tavern offering a splendid *kavarna* (full meal under US$2) with home-cooking and a cozy atmosphere (open 8am-til last person leaves). **Pod Starata Krusha** (Под Старата Круша; tel. 2163) at the bus station, is undisturbed by traffic in the evenings—only birds, frogs, and an occasional dog may accompany your meal. The specialty, *pileshka purzhola s drobcheta* (пилешка пържола с дробчета, chicken steak with liver; 240lv) goes well with a salad (50-70lv) and wine (250-450lv a bottle). The **food market** by the stream, past the buses and post office, is well stocked. A **bakery** lies nearby (delicious bread; 25lv).

Sight Old houses are Koprivshtitsa's main attraction. Masterpieces of three distinct stages of National Revival architecture remain wonderfully preserved and open their doors to tourists. The first settlers' houses are low plank structures. The second type are sturdy, half-timbered, early 19th-century homes with open porches, high stone walls, and sparse ornamentation. The third, and most common type, features enclosed verandas and delicate woodwork reflecting the mercantile prosperity of the mid-19th century. Many homes of the 1876 Uprising leaders have become museums. A 120lv ticket valid for all museums may be purchased at any one of the houses or at a *kupchiinitsa* (купчийница) booth nearby. English and French tours are also possible (ask at the Museum Administration office in the main square; tel. 21 80 and 21 14). All

---

More Precious than Gold

More expensive by weight than gold, rose oil drips from the fertile valleys of Bulgaria, producing over 70% of the world's supply. A single gram of "attar of roses" (rose oil) requires 2000 petals snatched before sunrise, and from late May to early June, workers pick furiously flower-by-flower to supply enough rose juice for the world to keep feeling fresh. Apart from perfume and rose water, Bulgarian rose petals have been used in medicine, jam, tea, vodka, sweet liquor, and syrup. Picking season ends with the annual rose festival (Прозник на Розата; *Proznik na Rozata*), held the first June weekend in Karlovo and Kazanluk.

are easy to find with a map. The 1845 house of **Todor Kableshkov** (Тодор Каблешков) is one of the third stage's grandest achievements dressed with an impressive façade, ingeniously carved ceilings, and the hero's personal possessions—all soaked in revolutionary spirit (tel. 20 54; open Tues.-Sun. 8am-noon, 1:30-5:30pm). The **Georgi Benkovski House** (Георги Бенковски; tel. 28 11; built 1831), near the statue of Benkovski, immortalizes the life and deeds of the leader of the "Flying Troop" of horsemen, more a symbolic than effective battle force in the April Uprising. Look for Benkovski's unusual rifle (closed Tues.). The **House-Museum Dimcho Debelyanov** (Димчо Дебелянов; tel. 20 77) shows the birthplace of one of Bulgaria's best lyric poets. Debelyanov died in the First World War, and, in the yard, sits a sculpture of his mother—vainly awaiting his return (closed Mon.). The houses of two merchants—**Oslekov** and **Lyutov**—are examples of the most prosperous Revival houses. Besides ornate ceiling work, the **Lyutov house** (tel. 21 38; closed Tues.) has original exhibits of non-woven carpets. The **Oslekov House,** supported by three columns of imported Lebanese cedar, has some stunning murals and wood carvings (closed Mon.). The 1817 **Assumption Church** (Успение Богородично; *Uspenie Bogorodichno*) was built in 11 days, according to legend, but looks much better. Inside you can find some masterpiece icons by **Zahari Zograf.**

■ Kazanluk (Казанлък)

Kazanluk has always been the center of Bulgaria's rose-growing world. Rather undistinguished throughout the year, the town acquires a sweet scent with the Rose Festival (the first week of June), which envelops the performances of traditional song-and-dance troupes, comedians, and soccer stars.

Orientation and Practical Information Take a **train** from Sofia (5 per day, 3hr., 208lv), Burgas (5 per day, 3hr., 210lv), Karlovo (10 per day, 1½ hr., 59lv); or a **bus** from Plovdiv's Sever station (2 per day). **Store luggage** at the train station (opens only 10min. within arrival or departure of trains; 10lv). From the train, bul. Rozova Dolina (Розова Долина) leads to the main **pl. Sevtopolis** (Севтополис). The main street runs west as the longest street name in Bulgarian history: Dvaisetitreti Pehoten Shipchenski Polk (Двайсетитрети Рехотен Шипченски Полк). It continues east as a more sane Knyaz Aleksandr Batenberg (Княз Александър Батенберг). The first floor of the massive **Hotel Kazanluk,** in the square, houses **Balkantourist** (tel. 210 87), where you can ask in English about private rooms and general info (open Fri. 8am-noon and 1-5pm). **United Bulgarian Bank** (tel. 512 79), Akad. Petko Stainov 7 (Акад. Петко Стайнов), on Dvaisetitreti, **changes cash** only (open Mon.-Fri. 8am-noon, 1:30-4:30pm). **Bookstore Tezi** (Тези; tel. 490 58), Dvaisetitreti 16, stocks useful English maps of town (55lv; open Mon.-Fri. 9:30am-7:30pm; Sat. 10am-1pm). The **post office** (fax 256 05) lies a bit farther on Dvaisetitreti (open Mon.-Fri. 7:30am-6:30pm, Sat. 8am-1pm; **telephones** open 7am-10pm; **faxes** open 7:30am-8pm). **Postal code:** 6100. **Phone code:** 0431.

Accommodations and Food Accommodation options are limited. Be sure to make reservations for the Rose Festival. **Hotel Voenen Klub** (Военен Клуб), bul. Rozova Dolina 8 (tel. 23 95 or 24 15), 30m down the street from Pl. Sevtapolis toward the train station in the big army club building, offers clean tiled rooms with private showers and hot water (singles 800lv, doubles 600lv per person). The **Hotel Vesta** (Веста; tel. 477 40), Chavdar Voivoda 3 (Чавдар Войвода), behind the monolithic cultural center, offers much newer rooms for similar prices (singles US$34, doubles and triples US$23 per person; private showers with 24-hr. hot water). **Campground Krunsko Hanche** (Крънско Ханче), 3km away, is open year-round. Take a bus to Gabrovo and ask the driver to stop there. Part of the new Tourist Complex Moshy (Туристически Комплекс Моши; tel. 242 39 or 270 91), the campground has two refurbished bungalows (sleeping two) at US$6 per person. Pitch a tent at the same price. The **Women's Monastery** (Женския Манастир; *Zhenskiya Manastir*), Tsar Osvobooditel 9, may offer shelter if you're stranded. For budget dining, search out **Starata Keshta** (Старата Къща), Dr. Baev 2 (Др. Баев; tel. 212 31). From pl. Sevtapolis, take the second left on Gen. M. Skobelev, then the first right on Gen. Gurko. Dr. Baev is the first right. Try the 60lv a piece *shishche* (шишче), a Bulgarian shish kebob, or a 137lv *kavarma* (open 24hr.).

Sights Kazanluk's **Thracian Tomb** (Тракийска Гробница; *Trakiiska Grobnitsa*) resides in Jyulberto Park, a 10-minute walk from pl. Sevtopolis. Climb the stairs to the top of the park's hill, the resting place of the original tomb dating from the turn of the 3rd century BCE. The interior has been re-created 20m away. The frescos in the corridor and dome chamber are the original early-Hellenistic; those in the replica are from the late-Socialistic period and, unsurprisingly, the paint has leaked. Both depict scenes from the life of the nobleman buried in the tomb. (tel. 247 50; open daily 8:30am-noon and 1:30-6pm; closed Nov.-Feb.; US$1, students US$0.50).

As you walk down the stairs out of the park, take a left on General Radetski (Генерал Радецки) and the first right onto the cobbled Knyaz Mirski (Кряз Мирски) which leads into the heart of the oldest part of Kazanluk—the **Koulata District** (Кулата), preserving the architecture and traditions of the National Revival. 20m down the street on the left is a **violin-maker's workshop**. On the right, a **coppersmith** still toils away at his ancient craft. Behind his ship, in the enclosed courtyard, the **Koulata Ethnographic Complex** (Етнографски Комплекс Кулата; tel. 217 33) displays two buildings—a village house and a city dwelling from the Revival years—and is probably the only museum that will treat you to a shot of genuine rose brandy and jam. In its wonderfully sculpted garden courtyard, a primitive distillery shows how rose oil and liquor are made the old-school way. Cheers! The English-speaking caretaker can also arrange for you to participate in **rose-picking** (May 15-June 15), and knows where to find authentic folk-singing. Ask her about private hotels and dorms (complex open daily 8:30am-noon and 1:30-6pm; US$2, students US$1). The **Art Gallery and Historical Museum Iskra** (художествена Галерия и историчски музей искра; tel. 263 22), Pr.R. Slaveykov 8, features a historical exhibit on ancient history, Thracian culture, and the rose in the life of Kazanluk. The gallery contains a rich permanent collection of Bulgarian masters and some icons (open daily 9am-noon and 1-5:30pm; US$1; polyglot guides 80lv). For those who still hunger for info on the oil-giving rose, a half-hour away from pl. Sevtopolis sits the **Rose Museum** (Музей на Розата; *Muzey na Rozata*; tel. 260 55). From the square, take Gen. Skobelev, go right at the fork and continue on bul. Osvobozhdenie (Освобождение) towards Gabrovo. If you're lucky, you may catch the irregular buses #5 or 6 across from Hotel Kazanluk (10lv). Located next to the **Scientific Research Institute of the Rose, Essential Oil-Yielding, and Medicinal Plants**, the museum displays, with the help of tools and black-and-white photos, the technology used over the centuries to produce rose oil. The institute's experimental **gardens** are home to over 250 rose varieties. The souvenir shop sells English brochures (40lv) and some indispensable rose products —liquor (100lv) and jam (open in summer 8:30am-5pm; US$1, students US$0.50). 10km south of Kazanluk, the man-made **Lake Koprinka** (Копринка), floods the remains of the Thracian city of Sevtopolis. Bus #3 shuttles from the train station.

■ Near Kazanluk: Etura (Етъра)

Etura is a worthwhile two-hour stop en route from Kazanluk (8 buses per day, 40min.) to Veliko Turnovo, or vice-versa (7 buses per day). **Buses** stop in **Gabrovo**. Once there (**store luggage** at the bus station for 24lv), take **trolley** #32 or bus #1 to the end-stop at Bolshevik (15min., 5lv), then **bus** #7 or 8 and ask to be dropped off at Etura (5min., 15lv). The big **Hotel/Restaurant Etura** (tel. 424 19 or 420 26) overhanging the street offers comfy rooms with private bath (singles US$30, doubles US$45). Downstairs, a small *mehani* is open 11:30am-5:30pm. The steps leading there also go to the miniature valley surrounding Etura; cross the bridge and head to the ticket kiosk. The village consists of a little **outdoor museum** (open daily summer

8am-8pm, winter 8am-4:40pm; 390lv, students 15lv). Continue down the path, past a wooden water mill, to the fairy tale's center. Climb through tiny doors and narrow staircases into workshops that look as if time had stopped a hundred years ago. Visit the candy store for sweet, sticky, and fresh sesame and honey bars (30lv), or the bakery for fresh sweet breads and pastries (60lv a piece).

■ Shipka (Шипка)

At the Rose Valley's northern edge looms the legendary **Shipka Pass,** site of the bloody and pivotal battle which lasted an entire winter and ultimately liberated Bulgaria from the Turks in 1878. The village at the base lies overshadowed and struggling—this time with the new cutthroat economy. Ten minutes up a little road from the main village square leads to the memorial **St. Nicholas,** built in honor of the Russian soldiers who lost their lives here. The golden cupolas glisten proudly over the trees, while the icon-filled interior is reminiscent of Russia's Golden Ring temples (open daily 8:30am-5:30pm; 100lv, students 50lv). Shipka Pass (Шипченски Проход; *Shipchenski Prohod*) is 20km up the paved road to Gabrovo. A hike starts at the memorial church (about 1½hr.), but locals don't recommend it. **Buses** run from Kazanluk to Gabrovo pass through (2 per day). Views of the Rose Valley extend from the top of the **Monument to Liberty** (Паметник на Свободата, *Pametnik na Svobodata*), crowning the famous battle site since August 26, 1934, in memory of the Russian and Bulgarian dead. Inside the basement is a sarcophagus built over the soldiers' graves, overlooked by a statue of Nike, and six floors of paintings depicting battle scenes, portraits of generals and wartime objects, and battlefield maps. Many of the writing fragments come from the legendary poem, "Shipka," by Ivan Vazov (see Literature, p. 107). Most Bulgarian students learn it by heart (open daily 8:30am-5pm; 50lv, students 20lv).

From Kazanluk, take **bus #6** from the train station or across from Hotel Kazanluk, in the direction away from the post office (every ½hr., 15min., 25lv). Buses also arrive from Gabrovo, dropping their human loads off in the lot in front of Hotel Shipka. You **cannot exchange currency** here. The **post office** is to the right on Hristo Patrev (Христо Патрев), the cobbled street above the square (open Mon.-Fri. 8am-noon and 1-4pm). **Postal code:** 6150. **Phone code:** 94324.

A **grocery** hides under the remains of old Hotel Shipka. **Restaurant Pronto** (Пронто; open daily 7am-midnight), across the square, conjures up a meal with some kind of *chorba* (чорба; soup), grills, *shopska salat*, and a tall, cool one for less than US$2. Closer to the pass, the other **Hotel Shipka** (tel. 247 50) has doubles (US$9), which can become singles (US$5) with shared floor bath, and three-person apartments with private bath (US$15). The **Hotel Sv. Nikola** (Свети Никола; tel. 246 09 and in Kazanluk 265 26; fax 266 11) has simple rooms, private baths, great views, and home cooking. Ask about the availability of hot water (US$10 per person including breakfast; open daily 8am-11pm). **Grills** and **souvenir stands** huddle at the foot of the 894 steps leading to the monument.

NORTHERN BULGARIA

■ Pleven (Плевен)

With 150 memorials to the Battle of Pleven, this town is a living monument to the Russian-Turkish War of 1877-78. But not to worry—Pleven offers its share of history in a fresh, relaxing atmosphere of parks, fountains, and flowerbeds. The per capita share of cafés is staggering, proof of the youth of Pleven's inhabitants.

Orientation and Practical Information Take a **bus** (1 per day, 4hr., 370lv) or **train** (9 per day, 3hr., 142lv) from Sofia; bus (1 per day, 3hr., 250lv) or train

(1 per day, 3½hr., 160lv) from Ruse; train from the Gorna Oryahovitsa international station (9 per day, 1½hr., 70lv) or Plovdiv (1 per day, 5½hr., 286lv). **Store luggage** both at the train station (left of main entrance; closed 8:15-8:45 am and pm) and the bus station (open 6:30am-7:30pm; 15lv per day). The focal points of Pleven are its two squares—**pl. Svobodata** (Свободата) and **Vuzrazhdane** (Възраждане)—connected by the pedestrian **Vasil Levski** (Васил Левски) and rows of trees and fountains. From the train station, walk down **Danail Popov** (Данаил Попов), which turns into **Osvobozhdenie** (Освобождение) and eventually hits Svobodata. Or, take **Asen Halachev** (Асен Халачев) to the right of the train station and turn left on Vasil Levski, Pleven's commercial and culinary artery. Buy an excellent **map** from the kiosk to the left of the ticket windows at the train station (50lv). **TSBank**, pl. Svobodata (tel. 310 48; fax 311 90), **exchanges money** and AmEx traveler's checks (US$4 charge) and gives Visa cash advances at a 5% commission (open Mon.-Thurs. 9am-3pm, Fri. 9am-1pm). **Orbita,** Zamenhof 3 (tel. 265 27; tel./fax 332 88), specializes in youth tourism and tourist info, gives away English brochures, issues ISICs, and arranges dorms in July and August (US$6-10 per person; open Mon.-Fri. 8:30am-5pm). The **post office** is in pl. Svobodata (open daily 7am-6pm). **Postal code:** 5800. The **phone office** is across the hall (open daily 7am-10pm). **Phone code:** 064.

Accommodations and Food Private Balkantourist rooms used to be the cheapest option, but Orbita student dorms are providing stiff competition. Otherwise, you'll have to choose among overpriced high-rises. Two-star **Rostov na Don** (Ростов на Дон), Osvobozhdenie 2 (tel. 238 92) on the left as you enter pl. Svobodata from the train station, has acceptable singles (US$17) and doubles (US$14 a bed) with clean bathrooms, and apartments (US$34) with TV and tub (MC and Visa accepted; bar, restaurant, exchange office, and disco). To get to **Hotel Balkan,** bul. Ruse 68 (Русе; tel. 222 15, 370 21, or 370 22; fax 370 23), take St. Cyril and Methodius from Vuzrazhdane, then turn left on Hristo Botev and walk until you see the tall white building on the right. As luxurious as Pleven gets—three stars, but with a 30% ISIC discount on lodging and 10% off on food. You must eat there to get sleeping discount (satellite TV, fridge, and tubs; Diner's Club, MC, Visa accepted; singles US$25, doubles US$22 after discount). The pricier **Hotel Pleven** (reception tel. 301 81; director tel. 383 13 until 5pm), near the bus/train station, has singles for US$27 and doubles for US$25 per person (Diner's Club, MC, and Visa accepted).

The well hidden **Old Walnut Tavern** (Механа Старият Орех; *Mehana Stariyat Oreh;* tel. 228 05), on Vasil Levski, serves memorable meals. Grab a seat in the garden and indulge in the specialty, the "Old Walnut" pork filet stuffed with mushrooms, cheese, and sausage (239lv; open daily 11:30am-midnight). The famous **Peshterata** (Пещерата; tel. 225 72) is 3km from town in **Kailuka Park.** Built in a sandstone cave, the loud restaurant has outdoor tables and plenty of space. *Kavarma* with eggs costs 120lv. Take trolley #3, or 7 from San Stefano (10lv), behind the post office, going away from the main square (5lv). From the end, follow the main street along the green park 20 minutes (open daily 10am-late).

Sights The granddaddy of Pleven's sights, the **Panorama** (Панорама; tel. 373 06), depicts the third Russo-Turkish Battle of Pleven and the liberation of Bulgaria (150lv, English guide 250lv, bother them about a student discount, and you might get it (open Tues.-Sat. 9am-5:30pm). Hire a guide or it'll just be a bunch of beautiful pictures. From the center, take bus #1, 9, or 12 to the second to last stop, then hike up. Down the alley from the main entrance is the old battlefield, now **Skobelev Park** (Парк Скобелев). Some wild greenery, guns, and an ossuary make for a spooky walk.

In the center of the first park-graced space left of Vasil Levski lies the small **Museum of the Liberation of Pleven** (Музей Освобождението на Плевен; *Muzeh Osvobozhdneito na Pleven;* open Tues.-Sat. 9am-noon and 1-6pm). Next door, outside the park, stairs lead down to the 1834 **Church of St. Nikolai** (Св. Николай; tel. 372 08), built two meters underground in compliance with a requirement that no church be higher than the local mosques. Holes in the walls and ceiling hold more than 600 clay pots to enhance acoustics (open daily 7:30am-6:30pm, services at 8am and 5pm). Midway between the two main squares on the right (coming from the train station), the **Turkish Baths** occupy a white building with brick stripes and keyhole-shaped doors and windows. The building is currently receiving a facelift *en route* to becoming an art gallery. At the end of pl. Svobodata is the **Mausoleum** of Russian and Romanian soldiers, built between 1902-04. The outside resembles the bathhouse; inside are socialist murals, ancient icons, and a vault holding the remains of many soldiers. Call ahead (tel. 235 69) to arrange a tour in English for 100lv (mausoleum open Tues.-Sat. 9am-noon and 1-6pm; free). The huge **historical museum,** St. Zaimov 3 (Св. Заимов; tel. 235 69), is minutes from the center. Go through the park at the end of pl. Vuzrazhdane or walk down Vardar (Вардар) and take a left on Zaimov. Two floors take you through archeology, ethnography, and National Revival exhibits, ending with the Russo-Turkish war and early 20th century history (open Tues.-Sat. 8am-noon and 12:30-5:30pm; Bulgarian-only signs make the 250lv English guide a must—call in advance). Across the street is the **City Art Gallery "Iliya Beshkov"** (Художествена Галерия "Илия Бешков"), bul. Skobolev 1 (tel. 300 30), named after a famous Bulgarian caricaturist. Temporary exhibits have seen the likes of Rembrandt and Picasso (open Mon.-Sat. 9am-5:30pm; free German tour and admission). Rent rowboats or *pedallo*s at the small pond in **Kailuka Park. Troyanski Manastir** (Троянски Манастир), was built in the Middle Ages and revived in the 17th century. Wall-paintings by Zahari Zograf adorn the walls. Vendors hawk Troyan **pottery** outside. Troyan can be reached via Levski by bus (2 per day, 2hr., 150lv) or train (2hr., 98lv). Buses connect the town and monastery (1 per day, 15min., 25lv)

■ Veliko Turnovo (Велико Търново)

Perched on steep hills above the twisting Yantra River, Veliko Turnovo has been watching over Bulgaria for 5000 years. The town has given the country revolutionaries, kings, and, after the overthrow of the Turks, the first Bulgarian constitution. The spirit of historical significance still lives in the Old Town's narrow streets. Lined with cafés and workshops, the lantern-lit streets of today's Veliko Turnovo wind from church to church through Bulgaria's biggest treasure trove of ruins.

ORIENTATION AND PRACTICAL INFORMATION

Maika Bulgaria Square (Майка България) is the town center. Bus #10 takes you there down **Nikola Gabrovski** (Никола Габровски) from both the **bus station** and the **Gorna Oryahovitsa international train station,** 7km east of town (15lv). The ever-changing Nikola Gabrovski has a host of different names: **Vasil Levski** (Васил Левски), **Nezavisimost** (Независимост), **Stefan Stambolov** (Стефан Стамболов), and **Nikola Pikolo** (Никола Пиколо). From the main square, **Hristo Botev** (Христо Ботев) leads towards the river. The National Revival Museum sells **maps** (20lv).

Currency Exchange: Balkan Bank, pl. Maika Bulgaria 2 (tel. 369 14; fax 378 06). Cashes traveler's checks (US$2 fee) and Visa cash advances (7% commission). Open Mon.-Fri. 7:30am-7pm, Sat.-Sun. 9:30am-1:30pm.

Trains: In **Gorna Oryahovitsa** (tel. 560 50), 7km from Veliko Turnovo. Trains to Pleven (16 per day, 1½hr., 70lv), Plovdiv (5 per day, 5hr., 230lv), Sofia (12 per day, 4½hr., 208lv), Tryavna (11 per day, 1½hr., 50 lv), and Varna (7 per day, 3½hr., 184lv). Take bus #10 (15lv) or a minivan taxi (50lv) from the outdoor market. The smaller **Veliko Turnovo** station, on bus #4 route, sees direct trains from Sofia (7 per day).

Buses: Nikola Gabrovski. Five stops from the center by bus #7 or 10. To: Gabrovo (hourly, 45min., 120lv). Longer distances are torture in dying Bulgarian-made buses. **Group Travel** (tel. 282 92) in the Hotel Etur building. To: Sofia (3 per day, 3hr., 420lv), Varna (2 per day, 3hr., 380lv). Open Mon.-Fri. 9am-6:30pm, Sat.-Sun. 10am-noon and 3:30-6pm. **ETAP** in the lobby of Hotel Etur (tel. 305 64) sends daily buses to: Shoumen (2hr., 300lv), Sofia (420lv), Varna (400lv). Open daily 7:30am-6:30pm. All buses leave from outside the hotel.

Taxis: Okay (tel. 221 21) charges 27lv per km and 13lv to start.
Luggage Storage: At the public bus station. Open 6:30am-7:30pm (10lv per day).
Pharmacy: ul. Vasil Levski (Левски). Open daily 7am-9pm.
Post Office: pl. Maika Bulgaria. Open Mon.-Fri. 7am-noon and 12:30-6:30pm, Sat. 8am-noon and 2-5:30pm. **Poste Restante** down the stairs 30m to the left of the main entrance. Open Mon.-Sat. 7am-noon and 1-6pm. **Postal code:** 5000.
Telephones: At the post office. Open daily 7am-10pm. **Faxes** (fax 298 77) can be sent and received here. Open daily 7am-7pm. **Phone code:** 062.

ACCOMMODATIONS

Finding a place to sleep should not be a problem...

Hotel Orbita (Хотел Орбита), Hristo Botev 15 (tel. 220 41), on the way to hotel Etur. Backpacker-oriented triples and quads on the 4th floor share a functional floor bathroom with 24-hr. hot water. 500lv per person.

Hotel Trapezitsa (HI; Хотел Трапезица), Stefan Stambolov 79 (tel. 220 61). Called "Edelweiss" by the locals. Excellent youth hostel. From the post office, walk straight, and turn right with the street. Fresh, new rooms with private bathrooms. Apartments for 2 (3300lv; TV and fridge) and singles (1900lv). Doubles are 940lv, nonmembers 1300lv. Triples and quads 835lv per person, nonmembers 1170lv. Lockout midnight. Ask for a quiet room with river view.

Hotel Komfort, (tel. 287 28), Panayot Tipografov 5 (Панайот Типографов). From Stambolov, walk left of Rakovski, turn left on the small square, and search for the street sign. Well-hidden in a private house. Clean rooms, beautiful bathrooms, and amazing views. US$10 per person. The luxury top floor apartment sleeps four and its balcony affords a great view of the nightly light show (US$48).

Hotel Etur, Aleksandr Stamoliiski 2 (tel. 218 38; fax 218 07), off Hristo Botev in the center. Shared bathrooms in good condition. Foreigners pay more than Bulgarians but get better rooms. Check hot water schedule. Clean, big rooms US$13 per person, with bathroom US$23 per person. Breakfast included. Visa accepted.

FOOD

A large **outdoor market** sells fresh fruit and veggies daily from dawn to dusk at the corner of Bulgaria and Nikola Gabrovski. Multiple **taverns** capitalize on the balconies of old houses overlooking the river. **Mehana Medovina** (Механа Медовина), Ivan Panov 5 (Иван Панов; tel. 201 90), off Stambolov to the right of Hotel Trapezitsa, serves great veal "medalion" with mushrooms (240lv). Other main courses run 110-240lv, wine 220-260lv (open daily 11am-2:30pm and 4pm-1am). **Starata Mehana** (Старата Механа), Stambolov, five minutes from Hotel Trapezitsa, is small and friendly with animal skins on the wall (*kavarma* 220lv, soups 35-40lv; open 10am-midnight). **Samovodska Sreshta** (Самоводска Среща), ul. Rakovski 31 (tel. 239 10), is a few minutes past Hotel Trapezitsa, in a dark wooden house on the left. Prepares entrées in front of the clients. The specialty is *zaek po lovdzhiiski* (заек по ловджийски, rabbit "hunter's style"; 185lv; open daily 10am-late, sometimes closed Sun.). **Sladkarnitsa Lotos** (Сладкарница Лотос), next to Hotel Trapezitsa, offers oodles of cake: try the chocolate *garash* (гараш; 32lv). Cappuccino's cheap at 35lv on the view-packed terrace (open daily 6am-11:30pm).

SIGHTS AND ENTERTAINMENT

The ruins of the **Fortress Tsarevets** (Царевец), which once housed the royal palace and a cathedral, stretch across an overgrown hilltop overlooking the city. Nikola Pikolo leads to the gates (open in summer daily 8am-7pm, off-season 8am-5pm; 100lv, students 50lv). From the heights near **Baldwin's tower,** you'll be standing where the imprisoned Latin emperor Baldwin of Flanders spent his last days after an unsuccessful attempt to conquer Bulgaria in 1205. Climb up the hill to **Ascension Church,** restored in 1981 on the 1300th anniversary of the Bulgarian state. One of the fortress gates plays host to a long-running **puppet troupe**—gypsy woman, monkey, and gremlin—performed daily in summer. Near the fortress off ul. Ivan Vazov, the **Archeological Museum** traces the region's history from the stone age to the middle ages with Thracian pottery, a collection of medieval crafts from Turnovo, and copies of religious frescos (open Mon.-Fri. 8am-noon and 1-6pm; US$1, students pay half). Next door, the **Museum of the National Revival** (Музей на Възраждането; *Muzey na Vuzrazhdaneto*) teaches about Bulgaria's 19th-century cultural and religious resurgence, but the Bulgarian-only signs and inscriptions make the lesson difficult for foreigners. The basement contains a rich collection of Tryavna School icons, and the ground floor celebrates anti-Ottoman uprisings and church and literary struggles, while the second floor is a snapshot from the day the Turnovo Constitution was signed in 1879. Call 298 21 to arrange an English guide for either of the museums (400lv per group; open Wed.-Mon. 9am-noon and 1-6pm; 70lv, students 20lv). On summer evenings there is often a **sound and light show** above Tsaravets Hill: five different-colored lasers play out Bulgarian history in symbols; check with **Interhotel Veliko Turnovo** off Stamboliiski for dates. They will charge you 800lv for a spot on their terrace, but there are plenty of places to see it for free. The Interhotel's indoor swimming pool is also open to visitors (100lv per hr.). The building identifiable by the big "БАР ПОЛТАВА" sign in the main square houses a **disco** (30lv, half dead except on weekends) and a **movie theater** (60lv).

■ Near Veliko Turnovo

ARBANASI (АРБАНАСИ)

Fifteenth-century **Arbanasi** lies 4km from Veliko Turnovo, with beautiful hill-top mansions turned museums. The restored white houses resemble fortresses, with indoor murals dripping with color, and intricately-carved wooden ceilings and furnishings. Todor Zhivkov, Bulgaria's long-time Communist leader, had a residence here, and the town is now a luxury resort. From Veliko Turnovo, take the **bus** (3 per day, 30min., 30lv) from the *pazar* (пазар) on Vasil Levski. **Minivans** to Gorna Oryanovitsa will also drop you off nearby (50lv). A **cab** costs about US$1. The 45-minute walk back down the hill uncovers some dizzying sights. The town is too small for street names. One ticket lets you into **Hadzhi Iliya House** (Хаджи Илиевата Къща), **Constantsaliev House** (Константцалиевата Къща), and two **churches**—the **Church of the Nativity of Christ** (Рождество Христово) and the **Church of Archangels Gabriel and Michael** (Архангели Гавраил и Михаил; open daily 9-11:30am and 1-4:30pm; US$1, students US$0.50). Unfortunately, the former of the two houses and the latter of the two churches are often closed, as the museum is understaffed. Nevertheless, ask at the kiosk for an English guide (400lv per group), and peek at the free-standing map. To spend the night, go to **Restaurant Galeria** (tel. 305 54) and ask for a recommendation. There are 13 **private hotels**. The owner of Galeria knows them all, together with prices and location (price range US$3-10). The restaurant has excellent meals—they will cook (almost) anything you want. Main courses run 120-190lv. Baked lamb is worth the 330lv (open Mon. 6pm-2am, Tues.-Sun. 10am-2am). There are several other **taverns** lining the main drag (all with fresh trout); don't miss the **bazaar**—a bargain-hunter's dream come true.

TRYAVNA (ТРЯВНА)

Fiercely independent during the centuries of Ottoman occupation, Tryavna was an important center of the National Revival. Works of the 17th-century Tryavna School of Woodworking and Icon Painting remain to remind us of the settlement's greatest years. The 12th-century **Church of the Archangel Mihail** (Църква на Свети Архангел Михаил; *Tsurkva na Sveta Arhangel Mikail*), Angel Kunchev 9 (Ангел Кунчев), is across the street from the post office. Inside, wood carvings and icons by Tryavna masters of the Vitanov family adorn thick columns beneath a low ceiling. The church's treasure is the Tsar's Crucifix (Царският Кръст; *Tsarskiyat Krutst*), a wooden relic with 12 Gospel scenes carved on it—ask the priest to unlock it and show it to you (open daily 7am-noon and 3-6pm). The **Shkoloto Museum** (Школото; the old school) stands at #7 pl. Kapitan Dyado Nikola (Капитан Дядо Никола), the only preserved National Revival square in Bulgaria. The museum displays timepieces, art, and "graphicatures" (open in summer daily 9am-6pm; off-season 8am-noon and 1-5pm; US$1). Cross the little arched bridge by the clocktower, and turn left to get to **Daskalovata House** (Даскаловата Къща), Slaveykov 27 (Славейков). A wood-carving museum (including portraits of famous historical figures) occupies the first floor. The second exhibits the carved ceilings of competing masters. Don't look for beds—they came to Bulgaria only late in the 19th century. A guide (French only, 200lv) or the free brochure might be useful (open in summer daily 9am-6pm; off-season daily 8am-noon and 1-5pm; US$1, Mon. free). Backtrack 30m on Slaveykov then take a left (toward the hill), cross the train tracks via the asphalt road. Take a left on Breza (Бреза) and after the buildings end, look for stairs on the right to take you up to the fenced-off yard of the **Museum of the Tryavna School of Icon Painting** (Музей Тревнинска Иконописна; *Muzey Trevninska Ikonopisna*). It contains works by members of six famous families of Tryavna masters. Over 160 icons tell the story of the oldest icon-painting school in Bulgaria. Don't miss the exhibit of **Zograf's** (зограф) instrumentarium and the stages in an icon's creation. Taped tours in *Bulglish* (open in summer daily 8am-6pm; off-season 8am-noon and 12:30-4:30pm; US$1, Thurs. free; English guide 200lv.) All three museums sell an English city **guide-map** (100lv).

Take a **bus** from Gabrovo (1 per hour, 45min., 100lv) or a **train** from Veliko Turnovo (6 per day, 45min., 42lv). Cross the little square in front of the bus/train station to get to Angel Kunchev, turn right, and religiously follow its fickle turns; it's 10 minutes to the center, marked by a big library on the right. Continue along Angel Kunchev to its seeming end—it continues to the right at the T-intersection. On the right (after the turn), **Private Agricultural Investment Bank** changes cash only (open Mon.-Fri. 9am-12:30am and 1-4:45pm). Ahead is the **post office** (open Mon.-Fri. 8am-noon and 1-5pm). **Postal code**: 5350. **Phone code**: 677.

Accommodations are hard to come by, and English language maps are practically nonexistent. **Hotel/Restaurant Tryavna**, in the town center has small, basic, clean rooms with bathrooms and phones (tel. 34 48; fax 25 27; singles US$14, doubles US$18 per person, triples US$16 per person, apartments US$50). Hot water runs 6-9am and 6-9pm. The restaurant serves dishes daily 4pm to 1am. **Private hotels** are popping up as well—follow signs from the center; chances are they are better and cheaper than more established establishments. Locals praise **Restaurant Pri Maistora** (При Майстора; tel. 32 40). The chef's specialty is a dish of veal and pork filet with cheese in the shape of a pyramid (315lv). Five types of *kavarma* (112-224lv) and salads (35-72lv). Paintings by the owner's talented son grace the cozy interior (open daily 11am-midnight). Take Chuchura (Чучура) from the old square, bear left at the fork and turn right on Kaleto.

■ Ruse (Русе)

For centuries, foreigners have drifted down the Danube, bringing in music, art, and architecture. Clever Ruse made the most of all the attention. Even in modern times this city lives or dies with the river and its ships. Recently, the Yugo embargo cut important links with Central Europe and affected Ruse's all-important shipping livelihood. Most of its museums are closed because the new private owners have no money for maintenance and renovation. But still, Ruse's center remains one of the liveliest and most beautiful in Bulgaria, reminding the traveler of its better known Danubian brothers and sisters.

ORIENTATION AND PRACTICAL INFORMATION

Despite its size, Ruse offers very easy orientation. The **train station** and **bus station**, far from the center, are connected to the main **pl. Svoboda** (Свобода), by **Borisova** (Борисова). The main street is **ul. Aleksandrovska** (Александровска), which cuts through the main square. The **statue in the main square** looks towards the Danube river, which runs parallel to Aleksandrovska, a five-minute walk away.

Tourist Office: Dunav Tours (Дунав Турс), pl. Han Kubrat (Хан Кубрат; tel. 22 42 68; fax 27 71 77), from pl. Svoboda, take Aleksandrovska in the direction indicated by the statue's left hand. They arrange private rooms (singles US$8, doubles US$12), provide maps and brochures, and sell tickets to the opera and theater.

Currency Exchange: TS Bank, in the main square, cashes traveler's checks. Open Mon.-Fri. 8:30am-3:30pm. Visa/Plus **ATM** outside. **Balkanbank,** Aleksandrovska 28, cashes traveler's checks and gives Visa cash advances. Open Mon.-Fri. 8am-12:30pm and 1:30-6:30pm, Sat. 8am-12:30pm. Private change bureaus line Aleksandrovska.

Trains: To: Bucharest (1 per day, 6hr., 296lv); Sofia (4 per day, 7hr., 350lv); Varna (2 per day, 4hr., 210lv). **Rila,** Knyazheska 33 (tel. 22 39 20), sells international train tickets. Open Mon.-Fri. 7:30am-6:30pm, Sat. 8am-1pm.

Buses: Ruse can be reached by bus from Burgas (1 per day, 5½hr., 450lv), Pleven (1 per day, 3hr., 250lv), Shoumen (2 per day, 3hr., 245lv), and Varna (1 per day, 3½hr., 300lv). **Group Travel,** pl. Svoboda (tel. 23 20 08), at Dunav Hotel, sends buses to Sofia (2 per day, 5hr., 550lv). Open Mon.-Fri. 7:30am-noon and 1-4:30pm. Sat.-Sun. 7:30am-noon and 1-4:30pm buy tickets from the hotel desk.

Public Transportation: Buy 15lv tickets on board for the **buses** and **trolleys.**

Taxis: tel. 142 or 189. 27lv per km.

Pharmacy: Apteka Nikolovi, Aleksandrovska 69 (tel. 27 03 86). Open Mon.-Sat. 8am-8pm, Sun. 8am-2pm. **Night pharmacy,** Aleksandrovska 97 (tel. 23 70 51).

Post Office: Sredets 1 (Среден), on the "left hand" side of Svoboda. Open Mon.-Fri. 7:30am-7pm; Sat. 7:30am-6pm. **Postal code:** 7000.

Telephones: At the post office (open daily 7am-10pm). **Faxes** (fax 23 36 00) can be sent and received 7am-7pm. **Phone code:** 082.

ACCOMMODATIONS AND CAMPING

Private rooms are the best option; go to Dunav Tours (see Tourist Office, above). Small hotels are few, and the former state ones, like the museums, fall into ruin while they're being privatized.

Hostel Prista (Хижа Приста; tel. 23 41 67), 8km from the city center, in the park above the Danube. Buses #6 and 16 run here from the center with unpredictable frequency (10min, 15lv). A taxi from the train station costs about 200lv. Bare rooms with big beds. Private baths of suspicious cleanliness—you may feel cleaner by avoiding the shower. Lockout 11:30pm. 500lv per head.

Hotel/Restaurant Petrov (Петров; tel./fax 22 24 01), near Hostel Prista. Small, private hotel with a restaurant and great views. Doubles with private bathroom at US$20 per person. **Laundry,** ironing board, even complimentary slippers. Restaurant open daily 8am-midnight. English spoken.

Hotel Helios (Хелиос), ul. Nikolaevska 1 (tel. 22 56 61). At the end of Aleksandrovska (left side of square) across the small park, then to the left. Bland rooms, small private bathrooms with showerheads right above the toilet and a sink in between. Singles US$25, doubles US$15 per person. Bring your own Bulgarian—the only language they speak. An unidentifiable smell may be lurking around.

Campground Ribarska Koliba (Рибарска Колиба; tel. 22 40 68). Bus stops at "Camping". Spartan but clean bungalows and caravans at US$5 per bed (get one in shade—the others may cook you alive). Pitch a tent for US$3 per person. Outdoor bathrooms and mosquitoes included. Restaurant down the road (see below).

FOOD

Food in Ruse centers around **Aleksandrovska,** with the Asko-Denitsa (Аско Деница) **grocery** at one end (open Mon.-Fri. 8:30am-7pm, Sat. 9am-2pm). **Leventa** (Левента; tel. 282 90), underneath the tallest TV tower in the Balkans (take bus #17), serves main courses (150-260lv), salads (30-70lv), omelettes or cheese vegetarian dishes (60-150lv). The house gypsy orchestra plays nightly if there's a crowd (open daily 11:30am-midnight). Try the **café-bar** on the top of the TV tower for delicious chocolate *torta garash* (50lv). Coffee is a meager 25lv. Ask them for binoculars—you can see the whole town from above (open daily 4-11:30pm; reservations suggested). **Restaurant Alibi** (Алиби), Aleksandrovska 128 (tel. 22 23 51), a long walk from the center, has a relaxing atmosphere, outdoor tables, and fancy meals on fancy plates with fancy prices. A full meal can be had for US$4 (open daily 10am-midnight). **Restaurant Ribarska Koliba** (tel. 22 43 57), 15 minutes down the road from the eponymous campground (take a right at the auto shop), is a Ruse institution known for fish soup (рибена чорба; *rybena chorba;* 60lv). Fish delicacies average 300lv, salads 50lv (open 10am-until last customer leaves).

SIGHTS AND ENTERTAINMENT

Ruse, marked by beautiful and colorful Baroque, Renaissance, and Art Deco architecture, centers around the **Pl. Svobod**. This peaceful square is full of places to sit and rest in the coolness of fountains and trees. On the right side of the square stands the **Opera House** and **Holy Trinity Church** (Света Троица; *Sveta Toritsa*), erected in 1632 during the Ottoman occupation (open Sat.-Sun. 6am-8:30pm). One of the few Catholic churches in Bulgaria—**St. Paul's** (Свети Павел; *Sveti Pavel*), is found on a small street off Knyazheska. In the evening, come for a stroll in the popular **Mladezhki Park** (Младежки Парк) on the east side of the city, complete with an **outdoor swimming pool**. At night, try one of the three **movie theaters** on Aleksandrovska or the **discos** in the Riga and Dunav Hotels. Buy **opera** and **theater** tickets through Dunav at the ridiculously low price of 100lv. And don't forget the **March Music Days,** Bulgaria's symphonic music festival. Tickets through Dunav Tours are 500lv. Close by is **Bassarbovo Monastery** (Басарбово); take bus #8 from Iv. Dimitrov. Ask at Dunav Tours for more information (see Tourist Office, p. 132).

■ Shoumen (Шумен)

Relaxing and pleasant, Shoumen is notable mainly for its proximity to Bulgaria's treasured archaeological sites at Preslav, Pliska, and Madara. Monolithic historical monuments, a busy main street, and some surprisingly well preserved specimens of early 20th-century architecture keep a traveler's tired eyes busy.

Orientation and Practical Information Shoumen can be reached by **train** from Pleven (7 per day, 3½hr., 184lv), Ruse (1 per day, 3hr., 122lv), Sofia (6 per day, 6hr., 302lv), Varna (11 per day, 1½hr., 86lv). **Group** (tel. 627 13) has a kiosk outside the train station with **buses** to Sofia (4 per day, 6hr., 600lv), Veliko Turnovo (4 per day, 2½hr., 220lv), and Varna (2 per day, 1hr., 250lv). **Store luggage** at the train station (10lv; open 24hr.). Buses #4, 6, 8, 9, 10 (15lv, buy ticket from kiosks and stamp on board) run to the central pl. Oborishte (Оборище). Get off at "Hotel Shoumen". To get to the main **bul. Slavyanski** (Славянски), a two-level walkway with cafés, trees, and benches between levels, take Hristo Botev from pl. Oborishte to the train/bus stations. The **tourist office**, pl. Oborishte 6a (tel. 553 13), arranges **private rooms** at US$5-8 per person and provides maps and brochures (open Mon.-Fri. 8:30am-noon and 1:30-6pm, Sat. 10am-3:30pm). **Balkanbank,** bul. Slavyanski 64, on 2nd floor (tel. 573 42), accepts cash, traveler's checks (US$2 fee), and Visa (5% commission; open Mon.-Fri. 8am-noon and 1:30-4pm). The **post office** is at the start of bul. Slavyanski (open Mon.-Fri. 7:30am-noon and 1-6pm; **telephones** open daily 7am-9:30pm). **Postal code:** 9700. **Phone code:** 54.

Accommodations and Food Other than **private rooms** (US$5-8), options for lodging are slim. Try **Hotel Orbita** (tel. 523 98) in Kyoshkovete Park (Кьошковете парк), near the Shoumen brewery. Take bus #10 from the train/bus stations to its last stop. You're in the right place if everything smells like beer. Enter the park, and walk down the alley. Fresh white paint gives away the renovation by its new owners. Clean rooms boast showers, shaded terraces, and firm mattresses (DM15 per person,

4-person suite DM60). Three-star **Hotel Madara** (tel. 575 98), at the beginning of bul. Slavyanski, has rooms with a view, TV, fridge, bath, and an occasional cockroach. (singles US$31, doubles US$19 per person; breakfast included).

Bul. Slavyanski is lined with places to eat and relax. **Popsheytanova Kushta** (Попше-йтанова Къща), pl. Oborishte (tel. 574 02), has an outdoor garden overgrown with ivy. A touristy folk tavern, it offers live music nightly, and prepares exotic salads and *starata kushta* (старата къща), a filet with cheese, mushrooms, and tomatoes (280lv; open Mon.-Fri. noon-2:30pm and 6pm-midnight, Sat.-Sun. 6pm-midnight; music after 7pm; English menu). For a real treat, drop by the **Shoumen Brewery** restaurant across from Hotel Orbita, home of the famous Shoumen beer. Rattan chairs and a grand piano welcome guests to try mixed grills (220lv) with fresh *"shoumensko special"*—a 0.5L draft beer (50lv; open daily 11am-11pm). **Mehana Orhideya** (Орхидея; tel. 569 71), up Hristo Botev 14, has a private table with stylish table cloths in a cool, brick wine-cellar-like basement room. The local *kareta po shoumenski* (карета по шуменски; pork with melted grated cheese in a mushroom sauce; 180lv) goes great with fries and feta cheese (*purzheni kartofi sus sirene*; 55lv; open daily 11am-2am).

Sights and Entertainment The 1744 **Tombul Mosque** (Томбул Джамия; tel. 568 23) minutes from Hotel Shoumen (above), away from the center, features a beautiful stone courtyard with a water fountain where believers wash before Friday services (open daily 9:15am-4:15pm; 80lv, students 45lv). The history of Shoumen, named for Bulgarian King Simeon (864-927CE) reaches back to the early 10th century, but its monuments date from still earlier. Three buses per day (15lv) run by the mosque to **Shoumen Fortress** (Шуменска Крепост; *Shoumenska Krepost*). Built by Thracians in the 5th century BCE, the fortress was later used by Romans and Byzantines. By foot, take the asphalt road by the last stop of bus #6 and 10 (½hr.; open Mon.-Fri. 9am-5pm, Sat.-Sun. 8am-2pm). A map outside the main gate exhibits suggested **hiking** routes (1½-3hr.) in the area. One of them (1½hr.) leads to the tall hilltop structure overlooking Shoumen, the **Monument to the Founders of the Bulgarian State** (tel. 625 98), erected in 1981. Exactly 1300 steps, to commemorate the 13 centuries of Bulgaria, get you there from the middle of bul. Slavyanski—the tiresome hike is rewarded with a view and beautiful mosaics, representing scenes from medieval Bulgarian history (open in summer daily 9am-7pm, off-season 9am-5pm). Dance the night away under the stars in open-air disco **La Strada**, next to the station (open daily 10pm-3am). Or choose the refined **Terminator 2** disco at Hotel Shoumen (open daily 9am-5am). If you're in the mood for something more relaxing, stroll up and down bul. Slavyanski and chill out with a *shoumensko* and all of Shoumen's youth in one of the numerous cafés along the boulevard.

■ Near Shoumen

PLISKA (ПЛИСКА) AND VELIKI PRESLAV (ВЕЛИКИ ПРЕСЛАВ)

Pliski (681-893CE) and Veliki (893-972CE), first and second capitals of Bulgaria, remain mute witnesses to Bulgaria's history from its birth to its greatest might. They share similar maps: a walled "inner city" circled by a lightly defended "outer city." They also share the tragic neglect of a country too poor to care for its treasures.

Pliska lies 23km northeast of Shoumen, accessible by an hourly **bus** (½hr., 45lv). A huge archaeological **excavation** has unearthed parts of palaces and fortifications 3km from the village. No public transportation goes there; some walk or ask around for a ride. Unmarked remains of round fortress towers and the somewhat rebuilt **king's palace** struggle to stay above the top of upstart grasses and bushes.

Preslav, 18km south from Shoumen can be visited in a daytrip from Shoumen by **bus** (10 per day, ½hr., 45lv). Walk up from the hotel to find the *pazar* (food market). From there, a walk uphill leads to the **Archaeological Museum** (tel. 32 43) and a complex of medieval ruins. The vandalized English map is the only one available. Enter the park, walk to the café, then take a left onto a paved alley (½hr. from center). The museum has exhibitions of ancient artwork and craftsmanship, and a 15-minute English film on the town. Emphasis is placed on some Preslav trademarks: painted floors and decorative tiles, stone-carved capitals, and objects from the Preslav School of Letters. Ask for an English guide (open daily in summer 9am-5pm; off-season 8am-4pm; 100lv, students 50lv). Walk down from the museum through a stone gate to find the poorly marked ruins. Make sure to see the **Golden Temple** ruins (built in 908) and its well preserved floor mosaic. The king's palace is marked by a column, and parts of the **fortress wall** of the inner-city remain.

MADARA (МАДАРА)

Madara, 16km east of Shoumen, is home to the famous stone relief **Madara Horseman**. On a vertical cliff 25m above ground, the life-size relief features a horse with rider, lion, and dog—an ensemble so legendary it graces e the backs of all *leva* coins and the front labels of Shoumen beer. The artist is unknown, but the work was done in the 8th century and supposedly symbolizes the victories of Bulgarian ruler Han Tervel over the broken Byzantine empire. Since August 1995 the horseman has been covered by a huge scaffolding—for evaluation of possible repair. In some ways, this has been fortuitous, as tourists often forget to see Madara's other riches. A path leads one methodically through prehistoric Stone and Copper Age people's caves (3500BCE). The largest one became the **Temple of Three Thracian Nymphs** (4th-1st centuries BCE) and now houses the annual festival **Madara Music Days** (Мадарски Музикални Дни; *Madarski Muzikalni Dni*) every June. More than 150 cells are carved into the rock, the one-time home of ascetic monks and heretics—proof of Madara's importance as a perennial cult center. On top of the plateau sit the remains of the **Madara Fortress** (4th-century) which once worked with the Shoumen Fortress to guard the way to Pliska and Preslav. Nearly 400 exhausting steps get you to the top (open daily in summer 8am-6pm; winter 8am-5pm; 80lv, 40lv if horseman is covered). To get to Madara, take a **bus** (4-5 per day, 20min., 40lv) or a **train**—any *putnicheski* (slow) one to Varna will do (9 per day, 3 stops away, 20min., 24lv). From the train station follow the crowd toward the village center then turn left on the street that runs along a little creek—it gets you to the main road to Madara (go left and up; whole walk 20min.). The tourist office in Shoumen can provide more info.

BLACK SEA COAST

The Black Sea is a sentimental journey through the sweet stuff of every Bulgarian's life: bare-bottomed childhood vacations, summer jobs flipping *kebabche*, first loves, second loves, and… The many campgrounds and international youth centers have long been popular with young party-bound backpackers; for years, the coast was the only place Bulgarians could come in contact with "the West." Today, ancient ruins, modern resorts, fishing villages, sandy beaches, and every sport from para-sailing to horseback riding remain within the budget traveler's reach. Go north for rocky cliffs and small villages; go south for popular resorts and beautiful beaches.

■ Varna (Варна)

Varna was crawling with sunburned Greek sailors as early as 600BCE, when it was a young port city known as Odessos. By the time Romans arrived in the 2nd century CE, Varna was busy trading and doing the things that cosmopolitan cultural centers do. These days, Bulgaria's third-largest city and sea capital harbors an alluring Old Town, Roman ruins, and an ideal beach backdrop for rollerblading. Long experience as a tourist hub has taught the city countless ways to squeeze out a traveler's last cent.

Central Varna

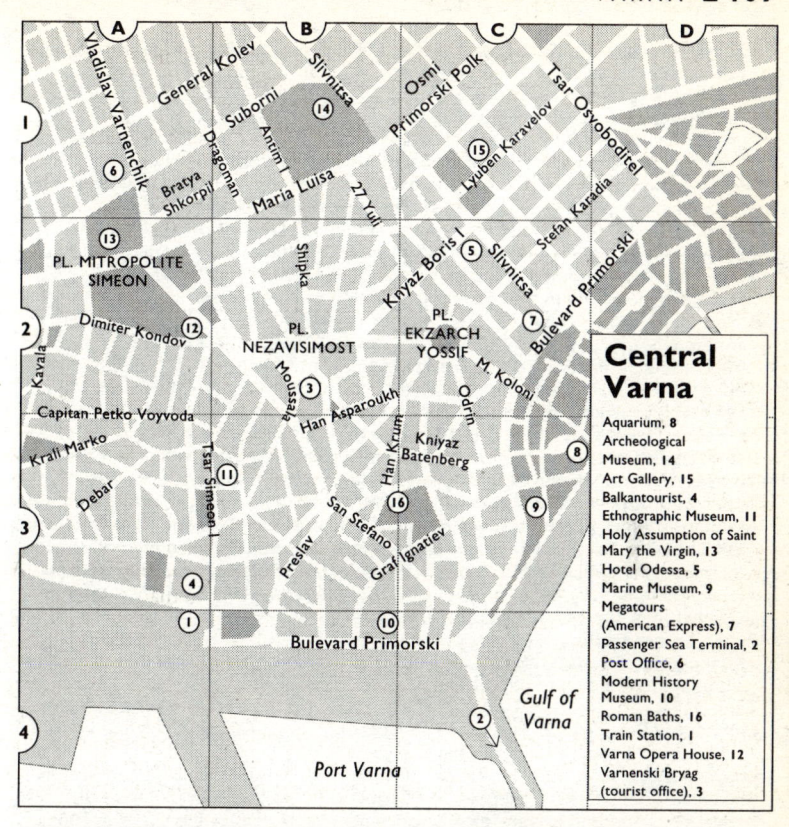

Aquarium, 8
Archeological Museum, 14
Art Gallery, 15
Balkantourist, 4
Ethnographic Museum, 11
Holy Assumption of Saint Mary the Virgin, 13
Hotel Odessa, 5
Marine Museum, 9
Megatours (American Express), 7
Passenger Sea Terminal, 2
Post Office, 6
Modern History Museum, 10
Roman Baths, 16
Train Station, 1
Varna Opera House, 12
Varnenski Bryag (tourist office), 3

ORIENTATION AND PRACTICAL INFORMATION

Although Varna is a sprawling city, the major sights are close together, and the Latin script on street signs makes the city easier to navigate. To get to central **pl. Nezavisimost** (Независимост), go through the underpass to **Tsar Simeon I** (Цар Симеон I). Varna's main artery, **bul. Knyaz Boris I** (Княз Борис I), starts at pl. Nezavisimost. Both **Slivnitsa** (Сливница) and **Tsar Osvoboditel** (Цар Освободител) connect bul. Knyaz Boris I with a multi-name parallel street that shows up as **Osmi Primorski Polk** (Осми Приморски Полк), **Maria Luisa** (Мария Луиза), and **Hristo Botev** (Христо Ботев). **Preslav** (Преслав), near Maria Luisa, continues past pl. Nezavisimost to the **train station**, forking at one point to form **San Stefano** (Сан Стефано), which leads to the **passenger port** and **beach**. Walk up Preslav from pl. Nezavisimost to the **Sv. Bogoroditsa cathedral**, a major stopping point for buses.

Tourist Offices: Varnenski Bryag (Варненски Бряг), Musala 3 (Мусала; tel. 22 55 24; fax 25 30 83), between Preslav and Knyaz Boris I off pl. Nezavisimost. Staff dispenses transportation info and arranges **private rooms** (US$8-9). Open daily in summer 8am-9pm; winter Mon.-Sat. 8am-6pm. Another branch (tel. 22 22 06) is at pl. Slaveykov 6, across from the train station.

Currency Exchange: Balkan Bank, Preslav 53 (tel. 60 26 99), across the park from Varnenski Bryag at Musala. They accept traveler's checks and give cash advances on Visa and MC. Open Mon.-Fri. 8:15-11:45am and 1-3pm. **TSBank,** Sheinovo 2 (Шейново). Visa cash advances given and traveler's checks cashed. Open Mon.-

Thurs. 9am-3pm, Fri. 9am-1pm. Outside **TSBank** is a Plus/Visa **ATM**. **PExchange bureaus** litter the city, but rates are much higher in summer and on weekends.

American Express: Megatours, Slivnitsa 33 (tel. 22 00 47; fax 22 00 61), in the Hotel Cherno More. They hold mail, sell traveler's checks, cash them (3% fee), and give cash advances for a 4.5% commission. AmEx, Diner's Club, MC, Visa accepted. **Free maps** of downtown. Open Mon.-Fri. 9am-6:30pm, Sat. 9am-noon.

Flights: From the airport (tel. 442 32), take bus #409 to the cathedral. **Balkan Airlines,** Knyaz Boris I 15 (tel. 22 29 48). There are flights to Sofia, Kiev, and Odesa.

Trains: Near the commercial port by the shore. To: Sofia (7 per day; 7hr.; 422lv, 200lv extra for *couchette*); Plovdiv (2 per day, 5½-7hr., 336lv); Burgas, and Ruse. **Rila** international trains bureau, ul. Preslav 13 (tel. 22 62 73 or 22 62 88), sells tickets to Budapest, Athens, and Istanbul. Open Mon.-Fri. 8am-6pm, Sat. 8am-2pm.

Buses: ul. Vladislov Varnenchik (Владислов Варненчик). Buses are the best way to and from Burgas (6 per day, 3hr., 330lv). **Group Travel,** ul. Knyaz Boris I 6 (tel. 25 67 34), hidden under a SONY sign, sends buses to Sofia (2 per day, 6½hr., 700lv; open daily 8:30am-5pm). International buses run to Warsaw (Tues. 6pm, 40hr., DM100). Buy tickets in advance. 10% discount for students and seniors.

Ferries and Hydrofoil: At the passenger port (Морска Гара; *Morska Gara;* tel. 22 23 26). Ferries go between coast resorts and are a pleasant alternative to hot, crowded buses. Cashier open 1hr. before departure. **Information kiosk** open Mon.-Fri. 7am-7pm. Daily **ferries** (hydro-buses) depart from Varna at 8:30am for Sveti Constantin (40min., 130lv), Golden Sands (1½hr., 220lv), and Balchik (2½hr., 370lv). **Black Sea Shipping,** Tsaribrod 46 (Царибрoд; tel. 60 04 59), runs a **hydrofoil** service with their luxury ship, the *Seacat*. To: Nesebur (Wed., Sat., Sun.; 1½hr.; 480lv), Sozopol (Sun., 2½hr.,US$12), Istanbul (4hr., US$70). Children under 12 get a 50% discount. Cashier open 1hr. before departure.

Public Transportation: City buses cost 15lv (pay on bus). Look for the resort name on the front of the bus or minivan at the cathedral. Take bus #1 or trolley #82 or 86 from the train station to the cathedral, or walk.

Taxi: Outside train station. Or call 25 87 16. Cutthroat fixed rates to resorts.

Car Rental: Europcar, at AmEx (see above). Unlimited mileage US$65 and up; otherwise US$24 plus US$0.24 per km and up. 22% VAT not included.

Luggage Storage: At the train station. 20lv. Open daily 6-11:30am and noon-10pm.

Photocopies: Slivnitsa 41 (tel. 23 74 92; fax 60 00 36), off Knyaz Boris I. 8lv per page. They also find **private rooms** (price negotiable). Open Sun.-Fri. 8am-10pm.

Pharmacy: Knyaz Boris I 29 (tel. 22 22 87). Open Mon.-Fri. 7:30am-8pm, Sat.-Sun. 10am-5pm. Debur 2 (Дебър), off Tsar Simeon I. Open 24hr.

Post Office: bul. Suborni (Съборни). The office is across the street from the cathedral. Open Mon.-Fri. 7am-7pm, Sat. 7:30am-7pm, Sun. 8am-noon.

Telephones: At the post office. Open daily 7am-10pm. **Faxes** (fax 24 40 30) open Mon.-Fri. 7am-8:30pm, Sat. 8am-1pm. **Postal code:** 9000. **Phone code:** 52.

ACCOMMODATIONS

There may be more **private room bureaus** in Varna than private rooms. Reserve ahead in July and August. It is generally easier to find rooms in Varna or Burgas than in the resorts. Location determines the price. Aside from **Varnenski Bryag's** two offices (see above), **Isak** (Исак; tel. 60 23 18), at the train station, finds rooms for US$5-7 per person (open daily 6am-10pm).

Hotel Musala (Мусала), Musala 3 (tel. 22 39 25), next to Varnenski Bryag, is mediocre but affordable. Spartan but clean rooms and tiled-floor bathrooms. Singles with sink US$20. Doubles with basin US$15 per person.

Hotel Orel (Орел), bul. Primorski 131 (Приморски; tel. 22 42 30; fax 25 92 95), along the seaside gardens. Cool double and triple rooms with shared baths US$20 a person. The beach is 150m away. 24-hr. café to indulge cravings for *Astika* beer.

Hotel Orbita (Орбита), Tsar Osvoboditel 25 (tel. 22 51 62 or 22 13 04). So-called "luxury" rooms have satellite TV, fridge, phone, and radio with a private shower. Doubles US$30 per person. Singles US$45. Ask for 10% ISIC discount.

COASTAL TOWNS

1. Periprava
2. C.A. Rosetti
3. Sulina ⚓
4. Dunevăţo de Jos ▲
5. Babadag
6. Jurilovca
7. Sinoie
8. Istria
9. Săcele
10. Corbu
11. Mamaia-Sat ▲
12. Mamaia Băi ⚓
13. Constanţa ⚓
14. Cumpăna
15. Agigea ⚓
16. Eforie Nord ⚓
17. Eforie Sud ⚓▲
18. Vasile Roaită
19. Costineşti
20. Neptun ⚓
21. Jupiter ⚓▲
22. Venus ⚓▲
23. Saturn ⚓
24. Mangalia
25. Vama Veche
26. Durankulak
27. Krapets ▲
28. Shabla ▲
29. Tyulenovo
30. Kamen Bryag
31. Sveti Nikola
32. Rusalka ⚓
33. Bulgarevo
34. Tuzlata ⚓▲
35. Balchik ▲
36. Albena ⚓▲
37. Kranevo ▲
38. Zlatni Pyasutsi ⚓▲
39. Sveti Konstantin ⚓▲
40. Varna ⚓
41. Galata ▲
42. Kamchiya ⚓▲
43. Novo Oryahovo ▲
44. Shkorpilovtsi ▲
45. Byala ▲
46. Obzor ⚓▲
47. Emona ▲
48. Slunchev Bryag ▲
49. Nesebur ⚓▲
50. Ravda
51. Pomorie ▲
52. Saratovo
53. Burgas ⚓
54. Kraimorie ▲
55. Chernomorets ▲
56. Sozopol ⚓▲
57. Primorsko ⚓▲
58. Kiten ▲
59. Lozenets ▲
60. Tsarevo ▲
61. Varvara
62. Ahtopol ▲
63. Sinemorets ▲
64. Rezovo ▲

⚓ Towns with beach   ▲ Towns with campsite nearby

Hotel Odesa, bul. Slivnitsa 1 (tel. 22 53 12/13; fax 25 30 83). Walk toward the beach; it's on the right. Satellite TV, direct international phones, big bath, and balconies with views of the sea. Singles US$40, doubles US$30 per person.

FOOD

Pedestrian **Knyaz Boris I** and **Slivnitsa** swarm with cafés, kiosks, and vendors selling everything from foot-long hot dogs to corn-on-the-cob and cotton candy. Varna is a great place to pick up a bottle of locally produced *Albena* champagne (US$1 per bottle). The many restaurants along the beach have great seafood and are full of young people. The **"Happy" English Pub** (tel. 25 01 69; tel./fax 25 01 71), bursts with youth—staff and clientele. Walk down Preslav nearly to the end. "Happy" serves all your favorite Bulgarian dishes at moderate prices; the chef's specialty is pork filet stuffed with ham and mushrooms (210lv). *Pupesh s med* (Пъпеш с мед; melon with honey; 60lv) is a great finale (open daily 8am-midnight). The bright **Restaurant Musala** (Мусала; tel. 60 19 28), pl. Nezavisimost, stirs up goulash for 350lv, *purzheni tikvichk* (fried zucchini with milk sauce; 140lv). Imaginative cocktails like the Zombie run 160lv, and desserts 89lv—try the *crème caramel* (open daily 9am-11pm, music from 8pm). **Café Casablanca,** Krustyo Mirski 1 (tel. 22 82 79), off Preslav, has wonderful cake (80-90lv) and huge *melbas* (мелба; ice cream; 150lv) in a setting reflected in the prices—treat yourself (open 8am-midnight). **Baba Tonka** (Баба Тонка), a tiny sweets booth without tables on Tsar Simeon, cooks up delicious *palachinkas*—thin pancakes filled with apple jam (15lv). Various pastries (20-30lv) make a great breakfast for under US$0.50 (open daily 6am-8pm).

SIGHTS AND ENTERTAINMENT

As you stroll along the **Seaside Gardens,** peep inside the **Marine Museum** (Военноморски Музей; *Voennomorski Muzej*; tel. 22 26 55), which presents the history of navigation on the Black Sea and the Danube River. Rusty ships, torpedoes, and even a helicopter clutter the yard. Look for the periscope of the first Bulgarian submarine (open 10am-6pm, tickets sold until 5:30pm; 70lv, students 40lv, photos 100lv). The **Akvarium** (Аквариум) features a stuffed monarch seal and some lively fish (open Mon. noon-5pm, Tues.-Sun. 9am-7pm; 80lv, children 60lv). The **Dolphinarium** (tel. 82 60 69), in the north part of the park, has half-hour shows at 11am, 2pm, and 3:30pm (open Tues.-Sun.; 740lv, children 2-10 370lv; ticket office open Tues.-Sun. 10am-4pm). Take bus #8, 9, or 14 or walk through the Seaside Gardens. On the way, you'll pass by the **zoo.** Hidden among the fountains and trees is a vine-covered **open-air theater,** home of international ballet competitions and festivals (May-Oct.). Buy tickets at the gate or the ticket office near Hotel Cherno More (Хотел Черно Море).

In the city's old quarter—**Grutska Mahala** (Гръцка Махала)—stand well preserved **Roman Baths** (Римски Терми; *Rimski Termi*) on San Stefano (open Tues.-Sun. 10am-5pm). Bulgaria's second-largest cathedral, **Sv. Bogoroditsa,** is in the city center across from the post office between Maria Luisa and Saborni. It was built in 1882-86 in honor of Russian soldiers who fought for the liberation of Bulgaria. At ul. L. Karavelov 1 (Л. Каравелов) near the cathedral, an exquisite **art gallery** hosts chamber concerts; get a schedule at the tourist bureau (the sign "free day Monday" means it's closed then). **Ethnographski Museum** (Етнографски Музей), Panagyurishte 22 (Панагюрище), in a traditional National Revival structure, makes for a cool break from the hot summer sun (open Tues.-Sun. 10am-5pm).

The **Opera House** (tel. 22 33 88, reservations tel. 22 30 89) on the main square, has a reduced summer schedule: inquire at the ticket office. Performances (50lv) start at 7:30pm. The beautiful, sandy, family dominated **beaches** can be reached through the Seaside Gardens (30lv). **Nightlife** centers around pl. Nezavisimost and ul. Knyaz Boris I. A popular hangout for younger crowds is the **festival complex,** with a cinema and disco. The music festival **Varnensko Lyato** (Варненско Лято) goes on for about six weeks, beginning in mid-June. Hotel Orbita's **disco** is popular with students (open nightly 11pm-sunrise). In summer, a good number of discos and bars open by the beach. Try **Spider** (tel. 25 00 22), close to the port. Dance the night away under glowing arachnids (gets better after midnight). Every August, Varna chills out during its **International Jazz Festival;** for the cynical, the **"Love is Folly" film festival,** takes place in the halls of the festival complex.

■ North of Varna

BALCHIK (БАЛЧИК)

An underrated jewel among the northern seaside resorts, **Balchik** captivates with its simple and spontaneous beauty, dotted with orange roofed white houses carved into rocky cliffs. Winding roads and crooked stairways lead to sun-kissed beaches. This sleepy fishing village is a perfect base for a Northern Black Sea Coast vacation, with most conveniences of a resort but not the high prices and crowds. Right before you reach the beachside Fisherman's square (Рибарски, *Ribarski*), you will find a lively **outdoor market,** and vegetarian heaven. The **public beach** at Balchik is small but clean (30lv). Showers, changing rooms, bar, volleyball, umbrellas (100lv), and *pedallo* rental (300lv per hour). At Romanian Queen Marie's summer **palace,** sit in her marble throne, gaze at the sea, then tour the **Botanical Gardens'** rose garden and the largest cactus collection in the Balkans (open daily 8am-8pm; palace open daily 10am-5pm; 200lv, student ID 50lv). At night, relax at a beachside café or dance at **Cariba disco** right on the beach (10pm til sunrise; free).

Take a **bus** from Varna (7-9 per day, 1hr., 100lv); **minivans** next to the Varna bus station make the trip faster and charge the same price (they leave when full). From Balchik's bus station, walk downhill on Cherno More (Черно Море) to the main square, **Nezavisimost** (Независимост). Ul. Primorska (Приморска) runs to the shore. **Balkan Bank,** Nezavisimost 7 (tel. 24 55), accepts traveler's checks (5% commission; open Mon.-Fri. 8:15am-4pm). **Dobroudzhanska Banka** (Добруджанска Банка), Cherno More 17, also changes money (open Mon.-Fri. 9-11:30am and 2-4pm). In the main square lies the **post office** (open Mon.-Fri. 8am-7pm, Sat. 8am-1pm, **telephones** and **fax** open daily 7am-9:30pm; fax 31 00). **Postal code:** 9600. **Phone code:** 0579.

Hotel **Esperanza** (Хотел Есперанса), Cherno More 16 (tel. 51 48), is small with spacious rooms and shared baths (US$7 per person). A satellite TV plays in the common room, and a kitchen is available. Hotel **Dionysopolis** (Хотел Дионисополис), Primorska 1 (tel./fax 21 75), the street parallel to the beach, sports rooms with baths, phones, balcony views of the sea, and an occasional cockroach. Pay in US$ or DM only (doubles US$24-30, apartments sleep three for US$42). Dozens of nameless food joints advertise their menus on chalkboards along the beach (250lv assures a healthy meal). One eatery worthy of note is **Emona** (Емона), Emona 14. From the beach, work up an appetite by climbing the ivy-covered stairs to the restaurant. A sign leads the way 15m down Cherno More from Hotel Esperanza, to delicious fish and chicken dishes and unrivaled view of the harbor from the ship-like building. A full meal runs less than US$3 (open daily 10am-midnight).

GOLDEN SANDS (ЗЛАТНИ ПЯСЪЦИ)

Golden Sands (*Zlatni Pyasutsi*), 17km north of Varna, has exquisite, though crowded (July-Aug.), beaches. A tourist trap in every sense of the word, it is a monstrous labyrinth of 74 hotels, numerous campgrounds, 30 restaurants, 30 discos, and 70 stores all built in Stalin's favorite architectural style. The beach is lined with attractive ways to lose your money: dip into a massaging **jacuzzi** (200lv per 5min.), play **tennis** (900-1500lv per hour; equipment included), rent a **bike** (500lv per hr.), go **horseback riding** (around US$15), **windsurf** (340lv per hr.), or rent a **pedallo** (300lv per hr.). A number of boats at the marina offer 30-hour **fishing excursions** (US$18 per person), **night cruises** (US$10), or trips to Balchik (US$26). Water-sports facilities are provided by **Sirena Sport and Animation Center** (tel. 85 62 38; 150lv), among others. A run down their winding **water slide** goes for 100lv.

From Varna, take **bus** #9, 109, 209, 309, and 409 (every 15min., 40min., 45lv) from the cathedral. Private minivans *en route* to or from Albena, Balchik, or Kavarna leave from the Varna bus station. Stop first at the 24-hour **reception** and **accommodations office** (tel. 85 56 81; fax 85 55 87), the last building on the lane with the **police station,** to obtain an invaluable resort **map,** and arrange for pricey **hotel rooms** (bed in double US$20-32) or more affordable **bungalows** (at Panorama US$7, at Oasis US$13). Many **currency exchanges** on the beachfront accept traveler's checks. **Business Bank** (tel. 88 60 70), next to Restaurant Casino, does MC/Visa/Diner's Club credit card advances (7% commission) and cashes traveler's checks for a 5% fee (open in summer daily 8:30am-11pm). **Laundry** facilities can be found in most hotels. The post office is on the beachfront, featuring international **phones** and **faxes** (open daily 8:30am-8pm; phones and faxes open in summer daily 8am-10:30pm, off-season Mon.-Fri. 8:30am-4pm; fax 85 61 40). **Postal code:** 9007. **Phone code:** 052.

Dozens of beachside restaurants compete for tourists' attention like contestants in a beauty pageant; unfortunately, competition hasn't driven prices down. Expect to pay around US$10 for a full restaurant meal. **Restaurant Kaliakra** (Калиакра; tel. 85 52 45), coexists with the beer hall **DAB**; the German/Bulgarian cuisine is quite expensive, but, so is the whole resort—a meal with wine is around 2000lv (US$12; open daily 11am-midnight; live music after 7pm). Warm beer flows at **Golden Lion,** an English pub; spin the roulette wheel at **Shipka Casino.** The organized **Equestrian Picnic** at **Bear's Meadow** includes entertainment and food (all you can eat and drink; US$23). Opportunities for nightly entertainment abound—find a floor show or stage a show of your own at the **disco Malibu** by the beach til sunrise (men pay 200lv).

ALADZHA MANASTIR (АЛАДЖА МАНАСТИР)

Known as the *skalen* (rock) monastery, **Aladzha Monastery** (tel. 85 54 60) was carved out of a mountain side 14km from Varna in the 13th-14th century (open June-Oct. 9am-6pm; Nov.-May Tues.-Sun. 10am-5pm; 150lv, students 80lv). No written source about the monastery exists, and its Christian name remains a mystery (*"Aladzha"* is Turkish for "patterned"). The monastery's two levels were carved in the 40m limestone cliff. The second level chapel, once reachable by a wooden corkscrew stairwell, preserves a likeness of Madonna with child and other frescos. 800m northeast you will find the **catacombs,** a group of three-level caves, the former homes of hermits. An **art gallery,** to the left as you enter the premises of the monastery, exhibits medieval mural paintings. An excellent guide and picture book (100lv) in English is available at the ticket office. Take **bus** #29 from the Varna cathedral to the foot of a hill, minutes from the monastery (only 2 per day, ½hr., 35lv). If you miss it, take #53 and get off at the fork "Golden Sands—Aladzha monastery". Going left and up it's a 15-minute hike. On the way down, have a snack at the small **café** serving crab cocktail and fried fish, or dine at **Lovna Sreshta** (Ловна Среща; tel. 85 51 90), for thrice the price. Wild boar (520lv) and various fish (240-520lv) top the menu, and when a large group wishes, mind-boggling outdoor folk shows feature *"Nestinari dancers"*—dancers prancing barefoot on hot coals (open daily 11am-2am; show 9:30-10:30pm, call ahead to see if the show will go on).

■ Burgas (Бургас)

Burgas, used mainly as a transport link to the villages and beaches of the south coast, is decidedly underrated by tourists. More industrial than Varna, Burgas more honestly represents a typical Bulgarian city with its lively and attractive center, connected to the beach via fresh Seaside Gardens. Approaching the outskirts, the salty breeze mixes with the scent of the largest oil refinery in Bulgaria—stick to the center.

ORIENTATION AND PRACTICAL INFORMATION

The Burgas **bus** and **train stations** are near the port at **Garov pl.** (Гаров). Across the street is the main pedestrian **Aleksandrovska** (Александровска). The tourist office is on the corner. To the right, pedestrian **Aleko Bogoridi** (Алеко Богориди) leads to seaside **Demokratsia** (Демокрация), beyond which are the seaside gardens and beach. On the other side is **Ferdinandova** (Фердинандова).

Tourist Office: Menabria Tours, ul. Aleksandrovska 2 (tel. 472 75), at the corner of pl. Garov, arranges private rooms (800lv per person), provides free outdated maps, sells **bus** tickets to Sofia (1 per day, 6½lv, 600lv) and Istanbul (1 per day, 10hr., 3000lv), and organizes boat trips to Istanbul (US$195 and up).

Currency Exchange: Balkan Bank, pl. Svoboda 2 (tel. 485 61), exchanges cash, accepts traveler's checks (3% fee, only leva returned), and gives Visa advances. Open Mon.-Fri. 8:30-11:30am and 1:15-3:30pm, Sat.-Sun. 1-8:30pm. Many private bureaus take AmEx traveler's checks. **United Bulgarian Bank** (Обедине на Българска Банка), runs a Maestro **ATM** on the left side of Aleksandrovska as you approach pl. Svoboda from the trains.

Trains: To: Ruse (1 per day, 6hr., 244lv); Sofia via Plovdiv or Karlovo (1 per day, 7hr., 314lv; express 6hr., 364lv); Varna (1 per day, 4½hr., 160lv).

Buses: Station **Yug** (Юг) by the train station serves the Black Sea coast. Station **Zapad** (Запад), take bus #4 from the train station, sends buses inland. To: Ruse (1 per day, 4hr., 560lv); Sofia (1 on Mon., Wed., and Fri.; 6½hr., 244lv); Varna (6 per day, 3hr., 330lv). In the lobby of Hotel Bulgaria tickets are sold for the Group, Kalea, and Turserviz bus lines to Sofia, Odesa, and more. Open daily 9am-6pm.

Taxi: tel. 145. (35-45lv per km).

Pharmacy: Bogoridi. Open Mon.-Fri. 8:30am-8pm, Sat.-Sun. 10am-8pm.

Luggage Storage: Near bus and train station. Look for the big "Гардероб" sign. 20lv per day. Open daily 6am-10:30pm.

Post Office: ul. Tsar Petur (Цар Петър), parallel to Aleksandrovska. Open Tues.-Fri. 7am-8pm, Sat. 8am-6pm, Mon.7am-8pm.

Telephones: At the new post office, bul. Osvobozhdenie 70 (Освобождение). From the bus/train station, ride 4 stops on bus #211. Open 24hr. **Phone code:** 052.

ACCOMMODATIONS AND FOOD

Private rooms in Burgas are plentiful, affordable (about 800lv), and often conveniently located. Secure them at **Menabria Tours** (see above) or other accommodations bureaus. Burgas is not a haven of cheap youth hostels, but should you shun a private room, try one of the two not-too-expensive hotels. **Hotel Park** (tel. 319 51), in the Seaside Gardens (take bus #4 from the center), offers clean rooms with balcony, shower, and phone (doubles 6240lv, single travelers in doubles 4920lv; restaurant on premises). **Kraimorie Campground** (Къмпинг Краймориe; tel. 240 25), 10km from Burgas by hourly bus #17, rents out motel rooms by wide, clean beaches and tennis courts (doubles US$10, bungalows US$8).

Ul. Bogoridi is full of restaurants and cafés. If you choose to feast near the waves, walk up the alley along the beach and look around. There are many places—from homely kiosks to refashioned ships—serving fish and seafood, especially at the north end of the Seaside Gardens, opposite the train station. Aleksandrovska and Bogorodi are awash with hamburger joints and ice cream stands. **Art Restaurant** (Арт Ресторан; tel. 422 39), on Bogoridi in the courtyard of the "CDC" building, cools you off with the shade of a huge fig tree and a mini fountain to get you ready for some healthy fish portions (130-250lv). A great place for dessert—try a Bulgarian interpretation of the banana split (106lv) or some *palachinki* (pancakes) with fruit, cream, and chocolate (98lv; 5% service charge; English menu; open daily 10am-midnight). Even further down Bogoridi, on the right just before the Seaside Gardens, the loud **Restaurant Odesa** (Одеса) serves national specialties (159-329lv), salads (45-75lv) and *mish-mash* (a local vegetarian specialty of peppers, eggs, and cheese; 80lv), on a terrace overlooking the stream of people at night. Live music gets especially lively on weekends. **Starata Gemiya** (Старата Гемия; tel. 457 08), aboard a ship behind Hotel Primoretz, specializes in seafood (150-250lv). Mackerel baked on a clay shingle with homemade sauce, onions, and spices (*skumriya na kremida,* скумрия на кремида) wets mouths at 150lv (open daily 10am-midnight).

SIGHTS AND ENTERTAINMENT

The center of Burgas—Aleksandrovska and Bogoridi—is colorful, friendly, unimposing, and filled with happy foreigners and young Bulgarians. The walkway along the beach affords a pleasant stroll, and the sand strip is nowhere near as overrun as in Varna—although ecologically it leaves something to be desired. When you have a sea next door, you don't worry much about creating other sights. One of them, the **Armenian Church,** Bogoridi, behind Hotel Bulgaria, shelters bells which awaken the neighborhood each morning (open Tues.-Fri. 9am-2pm and 4-6:30pm, Sat. 9am-noon and 4-6pm, Sun. 9am-noon). The **Archaeological Museum,** Bogorodi 21 (tel. 452 41), houses the oldest marble statue found in Bulgaria (5th century BCE; open Mon.-Fri. 9am-noon and 2-5pm; 60lv, French guide 150lv). At night, try the **Black Sea Nightclub** near Hotel Primoretz (open 24hr., nightly live performances).

■ Near Burgas

NESEBUR (НЕСЕБЪР)

Nesebur, a museum town atop the peninsula at the south end of Sunny Beach, is a sweet alternative to generic coastal tourist ghettos, though it gets crowded in high season. Medieval churches and Thracian, Byzantine, and Roman ruins dot the town, sometimes referred to as the jewel of Bulgaria's Black Sea coast. A walk through Nesebur's **Old Town** is a genuine walk through time. Stone **fortress walls** (3rd century CE) survive on the north shore. The Byzantine **gate** and **port** date back to the 5th century. A 6th-century **Metropolitan Church** survives roofless in Nesebur's center. The temple of **John the Baptist,** now an art exhibit, has been around since the 10th century. The 11th-century **Church of St. Stephen** is plastered in 16th-century frescoes. The **Church of Jesus Pancrator** in the main square dates from the 13th century, and in summer doubles as an art gallery (open daily 9am-11pm; free). The **Church of St. Spas** (1609) on Mitropolitska, offers a written tour in English about its 17th-century frescos. The gravestone of a Byzantine princess is found inside (open Mon.-Fri. 9:30am-5pm, Sat.-Sun. 9:30am-1:30pm; 50lv). The **Archaeological Museum** (tel. 60 18), to the right of the town gate, exhibits a fascinating collection of ceramics, coins, icons and naval implements (English tours arranged; 200lv per group; open daily 9am-1:30pm, 2-7pm; 90lv). The **Ethnographic Museum,** Mesembria 32, in a two-story National Revival house (first floor made of stone, second made of wood with bay windows and carved ceilings) has an exhibit on clothes and fabric from the Burgas region. **Artists** sell wares along the alleys and in front of churches and ruins.

Get to Nesebur by **bus** from Burgas (every 40min., 40min., 100lv) or Varna (6 per day, 2hr., 230lv) or by **hydrofoil** from Varna (see Varna, p. 138). Buses stop at the Old Nesebur port and gate leading to town. The main **Mesembria** goes right while **Mitropolitska** goes left at the central square fork. The town is small but intricate, so stop by **Tourist Bureau Mesembria** (tel. 28 55; fax 60 11), and get a map; from the bus stop, walk right (facing the town). The staff sells bus tickets to Sofia (1 per day, 7hr.) with **Adress** (900lv) and **Kalea** (850lv) and arranges **accommodations** (US$10-11 per person; open in summer daily 8am-8pm, winter Mon.-Fri. 8am-5pm). At the city entrance on Mesembria, **TSBank exchanges currency,** gives Visa cash advances, and cashes traveler's checks (open 9am-3pm). **Commercial Bank Biochim,** Mesembria 19 (tel. 3229), gives cash advances on Diner's Club, MC, and Visa (5% commission; open Mon.-Fri. 8:30am-4:30pm). **Private exchange offices** accept traveler's checks with better rates. The **post office** is in the main square (open daily 8am-6pm; **phones** open daily 7am-10pm). **Postal code:** 8231. **Phone code:** 0554.

In high season, it may be difficult to find a room for less than a three-night stay. **Mesembria Hotel,** Mesembria 14a (tel. 32 55), near the post office, has singles for US$32, doubles for US$24 per person. People will approach you on the street with rooms to let for US$3-5. It is cheaper and easier to find a bed across the isthmus on the mainland. **Hotel Panorama** (Панорама; tel. 32 83) has clean doubles with bathrooms and terraces (US$12 per person; breakfast included). For the hotel, follow the left street at the fork coming out of the Old Town and walk uphill for five minutes.

Along the harbor, munch on fresh fish with fries and *shopska* salad for US$3 at street **kiosks**. Or order steaming-hot seafood and add fresh veggies from the **farmers' market**. **Captain's Table** (Капитанска Среща; *Kapitanska Sreshta*), Chaika (Чайка; tel. 34 29), serves up superbly prepared treasures of the sea. "Breakfast for the hungover with spicy sauce" goes for 485lv, and the specialty, "Captain Peter's fiery mixture", is 460lv. Groove to the nightly live music from 6-11pm (open daily 8am-midnight). All the way up Mitropolitska, **Neptun** (Нептун; tel. 41 33), overlooking the sea, serves delicate rabbit "hunter's style" (430lv; open daily 10am-midnight).

SOZOPOL (СОЗОПОЛ)

Sozopol was formerly the resort of choice for Bulgaria's artistic community, and still caters to a more creative set than its Black Sea neighbors. The town is quieter and less expensive than Nesebur or Golden Sands and works to fill the needs of visitors who don't travel in tour buses. Sozopol, 34km south of Burgas (hourly **buses**, between 5am-8pm, 45min,80lv), is Bulgaria's most ancient Black Sea town, settled in 610BCE. Its **Old Town** sits on a rocky peninsula; century-old houses line its cobbled streets. The **bus station** is in the middle of a park connecting the Old and New Towns. At the end of the park, turn left on Republikanska (Републиканска) toward the New Town. Tourist bureau **Lotos** operates at the bus station (tel./fax 282) and in the New Town main square, Ropotamo 1 (Ропотамо; tel. 429). The staff arranges private rooms (US$7 per person) and organizes trips (open daily 8am-5pm). **TSBank**, opposite, cashes traveler's checks and gives Visa card advances (open Mon.-Fri. 9am-3pm). The **post office** is in the Old Town, a block past the bus station on main **Apolonia** street (open Mon.-Fri. 7am-8pm; Sat.-Sun. 7-11am and 2-8pm); **phones** daily 7am-9:45pm; send or receive **faxes** at fax 306 daily 7:30am-8pm). **Postal code**: 8130. **Phone code**: 5514.

Private rooms abound and can be arranged at tourist agencies (see above) or with locals (US$3-5 per person); rooms get scarce in high season, and it is almost impossible to get one for less than a three night stay. **Zlatna Ribka** (Златна Рибка) camping is a five-minute bus or ten-minute boat ride away. **Camping Kavatsite** (Каваците; 3km away; tel. 354), **Chernomorets** (Черноморец; 10km away) and **Gradina** (Градина; halfway between the two) can be reached by bus. Contact **Lotos** (see above). **Hotel Radik** (Радик), Republikanska 4 (tel. 17 06), offers doubles, floor baths, and a panoramic view for US$6 per person. Across the street, **Hotel Alpha-Vita** (tel. 18 52) offers similar accommodations and prices. Apolonia is the site of an **artists' park** and home to many **kiosks** offering fresh fried fish and calamari. For a delicious meal, walk to **Restaurant Vyaturna Melnitsa** (Вятърна Мелница), Morski Skali (Морски Скали; tel. 844), the street running along the tip of the peninsula. The specialty *gyuvech* is a meat and potato dish served over a live flame in exquisite clay pots (215lv; nightly folk show; entrées 130-250lv; open daily 8am-midnight). **Restaurant Orpheus** (Орфей), Kiril i Metodii (tel. 1749), has tables in the privacy of a courtyard overlooking the sea. Get a vitamin fix with their vegetable soup (60lv) and colorful "south coast" salad (200lv; open daily 11am-late). For a little pre-dinner adventure, take a **boat cruise** (1hr., 200lv) from the seaport around Sozopol and take a peek at the two adjacent islands, St. Peter and St. Ivan. The best time to go is around sunset. One of the most popular night spots is the misleadingly named **Country Club,** right on the beach. Look out for rave nights (open daily 10pm-sunrise; men pay 50lv). Every September, Sozopol hosts the **Arts Festival Apolonia**—artists, actors, and their friends move here for a while.

PRIMORSKO (ПРИМОРСКО)

Young Bulgarians think of Primorsko as site of the **International Youth Center**, where the best *komsomoltsy* and pioneers were once sent to strengthen international comradeship. Today, premier Zhivkov would blush at this rocking, inexpensive resort with scantily-clad foreign youths. At the manicured **beach,** equipped with dunes and some of the cleanest Black Sea water, you can rent *pedallos* at 200lv per hr.; in the oak forest, play **tennis** (US$6 per hr., equipment US$2), volleyball, basketball, or handball (fields cost US$5 per hr.). The complex also has a **medical center**, open-air **theater, cinema, and mini-casino**. The **tourist office** (tel. 21 01) in **Hotel Druzhba** (Хотел Дружба) has maps and books hotel rooms (doubles US$20) and bungalows (US$4-10 per person). People will also approach you with **private room** offers (300lv per person). To reach the **Youth Center**, walk beyond the post office then take a left at the big intersection. Cross the bridge over Devil's River (Дяболска Река) and keep going for another 10 minutes to reach the entrance to the center (30-min. walk; a cab shouldn't cost more than US$1). Behind the shopping center **Stop**, the **information office** (tel. 2101) has maps and books hotel rooms (US$13 per person) and bungalows (US$4-10 per person; US$13 with bath). If all are full, they'll try to arrange a private room (open daily 8am-5pm). Take a southbound coastal **bus** from Burgas (on the hour, 1½hr., 134lv) to the main street, **Cherno More** (Черно Море). **Exchange money** at a kiosk near the bus station (cash only; open daily 8am-8:30pm). The **post office** and phones are nearby (open Mon.-Fri. 7:30am-noon and 2:30-6pm; phones daily 7am-9am). **Postal code:** 8290. **Phone code:** 5561.

АНТОРОL (АХТОПОЛ)

Ahtopol, 25km from the Turkish border, is a humble town of 1400 inhabitants. The man-made attractions are few. Yet hidden rocky bays with crystal clear water and the highest seawater temperature of all Bulgarian resorts more than make up the difference. The public **beach** (40lv) competes with several small bays (try the one at the lighthouse). Watch fishermen throw their bait off the quay. A couple of **discos** operate til sunrise by the beach. Get there by **bus** from Burgas (4 per day, 2½hr., 210lv). The bus station is on the main **Trakia** (Тракия) street. All points of interest are within a 15-minute walking radius. **Tourist bureau CREDO-OK** is at the bus station (tel. 340). Helpful staff provides free **maps, private rooms** (US$3-4 per person), and sells **bus tickets** to Sofia (2 per day, 7½hr., 900lv). Bus excursions to Istanbul also arranged (US$50). An **exchange bureau** is on the way to the post office (open daily 9am-1pm and 4-7pm). The **post office** is at the end of Trakia (open Mon.-Fri. 7:30am-noon and 2:30-6pm; phones daily 7:30am-10pm). **Postal code:** 8280. **Phone code:** 995563.

Private rooms are the accommodations of choice (US$3-4), but a few private hotels also exist. Try **Valdi** (Валди; tel. 320), Mitko Palauzov (Митко Палаузов). Take a left on Veleka (Велека) from Trakia, then a right on Cherno More (Черно Море). You'll see it on the right. Clean doubles with shower US$7-8 per person. The small town leads a surprisingly active culinary life. It is busiest along **Kraimorska** (Крайморская)—left and right off Trakia at the quai. On the other side of Trakia, **Restaurant Sirius** (Сириус; tel. 413), Kraimorska, offers cheap grills (40-80lv) and fish (50-350lv) amid mythic Greek scenes painted on the fence and live music (open daily noon-2am). Left and up the street is **Chetirimata Kapitana** (Четиримата Капитана; tel. 366), Kraimorska 29. Draped in fishing nets, it offers imaginatively named and prepared dishes (160-430lv; open daily noon-midnight).

CROATIA (HRVATSKA)

US$1	= 5.23kn (Kuna)	1kn =	US$0.19
CDN$1	= 3.81kn	1kn =	CDN$0.26
UK£1	= 8.16kn	1kn =	UK£0.12
IR£1	= 8.48kn	1kn =	IR£0.12
AUS$1	= 4.13kn	1kn =	AUS$0.24
NZ$1	= 3.64kn	1kn =	NZ$0.27
SAR1	= 1.18kn	1kn =	SAR0.85
DM1	= 3.54kn	1kn =	DM0.28

Country Phone Code: 385 **International Dialing Prefix: 00**

Although Croatia's capital lies in the country's flatlands, most tourists flock to the ancient cities and enchanting islands of the lengthy coast. Only a few of them find sand, but the beauty of the rugged mountains rising up from the clear water more than compensates. An Italian influence can be felt in the food and architecture of the coastal cities, and there is a sizeable Serbian minority inland, but national pride is in evidence everywhere, from the discos to the cafés.

CROATIA ESSENTIALS

Irish and U.K. citizens don't need visas, but Americans, Australians, Canadians, New Zealanders, and South Africans do. Visas are valid for three months—free for Australian, Canadian, New Zealanders, and U.S. citizens, US$10 by personal check or money order for South Africans. If applying by mail, send an additional US$13.50 for FedEx return. See Essentials: Embassies and Consulates, p. 5. Single-entry visas take two days (regular service) or one day (rush service) to process; multiple-entry visas take up to ten days. Australian, Canadian, Irish, British, and U.S. nationals may procure single-entry visas at the border, but for expediency's sake, travelers are advised to obtain one prior to arriving. Visas can be renewed at a local police station.

GETTING THERE AND GETTING AROUND

By plane or train, Zagreb is the main entry point. **Croatia Airlines** flies there from many cities, including Chicago, Frankfurt, London, New York, Paris, and Toronto, before continuing to Dubrovnik and Split (info and reservations tel. (041) 451 244; fax 451 415). **Trains** travel to Zagreb from Budapest, Ljubljana, and Vienna, continuing to many additional destinations in northern Croatia. On the schedules posted around the stations, *odlazak* means departures, *dolazak* arrivals.

Slow, stuffy, and hellishly crowded, **buses** are sometimes more convenient than trains, and occasionally the only option. From Zagreb, they run to Dubrovnik and Split. To reach Istria, travel from Koper or Portorož in Slovenia to Poreč or Pula. Tickets are sold on the bus, as well as at the station. In theory, luggage (including backpacks) must be stowed—and paid for—separately. Consider being brash and bringing it on; everyone else does, though it may be tight if the bus gets crowded.

Ferry service is run by **Jadrolinija.** Boats sail the Rijeka-Split-Dubrovnik route, stopping at some islands along the way. Ferries also float from Split to Ancona, Italy, and from Dubrovnik to Bari, Italy. Although even slower than buses, they're much more comfortable. The basic fare provides only a place on the deck. Cheap beds sell out fast, so purchase in advance for overnight international trips. Sometimes, the agency will only offer a basic ticket; in that case, *run* to get a bed. The second-best are reclining seats imported from the airport. There's a charge for these, but locals rarely pay. Heavy sleepers can snooze in the bar, or at least watch TV. Additional local ferries and more expensive **hydrofoils** are run by private companies.

TOURIST SERVICES

Most major cities and sites have a public tourist office *(turist biro).* Some private agencies also crop up, like the two conglomerates **Kompas** and **Atlas,** associated with American Express. They exchange money and find private rooms, but have suffered from the war. Tourist offices are usually open weekdays 8am-6pm and Saturdays 8:30am-1:30pm; on the crowded coast, they may take a mid-day break and then stay open until 10pm, even on Sundays.

MONEY AND COMMUNICATION

Most banks, tourist offices, hotels, and transportation stations offer **currency exchange,** but **traveler's checks** are accepted by only a smattering of banks; even American Express offices in small cities refuse them. Croatia's monetary unit, the **kuna**—divided into 100 **lipa**—is theoretically convertible, but impossible to exchange abroad (except in Hungary and Slovenia). To change any leftover kunas back, ask a local friend who will do it for you or go to a private exchange (never a bank) that might bend the rules. **ATMs** are still rare, but their number is on the rise. Most banks give **MasterCard** or **Visa** (or both) **cash advances,** but only pricey stores, restaurants, and hotels accept plastic.

Mail from the U.S. arrives in 7-10 days; if addressed to *Poste Restante*, it will be held for 90 days at the main (not always the central) post office. **Post offices** usually have **telephones** available to the public; pay after you talk. Dial 993 85 42 88 for **AT&T Direct,** or 99 38 00 44 for **British Telecom Direct.** Technically, this operator assistance is free, but some phones demand a card or token, and actual calls to the United States are expensive (about 20kn per min.). Phones requiring a **telekarta** (phone card), available at newspaper stands and the post office, are replacing token phones.

LANGUAGE

A Slavic people, the Croats speak almost the same language as the Serbs, but write in Latin rather than Cyrillic characters. Words are pronounced exactly as they are written; *"č"* and *"ć"* are both pronounced "ch" (only a Croatian can tell them apart), *"š"* is *"sh",* and *"ž"* is a "zh" sound. The letter *"r"* is rolled, but when not next to any vowels, makes a sound as in "Brrrr!" In Zagreb and tourist offices, many know **English,** but the most popular coastal languages are **Italian** and **German.** Almost everyone involved in the tourist industry speaks the latter, and a few German phrases might prove invaluable in communicating with private room renters. For a little Croatian vocabulary help, see the Glossary, p. 774.

Street names, especially those christened after Communist officials, are changing, and *Tito* is now taboo. More mundanely, street designations on maps often differ from those on signs by *"-va"* or *"-a"* because of grammatical declensions.

HEALTH AND SAFETY

> **Emergency Numbers: Police:** tel. 92. **Fire:** tel. 93. **Ambulance:** tel. 94.

The **climate** is mild and continental around Zagreb, and Mediterranean along the coast. The palm-tree-lined Adriatic shoreline once served as a poor man's Italy.

Although Croatia is currently at peace, travel to areas once held by rebel Serb forces—the Slavnija and Krajina regions—is still extremely dangerous due to unexploded mines. Travel to the coast and islands is considered safe, but always check in advance. Many cities, including Dubrovnik, are only a few miles from the Bosnian border. Be careful; the peace is not an easy one. The **police** require foreigners to register with them within 24 hours of arriving in a new city. Hotels, campsites, and accommodations agencies should do this for you, but if you're staying with friends or finding your own room, you'll have to do it yourself. Failure to do so has led to arrest, imprisonment, and fines. Police may check foreigners anywhere, but are more likely to do so in areas that have seen war, including Zagreb and Dubrovnik. Otherwise, **crime,** especially violent crime, is quite low. Emergency numbers for the entire country are listed in the above white box.

Croatians are generally friendly toward foreigners, including Americans. Traveling for **women** is usually safe, though having a companion may help ward off an unreasonably large number of pick-up lines. Croatians are just beginning to accept the presence of **homosexuals** in their own society; discretion is still wise.

ACCOMMODATIONS AND CAMPING

Most **hotels** are expensive, with a 20-50% tourist surcharge, that can often be avoided by asking to pay in kuna. Special deals are supposed to entice vacationers to the Southern Adriatic. *Sobe* (rooms to let, synonymous with *Zimmer*) can be great, but prices are increasing. Sharing a double room with someone is significantly cheaper than trying to find a single. Agencies generally charge 30-50% more if you stay less than three nights. Bargain them down to a price 20% less than tourist offices charge, and check the room before paying. Organized **campgrounds,** open April or May to September or October, speckle the country and are usually packed. All accommodations are subject to a **tourist tax** of 5-10kn (another reason the police require foreigners to register). Arriving on a weekend may cause lodging problems.

FOOD AND DRINK

Because of the paucity of tourists, the supply of **restaurants** is smaller than before, but the war has multiplied the already plentiful **kiosks** offering fast food and Balkan specialties like *burek*, a layered pie packed with *sir* (cheese) or *meso* (meat). *Purica s mlincima* (turkey with pasta) is the national dish. Along the coast, try *lingje* (squid) or *prt* (smoked Dalmatian ham). *Pljeskavica* (a spicy meat pattie), a Bosnian Croat specialty, and *čevapčici* (ground beef dumplings) are also popular. *Sladoled* (ice cream) is always a welcome delight (2-3kn for a small scoop). Beware of the price of drinks, though—a small glass of Coke may set you back 10kn. You'll also be charged, per slice, for any bread eaten at restaurants.

CUSTOMS AND ETIQUETTE

Tipping is not expected, and when paying or receiving change for anything, money should be set on the counter, not passed hand to hand. **Clothing** is unpretentious in northern Croatia, but style becomes increasingly important as one moves farther south. Likewise, the rhythms of life change; on the southern islands, it is common to see people eating dinner at 10pm. If you ask someone how they're doing, they'll invariably answer, "thank you," often without answering the question. Many stores don't close until 8pm, with shorter weekend stints, but in warmer areas they may pause from noon to 6pm, re-opening for several hours in the evening. Generally, only restaurants are open between Saturday at noon and Monday at 8am.

LIFE AND TIMES

HISTORY

The ancestors of Croatia's modern day inhabitants settled the Adriatic's shores in the 6th-7th centuries. They were **Slavs** who followed an largely unknown native religion until **Catholicism** arrived slowly over the next two centuries. The Croats successfully resisted Charlemagne's attempts to gain control of their area, and King Tomislav (910-28) earned his country papal recognition, consolidating Croatian independence. King Zvonimir expelled the Byzantines and was crowned by Pope Gregory in 1076, decisively strengthening Croatia's orientation toward Catholic Europe.

In 1102, the Kingdom of Croatia-Slavonia entered as a junior partner into a dynastic **union with Hungary,** in which it preserved some independence in the form of *sabors* (noble assemblies) and *bans* (viceroys). This partnership would tie Croatia's history with that of Hungary for the next 800 years. Instability prevailed after 1241, when **Mongol** invaders swept through Eastern Europe, crushing the Hungarians at the Sajo River. Local rulers became more powerful at the expense of the Hungarian king of Hungary-Croatia until the kingdom's recovery in the late 14-15th centuries. During this period, other Balkan kingdoms—Serbia, Bulgaria, Albania, Moldova, Greek Constantinople, and Wallachia—fell to the Turks. After the Turkish victory over Hungary at Mohács in 1526, Croatia became an embattled, divided border region. Over the centuries, Turks and Hungarians tugged at the region, but Croats did not raise a unified cry of protest until the 19th century. After Hungarian was declared the official language and minority rights were curbed in the 1830s and 1840s, an **independence movement** began to emerge. When Hungary revolted against Austria in 1848, the Croats sided with the latter and convened a diet in Zagreb demanding self-government. **Josip Jelačic,** chief of the Zagreb diet, ordered Croatia to break with Hungary, proclaimed loyalty to the Austrian Emperor Franz Josef, and led an army toward Budapest to "end the rebellion in Hungary." Though defeated by the Hungarians at Pákozd in 1848, the struggle continued into 1849; Croat participation on the Habsburg side helped defeat the Magyars. But following a devastating defeat by Prussia in 1866, Austria was forced to grant a constitution and more independence to Hungary.

With the compromise of 1867, the empire became known as the **Austro-Hungarian Dual Monarchy,** though the Habsburgs retained the upper hand. Croatia-Slavonia, including Zagreb and Rijeka, became part of the **Hungarian kingdom,** while most of the coast, including Istra, Zadar, and Dubrovnik, was incorporated into the Austrian half of the kingdom. Initially, the Hungarian government adopted a liberal attitude, but between 1875 and 1890, Tisza's Liberal Party campaigned to Magyarize Hungary, re-instituting Hungarian as the only official language.

During **WWI,** Croatian troops fought on the side of the Germans along with the rest of Austria-Hungary, but from November 1914, political exiles proposed the idea of political unity between the Serb, Croat, and Slovene nations as a way to further independence. On October 29, 1918, after the collapse of the Central Powers, Croatia broke with Hungary and the Dual Monarchy. Austria-Hungary sued the Allies for peace on November 3, and on December 1 the **Kingdom of the Serbs, Croats, and Slovenes** (the original name for **Yugoslavia**) declared its independence, with two rival governments: the National Council in Zagreb and the Serb royal government in Belgrade. Croats and Slovenes demanded a federal state, but the Serbian monarch, King Alexander, failed to work for reconciliation, and proclaimed a dictatorship in 1929. In 1934, he was assassinated by Croat nationalists during a visit to Marseille.

In 1939, Croatia finally achieved **autonomous** administration and government. Neutral at the outbreak of WWII, Yugoslavia nearly joined the Axis for protection, but British-assisted Greek triumphs over Italy provoked a pro-Allied coup in Belgrade in 1941. Hitler diverted forces to smash Yugoslavia, and German bombers reduced Belgrade to rubble with the help of Hungary and Bulgaria. Italy annexed Split and parts of Slovenia, while Croatia and Serbia were occupied. WWII saw savage fighting between Serbs and Croats. The puppet state created by Croat **Ustaši** fascists under Ante Pavelić collaborated with the Germans and planned to exterminate the Serbian population. The Četniks, Serb royalist partisans—who included **Josip Broz Tito** in their ranks—fought against the Croats. Partisan resistance in Yugoslavia was fierce, led by effective Communists receiving Allied assistance, and headed by Tito, a half-Croat. Yugoslavia owed its liberation from German and Ustaši rule to these partisans, though so many groups contested control that Tito was unable to enter Zagreb til May 9, 1945, the day after German capitulation.

Yugoslav Croatia recovered Istra, Rijeka, the Adriatic islands, and Zadar from Italy after the war and became part of the Socialist Republic of Yugoslavia. In 1945, **Tito** placed all industry and natural resources under state control. Under his unchallenged rule Yugoslavia broke with Stalin in 1948, decentralized the administration, and proclaimed a federal republic in 1963. Ethnic rivalries were suppressed, and Yugoslavia became a relatively tolerant, prosperous Communist country. In 1971, the Croatian Communists asked for greater autonomy within Yugoslavia, and Tito, under pressure from the army, dismissed and replaced the entire leadership with more obedient Communists. Tito ruled until his death in 1980. Yugoslavia, with its volatile ethnic mix, proved highly susceptible to quick disintegration and descent into violence after Communism's wholesale defeat and collapse in Europe. In April 1990, the nationalist Franjo Tudjman was elected president of Croatia and the people of Croatia, following quickly on the heels of Slovenia's declaration, approved a referendum for **independence** on May 19, 1991. Autonomy was declared in April and tensions began to rise with the significant Serbian minority in the country which began to fear for their rights in the new country; Tudjman did little to allay these fears and a war broke out in the Serb-controlled **Krajina** that lasted until August. On January 15, 1992, Croatia was recognized as an independent country by the EC and an UNPROFOR presence kept any further fighting at bay. In early May of 1995, Croatia, frustrated with the continued lack of control of over one-half of its nominal territory, began an operation in Western Slavonia, and in August, seized the Krajina, expelling over 150,000 Serbs. Since a late-1995 agreement with the Serbs, there has been relative peace in Croatia, although tension is still high.

LITERATURE

The first Croatian texts date from the 9th century, and for the next six centuries, literature in Croatian confined itself almost entirely to translations of Europe's greatest literary hits. Renaissance influences from the West made their way to the Dalmatian coast in the 1500s when the first Croatian poets, such as **Marulić**, finally moved from devotional to secular writing. The 16th-century dramatist **Držić** and the 17th-century poet **Gundulić** raided Italy for models (of the literary type), combining them with influences from the oral traditions back home. After Dubrovnik's devastating 1667 earthquake, the focus of Croatian literature shifted north.

The largely German-speaking middle class and the constant fear of attack from the Ottoman Empire left little room for Renaissance and Reformation ideas. Then the Counter-Reformation hit the area with the work of the Franciscans and the Jesuits. Not only did these two orders expand education and establish Zagreb as a cultural center, but the most important Croatian authors in the 18th century were two Franciscans, **Filip Grabovac** and **Kačić-Miošić,** and the Slavonian **Matija Reljković.** The political domination of Croatia by Germany and Hungary threatened to become a linguistic domination in the following century—**Ljudevit Gaj** led the movement to reform and codify the vernacular as the standard literary language. It was with the work of the poet **Mažuranić** that the Revival of Croatian literature was established at last. **Šenoa**, 19th century's most important literary figure, played a key part in the formation of a literary public and in completing the work that Gaj had begun—ending the trend of the seemingly requisite terminal "c" in the family names of Croatian literary figures. Mirroring European trends of the later 1800s, prose dominated, especially that of **V. Novak** and **Kovačić.**

Poetry returned in multiple reincarnations in the 20th century, the first stimulated by Croatian Modernist **Matoš** and then by interwar avant-garde writers **Šimić, Ujević,** and **Krleža.** After WWII, Krleža fought to prevent **Socialist Realism** in the Socialist Republic. Following this rejection of outside influence, Croatian literature, led by the circle of writers around the journal *Krugovi (Circles),* returned full circle to its origins—exploitation of foreign models. In recent decades, post-modernism and feminism have had their influence as well.

CROATIA TODAY

The Bosnian Serbs' loss of Krajina to Croatia may cause increasing tensions, particularly as NATO, Russia, and the United States increase their presence in the area. As Croatia copes with the effects of the war, a burdened economy, and thousands of refugees from Bosnia, the euphoria of independence is long gone. Popular discontent with deteriorating standards of living is increasing, though the future seems increasingly brighter as Croatia continues with the necessary reforms, and trade and foreign investment in the country expands. In October 1995, an election was called and the Croatian Democratic Community party (HDZ) was re-elected; Tudjman remained president and Zlatko Matesa became the new prime minister. Croatia is trying to cozy up to the European Union, and most Croats are friendly to foreign tourists, even though many feel the U.S. let them down by not recognizing their independence for two years. With the problems associated with the war and exorbitant taxes, the cost of living remains high. Prices in Croatia are close to those in Italy—still not as high as those in much of northern Europe, but higher than those Central Europe.

Zagreb

After bearing much of the weight of the war, Croatia's "victory" has brought few rewards to Zagreb. Still, the city bears its burden well: the buildings are still brighter than those throughout much of Eastern Europe. Few foreigners, except for the military, venture here, but those who do are rewarded with wide streets opening into green parks and busy public squares. If many of the museums are still closed, shops

ZAGREB ■ 153

Zagreb

Arts and Crafts Museum, 6
Art Museum, 10
Bus Station, 23
Dolac Marketplace, 16
Ethnographic Museum, 5
Funicular, 8
Hotel Inter Continental, 3
Jelačić Palace, 13
Lotrešćak Tower, 11
Mimara Museum, 4
National Theater, 7
Post Office, 22
Priest's Tower Observatory, 15
Rauch Palace, 12
Rudolfova Vojarna, 1
St. Catherine's Church, 9
St. Mark's Church, 14
St. Stephen's Cathedral, 17
Studentski Center, 2
Train Station, 21
Youth Hostel Omladunski, 19

CROATIA

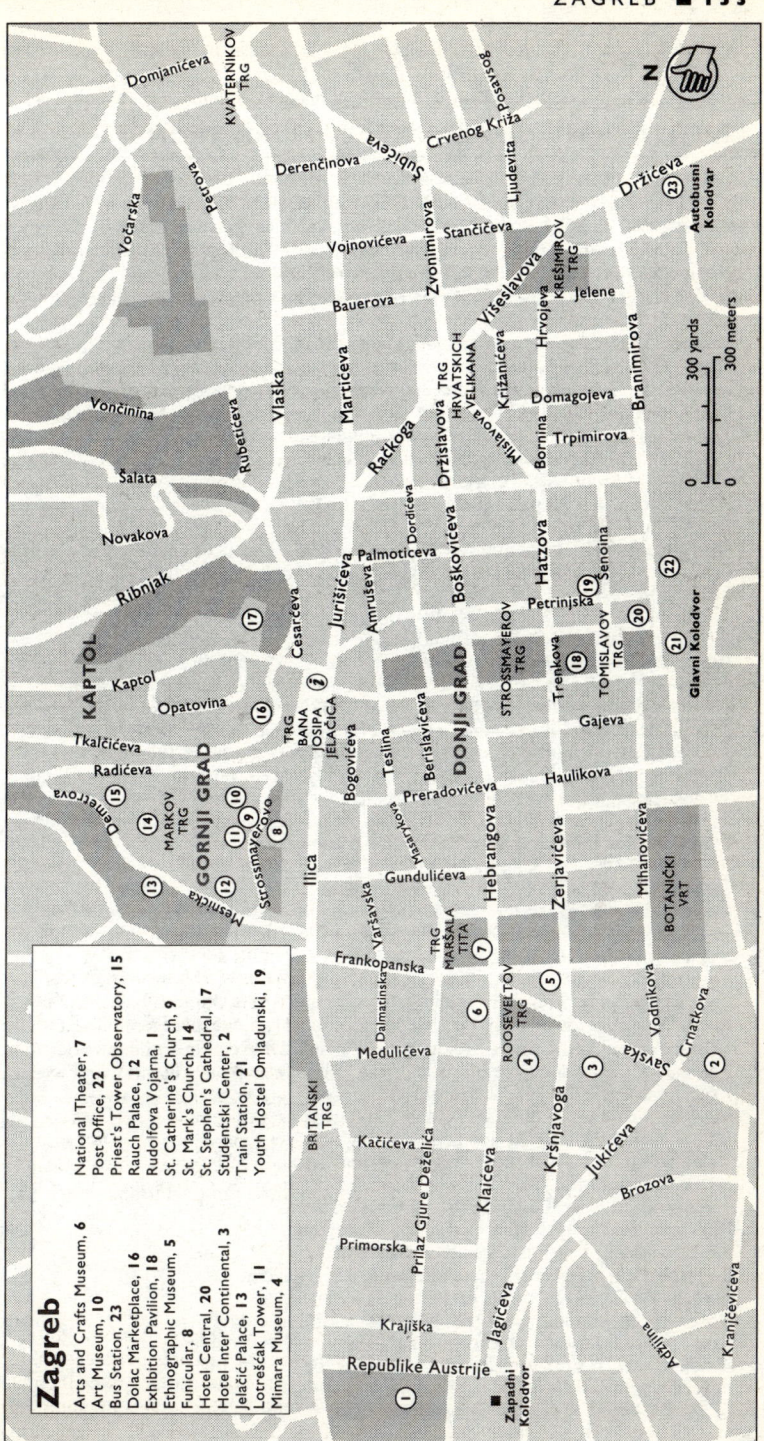

are generally open, selling everything from local rock music to neckties—invented by Croatians. A huge student population thrives on the lively cafés and beer halls, and youthful *joie-de-vivre* makes Zagreb exciting almost every night of the week.

ORIENTATION AND PRACTICAL INFORMATION

Zagreb is 30km from the Slovene border; Austria and Hungary are about 100km away. **Trains** arrive here from many European capitals, via Ljubljana or Budapest. **Buses** expand Zagreb's connections to the unstable lands south and east. To reach the main square—**Trg bana Josipa Jelačića** (formerly Trg Republike)—from the train station, walk north along the parks, then on **Praška**. Uphill are the cathedral and cobblestone streets of the **Old Town**; nearby is the main shopping street, **Ilica**.

- **Tourist Office: Tourist Information Center (TIC),** Trg J. Jelačića 11 (tel. 272 530; fax 274 083), in the southeast corner of the square. Helpful staff distributes maps *gratis*. Catch the huge map outside. Open Mon.-Fri. 8am-8pm, Sat.-Sun. 9am-6pm.
- **Embassies and Cultural Centers: Australia,** Mihanovićeva 1, Esplanade (tel./fax 451 663). Open Mon.-Fri. 8am-4pm. **Canada,** Mihanovićeva 1, Esplanade (tel. 450 785; fax 450 913). **U.K.,** Tratinska 5/II (tel. 340 311; fax 338 893). Open Mon.-Fri. 8:30am-4:30pm. **U.S.,** Hebrangova 2 (tel. 455 550, Citizen Services ext. 276; fax 274 083). Open Mon.-Fri. 8am-4:45pm. An **American Cultural Center,** Zrinjeva 13, is around the corner. Open Mon.-Wed. and Fri. 9am-4pm, Thurs. 9am-6:30pm.
- **Currency Exchange: Zagrebačka Banka** has several branches throughout the city; the convenience outweighs the slight gains made by those who find a better *menjavnična* (private exchange office). Traveler's checks cashed at a 1.5% commission. Open Mon.-Fri. 7:30am-7pm, Sat. 7:30am-noon.
- **ATMs:** Several **Zagrebačka Banka** locations have Cirrus-linked machines.
- **American Express: Atlas,** Zrinjeva 17 (tel. 427 623). Mail held and cards replaced, but no traveler's checks accepted Open Mon.-Fri. 8am-7pm, Sat. 8am-noon.
- **Flights: Croatia Airlines,** Teslina 5 (tel. 427 752; fax 427 935). Flies to selected destinations in Europe and America. Other airlines make the journey here as well. Buses depart from the bus station to the **airport** (tel. 525 222 or 525 451) on the half-hour and the hour (Mon.-Sat. 3:30am-7:30pm). Sun. schedule differs a bit.
- **Trains:** Though not well connected to coastal Croatia, trains provide fast, efficient service to countries to the north and west. All passenger trains arrive and depart from the **Glavni Kolodvor** (main station), Tomislava 12 (tel. 272 244). To: Budapest (3 per day, 7hr., 165kn); Ljubljana (3 per day, 2½hr., 41kn); Venice (1 per day, 8hr., 152kn); Vienna (2 per day, 6½hr., 257kn).
- **Buses:** Croatia's bus system is better developed than its rails. The **bus station** (tel. 615 7111) is just south of the railway tracks on Držićeva Cesta. Information and tickets are on the 2nd floor. Many distant destinations are given in DM and converted on the spot. To: Frankfurt (5 per week, DM150); Ljubljana (6 per day, 3hr., 55kn); Sarajevo (2 per day, 11hr., DM65); Vienna (every other day, 8hr., 200kn).
- **Public Transportation:** You may see an occasional **bus,** but **trams** rule Zagreb. Buy tickets at any newsstand (3.70kn); punch 'em in the boxes near the tram doors.
- **Taxis:** Fares are expensive but usually fair. Larger companies like **Radio Taxi** (tel. 682 505 or 682 558) are the most reliable.
- **Luggage Storage:** At the train station. 9kn per piece per 24hr.
- **Laundromat:** No self-service laundromats exist yet; one of the most reliable **dry cleaners** in town is at the **Hotel Intercontinental,** Kršnjavoga 1 (tel. 453 411, ext. 1749), around the back. Laundry is priced per item, 50% more for fewer than 3 items or for 24-hr. service. Shirts 9kn. Open Mon.-Fri. 8am-4pm.
- **Photocopies: Super Copia,** Petrinjska 32a (tel. 430 619). 0.5kn per page; color and bulk copying available. Open daily 8am-6pm.
- **24-Hour Pharmacy: Centralna Ljekarna,** Trg J. Jelačića 3 (tel. 276 305).
- **Medical Assistance:** Dordićeva 26 (tel. 444 444).
- **Post Offices:** Branimirova 2 (tel. 271 593) and Junišićeva 13 (tel. 277 112), a block east of Trg J. Jelačića. Open Mon.-Sat. 7am-8pm. **Postal code:** 1000.
- **Telephones:** Located outside the post office, or use the ones inside and pay afterward. **Phone code:** 41.

ACCOMMODATIONS

To stay in Zagreb, you'll have to open that wallet (or moneybelt) and pay, pay, pay. Hotel prices are on par with much of Eastern Europe, but with so few young vacationers, there has been little to no demand for true budget accommodations. For help with private rooms you can contact **Staza,** Heinzelova 3 (tel. 213 082), near Kvaternikov trg. From the train, take tram #4 to Dubrava. Rooms run about 150kn per person, plus a 50% fee for stays fewer than three nights (open Mon.-Fri. 9am-4pm). **Di-Prom,** Trnsko 25a (tel. 523 617), also offers accommodations from 200kn per person, with the same bulk-pricing deal (open Mon.-Fri. 9:30am-4pm). The TIC (see Tourist Offices, above) no longer makes reservations, but may be willing to call Hotel Cvjetno or Stjepan Radić (see below) to see where there is a room.

- **Hotel Central,** Branimirova 3 (tel. 425 777; fax 420 547). Rooms facing the train station are a bit noisy, but it's the best deal near the center. The tiny rooms (with shower and cable TV) are so clean even yo' grandma would approve. Singles 230-340kn. Doubles 320-560kn. Breakfast included. AmEx, Diner's Club, Visa.
- **Student Hotel Cvjetno,** Odranska 8 (tel. 530 722). Converted dorms—from cheap to costly. Singles 200kn. Doubles 270kn. Open July 15-Oct.1.
- **Hotel Stjepan Radić,** Horvaćanski Zavoj (tel. 530 722). Relatively cheap student housing far from the center. Singles 80kn. Doubles 130kn. Open July 15-Aug. 30.
- **Omladinski Turistički Centar (HI),** Petrinjska 77 (tel. 434 964; fax 434 962). Clean rooms with tiny bathrooms. Loiterers may make some feel uncomfortable. You'll see more down-on-their-luck Croatians than students. Check-out 9am. Hostel beds 70kn. Singles 190kn, with shower 245kn. Doubles 255kn, with shower 310kn.

FOOD

Along with bars and cafés, **slastićarnas** play an important part in the Zagreb experience; their cakes are as low-priced and delicious as their Budapest counterparts, and the ice cream is well worth 2kn a scoop. Suffering from a lack of tourists, many restaurants have shut their doors for good, but a truly inexpensive meal may be at your feet; across the street from the railway station, an escalator leads to a huge **underground mall,** replete a food court—inexpensive cafés, bakeries, sandwich shops, and pizzerias. Behind Trg J. Jelačića is a daily **market** (open Mon.-Sat. 6am-2pm, Sun. 7am-noon). Also check out the **delicatessen** at the corner of Ilica and Frankopanska (open Mon.-Fri. 6:30am-8pm, Sat. 6:30am-4pm).

- **Matovilec,** Petrinjska 2 (424 564; fax 455 346). Delicious vegetarian *à la carte* options in this airy eatery. Selections change daily, with occasional meat options for a bit of protein. Mushroom lasagna 25kn. Open Mon.-Sat. 8am-11pm.
- **Vincek Slastićarna,** Ilica 18. As popular as they come, and with reason. But watch out—the cherry strudel is the pits…or rather comes with the pits. It's scrumptious, honest. Romantic seating in back. Open Mon.-Sat. 8am-11pm.
- **Restaurant Četvrti Lovac,** Dežmanova 2, just off Ilica. Various tasty pizzas starting at 22kn. *Ožujsko* beer 11kn. Espresso 4kn. Some English spoken. Open Mon.-Fri. 7:30am-10pm, Sat. 3-10pm.
- **Bistro Fulir,** Ilica 13 (tel. 424 731). Get fuller at Fulir where fat comes in many forms: ice cream, burritos, fried cheese. Sandwiches (tuna salad 12kn), salads (Caesar 11kn). Open Mon.-Sat. 9am-midnight, Sun. 10am-midnight.
- **Manta,** Petrinjska 44. The greasy spoon of Zagreb. Great food, but watch the bill—and ask for prices if they're not on the chalkboard. *Bečki Šnicl* (schnitzel) 20kn. Fries 5kn. *Karlovačko* beer 7kn. Only Croatian spoken. Open Mon.-Sat. 9am-9pm.
- **Centar,** Jurišićeva 24. It's small, so don't miss it. Cakes, shakes, and more flavors of ice cream than any two shops put together. You're in Ice Cream City, baby! Pastries and baklava 6kn. Open daily 9am-11pm.

SIGHTS

Strolls through old Zagreb generally begin and end around the huge statue and beautiful façades of **Trg bana Josipa Jelačića.** The **Zagreb cathedral,** visible from many parts of the city, lies just around the corner. Neo-Gothic structures blend seamlessly with the remains of the 13th-century building. Tours (Mon.-Sat. 10am-5pm, Sun. and holy days 1-5pm) point out most of the interesting features of the structure, including an altar attributed to Dürer. This elegant building, however, is still much more a place of worship than a tourist attraction.

Today the former clerical city of Kapitol and the craftsmen's province of Gradec— the twin seeds which grew into modern-day Zagreb—comprise the area called **Gornji Grad.** The medieval core remains the same, including such structures as the **Kamenita Vrata** (Stone Gate), on Radićeva ulica, and the **Church of St. Mark,** with its Gothic entrance. Despite the other small churches on the hill, Zagreb's visitors tend to head straight for the **Lotreščakova tower,** Strossmayerovo šetalište 9 (tel. 421 887), and its splendid panorama of the city (open Mon.-Fri. 10am-6pm, Sat.-Sun. 10am-2pm; 7kn). The romantic **Strossmayerovo promenade** edges the west half of the hill. Follow it to its end to return to the heart of the city, or from the east side of the promenade, take the stairs or the funicular. All routes from Gornji Grad end on **Ilica,** the main shopping district. South of here is **Donji Grad,** or the Lower City.

For some years, Croatia has had a hard time showing off its many, well stocked **museums**—during war time their doors were closed and collections moved to safer places. Many are cautiously preparing to open again. Below is a list of the major museums, with their status in summer 1996. A more updated and complete list can be found in the free *Zagreb: Events and Performances,* published monthly and available at the TIC (see Tourist Offices, p. 154). It also lists numerous galleries and, as the title suggests, plays, festivals, concerts, and sporting events.

Mimara Museum, Rooseveltiv trg 4 (tel. 448 055). Strong collection combines history with globe-spanning art. With expansive halls and tasteful arrangements, this should be the museum to see. Most permanent exhibits were back by summer 1996. Open Tues.-Sun. 10am-6pm, Mon. 2-8pm. 20kn, students 10kn, Mon. free.
Museum of Modern Art, Katarinin trg 2 (tel. 425 227). Works by foreign and Croatian masters. Permanent exhibitions closed as of summer 1996. Open Tues.-Sat. 11am-7pm, Sun. 10am-7pm. Tues. free.
Ethnographic Museum, Mažuranićev trg 14 (tel. 455 8544). Open Tues.-Thurs. 9am-1pm and 5-7pm, Fri.-Sun. 9am-1pm.
Arts and Crafts Museum, Trg Maršala Tita 10 (tel. 455 4122). All exhibits on display. Frequent special exhibits. Open Tues.-Fri. 10am-6pm, Sat.-Sun. 10am-1pm.
Strossmayer Gallery of Old Masters, Trg Nikole Šubića Zrinjskog 11 (tel. 433 444). Open Tues. 10am and 5-7pm, Wed.-Sun. 10am-1pm.

ENTERTAINMENT

Those who care to imbibe are in luck: bars are a civic institution, busy from morning til night. Little distinguishes one from another, but beware, this is definitely male territory. The one exception to the pub-full-of-dark-wood-and-middle-aged-men is the **Hard Rock Caffé,** Gajeva 10, reputedly a branch of the famous chain regardless of the second "f", replete with records, memorabilia, and a pink Cadillac (t-shirts 219kn; open daily 9am-midnight). In the same hallway is the **BP Club,** Teslina 7 (425 520), the venue for jazz in Zagreb (open daily 10am-2am; cover varies).

The numerous sidewalk cafés along **Tkalčiceva ulica,** in the Old Town, beckon a young, mixed crowd. For a more rousing time with equally fab people-watching possibilities, a visit to Zagreb's **discos** is in order. Most are empty early in the week, but for a good time on the weekend, **Disco Amazona,** av. Dubrovnik 2 (tel. 522 010), boasts a lively crowd with frequent theme nights (open Fri.-Sat. 9pm-4am). The **Big Ben,** Bogovićeva 7 (tel. 425 706), is a good bet near the center of town (open Fri.-Sat. 10pm-4am). At Petrinjska 4, the **Media Music Club** (tel. 277 608) manages to stay open seven nights a week by virtue of its slightly quieter music and high table-to-dance floor ratio (open nightly 10pm-4am). The **Sokol Club,** Trg Maršala Tita 6 (tel. 410 012), boasts live Latin music on Wednesday nights and frequent other live acts in addition to the standard fare (open Weds.-Sun. 10pm-4am; cover 300kn).

In the realm of sports, **17 Ilica** is a popular but testosterone-heavy pool hall. Zagreb is arguably the most fanatical of **basketball**-mad Croatian towns. **Cibona,** the local team, has twice been the European champions—as well as the only team to seriously challenge the legendary American "Dream Teams". The season lasts from mid-October through May; tickets are available at the silver-towered stadium south of Savska (tram #4 from the train station, #14 or 17 from Trg Jelačića).

In the middle of June, Zagreb hosts the annual **World Festival of Animated Films** in the Vatroslav Lisinski Concert Hall on Trg S. Radića 4. Films range from the best of Disney to abstract American works to high-tech Japanese sci-fi. Folklore fetishists flock to Zagreb toward the end of July for the **International Folklore Festival,** a premier gathering of European folk dancers and singing groups. July and August see open-air concerts and theatrical performances during the **Zagreb Summer Festival;** some of the best concerts take place in the Museum Gallery Atrium. **Zagreb Fest,** in November, balances the offerings with a festival of pop.

ISTRIA

Although it claims few of the islands that are so prominent farther south, this Croatian peninsula attracts a huge tourist population to its Roman cities, crystalline waters, and, most of all, its proximity to the landlocked north.

■ Poreč

Though Poreč has been a municipality since before Caesar's time, it has never been as lively as it is today. Along the polished stone pavement, the buildings glisten, the ice-cream vendors juggle their wares, and live bands play on every corner, each proud to be a small part of the reason that Poreč and its beaches are the most visited tourist region in Croatia. Somewhere, the Roman gods must be smiling.

Orientation and Practical Information Buses link Poreč with the rest of Croatia. Ten minutes south of the town center, the **station,** Rade Končara 1 (tel. 432 153), sends buses to Ljubljana (2 per day, 4½hr., 71kn), Pula (12 per day, 45min., 22kn), and Zagreb (10 per day, 5hr., 70-103kn). **Store luggage** there (open Mon.-Sat. 6-9am, 9:30am-5:30pm, and 6-8pm; 2kn per piece). **Turistička Zajednica,** Zagrebačka 11 (tel. 451 458; fax 451 665), provides free maps and pamphlets (open in summer daily 8am-10pm; off-season 9am-4pm). To reach the main **Trg Slobode,** walk toward the water and head right on Bože Milanovića, Petra Kandlera, or Maršala Tita. **Exchange currency** at **Zagrebačka Banka,** Maršala Tita (tel. 451 166), by the harbor. Rates here are better than at most tourist offices but not as good as in Rovinj or Pula (open Mon.-Sat. 8:30am-7pm). A MC/Cirrus **ATM** and automatic bill changer wait outside. An **apoteka** is t Trg Sloboda 12 (pharmacy; open Mon.-Sat. 7:30am-10pm, Sun. 8am-9pm). The **post office** sits in Trg Slobode 14 (tel. 431 808; open Mon.-Sat. 7am-9pm, Sun. 9am-noon). **Postal code:** 51440. **Phone code:** 52.

Accommodations and Food Poreč possesses several accommodations options, most with a DM2 daily **tourist tax,** and a 30-50% surcharge for fewer than four nights. Although prices are quoted in DMs, they can be paid in the kuna or dollar equivalent. Check options first when traveling off-season; many institutions refuse visitors November to March. For private rooms, try **Atlas,** Zagrebačka 17 (tel. 432 27; fax 434 933), near the tourist office. Expect 82kn singles, 58kn-per-person doubles, and apartments from 206kn (open daily 8:30am-9:30pm). If their rooms are full, there are two agencies on every corner—shopping around is worthwhile. **Laternacamp** (tel. 443 088; fax 443 093), is far to the east, with good facilities (sites DM13 per night plus DM6 per person; open April-Oct.).

For fine Italian food on a quiet side street, go to **Barilla**, Eufraziana 26 (tel. 452 742). Pasta specialties, plentiful vegetarian selections (25-36kn) and special prices to lure in patrons make up for the less-than-generous portions (MasterCard accepted). On J. Voltica off Dekumana, **Restaurant Slavonija** (tel. 431 922) presents predictable fare, including schnitzel (32kn), spaghetti (24kn), and calamari (27kn; open Mon.-Sat. 11am-11pm). **Grill Sarajevo**, M. Vlačića off Dekumana, offers Bosnian and Croatian specialties such as *pljekavica* (32kn) and Sarajevo-style steak (48kn). Soup and beer both cost 10kn (open daily 11am-10pm).

Sights The Old Town's main street is the historic **Dekumana**, lined with shops, cafés, and restaurants. From Trg Slobode, walk past the **Pentagon Tower**, a relic of Poreč's Venetian days; the emblematic lion remains visible today on the **15th-century Gothic tower**. At Dekumana 9, the **Museum of Poreč** (tel. 431 585) is cluttered with collections of prehistoric, antique, medieval, and ethnographic knick-knacks. Founded in 1884 in the Baroque palace of the Sinčić family, the museum merits a stop if—and only if—the heat becomes unbearable (open Mon.-Sat. 7am-3pm). At Narodni trg, south of Dekumana, rises the **Round Tower**, another creatively named 15th-century edifice, from whose terrace one can view Poreč and the big, bad, blue Adriatic. The **Euphrasius Basilica**, one block north of Dekumana, is the city's most important monument. Composed of 6th-century foundations, late Gothic choir stalls, and a Renaissance belltower, the basilica contains a millennium and a half of art history—don't worry, there's no quiz at the end. The artifact-of-the-day prize goes, without a doubt, to the phantasmagorical Byzantine mosaics adorning the interior. The Byzantine take on perspective reveals a refreshing, simple, highly symbolic style—or maybe just the need for some better glasses.

The stores close down mid-day and people rush out to make it to the ancient Croatian tradition of the fun-in-the-sun summer afternoon—it's surf-time Dalmatia-style, baby! The best **beaches** are south of the Marina, around the **Plava Laguna** (Blue Lagoon) and **Zelena Laguna** (Green Lagoon). Don't waste your time looking for Brooke Shields, but there are some sights to see at the beaches marked "Naturists"—the self-conscious need not apply to these bare-it-all stretches. To escape the crowds, find the rocky areas where the tide has cut small coves into the base of a hill, each with room for two or three people—depending on how those people use the space. A **ferry** leaves every half-hour for the island of **Sveta Nikola** (Saint Nicholas). Hop aboard (roundtrip 9kn) beside the Hotel Rivera for less exciting, but quieter, beaches. If an area of the coast line has a name, it also has its own hotel complex and **disco** (generally open nightly 10pm-4am). If a walk down the beach sounds too strenuous, join the crowd at **Capitol**, Vladimira Nazora 9, smack in the Old Town. **Club No. 1**, Marafor 9, has a higher bar-to-dance floor ratio (open nightly 9pm-4am). If you're no John Travolta, stores and boutiques in the Old Town are open as late as 11pm—Svetlana sells seashell chandeliers and more by the sea shore. **Pubs** are crowded and open late. The **Casablanca**, Eufrezijeva 3, doesn't close until 2am. **Bar Ulixes**, Dekumana 2, hides from tourists in a narrow alley just off of Deukmana, but the cool cellar and outdoor garden make it a rocking all-weather choice.

■ Rovinj

For almost 1300 years, Rovinj's narrow, labyrinthine stone streets have separated the townspeople from the visitors. Laundry flaps between the sunwashed buildings of the five-story medieval quarter, where thousands of people still live. The Italian connection is clearly felt here, and the entire town seems bilingual, with "Rovingo" in evidence as often as "Rovinj". *Capice?*

Orientation and Practical Information With no train station, Rovinj depends on **buses** (tel. 811 453) to get to Poreč (7 per day, 1hr., 16kn) and Pula (18 per day, 1hr., 15kn). There are no platforms, so watch carefully. To reach the Old Town, proceed up the busy pedestrian street. **Taxi** drivers hold amateur chess tourneys as they wait for fares in front of the bus station; if none are there, call 811 100. **KEI Istra** (tel. 811 155; fax 816 012), on Nello Quarantotto across from the bus station, will serve you a tall, cool glass of that favorite summer cocktail: "info 'n' pamphlets" (open daily 9am-7pm). **Exchange currency** at **Istarska Banka,** along the water north of KEI Istra, with decent rates but inefficient service (open Mon.-Fri. 7:30am-7:30pm, Sat. 7:30am-noon). Use the **post office** (tel. 811 466) next to the bus station on M. Benussi-Cio, or the numerous **telephones** outside (open Mon.-Sat. 7am-10pm, Sun. 8am-noon). **Postal code:** 52210. **Phone code:** 052.

Accommodations and Food With its well developed tourist industry, Rovinj has much to offer in terms of accommodations. A DM2 tourist tax and 30% surcharge for one-to three-day stays is standard; the good news is that the high prices of the peak season only last from mid-July to mid-August. **KEI Istra** (see above) arranges private rooms from DM13-24 per person, double apartments from DM68. **General Turist,** Trg Maršala Tita 2 (tel. 811 402), on the waterfront, accepts MasterCard and Visa for its rooms (singles 76-105kn, doubles 116-174kn; open daily 9am-9pm). Rovinj is a popular resort for nudists—ask around town to find the covert games of mini-golf in the buff; we've only seen pictures. If you prefer camping with your clothes on, visit **Camping Polari,** (tel. 813 441; fax 811 395), east of town with hot and cold water, a supermarket, and nearby bars. Take the hourly bus to Polari, and buy a ticket (DM5 per person; DM9.5 per campsite; off-season prices 10% less; closed Nov.-March).

Fish and seafood are frequent themes, and the Adriatic's squid and calamari are highly esteemed, but pasta comes cheaper. For a grocery store, look next to the bus station (open Mon.-Sat. 6am-9pm, Sun. 7am-11am). **Cisterna Gostionica Osteria,** in the heart of the medieval quarter on Trg Matteotti, has many entrée options (squid/calamari 35kn, schnitzel 32kn, salads 10kn; open daily 10am-11pm). The cheapest *menü* at **Amfora Riblji Restaurant,** Rismondo 23 (tel. 815 525), one of Rovinj's most celebrated fish restaurants, includes spaghetti, soup, and crepes (75kn; Diner's Club and MC accepted; open daily 11am-midnight).

Sights and Entertainment Half the fun of Rovinj lies in exploring the **medieval quarter,** inland on the jutting peninsula. Most of the narrow alleys and hilly cobblestone streets eventually lead to **St. Euphemia's Church,** whose Baroque Venetian tower dominates the town; if you're afraid of getting lost, just follow the signs. Or, try to find the tower blindfolded if you're really trying to kill time. The church's sheer size and its Italianate exterior are impressive, though most come to see the 5th-century Byzantine sarcophagus, containing the remains of Euphemia. Miraculously transported here in 800CE, it now lies behind the right-hand altar. You can also climb the **bell tower,** 50 years older than the rest of the church (5kn), for a quick cure for Stairmaster-withdrawal. The only other real sights in town—the occasional medieval chapels and Renaissance arches—don't merit a special trip, but you could try the **Museum of National Heritage,** Trg Maršala Tita 11. It contains the work of local masters from 1100BCE to the present (open Tues.-Sat. 9am-noon and 7-10pm, Sun. 7-10pm; 5kn). **Beaches** are visible from the Old Town.

At least in the non-nudist sections, Rovinj is not nearly as boisterous at night as nearby Poreč and Pula. Check for shows at **Gandusio Theater,** Valdibora 17 (tel. 811 588), or visit a **café** after dark. There seem to be enough tourists to keep **Discoteca Monte Mulini,** in the eponymous hotel, hopping (open nightly 10pm-5am).

▓ Pula

At Istra's south tip, 3000-year-old Pula was founded by sailors who had failed in their quest to retrieve the Golden Fleece and defeat the Argonauts. Legend says that since the unlucky seafarers couldn't bear the shame of returning home empty-handed, they founded Pula instead. However fantastic the myth, Pula is home to a fascinating array of Roman ruins. Handsome tree-lined avenues from the Habsburg days and narrow winding streets of its medieval quarter combine with Pula's ancient heritage and modern energy to make it an eminently worthwhile destination.

Orientation and Practical Information From the **train station**, exit and turn right. Keep walking down **Vladimira Gortana** until it turns into **Istarska**, near the amphitheater. When it becomes **Giardini**, the circular **Old Town** will be on your right. The **bus station** is downtown between Istarska and Balote Mate. **Luggage storage** here is cheaper, more convenient, and more accessible than at the train station (open daily 5-9am, 9:30am-5pm, and 5:30-11pm; 5kn per item per day). **Buses** run every few hours to Rijeka (19 per day, 2½hr., 41kn) and Zagreb (15 per day, 5-6hr., 74-103kn). **Trains** to Rijeka (4 per day, 2½hr., 22kn) and Zagreb (4 per day, 7hr., 69kn) are slow and expensive, and even the domestic routes cross through Slovenia, which may pose visa problems. Brave the sometimes cantakerous transportation officials—train or bus—and confirm the posted times, which are old and not entirely correct. For **taxis,** call 23 228, or try the taxi stand at Giardini and Balote Mate. The helpful staff at the **Tourist Information Center,** Istarska 13 (tel. 33 557; fax 41 855), provides free maps and cultural programs (open daily 8am-1pm and 2-8pm). **Istarska Banka,** Istarska 12, and elsewhere throughout the city, **exchanges cash** and has a Cirrus/MC **ATM** outside (open Mon.-Fri. 7:30am-7:30pm, Sat. 7:30am-1pm). At Istarska 5 stands the **post office, telephones** and all (open Mon.-Fri. 7am-8:30pm, Sat. 7am-4pm). **Postal code:** 52000. **Phone code:** 052.

Accommodations and Food A plethora of travel agencies, many on Giardini, help tourists find overpriced hotels, somewhat expensive apartments, and reasonably-priced private rooms. **Arenaturist,** Giardini 4 (tel. 34 355; fax 42 277), may seem a bit brusque, but their rooms are in the tonniest locations (singles: 1 night 86kn, 2-3 nights 70kn per night, 4 or more nights 56kn per night; daily tourist tax 7kn; registration fee 6kn; doubles run about 50% more per room). South of Pula, youth hostel **Ferjalni Savez Valsaline,** Verudela (tel. 34 595), often fills to capacity, thanks to its pleasant rooms and its own beach area (68kn per night; breakfast included). To get there, take bus #2 or 4 towards Verudela, then exit at Draomirica ul. Call first to see if they have space. **Stoja Camping** (tel. 24 144), west of Pula, lies on the tip of Pula's western peninsula. From Giardini, take bus #1 towards Stoja to the end (DM6 per person and DM3 per tent or car, plus a DM2 daily tourist tax and DM1.2 registration fee).

Well-stocked **grocery stores** abound in Pula (generally open Mon.-Sat. 6am-8pm and Sun. 8-11am). **Dolce Vita,** just to the left on Prvomajska ul., after you enter the Old Town through the Roma arch, serves pasta (15-20kn), pizza (25-30kn), sandwiches (10kn), and salads (8kn). **Restaurant Istra,** Giardini 6, has an extensive selection of entrées, from spaghetti (20kn) to schnitzel (35kn), supplied by its unilingual staff (open Mon.-Sat. 10am-5pm). **Pizzeria Orfey,** Gorana Kovačića 8, in the medieval quarter, supplements small pizzas (20-25kn) with a wide variety of desserts (open Mon.-Sat. 11am-11pm). **Restaurant Delfin,** Gorana Kovačića 17 (tel. 22 289), across from the 4th-century cathedral visible from the restaurant terrace, predictably provides Adriatic fish and seafood entrées (open daily 11am-10:30pm).

Sights and Entertainment Visitors to Pula are understandably enchanted with the Roman ruins. The number one, must-see sight is the **amphitheater,** a wonder of ancient Roman architecture built in the first century CE, now used again for concerts. From the bus station, walk south along Istarska, then Giardini—a tree-lined boulevard recalling the era of Habsburg influence. At the southern tip stands the 27-BCE **Arch of the Sergians.** Pass through the gates to stroll along narrow, shop-crammed **1 Maja ul.,** a little street that comes alive in the evening. Trg Republike, at the end of 1 Maja ul., contains the columned **Temple of Augustus.** As well preserved as Elizabeth Taylor, it was originally constructed over a 16-year period (2BCE-14CE).

Smile back at the worn faces on the Roman statuary inside (open daily 9am-9pm; 4kn). More 2000-year-old stone structures await in the **Galeria Capitolium,** inside the 700-year-old Italianate building next door (open Mon.-Fri. 10am-1pm and 6-9pm, Sat. 10am-1pm, Sun. 6-9pm; free). Pass through the **Twin Gate,** just north of the bus station, and climb the hill to the **Archaeological Museum of Istria,** Mate Balote 3 (tel. 33 488). Some prehistoric and medieval exhibits have been thrown in for good luck (open May-Sept. Mon.-Sat. 9am-8pm, Sun. 9am-3pm; Oct.-April Mon.-Fri. 9am-2pm).

Looking from the Old Town to the shipyards, you wouldn't guess that Pula had **beaches** at all. Purchase a bus ticket from the magazine stand on Giardini (8kn; punch on one side getting in and on the other getting off) to hop a bus to where the real sand castles stand. All the southbound buses pass a beach or two—just follow the crowds holding towels and buckets.

For the scoop on Pula's **entertainment** scene, pick up a copy of *Istrien Live,* available at any tourist agency. It's a lot easier to understand if you speak some Croatian, German, or Italian. Pula is a city of **cafés,** though during the evenings most also serve as pubs. Several first-rate ones inhabit Trg Republike; if they appear dormant during the day, return after 8pm. Those worth mentioning include **Bistro Sirena,** serving coffee (2kn), desserts, and beer (10kn; open daily until midnight), and **Café Carius,** central and always buzzing with espresso-energized conversation (open daily until 11pm). Of those in Narodni trg, **Caffé Milan** is smack in the middle. Enjoy an espresso (2kn) or a pint of *pivo* (10kn; open daily until 11pm).

■ Rab

Isolated in the Gulf of Kvarner, Rab is the main urban center on the eponymous island. While the island's north coast appears a rocky and desolate moonscape, the south side luxuriates amid lush Mediterranean vegetation. Guarding a harbor on the south coast, the fortified medieval town is home to several well preserved buildings, whose fine restaurants and cafés attract visitors. Most of Rab's sights lie on its elevated, southernmost street, **Gornji ul.** (High St.). Begin your stroll at the easternmost point, near **St. Anthony's Monastery,** a 15th-century complex of medieval buildings surrounded by 20th-century overgrown grass. The monastery's neighbor is the 12th-century **Virgin Mary Cathedral. St. Justin's Church** today houses a **museum** dedicated to local art (open Mon.-Sat. 9-11am and 7:30-9:30pm; 5kn). If you haven't had your fill from the road, a nearby **tower** offers an even better view of the sea (open Mon.-Sat. 7:30-10pm; 5kn). Gornji ul. ends its tour at **St. John's Church.** There are real **beaches** on the island, but to get to places with names like "Sahara", you'll have to board a bus to Lopar, on the island's northwest corner (every 2 hours, 15kn).

The **tourist office,** Donja ul. 2 (tel. 724 064) rents **private rooms. Merkurtourist,** M. Dominisa 7 (tel./fax 724 885), facing the harbor as you enter the Old Town, offers singles or doubles for 49-65kn per person. **Camping III Padova** (tel. 724 012; fax 724 355), 1km east of the bus station, is close to town without being co-dependent (DM6 per night plus DM6 per person). The **supermarket** is at the beginning of the peninsula (open daily 7am-10pm). Try *pljeskavica* (35kn) or the Šibenik cutlet (35kn) at **Gostiona Labirint,** one block from Stjepana Radića (open daily 11am-2pm and 6-11pm). **Buffet Harpun,** Donja ul. 15, probably refers to the implement and not the beer. It serves Adriatic calamari (35kn) and spaghetti (25kn; open Mon-Sat. 10am-11pm). To **exchange currency,** stop by **Riječka Banka,** Trg Municipium Arba (tel. 724 099; open Mon.-Sat. 8am-noon and 5-9pm). **Buses** run to Rijeka (4 per day—2 leave before 7am, 3hr., 74kn) and Zagreb (2 per day, 6hr., 188kn). Schedules aren't posted, but the friendly staff will help. **Hitchhikers** report success getting off a Split-bound bus at Jablanac, catching a ride to the ferry (9kn per person), and staying on until Rab (the ferry is accessible only by car). The **bus station** stands next to the tourist office (see above; open Mon.-Sat. 5:30am-7:30pm, Sun. 11am-6pm).

THE DALMATIAN COAST

■ Split

Even with tourism at a low, the residents of Dalmatia's largest city are energetic, stylish, and happy to enjoy the long-awaited peace near blue Adriatic waters. Founded in the 7th century by Salonians fleeing a previous war in the Balkans, this lush peninsula has attracted people ever since. With an Old Town wedged between a high mountain range and a palm-lined waterfront, Split lures visitors with Roman ruins, multiple museums, and, above all, tear-inducingly lovely natural beauty.

ORIENTATION AND PRACTICAL INFORMATION

The **train** and **bus stations** lie across from the ferry terminal on **Obala kneza domagoja**. Leaving the stations, follow Obala kneza domagoja to the waterside mouthful **Obala hrvatskog narodnog preporoda**, which runs roughly east to west. To the north lies the **Old Town**, built inside the walls of **Diocletian's Palace**.

- **Tourist Office:** Obala hrvatskog narodnog preporoda 12 (tel. 342 142). Staff knows it all. Free English maps. Open Mon.-Fri. 7:30am-8pm, Sat. 8am-12:30pm.
- **Budget Travel: Croatia Express,** Obala kneza domagoja 9 (tel. 342 645; fax 326 408). Youth discounts for bus, train, and plane fares. Also sells Eurorail and B.I.J. Wasteels tickets. Open daily 6am-9pm.
- **Currency Exchange: Banka Splita,** Obala hrvatskog narodnog preporoda 10. Has good rates, takes Visa and MC, and cashes AmEx traveler's checks. Open Mon.-Fri. 7am-12:30pm and 2-8pm, Sat. 7am-noon.
- **ATMs:** A Cirrus/MC/Visa sits in front of the **Zagrebačka Banka,** next door to the Banka Splita (see above), which also exchanges money.
- **American Express:** Trb Braće Radnića 7 (tel. 43 055). Cash advanced, traveler's checks cashed, and mail held. Open Sun.-Fri. 8am-8pm, Sat. 8am-1pm.
- **Trains:** (tel. 355 388). Trains running north out of Split offer fewer choices but cheaper prices than buses. To: Zagreb (3 per day, 9hr., 66kn).
- **Buses:** Domestic tickets are sold at the outside ticket counter; international tickets are sold inside. To: Dubrovnik (6 per day, 4½hr., 67kn); Sarajevo (2 per day, 8-9hr., 130kn); and Zagreb (27 per day, 6½-9hr., 86-99kn; 3 overnight departures).
- **Ferries:** (tel. 355 557). **Jadrolinija,** south of the stations, sells tickets to Italy and domestic cities. To: Ancona (daily, 9hr., DM80); Dubrovnik (daily, 8-12hr., 67kn).
- **Public Transportation:** Tickets for **buses** are good for 2 trips; buy them from the driver for 8kn and punch them on board. Most buses run every ½hr.
- **Taxis:** Call 47 777. Average fare runs 15kn, plus 7kn per km.
- **Luggage Storage:** At the bus station (7kn per day). Open daily 6am-10pm. Or at the train station—follow *"garderoba"* signs (8kn per day). Open daily 5am-11pm.
- **24-Hour Pharmacy:** The numerous private pharmacies take turns staying open 24hr. Find one, and a sign will indicate the nearest nightly pick. Try the **Ljekarna,** Istarska 2, north of the market. Open Mon.-Fri. 7am-8pm, Sat. 7am-1pm.
- **Post Office:** ul. kralja Tomislava 9, north of the Old Town. Go straight in the main doors to send mail, through the left-hand doors for **telephones, fax,** and **telegrams,** and through the doors on the right for **Poste Restante.** Open Mon.-Fri. 7am-8pm, Sat. 7am-2pm. **Postal code:** 21000. **Phone code:** 021.

ACCOMMODATIONS

Accommodations in Split tend to be of the same quality as in the rest of Dalmatia. Prices also tend to be higher. The tourist office (see above) finds **private rooms** (singles 72kn, doubles 100kn; tourist tax 6kn per night). Old ladies at the bus station offer rooms that are held to a somewhat lower standard, but may be cheaper. When summer school students haven't filled **Bevno Bušić,** Spinutska 37 (tel. 342 580), this student dorm rents nice, clean rooms. Call ahead and ask to speak with the *upravnik,* who should speak English, German, or both (50kn per night). **Penćište Slavija,** Buvinova 2 (tel. 47 053), in the Old Town, east of Trg Braće Radnića, has seen better days, but is sparkling clean (singles 160kn, with bath 200kn; doubles 200kn, with bath 240kn; tourist tax 5kn).

FOOD

Fast food joints offering hot sandwiches and *ćevapi u lepinji*—delicious grilled sausages in pita-like bread—are a staple here. Split also claims enough fine restaurants to satisfy the most demanding diners. A lively **market** sprawls east of the Old Town (open daily 7am-9pm; produce area open daily 7am-2pm). **Restaurant Sarajevo,** Dolmadova 6 (tel. 47 454), is the oldest restaurant in the Old Town for a reason—class, candlelight, and delicious grills. Scan the menu for a few surprisingly inexpensive entrées. The stuffed *pljeskavica* (spicy beef pattie) puts a whole new twist on an old standby (30kn). Open daily 9am-11pm. The fixin's are free, **Delta,** Trumbićeva Obala 12, at the only sandwich-maker with piles of toppings from tomatoes to boiled egg. It's a budget eater's delight at 10kn per sandwich. Open daily 6am-8pm. **Hotel Central,** Narodni trg 1, provides worthy dining at any hour, but the time to come is before 11:30am, when the brunch prices are an absolute steal (stuffed peppers 18kn; open daily 9am-midnight). **Kavana Luxor,** in front of the cathedral, seems to good to be true—do it in the morning for a happy wake-up. Espresso runs 5kn. It is sometimes closed in the evenings when the space is used for outdoor performances.

SIGHTS

Split's Old Town, the eastern half of which inhabits the one-time fortress and summer residence of the Roman Emperor Diocletian, is a living, thriving museum of classical and medieval architecture. The best entrance is easily overlooked—it sits just past the line of taxis on the south side of the city. This small **portal** (open daily 9am-10pm) leads into the **cellars** of the city. At the entrance, turn either direction to wander around this labyrinth. The dark stone passages originally created a flat floor for the emperor's apartments; the 1700 years of trash stored here has metamorphosed into an archaeologist's paradise. Some of these archaeological finds are displayed in hallways to the left of the entrance, which also hold a complex of dripping domes. The airier right side—just opened in '96—is used as a space for **modern art** displays. Tickets to either side cost 3kn.

Straight through the cellars and up the stairs, you will find yourself in the open-air **peristyle,** a colonnaded square used for outdoor operas and ballets. Up a few stairs and behind you is the open-domed **vestibule,** which becomes the backstage during the Summer Festival. Explore it freely during the day. The **cathedral** on the west end of the peristyle is one of architecture's great ironies—it was originally the mausoleum of Diocletian, an emperor known to history primarily for his violent persecution of Christians. This ancient genealogy makes it the world's oldest Catholic cathedral—and one of the strangest. Its small, circular interior with intricately wrought stonework leaves almost no room for the faithful or the tourists who come to gawk at the magnificent inner door and altar. The adjoining **belltower of St. Domnius,** begun in the 13th century, took 300 years to complete. The views aren't quite as breathtaking as its 60m would suggest, but there's a cool sea breeze at the top (cathedral and tower open daily 7am-noon and 4-7pm; entrance to tower 5kn).

Walk north from the peristyle along ul. Dioklecijana, then right on ul. Paplićeva to the **City Museum,** Paplićeva 1 (tel. 341 240). The assorted collection inspires less than the rich medieval palace housing it, but it's a good way to beat the heat (open Tues.-Sun. 9am-1pm and 5-8pm; 10kn, students 5kn).

Several gates exit from the Old Town, so choose your own adventure. Exiting by the east **Silver Gate** leads to the main **market.** Outside the north **Golden Gate** thunders a huge statue of **Gregorius of Nin,** the 10th-century Slavic champion of commoners' rights. In Ivan Meštrović's rendering, he looks like a grandiose wizard. Or, exit the palace's walls through the western **Iron Gate.** You'll still be in the Old Town on Narodni trg. The 15th-century, Venetian former **town hall** sits on the north side; a sign designates it as the Ethnographic Museum, but it no longer serves that function either. Though this side of town lacks the otherwise omnipresent excavations, medieval architecture still dominates. Browsing through the many boutiques, it's hard not to run into a centuries-old church or an equally old residential section.

Headless statues meander in a beautiful garden north of the Old Town—visitors are welcome join them. Or dig up the **Archaeological Museum,** Zrinjsko Frankopanska ul. 25 (tel. 44 574; open Mon.-Fri. 10am-1pm; 10kn). Sadly, the nearby **Gallery of Fine Arts,** Lovretska ul. 11 (tel. 341 250), was still closed in 1996 to protect its treasures from war-related disaster. Similar worries plague the **Meštrović Gallery,** Šestalište Ivana Meštrovića 46 (tel. 342 483), west of town.

The rocky cliffs, green hills, and sandy beaches on the west end of the peninsula now make up a **city park,** and serve as reminders of why Diocletian once vacationed here. The trails and the roads are almost completely abandoned in summer, but those who love the smell of evergreens and prefer to simply *see* the sea will appreciate this area. Paths are indicated on the tourist map; you can find your own, but watch for signs indicating that a trail leads to private lands—the dogs do bite.

ENTERTAINMENT

Beaches flank Split, but the best ones require a bus ride (#60) outside the city. At night, the Old Town transforms into a teeming, vibrant mass of people spilling in and out of the local bars. In fact, Split's nightlife far surpasses that of its posher island rivals, with as many discos as Zagreb. From mid-July to mid-August, Split hosts its annual **Summer Festival.** Every night among the town's churches and ruins, the city's best *artistes* join international guests in presenting ballets, operas, plays, and classical concerts. At other times of the year, visit the **Croatian National Theater,** Trg. Gaje Bulata (tel. 585 999), to see and hear the same indoors (box office open daily 9am-noon and 6:30-8:30pm). Pick through the bi-weekly Croatian *Splitska Scena,* free at the Turistićki biro (see Tourist Office, p. 162), for more cultural listings.

- **Discoteque Shakespeare,** follow ul. Slobode to the town's souther shore, then turn left, walking along the beach. The most popular not because of technical wizardry, but because you can park your scooter on the sand and get drunk on the outdoor patio overlooking the sea. It'll bring you right back to ye olde Stratford-upon-Avon. Inside, the dance floor is packed on weekends. Live music Friday nights. Open nightly 10pm-5am. Thurs.-Sat. 25kn, Sun.-Wed. no cover.
- **Discoteque Form,** located by the northwest shipyards. Frequent foreign DJs and randomly titled nights (e.g., "Sexy Boxing") bring in students from the nearby dorms—just don't expect to see Sugar Ray disrobed. Open nightly 10pm-4am.
- **Puls,** Buvinova. The Old Town's trendiest bar flaunts steel and industrial music on 2 floors. Open daily 8am-1pm.
- **Jazz bar,** Grgura Ninskoga p. 3. Hidden on a tiny backstreet in the Old Town, the stone interior is so mellow it draws more people than the sunny outdoor tables. Open daily 7am-midnight.

■ Near Split: Hvar

Hvar touts itself as the sunniest spot in Croatia. Only its inaccessibility keeps most tourists away, meaning that the island, together with its eponymous main town, is one of the truly unspoiled jewels of the Adriatic. While this Venetian-styled town gleams enticingly against the water, no single building demands a visit. The **main square** sits northeast of the docks. Various museum-going thirsts can be quenched at the central **town arsenal** (open Mon.-Sat. 10am-noon and 9-11pm, Sun. 9-11pm) or at the **Last Supper Collection** of art in the **Franciscan monastery,** with the famous oil *Last Supper* by Matteo Ignoli (open daily 9am-noon and 6-7pm). The monastery also hosts the outdoor performances of the **Hvar Summer Festival.** The indoor ones take place in Europe's **oldest municipal theater,** above the arsenal and dating from 1612.

The towers at the Franciscan and the farther north **Domincan monastery** are off limits, but you can climb the **cathedral tower** (open daily 9am-noon and 5-7pm; 10kn).

A more enjoyable way to see the city from above is to climb the path to the 1551 **Venetian fortress.** To reward your efforts, it houses a **museum of underwater archaeology** (open daily 9am-3pm; 10kn). On the lower, western hill stands a pseudo-fortress whose outdoor patio plays soft dance hits in the early evening, disguising the fact that after midnight it morphs into a **disco** so loud and fast that it draws hordes of youth off the mainland (open nightly 10pm-5am; free). Some of the Adriatic's clearest and bluest water surrounds Hvar, but the gravelly **beaches** don't measure up. Leave them for the island's stone outcroppings, or, better yet, head to the small nearby islands of **Jerolim** and **Stipanska.** Boats in the harbor run a taxi service between them (roundtrip 10kn).

Walking north from the ferry landing will bring you to the **tourist office Pelegrin** (tel. 742 250; open Mon.-Sat. 9am-noon and 6-9pm, Sun. 6-8pm), which rents **rooms** (singles 70kn, doubles 120kn). Nearby is the friendlier **Mengola** (tel. 742 099), which offers more expensive rooms with private bathrooms (singles 98kn, doubles 132kn). Either *might* help you bypass the 30% per night additional fee for shorter stays, but it's probably easier to follow the women offering rooms at the ferry terminal for comparable prices. The **Hotel Bodul** (tel. 741 744), isn't exactly a steal, but it's the cheapest hotel in town, with singles at DM63 and doubles at DM102. Seafood restaurants, though arguably Dalmatia's best, are equally pricey. Try the **Jerolim,** on the west side of the harbor, which serves up spaghetti at 20kn and pork cutlets at 35kn (open daily 10am-11pm). Better yet is the well stocked **Razvitka market,** on the north side of the main square (open Mon.-Sat. 6am-9:30pm, Sun. 7-11am). Everything else you'll need is on the waterfront. North from the ferry, **Splitska Banka,** exchanges money and gives Visa cash advances (open Mon.-Fri. 7am-1pm and 2-8pm, Sat. 8:30-noon). Further on, the **Atlas** office will give you kunas on your **AmEx** card and cash traveler's checks (open Mon.-Sat. 8:30am-12:30pm and 6-8pm, Sun. 6:30-8:30pm). The only easy way to get to Hvar is the **Jadrolinija Ferry,** which visits the island in the morning four days per week on its trip from Split (1½hr., 50kn) to Dubrovnik (6-8hr., 60kn) and returns in the afternoon on the other three days. Three daily **buses** run from the station east of Hvar's main square to Stari Grad (10kn), where you can catch a local ferry back to Split. **Phone code:** 021.

■ Dubrovnik

Picturesquely sandwiched between the Dinaric Alps and the calm Adriatic, the city walls of Dubrovnik appear in every piece of Croatian tourist literature. Other, less idyllic images of the city appeared around the world as Dubrovnik suffered attacks during the war in the former Yugoslavia. Those expecting to see still-smoking ruins will be disappointed—this city brims with energy and pride.

Orientation and Practical Information The **bus station** (tel. 23 088) lies several kilometers north of the Old Town. **Buses** travel to Split (8 per day, 5hr., 67kn) and Zagreb (6 per day, 10hr., 134kn). The **ferry landing** (tel. 23 068) is a few hundred meters farther north. **Ferries** make their way to Rijeka (20hr., 120kn) and Split (5 per week, 8hr., 67kn). You can base yourself in this area, or catch a bus to the Old Town gates (dir. "Pile"; on board 5kn, at a kiosk 4kn). Or, walk down **ul. Ante Starčevića** from the bus station (20min.). To find **taxis** check outside the city gates, or call 24 343. Many of the tourist facilities are scattered on Lapad peninsula, to the west, but all the attractions wait within the city gates. Unfortunately, Old Town street names are nearly invisible. The **tourist office** (tel. 26 355) is just through the main gates on the right (open daily 8am-2pm and 3:30-9pm). Keep walking down the main pedestrian street; on your left you'll see the **Dubravačka Banka** (tel. 412 967), the best place for **currency exchange,** as well as AmEx and Visa cash advances (open Mon.-Fri. 7:30am-1:30pm and 2-8pm, Sat. 7:30am-1pm). **ATMs** are available at the banks around the bus station. At the end of the street, exiting from the gates to the left, you'll find **Atlas**

tourist agency, which can serve all of your **AmEx**-related needs and runs city tours (70kn; open Mon.-Sat. 8am-8pm). The **post office,** Ante Starčevića 2, is up the street from the main gate. **Telephones** and **Poste Restante** are found here (open Mon.-Fri. 7am-9pm, Sat. 7am-5pm, Sun. 8am-2pm). **Postal code:** 2000. **Phone code:** 050.

Accommodations and Food With the special police having barely moved out, the **HI youth hostel,** Bana J. Jelačića 15/17 (tel. 23 241; fax 412 592), is ultra-clean, friendly, and ready to host its new, less-sinister guests. Up a quiet alley, but still within reach of some happening bars, its 82 beds are a steal at 50kn, including breakfast. To get there from the Old Town gates, walk up the main street (Starčevića) for about 15 minutes, or follow the same street from the bus station. Women will meet you at the transportation terminals to offer **private rooms** in the area (singles 70kn, doubles 120kn). **Atlas** (see above), has rooms for the same price. **Globtour** (tel. 28 992), a few minutes down Starčevića, offers higher quality private rooms—including bath and breakfast—for DM20 per person (open daily 8am-3pm and 5-8pm). Not its fanciest, but definitely Dubrovnik's least expensive hotel sits right across from the ferry terminal. **Hotel Petka,** Obala S. Radića (tel. 24 933; fax 23 851), charges 175kn for a single and 320kn for a double, including breakfast. Yes, those are bullet holes on the outside. Farther in on the peninsula, **Hotel Zagreb,** Šestalište Kralja Zvonimira 27 (tel. 431 011; fax 23 581), has airy rooms with long, white curtains and breakfast included in its price (singles 195kn; doubles 335kn). **Camping Solitude** (tel. 448 310), on the Loped peninsula, was closed in 1996 after being hit in the 1991 attack, but they should reopen once they feel safe enough.

If you're outside the Old Town, look around your neighborhood; you'll probably find some cheap eats, even if they're not as stylish as their more central counterparts. **Raguse 2,** Zamanjina 2 (tel. 22 435; fax 34 727), cooks up spaghetti (30kn) and mussels (30kn; open daily 8am-11pm). **Lokrum,** Široka 4, is located on the sixth street on the right, off the Old Town's pedestrian way. The calamari risotto (35kn) is delicious, but leaves you a bit peckish (open daily 10am-11pm). Your cheapest option may be the **Buffet Laus,** near the end of the same pedestrian road up a left-hand street, offering American and Croatian fast food for 10-25kn (open daily 9am-10pm).

Sights and Entertainment Dubrovnik's **Old Town** resembles no other on the Croatian coast. It's streets run at right angles to each other, and the store buildings seem unshakeably solid. The most impressive legacy of this former naval city-state are the awesome **city walls.** Stretching up to 25m, they were mostly completed by the 14th century, but didn't receive their finishing touches until the 17th. You can climb on top for 5kn, but count on an hour to walk all the way around (2km; open daily 9am-9pm). If you can't make it to China, by all means, come here. Entering the Old Town on its main street, the **Franciscan monastery** will be on the left, and the **Dominican monastery** at the other end. For all you mortar-and-pestle fans, the Franciscan one holds Europe's third oldest working pharmacy (exhibition open daily 8am-noon and 4-7pm; 5kn). Its Dominican partner in penance has an especially rich collection of Renaissance paintings, art, and books (open daily 9am-6pm; 5kn). Nearby, the street opens into a large square, with **St. Blaise's church** sitting on the same side as the **cathedral.** The town's main museum, the 1441 **Rector's Palace,** between the two, was unfortunately still closed as of summer 1996. The 15th-century **synagogue** hides at ul. Žudioska 5 (open daily 10am-noon; donation requested). To find the other medieval churches and nunneries that dot the city (many now converted for other uses), check out *Gradski Vodič,* a free English tourist guide available at the tourist office (see above). For something a little less pious, many visitors lie out on the **rocks** east of the Old Town. The steep descents into the sea make for great diving, but you may instead want to take the ferry from the Old Town's harbor to **Lokrum island.** It's more beach-like and the view of Dubrovnik on the return trip is well worth the 15kn. For Dionysian **disco** deca*dance,* follow the noise in the Old Town to the **Arsenal** (open nightly 10pm-5am).

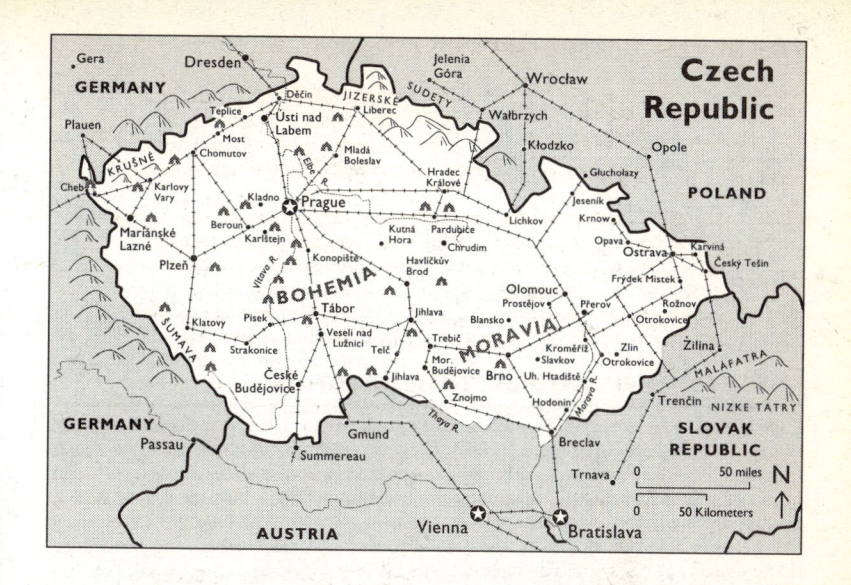

CZECH REPUBLIC (ČECHY)

US$1 = 26.15kč (koruny)	10kč = US$0.38
CDN$1 = 19.05kč	10kč = CDN$0.53
UK£1 = 40.76kč	10kč = UK£0.25
IR£1 = 42.36kč	10kč = IR£0.24
AUS$1 = 20.61kč	10kč = AUS$0.49
NZ$1 = 18.18kč	10kč = NZ$0.55
SAR1 = 5.88kč	10kč = SAR1.70
DM1 = 17.67kč	10kč = DM0.57
Country Phone Code: 42	**International Dialing Prefix: 00**

On New Year's Day, 1993, after more than three quarters of a century of relatively calm coexistence, the Czech and Slovak Republics, formerly known as Czechoslovakia, split, bloodlessly. The notion of self-determination is new to the Czech people; from the Holy Roman Empire to the Nazis and the Soviets, foreigners have driven their internal affairs; even the 1968 Prague Spring was frozen by the iron rumble of Soviet tanks. Today, the Czech Republic is facing yet another invasion, that of enamored tourists sweeping into the country to savor the historic towns, magnificent capital, and the world's best pilsner beer.

CZECH REPUBLIC ESSENTIALS

Citizens of the U.S. may visit the Czech Republic visa-free for up to 30 days, of the U.K. or Canada for up to 180 days, and of Ireland for up to 90 days. Australians, New Zealanders, and South Africans need visas, valid for 30 days. Visas may be obtained at three border crossings: Rozvadov, Dolní Dvořiště, or Hatí, or at an embassy or consulate. See Essentials: Embassies and Consulates, p. 7. Processing takes three days by mail or are processed within 24-hrs. when application is made in person. With the application you must submit your passport, two photographs (for a double-entry visa send two applications and four photos; for multiple-entry, two photos), a self-addressed, stamped envelope (certified, or any of the overnight mail services), and a visa fee by cashiers check or money order. Single-entry and transit visas cost US$22 (the price jumps to $60 if you buy it at the border), double-entry US$36, and 90-day multiple-entry visas go for US$50 (180-day ones for US$90). South Africans willing to settle for a 30-day, single-entry visa can get it gratis. Fees must be paid by cashiers' check or money order. You may extend your stay for up to six months by applying for a extension at the local Passport and Visa Authorities.

GETTING THERE AND GETTING AROUND

Eastrail has been accepted in the Czech Republic since 1991, but **Eurail** is not yet valid here. Railpasses are not a necessity, however, because after one ride on a Czech train you'll opt for bus travel. Although cheap, trains are very slow, rarely direct, and in the middle of any ride the conductor might announce that the stretch from X to Z has to be done by bus—a head-spinning affair (just imagine the contents of ten wagons pouring into twenty buses and driving to the next stop, where the procedure occurs again, in reverse). The fastest trains are the *expresný*. The *rychlík* costs as much as the express, while the few *spešný* (semi-fast) trains cost less; avoid *osobný* (slow) trains. **ČSD,** the national transportation company, publishes the monster *Jízdní řád* (train schedule, 74kč), helpful if only for the two-page English explanation in front. *Odjezd* (departures) are printed in train stations on yellow posters, *přijezd* (arrivals) on white. **Čedok** gives ISIC holders up to 50% off international tickets bought at their offices. If heading to **Austria** or **Hungary,** it's generally less expensive to buy a Czech ticket to the border, then, once inside the country, buy a separate ticket to your destination. Seat reservations (*místenka*, 6kč) are required on almost all express and international trains and for all first class seating; snag them at the counter labeled with a boxed "R". A slip of paper with the destination, time, date, and a matching "R" expedites the transaction.

    Buses can be significantly faster and only slightly more expensive than trains. **ČSAD** runs national and international bus lines. From **Prague,** buses run a few times per week to Munich, Milan, and other international hubs; buses depart from **Brno** to **Linz,** in Austria. Consult the timetables posted at stations or buy your own bus schedule (25kč) from kiosks.

    Because of the inherent risks, *Let's Go* does not recommend **hitchhiking** as a safe means of transportation. However, hitchhikers report that it still remains a popular option in the Czech Republic, especially during morning commuting hours (6-8am).

TOURIST SERVICES

The importance of **Čedok,** the official state tourist company and a relic of centralized Communist bureaucracy, has largely diminished since 1989. **CKM,** its junior affiliate, remains helpful for the student and budget traveler, serving as a clearinghouse for youth hostel beds and issuing ISIC and HI cards. The quality and trustworthiness of private tourist agencies varies; use your instincts. **Tourist offices** in major cities provide heaps of printed matter on sights and cultural events, as well as lists of hostels and hotels. City maps (*plán města*) are available for 28-60kč. Bookstores sell a fine hiking map of the country, *Soubor Turistických Map*, with an English key.

MONEY

The black exchange market is singing its death aria at the moment of prinint while banks are bearing unending litters of **ATMs. Traveler's checks** can be exchanged in every town, if only because **Komerční banka** operates wherever a human being earns cash; its every branch accepts all sorts of checks. Banks generally work weekdays from 9am to 5pm and close for the weekend.

COMMUNICATION

The Czech Republic's **postal system** has been converted to capitalist efficiency; letters reach the U.S. in under ten days. When sending a package by air mail, stress that you're sending it by air (*"letecky"* in Czech, but *"par avion"* works if you say it without a Southern drawl)—the postmaster might be surprised that anyone wants to spend so much money on mail.

To make calls within the country, a phone card (100kč for 50 impulses) is a must and a godsend. It's used in new blue phones and gray ones—the old blue ones demand coins but usually choke on them. Local calls cost 2kč regardless of length. Making calls abroad through an operator does not even require a card—just dial the toll-free number of an international long-distance system (avoiding the hefty charges of the Czech telephone bureaucracy). Calls run 31kč per minute to the U.K.; 63kč per minute to the U.S., Canada, or Australia; and 94kč per minute to New Zealand. To reach the **AT&T Direct operator**, dial tel. 00 42 00 01 01; **MCI WorldPhone operator,** tel. 00 42 00 01 12; **Canada Direct operator,** tel. 00 42 00 01 51; **British Telecom Direct operator,** tel. 00 42 00 44 01.

LANGUAGE

Russian *was* every student's mandatory second language. These days, **English** will earn you more friends. A few **German** phrases go further, especially in the western spas, but might gain you some enemies. English-Czech dictionaries are indispensable; before you leave home, pick up a *Say it in Czech* phrasebook. A handy phrase is *"Zaplatíme"* (ZAH-plah-tyee-meh—We're ready to pay). If you've learned Czech abroad and arrive in Prague ready to romp, beware the Prague cockney—or just allow for some imaginative "mispronunciations." See the Czech Glossary, p. 775.

HEALTH AND SAFETY

> **Emergency Numbers: Fire:** tel. 150. **Ambulance:** tel. 155. **Police:** tel. 158.

The greatest risk of ill-feeling comes from food—it's cheap and stodgy. **Pharmacies** (*lékárna*) and supermarkets together carry a sufficient variety of hygiene and health products. Most pharmacies list a town's 24-hour ones on the front door. **Crime** has climbed dramatically since 1989; beware purse-snatchers and pickpockets prowling among the crowds in Prague's Old Town Square, on the way to the Castle, and on trams. There is some moral code: lost wallets and purses sometimes appear at embassies with only the cash missing. In **emergencies,** notify your consulate—police may not be well versed in English. There is less danger of crime in smaller towns. There is a toll-free **AIDS** emergency number (Mon.-Fri. 1-6pm): 0606-44444.

ACCOMMODATIONS AND CAMPING

Converted **university dorms** rented by **CKM** are the cheapest option in July and August. Comfy two- to four-bed rooms go for 200-400kč per person. CKM's **Junior Hotels** (year-round hostels which give discounts to both HI and ISIC cardholders) are

> ### The World's Most Difficult Sound
>
> Not quite a Spanish "r" and simply not the Polish "rz" (pronounced like the second "g" in "garage"), Czech's own linguistic blue note, the letter "ř," lies excruciatingly in between. Although many of Prague's ex-pats would sacrifice a month of Saturdays at Jo's Bar to utter the elusive sound just once, few manage more than a strangely trilled whistle. Most foreigners resign themselves to using the "ž" (akin to the Polish "rz") in its place, but what we consider a subtle difference, often confuses Czechs. For all those linguistic daredevils in the audience, here's a sure-fire method of tackling the randy Mr. Ř: roll your tongue and quickly follow with a "ž", repeat. Oh, yeah—and start when you're two.

comfortable but often full. Private youth lodgings have usurped CKM's monopoly, but have not necessarily surpassed its reliability. Showers and bedding are usually part and parcel, breakfast occasionally too, especially outside Prague.

Across the country, **private homes** have become a legal and feasible option. In Prague, hawkers offer expensive rooms (US$16-30, but don't agree to more than US$25), often including breakfast. Scan train stations for "hostel," *"Zimmer,"* or "accommodations" ads. Quality varies widely, so do not pay in advance. Make sure anything you accept is easily accessible by public transport, also at night for day transport stops running at midnight; be prepared for a commute to the town center. Outside of Prague, **Čedok** handles private room booking, although private agencies are burgeoning around train and bus stations.

If you're sticking to **hotels,** reserve ahead from June to September in Prague and Brno, even if pre-payment is required. It's easier to find a bed in smaller towns.

Inexpensive **campgrounds** are available throughout the country, ranging from 60-100kč per person (most sites are open only mid-May to September). The book *Ubytování ČSR,* in decodable Czech, comprehensively lists the hotels, inns, hostels, huts, and campgrounds in Bohemia and Moravia.

FOOD AND DRINK

Anyone in the mood for true Czech cuisine should start learning to pronounce *knedlíky.* The thick pasty loaves of dough, feebly known in English as dumplings, serve as staples of Czech meals, soaking up *zelí* (sauerkraut) juice and the unbelievably schmaltzy sauces that smother almost any local dish. The Czech national meal is *vepřové* (roast pork), *knedlíky,* and *zelí,* but *guláš* (stew) runs a close second. Subsidies on meat and dairy products managed to strip most meals of fruits and vegetables, and the main food groups have become: *hovězí* (beef), *sekaná pečeně* (meatloaf), and *klobása* (sausage). Meat can be *pečené* (roasted), *vařené* (boiled) or *mleté* (ground). *Kuře* (chicken) is eaten less often here than in North America. *Ryby* (fish) include *kapr* (carp) and *pstruh* (trout). If you are in a hurry, you can grab a pair of *párky* (frankfurters) or some *sýr* (cheese) at either a *bufet, samoobsluha,* or *občerstveni,* all variations on a diner. Vegetarian restaurants serve *šopský salat* (mixed salad with feta cheese) and other *bez masa* (no meat) specialties. *Káva* (coffee) is almost always served Turkish-style, with a layer of grounds at the bottom. *Koblihy* (doughnuts), *jablkový závin* (apple strudel), and *palačinky* (pancakes) are favorites, but possibly the most loved is *koláč*—a tart filled with either poppy-seed jam or sweet cheese. If you love ice cream, master the consonants of *zmrzlina.*

Produced chiefly in Moravia, Czech wines are worth a try. *Rulandské* from Znojmo in South Moravia is good, but the quality of *Müller-Thurgau* varies. Any *Welschriesling* is drinkable. People typically drink wine at a *vinárna* (wine bar). Charles IV planted Burgundy wines in Mělník in the 14th century. Since then, Mělník has attracted visitors year-round, but particularly during its wine festival in the last week of September. Wine bars also serve a variety of hard spirits, including *slivovice* (plum brandy) and *Becherovka* (herbal bitter)—the country's favorite drink next to *Plzeňský Prazdroj* beer.

CUSTOMS AND ETIQUETTE

Everyone in the country addresses all of their friends, family, and foes with *"ty vole"* (you ox). This does *not* mean, however, that you should do here as oxen do: screw all the cows and crap on public lawns. Although by no means uptight, the Czechs do have certain rules of etiquette, most of which relate to dinner table behavior. When beer is served, wait until all raise the common *"na zdraví"* toast, then drink. Similarly, before biting into a sause-seeped knedlík, which everyone *"dobrou chut'"* and when wished that by others, answer *"děkuji."* At the end of the meal, the Czechs don't **tip** waitrons but round upward the amount to the nearest whole and tell the waitron how much they're paying. So learn your numbers.

LIFE AND TIMES

HISTORY

A fertile plain protected by a ring of mountains, the area now known as the Czech Republic has always been a great place to start a culture. **Paleolithic** tribes hunted mammoths here, and a few millennia later, **Neolithic** farmers in Bohemia made a big splash in the European fashion scene; their Linear pottery decorations dominated Central European art for 2000 years. The **Unetice** and **Tumulus** cultures crafted gold and bronze treasures to hide in tomb-mounds, until **Celts** arrived around 1300BCE, bringing improved trade, a warrior aristocracy, and a fetish for cremation. **La Tène Celts** introduced iron weapons and urban civilization around 450BCE.

In the 5th century CE, arrived the **West Slavs:** Moravians in the southeast, and Bohemians (Czechs) in the west. Peaceful for three centuries, the area became a hot property in the 800s. Charlemagne conquered and converted the Czechs in the 8th century. But the Moravians fought fiercely against the western catholic tide, until 830 when they gained a measure of security by converting to Greek Orthodoxy. They reconverted to Catholicism in 880, buckled under the Magyar invasions in 906, and were traded between Poland, the Holy Roman Empire, and Bohemia for hundreds of years.

The Czechs had more luck, although theirs is also a tale of thwarted ambition. In the 9th century, the **Přemysl Dynasty** united the Czechs and quickly created a strong autonomous state. The legendary **Václav (Wenceslas) I** (c. 903-935), later patron saint of Bohemia. Bohemia escaped the Holy Roman Empire's yoke during the **Slavic Wars** of 928-929, but fell in 1004. In 1140, the region became a hereditary kingdom under **Vladislav II,** and reached a peak under Přemysl Otakar II (1253-1278), who conquered Austria and Slovenia before falling to the Holy Roman Emperor. Bohemia and Moravia remained in Přemysl hands until 1306, when they reverted to imperial estates.

Holy Roman Emperor Karel (Charles) IV (1346-1378) made Bohemia the center of Imperial power, and Prague experienced its **Golden Age.** Charles established Prague as an Archbishopric, founded the first university in Central Europe, and constructed hundreds of buildings, including the Hradčany Castle. Charles's son Václav "the Lazy" was clearly not as productive. During his reign, **Jan Hus** (1369-1415) spoke out against the corruption of the Catholic hierarchy and was burned to death as a heretic. The thus created Hussite movement (later the Community of the Bohemian and Moravian Brethren) led to the **first Defenestration of Prague,** a significant precursor of the Protestant Reformation. The **second Defenestration of Prague** launched the **Thirty Years War** (1618-1648), during which Bohemian losses led to massive land confiscations, forced Catholic conversion, coerced German emigration, and the utter destruction of Bohemia, resulting in the deaths of over one-third of its inhabitants. While the Counter-Reformation inspired the building of magnificent churches, the absorption of Czech territory into the **Austrian Empire** turned into the three centuries of oppressive rule that directly inspired Franz Kafka's nightmare world.

As the spirit of national invention swept Europe from west to east, Bohemia became the home of Czech nationalism, and Josef Dobrovský and Josef Jungmann revived and standardized the Czech language. During the **1848 revolutions,** Czech nationalism was crushed by imperial conservatism. Unquenched nationalism congealed into extremist groups in the late 19th century, including Pan-Slavs, Young Czechs, and Pan-Germans. **WWI** did nothing to increase harmony among the nationalities of the Habsburg Empire, though in the post-war confusion, **Edvard Beneš** and **Tomáš Masaryk** convinced the victorious Allies to legitimize a new state which united Bohemia, Moravia, and Slovakia into **Czechoslovakia.** Unique in Eastern Europe, Czechoslovakia remained a parliamentary democracy between the wars, only to be torn apart as Hitler exploited the Allies' appeasement policy in the infamous 1938 **Munich Agreement,** whereby Czech territory was ceded to Germany.

The following year, Hitler brutally annexed Bohemia and Moravia as a protectorate and turned Slovakia into an independent fascist state. Despite protection from Czech Christians, most of Czechoslovakia's Jews were murdered by the Nazis during the five-year occupation. In 1945, Soviet and American troops met in Czechoslovakia. The Communists won 38% of the vote in the 1946 elections and, led by **Klement Gottwald,** seized power two years later. In 1968, Communist Party Secretary **Alexander Dubček** sought to implement "socialism with a human face," dramatically reforming the country's economy and easing political oppression during the **Prague Spring.** Not pleased with the new developments, the Warsaw Pact states suppressed Dubček's counter-revolution. Gustáv Husák introduced an even more repressive system that lasted 21 years. After the demise of the Communists in Hungary and Poland, the **Velvet Revolution** came to Czechoslovakia. Despite crackdowns, Czechs increasingly demonstrated in Prague and other cities in November, and within a month, the Communist government had resigned and **Václav Havel** emerged as the political leader. He attempted to preserve the Czech-Slovak union, but three years of debate and a popular vote resulted in the separation of the two nations on **January 1, 1993.** Although Havel temporarily stepped down during the divorce with Slovakia, Czechs today have much respect for their playwright-president and for the most part are embracing the economic transition process.

LITERATURE

In the Czech Republic, literature and life are inextricably intertwined. From former foreign minister **T.G. Masaryk** to current president **Václav Havel,** writers have retained an immense influence over the political process, posing a real threat to the terrors of totalitarianism and Communism. This is not because they have proposed alternative programs. Instead, as Havel himself opines in *The Power of the Powerless,* authors expose ideology and propaganda for what they are merely by describing life in all its intricacies.

The themes, those of justice and technology pervade Czech literature, tempered by characteristic humor. From the Defenestration of Prague to the less elegantly labeled one of T.G. Masaryk, the Czech government has almost always meant corruption. Obliged to face this fact in their daily life, Czech writers mused on paper about what was fair, and came to their own conclusions. Authors also expressed ambivalence about the Czech Republic's rapid industrialization—the result of its location at the border between East and West. Science fiction prose and dramas served to satirize and debunk the grandiose ideas of the Party line.

Music also reappears frequently, in Czech literature. Twentieth century novelist **Josef Škvorecký** writes in his foreword to *The Bass Saxophone,* "jazz was a sharp thorn in the sides of the power-hungry men, from Hitler to Brezhnev, who ruled in my native land." A popular and spontaneous form of emotional expression, jazz threatened the powers that be—just as in the American movie *Swing Kids.* Havel himself began the human rights organization "Charter 77" when a rock group was put on trial under the Soviet system, and **Milan Kundera,** among others, writes of music in *The Book of Laughter and Forgetting.*

Swing Kids is not the sole American movie that resembles a work of Czech literature. Indeed, more icons of foreign culture have been co-opted from Czech literature than you might think. The renowned South American poet Pablo Neruda adopted his pseudonym in emulation of the Czech poet **Jan Neruda,** while the replicants of the 80s film *Blade Runner* distinctly ressemble the robots in **Karel Čapek's** *Rossum's Universal Robots.*

In terms of early literary development, two works stand out: the **Unitas Fratrum scholars'** translation of the bible, dubbed the *Kralice Bible* (1579-93), which set a standard for the Czech language, and **Jan Ámos Komenský's** *Labyrinth of the World and Paradise of the Heart* (1631), composed after the author had been sent into exile by the Habsburgs. While other Czech literary production did occur elsewhere during the period of Habsburg oppression, as the indigenous tradition was stiffled, it was not until the 19th century that a literary renaissance (Romanticism) took place.

Fueled by scholarly endeavors to revitalize the language, **Karel Hynek Mácha** created his lyric epic *Máj* (1836, May). Considered one of the masterpieces of Czech poetry, these verses recounted the age-old tale of seasonal death and rebirth. The simple theme finds perfect expression in Mácha's consummate artistic work. The respect that it commanded throughout Czech literary circles prompted a later 19th century circle of writers christened themselves the "Máj group," despite their rather different aims. Besides novelist Karolina Světlá and poet Vitězslav Hálek, poet and story-teller **Jan Neruda** was the principal player in "The Máj Group."

In the 1870s, **Jaroslav Vrychlický** and his companions clustered around the periodical *Lumir* tried to steer Czech culture toward that of the rest of Europe. **Svatopluk Čech**, representative of the rival publication *Ruch*, disagreed, claiming that Czech writing should deal with subjects of national importance. Political leader **T. G. Masaryk** followed in this vein with his newspaper articles and other compositions. German oppression supplied an incessant theme for **Petr Bezruč**, and **Otakar Březina** retained a lyrical style verging on the mystical style.

The next generation of authors included **Franz Kafka, Karel Čapek, František Langer, Jaroslav Hašek,** and **Vladislav Vončura**. Although he never explicitly discussed politics, Kafka alluded to the evils of the state in all his novels. Karel Čapek explored similar themes in his *Pocket Tales,* masterpieces of short fiction which emulate the detective story style of the likes of Arthur Conan Doyle.

Today, the novels of **Milan Kundera** and **Josef Skvorecký** and the dramas of **Václav Havel** remain part of the Czech Republic's daily life, and continue to serve as introductions for readers new to the Czech tradition. The streets that Czech writers have so affectionately depicted, in Prague and other cities around the country, now bear their names.

CZECH REPUBLIC TODAY

Czech Republic is enjoying its status as the ex-communist pet of Western investors and politicians. Foreign money is pouring in faster than the Czechs can build new dumpling factories or breweries, although some national economists voice doubts about the soundness of the transformation's fundaments. Václav Klaus's government has been ruling the economy with an iron hand since its democratization. Although the 1996 elections changed the parliament's spectrum, taking away a full majority position from the Klaus-led coalition, the political, social, and economic process will continue to evolve in the same, capitalistic direction. Meanwhile, Václav "God" Havel, the president, keeps careful watch.

Although Czechs have resolved most of their political and economic problems, they are still struggling in ethnic affairs. In the past years, incidents of violence aimed at the small Romany population have increased. The government has tried to establish stiffer penalties, but newspapers still report isolated ethnic violence. On another note, Germans want the Czech government to condemn the "Beneš decrees" which expelled Sudetenland Germans from the country after WWII. Czechs still view Beneš as a national hero, and harbor some resentment about Germany's seizure of the region during the war. Both sides are looking to compromise. By summer of '97, chances are all will be solved and one of the last obstructions to the Czech Republic's membership in the EU and NATO will be removed.

Prague (Praha)

> *I see a city whose glory will touch the stars; it shall be called Praha.*
> —Princess Libuše

From its mythological inception to the present, benefactors have placed Prague on the cusp of the divine. Envisioning a royal seat worthy of his rank, King of Bohemia and Holy Roman Emperor Karel IV refashioned Prague into a city of soaring cathedrals and lavish palaces. Legends of demons, occult forces, and mazes of shady alleys lent the "city of dreams" a dark side and provided frightening fodder for Franz Kafka's 20th-century tales of paranoia. Be it benevolent or evil, a dreamy spell stands over Prague, whose clocks run backwards or not at all. In recent years, the spell has begun to break. After the Wall fell in Germany, hordes of Euro-trotting foreigners rose over the "threshold," and flooded the venerable capital. They sought history and cheap beer. Now, seven years after the fall, tourism has become the ideology of choice. In August, most of central Prague's citizens leave for the country as the foreigner to resident ratio soars above nine to one. Some contend that the only thing distinguishing central Prague from Disneyland is an admission fee, which also means the city can't control its numbers. Masses pack some streets so tightly that crowd-surfing could become a summer pastime. Although today's tourists chase day-ghosts away, at night Rabbi Loew's *golem* still runs amok and a phantom baby cries under Charles Bridge. Meanwhile drunken mobs of foreign youths roam the city seeking cheap hash and mythical 6kč beers. A growing number of international expats has chosen to savor the city before the magic is gone. Some believe it already is, but those willing to explore for themselves might find a bit of stardust left in the cobblestone cracks.

ORIENTATION AND PRACTICAL INFORMATION

Straddling a bend in the Vltava, Prague is a gigantic mess of suburbs and curvy streets. Pick up a map and study it. **Staré Město** (Old Town) lies along the southeast riverbank. Across the Vltava sits **Hradčany** castle with **Malá Strana** at its south base. Southeast of the Old Town spreads **Nové Město** (New Town), and farther east across **Wilsonova** lie the **Žižkov** and **Vinohrady** districts. **Holešovice** in the north has an international train terminal. **Smíchov**, the southwest end, is the student-dorm suburb. All train and bus terminals are on or near the **metro** system; Metro B: nám. Republiky is closest to the principal tourist offices and accommodations agencies. *Tabak* stands and bookstores vend indexed *plán města* (maps). The **Praha** booklet (190kč) contains maps of the city by suburb including up-to-date transport links and a comprehensive street index. The **English-language** weekly *The Prague Post* provides numerous tips for visitors, as well as the usual news.

> Prague is in the process of carrying out a telephone-system overhaul; throughout 1997 many numbers will change, though the 8-digit ones should not.

Useful Organizations

Tourist Offices: The "i"s of Prague indicate the myriad tourist agencies that book rooms, arrange tours, and sell maps and guidebooks. Be wary: with money on their minds, these private firms didn't pop up just to aid tourists.

Pražská Informační Služba (Prague Info Service), Staroměstské nám. 1 (tel. 54 44 44; fax 24 21 19 89). Happily sell maps, arrange tours, and book musical extravaganzas. Open Mon.-Fri. 9am-7pm, Sat.-Sun. 9am-6pm. Other offices at Na příkopě 20 (open Mon.-Fri. 9am-7pm, Sat.-Sun. 9am-5pm), Hlavní Nádraží (open Mon.-Fri. 9am-7pm, Sat. 9am-3pm), and in the tower on the Malá Strana side of the Charles Bridge (same hours as Na příkopě 20).

Čedok, Na příkopě 18 (tel. 24 19 73 50; fax 232 16 56). This Communist relic once controlled all of Czech tourism. Answers to the trickiest travel and transportation questions, but for more banal requests the bureaucracy isn't worth it. Open Mon.-Fri. 8:30am-6pm, Sat.9am-1pm.

Budget Travel: CKM, Jindřišská 28 (tel. 26 85 32; fax 26 86 23). Sells ISICs (150kč) and HI cards (350kč) and arranges trips to Scandinavia. Open Mon.-Fri. 9am-6pm. The office at Žitná 12 (tel. 29 12 40; fax 24 22 18 13) handles bus, rail, and train tickets. Open Mon.-Fri. 9am-6pm. Not to be confused with its predecessor, **KMC**, Karoliny Světlé 30 (tel. 24 23 06 33; fax 855 00 13), which sells HI cards (300kč) and can book HI hostels all over the world, not to mention in Prague. Open Mon.-Fri. 9am-noon and 2-4pm.

Passport Office: Foreigner police headquarters at Olšanská 2 (tel. 683 17 39), Metro A: Flora. Walk down Jičinská, turn right onto Olšanska. Or take tram #9. Come here

ORIENTATION AND PRACTICAL INFORMATION ■ 175

for a visa extension. Open Mon.-Tues. and Thurs. 7:30-11:45am and 12:30-2:30pm, Wed. 7:30-11:30am and 12:30-5pm, Fri. 7:30am-noon.

Embassies: Canada, Mickiewiczova 6 (tel. 24 31 11 08, after hours 06 01 20 35 20). Metro A: Hradčanská. Open Mon.-Fri. 9am-noon and 2-4pm. **Hungary,** Badeniho 1 (tel. 36 50 41). Metro A: Hradčanská. Same-day visas for citizens of Australia and New Zealand for US$80 plus three photos. Open Mon.-Wed. and Fri. 9am-noon. **Poland,** Valdštejnská 8 (tel. 53 59 51). Consulate, Václavské nám. 49 (tel. 24 22 87 22). Same-day express visas for citizens of Australia and New Zealand for 2470kč; citizens of Canada 2860kč. Open Mon.-Fri. 9am-noon. **Russia,** Consulate, Korunovačni 34 (tel. 37 37 23) around the corner. Metro A: Hradčanská. Open Mon., Wed., and Fri. 9am-7pm. **Slovakia,** Pod hradbami 1 (tel. 32 05 07). Metro A: Dejvická. Open Mon.-Fri. 8:30am-noon. **South Africa,** Ruská 65 (tel. 67 31 11 14). Metro A: Jiřího z Poděbrad. Open Mon.-Fri. 9am-noon. **U.K.,** Thunovská 14 (tel. 24 51 04 39). Metro A: Malostranská. Open Mon.-Fri. 9am-noon. Travelers from **Australia** and **New Zealand** should contact the British embassy in an emergency. **U.S.,** Tržiště 15 (tel. 24 51 08 47, after hours 53 12 00). Metro A: Malostranská. From Malostranské nám., turn onto Karmelitská then right on Tržiště. Open Mon.-Fri. 9am-noon and 2-3pm.

Currency Exchange: The best rates go to AmEx and Thomas Cook's traveler's checks holders who incur 0% commission at their respective offices. On weekends and holidays, exchange counters in large hotels will convert money.

Komerční Banka, main office Na příkopě 33 (tel. 24 02 11 11; fax 24 24 30 20; open Mon.-Fri. 9am-5pm). 2% commission on traveler's checks and cash. Private firm commissions can be much higher. Open Mon.-Fri. 9am-5pm.

Živnostenská Banka, Na příkopě 20 (tel. 24 12 11 11; fax 24 12 55 55). Cash advances on MC and Visa. Commission 1% on cash, 2% on traveler's checks. Open Mon.-Fri. 8:30am-5:30pm.

Chequepoint, in highly-touristed areas. About 10% commission on top of a service charge. The counters at Staroměstské nám. 21 and the intersections of Václavské nám. and Vodikčová are open 24hr.

ATMs: Popping up everywhere. The one at Krone supermarket on Václavské nám. is connected to the Cirrus, Eurocard, Eurocheque, MC, Plus, and Visa networks.

American Express: Václavské nám. 56 (tel. 24 21 99 92; fax 24 22 77 08). Metro A or C: Muzeum. If the line extends out the door, just walk 5min. up Václavské nám. to the banks listed above. Address mail to: "Peter Peartree, American Express, Client Letter Service, Václavské nám. 56, 113 26 Praha 1, Czech Republic." Mail held at "Cardmember services." MC and Visa cash advances at 3% commission. ATM-machine. Exchange office open May-Sept. daily 9am-7pm; Oct.-April Mon.-Fri. 9am-6pm and Sat. 9am-3pm. Travel office open May-Sept. Mon.-Fri. 9am-6pm, Sat. 9am-2pm; Oct.-April Mon.-Fri. 9am-5pm, Sat. 9am-noon.

Thomas Cook: Václavské nám. 47 (tel. 24 22 86 58; fax 26 56 95). Cash Thomas Cook's Eurocheques here. Flexible hours for clients. MC cash advances. Emergency card replacement. Open Mon.-Fri. 9am-6pm, Sat. 9am-5pm.

Post Office: Jindřišská 14. Metro A or B: Můstek. Address **Poste Restante:** "Dr. Judith Driver, POSTE RESTANTE, Jindřišská 14, 110 00 Praha 1, Czech Republic." Poste Restante at window #28 (open Mon.-Fri. 7am-8pm, Sat. 7am-1pm), stamps at windows #20-23, letters and parcels under 2kg at windows #10-12. Open 24hr. Parcels over 2kg can be mailed only at **Pošta-Celnice,** Plzeňská 139. Take tram #9 west. Airmail should arrive within 10 days from the U.S. Open Mon.-Tues. and Thurs. 7am-3pm, Wed. 7am-6pm, Sat. 8am-noon.

Telephones: Jindřišská 14, in the post office. Open daily 7am-11pm. If using coins at one of the many phones, be sure not to use an emergency phone or one whose money slot is blocked. Buy phone cards at kiosks, the post office, or from the Telecom man at *Hlavní pošta.* Beware: some kiosks, mostly near Malá Strana and Staré Město, charge above the usual 100kč for 50 units. **Phone code:** 02.

Transportation

Flights: Ruzyně Airport (tel. 334 33 14), 20km northwest of the city center. Take bus #119 from "Dejvická" or #176 from Metro B: Nové Butovice. Private companies offer expensive buses from the airport to locations in downtown Prague (90-400kč). 15 carriers operate out of the airport, notably **Air France** (tel. 24 22 71

PRAGUE (PRAHA)

HOSTELS
1. Hostel Sokol
2. CKM
3. Junior Hotel Praha
4. Hotel Juventus

Prague
1. Canadian Embassy
2. Palace Belvedere
3. National Gallery
4. St. Vitus Cathedral
5. Royal Palace
6. Basilica of St. George
7. Lobkovic Palace
8. U.K. Embassy
9. Wallenstein Palace
10. St. Nicholas Church
11. U.S. Embassy
12. Church of Our Lady Victorious
13. Charles Bridge
14. National Theater
15. New Town Hall
16. National Museum
17. Smetana Theater
18. Praha hlavní nádraží
19. Church of Our Lady of the Snows
20. Bethlehem Chapel
21. Kafka's Birthplace
22. Maislova Synagóga
23. Vysoká Synagóga
24. Staronová Synagóga
25. Old Town Hall
26. Týn Church
27. Church of St James
28. Powder Tower
29. Masarykovo nádraží
30. Florenc Bus Station
31. Pražská Informační Sluzba (PIS)
32. Čedak Office
33. Main Post Office
34. Anežský klášter (St. Agnes Convent)
35. American Express Office
36. Kafka's Grave

ORIENTATION AND PRACTICAL INFORMATION ■ 177

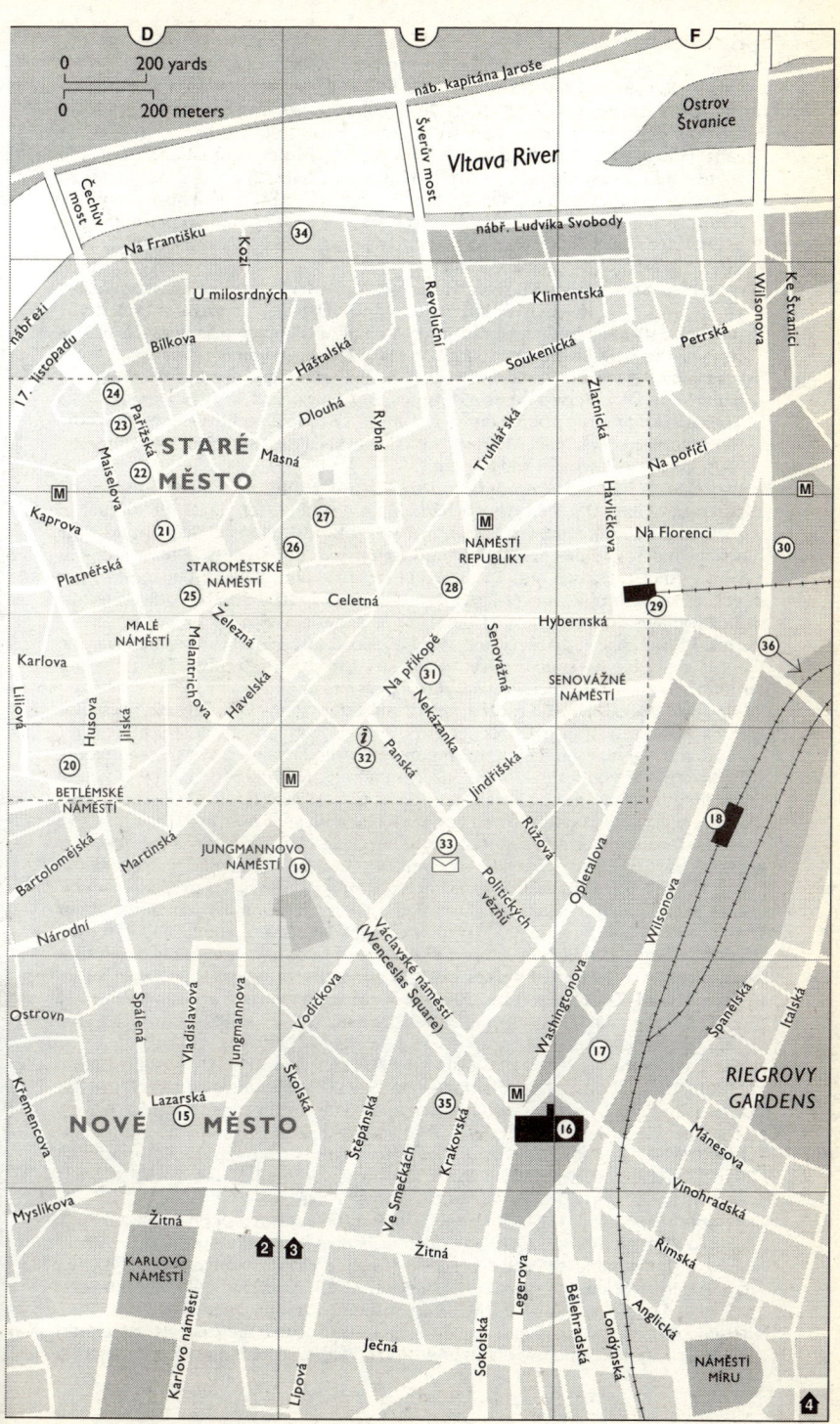

64), **British Airways** (tel. 232 90 20), **Delta** (tel. 26 71 41), **KLM** (tel. 26 80 56), **Lufthansa** (tel. 316 74 38), and **Swissair** (tel. 24 81 08 90). **ČSA** (Czech National Airlines), Revoluční 1 (tel. 24 80 61 11 or 24 80 62 25). Metro B: nám. Republiky.

Trains: (24-hr. info in Czech tel. 24 21 76 54). Prague has 4 train depots; always ask what your departure point is. Čedok efficiently books seats and couchettes.

Praha Hlavní Nádraží. Metro C: Hlavní Nádraží. International and domestic routes. **B.I.J. Wasteels** (tel. 24 61 50 54; fax 24 22 18 72) offers those under 26 train tickets for 20-40% off. Open Mon.-Fri. 8:45-11:30am and 12:30-5:45pm. To: Berlin (6 per day; 6hr.; 1301kč, Wasteels 1123kč); Budapest (6 per day; 9hr.; 906kč, Wasteels 670kč); Vienna (4 per day; 5hr.; 638kč, Wasteels 460kč); Warsaw (3 per day; 10hr.; 625kč, Wasteels 413kč).

Praha-Holešovice Metro C: Nádraží Holešovice. A large international terminal—you'll probably arrive here or at Hlavní Nádraží. Five daily departures to Berlin, 5 to Budapest, and 2 to Vienna. The international ticket office sells Wasteels tickets (open 24hr. with 4½-hr. breaks for breakfast, lunch, and dinner).

Masarykovo Nádraží (formerly Střední), at Hybernská and Havlikčova. Metro B: nám. Republiky. Serves domestic routes, in Central and West Bohemia (Česká Třebova, Chomutov, Kolín, Louny, and Žatec). **Praha Smíchov,** south across the river, opposite Vyšehrad. Metro B: Smíchovské Nádraží. Serves nearby domestic routes, such as Karlštejn and Beroun.

Buses: ČSAD has 3 *autobusové nádraží* (bus terminals). **Praha-Florenc,** Křižíkova, behind the Masarykovo Nádraží train station (tel. 24 21 49 90, info in Czech 24 21 10 60, Mon.-Fri. 6am-8pm). Metro B or C: Florenc. Staff speaks little English, but schedules are legible and extensive. Buy tickets at least a day in advance; they often sell out. To: Berlin (1 per day, 6hr., 820kč); Budapest (5 per week, 8hr., 740kč); Vienna (1-2 per day, 8hr., 810kč). The Tourbus office upstairs sells **Eurolines** tickets (tel. 24 21 02 21; open daily 8am-8pm).

Ferries: PPS, Rašínovo Nábřeží (tel. 29 83 09; fax 24 91 38 62) to Vyšehrad and the zoo; if you have no specific destination, try the dancing cruise (50kč). A tour around Vltava's Prague bends costs 200kč per person.

Public Transportation: The **metro, tram,** and **bus** systems serve the city well. Bus routes frequently shift for street repairs. Tickets, available at newsstands, "DP" kiosks, and machines in the metro stations, are valid on all forms of transportation. 6kč tickets are good only 15min. after punching, and only for 1 ride. If you're switching trains, trams, or buses, get a 10kč ticket (valid for 1hr.). Baggage costs 5kč per piece, but you're allowed one large bag with your personal ticket if you've got one for 24hrs. or more. Infrequent controls lead to 200kč fines for ticketless passengers. The metro's 3 main lines run daily 5am-midnight: on city maps, line A is green, line B is yellow, and line C is red. "Můstek" (lines A and B), "Muzeum" (lines A and C), and "Florenc" (lines B and C) are the primary junctions. **Night trams** #51-58 and **buses** #500-510 run midnight-5am (every 40min.); look for the dark blue signs at transport stops. **DP** (*Dopravní Podnik*), the municipal transit authority, also sells **tourist passes** valid for the entire network (1 day 50kč, 3 days 130kč, 1 week 190kč, 2 weeks 220kč). **DP offices:** Jungmannovo nám. (tel. 24 22 51 35, Metro A and B: Můstek) and Palackého nám. (tel. 29 46 82, Metro B: Karlovo nám.). Open daily 7am-9pm.

Taxis: Taxi Praha (tel. 24 91 66 66) and **AAA** (tel. 312 21 12) are 24-hr. Before entering the cab, ensure that the meter starts at 0. On shorter trips, check that the meter is running by saying *"Zapněte taxametr";* for longer trips set a price beforehand. Ask the driver for a receipt *("Prosím, dejte mi paragon.")* stating the distance traveled and the price paid. The official fare is 12kč per 1km atop the flat 20kč for getting in. Downtown to the airport costs about 500kč. Locals strongly distrust cab drivers and warn foreigners against using taxis.

Car Rental: Hertz (tel. 312 07 17 or 36 59 98) at the airport, is open daily 8am-8pm; Karlovo nám. 28 (tel./fax 29 78 36), open daily 8am-8pm. Minimum age 21. A Ford Fiesta with unlimited mileage costs 2160-3510kč a day. Insurance 198-1044kč per day. Special weekend deals. **Czechocar** (tel. 24 19 76 42; fax 24 22 23 00) rents Škodas at Čedok for 1470kč per day with insurance at 200kč per day.

Hitchhiking: Hitchhiking in and around Prague has become increasingly dangerous; luckily, cheap and extensive train and bus service renders it an unnecessary risk.

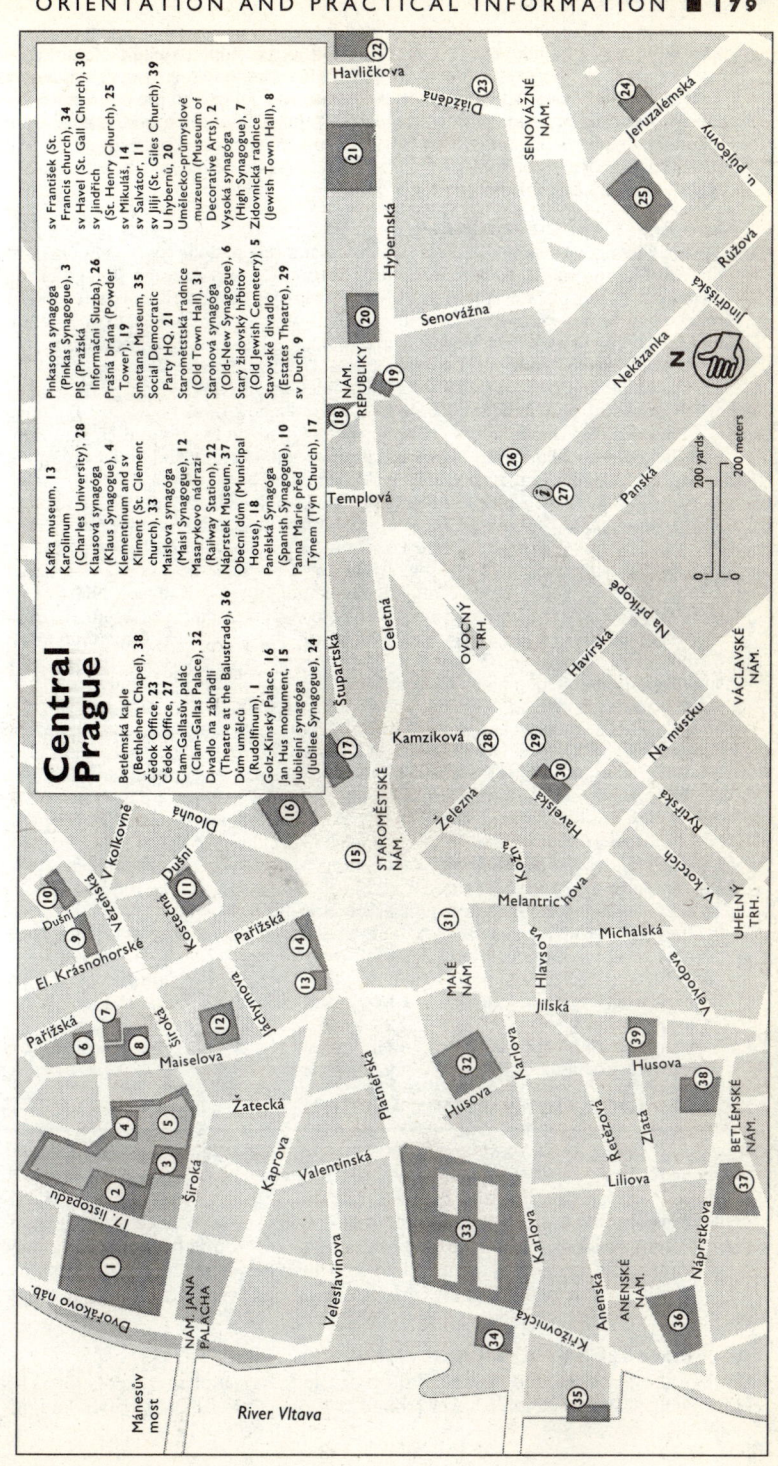

ns AND PRACTICAL INFORMATION ■ 179

Central Prague

Betlémská kaple (Bethlehem Chapel), **38**
Čedok Office, **23**
Čedok Office, **27**
Clam-Gallasův palác (Clam-Gallas Palace), **32**
Divadlo na zábradlí (Theatre at the Balustrade), **36**
Dům umělců (Rudolfinum), **1**
Golz-Kinský Palace, **16**
Jan Hus monument, **15**
Jubilejní synagóga (Jubilee Synagogue), **24**
Kafka museum, **13**
Karolinum (Charles University), **28**
Klausová synagóga (Klaus Synagogue), **4**
Klementinum and sv Kliment (St. Clement church), **33**
Maislova synagóga (Maisel Synagogue), **12**
Masarykovo nádraží (Railway Station), **22**
Náprstek Museum, **37**
Obecní dům (Municipal House), **18**
Panělská synagóga (Spanish Synagogue), **10**
Panna Marie před Týnem (Týn Church), **17**
Pinkasova synagóga (Pinkas Synagogue), **3**
PIS (Pražská Informační Služba), **26**
Prašná brána (Powder Tower), **19**
Smetana Museum, **35**
Social Democratic Party HQ, **21**
Staroměstská radnice (Old Town Hall), **31**
Staronová synagóga (Old-New Synagogue), **6**
Starý židovský hřbitov (Old Jewish Cemetery), **5**
Stavovské divadlo (Estates Theatre), **29**
sv Duch, **9**
sv František (St. Francis church), **34**
sv Havel (St. Gall Church), **30**
sv Jindřich (St. Henry Church), **25**
sv Mikuláš, **14**
sv Salvátor, **11**
sv Jiljí (St. Giles Church), **39**
U hybernů, **20**
Umělecko-průmyslové muzeum (Museum of Decorative Arts), **2**
Vysoká synagóga (High Synagogue), **7**
Židovnická radnice (Jewish Town Hall), **8**

Those hitching east take tram #1, 9, or 16 to the last stop. To points south, they take Metro C to "Pražskeho povstání," walk left 100m, crossing nám. Hrdinů to 5 Května (highway D1). To Munich, hitchers take tram #4 or 9 to the intersection of Plzeňská at Kukulova/Bucharova, then hitch south. Those going north take a tram or bus to "Kobyliské nám.," then bus #175 up Horňatecká. German drivers are rumored to be the most willing to pick up hitchers. *Let's Go* does not recommend hitchhiking as a safe form of getting around.

Other Practical Information

Luggage Storage: There are lockers in all train and bus stations (two 5kč coins). In the main train terminal they're often full, so try the 24-hr. baggage storage in the basement (25kč per day for first 15kg). Beware of nimble thieves who might relieve you of heavy baggage as you set your 4-digit locker code. The bus station luggage room charges 10kč per bag (up to 15kg) and is open daily 5am-11pm.

Lost Credit Cards: American Express, tel. 24 21 99 92; **MasterCard,** tel. 24 42 31 35; fax 24 24 80 37; **Visa** and **Diner's Club,** tel. 24 12 53 53.

English Bookstores: The Globe Bookstore, Janovského 14 (tel. 66 71 26 10). Metro C: Vltavská. From the Metro, walk under the overpass on the right, then turn right onto Janovského. Many used books and job, accommodation, and bungee-jumping listings. Open daily 9am-5pm. **Big Ben Bookshop,** Rybná 2 (tel. 232 82 49). Metro A: nám. Republiky. Current editions and travel books. Open Mon.-Fri. 9am-6pm, Sun. 10am-5pm. **U Knihomola International Bookshop,** Mánesova 79 (tel. 627 77 70; fax 627 77 69). Metro A: Jiřího z Poděbrad. Open Mon.-Thurs. 10am-11pm, Fri.-Sat. 10am-midnight, Sun. 11am-8pm. **American Center,** Hybernská 7a (tel. 24 23 10 85; fax 24 22 09 83). Open Mon.-Fri. 11am-5pm, but closed in late summer.

Cheap Clothes: Milady Horákové is a street lined with rag boutiques. From Metro C: Vltavská, take tram #1 or 25 to "Letenské nám." and walk back. **Obchodní Dům Letná,** Milady Horákové 62, stores its *prêt-à-porter* in wire baskets that you may rummage though. Open Mon.-Wed. and Fri. 9am-7pm, Thurs. 9am-9pm.

Laundromat: In some private flats, travelers ask to include their laundry with the family's. Often underwear returns darned and ironed. Otherwise, go to **Laundry Kings,** Dejvická 16 (tel. 312 37 43), 1 block from Metro A: Hradčanská. Cross the tram *and* railroad tracks, then turn left onto Dejvická. Wash 50kč. Dry 15kč per 8min. Soap 10-20kč. Full-service is 30kč more and takes up to 2 days. Beer 11kč. Filled with similarly soiled and thirsty travelers. The noteboard has become a mecca for apartment seekers, English teachers, and those trying to locate friends. Use the spinner to save on drying. Open Mon.-Fri. 6am-10pm, Sat.-Sun. 8am-10pm. **Laundryland,** Londýnská 71 (tel. 25 11 24). Wash 45kč. Dry 10kč for 8min. Soaps 10-20kč. Full-service 30kč more. Open daily 8am-10pm.

Pharmacies: Pharmacies are plentiful in Prague and offer a variety of foreign products at very foreign prices. Don't hesitate to ask for *kontracepční prostředky* (contraceptives), *náplast* (bandages), or *dámské vložky* (tampons). **24-hr. pharmacies,** Koněvova 210 (tel. 644 18 95) and Štefánikova 6 (tel. 24 51 11 12).

Gay Information Center: tel. 692 63 59—a private number. English spoken.

Emergencies: Medical Emergency Aid in English: tel. 29 93 81. **Na Homolce** (for foreigners), Roentgenova 2 (tel. 52 92 21 46, after hours 52 92 21 91).

ACCOMMODATIONS AND CAMPING

While hotel prices rise beyond your wildest dreams, the hostel market is glutted, and prices hover between 200-300kč per night. The smaller hostels provide a friendly, communal atmosphere, but they're often full. The Strahov complex and other student dorms bear the brunt of the summer's backpacking crowds, but a growing number of Prague residents have begun renting rooms. Year-round hostels are popping up in some of the most convenient and inconvenient places, so weigh your options. A few bare-bone hotels still keep low prices. Campgrounds are the last option. Sleeping on Prague streets is too dangerous to consider.

Accommodations Agencies

Many of the hawkers who besiege visitors at the train station are agents hired by other people. The going rates hover around US$15-30 (500-1000kč), depending pri-

Prague Metro

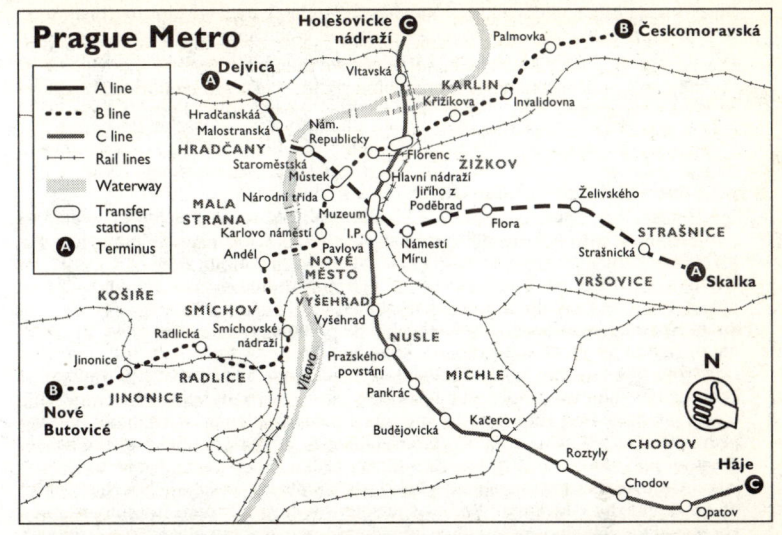

- —— A line
- ••••• B line
- ▬▬▬ C line
- ┼─┼ Rail lines
- ▓▓▓ Waterway
- ⓐ Transfer stations
- Ⓐ Terminus

marily on proximity to downtown. Try haggling. Arrangements made in this way are generally safe, but if you're wary of bargaining on the street, you can try private agencies (sometimes with low group rates). Make sure any room you accept is close to public transportation and that you understand what you are paying for; have the staff write it down. Payment is usually accepted in Czech, German, or U.S. currency.

Hello Travel Ltd., Senovážné nám. 3, between Na příkopě and Hlavní Nádraží (tel. 24 21 26 47). Arranges any sort of housing imaginable. Rooms in apartments start at US$14, hotels at US$35, and hostels at US$8. Payment in kč, DM, or by credit card (AmEx, Diner's, MC, Visa). Open daily 10am-9pm.

Konvex 91, Ve Smekčách 29 (tel. 26 49 01; fax 24 21 49 37). The professional staff books hostels from 295kč and central apartments with kitchen and bathroom from 540kč per person. Open Mon.-Fri. 9am-12:30pm and 1:30-6pm.

Ave., Hlavní Nádraží (tel. 24 22 32 26; fax 24 23 07 83), left from the main hall of the train station. The burgeoning firm offers hundreds of rooms (shared and private) starting at 440kč a person and hostels from 170kč. Open daily 6am-11pm.

Hostels

Next to the Olympic stadium in the Strahov neighborhood west of the river, an enormous cluster of dorms/hostels frees up for travelers July-August. These rooms may be the best bet for travelers who arrive in the middle of the night *sans* clue. For those who prefer a more intimate setting, a number of hostels around town provide fewer beds with more tender loving care. Call ahead.

Hostel Sokol, Hellichova 1 (tel. 57 00 73 97; fax 54 74 47), at the end of Karmelitská. Metro B: Malostranská, then tram #12 or 22 to Hellichova, and walk straight another 100m. It's on the left in the passage 5min. from the Charles Bridge. The all-play-no-sightseeing crowd choose this over more comfortable hostels because of the staff's friendliness. Day-long bar in summer (until 12:30am) where you can grab breakfast. Mega-hip receptionists will fill you in on "the scene" when asked. It's not sparkling, but guests like it that way. Kitchen facilities. 40 beds, 80 in summer. Lockout 10am-3pm. Curfew 10:30am. 179kč per person in 10-bed rooms. 54kč for pillow, sheets, and blanket for the whole stay.

Slavoj Wesico (a.k.a. **Hostel Boathouse**), V náklích 1a (tel. 402 10 76). Metro A: Staroměstská, then tram #17 to "Černý Kůň". Descend by the balustrade on the river side and walk all the way to the Vltava; be sure to look for it in the daytime.

From a yummy breakfast to the motherly figure in charge, this former boathouse feels like pre-school. Clean rooms for 3 and bathrooms scrubbed sparkling clean. No curfew or lockout. 190kč per person or 120kč for a bed in the hallway. 50kč deposit. Hearty meals 50kč, breakfast 30kč, laundry 50kč. Call ahead.

Domov Mládeže, Dykova 20 (tel. 25 06 88; fax 25 14 29). From Metro A: nám. Jiřího z Poděbrad, follow Nitranská and turn left on Dykova. Possibly the most enjoyable hostel trek in Prague. 60 beds in the tree-lined Vinohrady district. So peaceful you might forget you're in Prague. 2- to 7-person rooms; clean but not sterile. 300kč per person includes breakfast—different each morning.

V podzámčí, V podzámčí 27 (tel. 472 27 59). From Metro C: Budějovická, take bus #192 to the third stop—be sure to request *"stop penzion."* A very popular home away from the hectic pace of Prague. No curfew. Laundry service available. Kitchen facilities. No bunkbeds. 2- to 4-person rooms. 225kč per person. Call ahead, as it often fills up with touring groups.

Hostel Hostel, Malá Veleslavínova (tel. 232 89 37). Metro A: Staroměstská and walk south (left as you face the river) on Křížovnická. On a small street just off a main one, round the corner from Charles Bridge, the nameless hostel gets the best of both worlds: quiet and centrality. In an alleyway to the right behind Křížovnická 7. Keeps 46 beds in 4 rooms of 11 and one double (for emergencies), all in what seems to be a converted kindergarten. Funky local anglophones run the house. Lockout noon-5pm. Beds 200kč, deck chairs 150kč. Open June 28-Sept. 2.

Hostel Unitour, Senovážné nám. 21 (tel. 24 10 25 36; fax 24 22 15 79). Near Hlavní Nádraží and the Old Town. Right of the station, turn left onto Bolzánova. 4-bed rooms on the 3rd floor of an office building. Impersonal but clean. 290kč per person in rooms of 3 and 4. 40kč deposit. Call ahead.

ESTEC Hostel, Vaníčkova 5, blok (building) 5 (tel. 52 73 44). Take bus #217 or 143 from Metro A: Dejvická to "Koleje Stranov"; or bus #176 from Metro B: Karlovo nám. to the end at "Stádión Strahov". 500 beds and a beer garden downstairs make for lively nights. Sterile rooms, but that means they're clean, as are the hall toilets and showers. Plush comforters and pillows. Exchange in the reception (3% commission). Check-in 4pm, check-out 9:30am. 150kč laundry service. Singles 360kč. Doubles 240kč. Breakfast 50kč. AmEx, Eurocard, MC, Visa accepted.

Traveller's Hostels: "New, Comfortable, Famous"—at least that's what the brochure says. 6 dorms become sleep factories in summer. The one at Husova 3 (D3-4; tel. 24 21 53 26) is the classiest, with singles at 390kč and doubles at 490kč. Smack dab in the Old Town. Take Metro A to Národní Třida, turn right onto Spálená (which turns into Na Perštýně after Národní), then Husova. All others are dorms. Střelecký ostrov (tel. 24 91 01 88) on the island off most Legii is the newest. Metro B: Národní třída. 270kč. Mikulandská 5 (tel. 24 91 07 39). Metro B: Národní třída. 240kč. Křížovnická 7 (tel. 232 09 87). Metro A: Staroměstská. 240kč. Růžova 5. Metro C: Hlavní nádraží. 200-240kč. U lanové drahy 3 (tel. 53 31 60). Tram #6,9, 12, or 22 to "Újezd" and up the stairs. 180kč.

Welcome Hostel, Zikova 13 (tel. 24 31 14 46 ext. 110; tel./fax 32 47 20). Take Metro A to Dejvická, and from the escalators, follow Šolinova to Zikova. A free beer welcomes weary travelers. No-thrill singles and doubles. Reception closed daily 9-10am. Check-in 2pm. Singles 300kč. Doubles 230kč per person.

Hotels and Pensions

With so many tourists infiltrating Prague, hotels are upgrading both service and appearance. Budget hotels are fading faster than you can say *damned Americans*. Beware that hotels may try to bill you for a more expensive room than the one you in which you stayed. Come armed with pen, paper, and receipts. The good and cheap ones require reservations up to a month in advance. Call, and confirm by fax.

Hotel Unitour, Senovážné nám. 21 (tel. 24 10 25 36; fax 24 22 15 79). Unbelievable find near the Old Town. Clean. Singles 470kč, with bathroom 820kč. Doubles 770kč, with bathroom 1200kč. Triples 1100kč, with bathroom 1420kč.

Penzion Unitas, Bartolomějská 9 (tel. 232 77 00; fax 232 77 09), in the Old Town. Metro B: Národní. A Jesuit monastery where Beethoven once performed, transformed by the regime into a state prison where Václav Havel spent time. Thoroughly renovated, though the iron prison doors remain. The dungeon rooms are understandably a bit damp. No alcohol. Check-in 2pm; you can leave bags here if you arrive earlier. Check-out 10am. Lockout 1-6am. Singles 920kč. Doubles 1100kč. Triples 1500kč. Quads 1750kč. Breakfast included.

Hotel Kafka, Cimburkova 24 (tel. 27 31 01; fax 27 29 84), in Žižkov near the TV tower. Brand new hotel in amid 19th-century architecture. Nearby restaurants and *pivnice*. In July, singles 1150kč, doubles 1600kč, triples 1950kč. In August, singles 1400kč, doubles 1900kč, triples 2300kč, quads 2500kč. Less off-season.

Hotel Standart, Přístavní 2 (tel. 87 52 58; fax 80 67 52). From Metro C: Vltavská, take tram #1,3,14, or 25 to "Dělnická", continue along the street, then make a left onto Přístavní. Very quiet neighborhood that gets very dark at night. Spotless hall showers and WC. 740kč per person. HI members 345kč.

Junior Hotel Praha, Žitná 12 (tel. 29 29 84; fax 24 22 39 11), right next to CKM. Decor on the cutting edge of 1970s revival. Private showers and baths. Singles 1200kč. Doubles 1900kč. Huge buffet breakfast included. Reserve in advance. The **hostel** in the same building charges 400kč a bed in rooms of 4, but often fills up with German school groups.

B&B U Oty, Radlická 188 (tel./fax 52 68 41). 400m from Metro B: Radlická. The affable owner, Ota, cooks a mean breakfast that comes with the room. Kitchen facilities and free laundry services available after 3 nights. Singles 450kč. Doubles 700kč. Triples 900kč. Quads 1200kč. 100kč per person more if staying only 1 night. Parking free, provided you won't use the car to travel while in Prague. Otherwise at cost. 12 beds in all.

Penzion U Medvídků, Na Perštýně 7 (tel. 24 21 19 16; fax 24 22 09 30). Very central. Upstairs from a popular pub, the renovated rooms somehow escape the noise. Hall showers and toilets. 599kč per person in doubles and quads. If you're alone, the price rises to 900kč.

Camping

Campsites have taken over not only the outskirts but even the centrally located islands on the Vltava. Their bungalows must be reserved in advance. However, tent space is generally available. Should one be all booked up, chances are another site lies across the fence. Tourist offices sell a guide to sites near the city (15kč).

Císařská Louka, a peninsula on the Vltava. Metro B: Smíchovské nádraží, then tram #12 to Lihovar. Walk toward the river and onto the shaded path. Alternately, take the ferry service from Smíchovské nádraží (5kč). **Caravan Park** (tel. 54 50 64 or 54 09 25; fax 54 33 05) sits near the ferry, and **Caravan Camping** (tel. 54 01 29 or tel./fax 54 56 82), near the tram. Both charge 85kč per person, 80-120kč per tent. Caravan Park rents 2-person bungalows at 400kč and 4-person ones at 600kč. Caravan Camping offers rooms at 265kč per person. Reserve by fax.

Sokol Troja, Trojská 171 (tel./fax 688 11 77). The largest campground north of the center in the Troja district. From Metro C: Nádraží Holešovice, take bus #112 to "Kazanka," the fourth stop, then walk 100m. 90-180kč per tent, 110kč per person. 2- to 3-person bungalows at 200kč per head. Often full, so reserve in advance, or check out one of the million other sites on the same street.

Na Vlachovce, Zenklova 217 (tel. 66 41 02 14; fax 66 41 04 28). Take tram #12 from Hlavní Nádraží towards Okrouhlická, get off, and continue in the same direction. If you've ever felt like crawling into a barrel of *Budvár*, this bungalow city provides 2-person barrels at 220kč per bed, and if you miss the beer, the pub in front pours it for 15kč. Great view of Prague. Reserve a week ahead.

FOOD

Restaurants in Prague eat careless travelers alive. After hidden charges are added, the bill can be nearly twice what is expected. *Anything* offered with your meal (even ketchup) costs extra, as will everything placed on your table, including bread. Check the bill scrupulously. The farther from Old Town tourist mobs, the less you'll spend. *Hotová jídla* (prepared meals) are the cheapest. For a quick bite, the window stands selling tasty *párek v rohlíku* (sausage in a roll) for 7-15kč are a bargain. Outlying metro stops become impromptu marketplaces in summer; look for the daily **vegetable market** at the intersection of Havelská and Melantrichova in the Old Town. A number of eateries serving vegetarian cuisine have also opened.

Supermarkets
K-mart/Maj department store (tel. 24 22 79 71), corner of Národní and Spálena. Metro B: Národní Třída. K-mart bought this formerly state-owned chain. Open Mon.-Wed. 7am-7pm, Thurs.-Fri. 7am-8pm, Sat. 8am-6pm, Sun. 9am-5pm.
Krone department store (tel. 24 23 04 77), on Wenceslas Square at the intersection with Jindřišská. Open Mon.-Fri. 8am-7pm, Sat. 8am-6pm, Sun. 10am-6pm.
Kotva department store (tel. 24 21 54 62), corner of Revoluční and nám. Republiky. Metro B: nám. Republiky. Consistently well stocked. Open Mon. 7am-7pm, Tues.-Fri. 7am-8pm, Sat. 8am-4pm.

Staré Město (The Old Town)
U Medvídků, Na Perštýně 7 (tel. 24 22 09 30), bordering on the Old Town. Upscale pub fare amid dark-wood furniture and yellow everything else. *Guláš* 77kč, finger-food 20-30kč. Vegetarian choices (79-89kč) are spaghetti with Rocquefort cheese, veggie plate with cheese, and fried cheese *extraordinaire*. Draft *Budvars* for 18kč per 0.5L. Open Mon.-Sat. 11:30am-11pm, Sun. 11:30am-10pm.
Klub Architektů, Betlémské nám. 59 (tel. 24 40 12 14). Walk through the gates and descend to the right. A 12th-century cellar thrust into the 20th century with sleek table-settings and fun copper pulley lamps. The menu mixes too, with traditional dumpling plates (55-60kč) and new-fangled vegetarian burritos (32kč). *Pilsner* on tap for 20kč a ha' liter. Open Mon.-Sat. 11:30am-midnight.
Pizzeria Rugantino, Dušní 4 (tel. 231 81 72). Hidden 50m from the Old Town square. Blaze-green exterior welcomes the weary with 50-150kč pizzas and 6 amazing salads (40-90kč). Open Mon.-Sat. 11am-11pm, Sun. 6-11pm.
Zlatá Ulička, Masná 9 (tel. 232 08 84). Metro B: nám. Republicky, follow U obecního dvory to Rybná, turn right, then left on Masná. Pricier than a commie buffet, but you get what you pay for. The 40kč veal broth is heaven; main courses cost upwards of 110kč. A guitar player having a coffee at an outside table might randomly strike up a tune. Open daily 10am-midnight.
Shalom, Maiselova 18 (D2-3; tel. 24 81 09 29; fax 24 81 09 12). Fine *košer* dining in the ancient Jewish Quarter. 600kč prix-fixe menu. Open daily 11:30am-2pm.

Nové Město (The New Town)
Velryba (The Whale), Opatovická 24 (tel. 24 91 23 91). Relaxed with a bit of chic, this café-restaurant stores a gallery in the back. Trendy expats without the cash enjoy inexpensive Czech dishes (50-80kč) and gallons of java (11-31kč). Can you see the whale on the sea-green wall? Open daily 11am-1am. Kitchen closes at 10pm. Last guests leave around 2am.
Góvinda, Soukenická 27. Rama and Krishna gaze upon diners and their delicious vegetarian stews. Cafeteria-style, serving a plate with the works for a 50kč donation. Menu changes daily so you won't get bored. Open Mon.-Sat. 11am-5pm.
U Rozvařlů, Na poříčí (tel. 24 21 93 57). The last of a Communist breed evolving to survive. The glass and steel remains—but shine has replaced the grit. Nowadays you can sit down with *guláš* (33kč) and Coke or beer (12kč). This is still as close as it comes to the red old days, so pay your respects. Open Mon.-Fri. 8am-7:30pm, Sat. 8am-7pm, Sun. 10am-5pm.
Pizzeria Kmotra, V jirchářích 12 (tel. 24 91 58 09). Some argue it's the best pizza on both sides of Italy. Watch your crust cook in the brick oven of a vaulted underground eatery. Huge pizzas 54-93kč. Moravian wine runs 19kč a glass. Beer 16kč per 0.5L. Open daily 11am-1pm.
Jáma (The Hollow), V Jámě 7 (tel. 26 41 27). Hidden off Vodikčova, Jáma attracts a diverse crowd with road rhythms and jazz shows on Sunday nights. Prices keep steadily rising, but the grilled chicken salad (89kč) might just be that ultra-light meal you've been looking for for ages. Weekend brunches (50-85kč) come with free coffee/tea refills. 3 beers on tap (22-24kč). Open daily 11am-1am.
Restaurace U Pravdů, Žitná 15 (tel. 29 95 92). Best *řízek* (schnitzel) in Prague. The wood and plaster decor, chandelier, and high ceiling take you back to a kinder,

gentler time. The garden in the back will do the same in hot weather. *Radegast* (15kč) and *Staropramen* (11kč) on tap. Open daily 11am-10pm.

Country Life, Jungmannova 1 (tel. 24 19 17 39). Veggie sandwiches and salads by a health-food store of the same name. The most popular concoction consists of carrots, endives, tomatoes, and a bulghar patty on a multi-grain bun (23kč). Prices drop 30-50% after 5:30pm. Open Mon.-Thurs. 9:30am-6:30pm, Fri. 10am-3pm.

Černý Pivovar, Karlovo nám. 15 (tel. 294 45 23). Metro B: Karlovo nám. An enormous mural runs the length of the wall, depicting comrades happily sweating in the restaurant's brewery. Locals sweat as the down Czech entrées for under 30kč. 0.5L of *Gambrinus* 10kč. Open Mon.-Fri. 7:30am-8pm, Sat.-Sun. 9am-8pm.

Česká Hospoda V Krakovské, Krakovská 20 (tel. 26 15 37). Tiny pub 60m from Wenceslas square. This is Czech! Aproned waiters scurry with 20kč beers and plates of tender *guláš* (73kč). But the Czech-est order, *vepřo-knedlo-zelo,* costs 76kč. Open Mon.-Fri. 10am-11pm, Sat.-Sun. 11am-11pm.

Malá Strana (Lesser Town)

Bar bar, Všehrdova 17. Left off Karmelitská walking down from Malostranské nám. A jungle jungle of salads salads with meat meat, fish fish, cheese cheese or just veggies veggies (49-69kč). The other choice is, surprisingly, not fried pork with french fries, but pancakes pancakes—sweet sweet (12-45kč) or savory savory (43-89kč). The stuttering eatery stuck a few tables in its spacious basement, but the whole area still fills with smoke to the last air-pocket. *Velkopopovický kozel* on tap at 15kč per 0.5L. Open Mon.-Fri. 11am-midnight, Sat.-Sun. noon-midnight.

Malostranská Hospoda, Karmelitská 25 (tel. 53 20 76), 2 blocks south of Malostranské nám. Chairs spill out onto the square from the pub's vaulted interior. The usual long table in the corner surrounded by beer and *becherovka* fans is made up of women. Good *guláš* (50kč), batman! Draft *Staropramen* 13kč per 0.5L. English menu. Open Mon.-Sat. 10am-midnight, Sun. 11am-midnight.

U zeleného čaje, Nerudova 19 (tel. 53 26 83), up from Malostanské nám. This teahouse on the tourist trail remains uncrowded thanks to the sparse 4 tables. The smoke-free space helps salad fans enjoy their cheap and tasty snacks (14kč for a small plate). The tea menu explains the curative qualities of each flavor. The *jablečný závoj* (apple strudel; 15kč) is hot—for an extra 5kč you can make it orgasmic by covering it in whipped cream. Open daily 10am-7pm.

U Švejka, Újezd 22 (tel. 52 56 29; fax 29 14 76). Touristy, but with large helpings. The gigantic "dinosaur leg" costs 100kč, smaller fare runs 40-90kč. *Pilsner* flows for 19kč a stein. Open daily 11am-midnight.

Café-Bar Bílý Orel (White Eagle), Minská 10, in Malostranské nám. If a child were to be brought up here, it would be murderously aggressive, given the screaming orange walls, abstract art, and chairs that look like chemical models. A très cool place for a 70-75kč small breakfast or a 30-35kč coffee. The radio tuned to BBC provides the accent of a snooty butler. AmEx and Visa accepted. Acid jazz is a frequent nighttime visitor. Open daily 8:30am-1am.

Jo's Bar, Malostranské nám. 7. You can bet the ranch house that everyone here speaks English (and after they grow out of their hippie hair or baseball caps will carry a *Fodor's*, have 2.6 kids, and an Oldsmobile). Burritos, quesadillas, and nachos 75-105kč. *Staropramen* 25kč.

On the Fringe

Na Zvonařce, Šafaříkova 1 (tel./fax 691 13 11), east of the New Town in Vinohrady. Czech dishes on a terrace over the city. 100 trees block the view, but diners feel like they're floating on air—until they eat the dumplings. Heavy, filling meat-and-*knedlíky* cuisine from 40kč. A 0.5L stein 15kč. Open daily 11am-11pm.

Bistro Bruska (tel. 32 05 78), corner of Dejvická and Eliášova. Metro A: Hradčanská. Catch a bite while doing laundry or during the commute to Strahov. As close to "tradition" as it gets with pink-lipsticked, bleached-haired, tight-tank-topped waitrons winked at by the flashing lights of gambling machines. Large veggie entrées 32-42kč. Daily specials only 40-50kč; the Ukrainian borscht is heavenly heavy (10kč). A half-liter of *Krušovice* 12kč. Open Mon.-Sat. 10am-10pm.

Restaurant U Holanů, Londýnská 10 (tel. 25 48 45), on tree-lined Londýnská in Vinohrady. 30-50kč *guláš* and other delights served under a timbered roof and plane trees. *Gambrinus* 12kč. Open Mon.-Fri. 10am-11pm, Sat.-Sun. 11am-11pm.

Deminka, Škrétova 1 (tel. 24 22 33 83), just southeast of Metro A: Národní muzeum. A staunch stickler for the old ways, Deminka's manager has kept the chandeliers, Victorian wallpaper, folded cloth napkins, and low-low prices. The *guláš* special runs at 45kč. Open Mon.-Fri. 11am-11pm, Sat.-Sun. noon-11pm.

Cafés

Dozens of dimestore *kavárnas* have opened up in the Old Town, but for more than an expensive one-bite stand, try the outskirts where sippers actually hang out. For *the* top-notch café, descend to **Velryba** (see Food: New Town, p. 184).

U malého Glena, Karmelitská 23 (tel. 535 81 15 or 90 00 39 67), just south off Malostranské nám. The "light entrée" choices top a plate of mixed salad with toast and tuna, meat, or cheese (95-115kč), but the best deals come with stuffed pita (veggie 55kč, shredded deli meat 60kč). A scary clay mask of the locale's patron ghost admires the tattoos and piercings of the young Czech clientele. Frequent live music at night—consult the schedule on the tables. Open daily 7:30am-2am.

U Knihomola, Mánesova 79 (tel. 627 77 70). Metro A: Jiřího z Poděbrad. An extended living room with 30ft. of comfy couch and coffee-table literature. Smooth jazz drifts in, lulling coffee-sippers to Nirvana (20kč). Carrot cake 65kč. Open Mon.-Thurs. 10am-11pm, Fri.-Sat. 10am-midnight, Sun. 11am-8pm.

The Globe Coffeehouse, Janovského 14 (tel./fax 66 71 26 10), inside Prague's largest English bookstore. Peruse *Let's Go* as you sip a hot beverage and contemplate literary self-reference. People come for the 0.4-L teas, a cigarette, and ex-pat gossip. Open daily 10am-midnight.

Derby, Dukelských hrdinů 20 (tel. 66 31 43 20). Metro C: Vltavská, then any tram that goes to "Strossmayerovo nám.". A block and a half north from there. Wood, wood, wood, and more wood. Black-clad waitrons with black hair. More wood. A large space that hosts occasional live concerts. Coffee 15-17kč. Salads 55-80kč. Quesadillas, fajitas, burritos (45-85kč). Open daily 11am-2am.

Nebozízek, Petřínské sady 411 (B4-5; tel. 53 79 05). Pricey but worth the view. A funicular runs from Újezd, between Všehrdova and Říční, to the midpoint of the Petřín summit (runs daily 9:30am-9pm). The lift stops only twice: at Nebozízek and at the miniature of the Eiffel Tower. Open daily 11am-6pm and 7-11pm.

Kavárna Medúza, Belgická 17. Antique shop masquerading as a café. Fluffed-up Victorian seats and 10 kinds of affordable coffee (15-25kč; 30kč if you like liqueur added, 30-60kč). Open Mon.-Fri. 11am-1am, Sat.-Sun. noon-1am.

SIGHTS

Central Prague is structured by three streets that form a leaning *"T"*. The long stem of the *T*, separating the Old and New Towns, is the boulevard **Václavské nám.** (Wenceslas Sq.). The **National Museum** sits at the bottom of the *T*. Busy and pedestrian, **Na příkopě** forms the right arm and leads to **nám. Republiky.** On the left, **28. října** becomes **Národní** after a block, leading to the **National Theater** on the river. A maze of small streets leads to Staroměstské nám. two blocks above the *T*. There are two prominent **St. Nicholas cathedrals**—in Malá Strana near the castle and in Staroměstké nám.—and two **Powder Towers**—one in the castle and another in nám. Republiky. Strollers will find that Prague has plentiful green space along Malá Strana's **Petřínské Sady.** Miles of pathways traverse the Kinsky, Strahov, Lobkowic, Schönborn, and Seminář **gardens,** but most are badly eroded. Many try the promenade on the banks of the Vltava south of **most Legií** along the New Town's **Masarykoro nábřeží.** Gorgeous greenery lies southeast of the Old Town in Vinohrady. The quarter's hills also offer great views of the town. Use common sense, and don't jog in polluted Prague.

Václavské Náměstí (Wenceslas Square)

> *I've taken my grandchildren to the top of Wenceslas Square where St. Wenceslas looks over the entire square. I tell them to imagine all the things St. Wenceslas might have seen sitting there on his horse: the trading markets hundreds of years ago, Hitler's troops, the Soviet tanks, and our Velvet Revolution in 1989. I can still imagine these things; it's the boulevard where much of our history, good and bad, has passed.*
> —Bedřich Šimáček, driver of tram #22, quoted in *The Prague Post*

Václavské nám., the festive heart of Prague, was designed as a quiet promenade in the late 19th century. The statue of the king and saint **Václav** (Wenceslas), in front of the National Museum, has presided over a century of turmoil and triumph, witnessing no less than five revolutions from his southeast pedestal. The perfectionist sculptor Myslbek completed Václav after 25 years of deliberation; as others gasped at its 1912 unveiling, poor Myslbek just mumbled, "It could have been bigger." The equestrian Sv. Václav is big enough for most and has stood for nearly a century as an encouragement to Czech independence. It was here that Czechoslovakia declared itself a nation in 1918, and here that in 1969 Jan Palach set himself ablaze to protest Soviet intervention in the Prague Spring.

Wenceslas Square sweeps down from the National Museum, past department stores, stately parks, and, at night, flashing neon signs. The view of the museum from Můstek's base is hypnotic at full moon, but keep your wits about you. Despite frequent police sweeps, the square has become one of the seediest areas in Prague. Behind the museum, across the Vltava all the way to Holešovice runs the monstrous six-lane **Wilsonova**, originally named Vitězného února (Victorious February) in honor of the 1948 Soviet-backed Communist seizure of power. In 1989, it was renamed after President Woodrow Wilson, who helped forge the ultimately doomed inter-war Czechoslovak state. The **Radio Prague Building** behind the National Museum, was the scene of a tense battle between Soviet tanks and Prague's citizens attempting to protect the studios by human barricade. The radio station succeeded in transmitting impartial updates for the first 14 hours of the invasion.

Stretching north from the Wenceslas monument, Art Nouveau, from lampposts to windowsills, dominates the square. The premier example is the 1903 **Hotel Evropa**. Since its construction, the hotel has been a socialite center with a side-street café of the same name. The post-revolution clientele is more kitchy than cultured, but people-watching possibilities still abound.

From the north end of Václavské nám., take a quick detour to Jungmannovo nám. and **Panna Marie Sněžná** (Church of Our Lady of the Snows). Founded by King Charles IV in 1347, this edifice was intended to be the largest church in Prague; the Gothic walls are, indeed, higher than any other house of worship, but the rest of the structure is still unfinished—there was only enough cash to complete the choir. It still feels tiny, despite the Baroque altar and magnificently vaulted ceiling (open daily 7am-6pm). Enter **Františkánská zahrada** through the arch at the intersection of Jungmannova and Národní. No one knows how the Franciscans who still tend the rose gardens have managed to maintain such a bastion of serenity in Prague's loud commercial district, but most friars would be too busy talking to the birds to answer questions (open daily 7am-9pm). Under the arcades halfway down Národní stands a **memorial** that honors the hundreds of Prague's citizens beaten on November 17, 1989. Marching in a government-sanctioned protest, they were greeted by a line of shield-bearing, truncheon-armed police. After a stalemate, the "protectors of the people" bludgeoned the marchers, injuring hundreds. This event marked the start of the Velvet Revolution, headquartered at the **Magic Lantern Theater**, Národní 4. Here, Václav Havel and others delivered press releases and developed a peaceful program to topple the Soviet-backed regime.

Staroměstské Náměstí (Old Town Square)

A labyrinth of narrow roads and Old World alleys lead to the thriving heart of the Old Town—**Staroměstské náměstí**. **Jan Hus**, the Czech Republic's most famous martyred theologian, sweeps across the scene in bronze. In summer, masses of travelers sit at the base of his robes, drinking, smoking, slinging woo, and performing a hundred other deeds upon which Jan can only frown. No less than eight magnificent towers surround the square; here the nickname "city of a thousand spires" takes on new meaning. The expansive cobblestone plaza leaves room for everyone, even the ranks of horse carriages (500kč for 20min.) and blacksmiths selling twisted metal for the price of a Trabant. The building with a bit blown off is the **Staroměstská radnice** (Old Town Hall). During the 1945 anti-Nazi uprising, the town hall was the first on the Fascists' list of buildings to demolish; luckily they never did. Prague's *radnice* has long been a witness to violence—**crosses** on the ground mark the spot where 27 Protestant leaders were executed on June 21, 1621 for a (failed) rebellion against the Catholic Habsburgs. The tourist office inside offers tours of the town hall's interior (20kč, students 10kč; open in summer daily 9am-5pm; off-season, only when there are tourists). The **Old Senate**, with a magnificent coffered ceiling, boasts a Baroque stove with a figure of Justice and a sculpture of Christ. The inscription reads, "Judge justly—sons of Man." Onlookers gather on the hour to see the town hall's fabulous **Astronomical Clock** (*orloj*) with 12 peering apostles and a bell-ringing skeleton representing death. The clockmaker's eyes were reputedly put out by his patron so he could not craft another.

Nám. Jana Palacha, next to the Staroměstská metro station, went by "Red Army Square" before 1989. Jan Palach was philosophy student at **Charles University** who set himself on fire to protest Soviet re-occupation. On the left corner of the philosophy department's façade is a copy of Palach's death mask, erected as a memorial of his self-immolation. Over 800,000 citizens followed his coffin from the Old Town Square to the Olšany Cemetery, where he is buried today.

Across from the town hall, the spires of **Panna Marie před Týnem** (Týn Church) rise above a huddled mass of medieval homes. The famous astronomer **Tycho Brahe** is buried inside; he over-indulged at one of Emperor Rudolf's lavish dinner parties. To the left of the church, the austere **Dům U kamenného zvonu** (House at Stone Bell) shows the Gothic core that lurks beneath many of Prague's Baroque façades. The flowery **Goltz-Kinský palác** on the left is the finest of Prague's Rococo buildings. **Sv. Mikuláš** (St. Nicholas Church) sits just across Staroměstské nám. (open Tues.-Sun. 10am-5pm). Kilian Ignaz Dienzenhofer built the church in only three years; Dienzenhofer and his dad then built the **St. Nicholas Church** in Malá Strana, right by the castle. Between Maiselova and Sv. Mikulaš, a plaque marks **Franz Kafka's** former home. For directions to his resting place see p. 193.

At Malá Štupartská, behind Týn Church, a thief's arm has been dangling from the entrance of **Kostel Sv. Jakuba** (St. Jacob's Cathedral) for five centuries. Legend holds that a thief tried to pilfer one of the gems from the **Virgin Mary of Suffering** statue, whereupon the figure came to life, seized the thief's arm at the elbow and wrenched it off. The monks took pity on the repentant, profusely bleeding soul by inviting him to join their order. He accepted and remained faithfully pious; the arm hangs as a reminder to the faithful (open daily 6:45am-4:30pm).

Karlův Most (Charles Bridge)

Head out of the Old Town square on Jilská and take Karlova at the fork to get to Charles Bridge, which bursts at the seams with beggars, tourists, and hawkers. Continue along Jilská to reach Betlémské nám. Imagine Jan Hus marching out of the **Bethlehem Chapel** after delivering a litany against the abuses and corruption of the Catholic Church. Being burnt at the stake by the Inquisition made him a martyr; many still regard him as a hero. Inside, the sect's hymns line the walls, inscribed in old Gregorian notation (20kč, students 10kč).

Karlův most is to Prague like sex is to Madonna: central, essential, and non-discriminating. Artisans and street performers fill Europe's most festive bridge day and night above a bevy of swans. The musical tradition is ancient; Austrian minstrel Dan von der Kuper once wandered the planks of the Charles asking for spare thalers. At the center of the bridge, the eighth statue from the right is a monument to legendary hero **Jan Nepomucký** (John of Nepomuk), confessor to Queen Žofie. At the statue's base is a depiction of hapless Jan, being tossed over the side of the Charles for faithfully guarding his queen's confidences from a suspicious King Václav IV. Torture by hot irons and other devices failed to loosen Jan's lips, so the King ordered him to be drowned in the Vltava. A halo of five gold stars supposedly appeared as Jan plunged into the icy water. The right-hand rail, from whence Jan was supposedly ejected, is now marked with a cross and five stars between the fifth and sixth statues. Place one finger on each star and make a wish; not only is your wish *guaranteed* to come true, but any wish made on this spot will at some point in the future whisk the wisher back to Prague.

King Karel (Charles) IV built his bridge to replace one that washed away in 1342. It is enormous—520m by 10m. The foundation stone was laid at 5:31am on the morning of July 9, 1357, the most significant astrological point for Leo—the mascot of Bohemia. Legend has it that the builder made a pact with the devil in order to complete the massive bridge. Satan was allotted the first soul to cross the completed bridge, but the builder's wife and newborn babe unwittingly traversed the finished structure first; the devil could not take the baby's pure soul, so he instead cast a spell over the bridge. In the evening, some hear the faint cry of an infant, the ghostly wails of a surrogate spirit child—or is it the whining of prepubescent hostel youth?

Climb the Gothic **defense tower** on the Malá Strana side of the bridge for a superb view of the city (open daily 10am-5:30pm; 20kč, students 10kč) or on the Old Town side (same hours, same prices, similar view). The stairs on the left side of the bridge (as you face the castle district) lead to **Hroznová,** where a mural honors John Lennon and the peace movement of the 60s. **Slovanský ostrov, Dětský ostrov,** and **Střelecký ostrov** islands are accessible from Janáčkovo nábřeží and the **most Legií** bridge. From the Charles, you can see rowboat outlets renting the vessels necessary to explore these islands and the remainder of the **Vltava** ("Kubík Tours" boat rental, tel. 231 99 52, rents rowboats and waterbikes at 50kč per hour; daily—depending on the weather—from 11am).

Josefov

Prague's historic Jewish neighborhood, Josefov, is located north of Staroměstské nám. along Maiselova and several side streets. Its cultural wealth lies in five well preserved synagogues. In 1179, the Pope decreed that all good Christians should avoid contact with Jews; a year later, Prague's citizens complied with a 12-foot wall. For the next five centuries, the city's Jewish community, when not expelled, perished within the confines of northwest Prague. With the walls came legends of intrigue, Frankenstein golems, and gift-giving goblins. The wall came down under Emperor Joseph II, for whom the quarter is named, but the persecution did not stop; it reached a height during WWII with pogroms, expulsions, and the Nazi annihilation of Josefov's population. A cemetery and five of the synagogues were saved by Hitler's perverse decision to create a "museum of an extinct race." The walls may be gone, but there is a steep admission fee (340kč, students 230kč) to see the synagogues and museum. This is reason enough to learn elementary Czech; if you can say *"jednou vstupenku [pro studenta]"* (YEHD-no VSTOO-pen-coo [proh STOOH-den-tah]) and are lucky enough not to be asked anything in return, pay only 25kč (Czech nonstudents 50kč). All monuments on the route for which the tickets are valid are open Sunday through Monday 9am to 6pm. At the ninety-degree bend in U Starého hřbitova, **Starý židovský hřbitov** (Old Jewish Cemetery) remains the quarter's most popular attraction. From the 14th-18th centuries, 12 layers of 20,000 graves were laid. Seven hundred-years old, **Staronová synagóga** (Old-New Synagogue) is Europe's oldest synagogue still in use. En route to the Old-New Synagogue, **Klausová synagóga** (Klausen Synagogue) displays rotating exhibitions, usually paintings on a common theme.

Next to the Old-New Synagogue, the 16th-century **Vysoká synagóga** (High Synagogue) holds exhibits of ceremonial items and religious tapestries. The neighboring **Židovská radnice** (Jewish Town Hall) was once the administrative control center of old Josefstadt, as Jews referred to Josefov in the early 19th century. Search out the Hebrew clock that runs counterclockwise in the pink Rococo exterior of the town hall. Walk down Maiselova and turn right on Široka until you reach the **Pinkasova synagóga** (Pinkas Synagogue). The synagogue's walls once again list the names of victims from four centuries of persecution, after Communists let damprot destroy them during their regime. A Torah from this synagogue is on permanent loan to Temple Beth Torah in Dix Hills, New York; many Central European synagogues have donated their scrolls to American and Israeli synagogues. Turning right onto Maiselova again, you can enter the ornate **Maiselova synagóga** (Maisel Synagogue), that exhibits the Jews' way of living and praying throughout the centuries.

Malá Strana (Lesser Side)

For nearly a century, the seedy hangout of criminals and counter-revolutionaries, the cobblestone streets of the Lesser Side have, in the strange sway of Prague fashion, become the most prized real estate on either side of the Vltava. Yuppies now dream of a flat with a view on St. Nicholas's Cathedral. Affluent foreigners sip beers in the haunts where Jaroslav Hašek and his bumbling soldier Švejk once guzzled suds. The current trends seem to fit the plans of the original designer, King Otokar II, who in the 13th century dreamed of creating a powerful economic quarter. This was not to occur until the 15th century, when Austrian nobility erected grand churches and palaces. However, as nationalism rose, the quarter became known as a rat's den of surly sailors, dealers, and drunken brawls. The 1989 revolution has brought a new appreciation for the district's architecture, and careful restorations have made it one of the most visitable and visited sections of Prague. Rising above the square's mess of Baroque frippery, **Sv. Mikuláš** (St. Nicholas's Church; tel. 53 69 83) impresses from the outside and simply frightens from within with its unbelievably high dome. Mozart's works are performed here almost nightly (open daily 9am-5pm; 20kč, students 10kč; concert tickets 300kč, students 200kč). Nearby on Karmelitská rises the more modest **Panna Maria Vítězna** (Church of Our Lady Victorious; tel. 53 07 52). The famous polished-wax statue of the **Infant Jesus of Prague,** which bestows miracles on the faithful, resides within. The figurine has an elaborate wardrobe of over 380 outfits; every sunrise, the Infant is swaddled anew by the nuns of a nearby convent. The statue first arrived in town in the arms of a 17th-century Spanish noblewoman who married into the Bohemian royalty; mysteriously, the plague bypassed Prague shortly thereafter. In 1628, the Barefooted Carmelite nunnery gained custody of the Infant and allowed pilgrims to pray to the statue; the public has been infatuated with it ever since (open daily 10am-7:30pm).

Designed by father-son Kristof and Kilian Ignaz Dienzenhofer, the duo responsible for the Břevnov Monastery's undulating façade (see Outer Prague, p. 193), the **St. Thomas Church** stands at Letenská off Malostranské nám., toward the Vltava. Rubens facsimiles await within, adjacent to the saintly reliquaries adorning the side altars (open daily 7am-6pm). A simple wooden gate just down the street at Letenská 10 opens onto **Valdštejnská zahrada** (Wallenstein Garden), one of Prague's best-kept secrets. This tranquil 17th-century Baroque garden is enclosed by old buildings that glow golden on sunny afternoons. General Albert Wallenstein, owner of the palace of the same name, held his parties here among Vredeman de Vries's classical bronze **statues**—when the works were plundered by Swedish troops in the waning hours of the Thirty Years War, Wallenstein replaced the original casts with facsimiles. **Frescoes** inside the arcaded loggia depict popular episodes from the Trojan War (open May-Sept. daily 9am-7pm). A 10m wall keeps the city out, and on sunny afternoons the grand buildings inside glow golden. Across the street from the Malostranská metro stop, a plaque hidden in a lawn constitutes the **Charousková Memorial,** the sole monument to those slain in 1968. It commemorates **Marie Charousková,** a grad-

SIGHTS ■ 191

Prague Castle

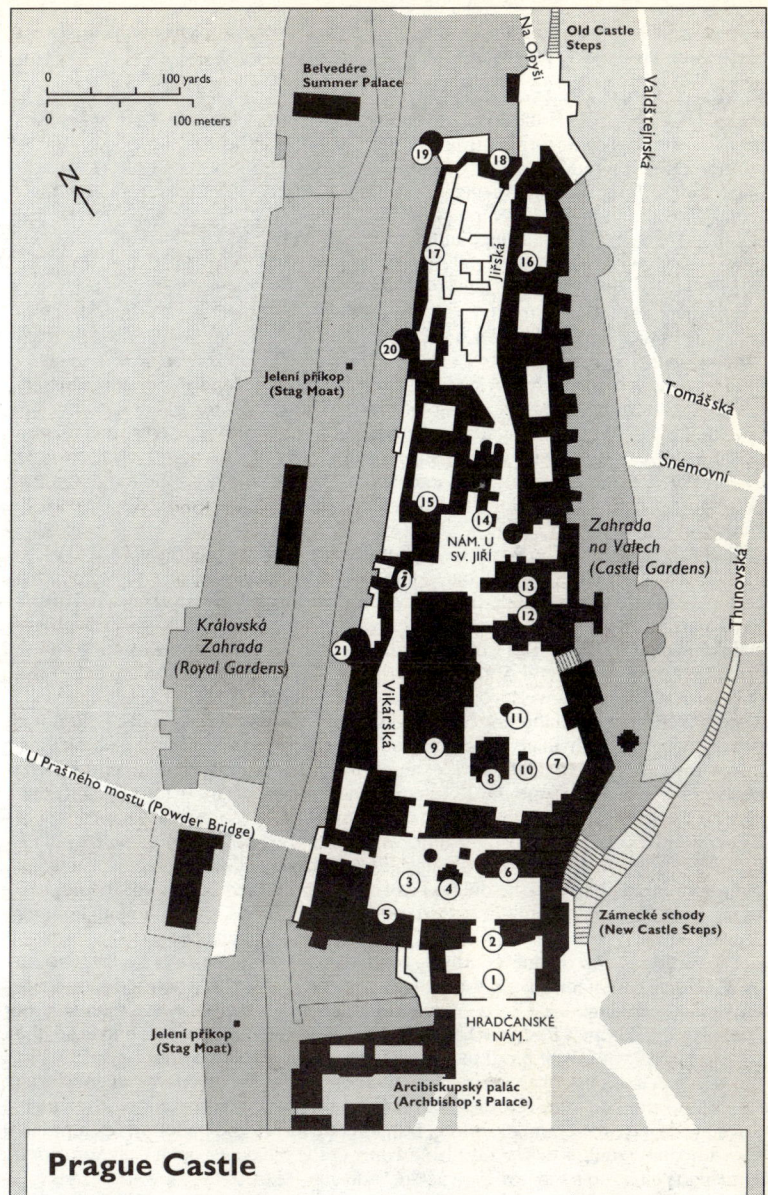

Bazilika Sv. Jiří (Basilica of St. George), **14**
Bílá věž (White Tower), **20**
Černá věž (Black Tower), **18**
Chrám Sv. Víta (St. Vitus's Cathedral), **9**
Daliborka (Daliborka Tower), **19**
I. nádvoří (First Courtyard), **1**
II. nádvoří (Second Courtyard), **3**
III. nádvoří (Third Courtyard), **7**
Jízdárna (Riding School; Art Gallery), **13**
Kaple Sv. Kříže s klenotnicí (Chapel of the Holy Rood), **6**
Kohlova kašna (Kohl's Fountain), **4**
Lobkovický palác (Lobkovic Palace), **16**
Matyášova brána (Matthias Gate), **2**
Monolit (Monolith), **10**
National Gallery of Bohemian Art, **15**
Prasná věž (Powder Tower), **21**
Socha Sv. Jiří (Statue of St. George), **11**
Španělský sál (Spanish Hall; Castle Picture Gallery), **5**
Staré probošství (Old Provost's House), **8**
Starý královský palac (Old Royal Palace), **12**
Zlatá ulička (Golden Lane), **17**

CZECH REPUBLIC

uate student who was machine-gunned by a Soviet soldier for refusing to remove a black ribbon protesting the invasion.

Pražský Hrad (Prague Castle)

Buried beneath carved stone and a millennium of legends, the original site of **Pražský hrad**—a simple pagan fortification—could give little indication of the sprawling contradiction it would become. Over the centuries, Hradčanská's walls saw Catholics replace Protestants, Protestants push out Papists (sometimes from very high windows), and in the last ideological struggle, a rebel playwright succeed the red regime. The castle and its surrounding town are a great place to spend a day, but bring everything you'll need for the day, don't come on Monday, and come early. The fortress houses the **National Gallery of Bohemian Art** (see Museums, below), but the primary attraction is the soaring **Chrám Sv. Víta** (St. Vitus's Cathedral), completed in 1930 after 600 years of construction. Past the sweating soldiers and through a second gate, the Czech Republic's largest church can't decide what style it wants to be. To the right of the high altar stands the **tomb of St. Jan Nepomucký,** three meters of solid, glistening silver, weighing two tons. The enormous silver sepulcher is crowned by an angel holding a silver tongue in her hand; supposedly, this tongue was the only part of Jan Nepomucký still recognizable when his body was discovered by fishermen in the spring after his execution. The queen placed the tongue in the notorious cathedral confessional to commemorate its silence; eventually, it was silvered and put on display.

Below the cathedral, the **Royal Crypt** is unusually calm, considering Charles IV and his four wives have been boxed together in a room for six centuries. A powerful spell cast by Charles's wizard curses unworthy souls who try on the royal crown; Hitler's Field Marshal Heydrick died a week after testing the magic. The walls of **Svatováclavská kaple** (St. Wenceslas Chapel) are lined with precious stones and a painting cycle depicting the legend of this saint. A large door leads from the chapel to the Bohemian coronation jewels; you'll have to ask President Havel for the keys.

Stroll across the third interior courtyard to enter **Starý královský palác** (Old Royal Palace), where gloomy halls have become the exhibition site for even gloomier art. Inside, the vast **Vladislav Hall** provides ample room for the jousting competitions that once took place here. Climb the 287 steps of the **Cathedral Tower** for a breathtaking view of the castle and the city (open daily 10am-4pm). In the nearby **Chancellery of Bohemia,** two Catholic Habsburg officials were lobbed out the window by fed-up Protestant noblemen in 1618 in the notorious **Defenestration of Prague.** Though a dungheap broke their fall, the die was cast, and war ravaged Europe for the next 30 years. Built in 1485 to enhance the castle's fortifications, the **Mihulka** (Powder Tower) houses a reconstruction of one protochemist's laboratories.

The vertical red-clay tennis court was erected in 921 as the **Bazilika Sv. Jiří** (Basilica of St. George). Immediately on the right as you enter, note the wood-and-glass tomb enclosing St. Ludmila's skeleton. When workmen were laying the first foundations, Ludmila's thigh bone vanished. One week later, the head mason was found dead; the two architects who were hired to complete the job both died within a year. Finally, the architect's son discovered the thigh bone among his father's personal effects; he snuck into the convent, returned the skeletal link, and thereby ended the curse. Roaming around the complex is free, but entering any of the buildings (except half the cathedral) requires tickets (available at any of the buildings; open daily 9am-5pm; some parts close up to 45min. early; 80kč, students 40kč).

The **Lobkovický Palác,** at the bottom of Jiřská, contains a replica of Bohemia's coronation jewels, and a history of the lands that comprise the Czech Republic (open April-Sept. Tues.-Sun. 9am-5pm; Oct.-March 9am-4pm; 30kč, students 15kč). Halfway up, the tiny **Zlatá ulička** (Golden Lane) served as the main research division of Rudolf's alchemy program; in the 20th century, Kafka conjured his own literary formulae in one of the lane's mini-offices.

Exiting the castle across **Prašný most** (Powder Bridge) you'll see the entrance to the serene **Královská zahrada** (Royal Garden), sculpted in 1534 to include the glorious and newly renovated Renaissance palace **Belvedér.** Devastated by Swedes and Saxons during the Thirty Years War, today the garden houses an **Orangery** and **Fig Garden** (open Tues.-Sun. 10am-5:45pm; 5kč, students 2kč). If you exit the castle through the main gate instead, and walk straight for 200 yards, the lovely **Loreto** (tel. 24 51 07 89) will be on the right. A medusa's garden of agonized statues guards the entrance to this popular pilgrimage site. Thousands of the faithful and curious pass through daily, admiring the shrine's many saints (open Tues.-Sun. 9am-4:30pm; 30kč, students 20kč). For more on the castle complex, seek out the **Informační středisko** (Information Center) behind the cathedral.

Outer Prague

The largest gardens in central Prague, **Petřínské sady,** provide some of the most spectacular views of the city. A cable car runs to the top (6kč; look for *lanová dráha* signs), leaving from just above the intersection of Vítězná and Újezd. It stops once to deposit visitors at Nebozízek, Prague's most scenically-endowed café. At the summit, a replica of the Eiffel Tower offers a few more meters of view (open daily April-Oct. 9:30am-9pm; Nov.-March 9:30am-6pm; 20kč, students 10kč). Next door, the wacky castle **Bludiště** (Hall of Mirrors) has become a favorite of both tots and hippies (open daily April-Oct. 10am-4pm). Just east of the park is **Strahov Stadium,** the world's largest, covering the space of 10 soccer fields.

Take tram #22 west of the castle to "Břevnovský klášter", and you'll find yourself staring down from the **Břevnov Monastery,** Bohemia's oldest Benedictine order. The monastery was founded in 993 by King Boleslav II and St. Adalbert, each independently guided by a divine dream to create a monastery atop a bubbling stream. **Kostel Sv. Markéty** (St. Margaret's Church), a Benedictine chapel, waits inside the complex. Beneath the altar rests the tomb of St. Vintíř, who, even in Bohemia, vowed to forego all forms of meat. On one particular diplomatic excursion, St. Vintíř met and dined with a German king, who was a fanatical hunter; the main course was an enormous pheasant slain that morning by the monarch's own hand. The saint prayed for delivery from the myriad *faux pas* possibilities, whereupon the main course sprang to life and flew out the window. The green bell tower and red tile roof of the monastery building are all that remain of the original Romanesque construction; the complex was redesigned in high Baroque by the Dienzenhofer father and son team. During the Soviet occupation, the monastery was allegedly used to store truckloads of secret police files. See if you can graft yourself onto a guided tour of the grounds, crypt, and prelature (tours daily 10am-6pm; 50kč).

Bus #112 winds from Metro C: Nádraží Holešovice to **Troja,** the site of French architect J. B. Mathey's masterful **château.** The pleasure palace, overlooking the Vltava from north of the U-shaped bend, includes a terraced garden, an oval staircase, and a collection of 19th-century Czech paintings (open Tues.-Sun. 9am-5pm). The tourist office carries schedules of **free concerts** in the château's great hall.

The former haunt of Prague's 19th-century romantics, **Vyšehrad** is clothed in nationalistic myths and the legends of a once-powerful Czech empire. It is here that Princess Libuše prophesied the founding of Prague and embarked on her search for the first king of Bohemia. The 20th century has passed the castle by, and Vyšehrad's elevated pathways now escape the shotgun tourists of Staré město. Quiet walkways lead between crumbling stone walls to a magnificent **church,** a black Romanesque rotunda, and the Czech Republic's most celebrated site—**Vyšehrad Cemetery** (home to the remains of Dvořák and Božena Němcová of the 500kč bill). Metro C: Vyšehrad. Even the subway stop has a movie-sweep vista of Prague (open 24hr.).

For a magnificent view of the Old Town and castle from the east, stroll up forested **Pohled z Vítkova** (Vítkov Hill), topped by the world's largest equestrian monument. One-eyed Hussite leader Jan Žižka scans the terrain for Crusaders, whom he stomped out on this spot in 1420. From Metro B: Křižíkova, walk down Thámova, through the tunnel, and up the hill.

Although less a pilgrimage destination than the Old Jewish Cemetery, the **New Jewish Cemetery,** far to the southeast, is one of Central Europe's largest burial grounds. Kafka is interred here; obtain a map and, if you're male, a mandatory head covering from the attendant before you start hunting for the tombstone. The main entrance is at Metro A: Želivského (open Sun.-Thurs.8am-5pm, Fri. 8am-3pm).

Prague's ancient wine-growing district, **Vinohrady** is short on history but wins the gold for greenest. Nature has overrun the streets with plane trees and vines, but the crumbling mansions never put up a fuss, and enjoy the shade of a luscious canopy. Tranquil terrace bars sprout up throughout the quarter, and it's worth the walk.

Museums

National Museum, Václavské nám. 68 (tel. 24 23 04 85). Metro A or C: Muzeum. Soviet soldiers mistook this landmark for a government building and fired on it; traces of the damage are still visible. Open daily 9am-6pm. Closed first Tuesday of the month. 40kč, students 15kč.

National Gallery: collections are housed in nine different historical buildings. The **National Gallery of European Art** is in the **Šternberský Palác,** Hradčanské nám. 15 (tel. 24 51 05 94), just outside the front gate of the Prague Castle. It includes works by Rubens, Breugel, Dürer, Picasso, and your favorite Impressionists. The **National Gallery of Bohemian Art,** ranging from Gothic to Baroque, is housed in **Basilika Sv. Jíří,** nám. U Sv. Jíří 33 (tel. 24 51 06 95), inside the castle. It showcases works by Czech artists including Master Theodorik, court painter for Charles IV. More Bohemian creations are exhibited at **Anežský areal,** at the corner of Anežská and Řásnovka; the structure was for centuries the Cloister of St. Agnes. All collections open Tues.-Sun. 10am-6pm. 50kč, students 15kč. Smaller temporary galleries dot the city (20kč, students 10kč).

Bertramka Mozart Museum, Mozartova 169 (tel. 54 38 93). Take Metro B to Anděl, take a left on Plzeňská, a left onto Mozartova. Housed in Villa Bertramka, where Mozart lived (and reputedly wrote *Don Giovanni*) in 1787. Open daily 9:30am-6pm. 50kč, students 30kč. Garden concerts July-Aug. Fri. 7:30pm; call ahead for tickets (220kč, students 120kč). The vast garden outside is free, and next to Prague's most haunting cemetery.

Muzeum Hlavního Města Prahy (Prague Municipal Museum), Na poříčí 52 (tel. 24 81 67 72). Metro B or C: Florenc. Holds the original calendar board from the town hall's Astronomical Clock and a 1:480 scale model of old Prague, precise to the last window pane on over 2000 houses and all Prague's great monuments. See what your hostel looked like in 1834. Other exhibits from the collection reside in the **House at Stone Bell,** Staroměstské nám., left of Týn Church. Both buildings open Tues.-Sun. 10am-6pm. 20kč, students 15kč.

Museum of National Literature, Strahovské nádvoří 1 (tel. 24 51 11 37). Walk from the castle's main gate and bear left. The star attraction here is the **Strahov library,** with its magnificent **Theological and Philosophical Halls.** The frescoed, vaulted ceilings of the 2 Baroque reading rooms were intended to spur enlightened monks to the loftiest peaks of erudition; great pagan thinkers of antiquity oversee their progress from the ceiling in the Philosophical Hall. Open Tues.-Sun. 9am-noon and 1-5pm. 15kč, students 5kč. Library 30kč, students 15kč.

Rudolfinum, Alšova nábř. 12 (tel. 24 89 32 05; fax 231 92 93). The Czech Philharmonic shares a building with one of Prague's oldest galleries. Rotating art exhibits in an immense Art Nouveau interior. The columned café at the end seems too elegant to be self-serve. Open Tues.-Sun. 10am-6pm. 30kč, students 15kč.

Museum of Decorative Arts, 17. listopadu 2 (tel. 24 81 12 41), across the street from Rudolfinum. Metro A: Staroměstská. Exquisite ceramics and bejeweled furnishings from Renaissance and Baroque palaces. The 2nd floor houses one of the world's largest glasswork collections. Open Tues.-Sun. 10am-6pm. 40kč.

ENTERTAINMENT

For a list of current concerts and performances, consult *The Prague Post* or *Do města-Downtown* (the latter is free and distributed at most cafés and restaurants). Most shows begin at 7pm; unsold tickets are sometimes available a half-hour before showtime (this is rare in summer). Most of Prague's theaters shut down in July and return in August only to provide tourists with re-running attractions. The selection is more varied off-season, with the peak mid-May to early June, when the **Prague Spring Festival** draws musicians from around the world. Tickets (300-2000kč) may sell out a year in advance; try **Bohemia Ticket International,** Salvátorská 6, next to Čedok (tel. 24 22 78 32; fax 24 81 03 68; open Mon.-Fri. 9am-6pm). Two film clubs run non-Hollywood movies (Sept.-June; 25kč pass for non-members). **Dlabačov,** Bělohradská 24 (tel. 311 53 28), tram #8 to Malovanka, and **Praha,** Václavské nám. 17 (tel. 26 20 35). Popular films sell out quickly, so think ahead.

- **Národní Divadlo** (National Theater), Národní třída 2/4 (C5; tel. 24 91 34 37). The "Golden Shrine" features drama, opera, and ballet. Tickets 100-1000kč. Box office open Mon.-Fri. 10am-6pm, Sat.-Sun. 10am-12:30pm and 3-6pm.
- **Stavovské Divadlo** (Estates Theater), Ovocný trh 6 (DE4; tel. 24 21 50 01). Metro A or B: Můstek. Reconstructed in 1992, this former Nostitz theater premiered Mozart's *Don Giovanni* in 1787 and continues to play "da' mann." Earphones for simultaneous English translation. Box office, in the Kolovrat Palace around the corner, open Mon.-Fri. 10am-6pm, Sat.-Sun. 10am-12:30pm and 3-6pm.
- **Státní Opera** (National Opera), Wilsonova třída, between the Metro A or C Muzeum stop and Hlavní Nádraží (tel. 26 53 53). Though not as famous as the National or the Estates Theater, the State Opera retains an impressive program. Box office open Mon.-Fri. 10am-5:30pm, Sat.-Sun. 10am-noon and 1-5:30pm.
- **Laterna Magica** (The Magic Lantern), Národní třída 4 (tel. 24 21 26 91). The theater which served as the headquarters of Václav Havel's Velvet Revolution now shows a unique integration of film, drama, and dance. Tourists welcomed with open arms. Performances Mon.-Fri. 8pm, Sat. 5pm and 8pm. Box office open Mon.-Fri. 10am-8pm, Sat. 3-8pm. Often sells out.
- **Divadlo na Starém Městě** (Old Town Theater), Dlouhá 39 (tel. 231 45 34). Relive your childhood at this theater that caters to the very young.
- **Říše Loutek** (National Marionette Theater), Žatecká (tel. 232 34 29), in the Old Town. A two-century-old Prague tradition. You won't find these creations on sale for 300kč on the Charles. Box office open daily 10am-8pm.

NIGHTLIFE

Prague nightlife is fluid—sometimes dark, quiet brews, sometimes shots of "screaming orgasm"—but always intoxicating and as fleeting as yesterday's hangover. Masses of frat boys do their best to take the "chic" out of Prague and thrust it into the mainstream. Many of the clubs listed below will become glossy tourist traps by mid-1997, so ask your ho(s)tel manager about *the* latest local favorite. The best way to enjoy the night is probably to while away the hours in a dark *pivnice* (beer cellar) or better yet, buy wine and head for the music at Charlie's Bridge.

Beerhalls and Pubs

- **Slovanská Hospoda,** Na příkopě 22. Duck beneath the passage. Christmas lights illuminate the leafy beer garden at night. Split in two by the invisible generation gap. A red-cheeked crowd of professionals enjoys 15kč brews on an organized terrace, while grunge thrives around discombobulated benches under tall tall trees. Open daily 11am-11pm.
- **Újezd,** Újezd 18 (tel. 53 83 62), near the hostels in Malá Strana. Their business card features a bespectacled smoker, but neither the basement beer cave nor the upstairs café-club shows a trace of pretense. A mid-20s crowd laughs the night away even on Mon., though only weekends feature (irregular) concerts. Beer… Maybe coffee's more "in" (10kč). Open Sun.-Thurs. til 2am, Fri.-Sat. til dawn.
- **Café Gulu Gulu,** Betlémské nám. 8. A hangout for the Czech university crowd. Fun-loving, from the graffiti by Salvador Miró to the frequent impromptu musical jams. By 11pm, people are hanging out of windowsills to get a place to sit. *Eggenberg* 20kč. Live music Fridays. Open daily 10am-1am.
- **U Hynků,** Štupartská 6 (tel./fax 232 34 06), just off the west corner of Staroměstské nám. The cigarette smoke has permanently inscribed itself into the brown-gray walls of this bar-*cum*-café. Many foreigners who come here look more local than the Czechs. The young, male, t-shirt-clad staff befriends only the cool clients, and

on request will play the tape you just bought. Light *Lobkowicz* beer 18kč per 0.5L, dark and *Fezané* 22kč. Open daily 11am-3am.

U Vystřeleného Oka, U božích bojovníků 3 (tel. 627 87 14), off Husitská. From Metro A: Flora or Metro C: Hlavní Nádraží, tram #26 goes to "Lipanská". Walk 1 block east of Seifertova, turn right on Chlumova through Prokopovo nám., turn left on Husitská and right on the tiny long-named street. All-Czech, all-student. A bright hangout for dark-clad, dark-souled folks, some of whom prefer to sit around the tables outside. *Radegast* 10kč. Open Mon.-Sat. 3:30pm-1am.

Café Marquis de Sade, a.k.a. **Café Babylon,** Templová 8 (tel. 232 34 06), between nám. Republiky and Staroměstské nám. Metro B: nám. Republiky. Enough breathing space, even if no seating space. The band on the central podium strikes up old pops when in full ensemble, but mellows out to jazz when only a couple of members show up. The "de sade" of the café shows up only on the walls, whose burgundy/orange color looks more like coagulated blood than paint. Beers 25kč. Open daily, officially til 1am, but often longer.

Molly Malone's, U obecního dvora 4. Irish prove they're the best fun at the cozy bar and washing room. Don't mind the drying drawers—they're just for show. A draft of *Staropramen* is 20 kč, and *Guinness* is cheaper than in Ireland at 60kč per pint. Open daily 11am-7am.

Taz Pub, U Obecního Domu 3. Metro B: nám. Republiky, on the street running along the right side of the county-house. A triptych, with sit-down spaces on the sides and a long bar in the middle. Go left for a yellow pizzeria-like atmosphere or right for a hellishly somber one. No Italian ovens here, though, just *Velkopopovický kozel* flowing freely in light and dark (15kč per 0.5L). Open daily til 2am.

Kecova Restaurace, Londýnská 51. Relaxed beer terrace on a quiet shaded street in Vinohrady. 5kč pistachio dispenser, but no monkeys to feed. *Gambrinus* and dark *Purkmistr* 15kč. Open April-Oct. daily 11am-11pm; closed Nov.-March Mon.-Fri. 11am-11pm.

U Sv. Tomaše, Letenská 12 (tel. 24 51 00 16; fax 53 37 19). Metro A: Malostranská. The mighty dungeons echo with boisterous beer songs and slobbering toasts. The homemade brew is 30kč as are the other six beers on tap. Live Czech folk music starts nightly around 8pm. Open daily 11:30am-midnight.

U Fleků, Křemencova 11 (tel. 24 91 51 18; fax 29 68 79). Founded in 1491, the oldest surviving brewhouse in Prague. A work of art, this beer garden boasts graffitoed walls, looming shade-trees, and a gazebo where bands play nightly. The 39kč per 0.4L of beer ensures no one gets drunk. Open daily 9am-11pm.

Sport Bar Praha, Ve Smečkách 30 (tel. 24 19 63 66). If you can't wait 2 weeks to see your next tennis match, check out the non-stop ESPN spouting from 3 wide-screen TVs. The schedule of what the baseball-capped masses will be watching is posted. Beer 20kč; pitchers 60kč. Open Sun.-Thurs. 10am-2am., Fri.-Sat. til 4am.

Clubs and Discos

Rock Club Bunkr, Lodecká 2 (F2; tel. 231 07 35). From Metro B: nám. Republiky, walk down Na poříčí, turn left on Zlatnická, then cross the parking lot diagonally. Hot Czech and foreign rock'n'roll bands in an erstwhile Communist-regime nuclear bunker. Absorb the graffiti, and add your own. 0.30L of *Gambrinus* 12kč. Open daily 8pm-6am. Cover 50kč, less on weekdays, women free. Concerts start at 9pm. Café upstairs is a respite from the energy below. Open daily 9am-3am.

Radost FX, Bělehradská 120 (tel. 25 69 98). Metro C: I.P. Pavlova. So alternative that only British tourists look straight. The downstairs disco seems caught in its own whirl but every now and then an exhausted particle man is ejected up to the spacious lounge or uptight café. Open nightly 9pm-5am. Cover 50-100kč.

Roxy, Dlouhá 33 (tel. 24 81 09 51). The former theater rocks on the ground floor and chills in the peanut gallery. Lots of space to do either, just don't fall over the edge. Good variety of reggae, ska, rock, tribal rhythms and—you just can't avoid it—techno. Beer 15kč. Open Tues.-Sun. 9pm-4am. Cover 20-40kč.

Agharta, Krakovská 5 (tel. 24 21 29 14), just down Krakovská from Wenceslas Square. The "Jazz Centrum" also operates a CD shop. Cramped space featuring nightly live jazz ensembles (starting at 9pm). Open nightly 7pm-1am.

Rock Café, Národní 20 (tel. 24 91 44 16). Same entrance as the Reduta. Anything but grunge. Marble counters, shiny steel chairs, and the bands that play are the best that pass through Prague. Nonetheless, look for the Communist mural in hot pink, and the punk dominatrix threatening with a whip: "The wages of sin are death." On live-musicless nights, dominatrix wannabes rule the dance floor. Open Mon.-Fri. 10am-3am, Sat.-Sun. 8pm-3am. Cover 30-40kč.

Lavka, Novotného lávka 1 (tel. 24 21 47 97). Tourists from around the world make Prague memories under the Charles Bridge. Otherwise devoid of character. The fluorescent disco downstairs pops eyeballs. Open nightly 10pm-5am.

Reduta, Národní 20 (tel. 24 91 22 46). Like everything "original" in Prague, the city's oldest jazz club has fallen to the tourists. But if you can get a seat in the tiny red velvet audience hall, the "jazz and not jazz" might blow your mind. Cover 90kč, but the cashier is not 100% resistant to sweet eyes pleading for a student reduction (50kč). Open nightly 9pm-late.

Hard Rock Café—Praha, Nepravda 69 (tel. 496 41 39), next to the Turkish baths. Metro D: Zabloudil jsi. Kafka once made "the Rock" his home, but now it's just bewildered tourists trying to buy a shirt. *Guinness* is 5kč, and the local *levné pivo* goes for the same price. Open daily 6am-6am.

THE FAGUE AND THE DRAGUE OF PRAGUE

If Prague had a desert, *Priscilla II* could be shot here. The scene is developing fast and in many directions: transvestite shows, stripteases, discos, bars, cafés, restaurants, and hotels aimed at gay and lesbian travelers can be found easily, although not by asking the random *babushka* selling cherries. At any of the places listed below, you can pick up a free copy of *Amigo*—the most comprehensive guide to gay life in the Czech and Slovak republics, published monthly. Most establishments also sell *Soho* and *Promluv,* Czech-language monthly magazines, the former full of fiction and scene listings, the latter a more scholarly, lesbian-oriented publication. Almost all gay life happens behind closed doors, but don't fear ringing the bell.

Penzion David, Holubova 5 (tel./fax 54 98 20). Take tram #14 to its end at Laurová (catch it by the main post office), take a left off the main street and then a right on Holubova. Some of the best and cheapest food in town on a quiet terrace surrounded by plants. Lunch specials go for 40kč, *guláš* 55kč, soyameat dishes 80kč. Beer 12-15kč. Open Mon.-Fri. 11am-11pm, Sat.-Sun. noon-midnight. The 3-star **pension** upstairs charges about US$50 per person.

L-Club, Lublaňská 48 (tel. 29 62 87). Metro C: I.P. Pavlova. Great fun for both the guys and the dolls with a dancing floor, bar, and café. Transvestite shows Wed. Strip shows Sat. No prostitutes. Open nightly 8pm-4am. Cover 35kč—the ticket gets you a small beer or Coke at the bar.

Tom's Bar, Pernerova 4 (tel. 232 11 70). Metro B: Křižíkova. Upon exiting, walk back, take a right on Křižíkova, a left at the square, and a right onto Pernerova. It's on you left (10min.). An all-around spot with a café, bar, disco, darkroom, and videoroom. The music is bearable, but in the disco-bar area downstairs it's hard to see anything but eyes and teeth, since the only lights are black. Open Mon.-Sat. 7:30pm-3am. Cover 20-50kč.

U Střelce, Karoliny Světlé 12, under the archway on the right. A bar that becomes more of a beerhall on Fri. and Sat. nights when transvestite actors perform anything from "Mein Herr" to "Total Eclipse of the Heart" and drag you onto the stage with them. Open nightly from 6pm; shows at midnight. Cover 60kč.

A Club, Milíčova 25, off Seifertova, "Lipanská" stop on tram #26 from Metro A: Flora or Metro C: Hlavní Nádraží. A nightspot for lesbians, although men come here too. The café is all-class with wire sculptures, soft light, and some comfy couches near the bar. Disco in the back starts jamming at 10pm nightly, but don't come before midnight if you want a crowd. 22kč beers. Open nightly 6pm-6am.

Near Prague

KUTNÁ HORA

One and a half hours east of Prague, the former mining town of **Kutná Hora** (Silver Hill) has a history as morbid as the bone church that made the city famous. Founded when lucky miners hit a vein, the city boomed with a hundred thousand gold diggers until the plague hit, and men who had rushed there like flies began dropping like them. What might have added most to the mess was a 13th-century wayfaring abbot who sprinkled the grounds with Jerusalem earth and created a mecca for those who wanted to be buried someplace cool and holy. Neighbors started to complain by about the 15th century, so the Cistercian order that ran the meadow of death built a chapel and started cramming in bodies. In a fit of whimsy, the monk in charge began designing flowers with pelvi and crania. He never finished, but the artist František Rint completed the project in 1870 with flying butt-bones, femur crosses, and a grotesque chandelier made from every bone in the human body. Some lucky corpse even got to spell out the artist's name (open daily 8am-noon and 1-5pm; 20kč, students 10kč). The *kostnice* lies about 2km out of town, and local buses leave from Kutná's bus station to Sedlec Tabák (4kč) every 45 minutes.

The 13th-century silver boom and subsequent bust in the 16th century left snapshots of a thriving medieval town replete with burghers' houses, cobblestone alleys, church spires, and a vaulted cathedral on a hill southwest of town. From Palackého nám., follow 28. října to Havlíčkovo nám. Originally a storehouse for Kutná Hora's stash, the imposing **Vlašský Dvůr** (Italian Court; tel. 28 73) got its name after Václav IV made a home out of it and invited the finest Italian architects to refurbish the palace with more than just silver. It also served a stint as the royal mint. The tour leads through only a few rooms but each one deserves a look. The **audience hall** witnessed the election of Vladislav II as King of Bohemia, and a life-size mural depicts the tense event. The **Chapel of St. Václav and Vladislav** has been draped with painted flowers and smirking saints since a 20th-century couple renovated the sanctuary in Art Nouveau (open daily 9am-5pm; tours every 15min.; 40kč, students 20kč; English sheet).

Behind the museum, a terrace looks upon the sweeping valley, and trails lead down to the garden **Letní scéna** below. Coming back around the Italian Court, Rutnardská leads past the ancient **St. James Church,** becomes a statued lane rivaling the Charles Bridge, and ends at the Gothic **St. Barbara's Cathedral,** one of Europe's finest (open Tues.-Sun. 8am-5:30pm; 20kč, students 10kč).

Informační Centrum, Palackého nám. 377 (tel. 23 78 or 755 56), a trip along Lorecká, then Vocelova, then Vladislavova from the bus station, sells maps (30kč), books private rooms for 200-1000kč per person (hostels starting at 60kč), and gives info on the concerts in Vlašský Dvůr and the cathedral (open Mon.-Fri. 9am-7pm, Sat.-Sun. 9am-6pm). **Buses** arrive from Prague's Florenc station (5 per day, 1 per day Sat.-Sun.; 1½hr.; 41kč) and station #2 at Metro A: Želivského (9 per day, 2 per day Sat.-Sun.; 1hr.40min.; 41kč). If you miss the last bus back, try catching one to Kolín, which has a bigger train station. **Lido,** opposite the post office, sells bread, butter, and *Dobra voda* (open Mon.-Fri. 6am-6pm, Sat.-Sun. 6am-noon). Near the cathedral, **U Kamenného Domu,** Lierova 147 (tel. 44 25), serves up pub fare for prices to warm a miser's heart (open Mon.-Sat. 10am-10pm). **Phone code:** 0327.

TEREZÍN

In the 18th century, Empress Maria Theresa had a **fortress** known as **Terezín** built at the Labe's confluence with the Ohře. Little did she know the miseries to which the fortress would bear witness. The Nazis established a concentration camp here in 1940 for 32,000 prisoners, many en route to death camps. Among the inmates were Jews, Poles, Germans, British POWs, and Communists. Nearby, the Nazis constructed the **Terezín ghetto,** a sham model village to satisfy a delegation from the International Red Cross, then murdered all of its residents after the visit. Following the Red Army's capture of the camp in May 1945, the Czech regime interred Sudeten and

Bohemian Germans in the camp. With zero development after the war, the town's history makes itself eerily felt, creeping under the visitor's skin.

The **bus** from Prague-Florenc (1 every 1-2hr., 1hr., 44kč) passes beside the ghetto before stopping at the central square. There, a **tourist bureau** sells panoramic maps of Terezín (40kč) that detail the town's gruesome sights (open Sun.-Fri. 9am-4pm). Retrace the bus route to the fortress's entrance (tel. (0416) 922 25) where the ticket (70kč, student 35kč; English guide 200kč; combined ticket for fortress and museum in the square 90kč, students 45kč) comes with a map of the complex, a suggested route, and explanations of each building's function. Many cells contain contemporary photographs of the corpses amassed in tiny rooms at the moment of Terezín's liberation by the Ukrainian Red Army Division. Bigger spaces have been converted into exhibition halls (admission included in the ticket). (Grounds open May-Sept. daily 8am to 6pm; April and Oct. 8am-5pm; Nov.-March 8am-4:30pm.)

Back in town, two more sights deserve a look. The **Muzeum ghetta** (tel. (0416) 925 76), in the central square at Komenského honors the memory of those whom it once imprisoned (open daily 9am-6pm). South of town lie the **crematorium** and **cemetery** (open March-Oct. daily 10am-5pm). Like most Nazi death machines, this crematorium was both built and operated by the imprisoned.

KARLŠTEJN AND KONOPIŠTĚ

The Bohemian hills around Prague contain 14 castles, some built as early as the 13th century. A train ride southwest from Praha-Smíchov (45min., 12kč) brings you to **Karlštejn**, a walled and turreted fortress built by Charles IV to house his crown jewels and holy relics. The **Chapel of the Holy Cross** (tel. (0311) 846 17) is decorated with more than 2000 inlaid precious stones and 128 apocalyptic paintings by medieval artist Master Theodorik. (Open Tues.-Sun. 9am-4pm. Admission with English guide 95kč, students 50kč; in Czech 25kč, students 10kč.)

Animal-rights activists might wish to avoid mighty **Konopiště**, south of Prague in **Benešov** (buses from Prague-Florenc leave at least every ½hr. 6am-6pm; 1½hr.; 52kč), a Renaissance palace with a luxurious interior from the days when Archduke Franz Ferdinand bagged game here—more than 300,000 stuffed animals. The Renaissance facade hides a castle-like Gothic body. The **Weapons Hall** contains a fine collection of 16th- to 18th-century arms (tel. (0301) 213 66; open Tues.-Sun. 9am-4pm; with guide 80kč, students 45kč; in Czech 25kč, students 10kč).

WEST BOHEMIA

Bursting at the seams with curative springs, West Bohemia is the Czech mecca for those in search of a good bath. Over the centuries, emperors and intellectuals have dipped in the waters of Karlovy Vary, Mariánské Lázné, and Františkovy Lázné, but more recently troops of German tourists have begun crossing the border for cheap sulphurous draughts. Karlovy Vary, the most famous spa town, is more commonly referred to as the German *Karlsbad*, while prices invariably come in DM, and *"bittes"* and *"dankes"* flow freely at the taps. Possibly punchier, the Czech Republic's two most popular drinks also have their home here—the spicy green herb-liquor *Becherovka* (known for its curative properties) and Plzeň's world-famous *Pilsner*.

■ Karlovy Vary

On a routine deer hunt, the Holy Roman Emperor and King of Bohemia Karel IV stumbled upon a fountain spewing hot water high into the air. So impressive was the sight that he built a personal lodge. Over the next 600 years, the spa developed into one of the "salons of Europe," visited by such diverse personalities as Johann Sebastian Bach, Peter the Great, and Sigmund Freud. It was during this period that present-day Karlovy Vary was built, largely by two tongue-twisting Viennese architects—Ferdinand Fellner and Hermann Helmer. The therapeutic waters continue to be the premier attraction, but perhaps the most beneficial of the springs is *Becherovka*, the secret alcoholic synthesis of selected herbs and just the right amount of sugar.

Orientation and Practical Information Trains run from the main **Horní nádraží** to Prague via Chomutov (3 per day, 3½hr., 80kč). From the station, take bus #11 or 13 (5kč per person or backpack—buy at the kiosk) from across the street to the last stop. Or, walk downhill from the bus stop bearing left; a right at the bridge leads straight to the post office at the start of **Masaryka**, the city's administrative street. Intercity buses leave from **Dolní nádraží**, on Zapadní, to Plzeň (25 per day, 1½hr., 54kč) and Prague (25 per day, 2½hr., 65kč). From Dolní Nadráží, turn left on Západní, continue past the Becher building, and bear right onto Masaryka, parallel to the other main thoroughfare, **Bechera**. The white booth of **City-Info,** Masaryka (tel./fax 233 51), across from the post office, packs an unbelievable stack of brochures and maps and books rooms starting at 270kč per person. The young staff knows about the newest nightlife and exchanges traveler's checks at 5% commission (open daily 9am-6pm). For written English-lingo info, consult *Promenáda* (12kč), available at every kiosk. It lists concert schedules, film showings, and hotel offers (with prices). There is a **pharmacy** at Bechera 3 (tel. 248 20; open Mon.-Fri. 7:30am-1pm and 1:30-6pm, Sat. 8am-1pm). **Komerčni Banka,** Tržiště 11 (tel. 322 22 05), cashes traveler's checks at 2% commission (open Mon.-Fri. 9am-5pm). A 24-hour Cirrus/MC **ATM** waits outside. A recently renovated **post office,** Zahradní 23 (tel. 322 49 30), opened in 1996 (open Mon.-Fri. 7:30am-7pm, Sat.-Sun. 8am-1pm). **Postal code:** 36001. 24-hr. **telephones** appear along the river. **Phone code:** 017.

> Many establishments are adding an initial "32" to their telephone numbers.

Accommodations CK-ACCOMM, Krymská 9 (tel./fax 322 84 37), books private rooms for 300-370kč per person plus a 15kč spa tax. From the bus station, follow Dr. Janátky off the main Západní, and turn right on Krymská (open Mon.-Fri. 9:30am-5pm). **Penzion Kosmos,** Zahradní 39 (tel. 322 31 68), scores big on location around the corner from the post office. Simply furnished rooms run clean and large. The hot water might flow from the blue-marked tap, not the red one (singles with sink 370kč; doubles and triples 310kč per person, with toilet and shower 350kč per person). The area around **Hotel Adria,** Západní 1 (tel. 322 37 65), can get hairy at night, but it's near the main nightclub strip and opposite the buses. The old hotel offers well worn but clean singles (752kč) and doubles (1168kč), with lower prices off-season. **Hotel Alice (HI),** Hamerská 1 (tel. 248 48), is a steal for HI-members in the quiet of the West Bohemian wilds (400kč plus 15kč tax per person for rooms that cost non-members 1400kč plus the 15kč; TV, shower, toilet). The bridge from the trains leads to a large bus stop, where buses depart for Březnová, stopping at "Hotel Alice" (the first stop after entering the Březnová village; 15min., 5kč).

Food Karlovy Vary's eateries serve either expensive or tasteless food—or the waitrons are rude. **Vegetarian restaurant,** Pavlova 25 (tel. 290 21), in the back of a building so follow the signs, is possibly the world's most angst-filled veggie restaurant. Slump, smoke, and order the fruitkebab (45kč) without cracking a grin, and you might fit in. The vegetable bowl is 28kč, beers 14kč (open Mon.-Sat. 11am-9pm). **Pizzeria Helvan,** Tržiště 41 (tel. 257 57), above the Plague Column, cooks up crazy pizzas and a few normal ones. Most arrive at the table for 38kč, but the luxurious "seafruit pizza", with oysters and shrimp, goes for 65kč. Those who want their stomachs bathed in sugar-goo should order the fruit pizza (37kč; open daily 10am-9pm). A more expensive eatery, with better service and a faithful crowd, **E&T,** Zeyera 3 (tel. 322 60 22), sits between Bechera and Masaryka. A leafy terrace and gleaming interior take in a mixed homo-hetero crowd that feeds on fried cheese (50kč), *šopský salát* (35kč), chicken dishes (80-90kč) and drowns it all in 20kč drafts of *Staropramen* (0.4L; open Mon.-Sat. 9:30am-midnight, Sun. 11am-midnight).

Sights and Entertainment Between Masaryka and the Teplá, **Smetanovy sady** (gardens) are noted for their spa house and plants arranged to spell the date. Masaryka and nabř. Osvobození fuse into **Zahradní**, which connects to **Dvořákovy sady**. The gardens are named after the Czech composer, a frequent visitor who premiered his "New World" symphony here. Along the Dvořák Gardens' south rim lies the Victorian **Park Colonnade**, where you can sip the curative waters of Karlovy Vary's 12th spring, **Sadový pramen**. The pedestrian **Mlýnské nábř.** meanders alongside the Teplá under the cool protection of shade trees. After Lázně (Bath) 3, the pavillion of **Pramen Svobody** (Freedom Spring) emerges, deep in the heart of the spa complex. In the bath (tel. 322 56 41; fax 322 34 73), travelers can treat their weary bodies with all kinds of **massages** (270-450kč depending on what parts of your body you need kneaded), including underwater ones (360kč; no prescription necessary). Otherwise, just buy one of the porcelain cups that everyone is carrying (40-200kč), and sample the precious liquids at no cost.

Next door, the imposing **Mlýnská (Mill) kolonáda** shelters six different springs. When mixing mineral draughts, just remember: nickle 'fore zinc, all's in the pink, zinc before nickle, you're in a pickle. Farther along the spa area, the former **tržištw** (market) appears with the delicate white **Tržní kolonáda,** where two more springs bubble to the surface. Across the Teplá, the dome of **Kostel Sv. Máří Magdaleny** towers over the town. Even for those who can't take another drop, the **Sprudel Fountain** nearby merits a look. The geyser can shoot over thirty liters off into the air, but don't touch: it's 72° (and that's not Fahrenheit!).

Follow Stará Louka until Marianská; at the dead end, a funicular rises to the **Diana Watchtower** (open Sun.-Thurs. 9am-6pm, Fri.-Sat. 9am-7pm; every 15min.; 20kč, roundtrip 30kč). If you want to horde your crowns or simply enjoy the forested hill's pathways, **hike.** The tower opens its spiraling staircase daily 10am-6pm (Fri.-Sat. til 7pm; 10kč, students 5kč). Stará Louka comes to a grand end at **Grandhotel Pupp.** Founded in 1774 by Johann Georg Pupp, the Grandhotel was the largest hotel in 19th-century Bohemia. The intricate façade you see today is the work of the Viennese Helmer-Fellner duo. The interior features luxurious suites, a concert hall, and multiple ballrooms. Cross the next bridge to reach Nová Louka, featuring **Karlovarské Muzeum** at #23 (tel. 26 252). Recently refurbished, the museum presents exhibits on *Becherovka* liquor, the manufacture of porcelain, and local zoology (open Wed.-Sun. 9am-noon and 1-5pm; 25kč, students 15kč).

Sipping and strolling to the mellow sounds of jazz bands seems to satisfy most of Karlovy Vary's temporary residents, but the spa also manages to thump if you're at the right place at the right time. Clubs are as temporary as the residents, so ask around. **Propaganda,** Jaltská 5, off Bechera, has a reputation for frequent brawls and unsafe drug-users, but mostly it's just urban legend. The disco gathers Karlovy Vary's 36001's equivalents of pre-university Brandons and Brendas (open Fri.-Sat. til 6am—gets thumping around 11-11:30pm; cover 30kč). **E&T** (see Food, p. 200) draws a mellow gay and lesbian pack of all ages. Free summer **concerts** take place under most colonnades. Karlovy Vary's biggest kick picks up at the first week in July; the resort's **international film festival** has begun to attract attention, but unlike other more suffocated fêtes, it still embraces locals and passers-by.

▩ Mariánské Lázně

In 1779 Dr. Nehr discovered a hundred curative springs, and Marianské Lázně sprouted up on peat bogs in half a century, straightaway taking on the shape we admire today. Heads of the world's political, cultural, and sexual life have all mingled here to gather up new energy and ideas. Young backpackers who have plenty of the above in store cross out this town from their itineraries, but the spa provides splendid grounds for quiet strolls for families and all those tired of raving youths.

Orientation and Practical Information Mariánské Lázně is linked by **train** to Cheb (16 per day, ½-1hr., 12kč), Karlovy Vary (9 per day, 1¾hr., 24kč), Plzeň (15 per day, 1hr., 32kč), and Prague (8 per day, 3hr., 80kč). **Buses** rush to the same: Cheb (17 per day, ½-1hr.); Karlovy Vary (2 per day, 1hr.); Prague (7 per day, 3½hr.). The **train station** (tel. 53 23) and the string of ten **bus stops** (tel. 33 11) next door lie a laborious 2km from the spa's compact center. **Trolley #5** connects the town and its train station (throw 4kč in the box on the trolley), but for the powerful and the poor: straight out of the station, take a right and turn left on the main **Hlavní třída,** which runs past the tiny steel and glass tourist booth and then leads to luxurious "hotel row." The staff of **City Service,** Hlavní tř. 626/1 (tel. 62 38 16; fax 62 42 18), books rooms starting at 365kč and sells maps and brochures (open Mon.-Fri. 9am-12:30pm and 1-5pm, Sat. 9am-12:30pm and 1-4pm, Sun. 10am-2pm). The good samaritans at **Komerčni Banka,** Hlavní tř. 132 (tel 6011), take only a 2% commission on currency exchange, but be ready for lines (open Mon.-Fri. 9am-5pm). **City Service** (above) and most banks charge 5%. The **pharmacy** lies at Tyršova 1 (tel. 27 64; open Mon.-Fri. 8am-6pm, Sat. 8am-noon). For a taxi, call 28 70. The **post office** is at Poštovní 17 (tel. 33 61; open Mon.-Fri. 7am-7pm, Sat. 7am-2pm). **Telephones** stand outside. If a phone number doesn't work, stick a 62 in front of it: many, but not all, will undergo this change in 1996-1997. **Postal code:** 35301. **Phone code:** 0165.

Accommodations Private rooms and cheap hotels bubble up everywhere. **City Service** (see above) books **private rooms** for 345-500kč. The only way to escape the sneaky 15kč tax is to sleep in the woods. Many hotels take DM. **Hotel Evropa,** Třebízského 101 (tel. 62 20 63; fax 62 54 08), is set in the ranks of "hotel row" without the rank prices. Climb Hlavní tř. to its end and take a left. The rooms are clean but antique: singles (400kč, with shower or bath and WC 600kč); doubles (600kč, with extras 900kč); triples (800kč, with the goods 1200kč; breakfast 60-70kč). Propped on a hill, **Hotel Suvorov,** Ruská tř. 76 (call the associated Hotel Kossuth at tel. 28 61 or fax at 28 62), enjoys panoramic views of the spa. Climb Hlavní tř. and take a left only after Ruská appears a second time, following it even through a 90° turn left. Huge rooms boast plush rugs and sofa-beds (singles 450kč, with bath 510kč; doubles 600kč, with bath 790kč; breakfast 70kč). **Junior Hotel Krakonoš (HI)** (tel. 26 24) lies in the forest to the northeast of town. Take trolley #5 to "Centrum" (40kč), then catch bus #12 to "Krakonoš" (infrequent, 5kč). If #5 isn't to come for more than a half hour, you might as well walk. Do a 120° turn right off Hlavní at the City Service. Then take a sharp right onto Angelická, taking the winding left branch up to the hotel. The cherubs outside have begun to crumble, but inside, winding staircases lead to small, spic-and-span singles through quads for 290kč a person (non-members 590kč). **Motel Start,** Plzeňská (tel. 62 20 62), offers 3-person rooms in dormitory-style "comfort" at 150kč per head. Take a right off Hlavní almost as soon as you enter it from the train/bus (before the Dyleň supermarket) and another right onto the busy Plzeňská. The steel motel sits on the left. Each two rooms share a bathroom.

Food Mariánské Lázně is famous for a distinctive sweet treat known as *oplatky*, wafers layered with either vanilla, chocolate, or almond fillings (25-40kč per box). Also try the popular *Chodovar*, brewed in a nearby village. A butcher, a baker, and an orange-juice maker sell groceries and a few prepared dishes at **Trio Občerstvení,** Hlavní tř. 30 (open Mon.-Fri. 7am-6pm, Sat. 8am-6pm, Sun. 9am-4pm). **Grill Terezie,** Hlavní třída 161 (tel. 57 46), in an alcove close to the roundabout with the spiky metal monument, lets you watch your chicken grill on the spit (60kč for a half), or bite into a chicken burger (20kč). *Gambrinus* beer flows at 15kč. Arrive around noon, when twenty watering mouths gaze as the first *kuře* comes off the grill (open daily 10am-7pm). **Tre Kronor,** Lidická 154/9 (tel 44 49), near Hlavní's intersection with Dykova (look for a sign), swims in blue and yellow. The Swedish enclave in Bohemia serves, logically, mostly pizza (35 kinds, most 50-60kč), but also Scandanavian and Czech concoctions (fried cheese 38kč). The "mixed" salad comes unmixed (30kč), and the beer comes only bottled (16kč; open daily 11am-11pm).

Sights Everyone seems to be on a prescription to stroll. Elderly ladies, stodgy old men, young tots and their sunny parents, all move like snails along Hlavní tř. sipping from porcelain and munching on *oplatky*. Grab some wafers, put on some shades, and get ready to meander. At the town's highest point, stately **Goethovo nám.** recreates the aura of Marienbad's heyday with well kept gardens, lawns, and 19th-century lampposts. In the center, a stone Goethe touches his chin and gazes at strollers; the famed author spent less pensive time in **spa-house #11** (tel. 27 40), tasting the waters with lascivious Ulrike. The house now displays minerals and depicts spa life (open Tues.-Sun. 9am-4pm; 30kč, students 6kč).

Across Goethovo nám.'s gardens, **Kostel Nanebevzetí Panny Marie** (Assumption Church) stands under a gigantic Neo-Byzantine dome. From the stairs of the church there is a good view of the spa town. The huge *kaisergelb* buildings on your left form the complex that houses the New Baths and the Casino. On the right, people sample the waters of **Karolina Spring** under a snow-white colonnade. Drops from the **Zpívající fontána** (Singing Fountain) land on steel spheres and make noise, or so the theory goes. The city council stopped trusting the fountain and plays music through loudspeakers on the hour while the spring undulates to its rhythm. Reconstructed in 1975-81, the nearby **Main Colonnade** resembles a mix of Neo-Baroque and '60s tie-dye. The ceilings' painter must have been tripping or living in a fish bowl with cherubs. Springs come in hot and cold. To rinse your mouth out afterwards, use a tap marked "trinkwasser" (taps open daily 8am-noon and 4-6pm).

Skalník Gardens descend from the *kolonáda* and connect to Hlavní tř. Grassy paths bend like spaghetti, but corner signposts keep the lost informed. At the colonnade's north end, a sweet old lady sells porcelain sippers in the **Křížový pramen** (Fountain of the Cross) building (open daily 6am-noon and 4-6pm).

Two chapels on Ruská warrant a look. The **Anglican Church** is Marianské Lázně's "little museum of obscure but brilliant art"—a motif in most Czech towns (open Tues.-Sat. 9am-4pm; 15kč). Farther up, the interior of the **Orthodox Church** (tel. 50 10) shines in porcelain icons and brass (open May-Oct. Mon.-Fri. 8:30am-noon and 1-4:30pm, Sat.-Sun. 8:30am-4:30pm; Nov.-April daily 9:30-11:30am and 2-4pm).

Cheb

Although Cheb is hardly huge by today's standards, a rich Old Town and brooding castle attest to its glory days as star of West Czechia. Sundays, a dynamic **market** (9am-3pm) in nám. Jiřího z Poděbrad sets the square's table with everything from watermelons to neon waterguns. Sitting to the sides, burgher homes join in the fun with festive Renaissance decorations and gold inlaid designs. **Špalíček,** translated simply as "the block," has presided at the head for over half a millenium and it's aged curiously; the teetering clump of wood-frame houses twists and bends as if in a carnival madhouse. Behind the iron gates of **Nová radnice** (New city hall), nám. Jiřího z Poděbrad, an exciting collection of modern art and a larger Gothic exhibit in **Galerie výtvarného umění** (tel. 224 50) warrant the 30kč admission (students 15kč; open Tues.-Sun. 9am-5pm). The collection at **Chebské muzeum**, nám. krále Jiřího 3 (tel. 223 86), depicts the many Bohemian castles of the too-rich-for-his-own-good Albrecht z Valdštejna, murdered in the Cheb castle by an Irishman (open Tues.-Sun. 9am-noon and 1-5pm; 5kč). The alley beside the *muzeum* leads to the twin-towered **Kostel Sv. Mikuláše** (Church of St. Nicholas), one of Bohemia's finest Romanesque structures. Although American bombers damaged the church in April 1945, the towering Gothic statues, Master Lukas's paintings, and the late-Romanesque west portal shine again. From the main square, descend Kamenná, turn left on Křížovická, and ascend the footpath to the left at the fortress walls. A cobblestone drawbridge leads to **Chebský hrad,** Frederick Barbarossa's imperial castle (open June-Aug. Tues.-Sun. 9am-noon and 1-6pm; May and Sept. 9am-noon and 1-5pm; April and Oct. 9am-noon and 1-4pm; 10kč). Looming over a cliff to the northwest of town, the *hrad* is one of the few Romanesque castles remaining in Bohemia. Inside, grass footpaths pass toppled statues and the stumps of stone walls. For the best sights, climb the 20m-high **Cerná věž** (Black Tower), from which a panorama of the Old Town and the castle unfolds.

Trains regularly depart *Hlavní nádraží* for Karlovy Vary (20 per day, 1hr., 44kč), Plzeň (7 per day, 1½hr., 50kč), and Prague (9 per day, 4hr., 100kč). **Buses** leave from in front of the station to Plzeň (8 per day, 2hr., 50kč). Exit along Svobody and **Čedok**, Májová 31 (tel. 43 39 51; fax 43 39 52), appears to the left, providing maps, brochures, and event schedules (open Mon.-Fri. 8:30am-5pm, Sat. 8-11am). **Komerční Banka**, Obměné brigády 20 (tel. 43 00 21; fax 43 03 81), takes a 2% commission on AmEx and other traveler's checks and has a 24-hour MC/Cirrus **ATM**. At the end of Svobody lies **nám. krále Jiřího**, with the **post office** at #38 (tel. 230 51; open Mon.-Fri. 8am-6:30pm, Sat. 8-11am). **Postal code:** 35099. **Phone code:** 0166.

Čedok might help get a **private room**, but, as they say, it's complicated. **Hotel Hradní Dvůr**, Dlouhá 12 (tel. 220 06; fax 224 44), is the best deal in town, with a beaming reception (open daily 2pm-8am) and well tended rooms (singles without shower 400kč, doubles with shower and WC 900-990kč, similar triples 1190kč). Hallway showers cost 40kč. **Hotel Hvězda**, nám. krále Jiřího 4/6 (tel. 225 49; fax 225 46), offers singles and doubles at 500kč and 900kč, respectively. The hall showers are clean, and bath-equipped doubles run 1200kč (breakfast included). *"Guten tag, zu trinken?"* is probably the first line you'll hear at an eatery. The **Grill-Lahůdky**, nám. krále Jiřího 37 (tel. 220 59), still gets local traffic with 44kč chickens. The small-stomached request mini-portions, but only big *velké piva* (big beers) are available at 13kč (open Mon.-Fri. 7:30am-6pm, Sat. 7:30am-noon). Stock up for picnics in any of a thousand **grocery stores**. There's also one across from Hotel Hvězda (open Monday to Friday 8am-6pm, Saturday 8am-3pm, and Sunday 9am-2pm).

■ Near Cheb: Františkovy Lázně

On a visit to his territories in 1803, Austrian Emperor Franz I spent a night at Eger's fountain and painted the town *gelb—kaisergelb* to be exact. Soon renamed Františkovy Lázně, the imperial springs began to attract Europe's elite. Goethe sipped from the Lázně's classical pavilions and contemplated *die Natur*, while Beethoven came for a break from the music industry. Of Bohemia's three main *lázně* (baths), only this one retains a cloak of woods, groves, and cooling lakes. Few tourists interrupt a leisurely promenade down the imperial streets and gardens. The origin of the present-day spa is at **Pramen František** (Franz Spring), but the most exciting source waits farther in the park (open daily 8am-noon and 1-5pm; plastic cups 1.20kč). The foaming **Dvorana Glauberových pramenů** shoots into aquariums right before your eyes (open daily 7-11:30am and 1-5pm; plastic cups 1.20kč).

Buses to the spa leave from the front of Cheb's train station (every ½hr., 20min., 4kč) but require exact change. The spa's bus stop straddles both sides of Americká, northwest of the center. Walk back, take the first left on Ruská, and turn right at **Národní třída**, the faint heart of the town. **Čedok**, Národní třída 5 (tel. (0166) 94 22 09), stocks maps (35kč for one of this "town") and will give you the low-down on accommodations but doesn't book rooms (open Mon.-Fri. 8:30-11am and 11:45am-4:30pm, Sat. 9-11:30am). 3km from the center, the lakeside **Autocamping Amerika** (tel. 94 25 18; fax 94 28 43) rents poppa, momma, and baby bear bungalows (2-4 people, 180-720kč). To set up a tent costs 80kč, plus 60kč per person. Walk down Národní třída as it becomes Klostermanova, and hang a right onto Jezerní.

■ Plzeň

Tell a Czech that you're going to Plzeň, and they might say "to je Škoda." The unfortunate pun both means "pity" and describes the auto plant that helped place Plzeň on the list of Bohemia's most-polluted cities. The region grossly underestimates the town, however, and not only in terms of architecture. Plzeň might just be the only enclave in the republic where all that is alternative thrives. As *Budvar* pushes *Pilsner Urquell* into the second-ranked beer and the stereotype of ugliness clings to Plzeň,

West Bohemia's capital is allowed to develop by itself, free of tourist throngs. Local students set the tone in pubs. If the highbrow is your game, hit Prague; come here for hard-jamming rock, dreads, and a pinch of soot.

ORIENTATION AND PRACTICAL INFORMATION

Náměstí Republiky—the central square—lies amid a rectangular grid of narrow streets. A couple blocks west and parallel to the square's east side runs **Sady Pětatřicátníků,** which becomes **Klatovská** farther south. At the name-change point, the busy street meets the perpendicular **Americká,** which runs east to the train station. From the **train station,** hang a right onto **Sirková,** dive into the underpass and emerge where the sign points to "Americká." Walk away from **Jungmannova,** which runs north to the square, morphing into **Smetany** before reaching it. From the bus station, follow any street east toward the spires. The beloved **tram #2** serves the train and bus stations, the central square, and the youth hostel.

- **Tourist Offices: MIS (Městské informační středisko),** nám. Republiky 41 (tel. 723 65 35 or 722 44 73). Helpful staff sells maps (48kč) and arranges 300-500kč private rooms. Open daily 9am-5pm. **Čedok,** Sedláčkova 12 (tel. 723 74 19; fax 722 37 03), a block west of nám. Republiky, offers free maps of the center and arranges private accommodations for 320-700kč. Open Mon.-Fri. 9am-6pm, Sat. 9am-noon.
- **Budget Travel: CKM,** Dominikánská 1 (tel. 723 63 93; fax 723 69 09), off the central square's northwest corner, books private rooms (400-500kč) and hostel beds (170kč), and sells HI and ISIC cards. Open Mon.-Thurs. 8am-6pm, Fri. 8am-5pm.
- **Currency Exchange: Komerční Banka,** Zbrojnická 4 (tel. 22 35 73), off nám. Republiky's southeast corner. 1% commission (min. 30kč) on traveler's checks. Open Mon.-Fri. 8am-noon and 12:30-5pm. A cash exchange machine outside of **Československá Obchodní Banka,** Americká 60, changes major currencies into kč. Open Mon.-Fri. 8am-noon and 1:30-5pm.
- **ATMs:** 24-hr. Cirrus/MC at Komerční Banka and Československá Obchodní Banka.
- **Trains:** Americká (info tel. 22 20 79). To: Prague (20 per day, 2hr., 48kč). International tickets and info on the 2nd floor. **24-hr. luggage storage:** 5kč.
- **Buses:** Husova 58 (tel. 22 37 04). Many cheap Eurolines buses pass through en route between Prague and France, Switzerland, and Germany. To: Prague (more than 1 per hr., 50kč; and a heap of West Bohemian spas.
- **Public Transportation:** Tram #2 serves the "practicalities route;" tram #4 the "fun route." The other means of transport are not nearly as exciting. 5kč per tram ride; backpacks ride for 2kč. Punch the ticket on board. Trams stop running around 11:30pm, at which time identically numbered **buses** take over their routes.
- **Taxis:** Big stands at the train station and Palackého 2.
- **AIDS Hotline:** tel. 27 36 60. Available 24hr.
- **Post Office:** Solní 20 (tel. 22 45 60). Open Mon.-Fri. 6am-8pm, Sat. 8am-2pm, Sun. 7:30am-noon. **Postal code:** 30100.
- **Telephones:** Outside the post office. **Phone code:** 19.

ACCOMMODATIONS

Prices are generally high. A few year-round hostels and summer dorms stick to the outskirts, but private rooms are the best bet. Try MIS, CKM, or Čedok (see above).

- **SOU (HI),** Vejprnická 56 (tel. 28 20 12). Take tram #2 to "Internáty", walk back 50m, and head left into the fenced compound. A former Škoda workers' house. No frills, make-your-own-bed rooms. Every 2 rooms share a bathroom. Chillingly quiet with long, hospital-type halls. 170kč per bed.
- **Penzion J. Bárová,** Solní 8 (tel. 723 66 52), a block from nám. Republiky's northwest corner. Immaculate showers in the middle of tidy rooms. Few rooms, so call ahead to reserve. Rooms have toilets, showers, and radios. Reception open daily 9am-6pm. Singles 510kč. Doubles 850kč. Extra bed 170kč. Breakfast 85kč.
- **Morrison Hotel,** Thámova 9 (tel./fax 27 09 52 or 27 54 50), off Klatovská (tram #4 to "Chodské nám."). Clean rooms with dark-wood beds and alabaster walls. Shower/

bath and WC. Reception open Mon.-Fri. 7am-10pm, Sat.-Sun. 7-11am and 5-7pm. Call ahead if you're arriving at a different hour. Breakfast included. Singles 560kč. Doubles 930kč. Restaurant and exchange office in the building.

TJ Lokomotiva Plzeň, Úslavská 75 (tel. 480 41). Turn left from the train station, take a quick left onto the right-curving Koterovská and one more left on Habermannova, which leads to the concrete building in a sport complex. Or tram #2 to "Habermannova". Plain rooms, many in full view of the soccer field. Occasionally filled with large groups, so call ahead. Shared bathrooms. 170kč per bed.

FOOD

If a meal in Plzeň has avoided a pint of *Prazdroj,* then it probably just included its dark equivalent, *Purkmistr.* The two combine in Czech-style black-and-tans (*Řezané*). The restaurants listed below also serve as entertainment spots. **K-mart,** Americká tř., is entered (at least the grocery section) from Sirková side (open Mon.-Wed. 7am-7pm, Thurs.-Fri. 7am-8pm, Sat. 8am-6pm, Sun. 9am-3pm).

U Dominika, Dominikanská, off the square's northwest corner. A tight crowd of students comes here mostly to chat over coffee (10-15kč) or beer (15kč). Offers the usual selection of ready-mades, ranging form pork to pork to pork, at around 50kč per dish. Open Mon.-Sat. 11am-midnight, Sun. 7pm-midnight. Its next-door beer garden is popular even on rainy days. Open nightly 6pm-1am.

Na spilce, U Prazedroje (tel. 706 27 54; fax 706 27 03). If Na spilce had been around in 1945 when armies marched through Plzeň, it probably could have fed the whole lot. The gigantic dining hall under Prazdroj Brewery now accommodates Plzeň's every guest with quality food and fast service. Soups (11-15kč) are not as salty as elsewhere. *Šopský salat* 33kč, apple strudel 26kč. House brew costs 15kč per 0.5L, but the water is free. English menu. AmEx and MC accepted. Open Mon.-Thurs. 11am-10pm, Fri.-Sat. 11am-11pm, Sun. 11am-8pm.

U bílého lva, Pražská 15 (tel. 722 69 98), entrance on Perlova. The "White Lion" rustles with the sound of fountain water in an open-air *orangerie.* Plants—each of a different species—lean at you from every corner, droop down from the walls, and tickle you around the tables. A glass corridor runs around the terrace for rainy days. Bulgarian-style salads 35kč. *Palačinky* (pancakes) 34kč. *Guláš* with *knedlíky* 55.50kč. Beer 14.50 per 0.5L. Open daily 10am-11pm.

U Salzmannů, Pražská 8 (tel. 723 58 55). Founded in 1637, Plzeň's oldest beerhall is back in business, and it's not just *pivo* anymore. The menu has everything from fried eel (81kč) to fried celery (33kč). *Pivovarská směs,* a slightly spicy *guláš* with dumplings, stuffs for only 61kč and you only have to add 17.50kč for 0.5L of beer. The "authentic" decor borders on the sterile, but loud locals provide a beerhall atmosphere. Open Sun.-Thurs. 10am-11pm, Fri.-Sat. 10am-11pm.

SIGHTS

Empire dwellings loom over the market place, but none out-tower the belfry of **St. Bartholemew's Church.** For a vertiginous view of the town, tourists can pay 17kč and climb 60 of the 103m to the observation deck. Assorted bells, named Matthew, Michael, and Pauline, line the way, but you won't find Bertha anymore. The unlucky bell had been cracked, removed, smelted in a fire, shot at, and cracked once more before being smelt for bullets during WWII. No one had the heart to put her up again. Inside, a rich collection of Gothic statues and altars bows to the stunning 14th-century polychrome **Madonna of Pilsen,** recalling Bohemia's glory days under Charles IV. In front, the soot-scarred saints of the **Plague Column** haven't let a plague in yet. Also in the square, Plzeň's golden-clock-topped Renaissance **radnice** (town hall) connects on the inside to the 1607 **Císařský dům** (Kaiser House).

From the northeast part of nám. Republiky, Pražská leads to **Masné krámy,** the former slaughterhouse, at #16, featuring changing art exhibitions (tel. 722 39 48; open Tues.-Fri. 10am-6pm, Sat. 10am-1pm, Sun. 9am-5pm; 15kč, students 8kč). Across the street, **Vodárenská věž** (Water Tower), Pražská 19 (tel. 722 01 40), stored the crystal-clear water needed for fine beer. The well's dried up, so the **Trigon Gal-**

lery (Plzeň's coolest—exhibiting independent artists) doesn't have to worry about water damage (open Mon.-Fri. 10am-6pm, Sat. 10am-1pm; free except for the upstairs exhibit; 10kč, students 5kč). The Water Tower and **Plzeňské podzemí** (Underground) can be visited on a tour that starts inside Perlova 4 near the tower and leads through the cellars, used for the storage and the covert mass consumption of beer, and features a collection of pottery and mugs (open Tues.-Sun. 9am-4:20pm; 30kč, students 20kč, Czechs 15kč).

Perlova ends at Veleslavínova, where **Pivovarské muzeum** (Brewery Museum), Veleslavínova 6 (tel. 723 55 74), exhibits beer paraphernalia from medieval taps to a collection o' coasters. The original malt-house room displays the Pilsner process (no cameras). The last room, labeled "miscellaneous," is probably the most fun, with gigantic steins, wacky pub signs, and a statue of Shakespeare's most famous drunk—that's Sir John Falstaff (open Tues.-Sun. 10am-6pm; 30kč, students 15kč).

Return down Veleslavínova to Rooseveltova, which becomes Františkánská on the other side of the square. The gate of the **Franciscan Convent and Church** leads into a quiet cloister garden, with statues in despairing Gothic poses. The church also houses a fine Baroque main altar and the renowned **Black Madonna of Hájek**, an 18th-century sculpture. The neighboring **West Bohemian Sculpture Museum** (open daily 9am-5pm), with a valuable collection of medieval works, stands on the site of old fortifications. People stroll and relax here in the shade of the trees as brass bands perform their repertoire of polkas, waltzes, and folk tunes. Moving west along the promenade, Kopeckého sady becomes Smetanovy sady, and at its intersection with Klatovská stands the Neo-Renaissance **Divadlo J. K. Tyla** (J. K. Tyl Theater). North of the theater along Sady pětatřicátníků lies the 1892 **synagogue,** an impressive monument to Plzeň's once-large Jewish community.

In 1840, over 30 independent brewers plied their trade in the beer cellars of Plzeň. Some of the suds were good, but some were awful, so the burgher brewers formed a union helping to create the best beer in the world. Many would agree that **Měštanský Pivovar Plzeňský Prazdroj** (Pilsner Urquell Burghers' Brewery; tel. 706 28 88) has succeeded with its world-famous *Pilsner Urquell*. The entrance to the complex lies 300m east of the Old Town, where Pražská becomes U Prazdroje. A huge Neo-Renaissance gate welcomes visitors into the pastel palace of the brewing arts. Guided tours run once each weekday at 12:30pm. After the stimulating "kaleidoscope" film (with Czech, English, and German subtitles) about Prazdroj's past and present, the group divides into Czech, German, English, and French subgroups. The English one gathers few people, so you'll be able to bombard the knowledgeable guide with questions (50kč, Czechs 20kč; the tour lasts 75min.).

ENTERTAINMENT

For early-evening high-brow entertainment, **Divadlo J.K. Tyla** (tel. 22 25 94) offers good **opera** cheap. The schedule's posted outside. Get tickets an hour before the performance (shows usually start at 7pm) in the theater or in advance at the Předprodej office, Sedláčkova 2 (tel. 722 75 48), a block southwest of the main square (open Mon.-Fri. 10am-5pm; best seats 60kč). To get to the theater, take tram #4 to "U synagogy" or, walk along Přešovská off nám. Republiky's southeast corner, and turn left along the main road (Sady pětatřicátníků, which becomes Klatovská).

Bars and Clubs

Thanks to West Bohemia University students, Plzeň booms with bars and late-night clubs. The young English-speaking summer staff at the tourist office eagerly advises. Some clubs have resorted to placing "members only" signs on the front door, but the doorpersons rarely ask for any cards. Things get hoppin' around 9:30pm.

Subway, Sady 5. května 21 (tel. 22 28 96). Descend left off the overpass at the end of Rooseveltova (off nám. Republiky's northeast corner). Students down 14kč beers in the hubbub you get by adding a hi-fi stereo to some kid's home-made, spray-painted playground. Bring some oxygen as this den of rock oldies often gets packed. Open Tues.-Thurs. 9pm-3am, Fri. 8pm-3am, Sat. 8pm-2am.

Pod lampou, Havířská 11 (tel. 27 30 10). Tram #4 to Chodské nám., walk back 50m, and turn left onto the small Havířská. Dreadlocks, dyed hair, tight jeans, and cliquish crowds pulsate to the loud rock—live or recorded. Character changes with the concerts. Live shows almost every day—often by foreign bands (schedule posted outside). Open Mon.-Sat. 8pm-late.

Bílej Měděd, Prokopova 30, off Americká. As much alternative-ness as Pod lampou—only at heart. Judging by looks, the "White Bear" hosts an average mix of locals. The apparently mellow beer-gulpers and coffee-sippers occasionally break into spasmatic slam-dancing. Sparse lighting and eardrum-bursting rock. Beer 10kč per 0.3L. Open Mon.-Thurs. 6pm-3am, Fri.-Sat. 6pm-4/5am, Sun. 8pm-2am.

Kapsa, nám. Míru 140, next to tram #4's stop. Lots of bright pine wood, lots of smoke, lots of graduate students, and lots of cheap beer—this time the gold-medalist of Pivinex '95: *Herold* (10kč per 0.5L). A terrace opens up in good weather. Open Mon.-Fri. 11am-2am, Sat.-Sun. 5pm-2am.

Moravská Vinárna, Bezručova 4 (tel. 723 79 72). Wine from wooden barrels (18kč per 0.2L glass) and bottles of white Moravian *Müller Thurgau* or red *Vavřinecké* (89kč). Wooden monks on the wall laugh with the tipsy crowd of mostly 40-50 year youngs. Open daily 10am-10pm.

Rumor has it that **gay discos** occur every other Saturday at Studna, Máchova 14-16. Those interested take tram #4 south to the end, walk back some 50m, and Máchova will be on the right.

SOUTH BOHEMIA

Rustic and accessible, South Bohemia is a rustic ensemble of scattered villages, unspoiled brooks, and ruined castles. Low hills and plentiful attractions have made South Bohemia a favorite of Czech bicyclists, who ply the countryside watching for wildlife, visiting ruins, and paying homage to the region's famous *Budvar* beer.

■ České Budějovice

No amount of beer will help you correctly pronounce České Budějovice. Pint-guzzlers world-wide can be thankful the town was known as Budweis in the 19th century when it inspired the name of the popular but pale North American *Budweiser*. But tourists come to Budějovice for more than just the town's malty *Budvar*. Mill streams, the Malše, and the Vltava wrap around the city's old center—a fascinating amalgam of Gothic, Renaisssance, and Baroque houses scattered along winding medieval alleys and impeccably straight 18th-century streets. České Budějovice is also a great launchpad for trips to South Bohemia's castles and natural wonders.

Orientation and Practical Information The Old Town centers around nám. Otakara II. Cheap rooms, generally found outside the Old Town's walls, are reachable by regular buses and trams (tickets 4kč at kiosks). The **train station** is 10 minutes from the main square. From the station, take the pedestrian **Lannova,** which becomes **Kanonická** after the moat, and finally pours out into the gigantic nám. Otakara II. **Turistické Informační Centrum,** nám. Otakara II 2 (tel./fax 525 89), arranges accommodations at 250-400kč (open Mon.-Sat. 9am-5:30pm, Sun. 9-11am and 3:30-5:30pm). **Komerční Banka,** Krajinská 1 (tel. 82 87 26), off nám. Otakara II, cashes traveler's checks for a 2% commission (min. 50kč). An **ATM** waits outside, and there are more 24-hour Cirrus/MC ATMs along Lannova and opposite the train station. **Trains,** Nádražní 1 (tel. 533 33), ply the rails to Brno (6 per day, 4½hr., 100kč), Plzeň (18 per day, 2hr., 56kč), and Prague (20 per day, 2½hr., 72kč). **Store luggage** at the station (5-8kč). **Buses** (tel. 544 44) congregate a few meters to the left and across the street from the train station, and spew smoke to Brno (3½hr., 125kč), Plzeň (2hr., 79kč), and Prague (2hr., 66kč). **Fun Sport,** Husova 41 (tel. 440 09), rents bikes at 180-200kč per day (open Mon.-Fri. 9am-noon and 1-5pm). The **post office,** Senovážné nám. 1 (tel. 782 49 11), sits south of Lannova tř. as it enters the Old Town (open Mon.-Fri. 6am-7pm, Sat. 7am-noon). **Postal code:** 37001. **Phone code:** 038.

Accommodations The town's hostels open exclusively in July and August, but inexpensive **pensions** flourish near the center year-round. The tourist office has a list and books rooms. At **Penzion U Výstavistě,** U Výstavistě 17 (tel. 724 01 48), baby-blue stairs lead to a corridor lined with stenciled clouds and homemade cartoons. Take bus #1, 13, 14, or 17 from the bus station five stops to "U parku", and continue 150m along the street that branches off to the right at the bus stop. The adorable pension is as clean as a new pair of diapers, and the rainbow pillows brighten the rooms. The common room contains a kitchen and lists of all the cheap restaurants in town. Call ahead (communal bathrooms; 250kč for the first night, 200kč afterwards; 10% off for ISIC holders). **Grandhotel,** Nádražní 27 (tel. 565 03; fax 596 23), sits directly opposite the train station. It's just one example of Budějovice's "less pricey" hotels. All rooms come with showers, and breakfast is included (singles 690kč, with toilet 800kč; doubles 800kč, with toilet 1120kč).

Food Despite the town's many decent restaurants, it's difficult to find anything but meat, dumplings, and *Budvar* at meal time. A 24-hour grocery, **Non-Stop Bartyzal,** sits in the mall on the corner of Opletala and Nedbala. Take bus #7, 13, or 15 from the train station to "Nedbala." **U paní Emy,** Široká 25 (tel. 575 76), near the main square, provides all four daily food groups with traditional meals (50-95kč), vegetarian dishes (30-50kč), and huge salads (60kč). At night, the 4-foot mountain of wax gets lit and the room flickers with candlelight (open daily 10am-3am). **U Hrušků,** Česká 23 (tel. 356 70), near the main square, has little to do with the eponymous associate editor of this travel guide. The complex contains three establishments: a non-intimidating sit-down buffet cooks up pork and potatoes for 20-30kč (open Mon.-Fri. 8am-3pm); a restaurant next door serves a wider range of dishes for a wider range of prices. Fish plates go for 40-50kč and more meaty dishes cost 50-100kč (open Mon.-Sat. 10am-11pm). The **vinárna** sells 85kč bottles of wine (open Mon.-Sat. 7pm-5am).

Sights and Entertainment Surrounded by an arcaded array of burgher dwellings, cobbled **nám. Otakara II** is the country's largest square. In the center, **Samson's fountain** doesn't flow with the local brew of the same name—maybe that's why the faces spewing water look so disappointed. The *náměstí's* impressive 1555 **radnice** (town hall) stands a full story above the other buildings on the square. Jazzed up in 1730, it bubbles with gargoyles and cherubs. Near the square's northeast corner, **Černá věž** (Black Tower; tel. 525 08) stands over the town. To taste all 72 meters and see all the bells costs nothing, but to get to the 360° balcony after the climb costs 6kč. Beware: the treacherous stairs are difficult even for the sober (open July-Aug. Tues.-Sun. 10am-7pm; Sept.-Nov. 9am-5pm, March-June 10am-6pm). The tower once served as a belfry for the neighboring 13th-century **Kostel Sv. Mikuláše** (Church of St. Nicholas), which became a cathedral when the town gained a bishop in the 18th century. **Sídlo biskupa** (Bishop's Residence) off the main square on Biskupská opens its courtyard to the public May to September (Mon.-Fri. 8am-noon and 1-2:30pm). The bishop's garden is only one of the city's attractive *sady* (orchards). The most scenic follows the former **Mlýnská stoka** stream at the Old Town's north edge.

The city's most famous attraction waits a bus ride from the center (bus #2, 4, or 5). The **Budweiser Brewery,** Světlé 4 (tel. 70 51 11), offers tours of the factory for groups of six or more (arrange them at the tourist office). The medieval meat market **Masné krámy,** Krajinská 13 (tel. 379 57), rings with clinking mugs and the *Nazdravi's* of a hundred tongues. Pricey finger food accompanies 15kč *Budvars*. Although dominated by old Germans, the market's a must for anyone who wants to say they saw České Budějovice (open Sun.-Thurs. 10am-11pm, Fri.-Sat. 10am-midnight). **Pivnice U Zlatého Soudku**, Široká 29, is one of the few places in town where *Samson* lager has survived (10kč per 0.5L; open Mon.-Sat. until 10pm). In summer, lakes around the town host open-air disco concerts (ask hipsters at the tourist office).

■ Near České Budějovice: Hluboká

Hluboká nad Vltavou is an ordinary town blessed with an extraordinary castle. This Disneyland of towers owes its success to Eleonora Schwarzenberg, who renovated the original Renaissance-Baroque castle into a Windsor-style fairytale stronghold in the mid-19th century. The English tour is highly informative, but if all you want is a glimpse of eccentric extravagance, take the cheaper Czech version. Although the palace contains 141 rooms, the tour leads through only the best half-dozen, all done in walnut reliefs, cooled by 17th-century air-conditioning systems, and decorated with magic mirrors and paintings of the Schwarzenbergs of Hluboká, who were once the most powerful family in Europe (tel. 96 50 45; English guides 100kč, Czech 40kč; students half-price). A shorter tour of the princess's quarters promises "interesting tinies and personal objects" (10kč, students 5kč; courtyard open July-Aug. daily 10am-5pm; April-May and Sept.-Oct. Tues.-Sun. 10am-5pm).

Buses run from České Budějovice to "Hluboká pod kostelem" (Mon.-Fri. 40 per day, Sat.-sun. 10 per day; 10min.; 7-9kč) and many have "Týn nad Vltavou" as their final destination. The most pleasant way of daytripping here is by bike (see **Fun Sport** p. 208). You can also walk it (2hr., free). Once at the bus stop, hike up the hill on any of the converging paths. **Štekl**—the greeting "lobby"—was superbly renovated in 1996, so don't mistake it for the real castle.

■ Český Krumlov

Built on a river in the bicycle-friendly plains of South Bohemia, the miniature medieval Český Krumlov attracts more than just train-bound tourists. Herds of ten-speeds wait outside cafés as their riders tank up for the road, while canoers and kayakers maneuver through the "Venice of Bohemia's" windy waterways. Bohemia's second largest castle presides over all the bustle, luring both sportsmen and more traditional tourists with scenic promenades and aging stone courtyards.

Orientation and Practical Information Located 16km southwest of České Budějovice, the town is best reached by frequent **buses** (Mon.-Fri. 10 per day, fewer on weekends; 35min.; 20kč). Most stop at two spots on the outskirts. The first stop, **"Špičak"**, is smaller, but just as close, and allows a downhill march to the tourist office. From "Špičak", pass through **Budějovice gate** and follow **Latrán** past the castle and over the Vltava. The street becomes Radniční as it enters the Old Town and leads into the main **nám. Svornosti**. The **tourist office**, nám. Svornosti 1 (tel. 56 70), in the town hall, books pensions and private rooms starting at 300kč. A wall of maps offers itineraries for bike tours (maps 55kč; open daily 9am-6pm). **Moravia Bank**, Soukenická 34, cashes AmEx traveler's checks at 1% commission (open Mon.-Fri. 7:30am-7pm, Sat. 7:30am-1:30pm). **Train station**, Nádražni 31 (tel. 88 01 11), is a 2-km uphill hike, and connections to České Budějovice take nearly twice as long as buses, but they're also cheaper, and on weekends, they run more frequently (8 per day, 1hr., 14kč). The **main bus terminal**, Kaplická 439 (tel. 761 11), lies to the southwest. A **bike rental**, Kájovská 62 (tel./fax 56 63), operates a block from the tourist office (200kč per 6hr., 300kč per day; open daily 8am-6pm). The main **post office**, Latrán 193 (tel. 22 71), has 24-hour **telephones** outside (open Mon.-Fri. 7am-6pm, Sat. 7am-11pm). Postal code: 38101. Phone code: 0337.

Accommodations Every street has a story, and every house a room to rent. **Moldau Hilton** sits at Parkan 116. Take Radniční from nám. Svornosti, turn right on Parkan, and pray for the "Goddamit! We have space!" sign to be hanging on the door. Even if it's not, they'll usually stuff weary souls in. Mattresses lie among antiques in a room reminiscent of grandma's attic, and those who stay a night find out what the disconnected bidet is for. Some lucky travelers even get to rough the Vltava in the makeshift "Mad Bastard". The Czechophobic Czech owner charges foreigners (200kč) less than natives (300kč; closed Jan. 15-April 30). **U vodníka,** Po vodě 55 (tel. 56 75), offers two quads (180kč per bed) a double (225kč per bed), a kitchen, laundry facilities (40kč per wash), a modern bathroom, and managers who speak native English. Get off at the main bus station, bear left toward the town spires, then hang a right into the town and follow the signs. They also offer an **English library** and rent two mountain **bikes** for 150kč per day (30kč per hour). **Ve věži,** Latrán 28 (tel./fax 52 87), has transfigured one of Krumlov's bastions into a hotel. White-washed rooms with lace curtains have candlesticks on the desks. Every pair of rooms shares a bathroom (singles cost 500kč, doubles 900kč, quads 1400kč; breakfast included). Get off at Špičak, and turn left off Latrán after the post office.

Food and Entertainment On weekdays or Saturday mornings, ask your ho(s)tel manager about the nearest store. The **supermarket** halfway between the main bus station and the town (where the road meets the cobblestones) offers an adequate selection of everything at low prices (open Mon.-Fri. 7am-5:45am, Sat. 7:30am-11:30am). Two food-and-beer houses vie for the greatest popularity. **Cikáanská jízba** (Gypsy bar) fills up with English-speaking expats and tourist-friendly locals. Good gulašes go for 50kč, and *Eggenberg* pours for 13kč per 0.5L (open Mon.-Fri. 4-11pm, Fri.-Sun. 4pm-1am). To get there take Másná off Horní and then follow the second street to the left. **U Matesa,** the other night-and-day house of laughter, sits near the water. Cross the bridge leading toward the cloud-bathed aqueduct, and stroll left along the Vltava. The Moravian owner serves good wine (20kč per 0.2L) in addition to the usual drafts (open Mon.-Thurs. 11am-11pm, Fri. 11am-1am, Sat. 10am-1am, Sun. noon-1am). Tables of satisfied customers spill out into the stone street at **Na louži,** Kájovská 66 (tel./fax 54 95). Flypaper hangs from the ceiling, newspapers hang from the wall, and after a meal here, you might have to rent a U-haul (dishes 40-100kč; open daily 10am-10pm). A summer-only midnight spot, **Myší díra** (Mousehole, a.k.a. The Boat Bar) makes its money by supplying booze to rafters, canoers, and kayakers who stop at the Vltava hut each time they drift by. Bottled beers (10-14kč), grog (rum with hot water and sugar, 20kč), warm wine (14kč), and hard liquors all help make the river a little more interesting (open whenever it's open).

Sights Strangely, pollution may have been Krumlov's biggest boon. In the early 20th century, an upstream paper mill began to putrefy the river, and most citizens moved to the outskirts. Under such benign neglect, the medieval "inner-city" escaped renovation. Now that the factory is gone, the citizens have returned, cleaned up the river, and restored a large part of the center—an effort which put Český Krumlov on UNESCO's distinguished World Heritage List. The town's most visited attraction clings to a cliff on the river. Originally a 12th-century fortress, the **castle** fell into the hands of wealthy families who had nothing better to do than fill it with fancy stuff. The length of stone courtyards is open to the public for free. Two separate tours cover the castle—the first visits the older wing preserved as it had been under the 19th-century Rožmberks, and the second leads past halls of antlers, Baroque ornaments, and the Rococo ballroom, whose walls sport life-size figures trying the latest step. The Czech tours cost 25kč (students 10kč), but to gain anything more than "Blah, blah, Schwarzenberg, blah," take the English tour (70kč, students 30kč; open May-Aug. Tues.-Sun. 8am-noon and 1-4pm; April 9am-noon and 1-3pm; Sept. 9am-noon and 1-4pm; Oct. 9am-noon and 1-3pm). The castle paths lead through pine gardens, a riding school, and a summer palace (open May-Sept. daily 8am-7pm; April and Oct. 8am-5pm). In summer, galleries in the crypts offer a cool break (5kč).

The Austrian painter Egon Schiele (1890-1918) found this place so enchanting that he decided to set up shop in 1911. Sadly, the citizens ran him out after he started painting burghers' daughters in the nude. Decades later, the citizens realized what genius they had run off, and converted Renaissance building, the **Egon Schiele Inter-**

national **Cultural Center,** Široká 70-72 (tel. 42 32; fax 28 20), displays hours of browsing material. Egon Schiele's works, including his infamous nudes, hang next to paintings by 20th-century artists. The collection's well worth the 100kč fee (students 60kč; open daily 10am-6pm). The **city museum,** Horní 152 (tel. 20 49; fax 22 49), covers Krumlov's history with bizarre folk instruments, bone sculptures, and log barges that once plied the river (30kč, students 5kč; open May-Sept. Tues.-Sun. 10am-12:30pm and 1-6pm).

MORAVIA

The word *"český"* grates on the ears in the wine-making eastern part of "Czech" Republic; it describes the *other* Slavic tribe to the west. Although some wanted the newly formed Czech Republic to be called Českomoravsko, there is no serious threat of Moravian separatism. The sub-regions of Moravia are equally finicky. Olomouc proudly describes itself as the capital of the Hanák region which eagerly distinguishes itself from the Horňáks and the "Moravian Slovaks" to the east.

■ Brno

The largest city in the Czech Republic's eastern half, Brno fulfills the role of a local Prague. Considering its much smaller size, the only Moravian town to have resisted the Swedish 17th-century invasion isn't doing a bad job. It's not only a matter of fancy architecture of which Brno has plenty. Rather, like Prague, Brno serves to incubate subcultures, cares for a happy student body, and brims with business life as traders fill up all accommodations during frequent fairs.

ORIENTATION AND PRACTICAL INFORMATION

Brno's compact center makes almost everything, excepting clubs and accommodations, accessible by foot. The tourist office has a branch in the Čedok building outside the train station. To get to the main office, cross the three tram lines and the packed **Nádražní** onto **Masarykova.** Continuing on Masarykova leads to the city's main square, **nám. Svobody.** To get to the tourist office, turn left before the square at **Zelný trh.** The tourist office is on **Radnická** in the old town hall.

Tourist Offices: Kulturní a Informační Centrum Města Brna, Radnická 8 (tel. 42 21 10 90; fax 42 21 46 25). The eager, multilingual staff books hotels, rooms, and concerts (10% fee), arranges trips to Moravian Karst and tours of the city, and sells guidebooks and city maps (29kč) from a veritable treasure trove of literature on Brno and the region. Open Mon.-Fri. 8am-6pm, Sat.-Sun. 9am-5pm.
Budget Travel: CKM, Česka 11 (tel. 42 21 31 47; fax 42 21 26 90). *Wasteels* train tickets, bus trips, and other travel tips. Open Mon.-Fri. 1-5pm. Around the corner at Skrytá (tel. 42 32 12 47), the staff books rooms and, in July and Aug., dorm beds for 320kč. Open Mon.-Thurs. 9am-noon and 1-6pm, Fri. til 5pm.
Currency Exchange: Komerční Banka, Kobližná 3 (tel. 42 12 71 11; fax 42 21 64 76). Provides Visa cash advances and cashes most traveler's checks. MC/Cirrus **ATM** on the 1st floor. Open Mon.-Fri. 8am-5pm. The non-stop exchange at **Taxatour,** at the train station, cashes AmEx traveler's checks with 5% commission.
ATMs: MC/Cirrus machine at Komerční Banka. 24hr. MC/Cirrus at Masarykova 15.
Trains: (tel. 42 21 48 03). To: Bratislava (10 per day; 2hr.; 73kč); Budapest (5 per day; 4½hr.; 754kč); České Budějovice (5 per day; 4½hr.; 100kč); Prague (12 per day; 3hr.; 110kč); Vienna (3 per day; 2hr.; 405kč). The international booking office handles *Wasteels* tickets. **Lockers:** 5kč. **luggage storage:** 5kč.
Buses: Zvonařka (tel. 33 79 26) behind the train station. Descend into the large area under the train station and follow "ČSAD" signs; 5min. past K-mart. To: Prague (12 per day; 2½hr.; 73kč); Vienna (4 per day; 2½hr.; 225kč).

BRNO ■ 213

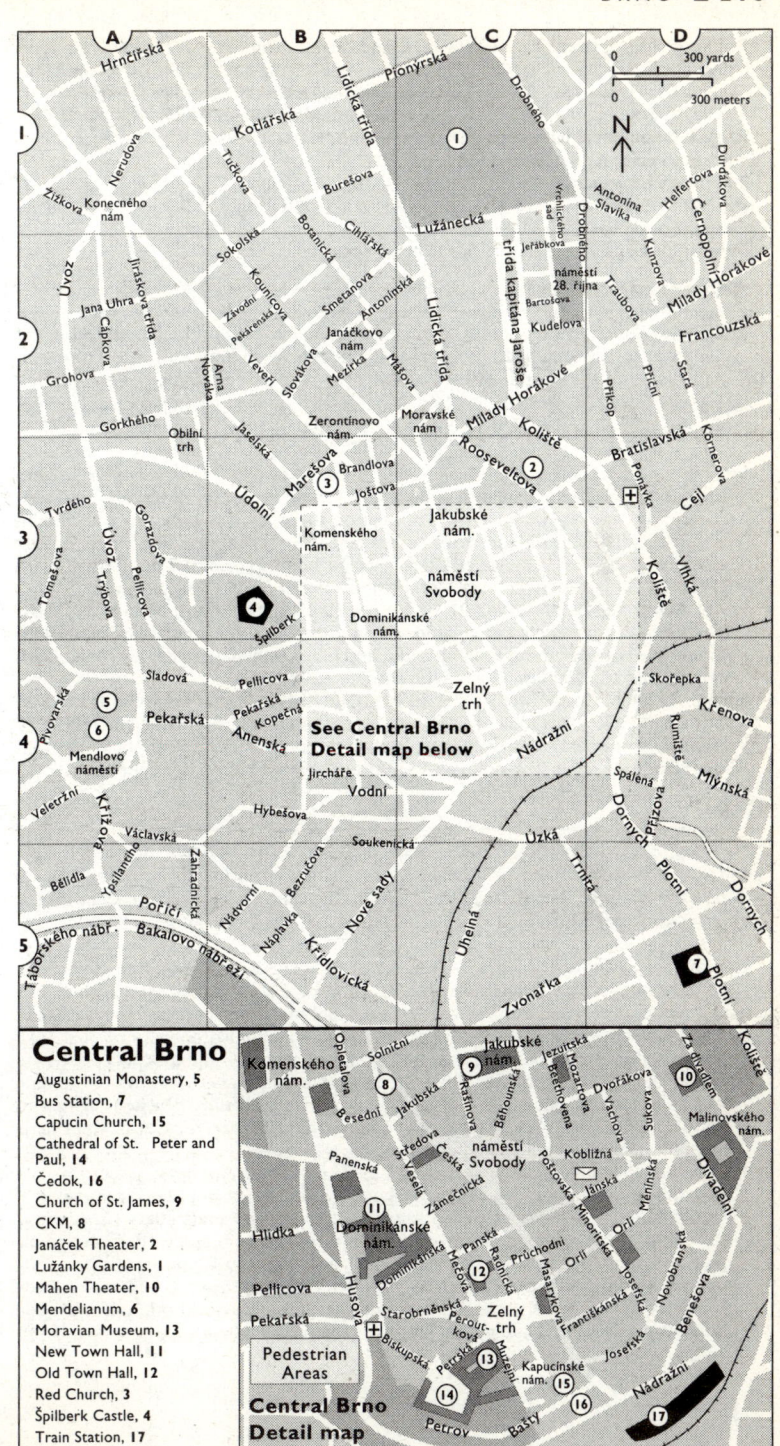

Central Brno

- Augustinian Monastery, 5
- Bus Station, 7
- Capucin Church, 15
- Cathedral of St. Peter and Paul, 14
- Čedok, 16
- Church of St. James, 9
- CKM, 8
- Janáček Theater, 2
- Lužánky Gardens, 1
- Mahen Theater, 10
- Mendelianum, 6
- Moravian Museum, 13
- New Town Hall, 11
- Old Town Hall, 12
- Red Church, 3
- Špilberk Castle, 4
- Train Station, 17

CZECH REPUBLIC

Public Transpotation: Trams, trolleys, and buses. Adult fare is 6kč. Luggage transport costs 3kč. Buy tickets at a *tabak*. Consider buying a day-pass that covers a specific 24-hr. period for 30kč at kiosks or Ćedok. Ticket checkers are relentless.
Taxis: Radiotaxi, tel. 33 33 33. At the train station and major hotels.
English Bookstore: Knihkupectvi, nám. Svobody 18 (tel. 42 21 09 30). Open Mon.-Fri. 8:30am-6pm, Sat. 9am-noon.
24-Hour Pharmacy: Koblížná 7 (tel. 42 21 02 22).
Post Office: Poštovská 3-5 (tel. 42 32 11 01). Open Mon.-Fri. 7am-9pm, Sat. 8am-1pm. **Postal code:** 65700.
Telephones: Inside the post office. **Phone code:** 05.

ACCOMMODATIONS

A walk around the city center will reveal a dozen hotels with prices beyond a budget traveler's worst nightmares. In most cases it's necessary to look for private rooms in the suburbs. Both the **tourist office** and **CKM**, as well as **Taxatour**, Nádražní 2 (tel. 42 21 33 48; fax 42 21 33 56; open 24hr.), at the train station, arrange such accommodations at 350kč per person. Most rooms lie 10 minutes from the center by tram.

Interservis (HI), Lomená 38 (tel. 43 32 13 35; fax 33 11 65). Take tram #9 or 12 from the train station to the end at "Komárov". Continue along Hněvkovského, and turn left onto Pompova. The hostel will appear on the right. The outgoing staff brightens up this high-class hostel with smiles and daily scrubbing. The 5-person flats consist of 2 doubles, a single, a kitchen, and a bathroom. 265kč per person, with HI or ISIC cards 190kč. Breakfast 29kč. Meals 45-55kč. MC, Visa accepted.

Hotel Avion, Česká 20 (tel. 42 21 50 16; fax 42 21 42 55), north of nám. Svobody. The inside of this 1920s avant-garde building has been semi-renovated in a 1960s Braun style with braun rugs, braun sinks, and braun wall-paper. Singles 565kč, with showers 845kč. Doubles 970kč, with shower 1200-1700kč.

Bulharský Klub, Česká 9 (tel. 42 21 10 63). One hall of double rooms with a shared shower and toilet that look like they're straight out of a house. Little amenities like a fluffy bath rug and patterned tiles. Well kept doubles and triples 300kč per person. Reception open 9am-noon and 5-10pm. There's a bar on the floor.

FOOD

Street-side pizza joints far outnumber traditional *párek* peddlers, and at noon, the fragrance of a thousand slices fills the Old Town. A daily **market** thrives on Zelný trh (Mon.-Sat. 9am-6pm). The **K-mart** right behind the train station has a **grocery** on the ground floor (open Mon.-Wed. 7am-7pm, Thurs.-Fri. 7am-8pm, Sun. 9am-3pm).

Restaurace U Minoritů, Orlí 17 (tel. 42 21 56 14). Class personified. Authentic Baroque statues, live flowers hanging in the terrace, and checkered marble floors. The waiters even seem to bow when they ask for your order. *Brněnská kapsa* (69kč) bursts with grilled meat, peppers, and sauteed mushrooms. *Radegast* 16kč per 0.5L. Coffee 17-24kč. Open Mon.-Sat. 11am-10pm. MC and Visa accepted.

Sputnik, Česka 1, right off Svobody nám. Self-serve on psychedelic trays to the tune of 30kč per *guláš*. The refined, thin-walletted go for the grilled chicken (half-a-bird 50kč). Entrées with fries 40-60kč, and *Starobrno* tastes the price at 8kč per 0.5L. Open Mon.-Fri. 7am-6pm, Sat. 7am-noon.

Restaurant Flora, Solniční 3a (tel. 42 21 29 83), near St. Thomas's. Generous servings amidst wood and wrought iron have made Flora a popular dining spot in Brno's center. Most prices below 100kč. Tasty mixed salads 40kč. *Gambrinus* 12.50kč per 0.5L. Smoking room open daily 11:30am-3pm and 6-10pm. No-smoking room open Mon.-Sat. 11:30am-midnight, Sun. 11:30am-10pm.

Stopkova Plzeňska Pivnice, Česká 5. Founded in 1554, this beerhall serves traditional *svíčková* (roast pork, 49kč). Order something else, though, if whipped cream is not what you like with your meat. Open daily 10am-11pm.

SIGHTS

Off Masarykova, one of Brno's most morbid attractions waits in the crypts of the **Capucin church**, Kapucínské nám. (tel. 42 21 32 32). In the 17th century, Brno's Capucin order discovered an ingenious method of ventilation which dried and embalmed corpses in the open air. The desiccated bodies still have all the fresh air they want, although they seem to need a bit to drink. Visitors pay 20kč (students 10kč) to see the original 24 monks and the 120 noblemen who thought the process cool enough to try it themselves (open Tues.-Sat. 9am-noon and 2-4:30pm, Sun. 11-11:45am and 2-4:30pm). Next door, the Dietrichstein Palace houses **Moravské Zemské Muzeum** in its never-ending halls. Mostly mushrooms, minerals, and mammoth bones, but the exhibits on the short-lived Great Moravian Empire and Moravian life in the Middle Ages are still worth a look. The museum's pride is the voluptuous Věstonice Venus (open Tues.-Sun. 9am-5pm; 12kč, students 6kč).

At Radnická 8, the **old town hall's** tower looms even larger over the vegetable market after a 1905 extension and the legends which surround the building give it added stature. The town hall's strangely crooked Gothic portal purportedly got its bent when the carver who created it spent his whole commission on too much good Moravian wine. Inside, legend says, the dismayed stone face looking on the hall is the petrified head of a burgher who met his doom behind the town-hall wall after siding with the Hussites in 1424. The most famous of the tales involves the stuffed "dragon" hanging on one wall. Sometime in the Middle Ages the reptile was ravaging the town; to stop him, a valiant knight stuffed quick-lime into an ox carcass and offered the venomous confection to the dragon. After devouring the bait, the dragon quenched his thirst in a nearby river, the lime began to slake, and the poor fire-breather's belly exploded—thus the seam that remains in his stomach today. The dragon is actually a crocodile from the Amazon Jungle offered to the town by Archduke Matthew to garner favor among the burghers (open daily 9am-5pm). Towering above Zelný trh on Petrov Hill is the **Cathedral of Sts. Peter and Paul.** Although destroyed in the Swedish siege during the Thirty Years War, the building has been re-Gothicized in the last two centuries. A neo-Gothic high altar and 14th-century Madonna and Child remain. The crypt museum hides around the back (open Mon.-Sat. 10am-4pm).

Biskupská curves from the Cathedral into Dominikanská which flows into Dominikanská nám. The **Dominican church** here remains closed, but coupled with the nearby **new town hall,** it's worth a glance. Directly across from the new town hall, an alley leads to **nám. Svobody,** Brno's largest square. Its partially gold **Plague Column** has successfully warded off infections for the last 300 years.

North of nám. Svobody along Rašínova, the great **Church of St. James** points its strangely thin tower ("the toothpick") into the skyline. Built for Brno's medieval Flemish and German communities, the church doesn't look a lick like it originally did after more than ten renovations. The French Huguenot Raduit de Souches, who helped save Brno from the Swedish armies in 1645, rests inside in a great stone monument. Following Jezuitská east from here, and turning right onto Rooseveltova, which becomes Divadelní leading into Malinovského nám, brings you to the grand **Mahen Theater,** erected in the late 19th century by Helmer and Fellner. The **Janáček Theater,** farther north between Koliště and Rooseveltova, was the pride and joy of the 1960s. From here, Rooseveltova runs northwest to a set of traffic lights. Turning left here, toward the center, conducts you to the **Kostel Zvěstování Panny Marie a sv. Tomáše** (Church of the Annunciation and of St. Thomas). Raised in 1350 as an Augustinian monastery, the church shelters the remains of its founder—the brother of Charles IV, yes, he of the bridge—right in front of the main altar. That location may be too good for anyone's bones, however, since the main altar contains a copy of the miraculous painting of "Virgin Mary of St. Thomas".

Down Joštova, the former **Seat of the Moravian Parliament** flanks the **Red Church,** a late 19th-century imitation of a medieval hall church by Heinrich Ferstel, the man who built Vienna's unabashedly neo-Gothic Votivkirche. The church commemorates the Protestant thinker, Jan Amos Komenský, who, incidentally turned down a rectorship at Harvard—the Florida State of the North. It figures.

Legends of outrageous torture surround the eerie walls of **Hrad Špilberk** (tel. 42 21 41 45): unfaithful wives walled up and subjected to slowly dripping water, criminals tied to underground "rat drains," and torture chambers from the Marquis de Sade's dreams. Špilberk served as a prison until 1855, hosting some of the Austrian Empire's most cantankerous criminals. Later used as military quarters, the castle has now become a museum of war and torture. The most popular display is the reconstructed torture room replete with knuckle clamps, shin clips, iron maidens, and devices for which only one's imagination could find a purpose. (Open June-Sept. daily 9am-6pm; Oct.-March 9am-4:45pm; April-May 9am-5pm.)

From Šilingrovo nám., a walk along Pekařská leads to the heart of Old Brno, **Mendlovo nám.** The high Gothic **Augustinian Monastery** contains the 13th-century *Black Madonna*, the Czech Republic's oldest wood icon, which purportedly averted the Swedes in 1645. The monastery's most accomplished monk, **Johann Gregor Mendel**, laid out the fundamental laws of modern genetics. It took the scientific world 50 years to appreciate his work, but as his words now accurately predict in stone, "My time will come!" The **Mendelianum** and the adjacent courtyard honor the order's son with a statue and a beehouse, used by the monk. Lamarckian Communists took the statue down in 1950, but it has since returned and remains happy as a pea in a pod.

A lengthy walk on Milady Horákové and a left on Černopolní will lead to the **Tugendhat Vila.** The Tugendhats were forced to leave the house in 1938 to escape the Nazi menace, and now it belongs to the city. A left on Schodová leads to **Lužánky Park,** the largest in Brno (open daily 8am-dusk). The 200-year-old trees and **St. Ignatius's Chapel** once belonged to the Jesuits but now please the public, providing paths and shade just to let visitors walk off dumpling-heavy lunches.

ENTERTAINMENT

The old town hall hosts frequent recitals and concerts (contact the tourist office), and the Janáček Theater presents operas and ballets (7pm; 30-100kč). Brno's teens seem to outgrow disco at the age of twelve, but a few rock clubs rumble in town. Surprisingly, it's easier to find a *pivnice* than a wine pub in the heart of wine-producing Moravia. Still, a *vinárna* does occasionally appear selling 80-100kč bottles.

- **Pivnice Minipivovar Pegas,** Jakubská 4 (tel. 42 21 01 04; fax 42 21 12 32). Founded in 1992, this microbrewery has acquired a loyal following among locals and visitors. Going straight up to the bar prevents a wait for the busy servers. Light and dark brews ferment right behind the bar. A pint goes for 10-17kč. The 5-sausage plate of *Pivovarská klobása* (43kč) is the house's suggested oily snack. Moravian food also served. Open daily 9am-midnight.
- **Mersey,** Minská tř. 14 (tel. 74 52 15), a ½-hour north along Veveří. Indie rock during the week, live bands on the weekends. The posters around town advertising this club as a venue for foreign and national bands' concerts make it clear that Mersey's worth the walk. Beer 15kč. Occasional discos. Open Tues.-Thurs. and Sun. 8pm-1am, Fri.-Sat. 8pm-late.
- **H46,** Hybešova 46 (tel. 32 49 45), a 10-min. walk west from the train station, or a couple of stops by tram #1 or 2. 300m down from the stop. If the door is locked, ring the bell. The inside is as black and cavernous as the outside is bright and bland. Get drunk on Moravian wine (18kč per 0.25L) or jittery on coffee (9-16kč). A poster board helps you find those met the previous night. Open nightly 5pm-4am.
- **Club Philadelphia,** Milady Horakové 1a (tel. 45 21 24 67). Smaller and lighter than H46. Philadelphia takes not nearly as romantic an approach to homosexuality as Tom Hanks. Packed and smoky by the bar. Open nightly 4pm-12:30am.

Near Brno

MORAVSKÝ KRAS

The traveler will spend a few hours waiting for bus connections in sleazy buffets to get to Moravský Kras, but no matter how much time is spent en route to and from Brno, the labyrinth of caves deserves a trip. Caverns, tunnels, lakes, and rocks spanning 92 km sq. of underground wonderland can be seen on an hour-long tour. If you're lucky, the guide will happen to speak English; otherwise, be ready for scattered German comments all over a Czech monologue. The visit comprises a 40-minute walking tour amid imaginatively named rock formations, such as "the rococo doll". Next, you're sent in a wobbly boat on a 20-minute ride through low-ceilinged limestone canals, some up to 40m deep. Just before entering the boat, the guide lets the spelunkers glance at the **Macocha (Stepmom) Abyss.** Legend has it that a stepmother from a nearby town threw her stepson into the gaping hole. When villagers found the boy suspended from a branch by his trousers, they saved him and threw the woman in instead. In the last 20 years, 50 people have committed suicide from the abyss's 1387m ledge. Buy tour tickets at Skalní Mlýn's bus stop or in the entrance booth. Bring a sweater; it gets chilly even in mid-summer. (Open April-Sept. Mon.-Fri. 7am-4:30pm, Sat.-Sun. 7:30am-4pm; Oct.-March Mon.-Fri. 7:30am-3pm, Sat.-Sun. 7:30am-4pm. 30kč, with ISIC 15kč.)

From Brno, take a **train** (or the railway service's **bus** to the left as you leave the train station) to **Blansko** (6 per day, ½hr., 10kč—be at the stop 40 minutes before departure time as the bus driver leaves as soon as the bus is full). Here, buses to **Skalní Mlýn** leave from the bus station's stop #6 (5 per day, 10min., 5kč). The bus station is to the right as you face the train station. Once in Skalní Mlýn, continue walking along the left-bearing yellow trail in the direction of the bus.

TELČ

Telč's Italian flair stems from a trip **Zachariáš of Hradec,** the town's ruler, took to Genoa in 1546. He was so enamored of the new Renaissance style, he brought back a battalion of Italian artists and craftsmen to fix up his humble Moravian castle. The town's thriving burghers asked the craftsmen to spruce up their houses too, and a heated battle-of-the-Joneses soon transformed the center into an Italian export, ultimately putting it on UNESCO's list of world heritage monuments.

Castle tours are Telč's most popular attraction. There are two options—*trasa* A (1hr.) and *trasa* B (45min.)—and each needs at least five people. Leading through magnificent rooms, 70% of *trasa* A consists of gazing at ceilings. A guidebook at the ticket office adds history to the already spell-binding visit (open May-Aug. Tues.-Sun. 8am-noon and 1-5pm; April and Sept.-Oct. Tues.-Sun. 9am-noon and 1-4pm; 40kč per tour, students 20kč; foreign-language guide 80kč per group). In the arcaded courtyard, a **museum** displays examples of Telč's folklore (same hours; 10kč, students 5kč; pick up an English leaflet). The **gallery** off the walled garden is a memorial to artist **Jan Zrzavý** (1890-1977), whose style recalls Magritte, Matisse, and…Pierrot posters (open May-Aug. Tues.-Sun. 8am-noon and 1-5pm; Sept.-April Tues.-Fri. and Sun. 9am-noon and 1-4pm, Sat. 9am-1pm; 10kč, students 5kč).

The **tourist office,** nám. Zachariáše z Hradce 1 (tel. (066) 96 22 33), in **Městský Úřad,** books hotel and private rooms (200-400kč). They also have info on the town's **cultural festival,** which takes place the first two weeks in August (open Mon.-Fri. 7am-5pm, Sat.-Sun. 9am-5pm). The **bus station** lies five minutes from the main nám. Zachariáše z Hradce. Follow Staňkova and turn left on Masarykova, which leads to the base of the Old Town. **Buses** between Brno and České Budějovice (7 per day, 2hr., 55kč to either). **Pod kaštany hostel,** Štěpnická 409 (tel. (066) 721 30 42), on an extension of Na posvátné off Staňkova, has clean, shower-equipped singles (400kč, with ISIC 250kč) and doubles (660kč, with ISIC 500kč) and accepts Mastercard. Call ahead; or be directed by the friendly staff to another hotel or *penzion*.

■ Olomouc

Capital of North Moravia, Olomouc won't stir any new emotions in the visitor's heart, but it will bring to mind the Czech Republic's best aspects. The masterfully rebuilt Old Town offers yet another network of promenades amid flaunts and friezes—perhaps even better than elsewhere. Although most tourism here is generated by antediluvian Deutschsprechers, foreign visitors are by far outnumbered by local students. The young scholars of Comenius and Hus do their best to infuse the eerily quiet, traffic-free squares with life, and if you come soon, the 99%-pure-nearly-free-of-guided-tours taste of Olomouc might still fill the air.

ORIENTATION AND PRACTICAL INFORMATION

All trams from the **train station** ride into the Old Town (4 stops). The **bus station** lies one stop beyond the trains on tram #4 or 5. The 5kč per ticket is a low price for this efficient way of getting into the center. Take the tram to the gigantic copper **Prior** department store and follow 28. října 50m to **Horní nám.**, the town's main square.

> **Tourist Office: A.T.I.S.,** Horní nám. (tel. 551 33 85; fax 522 47 88), in the town hall. Tons of info on Olomouc and the surrounding region. They help book hotels and private rooms (from 250kč per person). In summer, student housing fliers are posted at the desk. The staff also offers 5kč trips to the town hall tower's top (April-Oct. daily 11am and 4pm). Open in summer daily 9am-7pm; off-season Mon.-Fri. 9am-6pm, Sat.-Sun. 9am-3pm.
> **Budget Travel: CKM,** Denisova 4 (tel. 522 21 48; fax 522 39 39). English-speaking staff sells ISICs (150kč), books rooms, and sells tickets. Open Mon.-Fri. 9am-5pm.
> **Currency Exchange: Komerční Banka,** Svobody 14 (tel. 550 91 11). Charges 2% on most traveler's checks and handles MC cash advances. Open Mon.-Fri. 8am-5pm. Its annex, Denisova 47 (tel. 550 91 69), does the same. Same hours.
> **ATMs:** Komerční Banka's 24-hr. ATMs suck'n'spit your Cirrus and MC plastics at Riegrová 1, near the town square, and at the Prior bus stop.
> **Trains:** Jeremenkovo 60 (tel. 472 21 75). To: Brno (9 per day; 1½hr.; 44kč); Prague (6 per day; 2½-3½hr.; 140kč). **Lockers** 5kč. **24-hr. luggage storage** 5kč.
> **Buses:** Sladkovského 37 (tel. 332 91). To: Brno (1 per hr. 5:30am-8pm; 1½hr.); Ostrava (12 per day; 2hr.); Rožnov pod Radhoštěrn (4 per day; 1¾hr.).
> **Public Transportation:** The city's **trams** and **buses** all require a 5kč ticket sold at kiosks marked with a big yellow arrow. All trams run between the train station and the central Prior department store before branching off.
> **Taxis: 24-hr. service,** tel. 271 81 or 285 91.
> **Pharmacy: Lékárna-Epava,** 1. máje 12 (tel. 522 75 04). Open Mon.-Fri. 7:30am-5pm, Sat. 8am-noon.
> **Post Office:** nám. Republiky 2 (tel. 522 40 83). Open Mon.-Fri. 7am-7pm, Sat. 8am-noon. **Postal code:** 77100.
> **Telephones:** Outside the post office. **Phone code:** 068.

ACCOMMODATIONS

Cheap beds (50-100kč) appear in summer when **dorms** open to tourists, but it's possible to snag a bed by mid-June. A few dorms have vacancies year-round.

> **Vysokoškolská kolej 17. listopadu,** 17. listopadu 54 (tel. 522 38 41). Take any tram 2 stops from the station to "Žižkovo nám." One of the many student dorms that open up in summer. Surprisingly undamaged, considering the winter occupants. The polished halls resonate with the omnipresent voice of the desk attendant calling students to the phone. 3 beds per room. Communal bathrooms. Bring toilet paper. 170kč, with a valid university ID 51.60kč (ISIC not accepted).
> **Penzion Best,** Na střelnici 48 (tel./fax 28 506). Take 3 stops on bus #18 from the trains to "DPO". Only 3 years old—sleek white bathroom tiles to prove it. Views of St. Wenceslas Cathedral. Singles with shower and toilet 450kč. Doubles with shower and toilet 800kč. With ISIC 5% off. Eurocard, MC, and Visa accepted.

Hostel, Legionářská 11 (tel. 41 31 81; fax 541 32 56), at the swimming stadium. Take any tram from the train station to nám. Národních hrdinů. Backtrack through the bus park leaving left under the airplane and round the pool buildings. The chlorine in the air keeps the bathrooms sterile but makes the tiles crack. Communal bathrooms. Singles 180kč. Doubles 380kč. Triples 420kč. Cheaper for the comrades from the old SocBloc. The pool is free after 2 nights, or 20kč per day.

FOOD

Faced with the dilemma of stuffing poor scholars and satisfying finicky tourists, the eateries of Olomouc have succeeded in providing something for everyone. South of town at the ramparts' base, a shady park guards excellent picnic spots. **Večerka,** Riegrova 20 (tel. 279 94), sells the grub (open Mon.-Fri. 7am-9pm, Sat.-Sun. 8am-3pm).

Vegetka, Dolní nám. 39 (tel. 522 60 69). Despite the name, most of the restaurant's entrées include well seasoned chicken (50-70kč). The veggie menu advertises mainly eggs and tofu (40-50kč). The salad bar clears up the misunderstanding with a choice of 10 already-slightly-mixed vegetables (small 33kč, large 50kč). Outside seating available. Open Mon.-Sat. 10am-10pm.

Restaurace U Huberta, 1. máje 3 (tel. 522 40 17). The only non-traditional thing here is the sign in the dining room requesting patrons not to smoke from noon to 3pm. *Krušovice* brew 13kč per 0.5L. Those who need some fat with their alcohol order *knedlíky* (10kč) with some form of meat (30-50kč) smothered in gravy and *schmalz* (free). Open Mon.-Sat. 10am-10pm.

Café Caesar, Horní nám. (tel. 522 92 87), in the *radnice*. A million conversations rumble and echo in the gothic vaults, and when the dixie band plays every other Thurs. (10pm-1am; no cover), Caesar roars. The popular spot offers 31 flavors of pizza (50-150kč) and all kinds of pasta combinations (50kč). But to enjoy the mesmerizing low of mixed tongues, a simple cappuccino will do (19kč). AmEx, MC, and Visa accepted. Open Mon.-Sat. 9am-1pm, Sun. 1pm-midnight.

SIGHTS

The imposing spires of **Chrám Sv. Václava** (St. Wenceslas Cathedral) are probably the only reason anyone can find tiny Václavské nám., tucked away in the northeast corner of the Old Town. The high-vaulted church interior is in impeccable condition. Downstairs, the crypt museum exhibits Gothic statues, old books, and the gold-encased skull of Olomouc's protectress St. Pauline; read along with the free English guidebook for the full story (open Mon.-Thurs. and Sat. 9am-5pm, Fri. 11am-5pm, Sun. 11am-5pm; donations accepted). The **tower** commands a magnificent view (open for climbs April-Oct. Mon.-Fri. at 11am and 4pm; 5kč).

Descend Dómská and climb up Wurmova to reach Biskupské nám. On the east side is the Renaissance **Arcibiskupský palác,** erected between 1665 and 1685 by Peter Schüller. While Austria was engulfed in the turmoil of the 1848 revolutions, Franz Josef ascended the imperial throne in this building. For more historical background, follow Mariánská to nám. Republiky, where **Vlastivědné muzeum** (Museum of National History and Arts), nám. Republiky 5 (tel. 522 27 41), presents the history of *homo olomouciensis* from mammoth to noble, as well as the pre-Communist history of the town hall's astrological clock. The temporary exhibits are the highlight of the museum (open Tues.-Sun. 10am-5pm. Permanent exhibit 10kč, students 5kč; entire museum 30kč, students 15kč). From the museum, take a left on Univerzitní after the pretty (but closed) church to the copper-domed **Sarkander Chapel** which commemorates Jan Sarkander's life and death with an exhibit on his torture in 1620. The priest was accused of treason by the Protestants after he refused to divulge a confessor's secrets and was subjected to "three-fold torture." While he hung by his arms, evil inquisitors set burning candles near his armpits and tickled a wound in his chest with a feather (open Tues. and Thurs.-Fri. 9am-4pm, Wed. 10:50-12:30am). A right on Mahlerova leads to the bustling **Horní nám.** The massive 1378 **radnice** (town hall) and its spired clock tower dominate the center while fountains gush on both sides.

The astronomical clock set into the hall's north side got a Communist facelift in 1954, and now steelworkers, instead of mechanical saints, coast out on the hour and ding the bell. A close second to the *radnice's* tower, **Sloup Nejsvětější Trojice** (Trinity Column) soars over 35m in black-and-gold glory. North along 28. října, next to Prior's massive copper cube, the blocky Gothic **Chrám Sv. Morice** might well have been the minimalist eyesore of its day, but the rich interior is all decoration. Most of the sculptures date from 1399-1540. One of Europe's largest Baroque organs bellows on Sundays in St. Maurice's resonant hall. Olomouc's orchestra also performs here on occasion. South of Horní nám., stately homes line Dolní nám. The oldest building is the 1580 **Hauenschildův palác,** at the corner of Lafayettova, but the square's centerpiece is the Plague Column which gathers eight saints around "Madonna and Child".

ENTERTAINMENT

Starting the bar crawl at the Student Center's **Kavárna Terasa,** Křížovského 14, might allow you to meet some English-speaking locals willing to take you on a tour of the local fun spots. Although it's the terrace that's chic, the inside bar is what's cool. *Lobkowicz* flows on tap for 12kč per 0.5L (open Mon.-Thurs. 10am-midnight, Fri. 10am-2am, Sat. 2pm-2am, Sun. 2pm-midnight). Two premier underground bars neighbor each other on Denisová. **Hospoda u musea** (popularly known as Ponorka, "Submarine") gathers a long-haired crowd even when the beer's out. It's also reputed to be the best place to fill up on some form of hay (open Mon.-Wed. 10am-11pm, Thurs.-Fri. 10am-midnight). **Depo No. 8,** next door, lets you choose one of three rooms to feast your eyes on the metal decor and your taste buds on the "expensive" *Staropramen* or even dearer *Guinness* on tap (open daily and late). The toppest of the top, however, hides right before the Sarkander Chapel on Univerzitní. The year-old **Vitriol** lurks below street level, and its fumy air out-sweets its Turkish kava (8kč). Twenty-somethings huddle on benches or roll around wall-less boudoirs letting Indian chants and macabre drawings penetrate their senses. Only the grinding sound of Czech chatter holds your consciousness fast (open nightly 4pm-11pm...right...).

This Bud's for EU

Many Yankees, having tasted the malty goodness of a Budvar brew, return home to find that the beer from Budweiss is conspicuously unavailable. The fact that Budvar was Czech Republic's largest exporter of beer, beating out even Pilsner Urquell in 1995, makes its absence from American store shelves even stranger. About the only way to sip a Bud from the ol' country on a porch in New York, is to pack a few bottles for the journey home and pray they don't shatter in transit.

So, you might be asking, as many are, where's the Budvar? The answer lies in a tale of trademarks and town names. České Budějovice (Budweis in German) had been brewing its own style of lager for centuries when the Anheuser-Busch brewery in St. Louis came out with its Budweiser-style beer in 1876. Not until the 1890s, however, did the Budějovice Pivovar (Brewery) begin producing a beer labeled "Budweiser". International trademark conflicts ensued, and in 1911 the companies signed a non-competition agreement: Budvar got markets in Europe and Anheuser-Busch took North America. That explains why Americans can't find the "other" Bud at the local 7-Eleven. But the story continues...

A few years ago, Anheuser-Busch tried to end the confusion by buying a controlling interest in the makers of Budvar. The Czech government replied, "nyeh" for national historical reasons. Coincidentally, the following year Annheuser-Busch didn't order its normal one-third of the Czech hop crop. Annheuser-Busch is now suing for trademark infringement in Finland, while Budvar is petitioning the EU to make the moniker "Budweiser", a designation as exclusive as that of "Champagne", meaning that any brand sold in the EU under that name would have to come from the Budweiser region. As long as the battle continues on European fronts, there is little chance that a Budvar in America will be anything but an illegal alien, so fill up while you can (and take a few for the road).

ESTONIA (EESTI)

US$1 = 11.83EEK (Estonian Kroons)	10EEK = US$0.85
CDN$1 = 8.62EEK	10EEK = CDN$1.16
UK£1 = 18.44EEK	10EEK = UK£0.54
IR£1 = 19.17EK	10EEK = IR£0.52
AUS$1 = 9.33EEK	10EEK = AUS$1.07
NZ$1 = 8.22EEK	10EEK = NZ$1.22
SAR1 = 2.66EEK	10EEK = SAR3.76
DM1 = 7.99EEK	10EEK = DM1.25
Country Phone Code: 372	International Dialing Prefix: 800

Apart from the occasional *Lada* or *Volga* rolling down the street, one might not realize that Estonia was a Soviet republic only five years ago. Historically and culturally identifying with Scandinavia and Finland, Estonia faces an identity crisis, as 35% of its population is ethnic Russian. Visitors encounter ancient springs, meteor craters, and boulders connected with Estonia's mythic hero Kalevipoeg, a giant who fought bears, Germans, and other evil forces. Estonia's new-found independence has led to a resurgence of national culture. As the tiny nation strives to realize the benefits of free-market democracies while remaining true to its heritage, the legend of fierce Kalevipoeg remains alive in the thoughts and hopes of Estonians.

ESTONIA ESSENTIALS

Citizens of the U.S., Canada, the U.K., Australia, and New Zealand can visit Estonia visa-free for up to 90 days. Australians flock to Tallinn, since Estonia is one of the few East European nations that does not require visas of them. Estonian consulates can issue 90-day, single-entry (US$10) or multiple-entry (US$50) tourist visas, or transit visas (US$5) to citizens of Ireland and South Africa, who also need an original invitation. To obtain the visa, submit your passport, one photograph and fee (cash or personal check) with your application (see Essentials: Embassies and Consulates, p. 7). It is possible to obtain visas upon arriving in Estonia, but they are more than twice as expensive (single-entry 400EEK, multiple-entry 1400EEK, transit 160EEK). For a visa extension, apply to the Estonian Immigration Board in Tallinn at (22) 66 43 32.

GETTING THERE AND GETTING AROUND

Several **ferry lines** reach Tallinn from Helsinki. **Tallink** (tel. 640 98 08) is a popular line. Three boats per day run between Helsinki and Tallinn (3½hr., 225EEK, students 175EEK). The **Estonian New Line** (tel. 631 86 06) runs three hydrofoils, making six total roundtrips per day Monday through Saturday and at 4pm on Sunday (1½-2hr.; Mon.-Fri. 250EEK, Sat.-Sun. 400EEK). Look for visa-free tours at travel bureaus or the Helsinki office at Kalevankatu 1 (tel. 358 (0) 680 24 99, summer only). **Estline** (tel. 631 36 36) sails the *Mare Balticum* between Tallinn and Helsinki, and the *Regina Baltica* between Stockholm and Tallinn (one every other day, 13hr., deck space 500EEK, students 380EEK; one place in a cabin 126EEK). **Silja Line** (tel. 631 83 31) sails two beautiful boats per day between Tallinn and Helsinki (3½hr., 140 Finnish Marks and up). Reservations for all ferry lines are most easily made through **Baltic Tours**, in Tallinn (tel. (372) 631 35 55 or 43 06 63).

The **Baltic Express** is the only train from Germany and Poland that skips Belarus, linking Tallinn to Warsaw and Berlin via Kaunas, Rīga, and Tartu (Tallinn to Warsaw one per day; 20hr.; 381EEK, private compartment 624EEK).

Finnair (tel. 631 14 55) connects Tallinn to Helsinki (4 per day; one-way US$125, under 25 one-way US$43), and **SAS** (tel. 631 22 40) flies to Stockholm (1 per day, US$292). **Estonian Air** (tel. 44 63 82) also goes between Tallinn and Helsinki (4 flights per day; roundtrip US$108, under 25 US$86).

Buses and trains radiate to all points from Tallinn and Tartu. Only three **train** lines cross the Estonian border; one heads from Tallinn through Tartu to Moscow, another goes to Rīga, and the third goes through Narva to St. Petersburg. Major towns such as Pärnu and Haapsalu are all connected to Tallinn, but trains can be scarce. Diesel trains are express. Estonian rail tickets are the most expensive in the former Soviet Union. **Buses** thoroughly link all towns, often more cheaply and efficiently than the trains. It's even possible to ride buses direct from the mainland to towns on the islands (via ferry) for less than the price of the ferry ride alone. During the school year (Sept. 1-June 25), students receive half-price bus tickets. On the islands, where buses have up to 12-hour gaps between trips, bike and car rentals can be relatively inexpensive and an excellent way of exploring the remote areas. Those who **hitchhike** stretch out an open hand and wave it up and down. *Let' Go* does not recommend hitchhiking as a safe form of transportation.

TOURIST SERVICES

Unlike most of the former Soviet Union, Estonia has grasped the importance of providing tourist services; most **small towns** now offer city maps, while **larger towns** and cities may have well equipped tourist offices with loads of literature and armies of enthusiastic workers eager to help you find hotels, restaurants, free rides, and whatever else you may need. Info booths marked with a green (or sometimes blue) "i" sell maps and give away free brochures. They can answer questions in English. The main tourist offices arrange tours and make reservations.

MONEY

The unit of currency is the **kroon** (EEK), divided into 100 **senti**. Most banks *(pank)* cash **traveler's checks**. **Credit cards** are still a rarity, but American Express, Diner's Club, MasterCard, and Visa are arriving. Hotel Viru in Tallinn, as well as many other banks across the country, provides Visa cash advances. **ATMs** still come up short.

COMMUNICATIONS

A **letter** to the U.S. costs 4.50EEK. Within Tallinn, some **telephones** require a 20-senti coin for local calls (a 10-senti coin will often work also). Most phones accept digital cards. **AT&T Direct** is available in Estonia by dialing 8-00-8001001 from any phone. **Long-distance** calls within Estonia to points in Europe or elsewhere can be made at post offices. Calls to the Baltic states and Russia cost 6.50EEK per minute (8.50EEK with a card). Phoning the U.S. runs a steep 20EEK per minute from Tallinn and 24EEK from other cities (28.80EEK with a card). Cards come in denominations of 30, 50, and 100EEK. International calls can be ordered through the operator in the post office, after which you'll have to wait 10 minutes for the call to go through.

In an attempt to update and modernize their phone system, the Estonians have come up with a system that proves that the universe, despite everything, tends toward disorder. Indeed, Einstein probably couldn't figure this one out. Keeping everything in perspective, however, the following explanation should make the phone system seem less like the fourth dimension:

In Tallinn there are three systems for phones: a crude medieval system, a new digital system, and a cellular system. Each one has its own area code. For the old system, phone numbers have 6 digits, the area code is 22. For the new system, in which phone numbers have 7 numbers, the first of which is a 6 (often mistakenly placed in parentheses), the area code is 2. For cellular phones, the area code is 25. The digital system and the old system can call each other without the area code within a given city. Calling from a cell phone, however, means always having to dial using an area code (and never having to say you're sorry). To call Tallinn from outside Estonia on the old system, dial 37 22 and then the number; on the digital system, dial 372. To call a cellular phone, dial 37 25 (that's the same throughout Estonia). From Russia, where the phones are unlikely to work anyway, the old codes are still active, so dial 014 instead of 372, but include the final 2 or 5 as appropriate.

To call out of Estonia, on the old system dial 8, wait for the second more mellow tone, then dial 00, the country code, and the rest of the number. From digital phones, dial 8-00 without waiting for a tone. From a cell phone just dial 00 and the number. To call Eesti Telefon's **information** number dial 07. If you're really lost in the chaos Estonians call a phone system, physically lost in the middle of the street or need any other information, call the **Ekspress Hotline** at 631 32 22. Operators speak English and can answer any questions.

English-language **books** and **newspapers** are relatively easy to find in Estonia, especially in Tallinn. The English-language weekly, **The Baltic Times** (5EEK), has an excellent entertainment listing for all three Baltic countries, as well as detailed news and features about the tri-nation area. The English-language weekly *Baltic Independent* is a good source for info on the latest in Tallinn and Tartu.

LANGUAGE

Estonians speak the best **English** in the Baltic states; most young people know at least a few phrases, though **German** is more common among the older set. **Russian** was theoretically learned in schools, but Estonians in secluded areas are likely to have forgotten much of it since few, if any, Russians live there. Younger people (under 20) are not likely to know Russian at all. Younger Estonians who do know Russian may be averse to using it. Many know English, **Swedish,** German, or **Finnish.** Always try English first, making it clear you're not Russian, and then switch to Russian. Estonian is a Finno-Ugric language, with 14 cases and all sorts of letters. One popular Estonian rock group calls itself Jää-äär, meaning "on the edge of the ice." You won't master Estonian in a day, but basic words help: *bussijaam* (BUSS-ee-yahm; bus station); *raudteejaam* (ROWD-tee-yahm; train station); *avatud* (AH-vah-tuht; open); *suletud* (SUH-leh-tuht; closed). For more words, see the Estonian Glossary, p. 777.

HEALTH AND SAFETY

> **In Tallinn: Fire:** tel. 001. **Police:** tel. 002. **Ambulance:** 003.
> **Elsewhere: Fire:** tel. 01. **Police:** tel. 02. **Ambulance:** tel. 03.

The **toilets** *(tasuline)*, marked by "N" or a triangle pointing up for women and "M" or a triangle pointing down for men, usually cost 1EEK and include a very limited supply of toilet paper. Tap water in Estonia is theoretically safe, but it is very high in chlorine, making it smell and taste funky. While the **crime** rate is low, women should avoid going to bars and clubs alone or walking alone at night, even during white nights. The emergency numbers for the entire country are listed in the above white box, but for English-speaking help, you might want to contact your embassy in an emergency.

ACCOMMODATIONS AND CAMPING

Each **tourist office** will have listings of all accommodations and prices in its town and will often be happy to arrange a place for visitors. Between the range of US$100-per-night ex-Intourist abodes and the cheap, drab hotels with no hot water, a few companies have set up youth hostels and started to arrange stays at private homes. Tallinn's **Baltic Family Hotel,** Mere pst. 6 (tel./fax (2) 44 11 87), and **CDS Reisid** (Baltic Bed and Breakfast), Raekoja plats 17 (tel. (2) 44 52 62; fax 31 36 66), offers rooms in homes throughout the Baltic countries. BFH charges US$9-15 per person; CDS is computer-efficient but charges US$25. Many hotels provide **laundry** services. Some hostels are part of larger hotels, so be sure to ask for the cheaper hostel rooms. Also, even some of the upscale hotels have hall toilets and showers.

FOOD AND DRINK

It's hard to define Estonian food; go to any restaurant and you'll see the same assortment of drab sausages, lifeless schnitzel, greasy bouillon, and cold fried potatoes that plague the former European USSR. If there is a difference in Estonia, it is that there is more fish on the menu. Trout is especially popular, and often the ham-stuffed *soljanka* you knew as meat stew in Rīga and Moscow will undergo a sea-change here into a deliciously thick whitefish soup. Beer is the national drink in Estonia for good reason—not only is it inexpensive, it's also delicious and high-quality. The national brand *Saku* is downright excellent, especially the darker *Saku Tume*. Local brews like the *Saaremaa* beer available in Kuressaare can be volatile. Some restaurants and cafés take an hour break during the late afternoon. Most Estonian doorkeepers are friendly to Westerners, although you'll occasionally encounter a hard-headed Stalinist. Try smiling and speaking English, German, or French. If dining late, try to get in before 10pm. If possible, make reservations around lunchtime.

CUSTOMS AND ETIQUETTE

Businesses take hour-long **breaks** at noon, 1, or 2pm and most are closed on Sundays. No one **tips** in Estonia, although a service charge is sometimes included in the bill at some restaurants. **Women** traveling alone are a rarity, so expect some questions. Also, women in Estonia never go to bars or clubs alone, and in some towns, women dining alone might get some stares, especially if they order beer—and especially if it's anything but *Saku* original. **Homosexuality** is legal in Estonia, but public displays are not socially accepted, even in bigger cities. Much late-night entertainment in cities and resort towns caters to mafiosi and frat boys, and on weekend nights most clubs throw expensive erotic shows involving naked women on neon floors. On the islands you will encounter people dressed in folk costumes, but your jeans won't be the first pair they've ever seen.

LIFE AND TIMES

HISTORY

Archaeological evidence suggests that **Finnish** tribes settled here as early as 6000BCE and formed into farming villages by about 1500-1300BCE. **Viking** invasions beginning in the 9th century CE shook up the rural peace. King Canute of Denmark launched attacks in the 1000s, and after two centuries of diligent pillaging, Denmark conquered the coast under **King Valdemar II.** According to legend, Danes finally defeated the Estonian resistance after the heavenly appearance of a white cross on a blazing red background—the markings of the contemporary Danish flag. The Danes set about converting the pagans, but upon fierce Estonian resistance, appealed to the **German Teutonic Knights** for aid. The pact set a social structure that endured until the Great Northern War—the Scandinavians as theoretical monarchs, the Teutonic nobility as true wielders of power, and the Estonians as absolute serfs.

Once **Russia,** under Ivan III, began to throw off the Mongol yoke, the international situation became more complex. The Teutons at first turned to Sweden for help against the new Russian power, and were stunned when instead the **Swedes** took advantage of Teuton weakness to take over Estonian lands. The **Swedish interlude** (1692-1709) was a relative respite for ordinary Estonians—the worst abuses of the feudal system were curbed. In retaliation, the Teutons allied themselves with Russia, and thus began the **Great Northern War,** in which Russia's Peter the Great and Sweden's King Charles XII duked it out in Northern and Central Europe. Ultimately, Peter won the war, and, by the 1721 Peace of Nystad, gained the Baltics.

Russian rule did not change the prestige and economic situation of the nobility, but serfs lost almost all rights. The situation improved in the 1800s, when the region's peasants won the right to own private property (1804). Serfdom was soon abolished (1819), and laws of the 1860s banned forced labor and prohibited landowners from flogging tenants. By the end of the 19th century, peasants controlled 40% of the country's privately owned land. The 1848 revolutions inspired the **Young Estonian** movement, which opposed all foreign domination but focused on that by Germans. Under Alexander III, Russia clamped down, prompting a nationalistic Estonian backlash led by **Konstantin Päts,** the editor of a radical newspaper.

The **Russian Revolution of 1905** sparked rebellions in Estonia that were met by harsh reprisals. At the outbreak of **WWI,** Estonians were in a difficult position. Many were drafted into the Russian Army, while the Estonian-German population sided with Prussia. The **Russian Revolution of 1917** intensified the Estonian struggle for independence. After occupation by Germany, Estonia declared **independence** in

---

The Singing Revolution

In the past century, Estonia has done more with music than just sing away its blues. The Russian-dominated nation made its musical debut in 1869 as 10,000 patriots joined voices to praise Estonia at the country's first song festival. Over the decades as ruling Russia tightened its grip on the country, the sing-a-thons became focal points of protest for independence. If they did not immediately produce results, they at least increased national pride, and with them, the ever-feisty Estonian freedom movement gained momentum. Despite the country's twenty-year stint with self-rule (1920-1940), its plaintive song remained the same. Under Stalin's rule, singing certain patriotic hymns became a sure-fire pass to a Siberian wonderland, and so the sing-alongs continued underground. By 1988, Estonians couldn't keep the music in any longer, and at a raucous political rally, 10,000 voices raised together in singing a tune which had been outlawed for 40 years. That summer, rebellious hymns resounded throughout the country, as marches and political rallies united the disgruntled Estonians, frightened the Soviet government, and ultimately, in 1991, gained Estonia its freedom.

1918 but was subsequently taken by the Red Army. Only with British and Finnish help did Estonians recapture their lands and declare their right to self-rule. From 1919-33, a **coalition government** ruled. However, the decentralized government was unable to cope with economic depression and unemployment in the early 1930s, forcing President Päts to proclaim a state of emergency and rule as a sympathetic dictator from 1934-36 before resuming democratic elections. During **WWII,** Estonia was occupied by the Russians (1940) and then the Germans (1941-44). Under Soviet rule, Päts, other Estonian leaders, and parts of the Estonian population were arrested, deported, or killed. As the Red Army slowly pushed out the Nazis in mid-1944, tens of thousands of Estonians fled to Germany or Sweden; thousands more died at sea trying to escape their war-ravaged homeland.

The 1950s saw extreme repression and Russification under **Soviet rule;** deportations and immigration reduced the percentage of ethnic Estonians in the population from 90% in 1939 to 60% in 1990. Internal purges removed the few native Estonians holding seats in the Republic's Communist party. *Glasnost* and *perestroika* eventually permitted breathing room for an Estonian political renaissance. In 1988, a **Popular Front** emerged in opposition to the Communist government, pushing a resolution on independence through the Estonian legislature. Agitators for independence won a legislative majority in the 1990 elections; following the foiled Moscow coup of 1991, Estonia became truly independent.

LITERATURE

The first written work in Estonian, a translation of the Lutheran catechism, appeared in 1535, but Estonian literature did not come into being until the 19th century. **Anton Helle's** 1739 translation of the Bible helped create a common Estonian language out of the northern and southern dialects—announcing the **Estophile period** (1750-1840), which increased the volume of Estonian literature, especially lyric poetry rooted national folktales and Finnish epics. Folklore provided the basis for **Friedrich Reinhold Kreutzwald's** *Kalevipoeg* (1857-61). The epic's eponymous hero slays castlefulls of Teutons. Chained to the gates of Hell, he is prophesied to return, his own release bringing new life to the nation. This became the rallying point of Estonian national rebirth in the Romantic period, of which **Lydia Koidula's** poetry and drama, imbued with protest, marked the peak.

Deepening class barriers in the 1800s shifted the intelligentsia's attention away from national problems to social ones. Still, Realism's entrance into Estonian literature was painful. **Eduard Vilde's** novels about emancipated women and evil capitalists drew moral criticism. In the revolution of 1905, Vilde helped popularize Socialist ideas. At the same time, the pro-revolutionary **Noor-Eesti** (Young Estonia) movement appeared. Its writers focused their attention on literary form. **Gustav Suits's** stylistic experiments produced poems which called on youth to fight for liberty and truth. Suits's later work, however, reflected the poet's disillusionment, a pessimism justified by the outbreak of WWI.

The inter-war years saw the development of tragic poetry, haunted by visions of human suffering and war. Realism-starved poets protested against newly independent Estonia's bourgeois rule. **Anton Tammsaare's** prose evolved with the changing literary styles. A turn-of-the-century naturalist, he joined the Noor-Eesti group only to surprise the public again with realist novels in the 20s. Tammsaare's *Tõde ja Õigus* (*Truth and Justice,* 1926-33), a search for the meaning of life (without the thin mints and salmon mousse), canonized him in Estonia's literary hagiography.

The resurgence of Realism did not dampen the Estonian literati's interest in mysticism. **Maria Under's** earthy love *Sonnets* and **Heiti Talvik's** doomsday predictions gained popularity in the 1930s. The latter seemed to foresee WWII and the enlargement of the USSR; both hindered the growth of Estonia's literary tradition. After 1940, many novelists went into exile and used symbolic and erotic writing to confront their new life and contemporary society. Later emigrés penned ironic and self-critical verses. Socialist Realism at home sent many to temporary exile in Siberia. **Jaan Kross** managed to get away with criticizing Soviet reality in *The Tsar's Madman* (1978).

Aimée Beekman avoided head-on conflict with the authorities, shedding light on modern women's dilemmas in *The Possibility of Choice* (1978).

ESTONIA TODAY

Thousands are out of work, and the 1995 elections scaled back the government's mandate for change by electing **Tiit Vähi** of the Coalition Party as the Prime Minister. The recovery plan is working; Estonia is already within reach of Scandinavian standards of living, while prices, to the joy of the budget traveler, stay low.

Estonia's main foreign policy problem is its relationship with Russia. Russia promised to honor Estonian borders in the 1920 **Treaty of Tartu,** but annexed 5% of Estonia's territory after invading in 1940. Estonia refuses to accept the loss of these regions (east of Narva and around Pechory). Moscow unilaterally demarcated the borders in these regions, but legal wrangling continues. A problem even closer to home is the fact that nearly 35% of Estonia's residents are immigrants or the children of Russian immigrants who came during the Soviet period. In July 1996 Soviet passports, which most Russians in Estonia possess and use, expired, leaving Russian citizens without passports and forcing them either to opt for Estonian citizenship or to live as illegal citizens. The first option is complicated by two extremely difficult tests (language and citizenship) that all would-be Estonians must pass. The language test has been waived for some returning ethnic Estonians, which has caused protest among Russians who claim that the Estonians are trying to disenfranchise the Slavs. The Estonian government has been slow to respond to the problem, saying that Russians can live in Estonia without passports, though "foreigner" status brings with it difficulties with travel or even registering a car. Russians claim that the Estonians are leaving them in a Catch-22 in order to squeeze them out of the country. In 1995 elections, the Russian party Our Home is Estonia! won six seats in the parliament.

Tallinn

With medieval spires climbing into the pink skies of summer twilight, vendors pouring tall glasses of *Saku* in the Town Hall Square, and narrow cobbled streets that wind their way through wonders of history and architecture, Tallinn's ancient beauty and charming serenity mix perfectly with an up-beat, cosmopolitan pace. Despite its Benetton and McDonald's, Tallinn possesses a more of an Eastern feeling than any other Estonian city—Russians make up 40% of its population. Once the most renowned European city in the Hanseatic league, Tallinn is rapidly working its way back to its glory days while maintaining a sleepy village-like atmosphere.

ORIENTATION AND PRACTICAL INFORMATION

Tallinn's **Vanalinn** (Old Town) is an egg-shaped maze ringed by four main streets—**Põhja puiestee, Mere pst., Pärnu maantee,** and **Toom pst. Narva mnt.** runs east from the junction of Mere pst. and Pärnu mnt. to the looming **Hotel Viru,** Tallinn's central landmark. The Old Town peaks at the fortress-rock **Toompea,** whose 13th-century streets are level with church steeples in **All-linn** (Lower Town). To reach the Old Town from the **ferry terminal,** walk 15 minutes along Sadama to Põhja pst., then south on Pikk between the stone towers. From the train station, cross **Toom pst.** and go straight through the park along **Nunne**—the stairway up **Patkuli trepp** on the right leads directly to Toompea. In the Old Town, **Pikk tee** (Long street), the main artery, runs from the seaward gates of the Lower Town to Toompea through **Pikk Jalg** tower. **Raekoja plats** (Town Hall Square) is the scenic center of the Lower Town. The shop on Hotel Viru's second floor has free copies of *Tallinn This Week.*

> **Tourist Office: CDS Travel,** Raekoja Plats 17 (tel. 44 52 62; fax 631 36 66; e-mail cds@zen.estpak.ee). Gives walking English tours of the city May 15-Sept. 15 daily at 2pm (45EEK; tour lasts 1½hr.; open Mon.-Fri. 10am-6pm, Sat.-Sun. 10am-4pm).

The **info booth,** Raekoja Plats 18 (tel. 66 69 59), sells maps (25EEK) and a catalogue of farm accommodations (around 200EEK per night). Open Mon.-Fri. 9am-7pm, Sat.-Sun. 10am-5pm. The **tourist information center,** Sadama 25 (tel. 631 83 21), at the Tallinn Harbor (A terminal), offers info on smaller hotels in Tallinn.

Embassies: Canada, Toomkooli 13 (tel. (22) 44 90 56; fax (358) 298 11 04; emergencies 630 40 50). Open Mon.-Fri. 9am-4:30pm. **Latvia,** Tõnismägi 10 (tel. 631 13 66; fax 2 681 668). Open Mon.-Fri. 10am-noon. **Russia,** Lai 18 (tel. 60 31 66); visa section (fax 646 62 54). Open Mon.-Fri. 9:30am-12:30pm. **U.K.,** Kentmanni 20 (tel. 631 33 53; fax 631 33 54). Open Tues.-Thurs. 10am-noon. **U.S.,** Kentmanni 20 (tel. 631 20 21; fax 631 20 25). Open Mon.-Fri. 8:30am-5:30pm.

Currency Exchange: Five *valuutavahetus* (currency exchange windows) line the inside of the central post office, offering some of the best rates in Tallinn.

ATM: ATM and Visa cash advances at the **Hotel Viru,** Viru väljak.

American Express: Suur-Karja 15 EE090 (tel. (372) 631 33 13; fax 631 36 56). Sells and cashes traveler's checks, books hotels and tours, and sells airline, ferry, and rail tickets. It arrange visas to the Baltics, Russia and the CIS. Card members can receive mail and get cash advances (open Mon.-Fri. 9am-6pm, Sat. 9am-3pm).

Flights: Estonian Air, Vabaduse sq. 10 (tel. 44 63 82), flies 4 times per day from Tallinn to Helsinki and Stockholm (US$138, students under 25 US$43; open Mon.-Fri. 9am-5:30pm). **Finnair,** Liivalaia 14 (tel. 631 14 55), flies to Helsinki (4 per day; US$125, under 25 US$43). **SAS,** Roosikrantsi 17 (tel. 631 22 40; 7 per day to Helsinki, roundtrip US$248). Every 20min., Bus #2 runs from the **airport,** Lennujaama 2 (tel. 21 10 92; fax (6) 38 87 33), to near Hotel Viru.

Trains: Toom pst. 35 (tel. 45 68 51). Trams #1 and 2 travel to Hotel Viru. Trains are modern, with announcements in English and no shoving crowds. To: St. Petersburg (1 per day, 10hr., 110EEK, *coupé* 175EEK). Buy same-day international tickets at window #8, or buy them in advance window #8 upstairs. Domestic tickets (same-day only) at windows #15-18 located in the older building on the other side of the tracks. The *Baltic Express* goes to Warsaw via Rīga, Kaunas, and a change at Šeštokai, Lithuania (1 per day, 21hr., 381EEK, *coupé* 624EEK). Buy tickets at window #7. To Rīga on the *Baltic Express* (7hr., 143 EEK, 195 *coupé*).

Buses: Lastekodu 46 (tel. 42 25 49), just south of Tartu mnt., and 1.5km southeast of the Old Town. Tram #2 or 4 and bus #22 connect to the city center. Windows #1-9 sell domestic tickets. The "As sebe" window deals with international links. To: Rīga (8 per day, 7hr., 96EEK); and St. Petersburg (2 per day, 9hr., 122EEK).

Ferries: At Sadama's end, 15min. from center. Terminal A sends ferries to Finland; B terminal sends 'em to Sweden. Bus #90 runs from the ferry to the train station. **Estline,** Sadama 29 (tel. 631 36 36; fax 631 36 33), to Stockholm (every other day; 15hr.; deck 500EEK, students 380EEK). **Tallink,** Sadama 4 (tel. 44 24 40), to Helsinki (3 per day; 1½hr., 225EEK, students 175EEK). **Viking,** Sadama 25 (tel. 631 86 23 or 631 81 39), to Helsinki (6 per day, 1½hr., 250-400EEK).

Public Transportation: Buses, trams, and trolleybuses cover the entire suburban area; each category has separate stops marked with ideograms. All run 6am-midnight. Tram #2 connects the bus and train stations. Kiosks sell tickets (4EEK), or you can buy them from the driver (exact change only on the tram). If you're in Tallinn for a while, buy a 10-day transit card at a kiosk, which is good for unlimited rides on all public transportation. Ask for a "Kümne päeva kaart" (50EEK).

Taxis: Around Hotel Viru they might overcharge you. Find a *Takso* stand, or call 60 30 44, 639 59 59, 31 27 00, or 43 03 30. "Volga" model taxis have low rates. Cabs with meters may charge up to 5.50EEK per km.

Car Rental: Europcar, Magdaleena 3 (tel. 650 25 59, airport office tel. 638 80 31), at 900EEK per day, are less expensive than others. Make reservations two days in advance. Open daily 9am-5pm. When **parking,** buy tickets from the black boxes on street corners, and place ticket in a visible place inside the windshield.

Luggage Storage: Lockers downstairs in the train station (6EEK—one 3EEK token to open it and one to retrieve your stuff). Open 5am-12:30am. Store luggage at the bus station for 2-9EEK per day. Open daily 5am-noon and 12:30-11:40pm.

Bookstores: Homeros, Vene 20 (tel. 631 10 59), just off Raekoja plats, sells a wide variety of books and magazines in English. Open Mon.-Fri. 10am-7pm, Sat.-Sun. 11am-5pm. Buy reference materials, including city guidebooks such as the *Tallinn Travel Guide*

ORIENTATION AND PRACTICAL INFORMATION ■ 229

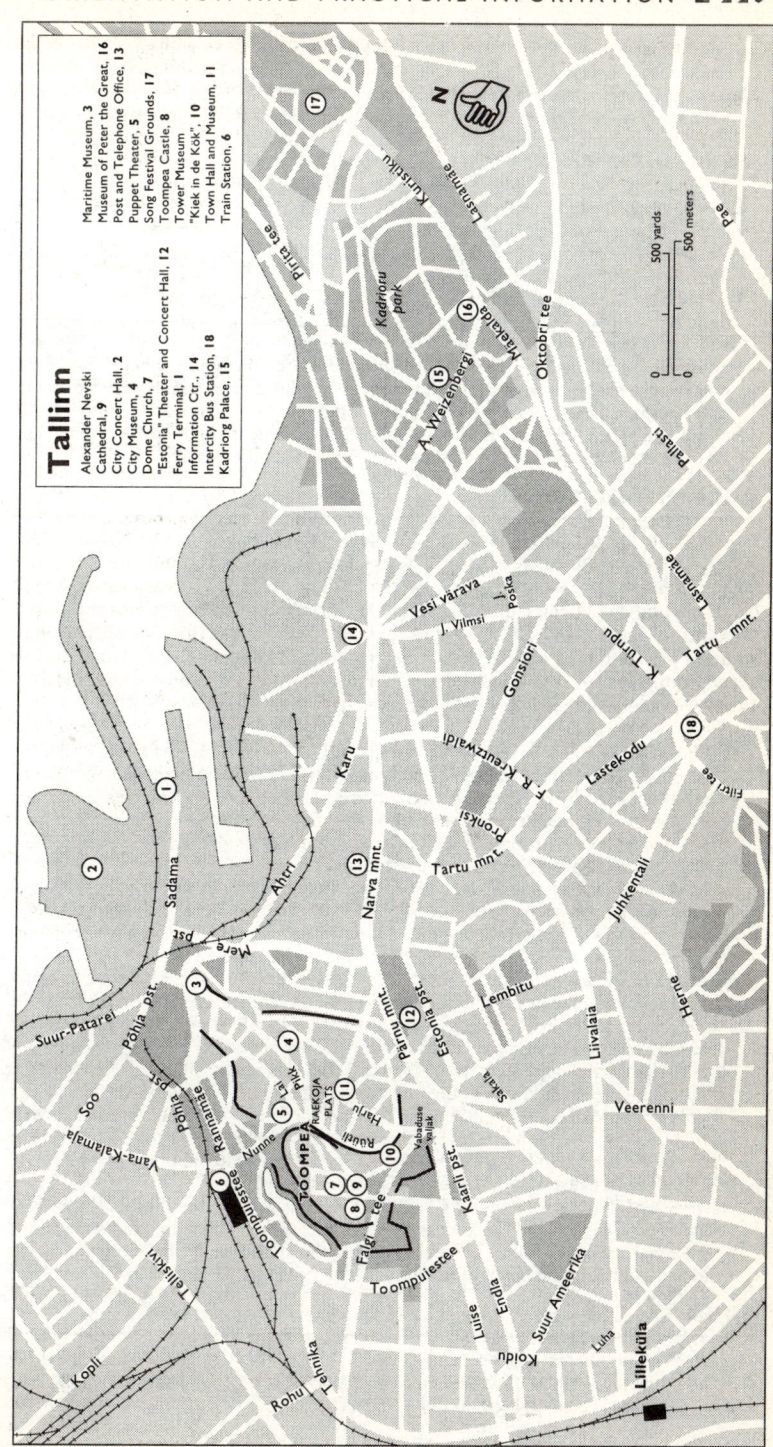

Tallinn

Alexander Nevski Cathedral, 9
City Concert Hall, 2
City Museum, 4
Dome Church, 7
"Estonia" Theater and Concert Hall, 12
Ferry Terminal, 1
Information Ctr.., 14
Intercity Bus Station, 18
Kadriorg Palace, 15
Maritime Museum, 3
Museum of Peter the Great, 16
Post and Telephone Office, 13
Puppet Theater, 5
Song Festival Grounds, 17
Toompea Castle, 8
Tower Museum
"Kiek in de Kök", 10
Town Hall and Museum, 11
Train Station, 6

(35EEK), at **Kupar,** Harju 1 (tel. 44 83 09) southeast of Raekoja plats. It also stocks travel books covering the Baltics. Open Mon.-Fri. 10am-6pm, Sat. 11am-4pm.
Laundry: Laundromat Seebimall, Liivalaia 7. One load (5½kg) washed and ironed 57EEK, without ironing 51EEK. Service usually takes 2 days, but is sometimes finished overnight. Open Mon.-Fri. 8am-9pm, Sat. 9am-6pm, Sun. 10am-4pm.
Pharmacy: RAE Apteek, Pikk 47 (tel. 44 44 08). A broad selection of Scandinavian medical supplies. Open Mon. 11am-6pm, Tues.-Fri. 9am-8pm, Sat.-Sun. 9am-3pm.
Express Mail: DHL, Jõe 5 (tel. (2) 631 24 04; fax 631 20 45; telex 17 38 01). A 10-page document to the U.S. costs 475EEK (open Mon.-Fri. 9am-5pm).
Post Office: Narva mnt. 1, 2nd floor, across from Hotel Viru. Open Mon.-Fri. 8am-8pm, Sat. 9am-5pm. **Postal code:** EE-0001.
Telephones: Telephone office: Narva mnt. 1, 1st floor. The phone office side of the building is closed indefinitely. For all phone services and inquiries go to window #45 in the post office next door. **Fax** services (fax from the U.S. +372 631 30 88). A 1-page fax to the U.S. costs 40EEK. Buy **phone cards** at any news kiosk or the postal store in the back of the post office. Local phones are sometimes free, sometimes require a 5-, 10- or 20-senti coin, and sometimes just don't work. **Phone code:** See Estonia Essentials: Communication, p. 223, for help with dialing. The short version: 22 or 2 for new digital lines; 25 for cellular phones.

ACCOMMODATIONS

Inquire at the information desk in the bus station, about beds (communal bathrooms; 80EEK). No reservations are accepted. **Karol Travel Agency,** Lembitu 4/7 (tel. 45 49 00; fax 31 39 18) sets tourists up in hostels for as low as 80EEK. In summer, make reservations one day ahead (open Mon.-Fri. 9am-6pm). **Baltic Family Hotel Service,** Mere pst. 6 (tel./fax 44 11 87), near Hotel Viru, off the street through the alleyway, arranges private rooms with access to bathrooms and kitchen. Call a couple of days ahead, though rooms can sometimes be arranged at the last minute (singles start at 198EEK; doubles in the center 335EEK; open daily 10am-6pm).

The Barn, Väike-Karja 1 (tel. 44 34 65), in the Old Town. This hostel has taken the concepts "clean" and "spartan" (excepting the microwave provided for guests' convenience) to heart. The thin foam mattresses might not appeal to all backs, but hey! they're spotless. Recently moved, so you may want to make further inquiries. Spacious, renovated rooms and spanking new plumbing. Bed, sheet, and pillow 150EEK, with blankets 160EEK. The 11th night is free.

Hotel Ookean, Paljassaare 39 (tel. 49 42 38). Take bus #59 from the train station or near Hotel Viru to the last stop, "Ookean"; walk straight after the bus stop. Cheapest hotel in town. Share toilets with another room and get a key for the communal showers. Singles 41EEK. The *baar* downstairs serves dinners for 16.55EEK!

Kuramaa 15 Hostel, Vikerlase 15 (tel. 632 77 81; fax 632 77 15). The hostel's major flaw is that you may never find it. Take the #67 bus from across the street from the Hotel Viru near the Baltic Tours Office to the last stop (7-10 min.). Go up the stairs and straight into the first courtyard of the building complex. The word "Hostel" is barely visible in a window toward the right that also reads "Juksuur". The office is on the left on the first floor of the entryway to the right. The hostel provides huge rooms with use of a full kitchen. Each apartment has two or three rooms each with 2 beds, many of which are queen size. Shared bathroom and toilets within the apartment. 100EEK per person, 90EEK with an HI card. Reception open Mon.-Sat. 9am-9pm, but call ahead and someone will wait for you.

Hotel Scard, Liivalaia 2 (tel. 44 61 43), left off Pärnu mnt. Institutional, standard-issue rooms, but clean. The toilets smell a little; worth it for the central location. No English spoken. 90EEK per person. The hostel door is locked between 11pm and 6am, but ring the bell and the administrator will let you in.

FOOD

Small restaurants in the Old Town offer low prices and large portions. Tallinn has many well stocked **supermarkets,** where you can see expat Americans weep with joy at the chance to buy Hawaiian Punch and Pop Tarts. The largest is **Kaubahall,** Aia

7, near the Viru Gates (open Mon.-Sat. 9am-8:30pm, Sun. 9am-8pm). The smaller **Kauplus Tallinn,** Narva mnt. 2 (tel. 64 01 10), stays open later and has lower prices (open daily 9am-10pm). When starved and broke, go to Hotel Ookean's *baar*.

- **Paks Margareeta** (Fat Margaret's), Pikk 70 (tel. 641 14 13), in the gate-tower housing the Maritime museum. American-style grease and subs that make mouths water. Chili dog 18EEK, Atomic Fries 35EEK, small subs 22EEK, large subs 42EEK. Climb up to the observation deck for a great view. Open daily 11am-11pm.
- **Sanjay's,** Rataskaevu 5 (tel. 44 02 54), on the 2nd floor of a four-restaurant complex. Palate-pleasing Indian and Chinese food served amid wingback chairs and white tablecloths. The Chinese menu is slightly less expensive, with vegetable spring rolls (28EEK), chef's chow mein (57EEK), and loads of vegetarian options. If you're set on Indian food, try the delicious *samosas* (26EEK) and fresh handmade *naan* (14EEK). MC and Visa accepted. Open daily noon-11pm.
- **Teater Restoran,** Lai 31 (tel. 631 45 18). One of the best affordable restaurants in Tallinn. This basement restaurant is romantic and just plain cool, with jazzy blues in the background. Choose which medieval cave you want to dine in and enjoy large portions of spicy creole food with a medieval Estonian touch. Fish dishes (60EEK), Chicken New Orleans (53EEK). Throw in a tall glass of *Saku* (17EEK). Bread and small salad come with the meal. Open daily 9am-1am.
- **Rüütli Baar,** Kohtu 2, in a portico across from the Toomkirik. An oddly irreverent restaurant-bar with fake stained-glass windows and the steady drone of slot machines. Pan-fried trout with fries and veggies 40EEK. *Seljanka* 9EEK. *Saku* to wash it all down 15EEK. Open daily noon-8pm.
- **Eeslitall,** Dunkri 4 (tel. 31 37 55). The "Donkey Stable" is the best place in Tallinn for Balto-Russian cuisine; there's been a restaurant in these halls since the 1300s. Throngs with tourists in summer, so call ahead for dinner. Sup on meat and vegetarian dishes (20-50EEK) or tasty omelettes (9-20EEK) in a crazy post-modern interior: wooden planks in the ceiling are painted in floral patterns and futuristic landscapes. Open Sun.-Thurs. noon-midnight, Fri.-Sat. noon-1am.

SIGHTS

Vanalinn (The Old Town)

Get acquainted with the Old Town by starting at Hotel Viru, walking down Narva mnt., then continuing along Viru through the 15th-century **Viru City Gate.** Along Uus, which runs north just inside the walls, a large **sweater market** sets up in summer; in winter, it moves into the flower stalls that line Viru. Continue up Viru to **Raekoja plats,** where handicrafts are sold on summer evenings, and folk songs and dances are performed on a small outdoor stage. **Vana Toomas** (Old Thomas), a 16th-century cast-iron figurine of the Tallinn's legendary defender, guards the **raekoda,** built between 1371-1404. Thomas has done a good job so far; this is the oldest surviving town hall in Europe. Behind the *raekoda*, the medieval town jail, **Raemuuseum,** Raekoja 4/6 (tel. 44 99 03), now displays early Estonian photography and contemporary Estonian sculpture (open Tues. and Thurs. 11am-5:30pm and Wed. 2-5:30pm; 7EEK, students and seniors 3EEK). On the north side of the square, the claustrophobic Saia kang (Bread alley) twists onto Pühavaimu, where the 14th-century **Pühavaimu kirik** (Church of the Holy Ghost) sports a 15th-century bell-tower and an intricate 17th-century wooden clock (open Mon.-Sat. 10am-5pm).

For a view of the medieval city's north towers and bastion, go up Vene from Viru, take a right on Olevimägi, and head up Uus. Along the way, bore yourself silly with roomfuls of 19th-century knick-knacks at the **Tallinn City Museum,** Vene 17 (tel. 44 65 53; open Wed.-Fri. 10:30am-5:30pm, Sat.-Sun. 10:30am-4:30pm; 5EEK, students 2.50EEK). Founded by Dominicans in 1246, **Dominiiklaste Klooster,** Vene 16 (tel. 44 46 06), across the street and through a courtyard, contains a Gothic limestone courtyard, two Catholic churches, a windmill, stone carvings, and a granary. The monastery's Church of St. Peter and St. Paul and the Church of St. Catherine (open daily 10am-6pm; 5EEK) border the cloister. In the large squat tower known as **Paks Mar-**

gareeta (Fat Margaret), a **Meremuuseum** (Maritime Museum), Pikk 70 (tel. 60 18 03), houses changing exhibits on Tallinn's history as a busy port (open Wed.-Sun. 10am-6pm; 6EEK, students 2EEK, seniors 3EEK). Grab lunch at the sub shop inside.

Going back down Pikk, **Oleviste kirik** (St. Olav's Church), the tallest church in town, rises to the right. The murals inside the adjoining chapel illustrate the architect's death; he fell from the tower (open Sun. 9am-noon and 5-8pm, Mon. 5-9pm, Thurs. 5-8pm). Go to the end of Pikk and hang a left on Rataskaevu to see **Niguliste kirik** (St. Nicholas's Church, tel. 44 41 40), frequent site of organ concerts, and its mighty spire. Inside is a fragment of Bernt Notke's medieval masterpiece, **Danse Macabre** (open Wed. 2-9pm, Thurs.-Sun. 11am-6pm). At the base of the hill WWII ruins lie undisturbed as a reminder of Russian bombing that gutted much of south Tallinn in 1944. Farther south along Rüütli, the **Kiek in de Kök** (Peek in the Kitchen; 1475CE) tower, Komandandi 2 (tel. 44 66 86), offered voyeuristic views into any Tallinnite's home in the 16th century. Take a peek at the tower, still pockmarked with embedded cannonballs, and the museum which keeps six floors of art and historical exhibits (open Tues.-Fri. 10:30am-5:30pm, Sat.-Sun. 11am-4:30pm; 10EEK, students and seniors 5EEK). Straight ahead, **Neitsitorni** (Virgin Tower), Lühike jalg 9a (tel. 44 08 96), features *hõõgviin* (hot mulled wine; open daily 10am-11pm; off-season the balcony closes, but the tower is open 11am-10pm).

Toompea

Following Lühike jalg uphill onto Toompea from St. Nicholas's Church leads to Lossi plats, a square dominated by **Aleksandr Nevsky katedral**, begun under Tsar Alexander III and finished a few years before the Bolshevik Revolution. A marble marker from 1910 recalls Peter the Great's 1710 victory over Sweden. The exterior renovations are not complete, but the rich interior is worth a look (open daily 8am-7pm). The **Toompea Castle**, present seat of the Estonian *riigikogu* (parliament), lies here, but the door is barred to prying eyes. Directly behind, a fluttering Estonian flag tops **Pikk Hermann**, Tallinn's tallest tower. The **Eesti Kunstimuuseum** (Estonian Art Museum), Kiriku plats 1 (tel. 44 14 78), across from Toomkirik higher up on Toompea, displays Estonian art from the 19th century to the 1940s, including a compelling exhibition of Art Nouveau/avant-garde book printing from independent Estonia (open Wed.-Mon. 11am-6pm; 7EEK, students and seniors 3EEK). There are three excellent viewpoints from Toompea, all framed by artists selling watercolor versions of the views—the best is at Kohtu's north end, on Toompea's west side.

Rocca-al-mare

In **Rocca-al-mare**, a peninsula 12km west of Tallinn, the **Estonian Open-Air Museum**, Vabaõhumuuseumi 12 (tel. 656 02 30; fax 656 02 27), collects wooden mills and farmsteads from the 18th-20th centuries. Most of the hay-covered houses were transferred to the museum from various farms in Estonia in the 60s. Now, visitors crawl into log cabins, see crocheted and macramé decorations, climb rickety stairs, and hide in horse stables, while intricately dressed enactors pretend to be ancient. Weaving machines, wooden clocks, and sheep abound. There are 68 buildings on 84 hectares, including a well, a mill, and **Sutlepa kabel** (chapel), where a choir sings in Estonian and Swedish during holidays. Estonian folk dance troupes perform regularly (open May-Oct. daily 10am-8pm, some buildings close at 6pm; 10EEK, students 3EEK). Eat at **Kolu kõrts**, which in the old days served as an inn and bar. From Tallinn's train station, take bus #21 (½hr.) or a taxi (66EEK).

ENTERTAINMENT AND NIGHTLIFE

Estonian Kontserdisaal, Estonia pst. 4 (40EEK; ticket office tel. 44 31 98; fax 44 53 17; open daily 1-7pm), holds symphonies almost every night. **Pühavaimu kirik, Niguliste kirik,** and **Toomkirik** also hold concerts (listings are posted outside Raemuuseum). During the **Organ Festival** (July 2-August 6), St. Nicholas's, Nõmme-Rahu, and Dome churches host performances. Tickets are sold in St. Nicholas's starting July 1, daily 2-8pm and at the door one hour before the concert. **Eesti**

Draamateater, Pärnu mnt. 5 (tel. 44 33 78), boasts the biggest shows in town (ticket office open Aug.-June Tues.-Sun. 1-7pm). **Estonia Teater,** Estonia pst. 4 (tel. 44 90 40), gives various performances including opera, ballet, musicals, and chamber music (ticket office open Aug.-June daily noon-7pm). Tallinn is home to **Tallinna Linnateater,** Lai 23 (tel. 44 85 79), in a medieval merchant's mansion, popular with local teens (ticket office open Mon.-Fri. 10am-7pm, Sat.-Sun. noon-6pm). Check *Tallinn This Week* for performance wheres and whens (free copies at Estonian Holidays in Hotel Viru, Viru väljak).

While Minsk, Moscow, and Kiev suffer between grim, vodka-doused cellars and slick, mafia-run nightclubs, Tallinn boasts a hefty pint of excellent drinking establishments. In July, **Rock Summer** draws students and bands from around the world to Tallinn for a week-long music fest. In 1996, over 30 bands from Estonia, the Baltics, and the West performed; the 300EEK tickets allowed entry for three days of ZZ Top. For more info contact Makarov Music Management (tel. 23 84 03).

George Browne's Irish Pub, Harju 6 (tel. 631 05 16), 300m south of Raekoja plats on the north edge of Vabaduse väljak. The posh lounge upstairs is out of the budget traveler's range, but the ground-level pub has live music in the evenings, several dartboards, and good snack bars. Excellent fries cure the drinking munchies (20EEK). Open daily 10am-2am. Live music Fri.-Sat. after 9pm; cover 20-25EEK.

Von Krahli Teater/Baar, Rataskaevu 10, (tel. 631 39 27), on the west edge of the lower Old Town. The avant-garde theater showcases Baltic talent from Lithuanian jazz to experimental dance and cutting-edge blends of Gregorian chant and techno. Attached split-level bar with *Saku* (17EEK) and a dance floor wiggling like nothing you've ever seen. Open Mon.-Sat. 10am-8pm, Sun. 10am-6pm. The theater has shows most nights 7-9pm (tickets 35-40EEK).

Mündi Baar, Mündi 5 (tel. 631 36 13) just off Raekoja plats. A dark network of cellar rooms favored by locals. Have a *Saku* (20EEK), and grab a corner table while your eyes adjust. Then stare at the boar skins on the wall. Open 24hr.

Hell Hunt (The Gentle Wolf), Pikk 39 (tel. 60 25 61). A rocking Irish pub with *Guinness* and *Killian's* on tap. The back room serves up a mean cottage pie (45EEK); wash it down with Irish Coffee (35EEK). In summer, an outdoor beer garden dispenses suds across the street as long as it's light. Open Sun.-Mon. 10am-1am, Tues.-Thurs. 10am-2am, Fri.-Sat. 10am-3am. Live music most nights, including "local" Irish bands. Nary a cover, which is why everyone is here.

Eeslitall Baar, Dunkri 4 (tel. 631 37 55), in the cavernous cellar of the restaurant. Sailors, tourists, and intellectuals wander through a labyrinth of colored lights, archways, nooks, and crannies to imbibe and dance the night away. *Saku Tume* on draft 17EEK. Imported beers 30-35EEK. Open daily 8pm-5am. Live music Fri.-Sat. after 10pm. Cover for men only Fri.-Sat. 25-30EEK, Sun.-Thurs. 20EEK.

Nimeta Baar (The Pub with No Name), Suur-Karja 4 (tel. 44 66 66), across from The Barn. Popular with ex-pats who love to buy a round of drinks for the house, which makes it popular with locals, too. The Irish bartender adds an authentic touch. The painting on the wall, entitled "Very Very Old Tallinn" is by a famous Estonian artist whose political message slips right by this rocking group's heads. Open 11am-whenever, but the place starts jumping at around 10pm.

■ Near Tallinn: Lahemaa National Park

Founded in 1971 as the Soviet Union's first, Lahemaa Rahvuspark is still Estonia's only national park. Nature trails lead over rolling hills from jagged coasts to forest bogs, while gargantuan boulders brought by long-melted glaciers punctuate the flat land. The park preserves more than just an ecological zone, it protects a way of life. The Soviet authorities that planned the park intended to protect the region's rural heritage. Rolling hills now hide villages, farmhouses, and crumbling castle walls.

Orientation and Practical Information Small villages pepper the plains. Some are connected by bus, others require a bike or walk to reach. Luckily most lie within two hours walking distance of each other. Buses from Tallinn travel to **Viitna** (12 per day, 1hr., 22EEK). There, check the schedule of buses to **Palmse mõis** (Palmse plantation). Transport rarely runs from Viitna to **Käsmu**, so hitching, biking, and hiking are the only ways to get there if you don't want to wait a few days for a bus. At Viitna, walk a bit past the bus stop, and take the first right under the wooden arch. In the trees, the **camping office** can set you up in the woods and give you info about the area. **Rent a bike** here for 15EEK per hour, but check the tires first. In Palmse plantation, the English-speaking **Palmse information center** has more info on Lahemaa Rahvuspark (Lahemaa National Park) than the one in Viitna (tel. (32) 341 96; fax 456 59; open Apr.-Aug. daily 9am-7pm, Sept. 9am-6pm, Oct.-March 9am-2pm).

Accommodations and Food The **camping office** in Viitna rents singles (100EEK) and doubles (150EEK) in log cabins with clean new hall toilets and showers. The **Park Hotell Restaurant** (tel. (237) 34 167), on the manor grounds, prepares fresh salads (15EEK), *soljanka* (18EEK), and Chicken Kiev (45EEK), and serves *Saku* (15EEK; open daily noon-10pm). For the best lodging, head for Käsmu. The sea-side **Merekalda Pansion,** Neema tee 2 (tel. (232) 99 451), offers rooms for 220EEK per person and a beautiful sauna at 150EEK per hour. The hostess also has three beds in a large room above the garage which she keeps for poor students. Use the shower and toilet in the main house and pay 150EEK, including breakfast. Rent a water bike (30EEK per hour), a yacht (150EEK per hour), or a **bike** (50EEK per hour) here. Make reservations a week early. Cheaper lodgings in Käsmu await at the end of Neema tee, the town's only paved road, at **Lainela Puhkebaas** (tel. (232) 991 33). Once a Soviet Pioneer camp, the hotel/campground offers singles for 90EEK without a shower, 110EEK with a shower and use of a kitchen. The **restaurant,** behind the hotel, serves chicken and rice (25EEK; open daily 1pm-5pm, baar open noon-midnight).

Park and Sights If the brown bear, lynx, storks, or swans you came to see don't show up, try a bit of history at **Palmse mõis**—a plantation turned **museum** (tel. 341 91; fax 324 45 75; e-mail teet@lklm.envir.ee). Between the years 1674 and 1923 (when the new regime reclaimed all private land), members of the German von der Pahlen family would while away the days among the manor's charming gazebos and swan ponds. Inside the restored main house, salvaged furniture and belongings re-create the landowners' lives. The chandeliers, particularly the 18th-century porcelain one on the second floor, win the "best-old-thing" award (open April-Aug. Wed.-Mon. 10am-6pm; 20EEK, students 10EEK; tickets sold inside the manor house).

In **Käsmu,** a well kept, brightly colored sea town, the **Käsmu Sea Museum,** Mere kooli 2 (tel. (232) 991 36), shelters a private collection of old ships built in Käsmu (open 24hr., donations requested). At the end of Neemetee and through the dirt path in the woods, the **stone hill** sometimes grants wishes to those who give the mound a good stone. **Boulder**-watchers will love Käsma. Brought from Finland by glaciers during the last Ice Age, some reach 25 feet above the sand. If the rockier beaches of Käsmu don't appeal to you, head east around the bay 7km to **Võsu** which has one of the most popular sandy **beaches** in Estonia. After drying off, travel further east 10km to **Altja,** an old fishing village turned Soviet military border look-out. The small island out at sea still holds a Russian border patrol station. The 100-150 year-old fishing huts in the town are part of a **museum** (open 24hr.).

Sagadi lies 5km south of Altja. The first white building on the left through the gates, the **Museum of Forestry** features exhibits on the park's plant and tree life, their historical uses, and the frightening effects that humans have had on the ecosystem (open Tues.-Fri. 11am-4pm, Sat.-Sun. 11am-6pm; 10EEK; students 3EEK). The restored **Sagachi mõis** (manor) holds, in addition to original artifacts from the household, a collection of Estonian folk costumes. Climb the spiral staircases to the attic, one half of which displays the manor's old furniture. The other part of the attic offers a look at the fauna the master of the house came back with after his hunts (open Tues.-Fri. 11am-4pm, Sat.-Sun. 11am-6pm; 10EEK, students 3EEK).

■ Tartu

First mentioned in the annals of history in 1030 after a Kievan prince ordered it burned to the ground, Tartu is the oldest city in the Baltics. You won't find many monuments to prove its age. Since that inauspicious date, 55 separate fires have turned Tartu to ashes, and destroyed any remnants of its medieval past. Instead, a youthful breeze blows through city as its tree-lined boulevards and colorful green parks buzz with the energy of 10,000 collegians.

ORIENTATION AND PRACTICAL INFORMATION

Tartu is a sprawling city, the second-largest in Estonia. Luckily, everything the traveler needs is located within a one km sq. bordered by the bus and train stations. **Vabaduse pst.** runs from the bus station along the **Emajôgi River** toward the northeast. **Raekoja plats,** the city's geographical, spiritual, and social center, runs west from the **Emajôgi** River toward the old castle hills. **Rüütli** heads north from the square; its end at Lai marks the boundary of the Old Town. Behind the town hall, **Lossi** meanders uphill between the two peaks of **Toomemägi** (Cathedral Hill). After passing under two bridges between the hills, Lossi dumps out into **Vallikraavi,** a crooked, cobblestone road that, together with von Baeri, follows the path of the old moat circling the hills. The stretch of Vallikraavi that goes south meets up with **Kuperjanovi,** which in turn continues southwest to the train station.

- **Tourist Office: Tartu Infobüroo Turistinfo,** 14 Raekoja plats. Provides info and organizes travel and transportation. Maps 22.20EEK. Open Mon.-Fri. 10am-6pm, Sat. 10am-3pm. Travel agency open Mon. 10am-6pm, Tues.-Fri. 10am-5pm.
- **Currency Exchange:** At the train station (tel. 39 22 87). Open daily 8am-10pm. **Pôhja-Eesti Pank,** Munga 18 (tel. 43 38 22). Cashes traveler's checks and gives credit card advances. Open Mon.-Fri. 9am-6pm, Sat. 9am-3pm. **ATMs** at **Rahvapank,** Raekoja plats 14, accept MC and Visa. Open Mon.-Fri. 9am-5pm.
- **American Express Travel Service:** Kompanii 2. Open Mon.-Fri. 9am-5pm.
- **Trains:** Vaksali, at intersection of Kuperjanovi, 1.5km from city center. Info booth open daily 7am-noon and 1-7pm. To: Moscow (1 per day, 18hr., 327.30EEK); Rīga (2 per day, 5hr., 226.50EEK); Tallinn (6 per day, 3hr., 61.90EEK).
- **Buses:** Vabaduse pst. (tel. 47 53 55), on the corner of Riia, 300m southeast of Raekoja plats along Vabaduse. The information booth is open daily 8am-1pm and 1:30-8pm. Virtually no buses to destinations outside of Estonia. To: Narva (4 per day, 3-4hr., 64EEK); Pärnu (9 per day, 4hr., 68EEK); Tallinn (34 per day, 2-5hr.—try to get the morning express bus, 61.90EEK); Valga (2 per day, 2hr., 30-40EEK).
- **Public Transportation:** Bus #5 and 6 go from the train station around to Raekoja plats, the central square, and the bus station. Bus #4 travels down Võru.
- **Taxis:** Outside the bus and train stations (4EEK per 1km within the city, 5EEK outside). A cross-town ride from the bus to the train stations runs 15EEK.
- **Luggage Storage:** Buy tokens inside a room marked *"Vaksali Korraldaja"* in main lobby (6EEK—one 3EEK token to open it and one to retrieve your stuff). 24hr.
- **Pharmacy: Raekoja Apteek** (tel. 33 528) on the north side of the town hall. Open Mon.-Fri. 8am-8pm, Sat. 9am-4pm.
- **Electronic Mail: Arvutuskeskus** (University Computing Center), Liivi 2, south of where Lossi meets Vallikraavi on the west side of Toomemägi. Hours vary with staff availability. Ask a student or staff member to use a computer for free. They prefer users to have some form of student ID.
- **Post Office:** Corner of Ulikooli and Vanemuise. Telephones, faxes, express mail. Open Mon.-Fri. 9am-7pm, Sat. 9am-3pm, Sun. 10am-3pm. **Postal code:** EE-2400.
- **Telephones:** Lai 29 (tel. 43 16 61; fax 43 39 93), at the corner of Rüütli north of the post office. Card-phones and **fax** machine. Open 24hr. Almost all the street phones take digital **calling cards** which can be purchased at the telephone office, main post office, or any kiosk for units of 30EEK or 50EEK. **Phone code:** 07.

ACCOMMODATIONS

Tartu's few budget options consist of standard Soviet hotel fare. The tourist office can help find cheap accommodations if those below are full.

- **Tartu Võõrastemaja (Hotel Tartu),** Soola 3 (tel. 43 20 91), behind the bus station. Hotel and hostel. Soviet-stamped rooms with communal showers. Sauna (100EEK per hour). Filling breakfast included. Private toilet with hot water. Negotiable prices for groups. AmEx and Visa accepted (singles 350EEK, doubles 550EEK).
- **Hotel Salimo,** Kopli 1 (tel. 47 08 88), 3km southeast of the train station off Võru. Take bus #4 to "Karete". Backtrack and take the first left (Sepa), then the second left (Võru). Kopli is the first right. The office is on the second floor. Generic rooms with bare-bones furnishings and no-nonsense dingy white paint. Doubles with private toilet and shower 150EEK. Triples 150EEK.
- **Hotel Rändur,** Vasara 25 (tel. 47 56 91). Take bus #4 or 9 on weekdays down Võru and onto Jalaka. Get off at the 2nd stop on Jalaka, walk down and make the first left, then a right on the path past the post office and pharmacy. The hotel is on the 5th floor. Mustard-colored paint and wallpaper and hospital-green floors make it the kind of place you want to just sleep in. Communal shower, but private toilet and sink, and a sauna downstairs. Singles 120EEK. Doubles 150EEK.

FOOD AND ENTERTAINMENT

It's strange that in a university town there aren't more cheap, downscale restaurants. The **supermarket Kaubahal** sells staples at the corner of Küüni and Riia (open Mon.-Fri. 9am-10pm, Sat.-Sun. 9am-8pm). See the **bulletin boards** just inside the entrance to the main university building (Ülikooli 20) for fliers on all the local events. Summer brings lots of folk music to Tartu, so be on the lookout for posters.

- **Taverna,** Raekoja plats 20 (tel. 43 12 22), in the cellar of a statue-cluttered Baroque building. An upscale Italian restaurant, it also offers outstanding Estonian dishes. *Antrekoot Grillastmega* (grilled steak; 74EEK). *Milaano aedviljasupp* (minestrone; 20EEK). And, for veggies, *Toma Tikastmega* (spaghetti with tomato sauce; 24EEK). Management can be picky about dress; don't wear shorts. Open daily noon-6pm and 6:30pm-midnight.
- **Püssirohukelder,** Lossi 28 (tel. 43 42 31; fax 43 41 29). This cavernous 18th-century gunpowder cellar in the side of Toomemägi now houses a two-level cellar bar and the jolliest restaurant in town. Clientele is evolving into the Mercedes-and-Rolex crowd; you may feel out of place in a t-shirt, but they'll let you in. Salads 15EEK; smoked eel 35EEK; veggie dishes 25EEK; and beer 20EEK. Make reservations. Open Mon. and Wed. noon-2am, Tues., Thurs., Fri., and Sun. noon-1am, Sat. noon-3am. Cover 10EEK after 8pm. If there is a show, cover is 20EEK. The variety/erotic show goes up every Wed., Fri., and Sat. at 10:15pm.
- **Pinguin,** Vabaduse pst. 2a (tel. 43 46 01), at the base of Raekoja plats. Ice cream 4EEK, pastries for 2-3EEK, schnitzel with fries 11EEK, pizza 11EEK, and sandwiches for 3.50EEK. Open Mon.-Fri 7:30am-10pm, Sat.-Sun. 10am-10pm.
- **Bistro,** just off Raekoja plats on Rüütli. Estonian fast food. Popular spot for an inexpensive meal. A salad, main dish, drink, and dessert runs about 25-30EEK. Open daily 9am-11pm.

SIGHTS

Strolling through the Old Town, stopping occasionally for a glass of *Saku* is one of the best ways to experience the charm of Tartu and see all the sights—in double. **Raekoja plats** (Town Hall Square), the center of Tartu, dates from 1775, when the medieval market which previously stood on the site burned down in a gigantic fire—the most recent of the conflagrations that razed Tartu. The **raekoda,** a late 18th-century edifice now painted pink and white, dominates the square. Most buildings rest on wooden pylons, and some are slowly sinking into the marshy ground. Raekoja plats 18, once the house of **Barclay de Tolly** (a Scottish mercenary who became famous in the war against Napoleon) slumps with the sulkiest of them.

Ülikooli runs behind the town hall. To the north, it passes **Tartu Ülikool** (Tartu University), founded in 1632 by King Gustavus II Adolphus of Sweden. The Great Northern War closed the school's doors in 1700, but when the dust settled 100 years later, Tsar Alexander I reopened it, and built the magnificent yellow-collonaded building at Ülikooli 20 to house it. The **Museum of Classical Art,** a small collection of Roman and Greek art, awaits inside (tel. 43 53 84; open Mon.-Fri. 11am-4:30pm; 6EEK, students 2EEK). The attic keeps a collection of students' detention-time doodles (4EEK, students 2EEK). The only Russian university with the right to have fraternities, Tartu U used its privilege well. The **Estonian National Awakening** began here, with the founding of **Eesti Üliõpilaste Selts** (Estonian Student Association) in 1870. The nationalists who made up the fraternity became so central to Estonia's struggle for independence that, when the country won its freedom in 1919, the frat's colors (blue, black, and white) became those of the national flag.

Farther up Ülikooli **Jaani-kirik** (St. John's Church), Lutsu 16-24 (tel./fax 43 38 60), completed in 1323, was unique in Gothic architecture with its thousands of terracotta saints, martyrs, and other figures. Unfortunately, the Russian recapture of Tartu in 1944 nearly destroyed the church, and only a few hundred figures remain in the scarcely standing edifice. Restoration was begun in the 1980s, but is still not completed. Across the street, the **Museum of the 19th-Century Tartu Citizen,** Jaani 16, displays town life during guess-which-era (open summer Wed.-Sun. 11am-6pm, winter Wed.-Sun. 10am-3pm; 4EEK, students, children, and seniors 2EEK).

If by this point, the beer hasn't taken effect, climb up the road or stairs to **Toomemägi** (Cathedral Hill), which dominates Tartu from behind the *raekoda*. On the west hump, the majestic 15th-century **Toomkirik** (Cathedral of St. Peter and Paul) remembers its stints as a granary (1600s) and university library (1800s). Today, it serves as the **Tartu University Museum** (tel. 43 53 35), an in-depth series of displays with descriptions in Russian, Estonian, and German (open Wed.-Sun. 11am-5pm; 5EEK, students and seniors 2EEK, cameras 5EEK). An English guide is available (70EEK, students 30EEK; after 5pm and Sat.-Sun. guides are 100EEK). Near the church, **Musumägi** (Kissing Hill), once part of a prison tower, is now a make-out spot and the site of an ancient pagan **sacrificial stone.** These days, students burn their notes here after exams. A **statue of Karl Ernst von Baer** (the famous embryologist who adorns the 2EEK note) tops this hill.

Two bridges lead to the east hump of Toomemägi—the pink wooden **Inglisild** (Angel's Bridge) built in the 1830s and the concrete **Kuradisild** (Devil's Bridge) from 1913. An annual competition between the university **choirs** takes place on these bridges: men on the Devil's Bridge, women on the Angel's Bridge. On this part of Cathedral Hill the 19th-century **Observatory** (tel. 43 49 32) houses what was once the largest telescope lens in the world. The observatory now houses a museum and the university's laboratory (museum open Mon.-Fri. 11am-4pm; 3EEK, students 2EEK). Down the hills, the **Estonian National Museum,** J. Kuperjanov 9 (tel. 43 03 87), gathers scads of ethnographic material and discusses the National Awakening begun in Tartu (open Wed.-Sun. 11am-6pm; 5EEK, students 2EEK).

■ Viljandi

At first glance, the town of Viljandi, located about 80 miles west of Tartu, appears as dead as the knights who founded the castle here in the 13th century, but its decorated wooden houses, surrounding forest, Lake Viljandi järv, and castle ruins make Viljandi a worthwhile daytrip. On Tasuja pst., a moat and suspended wooden bridge protect the medieval **St. John Church of Viljandi.** In 1466, Franciscan monks built a monastery onto the church, and although it was destroyed in the 1560s during the Livonian war, the monastery's ruins are still visible in the church's basement. Further down the road, a dirt path leads left to the **Viljandi Castle,** founded by the Knights of the Sword in the 13th century. Centerpiece of the town's history, the castle also affords the best view of the lake and surrounding forests. Children run through coves and climb walls as if the ruins were a jungle gym, so wear shoes suitable for playing. Cross the red and white **suspension footbridge,** built in 1931, and walk through the woods back into town. The **town hall** peers past the statue of Estonian artist **Johann Köler** to **Laidoneri plats,** the former market place. **Viljandi Museum,** Laidoneri plats 5, was closed in the summer of 1996. If the weather permits, a hut at the nearby **beach,** rents paddle boats. Or swim—the lake's clean.

Viljandi, easily accessible by bus from Tartu, is halfway between Tartu and Pärnu on the west side of Lake Võrtsjärv. Viljandi's main street, **Tallinna,** runs from beyond the bus station to the castle ruins. **Tartu** leads east off Tallinna towards the town square, called **Keskväljak.** At the bottom of Tallinna, **Vaksali** runs west toward the train station. **Buses** to Viljandi leave frequently from Tartu (9 per day, 1½hr., 23EEK). **Exchange money** at the **Tallinna Pank** in the Keskväljak (open Mon.-Fri. 9am-4pm, Sat. 9am-3pm). Both the **post** and **telephone office** are at Tallinna 11. (Open Mon.-Sat. 8am-6:30pm; 24hr. phones) **Postal code:** EE2900. **Phone code:** 43.

The **Motell Viljandi,** Tartu 11 (tel. 338 52), is centrally located on Keskväljak, with light, airy rooms and private bathrooms (including little packets of soap and shampoo). Singles cost 150EEK and doubles, 200EEK. For a sit-down meal with cloth napkins and friendly service, try **Restoran Iva,** Tasuja 3 (tel. 344 93), where Tallinna meets Tasuja at Vabaduseplats, just before the castle. Salads run 5-10EEK, crepes with various fillings 8EEK, and chicken Kiev (a popular choice) 45EEK (open daily 8am-9pm). The popular **Café Jsutuba,** Tartu 8A, just off Keskväljak, offers the basics. Sausage with fries costs 13.50EEK, and schnitzel with fries 16.60EEK (open Mon.-Fri. 7am-6pm, Sat.-Sun. 8am-3pm). **Hundinui,** on the far corner of Tallinna and Tartu, is a modern café selling hot dogs (9.40EEK), hamburgers (15EEK), various homemade pastries (3EEK), and *Saku* (10EEK; open daily 7am-10pm). The **grocery store** is on Keskväljak (open Mon.-Fri. 9am-8pm, Sat.-Sun. 9am-5pm).

▎Pärnu

Sun, seawater, sand…and mud. This resort has taken its natural bounty and translated it into free-market profit. Trendy stores and restaurants line Pärnu's main street, but interfere little with the overall charm of its parks and grand old summer residences. Best of all, the mud baths, built in the 19th century and famed throughout the Russian Empire, continue to cure weary traveler's ills.

Orientation and Practical Information Grab Pärnu maps and information at the **tourist office,** Mungu 2 (tel. 406 39; fax 456 33; open Mon.-Fri. 9am-6pm, Sat. 9am-4pm, Sun. 10am-3pm). You can **exchange money** at Hotel Pärnu (open 24hr.), but the rates are better at the post office. Exchange traveler's checks and obtain cash advances at **Eesti Ühis Pank,** across from the bus station (open Mon.-Fri. 9am-6pm, Sat. 9am-2pm). The **train station** (tel. 407 33) sits east of the city center, by the corner of Riia mtn. and Raja (take bus #40 from the central post office to "Raeküla Rdtj."). Trains choo-choo north to Tallinn (4 per day, 3½hr., 25EEK). But Pärnu is best reached by **bus;** the station, Ringi 3 (tel. 415 54), lies in the town center, a block down from the bus parking lot on the right. Buses go to Haapsalu (2-3 per day, 3hr., 42EEK), Kuressaare (2 per day, 3hr., 70EEK), Riga (5 per day, 4hr., 57EEK), Tallinn (40 per day, 2-3 hr., 46EEK), and Tartu (8 per day, 5hr., 68EEK). For a **taxi,** call 412 40. To **store luggage** in the bus station, go through the door opposite the ticket office inscribed "*Pakihoid*" (large bags 5EEK). The **post** and **telephone office,** Akadeemia 7, is at the west end of Rüütli, less than 1km from the bus station. Enter the telephone office around the corner to the right on Rüütli (post office tel. 403 81, open Mon.-Fri. 8am-6pm and Sat.-Sun. 9am-3pm; telephone office tel. 409 69, open daily 7am-10pm). **Postal code:** EE-3600. **Phone code:** 244.

Accommodations Hotell Pärnu, Rüütli 44 (tel. 789 11; fax 359 05), by the bus station, offers centrally located rooms with TV, private bath, and telephone. Most have balconies facing the town center (singles 490EEK, doubles 650EEK). The small, plain **Hotell Seedri,** Seedri 4 (tel. 433 50), near the beach, could smell better. It offers only hall showers and toilets, but has a fridge and sink in every room (singles 100EEK, doubles 220EEK, triples 290EEK, quads 345EEK; reservations recommended). **Hotell Kajakas,** Seedri 2 (tel. 430 98), provides a sauna (240EEK per hour for two), and has much cleaner, newer toilets and showers (singles 120EEK, with toilet and sink 180EEK; doubles 160EEK, with toilet and sink 300EEK). **Hotel Vesiroos,** Esplanaadi 42a (tel. 435 34), located between the town center and the beach, provides private telephone, television, and shower in each room, as well as free use of the hotel swimming pool (one person in a double 220EEK, double 400EEK, triple 575EE, sauna 80EEK per hour). Though not situated in the most attractive area, the **Hotell Yacht Club,** Lootsi 6 (tel. 314 20), boasts modern furnishings and bathrooms in every room. Some rooms have views of the port. English spoken (singles 200EEK, doubles 320EEK, sauna 100EEK per hour).

Food **Trahter Postipoiss,** Vee 12 (tel. 402 04), runs a courtyard café and restaurant in a former 19th-century post office. Dine on excellent roast chicken (15EEK per 100g), Estonian chicken salad (a tasty mix of chicken, pickles, pasta, cucumbers, and tomatoes; 20EEK), and cheese schnitzel (39EEK). All main dishes served with generous helpings of vegetables and fried potatoes (open daily 11am-midnight). **Restoran Jahtklubi Körts,** Lootsi 6, under the hotel, serves up large portions in a ship-like atmosphere *sans* sea-sickness. Chicken schnitzel with fries costs 48EEK, ham and cheese omelette 16EEK, steak and fries 55EEK (open 11am-midnight). One of the most popular spots in town for an inexpensive meal or quick snack is **Georg,** on the corner of Rüütli and Hammiku, a buffet-style restaurant offering *plov* (chicken and rice; 16.50EEK), salads (5.50EEK), and sausage or schnitzel with fries (21EEK; open Mon.-Fri. 7:30am-7:30pm, Sat.-Sun. 9am-7:30pm). A **turg** (market) is at the intersection of Sepa and Karja (open Tues.-Sun. 7am-1pm).

Sights and Entertainment With beaches and mud baths, Pärna has little need for man-made distractions. Nonetheless, two museums show their stuff. Facing Hotell Pärnu at Rüütli 53, the **Museum of the City of Pärnu** (tel. 434 64), displays traditional clothing and archaeological finds from the region (open Wed.-Sun. 11am-6pm; 4EEK, students 3EEK). The **Lydia Koidula Museum,** Jannseni 37 (tel. 416 63), across the Pärnu river, commemorates the 19th-century poet who led a revival in Estonian-language verse and drama (open Wed.-Sun. 10am-4pm; 3EEK, students 1EEK). South on Nikolai from Rüütli stands the rust-red **Eliisabeti kirik,** built in 1747. Farther west, at the corner of Uus and Vee a block north of Rüütli, the Russian Orthodox **Ekatariina kirik** is a multi-spired, silver-and-white edifice from the 1760s. Rüütli ends at an **open-air theater** dominated by a Swedish fortress from the late 1600s. The

---

The Dirtiest Bath This Side of the Baltics

Mud has never looked or felt better than at the **Mud Bath Establishment,** Rannapuiestee 1 (tel. 424 61 or 412 95), in Pärnu. Since 1838, when the mud baths and health resort were founded in Pärnu, the privilege of rolling around in gooey mud has not been limited to pigs and small children. In fact, workers at mud baths and many other health professionals insist that the sea mud in Pärnu has a curative effect on disorders of the bones, joints, and peripheral nervous system. There's even a special ward for patients with myocardial infarction and cardiovascular diseases. After a brief consultation, patients can choose between General Mud, Local Mud, and Electric Mud. And, for those tough-to-reach areas, there's the ever-so-popular mud tampon. No day at the mud bath is complete without a massage, a "curative" bath or shower, and a cup of restorative herb tea—no mud added. (Mud treatment, massage, and shower costs around US$7, but can vary with procedure length; open Mon.-Sat. 9am-6pm).

formidable **Tallinna värav** (Tallinn Gate), the only gate that led into the city under the Swedes, breaches the ramparts at their widest point. **Tallinna Baar**, a small, dark, stone tavern, sits atop the gate (open daily noon-11pm). The **Rannasalong**, Mere pst. 22 (tel. 432 78), is a 1930s-era dancehall that now hops to 90's grinds. The hall features different musical acts almost every night and pours *Saku* for 15EEK. The **movies** next door, usually shown in English with Estonian and Russian subtitles, cost 20EEK. Buy tickets inside. The Irish-Estonian **Rüütli Pub** on the corner of Rüütli and Ringi taps *Guinness* and *Kilkenny* for 11EEK in a cool, dark setting (open Mon.-Thurs. noon-midnight, Fri. noon-2am, Sat. 10am-2am, Sun. noon-midnight).

The broad, tree-lined street stretching south from the Tallinn Gate leads to a long pedestrian zone just behind the white-sand **beach**. There's a whirly slide open daily 11am-6pm in summer (5EEK a swoosh); be careful at the bottom—the pool is only one meter deep. A small **amusement park**, Jalaka 5 (tel. 421 01), including a ferris wheel (3EEK), lies just off the boardwalk (in summer open daily 11am-7pm). The beaches and water are clean, if not a bit cold before July. **Nude bathers** wander up the beach to the right, well past Rannasalong. The famous **mud baths**, Ranna pst., that started Pärnu on the path to greatness still function in the Neo-Classical bathhouse at the south end of Supeluse pst., where the pedestrian boardwalk ends. Pamper yourself with **massage**, sauna, mud baths (90EEK), and therapeutic silt water (tel. 432 47; open Mon.-Fri. 9am-2pm, Sat. 9am-1pm).

To play **tennis**, go to Ratta Sport, Ringi 14a (Mon.-Fri. 5pm-10pm; 80EEK per hour, Sat.-Sun. 60EEK; racket and balls each 25EEK; open daily 8am-10pm). **Diskoklubi "Hamilton,"** Rüütli 1, near the post office in the outdoor theater, hosts disk-spinners nightly from all over Estonia (open Fri.-Sat. after 9pm; cover 45EEK). Around **Jaanipäev** (Midsummer Night), Pärnu hosts the July 8-9 **FiESTa International Jazz Festival**, along with the **Baltoscandal**, a modernist extravaganza of Baltic and Scandinavian theater. An **outdoor café/beer garden**, Lootsi 6 (tel. 419 48), bustles next to the yacht club (open daily 11am-late). The bar **Väike Klaus**, Supeluse 3 (tel. 421 30), meaning "little saint," avoids the hammering techno heard on Estonian radio, opting for Western tunes. Foreigners and locals down glasses of *Saku* (15EEK), while filling up on the *fabulous* fries (5EEK; open daily 11am-midnight).

■ Haapsalu

Famed in the 19th century for its curative muds, Haapsalu was once the seat of the Saare-Lääne (or Ösel-Wiek) Bishopric, which encompassed much of West Estonia. Under the East Bloc, an airbase was the city's main distinction, but today the town is hardly recognizable as a Soviet stronghold. The old city center, built around the bishop's castle, defies its age with trendy bars and restaurants, while small decorated houses and yards in the outskirts maintain old-fashioned goodness.

Orientation and Practical Information Get the lowdown on Haapsalu maps, ferry reservations, or plane tickets at the **tourist office**, Läänemaa Reisid/Westland Travel, Karja 7 (tel. 450 37; fax 443 35; open Mon.-Fri. 10am-5pm). The info booth, Posti 39 (tel. 452 48; fax 451 01), hands out leaflets and sells maps. The free broadside *Two Weeks in Haapsalu*, usually available at Haapsalu Hotell, has got the goods on events in town. **Exchange money** at **EÜP**, Korja 27 (tel. 447 65), but make sure the bills are crisp (open Mon.-Fri. 9am-4pm, Sat. 10am-3pm). Hotels in Haapsalu change money 24 hours a day, but at a much lower rate. **Trains**, Raudtee 2 (tel. 576 64), are a rarity now in Haapsalu, though Tsar Nicholas II came here so often he had a massive covered platform built to make sure none of his party would get wet while disembarking. The station still stands, apparently left to rot, on Raudtee at the south end of town. The ticket office is open daily 5-6am, 9-10am, and 4-6pm; trains creep to Tallinn (3 per day, 3hr., 35EEK). From the (functioning) station, walk east on Jaama past the market, then turn left on Posti at the traffic lights to reach central Haapsalu. **Buses** (tel. 577 91) run from the rail station to Kärdla (4 per day, 3hr., 29EEK), Pärnu (8 per day, 2-3hr., 42EEK), Tallinn (6-8 per day, 2hr., 26-33EEK), and Virtsu (8 per day, 2hr., 20EEK). The bus ticket office is open daily 5-9am, 10-11:30am, noon-1:40pm, 2:10-5pm, and 5:30-7pm. The nearby town of **Rohuküla,** 9km west of Haapsalu, sends **ferries** (tel. 911 38) to Heltermaa (port tel. 942 12) on Hiiumaa (9 per day, 1½hr., 15EEK). Bus #1 runs to Rohuküla from stop #1 at the station in Haapsalu (roughly every hour, 25min., 3EEK). Keep in mind that it's significantly cheaper to take a bus from Haapsalu to Kärdla (Hiiumaa) or Sviby (Vormsi) than it is to ride the ferry and grab a bus once you arrive on the islands. For a **taxi,** call 453 30. Taxis cost 4EEK per 1km. The **post office** (*postkontor,* tel. 445 55) is at Posti 1 (open Mon.-Fri. 7:30am-6pm, Sat. 8am-4pm). The **telephone office,** Kalda 2 (tel. 552 57), near the post office, dot-dash-dots to all corners of the world (open daily 7am-10pm). **Postal code:** EE-3170. **Phone code:** 247.

Accommodations and Food Yacht season fills every cranny in town. One of the few budget options, the **Hotell Laine** (Hotel Wave), Sadama 9/11 (tel. 441 91), welcomes visitors on the shores of Väike-viik. It was the Sanatorium Laine in a previous life. No TV, but you can get a massage (70EEK per 25min., 130EEK per 45min.) or a pedicure. 250EEK singles and 380EEK doubles come with a bath, balcony, and breakfast in the airy restaurant. Follow Posti north until it ends near the castle, go two blocks west on Ehte, then two blocks north on Sadama; the entrance is at the rear of the building. Make reservations six months ahead for August and September. Ask for a room with a view towards the swan-filled sea. Otherwise, try **Haapsalu Hotell,** Posti 43 (tel. 448 47; fax 451 91), a renovated place that reeks of foreign money and, accordingly, accepts Visa. Even the doors open automatically. The meticulously kept rooms include new Scandinavian furniture, cable TV, and mini-bars with prices that'll make your eyes pop (singles 500EEK, off-season 420EEK; doubles 700EEK, off-season 600EEK; breakfast included; MC and Visa accepted).

Sit down to dinner in **Rootsituru Kohvik,** Karja 3 (tel. 450 58), a pink building on the corner of Ehte in the castle's shadow. The Estonian chef proves that a standard menu of borscht, schnitzel, and potatoes need not entail lukewarm, tasteless lumps. In fact, it's darn good—especially the mashed potatoes. Try the succulent salmon dish *kala taignas* (42EEK; open daily 11am-10pm). The new **Restoran Central,** Karja 21 (tel. 446 73), is bathed in shades of green. The town's older crowd loves the juicy *puljong pirukaga* (meat pancakes served with broth, 9EEK). Main dishes run 45EEK (open Mon.-Fri. noon-midnight, Sat.-Sun. noon-2am). The **turg,** or market, is one block from the train station on the corner of Jürlöö and Jaama (open April-Oct. 7am-3pm, Oct.-March 9am-2pm).

Sights and Entertainment The center of Haapsalu, the 1228 **Piiskopilinnus** (Bishop's Castle), offers its watchtower to adventure-starved mountain-climbers (open Tues.-Sun. 10am-6pm; 10EEK). Enter it from Lossiplats, the square just east of the north end of Karja. Home to the Bishop of Saare-Lääne until he moved to Saaremaa in 1358, the castle is now mostly a set of picturesque ruins surrounding the **cathedral.** The temple, which hosts occasional concerts, was thrice destroyed and abandoned, most recently by a storm in 1726, after which it was left unrepaired until 1887 (open Mon.-Fri. 11am-4pm, Sat. 9am-3pm; donations of 3EEK requested during concerts). On the night of the August full moon, Haapsalu's **White Lady,** the ghost of a woman walled up in the cathedral for crossing its threshold in the 1280s (a time when only men were allowed inside), makes an apparitional appearance in one of the cathedral windows. The event is celebrated by a week-long **festival.** The blustery **Aafrikarand** (Africa Beach) promenade, northeast of the castle at the end of Rüütli, runs 2km up to the yacht club—a great walk on sunny days.

Hot **Africa Discotheque,** Tallinna mnt. 1 (tel. 452 91), at the south end of Posti, is bigger and better than anything in Rīga, Vilnius, or other nearby cities. The disco boasts tuxedoed staff. Every kind of booze (except Southern Comfort) flows from the bar, and the *nouveau-riche* men sport cellular phones. (Open Sun.-Wed. noon-8pm and 9pm-3am, Thurs. noon-8pm and 9pm-4am, Fri.-Sat. noon-8pm and 9pm-5am;

cover Sun.-Thurs. 25EEK, Fri.-Sat. 70EEK; Wed. women enter free until midnight, men enter for 15EEK until midnight; MC and Visa accepted.)

■ Kuressaare

A major resort between the wars, the island of Saaremaa became off-limits to outsiders during the Soviet occupation. Consequently the island is reckoned to be more Estonian than Estonia itself, with much of the population still living in traditional Estonian farm houses, huddled around a palace abandoned since the 16th century, hardly concerned with the events of the mainland, or, for that matter, the world.

Orientation and Practical Information Kuressaare, an easy bus ride from Tallinn, rests on Saaremaa's south coast. Between the **Bishop's Castle** on the west side and the modern **bus station** on the east, the city spans a 15-minute walk. **Raekoja plats** is the narrow town square. The **tourist office,** Tallinna 2 (tel. 551 20), inside the *raekoda,* sells **maps** (6EEK; open Mon.-Fri. 9am-5pm, Sat. 10am-5pm). **Baltic Tours,** Tallinna 1 (tel. 554 80), on Raekoja plats, although not exactly a tourist office, will help with ferry info, English-language tours, and hotels (open Mon.-Fri. 9am-6pm, Sat. 10am-3pm). **Hansapank** on the north end of Raekoja plats, gives cash advances and **exchanges currency** (open Mon.-Fri. 9am-4pm, Sat. 10am-3pm). **Buses,** Pihtla tee 2 (info tel. 573 80, reservations tel. 562 20), at the corner of Tallinna go to Muhu (11 per day, 1½hr., 15EEK), Orissaare (11 per day, 1 hr., 12EEK), Pangu (3 per day, 2 hr., 11.50EEK), Pärnu (2 per day, 3hr., 70EEK), Tallinn (6 per day, 4hr., 90EEK). If you're going to the mainland, it's easier and cheaper to take a direct bus (which gets first priority on the ferries). There is a new **ferry** route that allows you to island hop between Saaremaa's Triigi port in the north of the island to Hiiumaa's Orjaku/Sadama port in the south of that island (3 per day, 45min., 45EEK). **Elvira Ella,** Kraavi 1 (tel. 552 42), rents older one-speed **bikes** for 60EEK per day. Take a left on Alee from Tallinna before the path to the castle, then another left on Rossamaare. Another left will bring you to Kraavi. A **post office,** Torni 1 (tel. 543 45), at the corner of Komandandi, a block north of Tallinna, offers **photocopying** (open Mon.-Fri. 8am-6pm, Sat.-Sun. 8:30am-3pm). **Telephones** are at the post office (open daily 8am-9pm). **Postal code:** EE-3300. **Phone code:** 0245; for faxes dial 5 instead.

Accommodations and Food New pensions and small B&Bs are sprouting as the city regains its inter-war reputation as a resort. Check with the tourist office to learn about the new crop. Hotel management students run **Mardi Öömaja,** Vallimaa 5a (tel. 574 36 or 558 78; fax 560 56), at the rear of the large white building, although some of the pupils have trouble making the grade. The hall toilets are clean, but you may want to bring your own toilet paper, and the showers in the basement also deserve an F for filthy. Otherwise tolerable with large, clean institutional-style rooms. Be explicit about asking for less expensive rooms (65EEK per person; breakfast 40EEK). A wooden turn-of-the-century B&B, **Lossi Hotell,** Lossi 27 (tel. 544 43) in the park, just meters from the Bishop's Castle, has only floor toilets and showers (singles 220EEK, off-season 120EEK; doubles 440EEK, off-season 240EEK; extra bed 120EEK, for those under 12 60EEK; breakfast included). **Võõrastemaja Kraavi,** Kraavi 1 (tel. 552 42 or 553 51), off Roomassaare, east of the castle, rents clean, cozy rooms with hall toilets and showers (singles 190EEK, doubles 380EEK; breakfast included; sauna 50EEK per hour). The family-run, **Suve Hotell,** Suve 6 (tel. 54 851), provides comfortable rooms with spotless toilets and showers (180EEK per person includes breakfast). **Kämping,** Mändjala (tel. 751 93), 8km outside Kuressaare at the "Kämping" bus stop, hides on a clean beach among secluded pine woods (4-bed rooms 120EEK per person, breakfast included; tent sites 40EEK a person; open May 30-Sept. 1).

The town's new-found cosmopolitanism means higher prices in restaurants. The bar at **Kodulinna Kohvik,** Tallinna 11 (tel. 541 78), downstairs off Raekoja plats, is inky black, but grope your way into the restaurant for pancakes full of rice and beef (10.45EEK), soups (9.70EEK), or ice-cold *Saare* beers (15EEK; open daily noon-2am).

Estonian Islands

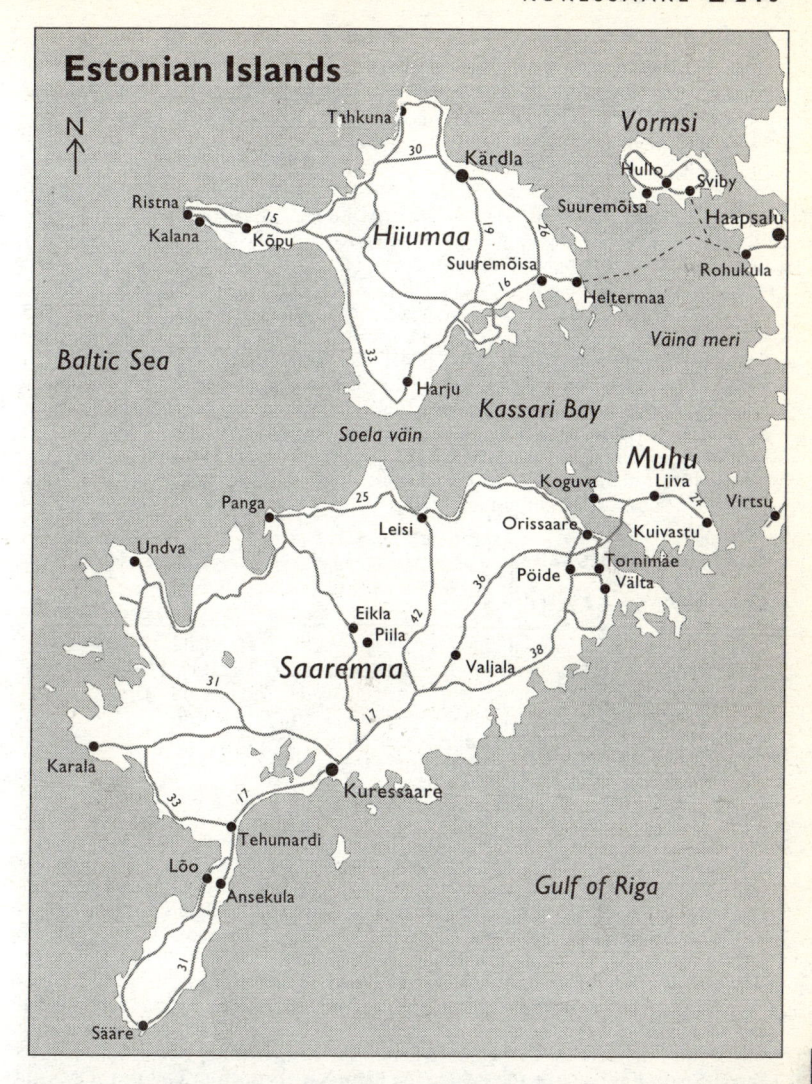

Sights and Entertainment Seventeenth-century buildings surround **Raekoja plats** (Town Hall Square)—most notably, the 1670 **raekoja**, a squarish building still serving as a town hall. Past the square's south end, a **monument** commemorates the 1918-20 struggle for independence from Russia. Farther down Lossi, the simple **Nikolai kirik** (St. Nicholas's Church) was built in 1790 for newly arrived Russian troops. The seat of the Saare-Lääne bishopric from 1358 until a 16th-century bishop sold the island to the Danes, Kuressaare keeps only the bishop's castle as a memento. Today, the pristine beaches and virgin woods define the city's feel.

Keep heading south on a mystical path with lily-covered ponds and white stone palaces on both sides, and soon the town's main attraction will come into view. **Kuressaare Linnus-kindlus** (Episcopal Castle), first built in 1260 shortly after the Teutonic Order subdued the islanders, was re-constructed from 1336-80 as the island home of the Bishop of Saare-Lääne; he liked it so much that in 1358 he declared it the bishopric's administrative center. The castle changed hands a number of times, starting in 1559 when the bishop sold it to the Danes. Later it became a Swedish, then a Russian stronghold. The tsar finally retired the venerable fortress from military use in 1899. The castle houses one of the more appealing museums in the Baltics, the **Saaremaa Regional Museum** (tel. 563 07)—an awesome collection of chariots, ceramic masks, furniture, swords, wooden sleds, stuffed wildlife, old bicycles, and trinkets from the 19th century and the 1918-20 War. The innumerable twisting and turning passages, stairwells, towers, and halls are enough to keep you busy all day; pick up a much-needed map (6EEK) at the entrance (castle and museum open daily 11am-7pm, last entry 6pm; 20EEK, students 10EEK). Be careful on the small, steep steps, but do visit **Tornikohvik,** a café with a view of the sea and castle (beer 18EEK; open daily 11am-6:30pm). Stomp on over to the **Citizen's Museum,** Pärgi 5 (tel. 563 07), a collection of dinosaur bones, dioramas, models, and pictures sure to please the first-grader in everyone (open Wed.-Sun. 11am-6pm; 20EEK, students 10EEK). At Pärgi 5a, the **exhibition hall** (tel. 596 71) features rotating displays, often of contemporary art (open Wed.-Sun. 11am-6pm; 2EEK). Stay long enough at **Disko Skala,** in the *kino* north of Raekoja plats on Tallinna, and you'll meet everyone ages 13-35 in Kuressaare (open Fri.-Sat. 10pm-whenever; cover 35EEK). For **Minigolf,** get clubs and balls at the bar to the right of the regional museum (open in summer only, daily 11am-3pm and 6-9pm; 10EEK per hour).

■ Near Kuressaare

SOUTHWEST SAAREMAA

Rent a bike and pedal south to the quiet, clean beaches of **Mändjala** and **Järve,** covering a stretch 8 to 12km west from Kuressaare. After the "Mändjala 1" bus stop, take the first left for a popular beach with sparkling water. The beach in **Järve** (turn left after the "Ranna" bus stop) has a **bar** (open daily 11am-10pm). More beaches dot the road south of here. At **Tehumardi,** a giant concrete sword with four faces chiseled into it marks the location of a 1944 battle. Across from it, rows of memorials have been built for the dead soldiers. Farther on, 17km out of Kuressaare, the town of **Salme** makes a good lunch stop. The restaurant **Ago & Co.,** on the main road (tel. 715 34 or 715 32), serves full meals (37-56EEK; open daily noon-midnight).

About 2km out of Salme, take the major turnoff to the right where a sign points to **Iide** along an unpaved road, and cut over to the west side of **Sõrve poolsaar** (peninsula), where the open Baltic makes for rocky beaches with bitchin' surf. At **Kaugatuma,** the locals make too much of the "cliffs", but there is a good lookout from the lighthouse and you can sunbathe alongside grazing cows on the fossil-strewn beaches. Five kilometers farther down the road rest the ruins of the WWII **Lõpe-Kaimiri kaitseliini rajatised** (defense line). Staying on the major gravel road, which now cuts inland, 12km of travel will bring you to the (real) cliffs at **Ohessaare.** At **Sõrve säär,** the very tip of the Sõrve Peninsula, clear weather opens up a vista to Latvia, 25km south across the Baltic. The **lighthouse** is open to visitors (5EEK, students 2EEK). **Warning:** the ride, especially on the one-speed bikes rented in Kuressaare, leaves many with sore rumps. Bring cushioning and plenty of mosquito repellent. On the trip back, take the road going through **Mõntu** (the opposite direction from Jämaja), which passes through the **national park** (look out for foxes and deer). If you're tired, take a bus back; ask the driver to put the bike in the luggage area (you'll be understood if you point first to the bike then to the back of the bus). The driver might charge for the luggage, but if he doesn't ask, don't offer.

NORTH SAAREMAA

If you're left unsatisfied by the cliffs to the south, try out the 60m wonders at **Panga,** on the north coast of Saaremaa, or just look at the picture on the back of the 100EEK note. **Buses** to Panga leave from and return to Kuressaare infrequently (3 per day, 2hr., 6EEK), so be careful not to get stuck. From Panga's cliffs cycle down about

12km to **Mustjala,** bearing right on the unpaved road to Võhma, and rolling along the coast. In Mustjala check out the village's **Anna Kirik** (Anna's Church), built in 1864 on the sight of a medieval burial ground. For an excellent **view** of the surrounding forest, sea, and fields, climb the steeple up to the bells. Hungry travelers should walk just a few meters down the road and follow the signs to **Käsitöösahver,** where a healthy portion of potato salad made with peas, carrots, tomatoes, and cucumbers could satisfy a giant (15EEK), and the heaping portions of chicken with rice (25EEK) might delay your bike trip, while you finish digesting them. Take a seat on a log bench and eat at a stone table in the woods (open daily 11am-7pm).

Continue down the road until Silla and go right on the unpaved road to **Pidula** where the natural **Odalätsi Springs** are said to bring eternal youth to young ladies who splash it on their faces. Apparently the local matrons haven't tried it. Farther south on the unpaved road, **Pidula Manor,** built in the 18th century, has an elaborate park, although the splendid manor is in poor condition. Further along the road, turn right down the hill into **Kihelkonna** where the 14th-century **Kihelkonna Kirik** holds choir concerts almost everyday in the summer. Only 2km down the paved road from Kihelkonna is the **Viki Farm Museum** (open Wed.-Sun. 10am-6pm; 10EEK). Also in the north of Saaremaa, not far from the Triigi port (6km) stand five preserved **windmills** in **Angla** (crawl around in them for 5EEK).

EAST SAAREMAA

From Kuressaare, take a bus towards Orissaare and get off in **Käo.** Bike 5km north to the turn to Tornimäe. Take that right to reach **Pöide.** Take the first left, onto a sandy path, and bike to the end of the road to **Pöidekirik.** First built as a Catholic church, it then became Lutheran, Russian Orthodox, and Lutheran again. The Teutonic Knights even used the edifice as a fortress against the locals. The outlines of the old church can still be seen (its small bottom windows remain). Get back on the main road and follow the signs north, then east to **Orissaare** (8km), the second biggest town in Saaremaa, with a population of about 1200. On the right is a series of tiny wooden houses and some castle ruins. Inside, a model table, chairs, clothing rack, and four beds make you want to ask for a room. Southwest of Orissaa in the small town of **Valjala** is the 13th-century **Valjala Kirik,** the oldest stone church in Estonia.

MUHU

From Orissaare, continue east, then north, and after 10km of pedaling through coastal splendor and over the causeway to Muhu island, take a sharp left turn to **Koguva.** At the end of the road (7km), the Koguva **open-air museum** consists of an old-fashioned town, complete with a well and houses made from hay (open summer daily 10am-7pm; 12EEK, students 6EEK). Pedaling back past the turning to Orissaare leads to **Linnuse,** where, on the left, you can crawl inside an old **windmill** (open daily 10am-6pm; 5EEK).

■ Hiiumaa

Closed off to outsiders and Estonians for 50 years, Estonia's second largest island is an all-but-forgotten land of hidden treasures and people who, emerging from their Soviet time capsule, want nothing more than to share these gems of nature, history, and culture with visitors. Hiiumaa's flat terrain and beautiful, peaceful forests and landscape make it ideal for biking. Native residents tell stories of spirits, giants, trolls, and devils who inhabited Hiiumaa before them; and doubtless the spirits of these creatures still haunt the island's enchanting sights.

ORIENTATION AND PRACTICAL INFORMATION

Hiiumaa is roughly cross-shaped, with the long end pointing west into the Baltic Sea. **Kärdla,** the only real city on the island (pop. 4000) is located on the north coast. **Käina,** with 200 residents, is the second-largest town, 16km away on the south coast.

Roads (mostly paved) ring the island, but the interior is made up largely of old farms—a woody wilderness unblemished by human habitation.

Tourist Office: Keskväljak 1, Kärdla (tel. 913 77; e-mail douglas@info.hiiumaa.ee; http://www.suba.com/hiiumaa). Run by Peace Corps volunteer Douglas Wells, this is one of the best-prepared tourist offices in the Baltics; Doug and his knowledgable staff can answer any query from ferry schedules to which species of tree grows in southern Hiiumaa. They are also a veritable font of information about hiking and wilderness possibilities. The *Hiiumaa Reisijuht* guide (15EEK), an excellent map of the island, is available here. Open in summer Mon.-Fri. 9am-6pm, Sat.-Sun. 10am-3pm; off-season Mon.-Fri. 10am-4pm.

Currency Exchange: Tallinna Pank, Keskväljak 7, Kärdla (tel. 912 78). Open Mon.-Fri. 9am-5pm, Sat. 10am-3pm.

Buses: Sadama 13, Kärdla (tel. 911 37; open daily noon-2:30pm and 3:30-6pm). To: Haapsalu (2-3 per day, 3hr., 14EEK); Kassari (2 per day Tues.-Sun., 50min., 15EEK); Tallinn (4-6 per day, 4hr., 70EEK).

Ferries: From **Rohuküla,** just south of Haapsalu on the mainland, ferries make the hour-long crossing to **Heltermaa** on the east tip of the island (in summer Mon.-Fri. 9-10 per day, Sat.-Sun. 4-5 per day; off-season 2 per day, depending on the ice that can make the journey take up to 36hr.; 10EEK). For info on **schedules,** especially off-season, call the ferry ports (tel. 919 80 in Hiiumaa, Haapsalu).

Public Transportation: Buses shuttle from in front of Heltermaa's port to Kärdla's bus station (4 per day, 45min., 14EEK). Theoretically, it's possible to take local buses to any point of the island with a house on it, since a mailbox is equivalent to a bus stop. But buses run to remote areas only once per day at best, and even between Käina and Kärdla, there can be 6-hr. gaps in service.

Taxis: It may be difficult to reach a taxi driver, but try these numbers: 992 78, 980 51, 980 91, 916 88, 911 39, 980 33, or 990 51. They cost 3EEK per km during the day, 4EEK at night. The catch is that all are based in Kärdla's central square, and you have to pay both directions of the driver's journey. In addition, waiting time costs 20EEK per hour during the day, 40EEK at night.

Car and Bike Rental: Dagotrans, Sõnajala 11, Kärdla (tel. 918 46), on the left in the little house at the gate that says not to enter on the left side of the street. Rent a car for 150-300EEK per day. They rent new Euro-type bikes with more gears than anyone knows what to do with (50EEK per day; open 24hr.).

Post Office: Posti 13, Kärdla, about 200m north of the bus station opposite the church. Open Mon.-Fri. 8:30am-4:30pm, Sat. 9am-1pm. **Postal code:** EE-3200.

Telephones: Leigri väljak 9 (tel. 915 37) in Kärdla. Open 24hr. **Phone code:** 0246.

ACCOMMODATIONS, CAMPING, AND FOOD

Fifty years of isolation means that Western prices haven't yet caught up with most of Hiiumaa's hotels.

Campground Puhkemajad (tel. 921 26 or 976 29), in Kassari (see Near Hiiumaa, p. 248), only a few km from Orjaku/Sadama port (ask the bus driver to let you off at Puulaid). The accommodations on this "campground" could compete with some of the nicer budget hotels in Estonia, with spacious rooms, modern toilets, a huge high-tech sauna and shower, use of a full kitchen, and a splendid view of the sea. 100EEK per person. Breakfast 40EEK. Supper 60EEK.

Võõrastemaja Kärdla, Vabaduse 13 (tel. 914 45), a white building near the corner of Vabaduse and Valli. Institutional, but meticulously clean rooms. The spotless single-sex toilets and showers offer a lot of privacy for communal facilities. The sexist sauna next door is open daily 11am-7pm, but only on Friday for women. Only room for 24 people, so arrive early. Doubles and quads 35EEK per person.

Hotell Sõnajala, Leigri väljak 3 (tel. 993 36 or 993 43), southwest of Kärdla's center, off Kõrgessaare mnt. Adjoining a tennis club, the rooms here are fairly plush and the sinks (not the showers) have hot water. The staff speaks Estonian, Russian, and German. Walk south on Rookopli from Keskväljak, turn right on Kõrgessaare mnt. (the major intersection with a big stone head on the corner), and left onto Sõnajala; the hotel is in the complex on the right (20min.). Singles 150EEK.

Lõokese Hotell, Lõokes 14, Käina (tel. 921 070), about 1km from Käina's center. The hostel is attached to a hotel and offers spacious rooms with modern furnishings, and bathrooms that come as a welcome change from the institutional rooms of other hostels. Doubles run 260EEK, doubles with sink 300EEK; quads 460EEK. Saunas 100EEK per hour.

In the hamlet of **Kõrgessaare** (also called **Viskoosa**), about 17km west of Kärdla, a large granite-block building, first a 19th-century silk factory and later a vodka distillery, houses the best restaurant on the island. The warm, homey **Viinaköök** (Vodka Kitchen; tel. 933 37) specializes in genuine Hiiumaa wild boar (54EEK). The salmon dishes are mouth-watering (20-30EEK; open Tues.-Sat. 11am-3am, Sun.-Mon. 11am-10pm). In Kärdla, **Priiankru,** Sadama 4 (tel. 962 95; fax 963 05), a pink wooden building at the corner with Posti serves well prepared helpings of *Praetud Lõhe Koorektames* (pan-fried salmon, 59EEK), thick *seljanka* (18EEK), or *puljong pirukaja* (broth with meat pie, 10EEK; open daily 8am-midnight). In Käina, **Lõokese Restoran,** Lõokes 14 (tel. 372 46), serves fresh smoked salmon (17EEK).

SIGHTS

Due to the variety of plants and waterfowl (more than two-thirds of all the plant species known in Estonia exist only on Hiiumaa), much of the island now belongs to the **West-Estonian Islands Biosphere Reserve. Hiking** and **camping** are permitted and encouraged ways of viewing the natural and man-made wonders of Hiiumaa, but be sure to pick up info on off-limits areas from the tourist office. Motor vehicles are not allowed on the seashore and certain core areas. Because of dry conditions, campfires are prohibited. The office also puts out *The Lighthouse Tour,* a guidebook to the 16 major sights on Hiiumaa (20EEK). Lighthouses dot the island, most notably the **Kõpu Lighthouse,** a beautiful, white towering structure on Hiiumaa's western peninsula. Constructed in the early 1500s by the Hanseatic League, the stairwell was an afterthought and was literally hacked out of the solid rock to provide access to the top. The 100m view from the top is an awe-inspiring panorama of the Baltic Sea, including all of Hiiumaa and, on a sunny day, the island of Saaremaa to the south (5EEK, but no one collects tickets, and the workers at the food stand/ticket booth forget to sell them). Farther west of Kõpu, there is an abandoned Soviet **radar facility** at the tip of the island, at what used to be the Soviet Union's northwesternmost point. Kärdla's **Pühalepa Kirik,** Pikk 26 (tel. 911 20), was built by the island's German Graf Sternberg in 1870. His smooth, shiny-gray grave is to the right of the church. The Frau is buried in the small red-roofed house next door. The **Tahkuna Lighthouse** also stands west of Kärdla. Built in Paris in 1874, the lighthouse was consistently ineffective in warning ships about the shallow waters of the northwest coast. Perhaps locals purposefully made sure the lighthouse never worked since they made a handsome profit by salvaging ships' loot and rescuing passengers. For a spectacular view, climb to the top of the lighthouse, which is usually left open. Near the Tahkuna Lighthouse stands a **memorial** to the Russian soldiers who fought a battle here during world WWII. The gun emplacement and bunkers still stand in the area. (The bunkers are open for people to look at, but it's not advisable to enter without a flashlight). Also notable and worth a visit are the **Contract Stones,** or, as locals call the sight, "Hiiumaa's Stonehenge". The large rocks were clearly placed by human (or divine) hands, but their purpose is still a mystery. Older islanders insist that a 6th-century Swedish King rests in peace under the carefully placed stones, and with him, his gold. Others argue that sailors carried a large stone to the sight before each voyage as a sort of show of faith in God, hoping he would grant them safe passage, hence the term "contract stones". Still other experts believe the stones served a religious purpose for worshippers of an ancient religion once practiced on Hiiumaa.

Near Käina, stands the **Suuremõisa Palace,** built in 1755 by Margerethe Stenbock, one of Hiiumaa's wealthiest landlords. The beautiful example of northern baroque architecture stands in disrepair, but the oak staircase is in excellent shape.

> **Crossed Paths**
>
> Legend claims that long ago at **Ristimägi**, "Hill of Crosses," on Hiiumaa, two wedding parties once met and, neither wanting to give way to the other, fought. The groom from one party and the bride from the other were killed in the scuffle. The remaining bride and groom decided to get married and, in memory of their dead loved ones, planted the first cross on this hill. Realistically, however, it is more likely that Ristimägi commemorates the last church service held there by Swedes who were forced to leave the island in 1781. Today, tradition holds that in memory of the departed Swedes, anyone who passes the spot must plant a cross constructed out of objects (such as grass, sticks, leaves, and rocks) that occur naturally in the surrounding area.

■ Near Hiiumaa: Kassari

The tiny island of **Kassari,** south of Hiiumaa, is home to even thicker woods and wilder sights. Visit the **Hiiumaa Koduloomuuseum** to see Hiiumaa's last gray wolf and exhibits on the island's history and wildlife. West of Sääretirp near the broken-down windmill, the museum (tel. 971 21) is a one-story orange-roofed barn-house (open Mon.-Fri. 10am-5pm; 6EEK, students 2EEK). The **Kassari Chapel**, a small white church on the sea, may be Europe's only church with a hay roof. From the campsite (see Hiiumaa: Accommodations, p. 248), go north and turn right at the "Kassari" store. Also check out the moss-covered **Devil's Stone**, near the **Suure-Maise Church.** According to legend, the Devil, intending to throw the stone at someone, accidently threw it here. Perhaps the most beautiful and wondrous of Hiiumaa's natural sights is **Sääretirp**, a 1- to 3m-wide peninsula extending over 3km out into the sea, lined with wild strawberries and juniper bushes. Legend holds that this is the remains of a bridge built by the giant Leiger between Hiiumaa and Saaremaa so that his brother Suur Töll could come for a visit. To get a full taste of life on Hiiumaa try the homemade Hiiumaa beer at **Humala Baar,** a tiny wooden pub on the main road just south of Partsi in eastern Hiiumaa (*Saku* 8EEK, homemade brew 3EEK; open daily noon-10pm).

HUNGARY
(MAGYARORSZÁG)

US$1 = 152 forints (Ft, or HUF)	100Ft =	US$0.92
CAD$1 = 111Ft	100Ft =	CAD$0.90
UK£1 = 238Ft	100Ft =	UK£0.44
IR£1 = 247Ft	100Ft =	IR£0.41
AUS$1 = 120Ft	100Ft =	AUS$0.83
NZ$1 = 106Ft	100Ft =	NZ$0.94
SAR1 = 34Ft	100Ft =	SAR2.92
DM1 = 103FT	100Ft =	DM0.97
Country Phone Code: 36	**International Dialing Prefix: 00**	

> As of summer 1996, inflation was running high in Hungary. Prices, listed in this section, will almost certainly change, but should give you a relative idea of cost.

Forty-five years of isolation and relative powerlessness under Soviet rule are a mere blip in Hungary's prolific 1100-year history, and traces of Socialism are evaporating with each passing iron-free day. Budapest dominates the country, though the capital by no means has a monopoly on cultural attractions. No provincial center is more than a three-hour train ride through corn and sunflower fields from Budapest. Try not to forsake the beauty of the countryside for a whirlwind tour of the capital—you'll have seen the heart of the country but missed its soul entirely.

HUNGARY ESSENTIALS

Citizens of the U.S., Canada, and Ireland can travel to Hungary visa-free with a valid passport for 90 days; U.K. citizens for 180 days; South African citizens for 30 days.

Australians and New Zealanders must obtain 90-day tourist visas from their Hungarian embassy or consulate; no border-control posts issue visas. See Embassies and Consulates, p. 7. For U.S. residents, visa prices are single entry US$40, multiple entry US $180, and 48-hr. transit visa US$38. Citizens of other countries who do not live in the U.S. pay US$65, US$200, and US$50, respectively. Obtaining a visa takes one day and requires proof of means of transportation, lodging arrangement, and financial means, as well as a valid passport, three photographs (5 for double visas), payment by cash or money order, and a self-addressed, stamped (certified mail) envelope. You will also receive an entry-exit form which you must keep in your passport. You can apply for a visa extension at police stations in Hungary, but most tourist visa holders cannot stay more than 90 days.

GETTING THERE AND GETTING AROUND

Hungary's national airline, **Málev**, has daily direct flights from New York's JFK airport to Budapest. Most **rail** lines swerve through the capital. Use **buses** to travel among the outer provincial centers. Hungarian **trains** *(vonat)* are reliable and inexpensive, although travelers coming from Vienna to Budapest should be especially careful with their bags, as theft is particularly high on that line. **Eurail** and **EastRail** are valid here. Travelers under 26 are eligible for a 33% discount on domestic train fares. An **ISIC** commands discounts at IBUSZ, Express, and station ticket counters. Book international tickets in advance. The student discount on international trains is roughly 30%, but sometimes you need to be persistent. Try flashing your ISIC and repeat "student," or the Hungarian, *"diák"* (DEE-ahk).

Személyvonat trains are excruciatingly slow; *gyorsvonat* (listed on schedules in red) cost the same and move at least twice as fast. Large provincial towns are accessible by the blue *expressz* rail lines. Air-conditioned *InterCity* trains are fastest. A seat reservation is required on trains labeled "R". Some basic vocabulary will help you navigate the rail system: *érkezés* (arrival), *indulás* (departure), *vágány* (track), and *állomás* or *pályaudvar* (station, abbreviated *pu.*)—see the Glossary, p. 778 for more. The platform for arrivals and departures is rarely indicated until the train approaches the station—and then the announcement will be in Hungarian.

The extensive **bus** system is cheap but crowded; it links many towns whose only rail connection is to Budapest. The **Erzsébet tér** bus station in Budapest posts schedules and fares. InterCity bus tickets are purchased on the bus (get there early if you want a seat). In larger cities, tickets for **public transportation** must be bought in advance from a newsstand and punched on board; they can't be bought from the driver, and there is a fine if you're caught ticketless. In smaller cities, you generally pay when you board; the standard fare is 70Ft. The Danube **hydrofoil** goes to Vienna via Bratislava. Eurail pass holders receive a 50% discount.

Either IBUSZ or Tourinform can provide a brochure about **cycling** in Hungary that includes maps, suggested tours, sights, accommodations, bike rental locations, repair shops, and recommended border-crossing points. Write to: **Hungarian Nature-Lovers' Federation** (MTSZ), 1065 Budapest, Bajcsy-Zsilinszky út 31, or the **Hungarian Cycling Federation,** 1146 Budapest, Szabó J. u. 3, for more information. Some rail stations rent bicycles to passengers.

TOURIST SERVICES

Knowledgeable and friendly **Tourinform** has branches in every county and is probably the most useful all-around tourist service in Hungary. **IBUSZ** offices throughout the country can make room arrangements, change money, sell train tickets, and charter tours, although they are generally better at helping arrange travel plans than providing information about the town that you are actually in. Snare the pamphlet *Tourist Information: Hungary* and the monthly entertainment guides *Programme in Hungary* and *Budapest Panorama* (all free and in English). **Express,** the former national student travel bureau, handles hostels and changes money. Regional agencies are most helpful in the outlying areas. The staff at Express generally speaks German, and sometimes English.

MONEY

The national currency is the **forint,** divided into 100 fillérs. In the first four months of 1996, inflation was over 25%. **Change money** only as you need it. Make sure to keep some dollars or Deutschmarks in hard cash to purchase visas, international train tickets, and (less often) private accommodations. **American Express** offices in Budapest and IBUSZ offices around the country convert **traveler's checks** to cash at about 6% commission. Cash advances on credit cards are available at most OTP branches, but with the already abundant and ever-increasing number of **ATMs,** many banks no longer give cash advances inside their doors. Machines which automatically change foreign cash into forints are popping up all over and tend to have excellent rates. They often spit back American currency, though, and may take a little while, so don't get impatient and walk away without your money. Major **credit cards** are accepted at expensive hotels and many shops and restaurants. **New Zealand dollars** cannot be exchanged here, so pack another currency. At exchange offices with extended hours, the rates are generally poor. The maximum permissible commission for cash-to-cash exchange is 1%. Allow a half-hour to exchange money, or go to IBUSZ for a marginally lower rate. Black market exchanges are common, but risky, illegal, and rarely favorable. Don't use them.

COMMUNICATION

English **press** is available in many Budapest kiosks and large hotels, but rarely in other cities. Hungary's *Daily News* is published weekly. The weekly *Budapest Sun* (250Ft) is oriented mostly towards news and hard business information, though its *Style* section will help one navigate through the cultural life of Budapest. English-language radio and TV programming is found in *Budapest Week,* which has excellent listings, survival tips, and articles about life in Hungary (published every Thurs.; 96Ft, free at AmEx offices and larger hotels). Also published weekly, the Magyar flyer *Pestiest* lists movies, concerts, and performances in Budapest; pick up a free copy in restaurants, theaters, and clubs. Used bookstores *(antikvárium)* often have English, German, and French books at fire-sale prices.

Three **radio** stations have anglophonic programming in Hungary: Danubius, Juventus, and Radio Bridge. The frequencies vary from region to region, but in the Budapest area they are 103.3, 89.5, and 102.1 FM respectively.

Almost all phone numbers in the countryside have six digits and begin with "3." For intercity calls, wait for the tone and dial slowly: a "06" goes before the phone code. **International calls** require red phones or new, digital-display blue ones, found at large post offices, on the street, and in metro stations. Though the blue phones are more handsome than their red brethren, they tend to cut you off after three to nine minutes. Phones suck money so fast you'll need a companion to feed them. Half of the public phones throughout the country require **phone cards,** available at kiosks, train stations, and post offices in denominations of 500Ft and 1000Ft. You don't save money either way, but the cards are convenient and seriously collectable. Direct calls can also be made from Budapest's phone office.

To call collect, dial 09 for the international operator. To reach the **AT&T Direct operator,** put in a 10- and a 20Ft coin (which you should get back), dial 00, wait for the second dial tone, then dial 80 00 11 11. For **MCI WorldPhone,** dial 80 00 14 11; **Sprint Express,** dial 80 00 18 77; **Canada Direct,** dial 80 00 12 11; **British Telecom Direct,** dial 80 04 40 11; **Mercury Call UK,** dial 80 00 44 12; **Ireland Direct,** dial 80 00 35 31; **Australia Direct,** dial 80 00 61 11; **New Zealand Direct,** dial 80 00 64 11.

The Hungarian **mail** system is perfectly reliable (airmail—*légiposta*—to the U.S. takes 5-10 days). Note that if you're mailing to a Hungarian citizen, the family name precedes the given name, as in "Pulliam Joel."

LANGUAGE

Hungarian belongs to the Finno-Ugric family of languages that includes Finnish and Estonian; even Hungarian and Finnish—probably the two most similar—are only as closely related as German and Italian. **English** is the country's very distant third language after Hungarian and **German**. *"Hallo"* is often used as an informal greeting or farewell. *"Szia!"* (sounds like "see ya!") is another greeting—you'll often hear friends cry: "Hallo, see ya!"

A few starters for pronunciation: *"c"* is pronounced "ts" as in "cats"; *"cs"* is "ch" as in "chimichanga"; *"gy"* is "dy" as in *"a*dieu*"*; *"ly"* is "y" as in "yam"; *"s"* is "sh" as in "shovel"; *"sz"* is "s" as in "Seattle"; *"zs"* is "zh" as in "pleasure"; and *"a"* is "a" as in "*a*lways". The first syllable usually gets the emphasis. See Glossary, p. 778, for more.

HEALTH AND SAFETY

> **Emergency Numbers: Ambulance:** tel. 04. **Fire:** tel. 05. **Police:** tel. 07.

Should you get sick, contact your embassy for lists of English-speaking doctors. Tap water is usually clean and drinkable (except in the town of Tokaj, where it bares an uncanny resemblance to the waters of the neighboring Tisza river).

ACCOMMODATIONS AND CAMPING

Most travelers stay in **private homes** booked through a tourist agency. Singles are scarce—it's worth finding a roommate, as solo travelers must often pay for a double room. Agencies may try to foist off their most expensive rooms on you; be persistent. Outside Budapest, the best and cheapest office will specialize in the region (i.e. Egertourist in Eger). These agencies will often call ahead to make reservations at your next stop. After staying a few nights, you can often make further arrangements directly with the owner, thus saving the tourist agencies' 20-30% commission.

Some towns have cheap **hotels;** most of these are rapidly disappearing. As the hotel system develops and room prices rise, **hosteling** will become more attractive, although outside of Budapest, it is difficult to find ones that are open year-round. Many hostels can be booked at **Express,** the student travel agency, or sometimes the regional tourist office. From late June through August, university **dorms** metamorphose into hostels. Locations change annually; register through an Express office in the off-season, or at the dorm itself during the summer. Offices can only book rooms for the city they're in. Hostels are usually large enough to accommodate peak-season crowds. **HI cards** are becoming increasingly useful. Sleepsacks are rarely required.

Over 100 **campgrounds** are sprinkled throughout Hungary. If you rent **bungalows,** you must pay for unfilled spaces. Most sites stay open May through September. Tourist offices offer the annual *Camping Hungary.* For more info and maps, contact **Tourinform** in Budapest (see Budapest, p. 256).

FOOD AND DRINK

Paprika, Hungary's chief agricultural export, colors most dishes red, and the food is more flavorful and varied than in much of Eastern Europe. In Hungarian restaurants, called *vendéglő* or *étterem,* you may begin with *gulyásleves,* a delicious and hearty beef soup seasoned with paprika. Alternatively, try *gyümölcsleves,* a delicious cold soup made from cherries, pears, or other fruit and often topped with whipped cream. *Borjúpaprikás* is a veal dish with paprika, often accompanied by small potato-dumpling pasta. Vegetarians can find the tasty *rántott sajt* (fried cheese) and *gombapörkölt* (mushroom stew) on most menus.

In a *cukrászda,* you can fulfill the relentless desire of your sweet-tooth for dangerously few forints. Pastries in Hungary are cheap and usually delicious. *Túrós táska* is a chewy pastry pocket filled with sweetened cottage cheese. *Somlói galuska* is a fantastically rich sponge cake with chocolate, nuts, and cream, all soaked in rum. After the Austrians stole the recipe for *rétes,* they called it "strudel" and claimed it as their own, but this delicious concoction is as Hungarian as Zsa Zsa Gabor. *Kávé* means espresso, served in thimble-sized cups and so strong your duodenum begins to unwind before you finish your first sip.

Hungary produces a diverse array of fine wines (see A Mini-Guide to Hungarian Wine, p. 283). Unjustly less famous, Hungarian *sör* (beer) ranges from the first-rate to the merely acceptable. *Dreher Bak* is a rich dark brew; good light beers include *Dreher Pils, Szalon Sör,* and licensed versions of *Steffl, Gold Fassl,* and *Amstel.* Hungary also produces different types of *pálinka,* hard liquor that resembles brandy. Among the best tasting are *barackpálinka* (apricot Schnapps) and *szilvapálinka* (plum brandy). *Unicum* is a very fine herbal liqueur that Habsburg kings used to cure digestive ailments.

CUSTOMS AND ETIQUETTE

General **business hours** in Hungary are Monday to Friday 9am-5pm (7am-7pm for food stores). Banks close around 3pm on Friday, but hours continue to expand with the market. **Tourist bureaus** are usually open Monday to Saturday 8am-5pm in summer (some are open until noon on Sunday); off-season, these hours shrink to Monday to Friday 10am-4pm. Museums are usually open Tuesday to Sunday 10am-6pm, with occasional free days on Tuesday. ISIC holders often get in free or pay half-price.

Rounding up the bill as a **tip** for all services, especially in restaurants but also for everyone from taxi-drivers to hairdressers, is standard for a job well done. Remember in restaurants to give it as you pay—it's rude to leave it on the table. Waiters often don't expect foreigners to tip—they may start to walk away while you're still fumbling for your money. The bathroom attendant gets 20Ft.

The frequency and extent of public displays of affection, among young and old, may be startling, or at least distracting. Every bus has an obligatory couple exchanging lesser bodily fluids. Taste in **clothing,** especially for men, is casual and unpretentious. Men rarely wear shorts, even in hot weather. Modesty is not a strong theme of women's fashions, though women in smaller towns dress more conservatively.

Hungarians love exercise—if they're watching others do it. They are serious about cigarettes, however. Dogs are family members, far bigger than the European average—no poodles here, thank you—and are spoiled rotten.

LIFE AND TIMES

HISTORY

After a long series of tenants—hunters, gatherers, Neolithic farmers, and cannabis-seed-burning Scythians—the same Celtic tribes who ravaged Greece and Rome settled Hungary in the 3rd century BCE. The **Celts** built a hill-fort on the site of what would later be Budapest's Citadel, but the city was officially founded by the **Romans,** who conquered Hungary in 10CE. Roman peace lasted until the 3rd century when waves of Vandals, Huns, Avars, and Franks trampled the remains of the Romano-Celtic civilization in Hungary for the next 700 years.

Magyars, mounted warrior tribes from Central Asia, arrived in the 9th century. After their entry in 896, the Magyars under **Prince Árpád** took only a few years to establish control over the Middle Danube Basin. Árpád's descendant, Stephen I, was crowned King of Hungary with papal benediction in 1001, after accepting the authority of the pope and decreeing the conversion of his subjects to Catholicism.

The Árpád dynasty ruled Hungary for another 300 years. In 1222, the **Golden Bull** officially recorded the rights of the various Hungarian classes. These rights were promptly revoked by the **Mongols** when they invaded in 1241. The Árpáds revived briefly, then died out in 1301, to be replaced by a variety of families from across Europe. One of these imported rulers, János Hunyadi, defeated the encroaching Turks in 1456 at Nandorfehérvár near modern Belgrade. His son, Mátyás Hunyadi, known as **Matthias Corvinus** (1458-1490), ruled as king over Hungary's Renaissance, building the great court at Visegrád, restoring prosperity and limited civil rights, and acquiring territory (Silesia, Moravia, and Lower Austria). Corvinus's death in 1490 was bad luck for the country. In the following century, it witnessed civil war, peasant rebellion (1514), civil rights setbacks, and Turkish invasion.

After destroying the Hungarian army at Mohács in 1526, the Turks occupied Hungary for almost 150 years. Divided between Habsburgs, Turks, and Turkish allies, the land fell to plague and persecution. More damage came with "liberation." The **Habsburg** hordes stormed through in the mid- to late-17th century, tearing the country away from the Turks only to usher in another era of foreign domination. A new **war of independence** began in 1848, led spiritually by the young poet Sándor Petőfi. The war resulted in the establishment of the **first Hungarian republic.** Led by Lajos Kossuth, the state held out for one year. In the summer of 1849, Habsburg Emperor Franz Josef I retook Budapest with support from Tsar Nicholas I of Russia.

Despite a period of repression, Hungary was granted its own government in 1867, in league with the Austrian crown; the Austro-Hungarian Empire came to be known as the **Dual Monarchy.** While the late 19th century witnessed economic development unseen before or since, Hungary adopted a language policy that favored Magyars over other linguistic groups. As a result, national movements emerged among Romanians, Serbs, Croats, Swabians, and Slovaks. The strife eventually erupted into WWI, which resulted in the permanent destruction of the empire and the loss of two-thirds of Hungary's territory. During WWI, many of these nationalities remained loyal to Hungary, and the post-war Trianon Treaty awarded political independence to only some of Hungary's nationalities at the expense of others. The Bourgeois Democratic Revolution which overthrew the monarchy in 1918 was followed by a short-lived republic and an even shorter-lived (133-day-long) Hungarian Soviet Republic. The latter was overthrown, and its leaders brutally repressed by the fascist government of Admiral Miklós Horthy de Nagybanya (1920-44). The depressed inter-war years were followed by a tentative alliance with Hitler in **WWII**, then by the year-long Nazi occupation and the almost total destruction of Budapest during the two-month Soviet siege of 1945. Two-thirds of Hungary's Jews, whose numbers had approached one million before the war, were murdered in WWII. Survivors fled the country.

Yet another Hungarian republic was replaced by a **People's Republic** in 1949. Communist Hungary was ruled by **Mátyás Rákosi** and the Hungarian Workers Party (later the Magyar Szocialista Munkáspárt—MSZMP), under which it became strongly tied to the USSR both economically and politically. Rákosi went out with the **"events of 1956,"** a violent uprising in Budapest during which **Imre Nagy** declared a neutral, non-Warsaw Pact government in Budapest.

Over the next two decades, borders were partially opened and the national standard of living improved, until inflation and a lack of economic growth halted the process in the 1980s. Democratic reformers in the Communist Party pushed aside Kádár in 1988, pressing for a market economy and increased political freedom. In autumn 1989, the Hungarian people fulfilled the aspirations of the previous generation and broke away from the Soviet orbit in a bloodless revolution. The 1990 elections transferred power to the center-right **Hungarian Democratic Forum,** led by Prime Minister József Antall and President Arpád Göncz, a former Soviet political prisoner. However, stalled progress led the renamed-and-revamped Socialists to again be trusted with power in 1994. Change continues at a dizzying pace, but Hungarians have adapted admirably since the last Soviet troops departed in June 1991.

LITERATURE

A non-Indo-European tongue brought by settlers in the 9th century, **Magyar** is a stranger in a strange linguistic land. The feeling of isolation created by such a unique and impenetrable language has defined the literary, social, and political history of its speakers. Since the Reformation, Magyar writers have dealt with the problems of Hungarian identity and establishing an independent role in the European system.

Before the 11th century, there is little record of literary Magyar, and not until Christian missionaries came to the region did the Hungarian language emerge from under the dominant Latin culture—Latin actually remained the language of state until 1844. The Ottoman occupation censored the Hungarian writers for over a century and a half and, as the Turks receded in the early 18th century, novels in French and German entered the country in translation. During the Enlightenment, French thinkers such as Voltaire and Rousseau influenced the memoirs of Hungarian nobility like **Count Miklós Bethlen** and **Countess Kata Bethlen**. As evidenced by the street names of post-Communist Hungary, the writers leading up to the revolution of 1848 played an important role in Hungary's history, as well as literature. **Kazincsy** organized language reform. Romantics like **Széchenyi** and **Vörösmarty** and the Populist anti-Romantic **Petőfi** provided the nationalistic rhetoric required for revolutions. This period bound together changing literary ideals with the quest for social reform and political independence. Outside of the poets **Arany** and **Kemény,** the 19th century produced less great works until the initiation of a new literary era with the founding of the Nyugat (West) literary journal in 1907. **Ady, Babits,** and **Kosztolány,** embraced Symbolism and psychoanalysis in their poetry. They expanded the creative field for Hungarian Expressionist writing and the free verse of **Kassák**.

László Németh was one of the most influential authors to emerge from the new Populist movements of the inter-war period in Hungary. He crafted plays that used a stark Realism that depicted the battle of the individual against the world—Németh remained in the political tradition of Hungarian literature with this clear demand for social reform. After WWII, Communism again silenced the Magyar writers who worked in the **Socialist Realist** style until a new generation appeared who more freely developed individualistic styles. **György Konrád** wrote both novels such as *The Case Worker* (Penguin Books, 1987) and important political treatises like *Antipolitics* (1984), which were crucial in defining the dissident movements all over Central Europe. Less concerned with social issues and more with the post-modern quest to redefine the meaning of use of words themselves, **Péter Esterházy** and his innovative book *An Introduction to Literature* (1986) founded a new movement in Magyar literature and brought it again to the world cultural scene. Since the end of Communism, the political motivations have had to be redefined, and the search is on for a new source of energy for this generation of Hungarian writers.

HUNGARY TODAY

Although still aglow with political triumphs, Hungarians have experienced an economic hang-over. High prices for daily necessities, widespread unemployment, and yawning inequities in income harshly remind Hungarians of the competitive side of liberty. However, along with Poland, the Czech Republic, and Slovakia, Hungary is one of the prosperous Visegrád Four, so-called after an economic pact signed in the city in 1991. Realizing that there are no quick solutions, most Hungarians are resigning themselves to a painful transition. The former Communists returned to power in 1994, winning control of parliament by promises of easier reforms, not a return to the past. Aside from economic woes, the most visible vestiges of the old regime are now benevolent: efficient public transportation, clean parks and streets, and a low incidence of violent crime.

Hungary is experiencing great problems controlling its rapidly increasing deficit. After a painful year of strikes and protests against cuts in Hungary's fat public sector, Prime Minister Gyula Horn remains firmly on track, bringing the economy into line with guidelines set out by international creditors and the EU. However, in the first four months of 1996, inflation was already over 27%, and foreign direct investment was predicted to be much less than it had been in previous years. A treaty with Slovakia concerning the treatment of the sizeable Hungarian minority has finally been signed and one with Romania was also announced. With a successful party conference in the spring of 1996 behind him, Horn is enjoying greater popularity and authority than ever.

Budapest

At once a cosmopolitan European capital and the stronghold of Magyar nationalism, two-million-strong Budapest has spirit after a 50-year Communist coma. Endowed with an architectural majesty befitting the Habsburg Empire's number-two city, the Hungarian capital's intellectual and cultural scene has often been compared to that of Paris. But unlike its western neighbors, Budapest retains a worn-at-the-elbows charm in its squares, cafés, and bath houses. WWII punished the city; Hungarians rebuilt it from the rubble with the same pride that fomented the ill-fated 1956 uprising, weathered the Soviet invasion, and overcame decades of subservience. Today, the city manages to maintain charm and a vibrant spirit—refusing to buckle under the relentless siege of glitzification—while pursuing the difficult course of modernization.

ORIENTATION AND PRACTICAL INFORMATION

Budapest straddles the **Duna** (Danube) in north-central Hungary 250km downstream from Vienna. Regular trains and excursion boats connect the two cities. Budapest also has direct rail links to Belgrade, Istanbul, Prague, Kraków, and other major cities. The old **Orient Express,** completely refitted, still chugs through Budapest on its way from Berlin to Bucharest.

Previously two cities, Buda and Pest, separated by the Duna, Budapest has retained a distinctive character on each side of the river. Buda is the source of inspiration for artists with its hilltop citadel, trees, and cobblestone Castle District. On the east side, **Pest** buzzes, the commercial heart of the modern city. Here you'll find shopping, banks, the Parliament, the Opera House, and theaters. The heart of the city, **Vörösmarty tér,** was once situated just to the north of the 4m-high, medieval town wall, still visible in many places.

Three central bridges bind the halves of Budapest together. Széchenyi lánchíd connects Roosevelt tér to the base of the cable car, which scurries up to the Royal Palace. To the south, the slender white **Erzsébet híd** departs from near **Petőfi tér** and **Március 15 tér;** it extends up to the colonnaded monument of St. Gellért at the base of Gellért Hill. Farther along the Duna, the green **Szabadság híd** links **Fővám tér** to the south end of Gellért Hill, topped by the Liberation Monument.

Moszkva tér, just down the north slope of the Castle District, is Budapest's bus and tram transportation hub. One metro stop away in the direction of Örs vezér tere, **Batthyány tér** lies opposite the Parliament building on the west bank; this is the starting point of the **HÉV commuter railway,** which leads north through Óbuda and into Szentendre (See Szentendre, p. 276). Budapest's three **Metro** lines (M1, M2 and M3) converge at **Deák tér,** beside the main international bus terminal at **Erzsébet tér.** Deák tér lies at the core of Pest's loose arrangement of concentric-ring boulevards and spoke-like avenues. Two blocks west toward the river lies **Vörösmarty tér.** As you face the statue of Mihály Vörösmarty, the main pedestrian shopping zone, **Váci u.,** is to the right.

If you feel like you're walking in circles, remember that many street names in Budapest occur more than once; always check the district as well as the kind of street: **út** is a major thoroughfare, **utca** (u.) is a street, **körút** (krt.) is a circular artery, and **tér** is a square. Addresses in Budapest begin with a Roman numeral that represents one of the city's 22 **districts.** Central Buda is I; downtown Pest is V. The middle two digits of the postal code also correspond to the district number. Also, streets arbitrarily change names from one block to the next. Because many have shed their Communist labels, an up-to-date **map** is essential. To check if your map of Budapest is *au courant,* look at the avenue leading from Pest toward the City Park (Városliget) in the east: the modern name should be Andrássy út. The **American Express** and **Tourinform** offices have good free tourist maps, or pick up *Belváros Idegenforgalmi Térképe* at any metro stop (100Ft). Anyone planning an exhaustive visit should look into purchasing András Török's *Budapest: A Critical Guide.*

ORIENTATION AND PRACTICAL INFORMATION ■ 257

Useful Organizations

Tourist Offices: Tourinform, V, Sütő u. 2 (tel. 117 9800; fax 117 9578), off Deák tér just behind McDonald's. M1, 2, or 3: Deák tér. This busy, multilingual tourist office provides information ranging from sightseeing tours to opera performances. Make room in your pack for all the free brochures. Open daily 8am-8pm. Sightseeing, accommodation bookings, and travel services are available at almost every private travel agency, including IBUSZ and Budapest Tourist (offices in train stations and tourist centers). Ask for their free and helpful quarterly *For Youth*. The **IBUSZ** central office, V, Apácsai Csere J. u. 1 (tel. 118 5776; fax 117 9000), a block west of Vörösmarty tér, patiently books airline tickets, arranges sightseeing packages (2900Ft per 3hr. tour; 12 languages), finds accommodations, and provides cash advances on DC and V. Open 24hr.

Tourist Police: KEO, V, Városligeti Fasor 46/48 (tel. 112 1537). M3: Nyugati Pu or M1: Oktogon. Two blocks southeast of Andrássy út. New visas and visa extensions. Open Tues. 8:30am-noon and 2-6pm, Wed. 8:30am-1pm, Thurs. 10am-6pm, Fri. 8:30am-12:30pm.

Budget Travel: Express, V, Szbadság tér 16 (tel. 131 77 77). Some reduced international air and rail fares for the under-26 crowd (train ticket reductions also available at train stations). Pick up ISIC for 500Ft. Open Mon. and Wed.-Thurs. 8am-4:30pm, Tues. 8am-6pm, Fri. 8am-2:30pm. Bring your own photos for the ISIC; there is a photo booth (4 for 400Ft) at the top of the escalators at the Moskva tér and other major subway stops. Amazing discounts for **youth** (under 26) as well as **standby** (purchase 2 days before flight) available at the **Malév office,** V, Dorottya u. 2 (tel. 266 56 16; fax 266 27 84) on Vörösmarty tér. Open Mon.-Fri. 7:30am-5pm.

Embassies and Consulates: Australia, XII, Kriályhágó tér 8/9 (tel.201 8899). Open Mon.-Fri. 9am-noon. **Canada,** XII, Budakeszi út 32 (tel. 275 1200). Take bus #22 five stops from Moszkva tér. Open Mon.-Fri. 9-11am. **U.K.,** V, Harmincad u. 6 (tel. 266 2888), just off the northeast corner of Vörösmarty tér. M1: Vörösmarty tér. Open Mon.-Fri. 9am-noon and 2-4:30pm. **New Zealanders** should contact the British embassy. **U.S.,** V, Szabadság tér 12 (tel. 267 4400). M2: Kossuth Lajos, then walk two blocks down Akademia and take a left on Zoltán. Open Mon.-Tues. and Thurs.-Fri. 8:30am-noon.

Currency Exchange: The bureaus open late often have less favorable rates. Most exchange offices will turn traveler's checks into hard currency for a commission.

General Banking and Trust Co. Ltd., Váci u. 19/21 (tel. 118 9688; fax 118 8230). Some of the best rates in town. Open Mon.-Fri. 9am-4:30pm.

IBUSZ, V, Petőfi tér 3, just north of Erzsébet híd. Cash advances on Visa. ATM machine for Cirrus. Open 24hr.

GWK Tours (tel. 322 9011), in the Keleti Station. Slightly off-beat. Excellent rates. Very convenient for rail travelers. Open daily 6am-9pm.

Citibank, Vörösmarty tér 4 (tel. 138 2666; fax 266 9845). Efficient and pleasant. Open Mon.-Fri. 9am-4pm. 24-hr. cash advances on Cirrus and MasterCard.

Magyar Külkereskedelmi Bank, V, Szent István tér 11. M: Deák tér. Two blocks north at the basilica's entrance. Perhaps the most comprehensive exchange place in town with very good rates. Open Mon.-Thurs. 8am-2pm and Fri. 8am-1pm. Two outdoor MasterCard/Cirrus ATMs. Another branch, V, Türr István u. 9, one block south of Vörösmarty tér. Open Mon.-Fri. 8am-8pm and Sat. 9am-2pm. They are among the few banks in the city to give Mastercard and Visa cash advances (forints only; go inside the bank if you don't have a PIN code) and cash traveler's checks in US dollars for a 2% commission.

ATMs: These machines have cropped up all over town. OTP Bank deals with MasterCard, while Posta Bank and IBUSZ handle Cirrus. Magyar Bank takes most major cards. Citibank and American Express also have ATMs.

American Express: V, Deák Ferenc u. 10 (tel. 266 8680; fax 267 2028). M1: Vörösmarty tér, next to Hotel Kempinski. Sells traveler's checks for hard cash, Moneygrams, or cardholders' personal checks. Cashes traveler's checks in US dollars for a 6% commission. Cash advances only in Ft. Free maps, and pick up the *Budapest Sun* or the free *Budapest Week* here. Holds mail; address mail as follows: "Bonnie BRENN-WHITE, American Express, Hungary Kft., Deák Ferenc u. 10, H-1052 Budapest, Hungary." Free pickup for AmEx cardholders or traveler's-check carri-

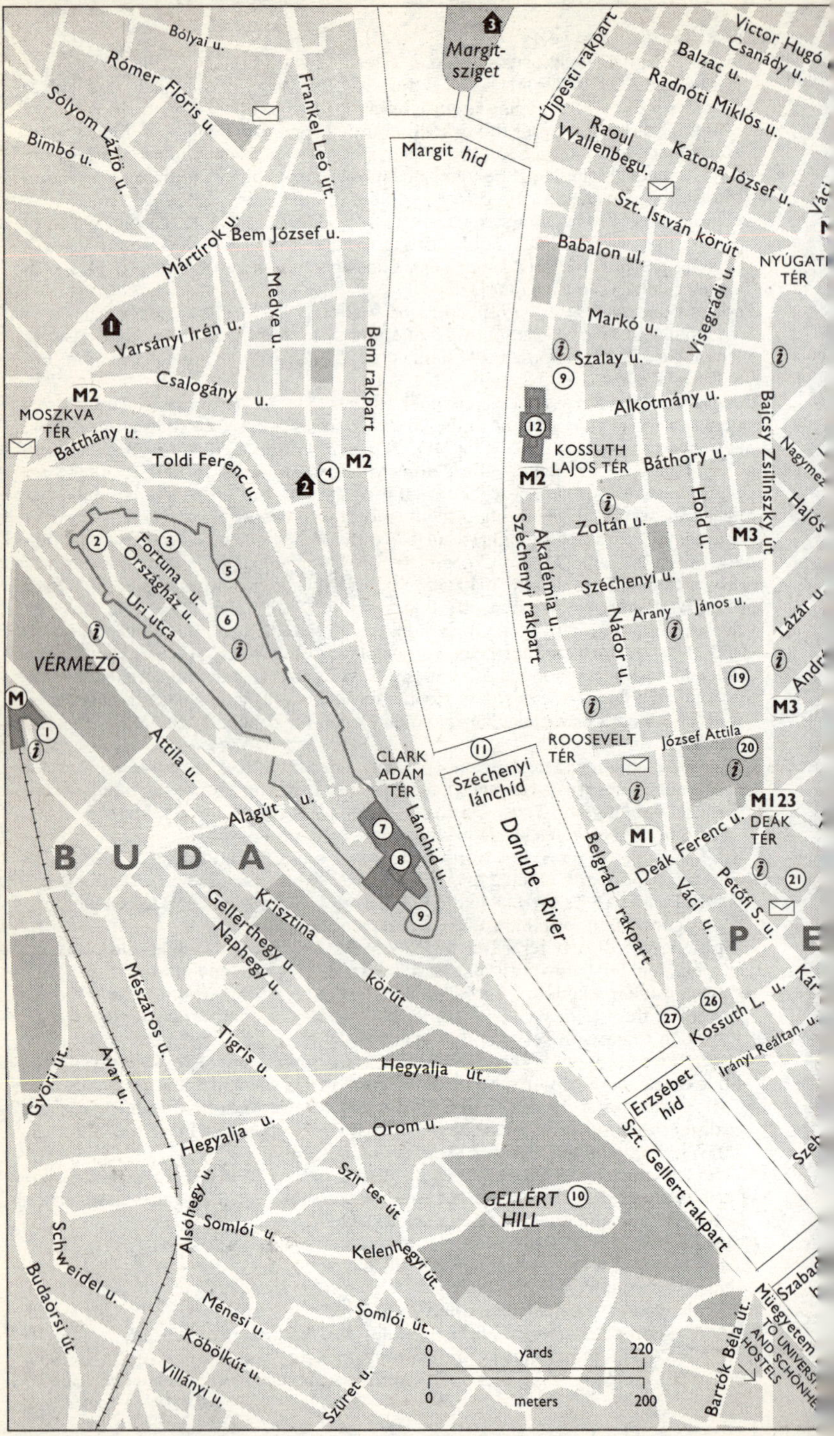

Bólyai u.
Rómer Flóris u.
Sólyom Lázió u.
Bimbó u.
Frankel Leó út
Margit-sziget
Margit híd
Újpesti rakpart
Victor Hugó
Csanády u.
Balzac u.
Radnóti Miklós u.
Raoul Wallenbegu.
Katona József u.
Szt. István körút
Váci
NYÚGATI TÉR
Mártírok u.
Bem József u.
Medve u.
Bem rakpart
Babalon ul.
Visegrádi u.
Markó u.
Varsányi Irén u.
Szalay u.
Csalogány u.
M2
MOSZKVA TÉR
Batthány u.
Alkotmány u.
Bajcsy Zsilinszky út
Toldi Ferenc u.
KOSSUTH LAJOS TÉR
Báthory u.
Fortuna u.
Országház u.
Uri utca
Zoltán u.
Hold u.
M3
Akadémia u.
Széchenyi rakpart
Széchenyi u.
Arany János u.
Nádor u.
Lázár u.
VÉRMEZÖ
Attila u.
CLARK ADÁM TÉR
Lánchíd u.
Széchenyi lánchíd
ROOSEVELT TÉR
József Attila
M123
DEÁK TÉR
Alagút u.
B U D A
Danube River
Belgrád rakpart
M1
Deák Ferenc u.
Váci u.
Petőfi S. u.
Krisztina körút
Gellérthegy u.
Naphegy u.
P E
Mészáros u.
Tigris u.
Kossuth L. u.
Irányi Reáltan. u.
Hegyalja út
Győri út
Avar u.
Erzsébet híd
Orom u.
Hegyalja u.
Szt. Gellert rakpart
Szir tes út
Alsóhegy u.
GELLÉRT HILL
Somlói u.
Kelenhegyi út
Schweidel u.
Budaörsi út
Ménesi u.
Somlói út
Műegyetem
Bartók Béla út
TO UNIVERSI AND SCHÖNHE HOSTELS
Kőbölkút u.
Villányi u.
Szüret u.
0 yards 220
0 meters 200

ORIENTATION AND PRACTICAL INFORMATION ■ 259

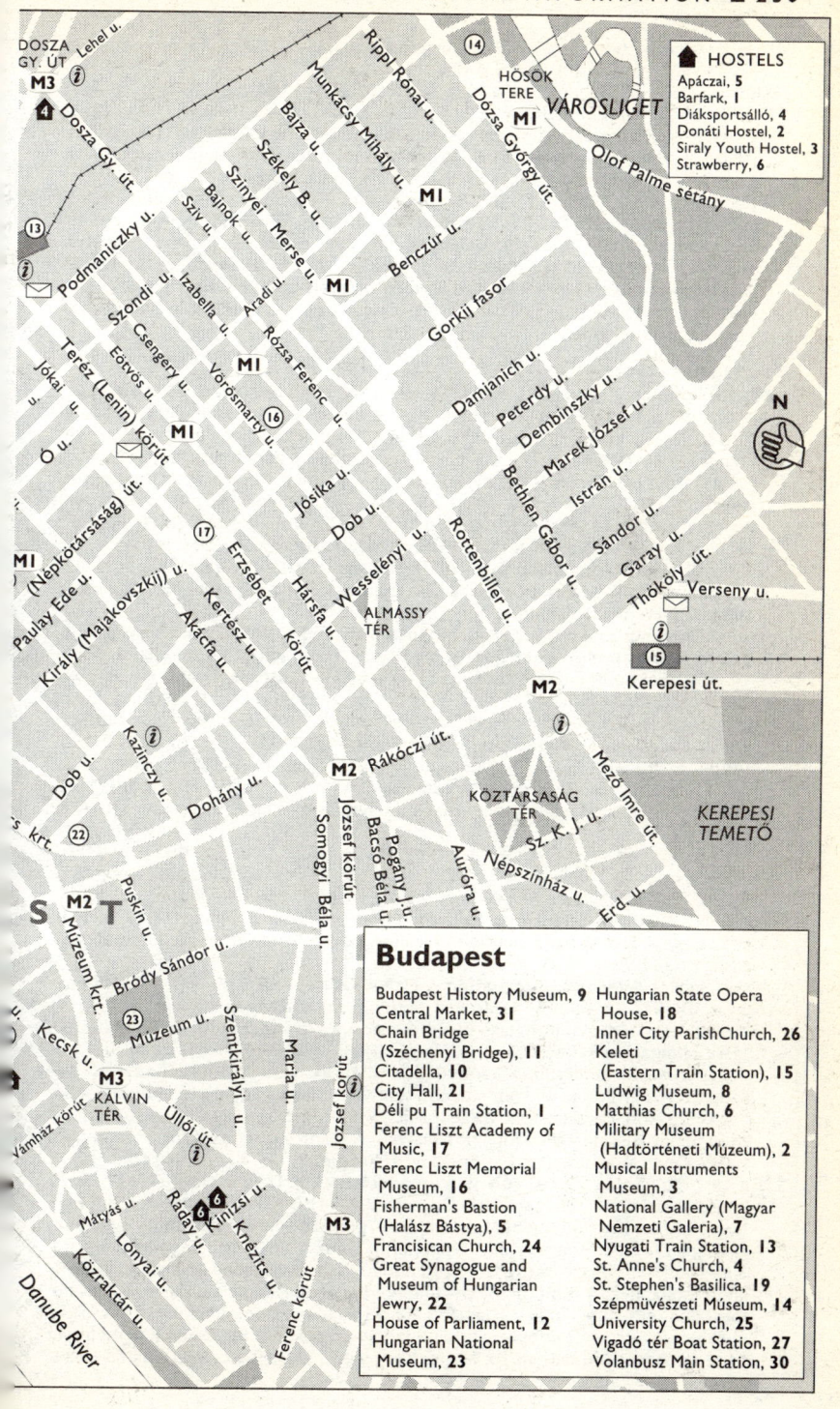

HOSTELS
Apáczai, **5**
Barfark, **1**
Diáksportsálló, **4**
Donáti Hostel, **2**
Siraly Youth Hostel, **3**
Strawberry, **6**

Budapest

Budapest History Museum, **9**
Central Market, **31**
Chain Bridge (Széchenyi Bridge), **11**
Citadella, **10**
City Hall, **21**
Déli pu Train Station, **1**
Ferenc Liszt Academy of Music, **17**
Ferenc Liszt Memorial Museum, **16**
Fisherman's Bastion (Halász Bástya), **5**
Franciscan Church, **24**
Great Synagogue and Museum of Hungarian Jewry, **22**
House of Parliament, **12**
Hungarian National Museum, **23**
Hungarian State Opera House, **18**
Inner City Parish Church, **26**
Keleti (Eastern Train Station), **15**
Ludwig Museum, **8**
Matthias Church, **6**
Military Museum (Hadtörténeti Múzeum), **2**
Musical Instruments Museum, **3**
National Gallery (Magyar Nemzeti Galeria), **7**
Nyugati Train Station, **13**
St. Anne's Church, **4**
St. Stephen's Basilica, **19**
Szépmüvészeti Múzeum, **14**
University Church, **25**
Vigadó tér Boat Station, **27**
Volanbusz Main Station, **30**

ers. 555Ft otherwise. AmEx **ATM.** Open July-Sept. Mon.-Fri. 9am-7:30pm, Sat. 9am-2pm; Oct.-June Mon.-Fri. 9am-5:30pm, Sat. 9am-1pm.

Thomas Cook: V, Vigadó u. 6 (tel. 118 64 66; fax 118 65 08), in IBUSZ.

Post Office: V, Városház u. 18 (tel. 118 48 11). Pick up **Poste Restante** here. Open Mon.-Fri. 8am-8pm, Sat. 8am-3pm. 24-hr. **branches** at Nyugati station, VI, Teréz krt. 105-107, and Keleti station, VIII, Baross tér 11c. After-hours staff doesn't speak English. You may be better off sending mail via AmEx. **Postal code:** 1052.

Telephones: V, Petőfi Sándor u. 17 (local operator tel. 01, international operator 09). English-speaking staff. Fax service. Open Mon.-Fri. 8am-8pm, Sat.-Sun. 8am-2pm. At other times, try the post office. Many of the public phones in Budapest now use **phone cards**, available at newsstands, post offices, and metro stations. 50-unit card 700Ft, 120-unit card 1500Ft. Use **card phones** for **international calls.** They will automatically cut you off after 10-20min., but it's more time than the coin phones will give you. **Phone code:** 1.

Transportation

Flights: Ferihegy Airport (tel. 267 4333, info 157 7155, reservations 157 9123, telephone check-in 157 7591). Terminal 1 is for foreign airlines and Malév flights to New York and Vienna. Terminal 2 is for all other Malév flights, Lufthansa, and Air France. Volánbusz takes 30min. to get to terminal 1 and 40min. to terminal 2 (300Ft) from Erzsébet tér. The most convenient journey, though, is by the **airport shuttle bus** (tel. 157 89 93), which will pick you up anywhere in the city at any time of day or night, or take you anywhere in the city from the airport (800Ft). Call for pick-up a few hours in advance. The cheapest way to the airport is to take the M3 to Köbanya-Kispest and then follow the signs to the Ferihegyi bus. It's well marked with lots of pictures of airplanes. This bus stops at both terminals and takes 40min. to terminal 1, 50min. to terminal 2.

Trains: (domestic info tel. 322 7860, international info 142 9150). The word for train station is *pályaudvar*, often abbreviated "pu." Those under 26 are eligible for a 33% discount on international tickets. You generally must show your ISIC and tell the clerk *"diák"* (student); English may not be understood, so try writing down your destination on a piece of paper and show that to the clerk. The three main stations—**Keleti pu., Nyugati pu.,** and **Déli pu.**—are also metro stops. The area around Keleti station can be dangerous at night. Trains to and from a given location do not necessarily stop at the same station; for example, trains from Prague may stop at Nyugati pu. or Keleti pu., although most international trains arrive at Keleti pu. Nyugati pu. serves east Hungary while Déli pu. serves west Hungary. Each station has schedules for the others. To: Belgrade (4 per day, 6½hr., 6003Ft); Berlin (5 per day, 12½hr., 14,779Ft); Bucharest (3 per day); Prague (7 per day, 7½hr., 7501Ft); Vienna (5 per day, 3½hr., 4819Ft); Warsaw (2 per day, 10hr., 8078Ft). The daily **Orient Express** arrives from Berlin and continues on to Bucharest. **Luggage storage** at Keleti pu. in yellow lockers across from the international cashier (60Ft).

Train Ticket Agencies: International Ticket Office, Keleti pu. Open daily 7am-6pm. **IBUSZ** (see p. 257). Generous discounts on other international rail tickets. Several days advance purchase may be necessary for international destinations. **MÁV Hungarian Railways,** VI, Andrássy út 35 (tel. 322 8275; fax 322 8405) and at ticket windows at all train stations. About 25% discounts for those under 26. Be insistent and whip out all your student/youth IDs. International and domestic tickets. Open Mon.-Fri. 9am-6pm. **Wagons-lits,** V, Dorottya u. 3 (tel. 266 3040), across from Malév just northeast of Vörösmarty tér. 25-50% discounts for seniors and youth. Open Mon.-Fri. 9am-12:45pm and 1:30-5pm.

Buses: (info tel. 117 2966). **Volánbusz main station,** V, Erzsébet tér (tel. 117 2562; international ticket office tel. 118 2122; fax 266 5419). M1, 2, 3: Deák tér. International cashier upstairs (open Mon.-Fri. 6am-7pm, Sat.-Sun. 6:30am-4pm). **Luggage storage:** 60Ft per item per day. Open Mon.-Thurs. 6am-7pm, Fri. 6am-9pm, Sat.-Sun. 6am-6pm. Buses to the Czech Republic, Slovakia, Poland, Romania, Turkey and Ukraine depart from the **Népstadion** terminal on Hungária körut 48/52, as do most domestic buses to East Hungary. M2: Népstadion. Domestic buses are usually cheaper than trains, but may take slightly longer. Buses to the Danube Bend leave from the **Árpád híd** station. To: Berlin (4 per week, 14½hr., 12,500Ft); Bratislava (1 per day, 3½hr., 1370Ft); Prague (4 per week, 8½hr., 2940Ft); Vienna (1 per day, 3hr., 2990Ft).

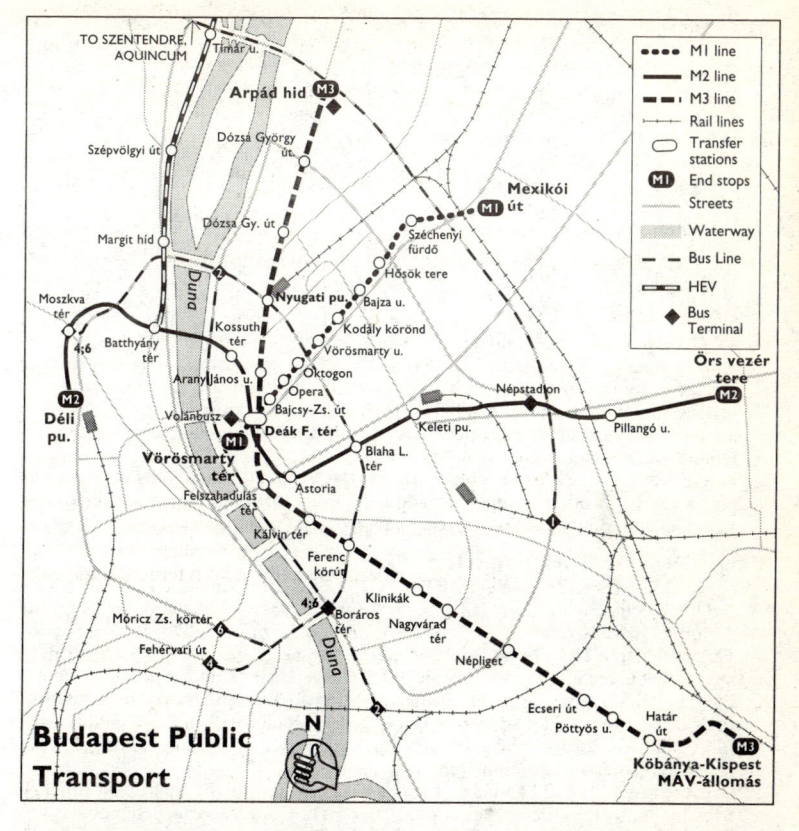

Public Transportation: Built in 1896, the Budapest **Metro** was the first in continental Europe and has been consistently rapid and punctual ever since. The subway, **buses,** and **trams** are inexpensive and convenient. The Metro has 3 lines: yellow, red, and blue (shown on our map and referred to in text as M1, M2, and M3 respectively). An "M" indicates a stop, but you will not always find the sign on the street; it's better to look for stairs leading down. All lines converge at the **Deák tér** station. Public transportation stops about 11:30pm; don't be surprised to find the subway gates locked 15min. earlier. Buses whose numbers are marked with an "E" continue to run along major routes 24hr. Bus #78E runs all day and night along the same route as M2. The subway, buses, and trams all use the same yellow **tickets** which are sold in metro stations and *Trafik* shops and by some sidewalk vendors. These tickets are valid through Óbuda on the HÉV; beyond that you'll have to buy one on the train. A single-trip ticket costs 50Ft; punch it in the orange boxes at the gate of the Metro or on board buses and trams. 10-trip tickets *(tíz jegy)* for 450Ft and 20-trip tickets for 850Ft, as well as passes lasting for different durations are available (passes: 1-day 400Ft, 3-day 800Ft, 1-week 875Ft, 2-week 1300Ft, 1-month 1950Ft). Tickets are checked mostly on the Metro and at the beginning of the month. It's a 600Ft fine if you're caught without a ticket; you'll pay 1500Ft if you can't come up with the cash on the spot. If you change metro lines or buses, you must use a new ticket. The **HÉV commuter rail** runs between Batthyány tér in Buda and Szentendre, 40min. north on the Danube Bend. Trains leave about every 15min.

Hydrofoils: MAHART International Boat Station, V, Belgrád rakpart (tel. 118 1704; fax 118 7740), on the Duna near Erzsébet híd. Has information and ticketing. Open Mon.-Fri. 8am-4pm. Or try **IBUSZ**, Károly krt. 3 (tel. 322 24 73). M2: Astoria. Open Mon.-Fri. 8am-4pm. Arrive at the docks 1hr. before departure for customs and passport control. Buffet and tax-free shopping on board. Eurailpass holders receive a 50% discount. To Vienna: April 8-May 19 and Sept.4-Oct. 29 daily 9am; May 20-Sept. 3 daily 8am and 4pm (6hr. via Bratislava; one-way 10,990Ft, students 8000Ft; round-trip 19,500, students 10,000Ft). Bicycles 1400Ft. All charges payable in Ft, US$, AS or with AmEx and Visa.

Car Rental: This is an expensive option in Budapest; most rental agencies charge over US$100 per day for their cheapest cars. If you must rent, try **Budget**, I, Krisztina krt. 41/43 (tel.156 6333; fax 155 0482), in Hotel Buda Penta; Ferihegy Airport terminal 1 (tel. 157 8197), terminal 2 (tel. 157 8481). Open Mon.-Sat. 8am-8pm, Sun. 8am-6pm. Their cheapest unlimited mileage option is the Opel Corsa at 11,170Ft per day. Minimum age 21. A much more economical option is to travel with **Kenguru**, VIII, Köfaragó u. 15 (tel. 138 2019). M2: Astoria. This is a **carpool** service charging 6Ft per km with both domestic and international service. If you're driving somewhere and would like to take passengers, notify Kenguru 3-4 days in advance. If you want to go somewhere, they'll need to know 4-5 days in advance. Open Mon.-Fri. 8am-6pm, Sat. 10am-2pm.

Taxis: Főtaxi, tel. 222 2222. **Volántaxi**, tel. 166 6666. 80Ft base plus 80Ft per km. Stay away from other companies, and especially avoid the Mercedes-Benz taxis, which charge double the jalopy fee. Taxis are more expensive at night.

Other Practical Information

English Bookstore: Bestsellers KFT, V, Október 6 u. 11 (tel./fax 112 1295), near the intersection with Arany János u. M: Deák tér or M1: Vörösmarty tér. Small but comprehensive. Literature, pop novels, current magazines, and local travel guides. They also carry **The Phone Book**, an English language "yellow pages" that can be an invaluable resource for people planning to spend an extended period of time in the city (US$4). Open Mon.-Fri. 9am-6:30pm, Sat. 10am-6pm. A few minutes away their other store, **CEU Academic Bookshop**, V, Nador u. 9 (tel. 327 3096), has a more erudite selection; particularly strong is their section on Eastern Europe. Open Mon.-Fri. 9am-6pm, Sat. 2pm-5pm.

Photocopies: V, Petőfi Sándor u. 11 (tel. 118 5484), near the main post office. A friendly photoshop that makes copies. 10Ft each. **Copy general**, Semmelweis út 4 (tel. 216 8880). 10Ft per page. Open Mon.-Fri. 7am-10pm, Sat. 9am-6pm.

Laundromats: Irisz Szalon, VII, Rákóczi út 8b. M2: Astoria. Wash: 5kg, 40min., 300Ft. Dry: 100Ft per 15min. Pay the cashier before you start. Open Mon.-Fri. 7am-7pm, Sat. 7am-1pm. **Mosószalon**, V, József Nádor tér 9. M: Deák tér. Head to József Attila u. on the north end of Erzsébet tér, then walk toward the river. After one block, turn left down Nádor tér. Look for the multicolored tile column in the window. Wash: 5kg, 350Ft per 15 min. Dry: 150Ft per 15min.Open Mon., Wed., and Fri. 7am-3pm; Tues., Thurs. 11am-6pm. Also, many youth hostels have washing machines, which you can use for a fee.

24-Hour Pharmacies: I, Széna tér 1 (tel. 202 1816). VI, Teréz krt. 41 (tel. 111 4439). IX, Boráros tér 3 (tel. 117 0743). IX, Üllői út. 121 (tel. 133 8947). At night, call the number on the door or ring the bell to summon the sleepy manager; you will be charged a slight fee for the service. State-owned pharmacies are the only source for all medicines, including aspirin; little is displayed and everything is dispensed from behind the counter. To find a pharmacy look for the tan-and-white motif with *Gyógyszertár, Apotheke*, or *Pharmacie* in black letters in the window.

Gay Hotline: tel. 166 9283. Open daily 8am-4pm. Try **Dohotourist**, VI, Jókai tér 7 (tel. 111 0406; fax 269 3645), for a free brochure with gay listings and a gay map of Budapest. Open Mon.-Fri. 8:30am-4:30pm. Also (see Gay Budapest, p. 275).

AIDS Hotline: tel. 166 92 83. Mon., Wed., and Thurs. 1pm-5pm; Tues. and Fri. noon-8pm.

Medical Assistance: tel. 118 8288. **Személyi Orvos Szolgálat**, VIII, Kerepesi út 15 (tel. 118 8012). English spoken. Open 24hr. Emergency medical care is free for foreigners. The U.S. embassy has a list of English-speaking doctors.

ACCOMMODATIONS AND CAMPING

Travelers arriving in Keleti station enter a feeding frenzy as hostel solicitors and proprietors huckstering their rental rooms elbow their way to tourists. Don't be drawn in by promises of free drinks or special discounts; the hostel-hawkers get paid by the customer and have been known to stretch the truth.

The easiest options are hostels, rooms in privately owned apartments, or family-run guesthouses. Get your bearings before you go with anyone. Always make sure that the room is easily accessible by public transportation, preferably by Metro, which runs more often than buses. Ask that a solicitor show you on a map where the lodging is located. Though the runners are generally legit, see the room before you hand over any cash.

Accommodations Agencies

Accommodation services are overrunning Budapest. The rates (800-3000Ft per person) depend on the location and bathroom quality. Haggle stubbornly. Arrive around 8am, and you may get a single for 1000Ft or a double for 1600Ft. Travelers who stay for more than four nights can obtain a somewhat better rate.

Pension Centrum, XII, Szarvas Gábor út 24 (tel. 201 9386 or 176 0057). A non-profit group that makes reservations in private rooms. Open daily 10am-7pm.

IBUSZ, at all train stations and tourist centers. **24-hr. accommodation office,** V, Apáczai Csere J. u. 1 (tel. 118 3925; fax 117 9099). An established service offering rooms in Budapest. Private rooms for 1600-3000Ft per person. Swarms of people outside IBUSZ offices push "bargains"; quality varies, but they're legal. Old women asking *"Privatzimmer?"* are vending private rooms.

Budapest Tourist, V, Roosevelt tér 5 (tel. 117 3555; fax 118 1658), near Hotel Forum, 10min. from Deák tér on the Pest end of Széchenyi lánchíd. A well established enterprise offering 1800-2400Ft singles and 4500Ft doubles. Open Mon.-Thurs. 9am-5pm, Fri. 9am-3pm. Same hours at branches through the city.

Duna Tours, Bajcsy-Zsilinszky út 17 (tel. 131 4533 or 111 5630; fax 111 6827), next to Cooptourist. Allows travelers to see rooms before accepting them. Doubles from 2000Ft. The English-speaking staff swears that their rooms are located only in districts V and VI. Open Mon.-Fri. 9:30am-noon and 12:30-5pm.

To-Ma Tour, V, Oktober 6 u. 22 (tel. 153 0819; fax 269 5715). Promises to find you a centrally located room, even if only for one night. Doubles 1800-3000Ft, with private bathroom 2800Ft. 20% off if you stay more than a month. Open Mon.-Fri. 9am-noon and 1-8pm, Sat.-Sun. 9am-5pm.

Year-Round Hostels

If you're eager to meet young people, hostels are the place to be. Most hostel-type accommodations, including university dorms, are under the aegis of **Express.** There is an office at V, Semmelweis u. 4 (tel. 117 6634 or 117 8600); leave Deák tér on Tanács krt., head right on Gerlóczy u., then take the first left. Or try the branch at V, Szabadság tér 16 (tel. 131 7777), between M3: Arany János and M2: Kossuth tér. Individual hostels advertise in the train stations and on billboards and flyers. You may also see the standard HI symbol outside buildings. Before accepting lodging, make sure you're not being brought to one of the new private hostels that cram hordes of tourists into tiny rooms. Within two minutes of arriving at Keleti pu., you're bound to be familiar with Traveller's Youth Hostels (formerly More Than Ways), Universam, and Strawberry—three companies that run youth hostels all over the city. Most rooms have linoleum floors which, despite avid cleaning, never quite look clean, and bunk beds. Many provide in-room refrigerators and TV rooms on each floor. Some offer laundry machines. Prices at the company run hostels are rising quickly in response to demand. The Traveller's Youth Hostels's Diáksportszálló is famous for its party scene. "Universam" hostels are usually quieter. One caveat with these large companies—they may quote you a price at the main train station only to claim later that all such rooms are taken.

Nicholas's Budget Hostel, XI, Takács Menyhért u. 12 (tel. 185 4870). Follow the directions to the Back Pack Guesthouse (see below), then continue a half block down the road. Not as corporate as their competition, but more spacious and clean, and just as friendly. TV, garden, kitchen, lockers. Reservations accepted. Laundry costs 400Ft per 5 kg. 800Ft per bed, bedding 400Ft.

Back Pack Guesthouse, XI, Takács Menyhért u. 33 (tel. 185 5089), a 20min. commute from central Pest. From Keleti pu. or the city center, take bus #1, 7, or 7A heading toward Buda and disembark at "Tétenyi u.", immediately after the rail bridge, 5 stops past the river. From the bus stop, head back under the bridge, turn left, and follow the street parallel to the train tracks for 3 blocks. Look for the small green signs and the most colorful house on the block. Carpeted rooms, clean bathrooms, and humor in every niche. The staff is young, friendly, and very helpful. 5- and 8-bed rooms. 800-900Ft per person. Showers, breakfast, private locker, and use of kitchen, TV, and VCR included. They also have a rotating day program. For only 1500Ft, try spelunking, horseback riding, paragliding, rock climbing, bungee jumping, or waterskiing, all in the Budapest area. The bulletin board lists special trips, programs, and information. Free bikes and tennis.

Diáksportszálló, XIII, Dózsa György út 152 (tel. 140 8585 or 129 8644). Entrance on Angyaföldi, 50m from M3: Dózsa György. Huge and hugely social, but not the best choice if safety, cleanliness, and quiet are major concerns. International crowd. It seems to have remained the same under new "Traveller's Youth Hostels" management, but they claim improvement is in the works. Check-out 9am. Bar open and occupied 24hr. Singles 1850Ft. Doubles 1750-1850Ft per person, with shower 1900Ft per person. Triples and quads 1550Ft per person. 8- to 12- person dorms 1100Ft per person. 10% discount with an HI card.

Summer Hostels

Almost all dorms of the **Technical University** (Műegyetem) become youth hostels in July and August; these are conveniently located in district XI, around Móricz Zsigmond Körtér. From M3: Kálvin Ter, ride tram #47 or 49 across the river to "M. Zsigmond". For more information, call the **International Student Center** (tel. 166 7758 or 166 5011, ext. 1469). In summer, the center also has an office in Schönherz. For bookings, you can try the **Express Office** (see Year-Round Hostels, p. 263).

Strawberry Youth Hostels, IX, Ráday u. 43/45 (tel. 218 4766), and Kinizsi u. 2/6 (tel. 217 3033). M3: Kálvin tér. Two converted university dorms within a block of one another in Pest, on a smaller street running south out of Kálvin tér. Check-out 10am. Spacious rooms without bunk beds. Doubles 1400Ft per person. Triples and quads 1260Ft per person. If you're lucky and the hostel isn't too full, you'll get a triple or quad room. Many rooms have refrigerators, sinks and drying racks. Breakfast 270Ft. Disco on premises. Use their old washing machines for free, or their new ones for 140Ft. 10% off with HI card.

Bakfark Hostel, I, Bakfark u. 1/3 (tel. 201 5419). M2: Moszkva tér. From the metro stop, stroll along Margit krt. and take the first side street after Széna tér. 78 beds in quads and sixes. Some of the coolest summer hostel rooms in town with lofts instead of bunks. Check-out 9am. Dorm beds 1100Ft. Sheets, locker, storage space, and use of washing machine included. No shower curtains. 10% off with HI card. Reservations recommended.

Apáczai, V, Papnövelde u. 4/6 (tel. 267 0311), 3 blocks south of M3: Ferenciek tér. Probably the most central summer hostel, with the usual amount of linoleum. Doubles 1680Ft per person. Quads and sixes (1500Ft per person), spacious dorms 980Ft per person. HI members get significant discounts.

Baross, XI, Bartók Béla út 17 (tel. 186 8365; fax 275 7046), 2 blocks from Géllert tér. Open late June-Aug. Lived-in college dorms—Madonna pin-ups and all. From simple singles to quads with sink and refrigerator in the room. Hall bathrooms. Check-out 9am. Triples and quads 1470Ft. 10% discount with an HI card. New Maytag washer (140Ft) plus washing powder (50Ft). Free parking.

Bercsényi, XI, Bercsényi u. 28/30 (tel. 166 6677), 3 stops after the river on tram #4 on the side street next to Kaiser's supermarket. 65 doubles with big desks, wood floors, fridge, and sink. Better-than-average hall bathrooms. 1400Ft per bed. Newly

Schönherz, XI, Irinyi József u. 42 (tel. 166 5460 or 166 5021). Take tram #4 two stops past the river near the BP station. This blue high-rise has some of the better summer dorms in town with well kept quads with bathrooms and refrigerators. A "Traveller's Youth Hostels" job. Disco and bar in the building, the noise isn't a problem because the rooms begin on the 7th floor. No curfew. 1550Ft per person. 10% off with HI card. Laundry: wash 140Ft, dry 70Ft.

refurbished. Laundry 160Ft (wash only). Free transportation from bus or train stations. 10% off with HI card.

Siraly Youth Hostel, on the southeast bank of Margit Island (tel. 302 3952; reservations 322 2205). Three rooms with 12 bunks each, one men only, one women only, one mixed. Kitchen. Near both Buda and Pest. Quiet area, but the island grows very dark and spooky at night. 800 Ft per person. 10% off with HI card.

Martos, XI, Stoczek u. 5/7 (tel. 463 37 76; tel. and fax 463 36 51; e-mail reception@hotel.martos.bme.hu), near the Technical University. The cheapest rooms in town at this independent, student-run summer hostel. Same quality as other university dorms, with free use of washers and dryers, phones on each floor for incoming calls, and communal kitchens. Guests can access the Internet. Hall bathrooms. No English spoken on weekends. No curfew. Check-out 9am. Singles 1400Ft. Doubles 990Ft per person. Plush 6-person apartment 1200Ft per person.

Universitas, XI, Irinyi József u. 9/11 (tel. 463 3825 or 463 3826). First stop after crossing the river on tram #4 or 6. Large square dorm with 500 beds. Check-out 9am. No curfew. In-room fridges. Communal bathrooms. Doubles on the shady side of the building 1850Ft per person, on the sunny side 1750Ft, directly over the disco 1100Ft. Wash 70Ft. A "Traveller's Youth Hostels" operation with satellite TV and a very active nightlife in the disco and bar.

Guest Houses

Guest houses and rooms for rent in private homes include a personal touch for about the same as an anonymous hostel bed (do not confuse these with pensions, or *panzió*, which are larger and rarely charge less than 3000-4000Ft per person). Owners usually pick travelers up at the train stations or the airport, and often provide services such as sightseeing tours or breakfast and laundry for a small extra fee. Most allow guests to use their kitchens, and are on hand to provide general advice or help in emergencies. Visitors receive the keys to their rooms and the house, and have free reign to come and go. Although proprietors spend much of their time looking for clients in Keleti station, they carry cellular telephones so they can always be reached for reservations. In stations, bypass the pushier hostel representatives and look for a more subdued group of adults hanging around in the background.

Caterina, V, Andrássy út 47, III. 48 (tel. 291 9538, cellular 06 20 34 63 98). At "Oktogon" (M1 or tram #4 or 6). The home of "Big" Caterina Birta and her daughter "Little" Caterina is in a century-old building on the grand Andrássy boulevard only a few min. from downtown Pest. Each bed is 1000Ft in a double, a small loft with two beds, and a large airy room for 8-10 people. There is one guest bathroom. Neither Caterina is fluent in English, but they compensate with enthusiasm. When the house is full, Big Caterina holds free goulash parties.

"Townhouser's" International Guesthouse, XVI, Attila u. 123 (cellular tel. 06 30 44 23 31; fax 342 0795). M2: Örs Vezér tere, then five stops on bus #31 to Diófa u. A quiet residential area 30min. from downtown in east Pest. Home of Béla and Rózsa Tanhauser, whose kind dog Sasha protects the family of guinea pigs living in the garden. The house has five large guest rooms, with two or three beds each, and two guest bathrooms. Béla speaks German, English, and some Korean, Japanese, and Spanish. Kitchen available and the cleanest bathrooms you'll find for the price. Béla transports guests to and from the train station. 1000Ft per person.

Weisses Haus, III, Erdőalja u. 11 (cellular tel. 06 20 34 36 31). Take bus #137 from Flórián tér to "Iskola". On a hillside in residential Óbuda, about 20min. from the city center, stands the house of Gaby Somogyi. With a panoramic view of northern Pest across the Danube, the four doubles and a triple are decorated more carefully than most rental rooms. Two guest bathrooms. 3600Ft per room. Breakfast included. German and some English spoken.

Ms. Vali Németh, VIII, Osztály u. 20/24 A11 (tel. 113 8846, cellular 06 30 47 53 48). 400m east of M2: Népstadion. Convenient for travelers arriving or leaving from Népstadion bus station. The first floor of a 4-story apartment complex in central Pest. Grocery stores and a cheap restaurant with an English menu are nearby. Two doubles and one triple. One guest bathroom. 1300Ft per person.

Mrs. Ena Bottka, V, Garibaldi u. 5, (tel. 112 4122), 5th fl. a block south of M2: Kossuth tér. Live the Bohemian life in the tiny rooms overlooking gabled rooftops and Parliament building. Small kitchen. Doubles 2900Ft. Also apartments. Call in the morning or evening to reserve. Mrs. Bottka speaks fluent French and *poco italiano* and *español*, while her son speaks flawless English and very good German.

Hotels

Budapest's few inexpensive hotels are frequently clogged with groups; call ahead. Proprietors often speak English. All hotels should be registered with Tourinform.

Hotel Goliat, XIII, Kerekes út 12-20 (tel. 270 1456). M1: Arpad hid. Then take the tram away from the river and get off before the overpass. Walk down Reitler Ferere ut. until you see the 10-story yellow building on the left. Clean, spacious rooms provide a step up from hostels at the same prices (singles 1800Ft, doubles 2300Ft). Bathrooms are still down the hall.

Hotel Citadella, Citadella Sétany (tel. 166 5794; fax 186 0305), atop Gellért Hill. Take tram #47 or 49 three stops into Buda to "Móricz Zsigmond Körtér", then catch bus #27 to "Citadella". Perfect location, built right in the Citadel. Spacious, with hardwood floors. Doubles, triples, and quads US$40-58. Usually packed, so write or fax to reserve. Safe deposit at reception 100Ft per day.

Hotel Flandria, XIII, Szegedi út 27 (tel. 129 6689). M2: Lehel, then either the #12 or 14 tram one street past Karoly Körut. Then a 5-min. walk down Szegedi út. Acceptable rooms and an inexpensive restaurant downstairs. Singles 3940Ft, doubles 5130Ft, quads 7000Ft.

Camping

Camping Hungary, available at tourist offices, describes Budapest's campgrounds.

Római Camping, III, Szentendrei út 189 (tel. 168 62 60; fax 250 04 26). M2: Batthyány tér, then take the HÉV commuter rail to "Római fürdő," and walk 100m towards the river. 2500-person capacity with tip-top security, a grocery, and tons of restaurants around. Disco, swimming pool, and huge park on the site; Roman ruins nearby. Bungalows open mid-April to mid-Oct. Common showers. Bungalows 1600-5000Ft. 650Ft per tent, students 500Ft.

Hárs-hegyi, II, Hárs-hegyi út 5/7 (tel. 115 14 82; fax 176 19 21). 7 stops on bus #22 from "Moszkva tér" to "Dénes u." Exchange for cash and traveler's checks and a good, cheap restaurant. Credit cards accepted. 510Ft per tent, students 460Ft.

Riviera Camping, III, Királyok u. 257/259 (tel. 160 82 18). Take the HÉV commuter rail from "Batthyány tér" to "Romai fürdő," then bus #34 10min. until you see the campground. 420Ft per tent. Bungalows 2000Ft. Open year-round.

FOOD

Even the most expensive restaurants in Budapest may be within your budget (see p. 268) though the food at family eateries may be cheaper and tastier. An average meal runs 600-800Ft. A 10% tip has come to be expected in many restaurants. Cafeterias lurk under **Önkiszolgáló Étterem** signs (meat entrées 160-200Ft, vegetarian entrées 80Ft). The listings below are just a nibble of what Budapest has to offer. Seek out the *kifőzés* or *vendéglő* in your neighborhood for a taste of Hungarian life. For the times when you want an infusion of grease or need to see a familiar menu late at night, the world's largest branch Burger King is located on the Oktogon, and McDonald's is everywhere. Travelers may also rely on markets and raisin-sized 24-hour stores, labeled "Non-Stop," for staples. The king of them all is the **Central Market**, V Kőzraktár tér u. 1 (M3: Kelvin tér). Marvel at the enormous display of fruit, vegetables, bread, cheese, meat, and just about any other kind of food you can imagine. Come for the aesthetic experience, stay for the best eating bargain around (open Mon. 6am-4pm, Tues.-Fri. 6am-6pm, Sat. 6am-2pm). Take a gander at the produce market, IX, Vámház krt. 1/3, at Fővám tér (Mon. 6am-3pm); the **ABC Food Hall**, I, Batthyány tér 5/7 (open Sun. 7am-1pm); or the **Non-Stops** at V, Október 6. u. 5, and V, Régi Posta u., off Váci u. past McDonald's.

Pest

Bohémtanya, V, Paulay Ede u. 6 (tel. 322 1453). M: Deák tér or M1: Bajcsy-Zsilinsky. Packed for its large portions of delicious and filling Hungarian food. Every part of the animal is served in a brooding setting. Full meals 290-780Ft. *Ropogös malacsűt* (crisp roast suckling pig) 390Ft. English menu and English-speaking staff attract lots of, well, English-speaking tourists. Open daily noon-11pm.

Vegetárium, V, Cukor u. 3 (tel. 267 0322). A block and half from M3: Ferenciek tere (on map Felszahadulás tér). Walk up Ferenciek tere (formerly Károlyi M. u.) to Irány u. on the right; a quick left puts you on Cukor u. A great place to detox after a week of meat. Elaborate and imaginative vegetarian and macrobiotic dishes 480-790Ft; tempura dinner 500Ft. Although they prepare a few ultra-healthy dishes that would meet even with Californian approval, the food still tends to be far from low-fat. Classical guitar in the evening from 7-10pm. Vigorously smoke-free environment. Menu in English. Open daily noon-10pm. 15% student discount with ISIC. 10% service charge.

Cafe Kör, V, Sas u. 17 (tel. 111 0053). Super friendly and only slightly pricey. Entrées 490-1180. Turkey breast filled with fruit 670Ft. The menu boasts that they will prepare any dish you want. Open Mon.-Sat. 8am-9pm.

Picasso Point Kávéhaz, VI, Hajós u. 31 (tel. 169 5544). Make a right onto Hajos u. two blocks north of M3: Arany János. A Bohemian hang-out for students, intellectuals and foreigners. The English/Hungarian menu is an eclectic mix of traditional Hungarian and everything else, including chili (200Ft), onion soup (100Ft), and crepes (150Ft). Dance club downstairs; when live bands play there may be a cover charge of 200Ft. Open daily from noon to some vaguely defined point after 4am.

Alföldi Kisvendéglő, V, Kecskeméti u. 4 tel. 267 0224). M3: Kálvin tér, 50m past the Best Western. Traditional Hungarian folk cuisine—even the booths are paprika-red. The spicy, sumptuous homemade rolls (40Ft) are reason enough to come. Entrées 320-680Ft. Open daily 11am-midnight.

New York Bagels (The Sequel), VI, Bajesy-Zsilinszky út 21. (tel. 111 8441). M3: Arany János u. Hungary's largest bagel shop, with nine more branches throughout the country. Assorted bagels baked hourly, freshly made spreads, sandwiches, salads, and Budapest's only chocolate chip cookies. Daily special bagel sandwiches (250Ft) or design your own. Owned by a former *Let's Go* Researcher-Writer and gleeful Wall Street escapee. Open daily 7am-10pm.

Marquis de Salade, VI, Hajós u. 43 (tel. 153 4931), corner of Bajzy-Zilinsky út two blocks north of M3: Arany János. A self-service mix of salads, Middle Eastern, and Bengali food in a cozy storefront the size of a large closet. The Azeri owner speaks English and posts notes about her regulars on the walls. She has also been known to mutilate vegetables into tantalizing dishes at her patrons' urging. Most dishes are 420-500Ft. Open daily noon-midnight.

Sancho, VII, Dohány u. 20 (tel. 267 0677). Walk up Károly krt. from M2: Astoria. "American-Mexican" pub and restaurant serving tacos, burritos, chimichangas, and their like (from 400Ft). Popular local bands perform evenings. At "tequila time" (11pm) the waiter puts on a sombrero and carries around a tray of half-price shots. English menu. Open Tues.-Fri. and Sat. 6pm-4am, Sun. 6pm-2am.

Apostolok, V, Kígyó u. 4/6 (tel. 267 0290; fax 118 3658). Visible from M3: Ferenciek tere, on a pedestrian street toward the bridge. An eclectic, swinging combination of Gothic ambience and superb food in an old beer hall. Most entrées 530-910Ft. Open daily noon-midnight.

Fészek Művész Klub Étterem, VII, Kertész u. 36 (tel. 342 6549), corner of Dob u. two blocks southwest of Erzsébet krt. M1: Oktogon, or tram #4 or 6 to "Király u." This was once the dining hall of a Golden Age private club for performing artists. Excellent Hungarian food and very low prices; the English menu is five pages single-spaced, and ranges from beef and fowl to venison and wild boar. Entrées from

400-900Ft but reckon on a 100Ft fee to get into the club. In warm weather, walk through to the leafy courtyard. Open daily noon-1am.

Bagolyvár, XIV, Allatkerti krt. 2 (tel. 351 6395; fax 342 2917). M1: Hősök tere. Directly behind the Museum of Fine Arts—a perfect and elegant place to deconstruct the chromatic schema presented on your supper plate. Exceptional Hungarian cuisine, yet remarkably affordable with a menu that changes daily. Entrées 560-1200Ft. Open daily noon-11pm. The Gundel Restaurant next door is Budapest's most famous—and most expensive.

Paprika, V, Varosáz u. 10. Cafeteria food from 210Ft, but come here for the bakery. Tasty snacks 35-60Ft. Open Mon.-Fri.11am-4pm, Sat. 11am-3pm.

Buda

Söröző a Szent Jupáthoz, II, Dékán u. 3 (tel. 212 2929). 50m from M2: Moszkva tér, with an entrance on Retek u. Venture down the modest stairway, then right back up into an open-air hall. Enormous portions and friendly staff. "Soup for Just Married Man" 190Ft. Entrées 350-900Ft. Open 24hr.

Remiz, II, Budakeszi út 5 (tel. 176 1896). Take bus #158 from "Moszkva tér" to "Szépilona" (about 10min.) and continue past three stores beyond the stop. Traditional and tasty Hungarian cuisine in a cosmopolitan setting. Frequented by Hungarian tennis-racket-wielding yuppies. Prices are average (entrées 600-1200Ft), but it's just fancy enough for special occasions. Outdoor seating in warm weather; live music; English menu. Call for reservations. Open daily 9am-1am.

Marxim, II, Kis Rókus u. 23 (tel. 212 4183). M2: Moszkva tér. With your back to the Lego-like castle, walk 200m along Margit krt. and turn left down the very industrial road. KGB pizza and Lenin salad are just a few of the revolutionary dishes served in structurally constrained, barbed-wire-laden booths. Food prepared by the staff according to their abilities, consumed by the patrons according to their needs. Join the locals in thumbing their nose at the erstwhile oppressive vanguard. English menu. Salads 100-170Ft. Pizza 200-520Ft. Open Mon.-Thurs. noon-1am, Fri.-Sat. noon-2am, Sun. 6pm-1am.

Marcello's, XI, Bartók Béla út 40 (tel. 166 62 31), just before Móricz Zsigmond Körtér on the river side. May be the only pizzeria in Budapest to use tomato sauce rather than ketchup. Classy to boot. Pizzas 300-420Ft. Small salad 200Ft, large 350Ft. Reservations suggested. Open Mon.-Sat. noon-10pm.

Cafés

A café in Budapest is more a living museum of a bygone era than just a place to indulge scrumptious desserts and coffee. These amazing establishments were the pretentious haunts of Budapest's literary, intellectual, and cultural elite. A leisurely repose at a Budapest café is a must for every visitor; best of all, the absurdly ornate pastries are inexpensive, even in the most genteel establishments.

Café New York, VII, Erzsébet krt. 9/11 (tel. 122 3849). M2: Blaha Lujza tér. One of the most beautiful cafés in Budapest, and the staff knows it. Velvet, gold, and marble, but still as affordable as it was for turn of the century artistes. Cappuccino 200Ft. Ice cream and coffee delights 20-400Ft. Filling Hungarian entrées (from 850Ft) served downstairs noon-10pm. Open daily 9am-midnight.

Művész Kávéház, VI, Andrássy út 29 (tel. 267 0689), diagonally across the street from the National Opera House. M1: Opera. The highly-acclaimed café draws pre- and post-Opera crowds with Golden-Age wood paneling and gilded ceilings. Together with Lukács Cukrászda and Gerbeaud Cukrászda it's considered Budapest's most elegant. Fabulous *Esterházy torta* 120 Ft. Open daily 10am-midnight.

Lukács Cukrászda, VI, Andrássy út 70. M1: Vörösmarty u., near Hősök tere. At this stunning café, dieters will wish the heavenly cakes and tortes were more expensive. Seated service is more expensive. Open Mon.-Fri. 9am-8pm.

Ruszwurm, I, Szentháromság u. 7 (tel. 177 5284), just off the square on Castle Hill. Confecting since 1826 and strewn with period furniture. Stop by to relax after the majesty of Mátyás Cathedral down the street. You won't be hurried on your way. Ice cream 30Ft per scoop. Cakes 90-130Ft. Open daily 10am-7pm.

Litia Literatura & Tea, I, Hess András tér 4 (tel. 175 6987), in the Fortuna Passage. Choose from an immense selection of teas in this airy gardenhouse café in a quiet courtyard. For the full literary experience, pick up some reading material in the adjoining artsy bookstore. Coffee 70Ft. Open daily 10am-6pm.

Café Pierrot, I, Fortuna u. 14 (tel. 175 6971). Antique clown dolls hang from the curvaceous walls. Espresso 120Ft. Crepes 320Ft. Open daily 11am-1am. Live piano music daily from 8:30pm.

Caffé Károlyi, V, Károlyi u. 19 (tel. 267 0206). South of M3: Ferenc krt. Around the corner from a law school, this café modern coffee shop is a favorite hangout for the Young and the Beautiful. Huge mirror is great for watching others—or yourself. Pastries from 40Ft. Cakes from 60Ft. Open daily 9am-1am.

Bécsi Kávéház, Apáczai Csere János u. 12/14 (tel. 117 8088), inside Hotel Forum on the Duna. Budapest's *crèmes de la cake* tantalize from glass cases. Give your life meaning for only 120Ft in the dark, wood-paneled, air-conditioned lounge. Cake 130-190Ft. Coffee 160Ft. AmEx, V, MC. Open daily 9am-9pm.

Café Mozart, VII Erzsébet kst 36. (tel. 267 0778). M2 to Blaha Lujza Tér. Newly opened café serves 75 different coffee drinks (110Ft-285Ft) and almost as many ice cream creations. Somewhat sterile environment and waitresses decked out in bizarre period uniforms, but the drinks are some of the best in town.

SIGHTS

In 1896, as part of Hungary's 1000th birthday party, Budapest received several architectural marvels. Though slightly grayer for the wear, they still attest to the wealth of the Austro-Hungarian Empire at the height of its power. Among the works commissioned by the Habsburgs were the Parliament and the Supreme Court Building (now the Ethnographic Museum), Heroes' Square, Szbadság Bridge, Vajdahunyad Castle, and continental Europe's first metro station. The domes of both Parliament and St. Stephen's Basilica are 96m high—vertical references to the historic date.

Várhegy (Castle Hill)

The **Castle District** rests 100m above the Duna, atop the 2-km mound called **Várhegy**. It houses a castle which has been of symbolic significance to the nation for over five centuries. Find one of the many paths up, or cross the **Széchenyi lánchíd** and ride the *sikló* (cable car) to the top of the hill (150Ft; open daily 7:30am-10pm, closed 2nd and 4th Mon. of the month). The upper lift station sits just inside the castle walls. Built in the 13th century, the castle was leveled in consecutive sieges by Mongols and Ottoman Turks. Christian Habsburg forces razed the rebuilt castle while ousting the Turks after a 145-year occupation. A reconstruction was completed just in time to be destroyed by the Germans in 1945. Determined Hungarians pasted the castle together once more, only to face the new Soviet menace—bullet holes in the palace façade recall the 1956 uprising. In the post-war period, sorely needed resources were channeled into the immediate reconstruction of the castle. During this rebuilding, extensive excavations revealed artifacts from the earliest castle on this site, which are now housed in the **Budapest History Museum** in the **Budavári palota** (Royal Palace). The castle walls, just to the left of the cable car peak station, also envelop numerous other collections (see Museums, p. 272) and statues lurk everywhere.

From the castle, stroll down Színház u. and Tárnok u. to reach **Trinity Square,** site of the Disney-esque **Fisherman's Bastion.** This arcaded stone wall supports a squat, fairy-tale tower, but you'll have to pay for the magnificent view across the Duna (50Ft). Behind the tower stands the delicate, neo-Gothic **Mátyás templom** (St. Matthew's Church), which with its multi-colored tiled roof is one of the most-photographed buildings in Budapest. It was converted into a mosque overnight on September 2, 1541, when the Turks seized Buda; it remained a mosque for 145 years. These days, high mass is celebrated Sundays at 10am with orchestra and choir (come early for a seat). On summer Fridays at 8pm, organ concerts reverberate in the resplendent interior (open daily 7am-7pm).

The holy edifice also conceals a **crypt** and a **treasury;** descend the stairway to the right of the altar. Besides the treasury's ecclesiastic relics, don't miss Queen Elizabeth's stunning marble bust, next to the entrance to **St. Stephen's Chapel.** The marble was hewn from the Italian Carrara mine, where Michelangelo shopped for rock (treasury open daily 9am-5:30pm; 60Ft). A second side chapel contains the **tomb of King Béla III** and his wife, Anna Chatillon; this was the only sepulcher of the Árpád dynasty spared from Ottoman looting. Outside the church is the grand **equestrian monument** of King Stephen, with his trademark double cross.

Next door, the brash **Budapest Hilton Hotel** incorporates the remains of Castle Hill's oldest church, a 13th-century abbey. Intricate door-knockers and balconies adorn the Castle District's other historic buildings; ramble through **Úri u.** (Gentlemen's Street) with its Baroque townhouses, or **Táncsics Mihály u.** in the old Jewish sector. You can enjoy a tremendous view of Buda from the Castle District's west walls. By **Vienna Gate** at the District's north tip, frequent minibuses run to Moszkva tér, though the walk down Várfok u. takes only five minutes.

Elsewhere in Buda

The **Liberation Monument** watches over the city and crowns **Gellért Hill.** The 30m bronze woman presiding over the city was created to honor Soviet soldiers who died while "libertating" Hungary, though the Communist star has since been removed. Hike up to the monument and the adjoining **Citadella**—built as a symbol of Habsburg power after the 1848 revolution—from Hotel Gellért or from beneath the St. Gellért statue on the other side. Bus #27 also drives up. The view from the top is especially spectacular at night, when the Duna and its bridges shimmer in black and gold. Overlooking the Erzsébet híd near the base of Gellért Hill is the statue of **St. Gellért,** accompanied by colonnaded backdrop and glistening waterfall. The Pope sent Bishop Gellért to the coronation of King Stephen, the first Christian Hungarian monarch, to assist in the conversion of the Magyars. Those unconvinced by his message hurled the good bishop to his death from atop the hill that now bears his name.

Fresh forest air awaits in the suburban Buda Hills, far into the second and twelfth districts. Catch bus #22 from "Moszkva tér", north of the Castle, and ride up to the "Budakesci ". There you'll find the **Vadaskert** (Game Park), where boar roam while deer and antelope play—here, people speak optimistically and the skies are supposedly cloudless. The **Pál-völgyi Caves** gape east of Vadaskert. Even first-time spelunkers enjoy the 15m-high caverns, remarkable stalactite formations, and such attractions as the Cave of the Stone Bat and the 25m-deep Radium Chamber. Be sure to wear your polar fleece, even in the summer—it's quite cool inside. Take the #86 bus from Batthyany tér to "Kolosyi tér". Then take bus #65 to the caves. Inquire at a tourist office for the irregular tour times and prices.

Between the caves and the castle, **Margit híd** leads over the Duna to the **Margitsziget** (Margaret Island). Off-limits to private cars, the island offers capacious thermal baths, luxurious garden pathways, and numerous shaded terraces. You can rent bikes here, go for runs along the river, or prance around the tennis courts. A little **zoo** adds a lovely aroma to the island's east part, while open-air clubs on the west half jockey for audiences in the evenings. According to legend, the *sziget* is named after

---

Like a Troubled Bridge over Water...

The citizens of Budapest are justly proud of the bridges that bind Buda to Pest. The four great lions that have guarded the **Széchenyi lánchíd** (The Chain Bridge; B4) since 1849 make this bridge one of the most recognizeable in the city. These exotic beasts were created by the master János Marschalkó in a naturalistic style, with the tongues resting far back in their gaping mouths. The anatomical correctness of their new city mascots did not impress the citizens of Budapest, and distraught by public ridicule over this apparently missing feature in his creations, Marschalkó jumped from the bridge to his death. Another version of the story has the king reprimanding Marschalkó—with the same result.

King Béla IV's daughter; he vowed to rear young Margit as a nun if the nation survived the Mongol invasion of 1241. The Mongols left Hungary decimated but not destroyed, and Margaret was confined to the island convent. Take bus #26 from "Szt. István krt." to the island.

Pest Cross the Duna to reach Pest, the throbbing commercial and administrative center of the capital. The old **Inner City,** rooted in the pedestrian zone of Váci u. and Vörösmarty tér, is a tourist haven. Filled with souvenir shops, Pest's riverbank sports a string of modern luxury hotels leading up to the magnificent neo-Gothic **Parliament** in Kossuth tér (arrange 1500Ft tours at IBUSZ and Budapest Tourist).

St. Stephen's Basilica, two blocks north of Deák tér, is by far the city's largest church, with room for 8500 worshippers under its massive dome. A very Christ-like depiction of St. Stephen *(István)* adorns the high altar. A 302-step climb up a spiral staircase to the Panorama tower yields a 360° view of the city from central Pest's tallest building (tower open April-Oct. daily 10am-6:30pm; 200Ft, students 125Ft). St. Stephen's holy **right hand,** one of the nation's most revered religious relics, is displayed in the **Basilica museum.** (Basilica open Mon.-Sat. 9am-5pm, Sun. 1-5pm. 70Ft, students 50Ft. Museum open April-Sept. Mon.-Sat. 9am-4:30pm, Sun. 1-4:30pm; Oct.-March Mon.-Sat. 10am-4pm, Sun. 1-4pm.)

Another grand religious destination is the **Great Synagogue,** at the corner of Dohány u. and Wesselényi u., the largest active synagogue in Europe and the second largest in the world. The Moorish-style building was designed to hold almost 3000 worshippers, with men on the ground floor and women in the gallery. The **Holocaust Memorial,** an enormous metal tree behind the Jewish museum, stands in the back garden directly over mass graves dug during 1944-45. Inscribed on each leaf of the dramatic sculpture is the name of a victim. The harmonies of organ and mixed choir float through the entire structure during Friday evening services (6-7pm). The synagogue is also open to visitors Monday to Friday 10am-6pm (off-season 10am-3:30pm; donation requested), but the building has been under perpetual renovation since 1988, and much of the artwork is likely to be blocked from view. The **Jewish Museum** devotes one haunting room to photos and documents from the Holocaust and the rest of the space to relics and artwork from Hungary's rich Jewish past. (Open April-Oct. Mon.-Fri. 10am-3pm, Sun. 10am-1pm, closed Nov.-March, although they are considering opening year-round—try your luck; 50Ft.)

Andrássy út, the nation's grandest boulevard, extends from the edge of Belváros in downtown Pest in the northeast corner of Erzsébet tér and arrives in **Hősök tere** (Heroes' Square), some 2km away. A stroll down Andrássy út from Hősök tere toward the inner city best evokes Budapest's Golden Age, somewhat tarnished by Soviet occupation. The most vivid reminder of this period is **Magyar állami operaház** (Hungarian National Opera House), VI, Andrássy út 22. M1: Opera. Laden with sculptures and paintings in the ornate Empire style of the 1880s, the building is even larger than it appears from the street—the gilded auditorium seats 1289 people. If you can't actually see an opera, make sure to take a tour. (English tours daily 3 and 4pm, 400Ft, students 200Ft.)

Andrássy út's most majestic stretch lies at the farthest end from the inner city between Hősök tere and Oktogon. M1 runs directly underneath Andrássy út. Hősök tere is dominated by the **Millennium Monument,** which showcases the nation's most prominent leaders and national heroes from 896 to 1896, when the structure was erected for the great 1000th anniversary celebration. The seven fearsome horsemen led by Prince Árpád represent the seven Magyar tribes who settled the Carpathian Basin. Overhead is the Archangel Gabriel, who, according to legend, offered Stephen the crown of Hungary in a dream. It was King (later Saint) Stephen, the colonnade's first figure, who made Hungary an officially Christian state with his coronation on Christmas Day, 1000.

Behind the monument, **Városliget** (City Park) contains a permanent circus, an amusement park, a zoo, a castle, and the impressive **Széchenyi Baths** (see Bath Houses, p. 274). The **Vajdahunyad Castle** was also created for the Millenary Exhibition of 1896. Originally constructed out of canvas and wood, the castle was redone with more durable materials in response to popular outcry. The façade, intended to chronicle 1000 years of architecture, is a stone collage of Romanesque, Gothic, Renaissance, and Baroque styles. The castle now houses the **Museum of Agriculture** (See Museums, p. 272). Rent a **rowboat** (June-mid-Sept. daily 9am-8pm) or **ice skates** (Nov.-March daily 9am-1pm and 4-8pm; 60Ft) by the lake next to the castle. Outside the museum broods the hooded statue of **Anonymous,** the secretive scribe to whom we owe much of our knowledge of medieval Hungary.

The ruins of the north Budapest garrison town, **Aquincum** (Szentendrei út 139; tel. 168 8241 or 180 4650; M2: Batthyány tér, then HÉV to "Aquincum"; the site is about 100m south of the HÉV stop), crumble in the outer regions of the third district. These are the most impressive vestiges of the Roman occupation, which spanned the first four centuries CE. The settlement's significance increased steadily over that time, eventually attaining the status of *colonia* and becoming the capital of Pannonia Inferior; Marcus Aurelius and Constantine were but two of the emperors to bless the town with a visit. The **museum** on the grounds contains a model of the ancient city as well as musical instruments and other household items. The remains of the **Roman Military Baths** are visible to the south of the Roman encampment, beside the overpass at Flórián tér near the "Árpád híd" HÉV station. From the stop, just follow the main road away from the river.

Museums

Though at times they may seem haphazardly thrown together, Budapest's museums are beautiful and, happily, extremely affordable. If you're in the mood to try to discover that up-and-coming new artist, there are galleries on both sides of the river; search for them in the **Budapest Panorama** and drop in a few.

Buda Castle, I, Szent György tér 2 (tel. 175 7533). Leveled by Soviet and Nazi combat, the reconstructed palace now houses an assortment of fine museums.

Wing A contains the **Museum of Contemporary History** and the **Ludwig Museum,** a collection of international modern art including the works of Zsigmond Kÿrolyi, Károly Keliman, Roy Lichtenstein, Robert Rauschenberg, and Andy Warhol. Frequent special exhibitions; get the exhibit calendars at a tourist office. Open Tues.-Sun. 10am-6pm. 100Ft, students 50Ft, Tues. free.

Wings B-D hold the **Hungarian National Gallery,** a vast hoard containing the best in Hungarian painting and sculpture over a millennium. Its treasures include a collection of Mihály Munkácsy, a founder of Hungarian Realism; Pál Mersei, a Hungarian Impressionist; and Károly Markó, a classical landscape painter. Open Tues.-Sun. 10am-6pm. 100Ft, students 40Ft. One ticket is valid for all 3 wings. English tour 120Ft.

Wing E houses the **Budapest History Museum,** a chronicle of the development of Óbuda, Buda, and Pest. Open Jan.-Feb. Tues.-Sun. 10am-4pm; March-Oct. 10am-6pm; Nov.-Dec. 10am-5pm. 100Ft, students 50Ft, Wed. free.

Szépművészti múzeum (Museum of Fine Arts), XIV, Dózsa György út 41 (tel. 343 6755). M1: Hösök tere. Simply spectacular. One of Europe's finest collections of artworks, from Duccio and Goya to Rembrandt and Bruegel, with a particular emphasis on Italian art. Highlights include an entire room devoted to El Greco and a display of Renaissance works. Paintings by all your favorite Impressionists, too. Open Tues.-Sun. 10am-5:30pm. 200Ft, ISIC-holders 100Ft. Tours for up to 5 people 1500Ft. English guidebooks for individual sections (around 100Ft).

Museum of Military History, I, Tóth Árpád Sétány 40 (tel. 156 9522), in the northwest corner of the Castle District just west of Kapisztrán tér. An intimidating collection of ancient and modern weapons, from the most functional to the most ornate. Some swords seem too splendid to sully with petty disembowelments. The upper floor presents the military history of WWII and a day-by-day account of the 1956 uprising; don't miss the severed fist from the massive Stalin statue toppled in the uprising. Open Tues.-Sun. 10am-5pm, Sun. 10am-6pm. 100Ft, students 50Ft, ISIC-holders free. English guide 500Ft.

Néprajzi múzeum (Museum of Ethnography), V, Kossuth tér 12 (tel. 132 6340), opposite the Parliament in the erstwhile home of the Supreme Court. Outstanding exhibit of Hungarian folk culture, from the late 18th century to WWI. Covers the whole cycle of peasant life and customs, from childhood to marriage (to taxes) to death. Though slightly skewed in presentation, the second floor houses an exceptional collection of cultural artifacts from Asian, African, and Aboriginal peoples. Open Tues.-Sat. 10am-5:45pm, Sun. 10am-6pm. 60Ft, students 20Ft.

Hungarian National Museum, VIII, Múzeum krt. 14/16 (tel. 138 2122). It chronicles Hungarian settlements and holds the **Hungarian Crown Jewels,** supposedly the crown and scepter used in the coronation of King Stephen on Christmas Day in 1000CE. Don't miss Mihály Munkácsy's enormous canvas *Golgotha* in the room at the top of the stairs. Open Tues.-Sun. 10am-6pm, cashier closes at 5:30pm. 150Ft, students 100Ft. English tour 100Ft. English guidebook 840Ft.

Vasarely Museum, III, Szentlélek tér 6 (tel. 118 7551). Take the HÉV commuter rail from M2: Batthyány tér to "Árpád híd." Room after room filled with Viktor Vasarely's arresting Op-art. Yes, it's modern and it's abstract.

ENTERTAINMENT

Performances

Budapest hosts a healthy amount of cultural events year-round. Pick up a copy of the English-language monthlies *Programme in Hungary* or *Budapest Panorama,* both available free at tourist offices; they contain listings of all concerts, operas, and theater performances in the city. The "Style" section of the weekly English-language *Budapest Sun* is another good source for schedules of entertainment happenings.

The **Central Theater Booking Office,** VI, Andrassy út 18 (tel. 112 0000), next to the Opera House (open Mon.-Thurs. 10am-1pm and 2-6pm, Fri. 10am-5pm), and the branch at Moszkva tér 3 (tel. 212 5678; open Mon.-Fri. 10am-5pm) both sell tickets without commission to almost every performance in the city. The gilded, Neo-Renaissance **State Opera House,** VI, Andrássy út 22 (tel. 131 2550), M1: Opera, is one of Europe's leading performance centers. An extravaganza here can be had for US$4-5; the box office (tel. 153 0170), on the left side of the building, sells tickets for operas and occasional ballets at discounts a half-hour before showtime (open Tues.-Sat. 11am-1:45pm and 2:30-7pm, Sun. 10am-1pm and 4-7pm). The **Philharmonic Orchestra** is also world-renowned; concerts are given almost every evening September to June. The ticket office, Vörösmarty tér 1 (tel. 117 6222), is on the square's west side; look for the Jegyroda sign. (Open Mon.-Fri. 10am-6pm, Sat.-Sun. 10am-2pm; tickets 800-1200Ft, 300Ft the day of the performance).

In late summer, the Philharmonic and the Opera take sabbaticals, but the tide of culture never ebbs; **summer theaters** are located throughout the city. In July, classical music and opera are performed nightly at 8:30pm in the **Hilton Hotel Courtyard,** I, Hess András tér 1/3 (tel. 175 1000), next to St. Matthew's in the Castle District. 300-800Ft tickets can be purchased from the reception; a little discount for those who buy just before the performance. The **Margitsziget Theater,** XIII, on Margitsziget, (tel. 111 2496), features opera and Hungarian-music concerts on its open-air stage. Take tram #4 or 6 to "Margitsziget." Try **Zichy Mansion Courtyard,** III, Fő tér 1, for orchestral concerts. **Mátyás templom,** Szentháromság tér, holds organ, orchestral, and choral recitals most Wednesdays and Fridays at 8pm (Wed. 600Ft, Fri. 500Ft). The **Pest Concert Hall** (Vigadó), V, Vigadó tér 2 (tel. 118 9903; fax 175 6222), on the Duna bank near Vörösmarty tér, hosts operettas almost every other night (cashier open Mon.-Sat.10am-6pm; tickets 3000Ft).

Folk-dancers stomp across the stage at the **Buda Park Theater,** XI, Kosztolányi Dezső tér (tel. 117 6222). Brochures and concert tickets flood the ticket office at Vörösmarty tér 1 (open Mon.-Fri. 11am-6pm; tickets 70-250Ft). For a psychedelic evening, try the laser shows at the **Planetarium** (tel. 134 1161; M3: Népliget). The multimedia sorcery even brings Floyd to life on occasion (Wed.-Thurs., and Sat. 6:30, 8, and 9:30pm; Mon., Fri. 8 and 9:30pm; Tues. 6:30 and 9:30pm). The **Budapest**

Spring Festival, in late March, is an excellent chance to see the best in Hungarian art and music. Autumn's **Budapest Arts Weeks** is another major festival.

Hungary has an outstanding cinematic tradition; most notable among its directors are Miklós Jancsó and István Szabó. **Cinemas** abound in Budapest, screening the latest Hungarian and foreign films. The English-language *Budapest Sun* lists a surprising number of reasonably current movies in English; check the kiosks around town. If *szinkronizált* or *magyarul beszélő* appears next to the title, the movie has been dubbed into Hungarian. Tickets are largely a bargain at 200-250Ft.

If you still miss international pop culture, many of the world's biggest shows come to Budapest, and prices are reasonable; check the **Music Mix 33 Ticket Service**, V, Vaci u. 33 (tel. 266 7070; open daily 10am-6pm). Touring companies *à la* Andrew Lloyd Webber also stop by—watch for Cats on roller skates. Tickets at the **Madách Theatre** box office, VII, Madách tér 6 (tel. 322 2015; open Mon.-Sat. 2:30pm-8pm).

Bathhouses

To soak away weeks of city grime, crowded trains, and yammering camera-clickers, sink into a **thermal bath**, an essential Budapest experience. The post-bath massages vary from a quick three-minute slap to a royal half-hour indulgence. Some baths are meeting spots, though not exclusively, for Budapest's gay community (see Gay Budapest, p. 275).

Gellért, XI, Kelenhegyi út 4 (tel. 166 6166). Take bus #7 to Hotel Gellért at the base of Gellért Hill. Venerable, segregated, indoor thermal baths, where you may soak nude if you like. This is the only spa with signs in English. An indoor pool surrounded by statues and enormous plants; rooftop sundeck and wave pool for the young or young at heart. Besides all this, there is a huge range of inexpensive *à la carte* options, from mudpacks to pedicures. Thermal bath 350Ft, with pool privileges 800Ft. 15-min. massage 250Ft. Open May-Sept. Mon.-Fri. 6am-7pm, Sat.-Sun. 6am-5pm; Oct.-April Mon.-Fri. 6am-7pm, Sat.-Sun. 6am-2pm. Pools open daily until 7pm except weekends Oct.-April, when they close at 5pm.

Király, II, Fő u. 84 (tel. 207 3688). M2: Batthány tér. Bathe in the splendor of Turkish cupolas and domes. Steam bath 250Ft. Thermal bath 170Ft. Massage 250Ft per 15min. Men only Mon., Wed., and Fri. 6:30am-6pm. Women only Tues. and Thurs. 6:30am-6pm and Sat. 6:30am-noon.

Széchenyi Fűrdő, XIV, Állatkerti u. 11 (tel. 121 0310), in *Városliget,* 7min. north of M1: Hősök tere. The city's public thermal baths (180Ft) command a devoted following among the city's venerable gentry, while the large **outdoor swimming pool** (180Ft) delights their grandchildren. Bring your swimsuit. Massage 500Ft per 30min. Open Mon.-Fri. 6am-6pm, Sat. 6am-noon. In August, the baths are men only on Mon., Wed., and Fri.; women only Tues., Thurs., and Sat.

Rudas, Döbrentei tér 9 (tel. 156 1322), right on the river under a dome built by Turks 400 years ago. Take the #7 bus to the first stop in Buda. The centuries haven't altered the dome, the bathing chamber, or the "men only" rule.

NIGHTLIFE

After a few drinks, you'll forget you ever left home. Global village alternateens wearing the usual labels and grinding to an electronic beat make the club scene in Budapest familiar to anyone who has ever partied in America or Britain. A virtually unenforced drinking age and cheap drinks may be the only cause for culture shock. As clubs become more and more technically endowed, the cover prices are rising—a night of techno may cost the same manageable price as a night at the opera.

Bars

Old Man's Pub, VII, Akácfa u. 13 (tel. 122 7645). M2: Blaha Lujza tér. Live blues and jazz under the newspapered ceilings. A classy and upscale environment. Kitchen serves pizza, spaghetti, and salads. Delicious cold fruit soup, 200Ft. Occasional free samples of beer. Open Mon.-Sat. 12pm-2am.

Jazz Café, V, Balassi Bálint u. 25 (tel. 269 5506). M2: Kossuth tér. Walk across the square past the Parliament. Live jazz under blue lights Tues., Wed., and Fri. Populated by a more mature crowd (at least in years). Open daily 6pm-2am.

Fat Mo's Speakeasy, V, Nyary Pal Utca 11 (tel. 267 3199). M3: Kalvin tér. Pricey food, but hip bands and reasonably priced beer (quart of *Guinness* 310Ft) combine well with the Prohibition-era decor. Open Mon.-Sun. 12pm-2am.

Morrison's Music Pub, VI, Révay u. 25 (tel. 269 4060), just to the left of the State Opera House. M1: Opera. Half pub, half hip dance club with 200Ft beer. A young, international crowd. This may be the one place in Europe where Jim's not buried. Functional English red telephone booth inside. Fri.-Sat. cover 200Ft. Open Mon.-Thurs. 7pm-4am, Fri.-Sat. 6pm-4am, Sun. 8pm-4am.

Discos

Bahnhof, north side of Nugati train station. M3: Nyugati pu. One of the most popular dance clubs and with good reason; no technical wizardry but two superb dance floors. Well ventilated. Cover 300Ft. Open Mon.-Sat. 6pm-4am.

Made-Inn Music Club, VI, Andrassy út 112. (tel. 111 3437), M1: Bajza u. Crowds come for the frequent live bands in this cavernous club. Cover varies. Open Wed.-Sun. 8pm-4am.

Véndiák (Former Student), V, Egyetem tér 5 (tel. 267 0226). M2: Kálvin tér. Walk up Kecskeméti u. Late-night bar with a lively dance floor. Popular with local students during school year. Really picks up around midnight. Open Mon. 9pm-2am, Tues.-Sat. 9pm-5am.

E-Play, by the McDonald's in the Nyugati Station. M3: Nyugati pu. More fog and more lights per person than any other dance club. Two floors of techno dancing, but little difference between them. Cover 500Ft.

Táncház. It might not be high-tech, but you can surely work up a sweat with these guys. An itinerant folk-dancing club, where you can stomp with Transylvanians. They have a beginners' circle and an instructor. Locate them in *Pesti Mősor* (Budapest's weekly entertainment guide, in Hungarian) or ask at Tourinform.

GAY BUDAPEST

For decades gay life in Budapest had been completely underground; it is only now starting to make itself visible. Budapest still has its share of skinheads, so it is safer to be discreet. If there are problems of any sort, you can call the gay hotline, open during somewhat irregular afternoon hours (tel.166 9283). **Dohotourist,** VI, Jokai tér 7 (tel. 111 0406; fax 269 3645), can provide a gay guide and map with listings and addresses of popular gay locations and organizations (open Mon.-Fri. 8:30am-4:30pm). Below are several locations are which are either gay-friendly or have primarily gay clientele.

Capella Cafe, V, Belgrád rkp. 23, (tel. 118 6231) An amicable bar just south of Erzsebet bridge. Different themes are set for each day of the week, and at times the candlelit, psychedelic walls transform into a disco.

Angel Bar, VII, Rákóczi út 51 (tel. 113 1273). Open daily 1pm-sunrise with a popular disco open Thurs.-Sun. Regulars complain of an increasingly mixed crowd. Take the M2 subway to Blaha Lujza tér.

Mystery Bar-Klub, V, Nagysándor József u. 3 (tel 112 1436), is a casual bar.

Baths: Király Fürdő, II, Fő u. 84 (tel. 201 4392). Open exclusively to men on Mon., Wed., and Fri., and popular among Budapest's gay community. Also try **Palatinus Strandfürdo** (tel. 112 3069) baths on Margit island.

THE DANUBE BEND

North of Budapest, the Danube sweeps south in a dramatic arc, called the Danube Bend *(Dunakanyar),* as it flows east from Vienna along the Slovak border. This lush and relaxed region is deservedly one of the great tourist attractions in Hungary. Ruins of first-century Roman settlements cover the countryside, and medieval palaces and fortresses overlook the river in Esztergom and Visegrád. An artist colony thrives today amidst the museums and churches of Szentendre. All this is within two hours of Budapest by bus, but the longer ferry ride is well worth the time for the relaxing, refreshing, and re-energizing rest it provides the weary traveler.

Szentendre

Szentendre is by far the most tourist-thronged of the Danube bend cities, but its proximity to Budapest, narrow cobblestone streets, and the artistic richness of its shops and museums keep the visitors coming. In June 1996, the town hosted the first Danube Carnival, a celebration of folk art dance groups from along the Danube; it may become an annual event. On Szentendre's **Templomdomb** (Church Hill) above Fő tér, sits the 13th-century Roman Catholic parish church. Facing it, the **Czóbel Museum,** houses works of Hungary's foremost impressionist, Béla Czóbel (open Tues.-Sun. 10am-4pm; 60Ft, students 30Ft). To the north across Alkotmány u., the Baroque **Serbian Orthodox Church** displays Serbian religious art (open Wed.-Sun. 10am-4pm; 60Ft). Szentendre's most impressive museum, **Kovács Margit Múzeum** at Vastagh György u. 1, exhibits brilliant ceramic sculptures and tiles by the 20th-century Hungarian artist Margit Kovács (open Mon. 10am-4pm, Tues.-Sun. 10am-6pm; 200Ft, students 100Ft). **Szabó Marcipán Múzeum,** Dumtsa Jenő u. 7 (tel. 311 484), puts the structural properties of this sticky sweet to the test; if the marzipan Parliament doesn't tempt you, the larger than life-size statue of Michael Jackson will. You can't beat it—it's a real almond-flavored thriller. Pick up a pastry from the shop (40-60Ft; open daily 10am-6pm; 100Ft, students and seniors 50Ft).

The HÉV commuter rail, train, and bus station is south of the Old Town; to get to Fő tér, use the underpass, and head up Kossuth u. HÉV travels to Budapest's Batthyány tér (every 20min., 45min., 128Ft). **Buses** run from Budapest's Árpád bridge station (every 10-40min., ½-1hr., 96Ft). At least once per hour buses continue to Visegrád (45min.) and Esztergom (1½hr.). **MAHART boats** leave from a pier 10-15 minutes north of the city for Budapest (3 per day; 320Ft, students 220Ft), and upriver toward Visegrád (2 per day; 320Ft, students 220Ft) and Esztergom (2 per day; 360Ft, students 250Ft). The helpful staff of **Tourinform,** Dumsta Jenő u. 22 (tel. 317 965 or 317 966), provides 35Ft maps and brochures (open Mon.-Fri. 9am-5pm, Sat.-Sun. 10am-2pm). **OTP Bank,** Dumsta Jenő u. 6, compensates for its excruciating slowness with great **currency exchange** rates and a 24-hour **ATM** (open Mon. 8am-5pm, Tues.-Thurs. 8am-3pm, Fri. 8am-12:30pm). **IBUSZ,** Bogdányi u. 4 (tel. 310 333), gives almost as good a deal, and finds private singles (2000-3000Ft), doubles (3000Ft), and triples (4000Ft; open Mon.-Fri. 8:15am-4pm). **Ilona Panzió,** Rákóczi Ferenc u. 11 (tel. 313 599), near the center of town, rents decent doubles with private baths for 2600Ft, breakfast included. **Pap-szigeti Camping** (tel. 31 06 97), 1km north of the center on Pap-sziget Island, rents small bungalows with three beds for 1200Ft, and larger bungalows with bath for 2390Ft for one person or 2690Ft for two; there is an additional 100Ft charge per person, waived for students. The campsite charges 890Ft for a space for two. The constant flow of tourists has made restaurants—especially in town—expensive by Hungarian standards. The budget traveler should return to Budapest or continue to Visegrád for dinner. **Grocery stores** wait near the rail station for those who just can't wait. **Phone code:** 26.

Visegrád

In medieval times, rural Visegrád served as the royal capital of Hungary. King Béla built a **palace** in this serene setting in 1259 to host elaborate feasts with the monarchs of Bohemia and Poland. The partially reconstructed **Royal Palace** (tel. 398 026; fax 398 252), at the foot of the hills above Fő u.'s west end has begun to resemble truly ancient ruins, with bleached stone and open-air mazes of rooms looking out over the river (open April-Oct. Tues.-Sun. 9am-5pm; 100Ft, seniors 50Ft, students free). In the second weekend of July, the town hosts the **International Palace Games,** on the palace grounds, complete with royal parades, knight tournaments, living chess, concerts, and medieval crafts (tel. 398 090 for more info).

Named for a king imprisoned here in the 11th century, the hexagonal **Salamon Torony** (Solomon's Tower), at the end of Salamontorony u., now keeps watch over the palace complex. The **King Matthias Museum** inside displays artifacts and stone carvings found in the ruins of the palace when it was re-discovered in 1934 (open May-Sept. daily 9am-5pm; 50Ft). High above the Danube, the 13th-century **Citadel** was built above a Roman outpost and commands a dramatic view of the river and surrounding hills (open April-Nov. daily 8:30am-6pm; 50Ft, students 30Ft). A bus (see below) or a demanding half-hour walk up Kalvaria (lined with stations of the cross) and along a ridge of the Pilis Forest brings you to the fortress's remains. Modern residents have built a **wax museum** inside devoted to medieval torture, and an exhibit on local life (open daily 9am-6pm; 140Ft, 90Ft students).

Visegrád Tours, Rév u. 13 (tel. 398 160; open June-Aug. daily 10am-8pm; Sept.-May 10am-6pm), between the pier and Nagy Lajos u., provides pamphlets and maps, and finds private doubles for 800-1500Ft. **Buses** to Esztergom (45min., 110Ft) and to Budapest's Árpád Híd metro station (1 per hr., 1½hr., 300Ft) pass through. **MAHART boats** run to Esztergom (2 per day, 2hr., 330Ft), Szentendre (2 per day, 75min., 320Ft), and Budapest (3 per day, 2½-3hr., 360Ft). Private **City Bus Visegrád** sends minibuses to the Citadel (900Ft; tel. 397 372 for service). **Phone code: 26.**

If you want to try your luck without an accommodation agency, *Zimmer Frei* signs line Fő u. The **Elte Guest House,** Fő u. 117 (tel. 398 165), charges 1232Ft per person. All rooms have a fridge, bath, and balcony. **Hotel Salamon,** Salamontorony u. 1 (tel. 398 278) offers simple but adequate singles, doubles, and triples for 1100 Ft per person. **Diófa Restaurant,** Fő u. 48 (tel. 318 131), serves Swedish and Hungarian dishes for 260-590Ft. **Gulás Csárda,** Nagy Lajos u. near Fő u., delivers tasty Hungarian fare in a room strung with paprika (400Ft and up; open daily 11:30am-10pm). The **ABC Supermarket,** 10 Rév u., sells beer for 90Ft (open Mon. 7am-4pm, Tues.-Fri. 7am-7pm, Sat. 7am-6pm, and Sun. 7am-2pm).

Esztergom

A hilltop **Cathedral** has shaped the Esztergom's 1000-year-old religious history and now offers a windy, awe-inspiring view of the Danube bend. A basilica was originally built here in 1010, but the present Neoclassical behemoth—Hungary's biggest church—was consecrated in 1856. On a smaller scale, the red marble **Bakócz Chapel** on the south side of the cathedral is a masterwork of Renaissance Tuscan stone-carving. Climb to the 71.5m-high **cupola** for a view of Slovakia (40Ft), or descend into the Egyptian-style **crypt** to walk among the ranks of Hungary's decaying archbishops (open daily 9am-5pm). The **Cathedral Treasury,** on the north side of the main altar, goes back a millennium as Hungary's most extensive ecclesiastical collection. The jewel-studded cross labelled #3 in the case facing the entrance to the main collection is the **Coronation Cross,** on which Hungary's rulers pledged their oaths from the 13th century until 1916 (open daily 9am-4:30pm; 60Ft, students 30Ft). Beside the cathedral stands the restored 12th-century **Esztergom Palace** (tel. 315 986; open summer Tues.-Sun. 9am-4:30pm; winter 10am-3:30pm; 60Ft, students 10Ft, free with ISIC). For an extra 10Ft, you can ascend to the roof to survey the kingdom. At the foot of the hill, **Keresztény Múzeum** (Christian Museum), Berenyi Zsigmond u. 2 (tel. 313 880), houses an exceptional collection of Renaissance religious artwork (open Tues.-Sun. 10am-6pm; 100Ft, students 50Ft).

The **train station** sits at the south edge of town. Get to central Rákóczi tér by walking up Baross Gábor út, making a right onto Kiss János Altábornagy út, and bearing straight as it becomes Kossuth Lajos u. **Gran Tours,** Széchenyi tér 25 (tel. 313 756), at the edge of Rákóczi tér, provides maps and finds 2300Ft doubles in private homes (open in summer Mon.-Fri. 8am-4pm, Sat. 8am-noon; off-season closed Sat.). **OTP,** Rákóczi tér, gives the best exchange rate in town. **Trains** connect to Budapest (12 per day, 1½hr., 225Ft). Catch **buses** a few blocks south of Rákóczi tér—take

Simor János u. straight up—to Budapest (every ½hr., 1½hr., 268Ft), to Visegrád (5 per day, ½hr., 134Ft) and Szentendre (1 per hr., 1hr., 198Ft). Thrice daily, **MAHART boats** (tel. 313 531) depart from the pier at the end of Gőzhajó u., on Primas Sziget island, stopping at Visegrád (1½hr.) and Szentendre (3½hrs.) on the way to Budapest (5hr.). Twice a day on weekends, a **hydrofoil** leaves from the same pier to Budapest (1hr.) and Visegrad (40min.). **Phone code:** 33.

One of several centrally located pensions, **Platán Panzió**, Kis-Duna Sétány 11 (tel. 311 355), between Rákóczi tér and Primas Sziget, rents vintage Socialist singles (1120Ft) and doubles (2464Ft) with shared toilets and bath. **Gran Camping**, Nagy-Duna Sétány (tel. 311 327), in the middle of Primas Sziget, within walking distance of all the sights, charges 2020Ft for a double in a pension, 1320Ft per person in a 6-bed room, and 290Ft per tent plus 580Ft per person at the campsite (prices higher July-Aug.). **Vadászkert Vendeglő**, Széchenyi tér (tel. 317 019), lets you relax on the terrace overlooking Esztergom's most attractive square. They do *sertés* (schnitzel) this way, that way, and the other way, starting at 410Ft (open daily 11am-9pm). **Halász Csárda** (tel. 311 052), at the Primas Sziget end of Bottyán Bridge, serves the catch of the day straight from the Danube for 300Ft (open daily noon-midnight).

NORTHERN HUNGARY

Hungary's northern upland is a series of six low mountain ranges running northeast from the Danube Bend along the Slovak border. The towns of the north are known for their skill at satisfying two of life's vital needs: recreation and alcohol. The Bükk and Aggtelek National Parks beckon hikers and explorers with their scenic trails and cave systems, while the dry volcanic soil of the hillsides yields the grapes for the famed white *Tokaj* and red *Egri Bikavér* wines.

■ Eger

In 1552, Captain Dobó István and his tiny army, holed up in Eger Castle, held off the invading Ottomans for an entire month. Credit for their fortitude is given to the potent *Egri Bikavér* (Bull's Blood) they quaffed before battle. Today, Dobó's name and likeness appear throughout the city, and the sweet red *Bikavér* still flows copiously and cheaply in Eger's tiny wine cellars. As if the wine wasn't enough to produce a warm, fuzzy glow, the 17th and 18th centuries brought a wealth of Baroque architecture, which has shaped the town's character ever since.

Orientation and Practical Information **Trains**, from Vasút u., go to Budapest's Keleti station (4 direct per day, 2hr., 676Ft), Füzesabony (12 per day, 20min., 70Ft) which connects to Budapest and Miskolc (1½hr., 324Ft), and Szilvásvárad (7 per day, 70min., 140Ft). Budapest trains split in Hatvan (a third of the way), so sure to be in the right car. **Buses** drive to Budapest (15-22 per day, 2hr., 550Ft), Szilvásvárad (every ½-1hr., 1½hr., 150Ft), Aggtelek (1 per day, morning departure, afternoon return, 3hr., 400Ft), and Debrecen (3-6 per day, 3 hr., 550Ft). From the **bus station** (tel. 410 552), five minutes west of the central Dobó tér, head right on the main street in front of the station, then turn right on the first street. Follow the stairs down and turn right at the "T" on **Széchenyi u.** A left down a side street will take you to Dobó tér. From the **train station** (tel. 314 264), 20 minutes south of the center, take bus #10, 11, 12, or 14 to the bus terminal or walk: a right onto **Deák u.**, a right and a quick left onto Széchenyi u. at the Cathedral, and a final right on **Ersek u.** The upbeat **Tourinform**, Dobó tér 2 (tel./fax 321 807), stocks brochures, English newspapers, good **maps** (50Ft), and accommodations info, and will research anything it doesn't already know (open in summer daily 9am-6pm; off-season Mon.-Fri. 9am-6pm and Sat.-Sun. 10am-2pm). **OTP**, Széchenyi u. 2 (tel. 310 866), gives advances on AmEx and MC, and charges no commission on traveler's checks. A **24-hour ATM**

takes Cirrus, EC, Eurocard, and MC (open Mon.-Tues. and Thurs. 7:45am-3:15pm, Wed. 7:45am-5pm, Fri. 7:45am-12:45pm). **Bank Posta,** Fellner u. 1 (tel. 313 540; fax 311 944), just south of Dobó ter, cashes traveler's checks, gives Visa cash advances, and has a **24-hour ATM** for Cirrus, EC, Eurocard, MC, Plus, and Visa (open Mon.-Thurs. 8am-4pm, Fri. 8am-3pm). The **post office** (tel. 313 232), is at Széchenyi u. 22 (open Mon.-Fri. 8am-8pm, Sat. 8am-2pm). **Postal code:** 3300. **Phone code:** 36.

Accommodations The best and friendliest accommodations are **private rooms;** look for "Zimmer Frei" signs outside the city center. There are several on Almagyar u. and Mekcsey u. near the castle. **Eger Tourist,** Bajcsy-Zsilinszky u. 9 (tel. 411 724; fax 413 249), arranges private rooms in the town center for about 1400Ft per person (open June-Sept. Mon.-Fri. 8:30am-7:30pm, Sat. 9am-1pm; Oct.-May Mon.-Fri. 8:30am-5pm). The agency also operates a very basic **Tourist Motel,** Mekchey u. 2 (doubles 1700Ft, with bath 2800Ft; triples 2100Ft, with bath 3300Ft; quads 2800Ft, with bath 3800Ft). At **Eszterházi Károly Kollégiuma,** Leányka u. 2/6 (tel. 412 399), east of the castle, charges 1500Ft per person in triples and quads (open July to early Sept.; call ahead). At **Autós Caravan Camping,** Rákóczi u. 79 (reserve through Eger Tourist) 20 minutes north of the center, camping is 240Ft per tent and 300Ft per person. Buses #5, 10, 11, or 12 go there (open April 15-Oct. 15).

Food For some of the town's best quick and inexpensive food, go to **HBH Bajor Söház,** Bajcsy-Zsilinsky u. 19 (tel. 316 312), in the southwest corner of Dobó tér, a Bavarian beer house that serves Hungarian specialties. The English menu-entrées run 389-529Ft (open May-Oct. daily 10am-10pm, Nov.-April Mon.-Sat. 10am-10pm). **Gyros Étterem,** Széchenyi u. 10, serves gyros (499Ft), souvlaki (450Ft), and small but tasty Greek salads (260Ft). In the Valley of the Beautiful Women, the vine-draped courtyard of **Kulacs Csárda Borozó,** Almási u. 51 (tel./fax 311 375), keeps the crowds coming for the goulash. Roasted fish with fries 370Ft, Parisian pork with green peas and rice 390Ft (open Tues.-Sun. noon-10pm). For caffeine and sugar, **Sarvari,** Kossuth u. 1 past the Lyceum (tel. 413 298), serves up pastries (35-60Ft) and espresso that javaholics will love (open Mon.-Fri. 6:30am-6pm, Sat.-Sun. 9am-6pm).

Sights and Entertainment Eger can be explored in a morning, but with good company you can spend an entire afternoon and evening in the wine cellars of Szépasszonyvölgy, the **Valley of the Beautiful Women.** Land on the volcanic hillside was sold cheaply by the town following WWII, and now holds some 25 open wine cellars, as well as hundreds more which are used for storage. Most open cellars consist of little more than 20m of tunnel and a few tables and benches, but each has its own personality: some are subdued and gentle, and, in others, rowdy Hungarians and Gypsies hold candlelit sing-alongs. Although locals also pride themselves on white wines, Eger is Hungary's red wine capital, and the most popular libations are the semi-sweet *Medina* and the sweeter *Bikavér.*

Little glasses for tasting are free, and 100mL ones are 25Ft. The valley is designed for people coming to buy (1L for 150-200Ft), but many spend hours in the friendly, smoky cellars, or outside chatting around the picnic tables in the small park. Visitors force small coins into the spongy fungus on the cellar walls—the legend says that if your coin sticks, you'll return. Most cellars are open from around 10am to 4pm and begin to close around 6 to 7pm, or whenever their owners have had enough. Some stay open as late as 10pm, but the best time to go is late afternoon. A South African woman at cellar #2 will give you a zany introduction to the area's wines if you descend into her cavern. Otherwise, you'll most likely be confronted with broken German. Get to the Valley by walking west from the 1956 monument on Deák u. down Telekessy u., which with a quick jog to the left becomes Király u. and then Szépasszonyvölgy u. About 15 to 20 minutes from Deák you will see the valley; walk past the buses and stands to the wine cellars. Don't just use this as an opportunity to imbibe wine freely; sip several samples, then buy a bottle of a variety you particularly like—you get good cheap wine, the cellars can continue to give those free tastings.

The yellow **basilica** on Eszterházy tér is Hungary's second-biggest church; it was built in 1836 by big-thinker Joseph Hild, who also designed the country's largest in Esztergom. Distinguishing the real marble from the painted illusions is a challenge—albeit not a particularly tough one. Half-hour **organ concerts** are held here April to mid-September (Mon.-Sat. 11:30am, Sun. 12:45pm; 120Ft, students 60Ft).

Opposite the cathedral is the Rococo **Lyceum.** The fresco in the library on the first floor depicts an ant's-eye view of the Council of Trent, which spawned the edicts of the Counter-Reformation (a slim lightning bolt at one end is blasting a pile of heretical books). Upstairs, a small **astronomical museum** houses 18th-century telescopes and instruments of the buildings' old observatory. A marble-line depression in the floor represents the meridian; when the sun strikes the line through a tiny aperture in the south wall, it is astronomical noon. There is also an observation deck with great views of the city and surrounding hills. Two floors up, a periscope projects a live picture of the surrounding town onto a table in a perilously stifling room (open Tues.-Fri. 9:30am-1pm, Sat.-Sun. 9:30am-noon; 120Ft, students 60Ft).

On the south side of Dobó tér stands the Baroque pink **Minorite Church,** built in 1773. It overlooks a statue of Captain Dobó and two co-defenders, including a possessed female poised to hurl a rock upon an unfortunate Turk. Hungarians revere the medieval **Eger Castle** (tel. 312 744). It was here that Dobó István and his 2000 men repelled the unified Ottoman army, halting their advance for another 44 years. The castle's innards include subterranean barracks, catacombs, a crypt, and, of course, a wine cellar (open daily 8am-7:30pm; 50Ft, students 20Ft). A 160Ft ticket (students 80Ft) buys admission to the three museums in the castle: a **picture gallery** showing Hungarian paintings from as early as the 15th century, the **Dobó Istvan Castle Museum,** which displays excavated artifacts, armor, and an impressive array of sharp, spiky, and pointy weapons, and the **Dungeon Exhibition,** a collection of torture equipment that inspires sadists and masochists alike (museums open Tues.-Sun. 9am-5pm; underground passages on Mon.; English tours 100Ft). The 400-year-old wine cellars are also open to the public (open Tues.-Sun. 10am-5pm).

Just north of Dobó tér, capture another Kodak moment from the 40m-tall **Turkish minaret,** the Ottomans' northernmost phallic symbol (open daily 10am-6pm; 30Ft). The steep spiral staircase is not much wider than the average 20th-century person. The 18th-century **Serbian Orthodox Church,** Vitkovics u. at the town center's north end, parallel to Széchenyi u., displays magnificent murals and an equally magnificent altar (open daily 10am-4pm; free).

Eger celebrates its heritage during the **Baroque Festival** held throughout July. Nightly performances of operas, operettas, and medieval and Renaissance court music are held in the Franciscan Church's yard, the basilica, and Dobó tér. Buy 250Ft tickets at the place of performance. An international folk-dance festival, **Eger Vintage Days,** is held daily throughout September. See Tourinform for schedules.

■ Near Eger: Aggtelek and Jósvafő

The **Baradla caves** are a 25km-long system of limestone tunnels that wind between Hungary and Slovakia. Each chamber is a forest of dripping stalactites, stalagmites, and fantastically shaped stone formations. Entrances (allowed only as part of tour) in Hungary are at **Aggtelek, Vörös-tó,** and **Jósvafő.** A variety of tours are available (tel./fax 350 006), including hour-long tours at Aggtelek (270Ft, students 135Ft; daily at 10am, 1, 3, and 5pm; tours are in Hungarian, but there are English pamphlets) and at Jósvafő (230Ft, students 115Ft; tours daily at noon, 5pm, and sometimes also 10am and 2pm). At Aggtelek, a large chamber with perfect acoustics has been converted into an auditorium, and spelunkers pause here for a light-and-sound show. Another hall is the site of the cemetery of the **Halstatt man,** with 13 people buried in a sitting position. The tunnels along the tour are all well lit, but the guide turns the lights off as you pass them in order to discourage stragglers.

The one daily **bus** leaves Eger at 8:40am, whizzes through Szilvásvárad at 9:20am, and arrives in Aggtelek at 11:20am (400Ft) in front of the Hotel Cseppkő, 200m uphill from the cave entrance. The bus back to Eger leaves at 3pm and to Miskolc at 5:30pm. **Baradla Camping,** at the mouth of the cave (tel./fax 343 073), has four- to eight-bed dorms for 450Ft per person (open Oct. 16-April 15; 520Ft), as well as bungalows and campsites (4-person bungalow 1680Ft; tent 310Ft per person, students 250Ft). The rooms in the dorms are acceptable, but don't count on hot water. Up the hill, at the two-star **Cseppkő Hotel** (tel./fax 343 075), the rooms all come with bath, TV, radio, and breakfast (singles 3000Ft, doubles 4000Ft, triples 4900Ft, and quads 6500Ft). The hotel also has **currency exchange.** The **phone code** for both cities is 48.

Ten minutes by bus (56Ft) past Aggtelek lies Jósvafő, a town of red roofs and roosters. From the first bus stop in town, walk back out of town by the main road and bear right at the sign to the cave. In 15 minutes, you will reach the Jósvafő entrance to the Baradla Cave. For overnight spelunkers, one of the only options remains **Tengerszem Szálló,** Tengerszem oldal 2 (tel. 350 006), where singles cost 1400Ft (2100Ft with shower-bath), doubles 2100Ft (2800Ft with shower-bath), and spare beds 560Ft. An additional tax of 50Ft per person is waived for students. **Tengerszem Étterem** has English menus and the standard Hungarian entrées for 320-630Ft. Buses run between Aggtelek and Jósvafő every two to three hours.

■ Szilvásvárad

Beloved for its carriages, Lipizzaner horses, and surrounding national parks, Szilvásvárad trots along at its own dignified clip, oblivious to the huge concrete factories 5km to the southwest. Recreational opportunities abound—the most popular being leisurely strolls in the Szalajka Valley or hikes in the fauna-filled Bükk mountains.

Orientation and Practical Information The town's one big street—**Egri út**—extends northeast from the Szilvásvárad-Szalajkavölgy train station (the first one in Szilvásvárad when coming from Eger) and bends north at the info cottage. **Szalajka u.** extends south from the turn and ushers you into the national park. Farther north, Egri út turns into **Miskolci út.** There is no bus station, so after you pass Bükkszentmárton with its looming concrete factories, Szilvásvárad is the next town. Don't get off at the first bus stop in town, unless you want to investigate the "Zimmer Frei" signs. The second stop is just north of the info cottage where from late June to September, **Tourinform,** Szalajka u. at Egri út, sells maps of the national park (250Ft). Off-season, Eger's Tourinform takes over responsibility. Laid-back, friendly, and eager to try their English, the staff can help find accommodations, but doesn't make reservations. Maps are also available from Dohány-Ajándék, a stand by the entrance to the park. A **currency exchange** and a few phones reside in the **post office,** Egri út 10 (tel. 355 101; open Mon.-Fri. 8am-4pm). **Hegy Camping,** Egri út 36a (tel. 355 207), five minutes southwest of Tourinform on the way to the trains, changes money 24 hours a day from May to October, but for only moderately good rates. **Trains** run to Eger (7 per day, 70min., 140Ft), and **buses** to Eger (every ½-1hr., 1½hr., 130Ft) and Aggletek (9:20am, 1¾hr., 324Ft). **Postal code:** 3348. **Phone code:** 36.

Accommodations Private rooms usually start at 600Ft per person without breakfast, but expect to pay a little more if you'd like water or heat. **Lipicai Hotel Szállására,** Egri út 12 (tel./fax 355 100), five minutes north of Tourinform, is the town's nicest budget option, a trifle gray, but clean— with breakfast and black-and-white TV on request, plus 100Ft tax per person, students exempt. Singles cost 1600Ft, doubles 3200Ft, triples 4500Ft, and quads 5600Ft. The rooms of the regal, hilltop **Szilvás Mansion Hotel,** Park u. 6 (tel. 355 211; fax 355 324), 15 minutes east of the main drag, are not as elegant as the building, but they are Szilvásvárad's cleanest, have showers, include breakfast, and are cloistered by trees and formal gardens. A double runs 3600Ft (4200 with TV, refrigerator, and bath), but you can have it for 3240Ft if you're alone. **Hegy Camping,** Egri út 36a (see above), offers great views of the valley from the grassy and groomed campground (tents 240Ft plus 400Ft per person, students 240Ft, no tax). If you'd rather have something with a roof, there are bungalows with shower and toilet (doubles 1800Ft, triples 2400Ft, quads 3000Ft; plus 100Ft per person tax, except for students; open May-Oct.).

Food **Szalajka Inn,** Egri út 2 (tel. 355 257), immerses the visitor in folk decor and cuisine. Try the Bükk-style wild boar with mushrooms for 650Ft or their forester's goulash soup for 290Ft (open daily 7am-midnight). **Csobogó,** Szalajka u. 1 (tel. (30) 415 249) on the road to the national park, lies among all sorts of *büfé* and little restaurants. In addition to traditional dishes made for the Hungary-seeking tourists, they offer random dishes from around the world and even have a salad bar (250Ft). Check out the Carpathian *borzaska* (450Ft), wild boar stew (500Ft), or the Indonesian pullet breast with nuts, curry, pineapple, and rice (450Ft; open daily 9am-8pm).

Sights and Entertainment Horse shows kick into action on weekends in the arena across from Tourinform on Szalajka u. (200Ft per person). Or you can get into the thick of things by learning how to drive a carriage, brandish a whip, or ride a steed—all with the 400-year-old race of Lipizzaner horses for which Hungary is famous. In July and August especially, many farms offer horse-riding. **Péter Kovács,** Egri út 62 (tel. 355 343), will let you borrow horses for 1000Ft per hour, and has two- and four-horse carriages for 1500Ft and 3000Ft respectively. Equestrians should also gallop to the **Lovas Kiállítas Szimbólkus Lótemető** (Horse Museum), Park u. 4 (tel. 355 155), which is chock-full o' riding paraphernalia from the region's horsey history (open Tues.-Sun. 9am-noon and 1-5pm; 150Ft).

Leafy walks through the **Bükk mountains** and the **Szalajka valley** are beautiful, but not always particularly relaxing. The most popular destination—and we do mean popular—is the **Fátiyol waterfalls,** whose rocks look like steps designed for giants. It only takes 45 minutes to walk here, or 20 minutes by the little open-air choo-choo train. Catch the train at the entrance to the park just to the right of the stop sign (70Ft, students 40Ft). This is not the place for solitude, but steeper hikes up the mountain attract fewer people. For those who want to cover more distance and enjoy bouncing over potholes, bike rental is available just past the stop sign at the entrance to the park. You can't miss the **bike rental,** Szalajka u. 28 (tel. (60) 352 695), thanks to the racks of fluorescent green mountain bikes lining the patio. The shop rents them and arranges trips to the local plateaus for groups of ten or more for the cost of a day's rental (250Ft per hr., 990Ft per day; open in summer daily 9am-dusk; off-season in good weather only). A half-hour hike beyond the waterfalls leads to the **Istálósk cave** that once sheltered a bear cult in the Stone Age. Talk about perfect acoustics—*La Traviata* sounds almost as good in here as in a tile bathroom. Most leave their bikes with the souvenir guy at the waterfall, follow the road (with the brook always to the right), and then scramble up the switchbacks. On the path to the waterfall, two museums are of moderate interest. The **Erdészeti Muzeum** shows logging techniques and life in the forest (open Oct. 16-April 15 daily 9am-2pm; April 16-30 Tues.-Sun. 8:30am-4pm; May-Sept. Tues.-Sun. 8:30am-4:30pm; Oct. 1-15 Tues.-Sun. 8:30am-3pm; 50Ft, students 30Ft), and the **Open Air Erdei Museum** exhibits typical huts of the types once used by the region's woodsmen.

The **Orbán-ház Museum,** Miskolci út 58, has a collection of all the archaeological treasures of the area. Fossils! (Supposedly open May-Oct. Thurs.-Sun. 9am-5pm; 30Ft, students 20Ft.) Just up the hill in front stands the white, rotund, and perfectly Classical **Keréktemplom**—a 19th-century reform temple, whose interior appears even more austere than most Protestant creations. Great views of the fields and valleys roll out from this vantage point.

In early September, the three-day **Lipicai Festival** ushers carriage drivers from all over the world for a grand international competition of horses and reins.

■ Tokaj

Locals say that King Louis XIV called Tokaj wine "the wine of kings and the king of wines." Tokaj itself is just one of the 28 small towns and villages that take advantage of the volcanic yellow soil and sunny climate at the feet of the Kopasz Mountains to produce unique whites, but it lends its name to the entire class.

Orientation and Practical Information Tokaj can be crossed on foot in about 15 minutes. The main **Bajcsy-Zsilinszky u.** becomes **Rákóczi u.** and, beyond the center at Kossuth tér, **Bethlen Gábor u.** Some pensions' brochures include street maps. **Tokaj Tours,** Serház u. 1 (tel./fax 352 259), at Rákóczi u., sells maps (200Ft), arranges private and hotel rooms, organizes tours of the region and wine-tastings, and can set you up with a horse or canoe (open Mon.-Sat. 9am-4pm). **Exchange currency** and traveler's checks at **OTP,** Rákóczi u. 35 (tel. 352 521; open Mon.-Thurs. 8am-3:30pm, Fri. 8am-2:30pm). **Trains,** Baross G. u. 18 (tel. 352 020), puff to Miskolc (14-15 per day, 1hr., 226Ft) and Nyíregyháza (10-11 per day, ½hr., 140Ft), which links to Debrecen (25min., 376Ft). The station sits 15 minutes southwest of town; walk east along the railroad embankment until an underpass, then north on Bajcsy-Zsilinszky u. At the Hotel Tokaj fork, stay on the left road. The only bus service is to local towns. The **post office,** Rákóczi u. 24 (tel. 352 417), is open Monday-Friday 8am-5pm, Saturday 8am-noon. **Postal code:** 3910. **Phone code:** 47.

Accommodations and Food Check the offerings at Tokaj Tours, but "Zimmer Frei" and "Szoba Kiadó" signs abound—your best bet is to walk along Rákóczi u. and venture down random streets to choose one you like. Singles go for 1200Ft-1400Ft, doubles 2400Ft. Don't be afraid to bargain, but beware: your host may well take you into a small wine cellar and talk you into sampling—and buying—her homemade vintage. The concrete and plexiglass-bubbled **Hotel Tokaj,** Rákóczi u. 5 (tel. 352 344; fax 352 759), has comfortable singles (3000Ft) and doubles (3600Ft) that include breakfast. **Makk-Marci Panzió,** Liget Köz 1 (tel./fax 352 336), facing Rákóczi u., provides small, bright rooms with bath (2016Ft for one person, 3024Ft for two, 4480Ft for three, and 5040Ft for four). There are only five rooms, so reservations are a good idea. If you feel tougher than the mosquitoes that control the banks of the Tisza, there are some options immediately across the river on the road to Nyíregyháza. Across the road, the best bet is **Camping Tisza,** on the right as you cross the river. Tent space costs 250Ft per person, for vehicles 450Ft plus 150Ft per person; Rover will run you an extra 80Ft. Or stay in a two- or four-person tiny bungalow for 450Ft per person. On the left, the extraordinarily friendly **Tisza Vízisport Centrum,** Horgász u. 3 (tel. 352 645), with an English-speaking proprietor, is expected to shed the drab Communist cover soon (350Ft per person in 4- or 12-person dorms).

Gödör, part of the Tisza Vízisport complex, cooks up heavy meat dishes and vegetarian entrées for 170-250Ft. English menu on weekends only—damn unions (open

---

A Mini-Guide to Hungarian Wine

Wine connoisseurs have been aware of the merits of Hungarian wines for years, and budget travelers have long appreciated the extraordinary prices. There have even been reported border crossings to get a bottle or two of the cheap—very cheap—beverage. But, the exotic names on the labels might intimidate those used to *Bordeaux* or *Chardonnay*. The main local products are *Furmint*, a basic dry white wine, and *Hárslevelű*, a slightly more complex white. *Szamorodni* is an aperitif that ages in barrels for a year and a half. *Aszú* is *Furmint* sweetened with "noble rot" grapes (which ripen and dry out more quickly than the others in the same bunch) and aged for three years. If you want to get even a little more technical, the sweetness is measured in three, four, five or six *puttony* (six being the sweetest), or units of *Aszú* grapes added. (1972, 1988, and 1993 are rumored to have been especially good *Aszú* years). *Fordítás,* another dessert wine, is made from *Aszú's* byproduct and aged three years. The real experts sample them in order from driest to sweetest and do not—this is important—do not ever swallow. But, we think it might go against the budget ethic to waste good wine, so go ahead. Drink up!

daily 7am-11pm). **Róna Étterem,** Bethen Gábor u. 19 (tel. 352 116), is more elegant, with entrées for 250-480Ft (open 11am-10pm).

Sights and Entertainment Wine's the word. Many signs herald private wine cellars—*Bor Pince*—as private accommodations. The owners of **private cellars** are generally pleased to let visitors sample their wares (for a fee)—walk on in, or ring the bell if the cellar looks shut. Many warn of the big flashy cellars on the main road. Explore the side streets for higher quality wines.

Serious **tasting** takes place at the well respected and largest of the lot: **Rákóczi Pince,** Kossuth tér 15 (tel. 352 009; fax 352 141), a French-Hungarian joint venture. Prices are the highest around, but they accept AmEx, MC, and Visa. This 1½km-long system of 24 tunnels was dug from volcanic rock in 1502. In 1526, János Szapohjai was elected king of Hungary in the elegant and surprisingly large hall, and the tunnel served as the imperial wine cellar for two centuries, until the end of WWI. Half-hour **group tours** of the cellar and its 25,560L barrel, along with wine-tasting sessions, are held on the hour, but can be pre-empted by tour groups. **Individual sessions** can also be arranged. The tunnel walls are coated with 500 years' worth of the dripping spongy fungus—it turns from cotton-ball white to sooty black with age—that keeps the cellar at a constant 10°C and 80% humidity. A jacket is a good idea down here, even in summer. Sessions are 100Ft for the tour alone, 200Ft for the tour and a glass of wine, and 650Ft for 6 glasses (open daily 10am-7pm, English-speaking guides available in July and Aug.). Another winery-museum hybrid, the **Borpince Museum,** Bem u. 2 (tel. 352 416), is run by the Várhelyi family, and is located in the 16th-century cellar of a former king. A chart lists good and bad years for Tokaji and other wine. Taste five wines here for 200Ft, although the one-room exhibit is free (flexible hours; the daughter speaks English).

The **Tokaji Múzeum,** Bethlen Gábor u. 7 (tel. 352 636), tells the history of the town through exhibits of the tools and equipment of wine production, and the glass bottles and porcelain decanters used for storing and serving wine over the last three centuries. Unfortunately, the lack of signs in English detracts from the interest-factor of the museum (open Tues.-Sun. 9am-5pm; 100Ft, students 50Ft). **Tokaji Galléria,** Bethlen Gábor u. 15, in an old red-and-cream Serbian Orthodox Church, puts on free exhibitions by local artists (open Tues.-Sun. 10am-4pm). The century-old **Great Synagogue,** Serház u. 55, guarded by a family of storks (look up!) one block behind the gallery by way of József Attila u., survived WWII by serving duty as German barracks. It is newly yellow outside, but awaits renovations inside.

Outdoor opportunities are multiplying as fast as cellar fungi. **Vízisport Centrum** rents bikes (400Ft per day) and canoes (1000Ft per day, 500Ft for ½-day), and suggests routes. **Camping Tisza** rents canoes (four-seater 1000Ft) and kayaks (500Ft).

NAGYALFÖLD (THE GREAT PLAIN)

Romanticized in tales of cowboys and mirages rising from its flat soil, the Great Plain is an enormous grassland stretching southeast of Budapest over nearly one-half of Hungary's territory. Also called the *puszta,* or "ravaged land," Nagyalföld was once a "Great Forest" until the Turks chopped down the trees. Much of the Great Plain is either pasture or farmlands, but a train ride through endless fields of sunflowers brings you to the beautiful towns of Debrecen, Kecskemét, and Szeged.

■ Debrecen

Protected by the Phoenix, Debrecen—one of the few cities in the world with neither natural waterways nor defensive physical features—has burned down 30-40 times in its history thanks to its scorching summers. It began as the bread basket of the Great Plain and later became a wealthy business center; even now, it's known as the unofficial capital of eastern Hungary. Once the "Calvinist Rome," the center of Protestantism during the 16th-century Reformation, Debrecen is even today more than 80% Protestant. Modern and 19th-century buildings alternate along the city's broad streets, and its position near the Romanian border draws a mix of shoppers.

Orientation and Practical Information The center of the city is **Kálvin tér,** and the inner city can be crossed by foot in 15 to 20 minutes. Running south from here, broad Piac u. ends at Petőfi tér and the **train station.** Piac u. becomes Péterfia u. at Kálvin tér and runs 3km north to **Nagyerdei Park** and the **Kossuth Lajos University.** Tram #1 (the one and only) runs from Petőfi tér through Kálvin tér into the park and then back. Ticket checks are frequent. Get the 45Ft ticket from the kiosk by the train station, or pay a 1000Ft fine. The tram is the best route to the town center from the train station; tourist offices are on the triangular Kossuth tér. The **bus station** lies 10 to 15 minutes southwest of the center, on Külsö Vásár tér. Walk east on Széchenyi u. to reach Piac u. just south of Kálvin tér. At **Tourinform,** Piac u. 20 (tel. 412 250; fax 314 139), English-speaking agents give away or sell city **maps,** provide info on concerts, and **rent bikes** for 1300Ft per day (open June-Aug. daily 8am-8pm; Sept.-May Mon.-Fri. 8:30am-4:30pm). **OTP,** Hatvan u. 2/4 (tel. 419 544), has fairly good rates, gives MC cash advances, accepts most traveler's checks, and has a **24-hour ATM** (open Mon.-Fri. 8am-3pm). **Trains** (tel. 326 777) ply the rails to Budapest (12 per day, 3hr., 988Ft; *InterCity* 5 per day, 2½hr., 1188Ft), Kecskemét (1 per day, 3½hr., 848Ft), Miskolc (3 per day, 2½-3hr., 592Ft), Oradea in Romania (destination Tîrgu Mureş; 1 per day, 3½hr. or more depending on border crossing, 2304Ft; 40% discount on return trip on international trains), and Szeged (through Cegléd, 7 per day, 3½hr., 1128Ft). Travelers can **store luggage** at the train station (100-200Ft; open 24hr.). Prices depend on size of luggage. **Buses** from the station (tel. 413 999), intersection of Nyugari ú. and Széchenyi ú., run to Tokaj (2 per day, 2hr., 478Ft), Szeged (2 per day, 4-5½hr., 1260Ft), Kecskemét (2 per day, 5½hr., 1260Ft), Miskolc (30 per day, 2hr., 530Ft), and Oradea in Romania (daily, 3½hr., 400-700Ft). For a **taxi,** dial 444 444 or 444 555. The **medical emergency** room (tel. 414 333), is just south of the bus station at the intersection of Erzsébet u. and Szoboszlój u. The **post office,** Hatvan u. 5/9 (tel. 412 374), lies west of Kálvin tér (open Mon.-Fri. 7am-8pm, Sat. 8am-2pm, Sun. 8am-noon). **Postal code:** 4001. **Phone code:** 52.

Accommodations and Food **Hajdútourist,** Kálvin tér 24 (tel. 415 588; fax 319 616), arranges central private singles (1000Ft) and doubles (1700Ft; open Mon.-Fri. 8am-5pm, Sat. 8am-12:30pm). **Ludas Matyi Panzió,** Batthyány u. 26 (tel./fax 411 252), a block east of Piac u., has singles on the top floor with slanted ceilings. Rugs and furnishings give a touch of home, with private bath 1500Ft; similar doubles 2600Ft; triples and quads without bath 3000-4000Ft; and six-bed dorms 1000Ft per person. **Hotel Stop,** Batthyány u. 18 (tel. 420 301), occupies a courtyard just north of Ludas Matyi Panzió (doubles with shower 2200Ft). Farther from the center, the youth hostel **West Tourist,** Wesselényi u.4 (tel. 420 891; fax 413 266), offers adequate doubles (1500Ft), triples (1800Ft), and quads (600Ft per person, 2500Ft with bath), but the bathroom awaits renovation in the wake of a sewer problem.

At the brick cellar of **Csokonai Söröző,** Kossuth u. 21 (tel. 410 802), waiters smother their customers with love and then allow them to try their luck with a roll of the dice for a free meal. The city's best menu includes English translations and photographs of the 475-960Ft entrées (open Mon.-Sat. noon-11pm, Sun. 4pm-11pm). **Régi Posta Étterem,** Széchenyi u. 6, named for an old stagecoach stop, has fried food and attentive waiters (entrées 270-470Ft; open daily 9am-midnight). **University Dining Halls** offer 300-500Ft lunches during the school year. Look for the building marked "Menza" behind the main university building on Egyetem tér (open daily noon-4pm, leftovers until approximately 6pm).

Sights and Entertainment Hungary's largest Protestant church, the 1863 twin-spired **Nagy templom** (Great Church; tel. 327 017), looms over Kossuth tér's north end. The T-shaped interior can hold 3000 people, and the huge organ threatening to crush the pulpit serves as the only major adornment. A great view extends from the bell tower (open Mon.-Fri. 9am-noon and 2-4pm, Sat. 9am-noon, Sun. 11am-4pm; 30Ft, students 15Ft). The **Reformed College,** Kálvin tér 16 (tel. 416 337), just in back, was established in 1538 as a center for Protestant education. The present 1819 building has housed the government of Hungary twice—in 1849 when Lajos Kossuth headed the Parliament in the Oratory, and in 1944. Today, it serves as the home for Calvinist schools, as well as a collection of religious art and an exhibit on the history of Protestantism in Debrecen. Hungary's second oldest, the 650,000-volume library displays 16th-century Bibles (open Tues.-Sat. 9am-5pm, Sun. 9am-1pm; 40Ft, students 25Ft; Hungarian and German explanations).

Two blocks west in Déri tér stands the **Déri Museum** (tel. 417 577), a collection that touches on everything from local history to Japanese lacquerware. See it for its exhibit on folkcraft since the 16th century and its marvelous collection of gold-and-silver work (don't lean on the cases—the alarm system is very sensitive). Upstairs in the **Munkácsy Gallery** are three awe-inspiring murals of Christ's trial and crucifixion by Mihály Munkácsy, who painted himself into *Ecce Homo* as the old man in the crowd, next to the arch (open Tues.-Sun. 10am-6pm; 180Ft, students 90Ft).

Debrecen is famous for its young population, and you'll find them all in **Nagyerdei Park.** There are thermal baths as well as bike lanes, paddle boats, bars, tattoo salons, and an overabundance of eligible men sitting either shirtless or in singlets. **Programs in Debrecen** is a series of summer events, ranging from equestrian exhibitions in the first weekend of July to musical performances to air shows, and culminating in the huge **Flower Carnival** parade on August 20 every year. In early September, **Jazz Days** feature well known musicians and bands. See Tourinform for the two fêtes' schedules and tickets. Every odd year (including 1997), the **International Military Band Festival** blows its horn in the last week of June. And every year, the **Béla Bartók Choir Festival** attracts great choirs from around the world in the first week of July. Master the unmasterable—the Debrecen summer school at Kossuth Lajos University offers cheap and popular **Hungarian language programs** for 500 students from over 35 countries. Contact Debreceni Nyári Egyetem, Egyetem tér 1, M-4010 Debrecen (tel./fax 329 117 or tel. 316 666, ext.3003).

■ Szeged

The easy-going charm of the Great Plain's cultural capital belies its status as the nation's only planned city; after an 1879 flood practically wiped out the town, streets were laid out in straight lines and orderly curves punctuated by large stately squares. Row after row of colorful Neo-Renaissance and Art Nouveau buildings now complement each other in shape and style. Equally colorful legends hold that Attila the Hun was buried here, where the Tisza and Maros Rivers unite.

ORIENTATION AND PRACTICAL INFORMATION

Szeged is split in two by the **Tisza River.** The downtown area sits on the west bank. **Újszeged** (New Szeged), on the east bank, is mostly parks and residences. A curved *körút* connects the streets that radiate from the center. The inner road, **Tisza krt.,** is a half-circle, with **Klauzál tér** in the middle, next to **Széchenyi tér,** which starts upriver and circles around to downriver. The outer road—named at different segments for the European cities that helped rebuild Szeged after the flood—is a nearly complete circle that crosses the river from the downtown's northeast section. Most travel bureaus are on or near Klauzál tér. **Tram #1** connects the **train station** in the south with Klauzál tér (5 or 6 stops away) and continues northeast to the **bus station.** Tickets (45Ft) can be purchased at the train station from a couple of guys standing at the exit and at the bus station kiosks. The tram stop is just north of the bus station on **Kossuth sugárút.** It's a 10- to 15-minute walk from the bus station to the center; the trains are a bit farther out.

Tourist Offices: Szeged Tourist, Klauzál tér 7 (tel. 321 800; fax 312 928). Maps, summer bus and boat tours (bus 300Ft, under 18 150Ft), international bus tickets with 10% student discount. Open Mon.-Fri. 9am-5pm, summer also Sat. 9am-1pm.
Currency Exchange: OTP, Klauzál tér 5. Open Mon. 7:45am-4:30pm, Tues.-Thurs. 7:45am-2pm, Fri. 7:45-11:30am. **K&H Bank,** Károly u. 2 by Széchenyi tér, has a **24-hr. ATM** for Cirrus, EC, Eurocard, MC, Plus, and Visa.
Trains: (tel. 421 821) one block east of the main drag, Boldogasszony sugárút that leads into town. To: Arad, Romania (1 per day with a change in Szolnok, 5½hr., 3995Ft); Budapest (*InterCity* 6 per day, 2½hr., 848Ft); Debrecen (7 per day with a change in Cegléd; 3-4hr.; 1128Ft); Kecskemét (dir. "Budapest"; 12 per day; 1hr.; 376Ft, *InterCity* 576Ft); Pécs (1 per day; 1128Ft). International cashier on the 2nd floor open daily 6am-6pm. **Luggage storage:** 100Ft; open 5am-11pm.
Buses: Mars tér (tel. 421 478) 10min. west of Londoni krt., along Merey ú. or Kossuth u. To: Budapest (7 per day, 3½hr., 946Ft); Debrecen (2 per day, 5¼hr., 1214Ft); Kecskemét (13 per day, 1¾hr., 478Ft); Pécs (6 per day, 4½hr., 1112Ft); Győr (2 per day, 6hr., 1238Ft); Miskolc (2 per day, 6hr., 1844Ft); Eger (2 per day, 5hr., 1410Ft).
Taxis: tel. 470 470, 490 490, 480 480, or 488 488.
English Bookstores: Kőnyvesbolt, Kárász u. 16 (tel. 312 328). Open Mon.-Fri. 10am-6pm, Sat. 9am-1pm. **Délhir I Bolt,** Dugonics tér (tel. 312 118). International magazines and newspapers. Open Mon.-Sat. 5am-8pm, Sun. 5am-7pm.
Pharmacy: **Kígyó Richter Referenciapatika,** Klauzál tér 3 (tel. 111 131). One of many (open daily 7am-8pm).
Medical Assistance: The center at Kossuth Lagos sgt. 15 (tel. 474 374) provides medical care. In an **emergency,** dial 04.
Post Office: Széchenyi tér 1 (tel. 476 276), at Híd u. Open Mon.-Fri. 8am-8pm, Sat. 8am-2pm, Sun. 8am-noon. **Postal code:** 6720. **Phone code:** 62.

ACCOMMODATIONS AND CAMPING

Szeged Tourist (see above) finds the best deals on rooms (singles 900-1800Ft; doubles 2400Ft). University dorms are generally cheapest, especially for solo travelers.

Béke Kollégium, Béke u. 11/13 (tel. 455 729), 5min. southwest of Klauzál tér. Fine rooms at good prices. Doubles 1100Ft. Quads 1700Ft. Open late June to early Sept.
Fortuna Panzió, Pécskai u. 8 (tel./fax 431 585). A serene neighborhood setting, across the bridge. Worth the walk and search—take a map. Air-conditioned, spacious rooms and sparkling bathrooms. Doubles with bath 3800Ft.
Napfény, Dorozsmai u. 4 (tel./fax 324 573), west of downtown. Hotel and campground. Take tram #1 to the last stop, then cross the overpass behind you and walk to the left. Hotel rooms are very expensive, but rooms in motel-like bungalows are more reasonable (doubles 1600Ft; campsites 200Ft per tent and 300Ft per person). Open May-Sept.

FOOD

Szeged is known both for university culture and food—it is the home of the famous Pick salami, the source of sweet paprika, and the best place for *halászlé,* a spicy fish soup. For those late-night cravings and supplies on weekends, there is a **non-stop ABC market,** Mars tér, near the corner of Londoni krt. and Mikszáth Kálmán u.

Roosevelt téri Halászcsárda (Lesőharcsa Étterem), Roosevelt tér 14 (tel. 480 117), on the square's southeast side next to the river. The place to sample the spicy fish soup for which Szeged is famous. Try any of the *"hallé"* dishes—they're only spicy if you add the green paprika served on the side (480-650Ft). The kitchen serves the catch of "the day" and other hefty entrées for 250-1000Ft. German menu. Open daily 11am-10pm.
Aranykorona Étterem, Deák Ferenc u. 29 (tel. 321 750), at the corner of Victor Hugo u., serves fish as well as vegetarian fried cheese and mushrooms (220-550Ft). Open Mon.-Thurs. 11am-midnight, Fri.-Sat. 11am-2am, Sun. 11am-4pm.

Csirke Étterem, Bocskai u. 3b (tel. 313 188). Shares the building with a *panzió*. Enter through a beer-barrel door for Hungarian cuisine (English menu; entrées 300-800Ft). Open Mon.-Sat. 11am-midnight.

Kisvirag Cukrasda, Klauzál tér (tel. 321 040). The entrance is crowded with the young and old intent on licking up their ice cream before the sun gets to it. Excellent pastries (70-120Ft), including *Somlói galuska* (98Ft), a regional specialty, and a dollop of ice cream (30Ft per scoop). Open daily 8am-10pm.

SIGHTS AND ENTERTAINMENT

The center of Szeged can be easily seen in an afternoon. Park-like **Széchenyi tér,** a block north of Klauzál tér, is near the geographical center of the city. The yellow **Old Town Hall** on the square's west edge was restored with red and green majolika ceramic tiles for shingles after the 1879 deluge destroyed most of the city. The bridge connecting the town hall to the drab building next door (which once held the tax office) was built for Habsburg Emperor Ferenc József's inspection of the reconstruction, to prevent His Majesty from having to go up and down.

To the east by the river, the huge Neoclassical **Móra Ferenc Múzeum,** Roosevelt tér 1/3 (tel. 470 370), exhibits folk art from the 18th century to the present. Keep an eye out for the waffle irons that look like giant salad tongs. The museum details the life of the long-vanished Avars, who occupied the Carpathian basin from the 6th through the 9th centuries. Exhibits include precise explanations in English (open Tues.-Sun. 10am-5pm; 40Ft, students 20Ft).

Oskola u. leads south to Dóm tér, where the red-brick **Votive Church** pierces the skyline with its twin 91m towers. Built by survivors of the great flood, the structure has too many tiny steeples and arches to be graceful. One of Hungary's largest churches, it houses an organ whose 10,000 pipes often exert themselves in afternoon or evening concerts (open Mon.-Sat. 9am-6pm, Sun. 12:30pm-6pm; known for closing haphazardly). Alongside the church stands the 12th-century **Demetrius Tower,** Szeged's oldest monument. Smaller and brighter than the Votive Church is the 1778 **Serbian Orthodox Church,** Somogyi Béla u. 3, across the street. Inside, the *iconostasis* holds 60 gilt-framed paintings, and the ceiling fresco of God creating the Earth swims in a sea of stars (open whenever there's someone around to collect the 40Ft admission fee). Just southwest of Dóm tér on Aradi Vértanuk tér stands the **Hősök Kapuja** (Hero's Gate), an arch erected in 1936 in honor of Horthy's White Guards, who brutally cleansed the nation of "Reds."

At the corner of Hajnóczi u. and Jósika u. lies the 1903 **Great Synagogue,** Jósika u. 8. Second in size only to the synagogue in Budapest, the structure's Moorish altar and gardens, Romanesque columns, Gothic domes, and Baroque façades combine to make this the most beautiful Jewish synagogue in Hungary. The cupola, decorated with designs symbolizing Infinity and Faith, seems to grow deeper the longer you look up into it. The walls of the vestibule are lined with the names of the 3100 members of the congregation who did not return from the concentration camps. English-speaking guides explain every detail of the building (open May-Sept. Sun.-Fri. 9am-noon and 1-6pm; 80Ft, students 40Ft). Next door, the **Old Synagogue** (now a theater) is disintegrating at the same speed as renovation progresses.

Frolic on the Tisza river on the summer-only disco boat **Szőke Tisza,** just off Roosevelt tér. *Kaiser* beer for 150Ft (no cover; open late daily—weekends until 4am). During the school year, join *Szegedi* students in their very own heavy metal joint at **Jate Klub,** in the Toldi u. entrance to the central university building on Dugonies tér, for a little taste of America—*Rolling Rock* for 120Ft. Party nights are Thursday, Friday, and Saturday (100-200Ft cover), and the doors don't close until 4am. One of the best pubs in town is the **HBH Beer House (Bajor Serfőzde),** in the heart of the city, Deák Ferenc u. 4 (tel. 313 934), where you can see how beer is made and promptly forget what you've learned for 111 to 178Ft per glass (open Mon.-Sat. 11:30am-midnight, Sun. 11:30am-11pm). The happening **Bounty Bar,** across from the Móra Museum on Roosevelt tér, closes up shop at 1-2am.

The **Open-Air Theater Festival** (Szegedi Szabadtéri Játékok), in mid-July to mid-August, is Hungary's largest outdoor theater festival. International troupes perform folk dances, operas, and musicals in an amphitheater with the Votive Church as a backdrop. Tickets (400-1500Ft) are sold at Deák u. 28/30 (tel. 471 466; fax 471 322).

Kecskemét

Nestled amid vineyards, fruit trees, and the plains *(puszta)*, Kecskemét lures tourists with museums and its famous apricot brandy—*barack pálinka*. On the old road between Istanbul and Hamburg, Kecskemét grew as the crossing point of traders' routes and was mentioned as early as 1368 as a great market town. The architecture captivates at every turn with everything from the town hall, made in Hungarian Art Nouveau style, to the synagogue, whose colorful tiles have a more romantic twist. The modern road between Szeged and Budapest passes near the *puszta* which surrounds Kecskemét with sandy lands populated by horses and cowboys.

ORIENTATION AND PRACTICAL INFORMATION

The town centers around a loosely connected string of squares. The town hall rises on **Kossuth tér,** which leads east into **Szabadság tér** and **Kálvin tér. Katona tér** is immediately south of the town hall, and **Jokai tér** and **Széchenyi tér** are two blocks north. The **train station** lies 10 to 15 minutes east of town along the main boulevard, **Rákóczi út.** The **bus station** is 2 minutes north of the train station. Local buses head into town from the train station. **Volán bus** will leave you next to the local bus station immediately north of Kossuth tér. Tickets available from the driver for 52Ft.

- **Tourist Offices: Tourinform,** Kossuth tér 1 (tel./fax 481 065), in the town hall's right-hand corner. Tons of free brochures organized by language. Basic maps free, detailed ones will cost you. Herds info on opportunities in the *puszta;* get it here, because obtaining it on the plains is harder than making a horse drink. Open summer Mon.-Fri. 8am-6pm, Sat.-Sun. 9am-1pm; winter Mon.-Fri. 8am-5pm, Sat. 9am-1pm. **Cooptourist,** Kettemplom kőz 9 (tel. 481 472), on the little pedestrian street between Szabadság tér and Kossuth tér. Good rates on private rooms. **Car rental** open Mon.-Fri. 8:30am-5pm. **IBUSZ,** Kossuth tér 3 (tel. 486 955; tel./fax 480 557), next to Hotel Aranyhomok. Private accommodations (approximately 800-1000Ft per person per night), and discounted international bus, train, and plain tickets, and visas. Open Mon.-Fri. 8am-5:30pm, Sat. 9am-noon.
- **Currency Exchange:** Numerous banks in the city center offer services and exchange rates similar to **Budapest Bank,** at the intersection of Nagykőrősi u. and Wesselenyi u. Forints for travelers' checks, and a **24-hr. ATM** for EC, Eurocard, Mastercard, and Cirrus. Open Mon. 8am-5pm, Tues.-Weds. 8am-4pm, Thurs. 8am-5pm, Fri. 8am-1pm.
- **Trains:** Kodály Zoltán tér, at the end of Rákóczi út (tel. 322 460). To: Budapest (hourly, 1¼hr., 508Ft); Szeged (15 per day, 1hr., 376Ft); Pécs (via Kiskunfélegyháza, 5hr., 988Ft). **Luggage storage:** 100Ft per day; open daily 7am-7pm.
- **Buses:** Kodály Zoltán tér (tel. 321 777). To: Balatonfüred (1 per day, 5hr., 1166Ft); Budapest (40 per day, 1½hr., 478Ft); Debrecen (2 per day, 5hr., 1260Ft); Eger (3 per day, 2½hr., 1410Ft); Pécs (3 per day, 5hr., 1112Ft); Szeged (13 per day, 1¾hr., 478Ft).
- **Public Transportation:** Take your pick between the private pink **CityBusz** (50Ft from driver, 40Ft from office by train station) or the normal large **Volán** buses (45Ft from kiosks, 52Ft from driver). Both have routes all over town and similar stops. Timetables are posted at most stops—both wind down around 10pm. The main bus terminal for the local Volán buses is just north of Kossuth tér.
- **Taxis:** 24hr. from stands around the city, or call 484 848.
- **Medical Emergency:** Call 04. Two facilities alternate for 24-hr. duty: Nyíri út 38 (tel. 486 511), northwest of town; Izsáki u. 5 (tel. 478 119) southwest of town.
- **Pharmacy: Mátyás Király Gyógyszertár,** Szabadság tér 1 (tel. 480 739) is open Mon.-Fri. 7:30am-8pm, Sat. 8am-5pm.

Post Office: Kálvin tér 10-12 (tel. 486 586; fax 481 034). Open Mon.-Fri. 8am-8pm, Sat. 8am-2pm, Sun. 8am-noon. **Postal code:** 6000. **Phone code:** 76.

ACCOMMODATIONS AND CAMPING

Summer offers all sorts of cheap accommodations in dormitories. Winter travelers will have considerably fewer options and will probably find the best deals in private rooms or pensions. Most tourist agencies (see above) locate private rooms. **Cooptourist,** Kéttemplom kőz 9 (tel. 481 472; open Mon.-Fri. 8:30am-5pm) rents singles and doubles (1600Ft per person), with a 30% additional fee on the first day for stays of less than 3 days. IBUSZ has rooms for 800-1000Ft per person.

Hotel Pálma, Hornyik János u. 4 (tel. 488 951 or 484 692), as close to the heart of the city as you could desire. Despite the name, it is the Reformed College's dormitory. Rooms are newly redone and super-clean. Bunk beds, showers, toilets, and telephones. The top floor is warm in summer. Singles 1700Ft. Doubles 2900Ft. Triples 3700Ft. Dormitory rooms for 4 to 8 (with lockers) 1100Ft per person.

Tantóképiz Kollégiuma, Jókai tér 4 (tel. 321 977), 2min. from Kossuth tér. A bed in spacious doubles, triples, and quads costs 700Ft; 1000Ft with bath and TV. There could be early check-out. Open July-Aug., but you can also try off-season.

Caissa Panzió, Gyenes tér 18 (tel./fax 481 685), on the 5th floor of a townhouse cloistered behind trees 5-10min. north of Kossuth tér. Head north from the northwestern corner of Jókai tér. Rooms are small, but clean and modern. Singles 2200-2700Ft, with bath and TV 3400Ft. Doubles 2700-3200Ft, with bath and TV 4200Ft. Triples 3500-4800Ft. Quads 4400-5200Ft. Quint 4800Ft. Breakfast 390Ft. Locked from 10pm-7am. German spoken. Call ahead.

Autós Camping, Sport u. 3 (tel. 329 398). A long haul southwest of town by minibus #101 or Volán bus #1 or 11. Tent sites 300Ft. 300Ft per person, 100Ft tax. Electricity and parking each 300Ft. Four-person bungalows 2700Ft. Open mid-April to mid-Oct.

FOOD

Numerous restaurants serve standard Hungarian food—lots of onions, flavorful sauces on meat, from goose to pork to beef, and the inevitable dish of paprika. The apricot brandy tastes great, but will put hair on your chest.

Őregház Vendéglő, Hosszú u. 27 (tel. 496 973), next to Széchenyi krt. Meat 'n' potatoes, Hungarian-style, in a neighborhood restaurant (entrées 270-420Ft). Open Sun.-Thurs. 11am-10pm, Fri.-Sat. 11am-midnight.

Borozó, Rákóczi út 3 (tel. 322 240). Head here for a quick swig of the local wines and apricot brandy. The wine pitchers are lined up waiting for you (only 20Ft for a 100mL glass). 85Ft for 50mL of *Barack pálinka*. Open Mon.-Thurs. 6:30am-7pm, Fri. 6:30am-6pm, Sat. 6:30am-noon.

Wéber Pince, Csongrádi u.2 (tel. 481 223), serves generous portions of German-style Hungarian food. Entrées 450-800Ft. Open Mon.-Sat. 11:30am-11pm.

SIGHTS AND ENTERTAINMENT

The salmon-colored **town hall,** Kossuth tér 1 (tel. 483 683), built in 1897 during the height of the Hungarian Art Nouveau movement, is clearly Kossuth tér's most impressive building (tours by appointment daily 7:30am-6pm; call 483 683 and ask for Földi Margit; 20Ft, in English 300Ft). The 1806 **Roman Catholic Big Church** brandishes its Neoclassical features on Széchenyi tér (Tues.-Fri. 9am-noon and 3-6pm). If you're not going to the *puszta*, visit the **Museum of Hungarian Folk Arts-Crafts,** Serfz u. 19 (tel. 327 203). In addition to clothes, furniture, and ceramics, the museum displays a sadistic collection of horse whips and painted Easter eggs. Don't worry; the eggs won't hurt you (open in summer Wed.-Sun. 10am-6pm; off-season 9am-5pm; 100Ft). The **Szórakaténusz Toy Museum,** Gáspár u. 11 (tel. 481 469), rotates exhibitions and a permanent collection of old miniature castles, soldiers, and dolls (open Tues.-Sun.

10am-6pm; 50Ft, students 30Ft). At the same address, the **Museum of Naive Artists,** Gáspár u. 11 (tel. 324 767), displays the sculptures and paintings of amateur artists from the area in a white 18th-century manor (open Tues.-Sun. 10am-6pm; 50Ft, students 30Ft, Thurs. free).

The Art Nouveau **Picture Gallery,** Rákóczi út 1 (tel. 480 776), displays the works of *Kecskeméti* artists (open Tues.-Sun. 10am-5pm; 50Ft, students 30Ft, Thurs. free). Inside the cupola-topped **synagogue** (now the Technika Háza), Rákóczi út 2 (tel. 487 611), sit 15 full-size copies of Michelangelo sculptures, including the head of *David* and the *Piéta* (open Mon.-Fri. 9am-6pm; 10Ft, students 5Ft). The **Katona József Theater,** Katona tér 5 (tel. 483 283), not only puts on excellent drama, but is also set in a magnificent 1896 building (off-season operettas 400-500Ft). For raucous disco fun, here's to you, **Club Robinson,** Akadémia krt. 2 (tel. 485 844; open 8pm-3am).

Kecskemét has produced such greats as the composer Zoltán Kodály (1882-1967) and author József Katona (1791-1830), and continues its artistic tradition each March with the **Kecskemét Spring Festival,** featuring music, theater, literature, and the visual arts. Late August and early September witness the "Hírös" Festival of food.

■ Near Kecskemét: Bugac

Bugac—where cowboys roam the *puszta* and rustle up goulash under the stars—brushes up against the Kiskunság National Park. The sand lizard and Orsini's viper share the park with gray cattle, twisted-horned sheep, and the Mangalica pig.

The area of Bugac is very large—start with information from **Bugac Tours,** Szabadság tér 1/A, Kecskemét (tel./fax 481 643), to make the most of your day. The most popular destination for fast-shutter cameras is the 45-minute horse show with whip tricks and flashy demonstrations (April-Oct. daily 1 and 3pm, or by request at the railing between the ticket collector and the barns). Tickets (1300Ft, students 650Ft) include admission to the park and a carriage ride and are sold at the info stand.

The national park itself offers some lovely hikes and bike rides in the hilly juniper forest. **Táltos Panzió** (tel. 372 633; fax 372 580), next to Bugaci Csárda in Bugac-Felső, is the best place to arrange horseback riding (DM8-12 per hour), carriage rides (DM5-6 per person per hour), bike rentals, and wintertime sledding. At the intersection of Beton út and Főld út, a summer souvenir shop offers **tourist information.** The **national park ticket office,** right before Bugac-Puszta, offers a lot of info, but their English ability depends on who is working that day. For hiking safety tips, see Essentials: Wilderness and Safety Concerns, p. 49.

If you want to spend the night, head for the **private rooms** in Bugac proper (about DM10 per person). Several *csárdas* in town serve the specialties of the *puszta* with dancing and Gypsy music to boot. Live the high life at the elaborate **Bugaci Csárda** (tel. 372 522), which sated—nearly—even the appetites of the horse-mad British royal family (hence the pictures). The house specialties are the ham-filled pancakes (350Ft), deep-pot goulash (300Ft), and for dessert, *palacsinta* (pancakes with apricot marmalade, 200Ft; open daily 8am-8pm).

Bugac Puszta, where you'll find the entrance to the national park and the horse shows, is about 6km north of Bugac. **Bugac-Felső** is about halfway between the two, a kilometer to the west. The best stop to get off at is Bugac-Felső, across from Táltos Panzió and the Bugaci Csárda. The **narrow-gauge train** (tel. 322 460) leaves from Kecskemét's little train station, Halasi u. down Batthyány u. from the center and over the overpass. The train (1hr.) stops four places in Bugac. The first—Bugac-Puszta—is not where the horse shows are. The next—**Bugac**—is best if you're looking for a private room. **Bugac-Felső** is closest to the riding school and Bugaci Csárda. Continue along the tracks until a sand path crosses the tracks, turn right, and follow the path 10 minutes. If your only destination is the *puszta* and you don't mind walking through fields, get off at **Móricgát-Tanyark** and walk west across the fields toward white houses in the distance. For a good daytrip, take the 8:15am train, which meanders through the countryside to Bugac (200Ft, students 100Ft; tickets can be bought on the train), and return to Kecskemét either by the 7:15pm train or a bus from Bugac-Felső (2 per day, 1hr., 210Ft).

TRANSDANUBIA

Transdanubia, the southwest half of Hungary, is known for rolling hills and expansive sunflower fields. Originally Pannonia, a Roman province, Transdanubia later witnessed the bloody battle of Szigetvár (1566) that ended the Ottoman Empire's push for Vienna. The Austro-Hungarian Empire rewarded the region with Baroque and Rococo architecture. Look to towns like Tata and Székesfehérvár, and Fertőd, home of the "Hungarian Versailles," for a glimpse of the Hungary beyond Budapest.

■ Pécs

Take two thousand years of history, add raucous collegians, and you have the recipe for Pécs. On the street, students and locals sit, sip, and stroll, while towering monuments recall Pécs's Roman foundations, medieval glory, Turkish occupation, and Habsburg yoke. Tourists have long appreciated the town's dynamic combo, and each year foreigners flock to admire ancient history over a cup of java.

ORIENTATION AND PRACTICAL INFORMATION

Pécs rests on the knees of the Mecsek mountain range; conveniently, north and south correspond to up and down the hillside. Tourists bustle through the historic **Inner City**, a rectangle bounded by the remnants of the city wall. The middle of the Old Town is **Széchenyi tér**, where **Hunyadi Janos u., Király u., Irgalmasok u., Ferencek u.**, and **Janus Pannonius u.** converge, and where most tourist offices are located. The Old Town is small enough for pack-toters to visit on foot; it takes less than 20 minutes to cross from north to south (more to get back uphill).

Tourist Office: Tourinform, Széchenyi tér 9 (tel. 213 315). The only office for all of Baranya county. Info on local entertainment and travel. Xeroxed maps (free), tourist **maps** (200Ft), and a guide discussing Pécs history building by building (50Ft). Open June-Aug. daily 9am-2pm; Sept.-May 8am-4pm.

Budget Travel: Mecsek Tours, Széchenyi tér 1 (tel. 213 300; fax 212 044). This travel agency specializes in trips out of Pécs, sells telephone cards and bus tickets, changes money, and arranges tours and private rooms. English spoken. Open June-Aug. Mon.-Fri. 9am-5pm, Sat. 9am-1pm; Sept.-May Mon.-Sat. 8am-3:30pm.

Currency Exchange: OTP, Király u. 1 (tel. 232 200), cashes traveler's checks. Open Mon.-Wed. 7:45am-3pm, Thurs. 9:15am-5pm, Fri. 7:45am-noon.

ATMs: 24-hr. ATM at **IBUSZ bank**, at Széchenyi tér's south end, takes most cards.

Trains: (tel. 312 443) just beyond the bottom of the city's historic district, 10min. by bus #30 or 34 from the center of town. *InterCity* trains (tel. 212 734) speed to Budapest (2 per day, 2½hr., 988Ft plus 200Ft reservation) for the same price as the slow train. Purchase tickets at the **MÁV travel office** in the station or at Rákóczi út 39c. Several regular trains chug daily from Budapest-Déli station (3hr., 988Ft). Four trains per day leave for various towns around Lake Balaton.

Buses: (tel. 415 215). Walking distance from the center, at the intersection of Nagy Lajos Király út. and Alsómalom u. To: Szigetvár (8-14 per day, 40min., 182Ft).

Public Transportation: City bus tickets cost 60Ft.

Bookstores: International English Center, Mária u. 9 (tel. 312 010). New and used books, an ESL section, and English newspapers. Open Mon.-Fri. 10am-6pm. The Center runs a café/library with *Newsweek* and *National Geographic*. Open July-Aug. Mon.-Fri. 10am-6pm; Sept.-June Mon.-Fri. 10am-8pm, Sat. 9am-1pm.

Post Office: Jókai Mór u. 10 (tel. 214 422). Open Mon.-Fri. 8am-8pm, Sat. 8am-2pm, Sun. 8am-noon. **Postal code:** 7621. **Phone code:** 72.

PÉCS ■ 293

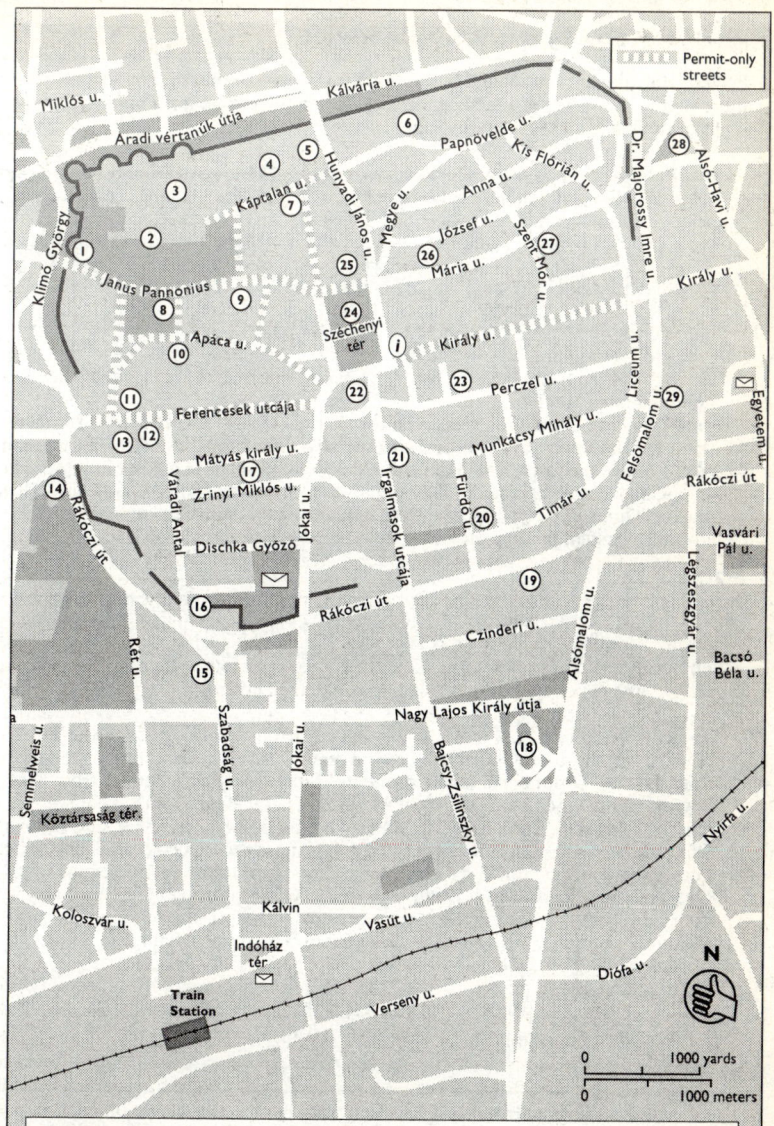

Pécs

Amerigo Tot Museum, 4
Barbakán (Barbican), 1
Belvárosi templom (Church of inner town), 24
Bóbita Bánszínház, 27
Bus Station, 18
Csontváry Museum, 9
Ferences templom (Franciscan Church), 13
IBUSZ, 22
Irgalmasok temploma (Church of the Brothers of Mercy), 21
Jakováli Haszán Museum, 14
Janus Pannonius Museum, 6

Kis Galéria (Small Gallery), 11
Liszt Ferenc Zeneművészeti Foiskola (Francis Liszt Academy of Music), 17
Mecseki Bányászati Múzeum (Mining Museum of Mecsek), 26
Memi pasa fürdöje--romok (Memi Pasha's baths--ruins), 12
Modern Magyar Képtár Kortás Gyüjtemény (Picture Gallery of Hungarian Modern Art), 15
Nemzeti színház, 23
Néprajzi Museum, 16
Ókeresztény mausóleum (Old-Christian Mausoleum), 8

Püspöki palota (Bishop's Palace), 2
Régészeti Múzeum (Archeological Museum), 25
Római sírkápolna (Roman Mausoleum), 10
Synagogue, 20
Székesegyház (Cathedral), 3
Szt. Ágoston-templom (St. Austin's Church), 28
Termeszettudományi Múzeum (Museum of Natural Science), 19
Várostörténeti Múzeum (Museum of the History of Pécs), 29
Vasarely Museum, 7
Zsolnay Museum, 5

ACCOMMODATIONS AND CAMPING

Private rooms can be arranged at the Old Town's tourist offices. For stays of under three nights, a 30% fee is added to the first night's price. **Mecsek Tours** (see above) seeks out singles (1100Ft) and doubles (1800Ft).

- **Janus Pannonius University Dormitory** has several campuses around Pécs; rooms are available during summer. **Universitas u. 2** (tel./fax 324 473). Take bus #21 from main bus terminal to the wooded "48-es tér." Sterile but clean rooms for up to three people (1680Ft). Laundry facilities. Call ahead Sept.-June. **Szántó Kovács u. 1** (tel./fax 251 203). Less central. Take bus #21 from the main bus terminal to "Nendtvich Andor u." The university is across the main road and to the left. Lower floors stay cooler. Laundry facilities. Neat triples with floor bathrooms for 560Ft per person, 605Ft after the first night. Available July-Aug.
- **Szent Mór Kollégium,** 48-es tér 4 (tel. 311 199). Take bus #21 to "48-es tér". Doubles in a gorgeous old building for 700Ft. Bathrooms in hall are cleaned daily. Sign up for laundry. Kitchen.
- **Hotel-Camping Mandulás,** Angyán János u. 2 (tel. 315 981). Take bus #34 from the train station directly to the hills above the city, where tent sites (DM12 for 2 people), 3-bed bungalows (DM35), and doubles with breakfast in a 1-star hotel (DM45) are located at the entrance to hiking trails into the Mecsek Hills. Discounts in low season. Open mid-April to mid-Oct. Call ahead for same-day reservations. For advance reservations, call Mescek Tours (see above).

FOOD

Pécs's countless restaurants, cafés, and bars lining the Old Town's touristy streets — especially Király u., Apáca u., and Ferencesek u.—offer varied menus and crowd-watching opportunities. **Konzum,** Kossuth tér, is an all-purpose grocery. Loaves of bread 70-240Ft (open Mon.-Fri. 6:30am-8pm, Sat. 6:30am-2pm).

- **Liceum Söröző** (tel. 327 284), in a cellar off Király u. 35 opposite the Liceum church, and through a courtyard. Low prices and a choice selection of beers make this a favorite with the student community. 140Ft *Gold Fassl.* Entrées from 310Ft. English menu. Open Mon.-Thurs. 11am-10pm, Fri.-Sat. 11am-11pm.
- **Caflisch Cukrászda Café,** Király u. 32. May be the best and trendiest café in town. Sit inside to savor Hungarian sweets, or enjoy the sun with a cold drink and watch Pécs go by. Pastries from 50Ft. Open Sun.-Thurs. 8am-10pm, Fri.-Sat. 8am-11pm.
- **DÓM Vendéglő Restaurant,** Király u. 3 (tel. 210 088), through the courtyard, last door on your right. The interior is an impressive two-level wooden reproduction of a church, complete with stained-glass windows. Many roasted meat dishes. German menu. English spoken. Entrées 420-800Ft. Open daily 11am-11pm.
- **Kolping,** Szent István tér 9 (tel. 324 712), just north of Ferencesek u. Good *borda* (cutlet) and a rainbow of colorful veggies, with a heavy emphasis on German food. Entrées 380-520Ft. 150mL beer 130Ft. Open daily 11am-10pm.

SIGHTS

The ornate buildings surrounding Széchenyi tér center around the **Gazi Khassim Pasha** (Inner City Parish Church), a converted and exorcised 16th-century Turkish mosque, built on the site of an earlier Christian church—a fusion of Christian and Turkish history emblematic of Pécs. A Rococo alien in the square, **Patika Múzeum** (Pharmacy Museum), Apáca u. 1 (tel. 315 702; open Mon.-Fri. 7:30am-4:30pm), is a testament to the belief that leeches and blood-letting were good and sound techniques to cure anything from stubbornness to political incorrectness. Stroll along Ferencesek u. to the **Franciscan Church,** whose eclectic exterior houses Baroque furnishings. **Jakovali Hassam Djami,** Rákóczi u. 2, is a functioning 16th-century mosque (no shorts; open Sun.-Wed. 10am-1pm, 2-6pm; 50Ft, students 25Ft).

Numerous trees shield Szent István tér, north of the Franciscan Church, from the hot afternoon sun. On the square's east side, 4th-century **Roman ruins** have been slowly decaying since Jupiter and Venus went out of business. Underneath lies the largest known burial site in Hungary (open Tues.-Sun. 10am-6pm). Rising above a **mausoleum**, across an open square, the **cathedral** stands proudly as Pécs's centerpiece. Masons have been piling on additions to the 4th-century foundation since the first bricks were laid (open Mon.-Sat. 9am-1pm and 2-5pm, Sun. 1-5pm; 120Ft, students 70Ft). To the west, the **Barbakán** is a popular walking spot and a vestige of the great double-walled defense of the 15th century.

East of the Old Town, the **Várostörténeti Múzeum** (History Museum), Felsőmalom u. 9 (tel. 310 165), chronicles Pécs' subordination under the Ottomans, Habsburgs, Nazis, and Communists. Pécs was above dreary labor productivity races, and programmed its conveyor belts to turn out elegance—porcelain, musical instruments, and champagne (open Tues.-Sun. 10am-4pm; 100Ft, students 50Ft, off-season students free). South of Széchenyi tér, a 19th-century **synagogue** stands on Kossuth tér (open Sun.-Fri. 9am-5pm; 40Ft, students 30Ft). The Jewish population in Pécs hovers at 300; 88% of the pre-war population did not return from Auschwitz.

ENTERTAINMENT

Nightlife in Pécs settles in the crowded, cheerful bars and restaurants near Széchenyi tér, especially on the first two blocks of Király u. For pierced body parts and loud music, the local alternative scene is the best outside of Budapest.

Rózsakert Sörkert/Rosengarten Biergarten, Janus Pannonius u., east of the cathedral, is the place to go for a sobering breeze and live music in a German-inspired outdoor setting. *Gold Fassl* 150Ft per 0.5L. Open daily 11am-11pm.

Kioszk Eszpresszo, opposite Janus Pannonius 1. A café/beer garden popular with lesbians, gay men, and heteros alike (open daily 11am-11:45pm).

Blues Pub, Apáca u. 2. On the weekends, this pub attracts slightly more mature Pécs youths who've learned to converse, carouse, and consume one cigarette after another. After a few *Stella Artois* (130Ft), you might begin to feel dizzy in this five-level Surrealist structure. Open daily 11am-1am.

Hard Rák Café, Ipar u. 7 (tel. 227 144 or 227 319), at the corner of Bajcsy-Zsilinszky u. Plays rock, alternative, and hard-core. The grotto inside comes complete with cave paintings. Don't get run over by the bands arriving by VW bus. Open Mon.-Sat. 7pm-past 4am. cover 200Ft Thurs.-Sat. when live bands play.

Gyár (Factory), Czinderi u. 3/5 (Czinderi u. isn't marked—find it between Bajcsy-Zsilinsky and Alsómalom u.). The tables are old tires from earth-moving equipment. One of the few places in Hungary where Marx and Lenin still grace the walls. A hard-core and alternative rock dance club with live bands on weekends. Open daily 6pm-dawn, but don't expect too much action in the early evening.

■ Near Pécs

SZIGETVÁR CASTLE

In 1566, 50,000 Turks besieged Miklós Zrínyi and his 2500 soldiers in **Szigetvár Castle.** After a month-long struggle, with their drinking water exhausted and the inner fortification in flames, Zrínyi's army launched a desperate attack against their aggressors. They were wiped out, but managed to kill a quarter of the Turkish force in the process. The **Zrínyi Miklós Museum** chronicles the siege, but the castle ruins are remnants of a structure built well after the battle and consist mostly of red brick walls with a pleasant park inside (museum open May-Sept. Tues.-Sun. 9am-6pm; April-Oct. 9am-4pm; closed Nov.-March; 60Ft, students 40Ft).

Buses from Pécs, 33km west (8-14 per day, 182Ft), stop at the town's south end. Walk north 15min. to the castle. The English-speaking reception at **Hotel Oroszlán,** Zrínyi tér 2 (tel. 310 116; fax 312 917), on the way, rents bath-outfitted rooms for 3100Ft (Nov.-April 2900Ft, except around Christmas). **Mecsek Tours** in the hotel (tel. 310 116) distributes 82Ft maps (open Mon.-Fri. 7:30am-4pm). **Phone code:** 73.

KAPOSVÁR

Located halfway between Pécs and Lake Balaton, Kaposvár is an easy daytrip destination. Surrounded by rolling hills and fields, the town is livelier than Pécs, but lacks its size and historical importance. Right on the pedestrian walkway, **Somogy Megyei Museum**, Fő u. 10, presents almost every aspect of the county's cultural life, ranging from archaeological finds from the Bronze Age to regional folk handicrafts (open daily 11am-5pm; 80Ft, students 30Ft). If you feel like getting out to the country lanes above the town, head for the **Rippl-Rónai Villa** in Róma Hegy. One of Kaposvár's most famous sons, József Rippl-Rónai (1861-1927) was a French-trained post-Impressionist painter. The 19th-century studio in which he spent his final years has been made into a museum for his collection and personal belongings (open Tues.-Sun. 10am-6pm; Nov.-March 10am-4pm; 50Ft, students 30Ft). Take city bus #15 (newsstands sell 45Ft tickets, but it costs 60Ft to come back. Who knew?) from the platform just south of the bus station, and ride about 12min. to the last stop; walk 300m farther, keeping to the paved road.

The **train station** and **bus station** are less than two blocks apart and five minutes south of the downtown area. **Trains** come and go to Siófok (6 per day, 3hr., 424Ft), and **buses** run back and forth to Pécs (12-15 per day; 1½hr.; 236Ft, students 118Ft). To reach the town center, **Fő u.**, from the stations, walk up **Teleki u.** to **Kossuth tér** and then take a hard right. Drop by the English-speaking **Tourinform**, Fő u. 8 (tel. 320 404), for maps, brochures, and lists of restaurants and cultural events (open in summer Mon.-Fri. 9am-6pm, Sat. 9am-1pm; off-season Mon.-Fri. 8am-12:30pm and 1-5pm, Sat. 8am-noon). Since relatively few tourists stay in Kaposvár, private rooms are rare and expensive. **IBUSZ**, Dózsa György u., (tel/fax 315 477), in a purple building just south of Fő u., offers private doubles (1600Ft for the first night, 1250Ft each night thereafter; open Mon.-Thurs. 8am-4:30pm, Fri. 8am-3pm). **Flamingo Panzió**, Füredi u. 53 (tel. 416 728), puts tourists up in singles (1300Ft) and doubles (2000Ft). **Nyári Szalló**, Bajcsy-Zsilinszky u. 6 (tel. 319 011), in the Kaffka Margit Kollegium, has dorm beds for 500Ft (students 300Ft). **Phone code:** 82.

■ Székesfehérvár

With its Old Town streets, 18th-century pastel buildings, and Baroque steeples, one would hardly guess that Székesfehérvár once served as Hungary's first capital. The one-time Basilica, built in the early 11th century, hosted all state events until the Turks occupied and ruined the town in 1543. Much of the architecture from the following century remains intact, and ongoing exploration continues to unearth artifacts from earlier periods. A concrete embrace of highrises has given new life to old Székesfehérvár, one of Hungary's friendliest and most unpretentious towns.

Orientation and Practical Information Pedestrian **Fő u.** bisects the Old Town. Central **Városház tér** and nearby **Koronázó tér** branch off Fő u. to the west and east, respectively. Székesfehérvár is a major transportation link for Transdanubia. **Trains** ply the rails to Budapest (33 per day, 1hr., 276Ft), Siófok (19 per day, 1hr., 176Ft), and Veszprém (11 per day, 1hr., 176Ft). **Buses** pass by wide fields of corn on their way to Budapest (12 per day, 1½hr., 340Ft), Siófok (6 per day, 1hr., 222Ft), and Veszprém (22 per day, 1hr., 222Ft). Trains generally run slightly more frequently than buses, but the central location of the bus terminal makes buses convenient. From the **bus station**, Piac tér (tel. 311 057), just west of Fő u., both **Liszt Ferenc u.** and **Megyeház u.** travel to Városház tér. From the **train station**, Béke tér (tel. 312 293), walk along **Prohászka Ottokár út** until it becomes **Várkör út**. The Old Town will be just to your left. The cheerful staff at **Tourinform**, Városház tér 1 (tel./fax 312 818), speaks English, gives out free brochures, and sells **maps** for 250Ft (open Mon.-Fri. 9am-1pm and 2pm-4pm). **OTP Bank,** corner of Fő u. and Várkapu u., is equipped with a Cirrus and MC **ATM** (open Mon.-Thurs. 8am-3:45pm, Fri. 8am-1pm). A 24-hour currency changer sits at Kossuth u. 14. The **post office** stands at Kossuth Lajos u. 16 (tel. 312 268; open Mon.-Fri. 8am-8pm, Sat. 8am-2pm, Sun. 8am-noon). **Postal code:** 8000. **Phone code:** 22.

Accommodations and Food The folks at **Albatours,** Kossuth Lajos u. 14a (tel. 312 494; fax 327 082), have a selection of private doubles for 1200Ft (open Mon.-Fri. 9am-5pm). The staff at **Tourinform** (see above), have no rooms of their own to offer, but know everyone in town who does, and will call and plead until they find an empty one within your budget. **Rév Szálló,** József Attila u. 42 (tel. 327 015; fax 327 061), at the corner of Bodai út, equips its doubles with TVs and refrigerators (1700Ft per room), but strips down its triples to the bare minimum (1500Ft). All rooms have shared baths. Call ahead, they are often full. The summer dorms of **József Attila Kollégium,** Széchenyi István u. 13 (tel. 313 155), cost 500Ft per bed. They might have space even before school lets out in late June. The dorms are cleaner than average, but still have no shower curtains. **Campground Székesfehérvári Kemping,** Bregyó-köz 1 (tel. 313 433), runs what could be the best campground in Hungary (269Ft per tent and 202Ft per person). Three-person bungalows run 471Ft per bed (open May-Sept). Athletic facilities abound near the campsite.

Pizza places are everywhere, but don't worry, the untouristed restaurants serving national cuisine are as inexpensive as the rooms. **Ősfehérvár Étterem,** Koronázó tér 2 (tel. 314 056), is a local favorite with German, French, and Russian menus, and a Hungarian list of daily specials. Outdoor tables are right over the basilica's excavation work (entrées 240-690Ft; open daily 11am-10pm). Come to **Arany Csengő Vendéglő,** Megyeház u. 10, for *galuska* (dumplings 120Ft) and tasty *káposztasaláta* (coleslaw 50Ft). Simple, good eatin', and not a tourist in sight (open Mon.-Sat. 5pm-8pm). **Maximka,** Ady Endre 4, has various types of good *pörkölt* (stews 210-390Ft; open daily, 10am-midnight). And, by the way, the **McDonald's** across from the bus station is open 24 hours. **Kaiser's** supermarket, minutes northeast of the Garden of Ruins on Kyegl György u., has everything you'll need and more (open Mon.-Fri. 8am-7pm, Sat. 8am-1pm).

Sights and Entertainment Start your walking tour of Székesferhérvár in **Városház tér,** the Old Town's center. The **fountain** in the middle represents the royal orb, which, along with the crown and scepter, serves as one of the three symbols of the Hungarian king's authority. The lime-green Baroque **városház** (town hall), was built in 1698 and enlarged in 1936-37.

Directly to the east, on Koronázó tér, spreads the **Garden of Ruins.** This courtyard contains the remains of Hungary's first **basilica;** St. Stephen, the country's first Christian king, built the basilica between 1016-38, while Székesfehérvár was the Hungarian capital. Here, 37 kings were crowned and 17 buried. Unfortunately, all that's left is some riveting rubble. When the Turks took the city in 1543, they used the basilica as a gunpowder storehouse; in 1601, an accidental explosion blew the building to smithereens. The excavation that has turned most of Koronázó tér into a sand pit is currently unearthing parts of the basilica that fared slightly better. Scattered throughout the garden and displayed near the walls are fragments of stonework and sculpture. Archaeologists now generally concur that the sarcophagus on the right as you enter once contained the remains of St. Stephen himself (open April-Oct. Tues.-Sun. 9am-6pm; 50Ft, students free).

Koronázó tér's long, yellow **Bishop's Palace,** built from 1790-1801, soon after the city became a bishopric, was constructed largely of stones from the old basilica. It is still the bishop's residence, but tourists can occasionally wheedle a glimpse of the 40,000-volume library. The twin-spired building to the south of the square on Arany János u. is **St. Stephen's Cathedral** (not to be confused with the **Church of St. János of Nepomuk,** which is also yellow and also has two towers, but is smaller and north of Varosház tér on Fő u.). It was built between 1759-78 on the site of the tomb of Grand Duke Géza, father of King Stephen and founder of Székesfehérvár. Unless mass is in session, visitors can go no farther inside than the glass doors in the vestibule, but from there they can see the airy hall with its Baroque frescoes. The white paving stones on the street in front outline the foundations of the 10th-century church thought to have contained Géza's tomb. The white 1470 **St. Anna's Chapel**, on the north side, was a mosque during the Turkish occupation. On the cathedral's east side is **Hősök tere**, dedicated to WWI heroes.

A courtyard off Jókai u. holds a wrought iron sign that says **Törökudvar** (Turkish Yard). From the street, it resembles a small vacant lot gone to weed, but it's the site of a 16th-century Turkish bath now under excavation. Stonework and brick arches are becoming visible as work progresses. The county-run **Szent István Király Múzeum** (King St. Stephen Museum) occupies several buildings in town and constitutes Hungary's second largest collection, after the National Museum in Budapest. The main building's **Permanent Exhibition of Archeology,** Fő u. 6 (tel. 315 583), spans the history of Fejér county from the first Transdanubian settlement to the 1600s, including a particularly large collection of Roman artifacts. There is even a small exhibition on the Turkish bath on Jókai u. (English explanations; open Tues.-Fri. 10am-4pm, Sat.-Sun. 1pm-5pm; 80Ft, students 40Ft). **Rotating art exhibitions** are shown in the branch of the King St. Stephen Museum at Országzászlo tér 3 (tel. 311 734; open Tues.-Sun. 10am-2pm; 80Ft, students 40Ft).

Budenz-ház, Arany János u. 12 (tel. 313 027), shelters the collection of the Ybl family, including 18th- to 20th-century Hungarian art and furniture. The house itself, named after the linguist József Budenz who lived here from 1858-60, was built in 1781, but its foundation dates to the Middle Ages (open Tues.-Sun. 10am-2pm; 80Ft, students 40Ft). The Jesuits built the **Fekete Sas Patikamúzeum** (Black Eagle Pharmacy Museum), Fő u. 5 (tel. 315 583), in 1758 and it remained a functioning pharmacy until 1971. All the original woodwork is still intact (open Tues.-Sun. 10am-6pm; donations encouraged).

One man's expression of artistic whimsy, the ferro-concrete-and-brick **Bory Castle**, at Bory tér on the city's northeast edge, could be the playground for the ultimate game of hide-and-seek. Architect and sculptor Jenő Bory (1879-1959) built it by hand over 40 summers as a memorial to his wife. The towers, gardens, crooked paths, winding staircases, incongruous statuary of historical figures, and stone chambers crowded with works of art were all meant for exploring. It is nearly deserted on weekdays (open Mon.-Fri. 9am-5pm, Sat.-Sun. 10am-noon and 3-5pm; 80Ft, students 40Ft). Take bus #26a from the terminal at Piac tér or #32 from the train station to the intersection of Kassai u. and Vágújhelyi u. (next to the white storefront with turquoise trim; tickets cost 60Ft on the bus and 40Ft at the terminal). Then walk north on Vagújhelyi u. to Bory tér. North of town, a chain of exceptionally well kept parks and lakes offers ample opportunity for relaxation. At the far end is a **sports park** with facilities for volleyball and tennis (250Ft per hour).

For late-night carousers, cold half-liters of draft *Dreher* run only 110Ft at **Dreher Maximka Söröző,** Ady Endre u. 4 (open Sun.-Thurs. 10am-midnight, Fri.-Sat. 10am-4am). **Vörösmarty Theater,** Fő u., and the **open-air theater,** Pelikán udvar, put on music and theater performances nearly every night. Get tickets (200-300Ft and up) and schedules at the box office at Fő u. 3 (tel. 314 591; open Mon.-Fri. 9am-6pm).

■ Szombathely

Big Szombathely likes to act small, as if it were still Claudia Savaria—its first-century Roman colony. Seat of Vas county and a major crossroads between Transdanubia and Austria, the city fills on weekends with clusters of people promenading among 2000-year-old ruins and Baroque façades. Szombathely's unparalleled selection of cafés, pubs, and restaurants provides welcome refueling for tired strollers readying for yet another crawl through the town's architectural treasures.

ORIENTATION AND PRACTICAL INFORMATION

The inner city of Szombathely can be crossed on foot in 20 minutes. The town focuses on several squares, the largest of which is **Fő tér,** its psychological center.

The main tourist offices are located around **Mártírok tere**, a few blocks north. The **train station** lies northeast of the inner city; to reach Mártírok tere, take **Széll Kálmán u.** straight down. The **bus station** is in the northwest part of the inner city; reach Mártírok tere by following **Petőfi Sándor u.** east, and **Király u.** south.

Tourist Office: For English information and maps, your best bet is Tourinform-licensed **Savaria Tourist**, Mártírok tere 1 (tel. 312 264). Open Mon.-Fri. 8am-5:30pm, Sat. 8am-noon. Wherever you go, avoid the blue and white covered map; not only does "Red Flag Street" no longer exist, even the bus station has moved.
Currency Exchange: Across the street from the tourist office, **OTP Bank**, Király u. 10. Open Mon.-Thurs. 8am-3pm, Fri. 8am-2pm.
ATM: Machine for Cirrus and MC at the OTP, Széll Kálmán u. 1.
Trains: tel. 312 050. To: Budapest (8 per day, 3½hr., 988Ft); Győr (2 per day, 3hr., 508Ft); Sopron (8 per day, 2hr., 276Ft); Veszprém (12 per day, 2½hr., 592Ft).
Buses: tel. 312 054. To: Budapest (1 per day, 3½hr., 1214Ft); Győr (4 per day, 2hr., 704Ft); Keszthely (3 per day, 3hr., 500Ft); Sopron (6 per day, 2hr., 424Ft); and Veszprém (2 per day, 2hr., 624Ft).
Post Office: Kossuth Lajos u. 18 (tel. 311 584). Open Mon.-Fri. 8am-8pm, Sat. 8am-2pm, Sun. 8am-noon. **Postal code:** 9700.
Telephones: Inside and outside the post office. **Phone code:** 094.

ACCOMMODATIONS AND CAMPING

There aren't many private rooms to rent in Szombathely, and they're difficult to discover on your own. **Savaria Tourist** (see above), offers centrally located doubles (1700-2000Ft) in the homes of people who could be your grandparents. **IBUSZ**, Fő tér 44 (tel. 314 141), has doubles for 1600Ft (open Mon.-Fri. 8am-4pm).

Orlay Hostel, central at Nagy Kar u. 1/3 (tel. 312 375). Charges 400Ft per person in an 8-bed room. More spacious than most, but still no shower curtains. Checkout 8am. Open daily in summer and on school-year weekends.
405 Kollégium, Holy tér 2 (tel. 312 198), next to the bus terminal. Holy college dorm, Batman! 460Ft per person in a room with 4 beds.
Hotel Liget, Szent István Park 15 (tel. 314 168). From the bus station, a #7 bus stops outside the hotel. A tourist hotel on the west side of town, features sparkling doubles with private baths, TVs, and breakfast for 5365Ft.
Péterfy Kollégium, just west of the inner city at Magyar László u. 2 (tel. 312 653). Rents 2- and 7-bed rooms at 450Ft per person. Summers only.
Camping: Tópart Camping, Kondics u. 4 (tel. 314 766). Four-person bungalows for 2800Ft (6000Ft with bath) and 5-person bungalows for 2800Ft. For campsites, it charges 200Ft per tent and 300Ft per person. Open May 1-Sept. 30.

FOOD

Szombathely offers a wide selection of top-notch restaurants and supermarkets. **Julius Meinl** supermarket, Fő tér 16, isn't the best stocked, but will gladly accept Visa and MasterCard (open Mon.-Fri. 7am-8pm, Sat. 7am-2pm).

Pince Étterem, Hollán Ernő 10. Serves exquisite Hungarian specialties for a more-than-reasonable price. Low ceilings, subtle lighting, and a classy staff make this Szombathely's top choice for a dinner date. The delicious *bakonyi sertésborda* (bakony schnitzel) is worth every forint at 440Ft. Entrées 400-560Ft. Have a glass of wine (51Ft) with this meal. Open Mon.-Sat. 11am-11pm.
Gyöngyös Étterem, Széll Kálmán u. 8 (tel. 312 665). Reliable and popular. Entrées run 320-690Ft, though there is also a cheaper daily set menu. Specialties include *pörkölt* (stew) and *sertésszelet* (schnitzel). Open daily 10am-10pm.
Király Bisztró, Király u. 3. Features cheap Hungarian sausages, sandwiches, and pastries for around 100Ft. Open Mon.-Fri. 6am-6pm, Sat. 6am-1pm.
Pannonia Étterem, Fő tér 29 (tel. 311 469). Centrally located and attached to a pub. Budget stews and schnitzels. Entrées 280-490Ft. Open daily 11am-11pm.

SIGHTS AND ENTERTAINMENT

The **Szombathely Cathedral** at Templom tér, built in 1797 as a cross between Baroque and Neoclassical styles, is adorned with frescoes and gilt ornaments. An Allied bombing raid in 1945 all but flattened the building, and so far the efforts at reconstruction have been slow: hence, the bare ceilings and no pews. Directly behind the cathedral stretches the north side of the **Garden of Ruins,** the center of the city's original first century Roman colony. The ruins from several different periods have been excavated, and visitors can walk among town walls, roads, a bathhouse, parts of a palace, official buildings, and floor mosaics, one of which is thought to have been part of the Caesar's audience hall. An English-speaking guide may be around to explain everything in copious detail (open April-Oct. daily 10am-6pm; Nov.-March 10am-4pm; 80Ft, students 40Ft).

The **Smidt Museum,** Hollán Ernő u. 2, is the collection of Dr. Lajos Smidt, who collected just about everything he could lay his hands on. The result is like a garage sale gone berserk—each case packed with weapons, watches, coins, clothing, tableware, Roman artifacts, and ancient maps. The museum vividly conveys 19th-century Szombathely life, and an antique beer mug's inscription "Bier ist Gift!" (Beer is Poison) warns of premature death from cirrhosis—and, what's the population of Germany these days? (open Tues.-Sun. 10am-5pm; 80Ft, students 40Ft).

Iseum, Rákóczi Ferenc u. 2, is the reconstructed remains of the Temple of Isis built by Roman legionnaires in the 2nd century. Touted as "one of Szombathely's best known monuments," it looks more like the wreck of an urban municipal building than a Roman temple; the Communists rebuilt all the missing parts using concrete, and the edifice stands in a weed-strewn lot bordered by an office block. Marx never actually wrote anything about bad architecture, but... The shed-like structure at the north side houses an exhibit about the temple (open daily 9am-4pm). Across the street at Rákóczi Ferenc u. 3 shoot up the two spires of the former **synagogue,** a late-19th-century, Moorish-revival structure. The unchanged façade hides an interior that has been remodeled into a modern concert hall. A **memorial** outside remembers the 4228 Jews deported to Auschwitz from that spot during the Holocaust.

The **Savaria Museum,** Kisfalvaly Sándor u. 9 (tel. 312 554), unearths the roots of Vas county. Natural history exhibits and archaeological artifacts from the Roman settlement and later are stored on the first floor. The basement level holds collections of medieval artifacts and Roman stonework, and the ground floor exhibits change regularly (open Tues.-Fri. 10am-5pm, Sat.-Sun. 10am-4pm; 80Ft, students 40Ft).

West of the inner city, at the end of Árpád u., spreads the **Vas County Village Museum,** the re-creation of a local village consisting of 150- to 200-year-old farmhouses transplanted from throughout the region. The three rooms of each home are decorated with authentic furnishings—the "owner's" clothes are even laid out. A blacksmith occasionally works at the village forge, and all maintenance is done using traditional techniques (knowledge of which is rapidly dwindling—a century ago, a thatched roof could last 60 years, but no one nowadays can figure out how to make them secure for more than 20). The English-speaking guide can explain everything, but is usually off on Saturdays. A visit here is worth the 25-minute walk from Fő tér (open April to early Oct. Tues.-Sun. 10am-5pm; 80Ft, students 40Ft).

On the west side of town, a series of **parks** provides opportunities for relaxation. Perhaps with Budapest in mind, Szombathely set a large, abstract **monument** dedicated to the 1945 "liberation" on the highest hill they could find. Farther north, a lake, complete with island, offers a more romantic atmosphere. Swimming is only allowed, however, in the huge **pool,** across the street at Jazsa m. u. 2 (open Mon.-Fri. 9am-8pm; 100Ft). Near the summer solstice, these parks host the season's festivities.

On weekends and evenings, **Fő tér** is the site of concerts, other performances, or primo people-watching. For something even sweeter get some tasty pastries at the **Rózsa Cukrászda,** Éhen Gyula tér 2, (open Mon.-Fri. 10am-8pm, Sat.-Sun. 9am-7pm). **Pince Söröző,** Hollán Ernő 10, is a popular pub housed in the cellar of the bishop's 19th-century brewery. Half-liters of *Amstel* draft only 100Ft (open Mon.-Sat. 11am-midnight). **Zipfer Söröző,** Aréna u. 1 (tel. 311 789), serves fine entrées (185-400Ft) and even finer lagers in the wood-and-plaster surroundings of the former Franciscan monastery's cellars (open Mon.-Sat. 11am-11pm). Wine drinkers will enjoy the vast selection of Hungarian vintages at the **Pannonia Borozó,** Fő tér 29 (tel. 311 469), a centrally located wine-pub (open daily 8:30am-9:30pm).

■ Near Szombathely: Kőszeg

Despite being surrounded by thriving farms, forested hills, and roadside shrines, Kőszeg is rarely visited by foreign tourists. It's their loss—Hungarians treasure this tiny fortification for its medieval cityscape, and especially **St. James' Church**—one of Hungary's best-known Gothic edifices. Between **Város Kapu** (City Gate) and its counterpart **Bécsi Kapu** (Vienna Gate), medieval burgher's dwellings line Rajnis and Schneller streets. **Trains** reach Kőszeg from Szombathely (1 per hr., ½hr., 70Ft); **buses** come less often, from Szombathely (6 per day, 45min., 114Ft) and Sopron (3 per day, 1½hr., 190Ft). The Szombathely-line bus from Sopron stops first at the train station and then closer to the center. Step off, and turn right on Kossuth Lajos u.; one block up is **Várkör** (Castle Ring), one of the main streets. From the train station, cross the little bridge and bear right up Rákóczi u. about 1km into the center. **Savaria Tourist,** Várkör 69 (tel. 36 02 38), offers doubles in **private homes** for 2000Ft (only German spoken; open Mon.-Fri. 7:30am-5pm, Sat. 8am-noon). **IBUSZ,** Városhaz 3 (tel. 36 03 76), has doubles from 1600Ft (open Mon.-Fri. 8am-4pm, Sat. 8am-noon). The upscale yet affordable **Bécsikapu Söröző,** Rajnis 3 (tel. 36 02 97), prepares pork according to recipes that hark from Kiev, Brassó, and Tokaj (360-850Ft; open daily 11am-10pm). Decipher the Magyar menu and enjoy local delicacies or plentiful beer with the locals at **Kiskakas Vendéglő** (open daily 9am-9pm), opposite the **Julius Meinl supermarket** on Rákóczi u. 25 (open Mon. 6am-6pm, Tues.-Weds. 6am-6:30pm, Thurs.-Fri. 6am-7pm, Sat. 6am-2pm). **Phone code:** 94.

■ The Őrség

In the far west corner of Hungary, low-flying storks guard the bucolic region known as the Őrség. During the Cold War, authorities discouraged visitors and Hungarian citizens alike from entering the Őrség, as it was too close to the capitalist Austrian and Titoist Yugoslav borders. And so a region that had always been a little behind the times—electricity didn't arrive until 1950—became more distanced from the step of the modern world. Tourists now arrive more frequently to catch this slice of timelessness, and the people of the Őrség hardly mind; here, hospitality is a way of life.

ŐRISZENTPETER

Rolling hills, cool forests, and beautiful countryscapes combine to make the Őrség a biker's and hiker's paradise. Centrally located **Őriszentpeter** makes an excellent starting point. Foremost of the tiny Őrség villages, the town still regulates its busiest intersection with yield signs. The bridgeless street running northwest-southeast will take you to a sign for **camping** up a short driveway to the left. The reception is **Savaria Tourist,** Városszer 57 (tel. 428 115); the same friendly folks run the **Fogadó,** the local inn, and can arrange **private rooms.** Camping is 200Ft per tent, 200Ft per person, and a room inside with a shared shower is 2000Ft. Hours, as with most places in the Őrség, are, well...whenever someone's around. You may be able to pick up a detailed **map** of the Őrség area at Savaria Tourist, or they may be all out and gamely offer you a hand-drawn one. Try to find maps in larger towns, before you arrive. The fine **Begnár Etterem,** Kovács Szer 99, dishes out entrées for 600Ft. **ABC Market** (open Mon.-Fri. 7am-noon and 1-5pm, Sat. 7am-noon) and a few **bars** cluster around the main intersection which is where the bus will let you off—no trains run here. The quickest way to get here is to take the **train** to **Körmend** (8 per day from Szombathely, 45min., 102Ft), and then turn left and walk parallel to the tracks until you reach the bus station (13 per day to Őriszentpeter, ½hr., 136Ft). Less frequent **buses** also arrive here from the nearby towns of Zalalövő and Sventgotthard (both on the rail line), as well as Sopron and Szombathely. The **bus station**, from which buses leading back out depart, is up the street to the northeast (the one with the bridge). **Postal code:** 9941. **Phone code:** 94.

Hiking, Biking, and Sights Hiking offers choice choices in the Őrség. The entrance to the trail network is just past Őriszentpeter's Savaria Tourist, up the stairs to your left—climb every mountain, ford every stream, follow... Wait! This is Hungary, not Austria. (For *The Sound Of Music*, see *Let's Go: Switzerland and Austria*.)

Bikers should turn right from the station in Őriszentpeter, then left on Petőfi u. until they see a trail off to the right at Petőfi u. 131 to reach **Borostyán lake**, the local **campgound** (tel. 92 371 467; tent 300Ft, 300Ft per person; 2-person bungalows 1600F) and **bike rental** (bikes 500Ft per day). Savaria Tourist (see above) rents bikes for only 400Ft per day. **Zalalövő** is the village closest to the lake.

The old saw about the "journey, not the destination" becomes clear in this scenic area. Select roads at random to feel the whole rhythm of life, as **museums** freckle the Őrség, and more medieval **churches** stand here than anywhere in Hungary. Visitors shouldn't be shy about knocking on nearby doors and asking for keys; this holds for the local **artisans' studios** (marked *"Fazekasház"* in the case of potters).

You might wish to "randomly" select the following routes. Leaving Őriszentpeter to the west, you will pass through the village of **Szalafő**. Before you reach the town, a sign to your left will point to a 13th-century **church**, one of the myriad of medieval churches here. Continue past the town and over the bridge, veer left, and at the top of the hill you'll find a model 19th-century **farm community**. Wander around the silent houses, and peek in the windows. The museum there is theoretically open March through November daily 10am-6pm (60Ft, students 30Ft). Farther past Szalafő lies **Fetete-to**, a huge peat bog home to a number of rare, insectivorous plants. South of Őriszentpeter about 12km, the villagers of **Magyarszombalta** stoke backyard kilns in which to fire plates, bowls, and jugs (so sturdy you can cook *gulas* in them). Or, approaching Őriszentpeter from the north, be sure to catch **Batthyany Castle** in Körmend and the 1256 **Romanesque church** in Jak.

If you're lucky enough to come at the right time, you may find a festival, such as June's **Őriszentpeter's Őrsegi Vásár** (Őrség Market).

Győr

Although most closely associated with the Rába truck factory, Győr maintains a certain charm. Some of Hungary's finest 17th- and 18th-century buildings crowd the inner city, and an occasional horse-drawn cart still plods through rush-hour traffic at the lazy pace of the Danube tributaries, which nourish timeless Győr.

Orientation and Practical Information Trains go to Budapest (12 per day, 2½hr., 592Ft), Vienna (6 per day, 2hr., 2912Ft), and Veszprém (6 per day, 2hr., 324Ft). **Buses** go to Budapest (every hr., 2½hr., 570Ft) and Veszprém (every hr., 2hr., 424Ft). The **train station** lies south of the inner city, and the underpass that links the rail platforms leads to the **bus station**. **Ciklámen Tourist**, Aradi Vértanúk u. 22 (tel. 317 601), sits one block north of the train station and offers free brochures and maps with the old street names (open Mon.-Thurs. 8am-4:30pm, Fri. 8am-3:30pm, Sat. 8am-12:30pm). A few blocks north, **IBUSZ**, Kazinczy u. 3 (tel. 311 700), is bigger, and gives away new maps if you look like you're lost (open Mon.-Tues. and Thurs. 8am-3:30pm, Wed. and Fri. 8am-3pm). **OTP Bank**, at the corner of Czuczor Gergely u. and Árpád u., has good rates on traveler's checks (open Mon.-Fri. 7:45am-3pm, Sat. 7:45am-1:30pm). The **ATM** at **Magyar Külkereskedelmi Bank**, Bajcsy-Zsilinsky út 19, links to Plus and Cirrus. The **post office** is at Bajcsy-Zsilinszky út 46 (open Mon.-Fri. 8am-8pm). **Postal code:** 9025. **Phone code:** 96.

Accommodations and Food In July and August, accommodations in downtown Győr overflow, and rooms can be scarce for those without advance reservations. **Ciklámen Tourist** (see above) makes various **private rooms** available, including singles starting at 1200Ft, and doubles for 1800Ft. **IBUSZ** (see above) has only doubles (1600Ft and up). If you stay for less than four nights with either agency, expect to pay a 30% surcharge. The English-speaking staff of **Hotel Szárnyaskerék,** Révai Miklós u. 5 (tel. 314 629), right outside the train station, rents clean doubles (with shared bath 2350Ft, private bath 3050Ft). **2sz. Fiú Kollégium** (Boys' Dormitory No. 2), Damjanich u. 58 (tel. 311 008), just north of the Mosoni-Duna River, charges 600Ft per bed in rooms with 3-4 beds (open mid-June to Aug. and weekends year-round). North of the river, **Széchenyi Istvan Főiskola Kollégiuma,** Hédevári út 3, entrance K4 (tel. 429 722 or 429 348), has dorm-room triples. The area is safe, unless you count mosquitoes; the large ones smashed on the walls should be warning enough to close your window at night. Checkout time is 9am (600Ft per bed, students 500Ft; open July-Aug. 15). Both dorms should be able to put you up when other places are full—even before school lets out in mid-June. The staffs don't speak English, but friendly students might. **Kiskút liget Camping,** Kiskút liget (tel. 318 986), has a motel open year-round and camping and bungalows open April 1 through October 15 (motel triples 3000Ft, quads 4000Ft, 6-bed 5000Ft; 4-person bungalows 2500Ft; campsites 300Ft per tent, 300Ft per person).

Napoleon Pince, Munkácsy Mihály u. 6 (tel. 320 314), just south of the Petőfi Bridge, is a French restaurant, slightly more upscale than the run-of-the-mill *étterem* (English menu; entrées 420-850Ft; open daily noon-midnight). The enthusiastic teen-age waitstaff at **Sárkányluk** (Dragon's Hole), Arany János u. 27 (tel. 317 116), runs a popular bistro whose seven tables fill up quickly. Entrées run 250-550Ft (open Mon.-Sat. 11am-9pm, Sun. 11am-3pm). The bar, **Vidam Barat,** 46 Apaca út (tel. 314 084), serves one different, cheap, and plentiful meal every day (180Ft). A first-rate **Julius Meinl** grocery store sits at the corner of Baross Gábor and Árpád (open Mon.-Fri. 6am-8pm, Sat. 6am-1pm).

Sights and Entertainment The **city hall** is the most magnificent building in Győr; it waits a few steps from the train station. Most sights, however, lie within a rough triangle between Bécsi Kapu tér, Káptalan-domb, and Széchenyi tér. Bécsi Kapu tér is the site of the yellow **Carmelite church** and the remains of a **medieval castle** built to defend the town from the Turks. A small branch of the **János Xanthus Memorial Museum,** built into the castle at Bécsi Kapu tér 5, contains a lapidarium with Roman stone carvings and monuments. The cool air makes it well worth the admission price (open Tues.-Sun. 10am-6pm; 60Ft, students 30Ft). To the east of the square at Kiraly u. 4, the house where Napoleon Bonaparte spent his only night in Hungary now contains an art gallery and music school called **Napoleon Ház.**

At the top of Káptalan-domb (Chapter Hill), the **Episcopal Cathedral** has suffered constant additions since 1030. Its exterior is now a not-particularly-coherent hybrid of Romanesque, Gothic, and Neoclassical styles. The Baroque splendor inside deserves more attention, with dozens of golden cherubim flying around magnificent frescoes. A priest fleeing Oliver Cromwell's regime in the 1650s brought the miraculous **Weeping Madonna of Győr,** all the way from Ireland. On St. Patrick's Day 1697, the painting is rumored to have spontaneously wept "blood and tears" for three

---

The Iron Rooster Crows Again

Unmarked against a corridor wall in the **János Xanthus Memorial Museum,** Széchenyi tér 5, leans an inconspicuous iron rooster weathervane with a half-moon at its base. When Turks invaded and occupied Győr, they erected it on the town's highest tower, and bragged that they would hold the town until the cock crowed and the half-moon changed phase. The Hungarians took the boast seriously, and crowed like cocks under a full moon as they began the siege that eventually retook the city (open Tues.-Sun. 10am-6pm; 160Ft, students 80F).

hours, ostensibly in compassion for persecuted Irish Catholics. The **Herm of King St. Ladislas,** a masterwork of Gothic goldsmithery in the Hédeváry chapel on the cathedral's south side, is a wide-eyed bust of one of Hungary's first saint-kings.

The **Diocesan Treasury,** also on the hill, presents an extensive assortment of ornate gold and silver religious accessories dating back to the 14th century, but the real eye-catcher is an impressive collection of 15th- and 16th-century illuminated texts. The exhibits are marked in Hungarian and English (open Tues.-Sun. 10am-5pm; 60Ft, students 30Ft). The way to Széchenyi tér leads through Gutenberg tér past the religious monument **Ark of the Covenant,** erected in 1731. Various stories circulate about its origin, but all agree that the king built it with funds levied on his mercenaries in order to keep them impoverished and in line.

To find the real summer hot spots in Győr, do as the locals do and spend less time in the musty museums and more time splashing in the water and enjoying the sun. Across the river from the Old Town, **thermal springs** serve as the basis for a large water park. Swimming, saunas, massages, and water slides—the price is based on the services you choose (open Mon.-Fri. 6am-8pm, Sat.-Sun. 7am-6pm; 130Ft, students 100Ft). Come work on your tan with a good portion of the city. Fishing, rowing, and swimming in the river are all popular, but if the murky waters don't appeal, there are several shady, though poorly-kept, parks south of the train station. Head straight down u. Zrinyi or út Tihanyi Arpád. The best park is one block east of the city hall. A peaceful resting spot of another kind is the cemetery at the southern edge of town; the most interesting memorials lie just inside the gates (open daily 7am-8pm). The white church at the west side of the cemetery deserves a peek; head out through the modern, sliding stained glass doors and back to town.

The **Imre Patkó Collection** in the **Iron Log House** (so named for the stump, into which traveling 17th-century craftsmen drove nails when they spent the night), Széchenyi tér 4, contains two floors of fine works by modern Hungarian artists, and a smaller room devoted to foreign masters such as Picasso and Chagall. The loft holds a collection of Asian and African works that Patkó amassed in his travels (open Tues.-Sun. 10am-6pm; 80Ft, students 40Ft). One of Győr's hidden treasures, the **Margit Kovács Museum** at Rózsa Ferenc u. 1, one block north of the square, displays the artist's distinctive ceramic sculptures and tiles (open April-Oct. Tues.-Sun. 10am-6pm; Nov.-March 10am-5pm; 80Ft, students 40Ft).

The market on the river transmogrifies into a **bazaar** on Wednesday, Friday, and Saturday mornings. Győr frolics away June and July with **Győri Nyár,** a festival of daily concerts, drama, and ballet. Buy tix at the box office on Baross Gábor út or at the performance venue. Schedules are found at Ciklámen Tourist and IBUSZ. Wine drinkers crowd the dark and mellow **Troféa Borozó,** Bajcsy-Zsilinszky 16 (open daily 6am-10pm), and beer-bellies gurgle in unison at the **Komédiás Biergarten,** in the courtyard at Czuczor Gergely u. 30. (Amstel 160Ft; open daily until midnight).

■ Near Győr: Pannonhalma Abbey

Eighteen kilometers southeast of Győr, the hilltop **Archabbey of Pannonhalma** (tel. (96) 370 191) crowns the region's shining fields and rolling hills. Established by the Benedictine order in 996, the abbey has seen 10 centuries of destruction and rebuilding, and now boasts a 13th-century Romanesque and Gothic basilica, a library of 360,000 volumes, a small art gallery, and one of the finest boys' schools in Hungary. The **Pope** was the most famous tourist in recent times when he visited here in September 1996, as part of the abbey's 1000th anniversary celebration. The Benedictine abbey at Tihany was established by a 1055 royal charter—the **oldest document bearing Hungarian words**—that is also kept here. If you walk back and forth in front of the painting *The Body of Christ* in the gallery, the body seems to rotate so that the feet always point toward the viewer. Somehow this has less immediate emotional effect than when a velvet Elvis follows you with his eyes, but it'll do. There is also a **Gregorian chant mass** every Sunday at 10am for the very chic and the very religious. To see the abbey, join an hourly tour group at the Pax Tourist office at the entrance.

English-speaking guides are usually available for the mandatory one-hour tour; otherwise, follow along with an excellent English brochure (abbey open daily 8:30am-4pm; 300Ft, non-Hungarian students 100Ft). Pannonhalma is an easy daytrip from Győr by **bus** (every 2hrs., 45min., 134Ft; ask for Pannonhalma vár), but bring a snack—there's nothing to eat or drink here.

■ Tata

The quiet vacation town of Tata stretches around lakes, canals, and a 14th-century castle, providing a restful training ground for the Hungarian Olympic team. A popular place for sunbathing, boating, and fishing, Tata's small size and few tourists make it a good place to visit, even you'd rather go for the beach than the gold. The still waters of the north tip of the lake reflect **Öregvár,** the Old Castle. The **museum** inside, holding two millennia of the area's history, is Tata's main tourist attraction. Breeze through the two lower floors and head for the third one, which hides the work of 18th-century master craftsmen in wood, metal, and porcelain (open Tues.-Sun. 10am-6pm; 120Ft, students 70Ft). The **Eszterházy mansion,** built in Baroque style in 1765 and now used as a hospital, sits between Kastély tér and Hősök tere. Nearby, a converted synagogue at Hősök tere houses the **Greek-Roman Statuary Museum,** a collection of copies of ancient statues and friezes that once lined the paths of Angol Park (open Tues.-Sun. 10am-6pm; 60Ft, students 30Ft). **Angol Park,** around Cseke-tó, was Hungary's first English-style park, and has managed to maintain its elegance *sans* statuary. On weekend nights, the lake comes alive. Live bands play outside on the southern tip; at the north end, the DJ pumps up dance mixes at the **Lovas Disco,** just off of Tanoda tér; follow the lights in the sky (open Fri.-Sat. 10pm-2am; no cover). Local youth party late at the **Zsigmond Vigadó** (tel. 247 746), a hip bar located in the underground caverns on the castle grounds. (Beer 160Ft per pint; open Mon.-Wed. noon-midnight, Fri.-Sat. 11am-2am, Sun. 10am-10pm).

You probably won't see the town name on the **train station,** but Tata's is the dilapidated yellow building. From the station, walk south on Bacsó Béla u., and make a right on Somogyi Béla u, which ends at Országgyűlés tér. Trains pass through on their way to Budapest (18 per day, 1½-2hr., 404Ft), but it might be wiser to avoid the mile-long hike into town by taking the **bus** from Budapest (4 per day, 1½hr., 380Ft). Most of the sights and stores lie along the northwestern shore of **Öreg-tó** (Old Lake). **Komturist,** Ady Endre 9 (tel. 381 805), located on the main drag, sells **maps** (120Ft; open Mon.-Fri. 8:30am-4pm). The **post office** is at Kossuth tér (open Mon.-Fri. 8am-6:30pm, Sat. 8am-noon). **Postal code:** 2890. **Phone code:** 34.

Komtourist (see above) can provide four-person lakefront houses (5600Ft), but more affordable rooms lie along the main street. The **Hattyú Panzio,** Ady Endre u. 56, supplies clean, well furnished singles with private shower and toilet (1600Ft per night) and equally beautiful doubles (2400Ft). The oh-so-helpful family cooks breakfast for 300Ft (7am-9:30am). If Hattyú is full, **Hotel Malow,** Erzsébet tér 8 (tel. 383 530), may have a stark but clean double available for 2000Ft—if you can find the proprietor. **Öreg-tó Camping,** Fáklya u.1 (tel. 383 493), has four-person bungalows (3000F) and campsites (400Ft per tent, 400Ft per person; open May 1-Oct. 1). Locals recommend the fish at **Halaszcsár da** (entrées 290-490Ft). One of many lakefront restaurants, it is located halfway down the eastern shore. Menus are in English.

■ Sopron

With its soaring spires and winding cobblestone streets, Sopron's medieval quarter feels decidedly German. Yet, as any local will remind you, Sopron is considered "Hungary's most loyal town." In 1920, the Swabians of Ödenburg (as Sopron was then called) voted to remain part of Hungary instead of joining their linguistic brethren in Austria. This fidelity notwithstanding, Sopron is deluged daily by Austrians drawn by low prices for medical care and sausage—especially sausage…

Orientation and Practical Information The historic town center is a 1km-long horseshoe, bounded by **Ógabona tér** and **Várkerület**. **Fő tér**, at the north end, is the center of town. The bus terminal is two blocks to the northwest, on Lackner Kristóf, and the train station is a 10-minute walk south on **Mátyás Király út**. **Ciklámen Tourist**, Ógabona tér 8 (tel. 312 040), is Tourinform-licensed (open Mon.-Fri. 8am-4:30pm, Sat. 8am-1pm). To **exchange currency**, skip the smaller agencies in favor of **Magyar Külkereskedelmi Bank**, Várkerület 16 (open Mon.-Thurs. 8am-2pm, Fri. 8am-1pm), or **Budapest Bank**, Színház u. 5 (open Mon.-Fri. 8am-1pm). **ATMs** outside are linked to Cirrus and Plus. A 24-hour machine that changes most currencies into forints can be found at **K&H Bank**, Ogabona tér 9 (open 24hr.). **Trains** dash to Vienna's Südbahnhof (17 per day, 1hr., 1582Ft), Budapest (7 per day, 3-4hr., 1168Ft), and Győr (7 per day, 1hr., 576Ft). **Buses** work their way to Budapest (5 per day, 4hr., 810Ft), Győr (about once per hour, 2hr., 410Ft), and many other destinations. The **post office**, Széchenyi tér 7/8, lies at the south edge of the Old Town (open Mon.-Fri. 8am-8pm, Sat. 8am-noon). **Postal code:** 9400. **Phone code:** 99.

Accommodations and Food Ciklámen Tourist (see above) finds **private rooms** (singles 1300Ft, doubles 1800Ft). **Locomotiv Turist**, Új u. 1, near Fő tér, arranges singles for 900Ft and doubles for 1600-3000Ft (open Mon.-Sat. 9am-5pm). **Talizmán Panzió**, Táncsics u. 15 (tel. 311 620), has small but impressively well kept doubles with TV and shower (but shared toilet) for 2000Ft. Checkout time is 10am. **Galéria Szálló**, Baross Gábor u. 4-6 (tel. 311 150), about 1km west of the inner city, is open all year and is often full (672Ft; no reservations). **Középiskolai Fiú Kollégium**, Erzsébet u. 9 (tel. 311 260), in the city center, and its sister dorm, **Középiskolai Leány Kollégium**, Ferency János u. 60 (tel. 314 366), just west of the city center, charge 470Ft per person in 4-bed rooms (available daily June 20-Aug. 20; during the school year weekends only). **Lővér Campground** (tel. 311 715), at the south end of town on Kőszegi u., has fun four-person bungalows (4000Ft), threesome ones (3200Ft), and huts for conservative couples (2000Ft). For campsites, it charges 350Ft per tent and 500Ft per person (open April 15-Oct. 15).

Puskás Restaurant, Várkerület 83 (tel. 319 286), near Széchenyi tér, serves up tasty *sertés pörkölt* (stews), homemade dumplings, and veggie entrées (340-680Ft). A half-liter of *Zipfer* or *Steffl* costs 160Ft. (English and German menu; open daily 10am-midnight). **Pince Csárda**, Széchenyi tér 4 (tel. 34 92 76), upholds its good reputation with a tremendous array of chicken, venison, and veal dishes for 400-750Ft (open Mon.-Thurs. 10am-11pm, Fri.-Sat. 10am-midnight). On Deák tér, **Deák Étterem**, Erzsébet u. 20 (tel. 311 686), houses an impressive beer garden that gets awfully crowded on hot summer days (entrées 300-550Ft; open Mon.-Sat. 10am-midnight, Sun. 10am-10pm). **Julius Meinl grocery**, Várkerület 100-102, is one of the town's best-stocked shops (open Mon.-Fri. 6:30am-8pm, Sat. 6:30am-3pm).

Sights and Entertainment The **Fire Tower** on Fő tér's north side consists of a 17th-century spire atop a 16th-century tower on a 12th-century base straddling a Roman gate. Its clock is the source of the chimes heard throughout town. Visitors squeeze up a narrow spiral staircase to the balcony for a view of Sopron's steeples and surrounding hills (open Tues.-Sun. 10am-6pm; 60Ft, students 40Ft).

Across the square, stands the **Bencés Templom** (Goat Church), built in the 13th century with funds from a happy herder whose goats found a cache of gold. Goats frolic on the heraldic design above the main entrance. The small **Franciscan Monastery** next door also dates from the 13th century. Visitors can enter its Chapter Hall, a room of textbook Gothic architecture enriched by ten sculptures of human sins and taped Gregorian muzak (church and hall open daily 10am-noon and 2-5pm).

The Gothic **Fabricius House**, Fő tér 6, is divided into three separate exhibits. The first and second floors hold a rather dry historical/archaeological collection called "3000 Years Along the Amber Route." On the third floor, are re-creations of domestic life in 17th- and 18th-century Sopron. Tour guides demand to know your native language as you enter each room, and thrust upon you a photocopied guide describing each article of the gorgeous antique furnishings. Inside the vaulted cellar—originally a Gothic chapel, and now the coolest place in town on a hot day—a **Roman Lapidarium** exhibits stonework and monuments dating to Sopron's start as the colony Scarbantia. The trio of Jupiter, Juno, and Minerva that once sat in the forum now adorn the hall (open Tues.-Sun. 10am-6pm; each exhibit 80Ft, students 40Ft; buy tickets for each exhibit from the cashier as you enter the house).

Just to the right at Fő tér 8, the **Storno House** may be the most interesting of the town's 13 museums. The Stornos were 19th-century Swiss-Italian restorers of monuments and cathedrals; their taste in restoration is often unimpressive, but their home and personal collection of furniture and artwork spanning the Renaissance to the 19th-century are exquisite. When you buy your ticket, the cashier hands you a ticket with a number on it and sends you up to the first floor, where there is a dry and poorly marked historical exhibit. Don't worry, that isn't the collection; the number on your ticket is the time your 40-minute guided tour on the second floor starts. The guide says almost nothing—instead, she carries around a tape recorder with narration in Hungarian or German and points out each item as it's mentioned, like a flight attendant doing a pre-flight safety instruction. English-speakers get a photocopied fact sheet (open Tues.-Sun. 10am-6pm; 100Ft, students 50Ft).

The **Angel Pharmacy Museum,** Fő tér 2, traces the history of the profession from the 15th- to 20th-centuries (open Tues.-Sun. 9:30am-noon and 12:30-2pm; 20Ft). Down Új u., once known as Zsidó u ("Jewish street"), stand two rare 14th-century synagogues which evoke the life of the local medieval Jewish community, expelled in 1526. The **Old Synagogue** at #22, first built around 1300, has been reconstructed to show the separate rooms for each gender, the stone Torah niche, the wooden pulpit, and the deep well used as the ritual bath (in a small building in the courtyard; open Wed.-Mon. 9am-5pm; 80Ft, students 40Ft). At #11, the **New Synagogue,** is new only because it was built 50 years later. After centuries of ignominy, it is now being restored. For a list of other museums, ask at Ciklámen Tourist (see above).

For a brief but thorough tour of **Old Sopron,** take a short walk down Templóm u. to the **Evangelical Church** with its late Baroque interior, especially the organ. Farther down Templón u. is the **Mór Kolbenheyer House,** where the famous 19th-century Hungarian liberal-cum-cleric lived. Return to Fő tér via Szent György u. and peek inside **St. George's Cathedral** to be amazed by the exquisite blend of Gothic and Baroque ornamentation concealed by the church's plain exterior.

Just north of the Old Town at Bécsi út. 5, the **Bakery Museum** illustrates the history of professional baking from the 15th to 20th centuries in the restored home and shop of a successful 19th-century baker (open Wed., Fri., Sun. 10am-2pm and Tues., Thurs., and Sat. 2-6pm; 50Ft, students 20Ft). Five minutes south of the Old Town at the corner of Deák tér and Csatkai Endre u., the **Liszt Ferenc Múzeum** (Franz Liszt Museum) houses a collection of folk crafts and has no apparent connection to the composer (open Tues.-Sun. 10am-6pm; 80Ft, students 40Ft).

Discos are few in Sopron, but the wonderful beer gardens and wine cellars more than make up for this when the weather is right. During the **Sopron Festival Weeks** (June-July) the town hosts opera, ballet, and concerts, some set in the **Fertőrákos Quarry** caverns, 10km away; there are hourly buses from the bus terminal (quarry 20Ft for students; concerts 500-600Ft). Buy tickets for all events from the **Festival Bureau** on Széchenyi tér across from the post office (open Mon.-Fri. 9am-5pm, Sat. 9am-noon). **Puskás,** Várkerület 83 (tel. 319 286), near Széchenyi tér, lets you carouse the night away in a beer garden at 160Ft per half-liter of *Zipfer* or *Steffl* (open daily 10am-midnight). **Kolostor,** Kolostor u. 9, south of Fő tér, has *Szalon* from the royal Pécs brewery on tap for a mere 70Ft per half-liter (open daily until 10pm). A 17th-century cellar houses **Cézár Pince,** Hátsókapu 2 (tel. 311 337), which quenches its guests' thirst with *Soproni Kékfrankos* (open daily 10am-9pm).

■ Near Sopron: Fertőd

In tiny **Fertőd**, 27km east of Sopron, stands the magnificent rococo **Eszterházy Palace**, Bartók Béla u. 2 (tel. (99) 370 471), nicknamed the "Hungarian Versailles." Miklós Eszterházy, known as Miklós the Sumptuous before he squandered his family's vast fortune, ordered the palace built in 1766 to hold his multi-day orgiastic feasts. Visit the inside of the mansion, now a museum, and see what time has done to the magnificent art (open Tues.-Sun. 9am–5pm; 150Ft, students 60Ft). Josef Haydn wrote and conducted here, and **concerts** still resound within. **Buses** leave every hour for Fertőd from stage 11 in Sopron's station on Lackner Kristóf (45min., 158Ft). Buses continue on to Győr every two hours (2hr., 370Ft). Fertőd has dorms and a few rooms, but groups often fill them. Book with Ciklámen Tourist in Sopron.

LAKE BALATON

Aspirations to become the glam Baywatch beach-land of Central Europe, shallow Lake Balaton has become one of the most coveted vacation spots in the area. Villas first sprouted along its shores during the Roman Empire, and when a railroad linked the lake to its surroundings in the 1860s, it mushroomed into a favored summer playground. Today, the region's rich scenery and comparatively low prices draw mobs of German, Austrian, and Hungarian vacationers. Once schools let out, the lakeside becomes raucous and crowded with young people, but at other times you will meet mostly retirees and kids.

> Storms roll in over Lake Balaton in less than 15 minutes, raising dangerous whitecaps on the otherwise placid lake. One minute, the shore resembles a colony of sleeping elephant seals; the next, thunder crashes, offspring are scooped up, and all run for cover. Amber lights on top of tall hotels and the Meteorological Research Center at Siófok's harbor give weather warnings; 30 revolutions per minute means stay within 500m of shore; 60 revolutions per minute means swimmers must be within 100m and boats must be tied on shore.

■ Siófok

Siófok is not only the largest town on Lake Balaton, but is also its main tourist center. The fact that more tourist offices per square mile congregate here than in any other Hungarian city says something about the numbers of surf- and bargain-starved German-speaking tourists who descend on Siófok each year. May to September, Siófok is abuzz by day at its beach and by night at its discos. Beware: in cooler months, especially October to April, tourists vanish and the town all but closes down.

Orientation and Practical Information Trains run to Budapest (7 per day, 3hr., 508Ft) and Pécs (5 per day, 3½hr., 848Ft). A **gyorsjárat** (fast bus) leaves for Pécs (3 per day, 3hr., 712Ft) and another goes to Budapest (4 per day, 2½hr., 624Ft). The quickest way to the north side of the lake is by the hourly **MAHART ferry** that docks next to the verdant **Jókai Park**, 10 minutes from the train station (Balatonfüred, 50min.; Tihany, 80min.; 300Ft to either port, 150 for Hungarian students, but you might squeak in with an ISIC). The **train** and **bus stations** are adjacent to each other in roughly the center of town, which runs east-west along Balaton's south shore. The main **Fő u.** is just south of the train station. A **canal** that connects the lake to the Danube bisects the town. The **Gold Coast** on the east side is the home of the older, larger hotels, while the **Silver Coast** on the west understandably has the newer, less expensive ones. **Tourinform**, Fő u. 41 (tel. 310 177), in the base of the wooden water tower, has English-speakers on staff and carries maps (open July-Aug. Mon.-Sat. 8am-8pm, Sun. 8am-1pm; Sept.-June Mon.-Fri. 9am-4pm). **IBUSZ**, Fő u. 176 (tel. 312

Lake Balaton

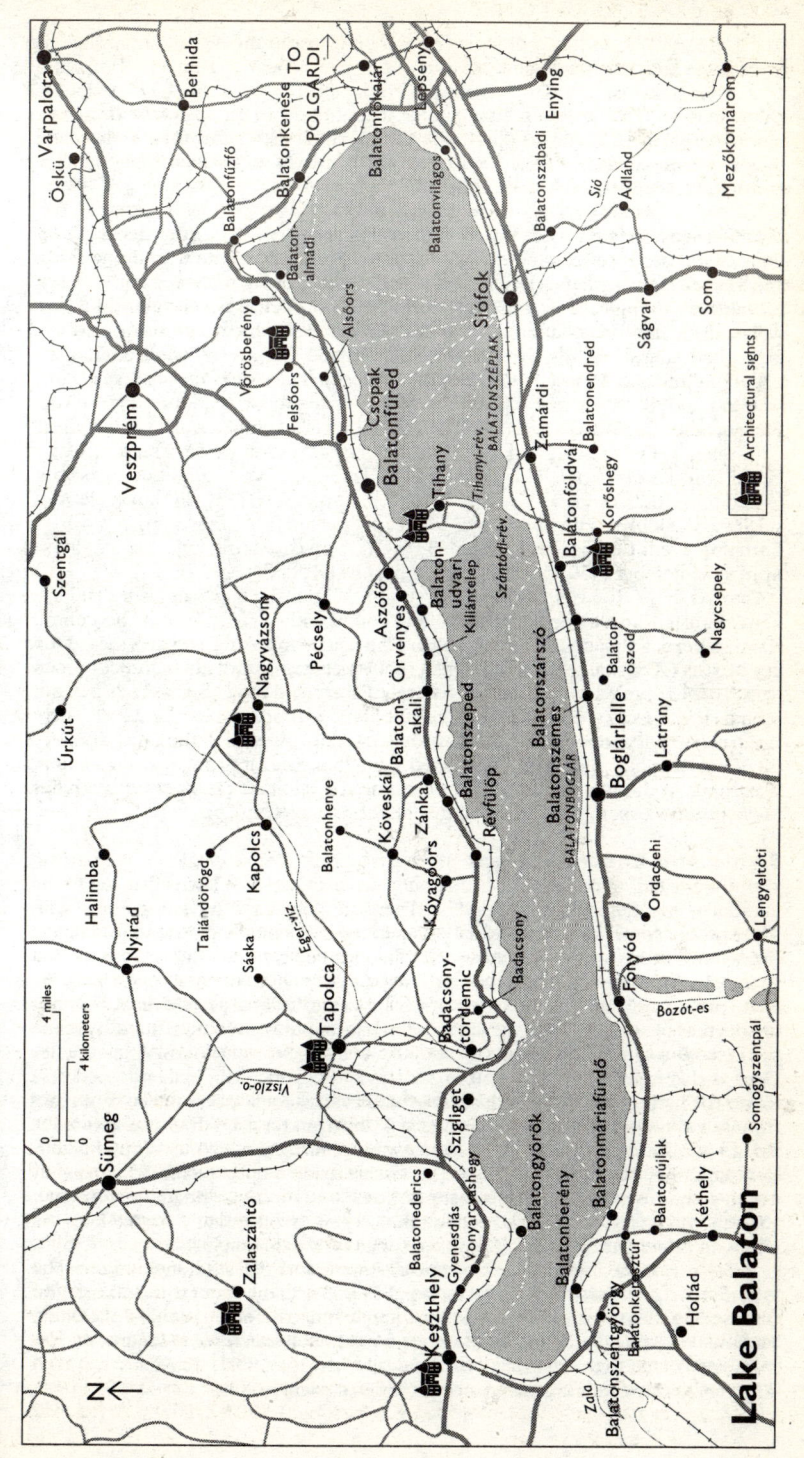

011; fax 315 213), on the 2nd floor. This is a bit closer to the bus and train stations (open June-Aug. Mon.-Sat. 8am-6pm, Sun. 9am-1pm; Sept.-May Mon.-Fri. 8am-4pm). To **exchange currency,** visit **Postabank,** Fő u. (tel. 174 176). An **ATM** and a **bill changer** lurks outside (open Mon.-Sun. 9:30am-noon and 12:30-7pm). There is a **pharmacy** at Fő u. 202 (tel. 31 00 41; open Mon.-Fri. 9am-3:30pm). **Telephones** stand outside the **post office,** at Fő u. 186 (tel. 310 210; open Mon.-Fri. 8am-6pm, Sat. 8am-1pm). **Postal code:** 8600. **Phone code:** 84.

Accommodations and Food A myriad of agencies offer private accommodations. If you prefer to search on your own, **Erkel Ferenc u.,** to the west of the canal, and **Szent László u.,** to the east, are residential streets close to the water with rows of *Panzió* and *Zimmer Frei* signs. **Tourinform** (see above) charges no commission and will mediate in the negotiation of rates. Doubles in the center of town average 2000Ft in July and August, slightly cheaper off season. **IBUSZ** (see above) offers doubles for 1700Ft in July and August. While they and other agencies offer quality apartments, bear in mind that there is a 30% surcharge for staying fewer than four nights. **Tuja Panzió,** Szent László u. 74 (tel. 314 996), provides well equipped singles and doubles with satellite TV, shower, and fridge for 2400Ft per person (less off-season). **Azúr Hotel,** Vitorlás u. 11 (tel. 312 033), off Erkel Ferenc u., offers bright doubles with bathrooms (1820Ft). **Hotel Korona,** Erkel Ferenc u. 53 (tel. 310 471), has pleasant singles and doubles, with breakfast at 3800Ft per person (less off- season). **Aranypart Camping,** Szent László u. 183-185 (tel. 352 801), 5km east of the town center, opens April to September (350-450Ft per person plus 1000Ft tax).

Csárdás, Fő u. 105 (tel. 310 642), serves up traditional Hungarian dishes and live native music. Entrées hover at 600-800Ft (open daily 11am-11pm). The central **Kálmán Imre,** Kálmán Imre sétány 1, near Fő u. and Mártírok u., prepares spiced turkey breasts (720Ft) and chicken paprika (530Ft); its taps run with *Steffl* beer (open daily 10am-10pm). Less expensive **Kristály Étterem,** Petőfi sétány 1, dishes out schnitzel with *lecsó* (pepper and tomato) for 380Ft and *Gösser* beer for 220Ft. There is a massive fruit and vegetable **market** south of Fő u. just west of the canal. Look for the **Vásárcsarnok** building (open Mon.-Fri. 7am-6pm, Sat. 7am-1pm, Sun. 7am-noon). Next door to the market, gourmands can find the choicest crumpets at the **Julius Meinl grocery** (open Mon.-Fri. 6:30am-8pm, Sat.-Sun. 6:30am-1pm).

Sights and Entertainment Most attractions in Siófok pale in comparison with the **Strand,** which is not a beach but a series of park-like lawns that run to the extremely un-sandy concrete shoreline. There are public and private sections, with some private spots charging at least 100Ft per person, depending on the location and the whim of the owner. The most centrally located section is the town park, but swimming isn't allowed. The largest private part lies right to the east (open Mon.-Fri. 8am-7pm; 120Ft). Most sections rent water bikes and sailboards. **Nightclubs** of varying degrees of seediness line the lakefront, while amphibious lounge lizards revel on the **Disco Boat** July 9 to August 21. For 450Ft, you too can frolic to ABBA and the Bee Gees as this funky craft takes you to Xanadu and beyond. The bell-bottomed boat leaves the harbor nightly at 9:30pm. Another boat, with a live pop music band, runs from July through August 21 and leaves at 7 and 9pm for a 1½-hour cruise (450Ft). Bring your Dramamine. Dance the night away at **Flört Disco,** Sió u. 4 (open nightly 9pm-5am). **Kajman Pub Disco,** Fő u. 212, swears it doesn't play techno (open nightly 10pm-4am; cover 150Ft). For a taste of home—if you're German—the **Sörbár,** Kálmán Imre étany, west of the pedestrian overpass, is a pleasantly shaded beer garden with *Zipfer* and *Wieselburger* on tap (open daily til midnight).

Siófok is also the hometown of composer Imre Kálmán. In his honor, an **operetta** is performed nightly in the Cultural Center, Fő tér 2, near the water tower. During the high season, the town's streets host the annual, four-day **International Folk Dance Festival.** For info on schedules and tickets, visit the **Kálmán Imre Múzeum,** Kálmán Imre sétány next to the train station (open daily 9am-5pm; 80Ft). The church at Fő u. 57 has biweekly evening organ concerts (350Ft, students 200Ft).

Keszthely

With 18th-century architecture and a large student population, Keszthely graces the west tip of Lake Balaton. The town's main claim to fame is the elegant and decadent Festetics Palace, but its parks and beaches are also worth exploring.

Orientation and Practical Information In summer, **ferries** run to and from Keszthely, and **boats** take passengers to Balatonboglár on the south shore of the lake (1 per day, 2½hr., 400Ft) and another to Badacsony on the north shore (1 per day, 2hr., 310Ft). **Express trains** run between Keszthely and Budapest (5 per day, 3hr., 848Ft). **Slow trains** make the route to Szombathely (3 per day, 2hr., 592Ft). **Buses** beat trains for local travel: Veszprém (15 per day, 2hr., 348Ft), Balatonfüred (8 per day, 2 hr., 370Ft), and Pécs (5 per day, 3hr.). Some buses leave from the terminal while others use stops in the town center at either Fő tér or Georgikan u. Each departure is marked with an "F" or a "G" to indicate which stop it uses. The **train station** and **bus terminal** are adjacent to each other, about half a kilometer from the water. The main **Kossuth Lajos u.** runs north-south with the **Festetics Palace** at its head. After **Fő tér**, it becomes a pedestrian street. To reach Kossuth Lajos u. from the train station, walk straight up **Mátírok u.** Turn right to head for Fő tér. **Tourinform,** Kossuth Lajos 28 (tel./fax 314 144), sits just north of Fő tér (open Mon.-Fri. 9am-5pm, Sat.-Sun. 9am-1pm). **IBUSZ** (tel. 312 951) occupies Kossuth Lajos 27 (open June-Aug. Mon.-Sat. 8am-6pm, Sun. 9am-1pm; Sept.-May Mon.-Thurs. 8am-4pm, Fri. 8am-3pm). The **OTP Bank** at the corner of Kossuth Lajos u. and Helikon u. **exchanges currency** (open Mon.-Thurs. 8am-3pm, Fri. 8am-1pm) and offers a Cirrus/MC **ATM.** An agency **rents bikes** at Kossuth Lajos u. 54 (750Ft per day). The **post office,** Kossuth Lajos u. 48 (tel. 314 232), lies two blocks south of Fő tér (open Mon.-Fri. 8am-7pm, Sat. 8am-noon). It may still be under construction in the summer of 1997; if so, the temporary location with the same hours and phone number is at 23 Georgikon u., near the palace. **Postal code:** 8369. **Phone code:** 83.

Accommodations and Food Tourinform (see above) finds four-person apartments at 3000-4500Ft. IBUSZ (see above) offers private doubles for 2200Ft. **Zalatour,** Kossuth Lajos u. 1 (tel. 314 301), has doubles for 1400Ft (open Mon.-Sat. 8am-9pm, Sun. 8am-noon). If those don't pan out, other agencies also help weary Teva-clad youths seeking shelter. **Hotel Amazon,** Kastily u. 11 (tel. 314 213), offers centrally located, clean doubles with private bathrooms for 3900Ft. If you'd rather strike out on your own, homes with *Zimmer Frei* signs are most common near the Strand, especially on Erzsébet Királyné u. **Mr. Athla Lukic's** cozy **panzió,** Jókai Mór u. 16 (tel. 311 232), has attractive doubles at 3000Ft per person. **Vajda J. Középiskola Kollégiuma,** Gagarin u. 4 (tel. 311 361), charges 600Ft for a dorm bed (open late June-Aug.). **Sport Camping,** Csárda u. (tel. 312 842), lies five minutes south of the train station and across the tracks; it has two-person bungalows (1000Ft, with bathroom 2000Ft), four-person bungalows (2000Ft, 3000Ft with bath), and tent sites (200Ft per tent, 200Ft per person; open May-Sept.). An additional 200Ft tax is levied on every group. Damn taxes.

The restaurants centered around Fő tér are obscenely overpriced, but there are more remote—and reasonably priced—eateries farther from the center. **Béke Vendéglő** (tel. 312 447), corner of Kossuth Lajos u. and Balaton u., offers tasty food in generous quantities in a shaded courtyard (entrées 450-850Ft). Drafts of good *Zipfer* run 170Ft (open Mon.-Thurs. 11am-10pm, Fri.-Sat. 11am-11pm). **Gösser Restaurant,** Erzsébet Királyné u. 23, north of the Strand, creates culinary delights out of the rich fish stocks of Lake Balaton. Carp and trout go for 260-560Ft (open Mon.-Sat. 11am-10pm). **Donatello,** Balaton u. 1b, brings Italian cuisine to Hungary with a plethora of pastas (230-510Ft) and pizzas (260-580Ft; open daily noon-11pm).

Sights Keszthely's pride is the Helikon Kastélymúzeum, the **Festetics Palace.** Built by one of the most powerful Austro-Hungarian families, the storybook palace does

Baroque architecture proud. Of the 360 rooms, tourists may visit only the central wing. The palace includes the 90,000-volume **Helikon Library,** an arms collection that spans a thousand years, and rooms full of artwork and period furniture. **Concerts** are often held in the mirrored ballroom during summer. Check your bag at the door and pad through the collection wearing tie-on shoe covers (open Tues.-Sun. 9am-6pm; 500Ft, students 200Ft). Get a guided tour (usually available in English or German) for a mere 2000Ft. The surrounding **English park** provides a vast and well kept strolling ground. To find the palace, follow Kossuth Lajos u. north until it becomes Kastély u. You can't miss it—it's the only one on the block.

Keszthely is very much alive during the day at the **Strand,** which covers much of the coast on the side of the train tracks opposite the town. With rocks instead of sand and swamp instead of waves, it's a wonder that it's still such a major people magnet (120Ft). The **Balaton Museum,** Kossuth Lajos u. 75 (tel. 312 351), corner of Mártirok u., displays Balaton's indigenous wildlife and ethnographic history (open Tues.-Sun. 10am-5pm; 80Ft, students 50Ft). **Georgikon Major Múzeum,** Bercsényi u. 67 (tel. 311 563), presents an amusing deification of György Festetics, who founded Europe's oldest agricultural university here in 1797. Exhibits detail the history of European agriculture (open April-Oct. Tues.-Sat. 10am-5pm, Sun. 10am-6pm; 50Ft, students 30Ft). And don't miss the **church** on Fő tér; its pastel green tower, built in 1896, hides the fact that the main part of the structure, dating from 1386, remains one of the most important standing works of Gothic architecture in Hungary. There are no Baroque frescoes here, but some beautiful stained glass, and, if they let you that far, 14th-century wall paintings in the sanctuary.

Eight kilometers northwest, **Hévíz** is home to Europe's largest **hot-water lake** (26-33°C or 77-91°F). Buses from Keszthely's Fő ter visit this gigantic hot tub hourly.

■ Balatonfüred

Although its dignified buildings and stately promenades remind one of yesteryear, Balatonfüred, Balaton's oldest spa, is still a popular destination for many Hungarians. Known for its mild climate, historical buildings, clean air, vineyards, and medicinal springs, Balatonfüred has been the site of a health resort for over 200 years. Though prices are high—especially for accommodations—Balatonfüred remains a refreshing destination, both as the largest town on the lake's north shore and as an excellent base for exploring nearby Tihany.

Orientation and Practical Information Most **buses** and **trains** on the lake's north side go through Balatonfüred. **Buses** to the Tihany peninsula run from the bus terminal (hourly, 20min., 76Ft), but also stop at Széchenyi u.'s corner with Jókai Mór u. and along Széchenyi u. Buses to Veszprém leave from the terminal (1 per day, 35min., 134Ft). **Express trains** leave for Budapest's Déli Station (7 per day, 2½hr., 592Ft). The train splits the town; almost everything of interest to tourists lies between it and the water. The main **Jókai Mór u.** runs northwest-southeast. From the **train** or **bus station,** walk east on Horváth Mihály u. The lakeshore promenade, **Tagore sétany,** is lined with shops and restaurants. **Balatontourist,** Tagore sétany 1 (tel. 342 822), has an excellent map of the Balaton region and offers helpful advice and information (open Mon.-Sat. 8:30am-6:30pm, Sun. 9am-12:30pm). To **exchange currency,** try the **OTP Bank,** Ady Endre u., just north of Petöfi Sándor u. (open Mon.-Thurs. 7:45am-4pm, Fri. 7:45am-2pm), which also offers a Cirrus/MC **ATM.** Summer **bicycle** and **scooter rentals** appear in parking lots near the water. Mountain bikes cost 200Ft per hour, scooters 500Ft per hour. Helmets are not mandatory within the town limits (but wear one). The **post office,** with adjacent **telephones** keeps in touch at Zsigmond u. 14 (tel. 342 115; open Mon.-Fri. 8am-6pm, Sat. 8am-noon). **Postal code:** 8230. **Phone code:** 86.

Accommodations and Food Private rooms here are pricier than in Budapest, and at the moment there is no hostel in town. **Balatontourist** (see above) has doubles for 2000-2200Ft (open Mon.-Sat. 8:30am-6:30pm, Sun. 9am-12:30pm). **Hotel Kelén,** Petőfi Sandor u. 38 (tel. 342 811; fax 343 702), offers reasonable doubles (3500Ft, with bathroom 3900Ft) and singles (1900Ft, with bathroom 2900Ft); prices drop a few hundred forints off-season. Ask the folks at Balatontourist if 500Ft dorm rooms are available at **Ferenc Széchenyi College,** Iskola u. Renovations may be completed by summer 1997. Agencies exact a 30% surcharge for those staying less than four nights. The beach-front bungalows at **Ficc-Rally Camping,** Széchenyi u. 24 (tel. 343 823), are priced out of sight, but you maybe able to afford space near the water for your car, camper, or tent (2500Ft per 60sq. m.).

Hotel Blaha Lujza Restaurant, Blaha Lujza u. 4 (tel. 342 603), is an affordable, centrally located class act. If you really need it, the staff will scrape up an English menu (entrées 400-700Ft; open Sun.-Thurs. 11am-10pm, Fri.-Sat. 11am-11pm). For Hungarian-style pizza, try the very popular **Spaten Pizza,** Zákony Ferenc u., just east of Széchenyi u. Pizzas run 210-410F, and beer 160Ft. Look for the terrace covered with a straw roof (open daily 11am-10pm), and be careful with your cigarettes! Even the groceries at the **Julius Meinl,** on the corner of Petőfi Sándor and Jókai Mór, are overpriced (open Mon.-Fri. 6:30am-8pm, Sat. 6:30am-2pm).

Sights **Jókai Mór Villa,** Jókai Mór u. 1, was home to actress Róza Laborfalvi and her prolific 19th-century writer and parliamentarian hubby Jókai Mór. The house-museum contains their personal belongings, open to inquiring minds that want to know, as well as a varied collection amassed by the couple themselves (open April-Oct. Tues.-Sun. 10am-6pm; 80Ft, students 40Ft). The **Kossuth Lajos spring** runs from a fountain in a pavilion in Gyógy tér. This was the first of six thermal springs discovered in the area. The water is drinkable, although it tastes slightly citric from the carbonic acid it contains, and is ever-so-slightly radioactive. This is supposedly a healthy quality on the mineral water circuit. The **State Hospital of Cardiology,** Gyógy tér 2, next door, makes full use of their resource; patients bathe in it to cure cardiovascular ills and drink it to relieve diabetes and liver and digestive problems. It seems to do the trick—the yellow **Sanatarium** has a collection of memorial plaques from prominent people cured by the spring's magical waters. The **Strand** can be entered through Tagore sétány's east end (120Ft). Here, there is actually a 5m-wide strip of sand favored by couples pushing the limits of foreplay. If you rent a bike, head up to **Siske,** a terraced slope of white-walled, thatched cottages—a world away from the Strand's crowded scene. You can see the lake from here, but not the attractions. Go up Jókai Mór u. to Aracsi út, then turn left up the hillside on Siske u.

For an evening (or morning) of tippling, try the 24-hour **Karaván Drink Bar,** Jokai Mór u. north of Zákony Ferenc u., for a great choice of mixed drinks, wine, and beer. For dancing and picking up Austrian and Canadian boys and girls, go to the **Jever Disco,** Zákony Ferenc u. just east of Széchenyi u. (open nightly until 5am).

■ Near Balatonfüred: Tihany

With its lush vegetation, luxurious homes, and extensive panoramas, the Tihany peninsula is the pearl of Balaton. Although every bit as touristy as the rest of the lake, Tihany has somehow managed to escape rampant commercialization. The main tourist attraction is the magnificent 1754 **Abbey Church,** with its Baroque altars, pulpit, and organ (open daily 9am-6pm; 100Ft, students 50Ft). Next door, an 18th-century monastery has been reincarnated as the **Tihany Museum,** with psychedelic dreamscapes, colorized etchings, and Roman inscriptions displayed in a cool, subterranean lapidarium (open March-Oct. Tues.-Sun. 10am-6pm; 50Ft). Follow the **"strand"** signs along the Promenade behind the church to get to the beach (open daily 7am-7pm; 80Ft). Clearly Tihany's strangest sight, the **garage-gallery** of "painter, artist, writer, professor" Gergely Koós-Hutás, Fürdőtelep 43, lies only a five-minute climb from the wharf, and includes massive canvases of didactic Lenins. Better yet, set out for a **hike** across the Peninsula (check out the map by the church first). It only takes an hour or two along the dirt roads and paths that pass through hills, forests, farms, and marshes.

Best of all, you may never see another person except the occasional worker pruning his vineyard.

A block from the bus stop (see below) is **Balatontourist,** Kossuth Lajos u. 12 (tel. 448 519). Should you decide to stay for another day of exploration in the "garage-museum", they can arrange a room in the village for 2500-3500Ft (open Mon.-Sat. 8:30am-6:30pm, Sun. 8:30am-1pm). It's expensive, but not as expensive as the lake-front rooms five minutes away (5000Ft or more!). For some nourishment, the outdoor terrace of the **Rege Coffeehouse,** Kossuth u. 22 (tel. 318 280), next to the church, sells drinks, ice cream, and what may be the best pastries along Lake Balaton. In summer, the **ferry** to Tihany departs from Balatonfüred's pier (every 20min., 20min., 150Ft). **Buses** frequently pass by the beaches at both Tihany and the more popular Tihanyi-rév. Ask them to stop before you jump off.

LATVIA (LATVIJA)

US$1 = 0.55Ls (lats)	1Ls = US$1.82
CDN$1 = 0.40Ls	1Ls = CDN$2.50
UK£1 = 0.85Ls	1Ls = UK£1.17
IR£1 = 0.89Ls	1Ls = IR£1.13
AUS$1 = 0.43Ls	1Ls = AUS$2.32
NZ$1 = 0.38Ls	1Ls = NZ$2.63
SAR1 = 0.12Ls	1Ls = SAR8.12
DM1 = 0.37Ls	1Ls = DM2.70
Country Phone Code: 371	**International Dialing Prefix: 810**

Battered by Swedish, Polish, German and Russian invaders since the 13th century, Latvia (pop. 2.6 million) is more than a little glad to finally have its independence. This expression of national pride ranges from patriotically renamed streets virtually bleeding with crimson-and-white flags to a reemergence of native holidays predating even the Christian invasions. The only real city in Latvia, Rīga is a westernized capital that serves as the base of operations for many corporations in the Baltics. The rest of the country is a peaceful expanse of deep green hills, dairy pastures, quiet settlements, and unbelievably fresh air.

LATVIA ESSENTIALS

U.K., Irish, and U.S. citizens can visit Latvia visa-free for up to 90 days. Citizens of Australia, Canada, New Zealand, and South Africa require 90-day visas, obtainable at a Latvian consular office (see Essentials: Embassies and Consulates, p. 7), at Rīga's airport, or at several other border-crossing points (you will pay the rush-processing price if you wait until the border). Single-entry visas cost US$15; multiple-entry cost US$30; there is a US$45 fee for 24-hour rush processing. Allow ten days for standard processing. Tourists may obtain only single-entry Latvian visas. For extensions, apply to the Ministry of Interior (see Rīga: Passport Office, p. 320).

GETTING THERE

Latvia is linked by **train** to Berlin, Moscow, St. Petersburg, Tallinn, and Vilnius. The efficient long-distance **bus** network has invaded Prague, Tallinn, Vilnius, and Warsaw. **Ferries** run to Rīga from Stockholm and Kiel—but from Stockholm, a train via Tallinn is cheaper, and from Kiel, just take a bus via Klaipéda. The least expensive way to reach Rīga from other Baltic locations is by train or bus, but if traveling by train, be sure to secure a *coupé* or first-class compartment. **Flights** to Latvia use the overworked Rīga Airport, whose only runway was short enough to cause safety concern when President Clinton visited in 1994. **Air Baltic, Czech Airlines, Finnair, Lufthansa,** and others make the hop to Rīga from their hubs.

GETTING AROUND

Trains are cheap and efficient, but stations aren't well marked, so get an idea of what time you should arrive at your destination to avoid missing it. The **suburban rail** system centered in Rīga qualifies almost the entire country as a suburb. The diesel trains, often express, stop only at towns marked by a white dot on the board in Rīga. **Buses,** usually adorned with the driver's bizarre collection of Christian icons, pornography, and nationalist symbols, go everywhere. They're quicker than trains but fond of stopping in places so isolated you'll wonder where all those waiting to get on came from. Beware the standing-room-only long-distance jaunt. **Hitchhiking** is common, and is considered more dangerous for drivers than passengers; hitchers may even be expected to pay. *Let's Go* doesn't recommend this as a safe means of transport.

TOURIST SERVICES

Look for the big green **"i",** marking some tourist-info offices across the land; they (the offices, not the "i"s) vary wildly in usefulness, as do their more subtly adorned brethren. In Rīga's forest of tourism, the **Tourist Club of Latvia** stands out for sheer quantity of info; and **Latvijas Universitātes Tūristu Klubs** plans nifty outdoor (and other) adventures, with prices geared to students rather than international businesspeople (see Rīga: Tourist Offices, p. 320).

MONEY

The Latvian currency unit is the **Lats** (100 santīmi = 1 Lats; abbreviated Ls). There are a few **ATM** machines in Rīga linked to Cirrus and MasterCard. In most towns, there are usually some nicer restaurants, banks, and hotels accepting **Visa** and **MasterCard**. **Traveler's checks** are harder to use; both AmEx and Thomas Cook can be converted in some Rīga banks, but Thomas Cook is a safer bet outside the capital.

COMMUNICATION

Buy **phone cards** for the newly digitalized telephones at the local post office (lowest denomination 2Ls). If you see a dot written within a phone number, wait for a tone before dialing the rest of the digits. Within Rīga's commuting range and in some Baltic coast spots, **digital telephones** are common; otherwise trek to the post office (or sometimes just across your hotel room) to make **international calls.** The **AT&T Direct** number in Rīga is 700 70 07; it's not a free call, but it's your best option. The gradual switch to digital phones leaves travelers trying to make a connection feeling like safecrackers—sometimes you must dial a 2 before a number, sometimes a 7, sometimes other assorted digits. An 8, followed by the old Soviet phone code from an analog phone zaps you across the fallen empire. If you tire of playing phone phreak, check a phone office or *Rīga in Your Pocket* for the latest in digit disaster.

LANGUAGE

A blend of German, Russian, Estonian, and Swedish influences, **Latvian** (see Glossary, p. 780) is, with Lithuanian, a member of the Baltic language group. However, life proceeds bilingually. Nearly 65% of the people in Rīga are Russians who speak little (if any) Latvian, while the populations of some cities are over 95% Latvian. A language law requires that signs, menus, and other public writing be in Latvian; this can seem obnoxious when, after struggling to order from a Latvian menu, you discover that your waiter speaks only **Russian.** Many young Latvians study **English,** but the older set know some **German.** Most speak some Russian, though non-Russians prefer not to. In smaller towns, Russian may bring immediate hostility, which can be softened by attempting it apologetically or as a last resort. *Alus* (beer) is a crucial word in any language. Key places are the *autoosta* (bus station), *stacija* (train station), *lidosta* (airport), *viesnīca* (hotel), and *pasts* (post office).

HEALTH AND SAFETY

> **Emergency Numbers: Fire,** tel. 01. **Police,** tel. 02. **Ambulance,** tel. 03.

Bathrooms are marked with an upward-pointing triangle for women, downward for men; interpret this at will. There are rumors that Rīga **tap water** is drinkable, but boil all water for 10 minutes to be safe. Many Latvian **drivers** seem aggressive enough to win international races, but don't be fooled; they'd all be disqualified for slamming on the pedal before the light turns green. Be very cautious around roadways. If you're **attacked,** it's better to speak Russian than English if possible. Since they don't necessarily know Russian, locals may not notice your accent. *"Ej prom"* (ey prawm) means "go away"; *" Lasies"* (lahsioos prawm) says it more offensively, and *"Lasies lapās"* (lahsioos lahpahs—go to the leaves), poetic though it may be, is even ruder. Emergency numbers are listed above, but your consulate is probably a better bet for English-speaking help than the local police.

ACCOMMODATIONS AND CAMPING

The **Tourist Club of Latvia** lists budget lodgings and makes travel arrangements. See Rīga: Tourist Offices, p. 320. **Patricia** provides English info and arranges homestays (average US$10 per night) and apartment rentals (see Rīga: Accommodations, p. 323). Many towns have only one **hotel** (if any) in budget range; expect to pay 3-8Ls per night, with price variations reflecting a monopoly in power not higher quality.

FOOD AND DRINK

Heavy and filling, Latvian food tries to fatten you up for winter. National specialties, tasty on the whole, include smoked *sprats* (once the fame of Rīga), the holiday dish *zirņi* (gray peas with onions and smoked fat), *maizes zupa* (bread soup usually made from cornbread, and full of currants, cream, and other goodies), and the warming *Rīgas (Melnais) balzams* (a black liquor great with ice cream or coffee). Dark rye bread is a staple, and homemade bread and pastries are deliciously worth asking for. Try *speķa rauši*—a warm pastry, *biezpienmaize*—bread with sweet curds, or the dark colored *kaņepju sviests*—hemp butter, which is good but unfortunately too dilute to have medicinal properties. Latvian beer, primarily from the *Aldaris* brewery, is pretty good and should cost 0.55Ls for 0.4L, 0.65Ls for 0.5L; *Porteris* is best. If imported beers aren't 1Ls or less, you're paying for the atmosphere.

CUSTOMS AND ETIQUETTE

Tipping is increasingly common; it will probably be expected in any restaurant accustomed to foreign patrons. As elsewhere in the region, expect to be bought a drink if you converse with someone for any length of time, and expect to repay the favor in kind. As in the rest of the Baltics, **stores** sometimes close for an hour or two between noon and 3pm, and restaurants may take a break between 5 and 7pm. **Staring** for short periods of time is rather common. **Flowers,** as gifts (in odd-numbered bunches), on monuments, and for no apparent reason, are everywhere. **Homosexuality,** though legal, may not be tolerated.

LIFE AND TIMES

HISTORY

Ancient Latvia was inhabited by the **Balts.** In the 9th century, fierce **Viking** ships swept down from the northwest, while **Slavic** invaders gnawed at the region's east frontier. In the 10th and 11th centuries, Latvia was threatened by Slavs to its east and **Swedes** to its west. During the 1100s and 1200s, German warriors known as the **Order of the Brothers of the Sword** subdued the area, beginning a long period of German hegemony. Missionaries rapidly Christianized the region, though the indigenous religions are still around. The Teutonic conquerors squeezed taxes, tithes, and forced labor from their Latvian peons; only Rīga remained temporarily free. The rest was under the unstable **Livonian Federation** until the 16th century.

The federation was divided by the 1619 Truce of Altmarkt, with Livonia and Rīga given to the Kingdom of Lithuania-Poland, and Vidzeme (the northern half of Livonia) to Sweden. **Russia,** which had tried to gain control of Latvia since the time of Ivans III and IV, under Peter the Great fought the **Great Northern War** with Sweden, taking Rīga in 1710 and Vidzeme in 1721. Latgale was acquired after the first partition of Poland in 1772, and Courland in 1795 after the third partition of Poland. By the end of the 18th century, Russia ruled all of Latvia.

Latvian peasants gained some freedom after the **Napoleonic Wars.** However, the issue of land ownership remained contentious, and unrest spread. When serfs were liberated throughout the Russian empire in 1861, Latvian peasants finally won the right to buy the lands their forefathers had farmed for centuries. Calls for independence were increasingly heard, particularly after the 1905 revolution in Russia.

Reacting to the Bolshevik coup of November 1917, the **Latvian People's Council** proclaimed independence on November 18, 1918. The new autonomous government in Rīga—a distant dream—was led by Kārlis Ulmanis. Over the next few years, Latvia was overrun by battling armies. Latvians, Germans, White Russians, British, French, Estonians, Lithuanians, and the Red Army fought for supremacy. When fighting ended in 1920, Latvians were in control. **Democratic coalitions** ruled the country, with Ulmanis serving four terms as prime minister. Proposed constitutional reforms created an uproar, however, and the Nazi movement spread in the minority German population. In 1934, Ulmanis established a dictatorship. In **WWII,** the country was incorporated into the USSR, and deportations began. Germany invaded in 1941, but by 1945 the Red Army had driven the Nazis out.

Latvia was one of the wealthiest and most industrialized regions of the Soviet Union. But under **Soviet rule,** it was torn by radical economic restructuring, extreme political repression, and a thorough Russification of its national culture. In 1949, the Soviets began deporting over 100,000 Latvians; meanwhile, immigrants from the rest of the Soviet Union poured into the country. Within four decades, ethnic Latvians accounted for only half the population, as compared to three quarters before the war. Most local party leaders were Russian immigrants.

Under **glasnost** and **perestroika,** Latvians protested *en masse* in 1987 over environmental protection, and created the Latvian Popular Front in 1988 to oppose the Soviet establishment. The opposition trounced the Soviets in the 1990 elections. On May 4, 1988, the new legislature declared Latvia **independent,** but Soviet intervention sparked violent clashes in Rīga in 1991. Finally, following the foiled Moscow coup in August, the Latvian legislature reasserted its independence.

LITERATURE

Written literature appeared in the 16th century in the form of religious treatises. Latvian fiction grew out of age-old *dainas*—folk songs, still widely known. In the 17th century, **Gotthard Friedrich Sender** first transcribed traditional oral Latvian literature. **Krišjānis Barons,** a 19th-century folklorist, collected and published over 20,000 *dainas*. Folklore also provided the basis for *Lāčplēsis the Bear-Slayer,* **Andr'js Pumpurs's** 19th-century national epic. A patriotic role-model and symbol of the National Awakening, Lāčplēsis kills a bear and conquers the German Black Knight—all only to fall into the Daugava River. Legend foresaw he would return to free Latvia. Some say *Lāčplēsis'* 20th-century reappearance in the form of **Māra Zālīte's** rock opera indeed affected Latvia's independence.

The National Awakening gave impetus to literary experimentation: **Juris Alunāns** became the first Latvian lyricist; **Reinis and Matiss Kaudzīte** defined a spectrum of Latvian character-types in *Mērnieku Laiki* (The Time of the Land-Surveyors)—a novel 20 years in the writing; **Aspazija Rainis** fought for women's rights, while her husband **Jānis Rainis** created a Symbolist current in a river of Realist poetry.

More new literary forms diversified Latvia's literature after the country achieved independence in 1918. **Jānis Akurāters'** romantic lyric exhibits Nietzschean themes—individual heroism and narrow aesthetic ideals. **Edvarts Virza** returned to Classicism, glorifying rural life and traditional (read: sexist) familial life. Others, like **Kārlis Zariņš,** were grappling with the effects of WWI. The folktale re-entered the scene as a context for analyzing modern Latvia; the ballad was used by **Aleksandrs Čaks** to caricature urban and suburban life. **Mirdza Bendrupe's** prose explored human psychology, watching modern society through a Freudian prism, and **Aleksandrs Upītis's** work, portraying class struggle and proletarian heroes, grew out of seeds sown by French and Russian naturalists.

After WWII, Upītis became a leading writer, thanks to the political correctness of his texts. Socialist Realism, however, failed to drown other trends. **Jānis Medenis,** exiled to a labor camp in Siberia, longed for a free Latvia in his poetry; **Imants Ziedonis** also managed to foster independent Latvian literature despite the authorities' tight censorship.

LATVIA TODAY

Latvia's transition to capitalism has been rocky. Industrial production has plummeted, and the standard of living continues to fall. Latvia still depends on Russia for its fuel and as a major market for its washing machines, refrigerators, motor scooters, radios, and solid organic fertilizer spreaders. However, the Latvian government has tightened its belt; fiscal austerity has been relatively successful at reducing inflation. In addition, banking has begun to boom as lax regulations have made the country a little Switzerland for the ex-communist countries. Latvia's second free elections in June 1993 handed conservative deputies a majority in the Saeima (parliament). Not all Latvians may vote, however; suffrage is limited to those who have been citizens since 1940 and their descendants. About 34% of all residents, mainly Slavs, are disenfranchised. Relations with Russia remain tense as Latvia demands a full withdrawal of Russian troops, while Moscow drags its heels and accuses Latvia of discriminating against the Russian-speaking minority.

A Midsummer Night's Eve

Everybody's favorite *Jogānu rituālus* (pagan-esque ritual), Līgo inflames Latvia on the June 23rd—Summer Solstice. Bigger than Christmas, New Year's, and even Lenin's Birthday, bonfires consume the hills as young lovers, sent to the woods by their parents to find the legendary fern flower that blossoms only on Midsummer's Eve, consume each other—passionately. Men don oak-leaf crowns to assert their fertility, and women wear flower wreaths; *dainas* (folk songs) fill the air, and the whole country stays up all night chasing *Jānu* cheese with rivers of beer and merriment. All of this results in a national hangover so severe that many establishments remain closed for the day after Līgo. When in Latvia...

Rīga

The largest city in the Baltics, cosmopolitan Rīga has a turbulent history of conquest that changed only in the 20th century. Just as the famed Art Nouveau architecture of the city reflects German influences, the city's population reflects the inescapable legacy of the Soviet era. Tensions between disenfranchised Russians, *nouveau-riche* "businesspeople" with cellular phones, and returning Latvians who fled in the 40s after Stalin's takeover make Rīga a hotbed of post-Soviet politics. But in the shade of the Old City's beer gardens, grievances and complications evaporate in the foam.

ORIENTATION AND PRACTICAL INFORMATION

Rīga's city center consists of an expanding series of concentric half-circles along the banks of the **Daugava River,** focused on **Vecrīga** (Old Rīga). **Kr. Valdemāra iela** to the north and **Marijas iela** to the south border Vecrīga, while **Pīlsētas kanāls** (the old city moat), surrounded by a park, marks the first circle—about a 15-minute walk across. Beyond the canal, a ring of parks and boulevards laid out in the 19th century make up the second circle; **Elizabetes iela,** 1km from the river, bounds this newer region. Beyond sprawls the noisy, dirty metropolis. Vecrīga has two sections, divided by **Kaļķu iela** in the Old Town, **Brīvības bulvāris** in the New City, and **Brīvības iela** out past Elizabetes iela. The **train** and **bus stations** sit on the southeast edge of the city center. With the trains behind you, take a left onto the busy Marijas iela; once you pass the canal's terminus, you are in the Old Town.

A city **map** (1Ls), widely available, is a must; you'll get lost in Vecrīga's wandering streets anyway, but it's a great city in which to get lost. *Rīga In Your Pocket* comes through, packed with up-to-date info on anything you could ask for (0.50Ls). The free *Rīga by Night* offers info on, well, things that happen at night.

Tourist Offices: The best bet for Baltics omniscience is the **Tourist Club of Latvia** (Latvijas Tūristu Klubs), Skārņu iela 22 (tel. 722 17 31; fax 722 76 80), behind St. Peter's Church. While they don't know everything, they can help with a Russian visa for US$15 given 10 days, US$60 in 1 (a sliding scale). The English-speaking staff is armed with a wealth of brochures, the entire *In Your Pocket* line, and smiles. English tours of old Rīga 4.50Ls per person. Open daily 9am-7pm. **Balta Tourist Agency,** Elizabetes iela 63 (tel. 728 63 49; fax 724 30 99), gives out maps, brochures, and flight timetables. Open Mon.-Fri. 9am-6pm, Sat. 10am-2pm. **Latvijas Universitātes Tūristu Klubs,** Raiņa bulv. 19, room 127 (tel. 722 52 98; fax 782 01 13; e-mail mountain@com.latnet.lv), arranges hiking and some canoeing trips in the Baltics. Trips run 17Ls for 2 days and include transport, a guide, accommodations, and any relevant museum admissions. Open Mon.-Fri. 9am-6pm.

Passport Office: Rīgas Centra Rajona Modaļa, Vogonera iela 5 (tel. 721 07 32). A visa extension will cost you 7.08Ls. Open daily 9am-4pm.

Embassies: Belarus, Elizabetes iela 2 (tel. 732 25 50; fax 73 22 89). Open Mon.-Fri. 10am-2pm and 3-5pm. **Canada,** Doma laukums 4, 3rd floor (tel. 722 63 15, emergency tel. 755 11 81). Open Mon.-Fri. 10am-1pm. **Russia,** Antonijas iela 2 (tel. 22 06 93), entrance on Kalpaka bulv. Open Mon.-Fri. 10am-1pm. **Ukraine,** Kalpaka bulv. 3 (tel. 33 29 56). Open Mon.-Fri. 10am-1pm. **U.S.,** Raiņa bulv. 7 (tel. 721 00 05). Open Mon.-Fri. 9am-noon and 2-5pm. **U.K.,** Alunāna iela 5 (tel. 733 81 26). Open Mon.-Fri. 9:30am-noon, also serves **Irish** citizens.

Currency Exchange: At any of the innumerable *Valutos Maiņa* kiosks or shops in the city. **Unibanka,** Kaļķu iela 13 (tel. 722 83 51), has generous hours (Mon.-Fri. 9am-9pm, Sat. 9am-6pm), gives MC and Visa cash advances (4% commission) and cashes AmEx and Thomas Cook traveler's checks (3% commission).

ATMs: Cirrus/MasterCard linked machine sits at the telephone office (see below).

American Express: Latvia Tours, Grēcinieku iela 22/24 (tel. 721 63 06 or 782 00 20), the Latvian AmEx representative, *doesn't* cash traveler's checks, but will hold mail. Open Mon.-Fri. 9am-7pm, Sat. 10am-3pm.

ORIENTATION AND PRACTICAL INFORMATION ■ 321

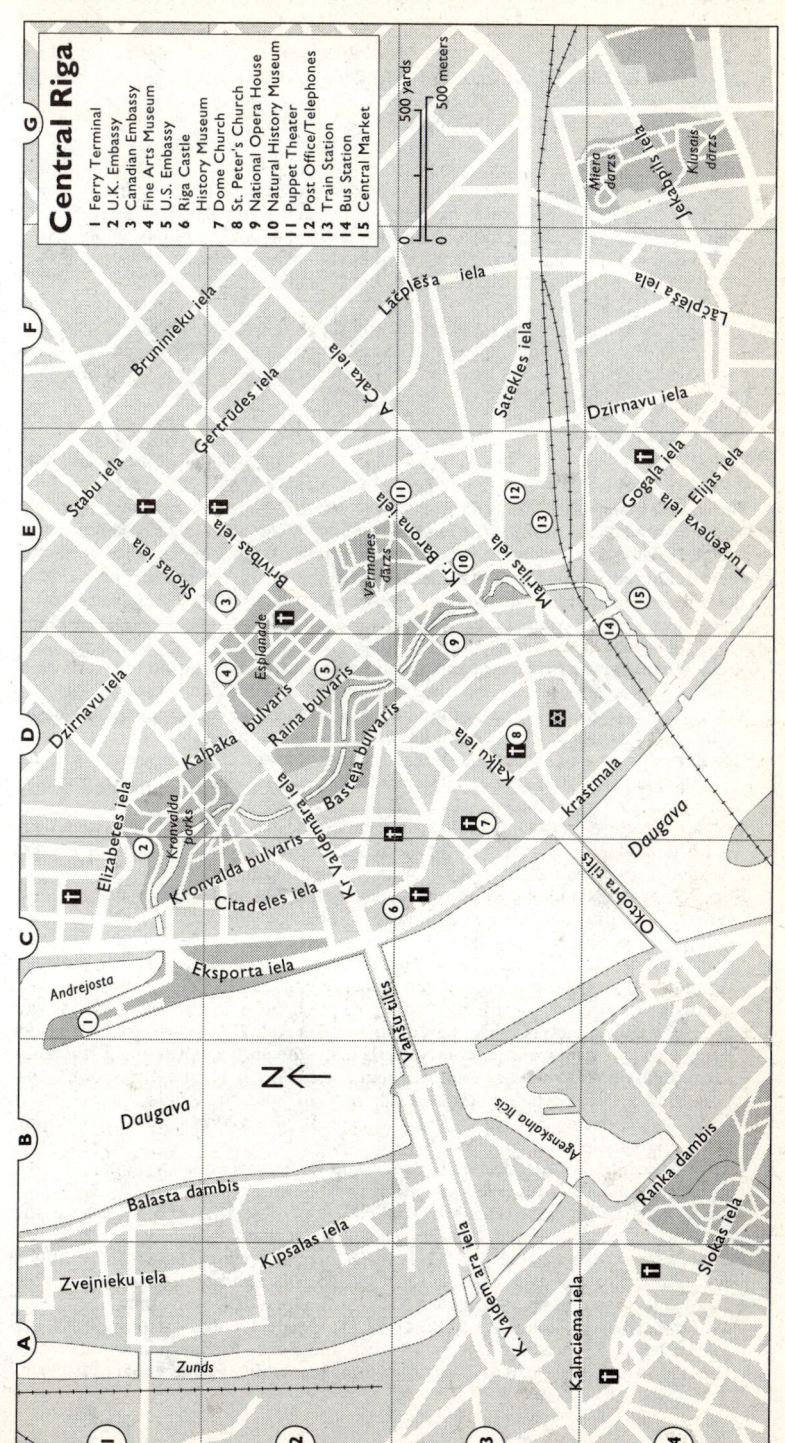

Central Riga

1. Ferry Terminal
2. U.K. Embassy
3. Canadian Embassy
4. Fine Arts Museum
5. U.S. Embassy
6. Riga Castle
7. Dome Church
8. St. Peter's Church
9. National Opera House
10. Natural History Museum
11. Puppet Theater
12. Post Office/Telephones
13. Train Station
14. Bus Station
15. Central Market

Flights: Lidosta Rīga (Rīga Airport; info tel. 20 70 09), 8km southwest of the Old Town. Take bus #22 from Gogol iela. **Air Baltic** (tel. 207 24 01) flies twice daily to Frankfurt and London, and once daily to Tallinn. **Lufthansa** (tel. 728 59 01; fax 782 81 99) and **Finnair** (tel. 720 70 10; fax 720 77 55) fly to most major cities.

Trains: Stacijas laukums (tel. 007, but don't ask for Mr. Bond), east of the Old City and north of the canal. It's really 2 stations, with **long-distance trains** located in the larger building to the left. Departures *(atiešanas)* listed on the board at right as you enter. To: Berlin (1 per day—via Hrodna, Belarus, so get your transit visa—31hr., *coupé* 57Ls); Moscow (2 per day; 17hr.; 11Ls, *coupé* 22Ls); St. Petersburg (1 per day; 15hr.; 9Ls, *coupé* 18Ls); Tallinn (1-2 per day; 8½hr.; 7.40Ls, *coupé* 15Ls); Vilnius (2 per day, 8hr., *coupé* 8.10Ls). **Suburban trains,** running as far as the Estonian border at Valga (Lugaži), leave from the smaller building. The Lugaži line includes Cēsis and Sigulda. Buy same-day tickets in the respective halls, and advance ones in the **booking office** off the right side of the suburban hall. Open Mon.-Sat. 8am-7pm, Sun. 8am-6pm. Tickets for **outside the former Soviet Union** must be purchased at the three windows at Turgeneva iela 14. Open Mon.-Sat. 8am-1pm and 2-7pm, Sun. 8am-1pm and 2-6pm.

Buses: (tel. 21 36 11) 200m south of the train station along Marijas iela, across the canal from the Central Market. To: Kaunas (2 per day, 7hr., 2.90Ls); Minsk (2 per day, 10hr., 5.85-6.90Ls); Prague (1 per day, 30hr., 38Ls); Tallinn (8 per day, 6hr., 3.80Ls); Vilnius (6 per day, 6hr., 3.60Ls); Warsaw (1 per day, 14hr., 11Ls).

Ferries: Transline Balt Tour, Eksporta iela 1a (tel. 232 99 03; fax 783 00 40), 1 km north of Rīga Pils (Castle) at the passenger port. The *Orion-II* floats to Slipte in Gotland, Sweden (one-way with hall shower and toilet Wed. 12.50Ls, Fri. 17.50Ls). It leaves Rīga at 6pm and arrives the following day at 10am, returning Thurs. and Sat. at 6pm, arriving in Riga at 11am. The "Sahalin" makes for Travemunde, Germany, Sat. 5pm, arriving Mon. 11am; it returns Thurs. 4pm, arriving in Rīga Fri. 11am. DM150 is the cheapest fare.

Public Transportation: Buses, trams, and **trolleybuses** take 15-santīmi tickets available at kiosks, post offices, and sometimes on board; punch tickets on board.

Taxis: State taxis (tel. 070) are outnumbered by private ones with a green light in the windshield. Haggle over price (under 3Ls crosstown at night).

Car Rental: Hertz (tel. 720 79 80), at the airport, has the cheapest rentals: 44Ls for a 100km day behind the wheel, 98Ls for 500km of weekend driving pleasure. Minimum age 19. Open Mon.-Fri. 10am-8:30pm, Sat.-Sun. noon-8:30pm.

Luggage Storage: In the bus station, on guarded racks (0.50Ls per bag). Open daily 5:30am-noon and 12:30-11pm. At the train station, lockers (0.30Ls) are in the tunnel under the long-distance tracks. Open daily 5am-1am.

Bookstore: Aperto Libro, Kr. Baronas iela 31 (tel. 728 38 10). With attached café where you can sip cappuccino and peruse your new *Moby Dick.* Open Mon.-Fri. 8am-1am, Sat.-Sun. and holidays 10am-1am. Attached **Café Osiris** has nifty breakfast combos for around 2Ls, free English newspapers, and everywhere Anglophones. MC and Visa accepted. Open Mon.-Fri. 8am-1am, Sat.-Sun. 10am-1am.

Laundromat: Yessiree—a real laundromat in the Baltics! Open 24hr. to wring out your traveling stench is **Miele,** Elizabetes iela 85a (tel. 271 76 96), about 2 blocks from the train station in the courtyard through the archway. Groaning machines take almost 2hr. to wash a load, so plan ahead. Wash 1.76Ls. Dry 0.60Ls. Discounted rates between midnight and 9am (wash 1.50Ls, dry 0.50Ls).

Pharmacy: Grindex, Audēju 20 (tel. 721 33 40). Open Mon. and Sat. 9am-5pm, Tues.-Fri. 8am-8pm.

Gay and Lesbian Centers: Latvian Association for Sexual Equality, Puškina 1a (tel. 22 32 93). **LASV,** Baznīcas iela 1924 (tel. 28 99 33).

Express Mail: DHL, Brīvības 55 (tel. 701 32 93; fax 701 32 98). Up to 50 pages to the U.S. in 1-2 days 23Ls. Open Mon.-Fri. 9am-6pm, Sat. 10am-2pm.

E-mail: Latnet, Raiņa 29 (tel. 721 12 41 or 782 01 53; e-mail darba@latnet.lv; http://www.latnet.lv). Opens an account for you for 5.90Ls per month (computers in the lobby if you want to try to borrow a password). Open daily 9am-5pm.

Post Office: Stacijas laukums 1 (tel. 721 32 57), near the railway station. EMS (10Ls for a 50-page letter to the U.S. in 2-5 days) and **Poste Restante** at window #16. Open Mon.-Fri. 8am-8pm, Sat. 8am-4pm, Sun. 10am-4pm. **Postal code:** LV-1050.

ACCOMMODATIONS ■ 323

Telephones and Telegraph Office: (tel. 733 12 22) Brīvības bulv. 21. Open daily 8am-10pm. Smaller office at the main post office by the train station. Open 24hr. With 24-hr. booths and a Cirrus/MC **ATM. Phone code:** 2 (8 for digital lines).

ACCOMMODATIONS

By some strange miracle, Rīga overflows with liveable, lustrously located hotels that loosen less Lati than like establishments in the countryside.

Arena, Palasta iela 5. So centrally located you'd think the Vecrīga was built around it. The door stays locked, so ring the bell. Tended by *babushki* and an incredibly fluffy cat, Arena's rooms are soaked in light, if a bit aromatic. Hall shower and communal kitchen for true budgeteers. Singles 3Ls. Doubles 5Ls. Triples 6Ls.

Hotel Baltija, Raiņa bulv. 33 (tel. 722 74 61), corner of Marijas near the train station, so it's perfect for daytripping. The old building has somehow held onto its beauty. Wrought iron staircase, high ceilings, an ancient (working) elevator, and natural light. Insects in 4th-floor bathroom never make it to a room. Friendly Russian staff. Singles with hall showers 3.50Ls. Doubles 5.60Ls. Triples 7.20Ls.

Saulite, Merķela iela 12 (tel. 22 45 46), across from train station. Surreal green spiral staircase reminiscent of one of Lex Luther's kryptonite constructions, branching off to truly clean halls, rooms, and communal showers and toilets. Singles 5Ls. Doubles 7-15Ls. MC and Visa accepted.

Aurora, Marijas iela 5 (tel. 722 44 79), across from the train station. A shade cheaper than Baltija, this dark, unrepentantly Soviet establishment isn't worth the extra pocket change you'll save. Hall bathrooms. Singles 3.20Ls. Doubles 5.40Ls.

Patricia, Elizabetes iela 22-26, 3rd floor (tel. 28 48 68; fax 28 66 50), 2 blocks from the train. Friendly and helpful English- and German-speaking staff arranges US$15 homestays in Vecrīga. Single room next to their office—clean and gorgeous with all the amenities—US$20. Open Mon.-Fri. 9am-7pm, Sun. 9am-1pm.

Viktorija, Čaka iela 55 (tel. 27 23 05), 8 blocks from the trains on Marijas iela (which becomes Čaka iela), or 2 stops on trolleybus #11 or 18. Pricier rooms pay for the new lobby and trappings of the renovated section, rather than the rooms themselves. Hall shower and bathroom cleaner than usual. Singles 8Ls. Doubles 10Ls. With private bath, TV, breakfast, and fridge 13-18Ls. MC and Visa accepted.

FOOD

Heavy competition means lots of spots serving good food at a good price—don't settle for less. Bleary-eyed women tend the 24-hour food and liquor stores of an insomniac's daydream. Pricey **Interpegro,** Raiņa bulv. 33 (tel. 722 45 57), at the corner of Marijas iela, is one of these. Stock up on pre-packaged goods on the first floor of the **Universālveikals Centrs,** Audēju iela 16 (open Mon.-Fri. 8am-8pm, Sat. 8am-6pm, Sun. 10am-4pm). **Centrālais Tirgus** (Central Market), in five immense zeppelin hangars behind the bus station, is an experience not to be missed. You can buy anything you want here at bargain prices, but shop around, as vendors' prices vary quite a bit (open Mon. 7am-3pm, Tues.-Sun. 7am-6pm).

Starburagas, Čaka iela 57. Fries it up Latvian style, complete with rugged wooden interior and a patriotic picture gallery. Big pig legs are a specialty (3.50Ls)—try them with stewed cabbage garnish (0.80Ls). Other dishes 1-2Ls. Open daily 11am-1am.

Rozamunde, Mazā Smilšu 8 (tel. 722 77 98), 1 block off Filharmonija laukums. A great pub run by the Rīga Jazz Company. Real live musicians play nightly 8-10pm in a classy candlelit room with white linen tablecloths. Delicious beef tenderloin stuffed with champignons and cheese 3.20Ls. Open daily 11am-11pm.

Fredis Café, Audēju iela 5 (tel. 21 37 31). Decent tunes disturb smoky air while tiny floodlights on wire arms flirt with each other, as do the carefully dressed patrons—when they take a break from acting cool. Subs 0.80-1.30Ls. Spaghetti with mushrooms 2.20Ls. *Aldaris* 0.5L for 0.65Ls. Open daily 9am-midnight.

Zilais putns, Tirgoņu iela 4 (tel. 722 82 14). The "Bluebird" boasts tasty thin-crust pizza downstairs or outside, the best pasta in Rīga and a great view of Doma laukums upstairs. Open in season daily 11am-1am; off season 11am-11pm.

Pica Lulū, Ģertrūdes iela 27. Thin-crust pizza is light on the cheese, but is the best in town. Loaded with toppings, a slice goes for 0.69Ls. Coke 0.40Ls. Psychedelic chalk menu and orange-tone interior wrestle with quality tunes for your attention.

Hotel Latvija Express Bar, Elizabetes iela 55 (tel. 722 22 11), at the corner of Brīvības bulv. past the Freedom Monument. Renowned breakfast joint with yellow tablecloths brighter than the mornin' sun. Pancakes with jam (0.99Ls). Or try one of the 23 varieties of omelettes (1-3Ls). Open daily 7am-11pm.

Pulvertornis, Vaņu iela 1 (tel. 21 68 80). Cafeteria-style dining in a roomful of silent people inhaling their food. Cheap and surprisingly good. Entrées for well under 1Ls. Open Mon.-Fri. 8am-8pm, Sat.-Sun. 9am-6pm.

Anre, Aspazijas bulv. 30 (tel. 722 99 15). One of the few places really welcoming you to sit alone with your work, your thoughts, and excellent coffee (0.25Ls). Gentle waitresses serve up the appetizing platters (2Ls). Open daily 8am-8pm.

SIGHTS

At the end of Audēju iela, **Sv. Pētera baznīca** (St. Peter's Church) prods the clouds with a green spire visible throughout the city. First built in 1209, the church now standing dates from 1408. At the top of the 72m tower, you can see the Baltic Sea. Inside exhibits cover the fire that destroyed the original tower in 1941 (open Tues.-Sun. 10am-6pm; church 0.30Ls; tower 1Ls, students 0.70Ls). Just behind at Skārņu iela 10/20 abides another church, the 1208 **Juras Kirik** (St. George's Church; tel. 22 22 35), the oldest stone edifice in Rīga. Constructed for the German Knights of the Sword, the church was secularized in the 1500s and carved into three warehouses by German merchants. Again altered, it now houses the magnificent **Museum of Applied Arts,** showcasing Latvian ceramics, jewelry, bookmaking, and tapestries (open Tues.-Sun. 11am-5pm; museum 0.40Ls, students 0.10Ls; exhibitions 0.50Ls).

Farther right on Skārņu iela at the intersection with Jāņa iela stands **Sv. Jāņa baznīca** (St. John's Church), a small 13th-century chapel embellished into the 1830s in a medley of architectural styles, from Gothic to Baroque to Neoclassical (open Tues.-Sun. 10am-1pm; for info call the office on Jāņa Sēta 7 at 722 40 28 or 722 75 73). Through a tiny alleyway at the left **Jāņa Sēta** (St. John's Courtyard) is the oldest site in Rīga, where the first city castle stood. Part of the old city wall is preserved here, and in summer a beer garden toasts the past. At Kaļķu iela's base, three granite soldiers guard **Latviešu Strēlnieku laukums.** Dedicated during Soviet times to the crack team of Latvian soldiers who served as Lenin's bodyguards after the revolution, the statues meant enough to the nation that they were some of the few Soviet monuments not torn down, but still offered flowers. Behind them, rise the ominous black walls of the **Latvian Occupation Museum,** Strēlnieku laukums 1 (tel. 21 27 15), probably Rīga's finest museum. Top-notch exhibits labeled in Latvian, English, German, and Russian take two hours to read through. The initial Soviet occupation is depicted so vividly you can almost hear the Red Army marching. A model gulag helps explain why the Germans were welcomed as liberators. Don't miss the shot of Latvian girls draping Hitler's soldiers with flowers as the invaders smile in disbelief.

North of the Occupation Museum along Kaļķu iela, **Filharmonija laukums** is bounded on the northwest by two ancient German guild houses and the felines of the yellow **Cat House.** Down Zirgu iela, between the two guild houses, **Doma laukums** oozes with the spirit of Rīga from every irregular cobble in its vast, beer-soaked expanse. Its 1226 foundations now well below the square, **Rīgas Doms** (Cathedral) adds looming mass to the relaxed elegance of the square. Inside, an immense German pipe organ resonates through the largest church in the Baltics (open Tues.-Fri. 1-5pm, Sat. 10am-2pm; concerts Wed. and Fri. at 7pm; church admission 0.30Ls). Behind the *dom*, at Palasta iela 4, the **History and Maritime Museum** thoroughly explores Rīga's complex Germano-Russo-Swedish-Latvian history, houses exhibits on the Latvian naval tradition, and—of course—has a veritable shrine to dancer Marta Lberinga (open Wed.-Sun. 11am-5pm; 0.50Ls).

Rīga Pils (Rīga Castle), Pils laukums 2 (tel. 32 30 11), at the street's end, defends three modest museums: the **Museum of Foreign Art** (open Tues.-Sun. 11am-5pm; 0.40Ls, students 0.20Ls), the **Museum of (Ancient) Latvian History** (open Wed.-Sun. 11am-5pm; 0.30Ls), and the **Raiņa Museum of Literature** (open Mon.-Sat. 11am-5pm; 0.40Ls). The apparently underfunded trio are labeled in Latvian only.

At Jēkaba iela 11, Latvia's **Saeima** (Parliament; tel. 32 51 35; fax (8) 83 03 33), was barricaded with trucks, barbed wire, sandbags, and nationalism during the 1991 struggle for independence. Call or visit the office at Maztrokšnu iela 2 a day in advance to arrange a free tour. The small street across Jēkaba iela from the Parliament, **Trokšņu iela** (Noisy Street), acquired its name because it ran just inside the city walls, where soldiers were always rowdy. A block down this passage is the **Swedish Gate**, built into the city walls in 1698 when Sweden ruled Latvia. Through it, Torņa iela leads to **Pulvertornis** (Powder Tower), one of Rīga's oldest landmarks and the only city tower still standing. Nine cannonballs are still lodged in its 14th-century walls; it's not clear why they're on the side facing *into* the city. Inside, the **Latvian Museum of War** (Latvijas Kara Muzejs), Smilšu iela 20 (tel. 722 81 47), shows Latvian resistance to Soviet rule; Latvians hated Communism so much that 200,000 enlisted in the German army during WWII (appeals to German heritage were apparently also a factor), and guerrilla bands continued fighting until the mid-1950s. The first floor is a national scrapbook of the 1991 independence struggle, while the 12 other rooms house displays on earlier conflicts, in a tone that varies from prideful joy to horror (open Tues.-Sun. 10am-5pm; 0.30Ls, students 0.10Ls).

In the park-ring near the Powder Tower, ruins of the old walls remain on **Bastejkalns**. Across and around the city canal, an old defensive moat, five red stone slabs stand as **memorials** to the dead of January 20, 1991, when Soviet special forces stormed the Interior Ministry on Raiņa bulv. The dead included a schoolboy and two cameramen recording the events. At the north end of the park on Kr. Valdemāra iela lies the **National Theater,** where Latvia first declared its independence on November 18, 1918 (open Mon.-Fri. 10am-7pm, Sat.-Sun. 11am-6pm). In the park, Kaļķu iela widens to become Brīvības bulv., where the beloved **Brīvības Piemineklis** (Freedom Monument) was dedicated in 1935, while Latvia was an independent republic. The Soviets left this standing, but Intourist craftily explained that the surmounting figure represented Mother Russia supporting the three Baltic States (it actually shows Liberty raising up the three regions of Latvia—Vidzeme, Latgale, and Kurzeme). The inscription reads "Fatherland and Freedom". Across the Esplanāde near Elizabetes iela, the **State Museum of Latvian Art,** Kr. Valdemāra iela 10 (tel. 32 50 21), features 19th- and 20th-century works by Kazaks, Tone, the colorful Rēriks, and others (open Wed.-Mon. 11am-5pm; museum 0.50Ls; exhibition 0.40Ls,).

Several other sights outside the city center are worth soaking up. On Zaķusalas island in the middle of the Daugava River, the **TV Tower's** (tel. 20 09 43) viewing platform and café loom 98m over the city, offering stunning panoramas of Old Rīga. To get there, take trolleybus #19. To the north, **Mežaparks**, a 6km-square woodland area at the end of tram line #11, houses the **city zoo**, pr. Meža 1 (tel. 51 80 35; open daily 10am-7pm; 0.80Ls), an open-air **concert shell,** and innumerable jogging paths. On the south end of this expanse, the three main cemeteries of Rīga assumed considerable symbolic significance in the struggle for Latvian nationhood. **Braļu Kapi** (Brothers' Cemetery) is dedicated to soldiers who fell in the two World Wars and the 1918-1920 struggle for independence. The poet Jānis Rainis rests in the smaller **Rainis Kapi,** along with other Latvian nationalists, literary figures, and important Communist stooges of the last 50 years. **Meža Kapi** (Forest Cemetery) is a peaceful area, filled with stones designed to reflect the personalities of the men and women they commemorate. All three can be reached by taking tram #11 to "Braļu Kapi", eleven stops from the starting point. **Etnogrāfiskais Brīvdabas Muzejs** (Open-Air Ethnographic Museum; tel. 99 41 06), on the shores of the Juglas Ezers (Lake), has collected nearly a hundred 18th- and 19th-century buildings from all regions of Latvia, including churches, complete farmsteads, and a windmill. On the first weekend of June, the annual crafts fair here brings together hundreds of artists. To reach the museum, take tram #6 to the end of the line, walk across the bridge, and turn right onto Brīvdabas iela (open daily May-Oct. 10am-5pm).

ENTERTAINMENT AND NIGHTLIFE

Bars

Rīga's pride, good bars, are abundant and inexpensive. Don't miss the vast beer gardens of **Doma laukums** or the smaller one at **Filharmonija laukums.**

- **Paddy Whelan's,** Grēcineku iela 4. You can wander through Vecrīga's bars until you wonder if you're the last surviving human and still have trouble finding a seat at Paddy's. Fast-flowing beer sates a noisy, friendly crowd of local students, backpackers, and the occasional businessman. Pint of *Guinness* (and other Irish brews) 1Ls. *Aldaris* 0.60Ls. Open nightly 5pm-midnight; food served until 8pm.
- **Ala** (Cave), Audēju iela 11, take a left onto Vecpilsētas iela, a left into the courtyard, and left immediately afterward. Subscribing to the "ant colony" school of bar design, tunnels and stairways connect little rooms filled with pool tables, bars, slot machines, and young cave-dwellers just hanging out. Open daily 3pm-4am.
- **M (Maksims) Bars,** Čaku iela 45 (tel. 27 54 41). Comfy black interior resembles a slightly cybernetic library—wood paneling, low leather booths, and a slightly higher grade of techno. *Shashliks* 2Ls—the chicken one is stuffed with mushrooms, red peppers, cheese, and taste. Beer starts at 0.40Ls per 0.5L. Open 24hr.

Dancing

For a city of around 800,000, Rīga has an awful lot of *diskotekas;* the unfortunate result is that clients get spread out pretty thinly. Some places still manage to pack 'em in, though. Keep in mind that Friday night is bigger and badder than Saturday.

- **Pulkuedim Neviens Neraksta,** Peldu 26/28. Coppery interior is a blackened combination of a modern art gallery and an alien spacecraft. Weekends, trendy youth pile over the backlit steel bridge, and a few even dance to the "alternative" (mainstream American rock) sounds. Days it's a top-notch restaurant with an exotic menu. Open Sun.-Thurs. noon-3am, Fri.-Sat. noon-5am. 1Ls cover after 9pm.
- **Bimini,** Čaka iela 67/69 (tel. 27 21 68; fax 27 73 00). Karaoke croons from downstairs after 11pm, or wander up for a large, full dance floor, a neon-soaked bar, and a crowd ranging from baby-fat to baby-boom. Enough camo-clad security to turn back the next Russian invasion. Open daily 8pm-6am. Cover men 2Ls, women get in with a smile; Wed. and Thurs. 50% discount with student ID.
- **Club Next** (Kabata II), Peldu iela 19 (tel. 22 53 34). Tumble down a long, grey spiral staircase to a room reminiscent of a high-school dance; the row of girls sitting against the left wall and the groups of *alus*-sipping guys at the tables on the right watch you make your entrance. The large dance floor is tragically underutilized, but if you could just leap that gender gap, this could be your lucky night… Open daily noon-5pm and 6pm-5am. Cover 3Ls minus the number of X chromosomes you have. Also an alternative theater.
- **Studentu Klubs,** Raiņa 23. A warm gathering of students in a low key, wood-toned subterranean playground. Fills up more on its theme nights (check posters around town). Open nightly 10pm-5am. Cover 1Ls, after midnight 2Ls.

Performances

Birthplace of Mikhail Baryshnikov, Rīga is home to the **Latvian National Opera** and the excellent **Rīga Ballet,** but with the opera house indefinitely under construction, both perform at the **Kongress zāle** (tel. 61 57 73), on the corner of Kr. Valdemāra iela and Kalpaka iela (tickets 0.35-2.00Ls). At the cathedral, **Ērģeļmūzikas koncerts** (organ concerts) employ the third-largest organ in existence. Purchase tickets at Doma laukums 1, opposite the main entrance at *koncertzāles kase* (tel. 721 34 98; open daily noon-3pm and 4-7pm). The **Latvian Symphony Orchestra** has frequent concerts in the Large and Small Guilds off Filharmonija laukums, while ensembles and artists from abroad perform in **Vāgnera zāle**, Vāgnera iela (open daily noon-3pm and 4-7pm). The ticket office, which sells tickets for nearly all concerts in Rīga, is on the first floor of the Large Guild, Amatu iela 6 (tel. 22 36 18).

■ Near Rīga

The beaches of **Jūrmala** (see below) or the forests and valleys of the **Gauja National Park** (see p. 335) are the most popular daytrips from Rīga. Sun-lovers who don't care for crowds should head to **Saulkrasti,** an hour north on the suburban trains (0.35Ls), with wider, sparser beaches that get direct sun far into the evening.

Electric trains travel frequently from Rīga to **Dārziņi** (*not* "Salaspils" on the Krustpils line; 14 per day, 20min., 0.18Ls), the site of the **Salaspils Memorial** where the Kurtenhof concentration camp was located during WWII. Blue and yellow signs point the way (20min.). At the entrance to the memorial dedicated to 100,000 victims, the overhead inscription reads, "Behind this gate the earth moans." A huge concrete museum-memorial and a field of immense statues depicting the suffering and courage of the camp's victims watch over barrack sites layered in flowers.

■ Jūrmala

Since the late 19th century, Rīgans have spent the summer on this narrow spit of sand between the Gulf of Rīga and the Lielupe River. In 1959, 14 towns were conglomerated into the city-resort Jūrmala (Seashore). To get there, take one of the frequent trains (every 15-20min., 4am-11pm) from Rīga, only 20km away. A handful of towns dot the coast—from Rīga, beachless Priedaine is the first stop in Jūrmala. The train then passes over the Lielupe River and quickly through Lielupe, Bulduri, Dzintari, Majori, Dubulti, Jaundubulti, Pumpuri, Melluži, Asari, Vaivari, and Sloka, before heading back inland to Kudra and Ķemeri. **Public buses** (15 santīmi) string together the towns of Jūrmala, each connecting two to four towns. The **commuter rail** runs one to two trains per hour in both directions from 5am to 11:30pm.

On the side facing the Gulf, the sand dunes of **Lielupe,** the first town with beach access (½hr., 0.23Ls), are the most dramatic in Latvia, but the places between **Bulduri** and **Dubulti** are more popular for sunning and swimming. Gulf water is reputedly polluted, and since 1987 all swimming has been prohibited. In the past few years though, taking a dip has made an unsanctioned comeback. The beaches are full of the young and old enjoying the sun; if it gets windy, just hide behind a dune.

Majori (35min., 0.32Ls), Jūrmala's center, sees trainloads of people busily relaxing after noon, when the cafés and restaurants throw open their gates. These establishments and their mushroom-selling streetside brethren line **Jomas iela**, Majori's pedestrian street. To the left, streets head for the beach; to the right, it's back to the parallel road and train tracks running the length of Jūrmala. The **Jānis Rainis Memorial Museum,** Pliekšāna iela 5/7 (tel. 76 42 95), displays the great poet's works, books, and photos in the villa where he died in 1929 (open Wed.-Sun. 10am-5pm; 0.20Ls). The **tourist office,** Jomas iela 42 (tel. 642 76), has maps (1Ls), a wealth of brochures, and a helpful director who speaks perfect English (open Mon.-Fri. 9am-5pm). **Exchange currency** on the same side of the street, at Jomas iela 2, in the **post office. Postal code:** LV-2015. The **telephone office,** Lienes iela 18 (tel. 76 25 71; fax 889 27 19), is parallel to the train tracks (open 24hr.).

If you adore the town, stay at **Hotel Jūrmala,** Jomas iela 47/49 (tel./fax 76 13 40). Showers may not have hot water, but every room comes with a toilet and a balcony (singles 8Ls, doubles 12-15Ls, triples 20Ls). **Orients,** 33 Jomas iela (tel. 620 82), is the Big Kahuna of local eateries; their tasty (though not Oriental) entrées will set you back 3-6Ls. At Jomas iela 66/3, **Barbara** smacks a big, bland omelette on your plate for under 1Ls and a Spanish main dish for under 3Ls. The interior and music seem a caricature of a Spanish restaurant.

At the end of Jūrmala, **Ķemeri** was once the prime health resort of the Russian empire, where therapeutic mud baths, sulphur water, and other cures have operated since the mid-18th century. The impressive white **Sanatorium** (tel. 76 53 88), built like an Art-Deco ocean liner, is an aging palace open to visitors (US$25-30 for up to 3 people). Be sure to check out the interior in any case, with a restored library complete with period furniture, tapestries, and acres of gardens. The #6 bus to "Sanitorija Latvia" brings you close; take the paved road next to the bus stop, following the street lights to the original, grand entrance.

KURZEME

■ Ventspils

Dusted by sand and seagull droppings, Ventspils reclines under the persistent Baltic sun. The natural slide of low buildings and open streets into windswept beaches is broken only by the swinging cranes and massive ocean liners of this ancient and active seaport, 200km west of Rīga.

Orientation and Practical Information Ventspils's central street, **Kuldīgas iela**, is highway-sized, and like **Ganību iela**, hugs the park; near the port side of the city, Kuldīgas iela curves away. Take a **bus** (0.15Ls) to the **town center**, a 40-minute walk from the train station. Or call a **cab** (tel. 639 50) and negotiate a 0.50Ls ride. The **train station**, Rīgas iela (tel. 692 64), has odd ticket office hours (Mon.-Fri. 6am-noon and 2-5pm, Sat.-Sun. 6-7am and 2-5:10pm). **Trains** run to Rīga (2 per day, 2hr., 2.90Ls), and **buses** to Rīga (9 per day, 3½hr., 2.15Ls) depart from the **bus station** at Kuldīgas iela 5 (tel. 227 89; open daily 5am-6pm). **Tobago**, a **tourist office** at Raina iela 16 (tel. 362 40 03) offers two-hour excursions in historic Ventspils for 5Ls and arranges for visas to Belarus (US$90; open daily 9am-5pm). **Exchange money** (but not traveler's checks) at the **post office**, Juras iela 9 (tel. 221 60; open Mon.-Fri. 7:30am-7pm, Sat. 7:30am-3pm), which also houses a **telephone office** (tel. 362 44 18; open daily 7am-10pm). **Postal code:** LV-3600. **Phone code:** 236.

Accommodations and Food To reach **Viesnīca Dzintarjūra**, Ganību iela 26 (tel. 221 79), turn left on Kuldīgas iela from the bus station and stay on the right side of the park. Clean rooms, hall showers with white floors and Howitzer-like hot water behind brand-new doors (singles 6Ls, doubles 8Ls).

Kaija (tel. 229 74) scoops out bucketloads of ice cream to bucketloads of locals and will deliver a tolerable pizza to your table or door (0.80-1.50Ls; open daily 10am-9pm). **Štrālzunde**, Plāta iela 7/9 (tel. 246 20), is a lively, somewhat formal, eatery smack in the center of things (live music Wed.-Thurs. 8:30pm-midnight and Sat.-Sun. 8:30pm-2am). Try the tasty "Wild Agaric" salad (1.21Ls) or the many fish snacks (caviar 4.40Ls), but leave the very salty beef steak for those who want to gargle (open Sun.-Thurs. noon-midnight, Fri.-Sat. 10am-2am). The **open-air market**, Tirgus iela, vends even cheaper stuff (open daily 8am-8pm), or stock up on imports at **Interprego**, Anna iela 1 (tel. 227 00; open daily 7am-2pm).

Sights To reach the Old Town center, follow any street north to Pils iela. Off Pils iela, a **Lutheran Church,** Tirgus iela 6 (tel. 227 50), flaunts several yellow Corinthian columns. In front, a large painting of Jesus in a red robe stands under a radial gold arc (open daily 9am-5pm; services Tues.-Sat. 9am-noon, Sun. 10am-noon). Undergoing repairs, a **Russian Orthodox Church** (tel. 210 16) menaces in shades of gray with black domes (open daily 9am-6pm; services Sat. 11am, Sun. noon). If it's closed, inquire at the little green house.

The **regional art and history museum,** Akmeņu iela 3 (tel. 220 31), is open Wednesday through Sunday noon-6pm. West of the hotel 3km, the impossibly broad **beach** meets the Baltic—its pale, wind-textured sand backed by dunes. Watch out for the barbed wire fencing off the industrial section. Turn left from the hotel, and catch bus #10 heading left. The outdoor **Sea Fishing Museum,** on the corner of Riņķu iela, features fishing and water accoutrements like a windmill (don't worry, the locals don't get it either). There's also a **memorial** to lost sailors where Pils iela nears the sea. Or visit the **open-air concert hall** on Vasarnīcu iela, where children, and the occasional adult, can ride the old, toy-like trains.

■ Kuldīga

Legend has it that Kuldīgas Rumba (the waterfall on the Venta River) formed after a rooster's call scared the devil out of the Devil, who dropped a sack of rocks into the river. The town's minuscule houses look Gothic and antique rather than old and worn-out. Outside the center, Kuldīga is populated by haystacks, and in summer, the air fills with dandelion fluff as dogs investigate the streets, fields, and your feet. The **Lutheran Church of St. Anne,** Dzirnavu iela 12, is a brick giant with green-coned tops (open daily 10am-5pm). Enter through the gate, and come around the church to the bright red house in the back. Be sure to notice the stained glass near the pipe organ. The front of the church has three stained-glass windows as well as a wooden mini-church with a golden statue of Jesus. The more famous church in Kuldīga, **St. Katrina's** decays in a large white building on Baznīcas iela (services Sun. 10am-noon). An old water mill still trickles down the hill. The **oldest house** (built in 1670) ages still further on the same street at #7. The town's ornate orange-and-brown building at the end of the street is the **town hall,** Rātslaukums. **Kuldīgas Rumba** lies across from the **regional museum,** Pils iela 5 (tel. 223 64), which features 19th-century ceramics, weather vanes, and a bit o' town history (open Tues.-Sun. 11am-7pm; 0.20Ls). Outside, a single-vaulted room of the Livonian Order castle remains, the top covered by earth and grass.

About 150km west of Rīga, Kuldīga's town center can be traversed in just 10 minutes. The main street, **Liepājas iela,** is a 15-minute walk on Rūpniecības iela from the bus station. With your back to the front of the bus station, turn right and walk to the big, brown-black barn. Take a left on Jelgavas iela, and follow it until it turns into Mucenieku iela, then take a right on Putnu iela to reach Liepājas iela. A touristy town without a tourist office? It's true. But **tours** of the town may be arranged in English at least two days in advance through the regional museum, Pils iela 5 (tel. 223 64). Only buses come to Kuldīga, arriving at the small **bus station,** Stacijas iela 2 (tel. 220 61; open daily 6am-5:45pm), from Riga (5-7 per day, 3hr., 1.80Ls). **Luggage storage** costs 0.10Ls (open daily 6am-6pm). The **post office** is at Liepājas iela 34 (open Mon.-Thurs. 8am-2pm and 3-6pm, Fri. 3-6pm, Sat. 8am-3pm). **Postal code:** LV-3300. The **telephone office** is upstairs from the post office (open daily 7am-10pm). **Phone code:** 0233.

Viesnīca Kuršu, Pilsētas laukums 6 (tel. 224 30), is the most prominent object in the wide main square. Shell out 8.48Ls (for a single, 13Ls double) for remodeled rooms with remarkably clean showers—remarkable, that is, until you realize there is no hot water. A selection of fine, reasonably priced restaurants outdo the many *kafejnicas* near the buses and the hotel. **Jāna Nams,** Liepājasiela 48 (tel. 234 56), serves up tasty but modestly proportioned entrées for 0.50-1.55Ls as each curtain-sculpture flutters in the orange-and-navy darkness. **Venta,** Pilsētas laukums 1 (tel. 249 66), offers dinner for 1.50Ls (open daily noon-midnight); crowded **Staburadze Kafejnica,** Liepājas iela 8 (tel. 235 99), prepares them for 0.70Ls (open Mon.-Fri. 7:30am-9pm, Sun. 10am-6pm).

■ Pilsrundāle

Built for the power-hungry Baltic-German Baron Ernst Johann von Bühren (Bīrons to the Latvians), the magnificent **Rundāles Pils** (Rundāles Palace). was designed by Francesco Rastrelli, the same famous Italian architect who did the Winter Palace in St. Petersburg. When construction began in 1736, Kurzeme (the west and south parts of modern Latvia) was a semi-independent duchy under Polish and Russian influence.

After the death of Peter the Great in 1730, his niece Anna inherited the Russian throne, and her marriage to the Duke of Kurzeme thrust the area into the spotlight. The Duke's untimely demise left Anna free to promote her lover, Bīrons, to Duke of Kurzeme.

Pilsrundāle was built in a year, and by 1738 the interior was almost finished. About that time, Bīrons decided that he should have a second palace in Kurzeme's capital, Jelgava, so he ordered Rastrelli to begin there before finishing the palace at Rundāle. Tsarina Anna's died in 1740, and the new power structure found the Duke more utilitarian in Siberian exile. In 1763, however, Catherine the Great ascended the throne, and Bīrons was allowed to return from his involuntary vacation. Over the next four years, the Baroque Pilsrundāle was completed by Johann Michael Graff in Rococo style. Bīrons held onto the palace until 1795, when Russia annexed Kurzeme, and he was forced to flee again.

Used variously as a grain storehouse, hospital, and primary school by the Soviets, the palace was in a dismal state when restoration began. Basketball hoops had been screwed into the walls of the parquet-floored dining room in 1953—you can still see the attachment points. On the first floor, there is a multi-room display on the original construction of the palace and of its restoration. With 138 rooms to refurbish, work continues, but the restored section includes the most opulent rooms. Upstairs is the **Zelta Zāle** (Gold Room), the marble and gold-leaf throne room, with dramatic murals on the ceiling—and soldiers' graffiti from as long ago as 1812. The **Baltā Zāle** (White Room) was the ballroom; plasterwork cherubim depict the four seasons and the four elemental forces (earth, air, fire, and water). The duke's chambers are huge, overlooking the vast gardens in back. The kitchen's immense fireplaces heated the ballroom above year-round and cooked an estimated 1200 eggs and one steer every day. It has been refurbished and houses a **café**.

The palace hosts occasional **concerts**—Museum Day (May 18), Christmas and Independence Day (Nov. 18). Around the third week in July there is an Early Music Festival (2Ls for a day of tunes; call the director's office at (239) 622 74 for details).

The palace is open Wednesday to Sunday 10am-6pm, off-season 10am-5pm. Admission is 1Ls, students 0.70Ls, 18 and under 0.15Ls; double that to add to your visit the excellent exhibit of art recovered from churches brutalized by the Soviets. Tack on 3Ls more to take photos. A 0.15Ls English guidebook is available, as are info-packed tours (1½-2hr., 8-10Ls; call (239) 621 97 in advance to arrange).

To get there, you'll have to go through Bauska, connected to Rīga by **bus** (22 per day, 1¾hr.). Then take one of the 8-10 daily buses to Jelgava, and ask the driver to drop you off at Pilsrundāle (25min., 0.20Ls). There are blue signposts. From that bus stop, go left at the big Pilsrundāle sign, and walk 1.3km. The palace is around a hedge to the left. Half the daily buses go all the way to the hedge.

LATGALE

■ Daugavpils

Founded in 1275 by Germans, what was then Dünaburg languished unnoticed until Ivan the Terrible swept through in 1577 during the 25-year Livonian War. For the next 50 years, Poles, Lithuanians, Russians, Germans, and Swedes fought over the city; in the end the Poles assumed control of what they called Dvinsk. Heavy fighting during WWI reduced the population by 80%. After WWII, the Soviets repopulated almost 90% of Daugavpils; even now it is now little more than a tenth Latvian. Ironically considered "Latvia's Second City", it betrays its size only by the westernized shops and chemically refined air (which, incidentally, makes for beautiful sunsets). Otherwise the idyllic pedestrian streets and quiet buildings are in harmony with the emerald peace of the Latvian countryside.

DAUGAVPILS ■ 331

ORIENTATION AND PRACTICAL INFORMATION

Daugavpils is an eminently walkable city carved in half by two hills and railroad tracks. From the train station, the pedestrian **Rīgas iela** leads to the commercial area, **Centrs.** North of the station, tram tracks follow **18. Novembra iela** through **Jaunbūve,** the residential area. A detailed map (0.60Ls) is easy to find at any kiosk.

Tourist Office: In Viesnīca Latvija (tel. 297 73). Open Mon.-Fri. 9am-5pm.
Consulates: Belarus, 18. Novembra iela 44 (tel. 306 92). Same-day Belarusian visas US$13. Open Mon.-Tues. and Thurs.-Fri. 10am-1pm and 2-4pm.
Currency Exchange: There's a 24-hr. exchange booth in the train station, but the ones speckling the town offer slightly better rates. Better rates than most of Latvia.
Trains: (info tel. 005) east of the commercial section. To: Rīga (5 per day, 3-6hr., 2.15Ls); St. Petersburg (5 per day, 11-12hr., 6-11Ls); Vilnius (4 per day, 4hr., 2.15Ls). **Luggage storage** downstairs (0.50Ls).
Buses: Viestura iela 26 (tel. 225 07, info 004). Open daily 5am-midnight, cashiers 4:45am-7:20pm. To: Aglona (3 per day, 1½hr., 0.79Ls); Vilnius (1 per day, 3hr., 3.25Ls); Warsaw (1 per day, 16hr., 10Ls).
Public Transportation: Trams and **buses,** but ignore the buses. Trams run daily 6am-1am. Tram #1 goes from the train station past the market and Viesnīca Latvija to Jaunbūve; #3 runs from the fortress past the market and Latvija to Jaunbūve. Buy tickets on the tram (0.07Ls) or bus (0.10Ls).
Taxis: State taxi service (tel. 254 50).
Pharmacy: Aptieka #1, Rīgas iela 54 (tel. 200 55), at Viesta iela. Open Mon.-Fri. 8am-8pm, Sat.-Sun. 10am-6pm.
Post Office: Cietokšņa iela 28 (tel. 223 55). A block east and 3 south of Viesnīca Latvija. Open Mon.-Fri. 8am-1pm and 2-7pm, Sat.-Sun. 8am-4pm. **Postal code:** LV-5401.
Telephones: Telephone and Telegraph Office, Cietokšņa iela 24, within the post office. Open daily 8am-11pm. **Phone code:** 254 (from Europe, drop the 2).

ACCOMMODATIONS AND FOOD

Even with only two hotels, there's an overabundance of rooms in Daugavpils, except in mid-August when the religious festival in nearby Aglona miraculously fills them. From the train station, walk 500m on Rīgas iela until the Soviet monstrosity **Viesnīca Latvija,** Ģimnāzijas iela 46 (tel. 290 03), rears its glass-and-concrete head (single 6Ls, with bath and breakfast 8.20Ls; doubles 10Ls, with bath and breakfast 15.20Ls). **Viesnīca Celtnieks** (tel. 325 10) hides deep in the residential section of town, take tram #1 up 18. Novembra iela to "Jelgavas". From here, make a right onto Jeglavas and another right on Strādnieku iela. It's the yellow brick building on your left, renting out clean cool rooms for 4Ls. Use the saunas for 3-5Ls per hour.

If the restaurant selection leaves you unimpressed, you're not alone. Fortunately, there are other options. The **tirgus** (market), Parādes iela just behind Viesnīca Latvija, has outdoor produce stalls and indoor meat and fish sections (open daily 7am-4pm). An **Interpegro** market (tel. 296 11) stands at Rīgas iela 22 (open daily 7am-midnight). **Mārtiņš,** Muzeja iela 2 (tel. 233 28), left off Rīgas near Imantas iela and the river, is easily the best restaurant in town, attentively serving respectable food in a comfortable basement (entrées 1-2.50Ls; open daily noon-midnight). Bands enhance the fishy main dishes from 8pm to closing (cover Tues.-Thurs. 0.50Ls., Fri.-Sun. 0.80Ls). The centrally located **Kafejnīca "Vecais Draugs,"** Vienības iela 22 (tel. 221 58), serves tolerable meat and cheese salads (0.20-0.35Ls) and soups (0.35Ls; open daily 11am-11pm).

SIGHTS AND ENTERTAINMENT

The **"four churches"** district, in the east half of Daugavpils, is the city's tourist highlight. Take tram #3 to "Lokomotīve", just past the bridge over the railway tracks. The huge **Borisa-Gļeba katedrāle,** Tartac iela 2 (tel. 535 44), is pure fantasy in rich purple, cobalt, and white, topped by starry blue onion domes with gold trim (mass Sun.

8am and 5pm). Inside, thousands of dark, classical icons clutter every available surface; a local belief held that every member of the congregation had to have a different patron saint. A block up on 18. Novembra iela, workers slowly refill the burnt-out shell of the **Luterāņu baznīca** after a 1987 fire gutted the church. Just a block further east at Andreja Pumpura iela 11a, is the more austere **Jaunavas Marijas katoļu baznīca**, still serving Daugaupils's 13% Polish minority (open daily 9:30am-noon). **Vecticībnieku baznīca** (Church of the Old Believers), on the corner of Pushkin and Tartac iela, reveals a more haphazard construction, the interior cluttered with aged icons surrounding rows of benches. It is home to a perennially persecuted Russian sect that fled to Latvia during Peter the Great's reign. Inside, women must cover their heads and are not permitted behind the wall of icons; everyone must always face the front. Contrary to Russian Orthodox tradition, worshippers cross with three fingers (Sun. service 8am). Abandoned by its spired comrades, **Sv. Pētera baznīca** (tel. 205 84) languishes near Viesnīca Latvija. Modeled after St. Peter's in Rome in the 1840s, it shadows spontaneous Hari Krishna concerts (open Mon.-Thurs. 8:30am-8pm, Fri.-Sun. 9:30-11am and 7-8pm).

Daugavpils' other attraction is the immense **Cietoksnis** (Fortress), abandoned by the Soviet air force in 1992. The Teutonic Order had a stockade on this same site as early as 1288, later replaced by a larger fort that Ivan the Terrible built in 1577. The current ring of bricks and earthen mounds, at tram #3's north terminus through the railroad trestle, only dates back to the early 19th century; the Nazis used the base as Stalag-340 in WWII. The immense network of military buildings has been totally stripped, though the families that remained behind in Latvia still live in the other half of the complex. A lone guard keeps nosy visitors out of the central courtyards. The **Regional History and Cultural Museum,** Rīgas iela 8 (tel. 227 09), contains one of the only two extant "polyphones." It looks like a midget piano without keys and plays minstrelish music when wound. Along with paintings, a tapestry, a statue, and a carriage, the museum houses a bottle collection (open Tues.-Sat. 11am-6pm; 0.30Ls, students 0.15Ls).

Aside from a few *diskotekas*, there isn't much **nightlife**. The disco **Vienības nams,** Vienības iela 22 (tel. 358 14), ensnares everyone under 20 (open Fri.-Sun. 9pm-2am; cover Fri. and Sun. 0.30Ls, Sat. 0.70Ls). In the same building, the **House of Culture** (tel. 262 68) hosts occasional concerts, ballets, jazz sets—you get the idea (tickets 0.30-1.50Ls); a **student theater** performs September to May. Motorcycle racing sometimes crops up from May to September.

■ Near Daugavpils: Aglona

About 40km north of Daugavpils, the town of Aglona is the site of the **Ascension Day pilgrimage** on August 15 every year; thousands of Catholics walk from all over Latvia, many carrying elaborately carved wooden crosses, to celebrate at its 17th-century cathedral. Buses run to Aglona from Daugavpils (see Daugavpils: Practical Information, p. 331), but don't get caught here overnight; there's not a rentable room in the village.

▓ Rēzekne

The only dustballs in this town spanning seven hills are those the infrequent visitors bring. The town is virtually immaculate—you can walk barefoot through the streets. Many locals live in 100-year-old houses, but they still manage to trim every stalk of grass around the central square. With plenty of places to swim, great fresh air, castles, and a fortress on a hill, Rēzekne will take the city out of any city slicker.

Orientation and Practical Information Rēzekne is 230km southeast of Rīga. From the train station, take bus #1 and get off at the fourth stop. The hotel on the main **Brīvošanas aleja,** near the statue of **St. Mara,** lies to the right, two churches rise to the left. Shortly before the hotel bus stop, Brīvošanas aleja intersects another large street, **Brīvības iela,** which parallels the bridge. **Tūrisma Firma "Ţēzeme",** inside the Vesnīca Latgale, sells maps (0.70Ls) and informs tourists about the region (what a novel idea!). Call three days in advance for a US$10 tour of Rēzekne (tel. 22 82; open Mon.-Fri. 9am-6pm, Sat. 10am-2pm). The Rēzekne II **train station** (tel. 721 01) sends trains to Rīga (5 per day, 3hr.). The **bus station,** Latgales iela 17 (tel. 220 45), has a daily bus to Rīga (5:30am, 5½hr., 3.60Ls). **City buses** are speedy, frequent vans that stop in front of the only hotel in town, and take you anywhere for 0.10Ls. Above the **post office,** Brīvošanas aleja 81/5 (open Mon.-Sat 9am-6pm), lurks the **telephone office** (open daily 7am-10pm). The **currency exchange** at the post office has better rates than the bank across the street (open daily 9am-5:30pm). **Postal code:** LV-4601. **Phone code:** 046.

Accommodations and Food The sparkling new **Viesnīca Latgale,** Brīvošanas aleja 98 (tel. 241 78; fax 221 80), is the only option; luckily it's a good one. Mirrors and paintings cover clean hallways, a short walk from the river. There is also a restaurant and indoor/outdoor café. Rooms vary in size and availability of hot water, TVs, phones, and fridges. The excellent bar downstairs, the restaurant, the café, and its location easily justify the prices (singles 5Ls, doubles 8Ls and up).

Try the old **tirgus** (market) on Latgales iela (open daily 8am-1pm), or the **supermarkets** lining the same street. **Kafejnica Senatne** (tel. 251 81) floats decorously above Brīvošanas aleja 100. Be prepared for perfumed waiters murmuring, *"Bon appetit,"* paintings of folk dancing couples, crocheted napkins, flowers, and Latvian dolls. Native Latvian and pan-flute songs are played. The second most expensive dish on the menu is only 1.38Ls and *solanka* is 0.50Ls (open daily 9am-11pm).

Sights and Entertainment Torn down repeatedly by the Germans and Soviets, the Latgale region's symbol, a **statue of St. Mara,** stands tall again on an oval of grass next to the hotel. Flanked by a huddling man and woman, she awkwardly holds a cross. **Latgales Kultūras Vēstures Muzeja,** Brīvošanas aleja 102 (tel. 224 64), has paintings, some historical material, and ceramics (open Mon.-Fri. 10am-5pm, Sat.-Sun. 10am-6pm; 0.30Ls). The blue-domed **Church of the Old Believers,** Brīvošanas aleja 99 (tel. 224 29), crams its gilded white interior with paintings (open Wed. and Fri.-Sun. 9am-noon; services Sat.-Sun. 6-8pm). Note the **two mini-churches** in front. One of the families that funded the metal one is buried within, while the wooden mini-church is dedicated to Tsar Alexander II. Take a right from Brīvošanas aleja onto Krasta iela, then a right onto Darzu iela. Go up the wooden stairs to see a view without a room and the two remaining stone walls of a **fortress** built by the Germans (1246-1324). Try to see the top of the **Russian Orthodox Church,** Sinicina iela 41, with its three bells. You may have to walk through patches of strawberries to get to it, but you'll agree with the locals that this— a fairy-tale edifice filled with icons and old books—is the most beautiful church in town.

Periodically, the **Russian theater** performs in the old building at Latgales iela 54. Placards announce performances. **Swimming** in the river is possible—away from the town center. **Lake Kovšy,** near the intersection of Latgales iela and Brīvošanas aleja, is also a popular spot. The **Nightclub-Cinema-Casino Rēvis,** Brīvošanas aleja 97 (tel. 228 85), plays movies for just 0.50Ls. (Pool tables and casino open Tues.-Sun. 6pm-3am. Nightclub open Fri.-Sun. 9pm-5am; cover 1.20Ls.) An insanely well stocked **bar** pours mixed drinks beneath the hotel for 1Ls. Check out their international money tree, but don't get your hopes up—the US$100 bill hangs on the alcohol's side, not the alcoholic's (open daily 3pm-midnight).

VIDZEME

■ Sigulda

Sigulda, 60km from Rīga, is a Latvian fantasy. The ridges of Turaida, aptly named the "Garden of God" by locals, tell the story of a mythic 400-year-old tragedy, while Gauja gorge beckons visitors to cross it by air (or plummet into it). Three castles, a monster-sized luge run, and extensive trails complete the dream, luring wide-eyed adventurers and die-hard romantics to plunge into the wilds of Gauja National Park.

Orientation and Practical Information From the **bus** and **train stations**, walk up **Raiņa iela** to the town center. Continue on as it transforms into **Gaujas iela**, then bears right as **Turaidas iela**. If you're tired, take bus #12 to Hotel Senleja, which provides a variety of valuable services; buy **maps** here (0.50Ls). Next door, **Makara Turisma Birojs**, Peldu iela 1 (tel. 737 24; fax 720 06), **rents bikes** (5Ls per day), canoes (8Ls per day), and boats (6Ls per day). They also organize raft, ski, and bike adventures and even supply ski instruction (Dec. 1-April 1). **Trains** run from Rīga by the suburban rail system (18 per day, 1hr., 0.53Ls). Both Sigulda and Cēsis are on the Rīga-Lugaži commuter rail line. **Buses** (8-10 per day, 1½hr., 0.36Ls) proceed from there to their *autoosta*. For a **taxi**, call 718 99. The **post office**, Pils iela 2 (open Mon.-Fri. 8am-noon and 1-5pm, Sat. 8am-2pm), contains the **telephone office** (open daily 7am-9pm). **Postal code:** LV-2150. **Phone code:** 29.

Accommodations and Food Gūtman's cave isn't for rent, but rooms across the way at **Hotel Senleja**, Turaidas iela 4 (tel. 721 62; fax 790 16 11), are (singles 8Ls, doubles 10Ls). To rough it out cold and toiletless, rent a double occupancy **cottage** near the river (4Ls). **Satezele,** Depo iela 28/33 (tel. 712 59), serves hearty mushroom omelettes (1.80Ls) and salads (0.50Ls)—10% less if you're still up after 2am. Two pool tables (0.70Ls per game) and other paraphernalia complement the meal (open daily 2pm-2am). For finer dining, the **hotel restaurant** (tel. 721 65) simmers up scrumptious entrées (1.5-2.5Ls; open daily noon-2am).

Sights Perched on a ridge to the right of Gauja iela on the near side of the gorge is the **Siguldas dome**, the new "castle." Behind it, the immense ruins of **Siguldas pilsdrupas** (Siguldas Castle) hint at their former magnificence. Constructed by the German Knights of the Sword in the 13th century and destroyed in the Great Northern War, the fortress invites exploration. At the end of the paved path opposite the Siguldas baznīca (Siguldas Church), the **cable car** hangs out (2 per hour, 5min., 0.50Ls). To the right of the terminal, stones still trickle from a small remnant of **Krimuldas pilsdrupas,** the bulk of it having fallen in the 1601 Polish-Swedish war. Down the slope and to the left along Turaidas iela about 500m, the chiseled maw of **Gūtmaņa ala** (Gūtman's Cave) continues to erode, inscribed with coats of arms and phrases by generations of Latvians and other visitors since the 16th century.

The wooden building nearby is the 1750 **Turaida Church,** now home to a small archaeological museum (tel. 95 16 20; open daily 9:30am-6pm). The sculpture park covering the surrounding hills is dedicated to Krišjānis Barons, a 19th-century scholar

---

Helen of Latvia Meets Paris of Poland

It's a tale too sad to tell. A wily Polish officer kidnapped Maija—Helen of Latvia—at Gūtman's Cave, and when all she did was pine for the palace gardener, the Pole married his sword with her lovely neck. As the gardener said his final farewells, he sought to shade her rest, making his grief immortal by planting a pair of linden trees. Near **Daiņa kalns** (Hill of Songs), two linden trees still bask in the scent of daisies and roses at the **grave of Maija,** "the Rose of Turaida".

who preserved 20,000 Latvian *daiņas* (folksongs). Farther out rise the towers and walls of **Turaidas pils** (Turaidas Castle). Restored earlier in this century, the skyscraping red tower is home to the **Sigulda History Museum,** Turaīdas iela 10 (tel. 97 14 02). The tower contains impressive displays on the history of the Liv people, from their immigration in the 3rd century to their near-elimination in the 12th-century crusades, complete with English descriptions and *faux* ancient music. Ascend the steep staircase for nauseatingly elevated views of the region and a chance to pretend you're watching a horde of enemy knights through an arrow slit in the 3m-thick wall (0.80Ls admission includes the adjacent buildings).

Sports and Entertainment Hiking options here are numerous. For safety info, see Essentials: wilderness and safety Concerns, p. 49. An excellent 2km walk follows the Gauja River to the steep **Piķenes Slopes,** where two caves, the deep **Velna Ala** (Devil's Cave) and the **Mazā velnala** (Devil's Little Cave), merit mention. The nearby spring is purportedly a **Font of Wisdom,** and ambitious mothers bathe their babies in it. Another good hike goes from the Sigulda castle down to the Gauja, then upstream to cross **Vējupite creek.** Upstream another 100m on Vējupīte, stairs rise to **Paradīzes Kalns** (Paradise Hill), where 19th-century Latvian painter Jānis Rozentāls made the valley view famous. The **Gauja National Park Center,** Raiņa iela 15 (tel. 740 06), has guided English tours. Call two days in advance to arrange. Visit the center in any case to see the stuffed wild boars in the office (open daily 9am-5pm).

Visible from the commuter rail, the Olympic-size **bobsled and luge run** plummets from Sveices iela 13, (tel. 739 44; fax 790 16 67). From October to March, you can take the plunge for 1Ls (open Sat.-Sun. 10am-8pm). Unfortunately, there's no action in summer. From the bridge incredibly thin rope supports a tiny, red cable car. This is the local **bungee jumping** thread for those itching to go one-on-one with gravity. Climb the wooden stairs any Saturday or Sunday 6-10pm; at the top, sign a release and jump away. Jump again for 7.50Ls (10% discounts for groups of five or more).

Vade Mecum, Pusas iela 12 (tel. 61 16 14; fax (8) 86 02 06), offers rides in a **hot-air balloon** (0.50Ls), and the **International Ballooning Festival** floats out of town in the third week of May. Next to the Turaidas Museum, Turaidas 10, **horses** are available, with or without a trainer (tel. 745 84; open Tues.-Sun. 10am-6:30pm; 5Ls per hour). Play **minigolf** on Parka iela (tel. 238 08; 0.50Ls before 2pm, 1Ls after) or **tennis** across the street (open daily 11am-9pm; 1Ls per hour before 2pm, 3Ls after).

■ Cēsis

Cēsis was once headquarters of the Livonian Order (a federation of German knights who controlled Latvia and Estonia in the 13th-16th centuries). But since a brief stint as a popular 1930s resort, Cēsis has declined in glory. It's rapidly becoming a suburb of Rīga. Center of Gauja National Park, it's a great base for hikes along the Gauja River; in late July the local brewery, the Baltics' oldest, hosts a massive beer festival.

Orientation and Practical Information Raunas iela darts to the town center, then empties into **Vienības laukums.** The streets heading downhill at the square's south end (Rīgas iela and Vaļņu iela) lead into the older section of town and meet at **Līvu laukums,** the original 13th-century heart of the city. Lenču iela, which runs away from Vienības laukums, travels to the old castle. Cēsis is easily reached via the suburban rail system. It's best to purchase all tickets in Rīga, for both **trains** (9 per day, 1½hr., 1.15-2Ls) and **buses** (17 per day, 2hr., 1.10Ls). The **bus station** is at one with the **train station** (tel. 227 62); ask the cashier to store your luggage. A brand-new **map** (0.50Ls) is available at the Don-Lat Hotel-Restaurant, Vienības laukums 1 (tel. 223 92). The **tourist service** of the hotel offers excursions of all sorts for DM3-36. Ask for Alex Rasmussen who speaks English, and call a few days in advance (open daily 9am-5pm). **Public transportation** consists of two buses (0.15Ls). bus #9 runs west to the Gauja river; catch it on Vienības laukums from the stop on the woodier side (Mon.-Sat.). **Exchange currency** at **Unibanka** (tel. 228 03) on Raunas iela. MC,

Thomas Cook, and Visa traveler's checks are accepted (open Mon.-Fri. 9am-5pm, Sat.-Sun. 9am-2pm). The **post** and **telephone offices,** Raunas iela 14-15, sit at the corner of Vienības laukums (post office open Mon.-Fri. 8am-7pm, Sat. 8am-6pm; telephones daily 7am-10pm). **Postal code:** LV-4100. **Phone code:** 0241.

Accommodations and Food **Cata,** Saules iela 23 (tel. 202 90), offers modest singles (2Ls) and rooms more up to budget-hotel standards for 3Ls. Doubles cost 4-6Ls. There's no bus, but to make the hike take Valmiera iela away from Vienības laukums, make a hard right onto J. Poruka iela, and another right onto the dirt Puķu iela, which leads to the hotel. **Kafejnīca Raunis** (tel. 238 30), where Rauna iela meets the square, presents plentiful if somewhat bland entrées for 0.50-1.60Ls (open daily 8am-10pm). **Don Lat Hotel-Restaurant,** Vienības laukums 1 (tel. 223 92), offers fancy food for 2-6Ls off an English menu (open daily noon-midnight). Rooms in the crowded, but sparkling clean, hardwood-floored hotel start at 12Ls.

Sights and Entertainment Cēsis was taken by the Livonian Order in 1209. During the battle, the **Latvian flag** was inadvertently designed. The Latvian leader died on a white sheet, staining it a deep crimson on two sides while leaving the middle section white. Begun the same year, the **castle** the Germans built to rule the region was a mighty fortress with walls 4m thick by its completion in the 1280s. By the late 16th century, the Order's power had lapsed, but when Russia's Ivan the Terrible laid siege to its fortress in 1577, the men preferred to fill the cellars with gunpowder and blow themselves up rather than surrender. Enough of the castle's wall remains for the locals to charge you 2Ls for a mandatory guide just to enter. Constructed with the new castle by a 19th-century baron, the surrounding **park** is mossy, shaded, and peaceful. A pool reflects families feeding ducks as a stone fisherman struggles with a water-spouting fish. Ask one of the museum attendants to point out the town Lenin, now resting under a giant wood crate resembling a coffin. **Cēsis Vēstures Muzejs** (Cēsis History Museum), Pils iela 9 (tel. 226 15), encompasses the two castles, with artfully arranged regional ephemera, coins, arrowheads, and jewelry (open Tues.-Sun. 10am-5pm; 0.50Ls).

Virtually next door, **Cēsu Alus Darītava** (Cēsis Beer Brewery), Lenču iela 9/11 (tel. 224 23), has produced fine products since the 1870s. The shop parts with its wares for 0.16-0.22Ls a bottle (open Mon.-Fri. 8am-7pm, Sat. 8am-5pm, Sun. 8am-1pm). Tours can be arranged in advance with the director. To access Cēsis's **Old Town,** take Torņa iela from the parking lot by the castle. The Gothic **Jāņa baznīca** (St. John's; built 1280-87) on Baznīcas laukums rises above narrow cobbled streets (open Mon.-Fri. 8-10am and 5-8pm; services Sun. 11am). The Gauja River flows on the east side of town, and a number of good **hiking** trails lead along the many cliffs lining the river. A 3-km journey along Gaujas iela leads to the base of the trails; take bus #9 in front of the hotel on Vienības laukums. The best cliffs are to the south.

Exit the bus or train station and cross the road to the large **bulletin board** on the right. Along with hand-written signs, like "I cure virtually all diseases: adults and kids in same way," there are **ballroom dance, disco,** and **movie** posters. Every late July to early August, Cēsis throws a massive **Beer Festival.**

■ Near Cēsis: Āraiši

Only **buses** run to Āraiši daily from Cēsis (7-9 per day, 15min., 0.15Ls). From the bus stop, follow the sign on the right to the **old mill.** Up 400m and left off the main road lie a reconstructed 9th- and 10th-century wooden **lake-fortress** and a ruined Livonian Order **castle** on the next peninsula. Some believe the Swedes keep maps of a secret underground road connecting this fortress and the one in Cēsis, and that they will guard the secret until they find a way to spirit the gold across the Baltic.

LITHUANIA (LIETUVA)

US$1 = 4.00Lt (Litai)
CDN$1 = 2.91Lt
UK£1 = 6.23Lt
IR£1 = 6.48Lt
AUS$1 = 3.15Lt
NZ$1 = 2.78Lt
SAR1 = 0.90Lt
DM1   = 2.70Lt
Country Phone Code: 370

1Lt = US$0.25
1Lt = CDN$0.34
1Lt = UK£0.16
1Lt = IR£0.15
1Lt = AUS$0.32
1Lt = NZ$0.36
1Lt = SAR1.11
1Lt = DM0.37
International Dialing Prefix: 810

Known by many for its Grateful-Dead-sponsored Olympic basketball team or the statue of Frank Zappa standing in its capital, little Lithuania occupies a bizarre niche in the annals of modern culture. The Baltic nation's current pop image may amuse some, but in no way is the tough republic a joke. Lithuania once rocked the house in Central Europe—spitting in the faces of proselytizing Christians, ruling over modern-day Ukraine, Belarus, and Poland, and generally getting medieval on its neighbors.

Ruined castles and fortifications stand as mute reminders of the glory days, while ancient Vilnius welcomes visitors with green parks, relaxed cafés, and an unassuming skyline. The Baltics' best beaches await at Palanga, also home to botanical gardens and mineral springs. The Curonian Spit offers more sunny fun, with dunes of fine white sand caught between dense forests and the mighty Baltic Sea.

LITHUANIA ESSENTIALS

Citizens of the U.S., Canada, the U.K., and Australia can visit Lithuania visa-free for up to 90 days. Citizens of Ireland, New Zealand, or South Africa who have visas from Estonia or Latvia do not need a visa for Lithuania; if they have not visited those countries, they will need regular 90-day visas. Got it? No border posts issue visas. Send one photograph, your passport, and application fee by money order, personal check, or cash to the nearest embassy or consulate (single-entry US$20; multiple-entry US$30; transit visa US$5). Regular service takes two weeks; rush service costs US$15 extra (24-hr. service), or US$10 (48-hr.). For visa extensions, contact the Migration Dept. at Šaltoniškų 19, Vilnius (tel. (222) 72 38 53). See Essentials: Embassies and Consulates, p. 7.

GETTING THERE AND GETTING AROUND

Klaipėda, Kaunas, and Vilnius are easily reached by **train** or **bus** from Belarus, Estonia, Latvia, Poland, and Russia. Most trains from Poland to Vilnius go through Belarus, requiring a transit visa (US$30). The daily *Baltic Express* departs Warsaw at 2:30pm, passing through Kaunas at 11:55pm, and arriving in Tallinn the next day at 1:10pm. There is also one overnight train running between Warsaw and Šeštokai, Lithuania; it arrives at 6:30am, two hours before a Šeštokai-Kaunas-Vilnius train departs. These two trains, as well as buses from Poland to Lithuania do not go through Belarus. Land travel often includes a lengthy wait at customs, especially at the Polish border. **Planes** drop by Vilnius from London, Warsaw, Frankfurt, and Moscow. **Ferries** connect Klaipėda with Sweden and Germany.

Trains are slow, noisy, and often crowded. Two major rail lines cross Lithuania. One runs north-south from Latvia through Šiauliai and Kaunas to Poland; the other runs east-west from Belarus through Vilnius and Kaunas to Kaliningrad, or on a branch line from Vilnius through Šiauliai to Klaipėda. Slightly more expensive and faster **buses,** however, radiate from all the cities of Lithuania.

TOURIST SERVICES AND MONEY

Litinterp, a network of interpretation and translation services, has also adopted the functions of a national tourist office without realizing that this may become its true vocation. Friendly staff arrange private accommodations and stock loads of city information. The big three Lithuanian metropoles publish detailed guidebooks on their respective scenes. *Vilnius in Your Pocket,* thoroughly updated every two months and available at newsstands (4Lt) is a best-seller. Check out its sister guides *Kaunas in Your Pocket* and *Klaipėda in Your Pocket.*

The unit of **currency** is the Litas (1Lt = 100 centų), Litai if you have more than one. Since March 1994, it has been tied to the U.S. dollar at US$1 = 4.00Lt. Still, private exchange bureaus might offer worse rates. Find a bigger bank which heeds the law. **Traveler's checks** can be cashed at most banks (usually for a 2-3% fee). Cash advances on a **Visa** card can usually be obtained with a minimum of hassle in certain banks; **Vilniaus Bankas,** with outlets in major Lithuanian cities, accepts all major credit cards and traveler's checks and charges 0%-0.5% commission.

COMMUNICATION

Local **phones** in Lithuania are mostly free. Long-distance calls can be made from some of the old gray public phones with the wide-grooved gold *žetonai* (tokens) sold at post offices (0.24Lt). For international calls, it is often best to use the Norwegian card phones that have been installed at main post offices and large railway terminals; cards are sold at the phone offices in denominations from 3.50 to 200Lt. Rates for international calls are: U.S. 10.50Lt per minute; Estonia and Latvia 0.95Lt; Europe 5.80Lt. You can book international calls through the operator at the central phone office (pay when finished), but you'll have to wait 20-45 minutes for the call to go through. You can ring only some countries directly. Dial 8, wait for the second tone, and dial 10 followed by the country code and number. Calls to cities within the former Soviet Union can be placed by dialing 8, followed by the old Soviet phone code. For countries to which direct dialing is not available, dial 8, wait for the second tone, and dial 194 or 195 (English-speaking operators available). To reach the **AT&T Direct operator,** dial (8) 196; to reach **Sprint Express,** dial (8) 197.

English-language books are cheap but not plentiful. The English-language *Lithuanian Weekly* covers Lithuanian events in fair depth (2Lt), but is increasingly hard to find and has never been available outside Vilnius. The Tallinn-based *Baltic Independent* and Rīga's *Baltic Observer* are both available in Vilnius, Kaunas, and Klaipėda.

In Vilnius, pick up **Voice of America Radio** at 105.6 FM, broadcasting 24 hours. If you can, tune into everyone's favorite radio program in Lithuania, *Sister Barbara's English Lesson;* Sister Barbara, a Lithuanian-American from New Orleans, comes on daily to teach Lithuanians important phrases in English like "Is this cheese hot?"

LANGUAGE

Lithuanians pride themselves on the fact that their national language is the most archaic of surviving Indo-European tongues, and one of only two surviving languages in the Baltic branch (Latvian is the other). All "r"s are trilled. Nearly all Lithuanians speak **Russian,** but attempts to use your college Russian will be better received after assays in **English** or **German** first. You may need the words *atidarytas* (ah-tee-DAR-ee-tass; open), *uždarytas* (oozh-DAR-ee-tass; closed), *viešbutis* (vee-esh-BOO-tees; hotel), and *turgus* (tuhr-GUHSS; market). See Glossary, p. 781.

HEALTH AND SAFETY

> **Emergency Numbers: Fire:** tel. 01. **Police:** tel. 02. **Ambulance:** tel. 03.

A **bathroom** door bedecked with a triangle whose point faces down indicates men; with the point facing up, women. Many restrooms are nothing but a hole in the ground. Well stocked **pharmacies** are popping up everywhere. Anything German with a picture of a man clutching his cranium is safe. Tylenol and Ibuprofen also dot the shelves. **Condoms** come in both familiar and unfamiliar packages; familiar will do you better. When thirsty, do not turn to the tap; everyone around you is drinking bottled mineral water. For info on **gay** life, contact the Lithuanian Gay League (tel./fax (22) 65 16 38), Vladimiras or Eduardas at P.O. Box 2862, Vilnius 2000, Lithuania.

ACCOMMODATIONS, FOOD, AND DRINK

Be sure to take advantage of the eight **Lithuanian Youth Hostels (LJNN/HI).** HI membership is nominally required, but an LJNN guest card (US$3 at any of the hostels) will suffice. The head office is in Vilnius (see Vilnius: Practical Information, p. 342). Grab a copy of their *Hostel Guide,* a handy booklet with info on bike and car rentals, advance booking, and maps showing how to reach the various hostels.

Lithuanian **cuisine** has miraculously survived Soviet-restaurant-blight; go into any restaurant and you'll see some evidence of an indigenous Lithuanian style. *Cepelinai* are heavy, potato-dough missiles stuffed with meat, cheese, and mushrooms, most prominent in West Lithuania. *Šaltibarščiai* is a beet and cucumber soup, not unlike cold borscht, prevalent in the eastern half of the country.

Lithuanian **beer** is passable. Although there is no national brew to recommend, *Kalnapilis Ekstra* is probably among Lithuania's best.

CUSTOMS AND ETIQUETTE

Reserve informal greetings only for those with whom you've bonded. A *"laba diena"* ("good day!") whenever you enter a shop ensures good feelings, and you can never say too many *"prašau"* (both "please" and "you're welcome"). Handshakes are reserved for men who've been introduced. Women nod or get their hands kissed. **Homosexuality** is legal.

LIFE AND TIMES

HISTORY

Lithuania's ancient inhabitants were the only **Balts** who succeeded in creating their own political state. At one point, Lithuanians ruled over parts of modern-day Ukraine, Belarus, Poland, and Russia. While Teutonic armies conquered other Baltic peoples, the Lithuanians, shielded by thick forests and natural moats of swampy marshland, held off the invaders. In the mid-13th century, the Teutonic menace prompted various tribes to unite under a single leader, **Mindaugas.** Crowned king by Pope Innocent IV in 1253, Mindaugas soon rejected Christianity and returned to paganism. Lithuania would not be Christianized for another century.

The Lithuanian empire was consolidated under the 14th-century ruler **Gediminas** (1315-42). Political anarchy broke out after Gediminas, Lear-like "in the infirmity of his age," unwisely divided his empire among his seven sons. The eldest, **Jagiełło,** finally defeated assorted brothers, uncles, and cousins—only to face a German invasion. Jagiełło chose to ally Lithuania with Poland, assuming the Polish throne as King Władysław V in 1385. By 1410, with the **Battle of Grunwald,** Jagiełło effectively crushed the marauding German armies. The new Polish alliance brought Roman Catholicism to Lithuania in 1387. Jagiełło reconciled with his brother **Vytautas,** who became monarch of Lithuania. Under Vytautas (1392-1430), Lithuania conquered vast tracts of territory. Meanwhile, Lithuanian culture, language, and religion were affected by Poland much more than by Russia, isolated under the Mongol Yoke. The Lithuanian empire reached its zenith in the mid-15th century, stretching from the Baltic to the Black Sea to within 100 miles of Moscow.

For the next 200 years, Lithuania successfully defended itself against Muscovite incursions. At the same time, political and cultural ties with Poland strengthened. But Lithuania's fortunes declined in the 18th century. Lithuania could not emerge unscathed from the **partitions of Poland** carried out by Russia, Austria, and Prussia during the course of the century. Gradually, bits and pieces of the empire slipped away to be engulfed mainly by the swelling Russian state, particularly after the Third Partition of Poland (1795) when Lithuania was split between Russia and Prussia.

Lithuanians repeatedly rose up against Russian rule during the 19th century; each revolt was met with repression and intensified Russification. The tsars closed the 250-year-old University of Vilnius, abolished the Lithuanian legal code, and banned the Lithuanian language in public places. But the Russian Revolution of 1905 thawed the freeze on Lithuanian liberties, prompting demands for independence.

World War I ignited a new power struggle in the region. German armies entered Lithuania in 1915, almost exactly 500 years after their last defeat. A Lithuanian congress made the rather futile gesture in February 1918 of declaring **independence,** but Germany continued to occupy the region until the end of the war. No sooner had Germany departed than the Soviets moved in. Lithuania managed to evict the Red Army in 1919, inaugurating a brief period of independence, and even joining the League of Nations. A fragile parliamentary democracy floundered, collapsing in a

1926 coup d'état. Under the dictatorship of **Antanas Smetona,** all opposition parties were banned. Meanwhile, Poland had taken Vilnius from the Red Army in 1919, and refused to give it back. Over the next few years, the Poles and the Soviets battled each other for the city. The Nazis, desiring a German empire, gazed covetously on the Lithuanian city of Klaipėda. In 1939, they seized the valuable port.

The façade of autonomy crumbled in 1939, when Moscow forced Lithuania to admit Soviet troops; in return, Lithuania got back Vilnius and about one-third of the territory that Poland had seized in 1920. A year later, Lithuania was entirely absorbed by the vast Soviet Union, ostensibly by a "unanimous" vote of the parliament. **Sovietization** entailed a total restructuring of Lithuania's government, economy, culture, and society. On the night of June 13-14, 1941, the Soviets began pulling Lithuanians from their homes; deportations eventually displaced 35,000 Lithuanians. The Nazis invasion in 1941 triggered a Lithuanian revolt against Soviet rule. In three years of German occupation, 250,000 Lithuanians died; the Lithuanian Jewish community was virtually wiped out.

When the Red Army expelled the Nazis in 1944, they initiated yet another period of forceful **Russification** and repression. But the iron fist of Soviet rule did not go unopposed; Lithuanian guerrilla fighters, at times 40,000 strong, badgered the Soviets into the early 1950s. Moscow's grip had relaxed by the early 1960s, and **Antanas Sniečkus** slowly transformed the republic's government into a nativized political machine. Unlike Latvia and Estonia, Lithuania resisted an influx of Russian immigrants; ethnic Lithuanians still compose 80% of the population.

The orthodox backlash of the 1970s and early 80s failed to quell Lithuanian nationalism; during this period, the republic generated more per capita *samizdat* (dissident underground publications) than any other in the Soviet Union. *Glasnost* and *perestroika* spawned a Lithuanian mass reform movement, imaginatively dubbed **Sąjūdis** (Movement). In March 1990, Lithuania shocked the world by declaring itself **independent** from the Soviet Union. Moscow immediately began reprisals, starting with a rather ineffective shutoff of all oil and gas supplies. In January 1991, Moscow launched an assault on Vilnius's radio and TV center, leaving 14 people dead. Only in the wake of the failed Soviet putsch of August 1991 did Lithuania achieve a measure of independence. Despite internal divisions, all Lithuanians rejoiced on August 31, 1993, when the last Russian soldiers left Lithuanian soil.

LITERATURE

Early Lithuanian literature was primarily religious in subject matter. The early 19th century saw a new literary movement focusing on Romantic themes and the early history of Lithuania. The first major Lithuanian work of fiction, **Kristijonas Donelaitis'** 1818 poem *Metai (The Four Seasons)* depicted scenes from village life throughout the year. In the wake of the French Revolution, Western influences triggered a renaissance in Lithuanian literature. From 1864, many writers violated the ban on publishing Lithuanian works in Latin letters (as opposed to Cyrillic), seeking to overthrow Russia's political control and Poland's cultural hegemony. One such author was **Jonas Mačiulis,** with his 1895 romantic *Pavasario balsai (Voices of Spring)*—the start of modern Lithuanian poetry. After independence in 1918, nationalistic trends intensified, but Soviet rule following WWII again gagged and shackled Lithuanian writers. **Vincas Mykolaitis-Putinas,** an ex-priest known for his novel *Altorių šešėly (In the Altars' Shadow),* is considered by some to be the 20th century's leading literary figure. Talented writers **Sigitas Geda** and **Judita Vaičiūnaitė,** challenged that ever-present, Eastern European phenomenon **Socialist Realism**—the first with poetry and drama, the second with a mix of realism and mythological ambience, and the third with urban romanticism.

LITHUANIA TODAY

Despite an early start—Lithuania began dismantling the Soviet economic system even before achieving independence from Moscow—Lithuania's economic reforms have run aground on rocky shores. Privatization has ground to a halt under new, restrictive government regulations. Lithuania is still heavily dependent on Russia for fuel, and trade with the EU has increased only slightly. In the face of declining production and high consumer prices, the standard of living continues to slide. Although Lithuania remains the least prosperous economic entity in the Baltics, its politics have become the most stable—if stable means reintroducing the former communists, now reorganized as the Lithuanian Democratic Labor Party. Lithuania saw most of its Russian population leave during Soviet withdrawal, and therefore escaped the citizenship questions which have plagued both Estonia and Latvia. The country's main tiff with Russia lies instead with border privileges. Russia wants the right to transport military equipment over Lithuanian soil to Kaliningrad—the ol' bear's separated republic—and tiny economically-dependant Lithuania finds itself in a dilemma: economic well being or independence?

Vilnius

Despite a history of foreign influence and a mix of Lithuanian, Polish, Russian, and Belarusian residents, Vilnius remains a staunchly Lithuanian cultural, social, and religious center. Cathedrals and churches on the Old Town's every corner hide the fact that Lithuania was the last European nation to embrace Christianity. And, although Jews have begun to trickle back to this 19th-century "Jerusalem of Europe," Vilnius is not just for the pious: boutiques and bars are sneaking into its revival.

ORIENTATION AND PRACTICAL INFORMATION

From the **train** or **bus station,** directly across from each other, walk east on **Geležinkelio g.** (to your left as you face the train station), and turn left at its end. This is the beginning of **Aušros vartų g.,** which leads north from the **Old Town's** south gates changing its name first to **Didžioji g.,** then **Pilies g.** At the north end, **Arkikatedros aikštė** (Cathedral Sq.) and the **Castle Hill** loom over the river **Neris's** banks. **Gedimino pr.,** the commercial artery, leads west from the square in front of the cathedral's doors. Pick up a copy of *Vilnius in Your Pocket* upon arrival. This bimonthly gem (4Lt), available at any self-respecting kiosk or hotel, includes everything you could ever want to know about the city—maps, a public transport grid, a handy glossary, a calendar of events, and more.

Tourist Offices: Litinterp, at Bernadinų g. 7/2 (tel. 22 38 50; fax 22 35 59; e-mail Litinterp@Omnitel.net). Arranges homestays, rent cars and bikes (20Lt per day), translates, and will guide you around the Old Town for US$10 per hour. Open daily Mon-Fri. 9am-6pm, Sat. 9am-4pm. **Lithuanian Youth Hostels Head Office,** Kauno g. 1a, room 407 (tel. 26 26 60; fax 26 06 31), a block south of the train station, next door to the "Inline Balt" sign, on the 4th floor. Countrywide hostel info, bike rentals, and student travel packages. Open daily 8am-6pm.

Passport Office: Imigracijos Taryba, Verkių 3 (tel. 75 64 53), 2km north of Old Town. Extends visas for 40Lt. Open Mon.-Fri. 9am-4:30pm.

Embassies: Belarus, Klimo g. 8 (tel. 65 08 71). Open Mon.-Fri. 9am-noon. **Canada,** Didžioji g. 8/5 (tel. 22 08 98). Open Mon.-Fri. 10am-1pm. **Latvia,** Čiurlionio g. 76 (tel. 22 05 22). Open daily 10am-noon and 2-4pm. **Russia,** Latvių g. 53/54 (tel. 72 78 68). Open Mon.-Fri. 10am-1pm. **U.K.,** Antakalnio g. 2 (tel. 22 20 70). Open Mon.-Fri. 9am-5pm. **U.S.,** Akmenų g. 6 (tel. 22 30 31). Open Mon.-Fri. 9am-1pm and 2-5:30pm.

Currency Exchange: Vilniaus Bankas, Gedimino pr. 12 (tel. 261 07 23; fax 262 65 57). Cash advances with no commission from your Diner's Club, MasterCard, or Visa. Also cashes AmEx and Thomas Cook traveler's checks. Open Mon.-Fri. 9am-1:30pm and 2:30-4:30pm, Fri. 9am-1:30pm and 2-4pm.

24-Hour ATM: At **Vilniaus Bankas** (see above) lurks a Visa-linked money-spitter.

Flights: The *aerouostas* (airport; flight info tel. 63 02 01 or 63 01 95) lies 5km south of town; take bus #2 (the airport bus) from the train station or from the third stop

ORIENTATION AND PRACTICAL INFORMATION ■ 343

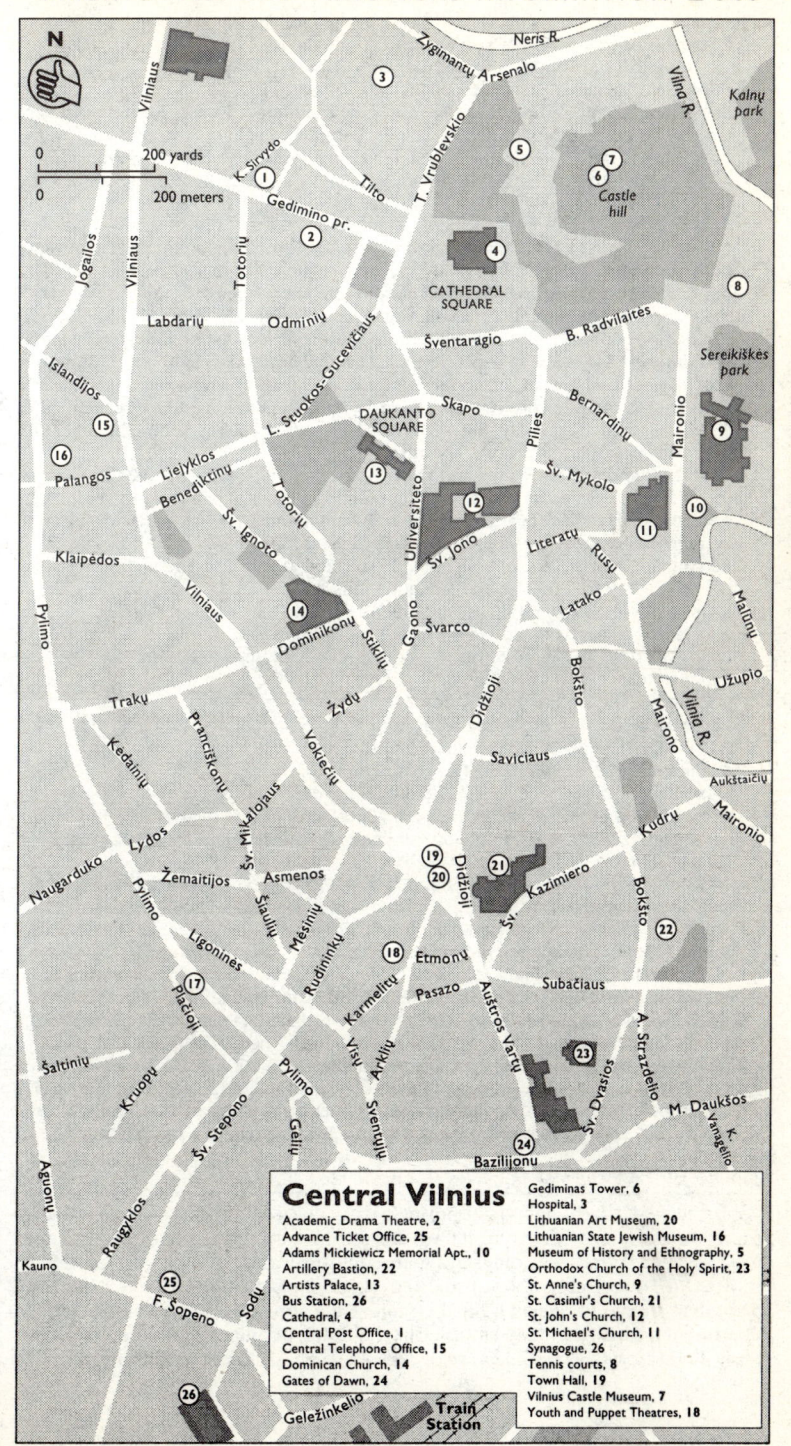

Central Vilnius

Academic Drama Theatre, 2
Advance Ticket Office, 25
Adams Mickiewicz Memorial Apt., 10
Artillery Bastion, 22
Artists Palace, 13
Bus Station, 26
Cathedral, 4
Central Post Office, 1
Central Telephone Office, 15
Dominican Church, 14
Gates of Dawn, 24
Gediminas Tower, 6
Hospital, 3
Lithuanian Art Museum, 20
Lithuanian State Jewish Museum, 16
Museum of History and Ethnography, 5
Orthodox Church of the Holy Spirit, 23
St. Anne's Church, 9
St. Casimir's Church, 21
St. John's Church, 12
St. Michael's Church, 11
Synagogue, 26
Tennis courts, 8
Town Hall, 19
Vilnius Castle Museum, 7
Youth and Puppet Theatres, 18

("Sparta") of trolley bus #16 on Kauno g. Daily flights: Warsaw by **LOT** (tel. 63 01 95); Moscow and Frankfurt by **Lithuanian Airlines** (tel. 75 25 88).

Trains: Geležinkelio g. 16 (tel. 63 00 86 or 63 00 88). Tickets for **local** trains are sold in a separate hall, to the left of the (pink) main building. Tickets for **long-distance** Lithuanian destinations (plus Daugavpils, Latvia) are sold at windows #1-4 in the main station. To get same-day tickets for trains **within the former Soviet Union,** go to the hall to the right of the main lobby. For advance purchases, contact the **Reservation Bureau** (tel. 62 39 27), in the station hall to the right (open Mon.-Sat. 8am-8pm, Sun. 8am-5pm). To: Berlin via Belarus (get that transit visa!—1 per day; 19½hr., *coupé* 323.21Lt); Kaliningrad (5 per day; 7hr.; 20Lt, *coupé* 24Lt); Minsk (1 per day, 5½hr., 32Lt); Moscow (2-3 per day; 17hr.; 80Lt, *coupé* 129Lt); Rīga (1-2 per day; 8hr.; 30Lt, *coupé* 49Lt); Warsaw via Belarus (1 per day; 12hr., 120.24Lt).

Buses: Sodų g. 22 (info tel. 26 24 82, domestic reservations 26 29 77, international reservations 63 52 77), opposite the train station. **Priemiestinė Salė,** to the left as you enter, is for buses to **local** destinations; **Tarpmiestinė Salė** covers **long-distance** buses and has an info booth open daily 7am-8pm. Windows #13-15 serve destinations **outside the former Soviet Union.** To: Kaliningrad (1 per day, 9hr., 33.90Lt); Minsk (9 per day, 6hr., 20Lt); Rīga (4 per day, 6hr., 30Lt); Tallinn (2 per day, 10hr., 61.30Lt); Warsaw (5 per day, 12hr., 75Lt).

Public Transportation: Buses and **trolleys,** packed like sardine cans, don't run in the Old Town but do an excellent job of linking Vilnius's train and bus stations, its suburbs, and the Old Town's edges (daily 6am-midnight). Buy tickets (0.60Lt), to be punched on board, or monthly passes (24Lt) at any kiosk.

Car Rental: Hertz, Rodūnės Kelias 2 (tel. 260 03 94), at the airport. Also at Ukmergės 2 (tel. 72 69 40). Starts negotiations at around US$28 per day for a Fiesta. **Litinterp** (see above) rents cars and microbuses with or without a driver.

Bike Rental: Filaretų Hostel (see below) made bikes available to its guests free of charge in 1996, but plans to make a little cash off the service by summer 1997.

Luggage Storage: At the **bus station.** Open daily 7am-10pm. Or in the tunnels underneath the **train station.** Open 24hr. 1Lt per bag.

International Bookstore: Penki Kontinentai (Five Continents), Stulginskio g. 5 (tel. 22 14 81; fax 22 61 15), off Gedimino pr. English, French, and German books. MasterCard accepted. Open Mon.-Fri. 10am-7pm.

Taxis: State Taxi Service (tel. 22 88 88). 1Lt plus 1Lt per km (double after 10pm). **Private taxis** show a green light in the windshield; debate the fare before you go.

Pharmacy: Vokiečių Vatstinė (German Pharmacy), Didžioji g. 13 (tel. 22 42 32), in the Old Town. Open Mon.-Fri. 9am-7pm, Sat. 10am-5pm.

Gay Information Line: tel. 23 92 82. Info about gay accommodations and events.

Fax Center: Universiteto 14/2 (tel. 62 66 49; fax 22 34 51). Open 24hr.

Photocopies: Xerox, Gedimino pr. 4 (tel. 22 70 57), in the Academic Theater Building. 0.30Lt per page. Open daily 9am-6pm.

Express Mail: DHL, Vytauto g. 6/4 (tel. 35 51 44). Open Mon.-Fri. 9am-5pm. **EMS,** Vokiečių g. 7 (tel. 61 80 24). Open Mon.-Fri. 8:30am-1pm and 2-5:30pm.

Post Office: Gedimino pr. 7 (tel. 61 67 59), west of Arkikatedros aikštė. Letter to the U.S. 1Lt. Open Mon.-Fri. 8am-8pm, Sat. 10am-5pm. **Postal Code:** LT-2001.

Telephones: Central Telegraph Office, Vilniaus g. 33/2 (tel. 62 55 08, directory info 09). Norwegian phones take phone cards (from 7.08Lt) and allow direct dialing abroad (to the U.S. 10.50Lt per min.). Office open daily 8am-10:30pm; phones open daily 24hr. **Phone code:** 22 (2 if calling from outside the ex-USSR).

ACCOMMODATIONS

For a town of its size, Vilnius is surprisingly weak on sleeping options. It's worth a try to ask for an "un-remodeled" room. All this usually means is no phone or TV. **Litinterp** (see above) arranges homestays with English-speakers and private apartments in the Old Town (reservations preferred; singles 60Lt, doubles 100Lt). They have a spotless room of their own for the same price and can also set you up with an apartment with kitchen and bath, starting at 200Lt per night. **Nakvynė Travel Services,** Kauno g. 8 (tel. 63 77 32), arranges rooms (US$10-35) just outside the city, with cheaper options (US$6-8) farther out, and some locations in Trakai and other nearby areas (open daily 7am-9pm).

Filaretų Hostel, Filaretų g. 17 (tel. 69 66 27), in a peaceful neighborhood on the Old Town's outskirts reached by bus #34 from the station (7 stops). Scarce hot water means you must time your shower. Curfew midnight. A bed is 24Lt the 1st night, 20Lt each additional with HI card or LJNN guest card. Doubles cost 64Lt for the 1st night and 56Lt thereafter. Skip the sparse 6Lt breakfast. Satellite TV in the common room. Seasonal excursions, including biking and canoeing trips.

Žaliasis tiltas, Vilniaus g. 2/15 (tel. 61 54 60, info and reservations 22 17 16). Small but clean rooms with shower, hot water, and toilet. Single 60-200Lt, double 120-280Lt. Breakfast included. AmEx, Diner's Club, MasterCard, and Visa accepted.

Žaliasis tiltas. No, it's not a typo; it's a different hotel located at Gedimino pr. 12 (tel. 61 54 50). Spacious, sumptuous lodgings from 90Lt. Single 90Lt. Double with hot water, toilet, shower, and a working TV 130Lt.

Hotel Gintaras, Sodų g. 14 (tel. 63 44 96), near train station. Liveable rooms with red bedspreads and a bathroom with a shower head attached to the wall. Enjoy the hot water. Single 49Lt. Double 69Lt. Reserve far in advance.

FOOD

Four French **Iki** stores stock loads of foreign goods. The one closest to the Old Town lies at Žirmūnų g. 68 (tel. 77 29 62), 1.5km north across the Neris. Bus #5 or 7 or trolleybus #10, 13, or 17 will get you there (open Mon.-Sat. 9am-9pm, Sun. 9am-8pm). Farmers offer the **fruits, vegetables,** and **dairy products** of their labor along the south half of Pylimo g., between Geležinkelio g. and Bazilijonų g. (opens daily at 7:30am). The street vendors at the corner of Vilniaus and Gedimino serve up killer personal pizzas at 1.50Lt a pop.

Restaurants

The days of US$4 multi-course meals are becoming a thing of the past. Vilnius now has a complex arsenal with which to bombard your taste buds; unfortunately, the quality-price correlation is getting stronger. A simple tip to save money: the more English words on the menu, the more you'll pay; visit a place with an extensive, translated menu, and take notes.

Ritos Slėptuvė (Rita's Hideaway), A. Goštauto g. 8 (tel. 62 61 17), west of Old Town along the Neris. *The* place to go if you've only got one night in Vilnius. Funky decor and "no sweat-suits allowed"—a subtle ban on the local mafia. Chicago-style 12" pizza (16-25Lt), great chili (8Lt), heaping plates of fresh pasta (5-10Lt), and bottomless cups of coffee (3Lt). Open daily 10am-2am.

Ritos Virtuvė (Rita's Kitchen; tel. 62 05 89). Rita trades her hideaway for a kitchen at this speedier branch with delivery until 2am. Medium pizza with 3 toppings 38Lt.

Literatų Svetainė, Gedimino pr. 1 (tel. 61 18 89), on the edge of Arkikatedros aikštė. Full of dark wood and velvet, with a view of the cathedral. Attentive service. An English menu of superb Lithuanian food plus imported beer equals a pleasant meal in the city's heart. Entrées 5-9Lt. Open daily 8:30am-midnight.

Stikliai Aludė (Beer Bar), Stiklių 7. Less pricey, equally good, and has a warmer atmosphere to boot. Entrées 16-40Lt. A nice spot for an excellent local brew or two: *Biržai Grafas* (4.50Lt) or *Kalnapilis Ekstra* (8.50Lt). Open daily noon-midnight.

Stikliai Restaurant, Gaono 7 (tel. 62 79 71), a block south of the university on the corner of Gaono g. and Stiklių g. Skylit, delicately luxurious red-and-green interior is extremely classy; it better be for entrées weighing in at 30-80Lt. MasterCard and Visa accepted, since you probably didn't bring enough cash.

Cafés and Coffeehouses

Visitors to Vilnius will soon begin to ask, "Where isn't there a café or coffeehouse?" Despite their similar menus, each café is unique; try a few to find your favorite.

Café Filharmonija, Aušros vartų g. 5 (tel. 22 13 83). Of the sidewalk cafés near the Gates of Dawn, this is the pick of the litter, marked by a golden *"Kavine"* sign over the door and a relaxed crowd outside. Once you drop in, you'll never just walk by again. Truly amazing fries (3Lt), entrées 7-12Lt. The ice cream desserts are incredible (5Lt). Open daily 10am-11pm.

Kavinė Romeda, Totorių g. 15 (tel. 62 48 25), at the corner of Odminių a block south of Gedimino. Dark, homey, with an old Italian feel. A brick-walled café in one half, and a bar in the other. This place deserves its crowds. The coffee's so strong it's hard to pour (1Lt). Tiny, rich cakes (2Lt). Open daily Mon.-Sat. 10am-8pm.

Pilies Menė, Pilies g. 8. Look for 2 bronze arms holding a plate of pancakes above the door. Not IHOP, but they do serve great meat or cheese *blynai* smothered in cream, butter, or other heart-stopping sauces (3.60-4Lt). Open daily 9am-8pm.

SIGHTS

Everywhere you turn there is an architectural wonder or an historic spot. The moment you reach the end of Geležinkelio g. and turn left, **Aušros Vartai** (Gates of Dawn) welcome you into the Old Town. Built in the 16th century, the gates are the only surviving portal of the old city walls.

Senamiestis (Old Town)

Through the gates, enter the first door on the right to ascend to the 17th-century **Aušros Vartų Koplyčia** (Chapel of the Gates of Dawn), built around an icon said either to have been captured in Ukraine by Grand Duke Vytautas or to be a portrait of a 16th-century princess. The shrine is usually packed with candles and locals praying...and selling holy paraphernalia. Going back down to the street and entering the doorway at the building's end, you'll reach **Šv. Teresės bažnyčia** (St. Theresa's church). An outpouring of Baroque sculptures celebrate beneath pale crimson, turquoise, and gold arches, a frescoed ceiling, and stained glass. A few steps farther down, a gateway leads to the shockingly bright 17th-century **Šv. Dvasios bažnyčia** (Church of the Holy Ghost), seat of Lithuania's Russian Orthodox Archbishop. A functioning monastery, the church is the final resting place of Saints Antonius, Ivan, and Eustachius, martyred in 1371. The usually red-clad bodies, well preserved in a glass case under the altar, are dressed in white for Christmas and black for Lent.

Beyond the gates, Aušros vartų g. turns into Didžioji g. and leads to the crown-topped **Šv. Kazimiero bažnyčia** (St. Casimir's church), named after the country's patron saint. Vilnius's oldest Baroque church, it was built by the Jesuits in 1604 to ape the Roman Il Gesù church, but its history is oh-so-very Lithuanian. In 1832, the church gained a Russian Orthodox dome; in WWI, the Germans made it Lutheran; and with their return in WWII, they tore down the dome. After "liberating" Vilnius, the Soviets turned the temple into a museum of Atheism, but it's been back in the Catholic fold since 1989. It's vast, plain salmon-colored interior encases an altar in gold and marble (open Mon.-Sat. 4-6:30pm, Sun. 8am-2pm).

Didžioji g. broadens into **Rotušės aikštė,** an ancient marketplace dominated by the columns of the 18th-century **town hall,** now home to the **Lietuvos Dailės Muziejus** (State Art Museum), with a collection rich in late 19th- and 20th-century Lithuanian paintings. Now undergoing restoration, the art it used to shelter is at Didžioji g. 4—the **Vilniaus Paveikslu Gallerija Lietuvos Dailė,** (tel. 22 42 58), in a former palace (open Tues.-Sun. noon-6pm; 2Lt, students 1Lt; Sept.-May Wed. free).

As Didžioji g. continues north, it passes **Šv. Mikalojaus bažnyčia** (St. Nicholas' Church), Lithuania's oldest church, built in 1320 for the city's Hanseatic merchants. Shortly after, Didžioji g. widens into a triangular square and merges with the pedestrian **Pilies g.,** lined with peddlers of amber, silver, and leather. At the corner of Pilies g. and Šv. Jono g. stands **Vilniaus Universitetas's** main entrance. Founded in 1579, the Jesuit university was a major player in the Counter-Reformation. On the main university courtyard's east side, the 1387 **Šv. Jonų bažnyčia** (St. John's church) served as a museum of science under the Soviets. Go through the arches opposite from St. John's to the remarkable 17th-century **Astronomical Observatory,** with zodiacal signs on its façade's frieze, once rivaled in importance only by Greenwich and the

Sorbonne. The university **library,** Universiteto g., was once among Europe's largest; with over 5 million volumes, it's still a contender.

Continue north on Pilies g. (or Universiteto g.) and you'll come out onto **Arkikatedros aikštė** (Cathedral Square), pictured on the 50Lt note. A church has stood here since 1387, when Grand Duke Jogaila converted his country to Catholicism to win the Polish throne. The present 18th-century **Arkikatedra** resembles a Greek temple (perhaps a reminder that this was also the site of the principal temple to Perkunas, the Lithuanian god of thunder). The contorted figures on the south wall depict Lithuanian grand dukes in religious fervor with suitably ecstatic poses. Inside, peek into the early-Baroque **Chapel of St. Casimir,** a marble-cake work which houses a royal mausoleum (open Mon.-Sat. 7am-1pm and 2:30-8pm, Sun. 7am-2pm). Back out in the square, the octagonal 1522 **clock tower,** atop one of the towers of the lower fortress, is one of the city's best meeting points. Behind the cathedral, walk up the long path of the Castle Hill to **Gedimino pilis** (tower) for a great view of Vilnius' spires—and you know what they say about the size of a city's spires...

When you descend the hill, meander through the park to the south until you reach Mairionio g., which leads south to Vilnius' Gothic treasure, **Šv. Onos ir Bernardinų bažnyčia** (St. Anne's Church and Bernadine Monastery). St. Anne's is a red-brick confection built at the height of the Gothic style, so beautiful that Napoleon is said to have exclaimed that he wanted to carry it back to France in his palm. Tough luck for him. The Bernadine monastery in back, part of the city walls in 1520, partly houses the Art Academy and Design School of the University of Vilnius. Across the street, the Renaissance **Šv. Mykolo** (St. Michael's), was built in 1625 to house a family mausoleum. The **Adam Mickiewicz Memorial Apartment,** Bernardinų 11, sits on the road back toward Pilies g. The famous Lithuanian-Polish poet lived here in 1822 (open Fri. 2-6pm, Sat. 10am-2pm; free).

Go south on Mairionio pr. to head south on Jogailos, later Pylimo. Off Pylimo between Kalinausko 1 and 3, a shimmering steel pedestal shoots skyward, topped by a **bust of Frank Zappa** erected in 1995—surely the most random monument in Eastern Europe. Lenin's gone, but Zappa's in the house.

The Old Jewish Quarter

Once a Jewish center on par with Warsaw and New York, Vilnius had a population of 100,000 Jews (in a city of 230,000) at the outbreak of WWII. Nazi persecution left only 6000 survivors by the time the Red Army retook the city in 1944. Only one of pre-war Vilnius's 96 **synagogues** remains, at Pylimo g. 39, 500m west of Aušros Vartai. The Nazis used it to store medical supplies; it's now undergoing its first exhaustive restoration. Despite 50 years of Soviet repression that stalled any immediate post-WWII rebirth, services are also being revived. Plaques memorializing this community have started to appear, especially around the Stikliai restaurants. Some street names also recall the past; Žydų g. (Jewish St.) runs south of Stiklių g. from the restaurants. The **Jewish State Museum,** in two buildings, offers testimonial to the vitality of Yiddish culture in Lithuania and homage to the victims of the Holocaust. An **exhibition on Jewish life,** Pylimo g. 4, houses rotating exhibits and a permanent display of items salvaged from the destroyed synagogues (open Mon.-Fri. 10am-5pm; donation requested). The **Holocaust Museum,** Pamėnkalnio g. 12, chronicles the destruction of Vilnius's Jewish community, including meticulous SS records of daily executions (open Mon.-Fri. 10-am-5pm; donation requested).

Soviet Vilnius
The tour guides in the **KGB Museum (Museum of the Lithuanian Genocide)** Gedimino pr. 40 (tel. 62 24 49), in the old KGB prison, were once prisoners of its cells. The prison is rife with torture and execution chambers; notice the mounds of documents partially destroyed by the KGB before they left in 1991 (open Tues.-Sun. 10am-1pm and 2-5pm; donation requested). Ask for the English guidebook. **Lietuvos Valstybės Muziejus** (Lithuanian State Museum), Studentų g. 8 (tel. 72 51 67), across the Neris off the riverside Upės g., offers exhibits on the January 1991 crackdown in Vilnius and the deportations to Siberia of the 1940s and 50s—stumps studded with Soviet medals and piles of USSR passports. (Open Tues.-Sun. noon-6pm; history museum 4Lt, students 2Lt; art section 2Lt, students 1Lt.) Wander by the **Parliament** at the west end of Gedimino pr., just before the Neris. In January 1991, the world watched as Lithuanians raised barricades to protect their parliament from the Soviet army. President Landsbergis later said that all of the deputies expected to become martyrs on the night of January 13, but the main attack came instead at the **TV tower,** where 14 unarmed civilians were killed as the Red Army put the station off the air. Crosses and memorials surround the spot today. The tower, visible from the city center, is reachable by trolleybus #11 going west from "Planeta" on Kalvarių bridge's south end toward "Pašilaičai" (14 stops).

East Vilnius
Above the Old Town's east side rises the **Hill of Three Crosses,** visible throughout Vilnius. White crosses were originally erected here in the 18th century to commemorate seven Franciscan friars crucified on the hill by pagan tribes in the 13th century. During Lithuania's first period of independence, a white stone memorial of three crosses appeared on the hilltop. Torn down by the Soviets in the 1950s, the present monument is a 1989 copy. A final must-see is the 1688 **St. Peter and Paul Church,** Antakalnio g., 10 minutes from the cathedral. (Or take trolleybus #12 or 13 from "Planeta" at the foot of the Kalvarių bridge three stops east to "Meno mokykla".) Carved figures levitate on the ceiling. The church's humble founder is buried next to the door; his tombstone reads *Hic jacet peccator (Here lies a sinner).*

ENTERTAINMENT

As if old churches weren't entertainment enough, new places to go out are popping up daily. Most **discos** seem to be nothing more than an excuse for an erotic show, but thank the dancing queen for **C.,** a Berlin DJ who organizes dances all over Vilnius. Check out posters around town or on Prie Parlamento's bulletin board. C.'s parties are low-key opportunities to have fun well into the night.

Gay entertainment is making its way into "the scene." A café by day and a gay disco after 6pm, **Ralda,** Basanavičiaus g. 18 (tel. 65 16 38), in the courtyard, welcomes every orientation to come by and hang out (open daily noon til at least 10pm; disco cover 5Lt).

> **BIX,** Etmonų g. 6. (tel. 62 77 91), in an unassuming white building. Surrealist to the nth power with a slanted ceiling, burning incense, and a mix of mad scientist and Tex-Mex decor. Quality tunes and a young cutting-edge crowd with nothing to prove. "Chicken with promise to fly" takes off for 15.60Lt. Owned by a local band, it will only get more popular. Open daily noon-4am.
>
> **N.A.T.O.'s,** Pasažo 2/3 (tel. 61 77 84). Find Bix's fantasy too tame? Head around the corner to N.A.T.O.'s, where you can wash down such items as the "Red Army" and "Remains of a Partisian"—smoked, boiled pig's ears—with *EKU Pils* (8Lt). It gets better. Set in a grey-and-black command post draped in missiles, guns, camo, and steel. Visa and MC accepted for your war debts. Open daily noon-3am.

Prie Parlamento, Gedimino pr. 46 (tel. 62 16 06). Café jolts you out of the haze at 8am. The restaurant attempts to serve English and American grills daily 11am-11pm, when the basement nightclub **Ministerija** kicks it techno-free 'til 2am.

The Pub (Prie Universiteto), Dominikonų 9 (tel. 62 35 68). Light food and *Pilsner Urquell* (10Lt per pint) in a huge (but full) courtyard and a romantic 2-story dungeon—we don't get it either. Open daily 11am-2am.

Vilnius is home to the internationally renowned **National Philharmonic Orchestra,** Aušros Vartų 5 (info tel. 62 71 65), and the **Opera and Ballet Theater,** Vienuolio g. 1 (tel. 62 06 36). Make learning fun at the **Planetarium,** Ukmergės g. 12a (tel. 41 48). Music and stars; what more do you need?

■ Near Vilnius

TRAKAI

The capital of the Grand Duchy of Lithuania in the 14th and 15th centuries, Trakai, 30km west of Vilnius, is an idyll of lakes and islands full of intricate wooden cottages, castles, and ruins. Though tourists seem to focus exclusively on the castle-museum, it's fun to explore the islands themselves and watch them be scenic.

At this intersection of Vytauto g. and Karaimų g., the first sight of interest is tucked down a dirt road, leading toward the lake. To the right down Kęstučio g. sprawl the untouched ruins of the **first castle,** built from 1362-82 by Grand Duke Kęstutis. This castle, repeatedly besieged by German knights, was captured twice, prompting Grand Duke Vytautas to build a new castle on the largest island of Lake Galvė in 1406. **Trakai Castle,** the picture-perfect result, is accessible by a footbridge 500m down Karaimų g. Getting to the bridge involves a right turn off Karaimų g.; to reach the castle, visitors must brave a flurry of kiosks and souvenir stands, almost as pesky as the crossbow arrows of centuries ago. The reward is a castle in remarkable condition and a truly tranquil setting. Restored thoroughly from 1952-80, the rooms of the 30m-high watchtower are stocked with historical displays about the castle. The **City and Castle History Museum** (tel. 512 86), in various castle rooms, houses an impressive but random selection of intricate glasswork, WWII memorabilia, 15th-century goblets, royal seals, 19th-century furniture, opera glasses, and an immense collection of tobacco and opium pipes in all shapes and sizes. (Open daily 10am-7pm. 4Lt, students 2Lt; cameras 2Lt. Tours to bring order to the chaos 30Lt, students 15Lt.) Rent a **rowboat** on the lakeshore for 6Lt per hour, or board a **yacht** for a tour of the islands (fees negotiable—try for about 20Lt).

Karaimų g. is the cottage-lined residential district of the smallest ethnic group in Lithuania, the religious sect of the **Karaites,** a fundamentalist Jewish sect adhering only to the Laws of Moses. Returning from campaigns in the Crimea, Grand Duke Vytautas brought a few hundred of this Turkic-speaking group back to serve as his royal guard. Today 150 Karaites live in Trakai; their **Kinesė** (prayer-house) stands at Karaimų g. 30. On your way back, refuel with 5-7Lt entrées in moody **Židinys,** Vytauto g. 91 (tel. 531 98; open daily 11am-midnight).

Along with eight daily **trains** from Vilnius (30 min., 1.30Lt), there are about 10 daily **buses,** the last departing Trakai at 8:30pm (30-50min., 1.20-3Lt). Trakai's train station is on Vilniaus g., 500m south of the bus station; follow the crowd into town, it's the only way to go. From the bus station, take a right, and follow Vytauto g. 1km to the intersection with Karaimų g., marked by a large column, topped by an ever-pious statue of a man in robes with a cross in his hands. **Phone Code:** 238.

PANERIAI

Just outside of Vilnius's city limits lies a former Nazi death camp. From July 1941 to July 1944, over 70,000 Jews from Vilnius and the surrounding area were murdered here by both Nazis and fellow Lithuanians. For fifty years, the site had been marked as a spot where "Soviet citizens" had lost their lives, but the truth about the past is revealed today in what is known as **Panerių Memorialas,** a stone monument in Hebrew, Lithuanian, and Russian, at the entrance to the death camp. From here, a trail leads into the woods to a monument dedicated to the Jewish dead. The Star of David tops the Hebrew inscription in front, while the back carries English, Lithuanian, and Russian translations of the text under the image of a man reaching up towards "1941-1944". About 50m from this new marker stands the star-marked Soviet obelisk. In all directions, paths lead to pits where prisoners were kept and murdered. Wildflowers have begun to cover them, but each is fenced off and marked with a stone block whose inscriptions remind visitors of the area's purpose.

Trolleys #4 and 12 (dir. "Žemieji Paneriai") run from central Vilnius to "Vaduvos", marked by a brick waiting area just after a railroad bridge. Ride **bus** #8 from here to "Aukštieji Paneriai" (3 stops). Take the footbridge over the railroad yard, then go right on Agrastų g. The site is 1km farther, at the road's end.

■ Kaunas

Kaunas is Lithuania's true heart and soul. Indeed, the city was the provisional capital during the Lithuanian independence of 1918-40. One need look no farther than the city's cobblestone avenues and florid parks to taste a slice of Lithuanian spirit. Unhurried citizens greet each other with a smile and handshake, and folk festivals flourish in the shadows of the city's graceful walls.

ORIENTATION AND PRACTICAL INFORMATION

On the confluence of the **Nemuna** and the **Neris** rivers, Kaunas is a peninsula pointing west, with the **Old Town** at the western tip, the bus and train stations at the southeast point, and the hilly suburbs of **Žaliakalnis** in the north. The **New Town** fills the middle, and the 2-km pedestrian **Laisvės al.** bisects it. At the fork in the road with **Šv. Gertrudos g.,** Laisvės al. gains new life as it connects with **Vilniaus g.** at the beginning of the Old Town, to lead directly to **Rotušės aikštė.** Magic **bus #7** heads from the stations west on **Kęstučio g.,** cuts between the Old and New Towns by going north on **Birštono Gimnazijos g.,** then heads east along the avenue formed by three connected streets: Šv. Gertrudos g., **F. Ožeškienės g.,** and **K. Donelaičio g.** It is never more than one block from Laisvės al. To get to the **tourist office,** take lucky #7 to the "S. Daukanto" stop and head one block to Laisvės al. The office lies 1½ blocks west. The city map in this book is oriented so that west is up.

Your pocket wouldn't be the same without *Kaunas in Your Pocket,* the loveable 4Lt guidebook with maps, restaurant listings, a public transportation grid, and humor that gets funnier as you go.

Tourist Offices: Migrovė, Laisvės al. 88 (tel. 20 49 11). Sells maps (3-8Lt) and dishes out info on accommodations and sights. Open Mon.-Fri. 9am-6pm, Sat. 10am-2pm. **Litinterp,** Kumelių 15, apt. 4 (tel./fax 22 87 18), deep in the Old Town. Golden-hearted staff answers questions, finds private rooms, and rents bicycles (20Lt per day plus US$100 deposit). Open Mon.-Fri. 9am-6pm, Sat. 9am-4pm.

Currency Exchange: Look for *"Valiutos Keitykla"* on Laisvės al. and Vilniaus g. Keep in mind the fixed 4Lt:US$1 rate. **Lietuvos Akcinis Inovacinis Bankas,** Laisvės al. 84, gives MC and Visa cash advances. Accepts AmEx and Thomas Cook traveler's checks (3-5% commission). Open Mon.-Fri. 10am-5pm, Sat. 9am-7pm.

Trains: Čiurlionio g. 16 (tel. 29 22 60 or 22 10 93), 1½km southeast of the New Town at the end of Vytauto pr. To: Kaliningrad (5:03pm, 5½hr., 19Lt); Rīga (1:23am, 6hr., 25Lt); Tallinn *Baltic Express* (12:09am, 12hr., 82/152Lt); Vilnius (18 per day, 1½-2hr., 5.30Lt); Warsaw *Baltic Express* (5:50am, 70Lt). **Advance Booking Office,** Šv. Gertrūdos 7 (tel. 29 24 08). Open Mon.-Sat. 9am-2pm and 3-7pm. Trolleybuses #3, 5, or 7 whisk you three stops from the train station to "Gedimino", a block south of Laisvės's end.

Buses: Vytauto pr. 24/26 (reservations tel. 29 24 55, international reservations tel. 29 24 46, info tel. 22 19 42 or 22 19 55). To: Klaipeda (9 per day, 4hr., 9Lt); Palanga (9 per day, 4hr., 26Lt); Vilnius (1-2 per hour 4am-9pm, 2hr., 10Lt).

KAUNAS ■ 351

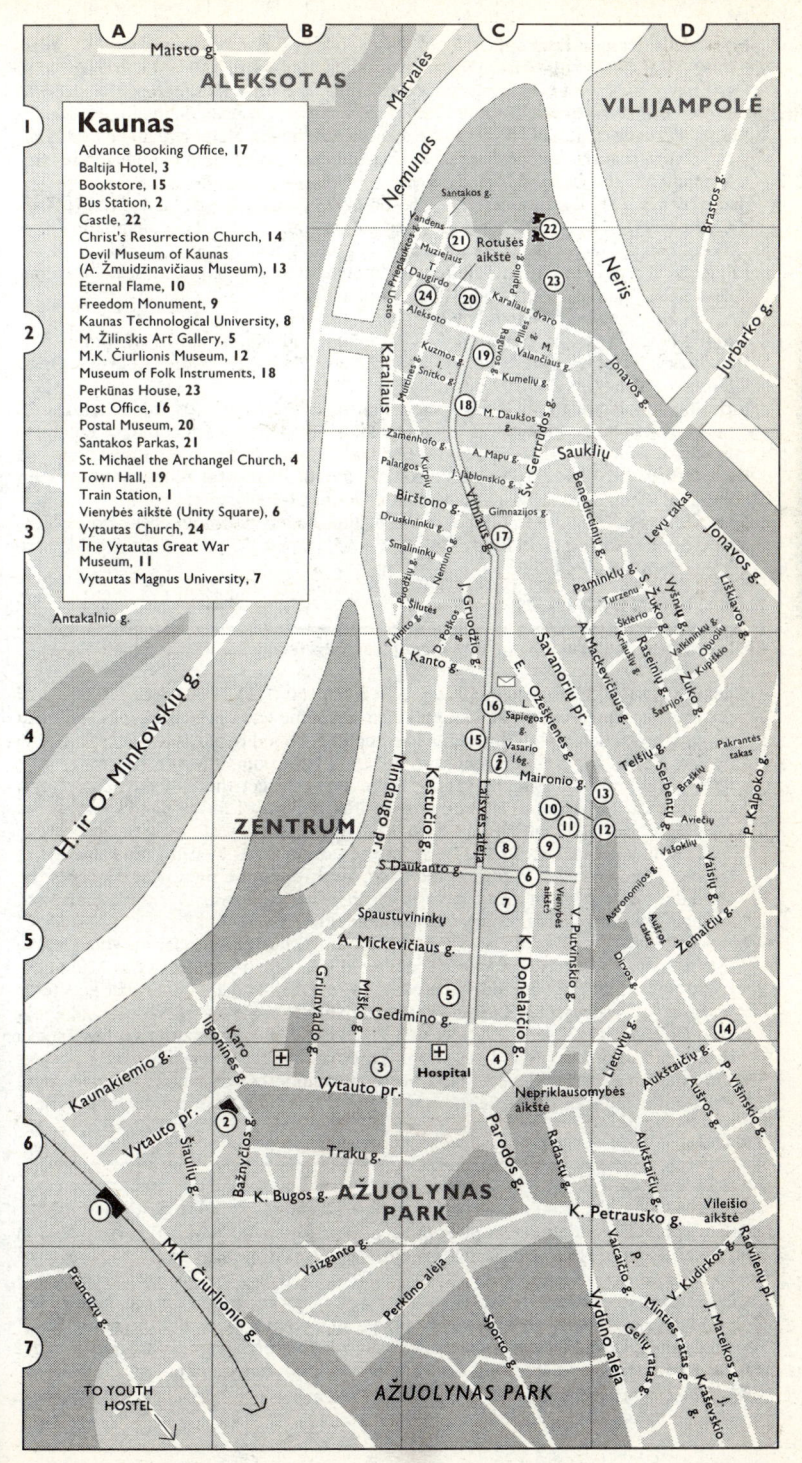

Kaunas

Advance Booking Office, 17
Baltija Hotel, 3
Bookstore, 15
Bus Station, 2
Castle, 22
Christ's Resurrection Church, 14
Devil Museum of Kaunas
 (A. Žmuidzinavičiaus Museum), 13
Eternal Flame, 10
Freedom Monument, 9
Kaunas Technological University, 8
M. Žilinskis Art Gallery, 5
M.K. Čiurlionis Museum, 12
Museum of Folk Instruments, 18
Perkūnas House, 23
Post Office, 16
Postal Museum, 20
Santakos Parkas, 21
St. Michael the Archangel Church, 4
Town Hall, 19
Train Station, 1
Vienybės aikštė (Unity Square), 6
Vytautas Church, 24
The Vytautas Great War Museum, 11
Vytautas Magnus University, 7

Hydrofoils: Raudondvario pl. 107 (tel. 26 13 48), in the trans-Neris town of Vilijampolė. Take trolleybus #7 from the train and bus stations, or #10 or 11 from the stop at Laisvės al.'s west end; get off at "Kedainių", the third stop across the river. In summer, *Raketa* hydrofoils link Kaunas to Nida via Nemunas (9am, 4hr., 39Lt).
Public Transport: Tickets (0.40Lt) are available at kiosks. Memorize all-powerful #7, the benevolent **trolleybus** that takes you from the train and bus stations to the ferry terminal, via the Old and New Towns.
Taxis: State Taxi Company (tel. 23 66 66 or 23 77 77). 1Lt per km. **Private Taxi Company** (tel. 23 98 80). Rates may depend on your clothes. Don't hand the driver more than the fare and ask for change if you didn't hear the price he asked.
Luggage Storage: In a tunnel under the train station (1Lt). Open almost 24hr., but closes 8-8:30am, 2:15-3pm, 8-8:30pm, so plan ahead.
English Bookstore: "Centrinis Knygynas," Laisvės al. 81 (tel. 22 95 72). English tomes at the far end. Open Mon.-Fri. 10am-2pm and 3-7pm, Sat. 10am-4pm.
Pharmacy: Vaistinė, Laisvės al. 100 (tel. 22 26 98), has its bottles in order. Open Mon.-Fri. 8am-8pm, Sat. 10am-5pm.
E-mail: Soros Foundation (Open Society Fund), Laisvės al. 53, 2nd floor (tel./fax 22 06 24; e-mail Rimas@kic.osf.LT). Send messages from Rimas's account, or receive if you have your Powerbook buddy. Write Attn.: (Your Name) in the subject line.
Post Office: Laisvės al. 102 (tel. 22 62 20). **Poste Restante:** Window #11. Open Mon.-Fri. 8am-7pm, Sat. 8am-5pm. **Postal Code:** LT-3000.
Telephone and Telegraph Office: In the hall to the left as you enter the post office; card-phones in the main lobby (tel. 20 33 15). Open daily 8am-10pm, desk 9am-9pm. **Phone Code:** 027.

ACCOMMODATIONS

Litinterp (see Practical Information) arranges B&Bs (singles 60Lt, doubles 100Lt).

Guesthouse (HI), Prancūzų g. 59 (tel. 7 74 89 72; fax 7 20 27 61). Head right out of the train station, cross the tracks, and turn left at the end of the bridge to Prancūzų g., which wanders uphill through a local neighborhood towards the guesthouse. A bit far. A bed in a double room with attached bathroom (shower, hot water, and toilet), kitchen, and balcony (24Lt). Make sure you get the HI 24Lt price. Ninth floor bar (tel. 7 74 89 50) is quite possibly the only place in the Baltics that stocks Diet Coke. Buy a 2L bottle (6.50Lt) to wash down all the lard.
Hotel, Kaunakiemio 1 (tel. 20 27 63), at the corner of M.K. Čiurlionio under the "Bravo" sign; entrance is around the back, go through the rightmost door, it's the third door on the left in the courtyard. Clean, hot hall shower. Average rooms with strange, couchlike beds. Single 40Lt. Double 60Lt.
Hotel Lietuva II, Laisvės al. 35 (tel. 22 17 91). If the hostel is too far for you, Lietuva II is near—very near. Rooms are decent-sized if less-than-sparkling. The 120Lt double, 160Lt triple price includes a broken TV, a toilet, and a shower that gets lukewarm if you wait awhile. Currency exchange in the lobby accepts AmEx.
Hotel Baltijos, Vytauto pr. 71 (tel. 28 32 02). Basic accommodations a few blocks from the end of Laisvės al. It's a prime candidate for renovation, but right now its tiny rooms can still be had for 60Lt per single and 94Lt per double. Showers available, but make sure you get a room with hot water and a door handle that works.

FOOD

Kauna's restaurant scene is benefitting from a recent boom. An open-air market operates across from the train and behind Vytauto 12 (open Mon.-Fri. 8:30am-6pm, Sat. 8:30am-3pm). For independent shopping, try **Parduotuvė SKALSA,** Laisvės al. 103 (tel. 20 29 66; open Mon.-Fri. 8am-8pm, Sat. 8am-6pm, Sun. 8am-2pm).

Gildija, Rotušės aikštė 2 (tel. 20 08 04). Kaunas's best restaurant for the money. The huge door and kingly high-backed chairs recall medieval glory, but the sparse selection and server's inflection tell a decidedly Soviet story. Entrées 8Lt, and a 0.20Lt bathroom fee. Open Mon. noon-6pm, Tues.-Sun. noon-midnight.

Eliza, Vilniaus g. 30 (tel. 20 75 93). Popular Eliza serves French food in an elegant atmosphere. The escape from Anglophonic to Francophonic pop comes at a price: entrées 20-30Lt. Open daily noon-midnight.

Pieno Baras, Laisvės al. at S. Daukanto. The name means "milk bar"—they're serious. Whipped milk 1.56Lt, whipped cream with chocolate sauce 1.40Lt, *Blyneliai* 3Lt. Ultraviolence not included. Open 8:30am-8;30pm.

Restoranas Davile, Vilniaus g. 56 (tel. 20 91 54). Unique, fresh salads from 5Lt. The Retro comes with mandarins, pineapples, chicken, olives, and a yogurt dressing (8.50Lt). Dishes include *Po serméga* (beef stuffed with sweet pepper and leeks in horseradish sauce, 22Lt), *Neptūnas* (halibut filet, coconut, lemon, asparagus, flowering cabbages, carrots, 19Lt). Interior is as classy as the food is delicious—they may even lift a polished silver cover from your plate. Open 11am-midnight.

Astra, Laisvės al. 76. Indeed the star of Laisvės al. Ask them to crank up their excellent music to drown out the zillions of kiosks blaring technotrash. Stewed macaroni with vegetables 8Lt, quail eggs 6Lt, "Sleeping" banana fried in dough with ice cream and cognac 8.60Lt. Divine cappuccino 2Lt. Breakfast specials 9-11am, a 10% lunch discount 4-6pm. Open Mon.-Sat. 9am-2am, Sun. 11am-2am.

SIGHTS

The massive **St. Michael the Archangel Church** commands Laisvės's east end. Built in the 1890s for the Russian garrison that came to man the nine forts placed around Kaunas in a period of intense Russification, the sumptuous neo-Byzantine interior is a feast for the eyes, although the exterior is currently undergoing renovation (open Mon.-Fri. 8am-5pm, Sat.-Sun. 9am-4pm; services Mon.-Fri. noon, Sat. 10am, Sun. 10am and noon). In the south shadow of the church is the **Mykolo Žilinsko Dailės Galerija**, with rotating exhibitions of modern art on the first floor and a collection of mummies, ceramics, and 19th-century paintings including works by Cézanne, Renoir, and Manet on the upper levels. Notice the well endowed statue of a "man" out in front—as if you could miss it (open Tues.-Sun. noon-6pm; 2Lt).

Walk two blocks down Laisvės al., turn right on Daukanto g., and after a block exit into **Vienybės aikštė** (Unity Sq.), depicted in etched glory on the back of the 20Lt note. On the south side, **Vytautas Magnus University** and the older **Kaunas Technological Univeristy** draw in a student population of more than 16,000. Across the street, in an outdoor shrine to Lithuanian statehood, busts of famous Lithuanians flank a corridor leading from the **Freedom Monument** to an eternal flame for those who died to win freedom in 1918-20. When Lithuania was annexed by the Soviet Union, these symbols of nationhood disappeared, only to re-emerge from their hiding place in St. Michael's in 1989.

Several museums surround the plaza. **Vytauto Didžiojo Karo Muziejus** (Vytautas the Great War Museum), Donelaičio g. 64 (tel. 22 27 56), behind two soccer-playing lions, isn't as bellicose as it sounds and houses the aircraft in which two Lithuanian-Americans, Darius and Girėnas, tried to fly from New York to Kaunas non-stop in 1933 (they crashed in Germany—check out the 10Lt bill; open Wed.-Sun. 11am-5:15pm; 2Lt, students 1Lt). The **M. K. Čiurlionis Museum**, Putvinskio g. 55 (tel. 22 14 17), displays pastels by the fanatic who sought to combine music and image to depict an idea in its pre-verbal state, as it might appear in a dream or subconscious reflection. Whooooa, dude. High-quality 20th-century Lithuanian works fill the other halls (open Tues.-Sun. noon-6pm, closed last Tues. of every month; 2Lt, students 1Lt). Across the street, the hellish **Devil Museum of Kaunas**, Putvinskio g. 64 (tel. 27 48 02), more properly known by its devilish moniker—the A. Žmuidzinavičiaus Museum—keeps a collection of nearly 2000 devils, most of them Lithuanian folk carvings. Other diabolic creations come from Africa, Siberia, the Urals, and South America. Don't miss Devil Hitler and Devil Stalin chasing each other across bone-covered Lithuania (open Tues.-Sun. noon-5pm, closed last Tues. of every month; English tours 15Lt; 2Lt, students 1Lt). Kaunas has taken the proper spiritual safeguards in case some bad voodoo leaks out. On a high hill behind the museum, **Christ's Resurrec-**

tion Church, a famous modernist creation, waits to be finished. Its construction ceased in 1932 on account of Stalin's meddlin' paws.

As you make your inevitable strolls up and down Laisvės al., stop and take a good look at the statue of Vytautas the Great, "creator of Lithuanian power." The four pillars of the statue are depictions of defeated enemies. History buffs can distinguish the Russian, the Pole, the Tartar, and the German crusader; but everyone gets a kick out of their expressions as the four enemies eternally curse the big guy on top.

Where Laisvės al. ends, Kaunas's Old Town begins; follow Vilniaus g. through an underpass and you'll be inside the medieval city walls. Two blocks farther, a left on Zamenhofo g. leads to the absorbing **Museum of Folk Instruments**, Kurpių g. 12, a collection of hand-carved fiddles, accordions, and strange Lithuanian sound-makers—a dried, inflated sheep's bladder on a string, for one (open Wed.-Sun. 11am-6pm; donation requested). Three blocks later, the **Kauno Arkikatedra Bažnyčia** (Kaunas arch-cathedral), one of Lithuania's largest churches, was first built in the 1908-13 Christianization of Low Lithuania, on the order of Vytautas the Great. Its shockingly vast interior is cut in sharp Gothic/Renaissance lines with blue and gold panels. On the south wall, the **Tomb of Maironis** holds a priest from Kaunas whose poetry played a central role in Lithuania's 19th-century National Awakening. West of the cathedral, the **town hall,** a confused stylistic concoction constructed in chunks from 1542-1771, crowns Rotušės aikštė. A gallows in the square's center helps keep the peace. Up Karaliaus dvaro off the north end of the square the Neris and Nemunas rivers meet at **Santakos Parkas**. Kaunas's 11th-century **castle** stands here.

Follow Aleksoto g. towards the river from the southeast corner of Rotušės aikštė to the 15th-century **Perkunas House,** a late Gothic masterpiece built for Hanseatic merchants on the site of a temple to Perkūnas, god of thunder. Kitty-corner to this electrifying edifice is the **Vytautas Church,** also built in the early 1400s. Next to the church, a bridge (note the hammer and sickle) creaks across the Nemunas; a **funicular** (0.15Lt) leads up the hill to an unrivaled panorama of Kaunas.

Kaunas's final jewel, the **Pažaislis Monastery and Church,** a vibrant Baroque ensemble with rich frescos, sits on the Nemunas's right bank 10km east of central Kaunas. Used as a KGB-run "psychiatric hospital," the monastery was returned to the Catholic Church in 1990 (open Mon.-Sat. 10am-5pm, Sun. 10am-6pm). Take trolleybus #5 from the train station to the end of the line; then walk 1km down the road. The church is just past a small beach.

Across the Neris from the castle lies the town of **Vilijampolė,** which gained infamy during WWII as the Jewish Ghetto of Kaunas, vividly immortalized in Avraham Tory's *Kovno Ghetto Diary.* The **Ninth Fort,** Žemaičių pl. 73, a few kilometers north of the ghetto, was one of the nine forts constructed in the 1880s around Kaunas as the first line of defense against the German Empire. During WWII, it became a Nazi concentration camp, and was later used by the KGB. The museum focuses on Nazi atrocities, but also includes newer exhibits on the mass deportations of Lithuanians in the 1940s and 50s, and the guerilla resistance which continued until 1952. Take bus #45 from the railway station to "IX Fortas" (open Wed.-Sun. 10am-6pm; 2Lt, Wed. free).

ENTERTAINMENT

Locals are especially proud of the city's theaters, and with good reason. Theater festivals occur at least two or three times a year. Even when they are over, **Akademinis Dramos Teatras,** Muzikims 11 (tel. 22 31 85), picks up the slack, with everything from classical to recent plays. The "small stage" at Kęstučio g. 64 covers alternative performances. For the music lover, **Muzikinis Teatras,** Lasvės al. 91 (tel. 20 09 33), says it with song; and **Kauno Filharmonija,** Sapiegos g. 5 (tel. 20 04 48), fills in the classical niche. Rotušės aikštė's outdoor bars offer live music in the evenings. Indoors, and often down a few flights, darker pubs offer local beer in excess.

> **Skliautai,** Rotušės aikštė 26 (tel. 20 68 45). Low-key staff is outdone only by the relaxed clientele whiling away the afternoon with chess and beer (4.50Lt). Even if

you miss the occasional live jazz, this is one of the phattest joints in town. Open 11am til everyone feels like calling it a night (between 10pm and midnight).

Vasaré, Vilniaus g. 40 (tel. 22 98 54). No one seems to care whether or not this courtyard café serves food. Most drop in to sit under the trees and have a drink on a summer evening. A good mix of comfortable café and friendly bar. Salad 4Lt. Sandwich 1.90Lt. Pancakes 3-5Lt. Open daily 11am-midnight.

Vilija, Varnių g. 41 (tel. 26 95 68), across the Neris in Vilijampolė. Admittedly high on the "goodfella" scale, this is Kaunas's hottest spot after midnight. If you've gotta rage and paint the town red, this bar is one step ahead of you. Open daily noon-3am. Cover 10Lt for men.

Disco, Mickievičiaus g. 8a (tel. 29 43 96). For more of what you want in a dance club, and less of what you don't, the nightly disco in this unassuming old building is worth checking out. Decent music and a friendly crowd. Themes vary (check the board outside), but Thursdays are "student night." Don't let the auditorium-like exterior fool you—this is the place. Open 8pm-2am. Cover varies.

Metropolis, Laisvės al. 68, is notable mainly for 7Lt 0.5L of *Guinness* and a modest disco after 8pm. Open noon-5pm and 6pm-midnight.

Baras Senas Stalčius, Laisvės al. 46A (tel. 20 25 67), rocks with live bands usually Thurs. night. Open Mon. noon-10pm, Tues.-Sun. noon-midnight.

Be on the lookout for **folk festivals.** Any excuse to revive traditional songs, dance, and dress is reason enough in Kaunas; when **Mindaugas's Day** comes around on July 6th, stand back and check out the jigs.

■ Near Kaunas: Druskininkai

"You hear the murmur of the pines, so solemn, as if they were trying to tell you something," mystic, avant-garde artist, composer, and resident Mikolojus Konstantinas Čiurlionis wrote in 1905. A few hours among the forest-town's still-whispering pines or by the pristine lake and you'll understand his inspiration. The town keeps his unique works alive at **M. K. Čiurlionio Memorialinis Muziejus,** Čiurlionio g. 41 (tel. 511 31), which tells the artist's story in four buildings, one of which is the house in which he worked. The museum has mostly prints and focuses on the artist's life and times; for the originals go to the M.K.C. Museum in Kaunas. Čiurlionio's evocative, mythical images are accompanied by recorded compositions, the other half of what he intended to be an integrated art form (open Tues.-Sun. noon-6pm, closed the 4th Tues. of the month; 1Lt, student 0.50Lt; color guidebook with English translations and excerpts from his letters 6Lt). Visitors should check out the 5m **statue** of Čiurlionis at the end of Kudirkas g., the other side of town from the bus station. The artist is depicted in a weary state caused by attempting to explain his paintings to everyone. There are **piano concerts** on Sunday evenings in summer featuring Čiurlionis's own compositions and those of such lesser-known figures as Bach, Debussy, and Ludwig B. (6pm, 1hr., 4Lt).

Druskininkai Hotel, Kudirkos g. 43 (tel. 513 45; fax 522 17), corner of Taikos g., offers comfort and tree-brushing balconies. In-room bathrooms have hot water, and offer a chance to brush up on your limbo skills as you struggle to get under the bizarrely low shower head (singles 25Lt, doubles 36Lt, quad 46Lt). Even if you're not hungry, stop by the **Baltoji Astra,** Vilniaus g. 10 (tel. 533 32), to ogle a purple-curtained, white-marble techno-temple to the triumph of ambition and funding over architectural taste (salads 4Lt, main courses 10Lt; open daily noon-midnight). Otherwise, there's always the pleasantly tacky, homey, and casual hotel restaurant, where a surprisingly good *karbonadas* runs 7.50Lt.

The bus station sends **buses** to Kaunas (7-11 per day, 3-4hr., 11.80Lt) and Vilnius (5 per day, 4hr., 11.80Lt), but be aware that the last buses leave before 5:20pm (Kaunas) or 4:25pm (Vilnius). **Store luggage** at the **bus station** (0.50Lt; open daily 5am-11pm; *kasa* closes 7pm). From the bus station, head left up Kudirkos g. to the intersection with **Čiurlionio g.,** the main street. Vilniaus g. is reached by going left on Čiurlionio g., then right after the parish church's yard. **Phone code:** 233.

THE BALTIC COAST

■ Šiauliai

On a sunny morn in 1236, German Knights of the Sword, returning after a campaign to Christianize Lithuania, were ambushed and massacred. The town that grew up on the site took its name from the shining *saulė* (sun) of that bloody morn, and to commemorate the bloodshed, people began a tradition of placing crosses on **Kryžių Kalnas** (Hill of Crosses), 10km northwest of the city. After the Lithuanian uprisings of 1831 and 1863, the collection grew as Lithuanians brought crosses to remember the dead and the deported. Under the Soviets, more crosses appeared for those killed or exiled to Siberia. During Soviet occupation, the hill became a mound of anti-Russian sentiment, and despite three bouts with a bulldozer, the memorial survived as Lithuanians stealthily replaced the fallen crosses. Independence has brought a new eruption of crosses as emigrated Lithuanians and relatives of the exiled have returned to place monuments of their own. After a day of religious imagery, there is still one last holy sight. In town, at the corner of Aušros al. and Tilžės g., the hilltop Renaissance/Baroque **Šv. Petro ir Povilo bažnyčia** (Church of St. Peter and Paul) looms over the city, thrusting its 17th-century steeple, the tallest in Lithuania, 70m skyward (4 daily services on weekends).

Buses running north to Joniškis, Meškuičiai, Rīga, or Tallinn pass by here (15 per day); ask the driver to stop at Kryžių Kalnas—it's not a regular stop. Don't take a bus to Kryžkalnis; it's 30km south of Šiauliai! A marked road leads down for about 2km. To get back, hike to where you got off the bus, cross the street, and take any bus that passes by. **Trains** shuttle to Kaunas (5 per day, 2hr., 6Lt).

■ Palanga

One of the former Soviet Union's prime beach resorts, Palanga entices visitors with fine sand, botanical gardens, mineral springs, and a relaxing small-town atmosphere. Despite a permanent population of only 22,000, in summers past, Palanga swam with more than 200,000 of the Union's luckiest elite. The *nomenklatura* of old is gone, but Lithuanians return, unable to forget the Baltics' best beach and its pine-scented sea breeze.

Orientation and Practical Information **Buses,** Kretingos 1 (tel. 533 33) run from the corner of Kretingos g. and Vytauto g. to Kaunas (7 per day, 4hr., 26Lt), Klaipėda (31 per day, 40min., 2Lt), Liepaja (3 per day, 2hr., 8Lt), and Vilnius (7 per day, 6hr., 30.70Lt). The *kasa* is open daily 6am-10pm. The bus station and post office mark the approximate center of town along **Vytauto g.,** the north-south boulevard. About 200m from the station, **Basanavičiaus g.** runs 1km west to the **beach** and the **pier.** The entrance to the huge **Botanical Park,** at the town's south end, is between Vytauto g. 21 and 19, 1km south. Farther north along Vytauto g., Palanga becomes a beach town. When heading north, any road to the left will lead to the shore. A 24-hour **tourist booth** (tel. 543 68) outside the bus station sells maps, suggests restaurants, finds accommodations, and helps stranded tourists willing to communicate in German, Russian, or frantic gestures. The green i-ed **Tourism Center,** Vytauto g. 106 (tel./fax 571 25) sells maps (1.50Lt) and brochures (5Lt) and parts with lodging, travel, and restaurant info (open Mon.-Fri. 9am-8pm, Sat.-Sun. 9am-4pm). Celebrate Westernization by renting **rollerblades** (3Lt per 30min., 5Lt per hour, 25Lt per day) at Basanazičiaus 4 (open 10am-midnight). The **Vaistine pharmacy** (tel. 540 54) is located at Vytauto 2 (open Mon.-Fri. 9am-7pm, Sat. 9am-2pm). The **post office,** Aušros al. 42, sits opposite the bus station and **exchanges currency** in cash (enter from the side; open Mon.Fri. 9am-2pm and 3-6:30pm, Sat. 10am-2pm). The **telephone** building behind the post office gives you a choice of direct or assisted international calls (tel. 534 47; phones and desk open 24hr.). **Postal code:** LT-5720. **Phone code:** 0236.

Accommodations and Food The sunny **Lithuanian Youth Hostel**, S. Nėries g. 23 (tel. 570 76; between #17 and 21, the street begins behind the post office), shelters ten rooms of two to three beds (20Lt per person). The communal kitchen and toilets are in a detached building. No lockout and no curfew make a stay here even more relaxing. There are no showers at the hostel, but you can get hot **showers** (3Lt) at **Palangos Miesto Sveikatos Rumai** (Health Palace), S. Nėries g. 44 (tel. 526 96), at the end of the street before the beach (massage 40Lt per hr.; pool 8Lt per hr.; sauna 10Lt per hr.; open Mon.-Fri. 9:45am-7pm, Sat. 10:45am-6pm). Klaipėda's **Litinterp** (tel. (26) 21 69 62; fax 21 98 62) arranges B&Bs in and around Palanga starting at 60Lt for a single, 100Lt for a double. Try to arrange a room ahead of time in Klaipėda.

Chalets and outside eateries line **Basanavičiaus g.** Similar façades hide differences in menus, prices, and quality. In the chalet called **Dasia Basanavičiaus 9** (tel. 545 06), mix food with alcohol—e.g. herring (*silke*, 5.30Lt) with vodka (3-10Lt)—to energize yourself after a day at the beach. Salads and other light dishes start at 5-8Lt, and entrées hover around 15Lt. *Pilsner Urquell* on tap for 5Lt may entice you to stick around and digest as you watch folks taking their evening walk. Breakfast is hard to find; the town is dead until 11am. If hunger hits before then, **Gaisra Kavine**, Vytauto g. 102, north of the bus station, lets you scrounge a decent morning meal out of yogurt, coffee, pastries, beer, and vodka. The tables outside bathe in the morning sun (open daily 8:30am-11pm).

Sights and Entertainment No arrowhead-and-rusty-teapot museums distract visitors from a pleasant day of strolling. The best way to spend a day here is at the **beach**, which runs unhindered from Girkeliai, 5km south of town, all the way to the border, 18km north. **Nude bathing** is allowed—women control the section starting 200m north of the pier, men head south. Say your brief good-byes in the middle. At the end of Basanavičiaus g., a fountain-bedecked plaza opens onto the **boardwalk** which stretches behind the dunes for the length of the town. Its cafés and beer gardens let you sip away the evening, and dance away the weekends.

On a cold day, or when evening comes, wander through the **Botanical Park** at Palanga's south end. In the early 19th century, Polish Count Tyszkiewicz bought the entire town, recognizing its growing popularity as a resort. He leveled half of it to lay out the 495-acre park surrounding the palace, and brought in a revolution-evading landscape architect from France. Well marked paths and flowering trails invite romantic walks around sunset. Back in the day, view-strewn **Birutės kalnas** (Birutės' Hill) was the site of a shrine to the sea goddess Jūratė; a late-19th-century chapel now controls the views. East of the hill, Count Tyszkiewicz's **palace** contains the glittering **Amber Museum** (tel. 513 19), a gargantuan collection of over 35,000 amber chunks, including a veritable Jurassic Park of amber drops that trapped insects millions of years ago. The definitive history of amber is presented here, with displays on mining and processing, and collections of jewelry. This may be Lithuania's best museum; don't miss it (open Tues.-Sun. 11am-7pm; 3Lt, students 1Lt).

In the evening, **Kavinė Fontanas**, Basanavičiaus g. 46 (tel. 53 504), tempts souls with beer (6Lt) and snacks (2-6Lt). Nightly live music in summer brings out the crowds. Candles after sundown are a nice touch. An **amusement park** whirls around in a flurry of lights and steel at the beach end of pedestrian Jūratės g. (off Vytauto). Everything from bumper cars to ringtossing-for-champagne is available for your, well, amusement. Interestingly, the park decided to name the roller coaster the "Tornado", instead of the more obvious and appropriate "Eastern European Geopolitics". (Open Mon.-Fri. 1-11pm, Sat.-Sun. 11am-11pm; rides 2-3Lt each.)

Klaipėda

Every time a German tourist calls Klaipėda "Memel", the citizens recall that for nearly 700 years Klaipėda was anything but Lithuanian. Yet this busy port was always the apple of Lithuania's eye, and through centuries of foreign control the country hoped one day to regain Klaipėda as its very own. In a few short years they have done wonders with the place. The blank slate left by fifty years of negligence following the city's destruction by the Red Army is being filled with comfortable cafés and elegant restaurants. The pace never gets too busy to forget about the peace and quiet by the river or the beaches across the lagoon.

ORIENTATION AND PRACTICAL INFORMATION

The **Danė River** divides the city into south **Senamiestis** (Old Town) and north **Naujamiestis** (New Town), while a lagoon cuts off **Smiltynė**, Klaipėda's Curonian Spit quarter. All of mainland Klaipėda lies close to the **bus** and **train stations**, separated by a parking lot. Follow **S. Nėries g.** away from the train to the end, then take a right on **S. Daukanto g.** to reach the heart of the city and **Litinterp**, 800m to the left off S. Daukanto g. Before reaching this oasis of aid, it's necessary to cross **H. Manto g.**, the main north-south artery which changes its name to Tiltų g., as it crosses the Old Town. Then Taikos g. **Liepų g.** (a.k.a. Naujoji sodo) is the main east-west street in the New Town. Most kiosks sell the *Klaipėda in Your Pocket*, an annually updated whimsical German and English guide, complete with maps and information on Palanga and the Curonian Spit (4Lt).

Tourist Office: Litinterp, S. Šimkaus g. 21/8 (tel. 21 98 62; fax 21 69 62), arranges private rooms in Klaipėda, Palanga, and on the Curonian Spit; rents bikes (20Lt per day, $100 deposit) and cars (175Lt per day with 200km, 0.35Lt per extra km, must be 21); sells maps and guidebooks; and answers *any* questions you may have. Open Mon.-Fri. 9am-6pm, Sat. 10am-4pm.

Currency Exchange: In kiosks surrounding the train station and the bus station, or in one of the city's multitudinous banks. If those 1Lt ferry rides start to add up, refuel at **Vilniaus Bankas,** Daržų g.13 (tel. 31 09 25), where the cashier will accept your Diner's Club, MC, or Visa card, or AmEx or Thomas Cook traveler's checks, while shuffling around huge stacks of US$100 bills (0.5% commission). Open Mon.-Thurs. 9am-1:30pm and 2:30-4:30pm, Fri. 9am-1:30pm and 2:30-4pm.

Trains: Priestočio g. 7 (tel. 21 46 14, reservations tel. 29 63 56). To: Kaunas (1 per day, 7½hr., 27Lt); Vilnius (3 per day, 5hr., 27Lt).

Buses: Butkų Juzės 9 (tel. 21 48 63, reservations tel. 21 14 34). To: Kaliningrad via Sovietsk (2 per day, 4hr., 20Lt); Kaliningrad via the Curonian Spit (first take the ferry to Smiltynė; 2 per day, 4hr.); Kaunas (13 per day, 4hr., 20Lt); Nida (2 per day, 2hr., 7Lt); Ventspils (1 per day, 4hr., 18Lt); and Vilnius (11 per day, 7½hr.).

Ferries: The **Smiltynė** ferry landing, Žueju 8 (tel. 21 22 24), sends ferries to (you guessed it!) Smiltynė; boats sail from 6am-1:30am (cashier open 5:45am-11:30pm; 1-2 per hour, 10min., roundtrip 1Lt). **International ferries** leave from the big boys' port at Perkėlos 10. To: Mukhran, Germany (odd dates at 3pm, 18hr., DM152); Kiel, Germany (Mon.-Thurs. and Sat. at midnight, Sun. at 7pm; 34hr.,; 510Lt). Call **Taurvita** travel agency, Taikos pr. 42 (tel. 21 78 00); open Mon.-Fri. 9am-6pm), or **Krantas,** Perkėlos g.10 (tel. 29 94 20), for info and tickets.

Hydrofoils: from the old ferry terminal at Žvejų g. 8. To: Kaunas via the Curonian lagoon and the Nemunas River (summer weekends only, 1 per day at 2:30pm, 29Lt); Nida (5Lt); Juodkrantė (4Lt). Tickets available 1½hr. before departure.

Public Transportation: City buses (0.50Lt per ride); the convenient **maršrutinis taksis** (route taxis) careen down the same routes. The latter pick up and deposit passengers anywhere along the way, with flexible fares (a.k.a. supervised hitch-hiking). They serve the Spit, going to Juodkrantė (5Lt), but rarely to Nida.

Taxis: The state company (tel. 000) recalls Soviet-style centralization, a private company (super-spy tel. 007) supports burgeoning Lithuanian business, and street taxis promote free-enterprise competition. 1Lt per km is the standard fare.

Luggage Storage: The lockers at the far end of the train station (0.30Lt) are safer than the racks at the back of the bus station (1Lt). Both open 5:30am-11:30pm.
Pharmacy: Vaistinė, Turgaus g. 8/10 (tel. 21 49 21) sells all those little white thingies that make you better. Open Mon.-Fri. 8am-8pm, Sat. 10am-5pm.
Hospital: Liepojus 15 (tel. 25 62 43).
Post Office: Liepų g. 16 (tel. 21 53 78), in a 1890 neo-Gothic brick fantasy. Open Mon.-Fri. 9am-6:30pm, Sat. 10am-2pm. **Postal Code:** LT-5800.
Telephones: Central Telephone Office, Liepų g. 1 (tel. 25 54 46). Pay the attendant or use magnetic blue card phones. Open daily 8am-11pm. **Phone Code:** 026.

ACCOMMODATIONS

Litinterp (see Practical Information) arranges B&Bs with local families at 60Lt for one, 100Lt for two (MC and Visa accepted).

Vėtrunge, Taikos g. 28 (tel. 25 48 01), occupies one of those eternally charming, gargantuan, inhuman residential blocks. Bright hallways—clean, but aged—and an ambience that is oh-so-Soviet, from the Russian staff to the lack of hot water. Singles (with two beds pushed together) 75Lt, doubles 90Lt.

Hotel Viktorija, S. Šimkaus g. 2 (tel. 21 36 70), on the corner with Vytauto g. offers a convenient location and the camaraderie that comes with simple lodgings… There's nothing *wrong* with it, but the small rooms and less-than-scalding water won't make you want to move in (singles 50Lt, doubles 70Lt).

Hotel "Jura," Malūnininkų 3 (tel. 39 98 57), in the northwest part of town. Lose those extra pounds walking from the Old Town to its remodeled lobby. Singles with phone, clean bathroom, and hot-water shower 95Lt. For just 5Lt more, a cavernous double comes with a couch, desk, phone, and fully equipped lavatory.

FOOD

A bonanza of **food-stalls** awaits in Turgaus aikštė, at the south end of Senamiestis. The grocery **Solvingė,** H. Manto g. 18, puts in a good effort daily 8:30am to 10pm.

Meridianas (tel. 21 68 51), on the Danė at the beginning of Tiltų g., 100m from the bridge that connects the Old and New Towns. If you eat only one meal in Klaipėda, you'll be really hungry. But if you eat it aboard this permanently docked three-masted schooner, you may not care. Extraordinary setting and precise service. The food doesn't quite match the brilliantly conceived locale, but it's reasonably good and reasonably priced (entrées 10-17Lt; food served noon-1am). Open daily 11am-1am. An occasional band performs to the percussion of crashing waves.

Resytė, Kepėjų g. 15 (tel. 21 71 67). A tiny outdoor café hidden by salmon-colored walls and a 19th-century archway. The courtyard within is another world. Shady and open, this is a great spot for a drink or a light evening snack (2-6Lt). A+ for presentation. Bistro/bar open daily 9am-9pm; café open daily noon-midnight.

Café Juoda-Balta, H. Manto g. 13/10 (tel. 21 57 97). True to its name, the café revels in black and white. Mirrors and excellent food further add to its chic. Go for the frozen treats, though, and catch on to Lithuania's sub-zero fever. The flaming ice cream (6Lt) is a liquor-coated burning mountain perfect for an afternoon indulgence. Open daily 11am-midnight.

Restoranas Luiza, Puodžių 40 (tel. 21 98 82), near the Hotel Viktorija. Your basic basement café, with cheap, fast, decent food, appreciated (isn't everything?) by tourist bunches. Warming rice soup 4Lt, entrées 10-14Lt. Open daily noon-midnight.

Baras Linas, Naujoji Sodo g. (tel. 21 99 62). Classy lace-and-roses table settings and food to match (goose filet, 19Lt), at not-too-painfully classy prices. Entrées stratified into 5-9Lt options, and more elaborate staples 14-29Lt. Open daily 11am-midnight.

Péda Galerija Kavine, Turgaus g. 10 (tel. 21 38 58). Bizarre brass fixtures and a gratuitous birdcage set the tone of this fashionable underground café that doubles as an art gallery—if the oddly coherent metal sculptures please you, the management will part with them for a mere 2000Lt. Snacks and entrées are less dear at 2-13Lt, drinks 4-14Lt.

SIGHTS

Mainland Klaipėda

Mažvydo Skulptūrų Parkas, by the train and bus stations between Liepų g. and Daukanto g., once served as the town's central burial ground. The city annually invites artists to use the park as a display area. The results peppers the old grounds. From Egyptian sun-dials to Chinese candle clocks and modern quartz watch-pens, every ticking contraption conceivable finds a place at **Laikrodžių Muziejus** (Clock Museum), Liepų g. 12 (tel. 21 35 31), in the New Town next to the main post office (open Tues.-Sun. 9am-5:30pm; 2Lt). Don't forget to get a good look at the old Post Office while you're sending off your mail or checking out the clocks. It's one of the few buildings in town that was not ruined in WWII.

Klaipėda Theater dominates the Old Town center, Teatro aikštė. Built in 1857, the theater was famous as one of Wagner's favorite haunts, and infamous as the site of the *Anschluss* (annexation) speech Hitler gave from its balcony in 1939. Today's main drama is renovation, but when it reopens, you can get tickets by calling 21 25 89 (open Tues.-Sun. 11am-2pm and 4:30-7pm). In front, the **Simon Dach Fountain** spouts water over the symbol of Klaipėda, a statue of Ännchen von Tharau. The Memel-born Dach wrote a song for the wedding of young Anna, expressing his love for her. You may wonder how the groom felt about Dach's calling Anna, "my soul, my flesh, and my blood," at the wedding. The original statue disappeared in WWII; the copy standing today was erected by German expatriates in 1989. Elsewhere, the fat lady sings at **Klaipedos Muzikinis Teatras,** Danės g. 19 (tel. 21 62 60, tickets tel. 21 62 60 or 21 59 37), which houses operas and other musical events (cashier open Tues.-Sun. 11am-2pm and 4-7pm). The **History Museum of Lithuania Minor,** Didžioji vandens g. (tel. 21 06 00), collects clothing, maps, rusty swords, coins and buttons from the Iron Age to the present (open Wed.-Sun. 11am-7pm; 1Lt). The museum's backyard conceals a **Lenin statue** which, before 1991, graced the square next to Hotel Klaipėda. **Aukštoji g.** is one of the best preserved areas of old Klaipėda. Craftsmen's quarters from the 18th and 19th centuries have been restored for use as shops, cafés, and boutiques. The **castle ruins** (half a moat and some grassy knolls) are worth a glance as you board for Smiltynė.

Smiltynė

The **Sea Museum and Aquarium,** Tomo g. 10 (tel. 39 11 01), housed in an 1860s fortress that protected the entrance to Klaipėda, now swarms with armies of parents and kids. The outer perimeter, buried deep in underground tunnels, displays the port's naval history. Sea lions now frolic in the inner moat, and for a scant 0.50Lt you can buy a fish to toss to them. Inside, Antarctic penguins press their noses to the glass, apparently confident they know which side of the glass holds the exhibit. Above the still-swishing specimens, the museum's second floor cringes in fear of the bad-ass Crab of Kamchatka and other stuffed seafood (open May-Sept. Wed.-Sun. 11am-7pm; June-Aug. Tues.-Sun. 11am-7pm; Oct.-April Sat. and Sun. 11am-6pm; 4Lt, students 2Lt, photos 5Lt). North sea lions kiss trainers and spectators in the **sea lion show** in an adjacent pool-theater at 1pm, 3pm, and 5pm (2Lt; photo of a sea lion kissing you 15Lt; photo of a sea lion kissing Helmut Kohl 15,000Lt). Right next door, the **Dolphinarium** shows off Flipper's friends three times per day (noon, 2 and 4pm; 10Lt, students 5Lt). Then, watch a sea lion nail unsuspecting audience members with a "USA" ball (a highly symbolic action to be sure, but we don't know exactly what it *means*). Both aquatic attractions are located in **Kopgalis** (Head), 1½km from the food-stall-lined ferry landing. Geography buffs will quickly realize that this is also where the Curonian Lagoon meets the Baltic Sea. Take a walk out on the pier, strewn with giant concrete tinker-toys, for a new definition of bleak. Several museums and displays line the road. The **Kuršių Nerija Nature Museum** (tel. 39 11 79) exhibits the Spit's fascinating natural and human history, including dioramas showing the locations of villages buried by the shifting dunes (open daily 11am-6pm; free). The **Veteran Fishing Boats,** four forlorn ships on concrete pillars, sit 20m from the water mainly to make visitors pause and wonder "How did they do that?" It helps to visit the Nature Museum before the **Ethnographic Coastal Fishermen's Village**, a reconstruction of a 17th-century settlement (open daily 24hr.; free). Forest paths lead west about 500m to the **beaches**. By walking north a ways before crossing over you can get a patch of sand to yourself. Signs mark gender-restricted areas for **nude bathing**—*moterų* is women, *vyrų* men. On blustery days, sunbathers retreat to the dunes to avoid wind chill and a good sandblasting.

ENTERTAINMENT

Reminisce about a day on the sand in one—or a dozen—of the Old Town bars. Some are well marked, others appear to be random doorways. All serve strong Lithuanian beer and salted, smoked, and dried fish to make you thirsty for more.

- **Žvejų,** Kurpių g. 10 (tel. 21 49 40). Dark, smoky, and loud with good, clean fun. "The Fishery's" salted herring fuels the thirst for more *Utenos* (3Lt), the local brew of choice. You might need more than one. Open daily from 10am-10pm.
- **Po Herbu,** Tiltų 1 (tel. 21 57 07). The buzzing bistro serves up ice cream (3-5Lt) in all shapes and sizes while the popular bar is an elegant wood-paneled watering hole. Sit outside and people-watch with a *Pilsner Urquell*, or stay inside and spy on the people-watchers. Bistro open daily 8:30am-11pm, bar noon-midnight.
- **Baras Senamiestis,** Bažnyčių 4 (tel. 25 18 44). Dark, velvety hunting lodge with huge wooden rafters and candles. An unobtrusively classy spot with an art gallery upstairs. Entrées around 10Lt, beer 5-10Lt. Open noon-midnight.

■ Kuršių Nerija (The Curonian Spit)

A 3km-wide strip of white dunes, unspoiled beaches, and thick pine forests, Kuršių Nerija is one of the best reasons to come to Lithuania. It's a world of tiny villages nestled in the sandy shores and shady trees where beach-goers emerge from fantastical forest paths to hike over 60m-high dunes for a personal audience with the Baltic Sea.

NIDA

If you're watching the sunrise from a high white dune as the crisp smell of smoked fish rises with sounds of a waking fishing village, you must be in Nida. Encircled by more unruffled sea than any one town has a right to be, Nida should not be missed.

Orientation and Practical Information Visitors make the 50km trip from Klaipėda by **hydrofoil** (5Lt) or by **buses** (2 per day, 2hr., 7Lt) which stop near the intersection of Nida's two main streets. **Taikos g.** heads inland from the ocean and shelters offices. **Naglių g.** follows the shore north to become Pamario g., which continues along the shore. The **tourist office**, Taikos g. 4, offers help and information. The **Tourist Information Center** of Neringa, Taikos g. 4 (tel. 52 34 59), opposite the bus and ferry stations, arranges homestays and has accommodation and transportation information about Nida and the rest of the Curonian Spit (open in summer daily 9am-1pm and 2-8pm; winter 9am-1pm and 2-6pm). **Lietuvos Taupomasis Bankas,** Taikos g. 5 (tel. 522 46), cashes AmEx and Thomas Cook traveler's checks, and provides cash courtesy of MC, Visa, and Western Union to help tourists cover smoked fish expenses. The **post office**, Taikos g. 13, lies up the road (open May-Sept. 10am-1pm and 2-6:30pm; Oct.-April 10am-1pm and 2-3pm). The adjacent **telephone office** (tel. 520 07) has cardphones (open May.-Sept. daily 7am-midnight; Oct.-April daily 8am-11pm). **Postal code:** 5870. **Phone code:** 0259.

Accommodations and Food The **tourist office** (above) is your best bet, arranging bed-and-breakfasts for 20-40Lt per person, per night. If you'll arrive after they close, call ahead, since prices jump quickly as you move to hotels. **Urbo Kalnas,** Taikos g. 32 (tel. 524 28 or 529 53), sprawls over a hill with big, balconied rooms furnishing clean hot showers (95Lt per person; breakfast included). **Rasyte,** Lotmiškio g.

11 (tel. 525 92), has a few rooms for 49Lt per person—book way in advance. If you can pass as a citizen of Lithuania or the CIS, you might get lower rates. If all else fails, call **Litinterp** in Klaipėda (tel. (26) 21 69 62); their usual 60Lt single, 100Lt double prices are hiked 10-15Lt in lovely Nida.

The local specialty, *rūkyta žuvis* (smoked fish), is great as a little meal, a big meal, or a tasty between-meal treat. The taste is, well, smoky, but selection varies from nondescript "fish" to delicate eel and perch. The motto of the now familiarly named restaurant **Rukyta Žuvis**, Naglių g. 18, is "if it swims, you can smoke it." Prices run 4-100Lt. Wash the seastuff down with a local beer (3Lt), and that's all you'll Nida (open daily 10am-10pm). At **Seklyčia**, Lotmiško 1 (tel. 529 45), servers speed delicious platefuls (10-20Lt) to dune-view outdoor seating or an adorable attic eatery, cruising to quality audio (Open Sun.-Thurs. 11am-11pm, Fri.-Sat. 1pm-3am).

Sights and Entertainment The **Drifting Dunes of Parnidis** are impossible to miss. Hikes pass surreal mountains and apocalyptic plains of white sand, suspended 60m above the sea and blowing gracefully into it. Farther south, the nature preserve is technically off-limits, but the footsteps of a few incorrigible tourists cross the line. The dunes here are even more spectacular, visibly in motion, and falling off at an incredible angle to the water below.

All of Nida's **wooden houses** clustered along Naglių g. and Lotmiškio g. are classified as historic monuments; another two whole villages of them are buried somewhere under the sand. From the town's north part, continue north and bear right onto Skruzdynės g. to reach the **Thomas Mann House** at #17 (tel. 522 60; open Tues.-Sun. 10am-5pm; 1Lt), where the famous writer spent three summers. Trails to the west lead to impressive **pine forests**.

The **pier** near Skruzdynės g. is one of the better places to catch twilight. The sunset lights up a cottony plane of clouds so solid and close that they seem climbable, as the Curonian Lagoon stretches to the edge of vision. When darkness finally wins, step back into **Savas**, Skruzdynės g. (tel. 528 32), for more artificial delights. Graffiti-covered windows hide the only youth bar in town, accordingly packed with tourists and locals sucking down 5Lt 0.5L of *Kalnapilis* (open daily 4pm-6am for travelers up past their bed-time).

FORMER YUGOSLAV REPUBLIC OF MACEDONIA (МАКЕДОНИЈА)

US$1 = 42dn (denars)	10dn = US$0.26
CDN$1 = 31dn	10dn = CDN$0.33
UK£1 = 65dn	10dn = UK£0.15
IR£1 = 68dn	10dn = IR£0.15
AUS$1 = 33dn	10dn = AUS$0.30
NZ$1 = 29dn	10dn = NZ$0.34
SAR1 = 9dn	10dn = SAR 1.06

DM1 = 28dn
Country Phone Code: 389

10dn = DM0.35
International Dialing Prefix: 99

Formerly a vacation hotspot in the Yugoslav federation, a free but frail Macedonia has been struggling under the weight of the trade embargoes which have damaged its economy. Despite the economic damage, Macedonia managed to stay entirely out of the latest war in the Balkans, and its treasures remain intact and accessible. Located along pivotal East-West trade and pilgrimage routes since Roman times, Macedonia offers sights and sites that run the gamut of history and geography—most notably the spectacular mountain basin which is home to Lake Ohrid.

> For the sake of brevity, *Let's Go* uses the name "Macedonia" throughout this chapter to refer to the Former Yugoslav Republic of Macedonia. *Let's Go* does not endorse any perceived claims of the former Yugoslav Republic to the Greek territory of the same name. Yes, we are toadies to Balkan irrationality.

MACEDONIA ESSENTIALS

Citizens of the U.K. and Ireland need only a valid passport. Citizens of Australia, Canada, and the U.S. can procure visas at any border crossing at no cost. New Zealanders and South Africans must submit their passport to an embassy or consulate (US$14 for 90-day single-entry). Allow 10 days for processing.

GETTING THERE AND GETTING AROUND

You can reach Macedonia by **air**, bus, or train. **Adria** (Slovenian), **Balkan** (Bulgarian), and **PALAIR** (Macedonian) fly to the capital, Skopje. Many people prefer to travel over land from Sofia, Bulgaria or Thessaloniki, Greece to gain access to a broader range of international flights and avoid the smog that causes frequent closures of the Skopje airport. A private **bus** company in Skopje located near the old train station is challenging the former monopoly of state run **Proleter**, which still runs international lines. Buses connect Istanbul, Sofia, Tirana, and other cities to various towns in Macedonia. Be warned: border crossings can take a long time, as there are often traffic backups for miles. The **train** system is not extensive and train tickets are usually more expensive than bus tickets. Luckily, buses run reliably and frequently to most destinations. Helpful words include билет (*bilet;* ticket), воз (*voz;* train), железница (*zheleznitsa;* railway), автобус (*avtobus;* bus), станица (*stanitsa;* station), повратен билет (*povraten bilet;* return ticket), линија (*linia;* track), перон (*peron;* platform), информација (*informatsia;* information), труганье (*trugvanye;* departures), and пристигнуванье (*pristignuvanye;* arrival). **Hitchhiking** in Macedonia is becoming increasingly dangerous, especially for foreigners.

As the country de-Communizes, street names change but old street signs remain. When asking for directions, use both the new and the old names; locals may be unaware of the change. Get a copy of a new map in English as soon as you arrive.

TOURIST SERVICES

The Macedonian government still operates **tourist bureaus** throughout the country which give out maps, often rent **private rooms**, and sell train and airline tickets. Look for the "i" signs. **Shops** are generally open 8am-8pm; weekend hours vary. Some **banks**, especially in tourist areas, are open all week. Expect an hour break starting around noon or 2pm at most offices and shops. In high season, many towns operate at a more frenetic pace, and services stay open later.

MONEY

The monetary unit is the **denar**, which comes in notes of 10, 20, 50, 100, and 500 denars, and in coins of one, two, and five denars. Exchange rates vary little from bank to bank. Hotels have worse rates, and changing money on the street is illegal. Most hard currency prices in Macedonia are given in **Deutschmarks (DM);** although most banks will readily accept U.S. dollars and British pounds and cash **AmEx** traveler's checks. Few places accept **credit cards,** and even some major hotels accept only cash. **ATMs** accepting MC and Cirrus have appeared in Skopje.

COMMUNICATION

Placing calls via Macedonia's **AT&T Direct** operator (tel. (99) 800 42 88) may be difficult. To get an international line, dial 99. Calls to the U.S. average US$2 per minute. At the post office, service is generally efficient, but employees, even in the capital, often have no idea that calling card or collect calls can be made from Macedonia. They may express disbelief at the absence of a charge on the telephone counter. Firmly insist that the counter is correct. To make local calls from public phones, you must buy a 4dn *zheton* (жетон, token) or a microchip phone card (75dn or 150dn) at a post office. Some kiosks also sell them, or lend their own phones at a small charge. When calling home, remember: Macedonia is one hour ahead of GMT.

Faxes can be sent at most phone centers for prices comparable to phone calls. **Photocopy** centers abound. Look for the sign "Фотокопир". Prices range from 2 to 8 dinars per copy. Some businesses in Skopje have access to **e-mail.** If you are desperate to log on, beg at the American Center in Skopje. There is **Internet access** (3.5dn per minute) at the Vardar post office in Skopje (window #22). Large hotels televise **CNN** in their lobbies, kiosks sell *Newsweek* and *Time,* the radio broadcasts **Voice of America** and **BBC,** and local TV features subtitled American movies.

LANGUAGE

Macedonian and **Bulgarian** are mutually intelligible. **Russian** is widely understood, as is **Serbian,** but it would be wise to ask before using either. **English** is quickly becoming the second language of choice in Macedonia, and many young people in urban areas are fluent. Macedonian-English phrasebooks (разговорник; *razgovornik*) are sold at bookstores and kiosks throughout the country for 150dn. The **head movements** for "yes" and "no" are reversed from in the U.S., although younger Macedonians may do it the familiar way; confirm everything with words. For more information, see the Cyrillic Alphabet, p. 771, and the Macedonian section of the Glossary, p. 782.

HEALTH AND SAFETY

> **Emergency Numbers: Police:** tel. 92. **Ambulance:** tel. 94.

Visitors should avoid traveling near the border with Serbia; relations between the two countries are tense, and shots have been fired by border patrols. Crossing into Albania can be dangerous at night with a private or rented car—bus travel is safer. Emergency numbers are listed above, but for English-speaking help, turn to your embassy.

Pack a small bar of soap and some toilet paper for the **public bathrooms.** Basic **medicines** are widely available in Macedonian **pharmacies** (аптека; *apteka*). *Analgin Cafetin* is aspirin, and *Arbid* is cold medicine. Bandages are *Flexogal.* **Condoms** are sold in kiosks and sometimes in pharmacies (10dn; neon green, purple, or red). If you are particular about brands, bring your own supplies, especially for **feminine hygiene products.** If you are taken seriously ill, the Faculty of Medicine at the University in Skopje is the best bet. Facilities may not be up to your home country's standards, but they are reasonable. You will be asked to pre-pay for treatment.

The **climate** in Macedonia is generally mild (see Appendices: Climate, p. 763). Mountain areas receive snow from early fall to late spring. Summers can be stifling while winters are often icy cold—especially when the heat is turned off for eight hours nightly.

ACCOMMODATIONS AND CAMPING

The hotel or hostel will take your passport at check-in: all businesses offering accommodations are required by law to **register** passports with the police. You'll get the passport back at the end of your stay; try to get it back earlier if you are expecting *Poste Restante* or plan to cash traveler's checks. If you are crashing with friends, they officially must do this as well, although this law is often ignored.

Private rooms outside Lakes Ohrid and Prespa are expensive (750dn) and difficult to find. Check with the nearest tourist office. In the resorts, you'll be met at the bus and train stations by room-renting locals. Prices improve with haggling. **Hotels** are exorbitantly expensive (2000-3000dn per person in summer). Service is better, and prices more reasonable at new private establishments (600-800dn per person). **Youth hostels** are usually outside urban centers; make reservations for most Macedonian hostels at the Skopje hostel. Many **campgrounds** are in a state of disarray with sacked or destroyed caravans. Call before heading out. Free-lance **camping** is popular, but you risk a fine and it's not safe. Camping in reserve areas is prohibited.

FOOD AND DRINK

Food is not cheap in Macedonia. Kiosks sell grilled meats (скара; *skara*), especially small hamburgers (плескавица; *pleskavitsa;* 35dn), and *burek* (бурек; delicious, warm filo-dough pastry stuffed with veggies, feta cheese, or meat; 30-35dn). Fruits and vegetables can be bought at outdoor markets or *pazar* (пазар). The standard *shopska* salad consists of cucumber, tomato, onion, and grated feta cheese. *Letnitsa* trout, found only in Lake Ohrid, is expensive. *Eyeyar* and *rindzur* are tomato-based pasta dishes. *Chorba* (чорба; a thick type of soup) is a popular mid-morning snack. Wash it all down with delicious Macedonian wine (вино; *vino*) or *rakiya*, a grape or plum brandy. The water is safe to drink, and there are fountains in touristed areas.

CUSTOMS AND ETIQUETTE

Tipping is not customary, but it is appreciated. When restaurants are crowded, share a table with the locals and practice your Macedonian. **Homosexuality** is illegal in Macedonia, and there is a general lack of tolerance towards lesbians and gay men. Life here will be easier if you do not express views or preferences openly.

LIFE AND TIMES

HISTORY

The **Greek Migrations** of 1200-1000BCE forced the Myceneans out of the Peloponnese and settled what is now the Republic of Macedonia with iron-wielding **Dorians**. The flourishing Greek culture to the south only seeped into the fringes of the area, then known as **Paeonia**. King Philip II of Macedonia (Macedonia was then situated just to the south of the modern Republic of Macedonia) joined Paeonia with his kingdom in 358BCE, incorporating it into the Empire which, under his son Alexander the Great, would stretch from Albania to the Indus. Following Alexander's death, Macedonia fell to General Cassander, whose kingdom was lost to invading La Tène Celts and the acquisitive **Antigonid** family after his death in early 3rd century.

Macedonia, including east Paeonia, was ruled by the Antigonids from 279 to 168BCE. Alliances with Carthage and Egypt led to losses to Rome in the first and second **Macedonian Wars,** while the third Macedonian War (171-168BCE) found Paeonia split from its southern neighbors. It remained an independent territory for some years before being incorporated into the larger **Roman** province of Macedon in 29CE. Under Roman rule, Paeonia enjoyed over five centuries of grazing cattle and quiet *pax,* while the Romans built the foundations of cities that exist today, notably Heraclea Lyncestis (present-day Bitola) and Skupi (present-day Skopje).

Change came in the 3rd century with the arrival of the rampaging Goths, Huns, Bulgars, and Avars. The Visigoths tore through the Balkans on their way to Italy and Spain, opening up Paeonia to settlement by **Balkan Slavs,** who arrived steadily over the next 300 years. These Slavs, the ancestors of the Republic's modern inhabitants, were soon re-incorporated into the Byzantine Empire under a system of tenuous military alliances that lasted well into the 13th century. The **Byzantines** and **Bulgarians** periodically warred over the territory from the 7th to 14th centuries, both empires treating the people as spoils and inserting their own nobles as feudal overlords. Serbian control from 1330 ended with the Battle of Kosovo in 1389, and over the next 70 years the territory was completely absorbed into the Ottoman Empire.

It is this **diverse heritage** of Greek and Slavic origins that has laid the foundation for contemporary conflict in Macedonia. The Christian government and culture brought by the Greek-speaking Byzantines competes with the traditions of the Slavs. The situation was complicated by the work of the 9th-century missionaries **Cyril** and **Methodius,** who by creating the Cyrillic alphabet brought Christianity into the vernacular, but were still tied to Constantinople. In addition, various Slavic groups (notably the Bulgars and the Serbs) claim Macedonia on historical grounds: the **Bulgars** were a dominant Balkan power under Simeon I (893-927) and later in 976-1014, and Bulgarian is linguistically similar to Macedonian; the **Serb** claims rest on the basis of their predominance in the area under the Serbian Nemanjić dynasty in the 14th century. Least disputed is the influence of the **Ottoman Turks** who controlled Macedonia from the end of the 14th century until 1913.

In the 19th century, the Balkan Slavs began agitating for independence. At the same time, the Great Powers (Austria-Hungary, Britain, France, Prussia, and Russia) became interested in the territories of the faltering Ottoman Empire. With Russian backing, the Slavs went to war in the late 1870s. After the fall of Pleven to Slavic forces, the Ottomans signed a truce on January 31, 1878, but Macedonia remained in Turkish hands. In reaction, Macedonians created the **International Macedonian Revolutionary Organization (IMRO)** in 1893, whose slogan was "Macedonia for the Macedonians." Twelve years later, every power in the Balkans fought over Macedonia in the **First Balkan War.** The Ottomans were quickly defeated, but the victors could not agree on how to divide the spoils. Bulgarian troops turned on their Serbian and Greek allies, causing the **Second Balkan War.** The Bulgarians were defeated and most of what would eventually become the Republic of Macedonia fell to Serbia. The **post-WWI** settlement confirmed this partitioning. In the years leading up to WWII, different Macedonias were artificially created (Vardar Macedonia and Aegean Macedonia) and countries fought for influence. During **WWII,** Macedonia was again partitioned, this time in 1941 between the Axis powers. Most of Macedonia was occupied by Bulgaria, though parts were combined with Albania and placed under Italian control.

When Macedonia was incorporated into **Yugoslavia,** an attempt was made to include each ethnic group in the government; each Balkan state was given republic status. Yugoslavia soon broke with the Soviet Union in favor of the non-Warsaw Pact Communism of **Tito.** Under Tito, Macedonian language, literature, and culture were revived, and the Church was brought back. In 1958, the archbishopric of Ohrid was restored, signifying a break with the Serbian Church. Macedonia was the least successful of the Yugoslav republics economically, though its loyalty to the federation remained unwavering even through debates over republican autonomy and the suppression of liberal Marxism in Macedonia. Eventually, however, popular support for independence could not be denied; on September 8, 1991, 96% of the population in Macedonia voted for **independence** from Yugoslavia.

LITERATURE

Tracing the roots of Macedonian Slav literature is as problematic as giving the fledgling country a politically acceptable name. So long occupied by foreign powers, the indigenous population (a portion of which occupies regions of modern-day Bulgaria) had little chance to bring their language to a literary level—Macedonian was not even officially recognized as a literary language until 1944, when Tito granted Macedonia republic status.

Until the 20th century, Macedonians and Bulgarians shared a literary tradition. Then, in 1903, **Krste Misirkov** published *Makedonskite Raboti* (On Macedonian Matters) in the Bitola dialect. This marked the divergence of the two, set the standard for later Macedonian writers, and set the stage for conflict between these writers and the reigning governments, who still opposed the language's literary use. One writer, **Bole Nedelkovski** (1912-1941), committed suicide rather than submit to arrest by Bulgarian authorities. Only three years later, the newly-formed Yugoslavia granted Macedonian official language status, and the legitimized tongue slipped into schools, theaters, and the mass media. **Yanevski** published the first Macedonian novel in 1953. The first works focused on the war and patriotic concerns, but soon diversified into themes ranging from the dream-lands of **Chingo** to the recent *Sok od prostrata (Prostratic gland juice)* by **Yovan Pavlovski**.

MACEDONIA TODAY

There are half a million more sheep in Macedonia than there are people. If only the people got along as well as the sheep! Ethnic tensions have risen among Slavic Macedonians, Albanians, Serbs, and Bulgars. Mosques mingle with Orthodox churches and nationalist propaganda is prevalent, the result of 50 years of brainwashing by Serbian leaders. Once weakened by U.N.-enforced embargoes from the north and Greek trade blockades from the south, Macedonia is now making a comeback. The U.S. is pumping aid into the strategically located nation, and the end of the war to the north is allowing trade routes to open. Most importantly, in January 1996, Greece, which originally contended that the new nation's name, currency, flag, and constitution, all implied pretensions to the Greek province of the same name, lifted its embargoes. In turn, the new republic may soon change its name to "New" or "North" Macedonia.

Skopje (Скопје)

The rolling hills, fields of sunflowers, and orange-roofed suburbs that surround Skopje lend the city an air of serenity. Contrary to popular misconceptions, Skopje is not a war zone, although in 1963, a disastrous earthquake did destroy 90% of the city's structures. As a result, international aid poured in to rebuild the city with some of the less repulsive examples of social futurism. Fortunately for those who prefer all things old, fate spared the town's mighty Old Bazaar, and old-school minarets still rise above the city's green parks.

ORIENTATION AND PRACTICAL INFORMATION

Despite being a city of half a million, Skopje has managed to keep most points of interest along a small stretch of the **Vardar River**. Several bridges, most notably the stone pedestrian **Kamen most** (Камен мост), connect the old and new sections of the city. The main **shopping center** (Трговски центар; *Trgovski tsentar*) is on the river next to **Macedonia Square** (Македонији). **Maps** of Skopje are sold at the tourist office and at some kiosks. Be sure the map has a decoder on the back; some only number streets, neglecting to include the names that the numbers stand for. While some street signs are in Latin script, most are printed in Cyrillic. To add to the confusion, city leaders have changed "red" names to democratic ones, though the signs have not been changed and people still refer to the streets by the old names.

> **Tourist Office: Tourist Association of Skopje** (Туристички Сојуз на Скопје), Dame Gruev, blok III, p.f. 399 (Даме Груев; tel. 11 84 98; fax 23 08 03). Runs information and tourist bureaus around town. Look for the "i" signs. One of the **tourist agencies** (Туристичка Агенција; tel. 11 68 54; fax 61 34 47), is around the corner from the bus station across from the low-lying domes of the Turkish Baths, in the building of

Skopje

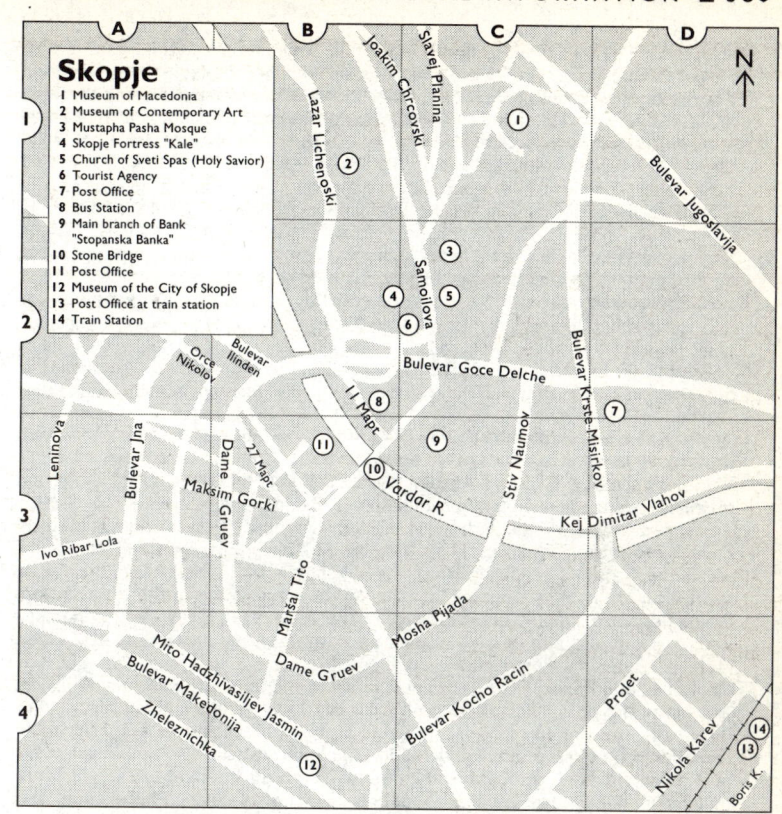

1. Museum of Macedonia
2. Museum of Contemporary Art
3. Mustapha Pasha Mosque
4. Skopje Fortress "Kale"
5. Church of Sveti Spas (Holy Savior)
6. Tourist Agency
7. Post Office
8. Bus Station
9. Main branch of Bank "Stopanska Banka"
10. Stone Bridge
11. Post Office
12. Museum of the City of Skopje
13. Post Office at train station
14. Train Station

shopping center "Most" (Мост). Cheery English-speakers provide maps of the city (100dn). Books rooms for 800dn including breakfast, private rooms for DM20-30. Polyglot guides for US$80-120. Up to 30% discounts on air tickets for travelers under 25. Open Mon.-Sat. 8am-8pm, Sun. 9am-2pm.

Embassies and Cultural Centers: U.K., Velko Vlakhovic 26, 4th floor (Велько Влах-овик; tel. 11 67 72; fax 11 70 05). U.S., British, and German flags out front. Citizens of **Australia, Canada,** and **New Zealand** should contact the U.K. office. Open Mon.-Thurs. 8am-4:30pm, Fri. 8am-1pm. **U.S.,** Bulevar Ilinden (Илинден; tel. 11 61 80; fax 11 71 03). Open Mon.-Fri. 8am-4:15pm. **American Cultural Center,** Nikola Vaptsarov 4 (Никола Вапцаров; tel. 11 66 23; fax 11 84 31), has an air-conditioned library replete with English newspapers and books. Open Mon.-Fri. 11am-4pm. Ask for the ex-pat newsletter chock-full of info on Macedonia.

Currency Exchange: Stopanska Banka, Tushinska (Тушинска; tel. 11 53 22; fax 11 45 03), across from the bus station, exchanges money and cashes traveler's checks. Open Mon.-Fri. 7am-7pm, Sat. 7am-1pm.

ATMs: Komertsialna Banka (Комерцијална Банка) operates 3 ATMs around town, the most convenient in the City Shopping Center. Cirrus and MC accepted.

Flights: Skopje Airport (tel. 11 28 75), 23km from downtown, is near the hamlet Petrovech. Slovenian **Adria** (tel. 23 55 31), Dame Gruev 11. Macedonian **PALAIR** (tel. 23 82 38), at the shopping center. **Balkan** (tel. 11 30 22), Lui Paster 5 (Луј Пастер). A taxi to Skopje airport is 800-1000dn.

Trains: (tel. 23 42 55) Bulevar Kuzman Yosifovsku (Кузман Јосифовски). International (меѓународна; *medzhunarodna*) tickets sold upstairs, domestic downstairs. To: Budapest (2 per day, 24hr., 3370dn); Thessaloniki (2 per day, 5hr., 560dn).

Buses: (tel. 23 62 54), at the entrance to the Old Town. From the train station, walk 3 blocks to the river, keeping the mountains on your left, then cross the 3rd bridge. **Tourist Agency Proleter** (Пролетер; tel 23 75 32) at the bus station also runs buses to Sofia (4 per day, 7hr., 440dn). The international terminal (Македонија сообракај; *Makedonija soobrakaj*), Mito Hadzhivasilev 1 (Мито Хациваcилев; tel. 11 17 20 or 11 63 45), left of the old train station. To: Sofia (3 per day, 7hr., DM15); Tirana (8-12hr., DM30); Istanbul (4 per day, 12 hr., DM40).

Public Transportation: Buy tickets for public buses from kiosks (20dn) or the driver (30dn), then stamp on board. Private buses run the same routes (10dn, pay on bus). In an effort to win back passengers and eliminate private competition, the public buses may have a seasonal bus fare of 10dn.

Taxis: Radiotaxi Vodno (tel. 91 91). Taxis crawl the streets with lost-people antennae. Relatively safe and reliable. 10dn to get in, 20dn per km (more if you look rich). **Radiotaxi Jambo** (tel. 91 81).

Car Rental: Avis Rent-a-car (tel. 22 20 46; fax 22 11 32), near Hotel Continental, in the same business center as DHL. One day rentals plus insurance (a good idea) start at around DM100.

Luggage Storage: Garderoba (Гардероба), at the domestic bus station. 40dn. Open daily 5am-10pm (often closes by 9:15pm).

24-Hour Pharmacy: Gradska Apteka (Градска Аптека; tel. 23 76 17). The second pharmacy in the main shopping mall hasn't closed in the last 20 years.

Medical Assistance: Contact a hotel receptionist. Skopje's best hospital is **Medical Faculty Hospital,** Vodnanska (Воднанска; tel. 11 42 44). **Emergencies:** tel. 94.

Post Office: Cross Kamen bridge from the bus station, take a right along the Vardar and follow the yellow signs to E.T.'s concrete space office in the train station. **Poste Restante.** Open daily 8am-8pm. **Postal code:** 91101. Also in the train station: passport and 2dn needed to pick up *Poste Restante* at window #20. Open Mon.-Sat. 7am-8pm. **Postal code:** 91000.

Telephones and Faxes: Next to the post office in the train station. Open Mon.-Sat. 7am-8pm. The post office along the Vardar has 24-hr. phone and fax service. For local calls, use the 4dn *zheton,* available at post offices and kiosks. **Microchip cards** for 5dn (100 impulses) and 150dn (200 impulses) can also be bought at the post office and used throughout the country (even for international calls). **Kiosk** owners often let people use their phones for a couple of dinars. **Phone code:** 91.

ACCOMMODATIONS

Accommodations are scarce and overpriced. Most hotels, still state-run, charge 3000-5000dn per person. Some private pensions are popping up, but the best bet may be private rooms booked through the tourist office (700dn, breakfast included). Although haggling will not help in the state-run hotels, it often gets you a cheaper room in private ones.

Youth Hostel Skopje (HI), Prolet 25 (Пролет; tel. 11 48 49; fax 23 50 29). From the train station, walk toward the river along Kuzman Yosifovski and take the second left onto Prolet to the big building with psychedelic murals. English-speaking reception. Recently refurbished with new fleet of beds. Doubles with shower and 3-bed apartments with shower and TV (830dn per person; nonmembers 1050dn), doubles, triples, or quads with hallway showers and stand-up toilet (549dn per person; nonmembers 610dn). Breakfast included. Provides info on nightlife.

Student dorm Gotse Delchev (Гоце Делчев; tel. 36 33 06), offers spartan rooms with shared showers for the standard fare of 350dn in July-Aug. It's 4km from the center. Take bus #5 from the train station and ask for *Studentski Dom Kuzman*.

Hotel Lackey (Хотел Лаки), Leninova 79 (Ленинова; tel. 23 55 97), is in the southwest. One of Skopje's first private hotels. Taller than they are wide, the rooms at least have private showers. Prices start at DM25 per person. Reception open daily 7am-midnight; check the restaurant downstairs if no one is at the desk.

Autokamp (tel./fax 22 82 46), on the river out by the stadium/park. English spoken. Rows upon rows of 4-person caravans at 300dn per person. 160dn per tent, 160dn per person. Stand-up toilets.

FOOD

You'll find Skopje's best dishes toasting over coals in the streets of the **Old Bazaar** (Стара Чаршија). Many locals start their day with a *chorba* (чорба; a thick soup of some kind or another), leaving the more substantial *shish kebabs,* grilled peppers, and the local *tavche gravche* (тавче гравче; greasy beans topped with *shish kebab* bits) to tempt strollers with spicy aromas. Kiosks specialize in inexpensive hot sandwiches. The Old Bazaar's north end hosts a huge vegetable market, and the adjacent **Bitpazar** (Битпазар; flea market) has everything else. Groceries stay open all week.

- **Bratstvo** (Братство), Pokriena Charshiya 82 (Покриена Чаршија; tel. 11 61 52). Tables on a busy intersection in the Old Bazaar with a great view of the Mustafa Pasha Mosque. Experience the buzz of a crowd and the whiz of antique motorcycle carts while digging into mousaka (100dn) or *tavche gravche* (120dn). English, Dutch, Russian, Turkish, and Albanian spoken. Open daily 6am-11pm.
- **Gostilnitsa Tourist** (Гостилница Турист; tel. 22 90 04), on the Old Bazaar's fountain square. For 85dn you can feast on a boiled head of lamb (eyeballs and brain included) or pay up to 300dn for a lamb's kidney, heart, and liver. For the less adventurous, there are more mundane salads (33dn) and grills (*kebabs*; burgers; 100dn). The *baklava* and *kadaif* (a pastry desert) give perfect closure to a good meal. Open daily 7am-until the last customer leaves.
- **Beerhouse An** (Пивница Ан; Pivnitsa An; tel. 22 18 17), down the steps and through the wooden gates in the Old Bazaar's fountain square. In the courtyard of a restored old house. Enjoy meat dishes like filet-mignon (Филе Мињон; 330dn) or less substantial grills (120-160dn). Desserts 60-100dn. English menu. Open 24hr.
- **Dal Metu Fu** (Дал Мету Фу), pl. Makedoniya (tel. 11 24 82). Imaginative pizzas, like the Indiana (tomato, cheese, chicken, and curry sauce, 169dn), pasta (148-169dn), and 25 kinds of chicken, beef, and pork dishes (290-390dn) served in a huge, bright joint. Open Mon.-Sat. 9am-midnight, Sun. 6pm-midnight.
- **Restaurant Simplon** (Симплон; tel. 23 32 53) operates out of a restored railroad car behind and a bit to the left of the old train station. The *shkembe chorba* (60dn), made of the lining of a lamb's stomach, is a love-it-or-hate-it affair with lots of garlic. Meat dishes (140-210dn); salads (30-70dn). Open daily 7am-midnight.

SIGHTS AND ENTERTAINMENT

Most of Skopje's historical sights are an easy walk from the bus station. The domes of the 15th-century **Turkish Baths** (Даут-пашин Амам; *Daut-pashin Amam,* tel. 23 39 04), now an art gallery with a different exhibition every month, are visible from the bus station. Perfect acoustics make the baths a desirable venue for concerts from the Festival Skopsko Leto (Скопско Лето; open Mon.-Sat. 8am-7pm, Sun. 8am-1pm; 30dn, students with ID free; call for concert schedule). The baths serve as a gateway to the **Old Bazaar's** enchanting streets. Largely Albanian and Muslim, the really Old Bazaar (Стара Чаршија) stands in stark contrast to the modern side of town. Bear left up Samoilova (Самоилова) to the **Church of Sveti Spas** (Свети Спас; tel. 23 38 12). Frescos of God and a few angels hover over marble floors and a masterful walnut iconostasis that took seven years to carve. Much of the interior is below ground level; Christian temples were once prohibited from being higher than mosques. In the courtyard a sarcophagus holds revolutionary Gotse Delchev, who died in 1903 (open Mon.-Fri. 7am-7pm, Sat. 9am-3pm, Sun. 9am-1pm; 50dn).

Farther up Samoilova, the **Mustafa Pasha Mosque** (Мустафа Пашина Џамија; *Mustafa Pashina Dzhamiya*) marks its 503rd year in this world, a miraculous survivor of the 1963 quake. Every Friday at 1:20pm, hundreds gather to listen to the Hodzha. The mosque's key-holder will let you in anytime he's around. The mosque with the insanely tall minaret belonged to Mustafa Pasha's brother, **Jaja Pasha,** who decided to match the height of Mustafa's temple despite the inferior valley site. Nearby, the elegant **Turkish Inn** (Куршумли Хан; *Kurshumli Han*) recalls five centuries of Ottoman occupation. Located in the Old Bazaar's former ironmongers' district, the inn served as a prison until it became part of **Muzey na Makedonia** (Музеј на Македонија). The museum's main building (tel. 11 60 44) gleams across a large courtyard with its three permanent exhibits—archaeological, ethnographic, and historical, each wing a nationalistic picture of the Macedonian past. English or Russian tour included in the ticket (100dn, students 50dn).

Even farther up Samoilova, the **Museum of Modern Art** (Музеj на современата уметност; *Muzey na sovremenata umetnost;* tel. 11 77 35; fax 23 63 72) occupies the highest point in central Skopje. Its collection does have a Picasso, but very little else. Nevertheless, the hike to the top of the hill is worth it, if only for the all-inclusive view of Skopje (open Tues.-Sat. 10am-5pm, Sun. 9am-1pm).

Walking back to Vardar's banks, you'll see that the crumbling **Turkish Fortress** (Кале; *Kale*) has turned into weedy pastures. On sunny afternoons, the base is covered with Yugos and the picnickers they transported to the vista. Backtrack to the 6th-century **Stone bridge** (Камен мост; *Kamen most*), one of the few structures to survive the 1963 earthquake. Monopolized by cheap t-shirt and fake-Marlboro peddlers, the aging thoroughfare leads to Skopje's New Town plaza. Since Macedonia's break with Yugoslavia, Marshal Tito Square sports a new name: Macedonia Square.

Follow Macedonia street to the city's **Old Railway Station.** Largely destroyed during the 1963 quake, the station has become the **Skopje City Museum** (Музеj на град Скопjе; *Muzey na grad Skopje*), Mito Hadzhivasilev Jasmin (Мито Хаџивасилев Јасмин; tel. 11 47 42), with more than 30 temporary exhibits per year of paintings, photographs, architectural, and archaeological articles. The world famous—at least among archaeologists—**Thracian Treasure** of Bulgaria is expected to be the highlight of 1997 (open Tues.-Sat. 9:30am-5pm, Sun. 9:30am-3pm).

Party-hungry Skopjeans gather at bars in the central mall to bar- and disco-hop until the wee hours. You can follow other disco-zombies to disco club **Playa Vista** at the outdoor swimming complex on the Old Bazaar side of the river (more or less opposite the stadium). The music is usually loud enough to be your guide from miles away (cover 50dn; open daily 9pm-whenever). **Club MNT** (МНТ Клуб) is underneath the City Cultural Center. Geared for a slightly older crowd, it opens only Friday and Saturday nights (cover 100dn; 10pm-morning).

LAKE OHRID

■ Ohrid (Охрид)

Ohrid is the lake's premier summer resort. A profusion of cafés fan out from the main square by the shore and give way to small shops on narrow streets up the sloping Old Town. Like so many Balkan towns, Ohrid changed hands several times. Romans, Slavs, and Ottomans left their mark, and for a while it was even Bulgaria's capital. Only the legacy of Yugoslav Socialism with its penchant for concrete is largely missing, thanks to UNESCO's designation of Ohrid as a protected town.

Orientation and Practical Information To get to the center from the bus station, make a right onto Partizanska (Партизанска). The collection of orange-roofed, white houses on the hill is the Old Town. At the foot of the hill, **Sveti Kliment Ohridski** (Климент Охридски) serves as Ohrid's pedestrian main street. The **tourist office AD Galeb-Bilyana** (АД Галеб-Биljана), Partizanska 3 (tel. 224 94; fax 241 14), one of many tourist bureaus in the center, finds **private rooms** (330-370dn per person; apartments from 1100dn) and sells new **maps.** Tour **guides** run 2000dn per day (open daily 7am-9pm; off season Mon.-Sat. 7am-8pm). **Buses** go to Skopje (10 per day, 3½-5hr., 235-270dn). The quickest route (3½hr., 235dn; via Kichevo); the longer west route winds through mountains (5hr., 270dn). **Exchange money** and cash AmEx traveler's checks at **Ohridska Banka** (Охридска Банка) on the corner of Makedonsk Prosvetiteli (Македонски Просветители) and Turistichka Blvd. (Туристичка; tel. 314 00; open high-season daily 7am-9pm; off-season Mon.-Sat. 9am-5pm). Store **lug-**

OHRID

gage at the bus station (50dn). The **post office**, on Makedonski Prosvetiteli, runs an **exchange** (open Mon.-Sat. 7am-9pm, Sun. 9am-noon). **Telephones** and **faxes** (fax 322 15) are in the post office (open Mon.-Sat. 7am-9pm, Sun. 6am-8pm). **Postal code:** 96000. **Phone code:** 096.

Accommodations and Camping Travelers getting off the bus in Ohrid are bombarded by offers of **private rooms**. The rates are good (270-400dn), but lower-end prices usually don't include the 80dn **registration fee**. In addition, some rooms will be far from the town center or high up a hill. Find out where the room is located and what exactly the price includes, then bargain. The shy can shun the madness by going to the **tourist bureau** (rooms 330-370dn). **Lyupcho Mileski,** Dame Gruev 37 (Даме Груев; tel. 322 17), offers a double with its own terrace and two triples with a common shower/bath for US$10/DM15 a head. The town's two **youth hostels** sit together 2.5km from the town center. **Hostel Magnus** (Магнус; tel. 216 71; fax 322 14) works as a hotel (no lockouts). Beds cost 850dn with meals included, 500dn with just breakfast (20% off-season discount). Rooms have two, three, or four beds, with clean bathrooms. A private beach, soccer area, and nightly live music amuse homebodies. **Hostel Mladost** (Младост; tel. 216 26) rents four-person caravans and two- to five-bed rooms. Full room and board is DM16, bed and breakfast DM13, and just a bed DM8. Take any bus headed for Struga (Струга; every 15min., 35dn) and tell the driver to stop at "Mladost", or walk up Gotse Delchev (Гоце Делчев) and take a left at the drugstore "Shkor" (Драгстор "Шкор").

Food A mini-market sells all you need on Sveti Kliment Ohridski (open daily 7am-11pm). The **town market** (Градско Пазариште; *Gradsko Pazarishte*) vends fruits and vegetables daily between Gotse Delchev and Turistichka. **Letnitsa** (Летница; tel. 224 96), on the left side of Sveti Kliment Ohridski as you walk towards the lake, occupies a huge building and three terraces (open daily 7am-midnight). A dish of the famous Ohrid fish runs 300dn, soups sell for 50dn on average, and meat dishes start at 160dn. Accepts AmEx, Diner's Club, MC, and Visa. **Pizzeria Cosa Nostra** (tel. 324 17), in the Letnitsa complex on a second-floor balcony, offers 24 kinds of pizza, including Cosa Nostra—a concoction of sauce, ham, cheese, mushrooms, bacon, eggs, mayonnaise, cream cheese, olives, and sausage (large 250dn)—and Erotica (210dn), which is consumed in large numbers by the curious and/or hopeful (open daily 9am-2am). Prices at **Restaurant Antico,** Tsar Samoil 30 (tel. 235 23),seem to include an involuntary contribution to the restoration of its UNESCO-protected house, home of the 180dn banana split. The two floors ensure your privacy amid old copper kitchenware and engraved wooden beams. Trout is 1300dn, meat dishes average 250dn, salads 30-80dn. English menu. Diner's Club accepted.

Sights and Entertainment **Sveta Sofia** (Света Софија), Ohrid's oldest preserved church, was built in the 9th century on the foundations of an even earlier church. In surprisingly good shape, the 11th-century frescos depict both Old and New Testament scenes. During the Ottoman Empire's domination of the town, the church served as a mosque. To get there, take Tsar Samoil and choose the left branch at the fork (open daily 9am-7pm; 100dn, students 50dn). Performances of the **Festival Ohridsko Leto** (July 12-Aug. 20) and the **Balkan Folklore Festival** (July 5-10) are held with the church as a backdrop. Up the hill from Sveta Sofia, go up Ilindenska then take a right toward the church of **Sveti Kliment** (Свети Климент), formerly devoted to the Virgin Mary. In one part, frescos are devoted to the holy teachers of the Christian faith, the Virgin, and the life of Christ (open daily 9am-8pm; 100dn, students 50dn). Across from the church sits the **Icon Gallery**, with works spanning seven centuries, including depictions of stoic saints enduring torture (open Tues.-Sun. 9-10:30am, 11am-2pm, and 5-8pm). The 13th-century **Sveti Yovan** (Свети Јован) perches on the lip of a cliff overlooking the lake. Take the steps behind Sveta Sofia (to the left as you exit) to Kocho Ratsin (Кочо Рацин), then follow the cliff path to the church. The sun sets in technicolor over the lizard-covered rocks. The **Archaeologi-**

cal Museum, Tsar Samoil, on the left as you descend from Sveta Sofia, contains largely pre-Roman and Roman items (open Tues.-Sun. 9-10:30am, 11am-1pm, and 6-10pm; 100dn, students 50dn).

Several **souvenir shops** flank the main street, and many artists with card tables display handmade jewelry crafted with the famed Ohrid pearl (Охридски бисер; *Ohridski biser*). The **flea market,** part of the larger town market, offers cheap flip-flops good for Lake Ohrid's often-rocky bottom. Ohrid's best beaches can be found on the lake's eastern side, starting at Hotel Park (Хотел Парк), 5km from town. They get even better farther, around Lagadin (Лагадин) where the wealthy and powerful erect their villas. **Water-taxis** wait on the town center's shores to transport sun-bathers to better beaches. It'll cost 40dn if you're willing to wait for the boat to fill up. Otherwise, hiring the whole boat runs 300dn to the first beach, 400dn to the second, and 500dn to the third (round-trip). You can also rent **bikes** on the left side of Gotse Delchev, near the entrance to the town market (300dn per day). If you feel like dancing, the **Disco Club** at Hotel Park stays open til dawn.

The exquisite 10th-century monastery of **Sveti Naum** (Свети Наум) stands 28km south. Buses connect Ohrid to Sveti Naum (6 per day, 45 min., 65dn).

▓ Struga (Струга)

In late-August, poets from around the world come to compete for Struga's golden wreath at the **Struga Poetry Evenings** (Струшки вечери на поезијата; *Strushki vecheri na poeziyata*). Past honorees include W. H. Auden and Allen Ginsberg. The festival commemorates Struga's favorite son—Constantin Miladinovil, founder of Macedonian lyric poetry and author of "Bulgarian Songs." He lived with his brother Dimitar in the **House of the Miladinov Brothers** on Brakya Miladinovi (Брака Миладинови; open daily 8am-3pm; free). Across the street from the Miladinov House, a **gallery** (галерија; open daily 9am-1pm; free) presents the works of Vangel Kodzoman (Вангел Коцоман) from the 1930s and 40s depicting scenes of life around the lake. The **Nikola Nezlobinsky Museum** (Natural Sciences; Никола Незлобински), Boro Kalajdzieski (Боро Калајджески; tel. 718 55), displays many past and present species of Struga's fragile ecological community. For once, preserved specimens of otherwise warring animals and insects "live" together at peace. A two-headed calf and a one meter *letnitsa* trout (16.5kg, the largest ever caught) top a marvelous show of insects, birds, reptiles, and mammals (open daily 7am-3pm and 4-8pm; 50dn). If you're in town in early August, you may be able to catch the **National Costume Festival,** a display of traditional Macedonian dress.

Fifteen km northwest of Ohrid town (buses every 15min., 30min., 35dn), Struga is a poor man's Ohrid. Centered a few hundred meters from the lakeshore, Struga may lack the charm of its more famous neighbor but still fills with tourists in July and August. To get to the beginning of Struga's main street, Marshal Tito (Маршал Тито), get off the bus or walk to one of the bridges over the Tsrni Drim (Црни Дрим) river—Marshal Tito starts on the second bridge from the lake. **Struga Tours,** Marshal Tito (tel. 751 46; fax 726 57), offers free brochures and **maps,** and arranges **private accommodations** for 300dn per person (open daily 8am-8pm). **Hotel Beograd,** Marshal Tito, (tel. 715 22), rents doubles with balcony and TV at DM30 per person; singles are DM40. **Campsites** are located several km from town (**Treska,** tel. 714 00; **As,** tel. 719 05; both charge DM30 for a caravan). **Exchange currency**—cash or traveler's checks—at **Stopanska Banka,** across the street from Struga Tours (tel. 718 00; open Mon.-Fri. 7am-3pm, Sat. 7am-2pm; branches throughout town may stay open as late as 7-8pm in the high season. Try a meat or cheese *burek* (pastry; 30-35dn) at one of a half-dozen fat joints inside the shopping complex opposite Hotel Beograd. Relax with a coffee (30dn), Coke (50dn), or whiskey (100dn) on one of the comfy rattan chairs at **Adagio** (Адацо; opposite Struga Tours; open daily 8am-1am). The **post office** is situated just over the bridge past Hotel Beograd on the left of J.N.A. St. (J.H.A.; open Mon.-Sat. 7am-8pm). **Telephones** are at the post office (open Mon.-Sat. 7am-9pm,

Sun. 9am-noon and 6-8pm). **Poste Restante** is at telephone cashier's window. **Postal code:** 96330. **Phone code:** 096.

■ Near Struga: Sveta Bogoroditsa (Света Богородица)

Five km from the center of town, near the village of Kalishta (Калишта), the churches of **Sveta Bogoroditsa** (Света Богородица) and **Sveta Atanasie** (Света Атанасие) are set into cliffs on the shores of Ohrid. To reach them, take the bus to Radozhda (Радожда; 5 per day, 15dn) and follow the signs for Hotel Biser—the Sveta Bogoroditsa complex is just beyond the hotel. The old Sveta Bogoroditsa consists of three caverns and a little chapel carved into a rock overhanging the lake. There, sometime in the 14th century, three Christian monks slept and fasted through their last days. The Ottoman oppressors discovered that the ascetic trio was preaching the forbidden faith and walled them inside their temple (open 6-10am and 5-9pm; 50dn; dress appropriately). Tiny Sveta Atanasie makes similar use of a cliff further up. A lakeside trail, which sometimes briefly disappears into the water, runs from Sveta Bogoroditsa's courtyard to the church. An overgrown path leads to the steps. What time has failed to do has successfully been done by vandals to the outside frescos, now adorned with those same vandals' names. Luckily, the door leading inside is locked. The caretaker of Sv. Bogoroditsa has the key.

CENTRAL MACEDONIA

■ Bitola (Битола)

Ringed by gray-brown apartment buildings and dotted with shiny glass-fronted banks, Bitola hides its heritage well. Macedonia's second city, founded by Philip of Macedon (father of Alexander the Great) in the 4th century BCE, can no longer rely solely on its strategic location for prosperity. In tourist eyes, the town relies singularly on **Heraclea Lyncestis,** the ruins of an ancient settlement about 2km from the city center. To get there, walk to the end of the park and turn left. Take the first right, after which signs on the right lead the way. You will walk by an abandoned zoo and an overgrown cemetery. At the turn of the millennium, Heraclea was an Episcopal seat; two basilicas and the Episcopal palace have survived, their floor mosaics intact. The amphitheater is being partially rebuilt with locally quarried stone to accommodate the **Hercalean Nights** (Хераклејски Бечери), a cultural event held every July (tel. 353 29; ruins open dawn to dusk). Many of Heraclea's precious finds sit in the **Zavod Museum and Gallery** (Завод Музеи Галерија; tel. 353 87), at the border of the park where Marshal Tito ends—opposite a bizarre white sculpture masquerading as a fountain (open Tues.-Sun. 5-8pm; 50dn). In the town center, the mosque **Yeni and Isak Dzhamiya** (Јени и Исак Џамија), is now a gallery of modern art (open Tues.-Sun.

The Secretive Christianity of the Balkans

After spelunking through your tenth church in the caves of far reaching Macedonia, you might wonder, "What were these crazy Christians thinking?" The answer lies not in monkish asceticism, but rather five centuries of Ottoman domination. The regime imprisoned or tortured Christian teachers and decreed that all churches remain physically, as well as symbolically, lower than mosques. Most churches from the Ottoman era still operate in cellars. To avoid persecution, congregations moved to secret grottos in the outskirts, but, as the three monks of Struga's Sveta Bogoroditsa found out, the empire had ears everywhere. Still, the hermit churches throughout the Macedonian countryside escaped the humiliation bestowed on their larger city "cousins" like Sveta Sofia in Ohrid, which had to carry a minaret until 1912.

CENTRAL MACEDONIA

9am-noon and 5-8pm; 30dn, students 10dn). If you take a right along the river (Први Мај; Prvi May) between the two mosques, you will eventually end up at the **Old Bazaar** (Стара Чаршија; *Stara Charshiya*), whose cobbled streets offer some of the largest concentrations of shops and cafés in town.

Trains chug to Skopje (5 per day, 2hr., 270dn), and **buses** run to Skopje (every 1½hr., 3½hr., 230dn) and Ohrid (every 1½hr., 1¾hr., 120dn). The **train** and **bus stations** are located across from each other, 10 minutes from the town center. To get to the center, follow the main road opposite the train station, then take a right on the main street. Note that although it is now officially called **Gotse Delchev** (Гоце Делчев), the signs and the people refer to it as **Marshal Tito** (Маршал Тито). **Exchange bureaus** line the thoroughfare. **Creditna Banka Bitola,** in the futuristic building at the intersection of Marshal Tito and Radoslavlyevik (Радославльевик), accepts traveler's checks (open Mon.-Fri. 9am-5pm, Sat. 9am-1pm). **Putnik Tours,** Gotse Delchev 77 (tel./fax 352 11; open Mon.-Fri. 8am-7pm, Sat. 8am-2pm), may have maps of the city. To get to the **post office,** take a right onto Ruzvelt (Рузвелт) from Marshal Tito immediately after the self-service restaurant (open Mon.-Sat. 7am-7pm). Make international **phone** calls or send **faxes** (fax 333 61) here daily 7am-8pm. **Postal code:** 97000. **Phone code:** 097.

A dearth of accommodations is reason enough to leave Bitola as a daytrip. **Dona Tours,** Gyuro Gyakovich 47 (Ѓуро Ѓаковиќ; tel. 426 34; open daily 8am-6pm), offers **private rooms** at 300-540dn a night. The only open hotel, **Epinal** (tel. 247 77; fax 247 78), rents unimpressive singles for 910dn or DM35, doubles 1200dn or DM60 (breakfast included). Reception speaks English. As bingo halls and cafés turn out greater profits than restaurants, Bitola offers few epicurean options. A 16th- to 19th century marketplace, the **Restaurant Kai Kuburot** (Кај Кубурот; tel. 246 55), in the building between the mosques in the city center, serves *bistrichka zhelka,* a pork filet stuffed with cheese and veggies (300dn). Macedonian wine is 100dn a bottle. Watch out for the mouth-igniting paprikas (open daily 7am-midnight).

MOLDOVA

US$1 = 4.60 lei	1 leu = US$0.22
CDN$1 = 3.35 lei	1 leu = CDN$0.30
UK£1 = 7.17 lei	1 leu = UK£0.14
IR£1 = 7.45 lei	1 leu = IR£0.13
AUS$1 = 3.63 lei	1 leu = AUS$0.28
NZ$1 = 3.20 lei	1 leu = NZ$0.31
SAR1 = 1.03 lei	1 leu = SAR0.97
DM1 = 3.11 lei	1 leu = DM0.32
Country Phone Code: 373	**International Dialing Prefix: 00**

Moldova is a bit like chocolate cake—everybody wants a bite. The "last bastion of healthy Communist order" survives in the Transniester Republic on the Russian-controlled left bank of the Nistru River. The south, dominated by the Christian Turks (*Gagauz*) has also effectively seceded. Over 70% of Moldova's land and people, mostly ethnic Romanians, are on the right bank of the Nistru. Despite—or perhaps because of—these divisions, the Republic of Moldova is one of the few European countries that defines itself as a multi-ethnic entity and not as a one-nation state.

MOLDOVA ESSENTIALS

Citizens of the U.S. need visas to stay in Moldova for one month or more. Citizens of Australia, Canada, Ireland, New Zealand, South Africa, and the U.K. need visas and invitations to enter the country. Single-entry visas (valid 1 month) are US$40 (U.S. citizens pay US$30), multiple-entry visas are US$90—depending on length of stay, and transit visas are US$35 (or US$50 for a double-transit). Regular service takes five days. One-day rush service is also available for an additional US$20. Together with a visa application, you must submit your passport, photograph, and fee by money order or company check. (See Essentials: Embassies and Consulates, p. 7.) Visas are also available at the airport in Chișinău. Travelers needing invitations can obtain them from acquaintances in Moldova, or from Moldovatur after booking a hotel in Chișinău. For a visa extension, visit the Ministry of Internal Affairs in Chișinău.

GETTING THERE AND GETTING AROUND

Trains connect Chișinău to Iași and Bucharest in Romania, Sofia in Bulgaria, Kiev and Odesa in Ukraine, Moscow in Russia, and many other former-USSR cities (generally via Kiev). The Iași-Chișinău trip takes about six hours, of which only two are spent in motion; border controls and wheel-changing (Moldovan rail tracks are of a larger gauge than Romanian ones) take up the rest. If you haven't seen bogies changed before, it's cool. Border guards will probably open your luggage.

Buses arrive in Chișinău from many directions, including Istanbul (via Romania). Beware the bus schedules posted at the station—they're often wrong. Ask the driver or the ticket salespeople instead. The efficiency of a bus driver's work is measured in number of heads per ride, so buses are always packed to bejezus. With such a frail railway system, they are almost the only way to get around.

TOURIST SERVICES, MONEY, AND COMMUNICATION

Moldovatur is the only show in town, and that town is Chișinău.

The monetary unit, the **leu** (plural lei), is worth 100 bani (often called by their diminutive form, *bănuți*). Unlike the currencies of many nearby countries, the Moldovan leu did not experience serious inflation in 1995-96. Do not confuse the Moldovan leu with the Romanian currency of the same name. Black market sharks are common, but take care: it's better to have receipts for all currency exchanged to tame nasty customs officials, who make you declare all the money you're carrying when you enter the country. Bringing some cash is necessary, since few places take traveler's checks or give cash advances.

AT&T Direct and similar **phone** services are not yet available. In fact, phones in general can be a bit sketchy. **Mail** is slower than average Eastern European mail. Tell your friends back home not to worry if they don't hear from you for some time.

LANGUAGE

As the official language of Moldova, **Romanian** is called **Moldovan.** Almost everybody speaks both **Russian** (see the Russian Glossary, p. 787, and the Cyrillic Alphabet, p. 771) and Romanian (see Romanian Glossary, p. 785, and Romania Essentials: Language, p. 476). For the first year after the fall of the USSR, it was unusual to hear Russian spoken on the streets of Chişinău. Most ethnic Russians, aware that the times were changing, either tried to leave or switch to Romanian, which they had avoided for decades. Nowadays, however, Russian is back and stronger than ever. In Chişinău and most of the urban centers, it dominates in all the tourist-oriented services, though you can get by with Romanian. Almost nobody speaks fluent **English,** but with perseverance you should get your message across. Most signs are bilingual (Romanian-Russian). Some Russians may refuse to answer if addressed in Romanian.

HEALTH AND SAFETY

Few travelers make it as far as Moldova. Consequently, most Moldovans treat foreigners with suspicion, those with questions might be sent to three or more different supposed answers. Women traveling alone will probably feel uncomfortable, as even in the capital, Chişinău, the streets feel unsafe, empty after 7 to 8pm, and are very dark.

LIFE AND TIMES

HISTORY

Present-day Moldova occupies the region known as **Bessarabia**—between the Nistru and Prut rivers. During the first millennium BCE, it was part of Scythia. Later, Romans acquired it in a combo with Romania. Kievan Rus (10th and 12th centuries), Galician princes (early 13th century), and the Tartars (1241-1300s) all took their turns at the "reign". In 1359 the **Volokhs**—the region's native inhabitants—formed an independent principality, but soon after, Bessarabia was annexed by its western neighbor, Moldova. The nation enjoyed a brief stint with victory in the 15th century, as Stefan **the Great** expanded Moldova's frontiers, pushing back Poles to the north and Turks to the south, and defeating Vlad the Impaler (a.k.a. Dracula), ruler of Wallachia. But Turks got their revenge, extracting tribute from Stefan's son, Bogdan the One-Eyed. For the next three centuries, greedy neighbors tore Moldova apart. Russia, Transylvania, Poland, Wallachia, and Turkey all took a bite. Finally, in 1812, after a **Russian-Turkish war,** the declining Ottoman Empire handed the region over to Russia.

Bessarabia's new rulers attempted to **Russify** the region's civil and religious institutions, but most peasants remained illiterate and culturally aligned with **Romania.** Bessarabia prospered; the region's agricultural produce found a market in the Russian empire. The birth of Romania as an autonomous kingdom (1881) fueled smoldering nationalist sentiment in Bessarabia. A quarter-century later, resentment erupted in a full-fledged nationalist movement following the Russian Revolution of 1905.

Although Moldovans fought alongside Russians in WWI, separatist sentiment remained strong; in early **1917,** Bessarabia declared itself an independent Moldovan republic. The Bolsheviks reacted by invading the region, but with Romanian help Moldovan forces drove them out. Alarmed by the German-sponsored government in nearby Ukraine, the new Moldovan state united with Romania in 1920. Frustrated, the Soviets decided to create their own **pseudo-Moldova;** in 1924, Moscow set up another tiny "Moldovan" state on Ukrainian territory, across the Nistru River from the "real" Moldova. Meanwhile, Moldova languished under Romanian control; its exports and had been geared toward Russia, not Romania, and the economy stagnated.

In **1939,** the Soviets invaded once again. They united traditional Moldova (central Bessarabia) with the miniscule Communist Moldova in the Ukraine. The Red Army expropriated Moldovan lands and expelled the German population. During most of **WWII,** Romania occupied the region as Germany's ally. Romania killed or deported many Bessarabian Jews, resettling the region with Romanian peasants.

By 1944, the Soviets had retaken the region. Moscow reintegrated the war-torn area into the Soviet empire as the **Moldovan Soviet Socialist Republic.** Under Communist rule, the Moldovan S.S.R. was radically collectivized and industrialized. Any kind of autonomous culture or society was stamped out, and the republic was thoroughly Russified, through the mass deportation of Romanian-speaking Moldovans to remote areas of the USSR and the resettlement of the area with ethnic Russians. The ethnic stratification of the Moldovan S.S.R. was intensified when Russian became the exclusive language of education and administration, with Romanian only sporadically studied as a foreign language. In the late 1980s, a new spirit of openness allowed open public debate to resume in Moldova. On August 27, 1991, amid political chaos in Moscow, the republic declared **independence.**

LITERATURE

Moldovan literature, like Moldovan history, is inextricably linked with that of Romania. *Let's Go* has continued this bond—to read about Moldovan literature, turn to the Literature section in the Romania chapter, p. 479.

MOLDOVA TODAY

When the Soviet Union disintegrated, a powerful nationalistic movement in Moldova gathered 600,000 people at a meeting in Chişinău. They forced the Communist leaders to reject the Cyrillic alphabet in favor of the Latin one and select the same national flag and hymn as Romania. The issue of Romanian influence or presence in Moldova remains contentious. Although the July 1994 constitution clearly declared Moldovan the official language, in April 1995 student strikes were held in favor of supplanting Moldovan with Romanian. February 1996 saw the parliament veto Moldovan's replacement with Romanian. Still, Moldova has granted citizenship to and tolerates the languages of all its ethnic minorities.

Moldova's pro-Russian and pro-Romania forcers were headed for a direct clash in the presidential elections scheduled for November 17, 1996. Though numerous candidates litter the race, the two front runners were incumbent Mircea Snegur, supported by pro-Romania and pro-Western forces, and Prime Minister Andrei Sangheli, a member of the former-Communist ruling party which claims to lead politics of independence from both Romania and Russia. The party's decision to join the CIS has led to fears of Russian influence. Economic reforms could finally be having an effect—1996 may see the first year of economic growth.

The **Transniester Republic,** backed by Russian ultra-nationalists, declared independence from Chişinău in September 1990, at the prospect of Moldovan union with Romania. The union has not yet materialized, and a poor economy is forcing Igor Smirnov, head of the self-styled republic, to take a more conciliatory position.

Chişinău (Kishinev)

The capital of Moldova, Chişinău has 700,000 inhabitants and looks like a Soviet provincial city. It is built on a rectangular grid, with large distances and concrete monsters on a Stalinest scale—yet there are glimpses of its past in pillared mansions along the main street. As a sign that times, they are-a-changin', a statue of the Romanian prince and national hero Ştefan cel Mare has replaced one of Lenin, and the main street is called bd. Ştefan cel Mare, instead of pr. Lenina. Most streets, in fact, now honor Romanian figures instead of Soviet ones, but apart from that, the only signs of incoming capitalism are the street vendors and tiny enterprises that have popped up since the "fall" of Communism. Lenin still casts a substantial shadow over this town.

ORIENTATION AND PRACTICAL INFORMATION

To get to the city center from the **train station,** walk up the park in front. On your left is the **trolley station** (near the vendors) with 25-bani tickets. Turn right, walk up to Hotel Cosmos, then turn left on **bd. Negruzzi;** after a few hundred yards it veers right and becomes **bd. Ştefan cel Mare.** This seemingly endless boulevard spans the city from southeast to northwest; most interesting sights are clustered around it. Most of the trolleys—such, as #8—from near the train station, travel along it.

ORIENTATION AND PRACTICAL INFORMATION ■ 381

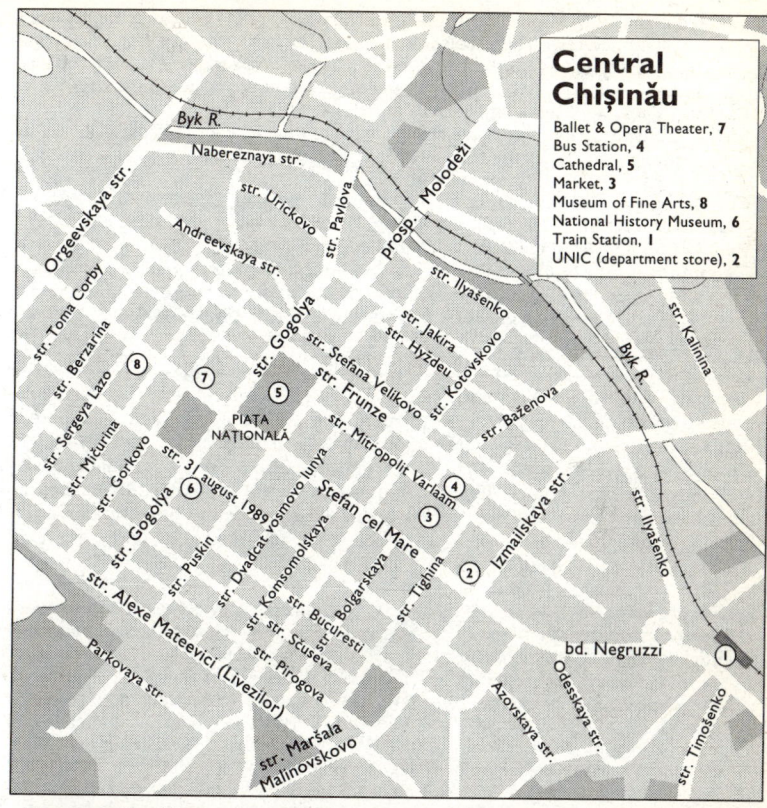

Central Chișinău

Ballet & Opera Theater, **7**
Bus Station, **4**
Cathedral, **5**
Market, **3**
Museum of Fine Arts, **8**
National History Museum, **6**
Train Station, **1**
UNIC (department store), **2**

Tourist Office: Moldovatur, bd. Ștefan cel Mare 4 (tel. 26 65 64), on the 2nd floor of Hotel Național's lobby. Arranges hotel reservations. Open Mon.-Fri. 9am-5pm.

Embassies: U.S., str. Alexe Mateevici 103 (tel. 23 37 72; fax 23 30 44), near the university. Take trolley #9 or 10 from the center. Open Mon.-Fri. 9am-6pm.

Currency Exchange: One of the few businesses booming in Chișinău. All accept DM and US$. Romanian lei work at bad rates. **Bancosind Bank,** at the corner of bd. Ștefan cel Mare and str. Pușkin, cashes AmEx, MC, and Thomas Cook traveler's checks. Honors Diner's Club and Visa cards. Open Mon.-Fri. 9am-4pm.

Western Union: Str. Pușkin 33 (tel. 24 10 23), way downhill. Window #24 in Banca de Economie al Moldovei. Open Mon.-Fri. 8:30am-6pm, Sat. 9am-5:30pm.

Flights: (tel. 52 54 12). The airport is 12km from downtown; take bus #65 from the train station. **Air Moldova,** bd. Negruzzi 3 (tel. 26 40 09, international tel. 26 13 98), near Hotel Național, flies to Athens, Bucharest, Frankfurt, Istanbul, Moscow, and Vienna. Most staff speak Russian only.

Trains: (tel. 25 27 35). Somewhat anarchic. You can buy international tickets at the 2nd floor Intourist booth, but they'll overcharge you (e.g. Chișinău-Iași one-way 18 lei); buying a roundtrip ticket in Romania saves about 50%. However, you will have to specify in advance which train you'll be taking back. Some save money by going to Iași, taking the train to Ungheni (6 per day, 2hr., 3.20 lei), then a bus to Iași (3 per day, 1hr., 4 lei). Those without a ticket in the waiting room pay a 25-bani fee. To: Bălți (4 per day, 7 lei); Bucharest (1 per day, 55 lei); Kiev (1 per day); Minsk (1 per day); Moscow (1 per day; 31hr.; 110 lei, with couchette 117 lei); Odesa (2 per day, 14 lei); Tiraspol (1 per day, 4.30 lei). **Luggage storage.**

Buses: (tel. 22 26 11). On str. Mitropolit Varlaam 58, a block to the right off the main street; take a left after the market. Beware the occasionally erroneous bus times posted in the lobby! Open daily 7am-7pm. The buses are old enough to be declared historical monuments. The 3 daily buses to Istanbul leave from the train station via a private coach (tel. 54 98 13). Crowded transports leave for Iaşi (3 per day, 10 lei), Bucharest (2 per day, 30 lei), Bălţi (10 per day, 8.40 lei), Tiraspol (2 per day, 5 lei), Odesa (5 per day, 11 lei), and Sofia (1 per week, 120 lei).

Public Transportation: Extensive **trolley** system; buy tickets (25 bani) at kiosks in the stations, and stamp them on board. Posters warn that fines for not having a ticket are up to 15% of the "minimum salary".

Taxis: State-run. Theoretically, 2 lei per km in the city, but, at least with foreigners, taxi drivers set the price in the beginning. Prices may vary a great deal.

Post Office: Bd. Ştefan cel Mare 34. **Postal code:** 277012.

Telephones: Corner of str. Tighina and bd. Ştefan cel Mare, 2 blocks from Hotel Naţional. Open 24hr., except for occasional coffee breaks. Calling internationally, dial 37 32. International service to the left as you enter. Open daily 8:30am-10pm. **Faxes.**

ACCOMMODATIONS

Coopertiva Adresa, bd. Negruzzi 1 (tel. 26 64 14), across from Hotel Cosmos rents **private rooms** for 16 lei per person (open Mon.-Sat. 9am-9pm, Sun. 9am-6pm). Approaching Cosmos from the train station, Adresa is in the first alleyway on your left as soon as you pass the traffic circle and enter bd. Negruzzi. Look for a small orange, blue, and white sign. Though not as cheap, hotels remain affordable. Remember all hotels have a hot-water schedule, so ask about the hours before you strip down for that long-awaited bath. Most, particularly the fancy grand-sounding ones, take Visa and have someone on hand who speaks a form of English.

Hotel Meridian, str. Tighina (tel. 26 06 20). As budget as they come. Noisy but good spot near the market. "Luxury" rooms have TV, fridge, and bath, while normal rooms have the "bear" necessities. If paying the luxury fee, be sure to get the luxury room. Singles 30 lei, luxury 45 lei. Doubles 40 lei, luxury 80 lei.

Hotel Chişinău, bd. Negruzzi 7 (tel. 26 63 41). The lobby resembles a tiny well kept train station with square marble columns and a dark-wood motif. The dim hallways are actually pink. Modest rooms with TV, phone, and bath. Restaurant, exchange office, and room service. Singles 57 lei. Doubles 96 lei. Triples 156 lei.

Hotel Cosmos, bd. Negruzzi 2 (tel. 26 44 57; fax 26 43 00). Parquet hardwood floors, dark checkerboard bedspreads, and golden wallpaper complete the ambiance. Singles 90 lei. Doubles 140 lei. Breakfast included. The mandatory 9-lei tax goes towards overhead, including a restaurant and bar (restaurant open daily 7:30am-midnight; bar til 4am), massage parlor, and an intimidating security guard who directs guests to the English-speaking hotel manager.

Hotel Naţional, bd. Ştefan cel Mare 4 (tel. 26 60 83). A former Intourist facility. Bright flowery rooms typical of well endowed Soviet hotels, with slightly dingy bathrooms. Barber shop, bar, and restaurant (open daily 8am-11:30pm). English spoken. Singles 100 lei. Doubles 150 lei. Reservations required (50% deposit).

FOOD

Finding good, cheap food in Chişinău is a problem. Try the **marketplace** (open summer Tues.-Sun. 6:30am-5pm, winter 7am-4pm), off the main street on str. Tighina.

Belluno, bd. Ştefan cel Mare 114 (tel. 26 03 42). Perhaps the best and most elegant eating establishment in town, serving so-called Moldo-Italian cuisine. *The* place to go if you want to impress your date. See his or her eyes widen when you pull out your huge Diner's Club card to pay for that 16-lei steak which tops the menu. Meals can easily reach 40-50 lei here. Open 24hr.

Butoiaş (Little Barrel), at the north end of town. Take trolley #11 to the last stop and look for the big barrel on the left. The restaurant inside has atmosphere but not much food. The choices: soup, pork, or chicken—but you can have the last for a mere 13 lei, which includes bread and mineral water *"Răcoarea Codrilor"* (Coolness of the Woods), synthetically produced at a Chişinău experimental plant. *En garde,* Evian. Open daily noon-4pm and 6pm-midnight.

Magic, across from the History museum. Bears a startling resemblance to a fast-food temple with its plastic red arches. And, indeed, they serve sandwiches, but with caviar (4.60 lei), boiled tongue (2.50 lei), and mushroom-stuffed chicken legs.

SIGHTS AND ENTERTAINMENT

To tour most of Chișinău's monuments, just walk up bd. Ștefan cel Mare. In front of Hotel Cosmos, the first statue you will see represents **Kotovski**—Robin Hood for Soviet apparatchiks, a bandit for Romanians. In the 1920s, he attacked Romania in flash raids from across the Nistru River. Not as dramatic as Lenin's accomplishments, but then Kotovski's statue is still up. Following the boulevard as it bears left and taking a left at Hotel Național (at the half-nude pillar statue pointing toward the Academy of Science) brings in view the sky-blue towers of the **Cioflii Church** (finished in 1876; open daily 8am-7:30pm), perhaps once the most beautiful in Chișinău. Look past the exterior's need for restoration to admire the icons inside, each framed by a different coverpiece-and-column combo.

Across the street on the corner of bd. Ștefan cel Mare is the **Art Expo** (open Tues.-Fri. 10am-6pm, Sat.-Sun. 11am-4pm), where 15-foot silver statues representing the classical arts—painting, writing, sculpture, etc.—stand outside the wall. All along the main boulevard, Stalinist blocks and Neoclassical buildings compete for attention. A few blocks up on the left are the Corinthian columns and orange façade of the **National Theatre.** The ticket office is on str. Pușkin. Close by, two gentle lions guard the **Organ Hall;** check the board for concert schedules (usually at 6:30pm). A flag crowns the small tower above the charming façade of the nearby **City Hall.**

Farther up, at the intersection of str. Pușkin and bd. Ștefan cel Mare, is **Piața Națională,** the main square, with an 1846 triumphal arch. Behind it lie a **park** and the temple-like **cathedral,** resembling a cross between the Lincoln memorial and R2D2. Both the inside and outside are being restored, but you can attend services amid the scaffolding. On the square's upper left corner stands the statue of the legendary **Ștefan cel Mare** (Stephen the Great). The statue, made in 1928, was moved here and there during WWII to avoid the Bolsheviks, but finally fell into Soviet hands in 1945, who modified its inscription. In 1972, it was set up in the park, but the 1990 national revival brought it back to its original resting spot. The park also contains an alley with statues from the classics of Romanian literature.

Several other monuments lie around the city. The **National History Museum,** str. 31 August 1989 121a (tel. 24 53 93), sits near Piața Națională. Take a left on str. Pușkin, then a right (open summer Tues.-Sun. 10am-6pm; winter 9am-5pm, closed last Fri. of the month; museum 50 bani, students 20 bani; treasury 1 lei, students 50 bani). In front of the museum, the statue of a she-wolf feeding the two founders of Rome, Remus and Romulus, stands as a reminder of south Bessarabia's Latin roots.

About five blocks left off the main street up str. Pușkin is the central **park,** complete with lake. On the way you'll pass by the **university;** many of the students who hang out at the cafés around here speak English and would love a chance to practice it on you. The department store **Lumea Copiilor** (Children's World), bd. Ștefan cel Mare 136 (tel. 22 34 23), five blocks up from Hotel Național on the corner of Piața Națională, is a living museum of pre-revolutionary Communism (open Mon.-Sat. 8am-8pm, Sun. 9am-4pm). For souvenirs, head for **Fondul Artei Plastice,** close to Hotel Național, which also has cool temporary exhibitions.

■ Near Chișinău

CĂPRIANA

Nestled in the hills 20km northwest of Chișinău, Căpriana centers around Moldova's most celebrated 14th-century monastery. Accessible as a daytrip, the village and the monastery provide a low-calorie glimpse of the countryside. From the bus stop, walk to the left of the only modern-looking building in sight to gaze upon the spires of the **old and new monastery churches.** The peach-and-light-blue main church has a bright interior with paintings in need of restoration. Meanwhile, in the monastery's far corner, the old church's gutted skeleton offers a glimpse of its former beauty, with silver towers melting into one high dome. Clad in scaffolding, this house of worship is now home to sparrows. Good picnic spots hide in the hills.

As with every other town in Moldova, getting there involves a fantastically cheap and overcrowded **bus** (daily at 11:30am and 4:45pm, Fri.-Sun. also 7:45am; 40min.; 5 lei). Since the only return buses leave the village at 9am, 1pm, and 4pm, you might broaden your transportation choices to include the 7-km hike to the Străşeni **train** station. Alternatively, some travelers hitch a ride into town (3-5 lei).

VADUL LUI VODĂ

About 12km northeast of Chişinău, the riverside resort Vadul lui Vodă—a collection of lodging and rest facilities—hosts hordes of Russian-speaking Moldovans in summer. Although water sports are not popular here, you can burn off a few calories with tennis, soccer, and other pastimes. The beach attracts a large Chişinău crowd, eager to quench its thirst at the kiosks in this wooded retreat. The hideous public toilets belong in the Outhouse Hall of Shame, but Vadul lui Vodă deserves a visit.

Bus #31 runs here directly from the center of Chişinău. Ride it to the very end (*plaja*), where you'll see globs of people in skimpy Speedos frolicking on the banks of the Nistru River. From the bus parking lot, take a right and walk until the first bend in the road to get to a **free campground.** Staying on the path through the first intersection leads to a "Baza de Odihnă" alley, where many state-run firms established rest areas for their employees. Some of these lodgings, such as **Păduricea Verde** (tel. 48 20 36), welcome tourists into their log-cabin houses (singles 30 lei, triples 105 lei). Their buffet offers reasonably priced food (open daily 9am-noon and 3-11pm). Adequate space, a sauna, and furnishings (including fridge and TV) make this shady little spot a great little deal.

■ Orhei

Now a desert purgatory, ages ago Orhei was home to a stone fortress built by Ştefan the Great. Destroyed by the Tartars in 1499, this ex-stronghold attracts neither armies nor many tourists. Those who come walk down str. Vasile Lupu past **St. Nicholas's Church** until it bears right. In the distance the gray roof and gold towers of the 1630 **Biserica Sf. Dumitru** church rise above the town.

You'll likely see a lot of Orhei's **bus station,** 50km north of the capital—all northbound **buses** out of Chişinău stop here (every ½hr., 80min., 2 lei). The last Chişinău-bound bus leaves at 5:50pm. Connections to Rezina, Trebujeni (for the Butuceni monastery), and Lalova (for the Ţipova monastery) are also available. To get to the center of town from the bleak bus station, head uphill on the footpath which bears left slightly and passes by the **Magazin Universul** department store (open Mon.-Fri. 8am-5pm, Sun. 8am-2pm). Take a right onto the main **str. Vasile Lupu.** Going a few blocks and taking a left onto **str. Ştefan cel Mare** at St. Nicholas's Church takes you to the tiny **telephone office,** str. Vasile Mahu 119 (a.k.a. Lenin; open Mon.-Sat. 7am-11pm). A few doors down is the **post office,** str. Vasile Mahu 129 (open Mon.-Sat. 8am-7pm). **Phone code:** 235.

In Orhei's case, "Accommodations and Food" should be called "Slim Pickings". The only hotel in town is **Hotel Codru,** str. Vasile Lupu 36 (tel. 248 21), whose spartan comforts and lack of running water don't thrill (singles 19 lei; doubles 29 lei, with bath 54.20 lei). The smoke-filled saloon-dungeonette called **Restaurant Rapid,** across the street from the hotel, serves full meals for about 7 lei (open daily in summer 8am-11pm; winter 8am-9pm). Or try the **market** behind Magazin Universul.

POLAND (POLSKA)

US$1 = 2.71zł (złoty, or PLN)	1zł = US$0.37
CDN$1 = 1.97zł	1zł = CDN$0.51
UK£1 = 4.22zł	1zł = UK£0.24
IR£1 = 4.39zł	1zł = IR£0.23
AUS$1 = 2.14zł	1zł = AUS$0.47
NZ$1 = 1.88zł	1zł = NZ$0.53
SAR1 = 0.61zł	1zł = SAR1.64
DM1 = 1.83zł	1zł = DM0.55
Country Phone Code: 48	**International Dialing Prefix: 00**

From the amber-strewn shores of the Baltic in the north to the snow-capped peaks of the Tatras in the south, Poland is shaking off the remnants of a half-century of Communism and reclaiming its heritage as one of the world's oldest democracies. Struggle has been a way of life for Poles, who have enjoyed only 27 years of freedom in this century; they have drawn strength from the Catholic Church and a rich intellectual tradition. Memories of WWII linger, but a new, headstrong generation is emerging, determined to rebuild the country in its own image. It has transformed the country into one large construction zone, diligently fixing the infrastructure so long neglected and renovating faded architectural treasures.

POLAND ESSENTIALS

Citizens of the U.S. and Ireland do not require a Polish visa for visits up to 90 days; citizens of the U.K. can stay visa-free up to six months. Make sure your passport is stamped when you enter the country. Australians, Canadians, New Zealanders, and South Africans all need visas. Single-entry visas (valid for 90 days) cost US$40 (children and students under 26 pay US$30); double-entry visas cost US$55 (students US$42); transit visas (valid 48hr.) cost US$20 (students US$15). A visa application requires a valid passport, two photographs, and payment by money order or cash. It is also possible to apply by mail. Regular service takes up to 14 days; rush service (24 hr.) costs US$35 extra (see Essentials: Embassies and Consulates, p. 7). If you want to extend your stay, apply for a new visa at the local voivodeship (province) office (*urząd wojewódzki*).

GETTING THERE

LOT, British Airways, and Delta **fly** into Warsaw and Kraków from London, New York, Chicago, and Toronto (among other cities). **Trains** and **buses** connect to all neighboring countries, but **Eurail** is not valid in Poland. ALMATUR offers ISIC holders 25% off international fares for the Polish portion of the trip and sells **Interrail** passes; for those under 26, **Wasteels** tickets and **Eurotrain** passes give 40% off international train travel fares. Discount international tickets for those under 26 are also sold at major train stations and ORBIS offices. Thefts have been known to occur on international overnight trains. **Ferries** run from Sweden and Denmark to Świnoujście, Gdańsk, and Gdynia.

GETTING AROUND

PKP trains scurry to most towns at bargain prices. Train stations have boards with alphabetical listings of towns, and posters with chronological listings of trains. *Odjazdy* (departures) are in yellow; *przyjazdy* (arrivals), in white. **InterCity** and *Ekspresowy* (express) trains are listed in red with an "IC" or "Ex" in front of the train number, respectively. *Pośpieszny* (direct; also in red) are almost as fast. *Osobowy* (in black) are the slowest but are 35% cheaper. All **InterCity,** *ekspresowy,* and some *pośpieszny* trains require seat reservations; if you see a boxed R on the schedule, ask the clerk for a *miejscówka* (reservation). Buy your ticket aboard the train for a surcharge; when doing so, find the *konduktor* before he or she finds you, or risk a fine. Train tickets are valid only on the day for which they're issued. Lines can be extremely long and move at a snail's pace; make sure you plan for enough time so you don't miss your train. Better yet, buy your ticket in advance at the station or an Orbis office. When traveling by bus or train, be aware that stations are not announced and are sometimes poorly marked. If you are getting off before the final destination, pay particular attention and ask someone if necessary.

PKS buses are cheapest and fastest for short trips. Like trains, there are *pośpieszny* (direct; in red) and *osobowy* (slow; in black). Purchase advance tickets at the bus station, and expect long lines. However, some tickets can only be bought from the driver. In the countryside, PKS markers (like yellow Mercedes-Benz symbols) indicate bus stops, but drivers will often halt wherever you flag them down. Traveling by bus with a backpack can be a problem (or at least uncomfortable) if the bus is full. Under-bus storage is rarely used and the overhead bins are so ridiculously small that they can barely accommodate coats.

Though legal, **hitching** is becoming increasingly dangerous for foreigners. Hand-waving is the accepted sign. The *Autostop Hitchhike Book* sold by PTTK, includes an insurance policy, an ID card, and vouchers that qualify drivers for compensation. *Let's Go* does not recommend hitchhiking as a safe means of transportation.

LET'S GO® TRAVEL

DISCOUNTED AIRFARES

EURAIL PASSES

1997
CATALOG
WE GIVE YOU THE WORLD...AT A DISCOUNT
1-800-5-LETSGO

TRAVEL GEAR

Let's Go carries a full line of Eagle Creek packs, accessories, and security items.

A. World Journey

Equipped with Eagle Creek Comfort Zone Carry System which includes Hydrofil nylon knit on backpanel and shoulder straps, molded torso adjustments, and spinal and lumbar pads. Parallel internal frame. Easy packing panel load design with internal cinch straps. Lockable zippers. Black, Evergreen, or Blue. The perfect Eurailing pack. $20 off with rail pass. $195

B. Continental Journey

Carry-on sized pack with internal frame suspension. Detachable front pack. Comfort zone padded shoulder straps and hip belt. Leather hand grip. Easy packing panel load design with internal cinch straps. Lockable zippers. Black, Evergreen, or Blue. Perfect for backpacking through Europe. $10 off with rail pass. $150

ACCESSORIES

C. Padded Toiletry Kit

Large padded main compartment to protect contents. Mesh lid pocket with metal hook to hang kit on a towel rod or bathroom hook. Features two separate small outside pockets and detachable mirror. 9" x 4¾" x 4¼". Black, Evergreen, or Blue. *As seen on cover in Blue.* $20

D. Padded Travel Pouch

Main zipper compartment is padded to protect a compact camera or mini binoculars. Carries as a belt pouch, or use 1" strap to convert into waist or shoulder pack. Front flap is secured by a quick release closure. 6" x 9" x 3". Black, Evergreen, or Blue. *As seen on cover in Evergreen.* $26

E. Departure Pouch

Great for travel or everyday use. Features a multitude of inside pockets to store passport, tickets, and monies. Includes see-thru mesh pocket, pen slots, and gusseted compartment. Can be worn over shoulder, around neck, or cinched around waist. 6" x 12". Black, Evergreen, or Blue. *As seen on cover in Black.* $16

SECURITY ITEMS

F. Undercover Neckpouch

Ripstop nylon with a soft Cambrelle back. Three pockets. 5¼" x 6½". Lifetime guarantee. Black or Tan. $9.95

G. Undercover Waistpouch

Ripstop nylon with a soft Cambrelle back. Two pockets. 4¾" x 12" with adjustable waistband. Lifetime guarantee. Black or Tan. $9.95

H. Travel Lock

Great for locking up your Continental or World Journey. Anondized copper two-key lock. $5

CLEARANCE

Call for clearance specials on a limited stock of travel packs, gear, and accessories from the 1996 season.

Prices and availability of products are subject to change.

1-800-5-LETS GO

EURAIL PASSES

Let's Go is one of the largest Eurail pass distributors in the nation.
Benefit from our extensive knowledge of the European rail network.
Free **UPS** standard shipping.

Eurail Pass (First Class)
Unlimited train travel in 17 European nations.
15 days	$522
21 days	$678
1 month	$838
2 months	$1148
3 months	$1468

Eurail Youthpass (Second Class)
All the benefits of a Eurail pass for passengers under 26 on their first day of travel.
15 days	$418
1 month	$598
2 months	$798

Eurail Flexipass (First Class)
Individual travel days to be used at your convenience during a two month period.
10 days in 2 months	$616
15 days in 2 months	$812

Eurail Youthpass Flexipass (Second Class)
All the benefits of a Flexipass for passengers under 26 on their first day of travel.
10 days in 2 months	$438
15 days in 2 months	$588

Europass
Purchase anywhere from 5 to 15 train days within a two month period for train travel in 3, 4, or 5 of the following countries: France, Germany, Italy, Spain, and Switzerland. Associate countries can be added. Call for details.

Pass Protection
For an additional $10, insure any railpass against theft or loss.

Call for details on Europasses, individual country passes, and reservations for the Chunnel train linking London to Paris, Brussels, and Calais. Rail prices are subject to change. Please call to verify price before ordering.

DISCOUNTED AIRFARES
Discounted international and domestic fares for students, teachers, and travelers under 26.
Purchase your 1997 International ID card and call 1-800-5-LETSGO for price quotes and reservations.

1997 INTERNATIONAL ID CARDS
Provides discounts on airfares, tourist attractions and more. Includes basic accident and medical insurance.

International Student ID Card (ISIC)	$19
International Teacher ID Card (ITIC)	$20
International Youth ID Card (GO25)	$19

See order form for details.

HOSTELLING ESSENTIALS

1997-8 Hostelling Membership
Cardholders receive priority and discounts at most international hostels.
Adult (ages 18-55)	$25.00
Youth (under 18)	$10.00

Call for details on Senior and Family memberships.

Sleepsack
Required at many hostels. Washable polyester/cotton. Durable and compact. $13.95

International Youth Hostel Guide
IYHG offers essential information concerning over 4000 European hostels. $10.95

TRAVEL GUIDES
Let's Go Travel Guides
The Bible of the Budget Traveler

Regional & Country Guides (please specify)
USA	$19.99
Eastern Europe, Europe, India & Nepal, Southeast Asia	$16.99
Alaska & The Pacific Northwest, Britain & Ireland, California, France, Germany, Greece & Turkey, Israel & Egypt, Italy, Mexico, Spain & Portugal, Switzerland & Austria	$17.99
Central America, Ecuador & The Galapagos Islands, Ireland	$16.99
City Guides (please specify)	$11.99

London, New York, Paris, Rome, Washington, D.C.

Let's Go Map Guides
Fold out maps and up to 40 pages of text

Map Guides (please specify) $7.95

Berlin, Boston, Chicago, London, Los Angeles, Madrid, New Orleans, New York, Paris, Rome, San Francisco, Washington, D.C.

1-800-5-LETS GO

ORDER FORM

International Student/Teacher Identity Card (ISIC/ITIC) (ages 12 and up) enclose:
1. Proof of student/teacher status (letter from registrar or administrator, proof of tuition payment, or copy of student/faculty ID card. FULL-TIME only.)
2. One picture (1 ½" x 2") signed on the reverse side.
3. Proof of birthdate (copy of passport, birth certificate, or driver's license).

GO25 card (ages 12-25) enclose:
1. Proof of birthdate (copy of passport, birth certificate, or driver's license).
2. One picture (1 ½" x 2") signed on the reverse side.

Last Name _____ First Name _____ Date of Birth _____

Street _____ *We do not ship to P.O. Boxes.* _____

City _____ State _____ Zip Code _____

Phone (very important!) _____ Citizenship (Country) _____

School/College _____ Date of Travel _____

Description, Size	Color	Quantity	Unit Price	Total Price

SHIPPING & HANDLING
Eurail pass does not factor into merchandise value

Domestic 2-3 Weeks
Merchandise value under $30 .... $4
Merchandise value $30-100 .... $6
Merchandise value over $100 .... $8

Domestic 2-3 Days
Merchandise value under $30 .... $14
Merchandise value $30-100 .... $16
Merchandise value over $100 .... $18

Domestic Overnight
Merchandise value under $30 .... $24
Merchandise value $30-100 .... $26
Merchandise value over $100 .... $28

All International Shipping $30

Total Purchase Price _____

Shipping and Handling (See box at left) _____

MA Residents (Add 5% sales tax on gear & books) _____

TOTAL _____

From which Let's Go Guide are you ordering?   ☐ Europe   ☐ USA

MASTERCARD ☐   VISA ☐   ☐ Other _____

Cardholder Name:

Card Number:

Expiration Date:

Make check or money order payable to:
Let's Go Travel
http://hsa.net/travel
67 Mt. Auburn Street • Cambridge, MA 02138 • USA • (617) 495-9649

1-800-5-LETS GO

TOURIST SERVICES

ORBIS, the Polish state travel bureau, sells international and domestic train tickets, and international bus, plane, and ferry tickets. **ALMATUR**, the Polish student travel organization, sells ISICs and helps find university dorm rooms in summer. Both provide maps and brochures, as do the **PTTK** and **IT** bureaus on the main street of every town. Since 1989, **private tourist agencies** have mushroomed all over Poland; their prices are competitive, but watch out for scams.

MONEY

The Polish **złoty**—plural *złote*—is fully convertible. For cash, private **kantor** offices, except for those at the airport and train stations, offer better exchange rates than banks. **Bank PKO S.A.** accepts **traveler's checks** and gives MasterCard and Visa **cash advances** all over Poland. **ATMs** (Bankomat) are becoming more common, mostly in large cities. **Wielkopolski Bank Kredytowy (WBK)** is affiliated with Plus and Visa, while Bank PKO S.A. accepts Cirrus and MasterCard (Eurocard).

In January 1995, the National Bank cut four zeros off all prices, and introduced new bank notes and coins. This is one case where new money is far better than the old—don't be a snob. As of January 1, 1997, only the new currency is valid. Learn the difference between the old and the new (posters at the airport and train stations show the currencies), and never accept old currency. When changing money, it is helpful to ask for smaller bank notes (10zł or 20zł). Often, businesses and hostels may not be able to give change for the larger notes (50zł or larger). Also, as there are nine types of coins, a change purse can prove extremely helpful.

COMMUNICATION

Mail is becoming increasingly efficient, though still plagued by theft. Airmail usually takes seven to ten days to reach the U.S. For **Poste Restante**, put a "1" after the city name to ensure it goes to the main post office. When picking up *Poste Restante*, it will usually, but not always, cost the amount of domestic postage (0.60zł).

There are two types of **pay phones** available. The older ones use *żetony* (tokens; "A" for local calls, "C" for intercity calls). Newer phones use **phone cards**, which come in several denominations. These phones have card slots and instructions in English. Both tokens and phone cards are available at any post office as well as some kiosks. Pay phones are becoming increasingly available throughout the country and are no longer constrained to the post office. To reach **AT&T Direct**, dial 01 04 80 01 11 (from outside Warsaw, dial a 0 and wait for a tone first); **MCI WorldPhone**, dial 01 04 80 02 22 or 00 800 111 21 22; **Sprint Express**, dial 01 04 80 01 15; **Canada Direct**, dial 01 04 80 01 18; **British Telecom Direct**, dial 044 00 99 48. To make a **collect call**, write the name of the city or country and the number plus *"Rozmowa 'R'"* on a slip of paper, hand it to a post office clerk, and be patient.

LANGUAGE

Polish varies little, apart from the regions of Kaszuby, whose distinctive dialect some classify as a separate language, and Karpaty, whose highlanders' accent has been affected by the rivers of goat's milk they drink. In west Poland, **German** is the most commonly known foreign language, though students may know **English**. Elsewhere, try English and German before **Russian**. Students may also know **French**.

The fully phonetic spelling is complicated by some letters not of the Latin alphabet: *"ł"* sounds like a "w"; *"ą"* is a nasal "o"; *"ę"* is a nasal "eh"; a dash above a consonant softens it; *"ó"* and *"u"* are both equivalent to an "oo"; *"ż"* and *"rz"* are both like the last "g" in "garage". The language also has consonantal clusters which are easier to spit out than they seem: *"sz"* is "sh", *"cz"* is "ch", *"ch"* and *"h"* are equivalent to each other, sounding like the English "h". See the Polish glossary, p. 783.

HEALTH AND SAFETY

> **Emergency Numbers: Police:** tel. 997. **Fire:** tel. 998. **Ambulance:** tel. 999. **AIDS:** tel. 958.

Public restrooms are marked with a triangle for men and a circle for women. They can be nasty, but don't get discouraged. Soap, towel, and toilet paper cost extra.

Polish **pharmacies** are well stocked. Hi-tech medical clinics are opening up around the country. The tap **water** is drinkable, although in some places it will taste strongly of chlorine. The latest fashion is bottled mineral water, which is available carbonated (*gazowana*) or not (*nie gazowana*).

Criminals feed off of naive rich western tourists; carry a bare minimum of cash. As unemployment grows, con-artists multiply. Always be on your guard at big train stations. Also, be on the lookout for pickpockets, especially when boarding or riding crowded public buses and trams.

ACCOMMODATIONS AND CAMPING

Grandmotherly **private room** owners smother travelers at the train station or outside the tourist office. Private rooms are usually safe, clean, and convenient, but are sometimes far from city centers. Expect to pay about US$10 per person.

PTSM is the national hostel organization. The average **HI youth hostel** (*schronisko młodzieżowe*) will likely be crowded, spartan, and uncomfortable. They're everywhere and average US$3 per night (less for "juniors" under 18 or 26, more for non-members). Hot water is chancy. **University dorms** transform into sparse but cheap tourist housing in July and August. These are an especially good option in Kraków. Ask at **ALMATUR;** the Warsaw office can arrange stays in all major cities (see Warsaw: Tourist Offices, p. 392). **PTTK** runs a number of hotels called **Domy Turysty**, where you can stay in multi-bed rooms for US$2-5. Many towns have a **Biuro Zakwaterowań**, which arranges stays in private homes. Rooms come in three categories based on location and availability of hot water (1 is the best).

Campsites average US$2 per person, with a car, US$4. **Bungalows** are often available; a bed costs about US$5. *Polska Mapa Campingów* lists all campsites. ALMATUR runs a number of sites in summer; ask for a list at one of their offices.

FOOD AND DRINK

Monks, merchants, invaders, and dynastic unions have flavored Polish cuisine—a blend of hearty dishes drawing from the French, Italian, and Jewish traditions. And, while Polish food is often loaded with cholesterol, it is less starchy than that of the Czech Republic and less fiery than that of Hungary or Bulgaria.

A Polish meal always starts with **soup.** From a typical menu, you should be able to choose between *barszcz* (beet broth), *chłodnik* (a cold beet soup with buttermilk and hard-boiled eggs), *kapuśniak* (sauerkraut soup), *krupnik* (barley soup), and *żur* (barley-flour soup loaded with eggs and sausage). *Bigos* (sauerkraut cooked with beef and mushrooms) and *flaczki* (tripe) can be eaten as either soup or entrée.

More filling **main courses** include *gołąbki* (cabbage rolls stuffed with meat and rice), *kotlet schabowy* (pork chops), *kopytka* (potato dumplings topped with buttered bread crumbs), *naleśniki* (cream-topped pancakes filled with cottage cheese or jam), and *pierogi* (dumplings with various fillings—blueberry are best).

Poland bathes in beer, vodka, and spiced liquor. *Żywiec* is the favorite strong (12%) brew, and *EB* is its excellent, gentler brother. *Wódka* ranges from potato to wheat to kosher. *Wyborowa, Żytnia,* and *Polonez* usually decorate private bars, though kosher vodka is rumored to be top notch. The herbal *Żubrówka* vodka comes with a blade of grass from the region where the bison roam; it's illegal in the U.S., so try it here. *Miód* and *krupnik*—two kinds of mead—are best loved by the gentry, and most idle grandmas make *nalewka na porzeczce* (black currant vodka).

CUSTOMS AND ETIQUETTE

Business hours tend to be Monday-Friday 8am-6pm and Saturday 9am-2pm. The Saturday hours are especially variable as all shops in Poland distinguish between "working" *(pracująca)* Saturdays, when they work longer hours, and "free" *(wolna)* ones, when hours are shorter. Unfortunately, each store decides for itself which saturdays is which, so there's no way of preparing a master shopping plan for any given weekend. Very few stores or businesses are open on Sunday. **Museum hours** are generally Tuesday-Sunday 10am-4pm. Museums are ordinarily closed on the day after a holiday. In restaurants, a 10-15% **tip** is expected, and usually given when paying the bill. When arriving as a **guest**, be sure to bring your host (only if it's a she) an odd number of flowers. You'll then be offered more than you can possibly eat; wolf it all or face eternal damnation. When addressing a man, use the formal *"Pan"*; with a woman use *"Pani"*. Most Poles eat meals at home, and when they do eat out, it is in the cafeteria-style *bary* and *bary mleczny*. It is not uncommon for restaurants to be mostly empty, especially in the evening. **Homosexuality** is legal and a frequent topic of media debate. Warsaw's **Lambda** offers info in English for both gays and lesbians.

LIFE AND TIMES

HISTORY

Present-day Poland's territory was settled around the 7th century by **West Slavs**. The country was named after the **Polanie** people, who lived near Gniezno in the 9th century. Prince Svatopulok introduced both Latin and Greek Christianity in the 9th century, but it was not until 966 that **Prince Mieszko I** officially converted to Catholicism. Under Mieszko's son, Bolesław Chrobry (the Brave), Poland fought Bohemia, the German Empire, and Kievan Rus with success. By the early 12th century, Polish kings had centralized administration and increased their hold on the land.

Though the Mongols succeeded in reaching the gates of Kraków and defeating a combined Polish-German army at Legnica in 1241, Poland escaped the Mongol yoke. The 14th century, particularly under **King Kazimierz Wielki** (the Great), was a time of prosperity and unprecedented religious and political tolerance; at this time Poland became a refuge for Jews expelled from Western Europe. Kazimierz rebuilt the country's defenses, made strategic peace pacts, and expanded Poland's territories. Scholars codified Polish law in 1347, and a university was founded at Kraków, the cultural center of Poland, in 1364.

After the death of Kazimierz in 1370, Poland experienced increasing international difficulties. The country had turned its attention to the Lithuanian Empire, and attempts to convert the Lithuanians to Christianity necessitated the cooperation with the **Teutonic Knights**. The Knights then turned on Poland, taking East Prussia and cutting off Polish access to the Baltic. An alliance was formed between the two former enemies, Poland and Lithuania, that was strong enough to resoundingly defeat the Teutonic Knights at the **Battle of Grunwald** in 1410. This established **Poland-Lithuania**—one of the greatest powers in Europe—and opened up the Baltic to the newly unified region.

Poland was a multi-religious state and avoided the religious warfare that plagued the rest of Europe. The Renaissance reached Poland under the rule of **King Zygmunt I Stary** (the Old). Under the reign of his son, **Zygmunt II August, Copernicus** created a new planetary theory, and the poet Kochanowski lectured in Kraków. In 1572, the *szlachta* (nobles) in the **Sejm** (Parliament) decided upon an elected kingship, which gave them the power to survey royal policy, the right to approve taxes, declarations of war, and treaties, and the right to resist the king's decisions. Elections became a major event, and too often an excuse for the highest ranking members of the *szlachta* to indulge in political intrigue and feuds.

In the early 17th century, one of the elected kings, **Zygmunt III Waza**, of a Swedish line, moved the capital to Warsaw. Soon after, the Wazas got their wazoos whipped during the bloody wars against Swedish invaders—the **"Swedish Deluge"**. **Jan III Sobieski** crushed the Turks and lifted the siege of Vienna in 1683, which further exhausted Poland and left it vulnerable to Prussia and Russia. Poland entered an unstable period, marked by increasing Russian influence and culminating in the three Partitions. The three **Partitions of Poland,** in 1772, 1793, and 1795, divided the kingdom among Russia, Prussia, and Austria, wiping Poland from the map for the next 123 years. While the 19th century was for most of Europe an age of empire, expansion, improvement, and progress, for Poland it was an ordeal. Russia suppressed the development of modern institutions in the 1820s, and bloody rebellions in 1831 and 1863 were crushed.

Poland did not regain its **independence** until 1918, when, under American President Wilson's principle of self-determination, the Allies returned Poznań and West Prussia, as well as access to the port of Gdańsk, to the newly independent country. From the 1920s until 1935, Poland was governed by the autocratic **Marshal Piłsudski**, with only formal preservation of parliamentary authority. Once Germany signed the Nazi-Soviet Non-Aggression Pact on August 23, 1939, Poland's defensive treaties with France and non-aggression pact with Germany were rendered worthless. The country fought courageously for a month against the raging Nazi war machine despite a simultaneous Soviet attack from the east. For six years, Poland was the site of massive destruction, unspeakable atrocities, and Nazi terror. Over 6 million of its inhabitants died, including 3 million Polish Jews. Liberated by the Soviet Union, which obstructed the return of the Polish government and installed Communist proxies after the war, Poland spent 45 years bound to Russia in the Soviet Bloc.

In 1979, **Karol Wojtyla** became the first Polish Pope, taking the name John Paul II. This helped to unite the still-overwhelmingly Catholic Poles and was an impetus for the events the next year. In 1980, **Solidarnosc** (Solidarity), the first independent workers' union in Eastern Europe, was born. Led by the charismatic **Lech Wałęsa,** a former electrician at the Gdańsk shipyards, Solidarity was to be one of the most important factors in bringing down Communism in the region. However, in 1980-82, it was still an isolated movement. Its actions resulted in the declaration of **martial law** in 1981, which was imposed by **General Wojciech Jaruzelski,** then head of the Polish government, allegedly as a means of protecting the Polish nation from a Soviet invasion. Wałęsa was jailed and released only when Solidarity was dissolved by the government in 1982. Officially disbanded and outlawed by Jaruzelski, the organization continued its fight underground.

The first of the 1989 Eastern European shakedowns unfolded in Poland. Solidarity members swept into all but one of the contested seats in the June elections, and **Tadeusz Mazowiecki** was sworn in as Eastern Europe's first non-Communist premier in 40 years. In 1990, the government opted to take the bitter dose of capitalism in one gulp, eliminated subsidies, froze wages, and devalued the currency in order to attract foreign investment. This threw the already antiquated economy into recession and produced the first unemployment in 45 years. The availability of consumer goods didn't compensate for the rise in prices and unemployment, a fact which led to the victory of the left in the elections of 1993. Wałęsa's popularity slowly declined as he made his own difficult transition from trade union president to President. Steadily rising crime, a fractured and fragile coalition government, and painful reform process also didn't help. Despite some serious setbacks, however, Poland has continued to inch towards economic prosperity and political stability.

LITERATURE

"Niechaj to narodowie wżdy postronni znają, iż Polacy nie gęsi i swój język mają (Let all other nations know that Poles are not geese and do have their language)."

—Mikołaj Rej

The oldest work written in Polish, the religious hymn *Bogurodzica*, dates back to the 14th century. The first author to write consistently in the language was the 16th century's **Mikołaj Rej**. His contemporary, **Jan Kochanowski**, hailed linden trees for their inspirational value in one of his many epigrams, *Na lipę* (On the Linden Tree).

Jan Chryzostom Pasek's prose tells no tales of geese or trees. Instead, his diaries, written in Baroque Poland's favorite literary style, recount the stormy life of his pet otter. An even greater passion sparked **King Jan III Sobieski's** unabashedly erotic letters written to his French wife, Marysieńka, who languished alone (as far as we can tell) during her hubby's unending military campaigns against the Turks. Diaries, letters, and all other forms of literary expression thrived during the 18th-century Enlightenment, under King Stanisław II August Poniatowski's patronage. The tireless, politically involved scribes even managed to compose a constitution.

The novel was first introduced in by **Ignacy Krasicki**, while international tensions and the partitions of Poland resulted in many political pamphlets and treatises. Poland's loss of statehood in 1795, followed by the failed 1831 uprising, ushered in Romanticism, which glorified the country, assigning it messianic significance. The works of the three *wieszcze* (national bards)—**Adam Mickiewicz, Juliusz Słowacki,** and **Zygmunt Krasiński**—depict Poland as a suffering martyr. Their poems are often set in the mystical scenery of Polish and Lithuanian folktales.

Like the Enlightenment, Romanticism also ended with a failed uprising in 1863. Disillusioned with the mood of the first half of the century, younger 19th-century authors ushered in **Positivism**. Characterized by naturalistic and historical novels, the new current advocated simple work and integration into one's community as the central goals of each individual. **Eliza Orzeszkowa** voiced such ideas in *Nad Niemnem* (On the Banks of the Niemen), a novel about a pauperized noble's interaction with peasants. A differently set story, **Henry Sienkiewicz's** Nobel-Prize-winning *Quo Vadis?*—a tale of early Christianity amid Roman decadence under Nero—pleads for every person's moral integrity as the foundation of a wholesome society.

The everyday grind provided inspiration only until the turn of the century. The early 20th-century **Młoda Polska** (Young Poland) movement did not have the previous generation's energy, and its work is laden with pessimism and apathy. In his mystery-filled *Wesele* (The Wedding), playwright **Stanisław Wyspiański** builds suspense towards the promised appearance of a miracle-bearing spirit. In place of a Polish messiah, the end introduces straw-men, symbols of weak national leaders.

Pessimism, as exemplified by the Surrealist drama of **Witos**, prevailed even after independence in 1918. Unlike Wyspiański, who settled for worrying about Poland's problems, Witos feared for the future of all people. His indignation at the soullessness of the mechanized society is seen in his sex-crazed, psychopathic characters.

The outbreak of WWII proved the relevance of Witos's catastrophic vision. The resulting chaos effected **Tadeusz Różewicz's** search for order. His failure to arrive at an attainable yet fulfilling level of existence pinned the term "nihilistic" to much of his pre-1956 poetry. In the late 50s, Różewicz and **Sławomir Mrożek** experimented with the theater of the absurd. Perhaps the best-known Polish play of this genre, Mrożek's *Tango* depicts the moral license of the intelligentsia, and the young generation's vain attempts to re-establish traditional values and familial peace.

POLAND TODAY

In Poland's election in November 1995, Lech Wałęsa—former leader of the Solidarity trade union and one of the most internationally recognized figures in Central European politics—was replaced by Alexander Kwasniewski. As the head of the Democratic Left Alliance, President Kwasniewski remains committed to further reform in Poland and strengthening relations with the west, including eventual Polish membership in international organizations such as NATO and the EU. Package 2000, announced in April 1990, calls for a cut in taxes, promotion of exports, and an attempt to bring the złoty back into single digit inflation. The economy is doing fairly well and the GDP is expected to increase by over 7% in 1996-97. March and April of 1996 saw the first new protests in Poland since its regime change, as people in cities and small towns across the country took to the streets in "silent marches" to protest the dramatic rise in crime.

Warsaw (Warszawa)

Warsaw's motto, *contemnire procellas* (to defy the storms), has been put to the test often in the city's long history. According to legend, Warsaw began when the lucky fisherman Wars netted a mermaid who begged him to release her, pledging to protect the new city that he and his wife Sawa would establish on the spot where the fantastic catch had been made. Warsaw has needed all the protection it can get; invaders from the north, east, and west have all taken a shot at this bastion of Polish pride. WWII saw two-thirds of the population killed and 83% of the city destroyed, but even that devastation was used as an opportunity to rebuild and revitalize. Once again the world's largest Polish city (a title long held by Chicago), Warsaw is quickly repairing the Communist legacy and emerging as an important international business center. Tourists come to see the city that rebuilt itself from rubble, relax in its parks, take in its museums, listen to its concerts, and feast in its restaurants. The city's university infuses Warsaw with young blood, which keeps the energy high and the nightlife lively. The mermaid appears to have kept her promise.

ORIENTATION AND PRACTICAL INFORMATION

Warsaw, Poland's principal air and rail hub, sprawls in east-central Poland, 150km from the Belarusian border and bisected by the **Wisła River.** The busy downtown area, known as **Śródmieście,** and most major points of interest are on the west riverbank. The main train station, **Warszawa Centralna** (a.k.a. **Dworzec Centralny**), is located near the center at the corner of **Aleje Jerozolimskie** and **ul. Emilii Plater.** From here, it is a short walk along Al. Jerozolimskie to the large intersection with **ul. Marszałkowska,** one of the city's two main north-south avenues. This busy intersection serves as a major stop for most bus and tram lines. Al. Jerozolimskie continues east to the other main north-south avenue, known as **Trakt Królewski,** which intersects Al. Jerozolimskie at **rondo Charles de Gaulle.** A left on Trakt Królewski runs north up **ul. Nowy Świat,** which becomes **ul. Krakowskie Przedmieście,** and leads directly to the Old Town. A right at rondo Charles de Gaulle puts you on **Al. Ujazdowskie,** which, by way of embassy row, reaches the Łazienki Palace. If you purchase a **map** (try WCIT, see below), buy one that covers the whole city, including the public transportation lines.

Useful Organizations

Tourist Offices: Warszawskie Centrum Informacji Turystycznej (WCIT), pl. Zamkowy 1/3 (tel. 635 18 81; fax 310 464), at the entrance to the Old Town. The friendly, busy staff runs an info line and provides maps, guidebooks, hotels and restaurant listings, currency exchange, and hotel reservations. Pick up a copy of the English-language newspaper, *The Warsaw Voice* (3.50zl), an entertaining and useful publication aimed at Warsaw's international population. Open Mon.-Fri. 9am-6pm, Sat. 10am-6pm, Sun. 11am-6pm. For info on cultural events, call tel. 298 489 (available Mon.-Fri. 10am-9pm, Sat.-Sun. 10am-6pm). **ORBIS,** ul. Bracka 16 (tel. 270 172; fax 277 605), entrance on Al. Jerozolimskie near ul. Nowy Świat. Sells train, plane, ferry, and bus tickets. Open Mon.-Fri. 8am-7pm, Sat. 9am-3pm.

Budget Travel: ALMATUR, ul. Kopernika 23 (tel. 263 512 or 262 639; fax 263 507), off ul. Nowy Świat. Often busy. Sells ISICs, international bus and ferry tickets, and plane tickets at student discounts. Sells vouchers to ALMATUR hotels in major Polish cities (US$15; students US$12). Open Mon.-Fri. 9am-6pm, Sat. 10am-2pm. **Room 3,** ul. Krakowskie Przedmieście 24 (tel. 269 980; fax 264 757), is ALMATUR's train ticket department. Go through the main university entrance to the 1st building on the right. **Interrail** and **Eurotrain** tickets. Open Mon.-Fri. 10am-

ORIENTATION AND PRACTICAL INFORMATION ■ 393

5:30pm. **PTTK,** Podwale 23 (tel. 635 27 25), in the Old Town. Info on budget hotels across Poland, and hitchhiker's guides (6zł). Open Mon.-Fri. 9am-3pm.

Embassies: Clustered around Al. Ujazdowskie. **Australia,** ul. Estońska 3/5 (tel. 617 60 81). **Belarus,** ul. Ateńska 67 (tel. 617 39 54). **Canada,** ul. Matejki 1/5 (tel. 629 80 51). Open Mon.-Fri. 8:30am-1pm and 2-5pm. **Russia,** ul. Belwederska 49, bldg. C (tel. 621 34 53). Open Wed. and Fri. 8am-1pm. **Ukraine,** Al. Ujazdowskie 13 (tel. 629 32 01). **U.K.,** ul. Róż 1 (tel. 628 10 01), also serves citizens of **New Zealand. U.S.,** Al. Ujazdowskie 29/31 (tel. 628 30 41). Open Mon.-Fri. 9am-noon.

Currency Exchange: Hotels, banks, tourist offices, and private *kantors* (which have better rates) throughout the city change cash. **24-hr. exchange** at central train station, Al. Jerozolimskie 54 (tel. 255 050), and the international airport departures area, ul. Żwirki i Wigury (tel. 469 624 or 469 694). For **traveler's checks** and **cash advances,** there are several branches of the **Bank PKO S.A. (Pekao)** including: pl. Bankowy 2 (tel. 637 10 61), in the blue skyscraper, ul. Mazowiecka 14 (tel. 661 25 59), and ul. Grójecka 1/3 (tel. 658 82 17), in Hotel Sobieski. AmEx and Visa traveler's checks cashed for 1% commission; MasterCard and Visa cash advances. All branches open Mon.-Fri. 8am-6pm. **Bank PKO BP,** ul. Marszałkowska 100 (tel. 260 061), opposite Hotel Forum, cashes Visa traveler's checks without commission. Open Mon.-Fri. 7am-8pm.

ATMs: Most **Bank PKO S.A.** branches have Cirrus/MC **ATMs. 24-hr. ATMs** are located at ul. Mazowiecka 14 and Hotel Sobieski, ul. Grójecka 1/3. There is also a 24-hr. AmEx ATM at American Express and the airport (see below).

American Express: ul. Krakowskie Przedmieście 11 (tel. 635 20 02; fax 635 75 56). Holds cardholders' mail and provides members with emergency cash advances. Exchange cash and American Express traveler's checks commission free. Postal code: 00-950. Open Mon.-Fri. 9am-6pm, Sat. 10am-2pm.

Western Union: ul. Krakowskie Przedmieście 55 (tel. 371 826), in Prosper Bank S.A. Open Mon.-Fri. 8am-6pm.

Express Mail: DHL, Al. Jerozolimskie 11/19 (tel. 627 23 23; fax 627 23 13). Open Mon.-Fri. 8am-6pm, Sat. 8am-2pm. **Federal Express,** ul. Obornicka 19A, in Hotel Marriott (tel. 630 63 47). Open Mon.-Fri. 8am-6pm, Sat. 8am-2pm.

Post Office: ul. Świętokrzyska 31/33 (tel. 204 551). For stamps and letters, push "D" when you enter, and go to the counter indicated when your number is called. For packages, push "F". **Poste Restante** can be picked up at *kasa* #12 or 13, after pushing "C" on the machine. **Fax** bureau (fax 300 021). To the U.S. 15zł a page. Open 24hr. **Postal code:** 00-001.

Telephones: At the post office (see above). Tokens and **phone cards** available. Open 24hr. **Phone code:** 0-22 for 6-digit numbers, 0-2 for 7-digit numbers.

Transportation

Flights: Port Lotniczy Warszawa-Okęcie, ul. Żwirki i Wigury (tel. 606 94 69), commonly referred to as Terminal 1. Take bus #175 to the center (after 11pm, bus #611). Buy bus tickets at the Ruch kiosk in the departure hall or at the *kantor* outside (1zł plus 1zł for every large suitcase or backpack). **Airport-City Bus** (4zł, 2zł with ISIC; luggage free) is a faster way to the center and back (daily 5:30am-11pm; weekdays 3 per hr.; weekends 2 per hr.). Buy tickets from the driver.

Airline Offices: LOT, Al. Jerozolimskie 65/79 (tel. 952 or 953), in Hotel Marriott. **British Airways,** ul. Krucza 49 (tel. 628 94 31), off Al. Jerozolimskie. Open Mon.-Fri. 9am-5pm. **Delta,** ul. Królewska 11 (tel. 260 257). Each carrier has at least 1 flight per day to London, and LOT flies directly to New York (6 per week).

Trains: Warszawa Centralna, the well organized central train station, is the most convenient stop for visitors to the city. Lines can be quite long, and most employees speak only Polish, so write down where and when you want to go, and ask them to write down which *peron* number to head for ("*Który peron?*" means "Which platform?"). To: Berlin (6 per day, 7-8hr., 90zł); Budapest (2 per day, 10hr., 170zł); Kiev (2 per day, 22-24hr., 88zł); Minsk (5 per day, 12hr., 50zł); Moscow (4 per day, 27-30hr., 160zł); Prague (3 per day, 12-14hr., 94zł); and connections to almost every corner of Poland.

Buses: PKS Warszawa Zachodnia, Al. Jerozolimskie 144 (tel. 236 494 or 236 495), shares a building, address, and city bus stop with the Warszawa Zachodnia train station, and sends buses north and west of the city. Buses from **PKS Warszawa**

394 ■ WARSAW (WARSZAWA)

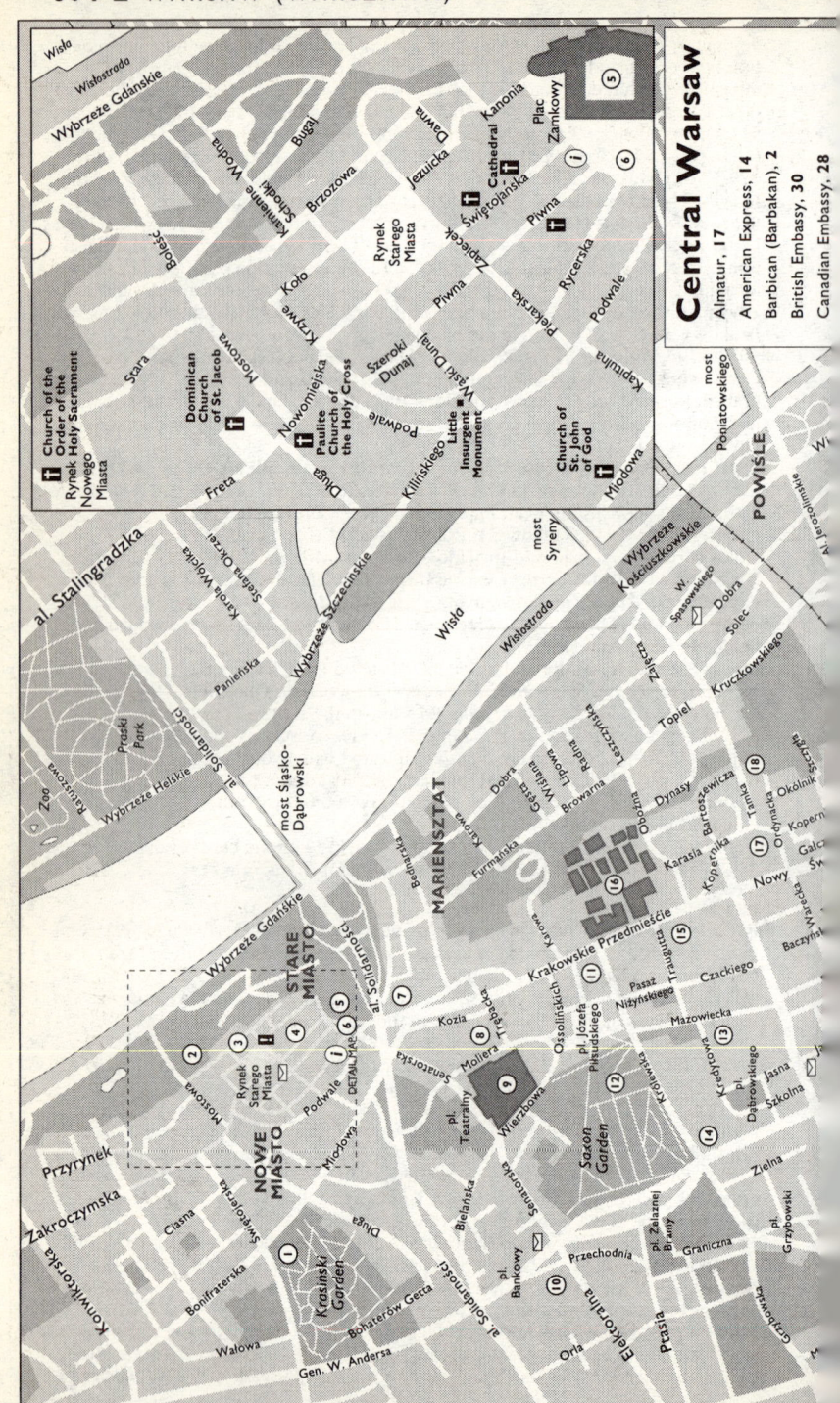

Central Warsaw

- Almatur, 17
- American Express, 14
- Barbican (Barbakan), 2
- British Embassy, 30
- Canadian Embassy, 28

ORIENTATION AND PRACTICAL INFORMATION ■ 395

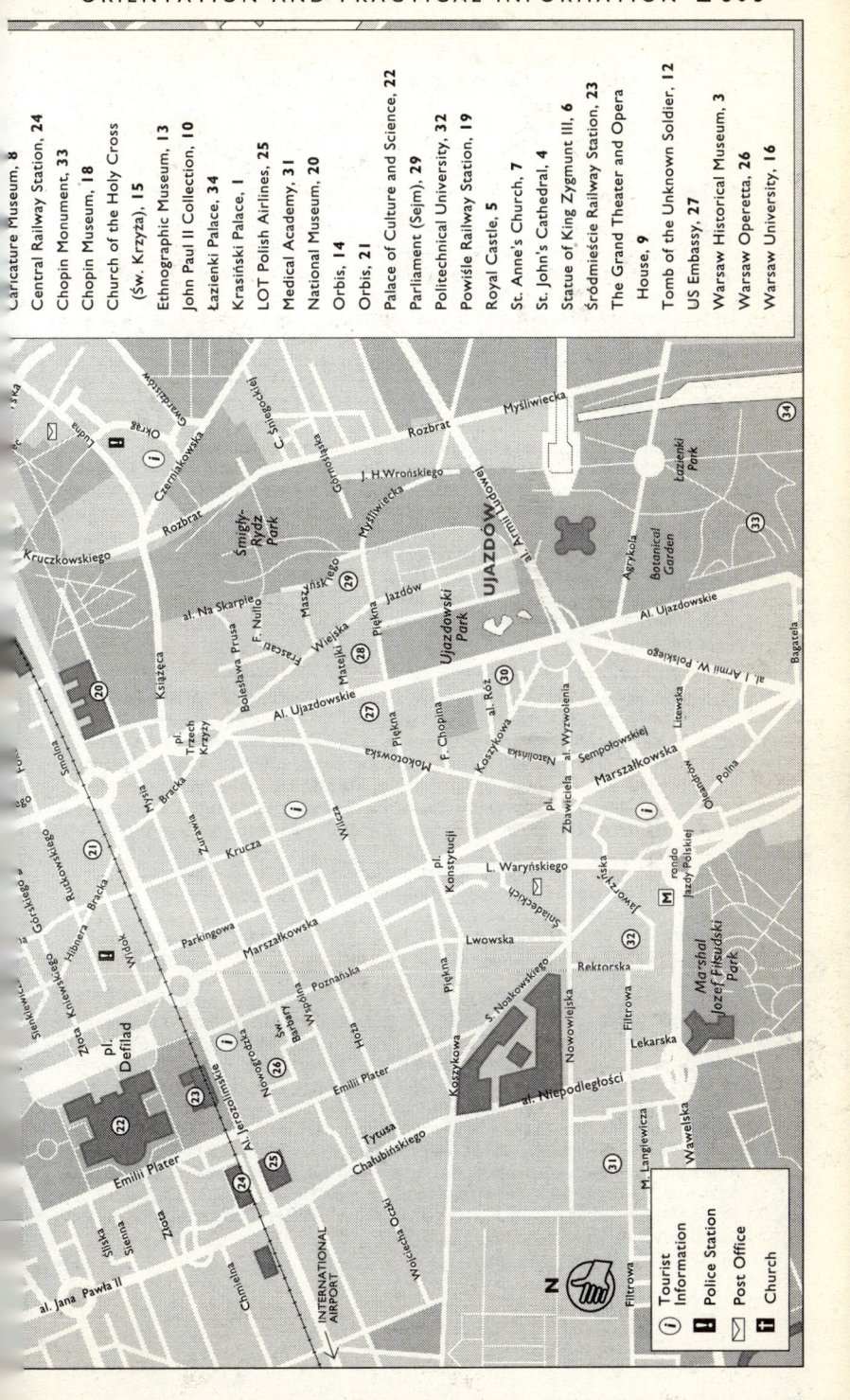

Caricature Museum, 8
Central Railway Station, 24
Chopin Monument, 33
Chopin Museum, 18
Church of the Holy Cross (Św. Krzyża), 15
Ethnographic Museum, 13
John Paul II Collection, 10
Łazienki Palace, 34
Krasiński Palace, 1
LOT Polish Airlines, 25
Medical Academy, 31
National Museum, 20
Orbis, 14
Orbis, 21
Palace of Culture and Science, 22
Parliament (Sejm), 29
Politechnical University, 32
Powiśle Railway Station, 19
Royal Castle, 5
St. Anne's Church, 7
St. John's Cathedral, 4
Statue of King Zygmunt III, 6
Śródmieście Railway Station, 23
The Grand Theater and Opera House, 9
Tomb of the Unknown Soldier, 12
US Embassy, 27
Warsaw Historical Museum, 3
Warsaw Operetta, 26
Warsaw University, 16

Warning: Theft is rising on international overnight trains (to Berlin and Prague) as well as in the train stations. Travelers should protect their safety and property.

Stadion, on the other side of the river, head to the east and south. Both stations are easily reached by taking the commuter train from the Warszawa Śródmiescie station (next to Warszawa Centralna; 1.60zł). Check with the International Bus Information window for ever-changing westbound schedules (open Mon.-Fri. 8am-4pm). **Polski Express:** Al. Jana Pawła II (tel. 630 29 67), offers faster and more comfortable bus service from Warsaw to Gdańsk (2 per day, 6hr.), Kraków (3 per day, 6hr.), Lublin (6 per day, 4hr.), and Szczecin (1 per day, 9½hr.).

Public Transportation: Bus and **tram** lines are marked on some city maps. Day trams and buses (including express lines) cost 1zł. Night buses 3zł. Large baggage 1zł per piece. Buy tickets at a Ruch kiosk or street vendors. Punch both ends of the ticket in the machines on board or face a 50zł fine. Bus #175 is the king of them all, going all the way from the airport to the Old Town by way of the central train station, the center of town, and ul. Nowy Świat. Warsaw's **Metro** is still in its early stages, and is not very useful. It costs 1zł (tickets available in Metro stations).

Taxis: Stands are marked by blue-and-white signs. For relatively cheap 24-hr. taxi service, call 919 or 96 22. Avoid cabs in front of hotels and at the airport, the train station, and the ul. Marszałkowska-Al. Jerozolimskie rotary; you'll be overcharged. Fares usually start at 3zł plus 1zł per km. Night rates are 50% more, plus whatever the driver thinks he earned. Cabs with a mermaid on the side are state-run and usually a safer bet.

Car Rental: Avis, at the Marriott Hotel (tel./fax 630 73 16). **Budget,** at the Marriott Hotel (tel. 630 72 80; fax 630 69 46). Open daily 8am-8pm.

Hitchhiking: Hitchers pick up *Książeczka autostopu* (The Hitchhiker's Book), at the PTTK office (see above). Locals are hitchhiking less in Warsaw, though it is still quite common in the countryside.

Helpful Services

Luggage Storage: At the main train station, below the main hall. Lockers come in 3 sizes: "A" (5zł per day), "B" (7zł per day), and "C" (12zł per day). Open 24hr.

English Bookstore: American Bookstore, ul. Krakowskie Przedmieście 45 (tel. 260 161). Lots of fiction, reference books, and periodicals, with a selection that will make you feel right at home. Open Mon.-Sat. 10am-7pm, Sun. noon-5pm.

International Newsstand: Empik, across from the Palace of Culture and Science on the ground floor of the Junior department store. Open Mon.-Sat. 9am-10pm, Sun. 11am-5pm.

Photocopies: Copy General, Al. Jerozolimskie 63 (tel. 628 62 52; fax 625 47 32), entrance on ul. Emilii Plater across from the train station. Self-service 0.13zł per page, otherwise 0.17zł. Open 24hr.

Laundromat: ul. Karmelicka 17 (tel. 317 317). Take bus #180 north from ul. Marszałkowska toward Żoliborz, and get off at ul. Anielewicza. Bring your own detergent. Wash and dry 12zł. Open Mon.-Fri. 9am-7pm, Sat. 9am-1pm.

24-Hour Pharmacy: Apteka Grabowski (tel. 256 984), at the central train station.

Crisis Lines: 24-Hr. AIDS: tel. 628 03 36; open Mon.-Fri. 10am-10pm. **Drugs:** tel. 96 33, 622 50 01, or 628 03 36; open Mon.-Fri. 9am-5pm. **Women's:** tel. 635 47 91; open Mon.-Fri. 4-8pm. **Psychological:** tel. 295 813, or 919.

Gay and Lesbian Hotline: tel. 628 52 22. The Lambda Center Information Line runs 2 weekly phone sessions: Wed. 6-9pm for women, Fri. 3-9pm for men. Both in English or Polish. They'll tell you what's up and where.

Medical Assistance: Medical Info Line, ul. Smolna 34/22 (tel. 278 962). Directs you to private doctors and dentists. Some English spoken. Open Mon.-Fri 8am-8pm, Sat. 8am-3pm. **24-hr. service** and **ambulance,** ul. Hoża 56 (tel. 999 or 628 24 24). **24-hr. dental service,** ul. Ludna 10 (tel. 635 01 02 or 625 01 05). **Marriott Hotel Medical Center,** Al. Jerozolimskie 6/7 (tel. 630 51 15).

ACCOMMODATIONS AND CAMPING

Warsaw's prices rise and rooms become scarce in July and August. The hostels are the first to go, so call ahead. For help finding **private rooms**, check in with **Syrena**, ul. Krucza 17 (tel. 628 75 40), off Al. Jerozolimskie (open Mon.-Sat. 8am-7pm, Sun. 8am-5pm). **Romeo i Julia**, ul. Emilii Plater 15/30 (tel. 292 993), directly opposite the central train station, also finds rooms. Singles run 50-70zł, doubles 60-80zł. **WCIT** (see Useful Organizations: Tourist Offices, p. 392) maintains a list of all accommodations in the city and can assist in making reservations.

Hostels

Schronisko Młodzieżowe (HI), ul. Smolna 30, top floor (tel. 278 952), across from the National Museum. A short walk from the train station, or you can take any tram headed east 3 stops to "Nowy Swiat". The optional rooms are clean, but the staff's English ability has empowered them to write up an imposing list of rules and regulations, including a 30-day max. stay, an 11pm curfew, and a 10am-4pm lockout. There is a kitchen and a baggage room, though only 2 co-ed showers. If you don't mind skipping the nightlife, this popular hostel is a good option. 12zł; nonmembers 15zł; sheets 2.50zł.

Schronisko Młodzieżowe (HI), ul. Karolkowa 53a (tel. 632 88 29). Take tram #22 or 24 west from Al. Jerozolimskie or the train station. Get off at "Okopowa". Go left on al. Solidarności, then right onto ul. Karolkowa. The hostel is hard to miss—it's the white building in the sea of gray blocks. Inside, it's well maintained and not as mobbed as the main one. Rooms are basic and clean. Kitchen and storage facilities. No showers. Lockout 10am-5pm. Curfew 11pm. 4- to 7-bed rooms 9zł, non-members 11zł. Doubles 40zł. Triples 18zł per person. Sheets 1.50zł.

Schronisko Młodzieżowe, ul. Międzyparkowa 4/6 (tel. 311 766), close to the river between two parks. Take tram #2, 6, or 18 northbound from ul. Marszałkowska to "K.K.S. Polonia". The hostel is across the street as you continue down the road. Definitely the least formal of the hostels in town, located in a tiny building in an old sports complex. The rooms go with the exterior (a bit rugged), but they do the job. Beds 10zł. Sheets 2zł. Open April 15-Oct. 15.

Hotels

Hotel Metalowiec, ul. Długa 29 (tel. 314 020; fax 635 31 38), 3 blocks away from the Old Town near the "Arsenał" stop. One of the most affordable hotels in the city, and a great location to boot. Spacious, comfortable rooms and clean communal bathrooms. TV in common area. Singles 30zł. Doubles 44zł. Quads 60zł.

Dom Literata, ul. Krakowskie Przedmieście 87/89 (tel. 635 39 20), at the entrance to the Old Town, over a café full of writers and artists. Lacks a sign or real reception desk, but this small hotel is worth hunting for. The rooms are spacious, and the bathrooms, though not private, are practically brand-new. All but one of the rooms overlook plac Zamkowy. 50zł per person.

Hotel Belfer, Wybrzeże Kościuszkowskie 31/33 (tel. 625 05 71; fax 625 26 00). From the train station take any tram east to Most Poniałowskiego, then go north (river on your right) along Wisłostnada, which becomes Wybrzeże Kościuszkowski. Overlooks a park, river, highway, and electric plant. Singles 50zł, with bath 76zł. Doubles 64zł, with bath 98zł. Triples with bath 128zł.

Hotel Garnizonowy, ul. Mazowiecka 10 (tel. 682 20 69). Hidden away a little more than a block from ul. Krakowskie Przedmieście off ul. Świętokrzyska, this is one of the most affordable hotels in the downtown area. Feels a bit like barracks, but the rooms are nice for the price. Singles 62zł. Doubles 84zł. Triples 102zł.

Hotel-Uniwersytet Warszawski, ul. Belwederska 26/30 (tel. 410 253). Take bus #131 or 180 from ul. Marszałkowska to "Spacerowa", south of Park Łazienkowski. Bright rooms and suburban surroundings. Singles 66zł, with bath 121zł. Doubles 82zł, with bath 152zł. Triples 110zł, with bath 183zł.

Hotel Aldona, ul. Wybrzeże Kosciuszkowskie (tel. 628 58 53), near the Most Poniatowskiego. This hotel is on a ship floating in the Wisła river. A great budget option, unless the thought of sleeping on a boat makes the land-lubber in ya' queasy. Communal bathroom. Singles 35zł. Doubles 45zł. Open May-Sept.

Camping
Camping Wisła, ul. Bitwy Warszawskiej 1920r. 15/17 (tel. 233 748). Down the road from the rotary by the main bus station. Take bus #127 to "Zachodnia" and cross the street. Closer to downtown, shadier, and less cramped than Gromada, it's also near a popular swimming pool. 6zł per person, 3zł per tent.

Camping Gromada, ul. Żwirki i Wigury 32 (tel. 254 391). Take bus #175 (dir. "Port Lotniczy") to "Akademia Medyczna". Cheerful signs welcome you to a crowded campsite. 7zł per person, 5zł per tent. Bungalows 12.50zł per person.

FOOD

For quick and cheap eats, most **food stands** are found along ul. Marszałkowska. You can blow your budget on roast duck or grilled salmon at any of Warsaw's best restaurants bunched around **Rynek Starego Miasta,** but proletarian **cafeterias** are infinitely cheaper and more colorful. There is a **24-hour grocery** at the central train station, as well as **Delikatesy,** ul. Nowy Świat 53. All are oases for late-night club crawlers and jet-lagged snackers.

Polish Cuisine
Bar Uniwersytecki, ul. Krakowskie Przedmieście 16/18, next to the university under a yellow awning. As Polish as it gets. Rice with apples 1.20zł. Soups 1.30zł. Pork chops 3.50zł. English menu. Open Mon.-Fri. 7am-8pm, Sat.-Sun. 9am-5pm.

Bar Pod Barbakanem, ul. Mostowa 27/29 (tel. 314 737), entrance on ul. Freta. A popular, cafeteria-style eatery between the Old and New Towns. A full meal runs only 6zł. English menu. Open Mon.-Fri. 8am-6pm, Sat.-Sun. 9am-5pm.

Bar Szwajcarski, ul. Nowy Świat 5, near the National Museum. Another traditional cafeteria, offering an extensive breakfast menu, as well as lunch options. Omelettes 1.50zł. Open Mon.-Fri. 8am-8pm, Sat.-Sun. 9am-5pm.

Zapiecek, ul. Piwna 34/36 (tel. 315 693), at the corner of ul. Piwna and ul. Zapiecek in the Old Town. Candle-light, German-style, but Polish cuisine rules the menu. *Barszcz* 3.50zł. Veal 10zł. Outdoor dining. Open daily 11am-11pm.

Restauracja Boruta, ul. Freta 38 (tel. 316 197), on the Rynek Nowego Miasta. Dine outdoors or in. Roasted duck 8zł. Open daily 11am til the last guest leaves.

Pod Herbami, ul. Piwna 21/23 (tel. 316 447). Looks like a medieval tavern, tastes like a Polish restaurant. Entrées hover around 10-15zł, while grilled salmon and other specialties run 20-30zł. Open Sun.-Thurs. 11am-11pm, Fri.-Sat. 11am-1am.

Restauracja Ekologiczna "Nove Miasto", Rynek Nowego Miasta 13/15 (tel. 314 379). Warsaw's first natural food restaurant. Organically grown vegetarian entrées 10-20zł. Whole grain desserts, health food soups, a variety of crêpes, and a whole salad theater. The 1996 salad repertoire included: *Bacchus' Triumph, King Lear,* and *L'Après-midi d'un Faun.* Encores of Polish beer and German wine. Outdoor seating available. Live music nightly. Open daily 10am-midnight.

International Restaurants
Pod Samsonem, ul. Freta 3/5 (tel. 311 788). Cheap eats on the way from the Old Town to the New, opposite Maria Skłodowska-Curie's museum. The Polish-Jewish cuisine is supposed to make you big and strong like Samson. You won't know unless you try it. *Cymes* salad 3zł. Open daily 10am-10pm.

Hoang Kim Restaurant, ul. Freta 18/20 (tel. 635 79 59). Ninety Chinese and Vietnamese dishes. Weekday lunch special includes soup, entrée, salad, and dessert for only 14zł. 10% off if you choose the take-out option. Open daily 11am-11pm.

Maharaja, ul. Szeroki Dunaj 13 (tel. 635 25 01). Thai cuisine hidden in a corner of the Old Town. The Polish and English menu showcases entrées for 12-17zł. Open daily noon-midnight. Their second location at ul. Marszalkowska 34/50 (tel. 621 13 92), serves up Indian specialties including Tandoori chicken and *Naan.*

El Popo, ul. Senatorska 27 (tel. 272 340). Yucca trees, colorful parrots, and desert-brown hues make it a real Mexican *casa.* Great place for a spicy snack. Nachos 7zł. Tacos 6zł. Salads 8-12zł. Latin rhythms free. Open daily noon-midnight.

Pizzeria Giovanni, ul. Krakowskie Przedmieście 37 (tel. 262 788). Over 25 kinds of pizza (7-13zł). Spaghetti 9.50zł. Delivery available. Open daily 11am-11pm.

Cafés

Kawiarnia Bazyliszek, Rynek Starego Miasta 3/9 (tel. 311 841). A relaxing outdoor café amid the restored splendor of Warsaw's Old Town and all the tourists who are here to see it. Tortes 3.50zł. Coffee 2.50zł. Open daily 9am-9pm.

Gwiazdeczka, ul. Piwna 40/42 (tel. 319 463), in the Old Town. The menu is full of innocent snacks and coffees (3-6zł), but beer and cocktails are ever-tempting alternatives. Open daily 9am-10pm.

Cyberia Internet Café, ul. Krakowskie Przedmieście 4/6 (tel. 627 14 47; e-mail: cafe@cyberia.com.pl; http://www.cyberia.com.pl). Envisaged as a communications center, drinks are served to spice up time on the 'Net (9zł per hour). Open daily 9am-midnight.

Lody W. Hoduń, ul. Nowomiejska 9, in the Old Town. Everyone in line knows what they are waiting for. The 0.50zł scoops of ice cream here are larger than anywhere else and the selection can't be beat. Open daily 10am-7pm.

SIGHTS

Razed beyond recognition during WWII, Warsaw was rebuilt from rubble by defiant survivors. Thanks to the wonders of Communist upkeep, most of the buildings look much older than their 50 years. The city requires time to explore, as sights are spread out, and some, quite distant.

Stare Miasto (Old Town)

Warsaw's postwar reconstruction shows its finest face in the narrow, cobbled streets and colorful façades of **Stare Miasto** (Old Town), at the very end of ul. Krakowskie Przedmieście. At the right side of the entrance to the Old Town stands the impressive **Zamek Królewski** (Royal Castle). In the Middle Ages, it was the residence of the Dukes of Mazovia, and in the late 16th century it replaced Kraków's Wawel as the official royal residence. Burned down in September 1939 and plundered by the Nazis, the castle became a symbolic martyr in the fight for Polish independence. Many Varsovians risked their lives hiding its priceless works in the hope that, one day, the *oeuvres* would be restored. After independence in 1945, the castle's plans and some of the treasures were retrieved, and for 30 years, thousands of Poles, Polish expats, and dignitaries worldwide sent contributions in hopes of restoring this symbol of national pride. Work began in 1971 and finished a few years later. The kingly abode is an impressive example of physical restoration, and visitors will marvel that anything like this could have been built in the 70s.

Kolumna Zygmunta III Wazy stands proud above the square in front of the castle. Constructed in 1644 in honor of the king who transferred the capital from Kraków to Warsaw, it stood here for 300 years before it was destroyed in WWII. For centuries, the king's crusading figure, now rebuilt, has watched over plac Zamkowy; his vigil continues with a silent view of the rollerbladers below.

Leaving the column behind and turning left past the castle onto ul. Świętojańska leads to **Katedra Św. Jana** (Cathedral of St. John), Warsaw's oldest church. Almost completely destroyed during the 1944 Warsaw Uprising, it was rebuilt after the war

---

Hey, Numbnutz!

The English word "numbnutz" makes no reference to the tactile abilities of certain organs, but rather is derived from the Slavic word *"nemets"* (немец), which originally meant "stupid" or "mute". The Slavs used this word as a moniker for the Germans and their tongue, as the foreigners seemed unable to communicate in a sensible Slavic way, but rather spoke in some odd gibberish: Nemetski. Needless to say, the Germans took this rather personally, resulting in a whole series of wars in which much of Eastern Europe was invaded, occupied, otherwise slapped around, and, eventually, touristed by the Germans. As a result, that crazy cacophony is not so inscrutable anymore, and nemetski makes perfect sense to a great many modern-day Slavs.

in Vistulan Gothic style. The 1339 case against the Order of Teutonic Knights, who had broken the pact made with Duke of Mazovia Konrad Mazowiecki, is hidden within the walls. The cathedral and its crypts are open to the public; the crypts shelter the graves of the dukes of Mazovia, and of famous Poles such as Henryk Sienkiewicz, winner of a Nobel Prize for his novel *Quo Vadis,* and Gabriel Narutowicz, first president of independent Poland. One side altar contains the tomb of Cardinal Stefan Wyszyński (open to visitors daily dawn to dusk, except during services).

Ul. Świętojańska takes you straight to the pristinely restored Renaissance and Baroque houses of **Rynek Starego Miasta** (Old Town Square). A stone plaque at the entrance memorializes its reconstruction, finished in 1953-54, and recalls the Old Town Square's pre-war history. On the *rynek's* southeast side at #3/9, **Dom "Pod Bazyliszkiem"** immortalizes the Old Town basilisk, whose stare brought instant death to those unfortunate enough to cross his path. Although most houses around the *rynek* were razed during the Warsaw Uprising, a few managed to survive WWII. The **house at #31** dates back to the 14th century. The *rynek* oozes with cafés, kitschy art, and tourists; for a mere 5-10zł, an ever-ready portrait artist will enter your image at least temporarily into the annals of art history.

In the northeast corner of the *rynek* starts ul. Krzywe Koło (Crooked Wheel St.). Ul. Krzywe Koło leads to **Barbakan,** a rare example of 16th-century Polish fortifications and a popular spot for locals and tourists to sit and rest their feet, while street performers provide a folk-music accompaniment. The **Little Insurgent Monument** honors the heroism of the youngest soldiers of the Warsaw Uprising. Around the barbican are the reconstructed remains of the walls that used to surround the entire Old Town; they are decorated by a statue of **Warszawska Syrenka** (Mermaid), the symbol of the city.

Nowe Miasto (New Town)

The Barbican Gate ushers you onto ul. Freta, at the edge of the New Town. In spite of its name, this is the city's second-oldest district. Also destroyed during WWII, its 18th- and 19th-century façades have enjoyed an expensive facelift.

Among the houses lining ul. Freta stands the former home of the Skłodowski family. The great physicist and chemist **Maria Skłodowska-Curie,** winner of two Nobel prizes, was born at ul. Freta 16 in 1867 (see Museums, p. 402).

Ul. Freta leads to **Rynek Nowego Miasta,** the site of **Kościół Sakramentek** (Church of the Order of the Holy Sacrament). The church was founded in 1688 to commemorate King Jan III Sobieski's 1683 victory over the Turks in Vienna. Its interior no longer shows its past glory, but the Baroque dome is a noteworthy sight.

Trakt Królewski (Royal Route)

The 4km-long **Trakt Królewski,** Warsaw's most attractive thoroughfare, begins on **plac Zamkowy** and continues along **ul. Krakowskie Przedmieście.** The "Royal Way", named for Kraków because it leads south toward Poland's former capital, is lined with palaces, churches, and convents built when the royal family moved to Warsaw. Traffic and crowds of tourists now distract from its once regal splendor. On the left as you leave plac Zamkowy, **Kościół Św. Anny** (St. Anne's Church) dates from the 15th century (open daily dawn-dusk). Farther down the street, the **Adam Mickiewicz Monument** gazes toward plac Piłsudskiego and Ogród Saski (Saxon Garden), which contains the **Grób Nieznanego Żołnierza** (Tomb of the Unknown Soldier). Urns hold earth from the graves of Polish soldiers murdered by the Soviets in Katyń and from battlefields marked by Polish blood. A ceremonial **changing of the guard** takes place at noon on Sundays and national holidays.

Fryderyk Chopin spent his childhood in the neighborhood near ul. Krakowski Przedmieście and gave his first public concert in **Pałac Radziwiłłów** (a.k.a. **Pałac Namiestnikowski**) at #46/48, the building guarded by four stone lions. The palace needs more active help these days in its new role as the Polish White House, and guards from the Polish military join the faithful felines out front. A block down the road, **Kościół Wizytek** (Church of the Visitation Nuns) once resounded with the romantic ivory-pounding of the mop-topped composer. **Czapski-Krasiński Palace,**

Chopin's last Warsaw home before he left for France in 1830, provided the setting for much of his composing. Now the palace houses the **Academy of Fine Arts** and **Salonik Chopinów** (The Chopins' Drawing Room; tel. 266 251; open Mon.-Fri. 10am-2pm; 1zł, students 0.50zł). Chopin died abroad at the age of 39 and was buried in Paris, but his heart was returned to Poland; it now rests in an urn in the left nave of **Kościół Św. Krzyża** (Holy Cross Church). And you thought he left it in San Fran.

In front of the Holy Cross Church, a complex of rebuilt palaces on the left belongs to **Uniwersytet Warszawski,** founded in 1816. **Pałac Kazimierzowski,** at the end of the alley leading from the main entrance to the university, now houses the rector's offices, but was once the seat of the School of Knighthood. Its alumni record includes General Tadeusz Kościuszko, who fought in the American Revolutionary War and later led an unsuccessful revolt against Russia.

The **Mikołaj Kopernik Monument,** a permanent seat for the image of the famous astronomer, and **Pałac Staszica,** the seat of the Polish Academy of Sciences, mark the end of ul. Krakowskie Przedmieście. The Royal Route continues, however, as **ul. Nowy Świat** (New World St.). The name of the street dates back to the mid-17th century, when a new settlement was started here, composed mainly of working-class people. It was not until the 18th century that the aristocracy started moving in, embellishing the area with ornate manors and residences. Eventually, ul. Nowy Świat became the main street of Warsaw. Today, there are wider and busier streets in the city, but none as charming or so enjoyable a place for a walk.

The Royal Route terminates with the **Botanical Gardens** (open daily 9am-4pm; 1.50zł, students 1zł), on the left side of Al. Ujazdowskie, and with **Park Łazienkowski,** summer home of the last Polish king, Stanisław August Poniatowski.

Łazienki

With its swans and majestic peacocks, the **Łazienki** (Baths; tel. 621 62 41, ext. 233 or 234, reservations tel. 621 82 12) park is an appropriate setting for the striking Neoclassical **Pałac Łazienkowski,** also called **Pałac na Wodzie** (Palace on Water). This, like most palaces in the park, is the progeny of benefactor King Stanisław August and his beloved architect Dominik Merlini. Galleries of 17th- and 18th-century art wait inside (open Tues.-Sun. 9:30am-3pm, barring rain; 3.50zł, students 2zł; guided tour in English 20zł). **Stara Pomarańczarnia** (Old Orangery; 1786-88) served not only as a greenhouse for orange trees, but also as a theater and servants' quarters (open Tues.-Sun. 9:30am-4pm; 2zł, students 1zł; guided tour in Polish 8zł, in English 20zł). **Teatr Stanisławowski** celebrated its grand opening on September 6, 1788. In 1791, Stanisław August donated the theater to Wojciech Bogusławski, an accomplished actor, director, playwright, "father of Polish theater," and all-around butt-kicker. Bogusławski accepted the gift and opened the theater to the general public. In the west wing of the Old Orangery, the 140 sculptures of **Galeria Rzeźby Polskiej** (Gallery of Polish Sculpture) illustrate the evolution of Polish sculpture from the end of the 16th century through 1939.

It's not just the monuments and museums that attract tourists to Łazienki; the serene greenery makes it an oasis of peace in the busy capital. Leave Warsaw behind, stroll down the shadowed, pebbled park alleys, and relax to the soothing sound of Chopin's music, performed at **Pomnik Chopina** every Sunday from at noon and 4pm from spring to autumn. The park is open daily from dawn to dusk.

Commercial District and The Warsaw Ghetto

In the center of Warsaw's commercial district, southwest of the Old Town, the 70-story "Stalinist Gothic" **Pałac Kultury i Nauki** (Palace of Culture and Science; a.k.a Stalin's Palace), ul. Marszałkowska, is a fitting monument to the man—larger-than-life, omnipresent, and tacky. Locals claim the view from the top is the best in Warsaw. Why? You can't see the palace itself (panorama open daily 9am-6pm; 7.50zł). The palatial eyesore houses over 3000 offices, exhibition and conference facilities, three theaters, two museums—**Museum Ewolucji** (Museum of Evolution; tel. 656 66 37) and **Muzeum Techniki** (Museum of Technology; tel. 656 67 47; both museums open Tues.-Sun. 9am-4pm; 1.50zł, students 0.80zł)—a swimming pool with a 10m-high diving tower, and several cinemas. Below, **pl. Defilad** (Parade Sq.), Europe's largest square (yes, even bigger than Moscow's Red Square), swarms with freelance bazaar capitalists.

Still referred to as "the Ghetto," the modern Muranów neighborhood of Warsaw holds few vestiges of the nearly 400,000 Jews who lived here—comprising one-third of the city's total population—before being deported to death camps during WWII. The Ghetto Uprising that took place here in 1943 was one of the most dramatic moments of resistance to the Nazi regime; a **monument** commemorating the heroes of this uprising can be found on ul. Zamenhofa. The beautifully reconstructed **Nożyk Synagogue,** ul. Twarda 6, lies north of Pałac Kultury i Nauki. **Cmentarz Żydowski** (Jewish Cemetery), ul. Okopowa, stretches for miles, a forest-covered treasure of gravestone art (open Mon.-Thurs. 9am-3pm, Fri. 9am-1pm). At **Umschlagplatz,** a monument marks the spot where Nazis gathered 300,000 Jews before being sending them to death camps.

Wilanów

After his coronation in 1677, King Jan III Sobieski bought the sleepy village of Milanowo, had its existing mansion rebuilt into a Baroque-style palace, and named the new residence Villa Nova (in Polish *Wilanów*). Over the years, a long line of Polish aristocrats made the palace their home. One of the bluebloods, Duke Stanisław Kostka Potocki, thought it might be nice to share it with his subjects—in 1805, he opened it to visitors, thus founding one of the first public museums in Poland. Since then, **Pałac Wilanowski** (tel. 428 101) has functioned both as a museum and as a residence for the highest ranking guests of the Polish state. To get here, take bus #180 or express bus B from ul. Marszałkowska to the end-stop "Wilanów". (Open Wed.-Mon. 9:30am-2:30pm; 3zł, students 1zł. Guides in English 20zł.) The gardens' landscaping will wow even the most experienced topiarist (open Wed.-Mon. 9:30am-2:30pm; 1.50zł, students 0.70zł). **Muzeum Plakatu** (Poster Museum; tel./fax 422 606), next to the palace, displays 50,000 **posters** from the last 100 years (open Tues.-Sun. 10am-4pm; 2zł, students 1zł).

Museums

Muzeum Narodowe (National Museum), Al. Jerozolimskie 3 (tel. 211 031). Poland's largest museum. Founded in 1862 as a museum of fine arts, converted into a national museum in 1915. Impressive illustration of the evolution of Polish art. Also houses a Gallery of Medieval Art and a Gallery of European Art, which includes Italian works from the 14th-18th centuries, German art from the 15th-16th centuries, and Dutch and Flemish paintings from the 17th century. Open May-Sept. Tues.-Wed. and Fri.-Sun. 10am-6pm, Thurs. noon-7pm; Oct.-April Tues.-Wed. and Fri.-Sun. 10am-4pm, Thurs. 11am-6pm; 5zł, students 2.50zł, Thurs. free.

Muzeum Wojska Polskiego (Polish Military Museum), Al. Jerozolimskie 3 (tel. 628 58 43). Polish weaponry through the ages. Documents Poland's fight for independence during WWII. Open Wed.-Sun. 10am-4pm; 2zł, students 1zł, Fri. free. Guided tours in English 20zł. Library open Wed.-Fri. noon-3pm.

Muzeum Historyczne Miasta Warszawy, Rynek Starego Miasta 28 (tel. 635 16 21). Chronicles the city's resilient past. The exhibit—"Seven Centuries in the Life of Warsaw"—illustrates the evolution of styles in architecture and clothing from the 13th century to the present. Open Tues. and Thurs. 11am-6pm, Wed. and Fri.-Sat. 10am-3:30pm, Sun. 10:30am-4:30pm; 2zł, students 1zł, Sun. free.

Zamek Królewski (Royal Castle), plac Zamkowy 4 (tel. 657 21 70). **Royal Suites** open to guided tours only; individual sightseeing possible in other parts. Open Tues.-Sun. 10am-6pm. Royal suites: 8zł, students 3.50zł. **Other interiors:** 5zł, students 2zł; Thurs. free—pick up your free passes at the *kasa*. English tours of the castle 30zł. The *kasa*, ul. Świętojańska 2 (tel. 657 23 38), across from the castle, is where you can purchase tickets and reserve guides. Open Tues.-Sun. 9am-6pm.

Muzeum Marii Skłodowskiej-Curie, ul. Freta 16 (tel. 318 092), in the Skłodowskis' former house. Founded in 1967, on the 100th anniversary of Maria's birthday, the exhibit chronicles Maria's life in Poland, emigration to France, and marriage to scientist

Pierre Curie, with whom she discovered radium, polonium, and marital bliss. Open Tues.-Sat. 10am-4:30pm, Sun. 10am-2:30pm; 1zł, students 0.50zł.

Muzeum Fryderyka Chopina in **Zamek Ostrogskich,** ul. Okólnik 1 (tel. 275 471, ext. 34 or 35). Portraits, manuscripts, letters, keepsakes, and a piano belonging to the great composer during the last 2 years of his life. Open Mon., Wed., and Fri. 10am-5pm, Thurs. noon-6pm, Sat.-Sun. 10am-2pm; 3zł, students 2zł.

Muzeum Etnograficzne, ul. Kredytowa 1 (tel. 277 641). Exhibits on folk costumes, customs, and handicrafts. Open Tues. and Thurs.-Fri. 9am-4pm, Wed. 11am-6pm, Sat.-Sun. 10am-5pm; 1zł, students 0.50zł, Wed. free. Guided tours 10zł.

Muzeum Archeologiczne "ARSENAŁ", ul. Długa 52 (tel. 311 537; fax 315 195). Among the artifacts that tell Poland's story are 1500 Roman coins and the armor of Poland's first leaders—the Piast dynasty. Open Mon.-Fri. 9am-6pm, Sun. 10am-4pm. Closed the 3rd Sun. of each month; 1.50zł, students 0.80zł, Sun. free.

ENTERTAINMENT AND NIGHTLIFE

Don't be fooled by people who tell you Warsaw doesn't have much nightlife outside of the **kawiarnie** (cafés) of the Old Town and ul. Nowy Świat. While these are excellent places to sit back and relax with a cold glass of *piwo* or a chic cup of *kawa*, the late-night student scene can be incredible, especially on weekends. Don't miss out on the sunrise hike up ul. Niepodległości from one of the student clubs back to the city center. Even if you decide not to party until 4 or 5am, there are plentiful pubs and outdoor beer gardens in summer; many offer live music and good, inexpensive grilled food to go with your *EB* or *Żywiec*.

Performances

Classical concerts fill the Gallery of Sculptures in **Stara Pomarańczarnia** near Pałac Łazienkowski on June and July Sundays. Inquire about concerts at **Warszawskie Towarzystwo Muzyczne** (Warsaw Music Society), ul. Morskie Oko 2 (tel. 496 856; tickets available Mon.-Fri. 9am-3pm and before concerts). **Pomnik Chopina** (Chopin Monument), nearby in Park Łazienkowski, hosts free Sunday performances by distinguished classical artists (May-Oct. noon and 4pm). **Teatr Wielki,** plac Teatralny 1 (tel. 263 287), Warsaw's main opera and ballet hall, offers performances almost daily. **Filharmonia Narodowa,** ul. Jasna 5 (tel. 267 281), gives regular concerts but is closed in summer. Classical music is also played in **Royal Castle's Sala Koncertowa,** plac Zamkowy 4 (tel. 635 41 95; tickets sold Tues.-Sun. 10am-3pm).

Jazz, rock, and blues fans have quite a few options as well, especially in summer. Other than the jazz mecca **Akwarium** (see Nightclubs, below), the cafés and pubs of the Old Town occasionally fill the restored streets with the sound of music. In summer, **Pałac Pod Blachą,** an open-air beer garden, offers nightly live music until 11pm right next to plac Zamkowy (down the steps in the direction of the river). **Sala Kongresowa** (tel. 620 49 80), in the Palace of Culture and Science on the train station side, hosts serious jazz and rock concerts. Most popular artists who make their way to Poland end up here. Enter Sala Kongresowa from ul. Emilii Plater.

Pubs

Warsaw's pubs are popular with both trendy locals and visitors looking for a comfortable nook where they can relax and have a relatively overpriced drink. However, the extra cost is often made up for by free concerts, making the atmosphere livelier and more enjoyable than the cheaper beer gardens.

The Irish Pub, ul. Miodowa 3 (tel. 262 533). Promotes folk and country music with free nightly concerts. Unsurprisingly, Irish music prevails, but some very un-Irish rock, jazz, and blues bands find their way on stage. The *Guinness* sign is no joke—it's on tap for 9zł (0.5L). Open daily 9am until the last guest stumbles out.

Harenda Pub, ul. Krakowskie Przedmieście 4/6 (tel. 262 900), at Hotel Harenda. Decorated like a British social club, complete with an exclusively leather-and-wood decor and plenty of pictures of the owners in bow ties doing "chummy" things like taking road trips and going on brewery tours. The friendly crowd usually stays til closing, but don't go for a Polish lesson. Open daily 8am-3am.

Pub Falcon That's It, ul. Marszałkowska 55/57 (tel. 621 96 75). Free rock and funk shows Thurs.-Sat. 6pm-10pm. More raucous than most pubs in town, it's worth checking out if the music is good. Food, too! Open daily 11am-midnight. That's it.

Nightclubs

These clubs are aimed at a young and energetic crowd. They're very hit-and-miss, usually based on where people feel like meeting for the night. Posters around town have the latest info about special club and disco nights.

Park, al. Niepodległości 196 (tel. 257 199 or 259 165). This international disco is one of the more popular student hangouts in Warsaw. At least once a week, Park packs 'em in for late-night fun. The crowd varies between crew-cut locals and dancing dervishes. Saturday nights are a relatively safe bet for a "disco" crowd. Open Wed. 10pm-2am, cover 5zł, students 2.5zł; Thurs. 10pm-3am, cover 5zł, students 2.5zł; Fri.-Sat. 9pm-3am, cover 10zł, students 5zł.

Club Giovanni, ul. Krakowskie Przedmieście 24 (tel. 269 239), on the premises of Warsaw University to the right and down the steps as you enter through the main gate. Or enter from the street by way of the narrow, unmarked stairway with the music at the bottom (the one right next to the main gates, which are often closed at night). As far from a disco as it gets, but still an all-student crowd. Rock music rules here, but if you want to hear something else, bring your own tapes. Seriously. They'll play it for you. Popular with the low-key student crowd. Plenty of beer on tap for 3zł. A good, friendly, hangout bar at all hours, complete with foosball and comfy leather chairs. Thurs. night live music (and outdoor grill in the summer) only make this place better. Vegetarian pizza 13.40zł, for a half 6.70zł, for a quarter 3.40zł. Open daily 10am until the last person leaves.

Jazz Club Akwarium, ul. Emilii Plater 49 (tel. 620 50 72). The top spot in the city for live jazz. Drinks and food served. Concerts daily. Various artists—stop by or call for their program. Shows begin at 8:30pm. The crowd is much older, but the love of be-bopping-good music knows no age limit. Open daily 11am til at least 11pm, depending on the show, Fri.-Sat. until 3am.

Stara Dziekanka, ul. Krakowskie Przedmieście 56. This entirely outdoor club has a permanent awning that protects revelers from the elements. This is a great place to meet both locals and foreigners and dance in the cool summer night. Grilled food, 3zł glasses of Żywiec, and lots of music blend together in a big open-air stir-fry. Picnic tables and stone terraces contrast with the pounding techno and dance mixes, but somehow it works. Drop by and see what all the fuss is about. Open daily 7pm-2am. Cover Sun.-Thurs. 4zł, Fri.-Sat. 10zł.

Hybrydy, ul. Złota 7/9 (tel. 273 763), near the commercial district. A major rager for foot-loose students. This club is loud, hot, and crowded even in the afternoon; the bar next door provides a place to cool off. It's open 7 days a week, but the schedule changes daily (check at the door or look for ads posted around town and in local papers). Reggae, metal, rock, hip-hop, rap, or techno, depending on the night. Cover Tues., Thurs., and Sun. 2zł; Wed. and Fri. 3zł; Sat. 6zł.

Klub Medyka, ul. Oczki 5/7 (tel. 628 33 76, ext. 12). The second closest of the student clubs to downtown, which makes the 4am hike home easier to bear. Sat. disco 8pm-4am, cover 10zł, students 4zł; Sun. Latino music 6pm-10:30pm, 3.5zł.

Klub Stodoła, ul. Batorego 10 (tel. 258 625 or 286 031). This dance-machine also has a pool in case things get a little slow. Only the disco madness around the corner at Park keeps the crowds down on Saturday, and there is a lot of cross-over between the two clubs. More local students here than international. Disco Fri. 8pm-4am, Sat. 8pm-4am—rock 'n' roll, reggae, hip-hop, techno. Cover Fri. 3zł, students free; Sat. 10zł, students 3zł.

GAY WARSAW

Unless a tourist has come to Warsaw for a black eye, he or she does not advertise their homosexuality. Warsaw is a community of conservative businesspeople, and gay clubs are few and ephemeral, but at least they're there. For the latest info, call the gay and lesbian hotline (tel. 628 52 22) on Fridays from 6-9pm. They'll tell you what's the best spot to hit and when, whether in- or outside the capital. Kiosks sell *Inaczej* and *Filo*—magazines that list gay entertainment providers throughout the country.

Między nami, ul. Bracka 20. A left off Al. Jerezelimskie when coming from the Palace of Culture. The 2nd restaurant with an outside seating area, on the right. Mixed during the day, mostly gay in the evening. Inside, the decor revives the Communist love of steel structures in a classy way. Salads 5-6zł, 0.2L of juice 4zł. Open Sun.-Thurs. til 11pm, Fri.-Sat. til midnight.

Koźla, ul. Koźla 10/12. One block left from the New Town Square, when facing away from the Old Town. There is no sign outside, but it's the only club on Koźla. A narrow staircase leads down to a small space that manages to combine the qualities of a beerhouse, a lounge, and a cruise bar. It's bound to remain here, too, since it's been operating since May 8, 1994. If you visit the pub on its birthday, you'll hit a party worthy of Victory Day. Open daily 5pm til the last person leaves.

Rudawka, ul. Elbląska 53 (tel. 633 19 99). Tram #19 or 33 to "Włościańska". Night bus #608 also runs here from the central train station. A yellow neon advertises the club on the main street, but the spot itself is some 300m on the alley that takes off to the left just before the neon. It's the Fri. hangout for gay men and lesbians. The DJ runs the same tunes over and over again, mixing in some annoying oldies—although they sometimes prove a welcome break from Brazilian disco hits. Vodka and tonic 5zł, beer 4zł. Cover 8zł. Arrive around 11pm.

Paradise, corner of ul. Wawelska and ul. Żwirki i Wigury, in the grounds of the "Skra" sports complex. Disco Fri.-Sun., but it's the place to hit on Sat. nights. A large, bright dance floor, mellow-out area, and a patio if you need a breather. Both men and women. Vodka and tonic 5zł, beer 4zł. Cover 10zł, Sun. 5zł.

■ Near Warsaw: Żelazowa Wola

Żelazowa Wola is the birthplace of Fryderyk Chopin. The cottage, surrounded by a small, maze-like park, is one more stop on the Chopin fan's dream itinerary, and weekly concerts draw quiet music lovers. At one time, Żelazowa Wola was the site of a large manor that belonged to the Skarbek family. The composer's father, a Frenchman named Nicolas Chopin, worked as a French tutor in the house of Count Skarbek. There, he met and married Justyna Krzyżanowska, a distant cousin of the count. They had four children—three daughters and a son, Fryderyk, born on February 22, 1810. The Chopin family did not remain at Żelazowa Wola for very long; they moved to Warsaw in October 1810.

The **cottage** (tel. (0494) 223 00) provides an interesting look at early 19th-century life. The interior, although lacking the family's original furniture, is maintained in the style of the era. Among the mementos on display are the composer's birth certificate and the first *polonaise* he wrote, at the age of seven. Every Sunday, and on Saturdays in July and August, at 11am and 3pm, music fans gather here to listen to concerts—probably the best reason to make the trip. Noteworthy Polish musicians perform Chopin's works and the crowds relax in the park as his music fills the air. The schedule of selected music and performing musicians, posted throughout Warsaw, is always available at the Chopin museum there (see Warsaw: Museums, p. 403); both change weekly. (Cottage open May-Sept. Tues.-Sun. 10am-5:30pm; Oct.-April 10am-4pm; 5zł, students 2.50zł; English labels; concerts 15zł.)

Żelazowa Wola, 53km west of Warsaw, is a short daytrip (or morning excursion) from the capital easily made by bus. Three **buses** a day pass through, but none of the signs in Warsaw mention it. Rest assured, it is a regular stop on the route to **Kamion,** although it may help to tell the bus driver that you want to stop at Żelazowa Wola. Buses to and from Kamion are limited, and only the 9:45am bus actually puts you in Żelazowa Wola in time (11:10am) to take it all in (the other 2 arrive after the museum has closed and there are no direct buses back after 4:30pm). If you want to get to Żelazowa Wola at any other time, take a **commuter train** to the small town of Sochaczew (at least 7 per day), where Sochaczew city bus #6 runs to "Żelazowa Wola" at least hourly. Each way, the entire trip costs 6-7zł and takes 1½-2½ hours, depending on transfers. The trip back to Warsaw can be done on the 12:40 or 4:30pm bus directly from Żelazowa Wola, or back through Sochaczew via #6.

POMORZE

Pomorze, literally "along the sea", sweeps over the murky swamps and wind-swept dunes of the Baltic coast. In the face of shifting sands and treacherous bogs, fishermen built villages here millennia ago. A few hamlets grew into monstrous ports—Szczecin on the lower Odra River, and Gdańsk and Gdynia in the east— but the landscape in between is still littered with coastal lakes, lagoons, small fishing ports, and the mysterious four-faced totems of Pomorze's ancient inhabitants.

■ Szczecin

Strategically situated on the Odra river, the port of Szczecin has witnessed power plays for centuries. All of this grappling has only increased the city's growth, and railways and waterways sprawl for miles around the center. It is Szczecin's tightly packed downtown that has the most to offer—the city's labyrinthine core commands fleets of historic buildings. These and the shipping port's friendly attitude have made Szczecin a popular starting point for tourists arriving from across the sea.

ORIENTATION AND PRACTICAL INFORMATION

Szczecin sits near the German border at the mouth of the Odra River, about 65km from the Baltic Sea coast. You'll need a map, so visit a **tourist office**. This is most easily accomplished by getting off the train at the **Szczecin Główny** train station (the bus stop is a block away) and following ul. Owocowa until it turns left and becomes ul. Dworcowa. Al. Niepodległości shoots to the right off ul. Dworcowa's end. Turn right onto ul. Wyszyńskiego. The **CIT** office is two blocks down, on the right. With map in hand, you will soon see that almost all sights lie in the rectangular area framed by the **Odra** to the east, **ul. Piłsudskiego** to the north, **al. Piastów** to the west, and the connected **ul. Krzywoustego, pl. Zwycięstwa**, and **ul. Wyszyńskiego** to the south. It's what's in between that calls for the map—including several traffic circles and divided roads that test your sense of direction at every turn.

Tourist Offices: Centrum Informacji Turystycznej (CIT), ul. Wyszyńskiego 26 (tel. 340 440; open Mon.-Fri. 9am-5pm, Sat. 10am-2pm) and **Szczecińska Agencja Turystyczna (sat)**, al. Jedności Narodowej 1 (tel. 339 253; fax 342 581; open Mon.-Fri. 10am-5pm), are both excellent sources for maps (1.20-3zł), brochures, and accommodations info. Each also sells little tourist books for 3.50zł.

Currency Exchange: Pomorski Bank Kredytowy S.A., ul. Bogurodzicy 5 (tel. 880 033). Branches located throughout the city. Cashes AmEx and Visa traveler's checks; gives AmEx, MC, and Visa cash advances. Open Mon.-Fri. 8am-6pm. Currency exchange at a slightly better rate available at *kantors* all over town.

Trains: Szczecin Główny station sits at the end of ul. 3-go Maja; take tram #1 or 3 north to the center. To: Gdynia (3 per day, 5hr., 20.70zł); Poznań (11 per day, 3hr., 13.80zł); Berlin (1 per day, 2½hr., express 50.28zł). **Antique steam trains**— *pociągi turystyczne Retro*—run weekends. Schedules posted at the train station.

Buses: Bus station, pl. Tobrucki, 2min. northeast of the train station. Tickets can be purchased either at the station or through ORBIS, pl. Zwycięstwa 1. Frequent daily connections to Świnoujście and Poznań starting at 12zł.

Public Transportation: The city's numerous **tram** and **bus** lines run along most major roads. Fares are 0.60zł for up to 10min., 1zł for 10-40min., and 3zł after 11pm. Schedules, route information, and tickets available at kiosks around town.

Taxis: Auto Taxi, tel. 919. **Radio Taxi**, tel. 96 22. **Super Taxi**, tel. 96 66.

24-Hour Pharmacy: ul. Krzywoustego 7a (tel. 336 673).

Baltic Coast of Poland

Medical Assistance: Pogotowie Ratunkowe, ul. Wojska Polskiego 52 (tel. 335 061; open Mon.-Sat. 9am-9pm). **Emergencies:** tel. 999.
Post Office: ul. Bogurodzicy 1 (tel. 346 124). Open Mon.-Fri. 8am-8pm, Sat. 9am-2pm. **Postal code:** 70-405.
Telephones: At the post office. Open 24hr. **Phone code:** 0-91.

ACCOMMODATIONS

For a complete list of summer youth hostels, contact **ALMATUR,** ul. Bohaterów Warszawy 83 (tel. 346 356). Budget accommodations in Szczecin become harder to find as summer months draw crowds to the city.

Youth Hostel (HI), ul. Monte Cassino 19a (tel./fax 224 761). Take tram #1 from the train station or the center to ul. Felczarka. By foot, a short hike through downtown along ul. Wojska Polskiego, followed by a right on ul. Felczarka, and a left onto ul. Monte Cassino. Often-crowded rooms of up to 12. Lockout 10am-5pm. Curfew 11pm. HI members only—10zł. Sheets 2.50zł. Offers **bike rental** and **luggage storage** to its guests (bikes 1zł per hr.; storage 0.70zł per day).

Hotel Piast, pl. Zwycięstwa 3 (tel. 336 622). Central ex-police barracks proclaims "Hotel," in black Gothic letters, above the oak-shadowed entrance. Scenic downtown location. Singles 46zł, with bath 54.50zł. Doubles 71zł, with bath 92zł.

Hotel Gryf, ul. Wojska Polskiego 49 (tel. 334 566; fax 334 030). Gryf offers some of the best-kept rooms in town for the money, all just 5min. from the sights. Popular with a younger crowd; the friendly atmosphere can't help but rub off. Singles 42zł, with bath 55zł. Doubles 72zł, with bath 92zł.

"Foundation in Support of Local Democracy" Hostel, ul. Marii Skłodowskiej-Curie 4 (tel. 70 472). In a white school building "Zachodniopomorska Szkoła Samorządu Terytorialnego." Take tram #9 to "Traugutta," continue two blocks, turn left, and walk to the end of the street. The service and facilities are worth the long trek northwest from the center of town. Dorms 10zł per person. Singles 21.40zł. Doubles 42.80zł, with bathroom 64.20zł. Triples 48.15zł. Quads 64.20zł.

FOOD

The invasion of western fast food chains is in full force, but local food still survives in both kiosk and restaurant environments. The 24-hour supermarket **Extra** is centrally located at ul. Niepodległości 27 (MC and Visa accepted). A quick meal can be had at one of the many **bars** around town for under 5zł. **Lucynka i Paulinka,** ul. Wojska Polskiego 18 (tel. 346 922), treats browsers downstairs with luxury food items and upstairs with sinful desserts, cups of coffee, and stiffer libations. Desserts and coffee start around 2.00zł (open Mon.-Fri. 9am-9pm, Sat.-Sun. 10am-9pm; MC and Visa accepted). **Pod Muzami,** pl. Żołnierza Polskiego 2 (tel. 347 209) connects to the expensive Hotel Victoria. Brass mirrors and pink lighting dominate the decor. Standard Polish fare runs 8-15zł (open daily noon-5am; dancing with live band every night at 9pm; cover 5zł, Sat.-Sun. 8zł).

SIGHTS

A millennium of history and a legacy of occupation, re-occupation, and invasion have left Szczecin's buildings with more than a few stories to tell. Some original structures remain, but much of the city's beauty lies in its restorations. A relic of the Prussian settlement, the Baroque **Brama Portowa** (Port Gate) marks the downtown area with a Prussian flavor. It features female figures blowing trumpets, a Latin inscription commemorating King of Prussia Friedrich Wilhelm I, a panorama of 18th-century Szczecin, and Viadus, the Odra's god, leaning against a jug from which the river's waters flow. Originally called the Brandenburg and later the Berlin Gate, it was built in 1725 and spared during the removal of the city fortifications in 1875 because of its architectural value. Friedrich Wilhelm would be proud.

Time has not been as kind to some of the other structures in downtown Szczecin. A block away on ul. Wyszyńskiego, the 13th-century **Katedra Św. Jana** (Cathedral of

St. James the Apostle) looms over the city. Destroyed during WWII, it was carefully restored to its original Gothic shape; however, it still patiently awaits the restoration of its stained glass windows.

For a good example of how Szczecin's past meets its present, head for the Old Town's 870-year-old **Kościół Św. Piotra i Pawła** (Cathedral of St. Peter and Paul). Visitors can relive the parish's past few decades through the photo collages inside, which include shots of a visit by the pope. On ul. Korsarzy, the giant, newly restored **Zamek Książąt Pomerańskich** (Palace of Pomeranian Princes; tel. 347 391) overlooks it all from the site of Szczecin's oldest settlement. The seat of Pomeranian princes until 1630, it later belonged to Swedes, Prussians, and Germans. These days it is under occupation by an opera and theater group. The large courtyard is often the site of performances and concerts (open daily 10am-6pm).

Behind the palace bravely stands the abandoned **Baszta Panieńska Siedmiu Płaszczy** (Maiden's Tower of Seven Cloaks), ul. Panieńska, the only one of the medieval fortifications' 37 original towers to survive WWII. Imagining that the cars speeding along the highway below are fearsome Nordic invaders will give you a good sense of the tower's historical importance.

If you head back to the Old Town market square from the palace, you will come upon the old **ratusz** (town hall), built in 1450. Rebuilt after WWII in the original Gothic style, it now houses one of **Muzeum Narodowe's** (National Museum) three branches; this branch illustrates Szczecin's history from stones to cups and saucers. Another branch—a chronicle of Pomeranian art—is in the Baroque palace of the **Pomeranian Parliament,** ul. Stromłyńska 27/28, north of Castle Hill two blocks west of St. Peter and Paul's. (All branches open Sat.-Sun. 10am-4pm, Tues. and Thurs. 10am-5pm, Wed. and Fri. 9am-3:30pm. 1 ticket gets you into 3 galleries.)

■ Świnoujście

Only a hop, skip, and jump from the clean sands of the Baltic coast, sunny Świnoujście does a good job of luring bathers from the shore with emerald parks and a tree-lined promenade watched over by elegant 20th-century villas.

Orientation and Practical Information Świnoujście occupies parts of two islands, **Wolin** and **Uznam,** linked by a ferry across the **Świna River.** The **train** and **bus stations** and the international **ferry terminal** are all located on the Świna's east bank near the **port** on Wolin Island. **Trains** travel to Szczecin (10 per day, 2hr., 12zł) and Warsaw (2 per day, 8½hr., 38zł). **Polferries,** ul. Dworcowa 1 (tel. 321 30 06), next to the main dock, sends ferries to Copenhagen (10:30am and 10:30pm, 9hr., 300 Danish kroner); and Malmö, Sweden (11:30am and 11pm, 10hr., 320 Swedish kroner). **Unity Lines** runs a ferry to Ystad, Sweden (10pm, 9hr., 300 Swedish kroner). To get to the main part of town, on the west side of the river, hop on the free **car ferry** (every 20min. 5am-11pm, every hour at night) across the street from the train and bus stations, five minutes up the road from the main ferry terminal; head left out of the ferry terminal on **ul. Dworcowa.** Disembark, take a left, and check out the map of the city to get your bearings. **PTTK,** ul. Paderewskiego 24 (tel. 321 26 13), sells 2.30zł maps (open Mon.-Tues. and Thurs.-Fri. 7am-3pm, Wed. 9am-5pm). **Orbis,** ul. B. Chrobrego 9 (tel. 321 44 11), vends maps, as well as ferry and train tickets (open Mon.-Fri. 10am-5pm). Two km west of Świnoujście, on ul. Wojska Polskiego, there is a pedestrian- and bicycles-only **border crossing** to Seebad Ahlbeck, Germany. In order to buy anything at the German market, be sure to change money on the Polish side before you cross the border. **Bank Pekao, S.A.,** ul. Piłsudskiego 4 (tel. 321 57 33), cashes traveler's checks, exchanges money, and does credit-card cash advances (open Mon. and Fri. 8am-6pm, Sat. 10am-2pm). A **24-hour pharmacy** (tel. 321 25 15) deals most drugs at ul. Piłsudskiego 23/25 (open Mon.-Sat. 8am-8pm, Sun. 8am-10pm; knock after hours). The **post office,** ul. Piłsudskiego 1 (tel. 321 20 15), has a **photocopier** on the premises (open Mon.-Fri. 8am-8pm, Sat. 8am-1pm). **Postal code:** 72-600. **Phone code:** 97.

Accommodations and Camping Reserve for summer. If you plan to spend a few nights in town, start the room hunt at **Orbis** (see above), which locates 21zł **private rooms. Hotel Wisus,** u. Żeromskiego 17 (tel. 321 58 50), has comfortable rooms near the beach for only 20zł per person. **Dom Rybaka** (Fisherman's Inn), ul. Wybrzeże Władysława IV 22 (tel. 321 29 43), is a budget option for those who want to stay near the car ferry; it's especially convenient for an early-morning departure. Well kept singles start at 24zł. **Hotel Hutnik,** ul. Żeromskiego 15 (tel. 321 55 11), provides singles at 31zł and doubles at 54zł near the beach. Follow the HI signs (5% discount for HI members). A short hike from the town center and beach, the **Youth Hostel (HI),** ul. Gdyńska 26 (tel. 327 06 13; reception 6-10am and 5-10pm) has good, clean rooms for 142zł per person (luggage storage 12zł per day). At **Camping Relax,** ul. Słowackiego 1 (tel. 321 39 12, for reservations 321 47 00), tents and sites cost 6zł, or relax in cozy cabins (triples 60-90zł, quads 68-98zł).

Food Kiosks clamor by the dozen along ul. Żeromskiego. Try the inexpensive and delicious *gofry*—hot Belgian waffles with whipped cream and strawberries. More substantial appetites can find a grilled *kiełbasa* and a *piwo* for only 4zł! In the main part of town, be sure to stop by the Greco-Polish eatery **Bar "Neptun",** ul. Bema 1 (tel. 321 26 43), across from the post office, where you not only feast on inexpensive Polish dishes and homemade carrot juice, but also get a chance to see the charismatic and multilingual Mr. Tomasz Strybel in action. Falter in your Polish and everything from German to Spanish could follow (open daily 9am-10pm). **Restaurant Thang Long,** ul. Rybaki 13 (tel. 321 55 22), serves authentic Vietnamese food prepared by Chef Pham Van Tinh. **Grocery Kama,** ul. Chopina 2 (tel. 327 04 73), features fresh bread, cheeses, and meats (open Mon.-Fri. 7am-10pm, Sat. 7am-9pm, Sun. 10am-8pm; no fresh bread or meat Sun.).

Sights and Entertainment Visitors flock to Świnoujście's main attractions: the shady parks and the Baltic shoreline with its grassy dunes and relaxed beachcombing. Even before you step off the ferry, you cannot help but see this town's seafaring side. Colorful tugboats sit at the port, while sailors walk the streets. The **beach** and the **promenade** along ul. Żeromskiego are sights in and of themselves.

As the sun goes down, the kiosks along ul. Żeromskiego transform into places for good times and cheap beer (2.0zł for 0.5L). Crowds of college-age fun-seekers move on from kiosk *piwo* to the **nightclubs,** which are within easy walking distance. For a real culture shock, check out the **Manhattan** nightclub, ul. Zeromskiego 1 (tel. 321 26 11), with its New York City US$100-bill decor (open nightly 11pm-6pm).

▌Woliński Park Narodowy

Amid the quickly developing coastal resorts, Woliński National Park protects a pristine tract of Wolin Island, containing glacial lakes, a bison preserve, and breathtaking views of the Baltic Sea. Vibrant greens and pine-scented breezes blow through its trails, erasing any memory of civilization, while dense woodland dampens the nearby road noise, leaving silence for distant eagle cries. Comforts are not far away, though, and a park visit begins in Międzyzdroje, a tiny village on the Baltic Sea.

Orientation and Practical Information The ideal point to begin a hike into the national park is Międzyzdroje, which can be reached either from Szczecin by **bus** or **train** (17 each per day, 1hr. 40min., 12zł); from Świnoujście by train (direction Szczecin, 17 per day, 30min., 2.70zł); or by a special **shuttle bus** (20 per day, 1.50zł). Obtain **maps** (2-3zł), **exchange currency** in cash, and get info about the park, budget travel, and accommodations at **PTTK,** ul. Kolejowa 2 (tel. 80 462; fax 80 086), in the center of town; go right out of the train station/bus stop and follow ul. Kolejowa to the center. Both the town and the park have very large maps posted at regular intervals—day-hikers will do just fine without a copy of their own, given the well marked trails. The **pharmacy** sits at pl. Zwycięstwa 9 (tel. 80 154; open Mon.-Fri. 8am-7pm, Sat. 8am-2pm). The **post office** is at ul. Gryfa Pomorskiego 2, around the corner from PTTK (open Mon.-Fri. 8am-8pm, Sat. 8am-1pm, Sun. 9am-2pm). **Postal code:** 72-510. **Telephones** are just inside. **Phone code:** 97.

Accommodations and Food Affordable accommodations still exist in Międzyzdroje, despite its rapid development. **PTTK** (see above) arranges stays in private rooms (singles 26zł, doubles 50zł, triples 46zł) and runs the well kept **PTTK Hotel** in their building (July-Aug. 38zł per person; Sept.-June 25zł per person). **Camping Gromada,** ul. Bohaterów Warszawy 1 (tel. 80 779, reservations 80 584) has cabins (9-16zł per person) and tent sites (6-9zł) only a few minutes from the beach. All three options lie within walking distance of both the park and town.

Perhaps the most obvious choice for food is the well stocked **supermarket Helios,** ul. Gryfa Pomorskiego 17, near the post office (open Mon.-Sat. 6:30am-9pm, Sun. 8am-6pm). Visitors who have had enough of the outdoors can slip into **Marina,** ul. Gryfa Pomorskiego 4 (open daily 10am-10pm), to feast on local and Italian fare. Entrées reach the 17zł range, but smart shoppers pick up dinner and a beer for less than 12zł in a relaxing and friendly atmosphere overlooking the town center.

Hiking While Międzyzdroje is rapidly drawing crowds as a prime beach resort, the true accolades still belong to **Woliński Park Narodowy.** The park is immaculately kept and has hut-like picnic areas off its three main **hiking trails** (red, green, and blue—marked on trees and stones every 30m); stick to them, or risk an encounter with park officials or worse. For general information on hiking, see Essentials: Wilderness and Safety Concerns, p. 49. All three can be accessed from Międzyzdroje—the red at the northeast end of **ul. Bohaterów Warszawy,** the green at the end of **ul. Leśna** (follow the signs to the bison preserve), and the blue just off **ul. Ustronie Leśne.** Each trail has something to offer ambitious or relaxed hikers. Before hiking, a visit to the **Park Museum,** ul. Niepodległości 3, provides information about the area and a preview of nearby wildlife (open Tues.-Sun. 9am-5pm; 1.5zł).

The **red trail** alone is worth the trip. Though it is part of a larger trek around Wolin Island, the 15km along the Baltic coastline, beginning at the end of ul. Bohaterów Warszawy, make up the prime hiking leg of the trail. Only a short climb from the trailhead, **Kawcza Góra** is the first of the red trail's many scenic outlooks high above the Baltic Sea. The sun on the water will dazzle your eyes as you step out of the shade. But look closely, and you just might see one of the park's famed eagles (*bielik*). Snaking along the cliffs, the trail never strays too far from the shoreline, and breezes off the water keep hikers refreshed.

The **green trail,** which heads into the heart of the park, offers the park's greatest variety of terrain and sights along its 15km length. The beginning is a steep climb up ul. Leśna (a left off ul. Norwida coming from the town center, a right coming from the train). Complete with a **bison preserve** (*Rezerwat Żubrów;* open Tues.-Sun. 10am-6pm; 1.80zł) and glacial lakes, the green trail has a slightly different feel from the red—grassy, bushy, forested, and, well, green. With the sea and the construction far removed, this path is also much quieter. Truly adventurous hikers sometimes combine the two trails into one mega-hike (they meet at the end), but even a short jaunt along the green route brings you to some fine-looking bison.

Rather than heading west to east like its counterparts to the north, the **blue trail** wanders south, covering more than 20km in its course towards the town of Wolin on the southernmost point of the island. This traipse heads into the park right off ul. Ustronie Leśne by the train station—go under the bridge, and take a right. Despite the path's location near the station, it is less traveled than the other two, a perfect escape from the mobs of tourists in town.

Of course, Międzyzdroje is virtually inescapable in any visit to Woliński National Park. For a glimpse of what makes the developers drool, check out the sandy **beach.** If you squint, you can almost block out the construction. Luckily, grassy dunes shield the beach somewhat from over-development, and as you head southwest, the sounds of progress quickly disappear.

TRÓJMIASTO (TRI-CITY AREA)

Trójmiasto, the Tri-City area in Pomorze on Poland's Baltic coast, is rapidly developing into a major tourist destination. Among the three cities of Gdańsk, Sopot, and Gdynia, there are numerous historic buildings, great restaurants, a wide selection of shops, exciting cultural events and nightlife, and the best beaches in Poland. Because of the area's efficient transportation, you can find a room in one city and visit the other two, as well as daytrip destinations such as Hel, Malbork, and Frombork.

■ Gdańsk

In 1997, Gdańsk celebrates its 1000th birthday. Celebrations are planned to highlight the city's historical significance and show the world that once again, Gdańsk is poised to be a center of European culture. Gdańsk's strategic location on the Baltic coast and at the mouth of the Wisła has helped it flourish architecturally and culturally by attracting diverse peoples and, less desirably, many battles. Centuries of prosperity were quickly destroyed in WWII. Gdańsk saw the first deaths of the war that devastated the city. At war's end, this port city put its heart into re-creating its previous appearance. This rebirth, though, did not quell Gdańsk's combative energy, and the city soon served as both the birthplace of the Solidarity movement and the workplace of its leader, Lech Wałęsa.

ORIENTATION AND PRACTICAL INFORMATION

Gdańsk, Poland's principal port, dips its toes in the Baltic Sea. From the **Gdańsk Główny** train station, the Old Town center lies a few blocks southeast, bordered on the west by **Wały Jagiellońskie** and on the east by the **Stara Motława**, a tributary of the Wisła River. For info and advice, take the underpass in front of the train-station McDonald's, go right, and walk until **ul. Heweliusza. Tourist offices** are just up ul. Heweliusza (head away from the train station). To get to the Old Town from ul. Heweliusza, go back toward the train station, and make a left on Podwale Grodzkie, which will turn into Wały Jagiellońskie. Turn left onto **ul. Długa** at the LOT building. Despite the fact that the tourist office is in a neighborhood called **Stare Miasto** (Old City), the real Old Town is a short walk south, in **Główne Miasto** (Main City), which contains most points of interest as well as the main avenue, the connected **ul. Długa** and **Długi Targ**.

- **Tourist Offices: IT Gdańsk,** ul Długa 45 (tel. 319 327; fax 319 572), in the Old City. Distributes info about sights and accommodations, and can arrange a Russian visa (US$30) for a jaunt to Kaliningrad. Open daily 9am-6pm. **ORBIS,** ul. Heweliusza 22 (tel. 314 425). International and domestic ferry, train, and plane tickets. Also an AmEx branch office. Open Mon.-Fri. 9am-5pm, Sat. 10am-2pm.
- **Budget Travel: ALMATUR,** Długi Targ 11, 2nd floor (tel. 312 931; fax 317 818), in the Old Town center. ISICs and information about youth and student hostels. Open Mon.-Fri. 10am-5pm, Sat. 10am-2pm.
- **Consulates: Germany,** Al. Zwycięstwa 23 (tel. 414 365). Open Mon.-Fri. 8:30am-11:30am. **Russia,** ul. Batorego 15 (tel. 411 088). Open Mon., Wed., and Fri. 9am-1pm.
- **Currency Exchange:** At hotels, banks, *kantors,* and certain post offices. the train station has a 24-hr. *kantor.* **Bank Gdański,** Wały Jagiellońskie 14/16 (tel. 379 222), cashes traveler's checks for a 1% commission. AmEx, Eurocard, MC, and Visa cash advances without commission. Branch at the train station. Open Mon.-Fri. 8am-6pm. ORBIS (see above) exchanges AmEx traveler's checks *sans* commission.

Central Gdańsk

- ALMATUR, 18
- Armoury, 23
- Bus Station, 3
- Chlebnicka Gate, 16
- Dwór Artusa, 20
- Ferry to Sopot and Hel, 12
- Gdańsk Główny Railway Station, 4
- Gdańsk Shipyards Museum, 1
- Golden Gate, 24
- Great Mill, 7
- Green Gate, 17
- Hala Targowa Market, 10
- Harbor Crane, 13
- High Gate, 25
- Holy Ghost Gate, 14
- Mariacka Gate, 15
- Neptune Fountain, 19
- Old Post Office, 11
- Old Town Hall, 6
- Solidarity Monument, 2
- St. Bridget's, 9
- St. Catherine's, 8
- St. Mary's, 22
- Tourist Office, 5
- Town Hall, 21

▯ Police
✉ Post Office

Flights: Rebiechowo airport (tel. 314 026), 22km south. The B bus links to the train station. **LOT,** Wały Jagiellońskie 2/4 (tel. 311 161). Open Mon.-Fri. 8am-6pm.

Trains: (tel. 311 112). To: Berlin (2 per day, 7hr., 76.75zł); Kraków (5 per day, 27.45zł); Prague (1 per day, 15hr., 73.10zł plus 47zł for optional sleeper); St. Petersburg (1 per day, 36hr., 250zł); Warsaw (July-Aug. 13 per day, Sept.-June 6 per day; 4hr.; 20.70zł);. **Commuter trains** run every 6-12min. to Gdynia (40min., 2.60zł) and Sopot (15min., 1.80zł). Punch your ticket at one of the *kasownik* machines before boarding. Commuter train schedule posted apart from main one. **Store luggage** at the train station. 0.50zł plus 1% of baggage value. Open 24hr.

Buses: (tel. 321 532). Behind the train station through the underground passageway. To: Chełmno (5 per day, 3hr.,12.68zł); Malbork (8 per day, 1hr., 4.20zł); Toruń (3 per day, 4hr., 16.70zł).

Ferries: Passenger ferries run to Sopot, Hel, and Gdynia (tel. 314 926). To: Oxelösund, Sweden (in high season 1 per day; off-season Mon., Wed., and Fri.; 17hr.; 380 Swedish kroner). Book through **Polferries Travel Office** (tel. 431 887; fax 436 574) or **ORBIS** (see above). Take the commuter rail to the Nowy Port terminal.

Taxis: Radio taxi, tel. 91 95. **Hallo Taxi,** tel. 91 97. **Super Hallo Taxi,** tel. 91 91.

Bookstore: English Books Unlimited, ul. Podmłyńska 10 (tel. 313 373). Watch for a black-and-gold sign. Open Mon.-Fri. 10am-6pm, Sat. 10am-5pm.

24-Hour Pharmacy: At the train station.

Medical Assistance: Ambulance service, ul. Nowe Ogrody 1/7 (tel. 411 000). **Private doctors,** ul. Podbielańska 17 (tel. 315 168). A big blue sign on the building says "Lekarze Specjaliści". Visit 25zł. **HIV tests** available. Open Mon.-Fri. 7am-5pm. **Emergency doctors,** al. Zwycięstwa 49 (tel. 323 929 or 323 924), or ul. Pilotów 21 (tel. 478 251 or 566 995), in Gdańsk Zaspa. Both are 24-hr. facilities that treat foreigners. Calling ahead is recommended. English spoken. Visit 25zł. **General Information on Health Emergencies:** tel. 323 944.

Post Office: ul. Długa 22/25 (tel. 389 139). Under construction in 1996, a sparkling new post office will be ready for the 1997 millennium celebrations. Open Mon.-Fri. 8am-8pm, Sat. 9am-1pm. **Fax** bureau. **Postal Code:** 80-800.

Telephones: Located both inside and outside the post office. Open daily 7am-9pm. **Phone Code:** 0-58.

ACCOMMODATIONS

With Gdańsk's somewhat limited tourist infrastructure and increasing popularity, it is best to reserve well in advance, especially in summer. **Gdańsk-Tourist (Biuro Usług Turystycznych),** ul. Heweliusza 8 (tel. 312 634; fax 316 301), across from the train station, arranges for stays in private rooms. Singles run 23zł, doubles hover around 38.50zł (open Mon.-Sat. 9am-5pm). **ALMATUR,** Długi Targ 11 (tel. 312 931), directs travelers to student dorms in July and August (25zł per person).

Schronisko Młodzieżowe (HI), ul. Wałowa 21 (tel. 312 313). Cross the street in front of the train station, head up ul. Heweliusza, and turn left at ul. Łagiewniki. Gdańsk's most conveniently located hostel. Escape the kiddie brigade in smaller rooms. Kitchen. Showers in basement. Reception on the 2nd floor. Lockout 10am-5pm. Curfew 10pm. 10-12zł, students 8-10zł. Sheets 1.50zł. Luggage storage 1zł.

Schronisko Młodzieżowe (HI), ul. Grunwaldzka 244 (tel. 411 660). Far from the center of the city, but near the commuter rail. Take the train to the Gdańsk-Zaspa station, then go across the tracks to ul. Grunwaldska. Immaculate and efficiently run. Reception open daily 5pm-9pm. Lockout 10am-5pm. Curfew 10pm. 8-10zł per bed. Sheets 1.50zł. Baggage room 1zł.

Hotel Zaułek, ul. Ogarna 107/108 (tel. 314 169). One of the few budget accommodations in town when the hostels get packed or when you want a little more privacy. Right off Długi Targ—so it's noisier than the hostels, but in a location that's tough to beat at the price. The carpetless floors can get chilly, but the rooms are clean, and the beds comfy. Singles 25zł. Doubles 35zł. Triples 40zł. Quads 45zł.

FOOD

For fresh produce of all sorts, try the **Hala Targowa**, ul. Pańska, in the shadows of St. Catherine's Church just off of Podwale Staromiejskie (open Mon.-Fri. and first and last Sat. of the month 9am-6pm).

Bar "Neptun", ul. Długa 33/34 (tel. 314 988). Hearty, homestyle meat dishes alongside vegetarian entrées in a cafeteria-style setting. A quick, basic break from sightseeing. A full meal for only 4zł. Open Mon.-Fri. 7am-6pm, Sat.-Sun. 9am-6pm.

Bar na Rybce, ul. Rybackie Pobreże. Moored in the Motława, downstream from the Harbor Crane, this floating restaurant serves fish 'n' beer at great prices. Visit its twin in Gdynia. Open daily 11am-9pm, but go early, to get the daily catch.

Pizzeria Napoli, ul. Długa 62/63 (tel. 314 146). Lives up to its "Best in Town" sign, with 30 varieties of tasty pizza (5-15zł) and spaghetti (7-10zł). Take-out and delivery available, but with a prime people-watching location like this one, why go elsewhere? AmEx, MC, and Visa accepted. Open daily 11am-10pm.

Royal, ul. Długa 40/42 (tel. 315 924). Ideal pastry shop with coffee and drinks. Apple pastry 1zł. Open Mon.-Fri. 10am-9pm, Sat. 11am-9pm, Sun. noon-6pm.

U Szkota, ul. Chlebnicka 10 (tel. 314 911). This Scottish restaurant with a history serves up salmon, eel, trout, chicken, and beef for around 15zł. Kilted waiters add to the red-and-green plaid experience. Open daily noon-midnight.

SIGHTS

Gdańsk was one of the first Polish cities to undergo an exhaustive postwar facelift. Only a few buildings have yet to be fully restored. The handsome market square, **Długi Targ**, forms the physical and social center of the Old Town, where the original 16th-century façade of **Dwór Artusa** faces out onto **Fontanna Neptuna**. The square hosts local artists and craftsmen, and visitors buy everything from original art to Gdańsk-themed t-shirts. Beer vendors and street musicians, on hand to keep the folks festive as they take it all in, should be in full force in 1997.

Next to the fountain where ul. Długa and Długi Targ meet, the 14th-century **ratusz** (town hall) houses **Muzeum Historii Gdańska**. Don't miss the fantastic Red Chamber with its ceiling covered in allegorical paintings by Baroque masters. Visit the museum's White and Winter Chambers to read a 1656 letter from Oliver Cromwell to Gdańsk authorities. Another more sobering exhibit shows the state of Gdańsk right after WWII—including some of the actual rubble (open Tues.-Thurs. 10am-4pm, Sun. 11am-4pm; 2zl, students 1zl).

One block north of Długi Targ is Gdańsk's grandest house of worship, the 14th-century **Kościół Najświętszej Marii Panny** (St. Mary's). Almost completely rebuilt after its destruction in WWII, the church reigns as Poland's largest brick cathedral. Visitors can climb the 405 steps up the steeple to rise above the din and clatter of the city (open May to mid-Oct. daily 9am-5:30pm; 2zł; binoculars at the tower's top 0.50zł). The church requests that visitors be respectful during Mass, for which hours are posted outside. In the foreground of the view on top stands the 14th-century **Kościół Św. Katarzyny** (St. Catherine's), ul. Wielkie Młyny, and farther behind, you'll see the 15th-century **Kościół Św. Mikołaja** (St. Nicholas's). Gdańsk's churches were often visited by the Polish monarchs: King Władysław III Łokietek, who unified Polish principalities in the 14th century, supervised court trials in St. Catherine's Church; King Zygmunt III, who moved the capital from Kraków to Warsaw, received his electorial diploma in St. Nicholas's Church. No matter where they ended up, however, St. Mary's was the starting point for all of the monarchs who visited Gdańsk. A look around inside the church will tell you why—its sheer immensity along with its white marble and towering columns create a setting fit for a king.

Ul. Mariacka, behind the church, is a tree-shaded, cobbled street that ambles from the church to the river. Street musicians play medieval music to complete the mood. After passing through the **Mariacka Gate,** the Motława river lies ahead, and you will be greeted by the numerous cafés and shops that line **ul. Długie Pobreże.** Check out the prices on silver and amber! Going left along Długie Pobreże leads toward the huge Gothic **Harbor Crane**, which once set the masts on medieval ships. This crane and the modern warship Sołdek are part of the **Centralne Muzeum Morskie** (Central Maritime Museum; tel. 316 938; fax 318 453; open daily 10am-6pm; 2zł, students 1zł).

Attend Sunday Mass at Lech Wałęsa's parish—the simple brick **Kościół Św. Brygidy** (St. Bridget's), ul. Profesorska 17, just north of the Old Town. Several blocks to the east, on pl. Obrońców Poczty Polskiej, lies the **Old Post Office**—the rallying point for Polish resistance during the German invasion and, since then, a patriotic symbol. Solidarity flags fly high once again at the **Gdańsk Shipyard** and at the **monument to the 1970 uprising**, pl. Solidarności, just north of the center at the end of ul. Wały Piastowskie. Take a ferry to the island of **Westerplatte** to visit the site of WWII's first shots. Boats leave from outside the Green Gate at the end of Długi Targ (tel. 314 926; May-Sept. 9 per day; 1hr.; roundtrip 14zł, students 9zł).

The most beautiful among Gdańsk's many suburbs is **Gdańsk-Oliwa**, with the lush green **Park Oliwski**, ul. Opata Jacka Rybińskiego (open May-Sept. daily 5am-11pm; March-April and Oct. 5am-6pm). Within the parks gates, visitors find the oldest church in the Gdańsk area, the 13th-century **Katedra Oliwska**. Rest and gaze at the golden stars of the high Gothic cross vaults or, if you arrive in August when the annual **Music Festival** is held, enjoy the strains of the magnificent 18th-century rococo organ.

ENTERTAINMENT

Of the three cities that line this little stretch of the Baltic Sea, Gdańsk draws the oldest and biggest crowds. The Długi Targ area is packed with tourists taking in the sights, buying amber, or relaxing at a café. However, even after the last tour bus leaves, a handful of **pubs** keep their doors open for some good beer and company.

Żak, Wały Jagiellońskie 1 (tel. 316 125; e-mail magrent@softel.gda.pl), in a multi-turreted mansion close to the Old Town, near the traffic circle at the intersection of ul. Hucisko. Gdańsk's one bastion of information on student culture and a most happening place. The best bet on any weekend night. It has a movie theater (4-5zł), a pub downstairs (open daily 2pm-2am), and a fashionably downtrodden café upstairs with an "English table" on Tues. beginning at 8pm (open daily 2pm-2am). Żak's free magazine describes upcoming events, including the weekend's live music—usually jazz and rock concerts by both local bands and well known stars.

Cotton Club, ul. Złotnicka 25/29 (tel. 318 813). Head here for jazz, or at least a jazzy atmosphere. Open daily 4pm-late. No cover.

Café "Piwnica U Filipa", ul. Długa 45 (tel. 310 800). Enter from around the back of the building. Fashionable pub-like café promising "muzyka life" (read Techno). Trendy salmon (12zł), chicken (11zł), margaritas (12zł), and other delectables. Open daily noon until the last customer leaves.

Irish Pub "Piwnica", ul. Podgarbary. Follow the signs from near the Golden Gate on ul. Długa. The brick and wood setting of this cellar pub is perfect for a bowl of Irish stew (9zł), followed by a glass of "snake mix" (*Guinness* and cider, 5zł). Also serves a full line of Irish beers and whisky (3-7zł). Open daily 1pm-midnight.

Palowa, ul. Długa 47 (tel. 315 532), in the town hall's basement. A popular pseudo-medieval café run by the students' union. Tortes from 2zł per slice. Coffee 2-4zł. Mixed drinks 3-8zł. Open daily 10am-10pm.

In celebration of the millennial anniversary of the city's founding in 1997, a posh partee has been planned. Festivities begin with a grand session of the Gdańsk City Council on April 18th—the councillors will be wearing traditional gowns that haven't been worn since 1793—and end with a premiere of a Symphony by **Krzysztof Penderecki** on October 31. Other events include exhibitions on the history of Gdańsk, a **craft fair** in July, and **Shakespeare week** in August. During Shakespeare week, the Prince of Wales will lay the cornerstone for the restoration of the Elizabethan Theater, of 17th-century vintage. Tourist offices can provide more information, including a detailed calendar of all events. During the first two weeks of August the **Jarmark**

Dominikański street fair erupts in Gdańsk. The **Jantar Jazz Festival,** which visits the city during July and August, ushers in the September **Polish Film Festival,** held in the LOT building next to Hotel Hevelius. ORBIS (see Practical Information, p. 412) has tickets and details.

■ Near Gdańsk

MALBORK

One of the many castles belonging to the Teutonic Knights, Malbork became the focal point of the Order in the 1300s. The Teutons first came to the region in 1230 at the request of the Polish duke, Konrad Mazowiecki, to assist the Poles in the struggle against the heathen Prussians. The Teutons used the invitation to double-cross the Poles, and establish their own state on conquered Prussian soil, making Malbork their capital in 1309. The great period of Teutonic castle-building lasted until the Order was defeated at the battle of Grunwald in 1410. Malbork, however, withstood several sieges, and the Poles finally defeated their arch-enemies in 1457 under the leadership of King Kazimierz Jagiellończyk. For the next 300 years, Malbork served as one of the major arsenals and strongholds of the Kingdom of Poland. After Poland's first partition (1772), Malbork was incorporated into the Prussian state. WWII heavily damaged the fortress, which was used by the Germans as a POW camp (Stalag XXB). With the fall of the Third Reich, Malbork returned to Poland, and reconstruction continues.

Malbork's layout is rectangular, like that of most Teutonic castles. It is unique, however, in that it is a complex of three huge castles. Construction began in the mid-1270s with the monastery that became the **Higher Castle.** It was to contain the main Church of the Virgin Mary, the Grand Masters' burial chapel, the chapter-room, the refectory, the brethren's dormitory, the treasury, kitchen facilities, a prison cell, and store-rooms. The Higher Castle was surrounded by a system of fortifications, and in 1335-1341 a tower and a bridge over the Nogat River were incorporated. The most splendid additions to Malbork were those of the Grand Master Winrich von Kniprode, who had the Rhenish architect Nikolaus Fellenstein design the magnificent **Master's Residence** in the **Middle Castle.** Guest lodgings lay in this part of the castle, along with the most magnificent hall, the **Grand Refectory,** where great feasts were once held. Finally, the 14th and 15th centuries saw the development of an enormous base, the **Lower Castle,** including an armory, a chapel, an infirmary, servants' quarters, stables, and storerooms. (Open May-Sept. Tues.-Sun. 8:30am-4:30pm; Oct.-April 9am-3pm; admission includes a 2½-hr. guided tour in Polish for 8zł, students 5zł; English-speaking tour guides available for 72zł extra.)

Malbork makes a perfect daytrip from Gdańsk by **train** (25 per day, 40min., 7zł) or **bus** (7 per day, 1hr., 4.20zł). With your back to the station, head right on ul. Dworcowa, then go left at the fork (dir. "Elbląg" on the sign). Go up and around the corner to a roundabout, cross the street at the first crosswalk (before the roundabout), and head towards the "Pizza" sign. The **Malturtourist office,** ul. Sienkiewicza 15 (tel. 722 614), sits near the traffic circle (open Mon.-Fri. 10am-4:30pm, Sat. 10am-2pm). To get to the castle, follow **Ul. Kościuszki,** and continue as it becomes **Ul. Piłsudskiego.** Make a right on **ul. Solina,** and follow it to the castle.

Close to the trains sits the **Youth Hostel,** ul. Żeromskiego 45 (tel. 722 511). Buy a bus ticket at a train station kiosk, and ride bus #6, 7, or 8 one stop or bus #1 or 9 two stops to Wielbark (9zł per person; showers, kitchen; reception open daily 8am-10am and 5-9pm; curfew 11pm). The shiny exterior of **Hotel Zbyszko,** ul. Kościuszki 43 (tel. 723 394), on the right as you head to the castle, leads to some very nice singles (35zł), doubles (50zł), and triples (65zł). **Café Zamkowa,** next to the castle entrance, prepares a regal feast amidst coats-of-arms (entrées 12-20zł, open daily 10am-8pm). **Phone code:** 0-55.

FROMBORK

Little Frombork is closely associated with the name and work of astronomer **Mikołaj Kopernik (Copernicus),** who lived here from 1510 until his death in 1543. It was in this town that Kopernik conducted most of his observations and research and composed the heliocentric *De Revolutionibus Orbium Coelestium.* The town is a tiny waterfront village with a scattering of buildings, all of which surround a truly breathtaking and well maintained cathedral complex perched majestically high atop a hill.

Follow the signs from the train and bus stops to get to the cathedral. Visitors enter the massive **Cathedral** area overlooking the town, on the south side. Once you cross the wooden bridge, the *kasa* on the left (tel. 73 96) sells tickets to **Muzeum Kopernika,** the cathedral, and the *wieża* (tower). The museum houses copies of *De Revolutionibus Orbium Coelestium* and various documents of Kopernik's life, including a scrap of paper that served as his Ph.D. diploma, circa 1503 (open Tues.-Sun. 9:30am-5pm; 1.20zł, students 0.70zł). Next door in the cathedral itself, the famous 17th-century **organ** has a seven-second echo and impeccable sound quality (opens Tues.-Sat. at 9:30am; 1.60zł, students 0.80zł; organ concerts twice daily). A climb up the tower provides a phenomenal view of the cathedral, the town, and the Vistula lagoon (open daily 9:30am-5pm; 1.5zł, students 1zł).

Frombork is best reached by **bus** from Gdańsk (5 per day, 2hr., 6.80zł). Bear in mind that the attractions close just as the third bus of the day leaves Gdańsk. If you take the **train** (7.30zł), you have to change in Elbląg, and the trip may easily take up to four hours, depending on the connection. Once in Frombork, the **train station** and the **bus stop** are along **ul. Dworcowa,** with the docks right behind them. Return bus tickets must be purchased from the driver.

In a parking lot opposite the train station stands a wooden hut with the familiar **IT** sign (tel. 75 00; open daily 8am-7pm). The main **tourist office, Globus,** ul. Elbląska 2 (tel./fax 73 54), sits across from the cathedral in the *rynek,* at the end of the path from the train station. Both offices have detailed info on local accommodations, the cathedral, and the museum. Either staff can arrange ferry trips to nearby Krynica Morska, a popular beach, and Kaliningrad.

The **Youth Hostel Copernicus,** ul. Elbląska 11 (tel. 74 53), sits in a quiet wooded area about 400m from the train station. As you leave the station, head right on ul. Dworcowa, and follow the blue and white signs. The white stone building's rooms are clean and adorned with plants and pictures of the great astronomer (5.20zł per bed, over 26 9.40zł). Camping behind the hostel costs 2zł. **Dom Wycieczkowy PTTK,** ul. Krasickiego 2 (tel. 72 52), on a hill near the cathedral area, offers singles (15zł, with bath 20zł), doubles with bath (28zł), dorms (10zł per person), and a home-style **restaurant** (open daily 7am-9pm). **Phone code:** 0-55.

Sopot

In Poland, there are numerous small towns, each centered around one main street. But when that "one main street" leads to the most incredible beaches in Poland, a 512-m pier, and renowned spas, it's hard not to take notice. With just as much fun in the sun as Gdańsk and a trendier image than Gdynia, it's no coincidence that each summer beach-goers and music lovers flock to little Sopot for a dose of seaside R and R. Whether it's on the beach, in a spa, or at the disco, it's all in the name of fun.

ORIENTATION AND PRACTICAL INFORMATION

Fifteen minutes north of Gdańsk and 25 minutes south of Gdynia by **commuter train,** Sopot can also be reached by the less frequent and more expensive **ferries** from Gdańsk, Gdynia, Westerplatte, or Hel. Sopot is on the Gdańsk **city bus** line, and buses arrive at the train station, a block from the main street, almost as frequently as trains. **Ul. Dworcowa** begins at the train station and leads to the pedestrian **ul. Monte Cassino,** which runs along the sea to the **molo,** the 512-m pier.

Tourist Offices: ORBIS, ul. Monte Cassino 49 (tel. 514 142; fax 512 492). Tickets for trains, planes, ferries, and concerts at Opera Leśna. The best place to get info on the Sopot scene. Exchanges currency and traveler's checks. Open Mon.-Fri. 10am-8pm, Sat. 10am-6pm. **IT**, ul. Dworcowa 4 (tel. 512 617), in a little wooden house next to the train station. Summer budget accommodations can be arranged, and maps of lil' old Sopot (2zł) and the Tri-City (4zł) can be bought. Open Mon.-Fri. 10am-8pm, Sat.-Sun. 9am-2pm.

Currency Exchange: Bank Gdański S.A., pl. Konstytucji 3 Maja 1 (tel. 510 299), opposite the train station. AmEx, MC, and Visa cash advances. Accepts traveler's checks of the same. Open Mon.-Fri. 8am-7pm. **Kantors** near the train station.

Commuter Rail: Over 80 per day to Gdańsk (15min., 1.80zł) and Gdynia (25min., 1.10zł). Basically, trains run every 6min. during the day and less frequently during the evening. Punch tickets in the yellow *kasownik* box before boarding.

Buses: To: Gdańsk by MPK city bus (every ½hr., 1.20zł); Gdynia (10 per day, 3zł).

Ferries: (tel. 511 293) at the end of the pier. To: Hel (roundtrip 20zł, students 15zł); Gdynia (8zł, students 5.50zł); Westerplatte (roundtrip 15zł, students 11zł). Open daily 8am-7pm.

Pharmacy: Pod Orłem, ul. Monte Cassino 37 (tel. 511 018). Convenient central location. Open Mon.-Fri. 8am-8pm, Sat. 9am-3pm.

Medical Assistance: ul. Chrobrego 18 (tel. 512 455), on ul. Mieszka I. Open 24hr.

Post Office: ul. Kościuszki 2 (tel. 515 951), the 1st street on the right heading down ul. Monte Cassino (open Mon.-Fri. 8am-8pm, Sat. 9am-3pm). **Postal code:** 81-701.

Telephones: Inside and outside the post office. Open Mon.-Fri. 7am-9pm, Sat. 9am-3pm, Sun. 11am-6pm. **Phone code:** 0-58.

ACCOMMODATIONS AND CAMPING

Sopot is one of Poland's most popular and expensive resorts, so summer reservations are a must. Consider renting a **private rooms;** stop by **IT** (see Practical Information, above) for help (singles 24zł; doubles 40zł; triples 44zł). To save money and escape the crowds, consider staying near the **Sopot Kamienny Potok** train station, one stop north of the main Sopot station. This part of town is just as near the sea as the pricier resorts and tends to be less crowded. Accommodations and the beach are reached by exiting the platform to the right and crossing ul. Niepodległości.

Hotel Miramar, ul. Zamkowa Góra 21/25 (tel. 518 011; fax 515 164). Although the sign is directly ahead as you cross ul. Niepodległości, the hotel is not the aqua-green structure you see before you (that's their restaurant and nightclub) but the moderately-sized brown building behind it. A perfect example of how to save money without sacrificing quality by going a bit away from the main part of town. Nice rooms in a park-like area a short walk from the beach. Singles with bath 67zł. Doubles with bath 100zł. Triples with bath 120zł. AmEx, Mc, and Visa accepted.

Camping: Nr 19, although technically at the same address and phone number as Hotel Miramar (see above), the campsite has a separate reception area and entrance, on ul. Niepodległości about 300m from the end of the path from the Sopot Kamienny Potok train station (go left). Showers. A billiards hall. 24-hr. Snack Bar "Amigo" next door. 6zł per person. Tents 4zł. 3-person cabins 48zł. Call for other options; they aim to please.

FOOD

Fish and beer can be found by the pier. A few spots stand out, even as ul. Monte Cassino grows more generic-looking with the invasion of chain restaurants.

Bar Rybny Pod Strzechą, ul. Monte Cassino 42 (tel. 512 476). Serves simple, yet amazing, fish dishes at unbeatable prices (2-7zł). Open daily 10am-11pm.

La Mela, ul. Monte Cassino 16 (tel. 511 544). At the entrance, huge sculptures of a man and a woman perpetually reach out towards you. Reward their eternal labor and visit the popular, sunny interior. Offers a wide selection of Italian dishes, including pizza and lasagna (5-10zł). Open daily 11am-9pm.

Kawiarnia Teatralna, ul. Monte Cassino 50 (tel. 514 241). The perfect place to enjoy a cup of good coffee and a coffee-time snack (2-5zł). Open daily 10am-11pm.

SIGHTS AND ENTERTAINMENT

Sopot gained prominence because of its **beach**—unavoidable and truly as impressive as they say. The most popular and extensive sands spread at the end of ul. Monte Cassino. This is also where the famous 512-m **molo** (pier) begins (Mon.-Fri. 1.20zł, Sat.-Sun. 1.80zł and a smile).

The city itself is just beginning to realize that entertainment doesn't have to come in with the tides, and the number of street-side **cafés, pubs,** and **discos** along ul. Monte Cassino continues to multiply. **Pub FM,** ul. Monte Cassino 36 (tel. 513 359), offers lots of fun for a student crowd. The house speciality is *pierogi ruskie* (dumplings with potato and cheese filling) for 4.5zł, but most folks come here for the beer and cider (open daily 12:30pm-2am). The Irish **Loch Ness Pub,** ul. Monte Cassino 45 (tel. 502 840), offers refreshing alternatives to Polish beer, including *Guinness* (open Sun.-Thurs. 12:30pm-1am, Fri.-Sat. 12:30pm-2am). The new discos and nightclubs are the latest nighttime rage by the pier. Especially popular are **Bunkier, Ground Zero, Non-Stop,** and **Fantom.** The open-air **Opera Leśna's** rock and pop music festival dominates the area in mid-August; call ahead for tickets and info on other festivals and shows (tel. 511 812). Concerts on the pier are frequent in summer; watch for ads for **Amfiteatr na molo** (tickets and info at the pier box office; tel. 510 481).

At ul. Ceynowy 5/7, **Sopocki Klub Tenisowy** (tel. 513 569) rents out 23 **tennis** courts (open daily 7am-10pm; 6-15zł per hr.).

■ Gdynia

Young Gdynia, much of it built only after WWI, is, thankfully, in no hurry to grow up. Although it lacks both the history and tradition of Gdańsk and the glitzy fame of Sopot, the town seems more than happy to be a spot for the simpler sides of maritime life: boats, sailors, and fish. Enticing evening strolls along the waterfront show boat-lovers a little slice of nautical heaven in Gdynia. Anyone who wants a no-frills visit to seaside life needs to look no farther.

ORIENTATION AND PRACTICAL INFORMATION

Despite its small size, the Gdynia Główna **train station** welcomes a large volume of traffic in both trains and **buses.** You can daytrip here from Gdańsk, thanks to the frequent **commuter trains** which connect the two cities. The **tourist office** is in the train station, but somewhat hidden in the back corner of the main lobby by the bus ticket area. Any of the three roads running away from the station will take you towards the beach and the pier. **Ul. 10-go Lutego** is the most direct. If you end up on **ul. Jana Kolna, ul. wójta Radtkiego,** or **ul. Starowiejska** (which parallel ul. 10-go Lutego), take a right at the end of the street onto **pl. Kaszubski,** then turn left on ul. 10-go Lutego where it runs into the fountain-filled **Skwer Kościuszki.** For shopping, continue along pl. Kaszubski to **ul. Świętojanska,** a 3km road full of things to buy and eat. The **beach** is off Skwer Kościuszki.

> **Tourist Offices: Mart-Tur,** pl. Konstytucji 1 (tel. 285 378 or 219 225), at the train station. Friendly and helpful. Sells maps (3-4zł each), helps with accommodations and camping, and maintains computerized lists of all bus connections from the Tri-City area to the European Union. Open Mon.-Fri. 9am-6pm, Sat. 9am-2pm.
> **Currency Exchange:** Many *kantors.* **Bank Gdański, S.A.,** Skwer Kościuszki 14 (tel. 204 135). Provides AmEx, MC, and Visa cash advances; also cashes AmEx and Visa traveler's checks. Open Mon.-Fri. 8am-6pm.
> **Trains:** To: Kraków (5 per day, 41.10zł); Poznań (7 per day, 31.20zł); Szczecin (6 per day, 20.70zł); Warsaw (13 per day, 31zł); and Wrocław (4 per day, 34.10zł).

Commuter Train: Peron I at the train station. The cheapest and easiest way to go to Gdańsk or Sopot. Prices posted in the station. Punch your stub in the yellow *kasownik* boxes before getting on the train. To: Gdańsk (2.60zł); Sopot (1.10zł).
Buses: To: Hel (24 per day, 2hr., 7zł); Świnoujście (2 per day, 8hr., 14zł); Warsaw (8 per day, 7hr., 25zł).
Ferries: al. Zjednoczenia 2 (tel. 202 642), on Skwer Kościuszki. To: Gdańsk (2 per day; 2hr.; 19zł, students 14zł); Hel (5 per day; 1hr.; 14zł, students 10zł; roundtrip 19zł, students 14zł); Sopot (3 per day; ½hr.; 8zł, students 5.50zł); Westerplatte (2 per day; 1¼hr.; roundtrip 19zł, students 14zł). **Lion Ferry,** ul. Kwiatkowskiego 60 (tel. 213 623; fax 213 620), sends 1 ferry per day to Karlskrona, Sweden (13hr., 180 Swedish kroner).
Taxis: Radio taxi, tel. 91 95 or 91 99.
Medical Assistance: ul. Żwirki i Wigury 14 (tel. 200 001). **Poliklinika EviMed,** ul. Bema 16 (tel. 203 235), has private doctors. Open 8am-10pm.
Post Office: ul. 10-go Lutego 10 (tel. 218 711), between the train station and Skwer Kościuszki. Open Mon.-Fri. 7am-8pm, Sat. 9am-3pm. **Postal code:** 81-301.
Telephones: At the post office. Open 24hr. **Phone code:** 58.

ACCOMMODATIONS AND CAMPING

Given fast commuter rail service and a slew of cheap sleeps, Gdynia is a good base for the Tri-City area. **Turus,** ul. Starowiejska 47 (tel. 218 265; fax 209 287), opposite the train station, finds private singles (25zł), doubles (40zł), and triples (42zł), but only for those staying at least three nights (open Mon.-Fri. 8am-6pm, Sat. 10am-6pm).

Youth Hostel (HI), ul. Morska 108c (tel. 270 005). Exit the station on the opposite side of the tracks (go through the tunnels under the platforms toward ul. Morska), then take the #22, 25, 30, 105, 109, or 125 bus 4 stops along ul. Morska. The entrance is in the back of the building marked 108b. Call to see if rooms are available. Basic, clean rooms. 132 beds. Reception open daily 8-10am and 5-10pm. Preference for Polish students and those with HI card. 11zł. Sheets 1.50zł.

Hotel Lark, ul. Starowiejska 1 (tel. 218 047), at the end of the road that begins to the right of the train station. This small hotel has decent rooms that are comfortable, but a bit dark. It's only a short walk from the sights and the beach. Communal bathrooms. Singles 49zł. Doubles 72zł. Triples 96zł. MC and Visa accepted.

FOOD

One of the most extensive markets in the Tri-City, **Hala Targowa** stretches between ul. Jana Kolna and ul. wójta Radtkiego (open Mon.-Fri. 9am-6pm, Sat. 8am-3pm). You can get everything from fresh fruit, vegetables, and meat to clothes, watches, and books, and numerous Russian vendors sell their goods at bargain prices. For a full sensory experience, check out the pungent "hall of fish." As in many seaside towns, there are also kiosks and food stands galore along the waterfront Hala Rybna, where a full meal can be had for less than 6zł. The prime areas seem to be around Skwer Kościuszki and the train station.

Chang Cheng, ul. Dworcowa 1/4 (tel. 208 107). A stone's throw from the train station. A surprisingly extensive menu. Entrées around 11zł. Open daily noon-10pm.

Bar na kutrze (tel. 243 165), marooned at Skwer Kościuszki next to the sailboat Dar Pomorza. This nautical eatery keeps things simple, but tasty, with 2 choices: fish and beer. The smiling fish on the ship will welcome you aboard for a meal that will run less than 5zł. Try the Baltic specialty, *dorsz*. Open daily 10am-9pm.

Róża Wiatrów, al. Zjednoczenia 2 (tel. 200 648). Serves tasty duck with apples for only 8zł and a good selection of Polish fare for 5-9zł. Wash it down with some gin (6zł) or rum (5zł). AmEx, MC, Visa accepted. Open daily 1pm-3am.

SIGHTS AND ENTERTAINMENT

The kiosks lining the **pier** on Skwer Kościuszki give it a carnivalesque atmosphere, and the crowds stay well after mealtimes to relax by the sea. For more seaside views, walk along shoreline **Bulwar Nadmorski im. F. Nowowiejskiego.** The stroll also includes a few popular places to sit and watch others do the walking. Check out **Café Bulwar,** with its outdoor stage, and the **Contrast Caffè,** with its fish net and sea-shell decor—two of the more prominent meeting places. Both await just south of Skwer Kościuszki and stay open until the last guest leaves.

Those who feel inspired to get nautical will not be disappointed by the pier. The warship **Błyskawica** docks here, complete with crew (open Tues.-Sun. 9:45am-12:30pm and 1:45-4:30pm; 2zł, students 1zł). The 1909 sailboat **Dar Pomorza** (tel. 202 371) served as a school at sea for the Polish navy between 1930 and 1981, and has won several sailing competitions (open daily 10am-4pm; admission and guided tour 3zł, students 1.50zł). The boat **Bożena** (tel. 510 685, ext. 206, after 3pm 57 56 13) gives tours of Gdynia's port (11 per day, 8am-10pm; 1-hr. tickets 9zł, students 6zł). **The Oceanographic Museum and Aquarium** at the end of the pier sheds some light on the surrounding sea, its history, and the multitudes of animals that call it home (open daily 9am-6:30pm; 4zł, students 2.50zł).

For more theatrical entertainment, **Teatr Muzyczny w Gdyni** (ticket info tel. 216 024 or 216 025) puts on several productions in the theater at pl. Grunwaldzki 1 (tel. 209 521). Call for shows and times. After the theater, become a disco **Tornado,** (tel. 202 305), below the restaurant Różu Wiatrów on the pier (open Fri.-Sat. 9pm-4am; cover Fri. 5zł, Sat. 10zł).

■ Hel

Go to Hel—really. For almost a millennium, the sleepy village of Hel has lived off the beautiful fish of the Baltic Sea and the booty from boats stranded on the Hel peninsula (Mierzeja Helska). Recently, the town has awakened to the sound of tourists walking its clean, wide, gorgeous beaches. Still an operating fishing town, Hel offers relaxation to those who make the daytrip from the mainland, serving up amazing fish and a pleasant change of pace from the crowded mainland resorts.

Orientation and Practical Information Frequent **trains** (9 per day, 2hr., 6zł) and **buses** (1 per hr., 2hr., 4zł) connect Hel to Gdynia. The trip is bordered (at times on both sides) by wind-swept dunes and awesome seaside views of the mainland. The **train station** (as well as one of the town's two bus stops) is a short walk from the main street **ul. Wiejska.** Simply take **ul. Dworcowa** to the right (with your back to the station) as it follows a small park to intersect ul. Wiejska. Make a left to head into town. If you take the bus past the train station to the last stop you'll be dropped off at the other end of ul. Wiejska. Hel can also be reached by **boat** from Gdańsk (in summer 2 per day, off-season 1 per day; 2hr.; roundtrip 28zł, students 19zł), Sopot (in summer 3 per day; 70min.; roundtrip 20zł, students 15zł), and Gdynia (in summer 5 per day; roundtrip 19zł, students 14zł). The ferry arrives at Hel's dock on **Bulwar Nadmorski,** a block from ul. Wiejska. Tickets can be bought at the waterfront in the white kiosk by the ferry landing (tel. 750 437; open daily 9am-5pm). The **PTTK tourist office,** ul. Wiejska 78 (tel. 750 621, ext. 44 01), in a 19th-century fishing hut, is staffed by super-friendly volunteers (the entrance to the office is in the back). Though their main goal is to organize trips for local youth, they also help find private accommodations for visitors and sell maps and brochures for around 3zł (open Mon.-Sat. 10am-2pm). **Exchange currency** at the **post office,** ul. Wiejska 55 (tel. 750 550; open Mon.-Fri. 8am-6pm, Sat. 9am-1pm; **kantor** open only 8am-10am and 2pm-6pm), or buy telephone cards and tokens. **Telephones** are available inside and outside. **Postal code:** 84-150. **Phone code:** 0-58.

Accommodations If you want to spend a few days in Hel, the PTTK (see above) arranges **private accommodations** in the houses of members. Room quality and location vary (15zł per person). If you have no luck there, get in touch with the director of Muzeum Rybołóstwa (The Fishing Museum), pani Hanna Bulinska, who may be able to put you up in her **pensionat,** ul. Plażowa 5 (tel. 750 848), a large, white cinderblock house a few hundred meters west of the museum (15zł per person). Private rooms are also offered by many of the shop owners along u. Wiejska; just look for the **"wolne pokoje"** sign in the window. These are usually group rooms above restaurants and shops, but because Hel quiets down at 10pm, noise is not an issue. The rooms themselves are fairly standard, but with so few options in town, they can get crowded, especially in summer when the mainland is jam-packed.

Food and Entertainment Hel feeds its guests well, and most eateries flank ul. Wiejska. The **supermarket "Marina",** ul. Wiejska 70, stocks groceries in a central location (open Mon.-Fri. 6am-6pm, Sat. 6am-2pm, and Sun. 10am-2pm). Restaurants and kiosks focus squarely on either fish or desserts. PTTK runs the tasty and inexpensive **Bar Turystyczny,** ul. Wiejska 78, a.k.a. **Jak U Mamusi** (The Way Mommy Cooks). This mommy serves tomato soup to fight off colds (1.80zł), grilled sausage to make you big and strong (1.80zł), and salmon to build those brain cells (2.50zł; open daily 11am-6pm). Farther down the street, **Izdebka,** ul. Wiejska 39—a white-and-brown fisherman's hut built in 1844 with a finely crafted street lantern in front—may be the only place in the world where salmon (2.80zł) is cheaper than tripe (3zł; open daily 10am-8pm). If you are in the mood for dessert, stop for coffee (1-2zł) and sweets (2-4zł) at **Maszoperia,** ul. Wiejska 110 (tel. 750 297), in a 200-year-old hut with a traditional fisherman's half-door. The name of this coffee house means "Fisherman's House" in the Kashubian dialect, but even vegans can enjoy this tiny eatery with its shady yard and homey interior. It's a popular meeting place, and if you ask nicely, they may take musical requests (open daily 10am-10pm).

Sights If you arrive by ferry, the first thing you'll see after the harbor is Hel's oldest building. The red-brick **Church of St. Peter** (1417-32), Bulwar Nadmorski, now houses **Muzeum Rybołówstwa** (Fishing Museum; tel. 750 552). An English history of the church waits just inside by the ticket window. Meanwhile, the museum provides a thorough history of the town through everything from stormy seas to Nazi invasions (open Tues.-Sun. 9:30am-4pm; 2zł, students 1zł). For an extra 1zł, climb the **wooden tower,** which commands a magnificent view of the Tri-City, Hel's harbors, and Hel town. The museum displays nets, canoes, boats, and fishing and boat-building techniques of the last 1000 years. Check out the fishermen's ice skates, the needles used for mending nets, and the giant metal combs employed in catching eel. The second floor details the development of Hel and exhaustively describes its role in WWII.

One of the Baltic Coast's best-kept secrets is the **beach** at the end of ul. Leśna (don't be discouraged by the small patch of sand by the ferry landing—it gets better). Ul. Leśna begins by the fishing museum and runs through a park to the other side of the *mierzeja.* It's a 15- to 20-minute walk through pleasant pine forest, and it's well worth it. **Ul. Wiejska,** the main artery, has retained much of its old character thanks to **19th-century fishermen's houses** at #29, 33, 39 and 110. These low-set, cellar-less huts are made of pine and bricks and face the street sideways. Following ul. Wiejska as it turns into ul. Kuracyjna eventually leads to a part of the Hel headland closed to visitors. This is the location of the **Headland Battery,** site of the Polish defense of Hel at the beginning of WWII. Concrete firing positions still exist to give evidence of the town's recent military history.

MAZURY

East of Pomorze, Mazury (pl.) are a region of woods and lakes; their nickname, "the land of a thousand lakes", is by no means an exaggeration—in fact, Mazury and the Suwałki region in the far northwest are home to about 4000 lakes. The largest and the deepest of the Polish lake, Śniardwy and Mamry are each over 100km sq. in area; Hańcza reaches 108m in depth. The lakeland's canals, rivers, and streams create excellent conditions for kayaking and sailing. Mrągowo and Augustów are the last outposts of civilization for tourists venturing out into the wild and beautiful waters.

■ Mrągowo

Toy-like, orange-roofed houses speckle the endless lakes and rivers where Germans and other tourists come to boat, fish, kayak, swim, water-bike, water-ski, and horse-back ride. Known as "Sensburg" before 1947, Mrągowo was named for Celesty Mrongowiusz, a patriot who fought the Germans so his countrymen could continue speaking Polish. His descendents have given up the fight, and now most respond to *Deutsch*. Shops and cafés crowd the central streets, while mosquitoes swarm hills and valleys, drawn by what once were part of a Scandinavian glacier (i.e., the lakes).

Orientation and Practical Information The locals do not seem to recognize the PKP train station as part of their town, although they will gladly direct you to the bus station, a.k.a. PKS. **Buses** run to Augustów (2 per day, 10.40zł), Gdańsk (1 per day, 19.60zł), Olsztyn (16 per day, 4.80zł), and Warsaw (7 per day, 19.60zł). The station separates **ul. Warszawska,** a leg of Mrągowo's main drag, from **ul. Wojska Polskiego,** which leads out of town. With your back to the blue "Mrągowo" sign, bear right on ul. Warszawska. Another right turn on **ul. Traugutta** drops down to **Jezioro Czos,** the biggest of the five *mrągowskie* lakes. With a little zig, ul. Warszawska becomes **ul. Ratuszowa.** The bookstore **Współczesna,** ul. Ratuszowa 8 (tel. 28 16; open Mon.-Sat. 10am-6pm, Sun. 10am-2pm), offers maps, *Let's Go* in Polish, and quick film developing. At the corner of ul. Ratuszowa and M. Rynek, the staff of **Eco-Travel,** M. Rynak 6 (tel. 36 61; open Mon.-Fri. 8am-5pm, Sat. 9am-2pm), speaks English. For **currency exchange,** try one of the common *kantors* or **Bank Polska Kasa Opieki S.A.,** plac Kajki 1 (tel. 32 72; fax 22 73; open Mon.-Fri. 8am-6pm, Sat. 10am-2pm), which also provides MC and Visa cash advances. **Hotel Orbis "Mrongovia,"** ul. Giżycka 6 (tel. 32 21; fax 32 20), rents boats, kayaks, water-skis, and even horses with or without buggy. In winter, cross-country skiing and ice boating become the hotel's sports of choice. After a left-right zag, ul. Ratuszowa reluctantly becomes ul. Królewiecka at a **pharmacy** *(apteka),* ul. Krówlwiecka 1 (tel. 33 46; open Mon.-Sat. 8am-7pm, Sun. 9am-3pm). Farther up the street lies a **post office** *(poczta),* ul. Krówlwiecka 34 (tel. 20 11; open Mon.-Sat. 8am-8pm, Sun. 9am-2pm). The **telephones** inside operate daily 7am-9pm. **Postal code:** 11-700. **Phone code:** 0-886.

Accommodations and Food The simple, clean **Hotel Meltur,** ul. Sienkiewicza 16 (tel. 29 00), rents doubles for 21.40zł, with shower for 37.45zł. From PKS, follow ul. Wojska Polskiego and turn right onto ul. Sienkiewicza. **Pensjonat Eva,** ul. Jaszczurcza Góra (tel. 31 16), has rooms with showers and color TVs (singles 64zł; doubles 80zł; under 26 20% off; off-season prices drop 40%; reception open daily til 10pm). Family-run **Pensjonat "To-Tu,"** ul. Jaszczurcza Góra 26 (tel. 39 77), offers luxurious lodgings near Jezioro Czos' shore. Follow the trail around Jezioro Czos to get here from PKS. Every room has a hot shower, and one of the apartments boasts a bath (singles 80zł, doubles 100zł, apartments 150zł; students 30% discount; off-season prices drop; breakfast in bed included; AmEx, MC, and Visa accepted). Each of the freshly furnished rooms at **Pensjonat "Maria,"** ul. Jaszczurcza Góra 20 (tel. 39 79), has a terrace and shower. Downstairs, grapes grow near a balalaika and a grill (singles 50zł, doubles 70zł; breakfast included; closed off-season).

Bars, snack shops, and ice cream joints pepper the town. The **Intercommerce supermarket,** ul. Brzozowa 10 (tel. 62 01), has got the groceries (open Mon.-Sat. 6am-8pm, Sun. 9am-1pm). **Restauracja Fregata,** just left of ul. Ratuszowa near ul. Dolny Zaułek (tel. 22 44), serves both international *plats* and local dishes. For a taste of the region, try *schab po mazursku* (pork, 9zł; open daily 9am-9pm).

Entertainment Every July 29 to August 1, an amphitheater on the shore of Jezioro Czos near Hotel Orbis, holds a **Country Picnic Festival. Miejski Dom Kultury "Zodiak"** (House of Culture), ul. Warszawska 26 (tel. 30 63), features weekend concerts at 6pm by both amateurs and Polish professionals: Fridays are for rock and amateur music, Saturdays for folk concerts and dance, and most Sundays for live Polish pop. The main **beaches**—Plaża Orbisu, packed with canoeists, and Plaża Miejska—are both on Jezioro Czos, next to Hotel Orbis.

■ Near Mrągowo: Święta Lipka

Sometime during the Middle Ages, a Prussian tribal leader was pardoned by the ruling Teutonic knights and thanked God by placing Mary's likeness in a local linden tree. Rumors of miraculous healing and epiphany soon attracted pilgrims to the Holy Linden (a.k.a. Święta Lipka)—so many that the Teutonic knights built a shrine to the arbor in 1320. Two hundred years later, the knights razed the Catholic chapel due to a religious reversal and slowed the flow of believers by installing threatening gallows (bodies included) round the tree. The gallows have since rotted away, and no deterrent blocks the annual flocks of Germans who come to visit **Sanktuarium Maryjne** (The Sanctuary of Our Lady). German brochures pack the gift stores, and German-speaking priests conduct most tours. Amid lakes, craft shops, and a flower-filled cemetery, the shrine guards an interior as breathtaking as its surroundings. Biblical paintings and a spiky gold recreation of the miraculous linden adorn the inside. When large crowds gather (i.e., all the time), glistening suns start swirling, baby-faced angels shake their golden bells, the archangel strums her balalaika, and golden trumpeters accompany the organ music—creating a religious trip. Special **concerts** are held every Friday at 8pm in July and August. A **bus** to Kętrzyn links Święta Lipka to Mrągowo (6 per day, 45min., 2.50zł); buy your ticket on the bus.

■ Augustów

Located on three lakes amid thick forests, bear-like Augustów sleeps in winter and wakes up in summer, when backpackers take possession of sailboats and kayaks. The scenery and the cool air welcome families swimming, young hordes camping, and older folks strolling along the lakeshore. The town, named after King Zygmunt August, who granted it a charter in 1557, celebrates its 400th year of privileges.

Orientation and Practical Information Augustów is curiously shaped, thanks to the lakes and forests around which it has grown. The main **Rynek Zygmunta Augusta** lies on the south side of the **Netta** River, which cuts the town in half and leads to **Jezioro (Lake) Necko.** The bus station sits on the *rynek's* southwest side and sends autocars to Białystok (16 per day, 2-3hr., 7zł), Druskininkai, Lithuania (2 per day, 5hr. plus time at border, 17zł), and Warsaw (4 per day, 4½hr., 16zł). A short walk through the park leads to **ORBIS,** whose staff cashes AmEx traveler's checks at 5% commission (open daily 9am-4pm). **Trains** arrive from Białystok (5 per day, 2hr., 12.90zł), Šeštokai, Lithuania (linked to Vilnius, 1 per day, 5hr.), and Warsaw (5 per day, 5hr., 19.80zł) but the station is at least a half-hour from town, so take **city bus** #1, 2, 6, or 10 from the stop on **ul. Turystyczna,** to "Rynek". Pick up a **map** of Augustów at Hotel Hetman (see below; 5zł) as accommodations and eateries spread over the whole town, and the paths, lakes, and streams become a maze after sunset. **Ferries,** ul. 29-go Listopada 7 (tel. 21 52 or 28 81), sail for other lake towns. Or, go-getters can **rent boats** of their own at **PTTK docks,** ul. Nadrzeczna 70a (kayaks and rowboats 13.50zł per day; sailboats 23zł per day). The **post office,** Rynek Zygmunta Augusta 3 (tel. 32 33 or 36 71), operates 24-hour pay phones outside (open Mon.-Fri. 8am-8pm, Sat. 8am-3pm, Sun. 9am-11am). **Postal Code:** 16-300. **Phone code:** 0-119.

Accommodations and Camping Despite the beautiful lakes and relaxing atmosphere, there is no real accommodations crunch, thanks to the endless number of campgrounds surrounding the town. To get to **Hotel Hetman,** ul. Sportowa 1 (tel. 45 345), take ul. Mostowa to ul. Partyzantów. At the end, head left on al. Wyszyńskiego until it bears left around a corner, after which the dashing cavalier on the hotel's sign will direct you left on ul. Sportowa. Or, catch bus #1, 2, 4, 6, or 8 headed out of the *rynek* and get off at "Krechowiak". It's the farthest hotel from the *rynek,* but that means quiet lakeside nights and the best beach in town. Average-size rooms with comfortable beds that make up for the mosquitoes that sneak in after visiting hours (singles 30zł, doubles 41zł, with bath 75zł; MC and Visa accepted). In a sailing center on the lake, **Ośrodek Żeglarski PTTK,** ul. Nadrzeczna 70a, is not so much a beachfront hotel as a near-dock hotel. Take the first left on ul. Mostowa before crossing the bridge. This well run, friendly building resembling a scaled-down ski lodge, offers clean, basic rooms just a short walk from the *rynek* on the Netta's south banks (doubles 26zł, Quads 48zł). In season, their **campground** offers 5-person cabins for 35zł, and sites at 3zł per person plus tent fees (double 5zł, triple 7zł, quad 9.50zł). The inside of sunny, central **Dom Nauczyciela,** ul. 29-go Listopada 9 (tel. 20 21), shouts out "new and renovated." The outside... Did we mention the amiable staff or the clean rooms? (Singles 25zł. Doubles 30zł.)

Food *Augustowskie* dining focuses on quick fixes in familiar packages. Fans of *łody,* grilled *kiełbasa,* and other push-cart provisions will be in heaven. Independent diners find their food shopping oasis at **Sklep Spożywczy,** Rynek Zygmunta Augusta 37 (tel. 27 77; open Mon.-Fri. 7am-8pm, Sat. 7am-6pm, Sun. 9am-4pm). What **Albatros,** ul. Mostowa 3 (tel. 21 23), lacks in character it makes up for with a varied menu, decent prices, and a prime location (entrées 4-10zł; open Sun.-Tues. noon-9pm, Wed.-Sat. noon-midnight; disco Tues. and Thurs. 8pm-1am, cover 4zł; dancing Fri.-Sat. 8pm-1:30am, Sun. 8pm-12:30am; cover 8zł). Sunnier than Albatros, **Restauracja Hetman,** ul. Sportowa 1 (tel. 45 345), serves up better food *and* breakfast (7.50zł). Bow-tied waiters dish out 8-15zł entrées (open daily 7am-11pm). **Pączki,** 3-go Maja 11 (tel. 31 94), across from Kościoła Najświętszego, serves the best *łody* in town plus *deser owocowy* (0.80 zł)—what jello should have been—with cream, blueberries, and chocolate. Open Mon.-Sat. 8am-6pm, Sun. 9am-5pm.

Sights and Entertainment Much of Augustów's appeal is that you don't feel forced to learn anything new and historical. Just sit by the lakes or have a glass of *piwo.* Two popular **beaches** lie on the lakefront across the bridge: one just to the left, the other behind Hotel Hetman (see Accommodations, above). Boat renters are free to go wherever their paddles take them, but sailors are at the mercy of the gentle Zephyr. For the most picturesque route, navigate northwest, where the lake opens up and islands invite explorer-types to sail on in. For the alcohol-inclined, indistinguishable **bars** litter ul. Mostowa.

PODLASIE

The entire region has been christened "Poland's green lungs," and is given maximum environmental protection. Known for small non-Catholic villages—not only Russian Orthodox and Jewish but also Muslim and Uniate—Podlasie also encompasses Puszcza Białowieska (Białowieża Forest). Once the favorite hunting ground of Poland's kings, the forest is now a national park, and the habitat of a huge variety of wildlife. The European bison reigns as undisputed king of the forest. Białystok, northwest of the forest preserve, is its hip urban center.

■ Białystok

The train station in Białystok hums with Belarusian, Russian, and Polish—most frequently with a cacophonous combination of the three. Travelers come here to buy and sell goods; the city caters to newcomers from the East with menus in Russian. Białystok is remarkably active and modern despite its less-than-central location. Boutiques line the streets, and visitors from distant lands add a cosmopolitan air.

ORIENTATION AND PRACTICAL INFORMATION

The downtown is organized along ul. Lipowa, which leads from the **bus and train stations** east to **Rynek Kościuszki**, the city center, and then on to **pl. Branickich**. If you arrive by train, cross the tracks via the overpass which leads to the bus station. From here, with your back to the bus terminal, go left on **ul. Bohaterów Monte Cassino**, then right on **ul. Świętego Rocha**, which leads directly to **ul. Lipowa**. Follow this street to the *rynek*. Other major streets are **ul. Sienkiewicza**, which heads northeast and south from the *rynek*, and **ul. Piłsudskiego**, which bows out to the left (from Św. Rocha), running parallel to ul. Lipowa.

- **Tourist Offices: ORBIS,** ul. Rynek Kościuszki 13 (tel. 421 627 or 423 047). Provides the usual—cash advances on MC and Visa, Western Union, and currency exchange. Open Mon.-Fri. 9am-5pm, Sat. 9am-2pm. In the bus station, the kiosk **Mapy** (tel. 22 461, ext. 32) gives out free info and carries a selection of maps (2.50-3zł). **PTTK,** ul. Lipowa 18 (tel. 517 173), sells maps, guides, and train and bus tickets. Also directs to local hotels and organizes trips to the Białowieża bison reserve. Open Mon.-Fri. 8am-4pm.
- **Budget Travel: ALMATUR,** ul. Zwierzyniecka 12 (tel. 28 943). Sells ISICs and has info on student travel and accommodations. Open Mon.-Fri. 9am-4pm.
- **Currency Exchange:** *Kantors* flank ul. Lipowa. **Bank PKO S.A.,** ul. Sienkiewicza 40 (tel. 436 626), cashes traveler's checks of all major brands for a 1.5% commission. MC and Visa cash advances at no fee. Open Mon.-Fri. 8am-6pm.
- **Trains:** ul. Kolejowa. To: Gdańsk (1 per day, 9hr., 23.10zł); Moscow (1 per day, 25hr., 150zł); Vilnius (2 per day, 9hr., 25zł); Warsaw (9 per day, 4hr., 15.90zł).
- **Buses:** ul. Bohaterów Monte Cassino (tel. 22 461, info 936). To: Minsk (2 per day, 18hr., 50zł); Vilnius (2 per day, 9hr., 35zł); Warsaw (4 per day, 4hr., 10zł).
- **Luggage Storage:** At the train station. 1zł. Open daily 8am-7pm and 8pm-7am.
- **Water Sports Equipment Rental: Ośrodek Sportów Wodnych,** ul. Plażowa, by Lake Dojlidy. Boats, kayaks, sailboats, surf boards, and water bikes. Take bus #15 from the center to Dojlidy, or bus #12 from the train station to the end-stop, then walk 5min. southeast on ul. Suchowola.
- **Pharmacies: Apteka,** ul. Lipowa 45 (tel. 423 365). Open Mon.-Sat. 7am-9pm, Sun. 10am-5pm.
- **Post Office:** ul. Warszawska 10 (tel. 435 325). Open Mon.-Fri. 8am-8pm, working Sat. 8am-1pm. **Postal code:** 15-001.
- **Telephones:** In the post office. Pay phones line ul. Lipowa. **Phone code:** 0-85.

ACCOMMODATIONS

PTTK (see Practical Information, above) directs tourists in trouble to the city's best steals.

- **Youth Hostel,** ul. Piłsudskiego 7b (tel. 524 250). A basic, crowded hostel offering backpackers a place to crash. Hang with Polish youth and not-so-youthful for 6-10zł. The *dyrektor's* understanding of "curfew" sometimes mean sharing drinks with guests into the wee hours. Lockout 10am-5pm. Curfew 11pm.
- **Hotel Rubin,** ul. Warszawska 7 (tel. 772 335), in a stylish building. Once part of Pałac Branickich, and still connected by an underground passage, it caters to East-

ern European visitors, price- and language-wise. Small but clean rooms. Communal bathrooms. Singles 13zł, doubles 20zł.

FOOD

Ul. Lipowa has some of the city's best eateries, both proletarian and posh. However, the mid-level lacks a bit. **Supersam,** ul. Skłodowskiej 14, is a full-blown supermarket (open Mon.-Fri. 6am-9pm, Sat. 6am-8pm, Sun. 8am-6pm).

Raj Smakosza (Gourmand's Paradise), ul. Malmeda 1 (tel. 26 042), on the corner of ul. Lipowa. A white-and-green oasis for weary travelers. Better than the average milk bar, with very tasty food. Fresh green salads 1.50zł, chicken 4.30zł, *bigos* 3.70zł, *chłodnik* 1.70zł. Open daily 7am-10pm.

Café Ratuszowa, Rynek Kościuszki 3 (tel. 454 804), outside the town hall. Packed with local hipsters sliding through the afternoon and evening with beer, frantic conversation, and endless furtive glances. Jazz and rock musicians add tunes. Seating: at a table 5zł, on the grass 3zł. *Tosty* (sandwiches) 2zł. Open daily 9am-1am.

Restauracja Cristal, ul. Lipowa 3/5 (tel. 26 245 or 25 800). Upscale, with a sparkling green-and-maroon setting and menu to match: caviar (15zł), duck (58zł), pears in red wine for dessert (8zł). Open daily 7am-11am and 1pm-3am.

Pizzeria Giorgio, ul. Lipowa (tel. 521 242). Saucy pizza and lusty, crusty aromas draw in crowds from the street for mongo treats topped with peppers, olives, and lotsa cheese (6.50zł). Open daily 11am-10pm.

SIGHTS AND ENTERTAINMENT

Although the interior of **Pałac Branickiego** is closed to tourists, this 18th-century mansion, which once belonged to a powerful aristocratic family, is still worth a visit. Easily the most impressive building in Białystok, it stands as a Baroque reminder of the city's glorious past. Today, it houses a bustling medical school. While the students have the edifice to themselves, you can enter far enough to see their test scores posted inside the door. The **palace park and gardens** are open to the public (April-Sept. daily 6am-10pm, Oct.-March 6am-8pm). Pass through the main gate on pl. Branickich, and walk down a long alley. The park and gardens await out back.

Muzeum Wojska (Military Museum), ul. Kilinskiego 7 (tel. 415 448), collects Polish weapons, military dress, and historical records. The rooms bristle with cruel daggers, improbably huge swords, and the arms of Poland's vanquished. The centerpiece lies in the main room on this floor: an exhibition of items relating to WWII, specifically the German march across Poland and the subsequent defeat of the Nazis. The museum displays posters and placards from the era, many praising the Red Army for its efforts. Most interesting, though, are the captured German objects including one dagger with "Alles für Deutschland!" inscribed on the blade. (Open Tues.-Sun. 9am-5pm. 2zł, students 1zł. English guidesheets available.)

A short walk to the west of the palace, the *rynek's* **ratusz** (town hall) originally served as a trade center. In 1940, it was demolished by the Russians, who planned to put a monument to Stalin in its place. This plan never materialized, and the site remained vacant until the present building was constructed in 1958. Inside, the ground floor of **Muzeum Okręgowe** (Regional Museum; tel. 21 473), is the **Gallery of Polish Painting,** with a small but impressive collection of paintings from the mid-1700s to the 1930s. The gallery is divided into three rooms: the first displays Neoclassical and Romantic works; the second exhibits paintings from the second half of the 19th century; and the third boasts paintings in various styles—Impressionism, Symbolism, Realism. The lower level of the museum hosts an **archaeological exhibit,** "The Ancient History of the Białystok Region," illustrating the history of the region from about 10,000 years ago to the early Middle Ages. (Open Tues.-Sun. 10am-5pm. 1.50zł, students 0.75zł, art students free.)

Watch the local gears grind to an industrial beat at **Klub Metro,** ul. Ireny Białówny 9/1 (off ul. Malmeda). The only hole in this ozone layer is the occasional musical lapse (beers 2.50zł). The pub **Bez Lokalu** (Without a Place), ul. Skłodowskiej 14 (tel. 20

466), also has occasional concerts and gives out info on local student life. The nightclub **Astoria** at ul. Sienkiewicza 3 has irregular live music and regular beer (3zł; cover 5zł; open Fri.-Sun. 8pm-3am). But the best nightspot in town has unresticted access—the square around the town hall (no cover).

■ Near Białystok

TYKOCIN

For an impressive and sobering reminder of Poland's Jewish past, take an afternoon bus trip to tiny Tykocin, home to one of the most beautiful Polish synagogues (16 per day, 1-1½hr., 2.50-3.20zł; pay on the bus). Turn left from the central square onto ul. Złota as it becomes ul. Piłsudskiego. A small bridge leads the final stretch to the tan **synagoga,** a 17th-century gem enclosed by unassuming walls. Of the three carved-wood entrances, only one, on ul. Piłsudskiego, is functional. Hebrew prayers and ornamental designs scroll around all four walls of the cavernous interior. During services, rabbis would occupy the central **bimah,** in front of which glass cases protect garments and one of the synagogue's original copies of the Torah. The synagogue once served 2300 Jewish residents of Tykocin, who accounted for almost 70% of the village's population. After the Nazis killed all but 150 Tykocin Jews, the edifice was abandoned until the 70s, when restoration began. Now, the building also provides exhibition space for Judaic artifacts—skillfully crafted silver menorahs and paintings chronicling Jewish struggles. The 4zł admission buys both entrance to the temple and to the museum next door, home to the pastels of Artur Markowicz (open daily 10am-5pm; off-season closed Mon.).

BIAŁOWIESKI PARK NARODOWY

Puszcza Białowieska (Białowieża Primeval Forest), a natural treasure of towering trees and **East European bison,** sprawls out over oceans of flatland. Exploration begins in the sleepy town of Białowieża. The preserve is reached by following a well marked four- to 5km path from the park entrance; you can rent a bike (see below). Stay on the trail, lest you catch a park official on a bad day. About 250 of the lumbering bison remain; many of their brethren were wiped out by hungry WWI soldiers. The strict bison preserve forms a small part of the park, that only guided tours may enter.

You can either take one of the two daily direct **buses** from Białystok. Or hop on one of the 20 to Hajnówka (1½hrs., 4.80 zł) and then one of 10 from Hajnówka to Białowieża (45 min., 2.50zł). Leave very early, as you may have to wait for some buses. From the bus stop and train station, the preserve entrance is over the bridge and up the hill, as is **Hotel-Restauracja Iwa** (tel. (0-835) 12 385; fax 853 253), home of the tourist office, **Guliver.** The office arranges three-hour **guided tours** of the park in horse-drawn carts (50zł; open daily 9am-5pm). Bikes go for 1.70zł per hour. Balconied doubles 45zł, with bath 50zł; triples with bath 66zł; quads without 50zł. Next door, **Dom Wycieczkowy PTTK** (tel. 12 505) offers two-hour group **tours** (50zł for a group of 25, 70zł in English) and lets comfortable rooms (singles 18zł; doubles 32zł, with bath 42zł; quads 60zł; MC and Visa accepted).

WIELKOPOLSKA (GREATER POLAND)

The *wielkopolskie* lowlands are a pastiche of fields and woods, gentle hills and lakes. A rainbow of wildflowers span the countryside, and afternoon breezes play with the tall grass that covers the fields. Signs of civilization come only at the irregular moments when a town or city suddenly seems to grow out of the rolling plain. Even then, the towns are little islands in a sea of green, soon replaced by lofty haystacks, cud-chewing cows, and country roads. Hardly just farmland, Wielkopolska has seen the crowning of Polish kings in its cathedrals, and important urban centers like Poznań continue to grow like weeds.

■ Poznań

Hundreds of international businesspeople are lured every year to Poznań's annual trade fair, musicians from around the world come to take part in the city's lively music scene, and tourists flock to sample the local food and architecture. Just off the main streets, locals meet in Old Town houses for quiet visits, and students seek out good beer in colorful watering holes. Located midway between Warsaw and Berlin and gaining recognition as a banking center, Poznań maintains its unique character after the last photo has been taken and the last briefcase closed.

ORIENTATION AND PRACTICAL INFORMATION

Most of the entertainment, sights, restaurants, accommodations, and services can be found in the central **Stare Miasto** (Old Town). The main train station, **Poznań Główny**, sits in the Old Town's southwest corner; the **bus station** is 500m down the road. Perhaps the best thing to do on arrival is to visit the train station's 24-hour **tourist office, Glob-Tour** (see below). From here, the sights, sounds, and smells of the Old Town are either a 20-minute walk or a short bus ride away. On foot, head out of the train station on **ul. Dworcowa** until it ends, and then take a right onto **ul. Św. Marcin.** Continue to **al. Marcinkowskiego.** From here, **Stary Rynek,** the Old Town's heart, is easily reached by going left, then taking the next right, **ul. Paderewskiego.** Or, catch any **tram** heading down Św. Marcin (to the right) from the end of ul. Dworcowa. Get off at the corner of ul. Św. Marcin and al. Marcinkowskiego for a short walk to the Old Town's wonders.

Tourist Offices: Glob-Tour, ul. Dworcowa (tel./fax 660 667), in the main lobby of the train station. Tourist info in English, maps of Poznań and the region (3-4zł), private rooms (from 35zł), and a **currency exchange.** Open 24hr. **Centrum Informacji Turystycznej (IT),** Stary Rynek 59 (tel. 526 156), in the heart of the Old Town. Sells maps of Poznań and surrounding areas (3-5zł) and provides information about sights and budget accommodations. Open Mon.-Sat. 9am-5pm.
Budget Travel: ALMATUR, ul. Fredry 7 (tel. 520 344; fax 537 105). This main branch offers discount plane, ferry, and bus tickets, as well as ISIC cards and information about hostels. Open Mon.-Fri. 10am-5pm, Sat. 10am-1pm.
Consulates: Germany, ul. Paderewskiego 7 (tel. 522 443). **United Kingdom,** ul. Kramarska 26 (tel./fax 532 919).
Currency Exchange: ORBIS, ul. Roosevelta 20 (tel. 558 000; fax 558 955), in Hotel Merkury. Cashes AmEx and Visa traveler's checks, provides cash advances on AmEx and MC (no fee), and Visa (1% commission). Open Mon.-Fri. 9am-5pm. There are numerous **kantors** and banks in the city, especially on ul. Św. Marcin.
ATMs: (Bankomat) Wielkopolski Bank Kredytowy, pl. Wolności 16 (tel. 542 900), has Visa and Plus ATM's at their many branches throughout the city.
Flights: Ławica airport, ul. Bukowska 285 (tel. 681 511), just west of the city center. All major airlines can be reached through **Blue Sky Travel,** ul. Libelta 26 (tel./fax 530 601). International flights to New York and other American destinations. Open Mon.-Fri. 9am-7pm. **LOT,** ul. Św. Marcin 69 (tel. 522 847), offers domestic and international flights. Open Mon.-Fri. 8am-7pm, Sat. 8am-3pm.
Trains: (tel. 661 212 or 693 499) ul. Dworcowa 1. To: Berlin (2 per day, 3hr., express, 92.50zł); Gdańsk (3 per day, 4hr.); Kraków (6 per day, 6hr.); Warsaw (11 per day, 3½hr.); and Szczecin (13 per day, 3hr.). 24-hr. **luggage storage** 1zł.
Buses: ul. Towarowa 17 (tel. 331 228), near trains. To: Gniezno (35 per day, 40min.-2hr., 5.20zł), Szczecin, Warsaw, and local towns. Open daily 5:30am-9pm.
Public Transportation: Tram and **bus** tickets within the city of are sold in blocks of time rather than on a "per ride" basis. Approximate times are given on the route maps around town (10min. 0.50zł; up to ½hr. 1zł; 1hr. 1.50zł; 1½hr. 1.50zł). As

Central Poznań

Hotel Wielkopolska, 2
Katedra Piotra i Pawła, 6
Kościół Farny Marii Magdaleny, 5
Museum of Historic Musical Instruments, 3
Ratusz, 4
Wojewódzki Ośrodek Metodyczny, 1

confusing as it can be, getting caught empty-handed could result in the nationally infamous 75zł fine for no ticket! From 11pm to 4am, the ticket price doubles.
Taxis: Radio taxi, tel. 919, 951, 222 222, or 51 55 15.
Car Rental: Hertz, at ORBIS (see above). **Avis,** ul. 23 Lutego 16 (tel. 517 778).
English Bookstore: Omnibus Bookstore, ul. Św Marcin 37. Wide selection of paperbacks, mostly novels. Open Mon.-Fri. 10am-7pm, Sat. 10am-2pm.
24-Hour Pharmacy: ul. 23-go Lutego 18 (tel. 522 625).
Crisis Lines: AIDS hotline: tel. 529 918; open Tues. and Thurs. 3-6pm. **Center of Information for Women:** tel. 520 170.
Medical Assistance: ul. Chełmońskiego 20 (tel. 661 235). Open Mon.-Sat. 3pm-7am, Sun. open 24hr.
Post Office: ul. Kościuszki 77 (tel. 697 060). Open Mon.-Fri. 6:30am-9pm, Sat.-Sun. 8am-9pm. **Postal code:** 60-942.
Telephones: Outside the main post office. **Phone code:** 0-61.

ACCOMMODATIONS

There are three year-round youth hostels. For similar prices and better locations in the summer, contact ALMATUR (see above), which has the scoop on **summer hostels.** During its fairs (March, June, Oct.), the city fills up quickly with tourists and businesspeople, and most prices rise by at least 10%. Getting a decently priced room upon arrival at these times is virtually impossible. Call ahead. For **private rooms,** contact **Przemysław,** ul Głogowska 16 (tel. 663 560; fax 665 163), for singles (28zł) or doubles (30zł; open Mon.-Fri. 8am-6pm, Sat. 10am-2pm).

Youth Hostel, ul. Berwińskiego 2/3 (tel. 663 680). Take a left out of the train station on ul. Głogowska; ul. Berwińskiego is the second street on your right, about 10min. down the road from the main part of town. Clean, split-level rooms in an old school, with two beds on each level. Curfew 11pm. Lockout 10am-5pm. Young "seniors" (18 and up) 5zł, juniors 2.50zł. Reception open daily 5-10:30pm.
Wojewódzki Ośrodek Metodyczny, ul. Niepodległości 34 (tel. 532 251). Spacious rooms located on a tree-shaded street just a short walk from ul. Św. Marcin (take ul. Niepodległości north about 15min. to the hostel) and the Old Town. By bus, take #51 away from the train station to Hotel Polonez and walk back a block. Bathrooms have been known to be less than sparkling. 15.40zł, students 10.20zł.
Hotel Royal, ul. Św. Marcin 71 (tel. 537 884; fax 517 931). Tucked away off ul. Św Marcin, a short walk from the *rynek*. The rooms are on the small side, but the prices are quite a value for the location. Singles 49zł. Doubles 75zł. Triples 110zł.
Hotel Wielkopolska, ul. Św. Marcin 67 (tel. 527 631; fax 530 880). Near the Hotel Royal, but in a noisier location. The hotel is deceptively large with very helpful staff. The rooms are comfortable and well kept, but there is a surprisingly small number of bathrooms. Singles 51zł, with bath 67zł. Doubles 81zł, with bath 91zł.

FOOD

They say food says a lot about a place, and whoever "they" are, they're right about Poznań. Two specialties capture the flavor of this city in edible form: *pyzy,* a cross between noodles and potato dumplings, and *rogale świętomarcińskie,* croissants with various fruit fillings sold by the kilo on November 11, St. Martin's Day. **24-hour grocery stores—Bonus Delikatesy,** ul. Libelta 6 (tel. 531 793), and **Aron,** ul. Wielka 8 (tel. 530 119)—provide a chance to pick up "just one more" 0.5L bottle of *Lech Premium,* the local brew of choice (2.50zł), as well as real food.

Cara Mia, Stary Rynek 51 (tel. 523 581), serves Polish and Italian food, specializing in pizza and outside dining. Entrées 4.40-13.50zł. Open daily 11am-11pm.
Bar Mleczny Pod Kuchcikiem, ul. Św Marcin 37. Traditional Polish food at unbeatable prices. A meal of *Żurek* (sour rye soup) and *pyzy* runs only 2.20zł. Open Mon.-Fri. 8am-7pm, Sat. 8am-4pm, Sun. 10am-4pm.

Cukiernia "U Marcina", ul. Św. Marcin 32 (tel. 526 788). Polish food in a pseudo-Greek atmosphere. They also run a small snack bar for a quick bite to eat. Entrées 1-6zł. Open Mon.-Sat. 9am-8pm, Sun. 9am-2pm.

Adria, ul. Głogowska 14 (tel. 658 374), across from the train station. Polish, Ukrainian, Georgian, and Alsatian dishes for 10-15zł. Open daily 10am-4pm. Dancing Tues., Thurs., Sun. 9pm-3am, Fri.-Sat. 9pm-5am. Disco nightly 11pm-4am. The cafeteria upstairs is open daily 10am-3pm. Is there anything they can't do!?!

SIGHTS

Poznań seems to be more about "doing" than "looking", but don't let all that action distract you from a number of noteworthy highlights. Downtown, in **Stary Rynek,** opulent 15th-century merchant homes frame the heart of the Old Town. Almost all are in fine form, with a rainbow of colors and architectural flourishes worth looking up from your dessert for. More importantly, they surround the multicolored pearl of Renaissance architecture: the **ratusz** (town hall). The original was built in the 13th century and reconstructed after a fire by the architect Giovanni Battista di Quadro in Renaissance style (1550-60). It is deemed to be the finest secular monument of the Renaissance period north of the Alps by those who take the time to decide such things. Locals and tourists alike consider it to be one of the finest places to sit and eat in the often-crowded *rynek*. Today, it houses the **Muzeum Historii Poznania,** Stary Rynek 1 (tel. 525 613). Built with the fines paid by maids who dressed to "sharply" for their masters, the **1535 whipping post** stands menacingly in front of the *ratusz*, (open Mon.-Tues. and Fri. 10am-4pm, Wed. 10am-6pm, Thurs. and Sun. 10am-3pm; 1zł, students 0.60zł, Fri. free).

Behind the town hall, on the *rynek's* northeast corner, starts **ul. Żydowska** (Jewish St.), the center of the pre-war Jewish district. Its 1907 synagogue was turned into a swimming pool in 1940. On the opposite side of the square, **Kosciół Farny Marii Magdaleny,** resplendent with frescos and pink marble, blesses the end of ul. Świętosławska. It is open to the devout, tourists, and devout tourists during most daylight hours whenever Mass is not being said (at which time, two of the three groups above are more than welcome). There are also organ concerts Monday to Saturday at 12:15pm. On a less Catholic note, the **Museum of Historic Musical Instruments,** Stary Rynek 45/47 (tel. 520 857), stars Chopin's own piano and a collection of instruments from Polynesia and Africa (open Tues. and Sat. 11am-5pm, Wed., and Fri. 10am-4pm, Sun. 10am-3pm; 1zł, students 0.60zł).

In the oldest part of town, **Ostrów Tumski,** stands the first Polish cathedral, **Katedra Piotra i Pawła** (Cathedral of St. Peter and Paul), with a ring of 15 chapels. The original building was constructed in 968, soon after the first Polish bishopric was established in Poznań. Burned down in 1945, toward the end of WWII, it was rebuilt after the war in neo-Gothic style. In the **Kaplica złota** (Golden Chapel) are the tombs of two famous Piasts: Prince Mieszko I (d. 992) and his oldest son, Bolesław Chrobry (the Brave), the first king of Poland (d. 1025). Again, visiting hours are whenever Mass is not being said (daily 9am-4pm).

One of the hardest sights to miss on ul. Św. Marcin provides a glimpse into more recent history. In 1956, workers protesting food prices clashed with government troops; 76 people died in the conflict. The bloody incident is commemorated in the **park** on pl. Mickiewicza by two stark crosses knotted together with steel cable and emblazoned with subsequent dates recalling workers' uprisings throughout Poland.

ENTERTAINMENT

Poznań's lively music and theater scenes change quickly. The monthly **Poznański Informator Kulturalny, Sportowy i Turystyczny (IKS),** contains info on all the cultural events and many useful phone numbers (2zł). It is available in English at bookstores and some kiosks. All questions about Poznań's music scene can be addressed to the Music Society—**Towarzystwo Muzyczne im. Henryka Wieniawskiego,** ul. Świętojańska 7 (tel. 522 642; fax 528 991), across from Kościół Farny. Those seeking less formal entertainment (or simply a place to hang out) have options from formal pubs to local yards with kegs and music to neon-and-smoke nightclubs. The *rynek's* restaurants provide a lively outdoor atmosphere in which to sip cappuccino or gulp beer surrounded by 15th-century wonders.

Harry's Pub, Stary Rynek 91 (tel. 526 169). Run by a Belgian, this international pub (the staff speaks Polish, English, German, and Belgian) is popular with locals and visitors alike. In fact, it is so popular that it has been reviewed by CNN and the New York Times—all this without any advertising! It makes sense considering they serve "the best steaks in Poznań", and have a prime location looking out at the town hall. Live music every Thurs. Open daily 10am til the last guest leaves.

The Dubliner, ul. Św. Marcin 80/82 (tel. 536 081, ext. 147), located in the "Zamek" (Poznańian Culture Center). The entrance is on al. Niepodległości. A true Irish Pub, run by real Irishmen, offering Irish food, beer, and whiskey, where they teach the Irish saying: "May you be in heaven half an hour before the devil knows you're dead." Disco every Sat. night. Open daily 11am-1am.

Dziedziniec Zamkowy, in the courtyard of the *Zamek*. The entrance is just past that of The Dubliner. Zamkowy is a spontaneous hang-out popular with the younger crowd. With kegs of 2zł-a-glass beer, loudspeakers, and some benches and trees surrounded by the *Pałac Kultury,* it's like a backyard party without a house to trash. The variable hours are posted outside.

Kawiarnia Arezzo, Stary Rynek 49 (tel. 526 253). Spend the evening out on the *rynek* under one of their pink and purple umbrellas eating ice cream (2-6zł) and sipping coffee (2-4zł). Open daily 9am-11pm.

Stajenka Pegaza (Pegasus's Little Stable; tel. 516 418), corner of ul. Fredry and ul. Wieniawskiego. If you like good beer and sudden musical uprisings, drop by and bring your favorite tape; they'll play it for you. A fun-loving mix of locals and tourists, and a number of draft beers make this somewhat out-of-the-way spot one of the places to be, especially on weekend nights. Open Mon.-Fri. from 11am, Sat. from 1pm, Sun. from 4pm til the last guest leaves.

For a quick dip in the hot summer months, go to **Jezioro Maltańskie** (Malta Lake). Take trams #1, 4, 6, or 7 eastbound from the center and get off at ul. Zamenhofa. There is a year-round artificial **ski slope** here if you want to get a jump on ski season.

Gniezno

Legend has it that Gniezno was built by Lech, the mythical founder of Poland, as a place to perch. The town's name—meaning "nest"—still holds true. The hamlet is a pocket of tree-lined neighborhoods, tiny shops, and a town square in miniature. What keeps the tourists coming is the massive **Katedra Gnieźnieńska,** at the end of ul. Chrobrego, past the *rynek* and a short walk up ul. Tumska. The 14th-century cathedral conceals a history of pre-Christian presence and at least four earlier churches. The first Polish king, **Boleslaw Chrobry** (the Brave), was crowned here in 1025, 25 years after Gniezno had become the seat of Polish archbishops. The bronze 12th-century door presents the life and martyrdom of **St. Adalbert** (Św. Wojciech) in 18 bas-reliefs. Inside, light coming in at odd angles illuminates the side altars but leaves the main altar, with its ornate spiraling columns, dark and somber (open Mon.-Sat. 10am-5pm, Sun. 1:30-5:30pm; English info available).

The serene yard which surrounds the parish buildings leads to the 12th-century **Church of St. George** and to the **Archdiocesan Museum,** ul. Kolegiaty 2 (tel. 263 778). Artifacts in the museum document the history of Catholicism in Poland. Especially impressive are the 14th-century ecclesiastical robes, which took over 20 years to create (open Tues.-Sat. 9am-4pm; 1.50zł, students 1zł).

Gniezno is linked to Poznań by **train** (21 per day, 40min., 7.05zł) and Toruń (6 per day, 1hr., 7zł) and **bus** (numerous buses daily, 20min.-2hr., 4-6zł). To reach the sights, head straight out of the train station onto ul. Lecha. Make a left onto ul. Chrobrego, and walk 10 minutes to the **rynek,** the center of town. The **Youth Hostel (HI),** ul. Pocztowa 11 (tel. 264 609), near the train station, is connected to the town's elementary school. Leaving the train station, go right on ul. Dworcowa, which leads to ul. Pocztowa. The basic five- to ten-bed rooms cost 12zł per person (students 9zł, sheets 3zł; lockout 10am-5pm, curfew 11pm). **Hotel Mieszko,** ul. Strumykowa 2 (tel. 264 625; fax 264 628), on a side street 10 minutes from the train (from ul. Lecha, go left on ul. Kościuszki, which will become ul. Dalkoska—ul. Strumykowa will be on the right), offers more privacy than the hostel. Reservations are recommended (singles 50zł, doubles with bath 58zł). The hotel accepts AmEx, MC, and Visa. In the third week of June, during the International Trade Fair, prices rise by more than 10%. Pub-like **Królewska,** ul. Chrobrego 3 (tel. 261 497; fax 264 692), located in a cellar, boasts sparkling red and white tables, a fireplace, and tuxedoed waitstaff serving pork, beef, and poultry (entrées 10-15zł; open daily 9am-10pm). Królewska also has a snack-bar upstairs for a quicker, cheaper meal.

■ Near Gniezno: Biskupin

The archeological site on Lake Biskupin contains well preserved artifacts of an early Iron Age settlement, including wooden fortifications, roads, and buildings. A daytrip to Biskupin should also include a ride on the narrow-gauge railway, complete with coal powered steam engine. On a sunny day, chug through plains with the breeze in your face for views of farms, wildflowers, lakes, and streams before reaching the Biskupin site, tucked in a wooded area.

Buses travel from Gniezno to Żnin (3.60zł). Take the 10 or 11am bus in order to have time to see the sights. Once in Żnin, the **narrow-gauge steam train** to Biskupin can be reached by facing the bus station and going left, then turning right on ul. Dworcowa (3rd stop; April-Sept. 9, 11:25am, and 2pm; May-Aug. also 10:10am and 12:40pm; 45min.; 2zł). To reach the **ticket booth,** walk across the train tracks and head under the wooden gate. (English guide 20zł; 3zł, students 2zł). A carved-wood **map** is near the gate. The last train back leaves at 3:26pm.

The archeological site is best appreciated by first visiting the **museum** in the white building at the end of the entrance road. Just inside the entryway to this little museum is a picture **timeline** that benchmarks Biskupin's history with other international events. You just might need to know that Nefertiti ruled Egypt when Biskupin was first fortified. The museum's **exhibit hall** contains info about Biskupin's culture as well as original tools, personal items, pottery, skeletal remains of Neolithic plant and animal species, and artifacts that show evidence of trade with places as distant as Egypt. The centerpiece is a detailed **model** of the fortified settlement as it would have appeared from 550-400BCE. The museum also presents human skeletal remains from the Neolithic Era and a large chunk of the original settlement. The settlement itself consisted of around 102 identical two-room houses, built so at 11am the sun would shine into every front room to allow for maximum use of daylight hours.

To get to the actual **reconstruction,** head out the front door and back to the main road. Face the ticket booth and go right, following the arrows along a tree-shaded walkway which passes by a reconstructed house from much later in Biskupin's history. At the fork in the road, follow the signs again to the left for the path that leads towards the reconstructed **tower,** which watches over the entrance where another carved-wood **map** diagrams the original site. This portion of the wall has been accurately reconstructed, right down to the posts set in the ground at 45 degrees to guard against rough waters and even rougher attackers. Once inside the reconstruction, there are two distinct rows of houses. The left-hand row leads to both a **photo exhibit** of the excavation's history and a **model of a house,** complete with bunk space, fire area, and entry room. Visitors lucky enough to be here at precisely 11am will see that yes, indeed, the sun does come a-shinin' in just as the museum said it would. On the right-hand row of houses, park employees wear the closest thing to period dress they could find and demonstrate some of the crafts that were practiced in the Neolithic era to present a model of a more lived-in home.

Before hopping back on the train, visitors to Biskupin can check out the **experimental archaeology exhibit.** Head back to the museum and go around to the right to get a look at re-created bread ovens and animals that are related to those which inhabitants of Biskupin may have raised or hunted. Even if none of this interests you, go simply to peek at the largest specimen of Polish red cattle you may ever see.

■ Toruń

Toruń extols itself as the birthplace and childhood home of Mikołaj Kopernik—Copernicus—the man who "stopped the sun and moved the Earth." After strolling along the medieval cobbled streets, visiting the museum, and resting on the promenade along the river, you'll wonder why he ever left. Students from the local university stroll along the Wisła and admire the 14th-century architecture and plush trees which line its banks. Within the Old Town, parishioners pray in 500-year-old churches, and children run in the ruins of a Teutonic castle. All the while, life moves on amid the sights and sounds of a town that has matured to a modern city, and yet has lost none of its medieval charm.

ORIENTATION AND PRACTICAL INFORMATION

Toruń lies 150km northeast of Poznań. The **Toruń Główny (train station)** lies across the Wisła from most of the city. To reach the center of town, it is easiest to take a city **MPK bus** across the river. Buy a bunch of tickets at any of the little booths outside the station (each 0.80zł, good for 2 validations). Toruń has an efficient and expansive public transportation system. Hop on bus #22 or 27; both start at the train station. Punch your ticket after you get on the bus (twice if you have a large piece of luggage). For the Old Town **tourist offices**, get off at the first stop over the river, **plac Rapackiego. PTTK** is only about 500 feet from the **bus stop.** Head through the little park area with your back to the bus you got off, and it's on your left. By foot, plac Rapackiego is reached by going left on **ul. Kujawska** from the train station, then going right on **ul. 700-lecia Torunia,** and hiking over the Wisła. Plac Rapackiego will be on your right after **ul. Kopernika.** The official Toruń tourist information center, **IT,** is located in the Old Town. From the *plac*, head under the archway (again walking away from the bus you got off) along ul. Różana until you come to **Rynek Staromiejski** (Old Town Market Square).

To reach the Old Town from the **bus station,** head away from the buses and through the small park that leads to **ul. Uniwersytecka.** Take a left on ul. Uniwersytecka until it intersects with **Wały Gen. Sikorskiego.** Go right on Sikorskiego until **plac Teatralny.** At plac Teatralny, go left on **ul. Chełmińska** into the Old Town.

Toruń spreads north away from the Wisła. Most of the sights, however, are located in the Old Town, centered around two main areas: Rynek Staromiejski and **Rynek Nowomiejski** (New Town Market Square). Rynek Staromiejski is the home of the Old Town hall, while Rynek Nowomiejski is primarily a location for farm stands and vendors. The two parts of the Old Town are divided by **ul. Podmurna.**

Tourist Offices: IT, Rynek Staromiejski 1 (fax 10 930), in the town hall. Info on Toruń and Copernicus. Helpful English-speaking staff. Open May-Aug. Mon. and Sat. 9am-4pm, Tues.-Fri. 9am-6pm, Sun. 9am-1pm; Sept.-April open Mon. and Sat. 9am-4pm, Tues.-Fri. 9am-6pm. **PTTK,** plac Rapackiego 2 (tel. 24 926; fax 28 228). Maps and brochures for 3-5zł. 2-hr. English tour of town 50zł. Open Mon.-Fri. 8am-4pm, Sat. 9am-1pm.
Currency Exchange: Bank PKO, ul. Kopernika 38 (tel. 10 915). Cashes AmEx and Visa traveler's checks for 1% commission (min. 5zł). Also AmEx, MC, and Visa cash advances. Open Mon.-Fri. 8am-6pm. Private *kantors* provide cash exchanges.
Trains: (tel. 13 044). To: Gdańsk (5 per day, 16.80zł); Poznań (5 per day, 14zł); Szczecin (2 per day, 20.70zł); Warsaw (3 per day, 17.55zł). The international *kasa* also sells Wasteels and Interrail. Open Mon.-Fri. 8am-5pm, Sat.-Sun. 8am-3pm.
Buses: (tel. 22 842). To: Warsaw (5 per day, 15.40zł); Gdańsk (3 per day, 15.40zł); Poznań (1 per day, 11.40zł).
Luggage Storage: At the train station. 1zł per item. Open 24hr.

Pharmacies: Apteka Królewska, Rynek Staromiejski 4 (tel. 10 017). Open Mon.-Fri. 8am-8pm, Sat. 8am-4pm.
Taxis: Radio Taxi tel. 91 93.
International Bookstore: Empik, ul. Wielkie Garbary 18 (tel. 24 895). Open Mon.-Fri. 10am-6pm, Sat. 10am-3pm.
Laundromat: ul. Glowackiego 2 (tel. 32 256).
Post Office: Rynek Staromiejski 15 (tel. 19 100). Open Mon.-Fri. 8am-8pm, Sat. 8am-1pm. **Postal code:** 87-100.
Telephones: At the post office. Open 24hr. **Phone code:** 0-56.

ACCOMMODATIONS AND CAMPING

Toruń has no particular "crunch season." Most visitors seem to be young adults who simply pile back on the bus at the end of the day. **IT** (see above) has info on accommodations in town and can arrange stays at student hostels (5-12zł per person).

Hotel Polonia, plac Teatralny 5 (tel. 23 028), opposite the municipal theater and down the street from the *ratusz*. On the edge of the Old Town, these surprisingly large rooms with surprisingly large beds are in a surprisingly shady building in a busy part of town. Singles 28zł, with bath 45zł. Doubles 38zł. Triples 48zł.

Hotel Pod Orłem, ul. Mostowa 17 (tel. 21 096; fax 25 024). Huge, comfortable rooms in a quieter corner of the Old Town. Meet that beloved 80s alien ALF on the second floor! Bathroom facilities are a bit spartan. Singles 35zł. Doubles 45zł, with bath 90zł. Triples 60zł, with bath 110zł.

Dom Wycieczkowy, ul. Legionów 24 (tel. 23 855). Take bus #10 outside the Old Town Gate away from the river to the 3rd stop. This PTTK hotel is an affordable option a short walk from the Old Town, and 3 blocks north of the bus station. The small rooms are well kept, and the neighborhood provides an escape from the late-night noise in town. Singles 26zł. Doubles 36zł. Triples 48zł. Quads 60zł.

Campground "Tramp", ul. Kujawska 14 (tel. 24 187 or 26 049), across from the train station. This campground rests in the wooded area across the Wisła from the city. Only a short walk from both the trains and the Old Town. Tent sites 5zł, tent rental 5-7zł. 3-person cabins 30zł. 4-person bungalows 35zł.

FOOD

Despite the gradual emergence of chains, Toruń has not dropped its centuries-old calling card: **ginger bread.** Originally sold by Corpernicus's father to put his son through school, it is now sold by the kilo. Whether covered in chocolate or shaped like old Copernicus himself, *pierniki* alone could feed the masses.

Groceries in town include **Delikatesy,** ul. Szeroka 29 (tel. 10 540; open Mon.-Fri. 7am-8pm, Sat. 7am-7pm, Sun. 9am-3pm), and **Serdelek,** ul. Szeroka 19 (tel. 27 654; open daily 8am-7pm). The large market **Targowisko Miejskie** sits behind the "Supersam," one block north of the Old Town on ul. Chełminska (open daily 8am-4pm).

Bar Mleczny, ul. Rożana 1. This clean, new "milk bar" serves up primarily vegetarian traditional Polish dishes, and a smattering of meat dishes. *Naleśniki,* the house specialty, come with a multitude of fillings. Try them with blueberries and cream (*z jagodami i śmietaną,* 2.3zł). Open Mon.-Fri. 9am-7pm, Sat. 9am-4pm.

Pizzeria at the Old Brewery, ul. Browarna 3. Perhaps the best pizza and the most options (46) in town. With creative names like "Tropikana," "UFO," and "Papa Joe," even ordering can be an adventure. Popular with the local college-age crowd, this building doubles as a night hangout. Pizzas start at 3.90zł for a plain cheese and peak at 8.50zł for the works and then some. Open daily 1pm-11pm.

Lotos, ul. Strumykowa 16 (tel. 10 497). Various Far-Eastern specialties. See what happens when Chinese food meets Polish cooks in a setting complete with bamboo and tropical-fish tank; you'll be pleasantly surprised. For a sure hit, try the "5 Flavored Chicken" (11.60zł; name those flavors…). Curried beef 10.20zł. Vegetarian dishes 5-8zł. Visa and MC accepted. Open daily noon-10pm.

WIELKOPOLSKA (GREATER POLAND)

Bufet Urząd Wojewódzki, plac Teatralny 2 (tel. 18 213). Enter at the "Bufet" sign and follow the enticing aroma through the underground passageways. A hearty meal for less than 5zł awaits you. Open daily 8am-6pm.

Kopernik Factory Store, ul. Żeglarska 25 (tel. 23 712), and Staromiejskie 6. Stock up on Toruń's delicious *pierniki* in almost every imaginable form. This place gets mega-crowded, so be patient, while visions of gingerbread dance in your head. Open Mon.-Fri. 10am-6pm, Sat.-Sun. 10am-2pm.

SIGHTS

An astounding number of attractions are packed into Toruń's medieval ramparts. The **Stare Miasto** (Old Town), constructed by the Teutonic Knights in the 13th century, saw the birth of renowned astronomer Mikołaj Kopernik (February 19, 1473). His birthplace, **Dom Kopernika,** ul. Kopernika 15/17 (tel. 26 748), has been meticulously restored, and visitors can get a peek not only into the life of Copernicus, but 14th-century Toruń in general (open Tues.-Sun. 10am-4pm; 2zł, students 1.50zł). Dom Kopernika also houses **Makieta,** a miniature model of 1550 Toruń (3zł, students 2zł). A traditional 16th-century sound and light show, in five languages, accompanies your visit to this museum.

The **ratusz** (town hall), Rynek Staromiejski 1 (tel. 27 038), stands in the center of the tourist district as one of the finest examples of monumental burgher architecture in Europe. The original Gothic four-winged building was built in the late 14th century, but various elements, such as the turrets, were added on throughout the centuries. The town hall now contains the **Muzeum Okręgowe** (Regional Museum), whose exhibits include the famous portrait of Mikołaj Kopernik from the late 16th century, portraits of wealthy and influential citizens of Toruń, and works of modern Polish art (open Tues.-Sun. 10am-6pm; 2zł, students 1.50zł). For an additional 2zł (students 1.50zł), you can climb the medieval 13th-century tower and survey the whole city. The friendly staff is eager to point out the most noteworthy sights: Kamienica Pod Gwiazdą, Dom Eskenów, and the Teutonic Knights' castle.

Opposite the *ratusz* stands the **Dwór Artusa** (Artus Court), Rynek Staromiejski 5, designed in the 1880s by Rudolf Schmidt. The house was erected on the site of the original Renaissance building—also called Dwór Artusa—which had been the seat of patricians belonging to the Hanseatic League. The building now houses the Toruń Orchestra. **Kamienica Pod Gwiazdą** (House Under the Star), Rynek Staromiejski 35 (tel. 21 133), originally a Gothic building, was later redone in Baroque style, with a finely modeled façade decorated with floral and fruit details. During the reconstruction of the late 1960s, interesting fragments of Gothic, late Renaissance, and Classical architecture were uncovered. This odd bird blends well with its equally varied neighbors. Check out the exhibits on the arts of the Far East (open Tues.-Sun. 10am-4pm; 1zł, students 0.50zł). **Dom Eskenów,** ul. Łazienna 16 (tel. 27 038, ext. 14), exhibits 20th-century Polish painting and military uniforms from medieval times to the early 20th century (open Tues.-Sun. 10am-4pm; 1zł, students 0.50zł).

The **Ruins of the Teutonic Knights' Castle,** ul. Przedzamcze, continue to fascinate visitors. The 14th-century **toilet tower** served its lords as indoor plumbing and a repository of smelly defense—back in the day, they didn't just *fart* in the enemy's general direction. The 13th-century castle was destroyed by a city-wide burghers' revolt on February 8, 1454, a mere 477 years before James Dean's birth (0.50zł). The **Leaning Tower,** ul. Krzywą Wieżą 17, is another unique building of Teutonic origin. Built in 1271 by a knight of the order as punishment for falling in love with a peasant girl, the 50-foot tower now deviates 5ft from the center at its top. Some call it "the leaning tower of Poland."

Among the tall Gothic churches which crop up everywhere, the **Cathedral of St. John the Baptist and St. John the Evangelist** is the most impressive of its kind. Built in the 13-15th centuries, it mixes Gothic, Baroque, and Rococo elements. Its 1407-33 tower contains Poland's second-largest bell, cast in 1500, and its chapel witnessed the baptism of Kopernik in 1473. From here, it's a short walk across the *rynek* to ul. Panny Marii and **Kościół Św. Marii** (Church of the Virgin Mary). Visitors are not allowed inside, but the view from the street, with an eerily high aisle and stained glass of geometric designs and pictures, is worth stopping by. At the end of a long day, stroll along the **Bulwar Filadelfijski**—named for Torun's sister city, Philadelphia—among lingering couples who line the stone steps to the river, where outdoor eating spots offer a place to sit and observe the local fisherman wait for a bite.

ENTERTAINMENT

The search for nightlife in Toruń doesn't require straying from the Old Town, but student life revolves around Miasteczko Akademickie—the campus—reached by bus #15 from ul. Odrodzenia 7 to the line's end at ul. Sienkiewicza. The entertainment is tucked away just off ul. Gagarina in the neighborhood by the bus stop. In the Old Town, music can be found at the **Blue Reflex Music Club**, ul. Browarna 1 (tel. 19 320), off Rynek Nowomiejski. The entrance for the club is around the corner from the Pizza place next to ul. Wielkie Garbary 1. (Open Sun.-Wed. 6pm-2am, Thurs. 8pm-4am, Fri. 8pm-4am, 5zł cover; Sat. 8pm-5am, 7zł cover). For daytime adventures, **Hotel Aeroklub Pomorski**, ul. Bielańska (tel. 22 474; fax 26 329), gives their guests an opportunity to **parachute** or fly **gliders**.

- **Pub Czarna Oberża** (Black Inn), ul. Rabiańska 9 (tel. 10 963). A favorite billiards and beer hangout of the local students. Impressive selection of imported beer, including Fosters (4.80zł) and Kilkenny (7zł). Open Mon.-Thurs. 1-11pm, Fri.-Sat. 1pm-midnight, Sun. 2-11pm.
- **Piwnica Pod Aniołem** (tel. 27 038, ext. 50) in the basement of the *ratusz*. A slightly older crowd in a much older building. Imbibe the history of Poland as you sip your vodka. Open daily 10am-1am.
- **Kawiarnia Pod Atlantem**, ul. Ducha Św. 3 (tel. 26 739). Waitresses in 14th-century period dress bring coffee, cakes, and ice cream to guests seated in truly royal plush chairs. Open daily 10am-10pm.

MAŁOPOLSKA (LESSER POLAND)

In Poland's southeast corner lie the uplands of Małopolska. This ancient province stretches from Wyżyna Krakowsko-Częstochowska in the west, strewn thick with medieval castle ruins, to Wyżyna Lubelska in the east, famous for its fertile brown and black earth. The region's Wiślanie tribe founded the Polish state along with Wielkopolska's Polanie. After King Kazimierz Odnowiciel (the Restorer) transferred the country's capital to Kraków in 1241, the area gained socio-political prominence and experienced an economic boom as 13th-century Rothschilds bet their gold on Kraków's fast development. Kraków remains Poland's heart and cultural focal point, thanks to little damage in WWII and two of the country's best universities.

■ Kraków

Kraków, it has been said, is now a smaller version of what Prague was a few years ago: trendy, international, and exciting without being overrun. Communism has left only a slight layer of gray sediment on many of the ancient city's architectural gems—an echo less grim than that still ringing through much of Poland. The huge main square—with its bright yellow centerpiece, the Sukiennice (Cloth Hall), is hemmed in by spires and cafés underneath zipping and diving birds.

ORIENTATION AND PRACTICAL INFORMATION

The city fans outward in roughly concentric circles from the large **Rynek Główny** (Main Market Square), at the heart of **Stare Miasto** (Old Town). The green belt of the **Planty** gardens rings *Stare Miasto*, and the **Wisła River** skims the southwest corner of **Wzgórze Wawelskie** (Wawel Hill). The **bus** and **train stations** sit adjacent to each other, 15 minutes northeast of the *rynek*. Pass the food stands and stores and head toward Hotel Europejski. The underpass leads diagonally across the street to the Planty. Across the gardens, follow **ul. Szpitalna** to the cathedral, then turn right to get to the *rynek*.

Tourist Offices: Dexter, Rynek Główny 1/3 (tel. 217 706 or 213 051; fax 213 036). The staff offers free pamphlets on the town and cultural events and organizes tours. Open Mon.-Fri. 9am-6pm, Sat. 9am-1pm. **ORBIS,** Rynek Główny 41 (tel. 224 035). Sells ferry, plane, and international bus and train tickets, including *Wasteels*. Arranges visits to Wieliczka and Oświęcim/Auschwitz. Open mid-June to mid-Sept. Mon.-Fri. 8am-7pm, Sat.-Sun. 8am-1pm; mid-Sept. to mid-June closed Sun.

Budget Travel: ALMATUR, Rynek Główny 7/8 (tel. 220 902), in the courtyard in back. International bus tickets and ISICs. Open Mon.-Fri. 9am-5pm.

U.S. Consulate and Cultural Center: ul. Stolarska 9 (tel. 221 400, 216 767, or 226 040). Open Mon.-Fri. 8am-5pm; **library** open Mon.-Fri. noon-4:45pm.

Currency Exchange: At *kantors,* ORBIS offices, and hotels. Rates vary widely. *Kantors,* except those around the train and bus stations, usually have the best rates; one at **Rynek Główny 40** stays open Mon.-Sat. 8am-10pm, Sun. 9am-7pm. **Bank PKO S.A.,** Rynek Główny 31 (tel. 226 022; fax 220 083). Accepts traveler's checks for a 1.5% commission and gives MasterCard and Visa cash advances. Open Mon.-Fri. 7:30am-7pm, Sat. 7:30am-1:45pm.

American Express: Rynek Główny 41 (tel. 219 880), in the ORBIS office and with the same hours (see above). Cashes AmEx traveler's checks with no commission, replaces lost checks, holds mail, accepts wired money, and sells traveler's checks.

Flights: The newly-renovated **Balice airport** (tel. 952) lies 11km west of Kraków. From the train station, take northbound bus #208 (40min.). **LOT,** ul. Basztowa 15 (tel. 953 or 952), flies to Frankfurt, London, Warsaw, and more. Office open Mon.-Fri. 8am-7pm, Sat. 8am-3pm. **INT Express Travel Agency,** ul. Św. Marka 25 (tel./fax 217 906), is a registered Delta, KLM, LOT, Lufthansa, and Swissair agent. Open daily 8am-8pm.

Trains: Kraków Główny, pl. Kolejowy (tel. 224 182, info 933), sends trains to Berlin (1 per day, 8hr., 111.80zł), Bratislava (1 per day, 7hr., couchette 78.40zł), Brno (2 per day, 6hr., 29zł), Budapest (1 per day, 11hr., couchette 153.40zł), Gdańsk (3 per day; 11hr., 28zł; 4 express per day, 10hr., 40zł), Kiev (1 per day, 12½hr., couchette 139.20zł), Lviv (1 per day, 10½hr., 62zł), Prague (1 per day, 8½hr., couchette 138.80zł), Vienna (1 per day, 9hr., couchette 152.50zł), Warsaw (9 per day, 4¾hr., 20zł; 14 express per day, 2½hr., 34zł), and Wrocław (14 per day, 4½hr., 19zł). Some trains to southeast Polish cities leave from **Kraków Płaszów,** south of the city center. Tickets are sold at train stations and travel offices (see above).

Buses: ul. Worcella (info tel. 936). International tickets are sold by **Sindbad,** in the bus station's main hall (tel. 221 238; open Mon.-Fri. 9:30am-5pm). To: Bratislava (1 per day, 8hr., 33zł); Budapest (1 per day, 11hr., 40zł); Lviv (1 per day, 10hr., 398zł); Prague (1 per day, 11hr., 128zł); Warsaw (3 per day, 6hr., 18zł).

Luggage Storage: At the train station. 1.40zł per piece per day. Open 24hr. **PTTK Dom Turysty** (see Accommodations, p. 442). 1zł per piece per day. Open daily 7am-10pm.

Car Rental: Budget (tel. 111 955, ext. 289), at the airport. Open daily 9am-5pm.

Public Transportation: Tickets must be bought at kiosks next to **bus** and **tram** stops (1zł) and punched on board. Large backpacks also cost a ticket. Express buses A, B, and C cost 1.30zł, and night buses 2zł. Day passes cost 4zł; week passes 10zł. Beware of violating the system—if you're caught, it's a 30zł fine.

Taxis: tel. 666 666, 919, or 96 33.

International Bookstores: Odeon, Rynek Główny 5. English, French, and German literature. Open daily 9am-midnight. **Jordan,** ul. Szeroka 2 (tel. 217 166), in the Kazimierz district. English maps, guides, and books on Jewish culture. Live music nightly at 8pm in the attached café. Open Mon.-Fri. 9am-6pm, Sat.-Sun. 10am-6pm.

Laundromat: ul. Piastowska 47, on the 2nd floor of Hotel Piast. 2-hr. drop-off available. Wash 4zł per load; dry 4zł per load. Open daily 8am-midnight.

Photocopies: Follow any "Xero" or "Ksero" signs or at the main post office.

Pharmacy: Everywhere. After hours, all post lists of the nearest open pharmacies.

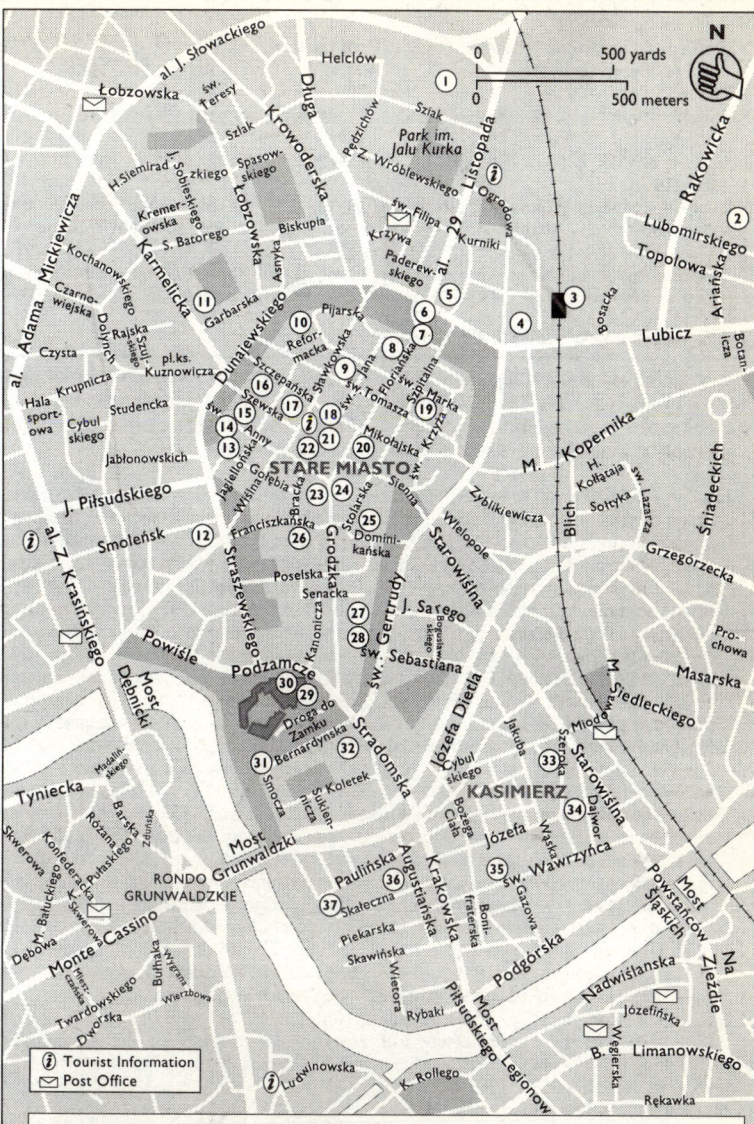

Central Kraków

Akademia Ekonomiczna, **2**
Almatur Office, **24**
Barbican, **6**
Bernardine Church, **32**
Bus Station, **4**
Carmelite Church, **11**
Cartoon Gallery, **9**
City Historical Museum, **17**
Collegium Maius, **14**
Corpus Christi Church, **35**
Czartoryski Art Museum, **8**
Dominican Church, **25**
Dragon Statue, **31**
Filharmonia, **12**
Franciscan Church, **26**
Grunwald Memorial, **5**
Jewish Cemetery, **33**
Jewish Museum, **34**
Kraków Główny Station, **3**
Monastery of the Reformed Franciscans, **10**
Muzeum Historii Fotografii, **23**
Orbis Office, **19**
Pauline Church, **37**
Police Station, **18**
Politechnika Krakowska, **1**
St. Andrew's Church, **28**
St. Anne's Church, **15**
St. Catherine's Church, **36**
St. Florian's Gate, **7**
St. Mary's Church, **20**
St. Peter and Paul Church, **27**
Stary Teatr (Old Theater), **16**
Sukiennice (Cloth Hall), **21**
Town Hall, **22**
University Museum, **13**
Wawel Castle, **29**
Wawel Cathedral, **30**

Medical Assistance: Private doctors at **Profimed,** Rynek Główny 6 (tel. 217 997), and ul. Grodzka 26 (tel. 226 453). Open Mon.-Fri. 8am-8pm, Sat. 9am-1pm.
Police: tel. 997.
Express Mail: DHL, ul. Racławicka 56 (tel. 338 096). **Express Mail Service,** in post offices at pl. Kolejowy 5 (tel. 224 026; open Mon.-Fri. 7am-8pm) and ul. Westerplatte 20 (tel. 226 696; open daily 7:30am-9pm, working Sat. 9am-3pm, free Sat. 8am-2pm).
Post Office: Main office ul. Westerplatte 20 (tel. 224 811 or 222 648; fax 223 606). Open Mon.-Fri. 7:30am-8:30pm, working Sat. 9am-2pm, free Sat. 9am-4pm, Sun. 9-11am. **Postal code:** 31-045.
Telephones: At the main post office (open 24hr.), and the office opposite the train station, ul. Lubicz 4 (tel. 221 485 or 228 635). **Phone code:** 0-12.

ACCOMMODATIONS AND CAMPING

Reservations are prudent in summer. Friendly neighborhood room-retriever **Waweltur,** ul. Pawia 8 (tel./fax 221 921), arranges for private accommodations (open Mon.-Fri. 8am-9pm, Sat. 8am-3pm; singles 32zł, doubles 54zł). Other locals gladly rent **private rooms;** watch for signs or solicitors in the train station.

Jan-Pol PTTK Dom Turysty, ul. Westerplatte 15 (tel. 229 566; fax 212 726), near the main post office. Big, brown, right on the park and near the *rynek.* The place to meet young travelers. Only one key per room, so the suites usually remain open. Make use of the hotel vault, or cuddle up with your money belt on in the low-slung beds. Reception open daily noon-10pm. 8-bed dorms 20zł per person.

Dom Wycieczkowy, ul. Poselska 22 (tel. 226 765; fax 220 439), 3 blocks south of the *rynek* off ul. Grodzka. Small, quiet rooms; rollercoaster hallways and clean hall bathrooms. Singles 50zł, doubles 80zł, triples 110zł, quads 150zł.

Schronisko Młodzieżowe (HI), ul. Kościuszki 88 (tel. 221 951), inside the convent gate a good 20-min. walk from the Old Town. Take tram #2 from ul. Westerplatte (direction "Salwator") and get off at the last stop. Run by nuns in a heavenly setting—a Renaissance courtyard tucked away behind the high convent walls. Reception open daily 8am-2pm and 5-11pm. Lockout 10am-5pm. Curfew 11pm. 8- to 36-bed rooms. 7zł per person, with HI 6zł. Sheets 2zł.

Schronisko Młodzieżowe (HI), ul. Oleandry 4 (tel. 338 822). Take bus #119 headed north from the train station, and get off once the main drag turns into ul. Mickiewicza. Oleandry parallels Mickiewicza outside the Old Town. Cheap but dingy. Flexible lockout 10am-5pm. Curfew 11pm. 350 rooms. Clean doubles 15zł. 4- to 5-bed rooms 14zł per person. 6- to 8-bed rooms 13zł per person. 8- to 16-bed dorms 12zł per person. HI members only; membership available for US$9.

Hotel Saski, ul. Sławkowska 3 (tel. 214 222; fax 214 830), a half-block from the *rynek* and nightlife. Comfy and full of international students. Singles 49zł, with bath 70zł. Doubles 76zł, with bath 108zł. Triples 86zł, with bath 123zł.

Pensjonat "Rycerska", pl. Na Groblach 22 (tel. 226 082 or 231 843; fax 223 399), in the shadow of the castle between ul. Straszewskiego and Powiśle. A clean and charming establishment with a quiet courtyard in a noisy city. Doubles with bath 95zł, with bath and TV 110zł.

Hotel Piast, ul. Piastowska 47 (tel. 374 933 or 372 176). Take bus #139, 159, 173, 208, 238, or 258 westbound to Piastowska. Popular with (mostly American) foreigners who come to learn Polish. Laundry. Singles 32.10zł first night, additional nights 29zł. Shared-bathroom doubles 42.80zł, additional nights 38.60zł. Doubles with bath 60zł, additional nights 55.60zł. Triples with bath 60.90zł, additional nights 54.60zł. Prices 50-67% lower during school year.

Hotel Warszawski, ul. Pawia 6 (tel./fax 220 622,) in front of the station off pl. Kolejowy. Not as gray as nearby hotels—at least on the inside. Singles 60zł, with bath 75zł. Doubles 85zł, with bath 120zł. Triples 100zł, with bath 120zł.

Camping Krak, ul. Radzikowskiego 99 (tel. 372 122 or 372 171; fax 372 532). Take tram #4, 8, 12, or 40 to "Fizyków" and walk north. Caravans 13zł, 8zł per person, no extra fee per tent. Open May 15-Sept. 15.

Camping Krakowianka, ul. Żywiecka 4 (tel. 664 191 or 664 192), south of the center. A long ride by tram #19 from the train station to "Borek Fałęcki". Get off when you see a post office and park on the right. Turn right onto ul. Kościuszkowców, then left onto ul. Żywiecka. 6-person bungalows 63zł. Tents 6.50zł per person. Caravans 8zł. Electricity hook-up 4.50zł for 24hr. Open May 1-Oct. 30.

FOOD

There are several **late-night grocery stores** in town: **Społem,** pl. Kolejowy, across from the train station; and **Non Stop,** ul. Szewska 10 (tel. 222 296), west of the *rynek* (open Sun.-Thurs. 7am-1am, Fri.-Sat. 24hr.). *Obwarzanki* (soft pretzels with poppy seeds), a street-stand specialty, sell for a mere 0.40zł. All the eateries listed below lie within a few blocks of Rynek Główny.

Restaurants

Bar Mleczny Barcelona, ul. Piłsudskiego 1 (tel. 223 247), across from Planty on the west side of *Stare Miasto*. A bastion of proletarian dining—a full meal for under 3zł. *Pierogi z truskawkami* (strawberry dumplings) 6zł. *Naleśniki z serem* (pancakes with cheese) 1.20zł. Lasagna 1.50zł. Open daily 8am-7pm.

Restauracja Hawełka, Rynek Główny 34 (tel. 224 753). Occupies an airy, white-and-green hall in the heart of *Stare Miasto*. Polish cuisine and English menu. Reserve in summer because this is where every tour group comes for its "folklore dinner." *Kiełbasa* 6zł, *pierogi ruskie* 7zł. Open daily 11am-11pm.

Restauracja Andalous, pl. Dominikański 6 (tel. 225 227), 1 block south of the *rynek*. Tasty Arabic and Spanish food, but loud due to the tram. Kebab 9zł. Veggie couscous 11zł. For a quicker, cheaper meal, stop by the grill, offering huge dishes with rice and salad (2-14zł). Vegetarian falafel 7.50zł. Open daily 9am-midnight.

Jadłodajnia u Stasi, ul. Mikołajska 16. A one-person operation—Pani Stasia is in charge. Definitely low-budget. Famous for its traditional Polish food, such as *pierogi z serem* (cheese dumplings) and *pierogi z mięsem* (meat dumplings). Open Mon.-Fri. 12:45pm until the food runs out—usually between 4 and 5pm.

Różowy Słoń (Pink Elephant), ul. Straszewskiego 24. Funky pop art decor and delicious salads. Bowls 1.20zł per 100g. Rice dishes 2.30-2.70zł. Huge plates of spaghetti 2.50-3.20zł. Open Mon.-Sat. 9am-9pm, Sun. 11am-9pm.

Restauracja Ariel, ul. Szeroka 17 (tel. 213 870), in the old Jewish district of Kazimierz, a 15-min. walk south of the *rynek*. Outdoor café-style seating and elegant interior with antique-style furniture and fresh roses on tables. Calls itself the "Jewish Artistic Café" and hosts concerts featuring Jewish, Russian, and Gypsy music nightly at 8pm. Jewish-style carp 9.20zł. Gefilte fish 9.90zł. Purim cake for dessert 1zł. Open daily 10am-midnight. Concerts 15zł.

Chimera, ul. Św. Anny 3 (tel. 232 178). The oldest and most famous in town. Especially popular with students between classes. A large plate of up to 6 varieties of their creative and delicious salads costs 6zł, a small one with up to 4 varieties, 4zł; small is large and large is huge. Open daily 9am-midnight.

Balaton, ul. Grodzka 37 (tel. 220 469). Its divine Hungarian cuisine always attracts crowds. Entrées 6-11zł. Menu in Hungarian and Polish; if that leaves you lost, the waitress will recommend *placki ziemniaczane po węgiersku* (potato pancakes with meat stew; 8zł) which is indeed delicious. Open daily 9am-10pm.

Pychotka, Rynek Główny 11 (tel. 212 512), in a little courtyard just off the *Rynek*. Big salads 6zł. Small salads 4zł. Veggie burgers 2.70zł. Five sorts of *pierogi* 2.60-3zł. Open daily 10am-8pm.

Chiński Pałac (Chinese Palace), ul. Sławkowska 3 (tel. 213 542), next to the elegant Hotel Saski. Lavishly decorated and permanently filled with Chinese tourists. Expensive specialties (10-35zł), cheaper egg rolls and fried rice (5.50zł). Take-out available. Open daily noon-10:30pm.

Cafés

Kawiarnia Jama Michalika, Floriańska 45 (tel. 221 561). Over a century old, this is one of Kraków's most famous—and surely best-decorated—cafés. Sip espresso (1.20zł), nibble on pastries, and attack elaborate ice cream specialties in the rarefied air of this former haunt of the Polish intelligentsia. Cabaret in the evenings.

Café Malma, Rynek Główny 25 (tel. 219 894). Popular spot, always crowded. American-, London-, or Kraków-style breakfast 9.90zł. Tortes 3-3.80zł. Slow service, but a great spot for people watching. Open daily 10am-midnight; cellar open for lunch and dinner daily 1-10:30pm.

Kawiarnia u Zalipianek, ul. Szewska 24 (tel. 222 950). Entertaining outdoor café in Planty, garnished with local folk art. Yummy tortes 1.90-2.60zł per slice. Open daily 9am-10pm.

Café Ariel, ul. Szeroka 18 (tel. 217 920), next to Restauracja Ariel, with similar decor. Tour groups descend regularly, but the staff is very friendly. Cup of coffee 3zł. Open daily 10am-midnight.

SIGHTS

Unlike Warsaw, Kraków was fortunate enough to be spared the destruction of WWII, but the fumes of the post-war Nowa Huta factory have eroded Kraków's monuments over the last four decades. Recently, the city has obtained UNESCO funds, enabling it to gradually regain its old beauty and character.

Stare Miasto (Old Town)

At the center of the Old Town spreads **Rynek Główny,** one of the largest and most distinctive market squares in Europe. At its northeast corner rises the asymmetrical red **Kościół Mariacki** (Cathedral of St. Mary). The two towers of Kościół Mariacki were each built by a brother: one rapidly and one with steady genius. The hasty brother realized over time that the work of his careful sibling would put his own to shame, and in jealousy he murdered his brother. The murder weapon remains in the Sukiennice (see below), although other legends remember it as an instrument once used to cut off the ears of thieves. The richly decorated interior of the cathedral holds a 500-year-old carved-wood altarpiece by Wit Stwosz, dismantled by the Nazis and rediscovered by Allied forces at the war's end. Reassembled, it is ceremoniously unveiled at noon each day (daily noon-6pm; altar admission 1.50zł, students 1zł). On every hour, a *hejnał* (trumpet call) blares from the towers—its abrupt ending recalls the destruction of Kraków in 1241, when the invading Tartars shot down the trumpeter. Polish radio broadcasts the noon call nation-wide. Across the square stands the lonely **Wieża Ratuszowa** (Town Hall Tower; open Mon.-Fri. 10am-5pm, Sat.-Sun. 10am-4pm; 0.70zł). Dividing the *rynek* in half, the yellow Italianate **Sukiennice** (Cloth Hall) is as mercantile now as it was in guild times; the ground floor contains an enormous souvenir shop. Upstairs, **Muzeum Narodowe** (National Museum; tel. 221 166) houses a gallery of 18th- and 19th-century Polish classics (open Tues.-Sat. 10am-6pm, Sun. 10am-3:30pm; 3zł, students 1.50zł). During the academic year, students cruise the area and look for inspiration around the **statue of Adam Mickiewicz,** Poland's most celebrated Romantic poet.

Running north from Kosciół Mariacki's corner of the *rynek*, **Floriańska** leads to the northern entrance of the new city and the Kawiarnia Jama Michalika (see Cafés, p. 399). The street was once part of the Royal Tract by which travelers made their way to the castle, and many houses date to the 14th century. At the northern end of the street, **Brama Floriańska,** the old gate to the city, is the centerpiece of the only part of the city walls still in existence. A local lover of historical monuments convinced someone that the wall would block the disease-carrying north wind, rescuing the gate from the 19th century destruction of most of the wall. A left onto ul. Pijarska from ul. Floriańska takes you to **Muzeum Czartoryskich,** ul. Św. Jana 19 (tel. 225 566), which shelters paintings from the Renaissance to the 18th century, including da Vinci's *"Lady with Ermine* and Rembrandt's *Landscape with a Merciful Samaritan* (open Tues.-Fri. 9am-5pm, Sat.-Sun. 10am-3:30pm; 3zł, students 1.5zł; Tues. 2zł, 1zł students; Sun. free). A few blocks southwest of the museum, the tiny **Kamienica Szołayskich,** pl. Szczepański 9 (tel. 227 021), which houses religious art from the 15-18th centuries, was undergoing renovations in summer '96.

Kraków's **Uniwersytet Jagielloński,** over 600 years old, ranks as the second-oldest university in Eastern Europe (after Prague's). Astronomer Mikołaj Kopernik (Copernicus) and drama scholar Agnieszka Marszałek are among its noted alumni. The university's oldest building, 15th-century **Collegium Maius,** ul. Jagiellońska 15 (tel. 220

549), west of the *rynek,* enchants with a bewitching Gothic courtyard and vaulted walkway (open Mon.-Fri. 11am-2:30pm, Sat. 11:30am-1:30pm).

South of the *rynek,* the **Franciscan Church** on Franciszkańska houses Stanisław Wyspiański's enormous "God the Father" stained glass window with its rippling colors and great fame. Pope John Paul II resided across the street in the **Bishop's Palace** when he was Cardinal Karol Wojtyła and influential in the creation of Solidarity. A statue in the courtyard commemorates his 60th birthday in 1980. To the south, on Grodzka, the **Church of St. Peter and St. Paul** is the first Polish church truly of the Roman Baroque style (open Mon.-Sat. 9am-5pm, Sun. 1-5pm). Right next to it, the older (11th century) Romanesque **Church of St. Andrew** provided shelter to many of Kraków's citizens as the city burned in the Tartar invasion of 1241. Slightly west of Grodzka, **Kanonicza,** like Floriańska, was once part of the Royal Tract. Several galleries line the path to Wawel, including **Cricot 2,** ul. Kanonicza 5 (tel. 228 332). A museum of the works of an avant-garde group once led by the late Tadeusz Kantor. Funky exhibit features eerie sounds and pieces—costumes, lights, etc.—of avantgarde shows (open Mon.-Fri. 10am-2pm).

Wawel (The Royal Castle)

Zamek Wawelski (Wawel Castle) is one of the finest surviving pieces of Renaissance architecture in Poland. Begun in the 10th century, the castle contains 71 chambers, a magnificent sequence of 16th-century tapestries commissioned by the royal family, and a series of arrases depicting the story of Noah's Ark. The castle is undergoing renovation—not all the quarters are open to the public. The **Crown Treasury,** within the castle, features swords, including the Szczerbiec (Jagged Sword), which was used in the coronations of Polish kings. Another separate exhibit, the **Oriental Collection,** displays vases and an enormous 17th-century Turkish tent, elaborately decorated with appliqué. (Tickets can be bought at the window inside Wawel; open Tues.-Thurs. 9am-4:15pm, Fri.-Sat. 9am-2:30pm, Sun. 10am-4:15pm. Royal Chambers open Wed.-Thurs. and Sat. 9am-2:30pm, Tues. and Fri. 9am-4:30pm, Sun. 10am-3pm; 4zł, students 2zł. Treasury open Tues.-Wed. and Fri.-Sat. 9am-2:30pm, Thurs. 9am-4:30pm, Sun. 10am-4:30pm; 4zł, students 2zł. Oriental Collection open Wed.-Thurs. and Sat. 9am-3pm, Tues. and Fri. 9am-4:30pm, Sun. 10am-3pm; 3zł, students 1zł. All exhibits free Wed.) At the entrance, a visitor's office (tel./fax 220 904) sells English guidebooks (open Mon.-Sat. 8am-4pm, Sun. 10am-3pm). A 3½-hour tour in English costs 55zł above the cost of tickets.

Poland's monarchs were crowned and buried in the **Katedra** (Cathedral) next to the castle. Its former archbishop, Cardinal Karol Wojtyła, now reigns as Pope John Paul II. The temple houses ornate tombs of kings and other dead white males—poets Juliusz Słowacki and Adam Mickiewicz, and Polish and American military leader General Józef Piłsudski. The sarcophagus of King Kazimierz Jagiellończyk was crafted by the creator of Kościół Mariacki's altar, while St. Maurice's spear, presented to the Polish prince Bolesław Chrobry (who later became the country's first king in 1025) by German Emperor Otto III in 1000, symbolizes Polish-German friendship. Atop the cathedral, **Dzwon Zygmunta** (Zygmunt's Bell) sounds only on rare occasions, but when it does, its tones echo for miles around the city (cathedral and bell open Mon.-Sat. 9am-5pm and Sun. 12:15-5pm; 3zł, with ISIC 1.5zł). Outside, the **statue of Tadeusz Kosciuszko** glorifies the Polish patriot who fought in the American Revolution and organized an anti-Russian revolution in Poland in 1794. The entrance to **Smocza Jama** (Dragon's Cave), home to Kraków's fire-breathing pet, hides in the complex's southwest corner (open daily 10am-5pm; 1.5zł).

Kazimierz (The Old Jewish District)

South of *Stare Miasto* lies **Kazimierz,** the 400-year-old Jewish quarter. In 1939, 64,000 Jews lived in the Kraków area, many of them in Kazimierz, but Nazi policies forced most out and the rest (15,000) into the drastically overcrowded Podgórze ghetto by 1941. All were removed by March of 1943, many to the Płaszów and Auschwitz-Birkenau concentration and death camps. The current Jewish population hovers around 600. Take tram #13 east from the corner of ul. Dominikańska and ul.

Grodzka one block south of the *rynek,* and get off when you reach the post office at the intersection of ul. Miodowa and ul. Starowiślna. Ul. Szeroka runs parallel to and one block west of ul. Starowiślna. By foot, the 15-minute walk from the center leads southeast on ul. Sienna, which turns into ul. Starowiślna. Turn right on ul. Miodowa, then take the first left on ul. Szeroka. You can still see the remnants of what was once a large and vital community: the beautiful **Remuh Cemetery** (Mon.-Fri. 9am-4pm) at Szeroka 40, and Kraków's two operating synagogues. In 1860-62, the Association of Progressive Israelis founded **Templ,** ul. Miodowa 24, which features a polychromed ceiling and 36 splendid stained-glass windows. Poland's oldest synagogue, **Stara Synagoga,** ul. Szeroka 24, houses **Muzeum Judaistyczne** (tel. 220 962), depicting the history and culture of Kraków's Jews. Particularly fascinating are the photos of pre-war Kraków and the appalling sequence of destruction in the 1940s (open Wed.-Thurs. 9am-3:30pm, Fri. 11am-6pm, Sat.-Sun. 9am-3pm; 4zł, students 2zł). The **Jewish bookstore Jordan,** ul. Szeroka 2 (tel. 217 166), organizes tours, including a two-hour tour of Kazimierz which traces the sites named in the film *Schindler's List* (open Mon.-Fri. 9am-6pm, Sat.-Sun. 10am-6pm; 2- to 6-hr. English tours (30-60zł) depart from the bookstore).

ENTERTAINMENT

Dexter (see Practical Information, p. 439) offers some brochures on the month's cultural events, and the **Cultural Information Center,** ul. Św. Jana 2 (tel. 217 787; fax 217 737), sells a comprehensive monthly guide, *Karnet,* for a few złotych (open daily 10am-7pm). **April** is reserved for stately organ music; **May** reviews the best international short feature films; **June** hosts the annual parade featuring costumed actors and the city's mascot—Lajkonik, the laughable Tartar; **August** brings to Kraków a series of festivals, including an international carnival of street theaters; **September** resounds with the sounds of jazz. Classical music buffs will appreciate **Filharmonia Krakowska** (tel. 220 958 or 229 477), which performs regularly in its hall at ul. Zwierzyniecka 1.

U Louisa, Rynek Główny 13 (tel. 218 092). Good, loud, live jazz and blues on weekends with no cover, as well as **internet access** for 3zł per hour. Beer 3.50-5.90zł. Open Mon.-Fri. noon-11pm, Sat.-Sun. 2pm-2am.

Pub Pod Papugami (Under the Parrots), ul. Św. Jana 18 (tel. 228 299). A self-declared Irish pub with cellars frequented by a quiet student crowd. Pool for 5zł per hour. 0.4L of *Guinness* 6.40zł. Open Mon.-Fri. noon-2am, Sat.-Sun. 4pm-2am.

Jazz Club "U Muniaka", ul. Floriańska 3. Café run by a well known Polish jazzman, who often invites his friends for jam sessions. Concerts Fri.-Sat. at 9:30pm. Open daily 3pm "to the end." The 15zł cover may scare off some.

Café and Gallery Krzysztofory, ul. Szczepańska 2 (tel. 229 360), in the cellars of the Krzysztofory House. Exhibits every 2 to 3 weeks, but month-long breaks from all the artistry usually occur in summer. The café also hosts **avant-garde theater** performances. 3zł for 0.5L of *Żywiec* beer. Open daily 11am-midnight; if the door is closed, push on in. Gallery open Tues.-Sun. 11am-4pm.

John Bull Pub, ul. Mikołajska 2 (tel. 231 168). A spot of England in the heart of Poland; everything inside was allegedly imported from Britain. Besides British beer, the pub also serves juices, coffee, and snacks. 8zł for 0.4L of beer. Open daily 11am until the last customer leaves, usually around 1am.

Bluebox, ul. Szpitalna 38 (tel. 139 960), between the main train station and the *rynek*. A popular disco thanks to the central location and A/C. Open nightly 8pm-5am. Cover Mon.-Sat. 5zł, Sun. 10zł.

Stańczyk (tel. 211 326), in the cellar under the town hall. Americans crowd this café. Comedy shows in Polish Tues.-Sun. 7:30pm. Jazz concerts Jan.-Feb. Open Mon. 10am-1am, Tues.-Sun. 10am-7pm and 9:30pm-1am. Cover 6zł.

Spartakus, Konopnickiej 20 (tel. 666 022), just across the bridge on bus #103, 104, 114, or 164 provides steam bath, Finnish sauna, a fitness center, a sun deck, and a cafeteria for 12zł per day to gay and straight men. Open daily 11am-11pm.

Near Kraków

OŚWIĘCIM: AUSCHWITZ-BIRKENAU

An estimated 1.5 million people, mostly Jews, were murdered and thousands more suffered in the Nazi concentration and death camps in the complex that encompassed **Auschwitz** (Oświęcim), **Birkenau** (Brzezinka), and Monowitz (a chemical plant). The first two names still conjure up the most vivid images of the Nazi death machine, due in no small part to the film *Schindler's List*, which was partially filmed in the camps. Prisoners were originally kept at the smaller **Konzentrazionlager Auschwitz I**, within the city limits. The red brick buildings, originally built as barracks for Polish soldiers, appear eerily normal until the irony of the inscription on the camp's gate—*Arbeit Macht Frei* (Work Makes Free)—slowly becomes clear. In fact, prisoners who made it to the horrifying conditions at Auschwitz were thought far luckier than the ones who lived in row upon row of overcrowded wooden shacks or were herded directly to the crematoria at Konzentrationlager Auschwitz II-Birkenau—the true death camp.

Visitors begin tours at the **Museum Oświęcim** at Auschwitz. Barracks and crematoria hold displays detailing Nazi atrocities, and many of the nations whose citizens were murdered here have erected their own exhibits or memorials. As you walk through the former barracks, separated only by glass sheets from enormous rooms holding remnants from the camp's storehouses at the end of the war—suitcases, shoes, glasses, over 100,000 pounds of slowly-decomposing women's hair—the sheer magnitude of the place slowly comes into focus. An English-language guidebook with maps of the camps is sold at the entrance for 2zł. Begin your visit with the terrifying **film** shot by the Soviet Army who liberated the camp on January 27, 1945— the black and white pictures of the near-dead survivors make it difficult to believe that these were the fortunate ones. There's at least one English showing per day (0.60zł); check the schedule at the movie ticket office. (Camp open 24hr.; museum open daily June-Aug. 8am-7pm; May and Sept. 8am-6pm; April and Oct. 8am-5pm; Mar. and Nov.-Dec. 15 8am-4pm; Dec. 16-Feb. 8am-3pm. Free).

The starker **Konzentrationlager Auschwitz II-Birkenau**, in the countryside 3km from the original camp, is a half-hour walk along a well marked route. Between April 15 and October 31, a bus shuttles to this site from the parking lot at the Auschwitz museum (6 per day, 0.60zł). Birkenau was constructed later in the war when the efficient killing of the Jews, Romani, Slavs, homosexuals, disabled people, and any others the Nazis deemed "inferior", was considered more important than the benefits of their labor. Begin with the central watchtower, where you can view the immensity of the camp—endless rows of barracks, watchtowers, chimneys, gas chambers, and crematoria. The Nazis tried to destroy the evidence of their mass destruction, and there remain only 45 brick buildings, 27 wooden ones, and what looks like a desolate forest of perfectly spaced brick chimneys. The gas chambers and crematoria are in ruins, having been dynamited by the retreating Nazis; the train tracks that led up to them, however, have been partially reconstructed and photos of the selection process make it all too easy to imagine the arbitrariness that once sent masses of people either directly to work or to their deaths. In the right corner of the camp lies a pond, still gray from the ashes deposited there half a century ago; fragments of bone are still found in the area near the crematoria.

Buses run here from Kraków's central bus station (11 per day, 1½hr., 4.80zł; get off at "Muzeum Oświęcim"). **Trains** leave from Kraków Główny (4 per day, 1¾hr., 5zł), although times are not particularly convenient. More trains run from Kraków Plaszów. Tourist offices in Kraków (see Kraków: Tourist Offices, p. 439) also offer tours including transportation and knowledgeable guides. From the train station in the town, buses #2, 3, 4, and 5 drop visitors off at the Museum Oświęcim bus stop, outside the driveway. By foot, turn right as you exit the station, go one block and turn left; the road stretches 1.6km to Auschwitz, which will be on the right.

WIELICZKA

About 13km southeast of Kraków rests a 1000-year-old salt mine at Wieliczka, ul. Daniłowicza 10 (tel. 782 653; postal code: 32-020), where pious Poles have carved an immense 20-chapel complex in salt 100m underground. The most spectacular one is the 180-ft. long and 33-ft. high **St. Kinga's Chapel.** Today UNESCO has declared the Wieliczka salt mine **one of the 12 most priceless monuments in the world.** In addition to the chapels, the tour covers the **underground museum** which gives a history of the salt mines and demonstrates the methods of salt extraction. High mass is conducted in St. Kinga's Chapel on July 24, Feast of the Miners on December 4, and Saturnalia on December 24. The tour is more interesting in theory than in practice—the second half of its 2½-hours drags. Those interested in a shorter tour can ask the guide to show them the exit about halfway through. (Open April. 15-Oct. 15 daily 8am-6pm; Oct. 16-April 14 8am-4pm. Obligatory guided tours; last leaves 1½hr. before closing; 16.50zł, students 8.50zł, cameras 5zł, videocameras 10zł. English guide upon request 20zł per person.) **ORBIS** organizes daily trips here (3hr.; 62zł, students 42.50zł); its bus leaves daily at 3:25pm from Dom Turysty at Westerplatte 15. Or choose a budget option: **trains** go to Kraków (1 per hr., 25min., 1.50zł), and **private minibuses** depart from the road between the train and bus stations (every 15min., 1.50zł). Once in Wieliczka, follow the tracks' former path and then the *"do kopalni"* (to the mine) signs. Local kiosks sell guidebooks in an intriguing version of English.

TARNÓW

A Roms town before WWII, Tarnów still manages to keep alive the Gypsy legacy. Dedicated to "all travelers, past, present and, I hope, future," **Muzeum Etnograficzne,** ul. Krakowska 10 (tel. (014) 220 625), traces the history of Polish Gypsies since 1401, when they first came to the area. WWII saw 35,000 Polish Gypsies perish; today, only 20,000 remain. The museum exhibits a display on their history, art, and culture. Painted caravans await riders, and the Gypsy flag—a red wheel against a green and blue background—symbolizes the people's wandering under the sky. The English brochure *The Gypsies: History and Culture* is worth its 1zł price (open Tues. and Thurs. 10am-5pm, Wed. and Fri. 9am-3pm, Sat.-Sun. 10am-2pm; 2zł, students 1zł). Tarnów lies 82km east of Kraków, connected to it by **trains** (38 per day, 1hr., 6zł) and **buses** (24 per day, 2hr., 8.20zł), both of which arrive at **plac Dworcowy,** southwest of the Old Town and 10 minutes from the center. From the main bus station, turn right on **ul. Krakowska,** which crosses **pl. Kościuszki** and ends at the *rynek*.

■ Częstochowa

Częstochowa is the Catholic Mecca of Poland. Every year thousands make the pilgrimage to the towering monastery on Jasna Góra to see the most sacred of Polish icons: the *Black Madonna*. Although now a spiritual center in a strongly religious country, evidence of the ideological conflict with the old Communist regime remains. Mismanaged industry left the city bleak and gray. The most striking example of the Communist response to the religious importance of the city is the hulking a smokestack seen by glancing back while headed to the monastery.

ORIENTATION AND PRACTICAL INFORMATION

Częstochowa lies about 100km northwest of Kraków. The main **train** and **bus stations,** connected at the south end of the railway station's platform #4, are located close to the town center and linked with **Jasna Góra** to the west by **al. NMP** (aleja Najświętszej Marii Panny—Avenue of Our Lady). The tourist office and the cheapest sleeps gather at the feet of the monastery.

Tourist Offices: WCIT, al. NMP 65 (tel. 241 360; fax 243 412). Fanatically organized, they provide a free map and detailed info on hotels. Open daily 9am-6pm. **Jasnogórskie Centrum Informacji (IT),** ul. Kordeckiego 2 (tel. 653 888; fax 654

CZĘSTOCHOWA ■ 449

343), inside the monastery near the entrance to the cathedral. Staff sells maps and English guidebooks (5zł), arranges monastery tours in English, and makes reservations for Dom Pielgrzyma. Open June-Oct. daily 7am-8pm; Nov.-May 8am-5pm.

Budget Travel: ALMATUR, al. NMP 37 (tel. 244 368; fax 244 378). Sells ISICs. Gives free directions to summer hostels. Open Mon.-Fri. 9am-5pm, Sat. 10am-2pm.

Currency Exchange: At *kantors* throughout the city. **Bank PKO S.A.,** ul. Kopernika 17/19 (tel. 655 060), several blocks south of al. NMP off ul. Nowowiejskiego. Cashes traveler's checks for a 1% commission and offers MasterCard and Visa cash advances. Open Mon.-Fri. 8am-6pm.

Trains: Częstochowa Główna, ul. Piłsudskiego 38 (tel. 241 337). To: Katowice (40 per day, 2hr., 6.70zł); Kraków (8 per day, 2hr., 12.90zł); Warsaw (7 per day, 3hr., 17.55zł); Wrocław (1 per day, 3½hr., 15.00zł).

Buses: al. Wolności 45/49 (tel. 246 616). To: Kraków (5 per day, 3hr., 14zł); Warsaw (1 per day, 4hr., 16.50zł); Wrocław (5 per day, 4hr., 12.60zł).

Luggage Storage: At the train station (2.50zł). Open 24hr. Also at the monastery. Donations set the prices. Open June-Sept. daily 6am-6pm; Nov.-May 7am-5pm.

Pharmacy: al. NMP 50 (tel. 246 274). Open Mon.-Fri. 8am-9pm, Sat. 8am-2pm.

Post Office: ul. Orzechowskiego 7 (tel. 241 342), between the bus and train stations. Open Mon.-Fri. 7am-9pm, Sat. 7am-2pm. **Postal code:** 42-201.

Telephones: At the post office. **Phone code:** 0-34.

ACCOMMODATIONS AND CAMPING

The best deals sit at the foot of Jasna Góra. The higher prices by the train station reflect only the convenient location. Reservations are strongly recommended all year, but are a must for early May and mid- and late August.

Dom Pielgrzyma (The Pilgrim's House), ul. Wyszyńskiego 1/31 (tel. 247 011; fax 65 67 28), outside the west gate of the monastery. A large operation with homey, spacious, and clean rooms. Religious paraphernalia proliferates. Singles with bath 40zł. Doubles with bath 42zł. Triples with bath 63zł. Quads 10zł per person.

Dom Pielgrzyma—Hale Noclegowe, ul. Klasztorna 1 (tel. 656 688, ext. 224), just southeast of Jasna Góra's west gate. A place for the ascetic pilgrim. Clean bedrooms and communal bathrooms, but no hot water. Friendly staff. 3- to 10-bed rooms. 7zł per bed regardless of the room.

Youth Hostel, ul. Jasnogórska 84/90 (tel. 243 121). From al. NMP go right on ul. Dąbrowskiego, then left on ul. Jasnogórska. At the Hostel sign, go to the end of the long alley. Lockout 10am-5pm. Curfew 10pm. 6zł per person. Sheets 1.50zł.

Hotel Miły, ul. Katedralna 18 (tel. 243 391), just off ul. Piłsudskiego near the train station. Look for the cheerful yellow and green signs. Convenient location, but a bit noisy. For a small hotel, the rooms are large. Communal bathrooms. Doubles 25.60zł, with bath 38.50zł. Quads 38.50zł.

Camping Oleńka, ul. Oleńki 10/30 (tel. 247 495; fax 251 479), across the parking lot from the west gate of the monastery near Dom Pielgrzyma. A sprawling complex with surprisingly clean and comfortable rooms. Kitchen facilities. Tents 5zł per

---

Let Them Eat Salt!

When Kinga, daughter of the Hungarian King Bela, married prince Bolesław Śmiały (the Bold), future monarch of Poland, the princess wanted her dowry to be a present not just to Bolesław, but to all the people of Poland. Upon questioning the delegates of the prince, she discovered that Poles had been supping on soulless stews and enduring flavorless foodstuffs for centuries. The reason? They had no salt. That night a mysterious voice came to Kinga and divulged the whereabouts of a magnificent El Dorado of salt. The next day, she asked her father to give her whatever her ring would touch. He agreed, and Kinga hurled the ring over the mountains separating Poland and Hungary. Upon arriving in Kraków, she ordered workers to start digging in the spot where the ring had fallen—after days of digging, the men found the ring stuck fast in an endless deposit of salt.

person. Bungalows: singles 10zł, doubles 22zł, triples with bath 39zł, quads with bath 52zł, quints with bath 65zł. Open year-round.

FOOD

Although food options are not as extensive as in other cities, you are not going to starve. Numerous kiosks sell cheap snacks, including *zapiekanka* (a pizza-like concoction) and hamburgers. **Solidom,** al. NMP 75, welcomes shoppers to its hallowed halls of post-Communist consumerism daily 6am-10pm.

Pod Gruszką (Under the Pear), al. NMP 37 (tel. 654 490), next to ALMATUR in a little courtyard. Popular student hangout with huge wax-dripping candles adorning the tables. Salads 2zł per kg. More of a café at night. Open daily 10am-10pm.

Bar Herbaciarnia, ul. Wyszyńskiego 1/31 (tel. 656 688, ext. 288), at Dom Pielgrzyma. Big, simple self-serve entrées (2-6zł), soups (1zł), and salads (1zł) dished up in a modern dining hall. Additional seating outside. Open daily 7am-8pm.

Klub Muzyczny Stacherczak, ul. Racławicka 3 (tel. 246 235), 1 block off al. NMP at the corner with ul. Dąbrowskiego. Chinese food and music in an incredibly posh setting. Entrées 5-25zł. MC and Visa accepted. Open daily noon-midnight.

Restauracja Polonia, ul. Piłsudskiego 9 (tel. 244 067), on the 1st floor of Hotel Polonia near the train station. A distinguished dining room with bearable prices. Chicken, fries, and salad 10.10zł. Steamed veggies and fried eggs platter 5.20zł. Open daily 7am-10pm. Dancing Tues.-Sat. 8-11pm.

SIGHTS

Klasztor Paulinów (Paulite Monastery), on top of **Jasna Góra** (Bright Mountain), is *the* sight in town. Begin a tour at the monastery's well stocked **tourist bureau** (IT; see Tourist Offices, p. 448). Everything in Jasna Góra comes free of charge, but donations are encouraged. The Paulite monastery, resembling a Baroque fortress was founded in 1382 by Duke Władysław Opolczyk, who also donated the epiphany-inducing painting of the Blessed Mother and Child in 1384. The masses of pilgrims travel here to view the miraculous **Czarna Madonna** (Black Madonna). A Byzantine icon from the 6th-8th centuries (though some believe it to be a painting by St. Luke), Czarna Madonna was desecrated in 1430 by Hussites and later restored. Two scars on the Madonna's cheek were left, however, as a reminder of the sacrilegious conduct of the Hussites and as proof to the faithful that the miraculous icon could not be destroyed. The ornate 15th-century **Bazylika** houses the icon inside **Kaplica Matki Bożej** (Chapel of Our Lady). Countless crutches, medallions, and rosaries strung upon the chapel walls attest to the pilgims' faith in the painting's otherwordly powers. (Chapel open daily 5am-9:30pm. Icon revealed Mon.-Fri. 6am-noon, 3-7:10pm, and 9-9:15pm, Sat.-Sun. 6am-1pm, 3-7:10pm, and 9-9:15pm.)

The monastery also houses a large **treasury,** containing invaluable art works, many of them donations by pilgrims: monstrances, chalices, candelabra, liturgical vestments, and jewelry (open daily 8am-4:30pm). The **Arsenał** exhibits weapons, military insignia, medals, and orders, including those from WWII (open daily 9am-5pm). **Muzeum Sześćsetlecia** (Museum of the 600th Anniversary) commemorates the founding of the church and monastery and contains an impressive collection of musical instruments from the 17th-19th centuries (open daily 9am-5pm). Also worth the time is a climb up the **tower** (open daily 8am-4pm) and a walk around the fortifications for views of the region extending from the battlements.

The largest pilgrimages and crowds converge on the monastery during the **Marian feasts and festivals.** These include: May 3 (Feast of Our Lady Queen of Poland), July 16 (Feast of Our Lady of Scapulars), August 15 (Feast of the Assumption), August 26 (the Feast of Our Lady of Częstochowa), September 8 (Feast of the Birth of Our Lady), and September 12 (Feast of the Name Mary).

SANDOMIERZ ■ 451

■ Near Częstochowa: Trail of Eagles' Nests

Along the narrow 100-km strip of land known as the **Kraków-Częstochowa Uplands,** numerous crags of Jurassic limestone erupt from rolling green hills. In the Middle Ages, these uplands served as a natural defensive barrier, with the limestone formations providing excellent lookout points. Beginning in the 12th century, **fortifications** were built along the uplands. The natural shape of the limestone was often preserved and incorporated into the design of the **castles,** whose perches high on the rocky crags earn them the appellation "eagles' nests". Beginning in the 16th century, the effectiveness of the castles' defenses declined as a result of advancements in artillery. By the 18th century, most of the fortresses had seriously deteriorated due to declining economic and political power; many were destroyed by the Swedish Invasions. Today, only a few castles remain, including **Wawel Castle** in Kraków, and **Pieskowa Skała,** just northwest of Kraków. The ruins of the rest still lie along the uplands and wait to be discovered by trail or by bus.

A **hiking trail** runs along the entire 100km, and takes about seven days to walk. **PTTK** in Kraków or Częstochowa can provide **maps.** A red blaze marks the trail, and the route has regularly posted maps. The route leads through many small towns where hikers can find tourist info, provisions, and accommodations. The two largest attractions of the trail, the **ruins at Olsztyn** and the Pieskowa Skala Castle, make easy daytrips from Częstochowa and Kraków, respectively.

To reach **Olsztyn castle,** take bus **#58** or **58bis,** from ul. Piłsudskiego, across from the Chęstochowa train station (30min., 1zł). The 14km would make an ideal bike ride, if only there were a rental in Chęstochowa—ride 'em if you got 'em. Once there, it's hard to miss the ruins, which still sit high above the town. The castle, originally constructed in the 12th-13th centuries, consisting of upper and lower parts, later supplemented by two outer castles. The Swedish army ransacked the complex in 1655, inciting its eventual ruin. In the 18th century, local residents appropriated bricks from the partially destroyed castle to rebuild the local church, farther reducing its glory. The sole preserved sections are in the **upper castle,** including a 20m cylindrical **tower** and the **Starosta's Tower.** Ghosts are rumored to haunt the castle; Maciek Borkowic, imprisoned here for his rebellion against King Kasimir the Great, and a young bride lost in the dungeon are the two most haunting apparitions.

■ Sandomierz

Another retreat into the *małopolski* countryside leads to Sandomierz. Named after Sudomir, its founder, the town suffered destruction by the Tartars in 1241-60 and a Swedish invasion in 1656. Only one fortification remains, but both the *rynek's* 15th-century apartments and the underground system of dungeon-like wine cellars survived. Their existence was threatened in 1967, when Sandomierz began sliding toward the river. Fortunately, timely restorations sidestepped the catastrophe, and the town remains solidly upon its hill, peacefully surveying the Wisła.

Orientation and Practical Information Trains roll to Przemyśl (2 per day, 3hr.) and Warsaw (3 per day, 4hr.). **Buses** run to Kraków (2 per day, 4hr.), Lublin (7 per day, 2½hr.), and Warsaw (16 per day). The **train station,** ul. Lwowska (tel. 322 374), sits in the outskirts across the Wisła River. To reach the center from the train, take bus #3 or 11. The **bus station,** ul. 11-go Listopada (tel. 322 302; open daily 4:30am-9pm), northwest of the Old Town, is a 15-minute walk from the center or a short ride on bus #10. Ul. 11-go Listopada links the bus station with the main drag, **ul. Mickiewicza.** Turn left on this street which leads past a park to **Brama Opatowska** (Opatowska Gate), which ushers you into the Old Town. The **PTTK tourist office,** ul. Rynek 25/26 (tel. 322 305; fax 322 682), has free maps of the town (open Mon.-Fri. 8am-3pm). **Exchange currency** at *kantors,* post offices, and banks throughout town. The **pharmacy** heals at ul. Rynek 14 (tel. 322 459; open Mon.-Fri. 7:30am-

4pm, Sat. 8am-2pm). The **post office** lies at ul. Rynek 10 (open Mon.-Fri. 8am-6pm, Sat.-Sun. 8am-1pm). **Postal code:** 27-600. **Phone code:** 0-15.

Accommodations Most accommodations are centrally located and reasonable in price. **Hotel Zajazd Pod Ciżemką,** ul. Rynek 27 (tel. 323 668), offers beds in bath-outfitted doubles (50zł), triples (60zł), quads (80zł), and quints (100zł), with the best location in town. **Hotel Dick,** ul. Mały Rynek 2 (tel. 323 591), one block north of the *rynek,* has carpeted rooms, clean communal bathrooms, and an unfortunate name in English (singles 30zł, doubles 38zł, triples 49zł, quads 60zł, 5-bed dorms 25zł per person). The smaller **Dom Noclegowy,** ul. Zamkowa 1 (tel. 322 219), just down the hill from the *rynek,* offers simple singles (10zł), doubles (20zł), and triples (30zł), each equipped with an antique furnace.

Food The main eateries in Sandomierz cluster around the *rynek.* **Snack Bar,** ul. Rynek 30 (tel. 322 838), offers salads for 3.50zł a bowl and healthy buckwheat for 1.50zł (open daily 10am-9pm). It's a point-and-serve operation, so non-Polish speakers won't be encumbered by unpronounceable words. The chef at **Pod Ciżemką,** ul. Rynek 27 (tel. 323 668), cooks up several specialties, including *śledź po sandomiersku* (herring; 2.70zł), *kociołek zbójnicki* (vegetable soup; 3.50zł), and pork roulade (11.40zł, open daily 11am-10pm). **Winnica** (Vineyard), ul. Mały Rynek 2 (tel. 323 591), serves tasty Polish fare plus a couple of "international" *plats* such as pizza (4zł) and beef stroganoff (6zł) in a traditional setting (open daily 11am-midnight).

Sights The Gothic **Brama Opatowska** (Opatowska Gate), the only remainder of the town's fortifications, marks the entrance to the Old Town. Steep stairs head to the top of the gate—and a fantastic view of Sandomierz (open daily 10am-5:30pm; 1.50zł, students 1zł). Ul. Opatowska continues past the gate and leads straight to the spacious, sloping, cobblestone **Rynek Starego Miasta** (Old Town Square). A right on ul. Oleśnicka, just before the *rynek,* leads to the entrance of the mysterious **underground tourist route,** traveling through stone and brick chambers inhabited by Tartar ghosts. In these 14th-century cellars, wealthy merchants stored grain and wine made from the grapes of the vineyards that covered the sunny slopes surrounding Sandomierz. The guide will also recount the story of the legendary Halina Krempianka, who sacrificed her life to save her hometown from the Tartars (tours on the half-hour daily 10am-5:30pm; 2.90zł, students 1.70zł).

In the middle of the *rynek,* the Renaissance **ratusz** (town hall) houses a division of the **Muzeum Okręgowe** (Regional Museum), which features a model of 18th-century Sandomierz (open Tues.-Sun. 9am-4pm; 1zł, students 0.50zł). Ul. Mariacka takes you to the town's grandest monument, the 14th-century **Katedra.** It has retained its Gothic structure, but its interior has been redone in Baroque style (open March-Nov. Mon.-Sat. 10am-12:30pm and 2:30-6pm, Sun. 3-5pm; Dec.-Feb. Mon.-Sat. 10am-noon and 2:30-3pm, Sun. 3:30-5pm). July and August bring weekly organ concerts to the cathedral. Ul. Mariacka continues to ul. Zamkowa and **Zamek Kazimerzowski** (Castle of Kazimierz). Built in the 14th century by King Kazimierz Wielki and destroyed by the Swedes in 1656, the castle has recently undergone restoration, and only its walls and skeleton reflect the original layout. Inside, the **archaeological exhibit,** ul. Zamkowa 14 (tel. 323 868 or 323 869), includes an 11th-century chess set (open Tues.-Sun. 10am-5pm; 1.50zł, students 0.50zł).

Kazimierz Dolny

Despite the 1712 sacking of Kazimierz Dolny's castle by the Swedish army, painters toting their canvases and brushes and tourists carrying their cameras flock to this bewitching and pristine Old Town. Tiny galleries crowd cobblestone streets, red-tile-roofed houses flank the market square, and the castle ruins stands watch on the hill—all attesting to the economic vitality of centuries past.

KAZIMIERZ DOLNY ■ 453

Orientation and Practical Information Some buses pass on the way from Puławy to Lublin (1 per hr., 1½hr., 4.40zł), making frequent stops in the countryside; others zoom to Warsaw (5 per day, 3½hr., 10.40zł). When coming from Lublin or Warsaw, Kazimierz will not be posted as the final destination. Ask to find out which buses pass through. When leaving Kazimierz by bus, don't assume that the driver will make the detour into the bus station—he may stop across the street just off the cobblestone **ul. Podzamcze.** If you've just arrived, continue up the incline to see the *rynek* on the left. The **PTTK tourist office,** ul. Rynek 27 (tel. 810 046), sells tiny guides and maps of town (1-2zł) and arranges private rooms (open May-Oct. Mon.-Fri. 8am-6pm, Sat.-Sun. 10am-5:30pm; Nov.-April Mon.-Fri. 8am-3pm, Sat.-Sun. 10am-2pm). The **pharmacy** stands at ul. Rynek 17 (tel. 810 120; open Mon.-Fri. 8am-6pm, Sat. 8am-3pm, Sun. 10am-2pm). The **post office,** ul. Tyszkiewicza 2 (tel. 810 515; fax 810 500), a block west of the *rynek* (open May-Oct. Mon.-Fri. 8am-8pm, Sat.-Sun. 10am-5pm; Nov.-April Mon.-Fri. 8am-8pm, Sat. 9am-1pm, Sun. 9-11am) offers a **currency exchange** (open Mon-Fri. 8am-8pm) and **telephones. Postal code:** 24-120. **Phone code:** 0-81.

Accommodations and Food Rooms in town are fairly limited, especially during summer weekends and during the **Ogólnopolski Festiwal Kapel i Śpiewaków Ludowych** (Festival of Folk Groups and Singers), which takes place during the last week of June. It is especially important to call ahead for reservations during these times. **PTTK** (see above) arranges private singles (11.48-17.90zł), doubles (10.41-16.83zł per person), and triples (9.34-15.23zł per person) around town and in the outskirts commission-free. There is a surcharge of 1.50zł for stays of only one night. The clean and conveniently located **Youth Hostel "Strażnica",** ul. Senatorska 23a (tel. 810 427), sits only one block southwest of the *rynek.* Its 50 beds come in 2- to 10-person rooms (doubles and triples 13.10zł, students 12.50zł; dorms 11.50zł, students 11zł; sheets 2.50zł).

A **grocery** lies just south of the *rynek* at ul. Klasztorna 5 (open Mon.-Fri. 6am-7pm, Sat. 6am-3pm, Sun. 9am-2pm). **Restauracja Staropolska,** ul. Nadrzeczna 14 (tel. 810 236), a block south of the *rynek,* is the town's culinary legend, serving Polish food at its best in the shade of spruce trees (open daily 11am-10pm). **Bistro "U Zbyszka",** ul. Sadowa 4 (tel. 810 723), just off ul. Nadwiślańska west of the *rynek,* invites its guests to cool off in their pool (2.50zł per hr.), but wait an hour after eating (salads 4zł, turkey breast 6zł; open daily 10am-10pm). An old-fashioned bakery with the freshest rolls in town, **Piekarnia Sarzyński,** ul. Nadrzeczna 6, a few steps from the *rynek,* also bakes bread to order, in any shape you want (bread roosters 3zł, delectable mini-pizzas 2.50-3.50zł, pastries 0.70zł; open daily 6am-8pm).

Sights and Entertainment Hike up to the **castle tower** that used to alert the residents to passing boats on which they could levy tolls. From this lofty vantage point, you can see not only a long stretch of the Wisła, but also the castle at Janowiec (open Tues.-Sun. 10am-5pm; castle ruins and tower 0.80zł, students 0.60zł). On your way up or down, stop by the 16th-century **Kościół Farny Św. Jana Chrzciciela i Św. Bartłomieja** (Cathedral of St. John the Baptist and St. Bartholomew) to survey one of Poland's oldest (1620) and best-preserved organs. **Muzeum Sztuki Złotniczej** (Museum of Goldsmithery), ul. Rynek 19 (tel. 810 289), displays European jewelry, silver and gold religious paraphernalia, and a large collection of Jewish silver dating back to the 15th century. Just southwest off the *rynek,* **Kamienica Celejowska,** ul. Senatorska 11/13 (tel. 810 104), houses a collection of paintings inspired by the town. The **Muzeum Przyrodnicze** (Museum of Natural Science), ul. Puławska 54 (tel. 810 326 or 810 341), displays fossils and rocks from the Kazimierz region. (Museums open May-Oct. Tues.-Sun. 10am-4pm; Nov.-April 10am-3pm; tickets valid for all museums and the castle 4zł, students 2zł; each museum separately costs 1.40zł, students 0.70zł.)

■ Lublin

Approaching Lublin, you pass a peaceful patchwork of colorful checkerboard of ploughed fields. An occasional horse-drawn cart climbs the winding, tree-lined road, and farmers cut the grass with the original lawn-mower—the scythe. Despite the slow pace of its setting, the region's capital is far from dull and anything but provincial. The center of Polish Reformation and Counter-Reformation in the 16-17th centuries, Lublin has been an incubator of social and religious movements. These days much of the city's efforts are aimed at restoring the old city to its past glory.

Orientation and Practical Information The city's main street, **ul. Krakowskie Przedmieście,** runs west from **Stare Miasto** (Old Town) and turns into **Aleje Racławickie** before reaching **Ogród Saski** (Saxon Garden) to the north and the **KUL** (Katolicki Uniwersytet Lubelski) to the south. You can hop a bus at the **bus station,** ul. Trsiąclecia 4 (tel. 776 649, info 934), to Warsaw (10 per day, 3hr., 12zł). From here, take bus #5 or 10 heading west into town; tickets can be bought at kiosks (10-min. ride 0.70zł, 20-min. 0.90zł). By foot, head to the castle and climb **ul. Zamkowa.** After changing names several times, it will emerge through **Brama Krakowska** (Kraków Gate). From the **train station,** pl. Dworcowy 1 (tel. 20 219, info 933), trains go to Kraków (2 per day, 4hr., 20.70zł) and Warsaw (10 per day, 2½hr., 15zł). Take tram #150 to get to the city center. **IT,** ul. Krakowskie Przedmieście 78 (tel. 24 412), carries maps (4zł) and brochures on the region (open Mon.-Fri. 9am-5pm, Sat. 10am-2pm). Another tourist office, **ORBIS,** ul. Narutowicza 31/33 (tel. 22 256; fax 21 530), handles plane, train, and international bus tickets and books hotels (open May-July Mon.-Fri. 9am-5pm, Sat. 10am-2pm; Aug.-April Mon.-Fri. 9am-5pm). *Kantors* around town have the best rates for **currency exchange. Bank PKO S.A.,** ul. Królewska 1 (tel. 21 016), accepts traveler's checks (1% commission) and offers cash advances (MC and Visa; open Mon.-Fri. 7:30am-6pm, Sat. 10am-2pm). A **24-hour pharmacy** sits at ul. Krakowskie Przedmieście 49 (tel. 22 425; from 8pm-8am, ring the bell). The **post office,** ul. Krakowskie Przedmieście 50 (tel. 36 400), has **fax** service (fax 25 061), and **telephones** (open Mon.-Fri. 7am-9pm, Sat. 8am-9pm, Sun. 10am-5pm; phones open daily 24hr.). **Postal code:** 20-930. **Phone code:** 0-81.

Accommodations Rooms in Lublin are abundant and relatively inexpensive. In the summer, **university dorms** serve as lodging, though they are quite a trek from the center. The tourist offices (see above) have information about these rooms. The helpful staff of **Horyzont** (tel./fax 315 846), upstairs in the train station, makes hotel and camping reservations (5zł fee)—good German and a bit of English spoken (open Mon.-Fri. 10am-4pm, Sat. 10am-1pm). **Schronisko Młodzieżowe (HI),** ul. Długosza 6a (tel. 30 628), west of the center near the KUL, has friendly owners, a clean kitchen, and informal camping facilities. Walk to the end of the Saxon Garden, and turn right on ul. Długosza (lockout 10am-5pm; curfew 10pm; triples 8zł per person, dorm rooms 7zł; sheets 2.50zł). Centrally located on ul. Krakowskie Przedmieście 56, **Hotel Lublinianka** (tel. 24 261) will end your quest for clean bathrooms (singles 33zł, with bath 40zł; doubles 54zł; quads 88zł; quints 90zł). **ZNP Dom Noclegowy,** ul. Akademicka 4 (tel. 38 285), sits next to the KUL. From the bus stop at the Saxon Garden, cross the street and follow ul. Łopacińskiego, which becomes ul. Akademicka (communal bathrooms; singles 27zł; doubles 33zł; 6-person rooms 13zł per person).

Food Eating establishments are limited—Lublin's *rynek* is practically devoid of cafés or restaurants. However, there are numerous **grocery stores,** mostly along ul. Krakowskie Przedmieście. **Jazz Pizza,** ul. Krakowskie Przedmieście 55 (tel. 736 149), sports walls adorned with portraits of Dizzy Gillespie. They host jazz concerts and cook up one helluva jazzy pizza (5zł plus 1-2zł for extra toppings, salads 3zł; English menu; 15% discount to Canadians, eh; open Mon.-Sat. noon-10pm, Sun. 3:30-10pm). A modern variation of fast food, **Bar Deli Rood,** ul. Krakowskie Przedmieście 21, offers a choice of healthy salads and soups or platters (under 5zł; open Mon.-Sat.

10am-8pm, Sun. 10am-6pm). **Bar Staromiejski,** ul. Jezuicka 1, in the Old Town, serves up cafeteria-style food at the lowest prices in town—soups 1zł, *pierogi* 2zł (open Mon.-Fri. 8am-5pm, Sat.-Sun. 8am-4pm).

Sights The 19th-century ocher façades of **ul. Krakowskie Przedmieście** introduce the medieval **Stare Miasto** (Old Town). A stroll east from pl. Litewski with its **obelisk** commemorating the 1569 union of Poland and Lithuania and its **Tomb of the Unknown Soldier** leads to pl. Łokietka and the 1827 **Nowy Ratusz** (New Town Hall), seat of Lublin's government. To the right starts ul. Królewska with the grand **Katedra Św. Jana Chrzciciela i Jana Ewangelisty** (Cathedral of St. John the Baptist and St. John the Evangelist; 1586-96). The cathedral's frescos and gilded altar are worth the visit. To the left runs **ul. Lubartowska,** the main artery of pre-war Lublin's Jewish district. **Plac Ofiar Getta** (Victims of the Ghetto Square), on the left side of the street, centers around the **Monument to the Murdered Jews.** At #10 stands **Bożnica,** an early 20th-century synagogue, which was the only one in Lublin to survive the war. The synagogue and former rabbinical academy also houses **Izba Pamięci Żydów Lublina,** a museum dedicated to Lublin's Jewish community. Ul. Krakowskie Przedmieście travels straight through pl. Łokietka to the fortified **Brama Krakowska** (Kraków Gate), which houses **Oddział Historyczny Muzeum Lubelskiego** (Historical Division of the Lublin Museum), pl. Łokietka 3 (tel. 26 001; open Wed.-Sat. 9am-4pm, Sun. 9am-5pm). Across the gate, ul. Bramowa leads to the **rynek,** lined with early Renaissance houses. In the middle of the *rynek* stands **Stary Ratusz** (Old Town Hall); redone several times, it finally settled for the 18th-century Neoclassical style. A walk along ul. Grodzka leads through the 15th-century **Brama Grodzka** (Grodzka Gate) to ul. Zamkowa, which runs to the massive **Zamek Lubelski** (Lublin Castle). Most of the structure was built in the 14th century by King Kazimierz Wielki, but was restored in the 19th century with a neo-Gothic exterior. Inside the castle walls, **Muzeum Lubelskie** (tel. 25 001) features archaeological and ethnographic displays; its most prized possession is Jan Matejko's canvas of the signing of the Polish-Lithuanian treaty, which occurred in this castle.

Entertainment Thanks to a large student crowd, Lublin has an impressive number of cafés and pubs and an active music scene. The **Old Pub,** ul. Grodzka 8 (tel. 73 7127), serves whiskey (2.20-13zł), beer (2-7zł), *wino grzane* (heated wine with spices; 4.50zł), and cappuccino (3zł) inside on antique sewing machine tables, or outside under umbrellas (disco upstairs; open daily 11am-11pm). Wallpapered with Poland's most famous daily newspaper—Solidarity's *Gazeta Wyborcza*—the **Bauhaus Café,** ul. Świętoduska 20 (tel. 22 136), is an über-creative hang-out for painters and art students run by an art-history grad and her husband (open Mon.-Fri. noon-midnight, Sat.-Sun. 4pm-midnight). The **18 Hester Café,** ul. Okopowa 20 (tel. 736 670), in a cellar two blocks south of ul. Krakowskie Przedmieście, is packed with and run by students (open Mon.-Fri. noon-midnight, Sat.-Sun. 4pm-midnight). For a little disco-dancin', check out **Graffiti,** at Teatr Scena Ruchu, al. Piłsudskiego 13 (tel. 27 542; open nightly Fri.-Sat. 8pm-3am). **Hades,** ul. Peowiaków 12 (tel. 28 761; fax 25 641), is home to a hella good nightclub, café, and restaurant. There's also live music—listen to it backwards (open nightly 5pm-midnight).

■ Near Lublin: Majdanek

Majdanek, the largest concentration camp after Oświęcim (Auschwitz), saw the gruesome murder of 360,000 people. The former cellblocks now house exhibits chronicling the operations of this death factory. The path takes the visitor to the bath-house, gas chambers, prisoners' barracks, assembly area, and crematorium, ending at the **Mauzoleum,** where the ashes of murdered prisoners have been deposited. Seeing the whole camp takes one-and-a-half to two hours by foot. A brochure describing the camp, its history, and the exhibits is available in English (1.50zł; open daily 8am-3:30pm). The **State Museum at Majdanek** (tel. 42 647) was founded in 1944 after the liberation of Lublin (open May-Sept. Tues.-Sun. 8am-6pm; Oct.-April 8am-3pm). The information booth shows a 15-minute film with 1940s footage from the camp (available in English; last show 3pm; 2zł per person). From Lublin, eastbound **bus** #28 from the train station, **trams** #153 and 158 from ul. Racławickie, and southbound tram #156 from ul. Królewska all stop at the huge granite monument marking the entrance to Majdanek at Droga Męczenników Majdanka 67.

■ Zamość

Designed by the Italian architect Bernardo Morando, Zamość sprang up in the 1580s as the dream-come-true of a young aristocrat, Jan Zamoyski. Having studied in Padua, Zamoyski wanted to recreate its beauty in his homeland and succeeded in conjuring up a perfect town with a palace, town hall, opulent houses, churches, an academy, and an immense *rynek*. Touted by locals as the "Padua of the North," this Renaissance pearl seems more akin to 16th-century Italy than 20th-century Poland.

Orientation and Practical Information Turn right outside the **train station,** ul. Szczebrzeska 11, and walk toward the spires of the Old Town, or take a **city bus. Trains** (tel. 386 944) run to Lublin (4 per day, 3hr., 10zł) and Warsaw (3 per day, 5½hr., 19zł). **Buses** (tel. 384 986) shuttle faster, also to Lublin (34 per day, 2hr., 7.80zł) and Warsaw (5 per day, 5hr., 20.20zł). For a **taxi,** dial 385 050. From the **bus station,** ul. Sadowa 6, **city buses** #0, 16 and 22 depart from the same side of the street as the station and circle around the Old Town. Otherwise, it's a 25-minute walk along ul. Partyzantów. Bus #0 connects the stations. Kiosks sell public bus tickets (0.70zł). The **IT tourist office,** Rynek 13 (tel. 392 292; fax 708 13), in the town hall, sells maps and brochures on Zamość for 0.20-2zł (open Mon.-Fri. 7:30am-5pm, Sat.-Sun. 9am-2pm). **Bank PKO S.A.,** ul. Grodzka 2 (tel. 392 040), cashes traveler's checks and provides MasterCard and Visa cash advances (open Mon.-Fri. 8am-6pm, Sat. 10am-2pm). There is a **24-hour pharmacy:** Apteka Rektorska, Rynek 2 (tel. 392 386). The **post office** and **telephones** are at ul. Kościuszki 9 (tel. 385 123; open Mon.-Fri. 7am-9pm, Sat. 8am-1pm). **Postal code:** 22-400. **Phone code:** 0-84.

Accommodations and Food The hostel-like **Dom Turysty "Marta",** ul. Zamenhofa 11 (tel. 392 639), in the Old Town, rents rooms for 15zł per person. **Ośrodek Sportui Rekreacji,** ul. Królowej Jadwigi 8 (tel./fax 386 011), next to the stadium, offers singles (41zł), doubles (53zł), triples (63zł), and quads (73zł), all with baths. They also have dorm beds (18zł per person). **Camping** facilities can be found at ul. Królowej Jadwigi 14 (tel. 392 499), in a wooded area past the stadium. Four-bed bungalows with bathroom and fridge are 20zł per person. If you prefer soft grass beds, campsites are 2zł per person, and 6zł per day will rent you a tent.

The culinary experience in Zamość is rather limited. **Ratuszowa,** Rynek 13 (tel. 71 557), in the town hall, serves traditional Polish fare in a relaxed café setting. Soups run 2-3zł, while only 8.50zł will get you the most expensive entrée (open daily 10am-11pm). **Café-Restaurant Muzealna,** ul. Ormiańska 30 (tel. 386 494, ext. 40), is a similar establishment with tasty *pierogi* (4.50zł) and outdoor dining (open daily 10am-midnight). The **Cukiernia,** Rynek 12 (tel. 392 873), will satisfy your sweet tooth with ice cream (0.50zł per scoop) and pastries (0.70zł; open daily 10am-5pm). There is a **24-hr. grocery,** at ul. Łukasińskiego 11, although the many 9-hr. stores open during the day in the Old Town are better stocked.

Sights and Entertainment The whole town is a monumental sight, with its Renaissance layout, imposing **ratusz** (town hall), peaceful cobblestone *rynek,* and the surrounding houses with painted façades. Especially worth seeing are the splendidly preserved **Armenian burgher houses,** ul. Ormiańska 22, 24, 26, 28, and 30, in the northeast corner of the *rynek*. House #30 is the headquarters of the **Muzeum Okręgowe** (Regional Museum; tel. 386 494), which displays regional art, including Lusatian jewelry from 1000BCE (open Tues.-Sun. 10am-4pm; 1zł, students 0.50zł).

Peep into the **Katedra,** ul. Kolegiacka, to see A. Allori's *Annunciation.* The region's religious riches—chalices, monstrances, and saints' relics—pack the adjoining **museum** (open May-Sept. Thurs.-Mon. 11am-4pm; 0.50zł). You can also climb the cathedral's bell tower for a panoramic view of the Old Town (open daily 10am-4pm; 1zł, students 0.50zł). Diagonally across from the cathedral, **Muzeum "Arsenał",** ul. Zamkowa 2 (tel. 384 076), houses war trophies and military artifacts (open 10am-3:30pm; entrance closes at 3pm; 1zł, students 0.50zł). Pool tables abound in Old Town bars, and many residents and tourists head to the *rynek* for an evening *piwo;* unfortunately, the good times begin winding down before midnight. Jazz is available year-round at **Jazz Club Kosz,** ul. Zamenhofa 3 (tel. 386 041), enter from the back of the building. Named after a local jazz pianist, Mieczysław Kosz, this is a popular concert spot and artsy hangout (open daily 1pm-1am). In May, jazz musicians from Poland, Ukraine, and Belarus jam for the **Jazz na Kresach** (Jazz in the Borderlands) festival. September gathers jazz singers for the **Międzynarodowe Spotkania Wokalistów Jazzowych.** Every summer, the town echoes with life during **Zamojskie Lato Teatralne** (Theater Summer), when experimental groups perform in theaters and on the streets. Contact **Wojewódzki Dom Kultury (WDK),** ul. Partyzantów 13 (tel./fax 393 887) for info.

■ Łańcut

The palace-castle complex of luxurious Łańcut—**Zamek w Łańcucie**—entices visitors with a glimpse into the lavish lifestyle of Polish nobility past. However, the impressive museum is not all that the palace offers; the extensive park grounds surrounding it offer a peaceful and serene setting for a walk, or a shady spot to sit and relax. Your trip will be more enjoyable if planned with the weather forecast in mind. Founded by King Kazimierz III Wielki in the mid-14th century, the town was fortified in 1610-20 by the Lubormirski family, who acquired the castle after the death of Stanisław Stadnicki—the "Devil of Łańcut". Although the Baroque fortress passed the tests of Swedish and Turkish sieges, it failed to please Elżbieta Lubomirska z Czartoryskich, an 18th-century lap-dog-loving duchess with French tastes and an eye for fine art. Under her direction, the castle was transformed into an aesthetically amiable edifice. The Potocki family inherited the palace and continued to expand it. Spared damage in WWII, palace's soul left when the last Lord of Łańcut fled Poland in 1944, taking 11 railway cars full of valuable artifacts with him. The new government turned the complex into a museum. Today, the **museum** showcases the rooms, furniture, architecture, and artwork of the complex. You'll find the ticket office (tel. 20 08; fax 252 012) next to the tourist office. (Open April 18-Sept. 30 Tues.-Sat. 9am-2:30pm, Sun. 9am-4pm; Feb.1-April 17 and Oct.1-Nov. 30 Tues.-Sun. 10am-2:30pm; 6.30zł, students 3.80zł). The guided tour (included with admission) outfits visitors with felt-soled shoes, before making the rounds of the palace. After returning the shoes, the tour continues with the **Orańżeria** (Orangery), inside the palace grounds, and the **Powozownia,** the largest display of carriages in Europe. Outside the palace gates—and not on the tour—stands a **synagogue,** ul. Paderewskiego, with impressive 18th-century polychromy (open June-Sept. Tues.-Sun. 10am-4pm, or by request; 1zł). The palace also hosts the mid-May **Festiwal Muzyki** and the June **Kursy Interpretacji Muzyczne,** both bringing musicians from around the world to play on the splendid grounds.

Buses (tel. 21 21, info 33 35) run to Przemyśl (12 per day, 1½hr., 6.80zł). **Trains** (tel. 23 17) zoom to Kraków (9 per day, 2½hr.), Przemyśl (23 per day, 1hr.), and Warsaw (1 per day, 7hr.). The **bus station,** ul. Sikorskiego, opposite the palace gardens, is a 10-minute walk along ul. Kościuszki to the *rynek.* Turn right as you leave the station. To get to the palace from the **train station,** ul. Kolejowa, call a **taxi** (tel. 20 00), or head along ul. Żeromskiego, across from the station, then right on ul. Grunwaldzka (½hr.). To reach the *rynek,* turn right where ul. Grunwaldzka meets ul. Kościuszki. The **Trans-Euro-Tours tourist office,** ul. Kościuszki 2 (tel./fax 30 16), provides information on hotels, operates charter bus lines, and has a **kantor** (open Mon.-Fri. 9am-

5pm, Sat. 9am-1pm). **Postal code:** 37-100. **Phone code:** 0-17. When calling from outside Łańcut, dial 25 before each number.

The quiet **Hotel Zamkowy**, ul. Zamkowa 1 (tel. 26 71), in the palace park, attracts an international crowd. The rooms are clean and remarkably well priced (doubles 20-30zł, with bath 50-70zł; triples 30zł, with bath 60zł). **Dom Wycieczkowy PTTK**, ul. Dominikańska 1 (tel. 45 12), occupies the old Dominican monastery. All rooms have been recently renovated and the bathrooms sparkle with Mr. Clean, twice as bald and half as pious (doubles 12zł per bed, dorms 10zł per bed). The four basic food groups are all available at the **grocery**, ul. Paderewskiego (open Mon.-Sat. 8am-8pm, Sun. 10am-6pm). **Restauracja Zamkowa**, ul. Zamkowa 1 (tel. 28 05), in the palace, fries up tasty potato pancakes with cream (4zł) in stately dining halls the color of clear *barszcz* (1zł; open daily 9am-10pm).

KARPATY (THE CARPATHIANS)

The Polish Carpathians attract millions of visitors each year, luring Poles and foreigners alike with great hiking and skiing. Karpaty's varied terrain—from the rounded hills of the Bieszczady in the east and Beskidy in the west to the sky-rocketing Tatry in the middle—offers recreational possibilities to satisfy every fancy. With armies of street stalls selling home-made everything, Tatran folklife hits visitors straight in the face. But to acquaint yourself with the locals' real world, don't confine your stay to touristy Zakopane; explore the gentler, less-frequented slopes in the east and west.

■ Sanok

The cultural and economic hub of the Bieszczady, Sanok sits proudly atop a hill, confident in its rich artistic heritage. Under Communism, much of the wealth of rural churches was looted and brought to Sanok. The icon museum houses priceless pieces of local religious art, and the open-air museum recreates village life destroyed by war and time. Sanok is also the ideal base for trips into the nearby mountains.

Orientation and Practical Information The **train** and **bus stations**, linked by an overpass, are a 15-minute hike from the *rynek*. **Trains**, ul. Dworcowa (tel. 30 516), huff to Kraków (4 per day, 18.30zł); and **buses**, ul. Lipińskiego, puff to Kraków (4 per day) and Przemyśl (8 per day). **Buses** #3 and 4 will take you near the center. A detailed map is posted across from the train station. To walk to the center, go left on ul. Dworcowa (facing the map), which will become ul. Kolejowa. Go right at the intersection with ul. Lipińskiego, which becomes **ul. Jagiellońska.** After a steep hill, the latter curves to the right and eventually turns into **ul. 3-go Maja** which heads straight into the *rynek*. **Ul. Kościuszki**, which houses banks, grocery stores, and the post office, jets out where ul. Jagiellońska meets ul. 3-go Maja. **PTTK**, ul. 3-go Maja 2 (tel./fax 32 512), sells maps and offers info on sightseeing in the area (open Mon.-Fri. 8am-4pm). **Bank PKO S.A.**, ul. Kościuszki 12, cashes traveler's checks and gives MasterCard and Visa cash advances (open Mon.-Fri. 8am-6pm, Sat.10am-2pm). If you're looking to **exchange** cash, *kantors* have the best rates. The **Mountain Rescue (GOPR)** headquarters is at ul. Mickiewicza 49 (tel. 32 204). The **post office** sits at ul. Kościuszki 26 (tel. 30 382; open Mon.-Fri. 7am-8pm, Sat. 8am-2pm, Sun. 9-11am). **Postal code:** 38-500. **Phone code:** 0-137.

Accommodations and Food Staying overnight in Sanok will cost a bit, but the rooms are all good value for the money. The fastidious owners of **Hotel Jagielloński**, ul. Jagiellońska 49 (tel. 31 208), near the station, some of the cleanest and most dignified rooms in town—spacious, fitted with oriental carpets, bathrooms, telephones, and TVs (singles 40zł, doubles 50zł, triples 65zł). If you've always wanted to know what Communist color coordination was all about, visit **Hotel PTTK**, ul. Mickiewicza 29 (tel. 31 013). This hotel offers a tourist office and midget baths in each room. To get here, take bus #0 from the stations and get off when the bus turns onto ul. Mickiewicza (singles 36zł; doubles 54zł; one double with bunkbeds 30zł). Hotel Błonie's **campground,** Aleje Wojska Polskiego 1 (tel. 30 257; fax 31 493), a 15-minute walk or a short ride on bus #0 from the train station, is set amid stadium lights to the right of the road and offers sites by the San River (3.40zł per person, tent rental 2.80-3.40zł per night; open June 15-Sept. 15).

While **grocery stores** abound—perfect for those stocking up for hikes—restaurant selection is quite limited. Traditional Polish cuisine in an upscale setting can be found at **Restaurant Max,** ul. Kościuszki 34 (tel. 32 254). Their selection is large and affordable entrées (3-9zł; open daily 10am-10pm). **Restauracja Jagiellońska,** at the hotel, is slightly more expensive, but not unreasonable (entrées 5-10zł). It lures clients with specialties such as Gypsy pork chop (8.30zł) as well as impeccable service (open daily noon-midnight). The **grocery store** with the longest hours is **Delta,** ul. Kościuszki 6 (tel. 36 808; open Mon.-Sat. 6:30am-8pm, Sun. 9am-5pm).

Sights and Entertainment Muzeum Historyczne, ul. Zamkowa (tel. 30 609), in the **zamek** (castle), is a must. The three-room **Muzeum Ikon** houses 15th to 19th-century Ukrainian icons and religious artifacts from the surrounding region. The adjoining **gallery** exhibits the surrealist works of local painter Beksiński—highly reputed throughout Poland (open Mon. 9am-3pm, Tues.-Sun. 9am-5pm; 2zł, students 1.50zł). Sanok's **churches** are also worth peeping into, especially on a Sunday, when they get mystical in a drone of ritual chants. The walls of the 14th-century **parish church,** in the *rynek,* still echo with the marriage vows of King Władysław Jagiełło—the founder of one of medieval Europe's most powerful dynasties.

The **Skansen** (Ethnographic Museum), 2km north of town and across the river San, recreates the village life of the region's main ethnic groups: the Łemks and Boyks. It surely rates among Europe's best open-air museums. A pleasant walk, the museum can also be reached by bus #3 from the *rynek.* Get off immediately after the bus crosses the river, take a sharp right onto ul. Rybickiego, and follow the signs to the Skansen (open May-Oct. daily 8am-6pm; Nov.-March 9am-2pm; April 9am-4pm; 2.50zł). While wandering around the site, make sure to visit the 150-year-old schoolhouse displaying old textbooks and maps.

Before dusk, the **Park Miejski** has outstanding views of the city and the valley. From the *rynek,* go southwest on ul. 3-go Maja, turn right on ul. Piłsudskiego, and follow it until the end. Or, enter the park next to the post office.

From Sanok, buses run regularly to the popular **hiking** destinations in the Bieszczady Mountains. The friendly staff at the information desk at Hotel PTTK (see above) will eagerly help to plan a trip to Ustrzyki Górne, Wetlina, Komańcza, or Solina Lake. They have maps, as well as information detailing accommodations and hiking routes. In the winter, cross-country and downhill skiers can be accommodated as well. Not to be missed is the **Bieszczady Park Narodowy,** with its well preserved forests and diverse flora and fauna. Included within the park is the highest peak in the Bieszczady, **Tarnicza,** which rises to an elevation of 1346m.

■ Zakopane

Zakopane is Poland's premier year-round resort. European tourists flock here for the Tatras's scenery and sporting opportunities without the inflated prices of Switzerland's Alps. Set in a valley surrounded by sky-high jagged peaks and soul-stirring alpine meadows, Zakopane buzzes with hikers and skiers clambering to be a part of the great outdoors. The streets are lined with local merchants selling everything from leather jackets to Russian army hip flasks.

KARPATY (THE CARPATHIANS)

ORIENTATION AND PRACTICAL INFORMATION

The **bus** and **train stations** lie across **ul. Jagiellońska** from each other, next to the street's intersection with **ul. Kościuszki**. It is a 10- to 15-minute walk west along the tree-lined ul. Kościuszki to the center and the perpendicular **ul. Krupówki**—the restaurant and shop hub. For Slovakia border crossing info, dial 662 65.

Tourist Offices: Centrum Informacji Turystycznej (IT), ul. Kościuszki 17 (tel. 12 211; fax 66 051), at the intersection with Sienkiewicza. They sell maps, brochures, and booklets and arrange private accommodations in town (20zł per person; open daily 7am-9pm). **ORBIS,** ul. Krupówki 22 (tel./fax 12 238). Sells plane, ferry, and bus tickets and organizes trips. The staff also cashes traveler's checks and provides MasterCard and Visa Gold cash advances with a maximum withdrawal of 300zł (tel. 14 609). Open June-Oct. Mon.-Fri. 8am-6pm, Sat. 9am-3pm; Easter-May and Nov.-Dec. 19 Mon.-Fri. 9am-5pm. **PTTK Biuro Usług Turystycznych,** ul. Krupówki 12 (tel. 15 848; fax 12 429). Arranges excursions of the Tatras. Guided tours in English: 4-hr. 20-120zł, full-day 180-345zł. Open in high season Mon.-Fri. 8am-4pm, Sat. 8am-2pm, Sun. 8am-noon; off-season closed Sun.
Currency Exchange: Bank PKO S.A., ul. Gimnazjalna 1 (tel. 68 505), north of and parallel to ul. Kościuszki (near the bus station). Cashes traveler's checks for 0.5% commission and offers Visa advances. Open Mon.-Fri. 8am-6pm, Sat. 10am-2pm.
Trains: ul. Chramcówki 35 (info tel. 14 504; daily 9am-9pm). To: Bielsko-Biała (dir. "Sucha Beskidzka"—20 per day, 3¾hr., 8.60-10zł); Kraków (26 per day, 2½-4hr., 9.30zł); Warsaw (4 per day, 7-10hr., 14.80-18.40zł).
Buses: ul. Kościuszki 25 (info tel. 14 603). To: Budapest (1 per day, 9hr., 25zł); Kraków (every 30-90min., 2½hr., 9zł); Poprad, Slovakia (5 per day, 2½hr., 8zł); and Warsaw (1 per day, 8hr., 23.20zł).
Taxis: Radiotaxi, tel. 919.
Bike Rental: Ital-Pol, ul. Piłsudskiego 4a (tel. 14 423). Rents Italian mountain bikes. 3zł per hr., 10zł for 4hr., or 25zł per day. Open Mon.-Fri. 10am-6pm.
Luggage Storage: At the train station 1zł per piece per day. Open 24hr. except 1-1:30pm. At the bus station, 1.5zł per piece per day. Open daily 8am-7pm.
Pharmacy: ul. Krupówki 39 (tel. 63 331). Open daily 8am-8pm.
Mountain Rescue Service: ul. Piłsudskiego 63a (tel. 63 444).
Hospital: ul. Kamieniec 10 (tel. 12 021).
Post Office: ul. Krupówki 20 (tel. 12 277). Open Mon.-Fri. 7am-9pm, Sat. 8am-2pm, Sun. 9am-11am. **Postal code:** 34-500.
Telephones: ul. Zaruskiego 1, near the post office. **Phone code:** 0-165.

ACCOMMODATIONS AND CAMPING

Since Zakopane sits at the summit of mountain tourism in Poland, it is crowded from July September, around Christmas, during the winter break in February, and around Easter. Prices skyrocket in high seasons by 50-100%. **IT** (see Tourist Offices, p. 460) is a popular source of private rooms and pensions (20-40zł per person). Or unload luggage at one of the stations and prowl around the town and its outskirts looking for **"pokój"** (private room) signs (10-15zł, with some haggling). Hikers often stay in **schroniska** (mountain chalets), but call ahead in the summer to avoid being stranded in the middle of nowhere with no roof over your head.

PTTK Dom Wycieczkowy, ul. Zaruskiego 5 (tel. 63 281). A large chalet in the very center of the town. Spacious rooms and reasonably clean bathrooms with 24-hr. hot water. Singles with bath 22zł. Doubles with bath 32zł. 4- to 8-bed rooms 9-10zł per head. 12- to 28-person dorms 8zł per person.

Schronisko Młodzieżowe (HI), ul. Nowotarska 45 (tel. 66 203). Walk down ul. Kościuszki toward the center, then take the 2nd right onto ul. Sienkiewicza and walk 2 blocks. The hostel sits across the street. Small rooms in a large, loud building. Showers open daily 5-10pm. Curfew 11pm. Doubles 17.50zł per person. Triples 16.50zł per person. Dorms 11.50zł. Breakfast included. The required HI card may be purchased for US$2 per night.

Student Hotel "Żak", ul. Marusarzówny 15 (tel. 15 706), in the south part of town on the Biały Potok stream close to all hiking trails. About 30min. from the train and bus stations. Head south on ul. Jagiellońska; after about 15min. turn right on ul. Witkiewicza which turns into ul. Kazimierza. Take a left on ul. Grunwaldzka, and follow ul. Marusarzówny to the end and around the bend. Small, fresh rooms with thin mattresses; only 2 toilets and 2 showers for as many as 50 guests. Hot water, except in the evenings. 6- to 8-bed rooms 10zł per person, with ISIC 9zł.

Schronisko Morskie Oko (tel. 77 609), by the Morskie Oko lake. A gorgeous, clean hostel in an ideal location—you won't mind the trek to the scenic lake. Both bunk and single beds available. 3- to 6-bed rooms 28zł per person. Reservations a must.

Camping Pod Krokwią, ul. Żeromskiego (tel. 12 256), across the street from the ski jump's base. From the train station, head south on ul. Jagiellońska; at the church, make a quick right on ul. Witkiewicza and an immediate left on ul. Chałubińskiego. Follow ul. Czecha from the roundabout, and turn right on ul. Żeromskiego. Bungalows 17zł per person, with shower 19zł. Hotel rooms 22zł per person, with shower 25zł. Tents 5-8zł plus 6.50zł per person, students 5.10zł; Off-season group discounts negotiable; prices expected to go up after June 1997.

FOOD

Highlanders sell the local specialty, *oscypek* (goat cheese) on street corners. From a distance, the salty cheese resembles carved wood, up close it looks like a little roll. Vendors have a poor reputation for refrigeration; watch out for anything that might spoil. For other supplies, head for **La Croissanterie**, ul. Krupówki 11, which has bread and sandwiches for 0.95-3zł (open Mon.-Sat. 9am-9pm, Sun. 10am-9pm); the grocery store **Delikatesy**, ul. Krupówki 41 (open daily 7am-8pm); or its competitor across the street, **Baca** (open daily 7am-10pm).

U Wandy, ul. Sienkiewicza 10. Heading northwest on ul. Kościuszki, turn right on ul. Sienkiewicza and walk to the footbridge on the left. Follow the bus driveway on the right. The menu is short, but the servings are so immense and tasty that guests need help getting up. The small-of-stomach should ask for half-portions. *Gołąbki* 5zł. Chicken cutlet 8zł. Open Tues.-Sun. 2-6pm.

Karczma Redykołka, ul. Kościeliska 1 (tel. 66 332), at the north end of ul. Krupówki. Irresistible tourist haunt fashioned after the traditional mountain huts. Food served by waitstaff in regional costumes. Veal 8.50zł. Open daily 10am-9pm.

Kolorowa, ul. Krupówki 26 (tel. 12 519). Delicious *pierogi* 6zł. Regional specialties such as *kotlet zakopiański* (pork stuffed with ham and veggies) 10-13zł. Pizzas 6-10zł. Live folk music some evenings. Open daily noon-midnight.

Karczma Obrochtówka, ul. Kraszewskiego 10a (tel./fax 63 987). Head southeast on ul. Krupówki, and continue when it merges with ul. 3-go Maja. After passing ul. Makuszyńskiego to the right, ul. Kraszewskiego is the first alley on the right. Worth the search for its fabulous kitchen and folk atmosphere, complete with candles and conversation. Soups 3-5zł. Entrées 4-15zł. Open daily noon-10pm.

ENTERTAINMENT

Chata Zbójnicka (Chateau Bad Night), ul. Jagiellońska, is by far the best place for raucous and intoxicating mountain nights. Five minutes south of the train station, a gravel path takes off to the left and leads directly up to the music-filled mountain house. The only way to be let in is to kick the door loud enough that the doorkeeper decides you're sufficiently hardy to endure an evening in the *chata*. He may tell you to go away on your first try. The more attitude you throw back, the more welcoming he'll be. A folk band provides dance music, and the staff serves a tea so potent its fumes alone will raise your spirits (8zł). Don't be surprised if the waiters tell their guests to serve or cook their own food—or if someone leaves with his tie cut off or with her face smeared with charcoal (open daily 7pm-midnight).

The **Antałówka Sports Center**, ul. Jagiellońska (tel. 63 917), offers hot springs for sore skiers, as well as tennis courts and a swimming pool in summer (day pass 9zł, students 5zł; open daily 6am-10pm). July ushers in the **Days of Karol Szymanowski's Music,** and August, the international **Festival of Highlanders' Folk Music.**

HIKING

Short mountain hikes are a specialty of **Tatrzański Park Narodowy** (Tatran National Park), whose entrances lie at the head of each trail (1zł, students 0.50zł; keep your ticket). For dramatic vistas, catch a bus to **Kuźnice,** (every 20min., 0.90zł) south of central Zakopane. Or walk along ul. Jagiellońska, ul. Chałubińskiego, or ul. Przewodników Tatrzańskich from the train station, and hop on the **Kasprowy Wierch** cable car. (Open July-Sept. daily 7am-6:30pm; June 7:30am-6:10pm; March-May and Oct. 7:30am-5:40pm; Dec.-Feb. 8am-4pm. Roundtrip 17zł, students 11zł.) Before hiking, buy the map *Tatrzański Park Narodowy: Mapa turystyczna* at a kiosk or bookstore (see Essentials: Wilderness and Safety Concerns, p. 49, for hiking info). For an overview of the Tatras, see the map in the Slovakia chapter, p. 650.

Giewont (1090m, 4½hr.): Giewont's silhouette looks like a man lying down, hence the mountain's starring role in so in many legends as the "Sleeping Knight." A traipse along the 6km-long moderately-hard blue trail leads to the peak. Begin at the lower chair-lift station in Kuźnice, and follow signs to the peak along Holy Brother Albert's Road and Piekło (Hell). Chains rooted into the rock help with ascending the final meters of the trail.

Morskie Oko (Sea Eye; 1406m, half-day): The mountain lake Morskie Oko dazzles herds of tourists who overrun it every summer; take a bus from Zakopane's bus station (11 per day, 45min., 2zł) to Polana Palenica (Burnt Clearing), a.k.a. Łysa Polana (Bald Clearing), then hike an easy 8km along the road (2hr. each way).

Czerwone Wierchy (Red Peaks; 2122m, 1 day): The red trail leads west from the top of the cable car at Kasprowy Wierch (see above) along the ridge separating Poland and Slovakia. If you tire quickly, 4 of the 7 peaks along the way have paths descending to Zakopane. From the last peak, Ciemniak, the trail descends to the exit of Dolina Kościeliska, connected to Zakopane in the east by bus.

Gubałówka (1120m): Go up a cable car north of the town center (3zł, students 1.50zł). Hike down (25min.) or walk to Butorowy Wierch and take a chairlift down to get a view of Zakopane and the slopes of Gubałówka (2.50zł).

Dolina Pięciu Stawów Polskich (Five-Lake Valley): One of the most beautiful hikes in the area. The 14-hr. summer-only option departs from Kuźnice and leads along the blue path to Hala Gąsienicowa, with Schronisko Murowaniec where hikers refuel, then Czarny Staw (Black Tarn). On the incline to Zawrat, you'll get to climb hand over hand up the chains. Another *schronisko* waits at Przedni Staw (Front Tarn), in the Five-Lake Valley, which shelters those exhausted by the hike or charmed by the scenery. The blue trail ends 200m north (sounds easy but it's several steep climbs and descents) at Morskie Oko, where you can eat, drink, or spend the night (see Accommodations, p. 460). From the lake, a road travels down to Łysa Polana, connected to Zakopane by bus. A shorter version of the hike (6-8hr.) begins at Łysa Polana. Head in the direction of Morskie Oko (see above). A green path takes off to the right about 45min. into the hike, after the waterfall Wodogrzmoty Mickiewicza and a parking lot. This heads to Dolina Pięciu Stawów Polskich. Once you reach Wielki Staw (Great Tarn), head east towards Przedni Staw and follow the trail up and down to Morskie Oko.

Rysy (2499m, 8hr.): To claim you've climbed Poland's highest peak, follow the red trail from Schronisko Morskie Oko (see Accommodations, p. 460) along the east lakeshore and up to Czarny Staw (Black Tarn). The arduous climb to Rysy begins in the tarn's southeast corner. Only for the fittest, and only in good weather.

Dolina Kościeliska (half-day): An easy and lovely hike crosses in a valley of Potok Kościeliski. A bus shuttles from Zakopane west to Kiry (every 40min.-2hr., 1zł), where a green trail takes off south toward Hala Smytnia and continues to Mała Polanka Ornaczańska. The valley makes a good biking route as well.

Dolina Chochołowska (Mulch Valley; 1 day): Take the westbound trail from the entry to Dolina Kościeliska, which turns south into the Mulch Valley after 3.5km. The trail follows Potok Chochołowski along an easy climb to a clearing.

■ Near Zakopane: Przełom Dunajca

A relaxing trip to the legend-packed Przełom Dunajec (Dunajec Gorge) suits those no longer craving Tatran thrills. The two- to three-hour float includes a Polish guide who navigates the cliff-bounded waterways, crossing the Polish-Slovak border for 1km of the ride. The sturdy wooden rafts avoid the rapids, and the guides wear traditional costumes. Look out for the place where the Slovak Robin Hood, Janosik, purportedly jumped 12m from bank to bank. The seven large stone slabs on the hill supposedly represent seven priests, turned to stone because of their trysts with a holy sister. Around the bend, the nun's silhouette is carved in the middle of a cliff.

The **rafts** travel from Sromowce to Szczawnica. Rafts run daily May to October. Tickets cost 19zł per person and per bag over 5kg (tel. (0-187) 50 221; office open May-Aug. daily 9am-4:30pm; Sept. 9am-3pm; Oct. 9am-2pm). A direct **bus** goes to Sromowce from Zakopane at 9am and another at 1:35pm (1½hr., 4.80zł). To catch a direct bus back to Zakopane (4 per day, 2hr., 6.80zł), walk 20 minutes down the riverside road to ul. Manifestu Lipcowego, which runs to the bus terminal.

■ Bielsko-Biała

Bielsko-Biała offers two of everything. A composite of two towns that used to belong to two duchies, it's one of the only places in Poland where two religions—Catholicism and Lutheranism—thrive. Thanks to its history of religious tolerance, Bielsko-Biała, the pre-war home of dynamic Jewish and German minorities, has always prospered. Today, the city proudly proclaims to travelers using it as a base for trips to the Beskidy mountains that it is "traditionally rich."

ORIENTATION AND PRACTICAL INFORMATION

Bielsko-Biała has two hearts: the Bielsko castle and center in the west and the Biała *rynek* in the east, a 10-minute walk apart along **pl. Chrobrego** and **ul. 11-go Listopada**. The train and bus stations are 15 minutes north of the Bielsko center along **ul. 3-go Maja,** the main thoroughfare. In-Tour lies right next to the bus station at **ul. Piastowska's** intersection with ul. 3-go Maja; ORBIS is opposite Hotel Prezydent.

- **Tourist Offices: In-Tour,** ul. Piastowska 2 (tel./fax 122 406). Cramped, but the staff are outgoing and helpful. They sell brochures and maps of the city and region (2-6zł). Open Mon.-Fri. 8am-5pm, Sat. 8am-noon. **ORBIS,** ul. 3-go Maja 9a (tel. 123 261; fax 20 784). Deals in international ferry, bus, and plane tickets; helps find hotels; and gives out maps and brochures. Open Mon.-Fri. 8am-6pm, Sat. 9am-2pm.
- **Currency Exchange: Bank PKO S.A.,** ul. 11-go Listopada 15 (tel. 127 231). Cashes AmEx, Thomas Cook, and Visa traveler's checks at 1% commission (minimum 5zł), and offers MC and Visa cash advances. Open Mon.-Fri. 7:30am-6pm, Sat. 9am-1pm. *Kantors* are primarily concentrated along ul. 11-go Listopoda.
- **Trains:** ul. Warszawska 2 (tel. 128 040, info 933), at the north end of ul. 3-go Maja. To: Bratislava (1 per day, 5½hr., 80.30zł); Katowice (27 per day, 1½hr., 4.70zł); Kraków (4 per day, 2¾hr., 7.30zł); Warsaw (4 per day, express 4hr., 31.30zł); Zakopane (2 per day, 12.90zł).
- **Buses:** ul. Warszawska 5 (tel. 123 125, info 228 25). Near the train station. To: Kraków (18 per day, 2¼hr., 8.20zł); Oświęcim/Auschwitz (4 per day).
- **Bookstore: "Pod Orłem",** ul. 11-go Listopada 60 (tel. 123 056), in an arcade. Magazines and books in English, French, German, Italian, and Spanish. Open Mon.-Fri. 10am-6pm, Sat. 10am-2pm.
- **Pharmacy: "Pod Św. Franciszkiem",** ul. Piastowska 4 (tel. 121 475). Open Mon.-Fri. 8am-6pm, Sat. 8am-1pm.
- **Mountain Rescue: GOPR,** ul. Armii Krajowej 220 (tel. 123 611).
- **Medical Assistance:** ul. Wyspiańskiego 21 (tel. 122 045).
- **Post Office:** ul. 1-go Maja 2 (tel. 151 001; fax 21 050). Open Mon.-Fri. 7am-8pm, Sat. 7am-1pm. **Poste Restante** at window #8. **Postal code:** 43-300.
- **Telephones and Fax:** At the post office. **Phone code:** 0-33.

ACCOMMODATIONS AND FOOD

Hotels are limited and spread out, but budget accommodations can be unearthed. **PTTK Dom Wycieczkowy,** ul. Krasińskiego 38 (tel. 123 019), 5 minutes from the bus station, rents spacious rooms and white-tiled bathrooms. Look for the stately green-and-white building to the left of ul. Piastowska (curfew 10pm; lockout 10am-6pm; doubles 35zł, with bath 50zł; triples 45zł, with bath 75zł; 5- to 7-bed dorms 13zł per person; sheets included). **Pod Pocztą** (Under the Post Office), ul. 1-go Maja 4a (tel./fax 124 730), just past the post office off ul. 3-go Maja, maintains decent but dark rooms with sinks (clean communal bathrooms; singles 40zł; doubles 50zł). **Youth Hostel "Bolka i Lolka",** ul. Komorowicka 25 (tel. 127 466), is a short walk off ul. 11-go Listopada. Populated by a younger crowd, these 8-person rooms go for 12zł per person (sheets 2zł; curfew 9pm; lockout 10am-5pm).

Restaurants abound around the central ul. 11-go Listopada. For a reasonably good meal at the lowest price in the town, try the **Bar mleczny** at the PTTK hostel (see above). Meals run under 6zł (open Mon.-Fri. 8am-6pm, Sat. 8am-4pm). **Restauracja Starówka,** pl. Smołki 5 (tel.122 424), off ul. 3-go Maja, displays a diverse menu in Polish and English, and dabbles in Polish, French, and Chinese cuisines. It's a bit pricey, but not unreasonable—drink in the screamingly bright Mardis Gras decor (entrées 8-15zł; open daily 10am-11pm). Bustling with a young crowd, **Pizzeria Margerita,** ul. Cechowa (tel. 125 161), off ul. 11-go Listopada, serves up pizzas (4-10.50zł) and a garden of salads (3zł; delivery available; open Mon.-Fri. 11am-11pm).

SIGHTS AND ENTERTAINMENT

Bielsko's modest 14th-century **castle** stands above pl. Chrobrego, though the entrance is located on its south end at ul. Wzgórze 16 (tel. 125 353). Its museum houses a collection of European paintings and sculptures. (Open Tues.-Wed. and Fri. 10am-3pm, Thurs. 10am-6pm, Sat. 9am-3pm, Sun. 9am-2pm. 1zł, students 0.50zł.) The simple, early 20th-century **Katedra Św. Mikołaja** (St. Nicholas's Cathedral), pl. Mikołaja 19 (tel. 124 506), just south of the castle, got bumped up from provincial church status only a few years back, when the pope fashioned the local parish into a bishopric. The grounds of **Kościół Ewangelicko-Augsburski** (Lutheran Church), pl. Lutra 8 (tel. 127 471), just northwest of the castle, feature Poland's only **statue of Martin Luther.** Bielsko's **Old Town,** just west of the castle, is perfect for strolling, with its crowded narrow streets and galleries. The grandest view of all, though, spreads along the main thoroghfare, **ul. 3-go Maja.** Thanks to the 19th-century architecture along the street, Bielsko has been likened to Vienna, despite a dreary Communist brown-gray color darkening many of the façades.

The tall towers of **Kościół Opatrzności Bożej** (Providence Church), ul. Ks. Stojałowskiego 64 (tel. 144 507), south of central Biała, are easily spotted. Peek in at its Baroque interior, and don't miss the small gold pulpit showing Jonah bidding the whale farewell. The **ratusz** (town hall), two blocks south of ul. 11-go Listopada next to the Biała stream, is a striking piece of Historicist architecture, modeled after a medieval hall. The portals in the northeast corner of the square merit a closer look.

In the south suburb of **Mikuszowice,** a grove of trees conceals the wooden **Kościół Św. Barbary,** ul. Cyprysowa 25 (tel. 145 481), typical of the Beskidy area. This well preserved 17th-century church also houses wall paintings depicting the story of St. Barbara. From the train station, take a southbound bus #2 and get off at Mikuszowice.

The repertoire of the experimental **Puppet Theater "Banialuka",** ul. Mickiewicza 20 (tel. 121 046), off pl. Chrobrego's northwest corner, ranges from folk tales to world literature (performances Wed.-Fri. 11am and 1pm, Sun. 4pm; closed during tours and July-Aug; every 8th show designed for adults; tickets 4zł). Across from the theater, relax at **Café Dziupla,** ul. Mickiewicza 15. This cellar pub offers a pool table as well as drinks and music (open Mon.-Fri. 11am-11pm, Sat.-Sun. 4pm-11pm). **John Bull Pub,** ul. 11-go Listopada 60/62 (tel. 1216 61), in Biała's second square just south of its main *rynek*, pours imported British beer, as well as the locally brewed *Tyskie* (0.4L for 2.8zł; open daily 11am-midnight).

For mountain thrills, hop on southbound bus #8 at the stop opposite the train station. At the end of the line, the road continues to a new high-tech **gondola,** ul. Armii Krajowej 366 (tel. 144 481; open May-Aug. daily 9am-5:30pm; Sept.-April 9am-4:30pm), which whisks vista-seekers up **Szyndzielnia** (1026m).

■ Szczyrk

A mouthful for the English tongue (mumble a "sh" sound with an "rk" at the end), Szczyrk's name comes from the sound that the Żylica stream makes as it passes through town—or so say the legends. Offering more hiking, mountain biking, ski jumping, and ski lifts than any other retreat in Poland, Szczyrk is a year-round tourist destination, and the second largest winter resort in the country.

Orientation and Practical Information Szczyrk is tucked away in a valley of the **Beskid Śląski** mountains, the westernmost part of the Carpathians. Frequent **buses** (43 per day, ½hr., 1.70zł) connect the town to Bielsko-Biała. The town stretches for 8km along the **Żylica,** although most services are concentrated in the 2km **Centrum** area. Bus stops line the main thoroughfare. Take the bus to "Szczyrk Centrum", and then go left on ul. Beskidzka for the **tourist office** at ul. Beskidzka 41 (tel./fax 178 187). They offer detailed mountain biking and skiing info, as well as **maps** of the town and hiking trails (open in summer Mon.-Fri. 8am-4pm, Sat. 9am-2pm; off-season Mon.-Fri. 8am-8pm, Sat. 9am-6pm). **Exchange currency** at **Bank PKO,** ul. Beskidzka 12 (tel. 178 358; open Mon.-Fri. 10am-4:30pm). There is a **pharmacy** at ul. Beskidzka 69. For those whose skills and precautions fail them, **GOPR,** a **mountain rescue** operation, is reachable at ul. Dębowa 2 (tel. 178 986). A **post office** with ringing **telephones** sits at ul. Beskidzka 101 (open Mon.-Fri. 7am-8pm, Sat. 8am-1pm, Sun. 9-11am). **Postal Code:** 43-370. **Phone code:** 0-30.

Accommodations and Food Lodgings span the entire range of hotels, hostels, pensions, and private rooms. Unfortunately, Szczyrk's restaurants are limited to the same, plus kiosks. To stock up on food before hiking, skiing, or biking, stop by the 24-hour grocery **Delikatesy,** ul. Beskidzka 4 (tel. 178 585). **Beskidy,** ul. Myśliwska 4 (tel. 178 878), offers rooms for 9-12zł, with shower 16-20zł, though prices are slightly higher in winter. Only a 10-minute walk from the center of town, **Dom Turysty PTTK,** ul. Górska 7 (tel. 178 321; fax 178 979), at the "Szczyrk PTTK" bus stop, rents its two-, three-, and four-person rooms with bath for 20zł per person. Farther from the town and the main hiking/skiing trails but connected by frequent buses to "Szczyrk Skalite" is **Camping Skalite,** ul. Campingowa 4 (tel. 178 760). Tent sites go for 5zł per person, tents for 3.50-5.50zł. Bungalows come in the usual permutations: doubles 32zł, with bath 41zł; triples 41zł, with bath 55zł. (Discount for longer stays. Reception open daily 8am-7pm.)

Sights and Hiking Although these mellow mountains flank both sides of the town with their own trails, most activity is focused on **Skrzyczne,** the highest peak in the region (1257m), and as unpronounceable as its namesake town. Ski lifts ascend the slopes of Skrzyczne and its neighbor, **Małe Skrzyczne** (1211m); many well marked **hiking** and **mountain biking** trails aim for the peak of Skrzyczne. For a full view of possible paths, buy a map or check-out the boards at the intersection of ul. Górska and ul. Beskidzka. The flatter bike trails are marked by circles; the steeper, hiking-only trails by lines. The longer green trails start by these signs at the base, while the more challenging red and blue trails begin by the "Szczyrk Kolejka" stop.

Szczyrk is an equal opportunity mountain, and the views from the top can be had by even the laziest traveler. From the base near the "Szczyrk Kolejka" bus stop, a **chair lift** operates, whisking panorama-pursuers to their destination. The lift, ul. Myśliwska 45 (tel. 178 620; fax 178 662), has two sections: upper and lower. Each part costs 2zł, making the full roundtrip 8zł. The lift operates daily from 9am-6:30pm.

Of the many **caves,** the most famous is **Jaskinia Malinowska** (Malinowski Cave). On the slopes of Malinowska Skała at an elevation of 1005m, the caves contain 132m of passageways—legend has it that in this maze, a treasure was hidden by the 16th-century outlaw Ondraszek—keep your eyes open. Take the bus to "Szczyrk Salmopol", and then follow the green trail. Taking the green trail from Szczyrk Centrum, you'll reach the cave—but only after climbing Skrzyczne, Małe Skrzyczne, Kopa Skrzyczeńska (1189m), and Malinowska Skała (1152m). For general info on hiking, see Essentials: Wilderness and Safety Concerns, p. 49.

DOLNY ŚLĄSK (LOWER SILESIA)

West of Kraków, Górny (Upper) Śląsk became Poland's industrial heartland when uncontrolled Five-Year Plans tore out the land's coal, iron, and zinc, and replaced these resources with heavy pollution. Farther west, Dolny Śląsk managed to confine heavy industry, protecting its castles and Sudety mountain spas. Both the Śląsks' collieries provided initial support for the Solidarity movement but, after the initial rush are now experiencing unemployment and stagnation. Fortunately, the heavy influx of German tourists coming to visit—and sometimes reclaim—the farms and tenement houses of their parents manages to keep the area economically afloat.

■ Wrocław

Wrocław, the capital of Lower Silesia, straddles the Odra River. Since the city's elaborate postwar reconstruction, only photographs recall the city's destruction in WWII, when it became Festung Breslau under the Nazis, one of the last battle grounds *en route* to Berlin. Recently, a similar post-communism restoration has been undertaken. Wrocław charms visitors with its many bridges, lush parks, and 19th-century buildings, which give this vast, yet graceful city an antique feel.

PRACTICAL INFORMATION

The political and social heart of Wrocław is its **rynek** (marketplace), site of the main tourist office. The **train** and **bus stations** are 15 minutes southeast, and cheap accommodations cluster by the train station. To get to the *rynek* from the bus station, cross **ul. Sucha,** and go through the station to the main entrance on **ul. Piłsudskiego.** Check out the **map** of the city at the train station's entrance. Then take ul. Piłsudskiego and turn right on **ul. Świdnicka,** which leads to the *rynek.*

Tourist Office: IT, ul. Rynek 14 (tel. 441 109; fax 442 962). Well stocked with useful maps. Answers all questions—well, almost all questions. Open in high season Mon.-Fri. 9am-5pm, Sat. 10am-2pm.

Budget Travel: ALMATUR, ul. Kościuszki 34 (tel./fax 443 951), in the student center "Pałacyk". Info about student hostels, ISICs, and international bus tickets. Youth fare bus tickets available here. Open Mon.-Fri. 9am-4pm, Sat. 10am-2pm.

Currency Exchange: At *kantors* throughout the city and in the trains station. **Bank PKO S.A.,** ul. Oławska 2 (tel. 444 454), cashes traveler's checks and gives MC and Visa cash advances. Open Mon.-Fri. 8am-6pm, Sat. 10am-6pm.

24-Hour ATM: Wielkopolski Bank Kredytowy, pl. Kościuszki 7/8 (tel. 443 241). Connected to the Plus and Visa networks.

Flights: Airport LOT, ul. Skarżyńskiego 36 (tel. 570 734 or 573 959). Students get 50% off domestic flights, seniors 20%. Open Mon.-Fri. 8am-6pm, Sat. 9am-3pm. A LOT shuttle operates between the office and the airport 50min. before domestic departures, 1½hr. before international, or take bus #406 from the train station. To: Frankfurt (1 per day; 1½hr.; roundtrip 786zł, student 655zł); Warsaw (3 per day, 1hr., 160zł).

Trains: ul. Piłsudskiego (tel. 360 31 or 360 35, infotel. 663 333). A true traveler's center with a 24-hr. exchange booth, pharmacy, and many eateries. Counters #17 and 18 deal with international links. To: Berlin (2 per day, 5½hr.); Budapest (1 per day, 12hr.); Dresden (3 per day, 4½hr.); Kraków (14 per day, 4hr., 18.90zł); Poznań (18 per day, 1¾hr., 15zł); Prague (3 per day, 6½hr., 60zł); Warsaw (10 per day, 5hr., 22.20zł). 24-hr. **luggage storage:** 5zł per day.

Buses: ul. Sucha 1 (tel. 610 177 or 617 256), behind the trains. To: Kraków (destination "Krosno"; 1 per day, 7hr., 23zł); Poznań (2 per day, 3hr., 14.50zł); Warsaw (4 per day, 8hr., 16zł); also connections to the West. Open daily 5am-11pm.

Public Transportation: Trams and **buses.** Tram #0 goes round in circles, so you can never really get lost. Tickets cost 1zł (students 0.50zł) per person and per backpack. A 1-day pass is also available (5zł).

Taxis: tel. 919, 633 737, or 210 303.

Car Rental: Hertz, ul. Rynek 29 (tel. 343 33 71; fax 447 946). A 5-seater costs up to 700zł per day with unlimited mileage. Open Mon.-Fri. 8am-4pm, Sat. 10am-2pm.
Avis, ul. Piłsudskiego 46 (tel. 723 567; fax 343 09 28). 3-day rental with unlimited mileage and insurance starts at 720zł. Open Mon.-Fri. 9am-5pm, Sat. 9am-1pm.

Pharmacy: ul. Kościuszki 53 (tel. 443 032). Open Mon.-Fri. 8am-9pm, Sat. 9am-3pm.

Medical Assistance: ul. Krasickiego 17a (tel. 481 819). Private doctors. Open 24hr.

Post Office: ul. Małachowskiego 1 (tel. 441 717; fax 447 419), to the right of the train station. Open Mon.-Fri. 7am-8pm, Sat. 9am-3pm. **Postal code:** 50-415.

Telephones: At the post office. Open 24hr. **Phone code:** 0-71.

ACCOMMODATIONS

Biuro Usług Turystycznych "Odra-Tourist", ul. Piłsudskiego 98 (tel. 343 00 35; fax 343 78 93), opposite the train station, finds private singles for 26zł and doubles for 43zł (open Mon.-Fri. 8:30am-5pm, Sat. 8:30am-2pm).

Youth Hostel (HI), ul. Kołłątaja 20 (tel. 33 856), directly opposite the train station on the road perpendicular to ul. Piłsudskiego. Fills up quickly due to its small size and prime location. Lockout 10am-5pm. Curfew 10pm. Doubles 13.70zł per person, with HI card 11.75zł. 6- to 7-bed rooms 13.10zł per person, with HI card 11.30zł. Sheets 2zł; baggage storage 0.50zł per day.

Hotel Piast, ul. Piłsudskiego 98 (tel. 343 00 33), near the train station. Clean. For a quieter stay, request a room that does not face ul. Piłsudskiego. With sinks: singles 27zł, doubles 55zł, triples 63zł, quads 77zł. Breakfast 7zł.

Hotel Podróżnik, ul. Sucha 1 (tel. 732 845), above the bus station. Comfortable rooms extremely convenient to both the bus and train stations. New as of summer '96. Doubles with bath 40zł. Triples with bath 50zł.

Dom Nauczyciela, ul. Nauczycielska 2 (tel. 229 268; fax 219 502). Take tram #4 from in front of Hotel Piast (direction "Biskupin") or #0 to plac Grunwaldzki, the 2nd stop after a large bridge. Go left off plac Grunwaldzki, and then turn left again at the gas station. Friendly reception. Communal bathrooms. Singles 29zł. Doubles 35.31zł. Triples 44.94zł. Quads 53.50zł. Quints 64.20zł.

Camping Stadion Olimpijski, al. Paderewskiego 35 (tel. 484 651). Take tram #17 from the train station and get off at the stadium. 5.35zł per person. Tents 1-2zł per person. Bungalow doubles 20zł, quints 8zł per person.

FOOD

There are two **24-hour grocery stores: U Pana Jana,** pl. Solny 8/9 (tel. 343 56 85), close to the *rynek;* and **Lokomotywka,** ul. Piłsudskiego 103 (tel. 343 31 56), across from Hotel Piast.

Bar Vega, ul. Rynek Ratusz 27a (tel. 443 934). 2 modern, spiffy floors of fast veggie relief. The menus differ by floor—head upstairs for an international flair. Even with a glossary, the imaginative dishes' names are hard to decipher. Full meal under 5zł. Spicy Japanese rice 2.50zł. Open Mon.-Fri. 8am-7pm, Sat.-Sun. 9am-5pm.

Bar Miś, ul. Kuźniczna 48 (tel. 342 49 63). The polar bear on the sign outside points the way to this bargain cafeteria. The crowds are a sure sign of its popularity. Savor a full meal for 4-5zł. Open Mon.-Fri. 7am-6pm, Sat. 8am-5pm.

Spiż, ul. Rynek Ratusz 9 (tel. 446 856 or 447 225; fax 445 267). Restaurant and microbrewery. Beer lovers lounge in this cool shelter on hot summer evenings. A frothy 0.5L of *Spiż* runs 4.30zł. The menu goes wild with Mexican *platos,* such as beef tortillas at 10zł. Prize-winning ox tongue in beer sauce 10zł. Gazpacho 5.50zł. Restaurant open daily noon-midnight; beer cellar open daily 10am-2am.

Tutti-Frutti, pl. Kościuszki 1/4 (tel. 444 306). Endless list of ice-cream desserts (3.50-8zł). Tortes 3-5zł. Bakery open Mon.-Sat. 9am-8pm, Sun. 9am-6pm. Restaurant open daily 10am-10pm. Take-out ice cream open daily 10am-11pm.

SIGHTS

The oldest neighborhood of Wrocław, **Ostrów Tumski** (Cathedral Island) ages peacefully across the river from the center next to the **Botanical Gardens,** ul. Sienkiewicza 23 (open Mon.-Fri. 8am-6pm, Sat.-Sun. 10am-6pm). The stately **Katedra Św. Jana Chrzciciela** (Cathedral of St. John the Baptist) gives this section its dignified character. Inside the cathedral, a nun shows you the amazing marble **Kaplica Św. Elżbiety** (Chapel of St. Elizabeth; donations suggested). Climb up the tower for a phenomenal view of the surrounding churches (open daily 10am-3:30pm; 3zł, students 1zł). The modern heart of the city, **Stare Miasto,** showcases the Renaissance and Gothic **ratusz** (city hall) on **Rynek Główny** (Main Market Square) and contains the **Historical Museum** (tel. 441 434). One exhibit focuses entirely on ul. Świdnicka, a street in central Wrocław so beautiful that the Germans tried to have its stones moved to their soil. Take time to look at the collections of armor and old silver, including an amazing scepter (open Wed.-Fri. 10am-4pm, Sat. 11am-5pm, Sun. 10am-6pm; cashier closes ½hr. earlier; 3zł, students 1.5zł, Wed. free).

The **University** occupies much of the city north and west of the *rynek.* A center for cultural life in the city, it contains architectural gems, the most impressive of which is **Aula Leopoldina.** This 18th-century lecture hall with its magnificent ceiling frescos is on the second floor of the main University building, pl. Uniwersytecki 1 (open Thurs.-Tues. 10am-3:30pm; 2.50zł, students 1zł).

East of the Old Town lies the **Muzeum Panoramy Racławickiej,** ul. Purkyniego 11 (tel. 442 344; fax 33 639). Its 120m by 15m *Panorama Racławicka* recounts the 18th-century peasant insurrection led by Kościuszko against the Russian occupation. Originally painted and displayed in Lviv in 1894, it was transplanted to Wrocław at the end of WWII, along with most of the city's residents. Head north from the *rynek* on ul. Kuźnicza and turn right on ul. Kotlarska, which becomes ul. Purkyniego (open Tues.-Sun. 8am-5pm; 9zł, students 4zł). Tickets are also valid for the **Muzeum Narodowe** (National Museum), pl. Powstańców Warszawy 5, in the dignified brick building across the street. Check out the medieval Silesian paintings and sculptures, 16-19th-century graphic art, and paintings by Canaletto and Grottger (open Tues.-Wed., Fri., and Sun. 10am-4pm, Thurs. 9am-5pm, Sat. 10am-5pm; 3zł, students 2zł).

The **Jewish Cemetery,** ul. Ślęzna 37/39, in a park, has recently been opened to the public. Pay your respects to famous citizens such as Ferdinand Lasalle and the family of Thomas Mann's wife (open only Sun. noon; 3zł). To reach the cemetery take tram #9 from the train station heading away from the center.

Wrocławskie Zoo, ul. Wróblewskiego 1, has gained its fame by torturing its feathered and fuzzy collection less than most zoos in Poland. Take tram #2 or 4 from the train station (dir. "Biskupin") and get off at ul. Wystawowa, next to a massive hall on the left (open daily 9am-6pm; cashier closes at 5pm; 3zł, students 2zł).

ENTERTAINMENT

In the city's south area, **Operetka** (ul. Piłsudskiego 72; tel. 343 56 52), **Teatr Polski** (tel. 343 87 89), and **Filharmonia** (ul. Piłsudskiego 19; tel. 442 001) are all on the same stretch of ul. Piłsudskiego. The month of May brings the international **Jazz nad Odrą** festival to Wrocław. Tickets are available at clubs **Pałacyk** (see below) and **Rura,** ul. Łazienna 4 (tel. 442 410), Wrocław's resident jazz club. Many student clubs are the places to go for live music.

Kawiarnia "Pod Kalamburem", ul. Kuźnicza 29a (tel. 447 528), in the theater building in the university area. A decadent, Art Nouveau artists' corner (read: spiffy keen). A large cup of viscous caffeine 2.50zł. Open Mon.-Sat. 10am-11pm, Sun. 4pm-11pm. Piano concerts every Fri. and Sat. at 9pm.
Night Club "Reduta", ul. Piotra Skargi 18a (tel./fax 723 522), at the end of ul. Teatralna. This popular new disco has danced its way into the late night scene. Could it be because there's no cover? Open nightly 9pm-5am.
Pałacyk, ul. Kościuszki 34 (tel. 38 094). A student disco, cinema, and billiard hall. Movie showings posted in the entrance hall. Billiards open daily 3pm-late. Disco open Sun.-Thurs. 10pm-2am, Fri.-Sat. 10pm-5am. Cover charge Fri.-Sat. 5zł.
Studnia, ul. Szewska 19 (tel. 343 15 13). A small pub near the university which expands its operation to 2 floors when school is in session. *Piast* 2.50zł per 0.5L). Open Mon.-Fri. 4pm-midnight, Sat.-Sun. 2pm-midnight. Concerts Oct.-June.
Internet Café "Baza", ul. Oświęcimskich 17 (tel. 445 431, ext.136; http://www.printy.wroc.pl). The local on-ramp to the information superhighway, and of course, beer and coffee. Computer usage, including e-mail (9.50zł per hour, students 7.50zł). Open Mon.-Fri. 9am-10pm, Sat.-Sun. noon-10pm.

In northeast Wrocław, the **Morskie Oko beach,** ul. Chopina 27 (tel. 482 717), has kayaks, tennis and volleyball courts, and a weight room (open daily 9am-7pm). There are three indoor **swimming pools,** ul. Teatralna 10 (tel. 441 656), in a pre-war building in the center of the town. The relaxing **Park Szczytnicki,** with the Japanese house on water, lies in the east part of the city.

■ Jelenia Góra

In Poland's southwest corner, the land buckles along the Czech border to form the Sudety mountains. The crisp air and mineral springs in the Jelenia Góra valley have provided a welcome respite for centuries of city dwellers, including Goethe, Marysieńka Sobieska, and Sienkiewicz. At the foot of the Karkonosze range (part of the Sudety), Jelenia Góra makes a perfect starting point for treks to loftier hiking, skiing, and cure-seeking. The charming Old Town has banned cars, and the renovated turn-of-the-century façades are some of the best preserved in the region.

Orientation and Practical Information The **Old Town** is ringed by a street that in the north and west bears the name **ul. Podwale,** and in the south, **ul. Bankowa.** The **train station,** ul. 1-go Maja 77 (tel. 23 936), 15-20 minutes east of town, sees trains off to Warsaw (1 per day, 8hr., 25zł) and Wrocław (7 per day, 3hr., 8.60zł). Most **buses** have a stop at the train station. The main **bus station,** ul. Obrońców Pokoju 16 (tel. 24 815), 10 minutes northwest of town, sends buses to Wrocław (often with a different final destination—check; 4 per day, 3hr.). From **ul. Obrońców Pokoju** head left out of the station, upon reaching the main ul. Podwale turn right, and make another left shortly on **ul. Jasna.** This comes to a T—take a quick left onto **ul. Grodzka** before continuing right on ul. Jasna, which travels to **pl. Ratuszowy.** If you remain on ul. Jasna, it turns into **ul. Konopnickiej,** and then **ul. 1-go Maja.** The **IT tourist office,** ul. 1-go Maja 42 (tel. 25 114; fax 24 054), is another 300m on the right. Well equipped with brochures, maps (2-4zł), and advice; the staff's German is better than their English (open Mon.-Fri. 8am-6pm, Sat. 8am-4pm, Sun. 9am-3pm). **Bank Zachodni,** ul. Bankowa 5/7 (tel. 25 407; fax 22 749), does Visa cash advances and cashes traveler's checks (open Mon.-Fri. 8am-5pm). The **post office,** ul. Pocztowa 9/10, lies 5 minutes south of ul. 1-go Maja (open Mon.-Fri. 7am-9pm, Sat. 9am-3pm, Sun. 9am-11am). **Telephones** are next to the post office (open Mon.-Sat. 7am-9pm, Sun. noon-5pm). **Postal code:** 58-500. **Phone code:** 0-75.

Accommodations If visiting both Karpacz and Jelenia Góra, consider staying in Karpacz, where hotels are cheaper. The cramped **Youth Hostel Bartek,** ul. Bartka Zwycięzcy 10, (tel. 25 746), off ul. Kochanowskiego two streets south of the train station, charges 8zł per bed. **Hotel Sudety,** ul. Krakowska 20 (tel. 29 300), has reasonably priced rooms close to the trains. Go left when leaving the station (singles 26.75zł, with bath 53.50zł; doubles 39.59zł, with bath 85.60zł; triples 50.29zł; quads 55.64zł). The clean and spacious **Hotel and Camping Park,** ul. Sudecka 42 (tel. 26 942; fax 26 021), 15 minutes southeast of town on the road to Karpacz, hides in a petite, pretty park (doubles 45zł, triples 50zł; tent sites 6.42zł per person, tents 4-6zł).

Food Relax beneath the gleaming-white arches of the pl. Ratuszowy arcade at one of three restaurants that rub shoulders on the square's west side. **Pokusa** (Temptation), #12 (tel. 25 347), and **Retro,** #14 (tel. 24 894), offer traditional Polish food; while **Smok** (Dragon), # 15 (tel. 25 928), prepares Chinese dishes. A meal at any one of these will cost about 10-20zł. Many cafeteria-type establishments on ul. 1-go Maja provide faster, cheaper options. For a cheapo feast, **Karczma Staropolska,** ul. 1-go Maja 33 (tel. 22 350), serves tavern chow for 4-8zł (open daily 8am-9pm). Excite your palate with a zesty Hungarian menu at **Tokaj,** ul. Pocztowa 6 (tel. 24 479), across from the post office, where entrées sizzle at 10-15zł (open daily 10am-10pm). **Kawiarnia Hortus,** pl. Ratuszowy 39 (tel. 26 968), brews a great cup o' joe (2-3zł) and chills cool ice cream concoctions (2-5zł; open daily 9am-8pm).

Sights and Entertainment The uniformity of the unassuming **pl. Ratuszowy** façades appears odd. Originally constructed at the turn of the 17th century, after the Thirty Years War, the market square had the fortune to survive WWII without any major damage. Recent renovation has only enhanced the Baroque appearance of the building. In the middle of all this, the 1747 **ratusz** (town hall) displays its unadorned Classicist architecture.

The many churches are worth a couple *Hail Marys.* Several steps northeast of the square, the **Church of St. Erasmus and Pancras** (tel. 22 160) becomes visible at pl. Kościelny 4. This basilica-style church boasts an elaborate 22m by 11m altar. At the intersection of ul. Konopnicka and ul. 1-go Maja, the locked **St. Anne's** is worth a glance as it originally formed part of the 16th-century town defenses. The 18th-century **Kościół Św. Krzyża** (Holy Cross Church), down ul. 1-go Maja, sits in a walled park. Built in the form of a Greek cross, the 1717 Baroque pulpit is composed of three pieces of limestone. The Michael Roeder **organ** here is one of Poland's largest.

To escape the crowds, an hour-long walk along the green-yellow path away from the bus station leads to the relaxing gorge, **Perła Zahodu** (Pearl of the West). Lose yourself in the amazing views over the reservoir and the silence that fills the air.

A lovely half-day trip to the south suburb of **Sobieszów,** 5 miles away, involves taking bus #7, 9, A, or B from the train station or from ul. Bankowa (every ½hr., 20min., 0.80zł—buy the ticket in the kiosk) and getting off after the bus turns right at Restaurant Pokusa. Head back and follow the signs to Chojnik across the river and south along dirt paths. The 14th-century **Zamek Chojnik** (Chojnik Castle) atop a wooded hill is the destination, left in ruins by a 17th-century lightning bolt. The red trail (45min.) is steeper and rockier than the half-hour blue and green routes. The castle tower offers stupendous views of the mountain ranges (open daily 9am-5pm; 1.20zł, students 0.60zł). If you've planned the trip two weeks in advance, you can stay at **Schronisko PTTK "Chojnik"** (58-570 Jelenia Góra-Sobieszów; tel. 53 535), within the castle, whose primary allure is location (10.20zł per person). The castle hosts the September **Knights' Crossbow Tournament.**

Other festivals in Jelenia Góra include the May 1st **Antiques and Oddities Market,** which crams pl. Ratuszowy with all sorts off odds and ends sheltered from daylight for centuries. The July week-long **InternationalStreet Theater Festival** fills the town's narrow streets with open-air performances of juggling and general clowning around. Starting at 16zł, **Aeroklub,** ul. Łomnicka (tel. 26 020), sends the adventurous gliding over the valley, and for 22-34zł per person, it loads groups of 3-12 into small airplanes and introduces them to the region from another angle.

Karpacz

The flies—non-biting—outnumber the Germans who outnumber the local Poles in this resort in the Karkonosze mountains. Winter tourists flock for the thrills of skiing, while summer rewards hikers with panoramic views above the treeline. Mineral springs and hang-gliding are not far off, and the town's many tourist establishments will delight your every culinary whim. The main draw, however, is the raw beauty of the landscape, especially Śnieżka (the highest peak in the Sudeten Mountains).

ORIENTATION AND PRACTICAL INFORMATION

The town meanders uphill from the train station along **ul. 3-go Maja**. Walking to the upper end of town by Wang Chapel takes 1½ hours and limber quads. Although there's no main **bus** station, buses stop at regular intervals along the hill. To get to a **tourist office**, get off at the first stop after the train station ("Karpacz Bachus") and either go uphill to the Karpacz tourist office or downhill to the IT.

Tourist Offices: Karpacz, ul. 3-go Maja 52 (tel. 619 547; fax 618 558). Exchanges currency, arranges private rooms for 20zł, and makes reservations at the town's pensions and hotels. Open Mon.-Fri. 9am-5pm, Sat. 9am-2pm. **IT,** ul. 3-go Maja 25a (tel./fax 619 716). A friendly, German-speaking bunch. Lots of brochures and maps (3zł). They organize private rooms for 15-25zł per person. Open Mon.-Fri. 10am-8pm, Sat. 10am-6pm, Sun. 10am-4pm.

Currency Exchange: Only a few *kantors*. **Bank Zachodni,** ul. 3-go Maja 43 (tel./fax 619 252), cashes traveler's checks at US$6 commission. Open Mon.-Fri. 8am-6pm.

Trains: ul. Kolejowa 1 (tel. 619 684). To: Jelenia Góra (4 per day, 35min., 1.80zł). **Luggage storage** 3zł; insurance 0.15zł per 10zł.

Buses: To: Jelenia Góra (17 per day, ½hr., 2.50zł).

Equipment Rental: Szkoła Górska Przewodnictwa i Narciarstwa, ul. Obrońców Pokoju 6a (tel. 619 711; fax 619 353), about 5min. off ul. 3-go Maja near the base of town. **Bikes** for groups of 5 or more 15zł per person per day. Mountain guides 100zł for 5hr. Horses 12zł per hr. Ski equipment 22zł, Feb. and Easter 30zł; ski instruction 30zł per hr., 130zł per day. Rock-climbing equipment 16zł; rock-climbing instruction 25zł per hr. In short, if you have a recreational need, these are your gurus. Reserve 2 weeks in advance. Open daily 9am-4pm.

Pharmacy: Pod Złotą Wagą, ul. 3-go Maja 82 (tel. 619 312). Open daily 9am-8pm.

Post Office: ul. 3-go Maja 24 (tel. 619 220; fax 619 585), opposite the IT office. Open Mon.-Fri. 7am-9pm, Sat. 9am-3pm, Sun. 9-11am. **Postal code:** 58-540.

Telephones: The telephone office is just uphill from the Karpacz tourist office. Open Mon.-Fri. 9am-9pm. All phones in Karpacz use **magnetic cards.** These can be bought at the telephone office as well as from most kiosks. **Phone code:** 0-75.

ACCOMMODATIONS AND CAMPING

Private rooms and **pensions** proliferate. The cost of an average pension (30-40zł) includes all meals, but hotels can be much cheaper options. Unfortunately, some of them are only open part of the year—inquire at the IT.

D.W. Szczyt, ul. Na Śnieżkę 6 (tel. 619 360), at the uphill end of town next to the Wang Chapel. Take the bus to "Karpacz Wang". At 860m, with views of the valley, Mt. Śnieżka, and the church, these comfortable rooms rule. Make reservations with the Karpacz tourist office. Clean communal bathrooms. 15zł per person.

FWP Piast, ul. 3-go Maja 22 (tel. 119 244), downhill across the street from the IT. Spacious singles, doubles, and triples, that err on the side of brown. Reasonably clean communal bathrooms. Free ping-pong. 15zł per person. With meals 30zł.

Dom Pegaz, ul. Karkonoska 17 (tel. 264), across from the "Karpacz Pegaz" bus stop. Ul. Karkonoska is the uphill continuation of ul. 3-go Maja. A newly renovated, modern, sparkling operation. Singles 15zł, with bath 30zł. Doubles 28zł, with bath 50zł. Triples 39zł, with bath 72zł. Quads 48zł, with bath 92zł.

Camping Pod Brzozami, ul. Obrońców Pokoju, off ul. 3-go Maja. Follow the signs toward Hotel Skalny. 5zł per person. 2-person tent 4zł, 6-person tent 6zł.

FOOD

Tourists not pressured into taking meals at their hotel can opt to taste the food at another pension or at one of the few operations catering solely to the palate. Downhill from the tourist bureau Karpacz, signs point down ul. Kościelna to **Wrzos** (Heather), ul. Kościelna 5c (tel. 618 160). Delicious, homemade Polish dishes fill the menu. Chicken cutlets run 5.50zł, and pork medallions with mushrooms 7zł (open daily noon-6pm). **Astra,** ul. Obrońców Pokoju 1 (tel. 619 314), just uphill from the IT, serves up large, finger-licking-good meals at slightly higher prices. Potato dumplings with meat and salad go for 6zł, chicken steak with fries and salad 10zł, spaghetti 6zł (open daily 9am-10pm). The grocery store **"Delikatesy",** ul. 3-go Maja 29 (tel. 619 259), stocks everything necessary to prepare a lunch for that dayhike to the mountains (open Mon.-Sat. 9am-9pm, Sun. 10am-6pm).

SIGHTS AND HIKING

Świątynia Wang (Wang Chapel), ul. Śnieżki 8 (tel. 228), is by far the town's most unexpected and wonderful draw. This Viking church was built in South Norway at the turn of the 12th century. In the early 1800s, it direly needed restoration no one could afford, so Kaiser Friedrich Wilhelm III of Prussia, out of his love for architecture, had it transported to Karpacz to serve the Lutheran community here. Gaping dragons' mouths, stylized lions, and intricate plant carvings ornament the temple. Organ concerts are held here on Saturday evenings in summer; check the schedule at the ticket office (open in summer Mon.-Sat. 9am-6pm, Sun. 11:30am-6pm; off-season Mon.-Sat. 9am-5:30pm, Sun. 11:30am-1pm; tours 1.80zł, students 0.90zł).

The main question visitors ask here is not where you're hiking to, but how you're getting there. Hikers of all ages aim for the crown of **Śnieżka** (Snow Mt.; 1602m), and there are several ways of getting there. Śnieżka and most of the trails lie within the **Karkonoski Park Narodowy** (1-day entrance fee 1zł, students 0.50zł; 3-day pass 2zł, students 1zł). To make it as quickly and painlessly as possible, take the **Kopa chair lift** from ul. Strażacka, just south of ul. Karkonoska, or follow the black trail from Hotel Biały Jar until you see the lift on the left (open daily 8:30am-5:30pm; one-way 7zł, students 5zł; roundtrip 10zł, students 8zł). From the top of the chair lift, the hike to the summit takes about one hour.

A longer and less crowded trek starts at Wang Chapel. Follow the blue route 50 minutes up to **Polana** (1080m) and then another 40 minutes up to the scenic **Mały Staw** lake. From here, it's 35 minutes to **Spalona Strażnica** (Burnt-down Guardhouse) and then an easy 25 minutes to the **Pod Śnieżką** pass (1394m). The ascent to the peak takes another 30 minutes (total 3hr.).

Another way to avoid crowds as thick as the swarms of flies involves taking the red path up from behind Hotel Biały Jar's parking circle. It's the most difficult ascent once you emerge above the tree line, but is still very manageable. Reaching Pod Śnieżką takes 1½ hours, and the summit rises another 20-30 minutes away.

Endurance hikers are usually rewarded by following the blue trail from the Wang Chapel to Polana, then the yellow path 25 minutes to the odd stone formations **Pielgrzymi** (Pilgrims; 1204m), and continuing along the yellow route to another petrified protrusion at **Słonecznik** (Sunflower; 1423m). Turning left here, the red trail travels to Spalona Strażnica and Pod Śnieżką (1hr.), one mound from Śnieżka.

There are two routes from Pod Śnieżką to the very top. The red "Zygzag" shoots straight up the north side—look for the cobbled path (20-30min.). The blue-trail road, "Jubilee Way," winds around the peak (30-45min.). Once there, climbing to the **observatory,** which looks like a building straight out of *The Jetson's,* costs 1zł, students 0.50zł (open daily 10am-5pm). The lure of most of these hikes lies in the expansive views when above the treeline. Be prepared for strange winds. See Essentials: Wilderness and Safety Concerns, p. 48 for tips on keeping healthy while hiking.

ROMANIA
(ROMÂNIA)

US$1	= 3161 lei (ROL)	1000 lei =	US$0.32
CDN$1	= 2302 lei	1000 lei =	CDN$0.43
UK£1	= 4926 lei	1000 lei =	UK£0.20
IR£1	= 5120 lei	1000 lei =	IR£0.20
AUS$1	= 2491 lei	1000 lei =	AUS$0.40
NZ$1	= 2197 lei	1000 lei =	NZ$0.46
SAR1	= 710 lei	1000 lei =	SAR1.41
DM1	= 2135 lei	1000 lei =	DM0.47

Country Phone Code: 40   International Dialing Prefix: EU: 00; USA: 011

Ensconced within the mysterious Carpathian Mountains, the fortified towns of Transylvania still look like an array of medieval woodcuts, and the green hills of Moldova remain as serene as the frescos on monastery walls. Here, in the surviving unspoiled villages, rural Romanians preserve folk traditions which the rest of Europe discarded centuries ago. The country's stains—ruined, soot-blackened towns and decades of forced resettlement in urban industrial nightmares such as Bucharest—date from the days when Romania was the poorest and most totalitarian country in the Soviet Bloc. Many of its tragedies and leaders remain; for the tourist, Romania is still untamed and unexplored, from the monasteries to the Danube Delta.

ROMANIA ESSENTIALS

Americans do not need a visa for stays of up to 30 days. Citizens of Australia, Canada, Ireland, New Zealand, South Africa, and the U.K. all need visas to enter Romania. Single-entry visas (US$22) allow for a two-month visit, and multiple-entry visas (US$68) for a six-month stay; a transit visa (US$22) is valid for four days. Obtain a visa at a Romanian embassy (see Essentials: Embassies and Consulates, p. 8) or at the border for no additional fee. To apply, submit a passport, payment by money order, and a letter stating the type of visa needed. Get a visa extension at a local police station.

GETTING THERE

You can **fly** into Bucharest on Air France, Alitalia, AUA, Delta, Lufthansa, Swissair, or TAROM. **TAROM** (Romanian Airlines) is currently trying to renew its aging fleet. So far, a few Airbuses and Boeings have been acquired, and TAROM flies direct from Bucharest to New York, Chicago, and to most major European cities. The recent renovation of the Otopeni International Airport has improved the notoriously bad ground services, but the airport is still far from ideal.

Daily **trains** head from Bucharest via Budapest to Munich and Vienna. There are also direct trains to and from Chișinău, Moscow, Prague, Sofia, and Warsaw. To buy **international tickets** in Romania, go to the **CFR** (Che-Fe-Re) office in larger towns. Budapest-bound trains leave Romania through either Arad or Oradea; when you buy your ticket, you'll need to specify where you want to exit. It is now possible, although complicated, to pay for international train tickets in lei. In this case, you will be given a special receipt at the counter saying how much you have to pay. You must change money at a nearby bank or bureau and then return with the validated receipt. An ISIC entitles you to discounts on international tickets throughout Eastern Europe, and if you're lucky, a 50% discount on domestic tickets. In any case, as a foreigner you'll pay twice as much as a Romanian on any international fare. The fine for being caught with a Romanian ticket eliminates any money you saved by being sneaky, so don't even think about it.

Buses connect Bucharest and Constanța to Athens, Istanbul, Prague, Varna, and various cities in Western Europe. Since plane and train tickets in Romania are often expensive, buses are often a good, if slow, option. Inquire at major tourist agencies about timetables and tickets. Buses depart from major Romanian cities.

GETTING AROUND

CFR sells domestic **train** tickets up to 24 hours before the train's departure. After that, only train stations sell tickets, generally only an hour before the train leaves. There is an info desk at the station (staffers will not necessarily speak English), where you can inquire about which counter sells tickets to your destination. Knowing the number of the train you want is crucial; get a copy of the train timetable *Mersul Trenurilor* (4000 lei; instructions in English and French). **Interrail** is accepted.

There are four **types of trains**: *InterCity* (indicated by an "IC" on timetables and at train stations), *rapid* or *expres* (in green), *accelerat* (red), and *de persoane* (black or blue). *InterCity* trains stop only at major cities such as Bucharest, Cluj, Iași, and Timișoara, and have two digits. *Rapid* trains have three-digit train numbers and are the next fastest. *Accelerat* also have three digits, but are slightly slower and dirty; and *de persoane* have four digits, are downright slow and dirty, and stop at almost all stations. The even slower *cursă* trains are also indicated by four-digit codes and stop at every single stop. The price differential between **first class** (*clasa-întîi*, wagons marked with a "1" on the side, 6 people per compartment) and **second class** (8 people per compartment) is small, but the comfort and security difference is significant. You should travel first class whenever taking an *accelerat* or slower. Second class is decent on a *rapid* or *expres*. If taking an **overnight train,** opt for first class in a *vagon de dormit* (sleeping carriage). During holiday periods or for all July and August trips to the beach, try to purchase tickets at least five days in advance.

Use the extensive local **bus** system only when trains are not available. Although buses cost about the same as trains, they are usually packed and poorly ventilated. Look for signs for the *autogară* (bus station) in each town.

Domestic flights use Soviet-made An-24 **airplanes.** Domestic flights connect Bucharest (Băneasa Airport, closer to downtown than Otopeni) to all major cities around the country. Foreigners are charged twice as much as Romanians. Fares here are still lower than in the EU, however. TAROM has a good safety record.

Hitchhiking, though popular, remains risky; *Let's Go* does not recommend it. Hitchers report that it works best in the mountains and Transylvania. A wave of the hand, rather than a thumb, is the recognized sign. Drivers generally expect a payment similar to the price of a train ticket for that distance for giving you a lift. Thus, it is really not worth the risk to hitch.

TOURIST SERVICES

ONT (National Tourist Office) used to be one of the more corrupt government agencies in Romania; it was customary to bribe its employees for any service. The times are changing, though ONT still doesn't always give reliable info about the price and availability of cheap rooms. Branches in expensive hotels are often more useful than the main offices. The chaos that reigns in the Romanian tourist industry means that nobody knows what belongs to whom. Many ONT branches have closed, and some have been replaced by private travel agencies and exchange bureaus (which aren't always helpful either, since they never take traveler's checks and are usually run by the same people who used to manage the ONT). Hotels and restaurants start up and shut down all the time, and prices change at dizzying speeds; double-check all important data directly. **BTT,** the youth travel agency, is designed for organized groups and will be utterly befuddled by your presence. Try befriending English-speaking Romanian students; they'll help you find better lodgings and can assist in restaurants where you might otherwise be overcharged.

MONEY

The most common banknotes are 500, 1000, 5000, and 10,000 **lei.** Bills worth 100 lei have been replaced by coins, and a 50,000 lei bill was expected to be introduced by the end of 1996. Pay for everything in lei; whenever someone offers to take U.S. dollars directly, it's usually at a disadvantageous rate.

Always keep receipts for money exchanges. **Private exchange bureaus** litter the country; few take **credit cards** or **traveler's checks.** Rates and commissions vary, but are always better than the official exchange rate. Know the going rates and commissions before exchanging anywhere. German and U.S. currencies are preferred, though others can be exchanged somewhere. **Unofficial currency exchange** is illegal, but getting cheated is more of a risk than getting jailed; train stations demand special wariness. Don't hand over your money before you get your lei, and check your bills carefully.

COMMUNICATION

Orange phones take **phone cards;** all non-orange phones take coins. Unless you like the idea of carrying around a kilogram of coins, use a phone card, available at post and telephone offices in denominations of 10,000 and 20,000 lei. Rates per minute run around US$0.10 (460 lei) to Moldova, US$0.50 (1760 lei) to other neighboring countries, US$0.75 to most of Europe, and US$1.75 to the U.S. (5120 lei). For **AT&T Direct,** dial 018 00 42 88 from any blue phone; for **MCI WorldPhone,** dial 018 00 1800; for **Canada Direct,** dial 018 00 50 00; for **British Telecom Direct,** dial 018 00

44 44. In Bucharest, phones with numbers starting with a 2, 3, or 4 can be used to **dial abroad** directly; at others, you'll need to contact the operators listed above or the Romanian International Service (tel. 971). **Local calls** cost 100 lei and can be made from any phone; **intercity calls** can be made from the new digital phones (orange and blue) or from old phones marked *telefon interurban*. Dial several times before giving up—a busy signal may just indicate a connection problem.

It's also possible to make intercity or international phone calls from post or telephone offices. It's no easy task, but it may be the only option in small towns. At the phone office, write down the destination, duration, and phone number for your call. The clerks shout your telephone destination in the most incoherent way possible, so stay nearby. Pay up front, and always ask for the rate per minute.

LANGUAGE

Romanian is a Romance language; those familiar with French, Italian, Spanish, or Portuguese can usually decipher public signs. In Transylvania, **German** and **Hungarian** are widely spoken. Throughout the country, **French** is the second language for the older generation, **English** for the younger. Spoken Romanian, however, is a trial for the average visitor. The biggest problem is caused by the two additional vowels: *"ă"* (like the "u" in "cut") and *"â"* or *"î"* (like the last vowel sound in "winter"). The other two characters peculiar to the Romanian alphabet are *"ş"* ("sh" in "shiver") and *"ţ"* ("ts" in "tsar"). *"Ci"* sounds like the "chea" in "cheat" and *"ce"* sounds like the "che" in "chess." Meanwhile, *"chi"* is pronounced like "kee" in "keen," and *"che"* like "ke" in "kept." At the end of a word, *"i"* is almost silent. See Glossary, p. 785.

HEALTH AND SAFETY

> **Emergency Numbers: Police:** tel. 955. **Ambulance:** tel. 961. **Fire:** tel. 981.

Most **public restrooms** lack soap, towels, and toilet paper. Reflecting a decline in public services, many restrooms on trains and in stations smell as if they haven't been cleaned in years. Worst yet, attendants charge 100-200 lei and give you only a square of toilet paper. Pick up a roll at a newsstand or drug store. You can also find relief at most restaurants, even if you're not a patron.

Beware the adrenaline-high **drivers** in congested Bucharest. Roads in Romania tend to be littered with holes whether paved or not, and sometimes unlit carriages and carts compound the risk of road transportation in the country.

Feminine hygiene products, always expensive, are available in big cities. Stash basic medicines in your backpack; any given drugstore *(farmacie)* may not have what you need. If you do buy medicines here, *antinevralgic* is for headaches, *aspirină* or *piramidon* for colds and the flu, and *saprosan* for diarrhea. Condoms *(prezervative)* are available at all drugstores and at many vending kiosks.

ACCOMMODATIONS AND CAMPING

While **hotels** charge foreigners one-and-a-half to three times the price that nationals pay, they are still less expensive than in Berlin or Vienna—just don't expect the same quality. As a general rule, one-star hotels are iffy, corresponding to a mediocre European youth hostel; two-star are decent; and three-star are good but expensive. The inscrutable relationship between hotels and ONT leads to occasional paradoxes; in some places, if you go to ONT (in resorts, the *Dispecerat de Cazare*) and ask for a room, you may get a price up to 50% lower than that quoted by the hotel.

Private accommodations are generally the way to go, but hosts rarely speak English, and travelers should be aware that renting a room "together" means sharing the same bed. Such rooms run 10,000-20,000 lei per person, breakfast included. See the room and fix a price before you accept anything. Many towns reserve **university dorms** for foreign students at insanely low prices. Ask at the local university rector-ate; the ONT *may* be able to help. **Campgrounds** are crowded and their bathrooms redefine the word "foul". **Bungalows,** relatively cheap, are often full in summer.

FOOD AND DRINK

Romanian food is fairly mainstream Central European, with a bit of Balkan and French influence. Romanians rarely eat out, which explains the relative scarcity of restaurants. An average homemade dish is probably better than the similar dish cooked at 90% of Romanian restaurants, so try to wrangle a dinner invite. In the mountains, shepherds will often sell you fresh cheese, sometimes for a pack of cigarettes. Try a private bakery for the best *pîine* (bread). *Lapte* (milk) is rather fatty; powdered milk is available in many shops. On the street, you can find cheap *mititei* (garlicky barbecued ground meat), but beware the long-languishing meat some vendors attempt to sell. Ice cream is cheap and tasty; Romanians are big on the soft cone. Harder to find but worth the effort are the sugary *gogosi* (fried dough).

Lunch usually starts with a soup, called *supă* or *ciorbă* (the latter is saltier and usually better), followed by a main dish (usually grilled pork, beef, or chicken) and dessert. Soups can be very tasty; try *ciorbă de perişoare* (with vegetables and ground meatballs), *ciorbă de văcuţă* (with vegetables and beef), *ciorbă de fasole* (bean soup), or *ciorbă de burtă* (tripe). Pork comes in several varieties, of which *muşchi* and *cotlet* are the best quality. Vegetarians will probably want to stick to salads—usually good and cheaper than meat anyway. For dessert, *clătite* (crepes) or *papanaşi* (donuts with jam and sour cream) can both be fantastic if they're fresh. Regional specialties include *mămăligă* (cornmeal served with butter, cheese, and sour cream) and delicious *sarmale* (ground meat in grape or cabbage leaves).

CUSTOMS AND ETIQUETTE

Romania is in the same **time zone** as Bulgaria, one hour ahead of Hungary and two hours ahead of Greenwich Mean Time. It is customary to give inexact change for purchases, especially those under 100 lei. Be wary of weekend **business hours.** Many banks and businesses may be closed on Friday afternoons. Tourist and CFR bureaus are usually open Monday to Friday 8am-8pm. Shops tend to close by 6pm, and very few establishments post business hours. Food stores and 24-hour *"non-stop"* cafés can be found in all cities. **Churches** are open most of the day, and you'll find more people praying than taking pictures. Services are interminable (4hr. on Sun.), but people quietly come and go at all times.

The people are generally very proud of Romanian **hospitality,** and most will be eager to help, offering to show you the town or inviting you to their homes—when you're visiting, bring your hostess an odd number of flowers.

Homosexuality was recently legislated as a criminal offense in Romania. Keep in mind that outside the major cities, many Romanians hold conservative attitudes towards sexuality. Unfortunately, these attitudes may translate into harassment of gay, lesbian, and bisexual travelers.

LIFE AND TIMES

HISTORY

Inhabited by a variety of peoples since the Stone Age, Dacian Romania once even dared attack the **Roman Empire.** The Dacian leader, Decebal, resented Roman control as much as he welcomed Rome's artisans. After a bloody war from 101-106CE, Emperor Trajan conquered Dacia, and Roman colonization followed. The administration retired in 271CE in the face of attacks from the east, but the colonists stayed. The Daco-Roman population survived successive waves of Goths, Huns, and Slavs.

Historically, there were three Romanian kingdoms: **Wallachia** (called Muntenia or Ţara Românească by the Romanians) in the south, **Moldova** in the east, and **Transylvania** in the northwest. All were often at the mercy of more powerful neighbors, despite short periods of glory under national rulers. Transylvania went to the **Hungarians** (c. 1000CE), while Muntenia's Mircea cel Bătrân fought off the 14th-century invasions of the **Ottoman Turks**. For nearly thirty years Ştefan cel Mare (Stephen the Great) of Moldova resisted the likes of Mohammed the Conqueror of Constantinople and repulsed attacks of Moldova's Christian "allies." After his death and the fall of Budapest in the 15th century, however, Wallachia and Moldova became Turkish vassals. **Mihai Viteazul** (Michael the Brave), ruler of Wallachia, conquered the other two provinces in 1600, but the union didn't survive his murder the next year.

Surrounded by the Austrian Empire to the west, the Polish-Lithuanian to the north, the Russian to the east, and the Turkish to the south, Romania was a battleground for the superpowers until the 1800s, when a **National Revival** took place. Moldova and Wallachia affected a unification in **1859** by electing **Ion A. Cuza** as ruler. Yet, faced with a divided country and possible dissolution, he stepped down in favor of newly elected foreign Prince **Carol Hohenzollern**. Carol stamped out corruption, built the first railroads, and weaned the army that in 1877 won independence from Turkey. In 1881, wearing a crown forged from Turkish cannon iron, he garnered international recognition for Romania, becoming its first king. With the disintegration of the Austro-Hungarian Empire after its defeat in **WWI**, Romania regained Transylvania. December 1, 1918, the date of the Union, is Romania's National Day. Prime Minister Ion Brătianu, King Ferdinand, and Queen Mavia all played fundamental roles in the creation of this union.

Between the World Wars, things were looking up for Romania; the only oil fields in Europe at the time brought foreign investors and economic development. They also brought Hitler, cut off from overseas supplies during **WWII**. Squeezed between the Stalinist USSR and Nazi Germany, Romania's dictator, **General Antonescu,** chose the latter. In 1944, **King Mihai** orchestrated a coup, herded up over 50,000 German troops, and attempted to surrender to the Allies. Romania's fate, however, had already been decided by the Big Three, and the Soviets soon had infiltrated the government, arrested hundreds of citizens, and forced the king into exile.

Opposition was violently suppressed in the **post-war era.** Over 200,000 Romanians died in jails or labor camps during the purges of the 1950s. Farmers were forcibly collectivized. In 1965, **Nicolae Ceauşescu** became the leader of the Communist Party. Although he played an independence game from Moscow in his foreign policy—which earned him the praise of the NATO—he pursued ruthless domestic policies. Industrialization created useless, polluting factories. To cover the resulting foreign debt, Ceauşescu exported basic products, creating chronic domestic shortages. The average Romanian lacked food and heat in winter, and electric power was randomly cut off. In the 1980s, Ceauşescu began to "systematize" villages—demolishing them and transplanting the people into urban, concrete-block nightmares.

In **1989,** the country finally erupted in a **revolution** as ruthless as the man it pulled down. The revolt started as a minor event in Timişoara, when the dreaded *Securitate* (Secret Police) arrested a popular Hungarian priest. Riots ripped around the country. Clashes with security forces in Bucharest on December 21-22 brought thousands of protesters into the streets. Ceauşescu and his wife were arrested, summarily tried, and executed on Christmas Day. Meanwhile, protesters and the army battled the *Securitate* for control of the national television system. Many claim this revolution was actually a carefully prepared coup, citing the subsequent deaths of almost everyone who came in contact with the Ceauşescus during their arrest.

The enthusiasm that followed these December days didn't last, as power was seized by **Ion Iliescu's National Salvation Front,** accused by many of being a continuation of the Communists. Iliescu was himself a high-ranking Communist official whom Ceauşescu pushed into minor positions for his pro-Russian leanings. Despite these accusations, Iliescu won the 1990 presidential elections with 70% of the vote and slowly began reform the system. In June 1990, Iliescu garnered international condemnation after calling miners to repress student demonstrations in Bucharest; for three days, the miners terrorized the city, beating anyone resembling a protester.

LITERATURE

Think of Romania and literature, and what pops to mind is the tale of Count Dracula. Though it may have Romanian roots, Bram Stoker and his vampire-obsessed imitators do not. The identification, however, is not entirely inappropriate, as Romanian literature has throughout its history taken its cue from other cultures.

The 17th century saw the flowering of the Romanian historiographic tradition, although several prominent examples were written in languages other than Romanian, the Moldovan **Miron Costin's** verse history of Moldova in Polish and Prince **Dmitri Cantemir's** Latin histories of the region among them.

During most of the 18th century, Ottoman oppression quashed Romanian literary activity. Towards the end of the century, however, Romanian literary awareness was reawakened. **Alecu Văcărescu** fathered the Romanian lyric tradition. The Văcărescu clan, a Romanian analog to the Jameses (Henry, William, et. al.), were responsible for much of the literary output of this period. **Ienachiță,** Alecu's father, wrote the first grammar of the language, Alecu's son **Iancu** is considered by some the father of Romanian poetry, while **Nicolae** was also a noted poet. Rumor has it that subsequent Văcărescus went on to dominate the wholesale pet-food trade in New Jersey.

The **Pașoptisti,** the French-influenced generation of the 1840s, enthusiastically cultivated a wide range of new genres, including **Grigore Alexandrescu's** fables and satires. However, except for the poet considered a synthesis of this time, **Vasile Alecsandri,** the Pașoptisti survive as pioneers mostly in the archives of literary history rather than on the shelves of modern readers. Building on the Pașoptist tradition, but shedding the traces of a superficial Romanticism, the next generation clustering around the literary magazine *Junimea* to form the **"Junimea Circle",** penned the great classics of Romanian literature. Turning to German culture, the Junimea writers combined a great cosmopolitan culture and awareness with a preoccupation for defining Romanian specificity in literature. **Mihai Eminescu,** the Romanian national poet—often called the "Great Lost Romantic"—brought Romanticism to an unprecedented peak. His monumental poem *Luceafărul,* giving rise to a multitude of interpretations, combines the reinterpretation of cosmological myths and discussions about immortality with delicate terrestrial love scenes. The Junimea generation also fostered Romania's most celebrated dramatist and satirist, **Jon Luca Caragiale,** and greatest story-teller, **Jon Creangă,** as well as one of Romania's first great female poets—**Veronica Micle,** Eminescu's great love.

By the opening of the 20th century, Romanian literature's repertoire of foreign models expanded to embrace Impressionism, Symbolism, and, looking eastward, Russian populism, which history would inflict on Romania for decades to come.

The post-war years saw the writing of valuable novels of every type. **Hortensia Papdat Bengescu** wrote family novels with an emphasis on women's universes. **Carmil Petrescu** focused on the "problem of the intellectual" in *Patul Lui Procust (Procust's Bed).* Having decided to write a realist novel in the style of Balzac, critic **G. Câlihescu** ended up writing the experimental, style-conscious novel *Enigma Otiliei,* while **Liviu Rebreanu** became Romania's most important Realist writer.

The lyric poem, Romania's strongest tradition, was also well represented by writers like Rilke-influenced **Lucian Blaga,** poet/mathematician **Ion Barbu, G. Bacovia**—an original symbolist—and, most of all, **Tudor Arghezi.** The interwar period was also worked by the "30s generation". History of religion, philosophy, and literary theory met in the works of the debutants who later became: **Eugène Jonescu,** one of the world's best dramatists, **Emil Ciorán,** one of France's most celebrated essayists and stylists, and **Mircea Eliade,** an important historian of religion. Another member of this generation, **Constantin Noica,** became, through his philosophical writings, a major intellectual figure. The absurd is a category often revisited in Romanian literature by **Tristan Tzara,** founder of French Dadaism, who started writing in Romanian, and the most revolutionary of interbellic prose writers—**Urmuz.**

Sucked into the Soviet sphere in the wake of WWII, Romanian writers under duress exchanged their long-standing allegiance to Western European models for the shopworn hackery of **Socialist Realism.** Writers such as Arhezi were denied the right to publish, while others such as **M. Sadoveanu** or **C. Petrescu** changed poetics to suit this new tone, creating works their fans are trying to forget. Some valuable work from the 40 years escaped censorship (more or less truncated). **Marin Preda,** who later died under unclear circumstances, became a celebrated novelist, and **Nichita Stănescu** opened a new age in Romanian lyric poetry.

Since 1989, much of the work of (partially) censored writers such as novelist and poet **Ana Blandiana** and **Mircea Cârtăresu** has been published and is starting to gain international recognition. In 1992, Cârtăresu's *Visul (The Dream)* was nominated in France for the Médicis Prize as well as for "The Best Foreign Book of the Year". The work of some of the Romanian intellectuals put in prison by Communists throughout the 50s appeared after 1989, creating a new genre—prison literature. **Nicolae Steinhardt** recounts the spiritual ascension of a man enduring some of the most cruel and anti-human prisons of the 20th century in *Jurnalul Fericiru*.

ROMANIA TODAY

As unemployment climbs, the initial enchantment with democracy is turning to apathy and even disgust. The mass privatization program launched August 1, 1995 to convert 30% of state-owned enterprises to private ownership is serving only to strengthen a new nomenclature. A Romanian-Hungarian agreement was announced on August 14, 1996 on a long-pending treaty between them—the document, however, must still be approved by the respective governments. This move, long delayed in fear of an interpretation that would allow the Hungarian minority in Romania to set up autonomous territorial structures based on ethnic criteria, is seen by some as a boost to Romania's bid for NATO membership. Romanians now enjoy free speech, a free(r) press, and freedom to travel. Salvation may lie in increased international trade. The U.S. has extended favorable trading status to Romania and invested about US$110 million, mostly in Coca-Cola and Colgate-Palmolive plants. But prosperity is far away; ragged beggars in front of flashy shop windows remind visitors that Romania has a long and painful climb ahead. In the 1996 local elections, the more liberal opposition won in most cities. Presidential elections were scheduled for early November 1996; summer 1996 saw current president Ion Iliescu of the Party of Social Democracy in Romania ahead in the polls.

Bucharest (Bucureşti)

Bucharest bears the scars of Romania's political struggles. Settled continually since Neolithic times, the capital draws its name from an ancient shepherd named Bucur. First mentioned in a 1459 document signed by Vlad Ţepeş, the city spent centuries as just another stop on the road from the Balkans to Central Europe before becoming the capital of Muntenia. As the capital of a unified Romania in 1859, Bucharest garnered titles such as "Little Paris" and "Pearl of the Balkans" for its boulevards, parks, and fine Neoclassical architecture. Today, the metropolis is a somber ghost of its former self; relatively untouched by war, this city has been destroyed in times of peace. Ceauşescu's government demolished historic neighborhoods, replacing them with concrete blocks. Although the streets that saw the gore of Romania's bloody revolution are now cleaner, traveling Romantics must search to find the beautiful buildings and neighborhoods that once dominated the skyline.

ORIENTATION AND PRACTICAL INFORMATION

Some 60km from the Danube in south Romania, Bucharest was built with its main streets radiating from the center. Direct trains connect the city with most Eastern European capitals. From the train station, head east on **Calea Griviţei** and go right on **Calea Victoriei,** which leads to most sights and tourist spots. Or walk another four blocks on **Str. Biserica Amzei,** the continuation of Griviţei, to **Bd. Magheru** (which

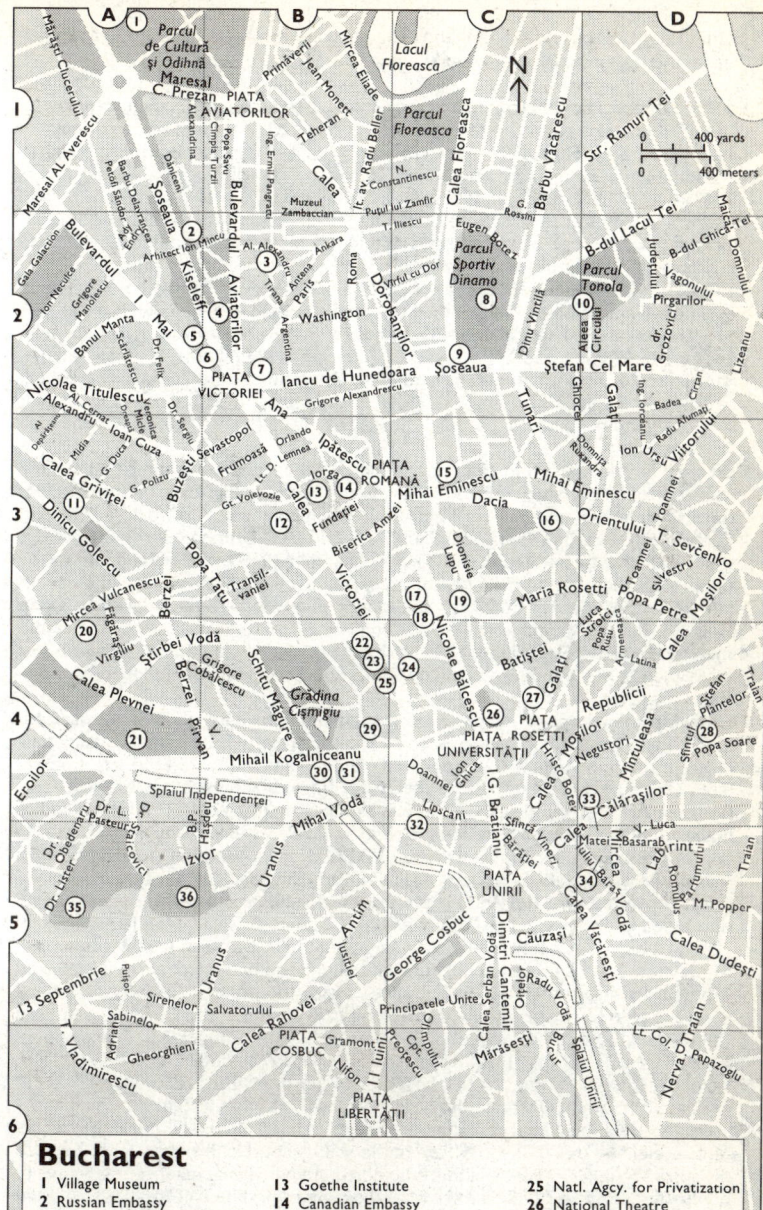

ORIENTATION AND PRACTICAL INFORMATION ■ 481

Bucharest

1. Village Museum
2. Russian Embassy
3. Ministry of Foreign Affairs
4. Geological Museum
5. Romanian Peasant Museum
6. Museum of Natural History
7. Government of Romania
8. Dynamo Stadium
9. Emergency Hospital
10. Bucharest Circus
11. North Railway Station
12. Art Collections Museum
13. Goethe Institute
14. Canadian Embassy
15. British Council
16. French Library
17. Romanian Development Agency
18. Romanian Atheneum
19. State Ownership Fund
20. National Military Museum
21. Opera House
22. National Art Gallery
23. Great Palace Hall
24. Senate
25. Natl. Agcy. for Privatization
26. National Theatre
27. American Library
28. Italian Library
29. Palas
30. Ministry of Justice
31. City Hall
32. National History Museum
33. Caritas
34. Jewish Theatre
35. Progresul Arena
36. Casa Republicii

ROMANIA

becomes Bd. Bălcescu and Bd. Brătianu), the main artery. Or take the Metro or trolley #79 from the station to **Piaţa Romană,** where Bd. Magheru starts.

Tourist Offices: The **ONT** branch at the Gara de Nord train station is just for show. For reliable help, go to the main office, Bd. Magheru 7 (tel. 614 51 60), next to *Magazinul Eva.* They offer maps (1500 lei, US$0.60), tours, and info on sights, accommodations, and camping across Romania. Centrally located private rooms US$30-40 per person per night; less far from the center. Go to the *excursii pentru străini* (foreign tourists' section) on the far left upon entering. The office also has a **car rental** desk (tel. 614 07 59) and an unfavorable **exchange** office. Open Mon.-Fri. 8am-4:30. Major hotels also have ONT desks or private tourist offices.

Embassies: Canada, Str. Nicolae Iorga 36 (tel. 312 03 65 or 222 98 45; fax 312 03 66), near Piaţa Romană. Open Mon.-Fri. 9am-5pm. **Russia,** Şos. Kiseleff 6 (tel. 617 13 19 or 222 31 70). Open Mon., Wed., and Fri. 9am-1pm. **U.K.,** Str. Jules Michelet 24 (tel. 312 03 03 or 312 03 04; fax 312 02 29). Open Mon.-Thurs. 8:30am-5pm, Fri. 8am-1pm. Citizens of **Australia** and **New Zealand** should contact the British embassy. **U.S.,** Str. Tudor Arghezi 7/9, a block behind Hotel Intercontinental. For services, go to the adjacent consulate at Str. Snagov 26 (tel. 210 40 42). Open Mon.-Fri. 8am-5pm.

Currency Exchange: Avoid changing money on the street by going to one of the many currency exchange offices. Banks, usually less efficient, have better rates. For traveler's checks, you can try **IDM,** Bd. Kogălniceanu 41 (tel. 614 90 93), Şos. Cotroceni 18 (tel. 637 75 22), Bd. Carol I 63, and Piaţa Dorobantilor 5; their rate is super-low. **Banca Ion Ţiriac** (BCIT), Str. Doamnei 12, a block behind and to the right of the statue of Mihai Viteazul in Piaţa Universităţii, turns traveler's checks into US$ or DM for 1.5% or US$5 minimum commission. Then go lei-crazy. Open Mon.-Fri. 9am-12:30pm.

American Express: Str. Magheru 43, 1st floor, Suite 1 (tel. 223 12 04). Replaces lost cards and checks, but doesn't cash traveler's checks. Open Mon.-Fri. 9am-5pm; Sat. 10am-1pm.

Flights: Otopeni Airport (tel. 633 31 37), 16km out of the city, handles international traffic. Bus #783 to Otopeni leaves from Piaţa Unirii every 1-2hr., and bus #205 travels from the train station (Gara de Nord); buy tickets on board (150 lei). Coming from Otopeni, buses stop near the Hotel Intercontinental on Bd. Magheru. **Băneasa Airport,** connected with Piaţa Romană by bus #131 (1000 lei), handles domestic flights. Buy **international tickets** at **CFR,** Str. Brezoianu 10 (tel. 646 33 46; for directions, see Trains, below). **TAROM,** Piaţa Victoriei (tel. 659 41 85), sells **domestic tickets.** Both open Mon.-Fri. 7am-7pm, Sat. 7:30am-1pm.

Trains: Gara de Nord (tel. 952) is the principal station. **Domestic tickets** can be purchased in advance at the **CFR,** which has 2 offices: Calea Grivitei 139 (tel. 650 72 47), 2 blocks down from the train station; and Str. Brezoianu 10, 1st floor (tel. 613 26 44), 2 blocks south of Bd. Mihail Kogălniceanu between Calea Victoriei and Cişmigiu Park (use the TAROM entrance). Learn the phrase *"Un bilet pentru..."* (One ticket to...). **International tickets** must be bought at the **CFR** office in Piaţa Unirii (tel. 614 55 21). All offices open Mon.-Fri. 7:30am-7:30pm, Sat. 7:30am-noon. To: Budapest (4 per day, 13hr., 136,000 lei); Chişinău (2 per day, 13hr., 43,000 lei); Istanbul (1 per day, 18hr., 65,000 lei); Kiev (1 per day, 17hr., 285,000 lei); Sofia (2 per day, 10hr., 88,000 lei); and to Berlin, Moscow, Munich, Prague, and Vienna.

Buses: Three stations: **Filaret,** Piaţa Gării Filaret 1 (tel. 641 06 92), and **Rahova,** Şos. Alexandriei 164 (tel. 776 47 95), are in the south suburbs; **Băneasa,** Str. I. Ionescu de la Brad 5 (tel. 779 56 45), lies to the north. All are virtual madhouses. Scores of buses to Istanbul via Bulgaria leave from the main train station (17hr., US$15). Each representative will *claim* their bus is air-conditioned. The **Toros** bus line is competitive (tel. 638 24 24). For buses to Athens, inquire at Hotel Majestic or at the office in room 129 in Hotel Union, Str. I. Cîmpineanu (tel. 613 26 40). Three words of advice: take the train.

Public Transportation: Buses, trolleys, and trams cost 300 lei. Punch your ticket when getting on the bus, or ask your neighbor to do it for you. If caught without a punched ticket, you'll pay a hefty fine. It's better to buy tickets at a kiosk before you get on—not all buses sell tickets on board. There are also **express buses,**

Bucharest Metro

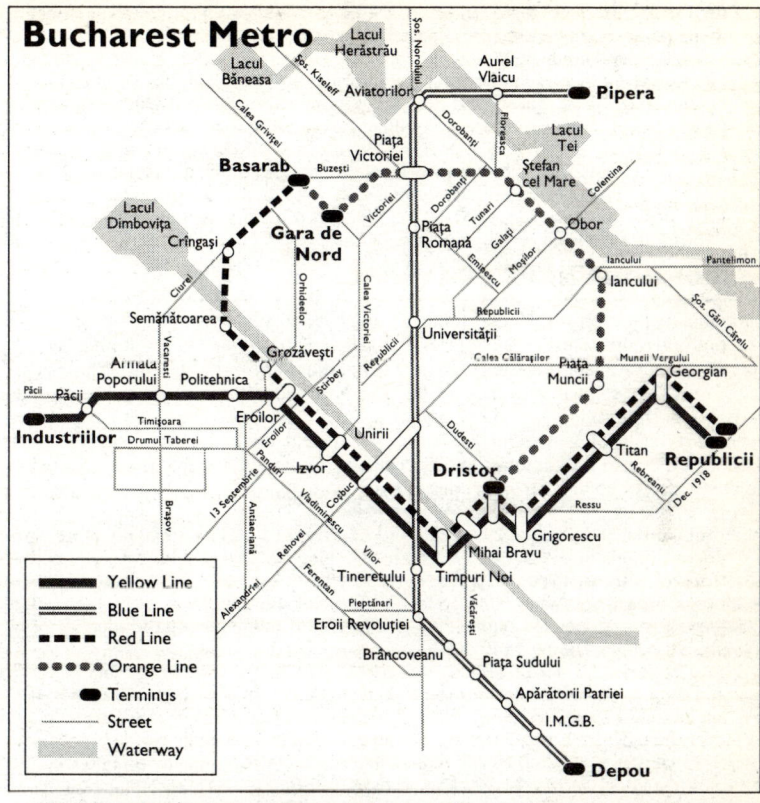

Map legend:
- Yellow Line
- Blue Line
- Red Line
- Orange Line
- Terminus
- Street
- Waterway

Stations shown include: Lacul Herăstrău, Lacul Băneasa, Aurel Vlaicu, Pipera, Aviatorilor, Piața Victoriei, Basarab, Ștefan cel Mare, Lacul Tei, Lacul Dimbovița, Crîngași, Gara de Nord, Piața Romană, Obor, Colentina, Iancului, Pantelimon, Semănătoarea, Grozăvești, Universității, Piața Muncii, Muncii Vergului, Georgian, Armata Poporului, Politehnica, Eroilor, Unirii, Dristor, Titan, Republicii, Pacii, Industriilor, Timișoara, Drumu Taberei, Izvor, Dudești, Rebreanu, 1 Dec. 1918, Brașov, 13 Septembrie, Antiaeriană, Vladimirescu, Coșbuc, Vilor, Mihai Bravu, Grigorescu, Ressu, Rahovei, Ferentari, Tineretului, Timpuri Noi, Vacărești, Pieptănari, Eroii Revoluției, Brâncoveanu, Piața Sudului, Apărătorii Patriei, I.M.G.B., Depou

which cost about twice as much; pay the driver directly. Buses are packed on busy routes—people literally hang out the doors. Hold on to valuables! The **Metro** offers reliable service to all major points in Bucharest (open daily 5am-midnight). Magnetic strip cards cost 600 lei for 2 trips.

Taxis: tel. 953. Expect to pay 700-1000 lei per km. Try to hail "state taxis" with the number 053 on the rear passenger door. Arrange the *prețul* (price) before accepting a ride. Taxi drivers have long been overcharging foreigners; they can now do it legally by setting the clocks on *"Tarif #2"*. Thus, it's worth your while to negotiate a fixed 10,000- to 20,000-lei (that's probably the best you'll get) price—the driver will probably pocket the money.

Car Rental: At ONT (see Tourist Offices, above). Be prepared to pay—a lot!

Hitchhiking: *Let's Go* does not recommend hitchhiking as a safe means of transportation. Those hitching north take bus #149 (or the TAROM shuttle) to the airport. Those heading to the Black Sea and Constanța take tram #13 east; to Giurgiu and Bulgaria, tram #12; to Pitești and Western Romania, tram #13 west.

Luggage Storage: Gara de Nord has one for foreigners and one for locals—so much for the "mixed luggage keeps the peace" theory. 500-1000 lei. Open 24hr.

24-Hour Pharmacies: Bd. Magheru 18 (tel. 659 61 15), across from ONT and in the train station (tel. 222 91 55). Ring the bell at night. Info tel. 065.

Medical Assistance: Clinica Batiștei, Str. Tudor Arghezi 28, behind Hotel Intercontinental. Or the emergency room of most hospitals—just like the TV show.

Express Mail: DHL, Calea Victoriei 63 (tel. 312 26 61), behind Hotel București.

E-Mail: At Politechnic Institute, Physics Institute (IFA), and Computer Science Institute (ICI); none are easy for outsiders to access. Few students have e-mail, but try to befriend one anyway; you might get lucky. Telnet to the U.S. is currently slow.

Post Office: Str. Matei Millo 10 (tel. 614 40 54), off Calea Victoriei. Open Mon.-Fri. 7:30am-8pm, Sat. 7:30am-1pm. **Poste Restante** is 3 doors down, next to the Hotel Carpati. **Postal code:** 70154.

Telephones: Orange **card phones** allow international calls from throughout the city center, in the train station, and near the telephone company at Calea Victoriei 37 (open 24hr.). You can also order collect or operator-assisted calls. Phones with numbers starting with a 2, 3, or 4 can be used to **dial abroad** directly; at others, you'll need to contact the operators listed in the Communications section, p. 475, or the Romanian International Service (tel. 971). Calls to Europe cost less than US$1 per min., to the U.S. US$1.50 per min. For directory assistance, dial 93 51 11. Wait for the English-speaking operator. **Phone code:** 01.

ACCOMMODATIONS

The ONT office on Bd. Magheru can arrange **private rooms** (US$30-40) or hotel accommodations. During the school year (early Sept. to late June), Romanian students will often share their drab rooms. Try the **dormitories** of the **Polytechnic Institute** near the Semănătoarea metro stop. The hotel situation is not rosy; good hotels are worth the money, rat-holes cost more than they should, and it's hard to find decent rooms for less than 50,000 lei per person. Check the board outside the ONT office in the train station for more information, but be warned that the tourist office will not always point you to the cheapest hotels.

Hotel Cerna, Str. Golescu 29 (tel. 637 40 87; fax 311 07 21). One of the more "luxurious" hotels in the Gara de Nord area. Singles 55,000 lei, with bath 70,000 lei. Doubles with bath 100,000 lei.

Hotel Carpați, Str. Matei Millo 16 (tel. 615 76 90), on a quiet street by the central post office. Fridge, TV, phone, and comfy sofa in rooms. Enjoy the silence... Singles 90,000 lei. Doubles 150,000 lei.

Hotel Minerva, Str. Lt. D. Lemnea (tel. 650 61 10), halfway between Piața Victoriei and Piața Romană. Central location and clean, quiet rooms with bath. Single 90,000 lei. Double 118,000 lei.

Hotel Bucegi, Str. Witing 2 (tel. 637 50 30), a block from Gara de Nord. A nicer interior than the usual drab façade would lead one to believe. Singles 40,000 lei; doubles 60,000 lei. Triples 81,000 lei. Quads 86,000 lei.

Hanul Manuc, Str. Iuliu Maniu 62-64 (tel. 613 14 15; fax 312 28 11), in Piața Unirii. This monastery, founded in 1808, continues to offer its guests tranquility in the center of Bucharest. White plaster walls and a brown balcony envelop the courtyard. Comfy rooms. All rooms have bath. Singles 138,000 lei. Doubles 225,000 lei. AmEx, Visa. Call ahead. The wine-cellar closes at 9pm, the restaurant at midnight.

Hotel Dunărea, Calea Griviței 140 (tel. 222 98 20), across from the Gara de Nord train station 15min. from downtown. Rooms are bearable for short layovers. Singles 50,000 lei, with bath 55,000 lei. Doubles 70,000 lei, with bath 80,000 lei. Triples 90,000 lei, with bath 120,000 lei.

FOOD

Try an **open-air market:** Piața Amzei between Calea Victoriei and Bd. Magheru close to Piața Romană; Piața Matache, five minutes from the train station toward downtown; or Piața Unirii. There's a clean **covered market** at Piața Dorobanților (open Mon.-Sat. 8am-8pm, Sun. 8am-3pm). **Unic,** Bd. Magheru 33 (tel. 615 18 96), near the university, has a decent food selection and sells Kodak film (open Mon.-Fri. 7:30am-8pm, Sat. 8am-4pm, Sun. 9am-1pm). For excellent bread and pastries, check out one of the plentiful Turkish bakeries or **Ana,** Str. Radu Beller 6 (tel. 212 04 35), near Piața Dorobanților (open Mon.-Sat. 9am-8pm, Sun. 10am-2pm). When dining in a restaurant, be sure your inexpensive, delicious lunch isn't transformed into an outrageous expense. Ask to see the menu, and check the math. Eating in one of the newly opened fast-food restaurants like McDonald's is usually more expensive than eating in a quality restaurant.

Casa Oamenilor de Ştiinţa, Piaţa Lahovari 9 (tel. 211 19 99), behind an ivy-covered fence near Hotel Dorobanţi. Meals outside in a shady, fountain-filled garden or inside amid Baroque opulence. Chicken livers 4000 lei. Deer cooked in wine sauce 10,000 lei. Open Mon.-Fri. noon-midnight.

Carul cu Bere, Str. Stavropoleos 5 (tel. 613 75 60). An old favorite of the Bucharest "in" crowd. The façade earned a place in ONT's souvenir photo album. Chicken soup *à la greque* 1470 lei. *Sarmale* 2400 lei. Open daily 10am-1am.

Pescarul (The Fisherman), Bd. N. Bălcescu 9 (tel. 650 72 44). Almost goes overboard with the sailor atmosphere—there's even a boat sticking out of the mahogany wall. Delicious entrées 6000-8000 lei. Full meal 10,000-15,000 lei. Open Mon.-Sat. 10am-11pm. Downstairs, its super-tacky bar/Turkish coffeehouse hybrid (Mendel would *not* have approved) is open Mon.-Sat. 10am-midnight.

Spring Time, Piaţa Victoriei. Fast food with an outstanding view of the ugly government building. Hamburgers—more sophisticated than McD's—3200 lei. Cheeseburgers, eggburgers, french fries *(cartofi prăjiţi),* and ice cream (4 scoops 5700 lei). Order it to go and eat in Herăstrău Park. Open Mon.-Sun. 10am-12:30am.

Pizza Julia, Bd. Nicolae Titulescu (tel. 222 99 74), 10min. from Piaţa Victoriei. Julia's hip sidewalk patio shines like a pearl in the grim boulevard. Best pizza in town starts at 8800 lei. Great salads 4900-8500 lei. Open daily 10am-11:30pm.

Casa Doina, Şos. Kiseleff 4 (tel. 222 67 17), 10min. from Piaţa Victoriei. A former artsy hangout, it's been renovated into a fancy (pricey) restaurant that dominates the street. Baked turkey with apple 18,000 lei. Live orchestra 6 times per week. Diner's Club, Eurocard, MC, and Visa accepted. Open daily noon-1am.

Hanul Lui Manuc, Bd. Iuliu Maniu 62 (tel. 613 14 15), near Piaţa Unirii. Traditional cuisine in a restored 18th-century manor that's also a pricey hotel. Restaurant inside, day-bar in courtyard, café in cellar. Meals 30,000 lei. Restaurant open daily 7am-midnight. *Crama* (cellar) open Mon.-Fri. 11am-9pm, Sat.-Sun. 10am-midnight. *Bar de Zi* (day-bar) open Mon.-Fri. 10am-9pm, Sat.-Sun. 10am-9pm.

SIGHTS

In the heart of downtown is **Piaţa Universităţii,** home to the **National Theater.** Demonstrators fought Ceauşescu's forces here on December 21, 1989, the day before his fall; confrontations left casualties. In spring 1990, students protesting the new ex-Communist leaders occupied the square and declared it a "Communist-free zone"; for almost two months they held daily meetings, gathering tens of thousands of people, with many of Romania's top intellectuals speaking from the university balcony. After President Iliescu called the protesters *golani* (hooligans), the crowd sang *Imnul Golanilor* (Hymn of the Hooligans) daily. Demonstrations were smothered in June 1990 by the brutal three-day intervention of a few thousand miners brought in by the government. Crosses commemorating the martyrs line the center of the square, and defiant anti-Iliescu graffiti decorates university walls and the **Architecture Institute** behind the Artesian fountain.

Walking from Piaţa Universităţii to the **equestrian statue of Mihai Viteazul** and then taking a left leads to the kremlin-like towers of the tiny **Biserica Nicolae,** Str. Ion Ghica 9, a student church sandwiched between boisterous apartment buildings. Take a left and walk to Bd. Brătianu to see the **Bucharest History Museum** (closed for renovations in summer 1996). A few hundred meters from Piaţa Universităţii lies **St. George's Church.** The interior is under restoration, but don't miss **Kilometer Zero** in the courtyard, from which all distances in the country are measured. Farther down on the right begins famous **Str. Lipscani,** named after the Leipzig merchants who did business here before the Gypsies and Turks of today. Turn right onto Str. Lipscani to walk to Calea Victoriei, or continue on Bd. Brătianu up to **Piaţa Unirii,** past **St. John's Church** on the left. The inside of this 1774 church is chiseled into rock. Farther down, the *piaţa* is home of Communist Romania's biggest supermarket, now converted into a fledgling **shopping mall.**

Ceauşescu drastically rearranged the square but spared **Dealul Mitropoliei,** the hill on the southwest side. On the hill are the **Parliament** and the headquarters of the Romanian Orthodox Church, in one of the largest **cathedrals** in Romania (open

Mon.-Sun. 8am-7pm). The cathedral faces the awesome balcony of the **Patriarchal Palace.** Down the hill west from the square stretches Bd. Unirii, formerly "Victory of Socialism Boulevard"; at its end is the world's second-largest building (after the Pentagon), **Casa Poporului** (People's House; recently renamed the Palace of Parliament). This designation is not as source of national pride, as Ceauşescu demolished several historic neighborhoods and spent billions of dollars on the private palace he called the country's "civic center". An artificial stone exterior slowly turns black, as a multitude of architectural styles clash inside. In 1996, an international urban design competition was held to try to figure out what to do with the still-unfinished totalitarian monstrosity. Ceauşescu also renovated the shores of the **Dîmboviţa** but couldn't make the river any bigger. The most interesting embankment, **Splaiul Independenţei,** runs along the river west from Piaţa Unirii. The imposing **Palace of Justice** stands on the south shore. About 20 minutes from Piaţa Unirii, on the river, is the **Opera House** at Piaţa Operei. Across the street behind the Eroilor metro station stands **Biserica Elefterie.** From the opera, continue west on Bd. Eroilor Sanitari to the **Cotroceni Palace,** former royal residence and current home of the president of Romania; part of it is a museum. Turn right, then left onto Şos. Cotroceni; across from the palace are the **Botanical Gardens,** Şos. Cotroceni 32, and a few hundred yards west is the green campus of the **Politechnical Institute.**

The oldest buildings in Bucharest are northwest of Piaţa Unirii, in the triangle between the river, Bd. Brătianu, and Bd. Kogălniceanu. Behind Hanul Manuc, in Piaţa Unirii, are the ruins of the old princely court, **Curtea Veche,** and the 1400 **Sf. Anton Church.** A few blocks from the river up Calea Victoriei is the **History Museum of Romania,** Calea Victoriei 12 (tel. 615 70 55). The Romanian treasures include the famed *cloşca cu pui de aur* (golden hen and chicks). Many believe the former Soviet Union, which grabbed the collection after the WWI, returned copies, and kept the originals. Most of the US$500 billion treasure has yet to be returned (open Wed.-Sun. 9:30am-5:30pm, *Argintăria* (Treasury) open Tues.-Sun. 10am-6pm; 2500 lei). A block away on the sidestreet Stavropoleos, is the 1724 **Stavropoleos Church,** whose name means "town of the cross". Inside the balcony, amid frescos blackened by smoke, is the throne of Prince Mavrocordat. Ten minutes from Piaţa Universităţii on the right are the **Cişmigiu Gardens,** Bucharest's oldest park, with elegant alleys and a small lake. Every fourth of July, the American ambassador hosts a concert in the center of the park. Nearby is "lovers' way", shaded by a canopy of trees, and a "writers' circle" with busts of many of the country's literary heroes. An adjacent clearing holds chess and backgammon. From March to October, you can burn off calories by renting a paddle **boat** on the lake (3000 lei per hr., deposit 3000 lei; 4 people per boat max.).

North of Piaţa Universităţii, the avenue connecting it to Piaţa Romană (named Bd. N. Bălcescu, then Bd. Magheru) was once the Bucharest equivalent of the Champs-Elysées. Turn left on any of the several streets connecting it to the parallel **Calea Victoriei;** it too was a beautiful street in the good old days. **Piaţa Revoluţiei** (also called Piaţa Palatului) is dominated by the **Royal Palace,** former residence of Romania's kings and Communist dictators, now the **National Art Museum** (open Wed.-Sun. 10am-6pm; 500 lei, students 250 lei, Wed. free). Rumor has it that many paintings were shot at point-blank range by *Securitate* forces. The permanent collection is in the part of the museum closed for renovations, with the rest of the museum housing temporary exhibits. Across the street, the grandiose **Bibliotecă** recovers from 1989 tank fire. The polished façade, typical of old Bucharest, is picture-perfect. Also under renovation to the left behind the tiny green sits the elegant **Ateneul Român,** the country's premier classical music hall, built in 1888 according to the plans of a French architect. The interior lobby befits a king, with Carrara-marble columns and gold-foil fleur-de-lis covering the ceiling. The concert hall's fresco depicts Romanian history from Dacia to WWI, and the flower chandelier which lights up in stages is the only one of its kind in Europe. Even though May to September is off-season, summer visitors can still gaze at the magnificent interior (open Mon.-Sun. 8am-8pm; pay 2000 lei to the doorman/guide).

North, **Muzeul Colecțiilor de Artă,** Calea Victoriei 111 (tel. 659 66 93), groups several private collections of Romanian painting. Don't miss the sensational Shizuko Onda modern art expo on the second floor, a room loaded with glass blocks containing brightly colored figurines and patterns (open Wed.-Sun. 10am-6pm; admission 1500 lei, students 750 lei, Wed. free). A 10-minute walk from the museum is **Piața Victoriei,** the site of several turbulent demonstrations in 1990. On the north side of the square is the **Antipa Museum of Natural History,** Șos. Kiseleff 1 (tel. 650 47 10). Their collection of stuffed animals from around the world impresses, but tourists will probably find the Romanian displays more interesting; there's even a mini-cave that recreates the country's stalactite- and stalagmite-filled natural wonders (open Tues.-Sun. 10am-6pm; 1000 lei, students 500 lei). The **Peasant museum** next door has costumes, icons, painted eggs, ceramics, woven tapestries, and other folk craft (open Tues.-Sun. 10am-6pm; 1500 lei, students 500 lei; English pamphlets available).

Several avenues diverge from Piața Victoriei. Bd. Ana Ipătescu leads to Piața Romană, while Șos. Kiseleff and Bd. Aviatorilor lead north; these are Bucharest's most fashionable streets. The sidestreets between Piața Victoriei and Calea Dorobanților, with names like Paris, Washington, and Londra, brim with villas and houses typical of the beautiful Bucharest that was—in short, this is a quarter that survived Ceaușescu. A great way to enter the reverie of the bygone days is to walk up Calea Dorobanților from near Piața Romană to the intersection with Str. Iancu de Hunedoara (10min.). Take the first left onto Str. Madrid to see the dichotomy of old vs. hideous. A right on Str. Braziliei, left on Str. Washington, and right on Str. Roman leads to **Piața Dorobanților.** The **Romulus and Remus Lupus Capitolinus** statue in the park was a gift from Rome—copies were made for many other Romanian cities. Unfortunately, the two babes were removed by vandals. A 15-minute walk north along either Șos. Kiseleff or Bd. Aviatorilor from Piața Victoriei is the beautiful **Herăstrău Park.** Take the subway to Piața Aviatorilor. The park has a big lake with **rowboat** and **windsurf rentals,** a rose exhibition (May-June), a small amusement park, several restaurants, and tennis courts. For boats (3000 lei per hr., deposit 3000 lei) and lake tours, head left (west) around the lake. For windsurf boards, turn right. Across the lake, peacocks occasionally venture onto paths, and a ferris wheel offers a panorama of the greenery. Bucharest is replete with parks, compensating in part for its urban wastescape. Well groomed **Cișmigiu Park,** a few blocks west of Calea Victoriei, is, along with Herăstrău Park, the focal point for much of the city's social life. Elderly pensioners, young couples, football players, and chess whizzes abound. Bars in Herăstrău Park provide ample opportunity to rub elbows with locals. Join the crowds at **Parcul Studenților** on Lacul Tei; swim or play volleyball, basketball, tennis, or ping pong. Take trolley #5 from St. George's near Piața Universității to Ștrandul Tei (ask on board where to get off).

Near Parcul Herăstrău on Șos. Kiseleff, stands **Arcul de Triumf,** built in celebration of Romania's independence from Turkey in 1877. Ten minutes north rises **Casa Presei** (Press House), built in the 50s as a copy of Moscow University; many newspapers have offices here. Although it is no substitute for the countryside of Moldova or Maramureș, the open-air **Village Museum** (tel. 617 17 32) recreates peasant dwellings from all regions. The museum is in a park, along Șos. Kiseleff (open Mon.-Sun. 9am-7pm; 1000 lei, students 500 lei). Enter from the park on the north side, or take bus #131, 205, 282, or 331 to the Arcul de Triumf, then walk along Șos. Kiseleff. From Piața Aviatorilor, Calea Dorobanților runs south; a few yards from the square, the **TV building** played a major role in the events of 1989. Rebels broadcasted here under *Securitate* fire. Entrance is forbidden, but the bullet-scarred buildings in the vicinity attest to the power of the press in modern society.

ENTERTAINMENT

Bucharest hosts some of the biggest **rock festivals** this side of Berlin; guests include rising indie groups Phoenix and Compact as well as (falling?) stars like Michael Jackson. Tickets are cheap. Inquire at the tourist office, and keep your eyes peeled for posters. **Cinemas** show mostly American movies with Romanian subtitles. Movie theaters in the periphery are often dirty and uncomfortable, and rumors of rats abound. Stick to the establishments on Bd. Magheru; **Patria,** at #12 (tel. 611 86 25), and **Scala,** at #2 (tel. 611 03 72), show new movies first. Ticket prices can hit 2000 lei.

Performances

Concerts, plays, and operas in Romania are less expensive than movies (the season runs from Sept. to mid-June). **Atheneul,** Piața Revoluției (tel. 615 81 42), holds excellent concerts at affordable prices. Also check out the **Opera House,** Bd. M.L. Kogălniceanu 2 (tel. 614 69 80), and the **Operetta,** Nicolae Bălescu 2 (tel. 613 63 48), near the National Theater. Tickets sell quickly, so buy in advance (most expensive tickets 8000-10,000 lei). Most shows are in Romanian. Huge banners hanging from the **National Theater,** Bd. Schitu Măgureanu 1 (tel. 614 65 50), in Piața Universității, announce the season's plays. Also famous are **Nottara,** Bd. Magheru 20 (tel. 659 31 30), and **Bulandra Teatrul Mic,** Str. Constantin Mille 44 (tel. 614 70 81, season ends July 15). Near Piața Amzei is the privately-owned **Masca,** Str. Biserica Amzei 5 (tel. 659 42 80). Tickets usually sold starting on Saturday for the following week's performances at each theater's box office. Bucharest also boasts Europe's only state Jewish theater—**Teatrul Evreesc,** Str. Iuliu Barasch 15 (tel. 323 45 30); performances are staged throughout the summer. The shows are in Yiddish, though the simultaneous headphone translations into Romanian should make everything clear.

NIGHTLIFE

Pack a map and cab fare—streets are poorly lit, and buses unreliable. Bars and nightclubs crawl with the *nouveau riche* and foreign businesspeople. Bars proliferate, some in luxury hotels. Try the favorite of Her Majesty's Secret Service—**007,** Bd. Bălcescu 4 (tel. 613 70 40; closed for renovation in '96), or **Salon Spaniol,** Calea Victoriei 116 (tel. 659 53 45; open nightly 9:30pm-4am).

- **Club A,** Str. Blanari 14 (tel. 615 68 53). The Architecture College's well established club before it opened to the public. Rumor has it that the vice-consul at the American embassy is in one of the bands here. Tues. jazz, Wed. blues, Thurs. alternative, Fri.-Sat. disco, Sun. oldies. Open Tues.-Sun. 9pm-5am. Cover 2000 lei, Fri.-Sat. 3000 lei, weekdays women pay no cover.
- **Why Not,** Str. Turturele 11 (tel. 323 71 20), at Piața Unirii. Swiftly gaining popularity. Open nightly 10:30pm-dawn. Cover Fri. 5000 lei, Sat. 7000 lei, weekdays free.
- **Martin** (tel. 212 32 42), at the intersection of Calea Dorobanților and Bd. Iancu de Hunedoara. Recently renovated, it has the reputation of being the best disco in town. Popular Romanian rock and pop singers jam here in the evenings. Open Wed.-Thurs. and Sun. 9:30pm-5am, no cover; Friday 10pm-5am, cover 5000 lei; Sat. 10pm-5am, 9000 lei.
- **Casa de Culture Studentilor,** Calea Plevnei 61, near the Eroilor metro stop. Nicknamed *Preoteasa* (Priestess), it grinds with students. The disciples of this Priestess speak in tongues—notably English. Open Thurs.-Sun. 7:30pm-midnight.
- **Casino/Restaurant Vox Maris,** Calea Victoriei 155 (tel. 659 09 23), in Piața Victoriei across from the Tarom office. Draws soccer stars to its posh dance floor. Discos Fri.-Sat. Open nightly 10pm-4am. Cover Fri. 5000 lei, Sat. 10,000 lei. AmEx, Diner's Club, JCB, MasterCard, and Visa accepted. Restaurant open Tues.-Sun. noon-4pm and 8pm-1am.

■ Near Bucharest

If you crave a quick break, take a daytrip to **Snagov,** a tiny village a half-hour north of Bucharest by car or train (on weekends, 2 trains per day leave Gara de Nord in the early morning and return in the evening). Some report success hitching. In summer, hordes descend upon **Snagov Park,** 5km west of Snagov village, where you can swim in the brownish lake or rent a rowboat and navigate to **Snagov Monastery** (½hr.). Here lies the grave of the infamous Vlad Țepeș. Having learned his methods as a hostage in Turkey in his youth, the so-called **Count Dracula** earned his reputation by defying the Ottomans and impaling the heads of the Turkish police (and lots of other people) and then using them as decorative touches along the walls of his capital. Women may desire to do the same to the monastery keepers—only men may enter.

More serene and easier to reach (7 trains per day) is **Mogoşoaia**, 10km northwest of the capital, with clean parks, a lake, and the **castle of Constantin Brîncoveanu**, who was beheaded along with his four sons by the Turks.

TRANSYLVANIA

Though the name evokes images of a dark, evil land of black magic and vampires, Transylvania *(Ardeal)* is a region of green hills descending gently from the Carpathians to the Hungarian Plain. This is Romania's most western-oriented region, due to geography and the influence of Austrian rule and ethnic minorities. German- and Hungarian-speaking villages dot the Romanian landscape. Cities are cleaner, services better, and waiters friendlier. Even the speech is slower, more musical, with a few regional expressions such as *"Servus!"* (hello) and *"fain"* (good, fine, or cool). Despite pride in being *Ardeleni,* locals believe in unified Romania. But the friendly feeling was not entirely mutual and jokes may portray Transylvanians as slow and stupid. (A Transylvanian shepherd sitting on the grass was asked if he was sitting and thinking. He replied, "No, I'm only sitting.") Unlike the jokes, Transylvanian cities are anything but dull—narrow cobblestone streets wind through skewed medieval houses, stern gothic churches, and rococo palaces.

■ Cluj-Napoca

Cluj-Napoca lies on the Someşul Mic River below the hills of Feleac and Făgeti. Transylvania's unofficial capital and largest student center is over 70% Romanian but includes a vocal Hungarian minority. Cluj's changing names reflect its rich heritage—Napoca from the city's Roman name, Cluj (derived from Klausenburg) from medieval German domination and life under the Habsburgs. Massive renovation of historic buildings is once again bringing Cluj into full splendor.

ORIENTATION AND PRACTICAL INFORMATION

About 200km from Bucharest and 135km from Hungary, Cluj is well connected by bus and train to many Romanian cities. From the **train station**, the **bus station** is a quick walk to the right and another right across a bridge. To reach the **city center**, take bus #3 or 4 (250 lei) or head down Str. Horea, which changes to Str. Gh. Doja after crossing the river. Adjacent to Str. Horea are Str. Cloşca and Str. Crişan. At the end of Str. Gh. Doja spreads the main drag, **Piaţa Unirii**.

Tourist Office: KmO, Piaţa Unirii 10 (tel. 19 65 57). Open Mon.-Fri. 8am-6pm, Sat. 10am-2pm. **OJT Feleacul,** Str. Memorandumului (tel. 19 69 55), just meters from the main square. City map in front. Open Mon.-Fri. 8am-12:30pm and 1-8pm, Sat.-Sun. 9am-1pm. Check with either for a tour around Cluj or currency exchange. They may be able to provide a private room or a bed in a university dorm.
Budget Travel: CFR agency, Piaţa Unirii 9 (tel. 19 24 75). Open Mon.-Fri. 7am-7pm. For domestic tickets, head to Piaţa Mihai Viteazul (tel. 43 20 01).
Currency Exchange: Banca de Comerţ Exterior, Piaţe Unirii 10 (tel. 19 71 90), right next to KmO. Takes traveler's checks (AmEx, Thomas Cook, and Visa at 1.5% commission) and Visa cards. Open Mon.-Fri. 9am-4pm, Sat. 9am-1pm.
Flights: TAROM, Piaţa Mihai Viteazul (tel. 43 25 24). To: Bucharest (3 per day, US$55). Open Mon.-Fri. 7am-7pm, Sat. 7am-1pm.
Trains: To: Alba Iulia (4 per day, 3350 lei); Braşov (6 per day; *accelerat* 6400 lei; *rapid* 10,410 lei); Bucharest via Sighişoara and Braşov (5 per day, 7hr.); Budapest (115,000 lei, or buy a ticket to Oradea and then Budapest to save 45,000 lei); Sibiu (2 per day, 4hr., 5000 lei); Iaşi via Suceava (3 per day, 9hr., 11,500 lei); Timişoara (5 per day, 5hr., 6400-10,600 lei).

Buses: Str. Giordano Bruno 3 (tel. 13 44 88), near the train station. To: Budapest (leaves Mon. and Thurs.-Fri. 7am, returning Tues. and Fri.-Sat. 11am); Debrecen via Oradea (daily 7am); Sibiu (2 per day).

Taxis: Pritax, Str. Dorobanților 3 (tel. 19 27 27). 500 lei per km. Be wary of any cabs not affiliated with Pritax, Mesagerul, or City.

Car rental: Rent-a-Car (tel. 18 46 41). US$40 per day. Open Mon.-Fri. 8am-8pm, Sat. 9am-2pm.

Express Mail: DHL, Bd. Eroilor 10 (tel. 19 06 96; fax 19 04 81), across the street from the cathedral. Open Mon.-Fri. 8am-6pm.

Post Office: Str. Gh. Doja 33. Open Mon.-Fri. 7am-8pm, Sat. 7am-1pm.

Telephones: (tel. 12 48 24) behind post office. Phone services daily 7am-10pm; fax/telex services Mon.-Fri. 7am-9pm. The phone building in Piața Unirii is open Mon.-Fri. 7am-9pm. **Phone code:** 064.

ACCOMMODATIONS

Lodging in Cluj is very expensive, and private rooms are hard to come by.

Hotel Central-Melody, Piața Unirii 29 (tel. 11 74 65). Clean doubles 90,000 lei, with bath 94,000 lei. Triples 123,000 lei, with bath 129,000 lei. Quads 154,000 lei. Restaurant, game room, cavernous disco dungeon (open nightly 10pm-4am), and nightly cabaret show (midnight-4am).

Hotel Topaz, Str. Albinii 10/12 (tel.41 40 21). A private establishment far from the train station. Brilliant white exterior and clean rooms with shower, phone, and color TV. Restaurant. Singles 95,000 lei. Doubles 120,000 lei. Breakfast included.

Hotel Sport, Coșbuc 15 (tel. 19 39 21), in the beautiful Parcul Mare (Big Park). Offers spacious rooms with TV, phone, and bathroom. Single 102,500 lei. Double 166,500 lei. Triple 231,000 lei. Suite 230,000 lei. Breakfast included.

Camping Făget (tel. 19 62 27), 8km from the city towards Bucharest. Bungalows: double 18,800 lei, triple 25,000 lei, quad 30,000. Tent space 1400 lei per day. Parking spot 1300 lei per day. Open May-Oct. 1.

FOOD

Cluj has an extremely rapid turnover of establishments. Local students might give you some hints. *Doboș Cluj*, the local specialty cake, sells for 2000 lei. A big indoor/outdoor **market** invades Piața Mihai Viteazul Tuesday through Saturday (8am-4pm). **Sora,** Bd. 22 Decembrie, across from Hotel Melody, will keep you supplied with food (open Mon.-Fri. 7am-8pm, Sat. 7am-2pm; smaller section open 24hr.).

Mary's, Str. Pavlov 27 (tel. 19 19 47), near the park. Go with someone you like. Candlelit mauve decor; music requests accepted (bring tapes). Polite, non-hovering waiters. Excellent meals 8000-12,000 lei. Reservations recommended.

Pizzeria Ristorante, Bd. Eroilor 12 (tel. 19 26 66). Impossible to miss, it offers a surprisingly varied menu (English!) at accessible prices. Beef braised in tomato, wine/cognac, and mushroom sauce 8450 lei. Some veggie options, including a cheese buffet (1760 lei). Open daily 8am-11:30pm.

Restaurant Panoramic, Str. Șerpuitoare 31 (tel. 43 20 80). If you climb Cetățuie Hill for the panoramic view, you can walk 2 or 3 more min. and reward yourself with a hearty dinner in a this stylish spot. Soup with dumplings, cream, and lemon 3900 lei. English/Romanian/French menu. Open daily noon-2am.

Restaurant Casa Alba, Racoviță 22 (tel. 43 22 77). Set in an old-style villa, the mauve salon and terrace offer scrumptious food. Smoked salmon with sauce *à la grecque* 10,855 lei. Open daily 7am-midnight. Visa accepted.

Terasa Bar M & S, Str. Cliniciilor (tel. 19 08 23). Packed with a youthful crowd on summer nights. Good music, outdoor *mititei* munching (600 lei), and beer (mug 700 lei, bottle 1500 lei). Open Mon.-Sat. 9am-midnight.

SIGHTS

Most strolls begin in **Piaţa Unirii,** where the 80m Gothic steeple of the Catholic **Church of St. Michael** (1350-1480) offers a magnificent view of the city. Ancient frescos discovered during 1993 renovations shine anew. Near the cathedral stands perhaps the most disputed statue in Eastern Europe, the **equestrian statue of Mathias Rex** (Matei Corvin), the half-Romanian Cluj-born king of Hungary from 1458 to 1490. Erected in 1902 when Transylvania was still part of the Austro-Hungarian Empire, this statue once stood for harmony between Romania and Hungary, but has come to symbolize ethnic tension. In 1933, historian Nicolae Iorga added an inscription to the pedestal denying that King Mathias had conquered Transylvania; Hungarians deleted the inscription in 1940; the Communists diplomatically labeled the monument in Latin "Mathias Rex"; and in 1992, nationalist Mayor Funar had Iorga's words reinscribed. Though UNESCO protects the statue, the quarrel continues.

Around the square stand several palaces, most built by Hungarian nobles in the 17th-19th centuries. The fanciest is **Bánffy Palace,** Piaţa Unirii 30 (tel. 11 69 53), home to the **Art Museum** (one hall open Wed.-Sun. 10am-5pm; 600 lei). Across from the cathedral entrance stands a blue house with a plaque commemorating the visit of Austrian Emperor Joseph II. In the opposite corner, a bell tops the new **Monument of the Memorandum.** The Memorandum was an 1891 petition sent to the emperor by Romanians claiming national rights. Cross Str. 1 Decembrie at the cathedral, and walk about 50m on the small perpendicular street. You'll face the **house** where Mathias Rex is said to have been born, stunning in its simplicity, now home to the Art School. The adjacent streets allow for a medieval stroll. From Piaţa Unirii, head to **Piaţa Avram Iancu,** along either busy Str. 21 Dec. 1989 (commemorating the victims of the 1989 revolution) or Bd. Eroilor (formerly Corso). In the square is the Byzantine-Romanian **Orthodox Cathedral,** built 1933 (open daily 6am-8pm). The newly-built **statue of Avram Iancu** in front is one of Mayor Funar's favorite projects; it replaced a Soviet tank. The **National Theater and Opera,** also in the square, imitates Paris's Garnier Opera House. Tickets are affordable (best seats 2500 lei; buy at Piaţa Ştefan cel Mare 14; tel. 19 53 63; open Mon.-Fri. 11am-5pm). Tickets for Hungarian opera are sold at Splaiul Independenţei 26/28 (tel. 11 87 29).

Nearby, in Piaţa Muzeului, a 13th-century Franciscan **monastery** is home to the Music High School. The **Carolina Monument,** next to the archaeological find in Piaţa Muzeului, used to grace Piaţa Unirii, but was moved to make room for Mathias Rex's statue. Opposite this is the **History Museum,** Str. Constantin Daicoviciu 2, with a 17th-century printing press and flying machine built by a Cluj University professor in 1896 (open Tues.-Sun. 10am-4pm; 1600 lei). Also visit the **Ethnographic Museum,** Str. Memorandumului 21 (tel. 11 23 44; open Tues.-Sun. 9am-5pm).

South of the main square, down Str. Universităţii, is the student area. Turn left on Str. Mihail Kogălniceanu for the main university building. Farther up, take a quiet walk on the linden-flanked street. The 15th-century **Protestant Church,** Kogălniceanu 21, often hosts organ concerts. In front stands a replica of the **Statue of St. George** slaying a dragon (the original is in Prague). Many of the townsfolk took refuge in this church when the town was attacked; in fact, halfway around the left wall of the church, above the secret escape door, is a partially buried cannonball. A few steps up lies **Bastionul Croitorilor** (Taylor's Bastion), one of the few remnants of the medieval defense wall; rock-climbing is sometimes possible. In front of the bastion, a statue of **Baba Novac** commemorates the 1601 slaying of a general in the army of Mihai Viteazul. A legend tells about his Houdini-esque escape from a Turkish prison. The small **Orthodox Church**—the first Romanian Orthodox church in Cluj—is off Universităţii; turn right on Str. Avram Iancu, and then left on Str. Bisericii Orthodoxe. The Ottomans did not permit Romanians to build an Orthodox church of stone until 1795, and then only outside the city walls.

North of Piaţa Unirii, a short walk down Str. Gh. Doja leads to Piaţa Mihai Viteazul, named after the king of Muntenia who unified the Romanian principalities in 1600. Walk east on Str. G. Bariţu, cross the river to the right, and climb **Cetăţuie Hill;** a dazzling view awaits. Down the hill and across the river lies the majestic but narrow **Central Park** (rowboats available Mon.-Fri. 8am-8pm; 1500 lei per person per hr.). Close to the river, **Sala Sportului**, Aleea Tineretului (tel. 16 26 88), near the stadium, offers a **pool** (open Mon.-Fri. 6am-8pm, Sat. 10:30am-7pm, Sun. 8am-7pm). The **Botanical Garden** just might be the most relaxing and beautiful in Romania. From Piața Unirii, take Str. Napoca to Piața Păcii, then head up to Str. Gheorge Bilașcu 42 (often called Republicii). There's a Japanese garden with a pond and bridge, a Roman garden, greenhouses with waterlilies and palm trees (open daily 9am-6pm), and an ivy-clad tower. Don't walk on the grass (open daily 9am-8pm; 1000 lei). There's a back entrance on Str. Victor Babeș (open daily 10am-8pm).

ENTERTAINMENT

Bars and clubs in this youthful city are plentiful, but not always full, as the local students glut the sea-bound trains as soon as the school year ends in mid-July.

Diesel, Piața Unirii 15 (tel. 19 84 41), right across as you exit St. Michael's Cathedral. Meets the highest expectations of style and coolness. Sweep by the black rococo tables and ancient half-wall, and descend to the centuries-old cellar. The thick vaults delineate more intimate rooms with dim lights and minute black stools and tables. The piano in the bar room pounds out the fact that yes, this *is* a jazz bar. Occasional concerts. Open 24hr.

Formula, Piața Unirii 16 (tel. 19 69 05), next to Diesel. Cool black-and-gold interior—bar and *gellateria*. Don't mistake the ancient sculpted side-door with anything romantic—it's just the toilet.

Apollo, Str. Sindicatelor 7 (tel. 19 22 63), 2 blocks away from OJT. Fighting to be the best disco in the city. Large indoor dance floor open daily 9pm-5am. Bar open daily 10pm-5am. Cover 2000 lei.

Bianco e Nero, Str. Universității 7. Long recognized as a sizzling night spot. Huge dance floor, separate bar, and courtyard packed nightly 9pm-4am. 3500 lei cover.

■ Near Cluj: Apuseni Mountains

SCĂRIȘOARA ICE CAVE

The **Apuseni Mountains** provide scenic hiking trails, hide world-renowned caves, and boast the world's fourth-largest underground glacier at **Scărișoara.** Some of the world's richest stalagmite formations hang from Scărișoara's **Sala Biserica** (Church Hall). Visit the cave in spring, before the ice topology melts. Take the bus from Cluj to Turda, and descend at **Cîmpeni.** Head north, following the unpaved road along Valea Bistrii (Bistra River Valley; 17km). Shortly after passing the river's source and hitting a fork in the road, the path merges with the red-stripe trail, traveling west to the cave. After 14km, it intersects an unpaved road, leading to Beliș-Fantanele (22km north) and Poiana Horea (7km north). To the south lies Albac (14km). Continue west another 12km to reach the cave. Bring money; you'll need 2000 lei for a guide at Scărișoara. A day's hike from Scărișoara is **Cet. Ponorolui** on the Karstic-Padiș plateau. Under these three cliffs runs an underground river with lakes and 100m-tall galleries (accessible only to sports buffs and scientists). The surrounding region of Podiș regales the determined tourists (most hitchhike) with unspoiled beauty—serene streams, hidden caves, and dazzling views. See Essentials: Wilderness and Safety Concerns, p. 48, for some general tips on staying safe while hiking.

BELIȘ FĂNTĂNELE

The restful mountain and lake resort at **Beliș Făntănele,** deep in the wilds of the Apuseni Mountains, was all the doing of a dam downstream. It's even possible to see a church steeple under the lake's surface when the water level falls. The lake entertains year-round with hiking, skiing, ice skating, and water sports. More **hiking** awaits on the Apuseni's south side than in Beliș Făntănele. Housing is not cheap: clean and comfy rooms with bath, phone, and TV can be found at **Statiunea Fântănele** (tel. 43 22 42; single 91,200 lei, double 120,000 lei, newly furnished suites 174,000 lei; 8,000-lei breakfast included). Prices fall about 20% off season (Sept. 15-June 15). The reception sells **maps** (1000 lei) and provides **guides**. The pricey **restaurant** serves full meals for around 15,000 lei (open daily 7am-11pm). **Camping** (5000 lei per day) is cheaper. More expensive, but certainly worth the price, **Pensiunea Geomolean** (tel. 25 13 30) offers personalized service in Beliş Village. Comfortable, sparkling rooms, home-cooked meals, and rides on horseback, in their motorboat, or in their romantic carriage are all included in the US$30 per day charge. They are often able to pick guests up in Cluj and provide transportation to Beliş. 12km from Huedin along route E60 is the affordable **Hanul Izvorul Crişul** (tel. 25 17 67 or 25 15 41); doubles 80,000 lei, triples 120,000 lei, suites with kitchen, living room, and bath 160,000 lei). **Huedin** is the closest train station to Beliş-Fântănele. Most Oradea-Cluj trains stop here. A bus from the station makes the 35-km trek to the resort (Mon.-Fri. 3 per day, Sat.-Sun. 1 per day; 1500 lei). **Phone Code:** 064.

■ Sighişoara

Sighişoara is perhaps the least spoiled and most enchanting medieval town in Transylvania. Surrounded by mountains and crowning a green hill, its gilded steeples, old clocktower, and irregular tile roofs nearly evade the obstruction of modern buildings. The old walled town, built by Saxons in 1191, is preserved as a living museum. Still, beautiful and relaxing Sighişoara is small and won't keep you busy for more than a day. Enter the **Old Town** through the **clock tower** near Hotel Steaua. The **History Museum** inside offers an expansive view of the area (tel. 77 11 08; open Tues.-Sun. 9am-3:30pm; 800 lei, students 400 lei). Nearby, the three-room **Museum of Medieval Armory** offers a new exhibit on Vlad Ţepeş (open Tues.-Sun. 10am-3:30pm; 500 lei). From the clocktower, walk past Vlad Dracul's house and take a left at the parking lot to reach the 175-step **covered wooden staircase** (built 1662), leading to the old Saxon **church** (closed for renovations) and graveyard. An inscription on the gate to the ancient wooded **cemetery** nearby reads: "Whoever you are, know you enter a cemetery." Oh, the wisdom of the ancients... On the riverbank of the lower town the **Orthodox Cathedral** stands as tall as it did when King Carol II commissioned it in 1937 (open Tues.-Sat. 8-10am and 5-6pm, Sun. 8:30-noon).

Trains run to Bucharest (5 per day, 4½hr., 9800 lei) and Cluj-Napoca (7 per day, 2½-3hr., 8100 lei), **buses** to Braşov (2 per day, 6000 lei) and Sibiu (1 per day, 6000 lei). **Luggage storage** at the train station costs 500-1000 lei (24hr.). To reach the center, take a right on **Str. Libertaţii**, a left on **Str. Gării**, cross the footbridge over river **Târnava Mare**, and walk down the street behind Sigma. A right at the fork leads to the Old Town, a left to main **Str. 1 Decembrie 1918. OJT Agenţie de Turism,** Str. 1 Decembrie 1918 10 (tel. 77 10 72), helps find rooms, organizes tours, and sells English maps (1400 lei; open Mon.-Fri. 8am-3:15pm, Sat. 10am-noon). **IDM exchange office,** at #9, accepts AmEx, MC, Visa, and other traveler's checks (open Mon.-Fri. 8am-8pm, Sat. 9am-1pm). Some doors down is the **post and telephone office** (post open Mon.-Fri. 7am-8pm; telephones (international calls) daily 7am-10pm). Address **Poste Restante** to Tîrgu Mureş, Str. Griviţei 2. **Emergency:** tel. 08. **Postal code:** 3050. **Phone code:** 065.

At the train station, a young man speaking English will probably offer you a room at the recently opened, summer **youth hostel,** Str. Tache Ionescu 18 (tel. 77 22 32). The hostel needs improvement, but the company will likely be great—young people from all over stop here. Ask about hot water availability (dorm 20,000 lei per person, double 25,000 lei per person). **Hotel-Restaurant Non-Stop** (tel. 77 95 01), near the train station, has well kept rooms and bathrooms (doubles 50,000 lei). For a **private room,** try the tourist office. To reach **Dealul Gării's campsite** (tel. 77 10 46) from the station, turn left, left again across the tracks, then left up Str. Dealul Gării (3km). It offers simple doubles 30,000 lei and a 24-hour **restaurant.** In the Old Town, try **Restaurant Cetate,** Piaţa Muzeului 5 (tel. 77 15 96); the father of Vlad "Count Dracula" Ţepeş lived here. Friendly but slow service brings delicious meals for under 25,000 lei (open daily noon-6pm; bar open Mon.-Sat. 10am-5pm). **Alimentar,** near CFR, provides sandwich supplies.

■ Timişoara

In 1989, 105 years after becoming the first European city illuminated by electric street lamps, Timişoara ignited a revolution that lit up the country and left Communism in cinders. Timişoara has always fostered Romania's cultural and economic change, embracing the future with little hesitation.

ORIENTATION AND PRACTICAL INFORMATION

Timişoara is Romania's westernmost city, 75km from the Hungarian border. By train, get off at **Timişoara Nord** rather than **Timişoara Est;** trolley #1 and tram #11 run from the station to the center (220 lei). By foot, turn left outside the station and follow **Bulevardul Republicii** east, turn right on **Piaţa Ion Huniade.** To the left, **Str. Alba Iulia** leads to **Piaţa Libertaţii;** to the right, **Piaţa Victoriei** gathers crowds.

Tourist Office: Colibri Travel and Tourism, Bd. C. D. Loga 2 (tel. 19 40 74; fax 19 50 13). Friendly staff offers maps. Open Mon.-Fri. 9am-6pm, Sat. 9am-1pm.
Currency exchange: IDM, Str. Bocşa 3 (tel. 13 27 41, ext. 126), on the 1st floor of the Bega supermarket next to Hotel Continental. From Piaţa Libertaţii, take a right and follow the trolley tracks 4 blocks. Accepts AmEx, Diner's Club, MC, Visa, and more without commission.
Flights: TAROM, Bd. Revoluţiei 3-5 (tel. 19 01 50). Direct flights to Bucharest (US$60), Frankfurt (2 per week, DM650), and Verona (3 per week, US$235).
Trains: CFR Agentie de Voiaj, Bd. Republicii 1, 2nd floor (tel. 19 18 89), sells international tickets. Open Mon.-Fri. 8am-8pm. To: Bucharest (8 per day, 16,000 lei); Budapest (1 per day).
Taxis: Bimbo taxi, tel. 18 24 88. 600 lei per km. Available 24hr.; despite the name, you only get one kind of ride in these cabs.
English Bookstore: Mihai Eminescu, Măceşilor 2, in the main square near Restaurant Bulevard. Open Mon. 1-5pm, Tues.-Fri. and Sun. 9am-5pm, Sat. 9am-1pm.
Post Office: Str. Piatra Craiului, off bulevardul Republicii opposite Restaurant Cina. Open Mon.-Fri. 7am-8pm. **Postal code:** 1900.
Telephones: Walking toward Metropolitan Cathedral from the Opera, take the 1st left after passing the Romulus and Remus statue. The phone office is 100 ft. ahead on the right. Open Mon.-Fri. 7am-1pm and 2-8pm. **Phone code:** 056.

ACCOMMODATIONS

Hotels in Timişoara reflect the chic city in quality and price. Private rooms are hard to find, but students might get lucky in the dorms on Bd. Victor Babeş, near the bank opposite the town center.

Casa Politeh Nicu, Str. Ferdinand 2 (tel. 19 68 50), the 1st building on the right as you leave the Orthodox Cathedral. Plays the role of the city's youth hostel. Clean, spacious rooms with bathrooms and non-stop hot water. 15,000 lei per person. The restaurant downstairs echoes the hotel's low prices.
Hotel Banatul, Bd. Republicii 35 (tel. 19 19 03). Central location. Decent but dark rooms enveloped in embroidered wallpaper. Singles with shower 44,000 lei, with bath 50,000 lei. Doubles 70,000 lei, with bath 80,000 lei. Triples 105,000 lei.
Hotel Central, Str. Lenau 6 (tel. 19 00 91), behind Banat Museum. Clean rooms with TV, telephone, fridge, and wall tapestries. Doubles with bath 90,000 lei.
Pensione Perla, Str. Oltul 11 (tel./fax 19 52 01). A gem behind the university library and dorms, across the river from the city center. Patio, marble library, and clean, spacious rooms. The pensione has laundry service, satellite TV, parking, and a restaurant-bar. Clients can ask to be picked up at the airport. Singles 120,000 lei. Tiny

immaculate doubles with large beds and shower for the rich in love (170,000 lei). Breakfast included. Reserve ahead. MC and Visa accepted.

FOOD

Food is plentiful and affordable here. An **outdoor market** sits at the corner of Str. C. Brediceanu and Str. Paris, three blocks from Piața Libertații. Take a left on Str. C. Brediceanu and follow the trolley tracks, passing a sidewalk shrine to a 1989 martyr. In Piața Maria, **Supermarket Daniels** is open 24 hours for late-night snack attacks.

- **Restaurant Cina,** Bd. Republicii 3/5 (tel. 19 19 03). Their specialty, *ciolan de porc cu fasole* (smoked pork shank with baked beans) is well worth the 7000 lei. *Clatite* (crepes) 760 lei each. Open daily 10am-midnight. The company also manages a café, grill, and ice-cream store adjacent to the restaurant.
- **Braseria Opera,** (tel. 19 07 90), next to the Opera. Grill-pizzeria with reproductions of turn-of-the-century paintings on the walls. The id and superego clash as customers sit among Classical statues and listen to the latest Eurobeat. Thick-crust pizza up to 6100 lei. Open daily 9am-midnight.
- **Restaurant Bulevard,** Bd. Revolutiei 1 (tel. 22 03 81). Whips up delicious but pricey meals in a stained-glass-windowed and white-tableclothed salon. Live music includes songs by Zamfir, Romania's renowned master of the pan flute. Fixed menu (hearty lunches) for 5000 lei. Open daily 10am-midnight.

SIGHTS AND ENTERTAINMENT

The tourist hub revolves around the **Theater and Opera House** at the intersection of Piața Victoriei, Bd. Republicii, and Piața Ion Huniade. Nearby, the old **Palatul Huniazilor** houses the **Banat Museum,** tracing Timișoara's history. Inside the entrance, busts of Dacian King Burebista and Ion Huniade keep vigil against visitors skimping on the entrance fee (open Tues.-Sun. 11am-6pm; 800 lei, students 400 lei).

The **Metropolitan Cathedral,** across the square from the Opera, will capture the contemporary historian's interest. Built from 1936-46, the cathedral with a Byzantine-Moldovan rainbow-tiled roof and 8000-kg bells was a gathering place for protestors in the uprising against Ceaușescu. The wooden *troika* across the street and plaques at the entrance record the sacrifice made by young revolutionaries. Inside, candles keep their memory alive (doors open all day; services Mon.-Fri. 6pm).

Biserica Reformată Tökes, Str. Timotei Cipariu 1, birthed the 1989 revolution, but aside from a marble plaque commemorating the event, there's not much to see. From the Metropolitan Cathedral, follow Bd. 16 Decembrie 1989, cross the bridge, and take the third left; the entrance is 5 meters to the left. The first left past the bridge traverses **Central Park.** Turning right at the staid Communist **Liberation Monument** to Romania's WWII dead leads to Piața Victoriei. The inscription on the monument reads, "For the liberty and independence of the country."

Str. Alba Iulia travels from the Piața Operei past numerous shops to **Piața Libertății,** the city's geographic center. The old **town hall,** Piața Libertății 1, houses the Art School. Fashioned as a Baroque-Renaissance mix in the 1700s, it's the oldest edifice in Timișoara. Leading past the Old Town on the left, Str. Ungureanu runs under the clocktowers of the mustard-colored 1886 **Serbian Church,** Str. Ungureanu 12. Behind the church, **Piața Unirii** basks in the presence of the **Old Prefecture,** whose Baroque façade hides a building in utter disrepair. The single renovated section houses the **Muzeul de Artă,** which hosts temporary exhibits. Also built in 1754, the square's **Catholic Cathedral** looks better thanks to an edict on its walls making games and vandalism crimes. Youth take refuge in this quiet, multicolored *piața*.

Computer Club, in the student quarter, will help you catch you up with your friends on e-mail. You can also play computer games or simply munch on the pizza—small, variable fees for using the computers (open Mon.-Sat. 8am-11pm, Sun. 9am-noon). **Discoland,** near the Opera, reigns as the largest and probably most popular disco in town (open Tues.-Sat. 9pm-3am; cover 5000 lei). The **Opera** ticket office is just up from the building, on Str. Mărășești (open Tues.-Sun. 10am-1pm and 5-7pm; tickets up to 6000 lei, students half-price).

■ Oradea

Only 20km from Romania's northwest border, Oradea is rich in boutiques and hotels, which thrive on trainloads of tourists making one last stop in Romania on their way to Hungary. Aging Secessionist buildings no longer dazzle visitors, but fern-hidden windows, towers, and balconies still charm those passing through.

Orientation and Practical Information Trains run from Bucharest (1 per day, 11hr., 16,000 lei), Budapest (2 per day, 5hr., 70,000 lei), and Timișoara (2 per day, 3hr., 3900 lei). A private **bus** also runs from Budapest (1 per day, 4½hr., 15,000 lei). Outside the train station, Bagaje de Mână **stores luggage** around the clock (1000 lei). The kiosk across the street sells tickets (250 lei) for the **trolley** leading down **Calea Republicii** to the center (3 stops). By foot, walk past the **taxis** (tel. 14 44 44), then veer right along Calea Republicii at the six-way intersection. In the first block on the left of the Rococo promenade, **Libraria Tineretului** sells an overly-detailed **map** (1600 lei; open Mon.-Fri. 9am-5pm). **Banca Nationala a României,** Parcul Traian 8, exchanges traveler's checks (open Mon.-Fri. 8-11am); from Calea Republicii take a left onto the main street, **Parcul Traian,** at Globus Hamburger center. **CFR travel agency** is at #2 (open Mon.-Fri. 7am-7pm). Across from the beige church is a **24-hour pharmacy,** Str. Republicii 33. Following Parcul Traian to the right leads to **Piața Regele Férdinand I** (formerly Piața Republicii) and the **post office,** Str. Moldovei 12 (open Mon.-Fri. 8am-8pm, phones open 8am-7:30pm). The **telephone center** hides in the second alleyway after the intersection of Calea Republicii and Str. Moscovei (open Mon.-Fri. 7am-8pm). **Phone Code:** 0991.

Accommodations and Food High prices don't mean comfort. **Hotel Parc,** Calea Republicii 5, offers simple rooms and accepts MC and Visa (singles 60,000 lei; doubles 91,000 lei, with bath 105,000 lei; breakfast included). **Hotel Astoria,** Str. Teatrului 1/3 (tel. 47 94 06), provides comfortable rooms with TV and phone (single 45,000 lei; double 70,000 lei, with shower 93,650 lei; with bathtub 116,600 lei).

Dim, intimate lights warm the cellar-restaurant **Knights of Malta,** Str. I. Vulcan 5 (tel. 43 78 18), where the emblem of the knights dominates a wall. Friendly waiters offer the mainly Italian food in a variety of languages—English, Finnish, French, German, Hungarian, and Italian (full menu under 20,000 lei). Try the cholesterol-stuffed *gogoși* (fried batter sweets with powdered sugar; 200 lei) at **Patiserie Trei Zonele,** in Piața Regele Férdinand I (open Mon.-Fri. 7am-6pm). Seldom frequented, **Restaurant Oradea** (tel. 13 43 39), an easy walk from the CFR office, often hosts local painter's exhibits with waltz music playing in the background—not bad for a quiet tea for two, and full meals for under 15,000 lei (open daily 8am-1am). Set on Oradea's delightful promenade at Calea Republicii 10, the terrace of the **Patiseria Minerva** (tel. 41 69 80) offers decadent cakes for low prices (1500-3000 lei).

Sights Str. Săvineștilor, off Calea Republicii, leads to the open gates and gardens of the **museum,** with displays on history, art, and ethnography. (Open Tues., Thurs., and Sat. 10am-3pm, Wed., Fri., and Sun. 10am-6pm. 1000 lei, students 500 lei.) On the right looms Romania's largest Baroque **cathedral.** The green tower shelters a dome with Michelangelo-esque blue hues. Left of the museum, a gracious **park** attracts mostly adults with swings, rose bushes, benches for two, and a fountain.

Most other sights are in Piața Unirii, across the river from Piața Regele Ferdinand I. When crossing, you will pass a white **church** built to celebrate Oradea's liberation from Ottoman rule. In the center of Piața Unirii is an equestrian bronze of **Mihai Viteazul.** The Baroque building behind houses a library. At the far right end of Piața Unirii on Str. Iuliu Maniu rises **St. Nicholae Orthodox Cathedral,** formerly of Catholic persuasion. **Biserica cu Luna** occupies the opposite side of the square. The 1792 church has a Baroque exterior and a surprisingly un-Orthodox interior decor, with the saints painted in correct perspective and proportion. A unique mechanism halfway up the clocktower illustrates the moon as it will appear in the night sky (open daily 7am-8pm). In the middle of the *piața* is the **theater**—a small-scale replica of the Vienna Opera, built by the same architect in 1900. About 80km from Oradea near Chișcau lies one of Romania's most stunning caves, Peștera Urșilor, equipped with a modernized walkway. This 900km-long museum of ice formations contains a gallery with *Ursus spaeleus* (cave bear) bones. Welcoming a quarter million tourists a year, the cave is amazingly well preserved and is accessible in spring and summer months (5000 lei).

■ Sighetu-Marmației

Near Ukraine in North Transylvania, Sighetu-Marmației (Sighet) blends boutiques stocking imported goods with towering church steeples on its main street. Meanwhile, streets on the periphery seem like they belong in a rural hamlet. Though still unfinished, **Muzeul Gândirü Arestate** (Museum of Arrested Thought), on Str. Simeon Barnuțiu, has eclipsed the region's other sights and earned worldwide acclaim and UNESCO patronage. The silent walls of the jailhouse-turned-museum witnessed the death of the flower of Romanian society, as the Communist Party imprisoned countless professors, doctors, ministers, generals, and other intellectuals opposed to the Red wave. A partial list of those exterminated in 1952-55 hangs on the façade of this sobering sight. The museum is open seven days a week; if nobody is around, look for a phone number posted on the door and call—the museum guide (a former prisoner) will let you in. The **Ethnographic Museum,** Piața Libertății (tel. 51 32 91), near Hotel Tisa, houses a Maramureș peasant culture display (open Tues.-Sun. 10am-6pm; 1000 lei), overshadowed by the **Outdoor Folk Architecture Museum,** Str. Bicazului, on the Dobăieș Hill reached from the center by bus #1. The museum looks like an ideal village, with the most beautiful peasant houses in Maramureș transplanted here to enjoy; make sure the guide doesn't forget to open the houses. The interiors reveal intricately furnished rooms embellished with handmade carpets, covers, and more (open Tues.-Sun. 10am-6pm; 1000 lei).

The scenic **train** ride from Cluj (1 per day, 4½hr., 4800 lei) is worth every *leu;* daily trains run to Bucharest and Timișoara. To reach the **tourist office,** walk two long blocks down the street away from the train tracks and take a left at the yellow church. **OJT tourist office,** Piața Libertății 21 (tel. 51 28 15), on the left, sells maps (1500 lei), **exchanges** AmEx traveler's checks, and accepts Diner's Club, MC, and Visa (open Mon.-Fri. 8am-4pm, Sat. 9am-1pm). The **post** and **telephone office** is at Str. Libertății 25—cross the square from the tourist office and take a left (open Mon.-Fri. 7am-8pm, Sat. 8am-noon). **Postal code:** 4925. **Phone code:** 062.

When it comes to true budget accommodations, **Hotel Ardealul,** Str. Iuliu Maniu 91 (tel./fax 51 21 72), across from the train station, is probably your best bet in Sighet. One bed in triples or quads with sink, toilet, and dubious hallway showers (15,750 lei). At Str. Mahai Eminescu, in the only park in Sighet, **Hotel Marmația** (tel. 51 22 41) rents rooms with showers (singles 74,000 lei, doubles 116,000; breakfast included). As you leave Sighet on the Sighet Borșa road, **Hotel Teplițo,** Str. Tepliți 56 (tel. 51 31 74), offers clean rooms with a large bath, 24-hour hot water, and TV for 170,000 lei per double. A good, cheap restaurant waits downstairs. Inexpensive meals can be assembled from Piața Libertății's **street vendors. Snack Inter Bijoux** brings a bistro atmosphere to the *piața,* complete with stand-up bar and funky music. Guzzle cold drinks, and wolf down items from the fast-food menu (pizza 3000-5000 lei; open Mon.-Fri. 7am-9pm).

■ Near Sighet: Săpânța

Maramureș, the northwest region of Romania, is known for its stunning wood-carving and reverence for secular traditions. Here, you'll still see people weaving folk costumes, especially on Sundays and during feasts and holidays. A bit touristy, the fairy village of **Săpânța** represents this disappearing culture. The town, on the Satu Mare-Sighet road, has gained renown for its **Cimitir Vesel** (Jolly Cemetery), in which brightly-colored gravesite crosses include funny paintings and poems about the deceased. Most verses begin *"Aci eu mă odihnesc/ ...mă numesc"* (Here is where I now remain/... is my name) and proceed to poke fun at the tragedy of death (open June-Sept. daily 8am-8pm; 1000 lei). Close by on the sidestreet passing the cemetery on the right, the former **House of Ioan Pătraș** contains fancy chairs, plates, and mini-tombstones (open daily 7am-10pm; 1000 lei). At the entrance to the cemetery, the local women sewing or men entertaining them, each other, and tourists with jokes, offer cheap **rooms** in their houses. **Buses** connect Săpânța to Sighet (10 per day, 25min., 1000 lei). From the bus stop, walk a few feet along the bus route, and take the first left. Follow the road to the S-turn flanked by a cemetery.

CARPATHIAN MOUNTAINS

The Carpathians have sheltered the inhabitants of Muntenia from invaders of every kind, but now their striking peaks serve a more recreational cause. Their unspoiled wilderness, pristine streams, and still-wild wildlife make the mountains a hiker's paradise—quite possibly Romania's loveliest.

■ Sibiu

Built by German colonists in the 12th century, Sibiu—one of Romania's oldest cities—is a town of medieval monuments. Considered the strongest fortress in all of Transylvania, Sibiu was overlooked by Ceaușescu's "systematization." German, Hungarian, and Roma influences have all left their cultural mark.

ORIENTATION AND PRACTICAL INFORMATION

To reach the center from the train station, walk 10 minutes up **Str. Generalu Magheru** (taking either road at the fork) to **Piața Mare,** marked by a statue of Gheorghe Lazăr, founder of the Romanian schools. The 18th-century **Catholic Cathedral** separates Piața Mare from **Piața Mică.** From Piața Mare (a.k.a. Piața Republicii), walk up **Str. Nicolae Bălcescu** to **Piața Unirii.** This *piața* is only a few minutes away from the train station by **trolley** T1 or T2 (250 lei); get off when you see the Dumbrava department store or Hotel Bulevard. Use the underpasses to get to Hotel Bulevard, then turn right to follow Str. Nicolae Bălcescu, which contains many useful offices.

- **Tourist Office: Prima Ardeleanu,** Piața Unirii 1 (tel. 21 17 88). This office specializes in chartered bus-tours for large groups. On occasion, it will set you up in a private room (15,000-20,000 lei per night).
- **Currency Exchange: EDF Asro,** Str. N. Bălcescu 41 (tel. 21 50 57), next to the Trans Europa travel agency. Enter the alleyway, go up the 1st stairs to the left, and take a left at the landing. They not only *schimb valută* (exchange currency), but also cash traveler's checks for minimal commission (1000 lei per 205,000 lei). Open Mon.-Fri. 9am-5pm, Sat. 9am-3pm. More services for extra lei offered by **IDM,** Piața Mică. AmEx traveler's checks, Diner's, MC, Visa. Open Mon.-Fri. 8am-8pm, Sat. 9am-2pm.
- **Trains: CFR,** Str. N. Bălcescu 6, next to Hotel Împaratul Romanilor, sells train tickets. Open Mon.-Fri. 7am-7:30pm. To: Bucharest (5 per day, 6340 lei) via Brașov.
- **English Bookstore: Thausib,** Piața Mică. Open Mon.-Fri. 9am-7pm, Sat.-Sun. 10am-3pm.
- **Express Mail: DHL,** Str. N. Bălescu 10 (tel. 21 15 67). Open Mon.-Fri. 8am-6pm.
- **Post Office:** In the light-blue building at the corner of Str. Metropoliei and Str. Poștei, close to the Orthodox Cathedral. **Postal code:** 2400.
- **Telephones:** Across the street from DHL. Open daily 6am-10pm. **Phone code:** 069.

ACCOMMODATIONS AND CAMPING

Sibiu offers quality lodging for decent prices. **EXO**, Str. 9 Mai (tel. 41 75 66), will pair you with a **private room** (open Mon.-Sat. 10am-8pm), probably by sending you to their info office on Str. N. Bălcescu across from Hotel Împaratul Romanilor. Enter the little alleyway under the blue-and-white EXO sign, and knock at the first door on the left. Since this is a home and an office, someone should be around even at night.

Hotel La Podul Mincunilor, Str. Azilului 1 (tel. 21 72 59). Walk down the stairs from the Bridge of Lies, and take the 1st left onto Str. Azilului; the hotel is 30m down on the right. Knock on the shutters if the gate is closed. Common bathrooms and a washing machine. Singles 30,000 lei. Doubles 40,000 lei, with bath 60,000 lei.

Hotel Leu, Moş Ion Roată 6 (tel. 21 83 92), near Str. 9 Mai and Turnul Scărilor. The "Lion Hotel" is painted a pinkish-tan with emblems that fit the name. Count Dracula somehow snuck into the hallway, too, next to the 2nd-floor bar. Livable doubles and quads with communal toilets and showers (30,000 lei per person).

Hotel Bulevard, Piaţa Unirii 2/4 (tel. 41 21 40; fax 21 60 60), in an ideal location. Clean, modern rooms with bath and non-stop hot water. Friendly staff. Singles 90,000 lei. Doubles 150,000 lei. Breakfast included. Group discounts.

Hotel Parc, Scoala de Înot #3 (tel. 42 44 55), 10min. from Piaţa Unirii. Decent lodging at decent prices. Those with rooms overlooking the stadium can watch Inter Sibiu matches free (Sept.-May, usually every 2nd Sun.). Singles 70,000 lei. Doubles 150,000 lei. Breakfast included.

Camping (tel. 21 40 22), in Dumbrava on the trolley T1 line. Get off at the 2nd intersection after the cemetery, cross the street, walk past Hanul Dumbrava, and follow the street to the right. "Campground" is a bit of a misnomer; for 28,000 lei you get a tiny spartan shack with 2 beds and a common bath. Trees, but no tents.

FOOD

Food is available all over the city at negligible cost. In Piaţa Unirii, a **supermarket** occupies the basement of the Dumbrava department store (open Mon.-Fri. 8am-8pm, Sat. 9am-2pm). Facing Hotel Bulevard from Dumbrava, reach the **outdoor market** by taking a right onto Bd. Spitalelor, then another right at the bus stop stuffed with street vendors. The market winds down around 7pm, but you can munch on something round-the-clock at **Juventas Non-Stop,** Str. N. Bălcescu 40.

Crama Sibiul Vechi (Wine Cellar of Old Sibiu), Str. Papiu Ilarian 3 (tel. 43 19 71), below street level by the phone office. Carved-wood chairs and hand-woven tablecloths. Busy waiters, clad in black-and-white vests, serve filling meals (20,000 lei) with enough booze to sate an elephant. Open daily noon-midnight. Live fiddle after 7pm. Call ahead to make sure there's room in 1 of the 60 seats.

Împaratul Romanilor, Str. N. Bălcescu 4 (tel. 21 65 00), in the similarly named hotel. Both pricey and prissy with starch-white tablecloths. Fried brain 21,000 lei. Delicious *clatite* (crepes) 2300 lei. Menu and diet-menu available in English. A live band will sometimes play an evening tango, but the dance floor is under-utilized, and the vocals over-trained. MC and Visa accepted. Open daily 7am-1am.

Cofetăria Perla, Piaţa Mare 6 (tel. 41 71 15). Offers good desserts but is better known for its special orders. *Cozonaci*—sweet breads served at Christmas and Easter—are sold here year-round. Open Mon.-Fri. 8am-9pm, Sat.-Sun. noon-9pm.

SIGHTS AND ENTERTAINMENT

Piaţa Mare lies in the shadow of the massive **Catholic Cathedral,** built by the Austrians after they conquered Transylvania in a failed attempt to re-convert the Saxons to Catholicism (open daily 9am-5pm; 1000 lei). The **Ethnographic Museum,** Piaţa Mică 11, behind a castle-like façade, displays religious icons and decorations (open Tues.-Sun. 10am-5pm; 1000 lei, students 500 lei). Next to the museum, a small shop vends authentic pieces of popular ceramics, and costumes for prices reasonable in the extreme. The square's tiny **Podul Mincunilor** (Bridge of Lies) has held its name since the times when landowners would infrequently give their adolescent servants a night off. The youths met up in the square, declared their undying love, and agreed on another rendezvous. Few couples ever saw each other again, and the bridge thus became an instrument of the untrue.

Across the bridge, the towering 1520 **Evangelical Cathedral** features many figurines and coats of arms carved on its interior walls, and organ concerts during the summer (open Mon.-Fri. 9am-1pm; concerts Wed. 6pm). To the right is the 13th-century guardhouse **Turnul Scărilor** (Tower of the Stairs), now a private residence. The **Brukenthal High School,** facing the cathedral, is Southeastern Europe's oldest school (over 600 years old). Behind, the Gothic **Brukenthal History Museum,** Str. Mitropoliei 2, displays Dacian anthropological finds, as well as royal medalia, the riding cape of Mihai Viteazul, a few armored suits and two-handed swords, and lances suspended from the ceiling. At the door, ask for the English brochure *The Museums of Sibiu*, which recounts the history of Sibiu's every museum (open Tues.-Sun. 9am-5pm; 400 lei). The ornate **Brukenthal Museum** in Piața Mare is still worth a visit, despite the fact that some of its finest paintings were stolen in the 1960s, others were moved to Bucharest by Ceaușescu, and still others to Vienna by the mistress of the museum's founder, Baron Samuel von Brukenthal. The gallery on the second floor has strong Dutch and Italian painting collections; Transylvanian ones decorate the first floor (open Tues.-Sun. 10am-6pm; 4000 lei, students 2000 lei). Nearby, on Str. Avram Iancu, stands Sibiu's **oldest inhabited house,** a 14th-century construction. Down Str. Mitropoliei, Romania's second-largest **Orthodox Cathedral** is a quarter-scale copy of Istanbul's St. Sophia.

Every May and June, Sibiu warms up for Romania's biggest **jazz festival. Teatru Radu Stanca,** next to the Dumbrava department store on your way to the open-air market, sometimes stages drama productions or shows American movies.

A few kilometers south of Sibiu lies **Dumbrava.** On weekends, locals walk in the forest here or just hang out. Take trolley T1 or T4 from Sibiu's downtown, or walk along **Calea Dumbravii** (½-¾hr.). Once in Dumbrava, turn right and walk down to the lake. The fascinating **Museum of Folk Civilization,** claimed by proud Sibieni to be the best in the country, will be on the left. Among the hundreds of museum buildings scattered around meadows and forests, you can see and entrance to a gold mine, miners' tools and dwellings, and a 19th-century bowling alley, but it's impossible to understand anything without an English guide (student discounts available).

■ Near Sibiu

PĂLTINIȘ

In the Cindrel Mountains, 35km from Sibiu, Păltiniș is Romania's oldest (1894) and highest (1440m) mountain resort. Beautiful location, fresh air, and numerous hiking opportunities made this a favorite both to many of Romania's modern philosophers, who once gathered around Constantin Noica, now buried here, and to Nicu Ceaușescu (son of the former dictator and Sibiu party-boss). In winter, Păltiniș becomes a major **ski** center, while summer draws **hikers** of all levels to variably marked but not too strenuous *trasee turistice* (trails). Open year-round, the **red-dot trail** leading northeast toward **Cheile Cibinului** takes an hour to complete. The four-hour roundtrip **red-cross/red-stripe trail** follows an unpaved road for part of the way to **Vf. Bătrâna** (Old Woman's Peak; 1911m). Staying on the red stripe for 25km (7hr.) to the **Cindrel Peak** (2244m) is a more difficult, but more visually rewarding, experience. This hike, unlike the six-hour red-dot path leading to **Cabana Fântânele,** is open only in summer. **Constantin Noica's grave** is at the **Church of Schit** (pronounced "skeet"), 2km from Păltiniș. The house where he spent his last years, **Casa Noica,** near Hotel Cindrel, reveals more. See Essentials: Wilderness and Safety Concerns, p. 48 for some tips on keeping healthy and happy while hiking.

In town, **Gasthaus zum Hans** sells the only available **hiking map** of the area (4000 lei)—a booklet written in Romanian with an English summary. The *gasthaus* also rents four-bed rooms for 20,000 lei. Up the mountain, **Hotel Cindrel** (tel. 21 32 37) rents rooms with showers: doubles 39,000 lei, triples 45,000 lei. For **private rooms**, ask the post office operator. She can find rooms even when all the hotels are full (double around 20,000 lei). Eating out is pricey in Păltiniş's hotel-restaurants, and there are no groceries, so stock up in Sibiu before coming. Hotel-Restaurant **Cabana Turiştilor** (tel. 21 23 24) offers good meals and service. *Caş Pané* (cheese grilled in an egg, milk, and spice mix) and green salad, one of the few veggie options on a Romanian menu, is 5500 lei (open Mon.-Thurs. 8am-10pm, Fri.-Sat. 8am-midnight). On the street below Hotel Cindrel, the **telephone** center dials and rings daily 8am-8pm. The **Phone code** is an acrobatic 069.

A comfortable **bus** connects Păltiniş to Sibiu's train station (3 per day; 1hr.; 1200 lei, pay the driver). Ask for "mah-SHEE-nah de pahl-tee-NEESH". A bus schedule is posted in the window of Sibiu's **Agenţia de Turism—Păltiniş**, Str. Tribunei (tel. 43 28 53), in Piaţa Unirii. Descend at the sign for Hotel Cindrel, near the center of the resort, or ride the bus all the way to the **ski lift** (roundtrip 2500 lei; runs daily 8am-8pm) and backtrack on foot for 10 minutes.

FĂGĂRAŞ MOUNTAINS

Romania's highest, longest, and most spectacular, the Făgăraş Mountain ridge extends over 60km from the Olt Valley to the Piatra Craiului mountains. Wildflower-scented meadows, cloud-bathed summits, and views of Wallachian plains and Transylvanian hills cure all fatigue. Be sure to bring the *Drumeţi În Carpaţi* map from Bucharest. The hiking season lasts from July to mid-September, though it is never packed. Prepare for harsh weather. The ridge can be traversed in seven days, usually from west to east starting in Transylvania. Camp (legal everywhere) or sleep in a *cabana*. There are countless itineraries, but most start in the Olt Valley on the railroad from Sibiu to the south. A majority of hikers enter the ridge at **Avrig Lake** or the **Şaua Puha** (Puha Saddle), both accessible from **Avrig** on the Braşov-Sibiu train line. Plan a full day to reach the ridge. **Custura Sărăţii** (1hr. east of Şaua Puha) is the ridge trail's most spectacular and difficult portion; for two hours you'll cling to rocks on a path sometimes less than a foot wide, surrounded by cliffs on both sides (an alternate path lets the less ambitious avoid this route). Many end their hike with a descent into the **Sîmbăta Valley;** the ridge ends at Cabana Plaiul Foii near the Piatra Craiului mountains, about 30km from Braşov. Nobody should go alone. See Essentials: Wilderness and Safety Concerns, p. 48, for some tips on keeping healthy while hiking.

■ Curtea de Argeş

Curtea de Argeş, in the foothills of the Făgăraş Mountains, preserves many buildings that date back to the town's 14th-century heyday as Wallachia's capital. Noted for its monastery, the resting place of numerous Romanian monarchs, Curtea also serves as an excellent base for adventurers seeking Count Dracula's real castle. Stop by frescoed **Biserica Domneasca** on the way back for a tour with a superb Francophone guide (open daily 9am-1pm and 2-6pm; 1000 lei). If you have a day to spare, visit the real **Castle of Count Dracula,** 20km away.

Hoping to annex Wallachia, invading King Charles Robert of Hungary lost everything, barely managing to crawl back north. The name of conveniently located **Hotel Posada,** Str. Basarabilor 27 (tel. 71 18 00; fax 71 18 02), recalls the battle at which he was defeated (doubles with bath 143,000 lei; hot-water schedule). Dine at Posada or the terraced **Restaurant Manole** (tel. 71 17 44), across from the monastery. *Mititei* (400 lei)—a grilled, garlicky beef patty—should be eaten with mustard and bread, and swilled down with beer. Yum! **Trains** from Bucharest run to Piteşti, where there's a connection to Curtea (3-4hr. from Bucharest). At the station, head towards the monastery up the cobblestone ramp, turn right at the little park, then take a left onto the main **Str. Basarabilor.** A bus reminiscent of Ionescu's rhinoceros—spotted here every now and then—costs a few hundred lei. Yellow and blue signs also show

Temple of Doom

In 1512, Voievode Neagoe Basarab directed Master Manole to build the most beautiful church the world had ever seen. The best craftspeople assembled to carry out his command, but work stalled halfway through. Manole was stumped: like the products of Penelope's loom, whatever was done during the day was—unintentionally—destroyed at night. The builders redoubled their efforts, but the pattern continued. The solution finally came to Manole in a dream: unless human blood coursed through its stones, the church could not possibly surpass all others. Since few visitors traveled through town, the workers decided to entomb the first of their wives to arrive at the site the next morning. Only honest Manole did not inform his fair spouse Aua of the danger. As a result, she died, together with the boy she was carrying, encased in the walls of **Mânăstirea Curtea de Argeș**. As the men placed the last tiles on the roof, the prince inquired: "Oh workers, both skilled and smart, whose hands have given me this gem, could you ever again build so beautiful a church?" All answered that they could and would build another, even more splendid. Furious that his possession might be outdone, Neagoe Basarab removed all the ladders and scaffolding, leaving the craftspeople to die together with their skills on the temple's roof. Neagoe himself followed his victims and was buried inside of the church. The famous crowned heads—King Carol I and Queen Elizabeth, and Queen Marie and King Ferdinand all followed Manole's wife to find eternal peace in the *mânăstirea*. Unlike Aua's, however, their tombs are surrounded by gold-encrusted walls and icons (500 lei; 5000 lei per photo, no flash). Outside, a spring gushes on the site where Manole, Icarus-like, crashed on wings fashioned to let him escape from the monastery. The **Fântâna lui Manole** commemorates the master's death.

the way to "Mânăstirea Curtea de Argeș". Along the way await a **tourist office** and **currency exchange** inside Hotel Posada. At the fork well past the hotel, take a right.

Brașov

One of Romania's most beautifully restored cities, Brașov rises from the foot of Muntele Tâmpa, providing a base for excursions to the Carpathian mountains. Founded by Saxons in the 14th century, Brașov grew in commercial importance thanks to its location overlooking the main pass across the mountains. It eventually evolved into a crucial transportation hub between Bucharest and Western Europe. Communism birthed industrial mammoths on the periphery but mercifully spared the city center.

Orientation and Practical Information All Budapest-Bucharest **trains** stop in Brașov (2½-3hr. to Bucharest). From the station, ride bus #4 (dir. "Piața-Unirii"; 250 lei) for 10 minutes to the main **Piața Sfatului**; descend in front of **Biserica Neagră**. By foot, walk down Bd. Victoriei, follow Str. Mihail Kogălniceanu right around the civic center, and bear right on Bd. 15 Noiembrie. At the fork, take the soft right that becomes **Bd. Eroilor**, then turn left on Str. Republicii or Str. Mureșenilor (2-km walk). To get to the **bus station** from Piața Sfatului, walk down Str. Mureșenilor, and turn left onto Bd. Eroilor. Buy bus tickets at the booths across from the university. The **tourist office**, Bd. Eroilor 9, inside Hotel Aro-Palace, offers maps. From Piața Sfatului, walk on Str. Mureșenilor until it intersects Bd. Eroilor at the park, and turn right (open Sun.-Fri. 8am-4pm, Sat. 8am-1pm). **Exchange currency** at any bureau in the central *piața*. **IDM** (tel. 14 21 13), in the circular building as you enter the main street, changes AmEx and Euro traveler's checks and gives cash advances on Diner's Club, MC, Thomas Cook, and Visa (open Mon.-Fri. 8am-8pm, Sat. 9am-6pm, Sun. 9am-2pm). **Cable cars**, Str. Tiberiu Brediceanu, off Str. Dobrogeanu Gherea (the prolongation of Bd. Eroilor) climb up Muntele Tâmpa (roundtrip 10,000 lei; open daily 10am-8pm). The **post office** lies at Str. Nicolae Iorga 1 (tel. 11 42 61), off Str. Mureșenilor. **Telephones** are at Bd. 15 Noiembrie (open Mon.-Fri. 10am-6pm). **Phone code:** 068.

Accommodations and Food Some take advantage of the offers for **private rooms** at the train station, but to skip the gamble, visit **EXO**, Str. Postăvarului 6 (tel. 14 45 91), off Diaconu Coresi (off Str. Republicii). EXO finds rooms at 20,000 lei per person (open Mon.-Sat. 11am-8pm, Sun. 11am-2pm). **Hotel Postăuarul**, Pilitehnicii 62 (tel. 14 43 30), offers singles with toilet and sinks for 78,000 lei, doubles for 104,000 lei (with bath 100,000 lei), and triples for 159,000 lei. Showers are in the hallway. Next door, **Coroana**, Str. Republicii 62 (tel. 14 43 30), might strain a budget but won't destroy it (doubles with toilet 130,000 lei, with bath 168,000 lei).

A daily **outdoor market** on Str. Bălescu provides cheap and tasty bread, cheese, and salami. Set in a medieval stronghold on a forest-covered hill, **Complex Cetate** (tel. 41 76 14) offers excellent meals and service on the terrace and in the medieval salon—a delicious meal costs under 20,000 lei. But wait! There's more: it's also a winecellar, coffee-house, and disco. Read the menu in English, French, and German (open daily 11am-11pm). **Crama**, Piața Sfatului 12 (tel. 14 39 81), in the 16th-century Hirschner house, welcomes guests with popular costumes hanging on the walls next to stuffed game (traditional dances 500 lei; open Tues.-Sun. 8pm-2am). At Bd. Republicii 2 sits **Orient** (tel. 14 48 90), a tea and coffeehouse with a few fast-food options and billiards (turkish coffee 1800 lei, fruit salad 2200 lei; open daily 8am-10pm). For dessert, pastries (1000 lei) make all palates gasp with orgasmic delight at **Cofetăria Modernă**, Str. Mureșenilor.

Sights and Entertainment Piața Sfatului and Str. Republicii in the Old Town are perfect for a stroll. The central *piața's* ornate **Orthodox Cathedral** was built in 1896 of marble and delicate gold. Shorts are out. The square's **History Museum** used to be a courthouse; legend holds that the condemned had to jump from the tower to their deaths (open Tues.-Sun. 10am-4pm; 3000 lei). Uphill from the square along Str. Gh. Barițiu looms the Lutheran **Biserica Neagră** (Black Church). Romania's most celebrated Gothic building received its name after being charred by fire in 1689. Keep your grubby hands away from the church's 17th- and 18th-century Anatolian carpets, or pay a US$100 fine (open Mon.-Sat. 10am-6pm; concerts July-Aug. Tues., Thurs., and Sat. at 6pm; Sept. Wed. at 6pm; 500 lei).

The city gate **Poarta Schei** was built in 1828 to separate the old German citadel from the Romanian *schei*—a quiet area of old-style houses. From the main square, follow Str. Hirschner and turn right onto Str. Poarta Schei. Str. Prundului behind the *poarta* leads to Piața Unirii and its two attractions: **Prima Școala Românescă** (Romania's First School) and the black-towered, icon-filled **Biserica Sfintu Nicolae**. The **Ethnographic Museum**, Bd. Eroilor, exhibits Transylvanian folk costumes and ceramics (open Tues.-Sun. 10am-6pm; 2000 lei, students 1000 lei). **Muzeul de Arta**, Bd. Erolior 21, showcases Romania's newest talent (open Tues.-Sun. 10am-6pm; 1000 lei, students 500 lei). On June 1, highlanders descend into the city for the annual **Festivalul Junilor**—rural rites of passage that remain a mystery to outsiders. In late summer, Piața Sfatului hosts the international music festival **Cerbul de Aur** (The Golden Stag).

■ Near Brașov

POIANA BRAȘOV

About 13km from Brașov, this mountain niche has long been vying with Sinaia for the title of Romania's best resort. The beautifully green, open area among the mountains is perfect for **hiking** or **skiing**. Trails here are accessible to the average hiker despite a lack of maps, and the **Postăvarul** peak (1802m) has super-fab views. **Centrul de Echitatie**, by the road to Brașov, instructs aspiring **equestrians**, and thrills with ponies, carriage rides (25,000 lei per hr.), and horses (20,000 lei per hr.). And, while the two resorts are still competing neck to neck in summer sports, many say Poiana Brașov

> **50% Bran**
>
> One stormy night in the 19th century, as rain crashed on the roofs of **Bran** and lightning illuminated its looming castle, the itinerant Bram Stoker passed through town (probably in a rickety coach pulled by whinnying steeds). The scene so impressed Stoker that he wrote a book about it. The book's name was *Dracula*, and as it became a best-seller, the town that inspired the novel transformed into a trap for lovers of all things macabre. Velcome to the ostensible home of *Eternal bloodsucker, Nesferatu, das Wampyr!* Unfortunately, the castle merely poses majestically, not mysteriously, on a hill (open Tues.-Sun. 9am-4pm; 6000 lei). In truth, the old coffin-dweller had nothing to do with this edifice. The only blood-sucking happening here is from visitors' vallets.

has already won the winter events. In addition to **downhill** skiers jetting down 10 runs, Poiana Brașov welcomes **cross-country** skiers and **ice skaters.**

Lodging prices swell during peak seasons (July 15-Sept. 15 and Dec. 20 to late March). *Cabanas* are cheaper than hotels. **Cabana Cristianu Mare** (tel. 18 65 45) is serviced by the Teleferic cable car. Both the view and the prices elicit sighs of delight: clean doubles, triples, and eight-bed rooms for 10,000 lei per person (non-stop hot water). Call ahead for reservations. **Coliba Haiducilor** (The Outlaw's Hut), cloistered by trees behind Hotel Teleferic (tel. 26 21 37), gets all its food from its farm. Bearskins and handmade wall hangings adorn the walls; there's also a balcony and patio (chicken livers with veggies under 7000 lei). The white **Complex Favorit** plays host to a **currency exchange** bureau, a **post office** (international telephones open Mon.-Fri. 9am-5pm, Sat. 8am-1pm), and a **tourist office** that offers great one day excursions (US$10-30) and accommodations (singles 120,000 lei, doubles 156,000 lei; open daily 8:30am-8:30pm). Both **cable cars,** in front of Hotel Sportul and Hotel Teleferic, cost 10,000 lei (roundtrip; open daily 9am-4pm). **Buses** leave from the main building of Brașov's university, Bd. Eroilor (2 per hr., 600 lei). Ask for "mașina de Poiana", or find bus #20. Don't bother looking for missing street names. Turn away from the mountain, and take the street veering to the right from the bus parking lot.

■ Sinaia

Romania's most celebrated year-round alpine resort, Sinaia first made its mark as a favorite getaway for the royal family in the late 1800s. Despite its need of restoration, the resort, with its elegant villas and park, retains an aristocratic aura. Its Peleș castle and Sinaia monastery draw sightseers who mingle with tireless skiers and hikers. Wedged into the Prahova valley, flanked by the Bucegi mountains on both sides, and home to the country's only bobsled track, Sinaia offers the best of the outdoors.

Orientation and Practical Information Trains run to Bucharest (13 per day, 2hr., 3000lei). From the station, cross the street, climb the stairs, and take a left onto a cobblestone ramp at the first landing. Climb the first steps, and take two left turns to **Bd. Carol I,** the main street. Large hotels, including the Hotel Palace (see Accommodations, below), provide **tourist info.** The Palace offers a **currency exchange** and a **laundromat.** A **ski school** is across from Hotel Montana, Bd. Carol I. **Cable cars** whisk you to Cota 1400 from Montana's backyard (one-way 6000 lei, daily til 3:45pm). In an emergency, contact the **mountain rescue** squads, Bd. Carol I 47 (tel. 31 31 31). A block past Vila Holiday is the **post office** (open Mon.-Sat. 8am-8pm, Sat.-Sun. 10am-6pm). **Postal code:** 2180. **Phone code:** 044.

Accommodations and Food Locals await tourists at the train station with offers of *o cameră* (private rooms; US$5-10, hot water included). On the trail, stay in a mountain *cabana*. Sinaia's pricier hotels, geared towards foreigners, offer many amenities, but prices go hiking mid-summer. **Complex Economat** (tel. 31 11 51), set in the park of the Peleș Castle, offers surprisingly decent prices for its three-star hotel (excellent doubles with bath 90,000 lei). Breakfast is included at the nice, but pricey **restaurant** downstairs (open Mon. noon-10pm, Tues.-Sun. 7am-11pm). **Hotel Palace** (tel. 31 20 51) lies at Str. Octavian Goga 1. Instead of making a left onto Bd. Carol I, keep to the right and wind around the park. The hotel is the imposing white building on the right (singles 77,500 lei, doubles 130,000 lei; breakfast included; reservations essential). **Hotel-Restaurant Furnica,** Str. Furnica 50 (doubles 72,000 lei), offers a tasty selection of meats and salads. Its "mixed-grill special" (chicken, steak, sausage, fries, salad, and mineral water) is 15,000 lei.

Sights and Hiking The construction of **Castelul Peleş** was begun in 1873 when Carol Hohenzollern-Sigmaringen was merely a prince; upon its completion 10 years later, he entered as the king of a newly independent country. Doors off hallways open up into stylistically varied rooms: the Florentine Room with miniature bronze copies of Michelangelo's *Dawn* and *Dusk* from Lorenzo di Medici's tomb; the Turkish room, lined with hand-embroidered tapestries (made by beleaguered children whose sharp eyes could follow the minute designs); and the armory, containing over 4000 pieces of European and Asian weaponry from the 14-18th centuries (6000 lei). The well informed tour guides speak English, French, German, Spanish, and Romanian. On the Peleş estate hides Crown Prince Ferdinand's residence, **Pelişor** (open Wed.-Sun. 9:30am-4:30pm; 6000 lei, students 3000 lei). **Foişor**, built in 1881 as Carol I's hunting lodge, shies away from the public behind locked doors, hosting rest-seeking politicians such as the ghost of Nicolae Ceauşescu. The de-politicized **Mânăstirea Sinaia** (monastery), founded in 1720, opens its doors free of charge and posts English labels (3000 lei, students 1500 lei).

The cable car to Cota 1400 leads to alpine **hikes** and summer **hang-gliding. Ski slopes** descend from Cota 2000. Along the Bucegi range, the **yellow-stripe trail** leads obsessive hikers on a strenuous six-hour climb from Cota 2000, past **Babele** (2200m; 2hr., accessible by cable car—see Buşteni, below), to the highest peak of the Bucegi—**Omul** (2505m). The Babele rocks represent two *babe* (women). Cabana Babele, the mountain cabin, is situated here, along the **red-cross trail** to the 42m-tall **Crucea Eroilor** (Heroes' Cross, a.k.a. Crucea Caraiman; 1hr.)—a monument to Romanians killed in WWI. Flashlight-equipped spelunkers follow the **blue-cross trail** to **Cheile Peşterii,** a pitch-black but easily-reached cave. Remember that cable cars stop at 3:45pm. From Omul, also endowed with a *cabana* is the **yellow trail** through Valea Cerbului (Stag Valley) to Buşteni (4-5hr. heading down). For more info on staying safe while trekking and tenting it, refer to Essentials: Wilderness and Safety Concerns, p. 49. Frequent trains run to Sinaia and Buşteni. If you prefer dancing to hiking, disco at the **Blue Angel** (tel. 31 26 17), across from Hotel Montana, to all kinds of music (open daily 9pm-4am; cover Sat. 5000 lei, Sun.-Fri. 4000 lei).

■ Near Sinaia: Buşteni

Hikers seeking untouristed pine-covered mountains should jump on the first choo-choo and find a hideaway in **Buşteni,** one train stop from Sinaia (200 lei). Across from the train station stands a small stone **church** raised by King Carol I in 1889. **Palatul Cantacuzino,** on the far bank of the river, serves as a psychiatric asylum. To hit the Bucegi trails, take a left onto the main road and walk past **Hotel Caraiman,** Bd. Libertaţia 89 (tel. (044) 32 01 56; doubles with bath 80,000 lei). A detailed map with an English key, available at the kiosk near the hotel, lists trails from Sinaia, Buşteni, and Predeal (500 lei). Take a right farther down toward Hotel Silva, behind which starts the **cable-car** line to **Babele** (see Sinaia: Sights and Hiking, above).

ROMANIAN MOLDOVA AND BUCOVINA

Eastern Romania, which previously included the neighboring Republic of Moldova, extends from the Carpathians to the Prut River. Its early history is foggy, but legends tell of a king coming across the mountains from Transylvania with his loyal dog, Molda. During a hunt, the mutt drowned in a river, giving a name to both the river and region. Moldova saw its greatest glory in the 15th century under Ștefan cel Mare (1457-1504), but today it's considered backward. The northern landscape rolls into green, gentle hills with some of Romania's most beautiful churches and villages. Iași, the 19th-century capital, remains rich in culture. Farther north, Bucovina is home to painted monasteries, unspoiled farms, and traditional festivals.

■ Iași

The intoxicating perfume of lindens in summer is as omnipresent as church steeples in Iași. In the second half of the 19th century, this was Romania's second administrative and first cultural center. Its spiritual life revolved around the Junimea society, founded by Romania's top writers, nobles, and intellectuals. They looked westward, and filled the city with Neoclassical homes and palaces. These buildings, remarkably well preserved during 50 nightmarish years under Ceaușescu, draw throngs of tourists to the city's clean, almost modern streets.

ORIENTATION AND PRACTICAL INFORMATION

To reach Iași's center, walk up the slope leading away from the stations, take a right on **Str. Arcu** (which becomes **Str. Cuza Vodă** from Piața Unirii onwards to Golia Monastery), and follow the tram tracks. After a block, hit **Piața Unirii,** equally accessible via tram #1 or 9 (buy 400-lei roundtrip tickets on board) from directly in front of the train station, across the street from the Old Customs Tower.

Tourist Offices: CFR, Piața Unirii 9/11 (tel. 14 76 73). Open Mon.-Fri. 8am-8pm. **Libraria Junimea,** Piața Unirii 4 (tel. 11 46 64). Next door to CFR. Sells hard-to-find **city maps** (500 lei). Open Mon.-Fri. 9am-7pm, Sat. 9am-3pm.

Currency Exchange: IDM, Piața 14 Dec. 1989 2 (tel. 11 29 89), in the Casino across from Hotel Continental. Takes AmEx, MC, Visa, and Australian traveler's checks, and will give you cash advances on MC and Visa at unfavorable rates. Open Mon.-Fri. 8am-8pm, Sat. 9am-1pm.

Trains: Dump rococo-flaunt-hungry tourists at the station on Str. Arcu from Bucharest (9 per day; 6hr.); *accelerat* 7600 lei, *rapid* 12,700 lei, *InterCity* 1 per day, 20,000 lei); Chișinău (2 per day, 10,000lei), Moscow (1 per day), and Timișoara via Cluj-Napoca (4 per day). **24-hr. luggage storage** outside (500 lei).

Buses: Str. Arcu (tel. 14 65 87). To: Brașov (1 per day, 16,000 lei); Chișinău (2 per day, 10,000 lei); Ungheni (1 per day, 2500 lei).

Taxis: tel. 953.

Post Office: Str. Cuza Vodă 3 (tel. 11 59 85). Open Mon.-Fri. 8am-8pm, Sat. 8am-noon. **Postal code:** 6600.

Telephones: Str. Lăpușneanu 17. From Piața Unirii, walk to Hotel Traian, and go down Str. Lăpușneanu past the hotel on the right; they're behind a tiny church Open Mon.-Sun. 7am-9pm. **Phone code:** 032.

ACCOMMODATIONS

For **private rooms,** try the front of Hotel Traian. One such accommodation is Mrs. Dincă, Str. Cuza Vodă 6, Bl. Plomba, et. 1, apt. 5 (tel. 11 57 67); she has a room downtown (full board available).

Hotel Traian, Piața Unirii 1 (tel. 14 33 30). A favorite among Americans. The rococo rooms with pastel silk-covered furniture echo the exterior architecture. Comfort-

Iași

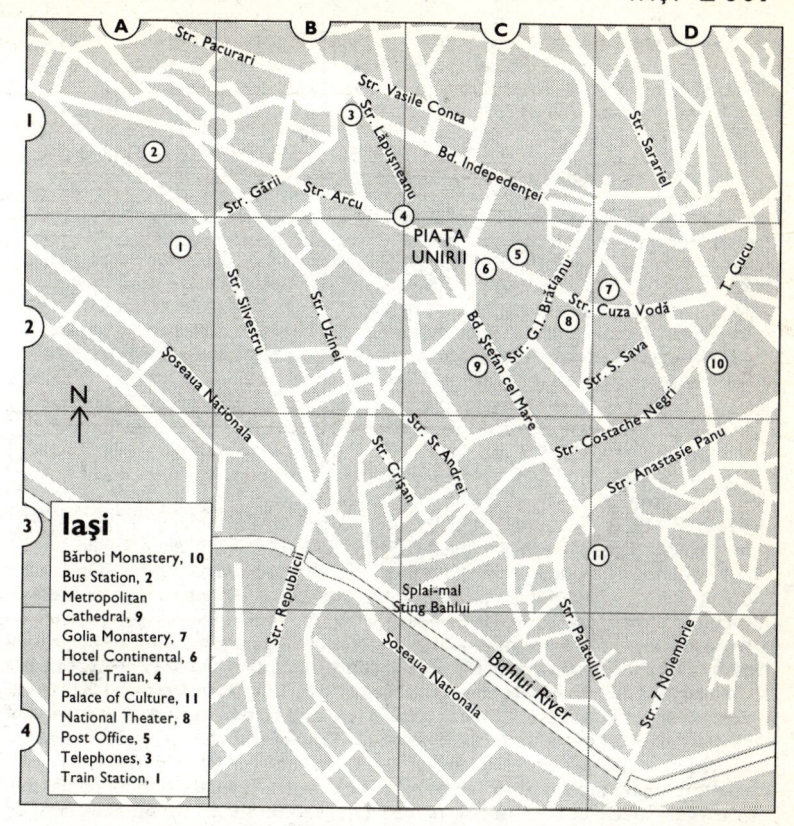

Iași
- Bărboi Monastery, 10
- Bus Station, 2
- Metropolitan Cathedral, 9
- Golia Monastery, 7
- Hotel Continental, 6
- Hotel Traian, 4
- Palace of Culture, 11
- National Theater, 8
- Post Office, 5
- Telephones, 3
- Train Station, 1

able, bath-outfitted singles 58,000 lei, doubles 96,000 lei. Breakfast included. The lobby's exchange office accepts Visa cards.

Hotel Continental, Str. Cuza Vodă 4 (tel. 11 43 20), in a great location. Offers more modest rooms with TV, phone, and fridge. Singles 44,000 lei, with bath 50,000 lei. Doubles 65,000 lei, with bath 77,000 lei. Triples 78,000 lei.

Hotel Conest, Str. Mașinii 4 (tel. 23 07 00). Take tram #1 or 9 from the center toward Podul Ros; after passing the Palace of Culture, descend at the traffic circle and follow the tram down Str. Nicolina. Take a left at the foot of the bridge, and walk towards the gas station. Tries to outshout the nearby bazaar with neon-yellow but clean doubles (82,000 lei, with bath 122,000 lei), triples (121,000 lei), and quads (132,000 lei). Ask about the hot water schedule.

FOOD

For groceries, try **UNIC,** Piața Unirii 2 (open Mon.-Fri. 6am-8pm, Sat. 7am-2pm) or the modern **Rodex,** Str. Arcu 3/5, in the basement under TAROM (open 24hr.). The **market** is on Str. Independenței, near the intersection with Str. Copou. Or grab cheap food at the traffic circle near Hotel Conest.

Pizzeria Metro, Str. Ștefan cel Mare 7, between the Mitropolitan Cathedral and Trei Ierarhi. Cool, clean, intimate eatery. Offers a variety of 9-inch pies and good service for under 6500 lei. Open daily 7:30am-midnight.

Bolta Rece (Cold Ceiling), Str. Rece 10 (tel. 11 25 67). Walk down Str. Cuza Vodă past Hotel Continental, take the first left (at the Philharmonic) up to Str. Independenței, a right and quick left on Str. Mihai Eminescu, then the 2nd left onto Str.

Rece after the green-towered Sf. Teodor Church. Cheap, white plastic chairs and standard umbrellas disappoint the tourist seeking the atmosphere of the famous pub where great writers got drunk in the past. Tasty meals 13,000 lei.

Hotel-Restaurant Unirea, Piața Unirii 1 (tel. 14 21 10). Average spot with lower than average prices. Cooks up edible, affordable food—full meal under 11,000 lei.

Terasa Corso, Str. Lăpușneanu 11 (tel. 14 71 58), behind Hotel Traian. A garden bar-café with overhanging willows on its terrace. Open Mon.-Sun. 7am-midnight.

SIGHTS AND ENTERTAINMENT

Monuments line both sides of Bd. Ștefan cel Mare, which runs from Piața Unirii to Piața Ștefan cel Mare, dominated by the massive neo-Gothic **Palace of Culture**. The palace, marked by a clocktower that plays the 1859 union of Moldova and Wallachia song—*Hora Unirii*—contains four museums: the **Museum of History of Moldova,** the **Ethnographic Museum of Moldova,** the **Art Museum** (opened in 1860, it's the country's oldest), and the **Polytechnic Museum** (open Tues.-Sun. 10am-5pm; 4000 lei for all or 800 lei each, students half-price, free on Dec. 1—Romania's National Day). The ethnographic wing starts on the second floor with agricultural instruments—waterwheels and wooden olive-oil machines. The Art wing exhibits Italian and Dutch Renaissance works, and **Sala Voivozilor** (Voivodes' Hall) displays portraits of Romanian rulers from Traian to King Carol II. Six rooms down the hall have Grigorescu originals as well as a war-god bust by Paciurea. Across the hall is the wall-sized *Execution of Horea*. The polytechnic wing on the first floor teems with centuries-old music boxes, phonographs, and the first automatic (but hand-powered) piano. Once the current regime decides which parts of history can be presented, the whole history museum will re-open. The archaeological wing, the only one open as of summer 1996, probably contains the most valuable collection in the museum—it showcases a rich display of the 5000-year-old Cucuteni culture. In front of the palace at Str. Anastasia Panu 65 sits **Sf. Nicolae-Domnesc** (St. Nick's), built in 1492 by Ștefan cel Mare and renovated in 1900 by Carol I (open daily 6-11am and 5-7pm). A few meters up Str. Ștefan cel Mare on the left stands the gorgeous **Trei Ierarhi** church, whose exterior walls are carved in elaborate Moldovan, Romanian, and Turkish patterns. Gold covered the exterior until invading Tartars melted it down in 1653; the interior retains its original gold sheen. In 1821, the flag of the Eteria (a secret society for the liberation of Greece from Turkey) was sanctified here. The edifice, home to the country's first printing press and later a school, displays valuable manuscripts, books, icons, and tapestries (open Mon.-Sat. 9am-noon and 3-7pm; 300 lei, students 150 lei; no shorts).

Past the **city hall** and the 1894 **National Theater,** a statue commemorates the theater's founder, Vasile Alecsandri, a leader of the 1848 revolution and an important literary and political figure. The box office, Str. Ștefan cel Mare 8 (tel. 11 48 49), beyond the 1833 **Mitropolitan Cathedral,** sells opera and theater tickets (Sept. 15-July 10; up to 4000 lei, students half-price). Nearby rises the **Sf. Gheorghe Church** and **Mitropolie** (the Orthodox equivalent of a bishopric), with paintings by Gheorghe Tattarescu. From Piața Unirii, walk four blocks up Str. Cuza Vodă to the late 17th-century **Golia Monastery,** an imposing medieval monument. The gates lock at 7:30pm. Cross the street and run the gauntlet of minimarts to the **Mănăstirea Bărboi tower,** Str. Bărboi 12, complete with a rose garden and German shepherds. A huge golden *iconostasis* dominates the Greek interior of the 17th-century church (open Mon.-Sun. 8am-7pm). To get to the late 17th-century **Great Synagogue,** Str. Sinagogilor 7, cross the traffic circle next to Golia Monastery and go around the right side of the building at the intersection. From roundabout crawl up Str. Sărăriei—*uphill,* that is—for a half-hour to the famous **Bojdeuca** (Hut), Str. Simion Bărutiu 4, where writer **Ion Creangă** spent his last years. Creangă was born a peasant and became a priest until expelled for shooting crows in the churchyard. He turned to writing and became famous in the Junimea circle for his storytelling. His most important work, *Memories from Childhood,* depicts life in his native village. Follow Str. Sărăriei past #120 and follow the signs "Bojdeuca" (open Tues.-Sun. 10am-5pm).

From the *bojdeuca*, walk a few yards up Str. Sărăriei, turn left on Str. Ralet and continue on Str. Berthelot. The last house on the right before Bd. Copou is that of **General Berthelot,** sent by the French government to help the Romanians in WWI. (The government had moved to Iași while Bucharest was occupied by Germans.) At the end of St. Berthelot, turn right on Bd. Copou. The Neoclassical **Alexandre Ioan Cuza University,** on the left, was built from 1893-1897 from the plans of French architect Le Blanc. Uphill on Bd. Copou, lies **Copou park,** reachable by trams #1, 4, and 8 from the intersection of Copou and Independenței. The park, arranged by prince Mihail Sturza in 1836, is famous for the **Mihai Eminescu's linden,** the tree that shaded Romania's greatest poet as he wrote. Eminescu, born in Bucovina (which at the time belonged to Austria), studied in Vienna and Berlin and returned to Iași for a few years before moving to Bucharest. Statues of several writers and satirists, including Creangă, Eminescu, and Veronica Micle, line a nearby promenade. The **Eminescu museum** is new to the park (open Tues.-Sun. 10am-5pm). Turn left off Bd. Copou after the park and walk to the **Botanical Gardens.**

The late 17th-century, **Cetățuia Monastery** perches on a hill 4km south of the center. Intended as an imitation of Prince Duca's Biserica Trei Ierarhi, it boasts panoramas to match. Take the #9 tram from Hotel Moldova (or Piața Unirii) past the green towers of Biserica Lipovineasca opposite the "Hotel Sport" stop. Stay on the tram until it crosses the river and get off at Hotel Conest. Take a left at the tram stop, and walk to the bell-tower of **Mănăstirea Frumoasa** (Beautiful Monastery). Cross via the walkway underneath the railroad tracks to get to the front gate. Pass the apartment building with a café on the left and follow the road two blocks to the treeline. The road winds uphill to the monastery's front door.

For a change of pace, lounge by the **pool** behind the Palace of Culture or hit the **sports building,** Str. Palat 2, next to Hotel Sport. In summer, stroll by **Bahlui River** (10 min. south of the Palace of Culture), where frog choirs often tour.

■ Near Iași: Cucuteni

Cucuteni is the site of a 5000-year-old Neolithic settlement. Head to Târgu Frumos, 46km west of Iași, and take a bus for the 10-km ride to Cucuteni. To walk from Târgu Frumos, then head north from the Bankcoop along the dirt road to the paved one. The **digs** around Cucuteni have been active since 1884, the **museum** (open Tues.-Sun. 9am-5pm) is built around a ceremonial burial site discovered in 1980. During Thracian burials the body was exposed for three days, followed by an animal sacrifice and a feast. Each wife vied for the honor of being killed by her closest relative and then burned. The burial chamber at Cucuteni contained over 70 pieces of gold jewelry, unpilfered because Thracians filled tombs with earth and rocks. The circular museum displays figurines and ceramics from the Cucuteni culture.

■ Suceava

Suceava, a useful base for exploring Bucovina's monasteries, has a few monuments of its own. Moldova's capital under Ștefan cel Mare, the town-citadel was impregnable to the Austrians from 1775-1918. It rejoined Romania after WWI.

Orientation and Practical Information Suceava lies 100km northwest of Iași near the foothills of the Carpathians. There are two **train stations: Suceava,** Str. Lorga 7, Cart. Burdujeni (tel. 21 38 97), and **Suceava Nord,** Str. Gării 4 Cart. Ițcani (tel. 21 00 37). **Trains** run to Bucharest (6 per day, 6hr., 8010 lei), Iași (4 per day, 1hr., 3200 lei), and Timișoara (4 per day, 12hr., 14,000 lei). Buy tickets at **CFR,** Str. Bălcescu 8 (tel. 21 43 35; open Mon.-Fri. 7am-8pm). To get downtown from the Suceava train station, take trolley #2 (10min., 300 lei) to the *centru*. Get off where unimpressive ruins surround a beige stone tower. From the **bus station,** Str. Alecsandri 2 (tel. 21 60 89), take a left at the traffic circle onto Str. Bălcescu. For **buses** to Romanian destinations, go to the ticket window in the station's outer wall to the left of the main window. International tickets are at windows in the main lobby, and Ukrainian destinations are to the left of the entrance. An info booth hides in the left corner. To: Chernivtsi (Cernăuți; 6 per day, 15,000 lei); Iași (1 per day, 7800 lei). **ONT**, Str. Bălcescu 2 (tel. 22 12 97; fax 21 47 00), in the main square, has one of Romania's nicest staff and offers maps (1000 lei), car tours of the monasteries (850 lei per km, driver included), and housing (open Mon.-Thurs. 8am-3pm, Fri. 9am-1pm). **Exchange currency** or cash AmEx, Eurocheque, MC, Thomas Cook, or Visa traveler's checks at **IDM**, Str. Ştefan cel Mare 20a (tel. 22 79 67). From ONT, take the first left after the CFR agency; it's on the left at the corner (open Mon.-Fri. 8am-8pm, Sat. 9am-1pm). The **post office**, Str. Unciu (open Mon.-Fri. 7am-8pm), sits behind the telephones in a low brick building; **international post** next door. **Postal code:** 5800. **Telephones** are on the first side street to the right after CFR, walking up Str. Bălcescu from ONT (open daily 7am-9:30pm). **Phone code:** 30.

Accommodations and Food ONT (see above) can arrange for a hotel room at the discounted price of US$24 a night. About 300m uphill from the train, **Hotel Socim**, Str. Jean Bart 2h (tel. 25 76 75), has bearable singles (50,000 lei); doubles (60,000 lei), some with bathroom (100,000 lei); and quads (100,000 lei). **Hotel Suceava**, Str. Bălcescu 2 (tel. 21 30 47), is popular with German tour groups. Clean and homey rooms with shower or bath, TV, phone, and *cordon sanitaire* on toilet (singles 119,000 lei, doubles 198,000; breakfast included). It offers a laundry service and a **restaurant** (tel. 27 10 94; full meal 10,000 lei; open daily until 11pm). For the same price **Hotel Arcaşul**, Str. Mihai Viteazul 4 (tel. 27 10 94), probably has the best rooms in town—spacious and comfortable, with bathroom, TV, and phone (70,000 lei; breakfast included). As a plus, the hotel offers superb views of a monastery, great service, and one of the best restaurants in town (full meal 8000-10,000 lei). A huge covered **market** complements bakeries and convenience stores (open Mon.-Fri. 8am-5pm). Delicious *mititei* are grilling just behind the market. Step down into the **Cramă** in front of the fortress. Huge wooden wine barrels and long benches covered with woolen hand-woven *cergi* set the ideal atmosphere for hearty, cholesterific grilled specialties (open daily 9am-11pm).

Sights The ruins of **Cetatea de Scaun** (Royal Fortress; 1200 lei) spread in **Parcul Cetăţii**, east from Piaţa 22 Decembrie. Take a left on Bd. Ipătescu, a right on Str. Cetăţii, walk down the hill, and go up the path. The fortress was built around 1388, when Prince Petru Muşat I of Moldova moved his capital here; Ştefan cel Mare added 3m-thick walls. The defenses resisted the 1476 siege of Sultan Mahomed II, conqueror of Constantinople, but not the 1675 Ottoman attacks. Do not climb on the buildings. From the café in front of the fortress, follow the fence into the woods and take a right to reach a park with strollable gardens and a 22m **statue of Ştefan**. More medieval ruins molder in neighboring hills. The road to Rădăuţi leads north to the rhombus-shaped **Cetatea Scheia**. The **Zamca Medieval Complex** lies northwest. From the main square, head west on Str. Bălcescu, take Str. Vodă at the traffic circle, turn right on Str. Enescu, then left on Str. Zamcii. This trapezoidal Armenian fortress built in 1606 combines Gothic, Classical, Ottoman, and crumble elements.

Back in town, check out the **Sf. Ioan cel Nou Monastery**. From the main square, turn right on Bd. Ipătescu, then left on Str. Ioan Vodă cel Viteaz. Thousands come from Bucovina for the June 24 **city festival**—a celebration of the local **Sf. Ioan cel Nou** (St. John the New)—in which the mummified body of the saint is removed from the monastery's church and paraded in a religious procession. According to legend, the saint was martyred at Cetatea Alba and brought back to Suceava by Prince Alecsandru cel Bun. The **History Museum**, Str. Ştefan cel Mare 53 (tel. 21 64 39), contains a French wax reconstruction of Ştefan cel Mare's throne room. The exhibit moves from 100,000-300,000-year-old mammoth bones to the vestiges of the archaeology goldmine at Cucuteni to the Daco-Roman era, and contains numerous paintings, coins, and wares; notice especially the green glass signifying the mixing of Dacians (who did not know how to make glass) and Romans (who did). (Open Tues.-Sun.

10am-6pm; 1600 lei.) Ask for the museum brochure (800 lei); it has a great town map. The **Ethnographic Museum,** Str. Porumbescu (tel. 21 37 75), displays paraphernalia of peasant culture from different parts of Romania—observe the painted eggs and funky masks (open Tues.-Sun. 10am-6pm; 1000 lei).

■ Near Suceava: Bucovina Monasteries

Bucovina's painted monasteries have napped away the centuries among green hills and forests, near rustic farming villages. Built 500 years ago by Ştefan cel Mare and his successors, the tiny structures serenely mix Moldovan with Byzantine architecture and Romanian soul with Christian dogma. Most of the monasteries are small, with stone walls and wooden roofs, surrounded by living quarters for monks or nuns and heavy stone walls that never managed to discourage looters. When visiting, always wear long sleeves and a long skirt or pants.

VORONEŢ AND HUMOR

Albastru de Voroneţ (Voroneţ Blue) is a phrase that haunts Romanian imaginations, from schoolchildren to experts feverishly looking for a modern equivalent of its 15th-century paint. The *albastru* that brought the monastery its legendary fame is also the source of its prolonged restoration, since most work has to be postponed until *albastru de Voroneţ* is produced once more. Voroneţ's frescos are stupendous, and the *Last Judgement* mural a masterpiece. The damned wear the faces of Moldova's enemies, the blessed look ethnically Moldovan, and angels sport regional musical instruments. God sits above Jesus at the very top of the wall, and angels roll up the Zodiac around him, showing the passing of earthly time. *Jesse's Tree,* on the south wall, displays the genealogy of Jesus, while the north wall depicts the Genesis and Adam's pact with the Devil. The church was built in 1488 by Ştefan cel Mare on the advice of **St. Daniel.** A copy of Ştefan's throne stands in the left nave (the original is being restored). The gold-covered *iconostasis* is made from *tiza* wood, which can last up to 1000 years (entrance 1500 lei).

To get here from Suceava, go to **Gura Humorului** by **train** (most any Cluj/Timişoara train will do; 4 per day, 1hr.) or **bus** (2 per day, 1hr., 1700 lei), then take a bus for **Voroneţ** (4 per day, 10min., 600 lei) from near the train station. By foot, walk straight from the Voroneţ station, then take a left on the main road. After less than 1km, take a left onto the road leading south toward Voroneţ (5km).

About 6km north of Gura Humorului, **Humor,** dating from 1530, can be visited on the same daytrip as Voroneţ. The south wall depicts the Virgin Mary's life. A fresco represents her saving Constantinople from a Persian attack in 626, based on a poem by the patriarch of Constantinople. With an eye towards contemporary threats, the painter substituted Turks for Persians and added weapons typical of the 16th century. He included himself as a faintly-painted cavalier running a Turk through with his spear. Nearby lies an older monastery built by Alesandru cel Bun. The open balcony provides an opportunity to study a *Last Judgment* fresco up close (2000 lei). Getting to Humor is no joke: **buses** leave Gura Humorului (see Voroneţ, above; 5 per day, 500 lei). By foot, take a right on the main road from the train station and walk to the heart of Gura Humorului. At the fork, near a park on the right and a market on the left, follow the soft left 6km to the monastery.

ARBORE AND DRAGOMIRNA

The tiny church of **Arbore** has some of the region's most beautiful frescos, though they badly need restoration. No monks or nuns remain here, and the small courtyard with time-worn gravestones with inscriptions in Cyrillic and symbols whose key may well be lost, lies off a rarely trodden secondary road. One daily **bus** to Arbore leaves from Suceava (1800 lei), and another from Gura Humorului (1½hr.).

Near Suceava lies the **Dragomirna monastery,** built between 1602 and 1627. While there are no exterior frescos, the building's sculpted tower is said to have inspired the exquisite exterior of Biserica Trei Ierarhi in Iași. The windows are pointedly Byzantine, the interior half-frescoed. Before the carved leafy *iconostasis* sits the throne of the ruling *domn* (prince) on the left and the *mitropolit* (bishop) on the right. The 1000-lei admission is for the church and the museum containing many old silver-gilded manuscripts. Fortified walls surround this forest-edge church, but did not prevent the Cossack troops of Khmielnitsky from looting the place in 1653. Not many visitors trek here, but a log-cabin **campground** is in the works. Access by car is easy, and a local bus makes the trip; get details at Suceava's bus station or ONT.

MOLDOVIȚA AND SUCEVIȚA

Moldovița is the largest of the painted monasteries, and its frescos are among the best-preserved. Built in 1532 and painted in 1537, it has another *Last Judgment,* another *Jesse's Tree,* and a monumental *Siege of Constantinople.* The siege of 626 painted on the exterior wall to the right of the entrance depicts the ancient fortress in an uncanny 16th-century light. The monastery was closed from 1785-1945, and the north wall is badly weathered. The *iconostasis* juts with elaborately carved grapevine columns painted with gold. As with most of the monasteries, the founder is painted "al fresco" inside the nave, presenting the church to Jesus. The museum houses the original wooden (now seatless) throne of Prince Petru Rareș. Opposite the throne in the main room is the *Pomme d'Or* prize awarded to Bucovina in 1975 in recognition of its touristic and artistic importance. Be sure to see the massive **religious tomb** donated by Catherine the Great (2000 lei; camera 4000 lei; video camera 10,000 lei). From Suceava, take a **train** to Vama and switch for the train to Vatra Moldoviței (3 per day, 5th stop), 2km east of Moldovița.

Sucevița is beautifully set in fortified hills, where its white walls shine on sunny days, making it appear more a citadel than a monastery. The frescoed south wall presents a *Genealogy of Jesus* and a *Procession of Philosophers* portraying Pythagoras, Socrates, Plato, Aristotle, and Solon in Byzantine cloaks. Plato is carrying a small coffin of bones on his head. The green you see is unique to Sucevița. Unlike the other monasteries' north faces, Sucevița's is well preserved. Souls climb a heavenly ladder of 30 rungs, each rung representing a virtue and a sin. The west wall remains unpainted— the artist fell from the scaffolding, and his ghost prevents completion. The blackstone head under the arch represents a woman who hauled stone for the construction in her ox-wagon for 30 years. Inside, a *Last Judgement* decorates the wall under the balcony's Zodiac ceiling next to an illustration of the martyred **Sf. Ioan cel Nou** returning from Cetatea Alba. The pro-nave depicts the deaths of 420 Orthodox saints, while the chamber contains an *iconostasis* carved from *tiza* wood. The **tomb room,** painted with scenes from Jewish history, houses the tombs of the **Movila** dynasty. A tiny door on the left leads to an emergency hiding place for relics and precious icons. The nave relives the life of Jesus, and the altar boasts two *iconostases* (2000 lei).

Roughly 3km south of Sucevița on the Moldovița road, lodging can be found March to December at **Popasul Turistic Bucovina,** set on a hill a few meters off the national road. The sparkling white houses with black-wood decorations seem more like prosperous Moldovan homes than standard inns. In the first house, the dry wood by the stove welcomes tourists to comfortable rooms (single 40,000 lei, doubles 50,000 lei; to reserve, call Sucevița's central phone office, ext.165). A terrace **restaurant** serves great meals (hearty portions of beef soup and *tochitijră* under 10,000 lei). As for the modern bungalows (25,000 lei for a double), hand-woven woolen carpets, immaculate bathrooms (with non-stop hot water), and reverence to old style Moldovan hospitality make you wish to stay longer. **Hikes** around Sucevița are gorgeous, but there is no map and the trails are badly marked (though it's hard to get lost in the hilly terrain). Sucevița lies 29km north of Moldovița (see above); **buses** run erratically between Sucevița and Rădăuți. Ask at Rădăuți's train station for the bus to Sucevița.

PUTNA

Immaculately white and beautiful in its simplicity, Putna has the marble-canopied **tomb of Ștefan cel Mare** (among others) and an interesting **museum.** It's also probably the best-kept and easiest to access of the monasteries. Ștefan decays down on the right, his sons occupy the nearer tombs. Built in 1469, Putna was the first of 38 temples founded by Ștefan, who built one church after each battle he fought. Ștefan left Putna's location up to God: he climbed a nearby hill marked by a cross, to the left of the monastery, and shot an arrow into the air. A piece of the oak it struck is on display at the museum (open daily 9am-7pm; 2000 lei). A part of Jesus's cross was apparently given to Ștefan by the Pope and placed for a time in this monastery; today, however, only a few monks know of its existence or whereabouts.

Quiet lodging can be found near the monastery at **Casa de Odihnă** (doubles 24,000 lei, 2-bed bungalows 15,000 lei). Both Casa de Odihnă and its **restaurant** are run by the local monks, so be prepared for monk's garb and monk's restrictions on food—no meat during fasting weeks. There are good hiking trails, but no map. Tourists flood Putna on July 2—St. Stephen's Day. For the scenic ride to Putna, catch direct **trains** from Suceava, 75km southeast (4 per day, 2½hr., 1500 lei). The last train leaves Putna in late afternoon. The monastery lies 2km from the train station. Exiting the platform, take a right, then a left at the first intersection; keep walking.

On the road between Sucevița and Putna, you'll pass through the potter's village of **Marginea,** famous for its black pottery. The studio is open to visitors, especially to ones who buy their pots at the ridiculously low prices (2000-10,000 lei). Just watch for the huge signs, **Atelièr de Ceramică** is right by the road. Next to the studio, a village house was converted into a shop that sells stunning 100-year-old, handmade popular costumes and carpets for a steal (open daily 7am-7pm).

NEAMȚ, SECU, AGAPIA, AND VĂRATEC

Fields of clovers and buttercups cradle **Mănăstirea Neamț** 12km northwest of Târgu Neamț. The monks offer unofficial housing in gorgeous rooms at negotiable prices; if you're not rowdy, these bathroom-less rooms are yours, along with a serenade from the crickets and frogs in the bubbling brook nearby. A throne worthy of Conan the Destroyer looks upon a 6th-century *Madonna and Child.* Presented to Alesandru cel Bun in 1424 by the Byzantine Empire, the icon was nearly lost in a Turkish attack. Legend has it that the Madonna's piercing eyes paralyzed the Turk who stole it, and he, stricken, swore to renounce Allah if the icon saved him. He died a monk at Mănăstirea Neamț. Be sure not to miss the chandelier holding eight ostrich eggs—symbols of eternal life. The **museum,** once home to the calligraphy school that nurtured Moldova's first historians, contains icons, priestly garb, Dimitrie Cantemir's 1825 *Descriptio Moldoviae* (the largest typed Old Romanian book; 45cm by 32cm), and the *iconostasis* from the older church built in 1375 by Petru Mușat. A **grocery store** sells goodies 2km away, but most bring food from Târgu Neamț. Târgu Neamț is on the Suceava-Buzău-Bucharest **train** line: switch at Pașcani onto a train to Târgu Neamț (5 per day). Getting between the **bus** and train stations is tricky; ask a cabby to take you to the *autogară* (US$2). Buses go to Agapia (5 per day, ½hr., 400 lei), Mănăstirea Neamț (7 per day, ½hr., 400 lei), Secu via the Sihastria bus (2 per day, ½hr., 400 lei), and Suceava (2 per day, 2½hr., 2500 lei).

Mănăstirea Secu, 10km southwest of Neamț, is the place to smell the roses. Inside the church, rarely visited by foreigners, are relics with excellent pedigrees. The gold coffin holds many a holy bone, including the right foot of **St. John the Baptist.** The wooden crucifix was presented to Ștefan the Great by the Pope, and has a black splinter from the cross on which Jesus died. Dazzled by these wonders, it's easy to forget the **museum** (2000 lei), containing old manuscripts, ornate crucifixes, and fine garments and tapestries sewn with silver and gold threads. The oldest of these (made in 1608) has deerskin hands and feet on all its characters and rubies in the halo of Jesus. Stolen in 1821 by the Turks, it was returned by Moldovan boyars.

From Secu, it's possible to hike to **Agapia**. Continue down the road 3km to the Sihăstria Monastery; 20m before reaching it, climb the hill on the left and follow the red stripe/white cross trail to Mănăstirea Sihla (40min.). In the bluffs by the humble church lived the hermit **Saint Theodosia**. To see her tiny cave, climb the stairs scaling the rocks on the right. Now it's only 8km downhill. Cross Sihla and take the trail behind the church across a stream. The road to the right leads to Agapia (take lefts at all major intersections). Built by Vasile Lupu's brother in 1642, Agapia was painted by Nicolae Grigorescu over 200 years later. The 20-year-old artist, with the assistance of Louis Girardelli, painted the icons and frescos on Renaissance themes of Raphael, Titian, and Da Vinci, but with a new (somewhat smoke-obscured) color scheme. A self-portrait of the artist as Daniel is in the last medallion in the upper left corner of the *iconostasis*. The 2000-lei admission covers the museum, with icons donated by the Patriarchs of Jerusalem, Constantinople, Africa, India, Moscow, and Bulgaria.

About 5km southwest of Agapia in a fir-studded crown of hills, roses, poppies, and pansies render **Mănăstirea Văratec** more an aromatic heaven than a monastery. The 1808 architecture distinguishes it from the other temples, and the museum's inscription of gold, silver, and deerskin tops the beautiful hike (2000 lei).

BLACK SEA COAST

The land between the Danube and the Black Sea has weathered a troubled history. Conquered by the Turks in the 14th century, it remained part of the Ottoman Empire until 1877, when it was ceded to Romania as compensation for losing South Moldova to its treacherous ally Russia. To the south stretch beautiful beaches. The interior, made up of dry valleys and rocky hills, holds Roman, Greek, and early Christian ruins, and produces some of Romania's best wines. Crowds packed the littoral in the past, but now prices are rising too high for many Romanians.

> For a map of the Black Sea Coast area, see p. 139 in the Bulgaria chapter.

■ Constanța

Though Ceaușescu's grandomania made into one of the largest—and largely unused—ports in Europe, the city started out as the simple Greek port of Tomis 2500 years ago. A crossroads between East and West, the town has been home, conquest, or place of exile for many, including Germans, Turks, and Romans—Constanța is named for the daughter of the Emperor Constantine. You may stumble across traces of eclectic charm in the dust- and sea-scented Old Town. This is one of Romania's largest cities, and the place to catch buses to Black Sea resorts.

Orientation and Practical Information Constanța is north of the Black Sea resorts, 225km from Bucharest by rail. Most **trains** from Constanța pass through Bucharest to Brașov, Cluj, Oradea, and Timișoara; tickets start at 4600 lei. There are also trains to Iași (1 per day), Suceava (1 per day), and Tulcea (2 per day). Chances are that trains will be packed in summer. Buy tickets in advance, and remember a seat reservation is needed to ride a *rapid* or *express*. Only on the *accelerat* can you squeeze in the hallway. The 8:05 and 8:41am *rapid* trains out of Bucharest's Gara Băneasa (behind Casa de Presei, a.k.a. Casa Scînteii) are one of the city's best-kept secrets; showing up 20 minutes early usually suffices. Constanța's **train** and **bus stations** are near each other; northbound buses leave from a third station, **Autogară Tomis Nord** (from the train station, ride 5 stops on tram #100). To get downtown from the train station, take trolley #40 or 43 and get off where Bd. Tomis intersects Bd. Ferdinand (4 stops). Cash **traveler's checks** at 6% commission or get a **cash advance** on Visa at 10% at **Trans Danubius**, Bd. Ferdinand 36 (tel. 61 94 81; open Mon.-Sat. 9am-9pm, Sun. 9am-2pm), a travel agency catering to foreigners with **tours**

DUNA PALOTA
Zrínyi utca 5.

DONAU — DANUBE
KONZERT

DONAU-SYMPHONIE-ORCHESTER

Melodies of
LISZT, BARTÓK, BRAHMS,
BERLIOZ, STRAUSS, LEHÁR,
KODÁLY, KÁLMÁN

DOHÁNY UTCA 2.
Synagogue

CULTURAL AND MUSICAL JEWISH HERITAGE IN BUDAPEST

BUDAPESTER KLEZMER BAND Concert

BUDAI VIGADÓ
Corvin tér 8.

FOLKLOR

HUNGARIAN STATE FOLKLOR ENSEMBLE

and

DANUBE FOLK ENSEMBLE

DUNA PALOTA
Zrínyi utca 5.

LET'S GO® TRAVEL

EURAIL PASSES

The most convenient and affordable way to travel in Europe. Save up to 70% off the cost of individual tickets.

EURAILPASS (FIRST CLASS)
Unlimited train travel for a specific duration of time. Accepted in 17 countries.
15 days • 21 days • 1, 2, or 3 months

EURAIL FLEXIPASS (FIRST CLASS)
Individual travel days that can be used at your convenience within a two month period.
any 10 days • any 15 days

EURAIL YOUTHPASS (SECOND CLASS)
The same as a Eurailpass, but for those under 26 years old.
any 10 days • any 15 days

EURAIL YOUTH FLEXIPASS (SECOND CLASS)
The same as a Eurail Flexipass, but for those under 26 years old.
any 10 days • any 15 days

FREE STANDARD SHIPPING

Call **1-800-5-LETS-GO** or mail in this card for an updated Eurail catalog and 1996 prices.

DONAU ▲▲ DANUBE
KONZERT

Tel./Fax: 117-27-54; 117-13-77
Tel: 117-27-90/extension 156
117-27-90/extension 115

PRICES: DANUBE CONCERT - from 16,50 US$
FOLKLOR - from 13 US$
Program JEWISH HERITAGE OF
BUDAPEST - from 24 US$

WITH THIS CARD WE ALLOW YOU A LET'S GO DISCOUNT OF 20%

KARTEN/TICKETS & INFORMATIO
☎ **117-27-54**
117-13-77
DUNA PALOTA
Zrínyi utca 5.

Please send my 1997 Eurail catalog
_____
_____
_____

LET'S GO
T R A V E L
67 Mt. Auburn Street
Cambridge, MA 02138
USA

to the Danube Delta. The **rent-a-car** (tel. 62 31 52) agency will get you a Dacia or Renault for US$20 per day plus US$0.20 per km and US$5 per day insurance (open Mon.-Thurs. 7:30am-4pm, Fri. 7:30am-1:30pm). At Bd. Tomis and Ștefan cel Mare are the **post office** (open Mon.-Fri. 7am-9pm, Sat. 8am-noon) and **phones** (open Mon.-Sun. 7am-10pm). **Postal code:** 8300. **Phone code:** 041.

Accommodations and Food While it is hard to find a cheap inn here, it isn't so difficult as elsewhere on the coast. **Hotel Continental's** location in the center of town at Bd. Ferdinand 20 (tel. 61 56 60) makes up for its unappealing exterior. In 1995, it was the cheapest; in 1996, it was under renovation for "one year, maybe two"—tempt fate! Actually, we're just leaving it in because all our directions depend on it. **Hotel Tineretului,** Bd. Tomis 20/26 (tel. 61 35 90), has decent rooms with shower, fridge, and TV (doubles 130,000 lei, suites 180,000 lei). The seaside **Hotel Palace,** Str. Remus Opreanu 5 (tel. 61 46 96), is reminiscent of Monaco. Fresh roses await you in the rooms, which are all budget-breakingly good with bath, TV, phone, and fridge (singles 152,500-155,700 lei, doubles 197,000-201,000 lei, suites 284,500-418,500 lei; laundry service 1000 lei per kg). **Restaurant** open daily 7am-midnight with an English menu and a beautiful terrace view of the sea. Closer to the sea than the Hotel Continental, the recently-opened **UFO International,** Bd. Tomis 17 (tel. 61 10 57), sets its fast food in a spacious black and metallic interior. Around the corner from Continental are a **grocery** and a **market.**

Sights and Entertainment Escape innumerable gray apartment blocks by exploring the **Old Town.** In the center, the main attraction of the **Folk Art Museum,** Bd. Tomis 32 (tel. 61 61 33), is the peasant glass icon exhibit. A small collection of costumes, tools, and artwork from all over the country places an emphasis on Dobrogean minorities (English labels; open daily 9am-8pm; 1500 lei). The **Naval History Museum,** Str. Traian 53 (tel. 61 90 35), stockpiles instruments, uniforms, documents, and models that dazzle even experts. An ancient tree-trunk canoe and Greek frigate are moored here (open Tues.-Sun. 10am-6pm; 1000 lei).

From Hotel Continental, take a right onto Bd. Tomis and follow it until it curves left and ends in Piața Ovidiu. The **Statue of Ovid** commemorates the Roman writer who penned his most famous poems while in exile here, ostensibly for writing *Art of Love*—the real reason was his affair with the Emperor Augustus's daughter. Ovid's epitaph on the statue asks you to pray for his tranquil slumber. The **Archaeology Museum,** Piața Ovidiu 12 (tel. 61 45 83), has several items from the Roman past, including an awesome snake-god statue of Sarpele Glycon-Divinitate (open daily 9am-8pm; 1000 lei). To the left of the museum, behind the Roman columns, are **excavations** of a Roman port with the **world's largest floor mosaic,** preserved from the 4th century BCE and discovered only in 1959—walk behind the museum to better admire it and the brickwork. Several walls still stand alongside a collection of amphorae and iron anchors (1000 lei).

The **mosque** on Str. Muzeelor is one of the few reminders of Turkish domination and has one of the largest **oriental carpets** in Europe (maybe to cover the mosaic?), woven in the 18th century on the island Ada-Kaleh in the Danube. The doors are constructed of black Italian marble, and banners bearing the name of the prophet hang from the walls. The 50m tower (140 steps) offers a bird's eye view of the town. Built in 1730, the mosque was reconstructed by King Carol I in 1910. If you come for services (Fri. 1pm), wash your hands, feet, and face in the courtyard (open daily 9am-5pm; 1000 lei). The less religious might prefer to relax among 2000-year-old Greek amphorae and Roman sarcophagi in the shade of the nearby **archaeological park.**

Closer to the sea is the **Orthodox Cathedral,** Str. Arhi Episcopiei 25, built in 1877, following Romania's independence from Turkey (open Mon.-Sun. 7am-7pm), and a beautiful, statue-lined waterfront promenade. Farther up, the **statue of poet Mihai Eminescu** gazes dreamily toward the sea. Behind him on Str. Remus Opreanu is the tiny **Farul Genovez** (Genoa Lighthouse), built in 1861. At the other end of the promenade, sailors procrastinate in the small passenger port. Ferry routes to Mangalia have been suspended, but you can charter a yacht for a few hours. It's cheaper for large groups; bargain directly with the owners.

Near Lacul Tăbăcăriei at Bd. Mamaia 255 (tel. 64 70 55), a **planetarium** and a **delphinarium** (dolphin show) coexist. Take trolley #41 from Bd. Ferdinand and get off after crossing the tram tracks (planetarium 6 daily shows, tickets 2000 lei; delphinarium 5 daily shows, tickets 2000 lei). The **Aquarium**, Bd. 16 Februarie 1 (tel. 61 12 77), has the world's largest sturgeon collection—oh-so-tasty (open daily 9am-8pm; 2000 lei; restaurant open 8am-1am; bar open until 4am). The asymmetric Baroque **Casino**, Str. Libertății 48 (tel. 61 74 16; restaurant open daily 8am-1pm; bar open until 4am), was built in 1910 and still smacks of the cosmopolitan high-life. The terrace serves up a stunning view of the sea, tasty food, and a nightly disco.

■ South of Constanța

The coast here is lined with sandy beaches and 1970s-revival tourist resorts. Buses run south from Constanța about every half-hour in the direction of Mangalia (40km, 1800 lei). More comfortable private minibuses have variable fares (2000-4000 lei). Trains are frequent, slightly slower, and only a bit more expensive. All of the resorts on the coast have the same postal and phone codes as Constanța (8700; 041).

MANGALIA, 2 MAI, AND VAMA VECHE

The **railway** terminus of Mangalia provides **luggage storage** (500 lei) and sees scores of trains dump beachgoers onto its sunburnt streets. Most Constanța-Mangalia (2000-4000 lei) and Olimp-Mangalia (600-1000 lei) **buses and minivans** stop here and turn around. If you're on a budget, Mangalia is ideal—you can grab groceries at the **market** and the adjacent **Gospodina** convenience store (open daily 7am-10:30pm), not too far from the station (walk down the Str. Ion Creangă sidestreet leading away from the station 1 block and take a left); then make your *adieus* to the venerable **Archaeological Museum**, Șos. Constanța (tel. 75 35 80), near the traffic circle (open Mon.-Sun. 9am-8pm; 2000 lei); and hightail it south 3km to **2 Mai** or 11km to **Vama Veche**, where housing is dirt cheap. These unspoiled villages offer tent space and **private accommodations** (set the price before you move in). In 2 Mai, a few Coca-Cola signs predict that its beauty might not outlive the first stage of Romanian privatization, while Vama Veche remains untouched. Most young people **camp** at the south end of the nude beach in 2 Mai (tent-space 2500 lei; parking 700 lei). Every night they light campfires and play guitar. Nearby, an old fisherman's cove comes complete with shacks, rotting boats, and straw umbrellas. 2 Mai is popular among intellectuals, artists, and free-spirited students. Dine at the definitely "in" **Șuberek's** (pizza 3000 lei, Turkish pie 600 lei; open daily 8pm-6am). The clothed **campground** (tents 5000 lei) with a beach lies in the north part of 2 Mai, a block away from the bus #14 stop.

VENUS AND SATURN

Venus rose from the foam of Saturn's seas to create one of the best **beaches** on the coast. Across the highway from the beach lies a popular **free camping** zone. Saturn's **Dispecerat de Cazare housing office** (tel. 75 58 42), behind Hotel Tosca and around the terrace restaurant, provides maps and rooms (doubles: 1-star 60,000 lei, 2-star 105,000 lei; bungalows 48,000 lei; camping available; open daily 5:30am-6:30pm).

Alternately, some vacationers accept offers of private room for 15,000-25,000 lei. For Saturn, take the train to Mangalia and walk up the beach a few blocks. From Saturn's *Dispecerat* (near Mangalia), it's a short walk through the resort to nearby Venus. Along the way you'll pass an under-used **amusement park**—a roller coaster, a few rides, and bumper cars. Or strike out under the mirrored ball at the **bowling alley** (dancing nightly 10pm-5am). Chow at **Grădina de Vară** amid billiards, video games, and loud music (under 15,000 lei; open daily 9:30am-1am).

NEPTUN AND OLIMP

This famous Roman god and his lesser-known brother have practically merged and are serviced by the Neptun train stop. **Neptun**, site of Ceaușescu's summer villa, is the more high-brow of the resorts with omnipresent roses, up-to-date services, and probably the best eateries on the coast. Its northern neighbor **Olimp** has excellent beaches but tends to be more expensive. **Phones** ring at the Neptun **post office** (open Mon.-Sun. 7am-9pm). **Siupa Exchange** (in the post office; open daily 9am-5pm) changes traveler's checks at 2% commission. Exchange Eurocheques and Visa at **Bance de Comerț Exterior** (tel. 73 15 33) for a 1% commission.

Neptun's **Dispecerat de Cazare housing office** (tel. 73 13 10), in the Topkapî shopping center, helps find rooms, often at prices lower than hotels' (singles in 2-star hotel US$10, 3-star hotel US$18; plus 10% commission; in summer open 24hr.). Locals may offer rooms for 20,000 lei. Two-star hotels, such as the Western, almost lakeside **Hotels Apollo** (tel. 73 16 16), and **Romanța** (tel. 73 10 23), offer clean, spacious rooms with showers (single 62,000 lei, double 124,00 lei). Romanța's stained-glass windows cast a surrealist aqua glow around the cozy, oh-so-blue couches. If not sparkling, they're at least close to the lakes. **Camping Neptun** (tel. 73 12 20) has wood and plaster houses as well as tent lots (2-bed wooden with or without running water 42,000-54,000 lei; 2-bed plaster with shower 80,000 lei; tent space 13,000 lei).

You can feast on grilled sturgeon with potatoes and quality wines while enjoying dance shows in the shade of the verdant trees at the **Rustic** (tel. 73 10 26). Reserve with your hotel's tourist office or directly with the Rustic (dinner and show under 20,000 lei; open daily noon-1am). **Restaurant Crama Neptun** (tel. 73 19 12) ages gracefully in a huge wine cellar with woven red-and-black cloths everywhere (entrées 10,000-22,000 lei; open daily 9am-4am). There are a few **grocery stores** on the main street. **Disco Clăbucet** (tel. 73 16 21), in an eponymous hotel, has a 3000-lei cover (open nightly 10pm-5am). Games and rides cluster near the bazaar at night.

EFORIE NORD, EFORIE SUD, AND COSTINEȘTI

Closest to Constanța are **Eforie Nord** and **Sud**, the first Black Sea resorts—still bejeweled with antique buildings and renowned for the mud baths near **Lake Techirghiol**. The lake water is rumored to be so salty you can't sink (do *not* test this rumor by purposely trying to sink). In Eforie Nord, **Hotels Bega** (tel. 74 14 68) and **Apollo** (tel. 74 18 73) are each 50,000 lei per person. At Apollo, you can bargain down the prices.

South of the Efories, **Costinești**, the hot spot on the coast, gets wonderfully crowded with young people. Some hitch the 3km from the bus station. The train drops you even closer; get off at Costinești Tabără and circle right around the lake to find **Albatros** and **Coral**, which provide decent doubles and a meal for only 33,000 lei per day (Albatros has in-room bathrooms). The super-budget *căsuțe* (little houses) run 12,000-16,000 lei (2 beds). One **cafeteria** advertises its cakes with the slogan: *"Prăjituri foarte proaspete. Serviți cu încredere."* (Very fresh cakes. Eat confidently.) **Grocery stores** gather near the train, as do many unofficial "backyard" campgrounds.

The heart of the littoral beats well into the night; **Disco Ring** is one of the largest outdoor dance clubs in Eastern Europe (open nightly 8pm-4am; cover 2000 lei). Also at 2000 lei, **Disco Tineretului** has live bands and features kick-ass UV/laser lights. The bar is non-stop, but the main activity at this mostly under-20 outdoor club is dancing (open nightly 9pm-4am). **Wanted** shakes under a geodesic dome across from an outdoor cinema—great music, though the DJ could jabber less at the twentysomething crowd (billiards and bar; open nightly 10pm-6am; cover 1000 lei).

DOBROGEA

Romania's most famous wines are made in the hills of Murfatlar in the heart of Dobrogea. Trans Danubius organizes wine tastings and tours of the Danube Delta (see Constanța, p. 514). Be warned that transportation in Dobrogea can be a hassle. Without a car, the only option is a slow and crowded bus.

■ Histria

A Hellenic colony mentioned by Greek historian Strabo in the 5th century BCE, the town of Histria was rediscovered in the early 20th century by Romanian archaeologist Vasile Pârvan. The excavations are about 30km north of Constanța, on the shore of Lake Sinoe (a lagoon separated from the sea by a thread of sand). Two daily **buses** leave from the Tomis Nord station in Constanța at 9am and 4pm; unfortunately they drop you off an all-too-invigorating 7km hike from the site.

The **museum** and continuing **excavations** follow the city's 14 centuries of recorded history, from the 7th century BCE to the 7th century CE. Most explanations are in Romanian, French, and German. The city is named in honor of the Danube (*Istros* in Greek), which returned the favor by ultimately causing its decay—blocking the city harbor with mud. So much for gratitude. Several walls and a few columns still stand, and the museum protects carved stones, statue fragments, and amphorae (museum open daily 10am-6pm; 1000 lei). **Bungalow** doubles run 10,000 lei.

■ Danube Delta

After winding its way through eight countries, the Danube empties into the Black Sea at the complex, enormous (almost 2000 square miles) biosphere known as the Danube Delta. This region provides a refuge for more than 300 species of birds and 110 types of fish, as well as supporting the only pelican colony in Europe. The delta is overgrown with more than 1000 species of plants, including the never-satiated carnivorous *Aldrovanda*. Villagers are tapping the delta's resources, and the expanding tourism has begun to affect the most traveled parts of the delta. Yet, the maze of lakes, channels, islands, tropical woods, and dunes has remained mostly pristine— due in part to its UNESCO designation as a "Reservation for the Biosphere"—and a site for fishing, boating, or simply observing an intricate eco-system.

Because of the difficulty of finding transportation around the area, the best place to start exploring the delta is not necessarily the town you'll want to spend most of your time in—be sure to arrive in the main access point of **Tulcea** early in the morning, as the **ferries** are few and far between (daily trips to: Galați and Brăila 12:15pm, Crișan, Sf. Georghe, and Sulina 1:30pm). Tulcea "caters" to travelers with expensive accommodations and a serious dearth of interesting sights; the buzz you hear will more likely be the hordes of stinging mosquitoes than the less-than-hopping nightlife. Arrangers of outings to the delta as well as hunting and fishing licences, the **Tulcea Tourism Agency** (tel. (040) 516 604) can also provide boarding house accommodation. The **Hotel Egreta,** 2, Păcii Str. (tel. (040) 51 71 03), offers blissfully bug-free rooms with phone and TV (singles US$38, doubles US$50).

From Tulcea, you can rent a boat and attempt to navigate the delta yourself, but it may be worth the money to sit in on an **organized tour** (see Trans Danubius, p. 514), and Tulcea Tourism Agency, above) or find a **tour guide/fisherman** willing to show you around. If you're anxious about paddling yourself, **rowers** available for a trip usually wait at the docks. Prices vary, but be ready to shell out 60,000 lei for three hours with an experienced guide—if you're lucky, he'll even speak a few words of English.

A popular destination within the delta is **Crișan,** reached by **ferry** from Tulcea. A caveat—the mosquitoes are huge and the water and food supplies may be small. Another option is to continue past Crișan on the ferry to the town of **Sulina,** which has lost some of the popularity it enjoyed during the Communist regime. Though not as inexpensive as it was during its heyday as a Red Retreat, its riverfront promenade and fine sand still make a romantic spot. It's also a good location to rent a private **boat** to explore the less well traveled parts of the delta. There are no truly budget hotels in Sulina, but **private accommodations** should be available. People will probably be waiting for tourists at the port; look for *Zimmer Frei* signs.

RUSSIA (РОССИЯ)

US$1 = 5181R (Rubles)		1000R = US$0.19
CDN$1 = 3774R		1000R = CDN$0.26
UK£1 = 8075R		1000R = UK£0.12
IR£1 = 8393R		1000R = IR£0.12
AUS$1 = 4084R		1000R = AUS$0.24
NZ$1 = 3601R		1000R = NZ$0.28
SAR1 = 1164R		1000R = SAR0.86
DM1 = 3500R		1000R = DM0.29
Country Phone Code: 7		**International Dialing Prefix: 810**

> In Russia's unstable economy, expect prices to have changed dramatically.

> *It is a riddle wrapped in a mystery inside an enigma.*
> —Winston Churchill, in 1939 on Russia

Many Russians claim they no longer recognize today's Russia, but Churchill is as right today as he was over half-century ago. Russia and the processes it is going through are mindboggling and incomprehensible. Though considered a world superpower, Russia is more of a chaotic bazaar with its own ever-changing rules and frustrations. Rapid economic change and the collapse of a legal infrastructure have led to a rise in poverty and a growing discontent with the new government system. As a result, many Russians have started to lend political support to old Communist leaders, making restructuring the system even more difficult. The collapse of the Soviet Union has allowed Russia's vast patchwork of autonomous regions and minority nationalities to tear apart, or at least fray. Still, Russians manage to endure with unique resourcefulness and a heavy dose of black humor, saving, bartering, growing vegetables on windowsills, and taking refuge around the kitchen table with homemade pickles and a pot of tea.

RUSSIA ESSENTIALS

Russian visas require an invitation stating itinerary and dates of travel and are thus inherently difficult to get without a Russian connection. Furthermore, once the invitation is obtained, the applicant must either present all papers to the consulate in person or through a registered travel agency (no mail). Fortunately, the following organizations specialize in supplying invitations and/or visas for individual tourists:

Russian Youth Hostels. In **Estonia:** Karol YHA Travel, Lembitu 4, EE0001, Tallinn (tel. (2) 45 49 00). In **Finland:** SRM—Finnish YHA, Yrjönkatu 38B, Helsinki (tel. (90) 694 03 77). In **Germany:** DJH—German YHA, Tempelhofer Ufer 32, D 1000 Berlin 61 (tel. (030) 264 95 20). In **Lithuania:** Lithuanian YHA, Kauno 1A-407, Vilnius (tel. (02) 262 660). In the **U.K.:** YHA Travel Store, 14 Southhampton St., London, WC2E 7HY (tel. (0171) 836 1036). In the **U.S.:** 409 N. Pacific Coast Highway, 106/390, Redondo Beach, CA 90277 (tel. (310) 379-4316; fax 379-8420, e-mail 71573.2010@compuserve.com). No, you don't have to be a youth.

St. Petersburg International Hostel (HI), 3rd Sovetskaya ul. 28, St. Petersburg, Russia 193036 (tel. (812) 329 80 18; fax 329 80 19; e-mail ryh@ryh.spb.su; http://www.spb.su/ryh/). Arranges visa invitations, registers you once you get to Russia, and sells air and train tickets.

Traveller's Guest House, 50 Bolshaya Pereyaslavskaya, 10th floor, **Moscow,** Russia 129401 (tel. (095) 971 40 59 or 280 85 62; fax 280 76 86; e-mail tgh@glas.apc.org). In **Hong Kong:** Global Union Express (H.K.) Ltd., room 22-23, New Henry House, 10 Ice House St., Central, Hong Kong (tel. 868 32 31; fax 845 50 78; e-mail guehk@netvigator.com). They arrange visa invitations, will register you once you arrive in Russia, make reservations, and get train tickets.

Russia-Rail Internet Travel Service (e-mail russia-rail@russia-rail.com; http://www.russia-rail.com). Provides visas, organizes accommodations, and books rail tickets on all railways in the former USSR, including the Trans-Siberian, Trans-Mongolian, BAM, and Moscow-Europe route.

Russia House. In the **U.S.,** 1800 Connecticut Ave. NW, Washington, D.C. 20009, attn.: Chris Poor (tel. (202) 986-6010; fax 667-4244). In **Russia,** 17 Leningradsky Prospekt, Moscow, Russia 125040 (tel. (095) 250 01 43; fax 250 25 03). Provides invitations and visas for all countries of the former USSR—visas are business visas, so your travels should be less restricted. No train tickets or hotel reservations.

Red Bear Tours/Russian Passport, Suite 11A, 401 St. Kilda Rd., Melbourne 30004, Australia (tel. (3) 98 67 38 88; fax 98 67 10 55; toll free in Aus. (800) 333 70 31; e-mail bmccunn@werple.mira.net.au; http://www.travelcentre.com.au). Also provides invitations to Central Asian Republics. Red Bear provides rail tickets for the Trans-Siberian/Manchurian/Mongolian and Silk routes and assorted tours.

IBV Bed & Breakfast Systems, 13113 Ideal Drive, Silver Spring, MD 20906 (tel. (301) 942-3770; fax 933-0024). Provides varied services for those going to Russia.

Host Families Association, HOFA, 5-25 Tavricheskaya, 193015 St. Petersburg, Russia (tel./fax 812 275 1992; e-mail alexei@hofak.hop.stu.neva.ru). Arranges homestays in more than 20 cities of the former Soviet Union. Visa invitations available for HOFA guests to Russia, Ukraine, and Belarus. Singles US$30, twins US$50. Breakfast included. 20% discounts for non-central locations and Russian-speaking students. Free nights for longer stays (1 night per week, 10 nights per month).

If you have an invitation from an authorized travel agency, the **visa** must be applied for in person at the Russian Embassy or Consulate. The Russian consulate provides a fax-on-demand list of authorized travel bureaus (U.S. tel. (800) 634-4296). For addresses, see Essentials: Embassies and Consulates, p. 8. Bring a photocopy of your invitation; a photocopy of the front pages of your passport; a completed application (U.S. fax-on-demand (800) 634-4296); 3 passport-size photographs; a cover letter with your name, dates of arrival and departure, date of birth, and passport number; and the visa fee to the embassy or consulate (a single-entry visa costs US$40 for 2-week processing, US$50 for 1-week service, US$120 for next-business-day; double-entry business visa US$120, multiple-entry US$140 for 3-day processing).

Most organizations (hotels, etc.) will **register your visa** for you on arrival, but if this service is not provided, go to the central OVIR (ОВИР) office (in Moscow called УВИР) to register; many ignore this step, but it's the law. This is also where you should attempt to extend your visa—a bureaucratic hassle; it's better to get a long one before you go. Officially, you can freely travel anywhere that isn't off-limits to foreigners (such as military bases and power plants), but the local administration may give you a hard time if their city is not on your visa. It's OK to enter Russia through a city not specifically listed on your visa.

Many organizations run special **educational tours** to Russia. Try contacting the **American Council of Teachers of Russian** (ACTR), 1776 Massachusetts Ave. NW, Suite 700, Washington, D.C. 20036 (tel. (202) 833-7522), which does educational exchange programs. **Volunteers For Peace,** 43 Tiffany Rd., Belmont, VT 05730 (tel. (802) 259-2759), has innovative work and language programs in the former USSR.

GETTING THERE

Flying on British Airways to St. Petersburg or Moscow is the most direct way to reach the former Soviet Union (student fares available). Other airlines generally make stops in various European capitals (i.e., Air France in Paris, KLM in Amsterdam). **Rail travel** from European capitals to Moscow and St. Petersburg is cheaper. Find out if you are going through Belarus, for which you may need a transit visa; sometimes you can get by with only a Russian visa. If you wait until the border, it may be more expensive, and you risk not returning to your train in time. (The Warsaw-Tallinn express goes through Lithuania instead.) Finnord **buses** leave for St. Petersburg four times per day from Lahti, Finland, and are cheaper than trains.

Customs

One day they'll tear your pack apart, the next they'll just nod and dismiss you. Always be polite. If you fly in, especially with a group, your baggage will probably not be inspected. You may encounter more difficulty if you arrive by train or car. If you have doubts about anything, bring a lot of documentation or check with the Russian embassy before you go. Politely answer the border officials' questions, but *do not* offer any information for which they don't specifically ask.

You cannot bring rubles into or out of the country. At the border, you'll be given a **Customs Declaration Form** to declare all your valuables and foreign currency. Don't lose it. Everything listed on the customs form must be on your person when you leave the country. You may not export works of art, icons, old *samovars* (pre-electric models), or antique books—technically, anything published before 1945.

GETTING AROUND

> As of summer 1996, the U.S. State Department issued a warning about the overnight train between Moscow and St. Petersburg, a popular route for tourists. See Essentials: Before You Go, p. 19, on how to find the latest travel advisories.

Be flexible. Expect airport delays, tour cancellations, hotel changes, cold showers, and bathrooms *sans* toilet paper. The rules have changed so often no one really knows what they are anymore. As a result, an authority figure can choose whatever version suits him or her best. While argument is often futile, at times battling the Russian sense of arbitrary confusion with your own sense of confusion can be beneficial *and* the only way to become tolerant of and accustomed to the chaos. Station clerks might have a panic attack if you try to ask where you should be buying tickets. Go instead to the "Справочное Бюро" *kassa* (касса; window). These too, will close the window on you, or answer only one question, even if you are paying up to 6000R for this Russian-speakers-only "service."

Ticket Restrictions
You are officially required to buy internal plane and train tickets at inflated Intourist prices. The actual enforcement of this rule varies. You will probably need to show your *dokumenty* (документы; your passport) when you buy train and plane tickets, as required by law. This makes it nearly impossible to get the Russian rate. With the help of a Russian friend, you may be able to circumvent this, but be warned: your name is printed on your ticket which will be checked against your passport on board—though bribery may help. If you buy your train tickets at the station like everyone else, you run the risk of only being able to get a 3rd-class seat. You cannot buy train tickets originating in a different city, so it is best to use Moscow or St. Petersburg as a base, and buy roundtrip tickets from these two cities.

Trains and Commuter Rail
Trains tend to be the cheapest way to get around. Fares for non-former-Soviet destinations must be paid in hard currency. Train cars are divided into many classes. The most popular are luxury 2-bed "L" (Л) compartments, 4-bed cozy *"koupé"* (К), and open-car *platskarty* "P" (П). Ask for a *koupé*. Women traveling alone might want to consider buying tickets for all the beds in a *koupé* for safety reasons. Recently, private businesses started buying rail time and renting trains for the Moscow-St. Petersburg route. These private trains, called *férmeny* (ферменый), offer a safer, more comfortable ride—the "er" and "more" are reflected in the price. *Elektrichka* (**commuter rail,** marked on signs as пригородные поезда; *prigorodnye poezda*) has its own platforms at each station; buy tickets at the *kassa*. These trains are often packed, especially on weekends; you may have to stand for an hour or more.

Planes and Buses
Russia boasts an extensive bus network and a vast, not-so-reliable air system monopolized by **Aeroflot,** with its aging fleet and history of disasters. **Buses** are slightly more expensive and less crowded than trains; they are a good option for shorter distances. Buy seats on *myakhky* (мягкий; soft) buses to get a seat assignment in a fairly comfy reclining chair. You can often store luggage in the undercarriage for a fee.

Public Transportation
Within Russian cities, overcrowded **buses, trams, trolleys,** and (in major metropoles) unbelievably efficient **metro** systems ferry citizens quickly and cheaply. In the Metro, buy *zhetony* (жетоны; tokens) at the *kassa*, then drop them into machines that let you onto escalators. Buy bus tickets at newsstands or from the *babushki* at metro stations. On the bus you must punch your ticket. Don't try to ride for free, especially in

city centers; the system is very energetic in searching out free riders, particularly in the last week of the month, and fines are punitive. It is customary for passengers to tap each other on the shoulder and ask if they are getting off at the next stop (Вы выходите?—sounds like "Vee vee-HOAD-it-yeh?") so everyone can push their way to an exit. Metro stations are labeled only in Cyrillic; if you don't read Russian, you can usually recognize stations by memorizing the first and last letters. When two lines intersect, there is often a different station name for each line. You'll want to know the words *vkhod* (вход; entrance), *vykhod* (выход; exit), *vykhod v gorod* (выход в город; exit to the city), and *perekhod* (переход; passage to another line). Metro stations are marked above ground by a fluorescent "M". Try to acquire the newest city map possible—stations and street names have been changing wildly in recent years as tastes in politics have spun. In Moscow and St. Petersburg, however, maps and street signs have all caught up with the times.

Taxis

Hailing a **taxi** is indistinguishable from hitchhiking, and should be treated as such. Most who stop will be private citizens trying to make a little extra cash. Those seeking a ride stand off the curb and hold out a hand flat, palm down, no thumb; when a car stops, riders tell the driver the destination before getting in. He will either refuse the destination and speed off, or nod his head, at which point haggling begins. Meters are non-operational. Non-Russian speakers will get ripped off. While this informal system might seem dicey, official labeled taxis can be expensive and dangerous, with reports of kidnappings and muggings

TOURIST SERVICES

Local "tourist" centers may not parallel those in other countries—no maps, brochures, etc. Russian tourist centers exist to make money on tours and tickets, not to help confused tourists. If you start asking questions about the city, the staff may get upset, as they prefer to work with large companies sending groups of tourists. Even though we list tourist offices in this chapter as we do elsewhere in the guide, remember that they are private travel agencies, not founts of information.

MONEY

Government regulations require your passport at exchanges. You'll have no problem changing rubles back at the end of your trip, but the exchange rate is unstable, so it's best not to change large sums at once. To effect the actual exchange, find an *Obmen Valyuty* (Обмен Валюты; currency exchange) sign, hand over U.S. dollars—many places will change Deutschmarks, and some French francs and British pounds, too—and receive your rubles. *Do not exchange money on the street.*

ATMs (банкомат; *bankomat*) are moving into most major cities, and big establishments now accept major **credit cards**. Main branches of banks will usually accept **traveler's checks** and give cash advances on credit cards—Visa is best. If you keep American currency on hand, be aware that most establishments do not accept the new US$100 bill or crumpled, written-on bills of any denomination.

COMMUNICATION

Mail, Telegrams, Faxes, E-mail, and Media

There is neither rhyme nor reason to the former Soviet Union's **mail service**. Delivery can take from two weeks to eternity. Domestic mail will usually reach its destination; send letters to Russian recipients via friends who are traveling there, and do the same to get mail out. **American Express** card- and traveler's check-holders can receive letters at the AmEx travel service bureaus in Moscow and St. Petersburg; this strategy is usually more reliable than Russian mail. They will hold your mail for 30 days. **DHL** operates in Moscow, St. Petersburg, Novisibirsk, and Nizhny Novgorod.

Central post offices are also now equipped to send and receive **faxes**. **E-mail** offers an instant and free connection to selected universities and institutes inside the country; ask student friends about setting up a trans-oceanic connection. The youth hostels in Moscow and St. Petersburg also offer e-mail services.

Most hotels stock *Time, Newsweek,* and the *International Herald Tribune* (US$2). If you plan on being in Russia for an extended period, a short-wave radio is invaluable. The BBC World Service comes in at around 1508MHz in west Russia.

Telephones

Local telephones in Moscow take special tokens, sold at metro *kassas;* in St. Petersburg they take metro tokens. In many small towns, pay phones are free for local calls. You can make **intercity** calls from private homes, telephone offices, your hotel room, or *mezhdugorodnye* (междугородные) phone booths. It will take awhile, but you can usually get through. Dial 8, wait for the tone, then dial the city code.

Direct **international** calls can be made from telephone offices and hotel rooms: dial 8, wait for the tone, then dial 10 and the country code. You cannot call collect. To make calls from the telephone office, you can buy tokens and use the *mezhdunorodnye* (международные) telephones; be sure to press the *otvet* (ответ) button when your party answers, or you will not be heard. If there are no automatic phones, you must pay for your call at the counter and dial it yourself (your money will be returned if you do not get through) or have it dialed for you by the operator. Several hotels in Moscow now have direct-dial booths operated by a special card or credit card. The cost is astronomical (at least US$6 per min. to the U.S.). For **AT&T Direct,** dial 155 50 42 in Moscow and dial 325 50 42 in St. Petersburg; **Sprint Express,** dial 155 61 33 in Moscow. Dial 8-095 before these codes when calling from another city; you pay for the phone call to Moscow in addition to the international connection. For **Canada Direct,** dial 810 80 04 97 72 33 in Moscow. Calling into the country can be equally frustrating. Most countries have direct dial to Moscow and St. Petersburg. For other cities, go through the international operator. It may take 30 tries, giving you ample opportunity to delve into *War and Peace.*

LANGUAGE

Take some time to familiarize yourself with the Cyrillic alphabet. It's not as difficult as it looks and will make getting around and getting by immeasurably easier. For more info on the Slavic script, see p. 771. Though more and more people speak **English** in Russia, come equipped with at least a few helpful phrases. See the Glossary, p. 787.

In the Slavic world, plurals of words are usually formed by adding the letter "ы" or "и" to the end, so the plural of *matryoshka* is *matryoshki*. Note that улица (*ulitsa;* abbreviated ул.) means "street", проспект (*prospekt;* пр.) means "avenue", площадь (*ploshchad;* пл.) means "square", and бульвар (*bulvar;* бул.) is "boulevard". Once you get the hang of the alphabet, you can pronounce just about any Russian word.

HEALTH AND SAFETY

> **Emergency Numbers: Fire:** tel. 01. **Police:** tel. 02. **Ambulance:** tel. 03.

Russian bottled water can be putrid. Boil or filter your own, or buy foreign **bottled water** (the Finnish kind is cheap) at a supermarket. Water in most parts of Russia is potable in small doses; however, water in Moscow and St. Petersburg should be boiled before drinking it. A gamma globulin shot will lower your risk of hepatitis. Check the expiration date before buying any packaged snack.

Men's **toilets** are marked with an "М", women's with a "Ж"—the 500-5000R charged for public toilets generally gets you a hole in the ground. Women will probably encounter drunk men on the Metro; try to avoid them or find a *babushka*.

Reports of **crime** against foreigners are on the rise, and it is important to remember that as a foreigner, you are a walking target—more so in Moscow and St. Petersburg than in small towns less used to tourists. Although it is hard to look Russian, try not to flaunt your true nationality. Your trip will be that much more pleasant if you never have to file a crime report with the local *militsia,* who will not speak English and will probably not help you. Reports of mafia warfare are scaring off tourists; unless you bring a kiosk for them to blow up, you are unlikely to be a target.

If traveling independently, leave a copy of your itinerary with your embassy, along with your name, address, date and place of birth, and passport number. If your passport or visa is stolen, go to your embassy or consulate immediately.

For **medical emergencies,** leave the country or get to a St. Petersburg or Moscow clinic for foreigners. Local ambulance drivers will speak no English and may have to be bribed to come get you. Be sure you have traveler's health insurance before you leave (ISIC provides some coverage; see Essentials, p. 25); you can then more easily use one of the foreign clinics here, or even be evacuated.

ACCOMMODATIONS AND CAMPING

American-style **youth hostels** have begun to appear in Russia, most frequently in St. Petersburg and Moscow. Some arrange visas. Reserve well in advance, especially in summer. Hotels offer several classes of rooms. "Lux," usually a two-room double with TV, phone, fridge, and bath, is the most expensive. "Pol-lux" is a one-room single or double with TV, phone, and bath. Rooms with bath and no TV, if they exist, are cheaper. The lowest price rooms are *bezudobstv* (безудобств), which means one room with a sink. Many hotels have restaurants on the ground floor, often the best eatery in town; all have at least a buffet or cafeteria—probably the worst food in town. In Russia, hot water—even all water—is sometimes turned off for pipe repair and conservation, so you may have to take cold showers. Water gets turned on only once every two weeks due to shortages in parts of south Russia.

University dorms offer cheap rooms; some take in foreign students for about US$10 per night. The rooms are liveable, but don't expect sparkling bathrooms or reliable hot water. Make arrangements with an institute from home.

FOOD AND DRINK

Russian cuisine is a menagerie of dishes both delectable and disgusting, where a tasty borscht can come in the same meal as a bit of *sala* (pig fat). The largest meal of the day, *uzhen* (ужен; lunch), is eaten at around noon or 1pm. The standard hotel **dinner menu** includes *salat* (салат), usually cucumbers and tomatoes or beets and potatoes with mayonnaise and sour cream; *sup* (суп; soup), either meat or cabbage; and *kuritsa* (курица; chicken) or *myaso* (мясо; meat), often called *kutlyety* (кутлеты; cutlets) or *beefshteak* (бифштек; steak). Ordering a number of *zakuski* (закуски; Russia's answer to Spanish tapas) instead of a main dish can save money and add variety to your diet. Dessert is *morozhenoye* (мороженое; ice cream) or *tort* (торт; cake) with *cofye* (кофе) or *chai* (чай; tea). Russian **cafés** (кафе) offer similar-quality food for lower prices; often the tables have no chairs. A *stolovaya* (столовая; cafeteria) will likely be unsanitary and should be viewed suspiciously.

One can find basic Russian eats on the street, from stores, or at the market. In the store category, **dietas** (диета) sell goods for people on special diets (such as diabetics); **produkty** (продукты) offer a variety of meats, cheeses, breads, and packaged goods; a **gastronom** (гастроном) sells a smaller range of meat and dairy products; and a larger **universam** (универсам), simulates a supermarket in its variety. The **market** (рынок; *rynok*) sells abundant fruits and vegetables, meat, fresh milk, butter, honey, and cheese. Wash everything before you eat it—Russian farmers use pesticides liberally. Furthermore, milk may not be pasteurized. **Bakeries** (булочная; *bulochnaya*) sell fresh black and white bread daily and, sometimes, sweet rolls, cakes, and cookies.

The **kiosks** found in every town are mini-convenience stores, selling soda, juice, candy bars, and cookies; all you have to do is point at what you want. You'll see a lot of the much-loved and consumed *shashlik* (шашлык; barbequed meat on a stick) and *kvas* (квас), a dark-brown drink. Kiosks often carry alcohol; imported cans of beer are safe (though warm), but be wary of Russian labels—you have no way of knowing what's really in those bottles. Buy booze in a foreign grocery store. *Zolotoye koltso, Russkaya,* and *Zubrovka* are the best vodkas; *Stolichnaya,* considered the best vodka in the world, is mostly made for export. *Moskovskaya* is another known name, and generic brands will get the job done.

Vendors do not provide **bags** for merchandise. You can usually buy plastic bags in stores, the market, and on the streets, but to ensure you won't have to carry around a smelly fish in your hands all day, bring your own bag or paper. The actual process of **purchasing** might be extended. In stores, decide what you want, then go to a *kassa* and tell the person working there the item, the price, and the *otdyel* (отдел; department) from which you are buying. The person there will take your money and give you a receipt. You then take the receipt back to the *otdyel*, give it to the person working there, and they will give you what you want—finally.

A final word of advice: take Pepto-Bismol®, Immodium®, and snack foods such as peanut butter, instant soup, and granola to tide you over on those days when you can't face another sour cream salad. *Bon appetit!*

CUSTOMS AND ETIQUETTE

Enforced egalitarianism has left the Russian people with a lack of respect for individual **comfort** and the environment. Forceful shoving is the rule of the game on buses, trams, and the Metro. Watch out for rubbish bin fires; cigarettes are rarely stamped out. **Tipping** is not expected, but with the frightful way foreign tourists throw money around, it may soon be. Most establishments, even some routes, close for a **dinner break** sometime between noon and 3pm.

The laws outlawing **homosexual** acts were taken off the books about six years ago. However, Russia is still not very tolerant of gays, lesbians, and bisexuals. In Moscow and St. Petersburg, a gay scene is starting to spring up.

Because of the recent influx of imports, token packs of cigarettes and ballpoint pens are no longer accepted as currency and don't make very good **gifts** for Russians. When visiting friends, bring flowers, cookies, or candy. A bottle of imported wine is a very special gift. Russians tend to dress up to go visiting or even across the street. Many locals say that criminals spot foreigners by their sloppy appearances, so dress up, don't smile when stared at, and don't address people by their last names (for polite requests, use first and middle names).

LIFE AND TIMES

HISTORY

The Eastern Slavs, ancestors of the Russians, began migrating from Central and Eastern Europe to present-day Russia around the **6th century** CE. Conversion to Christianity occurred during the course of the 9th and 10th centuries, a lengthy and gradual process initiated by the missionaries **Cyril and Methodius,** who also introduced the Cyrillic alphabet. The Slavic tribes established strong trade relations with the Byzantine Empire in the south and the Vikings in the north. Well aware of the abundance of natural resources and cheap labor that the Slavs had to offer, the Vikings set out to conquer their lands. In 862, Prince Rurik of Jutland founded Novgorod after unifying the areas under his control; this was the beginning of both the Rurikid dynasty and the Russian state. After Rurik's death, **Kiev** emerged as the dominant power and became the seat of the Russian Orthodox church in 988; the region became known as **Kievan Rus** ("Rus" probably derived from the name of a powerful Kievan clan).

The 12th and 13th centuries were Kiev's **Golden Age.** In the 1100s, Vladimir Monomakh founded the city of Vladimir to the north of Kiev and moved the capital from Kiev to Vladimir in 1169, when Vladimir became the main center of economic activity. **Mongols** came in 1236 and conquered the Russian lands by 1240. Russia remained isolated from the rest of Europe for 240 years, and during these years, developed in a direction which would for many centuries make Russia a step-sister to other European countries. Despite some autonomy under the Mongol yoke, culture and the arts stagnated. Cities had to pay protection money to their Mongol overlords,

HISTORY ■ 527

Eastern Orthodoxy flourished, and trade links multiplied. The Lithuanian-Polish Empire became interested in Russian territory but was defeated by the Mongols in 1370. In 1380, Grand Prince Dmitri attempted an uprising against the Mongols which the eastern horsemen brutally repressed.

Under **Ivan III (the Great)** Russia finally threw off the Mongol yoke and set out to make Moscow a dominant power; Ivan conquered Novgorod and other neighboring principalities. **Ivan IV (the Terrible)** was the first ruler to have himself formally called "tsar." He conquered neighboring Kazan and expanded into the European sphere, but also alienated his generals, suffered severe skeletal deformation, and killed his oldest son and heir with his own hands, a daft move that clipped the continuity Russia always fell short of enjoying—Ivan's second son, **Fyodor I,** was too weak to rule the empire. His brother-in-law, **Boris Godunov,** became the actual ruler. When Fyodor died childless in 1598, Boris became tsar of Russia, thus putting an end to the Rurikid dynasty. Conspiring against Godunov, the Russian *boyars* (nobles) brought forward a pretender named Dmitry, claiming he was the son of the deceased Fyodor I. After Godunov's mysterious death, the *boyars* succeeded in making the **"False Dmitry"** tsar. What followed was a decade of unprecedented instability and chaos, with the *boyars* continually striving for more power and control over the numerous tsars. Finally, in 1613, **Mikhail Romanov** was elected tsar, thus starting the Romanov dynasty that ruled until the Bolshevik Revolution of 1917.

Romanov **Peter the Great** dragged Russia to Europe. Tsar from 1682, he became known as the "Westernizer of Russia", although he was not intent on Westernization *per se,* but simply opposed to all things Russian. Peter created his own elite and built a trading capital on the Baltic. He killed innumerable workers in the process, hung the opposition, traipsed around Europe causing more damage than the average *Let's Go* traveler, killed his own son in anger, and in general precipitated a permanent crisis of cultural identity. He died in 1725, without a male successor. This ushered in a period of tsars and tsarinas under the control of the nobles until the advent of **Catherine the Great.** The meek, homely daughter of an impoverished Prussian aristocrat, Catherine came to Russia to marry Elizabeth's nephew, Peter III. Shortly after Peter became tsar, Catherine overthrew him in a coup. She raised Russia to an equal among European monarchies—and incited the building of the Potemkin villages (2-dimensional town façades) when she asked to see what Russia was *really* like.

Serfdom persisted in Russia up to 1861. In the late 1800s, famine, peasant unrest, and a wave of strikes culminated in the failed **1905 revolution.** Although the Tsar **Nicholas II** established a progressive congressional body, the *Duma,* and made attempts to address the demands of the people, WWI forced his abrupt abdication. The organizational genius of **V.I. Lenin** then led the bloodless coup of October 1917: a combination of a few well placed words to **Aleksandr Kerensky** and the provisional government, and a harmless shot from the old naval ship *Aurora.*

Thus began the great failed experiment. After the Bolshevik revolution came the **Civil War;** the White Army, backed by foreign powers, struggled with Bolshevik troops. A period of social liberation followed the Red Army's victory. 1922 witnessed the birth of the **Union of Soviet Socialist Republics (USSR).** Lenin died in 1924 without naming a successor. **Joseph Stalin** succeeded in eliminating his rivals, Trotsky, Zinovev, and Kamenev, and in 1929 became the sole leader of the Communist Party. The first wave of political executions and **Socialist-Realism** intellectual stifling began soon after. Five-year economic plans, forced collectivization of Russia's farms, and creation of Siberian labor camps formed the basis for a totalitarian regime headed by Stalin. Priority was given to national defense and heavy industry, which led to shortages of consumer goods. Numerous purges resulted in millions of casualties.

In international affairs, Stalin was able to find only one chum—Hitler. After trusting the Nazi dictator's promises of conquering the world together, USSR's government entered **WWII** unprepared. The Soviet Union won only thanks to the icy winter of 1943-44, which gave the German army frostbite and sent it packing.

In 1949, the Soviet Union formed the **COMECON,** which incorporated all the Eastern European countries, reducing them to satellite states and linking them closely to the Party's headquarters in Moscow. After Stalin's death in 1953, **Nikita Khrushchev** emerged as the new leader of the Union and all its satellite states. In his 1956 "secret speech," he denounced the terrors of the Stalinist period—a political and cultural **"thaw"** followed in the early 1960s. In 1964, Khrushchev was ousted by **Leonid Brezhnev,** who stayed in power until 1983, overseeing a period of monstrous political repression. **Yuri Andropov** and **Konstantin Chernenko** followed him in humorously quick succession. The geriatric government finally gave way to the much younger (56-year-old) controversial **Mikhail Gorbachev** in 1985. As the shedding of the aging elite consumed the political circle in Moscow, the army was becoming frustrated with their losses in the Afghanistan War. Gorbachev reflected this anxiety and desire to improve the deteriorating life in Russia. His political and economic reforms were aimed at helping the country regain the status of a superpower. The reforms began with the slow steps of *glasnost* (openness) and *perestroika* (rebuilding). The state gradually turned into a bewildering hodge-podge of semi-anarchy, deepening economic crisis, and cynicism. Ironically, Gorbachev was the architect of his own demise. Despite his great popularity abroad (and the 1990 Nobel Peace Prize), discontent with his reforms and a failed right-wing coup in August 1991 led to his resignation, the dissolution of the Union, and **Boris Yeltsin's** election as President of Russia. Fragments of the union have remained together under the **Commonwealth of Independent States** under threat of increased Russian trade tariffs, but other areas have gone their own way.

LITERATURE

In Russia's millennium-long history, ideology and theology have managed to isolate the country from West Europe. During the Middle Ages, Russia worshipped according to Byzantium and prayed in Old Church Slavonic instead of Latin. In the 13th century, invaders from the Far East took control, and two centuries of a Mongol yoke benched the bear. Russia watched from the sidelines while most of Europe witnessed a cultural rebirth and religious reformation, and though Peter the Great tried to pull the bear back into the game, Russia remained the most "eastern" nation in "Eastern Europe." Such isolation seems to have instilled in the Russian people a contradictory mixture of national pride and cultural envy, a feeling which pervades both Russian literature's evolution and its themes.

Christianity, that source of most early European writings, gave to Russia both an alphabet, Cyrillic, and a literary language, **Old Church Slavonic.** But the language was not their own, and though the **Archpriest Avvakum** wrote his autobiography in colloquial Russian, most literature was religious and strictly Church Slavonic. Commoners preserved poetry and folklore orally in epic *byliny*, while the elite wrote religious works and political propaganda praising the Muscovy princes.

In the 17th century, commerce between Russia and the West increased, and new ideas—religious, technological, and social—followed flourishing trade routes. Peter the Great embraced all this novelty, ordering the mass translation of western technical manuals. To expedite practical affairs, he relegated Old Church Slavonic to the clergy, and replaced Old Church characters with a simplified **civic alphabet.** In 1757, **Mikhail Lomonosov,** one of the first purely Russian poets, wrote a grammar that systematized the colloquial language into a literary medium. As Peter emulated Western Europe in technology, Russian writers found inspiration from French writers. In fiction, **Nikolai Karamzin** mastered the "sentimental" trend in *Letter of a Russian Traveller,* and in *Poor Liza* completed Lomonosov's reform by making the gentry's everyday speech the literary medium.

Some contend that Russian literature's greatest year was 1799, the birthdate of **Aleksandr Sergeyevich Pushkin.** In his 38 short years, the "Russian Shakespeare" mastered European literary technique, added his own brand of Russian spice, and became not only the greatest Russian poet, but also the central figure in all of Russian literature. Published in 1825, *Eugene Onegin* was his greatest novel. Though his sympathy with dissenters evident in this and other works created a stir with the Russian secret service, Tsar Nicholas, who had close ties with Pushkin's family, protected him. Unfortunately, the tsar's control did not extend to affairs of love; Pushkin died in a duel over his flirtatious wife's honor. **Mikhail Lermontov** became heir to Pushkin's literary legacy. Exiled to the Caucasus for a lament he wrote on Pushkin's death, Lermontov published *A Hero of Our Time* in 1840. A year later at age 26, he too died in a duel. Another follower of Pushkin, **Nikolai Gogol** (1809-52) wrote the satirical *The Government Inspector,* the first major Russian play, and *Dead Souls,* whose pessimistic attitude toward life inspired Dostoyevsky.

The prerequisite of a great writer in the 19th century seemed to be a stint in prison. **Ivan Turgenev** made the mistake of praising Gogol in an obituary, and yet another eulogizer was arrested. The tsarist government had other reasons for incarcerating the author. His most famous work, *Fathers and Sons,* condoned challenging authority (e.g., the tsarist government), and the hero Bazarov became a nihilist symbol for the December revolution. Russia's most morbid writer, **Fyodor Dostoyevsky,** further darkened his style after undergoing a mock execution and spending time in Siberia, which influenced in particular the ending of his novel *Crime and Punishment.*

Russian writers had originally borrowed many literary ideas from the west, and some critics believed that Russian literature was the result of a backwards nation mooching the thoughts of other countries. **Lev Tolstoy,** with his cutting psychological analysis and extensive use of the Russian idiom in *War and Peace,* convinced most that Russian literature was not only branching in original directions but also creating new work which could teach other European writers. Two other authors who managed to create a distinctly Russian literature were **Anton Chekhov** (1860-1904), author of *The Three Sisters* and *The Seagull,* and **Maxim Gorky** (1868-1936), author of *My Childhood.* The latter spent his childhood in the lower class, and as a Bolshevik sympathizer helped establish a role for literature in the new order that followed the revolution. Lenin tolerated literary objectivity, and works like **Mikhail Sholokhov's** famous *And Quiet Flows the Don* were permitted.

The political Revolution of 1917 led to a revolution in literature. Printing stopped, while political poetry readings exploded. Many authors fled the country. **Vladimir Mayakovsky,** the revolution's first mouthpiece, committed suicide as did **Sergei Esenin.** Authorities persecuted **Anna Akhmatova** into silence and exile, and banned the great satirist, **Mikhail Bulgakov,** author of *Master and Margerita.* As Trotsky put it, writers didn't have to be Marxists, but they did have to be "fellow travelers."

Largely championed by Gorky in the 1930s, **Socialist Realism,** a mix of historical fiction and cheerleader patriotism, became the model for party-authorized artists. After the war, freedoms that the state had allowed to boost embattled spirits were restricted, and most progress in the arts stopped. In 1953 Stalin died, Khrushchev atoned for his sins, and the literary scene thawed. The regime established official writers' journals—a good way of tracking literary dissidents. Unlike most authors, **Boris Pasternak** did not emigrate and suffered state persecution for such works as the world-famous *Dr. Zhivago.* Rejected in the USSR for its unbiased analysis of the civil war, the book was published instead in Milan. Russians prefer Pasternak's brilliant poetry. Khrushchev fell in 1964, controls became tighter, and previously tolerated authors like **Aleksandr Solzhenitsyn,** who published the accusatory *One Day in the Life of Ivan Denisovich* in 1963, couldn't get anything else to press. He received the Nobel prize in 1970, but in 1974, with *The Gulag Archipelago,* he was exiled and joined **Vladimir Nabokov** of *Lolita* fame. He returned to Russia in 1994.

In 1986, *glasnost* saw the circulation of previously banned books. Of recent fame are **Viktor Yerofeev** for *Russian Beauty,* translated into 27 languages, and **Tatyana Tolstaya** for *On the Golden Porch* published in the West in 1989.

RUSSIA TODAY

Russia's future is uncertain. Yeltsin, while trying to construct a new Russian economy, is continually engaged in a power struggle with the Russian Parliament, which includes such figures as right-wing nationalist Vladimir Zhirinovsky. At the same time, in the name of democracy, Yeltsin has at times assumed (or tried to assume) near-dictatorial prerogatives, such as ordering the national bank to release a large part of a billion-plus dollar loan from the IMC to aid his campaign for reelection. Shortly after Yeltsin won the 1996 presidential election (and appointed the outspoken General Lebed national security advisor), two bombs exploded on Moscow trolleys. At the time of publishing, Russian officials were still puzzled as to who—Communists, Chechens, etc.—might want to terrorize Moscow citizens now. Meanwhile, the war in Chechnya, renewed after a Chechen offensive on Yeltsin's inauguration day, may finally have ended with the August 31 signing of an agreement, brokered by Lebed with little to no input from the ailing Yeltsin, which puts off any permanent decision on Chechnya's independence until December 31, 2001.

Moscow (Москва)

Moscow is huge, apocalyptic, and compelling. Founded by Yuri Dolgoruki in 1147, the city's early peak came in 1571, when it had over 100,000 citizens and was probably one of the world's largest settlements. Originally built up by Ivans the Great and the Terrible, Moscow reigned as Russia's capital until 1714, and again after 1917, when it became the site of some of the 20th century's most watched political maneuvering. Home to one in fifteen Russians, the city throbs with energy and noise. Stalinist edifices make a gray backdrop, against which splash the gaudy colors of churches and monasteries. Behind anonymous walls, apartments full of books and beloved knick-knacks shine like pools of light at the end of the crumbling buildings' dank hallways. Out on the street, Moscow is a haphazard and anarchic conglomerate of peasant villages—a bazaar where careerists selling Japanese televisions out of a truck stand next to grandmothers offering potatoes and dill. Moscow is Russia's center of change, and as such, provides the visitor with a dizzying view of the country's possibilities. You may not love the city, but you won't regret seeing it.

ORIENTATION AND PRACTICAL INFORMATION

A series of concentric rings emanates from the **kremlin** (кремль; *kreml*). The outermost ring road forms the city boundary, but most sights lie within the inner **Garden Ring** (Садовое кольцо; *Sadovoe koltso*). **Red Square** (Красная площадь; *Krasnaya ploshchad*) and the kremlin mark the city center. Nearby start Moscow's popular shopping streets: **Novy Arbat** (Новый Арбат), running west parallel to the Metro's blue lines, and **ul. Tverskaya** (Тверская), extending north along the green line. Ul. Tverskaya was formerly called ul. Gorkovo (Горкого); the upper half, which leads to the Garden Ring, is now known as ul. Pervaya Tverskaya-Yamskaya (Первая Тверская-Ямская). Learn the Cyrillic alphabet, orient yourself by the **Metro**, and it's difficult to get lost. All buses and trams eventually stop at one of the stations, marked by a red neon "M". An extensive city **map**, including all public transportation routes and a street index, is sold at many kiosks for 10,000-20,000R. Many are outdated, so be sure the year 1997 is clearly marked. See this book's **color insert** for maps of Moscow and the Metro. *Let's Go* lists metro stops in their transliterated form.

Useful Organizations

Tourist Offices: Mainly excursion bureaus—snag a free city map (metro map on back) at a major hotel, such as the Olympic Penta Hotel at M4,5: Prospekt Mira.
Intourservice Central Excursion Bureau, Nikitsky per. 4a (Никитский; tel. 203 75 85 or 203 80 16; fax 200 12 43 or 203 56 19). M1: Okhotny Ryad. Credit cards accepted. Open daily 9am-7:30pm.
Moscow Travel Agency, ul. Pushkinskaya 14 (Пушкинская; tel./fax 956 54 46). M1: Okhotny Ryad. Plane tickets, visas, interpreters. Open Mon.-Fri. 10am-6pm, Sat.-Sun. 10am-5pm.
Moskovsky Sputnik (Московский спутник), Maly Ivanovsky per. 6, kor. 2 (Малый Ивановский; tel. 924 03 17 or 925 92 78). M5,6: Kitai Gorod. Student travel, visas, and tickets. Open Mon.-Fri. 9am-1pm and 2-6pm, Sat. 9am-1pm and 2-5pm.

ORIENTATION AND PRACTICAL INFORMATION ■ 531

Budget Travel: Student Travel Agency Russia (S.T.A.R.), 50 Bolshaya Pereyaslavskaya, 10th fl. (tel. 913 59 52; fax 280 90 30; e-mail star@glas.apc.org), in the same building as Traveller's Guest House. STA representative, soon to represent Council Travel, too. Sells discounted plane tickets worldwide, Interrail and Eurobus tickets, and ISIC and GO25 cards. Also books hostels 'round the globe.

Passport Office (UVIR): ul. Pokrova 42 (Покрова).

Embassies: Australia, Kropotkinsky per. 13 (Кропоткинский; tel. 956 60 70 or 246 50 12). M3: Smolenskaya. Open Mon.-Fri. 9am-12:30pm and 1:30-5pm. **Canada,** Starokonyushenny per. 23 (Староконюшенный; tel. 956 66 66). M1: Kropotkinskaya. Open Mon.-Tues. and Thurs.-Fri. 8:30am-1pm and 2-5pm. **Ireland,** Grokholsky per. 5 (Грохольский; tel. 288 41 01). M4,5: Prospekt Mira. Open Mon.-Fri. 9:30am-1pm and 2:30-5:30pm. **New Zealand,** ul. Povarskaya 44 (Поварская; tel. 956 35 78). M4,6: Krasnopresnenskaya. Open Mon.-Fri. 9am-5:30pm. **South Africa,** Bolshoy Strochinovsky per. 22/25 (Большой Строчиновский; tel. 230 68 69). Open Mon.-Fri. 9am-12:30pm and 1-5pm. **U.K.,** nab. Sofiskaya 14 (Софиская; tel. 956 72 00; fax 956 74 20). M1,3,8: Borovitskaya. Open Mon.-Fri. 9am-5pm. **U.S.,** Sadovaya-Kudrinskaya 6 (Садовая-Кудринская; tel. 956 42 32). M6: Barrikadnaya. Open Mon.-Fri. 9am-5:30pm.

Currency Exchange: Banks at almost every corner; check ads in English-language newspapers. The pamphlet *Moscow Express Directory,* updated biweekly and free in most luxury hotels, lists the addresses and phone numbers of many banks, as well as places to buy and cash traveler's checks. **Sberbank** (Сбербанк); pr. Mira 41/1 (Мира; open Mon.-Fri. 9am-7pm, Sat. 9am-6pm), and numerous other locations will cash AmEx, Thomas Cook, and Visa traveler's checks and issue Eurocard, MC, STB, and Visa cash advances for a commission.

ATMs: 24-hr. machines outside banks and in the AmEx lobby. **ATMs** also at Gostinitsa Mezhdunarodnaya (Международная), Krasnopresnenskaya nab. 12 (Красно-пресненская), and at Gostinitsa Metropol (Метропол), Teatralny pr. 1/4 (Театральний), M2: Teatralnaya. Some ATMs are more finicky than others.

American Express: ul. Sadovaya-Kudrinskaya 21a (Садовая-Кудринская; tel. 755 90 00; fax 755 90 04). M2: Mayakovskaya. Take a left onto ul. Bolshaya Sadovaya (Большая Садовая), which becomes ul. Sadovaya-Kudrinskaya. Travel assistance for all, and banking services for members. Mail service for members and traveler's-check holders. Office open Mon.-Fri. 9am-5pm, Sat. 9am-1pm.

United Card Service: Novocheremushkinskaya (Новочеремушкинская; tel. 256 35 56). M5: Alekseyevskaya. Call to cancel a lost or stolen Eurocard, MC, STB, or Visa; they will not replace cards.

Western Union: Rossysky Credit (Россыски Кредит), Usacheva 35 (Усачева; tel. 119 82 50), left entrance. M1: Sportivnaya. Exit to the right; it'll be on the right, next to the Global USA Shop. Open Mon.-Fri. 9am-8pm. Sat. 9am-4pm.

Faxes and Telegrams: Moscow Central Telegraph (see Post Offices, below) at window #1; immediate fax windows #7 and 8. Telegrams around 1400R per word to the U.S. **Fax** price per page is 9800R to Europe, 13,100R to the U.S., and 33,500R to Australia and Africa. Open daily 8am-9:30pm.

Express Mail: DHL: Radisson-Slavyanskaya, Berezhkovskaya nab. 2 (Бережковская; tel. 941 87 40). M3: Kievskaya. **GUM** (ГУМ) business center (бизнес-центр), 2nd floor (tel. 921 09 11; fax 921 46 09). Open Mon.-Sat. 8am-8pm. **Main Office,** Trety Samotechny per. 11/2, 3rd floor (3-ий Самотечный; tel. 956 10 00; fax 974 21 06). M4,8: Novoslobodskaya. Open Mon.-Fri. 8am-5pm.

Post Offices: Moscow Central Telegraph, ul. Tverskaya 7, a few blocks from the kremlin. Look for the globe and the digital clock out front. M1: Okhotny Ryad. **International mail** service open Mon.-Fri. 8am-2pm and 3-9pm, Sat. 8am-2pm and 3-7pm, Sun. 9am-2pm and 3-7pm. Address mail "Москва 103009, POSTE RESTANTE, JORGENSEN, Martin". **Poste Restante** also at the **Gostinitsa Intourist post office,** ul. Tverskaya 3/5. Address mail "HRUSCHKA, Thomas, До востребования, K-600. Гостиница Интурист, ул. Тверская 3/5, Москва, Russia". To mail **packages,** bring them unwrapped to the Intourist post office or to Myasnitskaya 26 (Мясницкая, formerly Kirova); they will be wrapped and mailed while you wait. The Intourist post office on the second floor is open Mon.-Fri. 9am-noon and 1-7pm, Sat. 9am-noon and 1-5pm. Window #32 sends letters, but not packages, abroad.

RUSSIA

Regular letters (3000R) are in transit 3 weeks; special delivery (заказное; *zakaznoe*; 6000R) takes 1 week. Express mail at window #6 (3-4 days). **Postal code:** 103009.

Telephones: Moscow Central Telegraph (see Post Offices, above). To **call abroad**, go to the 2nd hall with telephones. Open 24hr. You must prepay at the counter for how long you expect to talk. You will then be given a stall number from which to dial directly. It may take 5-10 tries to get through. To collect your money if you do not reach your party, you must stand in line again at the same counter. Depending on the time of day, calls to Europe run 6300R; to the U.S. and Australia about 14,700R per min.; to Africa 17,550R. Do not try to call collect or use your calling card here. Use the **international telephone cabinets** (международные телефоны; *mezhdunarodnye telefony*). Major hotels have direct-dial international phone booths at exorbitant rates (1min. to the U.S. US$6-15). International calls can also be placed from private homes (direct dial: 8-10-country code-phone number). If you have an AT&T calling card, simply dial 155 50 42. **Local calls** require plastic tokens (жетоны; *zhetony*), which are sold at some metro stations and kiosks (1500R). **Phone code:** 095.

Transportation

Flights: International flights arrive at **Sheremetyevo-2** (Шереметьево-2; tel. 956 46 66). M2: Rechnoy Vokzal. Take the van under the sign "автолайн" in front of the station (every 10min. 7am-10pm, 20min., 5000R). 24-hr. Visa ATM and MasterCard cash advances on the 1st floor. Most domestic flights originate at **Vnukovo** (Внуково; tel. 436 14 72), **Bikovo** (Биково; tel. 553 00 24), **Domodedovo** (Домодедово; tel. 234 87 27), or **Sheremetyevo-I** (tel. 578 36 10). Buy tickets in *kassy* at the **Central Airport Station** (Центральный Аэровокзал; *Tsentralny Aerovokzal*), a 2-stop tram (#23) or trolley (#12 or 70) ride from M2: Aeroport. Check the express-bus schedules posted outside the station. Taxis to the center charge more than you ever dreamed possible, up to 400,000R—consider arriving in St. Petersburg first.

Foreign Airline Representatives: Air France, ul. Korovy Val 7 (Коровий Вал; tel./fax 237 23 25). Open Mon.-Fri. 9am-6pm. At Sheremetyevo-2, 6th floor (tel. 578 31 56). Open Mon.-Sat. 5:30am-11pm, Sun. 1-6pm. **Austrian Airlines,** Krasnopresnenskaya nab. 12, 18th fl., office 1805 (Краснопресненская; tel. 258 20 20; fax 258 22 00). Open Mon.-Fri. 9am-1pm and 2-5:30pm, Sat. 9am-1pm and 2-5:30pm. At Sheremetyevo-2 (tel. 578 29 32). Open daily noon-7pm. **British Airways,** Krasnopresnenskaya nab. 12, 19th fl., office 1905 (tel. 258 24 92; fax 258 22 82). Open Mon.-Fri. 9am-5:30pm. At Sheremetyevo-2, 6th fl. (tel. 578 29 23). Open daily 11:30am-7pm. **Czech Airlines ČSA,** ul. Vtoroya Brestskaya 21/27 (2-я Брестская; tel. 250 02 40; fax 250 31 04). M2,4: Belorusskaya. Open Mon.-Fri. 10am-1pm and 2-5pm. **Delta,** Krasnopresnenskaya nab. 12, 11th fl., office 1102a (tel. 253 26 58—wait for tone, then 60). M3: Smolenskaya. Open Mon.-Fri. 9am-5:30pm, Sat. 9am-1pm. **Finnair,** Kuznetsky most 3 (Кузнецкий мост; tel. 292 17 62). M1,2,3: Okhotny Ryad. Open Mon.-Fri. 9am-5pm. **Hungarian Airlines Malev,** Kamergersky per. 6 (Камергерский; tel. 956 27 31; fax 250 71 86). M1,2,3: Okhotny Ryad. Open Mon.-Fri. 9am-4:30pm. **LOT,** ul. Kirovy Val 7, room 5 (tel./fax 238 10 36, in Sheremetyevo-2 tel. 956 46 58). M4,5: Oktyabrskaya. Open Mon.-Sat. 9am-5pm. **Lufthansa,** Olimpiysky pr. 18/1 (Олимпийский; tel. 975 25 01), in Hotel Olympic Penta. M4,5: Prospekt Mira. Open Mon.-Fri. 9am-5:30pm. Also at Sheremetievo-2 (tel. 578 31 51; open 24hr). **SAS,** Kuznetsky most 3 (tel. 925 47 47; fax 924 61 47; at Sheremyetievo-2 tel. 578 27 27). M1,2,3: Okhotny Ryad. Open Mon.-Fri. 9am-5:30pm.

Trains: (tel. 266 93 33). Unless going to nearby places such as Peredelkino, foreigners need to bring their passports to purchase the tickets in 1 of 2 places: in a building at the side of Yaroslavsky Vokzal, entitled "Central Train Agency" (Центральное Железнодорожное Агенство; *Tsentralnoe Zheleznodorozhnoe Agenstvo*), at windows #10 and 11. Open daily 8am-1pm and 2-7pm. Or, in the 24-hr. Intourist *kassy* on the 2nd floor of the Leningradsky Vokzal (entrance #3, windows #20 and 21). Tickets to places such as Smolensk in *platskartny* wagons on the slow trains are around 60,000R. Your ticket tells you at which *vokzal* (вокзал; station) to catch your train. Platform numbers for arriving trains are announced when the trains arrive. A list of departure times is posted on the building where the toilets are, across and to the left of the Yaroslavsky Vokzal's waiting room entrance. Trains to St. Petersburg use **Leningradsky Vokzal** (Ленинградский; tel. 262 91 43). M1,4:

ORIENTATION AND PRACTICAL INFORMATION ■ 533

Komsomolskaya. Opposite, **Kazansky Vokzal** (Казанский; tel. 264 65 56) sends trains to the east and southeast. **Yaroslavsky Vokzal** (Ярославский; tel. 221 59 14) sends wagons northeast. Other stations are reached by eponymous metro stops: **Paveletsky Vokzal** (Павелетский; tel. 235 68 07) and **Kursky Vokzal** (Курский; tel. 924 57 67) serve the south; **Rizhsky Vokzal** (Рижский; tel. 924 57 62) serves Riga (3 per day, 16hr.) and Estonia. Trains from Warsaw (5 per day, 24hr.), Minsk (3 per day, 11hr.), and Kaliningrad (3 per day, 26hr.) arrive at **Belorussky Vokzal** (Белорусский; tel. 251 60 93); trains to Bulgaria, Romania, Slovakia, and Ukraine use **Kievsky Vokzal** (Киевский; tel. 240 11 15).

Public Transportation: The **Metro** is large, fast, and efficient—a work of art in urban planning. It stops within a 15-min. walk of any place in town and is a continual reminder that 13 million people do live in Moscow and that all 13 million always ride the Metro. Passages to different lines or stations are shown with a blue and white sign of a man walking up stairs. A station which serves more than one line will generally have more than one name. Trains run daily 6am-1am (8000R). Rush hours are 9-10am and 5-6pm. **Bus** and **trolley** tickets are available in gray kiosks labeled "проедные билеты" and from the driver (1500R per ride). Be sure to punch your ticket when you get on, especially in the last week of the month when ticket cops come out. The fine for not doing so is 10,000R. *Edinye bilety* (единые билеты; month passes) let you ride on any form of transportation (180,000R). Buy them after the 20th of the previous month. Monthly metro passes are more cost-effective (90,000R). Purchase either from the *kassy*. Metro maps are on the wall inside the entrance to every station, or consult the maps (in Cyrillic and Latin) in the front and back of this book.

Taxis: Call 927 00 00. If you don't speak Russian, it's nearly impossible to get a fair rate. Ask around for the going rate (25,000R/km in July 1996) and agree on a price before you set off. Taxi stands are indicated by a round sign with a green "T". Meters are purely ornamental, although new Moscow law decrees that they must be used. In general, avoid taxis unless you know Moscow.

Train and Airplane Tickets: Intourtrans Main Office, Maly Kharitonevsky per. 6, (Малый Харитоньевский; formerly Griboyedova; tel. 262 06 04). M5: Turgenevskaya. Take a right off ul. Myasnitskaya (Мясницкая) and walk into the ancillary building on the right which handles foreigners. Open daily 8am-1pm and 2-7pm. Also in Gostinitsa Intourist. Same hours as main office. Limited tickets only. Purchase same-day tickets at the appropriate train station. Foreigners are required to purchase tickets from Intourist, though the lesser hassle and shorter lines make the main office a tempting option.

Lost Property: For the Metro, tel. 222 20 85.

Other Practical Information

English-Language Literature: Two free English-language daily newspapers are easy to find in hotels and restaurants across the city. *The Moscow Times* (more widely read and distributed) and *The Moscow Tribune* have foreign and national articles, sports, and the like for news-starved travelers. More importantly, they both have weekend sections (Sat. during the year, Fri. in summer) that list exhibitions, theatrical events, and English-language movies. The *Moscow Business Telephone Guide* and *What and Where in Moscow,* both free, are excellent info resources if you don't want to shell out 125,000R for *Information Moscow* (useful only if you are actually living here), published quarterly. For housing and job opportunities, the 2 free dailies are most useful. Most such publications are found in the lobby of Hotel Intourist. Foreign publications such as *Time, Newsweek,* and *The International Herald Tribune* (21,000R) are available in foreign supermarkets and major hotels. To get week- or 2-week-old magazines for a cheaper ruble rate, check at the stands at the bottom of ul. Tverskaya near the kremlin.

Photocopy Services: For a complete list, check under "Copy services" in *Moscow Business Telephone Guide,* free in most luxury hotels. **Intergraphics** (Интер-графикс), ul. Marksistskaya 5 (Марксистская; tel. 222 39 82; fax 232 93 64). M1, 4, 6: Taganskaya. Every possible business convenience: stamps, passport photos, color copies, and color laser printing. Copies 500R per page; price decreases for large orders. Open Mon.-Fri. 9am-6pm. AmEx, Diner's Club, Eurocard, MC, Visa.

Laundromat: Traveller's Guest House (see Accommodations, p. 534) does your laundry for 20,000R per load. Otherwise, your bathtub is the only option. Bring your own detergent or buy it at a supermarket (expensive) or at random kiosks stocking *Tide* or *"Nock"*.

24-Hour Pharmacies: Leningradsky pr. 74 (Ленинградский; tel. 151 45 70). M2: Sokol. **Kutuzovsky pr. 14** (Кутузовский; tel. 243 16 01). M3: Kutuzovskaya. **40-Letia Oktyabrya pr. 4**, bldg. 2, (40-летия Октября; tel. 350 05 94). M9: Lyublino.

Medical Assistance: American Medical Center, Vtoroy Tversky-Yamsky per. 10, 2nd fl. (Тверский-Ямский-II; tel. 956 33 66; fax 956 23 06). M2: Mayakovskaya. French joint-venture offering walk-in medical care for hard currency (US$150 per visit). Open Mon.-Sat. 9:30am-7pm. After-hours service. **Athens Medical Center,** Michurinsky pr. 6 (Мичуринский; tel. 143 23 87, emergency tel. 143 25 03; fax 147 91 22). Provides medical care for Euromedical Club members and emergency care for all. Open Mon.-Fri. 9am-6pm. **International Medical Clinic,** Grokholsky per. 31, 10th fl. (Грохольский; tel. 280 71 77). M4,5: Prospekt Mira. Australian, Canadian, and U.S. doctors charge US$80 for consultation, US$105 for gynecological consultation. Open Mon.-Fri. 8am-8pm, Sat. 9am-5pm.

Dentists: Intermedservice, ul. Tverskaya 3/5, 19th fl., room 1925 (tel. 956 89 88), in Gostinitsa Intourist. M1: Okhotny Ryad. Swiss-Belgian-Russian venture offering basic dental care. Open Mon., Wed., and Fri. 10am-2pm. **Mosta Dental,** Bolshoy Cherkassky per. 15 (Большой Черкасский) M1: Lubyanka. English-speaking Japanese clinic providing basic dental care. **US Dental Care,** ul. Shabolovka 8, kor. 3 (Шаболовка; tel. 931 99 09). M4,5: Oktyabrskaya. U.S. dental venture. Open Mon. and Fri. 9am-1pm and 2-6pm, Tues.-Thurs. 9am-1pm and 2-8pm.

Emergencies: Try the above centers for medical emergencies, call your embassy for passport and visa problems, and give up on legal retaliation. There is a number to report offenses *by* the police (tel. 299 11 80, no coins needed from pay phones). Also try the **U.S. embassy's emergency number,** tel. 230 20 01 or 230 26 01. **Lost children:** tel. 401 99 82.

ACCOMMODATIONS

Student travelers will have a hard time finding budget accommodations in Moscow. There are good ones to be had, but options are slim, so in summer, reservations are a must. Numerous women standing outside Kursky Vokzal rent **private rooms** or apartments (as low as 45,000R per night—don't forget to haggle). Look for the signs advertising rent of a room (сдаю комнату; *sdayu komnatu*) or an apartment (сдаю квартиру; *cdayu kvartiru*).

Traveller's Guest House, ul. Bolshaya Pereyaslavskaya 50 (Большая Переяславская; tel. 971 40 59; fax 280 76 86; e-mail tgh@glas.apc.org). M4,5: Prospekt Mira. Walk north along pr. Mira, and take the 3rd right on Banny per. (Банный), and a left at the end of the street. TGH is the white 12-story building across the street; take the elevator to the 10th floor. The administrator downstairs has nothing to do with TGH. If you arrive in Moscow speaking no Russian and knowing no one, TGH is all you'll ever need. Even if you do have some connections, TGH is a great place to meet other travelers, get tips, and find companions (and buy tickets) for that Trans-Siberian trip. The English-speaking staff is helpful and enthusiastic. TGH offers kitchen facilities, a laundry service (20,000R for a 3- to 5-kg bag, 1- to 2-day service), and a common room with TV and phone. Checkout 11am. Dorm beds 92,000R. Singles 179,000R. Doubles 230,000R. Reserve at least 1 week ahead; retain copies of all reservation forms and receipts. Calls to U.S. US$3 per min. MC and Visa accepted. *Moscow Times* free.

Tsentralnaya (Центральная), ul. Tverskaya 10 (tel. 229 89 57), next to Pizza Hut. M2,6,8: Pushkinskaya. Has escaped renovation and so still charges Soviet-era prices. Ideally located, standard Russian hotel, with a guard downstairs and floor women to keep your key. All rooms have sinks, but no bath or toilet; those are off the hallway. Cean and well lit. Singles 145,000R. Doubles 200,000R. Cash only.

American Academy of Foreign Languages, ul. Bolshaya Cheremushkinskaya 17a (Большая Черёмушкинская; tel. 129 43 00; fax 123 15 00). M5: Akademicheskaya.

From the metro station, turn left at the Ho Chi Minh sculpture and walk 15min. on ul. Dmitriya Ulyanova (Дмитрия Ульянова), then turn left on Bolshaya Cheremush-kinskaya. Unlike other dorms, this one will let you stay without any special papers/permission. The "single in a triple" (50,000R) will be one of 3 beds crammed head-to-head around a table. Shower in room. Stuffy but clean. Singles in a more spacious double 70,000R. 2-room "lux" suites (440,000R), as well as ½-lux available. Make reservations 2-3 days ahead. Cash only. English spoken.

Prakash Guesthouse, ul. Profsoyuznaya 83, bldg. 1, 3rd fl., (Профсоюзная; tel. 334 25 98). M5: Belyaevo. From the center, take the exit nearest the 1st car of the train, then go all the way to the left, exiting on the left side of the *perekhod*. The guesthouse is 1 block up on the right (they can meet you at the Metro). Don't pay attention to the guards for the big dorm in which this is ensconced; they don't know about the guesthouse and will say you need permission to stay in their dorms. Reception open daily 7am-11pm; call ahead if you're arriving later or earlier, and they'll have someone waiting for you. Shower, toilet, and telephone for local calls in each room. Nightly movies—Indian and American. Singles US$30. Doubles US$40. Breakfast US$5. Dinner US$10. Cash only.

FOOD

Eating out in **restaurants** is a luxury mainly enjoyed by wealthy foreigners and the new Moscow elite. Meals are outrageously expensive, and quality is no better than in the provinces. There are a few exceptions, but everybody knows them, so reserve ahead—a round of calls at noon will secure a table for the evening. Alternatively, adopt an early eating schedule; Russians tend to come later and linger until closing. However, this is becoming less common as the concept of business meals enters into Russian life. Restaurants with prices listed in dollars usually accept either credit cards or rubles; dollars are no longer legal tender for such transactions. This same law also decrees that rubles must be acceptable everywhere, opening foreign-goods supermarkets to all who can afford them. If you're going for ethnic fare, Georgian is both tasty and cheap. If you do go Russian, make sure that you're getting a *chisty stol* (clean table)—without a large assortment of appetizers for which you would pay dearly. **Cafés,** substantially cheaper than restaurants, often serve better food, offering one or two well prepared dishes rather than a selection of mediocre ones. They do it faster, brighter, and more casually. **Fast-food stands** selling hot dogs, pizza, and Pepsi guard almost every street corner—some are quite good, others may not be so kind to your stomach.

The Chains

Pizza Hut (Пицца Хат), ul. Tverskaya 12. M6: Pushkinskaya. Two guards outside protect the upscale interior—complete with requisite salad bar and Americans. Small cheese 25,400R. Medium veggie 64,600R. Apple pie 9400R. Open daily 11am-11pm. AmEx, MC, Visa. Outside counter sells 7500R slices.

McDonald's (Макдоналдс, not that you need the Cyrillic), ul. Bolshaya Bronnaya 29 (Большая Бронная; M6: Pushkinskaya) and ul. Arbat 50/52 (Арбат; M3: Smolenskaya). Centrally located fast-food machine. Big Mac 9500R. Large fries (большая порция картофель-фри; *bolshaya portsiya kartofel-fri*) 6000R. Open daily 8am-11:30pm.

Baskin Robbins, all over Moscow—on the Arbat, at Gostinitsa Rossiya, in bright pink kiosks dotting the city. The not-always-31 flavors are losing their appeal, due to the high prices and influx of other ice cream. But the familiar taste is still there. A tiny scoop 5000R. Open daily 10am-9pm.

Pinguin, Arbat 36, Okhotny Ryad 2 and ul. Nikolskaya 4/5 (Никольская). A Russian-Swiss ice-cream venture—one of the first in Moscow. Open daily 11am-11pm.

Red Square (North of the Kremlin)

Moscow Bombay, Glinishchevsky per. 3 (Глинищевский; formerly Nemirovicha-Danchenko; tel. 292 97 31; fax 292 93 75), just off ul. Tverskaya. M6: Pushkinskaya or M1: Okhotny Ryad. Small tables and plants should be familiar. Menu in English reveals vegetarian options. Veggie samosa US$8. Tandoori chicken US$7.50. *Naan* US$1.50. Reservations recommended. Open daily noon-11:30pm.

La Cantina (Ла Кантина), ul. Tverskaya (tel. 292 53 88), on the right of Gostinitsa Intourist. M1: Okhotny Ryad. The small booths, long bar, and mural of the "Moscow honky-tonk" spell a carefully designed Mexican restaurant with a Russian flavor. Popular with tourists craving Spanish guitar bands. Nachos and chili 40,000R. Large chicken enchiladas a whopping 75,000R. Open daily 8am-midnight.

Rostik's (Ростик'с), 2nd floor of GUM department store at the end nearest Kazan Cathedral. Moscow's answer to KFC, only here the birds are roasted. 2 pieces of chicken with roll 18,000R. 16 pieces 105,000R. Fried fish 25,000R. Shakes 7500R. English menu. Order and pay at one of the *kassas,* then go get your food. Take-out available. Open Mon.-Sat. 8am-8pm, Sun. 11am-6pm.

Gostinitsa Moskva, Manezhnaya pl. 8 (tel. 292 12 45), next to Red Square. Restaurant on the 3rd floor. Especially popular with the bureaucrats across the street at Gosplan. All the borscht, beet salad, fried potatoes, and *cutlety* you can eat for 35,000R. *Shashlik* 40,000R. Chicken *cutlety* 35,000R. Open daily 8am-11pm.

Copacabana Café, 2nd floor of GUM. Some call it the hottest spot north of Havana—it calls itself Brazilian, but the food is standard, quasi-foreign-café fare. Hot sandwiches, some salads, all 15,000-20,000R. Ice-cream sundaes 7300-21,500R. Notable for its breakfast. Open Mon.-Sat. 8am-8pm, Sun. 11am-6pm.

Aztec, ul. Tverskaya 3/5, 20th fl. (tel. 956 84 89), in Gostinitsa Intourist. M1: Okhotny Ryad. The super-friendly service and tasty Latin American food will entice you. And if they don't, the view from the large window in this tiny 2-story restaurant overlooking Moscow will—count the Stalinist buildings. If all you want is a quick snack or a margarita, stay downstairs. Cheese enchilada US$16. Free champagne or wine Sat.-Sun. noon-4pm. Open daily noon-4pm.

Spanish Bar, Manezhnaya pl. (Манежная; tel. 292 62 67), in Gostinitsa Moskva. 2 floors. Real Spanish food at French prices. Appetizers US$5-14. Omelette US$6. Paella for two US$42. Downstairs open daily noon-5pm; upstairs open Mon.-Fri. 4pm-midnight, Sat.-Sun. 2pm-midnight. AmEx, MC, and Visa rule.

West of the Kremlin

Aist (Айст), ul. Malaya Bronnaya 1/8 (Малая Бронная; tel. 291 66 92). M6: Pushkinskaya. Hearty soups and appetizers make this a cozy spot to sample solid Russian food. Wrap-around red velvet decor simulates a 70s opium den, and large, secluded booths make this better for groups. *Lobio* 18,000R. *Plov* 30,000R. Open daily noon-10pm. Contrary to the stickers outside, credit cards are not accepted.

Blinchiki (Блинчики), a kiosk on Strasnoy bul. (Страстной) off ul. Tverskaya diagonally opposite McD's. Scrumptious apricot-filled *bliny* (блины; pancakes) 2000R. The long line at midday means this is the real thing. Open daily 8am-8pm.

Russian Souvenir (Ресторан Русский Сувенир), Petrovka per. 23/10 (Петровка). M6: Pushkinskaya. Inside, it looks like a log cabin with folk paintings of roosters and maidens. Waiters wear traditional Russian raiment. Tender beef in a pot 30,000R. *Shchi* (cabbage soup) 15,000R. *Kvas* 2000R. Open Mon.-Fri. noon-11pm.

Café Oladi (Оладьи), ul. Pushkinskaya 9 (tel. 916 26 59), just past the Tchaikovsky Conservatory. The namesake dish are small, sweet pancakes with jam or sour cream (5500R). Yum! Open daily 9am-8pm.

Near Bolshoy Teatr

Uzbekistan (Узбекистан), ul. Neglinnaya 29 (Неглинная; tel. 924 60 53). M8: Tsvetnoy Bulvar or M6: Kuznetsky Most. A majestic hall for homesick Uzbeks, Kazakhs, and Tadzhiks. Enough Uzbek decor to pretend you've left Moscow for the evening. Specialties include *lagman* (a meat and vegetable soup), *tkhumdulma* (boiled egg with a fried meat patty), and Uzbek-style *shashlik.* Uzbek bread baked on the premises. Open daily noon-11pm. Reservations necessary at dinner. Some may feel uncomfortable alone in this area at night.

Around the Arbat

Café Margarita (Кафе Маргарита), ul. Malaya Bronnaya 28 (tel. 299 65 34), at the corner of Maly Kozikhinski per. (Малый Козихинский). An artistically painted door leads to this super-trendy café opposite the Patriarch's Ponds, where Bulgakov's *The Master and Margarita* begins. Enjoy the house speciality—tomatoes stuffed with garlic and cheese—or just sip a cup of tea and watch the artsy gossip and smoke the afternoon away. *Lobio* 17,000R. *Bliny* with mushrooms 36,000R. Open daily 1pm-midnight. Live piano music after 7pm (cover 15,000R).

Praga, Arbat 2, at the corner of Novy Arbat. M3: Arbatskaya. It's not the main course the traveler will crave. Creator of the infamous "Praga" chocolate torte sold all over Moscow, the bakery to the right of the restaurant sells scrumptious goodies for a few rubles. The stand out front sells yummy eclairs (2000R). Open daily from 9am.

Italian Bar, Arbat 49 (tel. 241 43 42). Although this restaurant serves pricey fare, you can have a seat at the snack bar outside and watch the hordes tramp past as you enjoy a cappuccino and sandwich in the shade. Beer 20,000R. Cappuccino 20,000R. Sandwich 25,000R. Open daily noon-2am.

Temple of Moon (Храи Луны; *Khram Luny*), ul. Senashko 1/12 (Сенашко; tel. 291 04 01). Ask to be seated in the candlelit room with ghostly paintings, incense, and ceramic Asian art. A bit pricey (entrées US$12-50, soups US$4-8), but the shrimp with bamboo shoots made with delicate, creamy white sauce will take your breath away (Креветки тушенные с бамбуком; *krevetki tushennye s babukom;* US$21).

Gyro Express (Джайро Экспресс), ul. Gertsena 15 (Герцена). Serves *shwarma* (1300R) and *chebureki* (meat inside greasy bread; 500R). You want cheap, come here; you want taste, don't. Open Mon.-Fri. 10am-11pm, Sat.-Sun. noon-1am.

Near the Pushkin Museum of Fine Arts

Patio Pizza, ul. Volkhonka 13a (Волхонка; tel. 201 50 00), opposite the Pushkin Museum of Fine Arts. M1: Kropotkinskaya. This place rocks, and everybody knows it—come before 7pm, when a line forms. Spacious and light, with impeccably fast service. International clientele. The food and prices, not the buzzing atmosphere, are the draw. Delicious thin crust pizzas and scrumptious desserts please the palate without excessively lightening your wallet. Well stocked all-you-can-eat salad bar 40,000R. 28cm pizzas 50,000R. Lasagna 55,000R. Chocolate mousse or sinful nutcake 30,000R. AmEx, MC, Visa. Open daily noon-midnight.

Krisis Genre, Bolshaya Vesinaya per. 22/4 (Большая Весиная; tel. 243 86 05), corner of per. Ostrovskovo (Островского). M1: Kropotkinskaya. Walk through a small opening in a gate across from the Danish Embassy on Ostrovskovo per. into the courtyard—it's the 3rd door on the right. A small café near the Arbat catering to pensive artsy types—bring your *Crime and Punishment*. Crowded and noisy in an abandoned-looking apartment building. Entrées 21,000-31,000R. Bloody Mary 10,000R. American coffee 3000R. Open Tues.-Sun. noon-1am.

West of Gorky Park

Guria, Komsomolsky pr. 7 (Комсомольский; tel. 246 03 78), corner of ul. Frunze opposite St. Nicholas of the Weavers. M1,4: Park Kultury. Walk through a courtyard to the left to enter this homey restaurant serving delicious Georgian fare for some of the city's lowest prices. It's one of the hottest eateries for both locals and foreigners. Vegetarian meal of *lobio* (beans), *khachapuri,* salad, and Georgian yoghurt costs 18,000R. *Satsivi* (turkey in walnut sauce) 12,000R. *Khachapuri* 10,000R. English menu. Bring your own drinks. Open daily 11am-10:30pm.

U Pirosmani (У Пиросмани), Novodevichi pr. 4 (Новодевичий; tel. 247 19 26; fax 246 16 38), across from Novodevichi Convent, with one of Moscow's best views. M1: Sportivnaya. Turn left, and walk straight until you see the pond; the restaurant is on the left. Specializing in delicately spiced Georgian cuisine, it's above the rest for flavorful dishes served with panache. See photos of Clinton, who ate here in spring '96. *Lobio* US$3. *Khachapuri* US$2. *Baklazhany* (eggplant) US$6. Reserve for dinner. AmEx accepted. Open daily 12:45-10:30pm.

Near M2: Mayakovskaya

Baku-Livan (Баку-Ливан), ul. Tverskaya 24 (tel. 299 85 06). M2: Mayakovskaya. Wait in line for *shwarma* (9000R) and other Middle-Eastern delicacies for deliciously low prices at the stand-up café on the right side. On the left, upstairs, is an elegantly set restaurant of the same name that serves tabbouleh US$6, hummus US$5, falafel US$7. Eurocard, MC, Visa accepted. Open daily 11am-11pm.

American Bar and Grill, Sadovaya Triumfalnaya ul. (Садовая Триумфальная; tel. 251 79 99), directly opposite M2: Mayakovskaya. Packed and, because no reservations are allowed, the wait can be 2hr. Most crowded 1-3pm. Despite the low-ceilinged *faux*-American decor (cowboy hats hang from the ceiling), the menu and prices are truly American. A good place for noisy fun—the bar is a scene in itself. New England clam chowder US$6. Chips and salsa US$4. BBQ ribs US$7. Cheesecake US$8. *Bud* US$4. American breakfast served daily 4am-11am. Free bottomless coffee or tea with breakfast. Accepts AmEx, MC, Visa. Open 24hr.

Near the Traveller's Guest House

Drop In and Try (Зайди и попробуй; *Zaydi i poprobuy*), pr. Mira 124 (Мира; tel./fax 286 81 65). M5: Rizhskaya, then take the trolley a couple of stops north. Entrance on Malaya Moskovskaya ul. (Малая Московская). Drop in you do, since the restaurant is below street level, through a dim entrance hall. The interior pleases with bright tablecloths and murals. The food is your favorite Russian cuisine, well prepared. *Borscht* 8000R. Entrées 35,000R. Open daily 11am-midnight.

Kombi's, pr. Mira 46/48. Clean sandwich shop with subs (12,500-21,000R), salads (6000-10,000R), and milkshakes (9000R). English menu. Open daily 9am-10pm.

Near Krasnaya Presnya

Café of Chinese Cuisine (Кафе Китайской Кухни; *Café Kitayskoy Kukhni*), ul. Krasnaya Presnya 30 (Красная Пресня; tel. 252 33 84). M6: Ulitsa 1905 goda. Turn left from the Metro; it's on the left, marked by yellow lettering that lights up at night. A small, dark café that looks just like so many across the city. The difference is that it serves cheap Chinese food. Not all the menu is translated into English, so look at what the Russian customers get and point. Fried emperor's chicken 21,000R. Boiled rice 2000R. Dumplings 24,000R. Open daily 10am-10pm.

Santa Fe, ul. Mantulinskaya 6 (Мантулинская; tel. 256 14 87). M6: Ulitsa 1905 goda. A hefty walk—exit onto ul. 1905 goda from the Metro, follow it straight to the Mezhdunarodny, and take a right. The restaurant is on the left. The New Mexican decor and bustling foreignness of this place make it a yummy oasis even for the budget traveler. Fast service with a smile. Black bean soup US$7. Cajun burger US$15. Large desserts US$8-22. AmEx, MC, Visa accepted. Open Sun.-Thurs. noon-2am, Fri.-Sat. noon-3am.

Markets

As Georgians, Armenians, Uzbeks, and peasants from all over cart their finest produce to Moscow, your best bet for fresh fruits and vegetables is a market. A visit to a market is worth it for the visual experience—sides of beef, piles of tomatoes, peaches, grapes, jars of glowing honey, and huge pots of flowers crowd together in a visual bouquet. The **Central Market,** next to the Old Circus, closed for reconstruction in summer 1996, is scheduled to re-open in September 1997. But enterprising Russians hawk their wares on the street nearby (M8: Tsvetnoy Bulvar and turn right). The alternative is the **Rizhsky Market** at M5: Rizhskaya. Exit the Metro and keep turning left until you see it. Otherwise, impromptu markets spring up around metro stations; some of the best are at M: Turgenevskaya, Kuznetsky Most, Aeroport, Baumanskaya, and Oktyabrskoye Pole. In general, people appear with their goods around 10am, and leave by 8pm, though a stragglers stick around until 10pm-ish.

Supermarkets

The number of supermarkets increases just as the need for them decreases. Many of the goods sold here can be found cheaper in kiosks and in even smaller markets selling Russian and foreign foods. Yet little beats the convenience of knowing you can find everything you need in one place—Mall of America, baby! Supermarkets accept rubles, but since the exchange rate is usually less than favorable, it's often cheaper to pay with plastic. Listed below are a few of the largest:

Gastronom #1, ul. Tverskaya 14 (tel. 209 07 60). Moscow's most famous grocery reflects the economic situation of the times. These days the shelves are packed with foreign goods, the lines long, and the prices lower than in the hard currency supermarkets. Remodeled in 1901, this landmark is endowed with stained glass, high ceilings, and chandeliers. Open Mon.-Fri. 8am-9pm, Sat. 8am-7pm.

Gastronom Tsentralny, ul. Bolshaya Lubyanka 12/1 (Большая Лубянка), behind Lubyanka Prison. This 24-hr. supermarket has all kinds of food, with a 20% elevation in price from 10pm-7am—you pay for that midnight snack. Clean, cheery, but considered expensive by locals. AmEx, Diner's Club, MC, and Visa accepted.

The Arbat Irish House, Novy Arbat 11, 2nd fl. (Нобый Арбат). M3: Arbatskaya. Also a clothing-electronics store with an Irish bar to boot. Open Mon.-Sat. 9am-10pm, Sun. 10am-8pm. A well stocked Russian supermarket, **Novoarbatsky Gastronom,** downstairs. Open Mon.-Sat. 8am-7pm, Sun. 9am-10pm. MC, Visa at both.

Stockmann, M2,4: Paveletskaya. Facing the station on the opposite side, walk left 2 blocks; past the *bliny* stand on your left; behind the white curtains is the glassed-in store. A Finnish grocery emporium accepting credit cards only. Prices are in dollars. *Moscow Times, Moscow Tribune,* and the *Career Forum* available. *PC magazine, Time,* and *The Economist* sold here. Open daily 9am-9pm.

Sweet, Sweet Way, ul. Tverskaya 12, past Gastronom #1 and Pizza Hut. M1: Okhotny Ryad or M6: Pushkinskaya. A sweet, sweet tooth's delight. Filled with candies of every sort, sold by weight. Gummy bears 50,050R per kg. Open Mon.-Sat. 10am-9pm, Sun. 10am-7pm.

SIGHTS

Moscow's museums, attractive neighborhoods, and parks cluster in its oldest region, surrounded by the Garden Ring. The city's sights reflect its strange history: the visitor may choose among 16th-century churches or Soviet-era museums, but little in between. Moscow is constantly under construction (Manezhnaya pl. in summer '96). And recent political upheaval has taken its toll; museums such as those for Lenin, Marx, and Engels are closed indefinitely while their historical significance is reassessed. Russia's capital also suffers from the 200 years during which St. Petersburg was the tsar's seat. Moscow has no grand palaces and fewer great art galleries and artists it can claim as native children. Still, there is plenty to do and see, and, with a little grit and a lot of humor, much to enjoy.

Red Square (Красная площадь; *Krasnaya ploschad*)

There is nothing red about it; *krasnaya* meant "beautiful" long before the Communists co-opted it. Red Square has been the site of everything from a giant farmer's market to public hangings to political demonstrations to a renegade Cesna's landing. It is a 700m-long lesson in history and culture. On one side the **kremlin** stands as both the historical and religious center of Russia and the seat of the Communist Party for 70-odd years; on the other **GUM,** once a market, then the world's largest purveyor of grim Soviet consumer goods, has become a bona-fide shopping mall. At one end **St. Basil's Cathedral,** the square's second oldest building, rises high with its crazy-quilt onion domes; at the other the **History** and **Lenin Museums** are both closed for ideological repair. Indeed, Lenin's historical legacy has finally come into question, and his name and face are coming down all over Moscow. The Party, so to speak, is finally over. But his mausoleum still stands in front of the kremlin—dejected and patrolled by several scowling teenage draftees. Now with a smaller entrance, Communist parades can never march into the square. The mayor of Moscow is trying to close this one down, too. He has built another church at the side of the kremlin. Begin your visit here; tradition has it that first-time comers must enter with their eyes closed so as to get the full effect. Remember, the first time only happens once.

Kremlin (Кремль; *Kreml*)

Like a spider in her web, the kremlin sits geographically and historically in the center of Moscow. Here Ivan the Terrible reigned with his iron fist; here Stalin ruled the lands behind the Iron Curtain. Napoleon simmered here while Moscow burned, and here the Congress of People's Deputies dissolved itself in 1991 ending the USSR. But despite the tremendous political history of the one-time fortress, the things to see here are largely churches. Buy tickets at the *kassa* in Aleksandr Gardens, on the west side of the kremlin, and enter through Borovitskaya gate tower in the southwest corner. Shorts and large bags are not allowed; there is a check-room.

Much of the kremlin is still government offices; the watchful police will blow whistles if you stray into a forbidden zone. Follow the people with cameras, and you will come to **Cathedral Square,** where the most famous gold domes in Russia rise.

The first church to the left, the **Annunciation Cathedral,** guards the loveliest *iconostasis* in Russia, with luminous icons by Andrei Rublev and Theophanes the Greek. Originally only three-domed, the church was elaborated and gilded by Ivan the Terrible. The second, southeast entrance is also his work; four marriages made Ivan ineligible to use the main entrance.

Across the way, the square **Archangel Cathedral** gleams with similarly vivid icons and frescos. But this temple has a more morbid attraction; it is the final resting place for many tsars prior to Peter the Great. Ivans III, the Great, and IV, the Terrible, are behind the south end of the *iconostasis;* Mikhail Romanov is in front of it.

The center of Cathedral Square is the **Assumption Cathedral,** where Ivan the Terrible's throne still stands by the south wall. The icons on the west wall are 15th-century; the others are from the 1640s. Napoleon, securing his excellent reputation with the Russians, used the place as a stable in 1812. To the east of the Assumption Cathedral rises **Ivan the Great Belltower.** Its tower is visible from 30km away thanks to Boris Godunov (the one pre-Peter tsar not buried in the kremlin—he's in Sergievsky Posad) who raised the tower's height to 81m. The ground floor has exhibits from the kremlin's collection. Behind the Assumption Cathedral stands the **Patriarch's Palace,** site of the Museum of 17th-Century Russian Applied Art and Life, and the **Church of the Twelve Apostles,** built by Patriarch Nikon in the 17th century as revenge against Ivan the Terrible's extravagant St. Basil's Cathedral.

Behind the Archangel Cathedral, the **Tsar Bell,** the world's largest, has never rung and never will: an 11.5-ton piece cracked off after a fire in 1737. Also open to visitors, the **Armory Museum** (tel. 221 47 20) lies just to the left as you enter. All the riches of the Russian Church, and those of the State that are not in the Hermitage, can be found in these nine rooms. Room 3, on the second floor, holds the legendary Fabergé eggs—each opens to reveal an impossibly intricate jewelled miniature. Room 6 holds thrones and other royal necessities: crowns and dresses (Empress Elizabeth is said to have had 15,000 gowns, only one of which is on display). Room 9 contains royal coaches and sleds—Elizabeth had her sled pulled by 23 horses (not one for understatement). The **Diamond Fund** (tel. 229 20 36), an annex of the Armory, has still more glitter, including a 190-carat diamond given to Catherine the Great by Gregory Onov, a special friend of hers. That's all of the kremlin you can actually go into, except for the **Kremlin Palace of Congresses,** the square white monster built by Khrushchev in 1961 for Communist Party Congresses. It's also a theater, one of the few open in summer for concerts and ballets. (Kremlin open Fri.-Wed. 10am-4pm. 12,000R, students 6000R, includes tour. Diamond Fund US$19. Armory free.)

Near the Kremlin

Aleksandr Gardens (Александровский Сад; *Aleksandrovsky Sad*) is more than just the place to buy kremlin tickets; this pleasant garden is a cool green respite from central Moscow's carbon monoxide fumes. At the north end, at the **Tomb of the Unknown Soldier,** an eternal flame burns in memory of the catastrophic losses the country suffered in WWII, the Great Fatherland War. Twelve urns containing soil from the Soviet Union's "Hero Cities" that withstood especially heavy casualties stand there as well. It used to be the trendy spot to get your picture taken on your wedding day—that and Lenin's mausoleum.

State Department Store GUM (Государственный Универсальный Магазин ГУМ; *Gosudarstvenny Universalny Magazin*), built in the 19th century, used to be a great place to come and be glad you didn't live in Russia. It is built to hold 1000 stores, and resembles a train station of the last century with its arched wrought-iron-and-glass roofs. During Soviet rule, it was a depressing experience; there's not much that's grimmer than a thousand empty stores. These days, it has been completely renovated and is a shopping mall of which any American metropolis would be proud. Most stores quote prices in US$ or DM, but you can pay in rubles. There are lines outside

SIGHTS ■ 541

Kremlin

Map Legend:

1. Armory Palace
2. Great Kremlin Palace
3. Terem Palace
4. St. Lazarus Church
5. Poteshny Palace
6. Palace of Deputies
7. Upper Saviour Cathedral
8. Church of the Deposition of the Robe
9. Granovitaya Palace
10. Cathedral of the Annunciation
11. Cathedral of the Archangel
12. Cathedral of the Assumption
13. Patriarch's Palace
14. Cathedral of the 12 Apostles
15. Tsar's Cannon
16. Ivan the Great Belltower
17. Tsar's Bell
18. State Council
19. St. Basil's Cathedral
20. Place of Execution
21. President's Cabinet Building
22. Lenin Mausoleum
23. Arsenal
24. Tomb of the Unknown Soldier
25. Historical Museum
26. Central Lenin Museum

KREMLIN WALL TOWERS

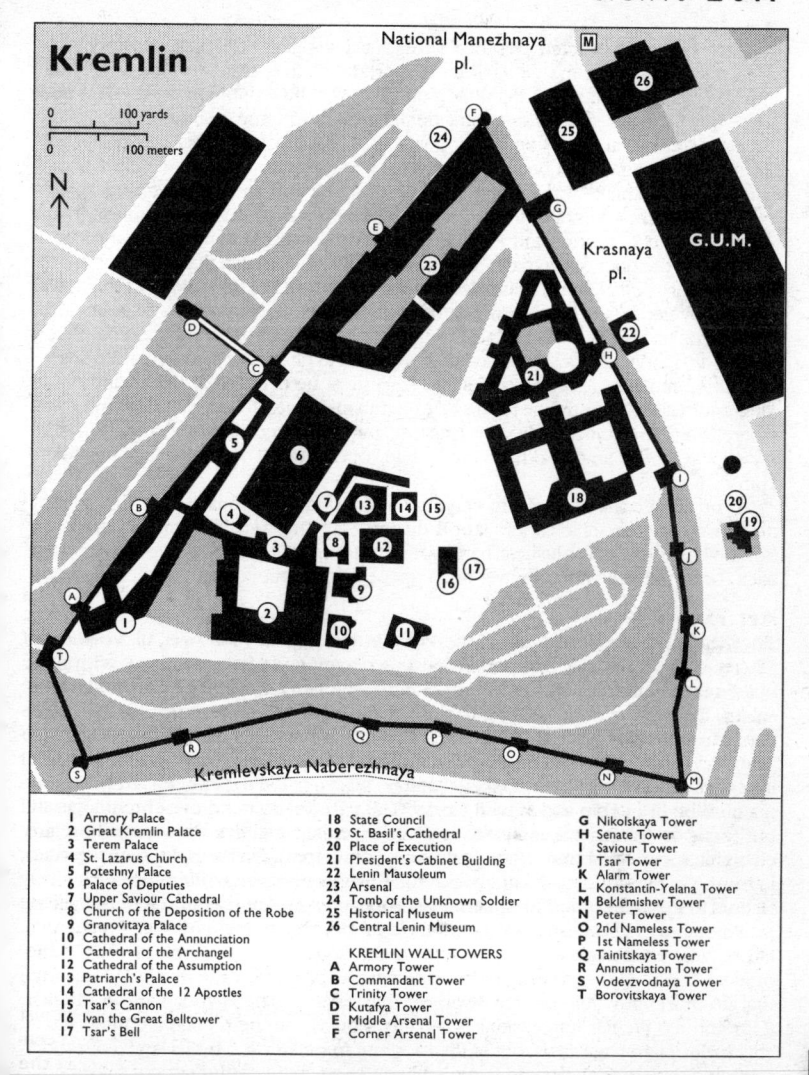

A. Armory Tower
B. Commandant Tower
C. Trinity Tower
D. Kutafya Tower
E. Middle Arsenal Tower
F. Corner Arsenal Tower
G. Nikolskaya Tower
H. Senate Tower
I. Saviour Tower
J. Tsar Tower
K. Alarm Tower
L. Konstantin-Yelana Tower
M. Beklemishev Tower
N. Peter Tower
O. 2nd Nameless Tower
P. 1st Nameless Tower
Q. Tainitskaya Tower
R. Annunciation Tower
S. Vodevzvodnaya Tower
T. Borovitskaya Tower

most doors. Kodak Express is on the first floor; a copy center, a DHL, and several decent restaurants on the second (see Food, p. 536). (GUM open Mon.-Sat. 8am-8pm, Sun. 11am-6pm.) Enter by the History Museum, and leave your credit card at home; the sight of so many consumer goods might mess up your brain.

There is perhaps no more familiar symbol of Moscow than **St. Basil's Cathedral** (Собор Василия Блажного; *Sobor Vasiliya Blazhnovo*; pictured on the cover of this guide). Completed in 1561, it was commissioned by Ivan the Terrible to celebrate his 1552 victory over the Tartars in Kazan. The nine main chapels are named after the saints' days on which Ivan won his battles, but the cathedral itself bears the moniker of a holy fool, Vasily (Anglicized to Basil), who correctly predicted that Ivan would murder his own son. Before the Kazan victory, Vasily died and was buried in the church that once stood on this ground. The grand cathedral that replaced it has seen the addition of a few minor domes since Ivan's time, as well as the 17th-century innovation of colorful patterns for which the domes are known. The interior is filled with intricate, but reconstructed, frescoes. Downstairs sits an exhibit on the history of the church and Ivan's campaign against the Tartars, all in Russian. (Open Wed.-Mon. 10am-4:30pm. To climb up 25,000R, students 15,000R; exhibition on the 2nd floor 300R. Buy tickets from the *kassa* outside the entrance before 4:30pm.)

Kazan Cathedral stands on the opposite end of the square. This orange-and-gold birthday-cake church has been reopened for services after being completely demolished in 1936 to make way for May Day parades. The interior is much plainer than in most Russian churches, and the *iconostasis* free from gold Baroque madness. There is a healthy mix of tourists and worshippers, so don't worry too much about the myriad rules on the door (open daily 8am-7pm; services at 8am and 5pm).

In the glory days, **Lenin's Mausoleum,** a squat red tomb in front of the kremlin, was guarded by fierce goose-stepping guards, and the line to get in was three hours long. The guards have now been replaced by one bored cop, and the line has completely vanished—getting in is a cinch...when it's open. No photos are allowed of Vladimir's embalmed remains, and backpacks and bags must be checked at the cloakroom in Aleksandr Gardens. Entrance to the mausoleum also gives access to the **kremlin wall** where Stalin, Brezhnev, Andropov, Gagarin, and John Reed, author of *Ten Days that Shook the World,* among others, are buried (open Tues.-Thurs. and Sat.-Sun. 10am-1pm).

As you admire the mausoleum on your stroll around Red Square, note the balcony on top where Russia's leaders stood during May Day and November 7 parades. Rumor has it that the plushest bathroom in Moscow is hidden somewhere in the back. Unfortunately, it has not yet been opened to the public.

Art Museums

Since the most recent revolution, the **Pushkin Museum of Fine Arts,** ul. Volkhonka 12 (tel. 203 95 78), M1: Kropotkinskaya, is becoming better organized, with new buildings to house its large collection of European Renaissance, Egyptian, and Classical art. The aquamarine building to the left of the main entrance houses the three-floor **Museum of Private Collections,** which exhibits famous foreign and Russian art from the 19th- and 20th-centuries. The museum began when Ilya Siberstein donated his collection to the state, and asked that it be placed in the old Prince Yard Hotel, frequented by Ilya Repin and Maxim Gorky. The exhibits do not move chronologically but focus on the private individual collector—a sign that even museums here are changing (open Wed.-Sun. 10am-5pm; *kassa* until 4pm). On the right, with a garden in front, the imposing main entrance to the **Pushkin Museum of Fine Arts** welcomes visitors to Russia's second most famous European art museum, after the Hermitage in St. Petersburg. The Pushkin was founded in 1912 by poetess Marina Tsvetaeva's father, who wanted his art students to have the opportunity to see Classical art in the original. It gained the majority of its impressive exhibits after the revolution ensured that no museum would be one of private possessions. The Egyptian art on the first floor and the French Impressionists (mainly Monets) on the second are understandably major pilgrimage areas, but as the museum frequently rotates its large collection, spending time in each section is probably more advisable. Although not as daunting as most museums of its caliber, this one still requires a day. Each floor has a detailed plan, and Walkmans (30min., 15,000R) help guide the way (open Tues.-Sun. 10am-6pm; 30,000R, students 15,000R; keep ticket for entrance to other museums).

Located in Moscow's inner south section of churches and 18th-century manor houses, Russia's premier **Tretyakovskaya Galereya** (Третьяковская Галерея), Lavrushensky per. 10 (Лаврушенский; tel. 230 77 88), M7: Tretyakovskaya, is unusual because Pavel Tretyakov collected this art himself before donating it to the state after the revolution. It exhibits some of Russian art's most important paintings and sculptures, as well as a magnificent collection of icons. The icons have come under some debate recently, as many of the churches from which they were taken wish to reclaim them. Although the works span to the present (including Malevich's infamous *Black Square*), the museum's Mona Lisa equivalent is the 12th-century Vladimir icon *God and Mother,* taken from Constantinople, which hung for centuries in the kremlin's Uspensky Sobor and allegedly protected Moscow from the Poles (open Tues.-Sun. 10am-8pm; 36,000R, students 18,000R).

There are numerous other museums of note in Moscow; many of the more renowned are listed below:

Manege (Манеж), Manezhnaya pl. (Манежная; tel. 202 93 04), west of the kremlin. This one-time riding school for the military is now the Central Exhibition Hall and often features interesting modern Russian exhibits. Enter from the north end, on the square. Open Wed.-Mon. 11am-8pm; *kassa* closes 1hr. before exhibitions. Closed due to construction in summer 1996.

State Tretyakovskaya Galereya (Государственная Третьяковская Галерея), ul. Krymsky Val 10 (Крымский Вал; tel. 928 41 06). M4,5: Oktyabrskaya. Directly opposite the Gorky Park entrance, on the right side. This museum, built to house newer works and exhibitions of Russian art, shares a building with the **Central House of Artists**; the Tretyakov is the building in back, with an entrance to the right side. Comprehensive exhibits on Russian artists: the ground floor usually hosts contemporary art and the 2nd floor, a 19th-century artist's life-work. The top floor contains the permanent exhibit, a huge retrospective of Russian art from the 1910s to the 30s, which intelligently shows the development of Socialist Realism. The fine depictions of the Russian body-ethic can be passed quickly. Open Tues.-Sun. 10am-8pm. *Kassa* open until 7pm. 25,000R, students 12,000R; Russians 6000R, Russian students 2000R. Behind the gallery to the right lies a makeshift graveyard for **fallen statues**. These huge black ghosts stand in disorder, staring into the distance. Stalin himself, nose broken, lies uncomfortably on his elbow and Khrushchev's unfortunate head rolls on the grass.

Central House of Artists (Центральный Дом Художника; *Tsentralny Dom Khudozhnika*; tel. 238 96 34), ul. Krymsky Val 10. M4,5: Oktyabrskaya. The only large museum which does not charge separate prices for foreigners, it houses numerous small exhibits—some for sale. Cutting-edge Russian art as well as fast-changing progressive historical exhibits. Consult *The Moscow Times* for info or go to the auction hall and start a private collection of your own. Open Tues.-Sun. 11am-7pm. 10,000R, students 5000R.

The Moscow Metro is worth a tour of its own. All stations are unique, and those inside the ring line are elaborate, with mosaics, sculptures, and crazy chandeliers. It's only 1500R—and with trains coming every 2min., you can stay as short or long as you like, with no *babushka* in the corner to yell at you. Stations **Kievskaya, Mayakovskaya,** and **Ploshchad Revolutsii** (with a staute on each step) are particularly good, as are **Novoslobodskaya, Rimskaya,** and **Mendeleevskaya**. Note the atomic-model light fixtures in the Mendeleevskaya station. Open daily 5:45am-1am.

All-Russia Museum of Decorative and Applied Folk Art (Все-российский Музей Декоративно-прикладного; *Vse-rossyisky Muzey Dekorativno-prikladnovo*), Delegatskaya ul. 3 (Делегатская; tel. 923 77 25), just north of the Garden Ring. M8: Tsvetnoi Bulvar. This is what the junk they sell on the Arbat is supposed to look like. The museum consists of 2 buildings. The 1st, where you buy your tickets, contains rooms of fine quality, contemporary painted and lacquered wood, 17th- and 18th-century textiles, and samovars. The 2nd, ul. Delegatskaya 5, is more interesting. The 1st room juxtaposes traditional Russian peasant costumes of the last century against what the St. Petersburg glitterati were wearing in the same period. More contemporary work includes pottery, wood carving, and incredibly intricate lacquered boxes. Open Sat.-Thurs. 10am-6pm. *Kassa* closes an hour before the museum. Closed last Thurs. of every month. 10,000R, students 3000R.

Museum of Folk Art (Музей Народого Искусства; *Muzey Narodnovo Iskusstva*), ul. Stanislavskovo (tel. 290 52 22). M6: Pushkinskaya. The sign for the museum is not on the door; the large black doors are the entrance to this 1-room museum. The exhibit changes continually, with the right half of the room simply for display and the left half for sale; there are often interesting pieces to buy. Open Sun.-Tues. 11am-5:30pm. 3000R, students 1000R. Art from 2000R.

Oriental Art Museum, Nikitsky (formerly Suvurovsky) bul. 12a (tel. 291 02 12). M3: Arbatskaya or M6: Pushkinskaya. A tiny museum that looks more like a gallery with knowledgeable curators. Often has excellent exhibits. The permanent exhibit includes art from the Far East, with somewhat mystical Russian explanations. Open Tues.-Sun. 11am-8pm. 25,000R, 2nd and 4th Wed. of the month free.

Historic Sights

The White House, M4: Krasnopresnenskaya. You can't visit this symbol of the 1993 political upheaval. But since you've probably already seen it on TV, you could stroll by and see what it's like in times of relative peace. Yeltsin climbed atop a tank here, brandishing the flag of the Russian Federation, and declared himself the only legitimate ruler of the country. Not long after, Yeltsin switched positions when he bombarded an anti-reformist Parliament with cannonfire during the October 1993 coup. The building has since been renovated, but if you look closely you can still see bullet-holes in the fence. From the metro station, take a left and follow the trail of red ribbons and makeshift monuments. Read the list of names of those killed and see if you can make sense of it. Not many can.

Muzey Revolyutsii (Музей Революции), ul. Tverskaya 21 (tel. 299 67 24). M6: Pushkinskaya. Housed in the former mansion of the Moscow English club, this museum could easily be called a history of 20th-century Russia as it covers everything since the revolution, although it often has exhibits from previous centuries. Amazingly, this Soviet archive has moved with the times, adding statistics on the ill-effects of socialism (in 1989, 40% of pensioners earned less than 60R per month) as well as eclectic documents such as those on 80s rock bands. Even their beat-up trolley has a recent story to tell: it was the one damaged in the August 1991 coup that clinched Yeltsin's support. But it's the museum shop on the 1st floor that reflects a revolutionizing Russia. One of the best places to buy Soviet medals, this store also stocks old posters and t-shirts with slogans like "The Party is Over" or "Хард Рок Кафе". Museum open Tues., Thurs., and Sat. 10am-6pm, Wed. 11am-7pm, Sun. 10am-5pm. 10,000R, English tour 150,000R.

Muzey Istorii Moskvy (Музей Истории Москвы), Novaya pl. 12 (Новая; tel. 924 84 90). M5,6: Kitai-Gorod. A Soviet-era museum where they still turn the lights on as you go through, and the collection consists of anything old and pretty enough to display. The ground floor houses archaeological finds from the area and old maps and plans, showing how Moscow expanded from the kremlin. Upstairs are Lev Tolstoy's desk chair and 19th-century knick-knacks. Open Tues., Thurs., and Sat.-Sun. 10am-6pm, Wed. and Fri. 11am-7pm. 10,000R, students 5000R.

Central Museum of the Armed Forces of the USSR (Центральный Музей Вооруженных Сил СССР; *Tsentralny Muzey Vooruzhennykh Sil SSSR*), ul. Sovetskaya Armia 2 (Советская Армия II; tel. 281 18 80). M4: Novoslobodskaya, then walk down ul. Seleznevskaya (Селезневская) to the square and go left. A block down on the right. Military paraphernalia from World War II, the most interesting item being the milepost 41 marker from the Moscow-Leningrad highway, the closest the Nazis came to Moscow. Otherwise, lots of tanks, guns, and propaganda posters. Visitors seem to be largely 8-year-olds and WWII vets. Open Wed.-Sun. 10am-5pm, closed the 2nd Tues. and last week of each month. 20,000R.

Borodino, Kutuzovsky pr. 38 (tel. 148 19 65). M3: Kutozovskaya, then 10min. to the right down Kutozovsky pr. A giant statue of Commander Kutuzov stands in front of the large circular building that houses the Borodino panorama and museum. Commemorating the bloody battle with Napoleon in August 1812, the 360° painting and accompanying exhibitions usually require you to wait in line along with the others eager to enter this bizarre memorial. 15,000R.

Monasteries, Churches, and Synagogues

When the grime and bedlam gets to you, escape to one of Moscow's hidden parks or monasteries. Among the most famous is **Novodevichy Monastir** (Новодевичий Монастырь; tel. 246 85 26), M1: Sportivnaya. Take the exit out of the Metro that does not go to the stadium, then a right on that street. The convent is several blocks down on the left. You can't miss the high brick walls, golden domes, and tourist buses. Tsars and nobles kept the coffers filled by exiling their well dowried wives and daughters here when they grew tired of them. Buried within the monastery's walls are some well known 16th-century Russians, such as the philosopher Solovyov, but all the truly famous folks are entombed at the cemetery next door. Wandering around the grounds is rewarding on a pleasant day, but a few of the buildings are also open. The **Smolensky Cathedral,** in the center of the convent, shows off some Russian icons. Unfortunately, due to staff shortages, it is closed in rainy weather when only the museum, housed in a white building to the left, is open. Other buildings of interest include the **Assumption Cathedral** (tel. 246 85 26), to the right of Smolensky, and a small three-room **exhibit hall** at the far end of the grounds. Entrance to the grounds is 2000R; to buy tickets to the other buildings, stop by the white *kassa* on the left once you enter the gate. (Open Wed.-Mon. 10am-5pm; closed first Mon. of the month. 25,000R, students 15,000R. Avoid Sun. when tour buses hog the place.)

Turning right and down the street, the convent's **cemetery** cradles the graves of Gogol, Chekhov, Stanislavsky, Khrushchev, Shostakovich, Mayakovsky, Bulgakov, and other luminaries. The tombstones are often highly creative representations—visual or symbolic—of the deceased. Once closed to prevent too many from flocking to Khrushchev's tomb (straight through the entrance at the back of the cemetery), it is now open to the public. The writers are conveniently clustered near each other. When tombstone shopping, Bulgakov's wife saw the stone and knew immediately this would be perfect for her deceased husband. Upon buying it, she learned it had originally been considered for Gogol, whom Bulgakov greatly admired. Buy tickets at the small kiosk across the street from the entrance; a useful map of the cemetery is also sold here, if you can read Cyrillic (open daily 10am-6pm).

Danilovsky Monastery, M8: Tulskaya, gains importance each day, as home to the head of the Russian Orthodox Church, the Patriarch. Although the grounds and building are stunning, there is little but the exterior to see. A map on the left side of the entrance explains the different buildings, and it is worth a visit simply to see the long-robed monks scurrying about their business. The Patriarch's office is hard to miss, due to an enormous mosaic of a stern-looking man watching over the visitors to his domain. The monastery itself is a pastel montage, with buildings freshly painted in soft pinks, yellows, and blues. Entrance is free; simply turn right from the Metro, and you can't miss the whitewashed walls and turrets (open daily 6am-7pm; services Mon.-Fri. at 7am and 5pm, Sat.-Sun. at 9am and 5pm).

Donskov Monastery, M5: Shabolovskaya (tel. 452 16 46), the least famous of Moscow's monasteries, is as a result the most authentic; those who stroll along its leafy paths believe in the serenity of this place. From the Metro, take a right onto Shabolovka until the second street, then turn right again. Since the fall of Communism, the red-brick Donskov has gained a congregation, but not quite the prestige it had in 1591. Still, on Russian Orthodox holidays the monastery teems with life, and on other days it sits peacefully in the golden sunlight. The church straight ahead from the entrance is cased in clearly painted frescos, while the smaller church to the right is also operational, but due to its greater age, less ornate (open daily 7am-7pm; services daily at 8am and 5pm; women should cover their heads).

Large, airy, and lovely, the **Moscow Synagogue,** Bolshoy Spasoglinishchevsky per. 10 (Большой Спасоглинишевский; former Arkhipova; Rabbi Pinchas Goldsmith, tel. 923 96 97), M5,6: Kitai-Gorod, feels very different from Russia's churches. In the yellow building with white columns on the right with the Hebrew over the door, services are held every morning and evening, during which time women are not allowed downstairs and men must cover their heads. Otherwise, it's open to the public (daily 9:30am-6pm). To get there, keep the double statue at your back, turn left on Solyansky Proezd (Солянский Проезд), and then take the first left.

Muzey Andreya Rubleva (Музей им. Андрея Рублева; tel. 278 14 89). From M8: Ploschad Ilicha, take ul. Sergia Radonezhskovo (Сергия Радонежского), turn right on Andronyevskaya pl. (Андроньевская) to pl. Pryanikova (Пряникова). The **Spaso-Andronikov Monastery** (Спасо-Андроников), across the street in the park, preserves life-size 16th-century icons and a biblical text from the 14th century. (Open Thurs.-Tues. 11am-6pm, closed last Fri. of the month. *Kassa* closes 5pm. 35,000R, students 5000R, free the last Thurs. of each month.)

An 18th century ecclesiastic gem, the **Church of Ionna Voina,** ul. Bolshaya Yakimanka 54 (Большая Якиманка; formerly Dimitrova), M4,5: Oktyabrskaya, takes its name from the patron saint of the tsar's musketeers (open Tues.-Fri. 8am-7pm, Sun.

> ### Hot Air
> The demise of Moscow's ill-fated swimming pool is an ironic mix of Soviet planning, Russian superstition, and hot air. A glorious cathedral twice the height of the Statue of Liberty once stood on the site of the modern-day pool. Stalin tore it down intending to erect a Palace of Soviets to rival the church in size, but fortunately for aesthetes worldwide, the ground proved too soft for such an edifice. Many muttered about a curse. Undaunted, Stalin ordered that an enormous, outdoor, heated swimming pool be built instead. The pool's first summer was a hit among the proletariat, but as winter approached, the heated pool began to steam, and a continuous fog beset the neighborhood. Of more concern to officials was the strange peeling and warping of paintings at the nearby Pushkin Museum. When city administrators discovered that steam from the pool was destroying their collection, they closed the pool, and left the gaping hole in the ground as yet another unintentional monument to Soviet planning.

7am-7pm; services Tues.-Sun. at 5pm). The inner south region is speckled with numerous, sometimes boarded-up, churches; simply walk around the neighborhood to find one you like. The **Yelokhovsky Cathedral,** ul. Spartakovskaya 15 (Спартаковская), M3: Baumanskaya, is Moscow's largest and perhaps most beautiful operational church. Built in 1845, only the gilded interior outshines the brilliant turquoise exterior. The cathedral has the grand honor of being one of the main administrative locations of the ever-growing Russian Orthodox Church (open daily; morning services 7pm; services Mon.-Sat. at 8am and 6pm, Sun. at 6:30, 9:30am, and 6pm).

The **Church of St. Nicholas of the Weavers** is one of Moscow's better known churches, mainly because it's very hard to miss. Located at the corner of Komsomolsky pr. and ul. Frunze (Фрунзе) across from the popular Café Guria (M1,4: Park Kultury), it looks like a church Hansel and Gretel's witch would have designed—whitewashed with deliciously artificial green-and-orange trimming. Enter the church off ul. Frunze to witness the low ceilings and colorful interior for yourself (open Mon.-Sat. 8am-7pm, Sun. and holidays 7am-7pm; service begins at opening).

The city government constructed the **Temple of Jesus the Savior** (Храм Христа Спосителя; *Khram Khrista Spositelya*), M1: Kropotkinskaya, to commemorate the cathedral which Stalin tore down in 1936 to build the **Moscow swimming pool.**

Regions for Walking
Several blocks away, at M3: Arbatskaya, the **Arbat,** a pedestrian shopping arcade, was once a showpiece of *glasnost*, a haven for political radicals, Hare Krishnas, street poets, and *metallisti* (heavy metal rockers). Now, it boasts a McDonald's, a Baskin Robbins, and a Benetton. With these forerunners of capitalism, this formerly infamous street has lost much of its political significance and life. Groups gather around guitar players and peddlers photograph tourists with their little monkey in a tutu. You can still buy Russian souvenirs from amber to *matroshka* dolls, but the commercial aspect once so unique has spread across the city. Midway up, on a sidestreet, is a graffiti wall dedicated to rocker Victor Tsoi of the Soviet group Kino, who served as an idol to many young Russian before his death in a car crash three years ago. Moscow youths still hang out, devoutly following rock-and-roll's three sacred precepts.

Intersecting but almost parallel with the Arbat runs **Novy Arbat,** a thoroughfare lined with foreign businesses like the Arbat Irish House and Sports Bar, and massive Russian stores like the famous **Dom Knigi,** a giant bookstore, and **Melodiya,** a top record store. Halfway up ul. Tverskaya from Red Square at M6: Pushkinskaya, **Pushkin Square** is Moscow's favorite rendezvous spot. Amateur politicians gather here to argue and hand out petitions, while missionary groups evangelize. All the major Russian news organizations are located in this region, perhaps one of the reasons the square is the center of free speech—though as the eight-story **Izvestia,** the formerly Communist-controlled newspaper, peers disapprovingly at Moscow's golden arches nearby, the changes are not so easy to read. Everything on the square is large—from the golden arches to the **Kinema Rossiya,** Moscow's largest, which brought *Termi-*

nator to the masses. Follow ul. Bolshaya Bronnaya, next to McD's, down to the bottom of the hill, turn right and follow ul. Malaya Bronnaya to the **Patriarch's Ponds,** where the action of Mikhail Bulgakov's *The Master and Margarita* begins. This region, known as the Margarita, is popular with artsy students and old men playing dominoes by the shaded pond.

Soviet and Old Russian architecture have their showdown on **ul. Razina** (Разина), one left turn past St. Basil's. The on- and off-ramp of the **Rossiya,** the world's largest hotel, snakes around a series of lovely churches. Turn right out of GUM down **Nikolskaya ul.** to reach **pl. Lubyanka,** currently site of the headquarters of the KGB and formerly of a huge stone Felix Dzerzhinsky, the organization's founder.

On the square's northeast corner sits **Muzey Mayakovskovo** (Музей им. В. В. Маяковского), a fascinating achievement in Futurist museum design. Chairs sit at an angle and hang from walls. Convoluted red metal in the shape of fire climbs with you on the spiral staircase; green paint spills everywhere. Look for the bust of Mayakovsky surrounded by huge crimson metal shards; the museum hides in the building behind it. The avant-garde poet and artist lived here in a communal apartment from 1919. His room is preserved at the top of the building, the eye in the storm of steel girders and shards of glass, chronicling his initial love affair with the revolution (Communist propaganda paper the museum) and his travels abroad. Mayakovsky shot himself in this flat in 1930, for reasons still unknown. The museum makes that chapter less clear than the others. (Open Fri.-Tues. 10am-6pm, Thurs. 1-9pm. *Kassa* closes 1hr. earlier. Closed last Fri. of the month. 3000R, guided tours well worth the 2500R in Russian, not necessarily the 70,000R in English.)

Moscow State University (МГУ; *Em Ghe Oo*), a hefty walk from M1: Universitet, lies within a single Stalinist edifice. To fully appreciate its size, you must go inside, which means persuading a student to take you. If you're desperate for fellow ex-pat company, hang out in the neighborhood: you're bound to run into some of the foreigners who come to "study". Near MSU, in **Lenin Hills** (a leafy enclave overlooking the city center), is one of the city's best viewing areas, from which you can see the **Luzhniki Sports Complex,** the **Lenin Stadium** (sites of the 1980 Olympics), and all of Moscow. Considered a highly romantic spot, this could be a Russian make-out point, except for the camera-toting tourists and the not-so-picturesque view—most of the golden splashes are lost in the sea of gray.

Houses of the Literary and Famous

Russians take immense pride in their formidable literary history, preserving authors' houses in their original state down to half-empty teacups on the mantelpiece. Each is guarded by a team of *babushki*, fiercely loyal to their master's memory.

Lev Tolstoy Estate, ul. Lva Tolstovo 21 (Льва Толстого; tel. 246 94 44). M1,4: Park Kultury. A hefty walk down Komsomolsky pr. toward the colorful Church of St. Nicholas of the Weavers; turn right at the corner on ul. Lva Tolstovo. The estate is 3 blocks up on the left. The famous author lived here between 1882 and 1901 in winter. He spent the summers at Yasnaya Polyana (a beautiful daytrip 200km south reachable only by car), a habit which may explain why he kept the large garden overgrown and wild; the current curators have left the lush dark green foliage as unkempt as in Tolstoy's day. The house itself is one of the most perfectly preserved house-museums in Moscow—one might imagine that the author and his family have just run into the garden, leaving the elegantly furnished wooden house exactly as it appears. Tolstoy was apparently a man of habit; he always drank barley or acorn coffee, dined at 6pm every evening, and wrote *The Resurrection* in the study here between exactly 9am and 3pm every day. But the personalities of Tolstoy's children, many of whom died young, are present in the house too, providing a more comprehensive understanding of the author as a father. Helpful explanations of each of the rooms are written in English on the doors. See the bicycle Papa Tolstoy learned to ride at the age of 60. The *kassa* is to the right of the entrance gate or, if that is closed, in the yellow house down a path to the left inside the entrance (open in summer Tues.-Sun. 10am-6pm; off-season 10am-3pm, closed last Fri. of the month; 20,000R, students 10,000R, Russians 5000R).

Tolstoy Museum-Apartment, ul. Spiridonovka 4 (Спиридоновка, tel. 290 09 56), next to Gorky's apartment. Like his books, there's always more. Tolstoy lived here between 1941 and 1945, finishing a few of his not-so-well known books. Grander than most museums in its collection of classical paintings and chandeliers. Placards in English explain each room, and so will the *babushki* guarding the rooms. Open Thurs. and Sat.-Sun. 11am-5:30pm, Wed. and Fri. 1-6pm. 5000R.

Dostoyevsky Museum-Apartment (Музей-квартира Достоевского; *Muzey-kvartira Dostoyevskovo*), ul. Dostoyevskovo 2, just off pl. Kommuny (Коммуны). M4: Novoslobodskaya. Dostoyevsky was born here—the flat lies on the grounds of the hospital where his father was a doctor. It is all preserved, and many of the contents are original. Each room is labeled (in Russian and English) with an excerpt from the memoirs of Fyodor's brother, Aleksandr, describing the room and what went on in it. The women working here revere the house's famous former resident and will gladly talk about him—in Russian. They even have the pen Dostoyevsky used to write *The Brothers Karamazov*. Undergoing renovations in '96. Open Thurs., Sat., and Sun. 11am-6pm, Wed. and Fri. 2-9pm, closed last day of the month.

Muzey Tropinina (Музей Тропинина), Shchetininsky per. 10 (Щетининский; tel. 231 17 99). M8: Polyanka. A superb 19th-century building owned by the serf Tropinin, chock-full of paintings by Russian artists. Often has exhibits on Russian 19th-century life. Open Mon. and Thurs.-Fri. noon-6pm, Sat.-Sun. 10am-4pm. 5000R.

Bakhrushin Theater Museum, ul. Bakhrushina 31 (Бахрушина; tel. 233 44 70), directly across from the Metro. M2,4: Paveletskaya, and turn left (across the street from the station). One of the surprisingly numerous theater-museums in Moscow, this one celebrates one of Russia's great art forms with a chronologically arranged permanent exhibit of costumes, dressers, programs, photos, and other intricately crafted theatrical creations. The pamphlet at the ticket desk will tell you, in English, all you need to know about the museum. Open Mon., Thurs., and Sat.-Sun. noon-7pm, Wed. and Fri. 1-8pm. *Kassa* closes 1hr. before the museum.

Gorky's Apartment, ul. Malaya Nikitskaya 6/2 (Малая Никитская; former Kachalova; tel. 290 51 30). M6: Pushkinskaya. A pilgrimage site more for its architectural interest than for its collection of Maxim Gorky's possessions. Designed by Shekhtel in 1906, this house is one of the best examples of Art Nouveau you'll find. The main staircase is modeled to project the feeling and movement of waves on the sea. Open Wed. and Fri. noon-7pm, Thurs. and Sat.-Sun. 10am-5pm, closed last Thurs. of the month. For an excursion, pay 30,000R. Wear the slippers.

Chekhov's House Museum, ul. Sadovaya-Kudrinskaya 6. M6: Barrikadnaya. Chekhov lived here 1886-90, both writing and receiving patients—but you won't really get a feel for the author/doctor here as he did for the Russian psyche. Open Tues., Thurs., and Sat.-Sun. 11am-6pm, Wed. and Fri. 2-8pm. *Kassa* closes an hour earlier. Closed last day of the month.

Shalyapin House-Museum (Дом-музей Шаляпина; *Dom-muzey Shalyapina*), ul. Sadovaya-Kudrinskaya (tel. 205 62 36). M6: Barrikadnaya. The home to opera singer Shalyapin from 1910-22, this tastefully furnished house was donated by the musician's son as a museum; it is better known as a concert hall for fall and winter performances. Open Tues. and Sat. 10am-6pm, Wed.-Thurs. 11:30am-7pm, Sun. 10am-4pm. 5000R, English tours 35,000R.

Stanislavsky Museum (Музей-дом Станиславского; *Muzey-dom Stanislavskovo*), Leontevsky per. 6 (Леонтьевский; formerly Stanislavskovo; tel. 229 24 42). M6: Pushkinskaya. Walk down ul. Tverskaya, and take a right on ul. Leontevsky. The respected theater director held lessons in his home, the rooms of which have different themes. More interesting than his upstairs apartment, however, are the collections of costumes in the basement used for such famous productions as Gogol's *Government Inspector* and Shakespeare's *Othello*. The *babushki* will proudly explain the director's importance and point out the vase offered to Stanislavsky by Isadora Duncan. Open Thurs. and Sat.-Sun. 11am-6pm, Wed. and Fri. 2-9pm, closed last Thurs. of the month. 5000R, with Russian tour 30,000R.

Literaturny Muzey Pushkina (Литературный Музей Пушкина; tel. 201 32 56), corner of Prechisterka ul. (Пречистерка; formerly Kropotkinskaya) and Khrushchevsky per.

(Хрущевский). M1: Kropotkinskaya. In case you haven't experienced Pushkin-worship first-hand, this carefully tended-to museum will convince you that Pushkin is indeed much beloved. If the first editions Pushkin owned don't thrill, his doodles should amuse. Unfortunately, it was closed in 1996 for renovations. Usually open Wed.-Sun. 10am-6pm, closed last Fri. of the month.

Muzey Gertsena (Музей А. И. Герцена), Sivtsev Vrazhek per. 27 (Сивцев Вражек; tel. 241 58 59), on a side street parallel to Arbat. Take a left off Arbat one street before the graffiti wall coming from M3: Arbatskaya, then turn right at the 1st street. The museum where the philosopher A. Gertsen lived from 1843-46 is on the left side. A fairly typical and well reconstructed 19th-century mansion with much of Gertsen's furniture and unique portraits. Aleksandr wrote the novels *The Thieving Magpie*, *Doctor Krovpo*, and *Who Is to Blame* in the 3 years he lived here. Open Tues., Thurs., and Sat.-Sun. 11am-6pm, Wed. and Fri. 1-6pm. 3000R, students 1000R.

Muzey Gogolya (Музей Гоголя), Nikitsky bul. 7 (tel. 291 12 40). M3: Arbatskaya. Gogol spent his last months here; you could spend your last days trying to find the museum. The "museum" is actually only 2 small rooms inside a library. But at least it provides a glimpse of the brilliant 19th-century writer's life and a look at his meager possessions without costing a ruble. Open Mon.-Thurs. noon-5:45pm. Free.

Lermontov House-Museum (Дом-музей Лермонтова; *Dom-muzey Lermontova*), ul. Malaya Molchanovka 2 (Малая Молчановка), off Novy Arbat. M3: Arbatskaya. One of Russia's much-loved and respected poets lived in this small house—appropriately preserved and guarded. Enter through the white gate to see another example of fairly well-to-do 19th-century life. Open Tues., Thurs., and Sat.-Sun. 11am-5pm, Wed. and Fri. 2-5pm.

Art Galleries

Moskovskaya Galereya (Московская Галерея), Kuznetski most 11 (tel. 925 42 64). M6: Kuznetski Most, then turn left. Not to be confused with the much larger **House of Artists** across from Gorky Park, this is a gallery of contemporary art, and unlike most museums, offers a picture of Russian cultural achievement that hasn't been spoiled by some state planner—it is what people are doing here, *now*. The works include sculpture, prints, lithographs, and paintings. Buy tickets at the *kassa* in the art supply store—stock up on cheap acrylics too. A bargain for a crash course in the latest Russian art. Four large rooms, informally hung with the latest stuff. Open Mon.-Sat. noon-6:30pm. 2000R, students 500R.

Exhibition Hall of the Russian Academy of Art, ul. Prechistenka 21/12 (tel. 201 74 25). M1: Kropotkinskaya, near the Pushkin Literary Museum. A well visited exhibit hall which displays the life work of trendy artists, also those from the Soviet period. Exhibits are changed periodically. Open Wed.-Fri. noon-8pm, Sat.-Sun. 10am-6pm. *Kassa* closes an hour earlier. 5000R, students 2000R.

MARS Gallery, ul. Malaya Filevskaya 32 (Малая Филевская; tel. 146 20 29; fax 144 84 26). M3: Pionerskaya. Widely known gallery for contemporary and avant-garde art. Check *The Moscow Times* for exhibits. Open Tues.-Sun. noon-8pm.

Photocenter, Gogolevsky bul. 8 (Гоголевский; tel. 290 41 88). M1: Kropotkinskaya or M3: Arbatskaya. Varying exhibits of photography. Check *The Moscow Times* to see if there's anything of interest. Open Tues.-Sun. noon-7:30pm. 10,000R.

Rosizo Gallery, ul. Petrovka 28/2, 2nd floor (tel. 928 14 45). M6: Pushkinskaya. One of the more centrally located galleries, it usually has small, eclectic exhibits. Summer '96 saw an exhibit of miniature lacquered art. Open Wed.-Sat. noon-7pm.

ENTERTAINMENT

Moscow is a large, fast-paced city, and it has the entertainment options to prove it. Renowned theaters, opera, and ballet provide a healthy injection of culture, while parks, baths, and green outskirts prescribe a relaxing dose of thought-free repose.

Performances

Summer in Moscow is the wrong season for theater. Those companies not on vacation are on tour, and the only thing playing in Moscow are touring productions from other cities. This being the capital, many do come, but the productions are of erratic quality. However, starting September and running well into June, Moscow boasts very good theater, ballet, and opera, as well as excellent orchestras. If you buy tickets far enough in advance or don't demand front row center, or both, you can go very cheaply. Just purchase them at the *kassa* in the theater, usually open from noon to 7pm, when performances start. All theaters have a labeled model in the lobby so you can identify your seats before you buy.

Scalpers and Intourist often snatch up tickets to performances at the Bolshoy and the Tchaikovsky Concert Hall, so if you have no luck at the box office, hang out outside the theater. Scalpers look around a lot and ask if tickets are needed, *"bilety nada?"* Always check back at the *kassa* to be sure you are not paying too much. Ask for the cheapest, *"samiy dishoviy"* at the *kassa* (25,000-50,000R for the Bolshoy Theater, 2500-20,000R for the Tchaikovsky Concert Hall).

Bolshoy Teatr (Большой Театр; tel. 292 00 50). M2: Teatralnaya Pl. Literally "Big Theater". Both the opera and ballet companies are still good, despite multiple defections abroad, and the theater itself is pure pre-revolutionary elegance. Champagne and caviar at intermission under crystal chandeliers—pretend you're Anna Karenina's suave Vronsky. Daily performances at noon or 7pm.

Maly Teatr (Малый Театр; tel. 923 26 21), just north of the Bolshoy on Teatralnaya Pl. The "Small Theater" shows a different drama production every night. Difficult for non-Russian speakers, it's fun if you can understand the language. *Kassa* is open Tues.-Sun. 12:30-3pm and 4-7:30pm. Daily performances at 7pm.

Tchaikovsky Concert Hall, Triumphalnaya pl. 4/31 (tel. 299 03 78). M2: Mayakovskaya. Popular venue for classical music that seats over 1600.

Vakhtangav Teatr, ul. Arbat 26 (tel. 241 07 28). M3: Arbatskaya. An actor's theater, formerly one of the most popular (helped partially by its prime location), and it remains good. Open late August-June.

Satire Theater, Triumfalnaya pl. 2 (tel. 299 36 42). M2: Mayakovskaya. One of the best, but over your head if you aren't fluent in Russian. Performances daily at noon and 7pm. *Kassy* open daily noon-3pm and 4-6pm. Tickets 20,000-50,000R.

Tchaikovsky Conservatory's Big and Small Halls, ul. Gertsena 13 (tel. 229 81 83). M6: Pushkinskaya. Centrally located and big. *Kassa* in big hall open daily noon-7pm. Concerts almost daily at 7pm plus Sun. at 2pm. Buy back-row tickets for the small hall (малый зал; *maly zal*) for just 2500R. During intermission, locals are known to sneak into the grander big hall (большой зал; *bolshoy zal*) to muse at its pipe organ and chandeliers. Scalpers may lie and say no tickets are available when the *kassa* will sell them more cheaply.

Luzhniki Sports Palace (Дворец Спорта; *Dvorets Sporta*), Luzhnetskaya nab. 24 (Лужнетская; tel. 201 09 55). M1: Sportivnaya. Huge. Rock concerts held here.

Leninsky Komsomol (LENKOM), ul. Chelchova 6 (tel. 299 96 68). M6: Pushkinskaya. The director of this theater is well known in Russia and attracts crowds. Drama such as *Figaro* and *Chaika*. Performances every other day at 7pm. *Kassy* open daily 1-3pm and 5-7pm. Tickets around 40,000R.

Mossoviet Theater, Bolshaya Sadovaya ul. 16 (tel. 200 59 43). M2: Mayakovskaya. Quite popular, depending on the performance. Usually possible to get tickets. *Kassa* open daily noon-5pm. Tickets 25,000R.

Stanislavsky Theater, ul. Tverskaya 23 (tel. 299 72 24). M2: Tverskaya. Named for the famous director. Avant garde productions, mostly. Closed in summer. *Kassa* open off-season daily noon-7pm.

Moscow State University Student Theater (МГУ), ul. Bolshaya Nikitskaya 3 (tel. 203 66 12). Performances oscillate wildly, but prices don't—they're usually low.

Children's Musical Theater, pr. Vernadskovo 5 (Версеневская; tel. 930 70 21). M1: Univesitet. Popular with the kiddies, and you'll be able to understand it too. *Kassa* open daily noon-3pm and 4-6pm.

Estrada Theater, Bersenevskaya nab. 20/2 (tel. 230 04 44). M8: Polyanka. Classical plays in a mid-sized theater. Open Aug.-late May. *Kassy* open daily 11am-6pm.

New Circus (Новий Цирк; *Novy Tsirk;* tel. 930 02 72). M1: Universitet. Look for the large, round building. Better than the Old Circus. *Kassas* open daily 11am-3pm and 4-7pm. Tickets (9000-13,000R) can be bought from "театры" kiosks.

Old Circus (Старый Цирк; *Stary Tsirk*; tel. 200 68 89). M8: Tsvetnoi Bulvar, turn right and walk half a block; it's on the right, newly renovated. It usually has animal acts in the first half and a glittery acrobatic performance in the second. Perfect for non-Russian speakers. *Kassa* open daily 11am-7pm. There are approx. 137 eager scalpers outside, so you can comparison shop. Performances Wed.-Mon. at 7pm, plus a matinee Sat. 3pm. Tickets 20,000R, under 6 free.

Taganka Theater (tel. 915 12 17). M4,6: Taganskaya. It's directly across the street from the ring line exit. This avant garde theater is the only excuse to come to this oppressive square on the loud and dusty Garden Ring Road. Closed in summer. *Kassa* open off-season daily 1-3pm and 5-7pm.

Parks and Baths

From M1,4: Park Kultury, cross the **Krimsky most** bridge to **Gorky Park,** or from M4,5: Oktyabrskaya, enter through the main flag-flanked gate on Krimsky Val. In summer, droves of out-of-towners and young Muscovites promenade, relax, and ride the roller coaster at Moscow's **amusement park** (30,000R, upside-down loop 20,000R). In winter, the paths are flooded to create a park-wide **ice rink.** A ride on the large **ferris wheel** in the center of the park affords a 360° look at the tallest of Moscow's landmarks: all the Stalinist sister buildings can be seen from the top. (Park open daily 11am-2am. General admission 10,000R. 150,000R for 12 rides.)

Izmailovsky Park (Измайловский Парк) is at M3: Izmailovsky Park—go left and follow the hordes. The main reason to come this far out from the center is not the park but the weekend market, which is colossal. Arrive late Sunday afternoon, when people want to go home and are willing to make a deal. And comparison shop, too—the first painted box you see will not be the last, guaranteed. If you're not buying, this is a window-shopper's paradise. Everything is on sale here, from carpets and samovars to military uniforms, pins, and old Soviet money. There are jewelry, shawls, old books, t-shirts tacky and cool, and Russia's favorite form of folk art: variations on the theme of painted wood—boxes, eggs, spoons, cutting boards, all decorated with designs and flowers. And, of course, the ubiquitous *matryoshki*—nesting dolls that used to be painted with pretty girls' faces, but now come in other themes. Find the tiniest Soviet premier, the seventh dwarf, and the shortest Chicago Bull. Some stalls even take orders, delivery in a week. (Open daily 9am-5:30pm.)

Another respite from Moscow's chaos is the tsars' **Kolomenskoe Summer Residence,** on a wooded rise above the Moskva River at M2: Kolomenskaya. Follow the signs to "к музею Коломенское". Walk about 400m south on ul. Novinka (Новинка) past *Kinoteatr* (Кинотеатр), and go right just before the long fence. Peter the Great's 1702 log cabin (same hours and admission as museum) and Bratsk Prison, where the persecuted Archpriest Avvakum wrote his celebrated autobiography, have been moved here from Arkhangelsk and Siberia respectively. The **Kazan Church** (tel. 112 03 42) holds services at opening and closing (open Mon.-Fri. 8am-1pm and 6-8pm, Sat.-Sun. 8am-8pm). At the complex's edge, overlooking the river, stands the 16th-century **Ascension Church,** the first example of a brick church built like a traditional wooden building (St. Basil's is a more famous example). Note the gold double-headed eagle at the top of the entrance gate: this emblem of the Romanovs, made of plastic, was installed in 1994. Red-coated guards with handy axes and swords patrol the grounds. (Grounds open daily 7am-10pm; free. Museums open Tues.-Sun. 11am-6pm; 4000R, buy tickets at the *kassa,* not the expensive tour bureau.)

Silver Pine-Forest (Серебряный бор; *Serebryany bor*) is the cheapest and fastest way to get into the countryside and relax. Take trolleybus #20, which starts at M1: Okhotny Ryad and stops at Pushkinskaya pl. (in front of Izvestia) and Mayakovskaya pl. on its way straight up ul. Tverskaya, to the very last stop (50min.). Join the groups of Russians heading to this gorgeous natural park and island, whose 2.5km sq. are criss-crossed with paths, making it possible to explore the countryside before taking your picnic down to the riverside and sunbathing. It is understandably one of Moscow's favorite weekend afternoon spots—*shashlik* stands and other signs of civilization cater to the frolicking urbanites. Much-loved by the tsars, the region now belongs to the bathing-suit-clad masses.

VDNKh (ВДНХ) lies, surprise surprise, near M5: VDNKh. Go left out of the Metro toward the pavilions. The **Exhibition of Soviet Economic Achievements** (Выставка

Достижений Народного Хозяйства; *Vystavka Dostizhenii Narodnovo Khozyaystva*) has changed since its original conception. Now that it has been fairly conclusively shown that there were no Soviet economic achievements, this World's Fair-esque park with its pavilions (each in a more garish architectural style than the last) has become, ironically, a large department store. Pavilions proclaim "atomic energy" and "education," right above signs reading "Stereos" and "Shoes." It's a fun place for a midday walk with lots of kiosks selling *shashliks* (8000R) and pizza. Open-air concerts make it a good picnic spot. On the extreme left and right, you can find a bit o' fun in the amusement park (open Mon.-Fri. 11am-8pm, Sat.-Sun. 11am-9pm). A small tent to the right hosts circus performances (Fri.-Sun. 1, 3, and 5pm; 15,000R, kids 10,000R) and young dancing fools (Wed.-Sun. 7-11pm; cover 10,000R). At the far end is the **Cosmos Pavilion,** where you can see the rocket that launched Sputnik. No shop opens before 10am, and visitors leave by dark.

Zoopark (Зоопарк; tel. 255 53 75), lies on both sides of ul. Bolshaya Gruzinskaya 1 (Большая Грузинская), M6: Barrikadnaya or M4: Krasnopresnenskaya. It's a depressing lesson for the kids and for you, but if you can stand the circus, you can survive this continually favored outing for young Muscovites. Fuzzy hand-made monkeys sell for 8000R (open Tues.-Sun. 9am-8pm; *kassa* closes at 7pm; 5000R, students 2000R).

Although Moscow is filled with serene green areas, one of the largest and most popular with small children is **Krasnaya Presnya** (Красная Пресня), M6: Ulitsa 1905 goda. Simply walk down ul. 1905 goda until the Mezhdunarodny and turn right for the leafy oasis, scattered with small playgrounds and wooden houses.

Sandunovsky Baths (Бани Сандуновских; *Bani Sandunovskovo;* tel. 925 46 31), M1,6: Kuznetski Most, just east of ul. Neglinnaya between the first and second Neglinny per. (Неглинный), occupy a restored green-and-white building bearing a sign "Бани". If the sometimes confusing, always exhausting life of a tourist in Russia has driven you to the edge, come here for a break and, simultaneously, one of the best windows on Russian culture. Saunas are Russia's chicken soup; taken regularly, they will make you live forever—at least so say the *babushki*. Certainly, the experience of sitting in oppressive, magnificent heat (perhaps while flogging yourself with birch branches) followed by intense cold is life-changing, if not life-lengthening. Russians love the public bathhouse, too— they will stay here for hours, gossiping and drinking. And visitors are welcome to join them; men enter at the corner marked "мужское отделение," women at the side marked "женское отделение" (open Wed.-Mon. 8am-10pm; 50,000R, super-fancy baths 100,000R).

SHOPPING

You can now buy anything in Moscow, from exercise machines to French perfume, but most imports will cost all you've got. As if GUM and all the Univermags were not enough, the monstrous crater now on Manezhnaya pl., whose destruction and construction can be viewed from a special ramp, will soon become a massive shopping complex. The only goods whose prices haven't gone through the roof (and the stratosphere) are books and records; in addition to the shopping possibilities listed elsewhere, a number are listed below. Typical tourist presents to take home, like *matryoshka* dolls and amber, are most easily found at the large markets like Izmailovski Park (see Parks and Baths, above). On the other hand, the hidden treasures usually lie buried in local gift shops where Russians buy cheap but often beautifully crafted birthday presents for their friends. At the **Melodiya** record store, Novy Arbat 40, you can find hard-to-get Russian classics and records by popular artists, often cheaper than in the U.S. Tapes cost 8000R, CDs 37,000-50,000R (open Mon.-Sat. 9am-8pm). **Dom Knigi** (Дом Книги), Novy Arbat 22, is a towering landmark, worth visiting for an understanding of the Russian love of books. Tourists and Russians alike scour the shelves for a wide variety of literature, but only maps are in English (open Mon.-Fri. 10:30am-7:30pm, Sat. 10am-6pm). Just north of Lubyanka pl., **Torgovy Dom Biblio-Globus** (Торговый Дом Библио-Глобус), Myasnitskaya 6, is a privatized bookstore also selling imported office supplies and electronic equipment. Here you can find art books and Russian literature, ancient and classical, at excellent prices (open Mon.-Fri. 10am-7:30pm). **Global USA Superstore,** ul. Usacheva 35 (Уса-чева; 254 56 57), M!: Sportivnaya, stocks electronics, clothing, some food, *Moscow Times,* and *Tribune* (open daily 10am-8pm).

NIGHTLIFE

Moscow isn't New York or Paris. But sometimes it thinks it is. While Moscow may seem the casino capital of the world, you won't be able to afford most of the exorbitant cover charges (usually above 125,000R), a dilemma which leaves finding advertised free nights your best option. Restaurants often transmogrify into nightclubs after dark, with 30,000R covers.

Nightclubs and Bars

Check the weekend editions of *The Moscow Times* or *Moscow Tribune* for music festival listings (the annual jazz festival thrills Moscow every summer) and club ads. *The Moscow Revue,* free at the Traveller's Guest House and sprinkled around the city, also includes good up-to-date listings of what's happening. Cheaper and more popular Irish bars on isolated streets may show a better time than the dark, half-empty, elegant, and expensive "bars" close to the center.

Sports Bar, Novy Arbat 10 (tel. 290 43 11). M3: Arbatskaya. Next to Melodiya and across from the Irish Bar. The 2 floors fill up fast for big games; otherwise, the 2nd floor is the place to be with pool tables, darts, and mafiosi with cellular phones. A true paradise for Eurosport lovers: 8 TVs at the bar and a large screen so you can catch every angle. The disco is one of the city's most popular. Live bands from 9-11pm. Bottled beer 12,000R, draft 25,000R. Tonya Harding and OJ Simpson burgers. Accepts AmEx, Diner's Club, MC, and Visa. Open daily 9:30am-midnight.

Shamrock Bar, Novy Arbat 13 (tel. 291 76 81). M3: Arbatskaya. A total scene on weekend nights, this place overflows with large groups of Americans, Irish, and Russians, many exhaling cigarette smoke. Chicken wings 25,000R. Bud 17,500R. *Guinness* 27,000R. AmEx, Diner's Club, MC, and Visa. Open daily 10am-1am.

Rosie O'Grady's, ul. Znamenko 9/12 (Знаменко; tel. 203 90 87). M8: Borovitskaya. Go right out of the Metro, then right on ul. Znamenko. Rosie's is on the left at the corner of ul. Marksa i Engelsa. Friendly Irish staff and largely ex-pat clientele. Loud and cheerful. Pub food and drinks, all somewhat pricey. Pint of *Guinness* 28,000R. Bottle of *Corona* 12,000R. Sandwiches 15,000R. Open daily noon-1am.

Club 011, ul. Sadovaya-Kudrinskaya 19, behind AmEx. Gets going around midnight. Open Thurs.-Sat. 10pm until everyone leaves. Cover US$10.

Manhattan Express (tel. 298 53 54), on the northwest corner of Gostinitsa Rossiya. M5,6: Kitai Gorod. One of the hippest clubs in town, this self-proclaimed New York supper club creates weekly extravaganzas—fashion shows, striptease, and performances by top Russian bands. This restaurant/bar doesn't even start discoing until 11:30pm, so make sure you can get a ride home. Open nightly 8pm-6am. Cover 50,000-250,000R, half-cover 8pm-10pm.

John Bull Pub, Kutuzovsky pr. 4 (tel. 243 56 88). M4: Kutuzovskaya. Take a left; it's behind the Ukraine hotel. An English pub with US$5 draft beers. Chinese, Russian, and pub food. Entrées US$6-30 with 50% discount noon-3pm. Lounge and conference room for private meetings or parties. Live pop bands, karaoke, blues, and jazz nights. Always some English-speaking staff. AmEx, Diner's Club, MC, and Visa accepted. Open Sun.-Wed. noon-1am, Thurs.-Sat. noon-3am.

Moosehead Canadian Bar, ul. Bolshaya Polyanka 54 (Большая Полянка; tel./fax 230 73 33). M8: Polyanka. Take a right coming out of the Metro, and hop on trolley #8. Canadian bar with *Tuborg* on tap (26,500 per pint). Indoor and outdoor bars with live music on weekends and a full menu of food, beer, and mixed drinks. The bartenders will make anything you request. Chicken fingers 37,000R. Moose steak US$25. Moosehead burger and fries 45,000R. Come in for breakfast (a hearty Canadian one 45,000R) or stay til then. Happy hours Mon.-Fri. 6-8pm with *Coors* 2-for-1. Open Mon.-Fri. noon-5am, Sat.-Sun. 10am-5am.

GAY AND LESBIAN LIFE

Because of the dangers of gay nightlife in a country where just six years ago homosexuality could land you in jail, many clubs, such as **3 Monkeys,** ul. Trubnaya (Трубная; tel. 208 46 37), M8: Tsvetnoi vul., have instituted a card-pass system: unless you know the right person and get a "pass," you will not be allowed in—no women allowed period. If you do get a pass (look for men selling the magazine *Ptyuch* (Птюч) in crowded areas such as the McDonald's on ul. Tverskaya, the cover (50,000R) is refundable at the bar (open nightly 6pm-9am). There is no sign outside, so ring the bell at the plain black door. **Club Ptyuch** has closed temporarily but still holds events—usually on Saturdays—in such places as the **Water Club,** Leningradskoe sh. 51 (Ленинградское), M2: Rechnoi Vokzal. Entrance is by invitation only. The best and probably only chance for real gay nightlife is **Chance** (Шанс), in Dom Kultury Serp i Molot (Дом Культуры Серп и Молот; tel. 298 42 67), M7: Pl. Ilicha. Walk on ul. Sergia Radonezhskovo all the way through the third open driveway on your right. When you come to a road where the tram tracks turn, walk up the stairs. It's on top of the hill, straight ahead on your right. Because of rave reviews in newspapers, the wait at the door may be as long as two hours on the weekends. This watering hole has three bars and aquariums. It's popular with everyone, but 99% gay. The women may seem straight, but… Although in summer '96 no invitation was required, the club is planning to institute a pass system soon. (Mon.-Wed. men boogie free before midnight, 30,000R after; women pay 50,000R all night; Fri.-Sat. men enter free 11:15pm-12:45am, 50,000R after; women pay 100,000R; Thurs. and Sun. men enter free before midnight, 40,000R between midnight and 2am, and 60,000R thereafter; women pay 60,000R. Open daily 11pm-6am.) Some numbers of general usefulness are: **Treugolnik** (Треугольник; general tel. 932 01 00)—a gay-and-lesbian social and lobbying organization and **AIDS Infoshare Russia** (tel. 110 24 60). Both carry info on gay and lesbian life in Russia.

■ Near Moscow

PEREDELKINO (ПЕРЕДЕЛКИНО)

An easy trip out of the city and into peacefully green *dacha* territory is Peredelkino, where Nobel Prize-winning writer and poet Boris Pasternak kept a country house. The area remained a dissident writers' colony well after Pasternak's death in 1960, and even when it was dangerous to do so, hundreds visited his grave annually.

The village of Peredelkino is a 25-minute *elektrichka* ride from Moscow's Kievsky Vokzal (1500R); buy a ticket from *prigorodnye kassy* (пригородные кассы), to the left as you exit M3,4: Kievskaya. To reach the cemetery, walk away from Moscow on the Peredelkino platform, turn right on the first road, and then take a left. Now hang a right so the cemetery entrance is on your left. Keep walking absolutely straightly onto a field. Take a left at the second-to-last break in the fence. Take the first right off this tiny path, and a glance straight and to the right will bring you to the simple, gray gravestone with Pasternak's profile in relief. Whoo…what a relief!

SERGIEVSKY POSAD (СЕРГИЕВСКИЙ ПОСАД)

Possibly Russia's most famous pilgrimage point, Sergievsky Posad attracts wandering Orthodox believers with the mass of churches huddled in its main sight—**St. Sergius's Trinity Monastery** (Троицко-Сергиева Лавра; *Troitsko-Sergieva Lavra*). Approximately 70km from Moscow, Sergievsky Posad, the Golden Ring town closest to Moscow, counts as one of the capital's outermost sights because of its ease as a daytrip. After decades of sanctioned atheism, the stunning monastery, founded in 1340, is again a religious center, and monks pace the paths between the colorful collection of churches and gardens. Although entrance into the *lavra* (the highest monastic order) is free, there are separate fees for the wall's ramparts, the folk art exhibit, the art museum, and the historical museum. Each church is exquisite, but

Russian Orthodoxy's opulent colors come out in the **Trinity Cathedral,** where the numerous covered heads and quickly crossing hands entrance the visitor as much as the gilded Andrei Rublev icons. The **Chapel-at-the-Well** has an appropriately superstitious history—one day, a spring with magical healing powers allegedly appeared inside a tiny chapel in the monastery—old women can still be seen coming here with empty bottles to carry this holy water home. The **Art Museum** (художественный музей; *khudozhestvinny muzey*) at the back of the complex contains numerous icons, and many have been returned to the interiors of the original churches (open Tues.-Sun. 10am-6pm; 25,600R, Russians 3000R). The **Historical Museum** next door includes artifacts from the region (open Tues.-Thurs. and Sat.-Sun. 10am-6pm; 10,240R, Russians 2000R).

To get to Sergievsky Posad, take the *elektrichka* from Moscow's Yaroslavsky Vokzal (every 40min., more on weekends; 2hr.; roundtrip 16,000R). Get tickets at the *prigorodnye kassy* (пригородные кассы), and check for departure times to the left as you exit. The announcement boards in front of the trains do not work, so you must look for a tiny strip on the side of the train that shows its destination.

■ Smolensk (Смоленск)

Since its origins in 863, the Tatars have sacked it, Moscow and Lithuania fought over it, Poland snatched it, Napoleon stormed it, the Nazis reached it, and the Soviet state demoralized it. Abroad, the town is known best for one of the Soviet Union's most infamous wartime crimes—the Katyn massacre. Only in 1990 did the authorities admit to killing 4000 Polish officers who had surrendered to the Soviet troops in nearby Katyn Forest in 1940; they had blamed the Nazis for the deaths. Tickets from Moscow on the overnight train are cheap, so if you need a place to sleep...

ORIENTATION AND PRACTICAL INFORMATION

Smolensk is one of the few hilly towns in Russia, thanks to the Dnieper River's eroding currents. Old city walls surround the center on the **south bank,** the location of all sights and hotels. A **train station** (tel. 215 20), north of the river, sends trains to Kaliningrad (5 per day, 16hr., 130,000R), Minsk (6 per day, 5hr., 47,000R), and other western destinations such as Berlin, Prague, Rīga, Vilnius, and Warsaw. Also across the river, **Kolkhoznaya pl.** (Колхозная) hosts a farmer's market. **Ul. Bolshaya Sovetskaya** (Большая Советская) leads from the square to the center, up the hill past the **Assumption Cathedral.** Trams #1, 4, and 7 run to the center—ul. Bolshaya Sovetskaya, the cathedral, and Kolkhoznaya. **Intourist,** ul. Konyonkova 3 (Конёнкова; tel. 314 92), near Gostinitsa Tsentralnaya, sells maps (6000R; open daily 9am-1pm and 2-6pm). **Store luggage** downstairs at the train station for 9100R per bag (open 24hr. except noon-2pm and 1-3am). **Telephones** at the train station serve intercity connections (open 24hr. except at mealtimes). **Exchange currency** at Обмен Валюты on the corner of ul. Lenina and ul. Bolshaya Sovetskaya (open Mon.-Sat. 10am-2pm and 4-8pm).

ACCOMMODATIONS

One of Smolensk's three centrally located *gostinitsas* should do you well. All double their rates for foreigners, but the prices are comparable. The breakfast in Gostinitsa Rossiya makes up for its peripheral location (well, sort of).

Gostinitsa Tsentralnaya (Центральная), ul. Lenina 2/1 (tel. 317 54). True to its name, this hotel is central, right near the Glinka Garden and about 10min. from the Assumption Cathedral. Recently renovated, so all rooms have baths and amenities. Sauna (open daily 11am-11pm; 54,000R per hour). Singles 180,000R, doubles 360,000R. 20,000R charge for reservation.

Gostinitsa Rossiya (Россия), ul. Dzerzhinskovo 23/2 (Дзержинского; tel. 339 70). Take tram #3 from the train station and get off at "Спартак" (Spartak Stadium). A monster of a hotel with all the conveniences. Singles 188,000R, doubles 228,000R with bath, toilet, phone, and TV. Swedish cooked breakfast included.

Gostinitsa Smolensk (Смоленск; tel. 918 66) corner of ul. Glinka (Глинка) and ul. Bolshaya Sovetskaya north of pl. Smirnova (Смирнова). Unlike the above hotels, this one serves more locals than foreigners, so local rules apply (leave key downstairs when going out). Ask for 3rd category for the cheapest rooms. The locks may be hard to open and the wallpaper peeling. Check-out noon. A bed in a quad 96,000R. Singles 144,000R. The prices listed are halved for Russians.

FOOD

Dark cafés squat on ul. Bolshaya Sovetskaya and ul. Lenina. The border town's large **market** (Заднепровский рынок; *Zadneprovski rynok*), ul. Belyaeva (Беляева) across the river directly downhill from the Assumption Cathedral, offers meat inside, and fruit and veggies outdoors.

Holstein 777, ul. Bolshaya Sovetskaya (tel. 308 30), just south of ul. Lenina. Look for the Holstein Beer sign, and enter the courtyard. This private-venture café—seemingly the only one of its kind in Smolensk—has American music, foreign beer, and fairly high prices, but better food than the hotel restaurants. Entrées 20,000-50,000R. Coffee 3500R. *Holstein* 14,000R. Open daily noon-3am.

Restoran Rossiya (Ресторан Россия), ul. Dzerzhinskovo, in the eponymous hotel. Lighter than most hotel eateries, with cloth napkins and flowers on the table in a grand hall. Reasonably priced, except for the 5000R live-music cover at dinner, which you may want to avoid anyway. Crab sticks 14,000R. Hot breakfast 6000R. Open daily 7-10am and noon-morning.

Dnepr (Днепр), ul. Glinka (tel. 391 11), to the left of Gostinitsa Smolensk. The chandeliered restaurant is on the 2nd floor. The peeling pink paint evinces a faded but nonetheless visible elegance. Lots of pork (швинина; *shvinina*) 14,000R. *Borscht* 4000R. Laser shows and modern music after 8pm (cover men 10,000R, women 5000R). Open daily noon-3am. Disco Thurs.-Sun. 8am-3am.

SIGHTS AND ENTERTAINMENT

The spectacular green-and-white **Assumption Cathedral** (Усненский собор; *Usnensky sobor*), one of Russia's largest, rises from Smolensk's highest hill. A flight of stairs leads from ul. Bolshaya Sovetskaya to the cathedral and the eye-crushing views from its terrace. A cathedral of one form or another has stood on this site since 1101. The latest model was completed in the early 18th century, and its gilded interior is said to have so impressed Napoleon that he had it guarded from pillaging by his own men. To the right as you enter, up a flight of steps, a 16th-century copy of St. Luke's *Virgin with Child* has returned after being stolen in 1923. Even today, masses of the devout ply it with candles in hope of the occasional miracle. (Open Mon.-Sat. 8am-8pm, Sun. 7am-9pm. Service Mon.-Sat. 9am and 6pm, Sun. 7am and 6pm; no photographs or loud noise; women may, men must, enter bare-headed.)

Apart from the Assumption Cathedral, the city's most striking architectural landmark is the 6km-long, 15m-high walls of the **Smolensk Kremlin.** They serve as a reminder of the many invaders the town has withstood. While the walls can be seen from many points in the city, the one spot you can actually scale a tower is off ul. Oktyabrskoy Revolutsii (Октябрьской Революции) to the left. The three towers on ul. Timiryazeva (Тимрязева) can be climbed, and a walk along the battlements provides a beautiful panorama (try to ignore the Brezhnev flats). Just follow the stream of artists.

The second floor of the **History Museum** (Исторический музей; *Istoricbesky muzey*), ul. Lenina 8 (tel. 338 62), is basic town-history fare: archaeological finds from the area, some 13th-century graffiti, 15th- and 16th-century icons, and local textiles and handicrafts. These last are unusually pretty—Smolensk is a huge flax-growing region, and as a result, home to skilled weavers and embroiderers (for more on the long and glorious history of Smolensk flax, see below; open Tues.-Sun. 10am-6pm; 1500R, students 1000R).

The **Smolensk Flax Exhibition** (Выставка Смоленский лён; *Vystavka Smolensky lyon*) sits on ul. Bolshaya Sovetskaya, in the pink Trinity Monastery (Троицкий монастырь; *Troytsky monastyr*) on the left side of the street two minutes uphill from the cathedral. This three-storied exhibit shows every aspect of Smolensk's main trade in full detail, with a Soviet touch. Two floors have photographs and models of linen-producing equipment of earlier times with the results—folk dresses—hanging in the final room. Many of the examples of textile craftsmanship are from the last three years, when such individual talent has been encouraged. The top floor seems like a strange anomaly, with exhibits of cooperative #2031's model worker #3567 supposedly illustrating the brilliant success of mass-produced Soviet clothing; no final clothing display is needed for this—you can see it on the old women on the street (open Tues.-Sun. 10am-6pm; 1000R, students 500R).

The footbridge over the train tracks leads to the **Church of St. Peter and Paul** (Петропавловская Церковь; *Petropavlovskaya Tserkov*), next to the train station. This 12th-century red-brick church, built in the Kiev-style and restored to its former glory thirty years ago, is currently a functioning church, but the plain whitewashed interior is not the lavish sort that tourists' jaded eyes have come to expect (open Tues.-Sun. 9am-5pm; services Sat. at 6pm, Sun. at 9am; enter on left side).

The **World War II Museum** (Музей Великой Отечественной Войны; *Muzey Velikoy Otechestvennoy Voyny*), ul. Dzerzhinskovo 4a (tel. 331 19). Walk past the busts of Soviet war heroes flanking the path to the main museum—yet another proof of the devastation WWII wreaked on this country. The German army reached Smolensk, and the personal possessions of Nazi soldiers are included here alongside photographs of Smolensk boys who died in the Great Fatherland War. The sign "Ещё не кончилась Война" over one exhibit reads "the war still hasn't ended," which, although referring to the situation at the time, could just as easily make a statement about Russia's attitude toward the war today. Come here only if you're a hard-core WWII buff (open Tues.-Sun. 10am-5pm; 1000R, students 500R).

Central House of Artists (Центральный дом художника; *Tsentralny dom khudozhnika*), ul. Bolshaya Sovetskaya 21 (tel. 335 36), is a contemporary art museum with monthly exhibits (some for sale)—check the poster outside to see if anything good is hanging (open Mon.-Sat. 11am-6pm; free; paintings can cost 1,000,000R).

In **Club "Discovery,"** ul. Kommunisticheskaya 4 (Коммунистическая), off Bolshaya Sovetskaya in Dom Molodyozhi (Дом Молодёжи), meet local youths at the dance floor's bar (open daily 8pm-6am).

GOLDEN RING (ЗОЛОТОЕ КОЛЬЦО)

To the north and west of Moscow lie a series of towns known as the Golden Ring with ancient churches and kremlins widely considered to be Russia's most beautiful. These towns gained importance in the 12th century as power shifted north with the weakening of Kiev. Vladimir and Sudzal were once Russian capitals and shine today as main attractions on Ring tours. Yaroslavl was the capital of its own principality in the 13th century, and Vologda was an important ally of Moscow after Aleksandr Nevsky freed it from Mongol control in 1252. After the tsar liberated Moscow in 1252, the entire region fell under this city's control. Today, the Golden Ring's architectural monuments and slower pace of life of the towns merit a visit.

■ Yaroslavl (Ярославль)

Yaroslavl acquired its wealth from 16th-century trade with the Middle East and the West, though even in its early days it rejected outside influence—setting a bear on Prince Yaroslavl the Wise when he considered founding a town on this spot. The citizens have fought as fiercely to keep out Soviet architectural monstrosities. With wide leafy boulevards, romantic river-view walks, numerous parks, and proximity to Moscow, Yaroslavl offers any tourist the best of two worlds—a provincial Russian feel with the comforts of Capital City.

ORIENTATION AND PRACTICAL INFORMATION

Yaroslavl lies on the **Volga's** west bank, 280km northeast of Moscow. It straddles the **Kotorosl** River, with most of the sights and churches off the north bank. Locals call the corner where the Kotorosl meets the Volga стрелка (*strelka*; the arrow). Many bus lines originate from **pl. Volkova** (Волкова). Ul. Kirova (Кирова) runs east out of this square towards the Volga. Ul. Komsomolskaya (Комсомольская) and ul. Pervomayskaya (Первомайская) lead south to **Moskovsky pr.** (Московский) and **Moskovsky Vokzal** (Московский Вокзал). The train station you will probably use, however, is **Glavny Vokzal** (Главный Вокзал).

- **Tourist Office: Excursion Bureau of the Monastery of the Transfiguration of the Savior** (tel. 30 38 69), inside the entrance to the left. An eager staff arranges tours of the monastery's museums and of individual churches and sights. Although the young employees don't speak English, they find guides who do. Tours of the city are 200,000R per group, tours of the Church of Elijah the Prophet 10,500R per person. Open June-Aug. daily 8:30am-5:30pm; Sept.-May Tues.-Sun. 8:30-5:30pm.
- **Currency Exchange:** In the post office (open Mon.-Fri. 9:30am-1pm and 1:30-4:30pm) or at **Intermedbank** (Интермедбанк), ul. Sverdlova 18 (Свердлова). Open Mon.-Fri. 9am-9pm, Sat. 9am-6pm. No bank in town takes traveler's checks.
- **Trains:** Foreigners must get their tickets (bring your passport) at the Intourist *kassa* #4 in the advance ticket office (кассы предварительной продажи железнодорожныхбилетов; *kassy predvaritelnoy prodazby zheleznodarozhnybbiletov*), pr. Lenina 11a (Ленина). Take trolley #1 to "Городской вал" (Gorodskoy val). At the lights ahead take a right, and at the next light take a sharp left. They charge 6000R to answer even the simplest questions. Open Mon.-Sat. 9:15am-1pm and 2-6pm. Find out from which station your train departs; there are several. To get to **Glavny (Central) Vokzal** (info tel. 29 21 11), take trolley #1 to the last stop on ul. Svoboda (Свобода). Trains leave for Moscow (every hr., 5hr., 52,600R) and St. Petersburg (2 per day, 14hr., 89,100R). 24-hr. lockers. Trains for Nizhny Novgorod (3 per week, 8hr., 66,200R), as well as daily passenger trains to Moscow and St. Petersburg, depart from **Moscovsky Vokzal,** Moskovsky pr., across the Kotorosl. Take bus #5 or 9 from just below pl. Volkova. *Kassa* #4 open 24hr. You are best off, though, buying a roundtrip ticket from Moscow.
- **Ferries:** To the north on the river on Volzhskaya nab. (Волжская), downstairs. Hydrofoils leave less than once a day to Golden Ring town Kostroma (1 hr., 23,000R); and Kazan (48hr., 60,000R), Moscow (36hr., 58,000R), Volgograd (5 days, 152,000R). Schedules are posted at the station, or call 22 42 50 or 25 43 25.
- **Public Transportation:** Yaroslavl's local transportation system is excellent, with trolleys and buses stopping every 2min. Trolley #9 runs up and down Moskovsky pr. through pl. Volkova to Leninsky pr. (Ленинский). Trolley #1 travels from the center to Glavny Vokzal. Buy tickets (500R) at the light-blue kiosks next to mains stops labeled "яргортранс продажа проездныхдокументов". Since the fine for being caught without a ticket is only 7000R, many locals don't bother buying them.
- **Post Office:** Podbelskovo pl. (Подбелского; tel. 22 37 28), across from the monastery (take trolley #9). **Fax,** telex, and a photocopier. Open Mon.-Sat. 8am-8pm, Sun. 8am-6pm. **Postal code:** 150 000.
- **Telephone Office:** In same building as the post office. Prepay at the counter, and get a booth. 3 tones mean the call has yet to go through. Press the "ответ" *(otvet)* button when your party answers. Buy tokens for local and intercity calls, and use phones labeled "международный автомат" *(mezhdugorodny avtomat)*. Open daily 8am-7pm. **Phone code:** 0852.

ACCOMMODATIONS

Always popular among Russians and foreigners, Yaroslavl offers the visitor more budget options than Moscow. Most hotels are of the large, pre-*perestroika* Intourist variety. Consequently, the staff is more likely to speak English but accommodations will be more expensive and not necessarily better.

Gostinitsa Yubilenaya (Юбиленая), Kotoroslnaya nab. 11(Которосльная; tel. 22 41 59, or call Intourist). From pl. Volkova, walk down Komsomolskaya ul. to pl. Podbelskovo, past the Church of the Epiphany on the left and turn right. Intourist's first choice and thus home to many tour groups. This 7-floor hotel is nonetheless a comfortable place to stay. English spoken. Private bathrooms. In summer, ask for a room on the back side; front ones have an attractive view but get incredibly hot. Singles 155,000R. Doubles 125,000R per person. Breakfast 10,000R.

Gostinitsa Yaroslavl (Ярославль), pl. Volkova 2 (tel. 30 50 75). Large and central. Impeccably neat, sparsely furnished rooms and friendly service. No personal bathrooms, but the communal toilets (without seats) are remarkably clean. Checkout 11am. Singles 174,000R, doubles 276,000R, triples 270,000R.

Gostinitsa Volga (Волга), ul. Kirova 10 (tel. 22 91 31). A small Soviet-era hotel ideally located off pl. Volkova. Spartan singles 64,000R. Doubles 100,000R, with bath and sitting room 234,000R. BYOTP—bring your own toilet paper. 4th-floor rooms are cheaper but above a noisy restaurant.

FOOD

Yaroslavl is not Moscow or St. Petersburg—there are no McDonald's or favorites that the locals brag about, so stock up on fruits and vegetables at the **market** on Moskovsky pr. just across the Kotorosl (open daily 9am-5pm) and bread at a bakery. The central **gastronom** on Kirova 13 sells 1-kg cheese wheels (25,000R), among other things (open daily 8am-noon and 1-11pm). The restaurant in **Gostinitsa Yubileynaya** and **Bear** serve acceptable fare.

Bear (Медведь; *Medved*), ul. Svobody (tel. 22 36 28), near pl. Volkova. A big wooden bear hangs out front. An old-style, characteristically undecorated, central eatery with edible food for surprisingly reasonable prices. *Beefshteak* 6800R. Omelet 1745R. Tea 147R. Open daily noon-11pm.

Staroye Mesto (Старое место), ul. Komsomolskaya 3, off pl. Volkova. High chairs in a whitewashed cellar room await through a beaded curtain and down a flight of stairs. Russian meals from a short menu. Vegetable salad 10,000R. Beef cutlet with mushrooms 17,000R. Open daily noon-10pm.

Café Lira (Кафе Лира), Volzhskaya nab. 43 (tel. 22 21 38), 1 block south of the river station. Entrées 17,000-25,000R. Try *zhyulene gribami* (жюльене грибами; creamy local mushrooms in a ceramic bowl; 18,000R). Open daily noon-11pm.

Yuta (Юта), ul. Respublicanskaya 79 (Республиканская; tel. 21 34 24), inside the Hotel Yuta. Nicknamed the candlestick *(svechka)* by the locals for its long, layered brick shape. This small, slick, black-and-white room serves entrées from 20,000R. *Okroshka voschnaya* (окрошка вошшая; typical Russian cold soup; 8000R). The 3-star entrées are the restaurant's own; try the *zamok struarta* with roquefort cheese (замок стюарта). Avoid the vinegary side-dishes. There is a 20,000R entrance fee at the guarded door which is 100% refundable at the restaurant, club, or hotel. Open Tues.-Sun. noon-11pm.

Chaika (Чайка), pr. Lenina 24 (tel. 23 46 91). Tastefully decorated Chinese restaurant serving a wide variety of salads and entrées with a somewhat Far Eastern feel. Salads 9000R. Chinese entrées 10,000-50,000R. Euro entrées 30,000R. *Baklazhany s gesnochny soysom* (Баклажны с гесночным соусом; vegetarian eggplant in garlic sauce; 16,000R). Open daily noon-11pm.

SIGHTS AND ENTERTAINMENT

Monastery of the Transfiguration of the Savior

Spaso-preobrazhensky sobor (Спасо-преображенский собор), pl. Podbelskovo, is crowded with tour groups in summer. Holding fort on the banks of the Kotorosl since the 12th century, the high white walls of Yaroslav's **kremlin** surround a number of buildings and exhibitions, which frustratingly all have separate entrance fees.

The most popular attraction, the **bell tower** in the rear entrance, offers a spectacular panorama of the town. The 15th-century church in the center, on the other hand, is usually passed over by visitors who head left to **Medveditsa Masha**, a seven-year-old

Russian bear found as a baby and installed in the monastery. The bear more than pays for its supper, delighting tourists by posing for cameras. She looks cuddly, despite being kept in an iron cage little more than six times her size.

A larger but deader bear also inhabits the monastery—in the **Natural History Department** (Отдел природы; *Otdel prirody*), housed alongside the more popular **History Department** (Исторический отдел; *Istorichesky otdel*) which focuses on local history, especially that of the monastery. The temporary exhibits are occasionally of interest. Enter the monastery grounds on the side facing the river. Grounds and monuments (Памятники спасского монастыря; *Pamyatniki spasskovo monastyrya*) 5000R. Exhibitions (Выставки; *Vystavki*) 5000R each. History and Natural History Departments 5000R each. (Have you noticed a pattern here?) Old-Russian and National-Applied Art exhibit (Древнерусское и народно-прикладное искусство; *Drevnerusskoe i narodno-prikladnoe iskusstvo*). Panorama from the belfry (звонница; *zvonitsa*) 6000R. (We spoke too soon.) (Monastery grounds open daily 8am-7pm. Museums open Tues.- Sun. 10am-5:15pm. Info tel. 30 38 69.)

Churches

Church of the Epiphany (Церковь Богоявления; *Tserkov Bogoyavlenia*), pl. Podbelskovo, across from the monastery. This large red-brick church requires an entrance fee, but is worth it to see the one frescoed room and a small exhibition of fragments of frescos taken from destroyed Yaroslavl churches. The main room has a simple, wooden 17th-century *iconostasis* and wooden benches; concerts are often held here at 6pm—ask at the monastery. The 3 other rooms allow you to examine the frescos up close. Open Wed.-Mon. 9am-1pm and 2-5pm. 5000R, students 2000R. Knock on the door if the place seems closed.

Church of Elijah the Prophet (Церковь Илья Пророка; *Tserkov Ilya Proroka*), Sovetskaya pl. (Советская), at the end of ul. Kirova. Widely considered Yaroslavl's most beautiful church, replete with glowing original frescos (the *iconostasis* is a partial restoration, though). Open Thurs.-Tues. 10am-1pm and 2-6pm. 8000R, Russians 4000R; photos 10,000R. Services Sun. 8:30-11am. **City maps** 5000R.

Church of the Archangel Michael (Архангела Михайла), across the park from the bottom right-hand corner of the monastery when facing its entrance. Similar to the more famous Church of the Epiphany with its red brick and green domes, but it is operational and old women pray before the mostly bare, wooden *iconostasis*. Open daily 9am-8pm. Services Sat., Sun., and holidays 9am and 5pm.

Church of the Savior On-The-City (Церковь Спаса на городу; *Tserkov spasa na gorodu*). Continue along the same road that overlooks the Kotorosl. Built in 1672, the church is closed, but its exterior is worth a brief stop. Continuing along the same road is the *strelka*, where the Volga and Kotorosl rivers meet. The view is spectacular and a garden has been built at the spot; bring a picnic lunch.

Museums

Muzey Metropolity Palaty (Музей Метрополиты Палаты), Volzhkaya nab. 1 (tel. 22 34 87) and 23 (tel. 30 34 95). Housed in an attractive 19th-century mansion, this museum displays the best of Yaroslavl's icons from the 13-16th centuries. 2 branches at #23 display 18th-century Russian paintings and sculpture in several media. Open Sat.-Thurs. 10am-5:30pm. *Kassy* close at 4:30pm. 10,000R.

Muzey Istorii Goroda Yaroslavlya (Музей Историй Города Ярославля) Volzhkaya nab. 17/2 (tel. 22 25 40), intersecting Sovetsky per. Small museum filled with engravings, furniture, photos, and clothes from numerous eras of Yaroslavl's history. Modern period exhibit focuses on the family that inhabited this building, down to their school textbooks and baby baskets. Open Thurs.-Mon. 10am-6pm. *Kassa* closes at 5:30pm. 5000R, students 2000R.

Music and Time Museum (Музей Музыка и время; *Muzey Muzyka i vremya*), Volzhskaya nab. 33. This tiny museum in a restored 19th-century brick house exhibits a collection of old clocks, musical instruments, and metronomes. Open Tues.-Sun. 10am-6pm. Join an organized tour. 10,000R.

Nightlife here involves much Russian pop. The dances at **Club Yuta** (Клуб Юта), ul. Respublikanskaya (Республиканская; tel. 32 97 86), in Gostinitsa Yuta, last from 9pm to 2am (Thurs.-Sun.). The well advertised but hard to find—it's downstairs—**Dzhoy-**

pati (Джойпати), ul. Naberzhnaya 2 (Набережная), has good hours and no cover for women Mondays through Wednesdays (open daily 10pm-5am). In the summer, many locals find it too hot to be cooped up in a club and instead drive to Volzhskaya nab., open their car doors, blast the radio, and simply stroll on the street.

■ Vladimir (Владимир)

Once the capital of all Russia and the headquarters of the Russian Orthodox Church, Vladimir suffered at the hands of the Tartars in the 13th century, and eventually fell to Moscow's dominance in the early 1300s. Until that time, it was a city to rival Kiev in size and splendor; since Vladimir became a province, its importance has declined, but the city has held on to some of the Golden Ring's most attractive churches.

Orientation and Practical Information Everything of interest to tourists is along **ul. III Internatsionala** (III-ого Интернационала), a five-minute walk uphill from the train station. Vladimir's **tourist office, Excursionnoe Byuro** (Экскурсионное Бюро), ul. III Internatsionala 43 (tel. 242 63), arranges English-speaking tours of Vladimir (33,000R plus 8,000R per person) and Suzdal (77,500R plus 8,000R per person). The bulletin board outside lists events and exhibits (open Mon.-Thurs. 8:30am-5:30pm, Fri.-Sun. 8:30am-3pm). For **currency exchange,** go to any *Obmen Valyuty* (Обмен Валюты) on the main street. The train station on Vokzalnaya ul. (Вокзальная) contains a 24-hour **telephone office,** which serves only Russian cities. **Trains** run go to Moscow's Kursky Vokzal (8 per day, 3hr., 20,000R) and Nizhny Novgorod (1 per hr., 4hr., 22,000R). **Store luggage** at the **bus station** (open daily 6:30-11am and noon-9:30pm; 3000R). **Postal code:** 600003. **Phone code:** 09222.

Accommodations and Food Uphill on the left path from the train station, **Gostinitsa Vladimir** (Гостиница Владимир), ul. III Internatsionala 74 (tel. 230 42) rents clean rooms with an occasional hole-y chair (cash only; bed in a triple 53,000R; singles without bath 73,000R; doubles 103,000R).

Café Blinchiki (Кафе Блинчики), ul. III Internatsionala 28 (tel. 23 691), sits directly opposite the trading arcades in a large square. Steaming-hot *bliny* come with lots of fillings and toppings. Eat here for every meal, and you may still hunger for more. *Blinchiki* stuffed with meat go for 2285R, topped with butter 2170R (open daily 10am-6pm). Unlike many Moscow eateries, **Café Slavianka** (Славянка), ul. III Internatsionala 24 (tel. 23 532), can call itself a "restaurant", cooking up yummy frog (23,500R), crab (10,600R), lobster (10,600R), and other exotic seafood in a tavernish little room. A cool cup of pear juice (*pear*; 10,000R) compliments the Slavic Surprise (Славянский Сюприз; *Slavyansky Supreez*; open daily 12:30pm-12:30am).

Sights and Entertainment The 1197 **Cathedral of St. Dmitry** (Дмитриевский Собор; *Dmitrievsky Sobor*) stands as the only surviving building of Prince Vsevelod III's palace. Painstakingly carved in stone, the cathedral's outer walls display the stories of Hercules, King David, and Aleksandr the Great, but locked doors prevent visitors from viewing the Byzantine frescos inside. Vladimir's **Assumption Cathedral** (Успенский Собор; *Uspensky Sobor*), to the right of Dmitrievsky Sobor, once guarded the famous Mother of God icon, now in Moscow's Tretyakov Gallery (see Moscow: Sights, p. 542). Fortunately, its interior still includes frescos by the renowned artists Andrei Rublyov and Daniil Chiorny. Looming large and white at the top of a small hill, the cathedral was begun in 1158, and in 1189 received four more domes and two more aisles (open Tues.-Sun. 1:30-4:45pm).

The **Museum of the History of Vladimir** (Музей Истории Владимирского Края; *Muzey Istorii Vladimirskovo Kraya*), ul. III Internatsionala 64, stocks its first floor with three-foot mammoth tusks, roosters in relief, and locks larger than most faces. The second floor keeps the tinies: statuette candle-sticks, old photos of Nicholas II, and a 1912 issue of Pravda (open Tues. and Fri.-Sun 10am-4:30pm, Wed.-Thurs. 10am-3:30pm, closed last Thurs. of the month; 7000R). Next door is the **Nativity Monas-**

tery (Рождественский Монастырь; *Rozhdestvensky Monastyr*)—Aleksandr Nevsky's former burial site. Peter I schlepped the poor guy's remains to Petersburg in the 1600s, and the town was left with an empty coffin (open Mon.-Fri. 9am-6pm).

The **Golden Gates** (Золотые Ворота; *Zolotye Vorota*) stand triumphantly in the center of ul. III Internatsionala, separating the center from the rest of town. Climb to the top (pay upstairs) for a view of Vladimir's central street through the low windows. The gates' appeal comes not from the model of the Mongol war of 1238, but rather the age of the 12th-century Russian fortification (tel. 225 59; open Mon. and Wed. 10am-4pm, Thurs.-Sun. 10am-5pm, closed last Fri. of the month; 7000R).

The church-like red-brick building beyond the Golden Gates houses an exhibit of **crystal and lacquer crafts** (Выставка: Христаль, Лаковая Миниатюра, и Вышивки; *Vystavka: Khristal, Lakovaya Miniatyura, i Vyshivki*; tel. 248 72), a large room filled with gorgeous gadgets from the surrounding region (open Wed.-Sun. 11am-6pm, Mon. 11am-5pm, closed last Fri. of the month; 7000R). **The Exhibit of Old Vladimir** (Выставка Старого Владимира; *Vystavka Starovo Vladimira*; tel. 254 51), in a water-tower near the Gates, displays regional archaeological finds (open Wed.-Thurs. 10am-4pm, Fri.-Sun. 10am-5pm, closed last Thurs. of the month; 2000R).

Down the hill to the right of the exhibit, an out-of-place monument demonstrates what can be done with U.S. investments in Russia. The weirdly familiar low fence, encircling lawn, and attached garage decorate the **American House** (Американский Дом; *Amerikansky Dom*), to be admired only from the outside, as it is inhabited—perhaps by Boris and Natasha Cleaver.

The **Vladimir Boys' Choir** gives concerts every Saturday at 7:30 pm. It is Vladimir's "living history"—singing old Russian hymns and folk songs (*kassa* open 9am-6pm; 2500R). Da boyz sing in an old church called the **theater** (Театр Хоровы ы Музыки; tel. 25 495), on ul. Georgievskaya (Георгиевская), a rock road rolling off ul. III Internatsionala around building 26. The **Drama theater** (Театр Драмы; *Teatr Drami*), ul. Moskovskaya (Московская), presents comedy, drama, musicals, and kiddie shows most days at 6pm (*kassa* open Wed.-Sat. 1-6:30pm; tickets 5000-8000R).

■ Suzdal (Суздаль)

Set in fertile countryside with lazy streams and dirt roads, miraculous Suzdal (pop. 10,000) looks much as it always has. Colorfully painted wooden houses and churches charm visitors, but just as the town withstood decades of Communism, it now stands strong as a historically protected landmark against the current tourist hordes. Until the 12th century, Suzdal's **kremlin** ruled over the Rostov-Suzdal principality. Although lush countryside now drowns the fortress' imposing power, inside, the **Church of the Nativity** (Рождественская Церковь; *Rozhdestvenskaya Tserkov*) still dazzles with its star-studded blue domes. Brightly colored frescos and ornately carved arches decorate the early 13th-century church. Two **museums**—art and history—occupy the church. (Open Wed.-Sun. 10am-6pm, closed last Fri. of the month. 7000R each; photography pass 3100R.) When the weather is good, a *troyka* trots around the ramparts for 10,000R per person (Sat.-Sun. noon-5pm). Most churches and monasteries stand near Suzdal's main axis, **ul. Lenina** (Ленина). The **Savior Monastery of St. Euthymius** (Спасо-Евфимиевский Монастырь; *Spaso-Evfimievsky Monastyr*), ul. Lenina, is Suzdal's largest monastery thanks to heavy fundraising by, among others, Ivan the Terrible. Inside are the 16th-century **Cathedral of the Transfiguration** (Преображенский Собор; *Preobrazhensky Sobor*) and the **Museum of Russian Decorative and Applied Art** (Музей самодеятельного творчества народов РСФСР; *Muzey samodeyatelnovo tvorchestva narodov RSFSR*). The former, though built in the 1590s, reflects the 12th-century style of the rest of Vladimir's and Suzdal's churches. Examine the before-and-after frescos—a vibrant upper-level and original untouched lower. The museum at the north end of the monastery, display 8th-century jewelry, old textiles, and haunting icons (complex open Tues.-Sun. 10am-5pm, Wed.-Thurs. 10am-4pm, closed last Thurs. of the month; 4000R, cathedral 4000R extra, museum 7000R extra). The **Museum of Wooden Architecture and Peasant Life** (Музей Деревянного Зогчества и Крестьянского Быта; *Muzey Drevyannovo Zogchestva i Krestyanskovo Byta*), across the river from the kremlin, is a bunch of 18th-century wooden houses and churches, complete with scythe-bearing peasant re-enacters (open May-Sept. Wed.-Mon. 9:30am-4:45pm, closed last friday of the month; grounds 3000R; buildings 8000R). The 17th-century **Aleksandr's Convent** (Александровский Монастырь; *Aleksandrovsky Monastyr*), ul. Gasteva (Гастева) off ul. Engelsa, stands on the grounds of a long-gone 13th-century church built by the legendary Aleksandr Nevsky.

Vasilevskaya ul. (Васильевская) runs from ul. Lenina to the **bus station** which sends buses to Vladimir (every hr., 40min., 3300R). The **Main Tourist Complex GTK** (Главный Туристский Комплекс, ГТК; *Glavny Turistsky Kompleks*) is a 40-minute walk from the center. Go north on ul. Lenina to the yellow belltower, and go left. Follow this road as it curves, and take a right when you come to a fork. The **Intourist** office inside GTK speaks Russified English and sells **maps** of Suzdal (2000R; open Mon.-Fri. 9am-5pm). The complex's lobby also houses the **post office** (open daily 8am-8pm). **Postal code:** 601260. The **telephone and telegraph office**, ul. Lenina 110, operates directly across from the yellow belltower (open 24hr. with a 1-2pm break)—only calls within Russia from here. For international calls, trot back to the expensive, credit-card phone at the GTK lobby. **Phone code:** 9231.

When you see the hotel prices in Suzdal, you'll be glad you're taking the bus back to Vladimir. Long fed on annual inundations of foreign tourists, Suzdal has more upscale Russian restaurants than cities ten times its size. **Pogrebok** (Погребок), Kremlyovskaya ul. (Кремлёвская), off Lenina, serves reasonably priced local specialties in clay pots (entrées 5000-20,000R, coffee 1080R; open Tues.-Sun. 10am-6pm).

■ Vologda (Вологда)

Deep in the north forests churns Vologda, self-proclaimed home of the world's best butter. A large trading city before the opening of the Baltic Sea to Russians, this town along the sleepy Vologda River is a wonderful escape from Soviet grayness— but not pollution. Despite its ornately carved wooden houses and brightly painted concrete ones, the town is tourist-free and unknown even to most egocentric Muscovites.

ORIENTATION AND PRACTICAL INFORMATION

Vologda is still a small town with everything you could need within a few blocks of **ul. Mira** (Мира). The town's **center** lies 10 minutes from the train station down ul. Mira. There are old, crowded, and frequent local **buses** (tickets 800R; those labeled "Центр" or "#1" run to the center). **Trains** leave from pl. Babushkina (Бабушкина; info tel. 72 06 73) to Moscow (12 per day, 11hr., 100,000R) and St. Petersburg (12 per day, 12hr., 100,000R). Next to the train station, **Buses** (info booth tel. 72 04 52; open daily 7am-1pm and 2-7pm) chug to places not worth going except Kirillov and Yaroslavl (2 per day, 4½hr., 18,000R), but the do have **luggage storage** (6300R; open daily 6am-10am, 11am-4pm, and 5-7pm). **Exchange currency** (US$ only) on the 1st floor of Vologdabank (Вологдабанк) at ul. Mira 36. Bring your passport (open daily 9am-1pm and 2-3pm). A **post office**, pl. Babushkina 1, lies across from the bank (open Mon.-Fri. 8am-noon and 1-7pm, Sat. 8am-noon and 1-5pm). **Postal code:** 160009. **Telephones** operate in the train station (open 24hr.). **Phone code:** 8172.

ACCOMMODATIONS

Choices are extremely slim, but mercifully suitable. Hot water is not available for one summer month, ironically, for "sanitation reasons." Always bring toilet paper.

Gostinitsa Spasskaya (Гостиница Спасская), ul. Oktyabrskaya 25 (Октябрьская; tel. 201 45). Sleepy cats outside this pastel-colored hotel welcome guests to the bright, carpeted, spacious rooms. Caters to businesspeople and has office equipment for rent (computers, fax, photocopiers, laminators!). Excellent service and clean rooms. Singles without bath run 100,000R. Doubles 80,000R per person.

Gostinitsa Sputnik (Гостиница Спутник), ul. Puteyskaya 14 (Путейская; tel. 72 27 52), just to the left of the front entrance of the train station. Clean but chipped floors line the small rooms and dark hallways. The lack of toilet seats, toilet paper, and doors to the hall toilets account for the price: 40,000R single, 60,000R double. Showers 6000R.

Gostinitsa Vologda (Гостиница Вологда), ul. Mira 92 (tel. 230 79). Spotlessly clean with an extremely friendly staff, this budget hotel contains a good restaurant and buffet. Tiles are chipped in the hall bathroom; there's no toilet paper, seat, or at times, soap, but there are doors. Singles with TV and telephone 77,600R, with bath 120,000R. Doubles 109,000R, with bath 200,000R. Outside showers 8000R.

FOOD

Several **markets** sit on ul. Mira—including the open-air fruit and veggie market behind ul. Mira 20-22. Take a left on the pedestrian shopping street off ul. Mira, then a quick right behind #20 (open daily 9am-4:30pm). **Kafe Lukomore** (Кафе Лукоморье), Lermontovaya 4 (Лермонтовая), is reason enough to come to Vologda. Turn right past ul. Mira 1 and stay right as the road curves; it's the big faux-diner building with a painting of a slick car on the side. Inside, the cheery café plays upbeat tunes and serves delicious *shashliks* (14,000R), salads (5000R), ice cream with syrup (2500R), and tea (100R). The paintings on the wall are for sale (open daily 10am-5:30pm and 6-11pm). The stand-up **Pirozhikovaya** (Пирожиковая), ul. Mira 9, cooks up under-1200R *pirozhki*, hand-size pizzas (1850R), and pastries. Avoid the triangular *pirozhki* filled with something resembling grass (open daily 8am-7pm).

SIGHTS

Follow the gold and silver domes to get to Vologda's sight center—Kremlyovskaya pl. (Кремлёвская). A monument here honors the poet **Konstantine Batyushkov**, Pushkin's teacher. On the left upon entering, the **kremlin** houses the **Vologda Region Gallery** (Вологдаская Областная Картинная Галерея; *Vologdaskaya Oblastnaya Kartinnaya Galerea*), Kremlyovskaya pl. 2. In summer 1996, it featured the graphic art of Yura Voronov (open Wed.-Sun. 10am-6pm; *kassa* closes at 5:30pm; 1000R). Behind the art museum rises the massive, multi-domed **Sofia's Cathedral** (Собор Софийский; *Sobor Softiysky*). Begun in 1568, it merits a look for the stunning, newly renovated frescos at the entrance (open Wed.-Sun. 10am-5pm). The 1869 green **Bell Tower** (Колокольня; *Kolokolnya*), to the left of the cathedral, rings its own bells at random hours. The kremlin's gate leads to a courtyard. In the back right corner, the **Vologda Museum** combines history and natural history, with stuffed ducks quacking next to samovars against a backdrop of WWII posters (open Wed.-Sun. 10am-5pm; 2000R, students 100R). To arrange a tour, call 22 51. A list of Vologda's smaller museums and their addresses is posted on the *kassa* of this museum. Several churches are visible from the Vologda River, but they are either closed or being renovated.

In a small park down Sovetsky pr. 47 (Советский) along the Vologda sits **Peter's House** (Петровский дом; *Petrovsky dom*; tel. 227 59). Bus #1 will take you from the center to the tiny house. The house saw one short visit by Peter the Great. It displays a collection of artifacts, mostly from St. Petersburg (open Wed.-Sun. 10am-1pm and 2-6pm; 2000R, 1000R students). Although it is illegal due to the polluted water, many townfolk swim in the river near Peter's House. The **Museum-House of Konstantin Batyushkov** (Музей-Дом Батюшкова; *Muzey-Dom Batyushkova*), ul. Batyoshkova 2 (tel. 207 30), shelters furniture and personal possessions interspersed with pictures of the poet and his family (open Mon.-Sat. 10am-5pm; 1000R).

A promenade through town leads to Vologda's most famous sight—its **18th-century wooden houses**. The most significant ones are labeled. To reach **Spaso-Prilutsky monastyr** (Спасо-Прилуцкий монастырь), stroll north for about an hour down ul. Chernyshevskovo (Чернышевского). To avoid the walk, take trolley #34 from the train station to its last stop. From there take bus #3, 102, 103, or 134 to the last stop. Along the way lie concrete flats, poorly located industry, and small wooden houses lacking indoor plumbing and phones. Begun in 1371, this monastery is a not-too-far escape into the countryside. The monastery basks on the banks of the Vologda, and the earthen ramparts are a perfect place on which to enjoy a riverside lunch. (Monastery open daily 7am-9pm. Morning liturgy 7 and 10am; evening services 5-8pm. Donations requested. Russian tour for less than 6 people 40,000R; to arrange, call 741 45.) The main church is open, and you may even be able to climb to the top of the lofty bell tower. From here extends one of the most phenomenal views in Russia. The lazy river Vologda moving beyond the lolling green countryside is barely touched by modern-day commerce.

■ Near Vologda: Kirilla-Belozersky Monastery
(Кирилла-Белозерск Монастырь)

This 14th-century monster of a monastery puts the smaller, poorer one in Vologda to shame. Even the two-hour **bus** ride to Kirillov (Кириллов; 5 per day, 20,000R) from Vologda is a visual delight—just try to find two farm houses with the same cut-out or color pattern in their windows. Get off the bus before the central Kirillov stop; watch for the white stone mass on your right and hop out there. According to legend, St. Kirill founded the monastery when the Virgin Mary came to him in a vision and showed him the towers of a new monastery—all are now privy to the vision in its spectacular physical form. Tourists of the present come to the monastery because princes of the past came here to leave their treasures. The luxurious clothes and icons that fill the museums and churches were, for the rich princes, a far smaller price to pay for salvation than years in purgatory. For only US$1 per building, you can ogle the above wonders as well as historical Russian folk valuables. (Open in summer daily 9am-5pm; off-season Mon.-Fri. 9am-5pm. Tours US$10 per person; to arrange a tour or for more info, call 314 79 or 312 59.)

THE TRANS-SIBERIAN RAILROAD

One of four lines falling under the label "Trans-Siberian," the all-Russian Trans-Siberian route, running from Moscow to Vladivostok, was for many years off limits to foreigners. Now, it's yours to enjoy, so pull back the curtains, and watch endless rivers, chiseled mountains, minute wooden cottages, and miles of grazing cows. Russian stations may not provide service with a smile, but fellow railers will chat about the changing times, where to get the cheapest goods and how to toughen up the kids. They might even ask you to join in a round of the card game, *durak* (fool).

Riding the Rails When arriving on the train, tickets and passport are checked to be sure the last name on the ticket matches the passport's. Keep the ticket; one attendant will come back when all are seated to collect them. She will ask if you want sheets for sleeping (*bilyo nada?;* 5000-10,000R). Say *"Da"*—if the rough boards don't kill ya' the cold nights will (carry-on sheets are not allowed). Keep the same sheets throughout the trip. Ask not to be put at the last seat (next to the toilet); the stench can be unbearable. Because the air-conditioned **restaurant** (ресторан; *restoran*) wagon—with movies in the evenings—charges twice the price, most locals bring bread, cheese, and meat to eat and share. Cover food when not eating: dust seeps through even closed windows and makes some travelers sick. Two **attendants**—*provodnik* (male) or *provodnitsa* (female)—sit at the front of each wagon. The provodnitsas provide you with glasses and sell tea and any other goods more cheaply than the restaurant. Across from their door, a large kettle heats water (free) for tea. The schedule on the attendant's door indicates arrival times and how long each stop (стоянка; *stoyanka*) will be. When stops are longer than 15 minutes, many locals come out to haggle and buy food from the *babushki* outside the train. The bathroom closes 30 minutes before and after any major stop. Usually, passengers may only use one of the bathrooms at each of the wagon's far ends—one is reserved for the attendants. Be sure to bring toilet paper, soap, and shoes that rise slightly higher than the ½-inch "wetness" on the bathroom floors.

For extra safety: don't drink tea or any other drinks offered by "friends" who know you're a foreigner. There have been reports of somnorific substances added to tea. Young women do travel alone and changes of seat may always be arranged by the attendants. To save money, be sure your tickets are not "фирменый" (*firminy*) —with carpeted floors, fake flowers, and toilet paper which lasts for the journey's first 30 minutes. Depending on the train, 29 hours separate Moscow and Yekaterinburg. Another 20 hours get you to Novosibirsk, and 32 hours more lead to Irkutsk. Ticket prices can as much as triple depending on the combination of types of trains and categories on the trains. For example, in summer 1996, the Traveler's Guest House (see p. 520) offered "second-class" seats to Irkutsk for US$198. Double that for "first-class." When traveling to Novosibirsk and Yekaterinburg, separate tickets must be ordered for each stop. For those wishing to take the train further, tickets to Vladivostok, first-class, sold for US$650 from the Traveller's Guest House. Tickets, as well as visas to China and Mongolia may be arranged here as well. For those wishing to stay longer in Siberia, homestays may be arranged (prices vary) with Youry Nemirovsky at Baikal Complex (tel. (3952) 46 47 62; fax 43 23 22); e-mail Youry@baikal.irkutsk.su).

> The Trans-Siberian snakes its way through eight time zones, but all train arrivals and departures are listed at the station according to Moscow time.

■ Yekaterinburg (Екатеринбург)

Both the birthplace of Yeltsin and the site of the Romanov's assassination, Yekaterinburg has most intimately experienced the end of empires. Many travelers consider Yekaterinburg to be the end of the world—industrial, gray, and empty. In the far reaches of Russia, the city's street signs haven't caught up to post-Communism yet, and most inhabitants still call their city by its Soviet name—Sverdlosk.

Orientation and Practical Information Set your watch two hours forward from Moscow time. Trolleys #1 and 9, or any other form of transport with "пр. Ленина" (pr. Lenina) written on the side run to the center (1000R). Buses with "ж.д. вокзал" (zh.d. vokzal) on the side go to the **train station. Exchange currency** on the second floor (open Mon.-Fri. 10am-2pm and 3-7pm, Sat. 10am-3pm). **Store luggage** (6000R; open 24hr.). Buy **maps** at **Knigi** (Книги), ul. Chelyuskintsev (Челюскинцев), just ahead and to the right of the train station (open Mon.-Fri. 10am-2pm, 3-7pm, Sat. 9am-2pm and 3-5pm). South of the train station, **Glavny pr.** (Главный, formerly Lenina), the main street, parallels two other central streets: **Pokrovsky pr.** (Покровский, formerly Malisheva, Малышева), and **Sibirsky pr.** (Сибирский, former ul. Kuybysheva, Кыйбышева). An **Intourist** office (tel. 51 90 13 or 51 81 34) is in Hotel Yubeleynaya (see below). A **post office,** pr. Lenina 39, **faxes,** telexes, and even **e-mails** (open Mon.-Fri. 8am-8pm, Sat.-Sun. 8am-6pm). The **telephone office** is on ul. Tolmacheva 25 (Толмачева), near the post office. **Postal code:** 620151. **Phone code:** 3432.

Accommodations and Food Foreigners pay double, but can still find cheap rooms. Try **Gostinitsa Bolshoy Ural** (Гостиница Большой Урал), ul. Krasnoarmeyskaya 1 (Красноармейская; tel. 55 68 96), behind the gray opera theater on pr. Lenina 46a. If taking a trolley to the stop "pr. Lenina", walk ahead to the tram tracks on pr. Lenina and turn left to get to the theater on you right. The elevator only travels up, most hallways are not lit, and the male guests are prone to harass women. Singles in a double of 4th category go for 70,000R. Pay a refundable 5000R on your floor to get the key. **Gostinitsa Yubeleynaya** (Юбилейная), pr. Lenina 40 (tel. 51 81 55), is not much different. Singles in 4th category go for 90,000R, and in 1st go for 225,000R.

Babushki haggle at the Chayniy (Чайный) **market** across from the train station. More systematic is the Soviet-style **Gastronom,** pr. Lenina 41 (open Mon.-Fri. 7:30am-9pm, Sat.-Sun. 7:30am-8pm). The restaurant **Harbin** (Харбин), Sibirsky pr. 39 (tel. 61 75 71), serves Chinese (30,000-60,000R) and European (50,000-60,000R) entrées in a

Trans-Siberian Railroad

> **Vam Kholodna, Baby?**
>
> Friendly fellow travelers are one of the best parts of riding the rails east, but beware geeks bearing gifts. Women in particular traveling alone on the Trans-Siberian may find themselves the recipients of just one too many concerned questions about their comfort. Male and female attendants have been known to pop into cabins at night to ask, *"Vam kholodna?"* ("Are you cold?") Beware lest their apparent will to warm you with extra sheets be a front for more heated desires. Once astrology catches on in Russia, undoubtedly they will emulate the Western world's pick-up artists with a subtle, "What's your sign?"

pagoda. Surrounded by wreckage on the street nearby, the place is usually empty (MC and Visa accepted; open daily 1-4pm and 6-11pm). Another marvel of decoration hides near the opera theater: **Teatralnoye Kafe** (Театральное Кафе), on one of the sidestreets off of Glavny pr. (tel. 55 30 25). Elegant burgundy walls, glass-pipe chandeliers, bronze pipes on the ceiling, and string designs complement entrées (15,000-50,000R; open daily 10am-4pm and 5-10pm). For cheaper options, check out the cafés on pr. Lenina, especially those hiding around the bridge.

Sights and Entertainment In a new era of political freedom, the small **Museum of the History of Yekaterinburg,** Voznesenski pr. 26 (Вознесенски; formally Karla Libknekhta, Карла Либкнехта; tel. 51 22 40), off Glavny pr., explodes with political satire blasting reigning prez Yeltsin. The requisite folk art and wax figure museum waits upstairs (open Tues.-Sat. 10am-5:30pm; 2000R, students 1000R; tours in Russian 10,000R; free last Wed. of the month). The **Fine Arts Museum** (Музей Изобразительных Искусств; *Muzey Izobrazitelnikh Iskusstv*), Voevodina 5 (Воеводина; tel. 51 03 05), just off Glavny pr. by the bridge, boasts a bevy of busts, bears, and belligerent bulls carved in black stone. The upstairs carries quartz and crystal; some is for sale (open Wed.-Sun. 11am-6pm; 5000R, students 1000R; Russian tours 25,000R).

The **Historico-Regional Museum** (Историко-краеведческий музей; *Istoriko-krayevedchesky muzey*), Pokrovsky pr. 46 (tel. 51 76 20), features changing exhibits—in summer 1996, it was clothing fashions from 1860-1956. The war exhibit, however, sticks with prison shirts, war photos, and declarations by Stalin (open June-Aug. Wed.-Mon. 10am-5pm; Sept.-May 11am-6pm; 3000R, students free). On Voznesensky pr., a simple stone surrounded by flags marks the spot where a firing squad ended the line of **Romanovs** (unless you believe in Anastasia). A tiny church serves as a faint memorial. Nearby the light-blue **Ascension Church** rises high above. Upon entering, women should take one of the head covers in the boxes labeled "косыний" (*kosiny*). Locals take a dip in the small pond behind the church and dry off at the white-gazeboed island in the middle. The **Circus,** Sibirsky pr. (Сибирский), near the Harbin restaurant brings on the clowns, as well as bears, monkeys, snakes, and horses (Fri., Sat., and Sun. at 2pm; *kassas* open daily 9am-6pm; 10,000R; kids 5 and under free).

Novosibirsk (Новосибирск)

Born only a century ago, the young city of Novosibirsk has grown faster than Aleksandr Karelin, and now competes with Moscow and St. Petersburg in population and political power. This is Siberia's biggest city, an example of Socialist ambition, the geographical center of Russia, and a good daystop for those who need more opulence than Yekaterinburg might provide.

Orientation and Practical Information Set your watch three hours forward from Moscow time. The **Metro** connects the city center, **pl. Lenina,** to the train station at stop "Гарина-Михайловского" (Garina-Mihailovskovo). From the train station, walk out into the city and then underground where you see the "M". Go one stop (1000R) to Sibirskaya (Сибирская), then walk upstairs to change stations. One more stop takes you to pl. Lenina. The Sibirskaya metro stop comes close to the circus, the Ascension Church, the market, and the stadium. Krasny pr. (Красный) runs through pl. Lenina. Buy a map (13,000R) in section "1" of **Tsentralny Dom Knigi** (Центральный Дом Книги), Krasny pr. 29 (open Mon.-Sat. 10am-2pm and 3-7pm). The **Siberia Travel Bureau** (tel. 21 38 52; fax 21 12 27) in Hotel Novosibirsk, second floor, across from the train station, arranges tickets and may give help, but no individual tours or maps (open daily 10am-7pm). **Store luggage** in the train station (9100R; open 24hr.). Different storage booths take different coffee breaks so pick the one that suits your departure time. **Sibirbank**, Lenina 4 (tel. 22 42 94), gives Visa cash advances, **exchanges currency,** and sends money **Western Union** (open daily 10am-1pm and 2-6pm, not as the sign outside indicates). The **post and telephone office,** ul. Lenina and ul. Sovetskaya (Советская), sends telegrams and **e-mail** (open Mon.-Fri. 8am-5pm), and still supports snail mail (open Mon.-Fri. 8am-7pm, Sat.-Sun. 8am-6pm; express mail til 3pm). **Postal code:** 630099. **Phone code:** 383-2.

Accommodations and Food

Hotel prices come as big as the city. Try to arrive in the morning, and leave by evening. **Hotel Novosibirsk** (Новосибирск; tel. 20 11 20), across from the train station, rents beds in triples (phone, toilet, TV, and hall showers) for 115,000R. The **Central Hotel** (Центральный), ul. Lenina 3 (tel. 22 72 94), rents similar beds in doubles for 110,000R. For **private rooms,** Yevgenia Prokofievna (tel. 24 83 17; Russian-speaking only) arranges singles at 50,000R, as well as doubles and apartments. To reserve places in English, call Inna Shmeriev at 22 88 84.

A large market covers nearly as much area as the stadium it borders on ul. Krylova (Крылова; open daily 8am-7pm). The **Gastronom,** Krasny pr. 30, offers indoor shopping (open daily 8am-8pm). The **Restaurant Druzhba** (Дружба), Lenina 3 (tel. 22 72 44), serves a full-course meal (*okroshka* soup, rice, stuffed meat, and tea) for 35,000R. Ask for *"kompleks"*. Music plays after 7pm (cover 30,000R; open daily noon-5pm and 6pm-2am). Inside the mall *Tsentralny Kompleks* (Центральный Комплекс), on the corner of ul. Lenina and Krasny pr., the **Café Virineya** (Виринея) sells small pizzas for 5000R, and *piroshki* with meat for 2000R (open daily 11am-5pm and 6-10pm). Upstairs, **Restaurant Tsentralny** (tel. 22 43 61) cooks up pricey entrées (30,000-40,000R). Live bands play nightly at 8pm; stripteases begin at midnight (cover 10,000R after 6pm; open daily noon-5am).

Sights and Entertainment

The well known opera and ballet theater companies on pl. Lenina leave for the summer. Nonetheless, traveling troupes come around in July and August, as do art exhibits. Novosibirsk boasts fewer museums than Yekaterinburg, but it compensates with good galleries. The popular **picture gallery,** Krasny pr. 5 or Sverdlova 10 (Свердлова; tel. 23 53 31), features a permanent exhibit of Russian artists of the 18th to 20th centuries (open Mon. 11am-6pm, Wed.-Sun. 11am-7pm; 20,000R, students 10,000R, locals 5000R). Across the street, the **Union of Artists Gallery** (Союз Художников; *Soyuz Khudozhnikov*), Sverdlova 3 (tel. 23 44 38), exhibits the work of local artists (paintings run US$400; open Mon.-Fri. 10am-5pm; 1000R). Near the galleries, the tiny, golden-domed **St. Nicholas's Church** supposedly sits smack dab in the middle of Russia (open daily 9am-7pm). The larger **Ascension Church,** on Gogolya ul. (Гоголя), flaunts a heavenly blue ceiling with classical paintings and a dazzling white and gold *iconostasis* (services held Mon.-Fri. at 9am and 5pm, Sun. at 7am, 10am, and 5pm). The **Regional Museum** (Краеведческий Музей), Vokzalnaya Magistral 11 (Вокзальная Магистраль; tel. 21 70 31), gears its aquariums, stuffed rabbits, and rhinoceros skulls toward pre-schoolers (open Mon.-Fri. 10am-6pm; 1000R, students 300R). The **Central Park** (Центральный Парк) further entertains kiddies with logwood playgrounds, a ferris wheel, and swings (5000R for 5min.). The **circus,** on the corner of ul. Narymskaya and ul. Chelyuskintsev (Челюскинцев; tel. 21 24 76), makes young'ns scream for more (Wed.-Fri. at 6pm and Sat.-Sun. at 3pm; 10,000-15,000R depending on rows; *kassas* open daily 10am-6pm).

Irkutsk (Иркутск)

A Siberian trading post for three centuries, Irkutsk is one of the few eastern metropoles which sprang up before the Trans-Siberian's tracks were laid. And the old-timer sure has stories to tell. A bazaar for fur-traders, a den for desperate gold-diggers, and a posh gulag for the empire's rebellious elite, Irkutsk developed as a feisty mix of high culture and window-smashing brawls. The pit of unchecked capitalism said "no" to the revolution in 1917, welcomed the retreating White troops, and only turned Red in 1920. Today, long tempered by the shackles of a restrictive regime, Irkutsk has lost much of its fire, but nearby, mighty Baikal beckons with wilds of its own.

Orientation and Practical Information Set your watch five hours forward from Moscow time. Trams #1 or 2 (1000R) cross the Angara river to connect the train station and center. The main streets, **ul. Lenina**, and **ul. Karla Marxa** run parallel to each other. The staff in **Hotel Intourist's** lobby, Sverdlova ul. (Свердлова; tel. 29 01 60), sell plane, train, and theater tickets, and arrange excursions (US$25 per person). They also sell **maps** (6000R) and **exchange currency** (open daily 8am-8pm). Get off at the first stop after crossing the bridge, turn right on bul. Gagarina to the right, and the hotel will be on your left. Irkutsk may be big, but only **Vneshtorgbank** (Внешторгбанк), ul. Sverdlova 40 (tel. 33 46 76), gives cash advances. **Store luggage** 'round the clock at the train station for 9100R. The run-down main **post office**, ul. Stepana Rezina 23 (Степана Резина), accepts **Poste Restante** (open Mon.-Fri. 8am-8pm, Sat.-Sun. 9am-6pm). The **telephone office**, ul. Proletarskaya 12 (Пролетарская), across from the circus, is open 24 hours. **Postal code:** 664000. **Phone code:** 3852.

Accommodations and Food **Amerikansky Dom** (Американский Дом), ul. Ovstrovskaya 19 (Островская; tel. 43 26 89; tel./fax 33 13 22), seems purposefully hidden on a tiny path surrounded by *dachas* and roosters. It's best to get there by taxi (negotiate for 20,000R outside the train station). The clean, small brick house offers a bed and breakfast for US$18. Some guest sleep on the floor for US$10 (hall showers). Reserve at least a week in advance. They also arrange visas to Mongolia (US$40) at no extra charge. The **Hotel Rus**, (Гостиница Русь), ul. Sverdlova (tel. 34 37 15), near the burnt-down Hotel Sibir, offers clean, carpeted beds in a double for 60,000R, with private toilets and hall showers. Reserve at least two weeks in advance. With a ticket handy, or 3000R, many locals spend the night at the train station's waiting room in rather uncomfortable chairs; beware, as some might just be waiting to swipe a bag.

One of the town's many **supermarkets** (супермаркет) stocks meats and cheeses at Stepina Razina 12 (open Mon.-Sat. 9am-2pm and 3-7pm. Sun. 11am-2pm and 3-7pm). The **central market** hawks fresh fruit, veggies, and meat (open daily 8am-8pm). Any form of transport that reads "рынок" *(rynok)* leads to the market. The wood-and-brick cabin, **Karlson Kafe** (Кафе Карлсон), ul. Lenina, serves tough and juicy *langet* (лангет; pork, 13,282R) and other equally edible entrées (4000-20,000R; open daily 11am-11pm). **Café Skaska** (Скаска), ul. Chritskovo 3 (Чрицково), off ul. Karla Marxa displays glazed witches and a puss-in-boots to entertain ice-cream eaters (2200R; open Mon.-Fri. 9am-2pm and 3-7pm, Sat. 9am-2pm and 3-6pm). The **Fihtelburg** (Фихтельберг), ul. Lenina across from the philharmonic (tel. 33 33 92), sets a more serious mood in a big wood hall. Entrées run 16,000-60,000R (open daily noon-midnight).

Sights and Entertainment The Decembrist Prince Sergey **Trubetskoy's house-museum** (Музей Трубецкого), ul. Dzerzhinskovo 64 (Дзержинского; tel. 27 57 73), exhibits his books, furniture, tapestried icons, silverware, and photos of the prince's jail cell. The extra 2000R for a tour makes the hall after hall of portraits more intriguing (open Thurs.-Mon. 10am-6pm; 8000R, Russians 6000R). Another Decembrist Dom, **Volkonsky's House** (Музей Болконского; *Muzey Vokonskovo*), ul. Volkonskovo 10 (Волконского; tel. 27 75 32), waits on a dusty side street just off of ul. Timiryazeva (Тимирязева; open Tues.-Sun. 10am-5:30pm; 8000R, Russians 6000R). The **Regional Museum** (Краеведческий музей; *Krayevedchesky Muzej*), ul. Karla

Marxa 2 (tel. 33 34 49), exhibits on its first floor the furs, snow skis, Buddhist masks, drums, woven icons, music shells, and pipes of local Siberian tribes. Antique clothes and furniture in old Russian styles wait next door (open Tues.-Sun. 11am-6pm; 10,000R, Russians 6000R). The local **Art Museum** (Художественный Музей; *Khudozhestvenny Muzey*), ul. Lenina 5 (tel. 34 42 30), copied some famous paintings from Moscow's and St. Petersburg's museums. The icons are real (open Wed.-Sun. 10am-6pm; 10,000R, Russians 3000R). The elegant gold-columned *iconostasis* in the **Znamensky Monastery's** (Знаменский) main church makes quite an impression. Note the door made of a cracked tree slice. Take trolley #3 here or walk along ul. Frank Kamenetskovo (Франк Каменецкого), and see some original log cabins. Bear right at the fork on this street, and carefully cross the street to the blue-green domes (open daily 8:30am-8pm; services daily 8:30 and 11am). The light blue **synagogue**, on ul. Karla Libknekhta 23 (Карла Либкнехта; tel. 27 12 45), off of ul. Karla Marxa holds daily services at 7am and 7pm. A **mosque** rises high at Karla Libknekhta 86.

As in other Russian cities, local theater troupes tour during the summer. Thus, the philharmonic, puppet theater, musical theater, drama theater, and even the circus hold only sporadic performances. At night, many youth head to aptly named Youth Island (Остров Уности; *Ostrov Unosty*), across the bridge near the regional museum. Although swimming is prohibited, rented **canoes/water-skis** contraptions ply the waters (5000R per 15min.; *kassa* open daily 10am-10pm). **Horse rides** await at the obelisk daily 5-7pm (15,000R with driver, 20,000R alone). The white spiky building hosts discotheques (Fri. and Sat. 11pm-3am; cover 15,000R).

■ Lake Baikal (Озеро Байкал)

A natural freak, a clear-blue oddity, mighty Baikal defies the definition of "lake", and dives into the realm of fantasy. At 1637m, it is the deepest freshwater body in world, and in those gaping jaws it guards one-fifth of the earth's unsalted water. Baikal is also the most ancient—25 million years old, when most lakes aren't more than 100,000. Surrounded by snow-capped peaks, its deep blue waters teem with species found nowhere else in the world—translucent shrimp, over-sized sturgeon, and deepwater fish that explode when brought to the surface. The *nerpa* freshwater seal lives 3000km from its closest relative, the Arctic seal—and no one knows how it got there. One deep-living fish has evolved into a gelatinous blob of fat—so fatty, in fact, that locals stick wicks in the lipidinous lumps and use them as candles.

In winter the lake freezes, and ferry routes become roads for trucks. During the Russo-Japanese war, the army even built train tracks over the ice, in order to send troops to the front lines faster. No engine ever made it across—the first one fell through the ice and sank to the watery graveyard of other trucks and vehicles that also had the ill fate to roll over thin ice.

Baikal's shores are no less fascinating. Reindeer, polar foxes, wild horses, brown bears, wild boars, and nefarious Siberian weasels hide in the forested surrounding mountains, while glacial lakes melt into ice-cold waterfalls. In some places, humans have left an idyllic imprint. Wooden villages and Buryat *ger* (tent) communities border the edges. Painted rocks and "wishing" trees strung with colored rags recall the locale's shamanistic heritage, and the Buryat region to the northeast, counts 45 high Buddhist monasteries. Deserted gulags (where many lamas and shamans spent their last days under an atheist regime) pepper the outskirts.

The human touch has not always been so gentle, though. Intense fishing has decimated some species, and pollution from upriver cities and shoreside factories has begun to disturb the balanced ecology. One of the lake's greatest threats could be the Irkutsk dam. Hundreds of rivers feed into Baikal, but only one, the Angara, flows out. Legend has it that poppa Baikal once threw a rock at his errant daughter Angara, in an attempt to steer her back. He failed for millennia, but with the Irkutsk dam, mighty dad might be getting his wish. Unfortunately, the dam has raised water levels, and begun to ruin the shallower feeding grounds of the Baikal trout (*omul*).

In recent years, authorities and international organizations have begun initiatives to preserve the region, but protected zones have been around for decades. One, the Barguzin National Reserve (Баргузинский Заповедник; *Barguzinsky Zapovednik*) on Baikal's east shore, was Russia's first national reserve. The **Pribaikalsky National Park** (Прибайкальский Национальный Парк) encompasses much of the lake's west coast, and is the closest reserve to Irkutsk. When fog doesn't obscure the forest tops, views spread over pine-trees and crystal clear water. Some days, visibility is better in the water (30m) than on land. **Olkhon island,** also part of the park, is a prime spot for seal watching.

Although **Listvyanka** (Листвянка), at the Angara's mouth, is not officially in the park—in fact, it is 100km from the reserve's southernmost border—many locals refer to their section of shore as "Pribaikalsky", as well. The scenes here are no less spellbinding. Rent **bikes** at Listvyanka's Hotel Intourist; ask the bus driver to drop you off near it. **Boats** tour the immediate lake (get off at the last stop near the shore). The log cabin three minutes back from the last stop sells **maps** and brochures of the area (10,000R). The 24-hour staff offers info on hiking, fishing, boating, motorboating, and skiing. The staff serves as the reception for a **hotel** (single 82,6000R). **St. Nicholas's Church,** built in thanks for a miraculous ship rescue, sits off in the hills with a dark green dome. Walk eight minutes back from the last stop and turn right when you see it. The cows of the surrounding villagers may moo and follow you unless you moo back. Plain white walls and detailed, golden-framed icons wait inside the church (open Mon.-Fri. 10am-6pm; services Sat.-Sun. 8:30am-noon and 1-7pm).

To get to Listvyanka, first make it on time to the bus station in Irkutsk (4 times per day, 2hr., 16,000R). Take tram #1 with "рынок" written on its front to the market stop and walk farther on ul. Timiryazeva. Or take tram #2 one stop farther after the market to get closer. Buses wait at platform #3 and may not be labeled.

THE VOLGA-DON REGION (ВОЛГО-ДОНСКАЯ ОБЛАСТЬ)

The fertile threesome of the Volga, Don, and Oka gave birth to Russian civilization around the 7th century. The Slavs prospered here, until the first wave of Mongol invasions forced them north. But even northern forests and powerful 'grads provided insufficient protection, and they were eventually overrun. It took a half-century before the Russians were able to push back south to Azov and reclaim their ancestral lands. The region of the *"chernozem,"* or fertile black soil, spreads around the crossroads of major trade routes to the Mediterranean and the Far East.

■ Nizhny Novgorod (Нижний Новгород)

Once on the edge of the Russian state, but now a center of privatization, Nizhny Novgorod (old Gorky) is immersed in three eras of Russian history. Privatized grocery stores and Baroque buildings share blocks with statues of Lenin. To shrug off the remaining edges of Soviet rule's stifling blanket, the city opened its gates to foreigners in late 1990, welcoming tourists with smiling, industrious citizens, more optimistic about their future than most Russians.

ORIENTATION AND PRACTICAL INFORMATION

Central Nizhny has two levels: the lower one includes the river station and **ul. Mayakovskovo** (Маяковского), and the upper, larger level boasts the Gorky museums, the kremlin, art museums, and the main walking street—**ul. Bolshaya Pokrovskaya** (Большая Покровская; formerly Sverdlova), which runs from the kremlin to **pl. Gorkovo** (Горького). It is a pedestrian street lined with stores, restaurants, and outdoor

NIZHNY NOVGOROD ■ 573

Volga Don Region

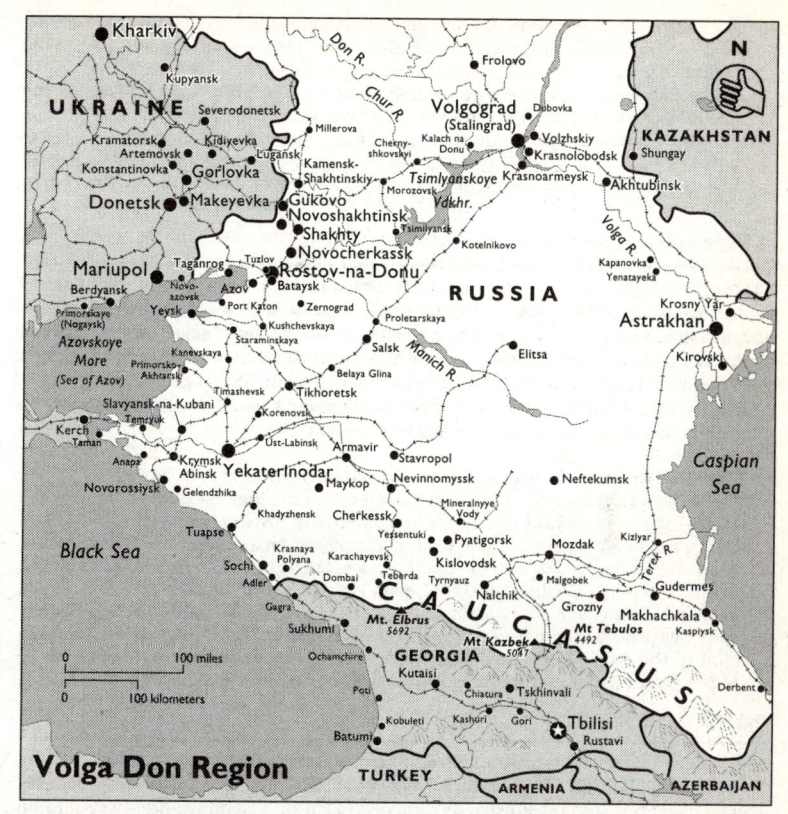

cafés. **Verkhne-Volzhskaya nab.** (Верхне-Волжская) originates near the kremlin and is perfect for strolling up to the top of a cliff overlooking the river.

Tourist Office: Intourist, pl. Lenina (Ленина), in Tsentralnaya Gostinitsa (Центральная Гостиница), rm. 814. Open when they want to be. Plane and rail bookings.

Currency Exchange: Gostinitsa Oktyabrskaya (Гостиница Октябрьская), Verkhne-Volzhskaya nab. 5. Cashes traveler's checks at a 6% commission. Gives cash advances on Eurocard and MC. Open daily 8:30am-1pm and 2-6pm. Take your Visa card to **Inkom Bank** (Инком Банк), Varvaskaya 32 (Варваская; tel. 37 94 42). Open Mon.-Sat. 8:30am-1pm and 2-8pm.

Trains: Moskovsky Vokzal (Московский Вокзал), across the river from the kremlin. Trains to Kazan (1 per day, 12hr., 50,000R) and Moscow (5 per day, 8hr., 64,900R), via Vladimir (4hr., 29,800R).

Buses: Coming out of the train station, the *avtovokzal* (автовокзал) is a 5-min. walk to the left. More crowded than trains. To: Moscow (9 per day, 9hr., 66,000R) and Vladimir (9 per day, 5hr., 38,000R). Open daily 6am-10:30pm.

Ferries: Nizhne-Volzhskaya nab. (Нижне-Волжская; tel: 34 04 25). Prices ascend by quality category (1-4) to Kazan (4pm, 19hr., 51,000-114,000R), Moscow (noon, 6 days, 66,000-709,000R), Volgograd (4pm, 90hr., 131,000-447,000R), Yaroslavl (noon, 20hr., 51,000-172,000R). Open daily 7am-6pm.

Public Transportation: Nizhny is clearly laid out but bigger than most Russian towns; you'd do well to use public transportation and confine your travels to central Nizhny. A 1-day pass costs 1200R at blue booths labeled "проездные карточки" (*proyezdeny kartochki*). Most destinations are clearly marked on the front of buses. Any bus or trolleybus labeled "Московский Вокзал" (*Moskovsky Vokzal*) goes across the river to the train station and stops at the ferry station and Tsentralnaya Gostinitsa. Any bus or tram with "#1 Минина" *(Minina)* on the side goes to the center of town.

Luggage Storage: Coins sold for 24-hr. lockers. 6400R. Turn the 4 buttons on the inside of any locker to pick your combination. Put the coin in the slot and close.

Post and Telephone Office: ul. Bolshaya Pokrovskaya 56, on pl. Gorkovo. Pay at window #4 (open daily 8am-9pm). The receipt lists your booth number. Dial 8 first; wait for the tone. Dial 3 when you hear an answer. Local calls are free. Open Mon.-Sat. 8am-10pm, Sun. 8am-6pm. **Postal Code:** 603000. **Phone Code:** 8312.

ACCOMMODATIONS

Nizhny Novgorod still hasn't forgotten the days when it was Gorky. Although Intourist has installed itself in Tsentralnaya Gostinitsa and both Gostinitsa Rossiya and Gostinitsa Oktyabrskaya take foreigners, the latter is well beyond budget prices, and the many other cheaper establishments will have nothing to do with imperialist infiltrators. So, as of yet, there are no budget choices in Nizhny. If you arrive during weekday office hours, you could try one of the many **dormitories;** for a small payment to the right person, it is rumored that they may let you stay.

Gostinitsa Rossiya (Гостиница Россия), Verkhne-Volzhskaya nab. 2a (tel. 39 19 71; fax 36 38 94). Walk toward the right when facing the kremlin and turn right at the river. Expensive, but it's one of only two games in town. A large, gray, drab hotel in a quiet neighborhood, close to the center, but farther than the Oka from the train station and without 24-hr. room service. Singles with no shower *(bez ooDObestv)* 150,000R. Doubles 300,000R, with view of Volga 360,000R.

Gostinitsa Oka (Ока), pr. Gagarina (Гагарина; tel. 65 86 40), inside the sports complex (дворец спорта; *dvorets sporta*). Take bus #26 or 43 from across the train station to the stop "Oka". Cockroaches have been spotted near the few shreds of waxed toilet paper in the bathroom. Singles with bathroom 162,000R.

FOOD

The recent private enterprise explosion has brought a slew of new cafés to town. Many flank ul. Bolshaya-Pokrovskaya. Do-it-yourselfers go to the **Dmitrievski grocery store** (Дмитриевский) off Bolshaya Pokrovskaya on ul. Piskunova (Пискунова; open Mon.-Sat. 8am-1pm and 2-7pm, Sun. 8am-1pm and 2-6pm). The **Mytny Rynok** (Мытный Рынок), between #2 and 4 on ul. Bolshaya Pokrovskaya, vends fruits and vegetables in the summer (Tues.-Fri. 7am-4:30pm, Sat.-Mon. 7am-3pm).

Gardinia (Гардиния), Verkhne-Volzhskaya nab. (tel. 36 41 01), near the art museum, a 5-min. walk along the cliff. You can't miss this large outdoor restaurant with flowered umbrellas and a mongo model airplane. Started by an American, this fast-food joint is frequented by wealthy Russians who can afford a taste of America. Chicken filet 25,500R, Cabbage salad 10,000R. Also fried potatoes, onion soups, spaghetti, and rice. Visa accepted. Open daily 10am-10pm.

Russkye Pelmeni (Русские Пельмени), ul. Bolshaya Pokrovskaya 24 (tel. 33 21 07). *Pelmeni* served in bouillon or with cheese, sour cream, or butter—all for less than 6000R. *Bliny* (yummy Russian pancakes) for 2700R. Open daily 10am-9pm.

U Shakhovskovo (У Шаховского), ul. Piskunova (Пискунова), one block off ul. Bolshaya Pokrovskaya in the Actor's House (Дом Актёра; *Dom Aktyora;* tel. 36 72 64). A fancy restaurant/jazz bar with prices to match. The management requires evening dress after 6pm to match the gleaming black-and-white decor. Jazz performances. Crab salad (салат "Острова Барвадос"; *salat "Ostrova Baravodoc"*) 63,470R. Chicken Kiev 16,500R. Imported beers 12,000-20,000R. Cover 10,000R when the band plays 6-11pm. AmEx accepted. Open daily noon-midnight.

Houston Bar & Café, across from the Gardinia and Gostinitsa Oktyabrskaya (tel. 36 02 00), lures Americanophiles with good food, good hours, and an English-speaking owner. Every meal comes with veggies and fries. Entrées run 18,000-50,000R and drinks 5000-25,000R (open Mon.-Fri. 1pm-2am, Sat.-Sun. noon-2am). Visa accepted.

NIZHNY NOVGOROD ■ 575

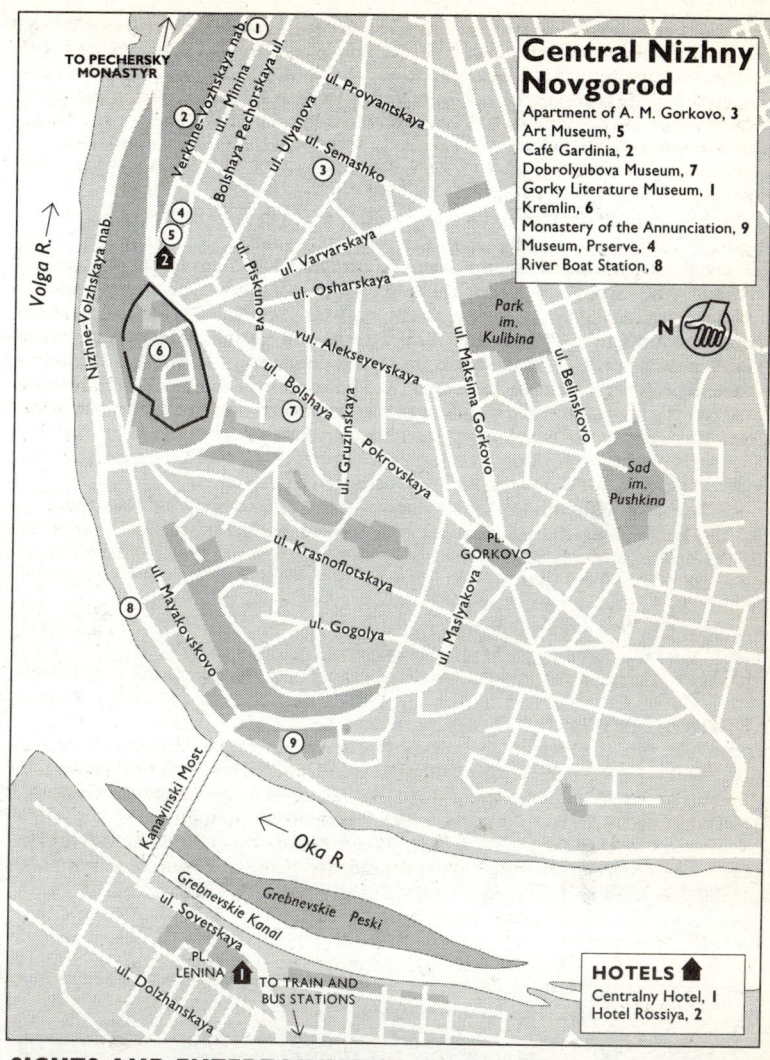

Central Nizhny Novgorod
Apartment of A. M. Gorkovo, 3
Art Museum, 5
Café Gardinia, 2
Dobrolyubova Museum, 7
Gorky Literature Museum, 1
Kremlin, 6
Monastery of the Annunciation, 9
Museum, Prserve, 4
River Boat Station, 8

HOTELS
Centralny Hotel, 1
Hotel Rossiya, 2

SIGHTS AND ENTERTAINMENT

Nizhny Novgorod's importance as a border town is most visible atop the **kremlin**. Resting upon one of Russia's few hills, the fortress surveys a vast expanse, making the town a perfect guard against the armies of Genghis Khan. Eight-meters-thick, the kremlin's walls still serve as a defense: the premises house a bank, the local governor and mayor's offices, and the 1631 **Archangel Cathedral** (Архангельский Собор; *Arkhangelsky Sobor*)—a museum of the city's history (open daily 10am-4pm; 8000R; closed for repair in summer 1996). The courtyard boasts an impressive collection of WWII-era tanks and other military vehicles. All can be climbed—pretend you're Patton. The governor's office was the site of an unwelcome visit from ultra-nationalist Vladimir Zhirinovsky in spring 1994; the local governor cleverly arranged to be out of town while Zhirinovsky sat in this office twiddling his thumbs. Since the current governor is Jewish, the chances of a return visit are slim.

The **Art Museum** (Художественный Музей; *Khudozhestvenny Muzey*) currently exhibits Russian art from the 15th-20th centuries in the kremlin while its home on Verkhne-Volzhskaya nab. awaits renovation. The works from before the 17th century, largely church art, are labeled in English as well as Russian. Art from the 18th-19th centuries includes portraits of tsars and other Russian VIPs; Russian artist Repin adds some color with, among other works, a vivid sketch of Ivan IV embracing the son after dealing his fatal blow. Russian peasants make a showing in Brueghelistic candor (open Wed.-Mon. 10am-5pm; 16,000R, students 8000R).

The best part of the **Gorky Literary Museum** (Литературной Музей им. А. М. Горького; *Literaturnoy Muzey imeni Gorkovo*), ul. Minina 26 (tel. 36 65 83), is the building housing it—a 19th-century mansion complete with mirrors, cherubs, velvet wallpaper, and carved dark wood. The inside supposedly shows the literary and cultural achievements of Gorky's contemporaries, with a sprinkling of his handwriting specimens. A photo of 19th-century Nizhny lends some historical perspective (open Wed.-Sun. 9am-5pm; 3000R; guided tours 2000R per person). To visit the **Museum-Apartment A. M. Gorkovo** (Квартира А. М. Горького; *Kvartira Gorkovo*), ul. Semashko 19 (Семашко; tel. 36 16 51), turn right off Verkhne-Volzhskaya nab., one street after Gostinitsa Oktyabrskaya, and keep walking for a couple of blocks; the museum is on the right. Gorky lived here for two years (1902-04). The apartment is under renovation in 1996 (open Fri.-Wed. 9am-1pm and 2-5pm).

The **Sakharov Museum** (Музей Сахарова; *Muzey Sakharova*), pr. Gagarina 214 (tel. 66 86 23), is reachable by trolley #13 from pl. Minina down pr. Gagarina to "Sakharov Museum" (about ½hr. from pl. Gorkovo). Cross the street, and it is a little to the right. The Nobel Laureate and physicist Andrei Dmitryevich Sakharov lived on the first floor of this typically Soviet apartment block while in internal exile. Guards watched him every moment; he was even forbidden to speak to people on the street (open Sat.-Thurs. 9am-5pm; 4000R; call to reserve English tours, 8000R).

There are two monasteries in Nizhny. The operational **Monastery of the Annunciation** (Благовещенский Мужской Монастырь; *Blagoveshchensky Muzhskoy Monastyr*), is located up the hill a short distance from where ul. Mayakovskovo ends and the bridge over the river begins. **Pechersky Monastyr** (Печерский Монастырь), on the lower banks of the Volga, is closed, but the crumbling building and overgrown foliage are refreshingly mind-numbing. Take bus #24 or 74 to "*avtovokzal*". Cross the street and walk all the way down the street directly across from the stop.

Museum-Preserve (Музей-Заповедник; *Muzey-Zapovednik*), Verkhne-Volzhskaya nab. 7, displays re-creations of pre-revolutionary Nizhny Novgorod apartments, including furniture and clothing, all housed in an attractive white stone building with statues carved into the façade (open Mon., Wed., and Sat.-Sun. 10am-5pm, Tues. 10am-10:30pm; closed for renovations in summer 1996). **Muzey na Dobrolyubova** (Музей на Добролюбова; tel. 34 22 49), ul. Lykova Damba 2 (Лыкова Дамба), off of Bolshaya Pakrovskaya, displays icons, porcelain, old money, and books (open Sat.-Wed. 9am-5pm; 3000R). **Katamaran Otdykh-1** (Катамаран Отдых-1), docked along

---

Watch Out for Grandma

They push harder than anyone on the buses and metro. They curse more frequently and fluently than Russian sailors. They bundle up to the ears on even the hottest days in scarves and winter coats, then strip down to teeny-weeny bikinis and sunbathe on the banks of the Neva. They are *babushki*, and they mean business. Technically, *babushka* means grandma, but under the Communist system, when everyone was family, Russians began using it as a generic term for elderly women. In any case, be warned: if a *babushka* gets on the metro, no matter how hearty she looks, and how weak and tired you feel, surrender your seat, or prepare for the verbal whooping of a lifetime.

---

the river, is a "boat for rest." Come by the river station around 6:30pm. The boat picks up not-so-sober Russians for a ride around the river (returns at 9:30pm).

■ Kazan (Казань)

Ivan the Terrible had such a hard time conquering the Khanate of Kazan, he had his top generals executed. Kazan eventually succumbed, and, in the following 400 years, the Tartar town was thoroughly Russified, becoming more famous for its university than for its dwindling Muslim population. Today the city is so typically Soviet that one would scarcely believe that Kazan is the capital of the autonomous Republic of Tatarstan, one of the more fractious regions of the Russian Federation. The predominantly Russian population is more concerned with surviving economic changes than with their leaders' separatist rhetoric.

ORIENTATION AND PRACTICAL INFORMATION

Kazan, a city of a little more than a million inhabitants, lies on the east bank of the **Volga** at the point where the river turns from east to south. Moscow is 700km to the west, Simbirsk 172km to the south. The city straddles the **Kazanka** (Казанка), which feeds into the Volga from the northeast. The streets of the old city on the south bank of the Kazanka splay out from the 16th-century **kremlin. Ul. Baumana** (Баумана), the main shopping street, links the kremlin with **pl. Kuibysheva** (Куйбышева), the city's commercial center. The only place you can buy a **map** of the city is in the lobby of Gostinitsa Tatarstan (Гостиница Татарстан), pl. Kuibysheva 2, for an extortionate 15,000R; be wary of its accuracy. To reach the center from the **train station**, catch tram #2 or 4 in front of the main building. From the **river station** (Речной вокзал; *Rechnoy vokzal*), take trolley #2 or tram #7.

- **Tourist Office: Intourist** (Интурист), ul. Baumana 9, 2nd fl. of hotel (tel. 32 41 95). Perpetuates the cycle of over-pricing. No maps, no free info—just tours for prices we aren't allowed to know for "commercial reason." Open Mon.-Fri. 9am-6pm.
- **Passport Office (OVIR):** ul. Gorodetskovo 1a, room 2 (Городецкого), around the corner from ul. Dzerzhinskovo (Дзержинского). The office is rumored to be moving soon. Stays longer than 2 days require registration. Open Tues. 10-11:30am.
- **Currency Exchange:** Spot an "Обмен Валюты" sign to change your US$ or DM. Cash only. Rates vary little, and there is generally no commission.
- **Flights:** The airport (tel. 37 98 07) lies southeast of the city and is accessible by taxi. Aeroflot flies to Russian cities, as well as to Tashkent in Uzbekistan.
- **Trains:** ul. Said-Galeeva (Саид-Галиева; tel. 39 23 00). Connections to Moscow (1 per day, 13hr., 96,000R), Nizhny Novgorod (1 per day, 12hr., 50,000R), Volgograd (1 per day, 37hr., 83,000R), and St. Petersburg (1 per day, 28hr., 110,000R). Buy all tickets on the 2nd floor, and check out the computerized info booths.
- **Public Transportation: Trams, trolleys,** and **buses** are cheap, frequent, and crowded. The faster the vehicle moves, the more packed it will be. You may be able to breathe on a tram. Tickets (600R) can be purchased in strips of 10 from the driver, or from light-blue kiosks at the stations and pl. Kuibysheva. Tickets are sometimes collected as you exit. Billboard maps of the tram and trolley routes are posted at the river station and in pl. Kuibysheva.
- **Taxis:** Many drivers are private citizens trying to make a few dollars. They habitually triple their rates for foreign passengers. Negotiate for 5000R per km.
- **Ferries:** ul. Portovaya (Портовая; tel. 37 97 00). Ferries (теплоходы; *teplokhody*) leave for Moscow (every other day, 83,000R-896,000R) and all points along the Volga. Cheap, fast **hydrofoils**—*rakety* (ракеты) and *meteory* (метеоры)—cover shorter routes at least once per day. Departures are often early in the morning.
- **Luggage Storage:** In the train station. Open 24hr. 6400R per day.
- **Post Office:** ul. Lenina 8 (Ленина). Use the hall on the left for **faxes** and letters (window #6). Open Mon.-Fri. 8am-8pm, Sat.-Sun. 9am-6pm. **Postal code:** 420111.
- **Telephones: Mezhdugorodny telefon** (Междугородный телефон), ul. Kuibysheva 17. Order international calls in advance. Open 24hr. **Phone code:** 8432.

ACCOMMODATIONS

The Tatarstan authorities have ruled that foreigners pay roughly 150% more than Tatars for hotel rooms. Don't take it personally: hoteliers will reassure you that Latvians, Lithuanians, Estonians, and Moldovans suffer the same fate. With a struggle, foreign students at Russian universities can pay the lower rate. Bring your student card and a letter from your institution. The best deal in town is with **Ida Pergishina** (tel. 37 41 55). For 50,000R, you can stay in one of her four rooms with bathroom and phone at ul. Kagalova 77 (Кагалова) on the tram #4 line about three stops from the center. Call her—she'll come and pick you up if you're not too far.

FOOD

There's a reason for the name "Steak Tartar." Red meat rules in Tatarstan, so the health-conscious must resign themselves to the **farmers' market** (колхозный рынок; *kolkhozny rynok*) on ul. Gabdully Tukaya (Габдуллы Тукая), one stop by tram #2, 4, or 7 from the end-stop at the train station, or three stops by tram #2 or 4 from pl. Kuibysheva in the direction of the train station. The bazaar covers all major food groups, including ketchup; arrive early and don't forget to haggle (open Tues.-Sun. 6am-6pm). **Groceries** can be found on ul. Baumana near pl. Kuibysheva.

- **Dom chaya** (Дом чая), ul. Baumana 64. Flowery cows, velvet cats, and outrageous tapestries of peasant life line the booths. A multi-course meal of local specialties costs 15,000R. Open daily 9am-8pm.
- **Restoran Kazan** (Ресторан Казань), ul. Baumana 9 (tel. 32 70 54). Black-faced lions with gold manes guard the entrance and set the tone. Moderately priced Soviet cuisine—bland and colorless, but it gets the job done. Entrées under 12,000R. A loud band spices up evening meals. Open daily 11am-5pm and 6-11pm.
- **Kafé Blinnaya** (Кафе Блинная), ul. Baumana 47. A vegetarian outpost with mosque drawings inside. *Bliny* with butter, honey, or sour cream for under 2000R, as well as fresh vegetable *salaty*. Open daily 7am-3pm and 4-8pm.

SIGHTS AND ENTERTAINMENT

To celebrate the destruction of the Mongol kremlin, Ivan the Terrible built the whitewashed one which now presides over Kazan. The main entrance at the end of ul. Lenina leads to government offices, which are closed to the public, and to the **Annunciation Cathedral** (Благовещенский Собор; *Blagoveschensky Sobor*), designed by Pskov masters in 1561, which now holds state archives. Across the square from the entrance to the kremlin, the **Tatarstan Museum**, Lenina 2 (tel. 32 09 84), displays an exhibit on the early history of Kazan, as well as local arts and crafts. Look out for the winking Satan against the back wall (open daily 10am-6pm; касса closes at 5pm; 3000R).

One block down ul. Lenina and downhill to the right, the 18th-century **Peter and Paul Cathedral** (Петропавловский Собор; *Petropavlovsky Sobor*) commemorates Peter the Great's 1722 visit to Kazan. Its Baroque octagonal central tower looks all the more colorful against the spare white walls of the nearby kremlin. The interior, featuring a 25m *iconostasis,* somehow survived decades of Bolshevik despoliation, including a brief stint as a pool hall, before being returned to the Orthodox Church in 1989. Pick up your copy of *"Popery and its Struggle against Orthodoxy"* on your way out, but leave quietly since this is a functional church—people will be praying (open daily 7am-noon and 3-7pm). A short walk further down ul. Lenina brings you to the campus of **Kazan State University.** A rare beardless statue of Lenin, easily recognizable by his trademark pout, honors the university's favorite expellee.

At one end is the pillared **Tatarstan Theater of Opera and Ballet** (tel. 38 46 08; box office open Tues.-Sat. 10am-7:30pm, Sun.-Mon. 3-7:30pm; 4 performances per week at 6 or 7pm; tickets 5000-15,000R). At the other end is the government of Tatarstan. Elsewhere in the city, two 200-year-old **mosques** stand on the banks of the first of three Kaban lakes along ul. Kayuma Nasyri (Каюма Насыри) but are closed to tourists. The **House of Culture** (Дом Культуры; *Dom Kultury;* tel. 32 63 28) exhibits war photographs at ul. Karla Marxa 26 (Карла Маркса). Security requires that you call in advance to see this "police museum." A large **park** sits on the shore of the Kazanka. The tall red-brick tower on ul. Baumana near pl. Kuibysheva, currently occupied by an eyeglass repair shop and two kiosks selling underwear and circus tickets, tops the **Revelation Church** (Церковь Богоявления; *Tserkov Bogoyavleniya*). Local believers are struggling to reclaim it from the city.

■ Simbirsk (Симбирск)

Twenty-five years ago, Soviet authorities threw their hearts, bulldozers, and concrete mixers into the construction of a memorial zone commemorating the birthplace of Vladimir Ilich Ulyanov, alias Lenin. What resulted was a monument to the man and the failed system. The town epitomizes Communist-era design: all gray concrete with a nuclear power plant spoiling an otherwise voluptuous view of the Volga. Unfortunately, after the town changed its name back from Ulyanovsk to Simbirsk, few visitors bother to make the pilgrimage to this Bethlehem of Bolshevism. The center sits on a hill above the west bank of the Volga to which **Ul. Goncharova** (Гончарова), the main shopping street, runs parallel. A short walk east from ul. Goncharova down any crossstreet takes you to the main Lenin sights. The first stop for Ulyanophiles is **Lenin's House** (Дом-музей Ленина; *Dom-muzey Lenina*), ul. Lenina 68 (tel. 31 22 22), next door to Ulyanovskturist (Ульяновсктурист). You will be asked to put on leather overshoes so as not to soil the holy ground. The carefully restored house holds a grand piano and other scandalous bourgeois touches (open Sun.-Mon. and Wed.-Fri. 9am-4:30pm; 5000R). Vladimir Ulyanov was actually born in a house on **100th Anniversary of Lenin's Birth Square** (100-летия со дня рождения В. И. Ленина; *sto letiya so dnya rozhdeniya Lenina*). The **birthplace** contains furniture typical of the period; the **room-museum** (квартира-музей; *kvartira-muzey*) is just a collection of family photographs. The surrounding concrete **Lenin Memorial** building (tel. 39 49 41) holds a concert hall and a rich collection of Bolshevik memorabilia, culminating in a glittering shrine to Ilich himself (open Tues.-Thurs. and Sat.-Sun. 9am-5pm, Fri. 9am-4pm; 1000R, students 500R). At the south end of the square, the **Classical Gymnasium,** Kommunisticheskaya 2 (Коммунистическая; tel. 31 28 68), graduated Vladimir Ulyanov, son of the regional school superintendent, at the top of his class. Note the glowing recommendation letter from the director of the school, whose son, Aleksandr Kerensky, went on to lead the Provisional Government after Lenin deposed him in October 1917 (open Tues.-Sat. 9am-5pm, Sun. 9am-4pm; 1000R, students 800R). The adjacent **Friendship of the Peoples Park** (Парк Дружбы Народов; *Park Druzhby Narodov*) was constructed by teams from each of the 15 Soviet republics.

Trains (tel. 37 07 03) chug to Moscow (3 per day, 17hr., 66,400R) and Volgograd (4 per week, 15 hr., 42,200R), but most tourists stop off during a **ferry** ride along the Volga. The dock is south of the center off ul. Kirova (Кирова; tel. 39 64 31). Take tram #1 or 4 from the center to the river station (речной вокзал; *rechnoy vokzal*), and walk down sp. Minaeva (Минаева) to the left of the tram. Trudge the main paved road for 15 minutes. The auxiliary building to the right sends *teplonody* (теплоходы) to Kazan (2 per day, 4½ hr., 45,600R), while the main building serves Moscow (every 2nd day, 4½ days, 120,000R) and Volgograd (every 2nd day, 2½ days, 99,000R). The sail from Simbirsk to Volgograd passes what some consider the Volga's most beautiful stretches. A short walk west along **ul. Lenina** takes you to **Ulyanovskturist** at #78 (tel. 32 64 12), which designed the tourist **map** of the city, but doesn't always have one to give away (open Mon.-Fri. 8am-4:30pm). **Inkombank** (Инкомбанк), Kuznetsova 5a (Кузнецова), accepts most traveler's checks (open Mon.-Fri. 9am-12:30pm and 1:30-5:30pm). The **post and telephone office** is on ul. Goncharova (Гончарова). **Postal code:** 432000. **Phone code:** 8442.

The town is best seen during a ferry stop, in large part because the government allows foreigners to stay only in select (expensive) hotels. **Intourist** (Интурист), Sovetskaya ul. 19 (Советская), rm. 304 (tel. 39 48 12; fax 31 97 35; open Mon-Fri 9am-

5pm), in **Gostinitsa Venets** (Гостиница Венец), offers singles (US$60). Take tram #4 from the rail and river stations. Try one of the **cafés** along ul. Goncharova and Karla Marxa (Карла Маркса). **Kafé Uyut** (Кафе Уют), ul. Karla Marxa 5, serves *pelmeni* (3000R) and pizzas (4000R) to local trendies (open daily 10am-7pm).

■ Volgograd (Волгоград)

Memories of World War II still haunt Volgograd. Here, in what was then Stalingrad, the remains of the Nazi Sixth Army surrendered to Soviet troops on January 31, 1943. But the 200-day battle that preceded had left 91% of Stalingrad in rubble and an estimated 1.8 million dead (1.5 million Russian). The center of Stalingrad was rebuilt with broad avenues, Neoclassical buildings, and countless monuments. But, as the diverse local population points out, the history of this sunny city didn't begin in 1943. Nearby lies a 200-year-old German colony, a Cossack settlement, and the medieval capital of the mysterious Khazar Empire sunk under a Soviet-era reservoir.

ORIENTATION AND PRACTICAL INFORMATION

The crescent-shaped Volgograd stretches around a bend in the Volga, 800km south of Simbirsk and 1000km southeast of Moscow. The **Volga-Don Canal,** which begins in Volgograd's southernmost part, links it with Rostov-na-Donu, 500km to the west, and with the Azov and Black Seas beyond. Most sights and hotels lie between the train and ferry stations. From the train station, head for the **Gostinitsa Intourist** (Гостиница Интурист) sign atop a large building. This hotel stands in central **pl. Pavshikh Bortsov,** and wide **alleya Geroev** leads from here to the river. The hill **Mamaev Kurgan**—102m tall according to military maps—rises several kilometers north. A kiosk in the basement of the train station sells city **maps.**

Tourist Office: The bureau (tel. 33 14 68) in **Gostinitsa Intourist,** ul. Mira 12 (Мира), carries no maps but has rousing brochure agents who help with trips. You might want to pretend that you'll be staying here. Open daily 9am-12:30pm and 1:30-6pm. Also in Gostinitsa Intourist is the **Valentina** (Валентина) travel agency (tel. 33 77 13), which arranges tours of the city for US$42, including car and driver (3hr.). Open Mon.-Fri. 9am-noon and 2-6pm.

Passport Office (OVIR): Registration is required for stays of longer than 3 days, but enforcement is spotty. Gostinitsa Intourist registers you automatically.

Currency Exchange: 1st floor of Gostinitsa Intourist. Open daily 9am-1pm and 2-8pm. 2½th floor of the **TSUM** store. Open Mon.-Sat. 9:30am-1pm and 2-5:30pm. Get Visa cash advances and exchange AmEx, Thomas Cook, and Visa traveler's checks for 2% commission at **Inkombank** (Инкомбанк), ul. Barrikagy 39 (Баррикагы). Take trolleybus #8 to pl. Titova (Титова), go uphill, and then right.

Flights: The airport is 35min. west of the city center (tel. 31 73 78). **Volga** (Волга), ul. Istoricheskaya (Историческая; tel. 39 62 26). Take trolleybus #7 or 10 to "Агентство Воздушных Сообщений". To: Moscow (2 per day, 2hr., 453,000R), Rostov-na-Donu (3-5 per week, 1½hr., 270,000R), Sochi (5 per week, 2hr., 500,000R), and other Russian cities. Open daily 8am-1pm and 2-7pm.

Trains: Volgograd-1 (tel. 005), northwest of pl. Pavshikh Bortsov. To: Astrakhan (2-3 per day, 13hr.); Moscow (2-3 per day, 20hr., 139,000R); Rostov-na-Donu (trains fill up fast; 2 per day, 13 hr., 123,000R).

Buses: Avtovokzal Tsentralny (Автовокзал Центральный), ul. Rokosovskovo 44 (Роковского; tel. 37 62 61). Cross the tracks behind the train station, and take a right onto the first road on the other side. To: Astrakhan (1 per day, 10hr., 88,400R); Rostov-na-Donu (4 per day, 12hr., 71,870R).

Ferries: Rechnoi vokzal (Речной вокзал), nab. 62-y Armii (tel. 44 52 09), near the foot of the steps at the end of alleya Geroev. Hard class is a bed in a quad on the lower deck; 2nd class a bunk-bed double on the middle deck; and 1st class a double with a basin, and a shower off the hall. Boats every other day to: Moscow (1 week; hard class 133,000R, 1st class 603,000R) and Nizhny Novgorod (5 days; hard class 98,000R, 1st class 447,000R). Hour-long boat rides (3500R) leave from near the river station on summer afternoons. On weekends, annoy local fishermen on the one-hour disco cruise (5000R). Ticket office open daily 8am-5pm.

Central Volgograd

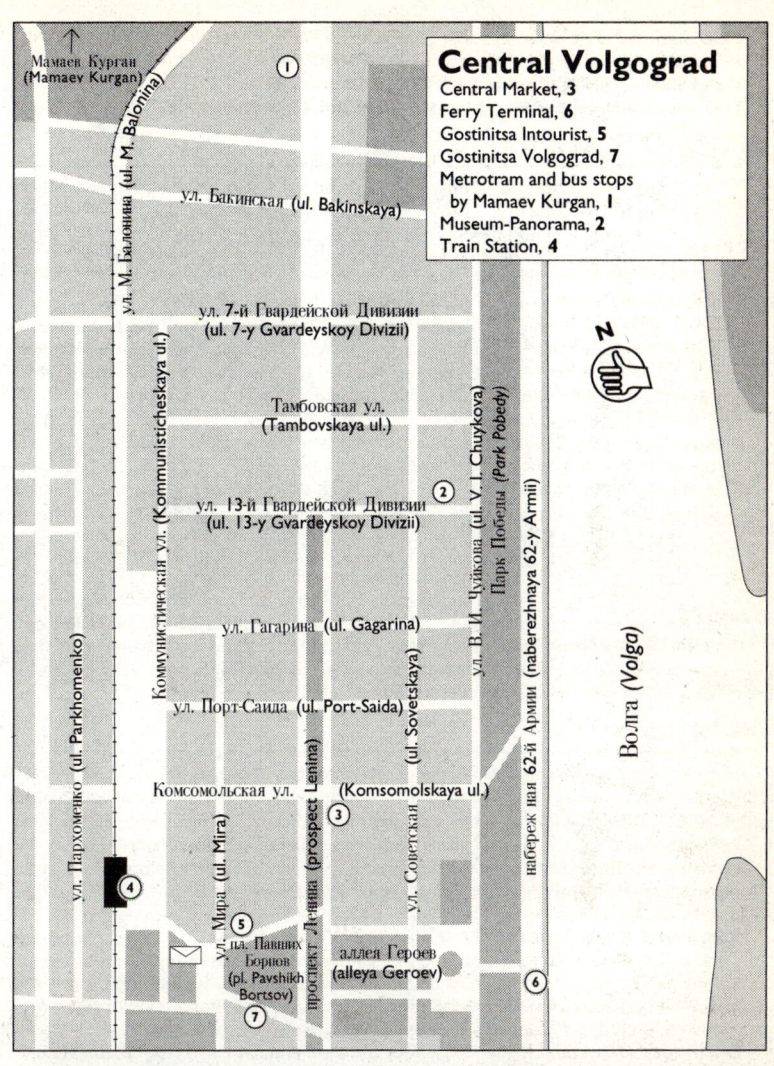

- Central Market, **3**
- Ferry Terminal, **6**
- Gostinitsa Intourist, **5**
- Gostinitsa Volgograd, **7**
- Metrotram and bus stops by Mamaev Kurgan, **1**
- Museum-Panorama, **2**
- Train Station, **4**

Public Transportation: The **metrotram** (метротрам) runs north from the center along pr. Lenina. It travels underground in the center but otherwise resembles a tram. Tickets (1000R) are sold at kiosks by the stops above ground and at ticket counters underground. The stop closest to alleya Geroev is "Комсомольская" (Komsomolskaya). **Buses** link the train station with the city's south and west regions. A ride costs 800R, but you have to find someone to pay first. The metrotram and buses supposedly run 'til midnight, but are scarce after 10pm.

Luggage Storage: Kamera khraneniya (Камера хранения), in the basement of the train station. 6400R per day. Open 8am-6:30pm, 7pm-7:30am. In the basement of the **ferry station** (1200R; open Tues.-Sat. 8am-1pm and 2-5pm); after hours, you can retrieve your bags by pestering the on-duty administrator in room 107.

Pharmacy: Apteka (Аптека), alleya Geroev 5 (tel. 36 19 75). Open daily 8am-8pm.

Post Office: pl. Pavshikh Bortsov (tel. 36 10 78), opposite Gostinitsa Intourist. Open Mon.-Fri. 8am-8pm, Sat.-Sun. 8am-6pm. Postcards show a sign above that used to read "V. I. Lenin's ideas are alive and will triumph." **Poste Restante** window #11. Telephone desk open daily 9am-9pm. **Postal code:** 400066.

Telephones: Phones take *zhetony* (жетоны; tokens), sold at the post office (400R). To make a long distance call or send a fax, go to **Mezhdugorodny telefon** (Междугородный телефон), ul. Mira 16 (tel. 32 78 10). Calls to the U.S. cost 24,500R per minute. Open 24hr., desk open daily 8am-7pm. **Phone code:** 8422.

ACCOMMODATIONS

Despite a large student community, Volgograd does not offer much in the way of accommodations for potential visitors. The presence of universities means that you can throw yourself at their students' mercy and pray for a room. If you make someone feel bad enough, they might send you to someone else who will give you a bed.

Volgograd State Pedagogical University Dormitory, pr. Lenina 78a. If you call Prorector Bolotov (tel. 36 64 59) ahead of time or catch him during the daytime at pr. Lenina 27, room 2-21, he might find you a room. If you miss him, take trolleybus #8 or 12 three stops past the university to Mamaev Kurgan. Take a right onto the drive headed toward the river, on the left of a huge vacant lot. Walk past the building adorned with a hammer-and-sickle to the one with balconies. The door with the black plastic sign "ОБЩЕЖИТИЕ" is the one you want. Talk to Nataliya Vasilevna on the 2nd floor. Singles with shower and hot water 50,000R.

Gostinitsa Volgograd, ul. Mira 12 (tel. 36 17 72; fax 33 99 24). Clean and central. If security lets you in the building, the front desk will reluctantly let you see a room with toilet and shower. Singles 287,500R. Doubles 387,500R.

Gostinitsa Intourist, ul. Mira 14 (tel. 36 45 53; fax 33 91 75), in pl. Pavshikh Bortsov. An unusually worthwhile Intourist hotel owned by its employees, who fully intend to bring the service up to world standards. The rooms are clean, the staff polite, and the hot water almost reliable. When the hotel is not crowded, a place in a double (MEST-o vdvookh-MEST-nom NOM-ere) can effectively be a half-price single. Singles US$36, US$65 with shower. Doubles US$50, US$80 with shower. AmEx, Diner's Club, MC, and Visa accepted.

FOOD

The **central market** (центральный рынок; *tsentralny rynok*), Sovetskaya ul. 17, has entrances on Komsomolskaya ul. and pr. Lenina, behind the Central Bank (open in summer Mon. 7am-4pm, Tues.-Sat. 7am-7pm, Sun. 7am-5pm; off-season Mon. 7am-4pm, Tues.-Sat. 7am-6pm, Sun. 7am-5pm). **Cafés** serving alcohol, coffee, and ice cream, abound near alleya Geroev on pr. Lenina and ul. Chuykova. Fish is the local specialty, but eateries serve mostly meat and spuds.

Kafé Mayak (Кафе Маяк), ul. 62 Armiya 1 (62 Армия; tel. 36 36 36), south of the river station in a short but conspicuous lighthouse. Outside seating looks upon the Volga. The interior is elegantly decorated, but the menu is limited. *Salat* 7,250-16,900R. Entrées 20,000-30,000R. Seafood *shashliks* 44,000-68,000R. Open daily noon-midnight. A band plays after 8pm every Tues.-Sun. evening.

Dormitory Cafe, pr. Lenina 78a, under the Pedagogical University dorm. Hoagies and grinders, Hoagies and grinders, navy beans, navy beans, meatloaf sandwich...welcome to lunchlady land. Meal 14000R. Open daily 8am-9pm.

U drakona (У дракона), pr. Lenina 12 (tel. 36 78 94). Squeezed between a café and a casino near alleya Geroev. Supposed to be a Chinese restaurant, but with the overdone purple-palace decor, the band, and the waitresses in tight, shimmering white blouses and short black skirts, you'd think they only served cheese. Entrées 10,000-34,000R. Open daily noon-4pm and 6pm-midnight.

SIGHTS

Despite a lack of stone Stalins, the grandeur of the monuments ensures that this city still is, and will remain for years to come, Stalingrad. Although some obelisks chronicle old Stalingrad's utter destruction, others glorify the good old days when the red Russians beat the snot out of those nasty ol' Nazis.

Mamaev Kurgan's strategic peak changed hands 13 times in the course of the battle, and the earth became so clogged with shrapnel that for two years nothing would grow on the mound. Today, trees dedicated to individual soldiers cover the slopes. The stairs to the peak crawl with graffiti shouting the Party's own slogans, like Stalin's murderous dictum "Ни шаг назад!" (Not a step back!). Farther up, statues of stoic Soviets carrying their wounded allow for no Communist rhetoric. Towering above all this, the 52m-tall **Motherland** (Мать Родина; *Mat Rodina*) wields her sword, calling troops into battle. Metrotram runs here, as do buses #8, 9, 12, and 13.

In contrast to the memorial complex, the dramatic **Muzey-Panorama** (Музей-Панорама), ul. Chuykova 2 (tel. 34 67 23), on the riverfront, is pure Soviet kitsch. The museum presents a blow-by-blow account of the Soviet counterattack, including photographs, uniforms, guns, and Communist Party membership cards retrieved from the dead. Supposedly the scene from the top of Mamaev Kurgan during one crucial day's fighting, the panorama is a polemic against Western historians who downplayed the Red Army's role in the defeat of Nazism. The painting is a bit overdone even by the lax standards of Socialist Realism, although the tour guides don't seem to care (open Tues.-Sun. 10am-5pm, closed last Fri. of each month; 5000R).

A gutted **mill,** preserved to show wartime destruction, crumble by the Muzey-Panorama. Across the street stand the remains of **Pavlov's House** (Дом Павлова; *Dom Pavlova*), where Sgt. Yakov Pavlov and 23 soldiers held out for 58 days against ceaseless German attacks. A nearby plaque promises a memorial for victims of political repression; one wonders if it will match the war monuments in size.

Southwest of the center lies the eerie **Bald Mountain** (Лысая Гора; *Lysaya Gora*), the scene of particularly fierce fighting where construction workers, collectors, and local children to this day find unexploded shells and mines. Farther south is **Sarepta,** a colony of Germans that dates back to the time of Catherine the Great. The **Museum of Old Sarepta** chronicles the history of the local community. Near the south edge of the city is the mouth of the **Volga-Don Canal,** guarded by a dapper Lenin on one side and a bare pedestal where Stalin once stood on the other. Near the triumphal arch of the canal's first lock, local teenagers jeer and spit at passing cruise ships. Those nostalgic for Five Year Plans can admire the city's industrial megaliths on hour-long **boat rides,** which include a close-up view of the massive hydroelectric power plant north of the city, and the sea resulting from it. Card-carrying Stalinists schmooze in the **Museums of the Metallurgical, Tractor, and Turbine Factories,** celebrating their wartime experiences and industrial achievements.

The city also has the inevitable **fine arts museum,** pr. Lenina 21 (tel. 36 39 06; open Thurs.-Tues. 10am-5:30pm; 3000R); a **railroad museum;** an **ethnographic museum,** pr. Lenina 7 (tel. 33 81 45; open Wed.-Mon. 10am-5pm; 2000R); a **museum of musical instruments,** ul. Bistrova 257 (Бистрова; tel. 42 10 56); and a **Cossack Museum** at Stanitsa Ilovlya, two hours by bus from the center (open by request; the tourist office can arrange a trip there).

ENTERTAINMENT

Volgograd youths get drunk in the shade of Mamaev Kurgan and other monuments. A park extends down alleya Geroev to the river, where couples stroll in the evening. The Stadium, one stop before Mamaev Kurgan, hosts Russia's top-league **soccer** team; game announcements are posted outside. **The New Experimental Theater (NET),** pl. Pavshikh Bortsov, boasts an internationally-known troop (*kassa* open Wed.-Sun. 2pm-7pm; tickets 90,000-130,000R). The marble-pillared **Planetarium,** ul. Gagarina 14 (tel. 36 41 84), has astronomy for children and astrology for adults, as well as films on Stalingrad's reconstruction (shows Tues.-Sat. 10am, noon, 2, and 4pm; 6000R). The **Puppet Theater** (Театр Кукол; *Teatr Kukol*), pr. Lenina 15 (tel. 33 06 49), stages performances (shows Sat.-Sun. 11am; 3500R; *kassa* open Tues.-Fri. 11:30am-2pm and 3-6pm, Sat.-Sun. 10am-1:30pm and 2:30-5pm). Stop at the big top, **Volgograd Circus** (Волгоград Цирк; *Volgograd Tserk*), ul. Krasnoznamensk (Краснознаменск; tel. 36 31 06; daily shows). Countless movie theaters show dubbed American movies. To reach the **beach** on the vast Volga's other side, take a quick ferry to

Krasnoslobodsk (Краснослободск) from terminal #12 at the river station (1 per hr. 6am-10:30pm, 12min., 2000R).

■ Rostov-na-Donu (Ростов-на-Дону)

For millennia, European merchants traveled to the mouth of the Don to trade with the tribes of south Russia's plains. In 1749, the Tsarist government decided to cash in on such commerce by establishing a customs post on the site of modern Rostov. Commerce and agriculture have attracted communities of Armenians, Greeks, and, most recently, Koreans to the area. The Chechen Communists moved out after losing a gunfight to the Russian mafia, but ethnic tensions remain.

ORIENTATION AND PRACTICAL INFORMATION

Rostov-na-Donu rises over the north bank of the Don, 1000km south of Moscow and 400km southwest of Volgograd. Thirty-five km west of Rostov, the Don feeds into the Taganrog Bay and the Azov Sea. Rostovskaya Oblast (Region) shares a long border with Ukraine, whose east edge is directly north of Rostov. The main street of the city's central grid, **ul. Bolshaya Sadovaya** (Большая Садовая; formerly and more commonly known as ul. Engelsa), starts at the **suburban train station** and parallels the river to the **Park of the October Revolution.** Rostov's quieter east region was, until 1928, the separate Armenian city of Nakhichevan-na-Donu. It still has a large Armenian community and several active Armenian Orthodox churches. The other main street, **Budennovsky pr.,** starts at the **river port,** climbs past the **Central Market** and across ul. Bolshaya Sadovaya. From the **train station,** take bus #7, 12, 62, or 80, or tram #9 or 22 up ul. Bolshaya Sadovaya to get to the tourist offices.

- **Tourist Offices:** The service bureau of **Gostinitsa Intourist,** Bolshaya Sadovaya 115 (tel. 65 90 66; fax 65 90 07), is willing to help you even if you're not staying at the hotel. They organize group and individual tours and sell brochures for 3000-10,000R. Open daily 8am-8pm. The tourist division of **Rostov State University,** Bolshaya Sadovaya 105, room 514 (tel. 64 87 00; fax 64 52 55), has maps and is used to dealing with young travelers. Open Mon.-Fri. 10am-5pm.
- **Passport Office (OVIR):** ul. Obarony 8 (Абароны; tel. 39 23 70). The officials don't speak English, so bring a local along if possible. Registration in Rostov is not compulsory if you have registered elsewhere in Russia, but some hotels appear to be unaware of this fact. Gostinitsas Intourist, Rostov, and Tourist register you automatically. Open Wed. 11am-noon. Arrive early, and take a place in line.
- **Currency Exchange: Gostinitsa Intourist** (see above) has a 24-hr. exchange bureau which cashes AmEx and Thomas Cook traveler's checks, and gives Visa cash advances at a 2% commission. A Visa **ATM** is in the lobby.
- **Flights:** The airport (tel. 54 88 01) is east of the town center. Conspicuously invisible on Soviet tourist maps, it's the large empty space next to Gostinitsa Aeroflot. **Aeroflot** flies to: Moscow-Vnuknovo (3 per day, 480,000R); Odesa (1 per week, 450,000R); Volgograd (3 per week, 250,000R). From the train station and ul. Bolshaya Sadovaya, take bus #7, express bus #62 or 93, or trolley #9. The Aeroflot **ticket office,** Sotsyalisticheskaya ul. 146 (Социалистическая; tel. 65 71 15), is open for foreigners Mon.-Sat. 8am-1pm and 2-5pm.
- **Trains: Glavny zheleznodorozhny vokzal,** pl. Pervoy Russkoy Revolyutsii 1905 goda 1/2 (Первой Русской Революции 1905-ого года; tel. 67 02 10). From the Central Market, take tram #1 to the line's end (heading right as you face the market). To: Moscow (even dates, 25-29hr., 168,000R). Make sure you get a train through Aiski (Аиски), because border officials will gladly send you back to Rostov if you don't have a Ukraine transit visa. To: Kiev (even dates, 23hr., 145,000R); Sochi (5-6 per day, 13-15hr., 85,000R); Volgograd (1 per day, 13hr., 67,000R). **Prigorodny vokzal** (tel. 38 36 00), a short walk from the main station, houses an info bureau on the 2nd floor and sends *elektrichki* (commuter trains) to nearby villages.
- **Buses:** pr. Siversa 1 (Сиверса; tel. 32 32 83), opposite the trains. To: Azov (every 20min., 1 hr., 3500R); Volgograd (4 per day, 10-12hr., 72,000R). Around Rostov,

ROSTOV-NA-DONU ■ 585

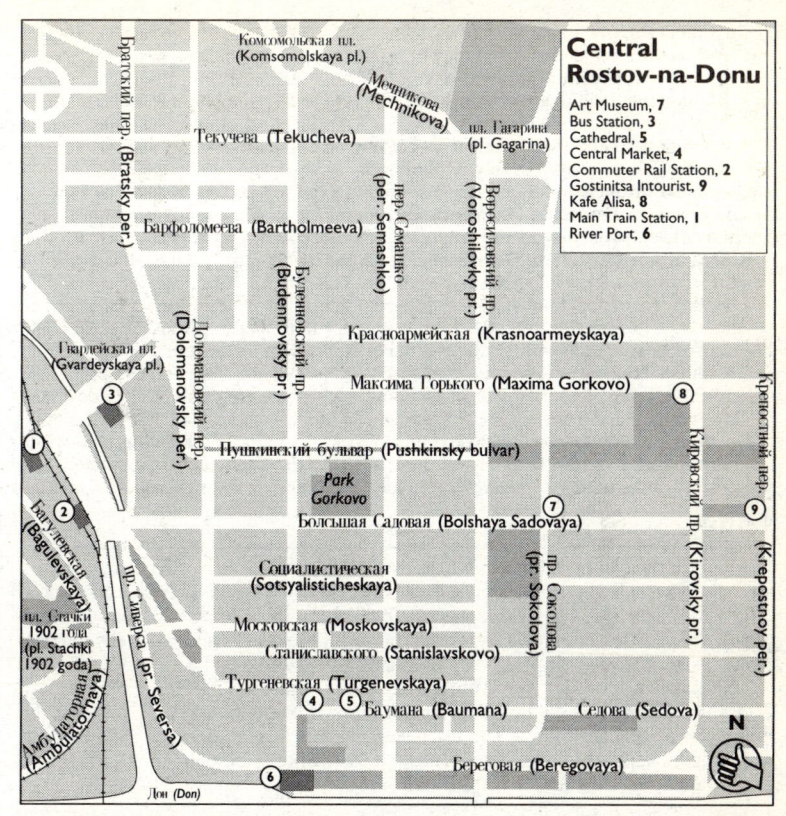

Central Rostov-na-Donu

Art Museum, 7
Bus Station, 3
Cathedral, 5
Central Market, 4
Commuter Rail Station, 2
Gostinitsa Intourist, 9
Kafe Alisa, 8
Main Train Station, 1
River Port, 6

buses are faster than the trains, and they tend to sell more tickets than there are seats. Get on the bus early and stake your claim.

Public Transportation: Trams, trolleys, buses (800R), and **express buses** (1200-1500R) run daily roughly 5am-1am, but get spotty on the outskirts at 8pm, and in the center after 11pm. The comfortable express buses, imported from Germany and Sweden, stop on request only. One-month tram and trolley pass 40,000R.

Ferries: Beregovaya ul. 10, at the foot of Budennovsky pr. **Cruise ships** bound for Volgograd (38hr.) and Moscow (9 days) leave every week. **Hydrofoils** zoom over the river to Starocherkassk (40min.) and Taganrog.

Luggage Storage: In the train station (6400R). Open daily 2am-1:10am. In the bus station (2500R per day). Open 4am-noon, 12:30-5pm, 5:30pm-2am.

Pharmacy: Apteka, Buddenovsky pr. 41 (tel. 66 63 97). Open Mon.-Sat. 8am-7pm, Sun. 10am-5pm.

Post Office: Pochtamt, Soborny per. 24 (Соборный; tel. 66 72 09). From the Central Market, walk away from the train station, and go left at the Russian Orthodox church. Open Mon.-Sat. 7:30am-7:30pm. **Postal Code:** 344007.

Telephones: Pay phones take 10R coins, which are, thus in desperately short supply. Make international calls from **Mezhdugorodny Telefon** (Междугородный Телефон), pl. Lenina 99, adjacent to the Gostinitsa Tourist. Open daily 8am-10pm. Token-operated phones in the train station, in Gostinitsa Rostov's lobby, and at Voroshilovsky pr. 77, serve domestic long-distance calls. **Phone Code:** 8632.

ACCOMMODATIONS AND CAMPING

The budget hotels in Rostov direct foreigners to the more expensive tourist hotels. The presence of several universities and institutes in the area means you can try to arrange something in advance or with someone nice you meet on the train.

Gostinitsa Rostov, Budennovsky pr. 59 (tel. 39 16 66). Take bus #6 or 58 two stops after the Central Market. Until they bring their prices up to those of the other tourist hotels, this central hot-bed of fun will be a viable option. Rooms are clean, although the toilet might not flush, and the refrigerator might not refrigerate. Bring toilet paper. Singles with cold shower, TV, fridge, and phone 102,000R. Similar doubles 192,000R. Don't panic if they take your documents—they just want to register you. Go to room 119 to get them back.

Gostinitsa Intourist, ul. Bolshaya Sadovaya 115 (tel. 65 90 65). Wicked nice place, with service bureau and **currency exchange,** but singles with TV, phone, toilet and cold shower run US$50. AmEx, MC, Visa accepted. Visa **ATM.**

Rostov State University Dormitory, ul. Zorga 28 (Зорга). Contact Prorector for International Relations, Nikolai Pelikhov (tel. 22 68 36; fax 24 43 11; e-mail rec@rsu.rostov-na-donu.su, attn.: international relations division) well ahead of time. A ½-hr. bus ride (#71, 71, 26, or express #4b to "Зорга") from the center, and not so cheap. Foreigners 75,000R, Russian skills might lower it to 25,000R.

Gostinitsa Tourist, pr. Oktyabra 19 (Октября; tel. 32 43 09). Take tram #13 ten stops from the trains. Rooms are clean and new, bathrooms are clean but not new. Singles with cold shower, phone, TV, fridge 170,000R. Doubles 340,000R.

Gostinitsa Moskovskaya, ul. Boshaya Sadovaya, in a grand old building with white plasterwork exterior. Bizarrely informal hotel on the 2nd floor lets absolutely cavernous vaults with TV and shower. Singles 140,000R, doubles 152,000R.

FOOD

Rostov is at the center of Russia's wheat-growing region, so it's worth tasting the local bread—especially the pastries on sale at street stands along **ul. Bolshaya Sadovaya.** The wine cellar, **Sun in a Wineglass** (Солнце в бокале; *Solntse v bokale*), Budennovsky pr. 25 (tel. 66 45 51), on the corner of ul. Bolshaya Sadovaya, sells regional wines— *sapfir gona* (сапфир гона) and *igristoe gonskoe* (игристое гонское); each 18,000R; open Mon.-Sat. 9am-1pm and 2-7pm). Numerous cafés line ul. Bolshaya Sadovaya and Pushkinsky bul. The **central market,** Budennovsky pr. 18, sits at the corner of ul. Stanislavskovo. The usual staples, plus Korean noodles and fresh fish (open April-Sept. Mon. 6am-1pm, Tues.-Sat. 6am-8pm, Sun. 6am-5pm; Oct.-March Mon. 7am-1pm, Tues.-Sat. 7am-7pm, Sun. 7am-5pm).

Kafe Valentina (Кафе Валентина), Budennovsky pr. 68 (tel. 34 65 66). Near Gostinitsa Rostov. High-backed seats allow you to make covert deals with your shady friends. Good, inexpensive entrées 10,000R-15,000R. Open daily 11am-11pm.

Lilia, ul. Mechnikova 75a, off Budennovsky pr., 4 tram stops north of ul. Bolshaya Sadovaya. An emotional experience for those who have forgotten the taste of seasoned food. Courteous if slow service. Entrées 15,000-30,000R. Open Mon.-Fri. noon-4pm and 5-11pm, Sat.-Sun. 4-11pm.

Kafe Randevu (Кафе Рандеву), ul. Bolshaya Sadovaya 53. A popular streetside spot to sit and sip a beverage in the afternoon shade of an unfortunate concrete block. Open daily 11am-11pm, indoor section open until midnight.

Kafe Stary Fontan (Кафе Старый Фонтан), in a particularly precious part of Park Gorkovo. Weeping willows part to reveal a fountain, pool, and garden humming with distant jazz. Unremarkable entrées 14,000-23,000R. Open daily 2pm-1am.

SIGHTS AND ENTERTAINMENT

Rostov itself does not have a lot to offer the visitor. The 1860 **Cathedral of the Birth of the Holy Mother of God,** next to the Central Market on ul. Stanislavskovo, is a startling sanctuary of peace amid the frenzied clamor of a transitional economy (open daily 7am-7pm). To reach the 1783 Armenian Orthodox **Surb-Khach,** ul. Myasnikyana (Мясникяна), now bizarrely stranded amid a bowl of Soviet-style apartment blocks, take express bus #77 from the central market to "Космонофт". It's the isolated green dome up the hill to the right. The **museum** inside has artifacts and writings in Russian and Armenian, with one panel of English explanation (open Tues.-Sun. 10am-7pm). The awkwardly symbolic memorial at **Snake Hollow** (Змейская Балка; *Zmeyskaya Balka*), in the northwest of the city, memorializes the spot where 27,000 citizens of Rostov were shot by the occupying Nazis. Surprisingly, there is no mention throughout the entire monument that more than half of those killed were Jewish. The lady in a strange position is Motherland summoning her strength to protect her child, and the guy in cuffs is a Red Army soldier. Take bus #6 from the Central Market; get off after you see the kooky lady to your left. Come between 10am-5pm for Tchaikovsky's 6th and a shoddy museum.

Locals stroll in **Park Gorkovo,** on Bolshaya Sadovaya near Budennovsky pr. Old guys match wits and trash-talking insults at the chess tables. Deeper in, shirtless youths battle at ping-pong while their grandparents swing to live jazz on the nearby dance floor. At the center, an **amusement park** spins and twirls (swings 2000R, bumper cars 3000R; open Tues.-Sun. 10am-10pm). On summer evenings, free open-air jazz and classical **concerts** take place 5-8pm, followed by a nightly **disco**. Don't miss the mosaics in the underpasses depicting idyllic Soviet life.

■ Near Rostov-na-Donu

STAROCHERKASSK (СТАРОЧЕРКАССК)

Cherkassk—now **Starocherkassk**—was the capital of the Don Cossacks from 1644 to 1806, during which time it played a role in nearly all of Imperial Russia's major peasant uprisings. Pushkin's visit here inspired *The Captain's Daughter* and a several-volume history of the Pugachev rebellion. Now a pleasantly stagnant *stanitsa* (farming village) on an island upstream of Rostov, its center has been preserved as a **museum of Cossack life and history** (open daily 9am-5pm). Bring your own lunch.

The older houses are constructed in typical Cossack style, with high cellars to protect the residents from the annual floods and meter-thick walls to defend against less frequent human attacks. The active nine-cupola **Resurrection Cathedral** (Воскресенщкий Собор; *Voskresnsky Sobor*) dates from 1706, and contains biblical frescos which are incomprehensible in parts due to age and neglect. By the cathedral's doors hang the chains with which authorities dragged legendary **Stepan Razin,** most famous of Russia's Cossack rebels, to Moscow to be executed in 1671. After the suppression of Razin's revolt, the previously independent Cossacks were made to pay homage to the tsar (open Thurs.-Tues.). In front of the cathedral lie the gateposts and weighing scales from the marketplace of Azov, trophies of the Cossack occupation from 1637 to 1644. Nearby stands the house where **Kondratii Bulavin,** another rebel leader, was murdered by treacherous Cossacks in 1708. His body—minus head and hands—was subsequently displayed in Azov as a warning to would-be revolutionaries. About 7km from the center are the ruins of the star-shaped **Petrine fort.** On the last Sunday of every summer month, the village holds a **festival of Cossack song and dance.** In Rostov, **buses** for Starocherkassk leave solely from the old bus station (tel. 51 08 67; take tram #1 or bus #1 or 9 to "старого автовокзал").

NOVOCHERKASSK (НОВОЧЕРКАССК)

Novocherkassk became the Cossacks' capital in 1806, after they gave up attempts to protect Cherkassk from flooding. Strategically located on a hill between the Aksai and Tuzlov Rivers, the city overlooks the surrounding steppe, and continues to house Cossacks and a large contingent of Russian troops. During World War II, the Nazis left the city largely intact in recognition of anti-Soviet collaboration. From the bus station, walk out and cross the street. Soviet propaganda, including the classic novel *And Quiet Flows the Don* by Mikhail Sholokhov, portrayed Cossacks as active supporters of the Bolshevik Revolution, but in fact Novocherkassk was one of the centers of White counter-revolutionary opposition during the Civil War. Bus #1 will take you to the **Ascension Cathedral** (Вознесенский Кафедральны собор; *Voznesenskii Cafedralny Sobor*), in the cobblestone pl. Yermaka (Ермака), Russia's third largest cathedral. Envisioned by the ataman Matvey Platov as a Russian version of St. Peter's in Rome, the cathedral ended up taking a century to build because the cupolas kept falling down. Now the cathedral is in a dismal state of disrepair. Inside are monuments to Cossack heroes in the defeat of Napoleon.

Next to the cathedral in pl. Yermaka is a **statue of Yermak Timofeevich,** who conquered Siberia for the tsar in the late 16th century. The original design of the monument had the tsarist two-headed eagle at Yermak's feet, but the authorities in St. Petersburg worried that the Cossacks might get the wrong idea and ordered the eagle removed. Apparently, the Cossacks got the idea anyhow, and the better part of the **Museum of the History of the Don Cossacks** (Музей Истории Донсково Казачевства; *Muzey Istorii Donskovo Kazachestva*), down pr. Platova (Платова) from the cathedral, celebrates the Cossacks' revolting ways. The bronze statue of an austere Stepan Razin, who was by all accounts a bad-ass, begins a collection of dangerously accessible chain armors, shields, and swords. "I came to give you freedom," said the rebel Razin. At each display, Marx and Lenin express their admiration for the Cossacks' resolve to fight for liberty. In the opposite room, the tsars are good guys again, as the feats of the Cossacks in wars with Napoleon are given their due. The museum also contains archaeological finds from Tanais. (Open Tues.-Sun. 10am-5pm; 1000R if you avoid the 800% tariff on foreigners; call (252) 241 14 in advance for a 30,000R group tour in English.) **Buses** (11 per day, 1hr., 6000R) and *electrichki* (9 per day, 1½hr., 2400R) connect the town to Rostov. Sit on the train's right side for views of the Don Steppe.

TANAIS (ТАНАИС)

Tanais is a **museum** and **archeological dig** at the site of a 2000-year-old Greek colony. Founded in the 3rd century BCE, the colony grew into a major trading center between Greeks and the nomadic steppe tribes. In return for olive oil, wine, cloth, and pottery, the Greeks bought fish, wheat, cattle, wool, and slaves. The city was destroyed and rebuilt several times before its abandonment in the 4th century CE.

Archaeologists took interest in the **ruins** over 170 years ago, initially sending most important finds to museums in Moscow and St. Petersburg. Systematic excavations began in 1955; every summer since, students from Moscow and Vladimir have come to work on the dig, enduring the scorching sun and Neolithic living conditions. Only a fraction of the city has been uncovered, but archeologists have already learned much about life and commerce in the city from the wealth of inscriptions, pottery, ornaments, and human remains they have unearthed. The on-site **museum** displays finds from the last 40 years, including elegant amphorae from the Mediterranean, statuettes of Greek gods, bronze oil-lamps, glass vials, and a pair of ancient handcuffs. A couple of the ancient buildings have been reconstructed to aid the imagination, but otherwise the original walls and foundations speak for themselves (closed off-season). *Electrichki* run from Rostov (11 per day, 1hr., 1600R). Sit on the left on the way there for an impressive view of the Don delta.

TAGANROG (ТАГАНРОГ)

Boasting a remarkable number of midday drunks and a vigilant militia, Taganrog is noteworthy if only because its most conspicuous monuments are not devoted to Communists. Instead, the birthplace of Anton Chekhov devotes its myths to the great playwright and master of the short story. The trip around Chekhov's haunts is easy. Climb the steps from the railroad station to Peter I, cross the street, and walk down ul. Chekhova (Чехова) to **Domik Chekhova,** ul. Chekhova 69, where Chekhov was born in 1860 (open Tues.-Sun. 10am-5pm). From here, walk out, take a right, a left, and another left (exactly a half-block), take the tram to "Спартовский" (pay the conductor or the driver) and walk to the end of the block. The **Literary Museum,** ul. Oktyabrskaya 9 (Октябрьская), up the steps in the gymnasium where Chekhov studied, contains reconstructed classrooms and a large collection of manuscripts, letters, journals, and early editions of Chekhov's works, interspersed with choice quotes from those literati, Lenin and Marx (open Tues.-Sun. 10am-5pm). **Lavka Chekovykh** (Лавка Чеховых), ul. Sverdlova 100 (Свердлова), was the Chekhovs' home and shop from 1869 to 1874. The front-room grocery store—which illicitly doubled as a pharmacy—has been restored (with emblematic food items). The rest of the house has been reconstructed on the basis of Chekhov's reminiscences, and includes paintings by Anton's brother (open Tues.-Sun. 10am-5pm). Getting to Taganrog is most of the fun—the 1½-hour **hydrofoil** takes you out into the Azov Sea, and the 2-hour *electrichka* provides an impressive view of the Don Delta (11 per day, 3200R).

THE CAUCASUS (КАВКАЗ)

> "The air is pure and fresh as a child's kiss, the sun is bright, the sky is blue. What more can one wish? What need have we here of passions, desires, regrets?"
> —Mikhail Lermontov, *A Hero of Our Time*

Lermontov may have wished to possess the soaring peaks and soothing waves of the Caucasus, but he was not alone. Since prehistoric times, the region bordering the Black Sea has been a meeting place for traders, tribes, and tourists. The three wars that have ravaged this region in the past five years are just the aftershocks of centuries of conflict among local groups. Over the past two hundred years, though, it is the ruling Russian regime that has manipulated and exterminated the peoples of this diverse and uneasy region. Lermontov first saw the *Kavkaz* as a visitor to a Black Sea spa, as many Russians do today in the country's premier holiday resorts. His novel, however, was inspired by his service in the Russian army, which brutally subdued a unified Caucasan force in 1859. Rule under the Soviet regime was no kinder. Resentment, founded in Stalin-era deportation and Russification, and nurtured by recent political oppression, boiled into guerilla warfare in 1991. Today the passions, desires, and regrets of the Caucasus make headlines, but the sun is just as bright and the sky as blue as it was for Lermontov and the traders who sailed into port millennia ago.

■ Sochi (Сочи)

In an earlier era, admirers dubbed Russia's Black Sea coast the "Caucasian Riviera," but Sochi now aspires to be the next Miami. The warm, opaque waters of the Black Sea, the subtropical climate, and the pebble beaches marred only by an occasional concrete slab make this resort a perpetual favorite among Russian vacationers. Once a bastion of the aged and decrepit, Sochi is increasingly attracting hip-hoppety youngsters and foreigners, and its facilities reflect it. Open late, incredibly modern, and preferring Latin over Cyrillic, Sochi is not the place to experience Russian culture—which may be precisely why so many Russians want to be here.

> The nearby mountains turn the resort into a potentially scenic adventure, but they also signal that the border with Georgia's breakaway republic, Abkhazia, is near. The crowds have returned to Sochi, but men with machine guns still keep many of the most beautiful mountain hikes and coastal cruises off-limits. If you do decide to savor the natural surroundings, take a guide.

ORIENTATION AND PRACTICAL INFORMATION

Greater Sochi extends 145km along the Caucasian coast of the Black Sea from Tuapse to the border of Abkhazia. The city center is roughly 1400km south of Moscow on the same latitude as Marseille and Buffalo. North of the center are the resort towns of Lazarevskoye and Dagomys; south are Khosta and Adler. The central section of the city, draped around several hills, bears little relationship to the two-dimensional grid shown on tourist maps. **Ul. Gorkovo** (Горького) links the train and bus stations with the seashore; **Kurortny pr.** (Курортный) runs along the coast from the **Park Riviera** (Парк Ривьера) towards the airport in Adler, crossing ul. Gorkovo at Gostinitsa Moskva and passing most of Sochi's sanatoria. **Ul. Moskovskaya** (Московская) runs from the train station past Gostinitsa Chaika to the Sochi River. **Ul. Vorovskovo** (Воровского) is the first left after Gostinitsa Chaika off ul. Moskovskaya. **Maps** are available from kiosks (1000R)—some show local bus routes.

Tourist Offices: Local tourist offices' most useful service, guided trips into the mountains, are costly for individual tourists. **Hotels Moskva, Zhemchuzhina,** and **Olimpiyskaya** (see Accommodations, p. 590) have English-speaking bureaus that hire guides and arrange transport. Local residents make the best guides. Excursion bureaus on the boardwalk have jaunts to the mountains (20,000-60,000R).

Tourist Police: (tel. 99 68 07). A single Russian- and Turkish-speaking official deals with crimes against foreigners.

Passport Office (OVIR): ul. Gorkovo 60 (tel. 99 97 69). Registration is desirable but not compulsory if you've registered elsewhere in Russia. Most hotels will register you automatically. Open Mon.-Sat. 8am-1pm and 2-5pm.

Currency Exchange: Currency exchanges are everywhere. **Gostinitsa Zhemchuzhina** and others have begun to give Visa cash advances at 4% commission.

Flights: The airport (tel. 44 00 55) is in Adler, a few km northwest of the Abkhazian border, just under an hour by bus #Jbə or 8Jbə from the bus station. **Aeroflot** flies to Istanbul, Moscow, St. Petersburg, and Volgograd. Charter companies fly irregularly (in all senses) to Turkey and Eastern Europe. Foreigners must use the plush "international hall," even for domestic tickets. Open daily 8am-2pm and 3-7pm.

Trains: Zheleznodorozhny vokzal, ul. Gorkovo 56 (tel. 92 30 44, reservations tel. 92 31 17). Foreigners must buy tickets on the lonely 2nd floor of the adjacent round building at *kassa* #12 (and pay for the privilege; open daily 8am-1pm, 2-7pm). To: Moscow (2-3 per day, 40hr., 230,000R)—choose one via Aiksi (Аикси), Russia not Kharkiv, Ukraine, or else you risk meeting dollar-hungry border officials. To: Kiev (3 per week, 40hr., 195,000R); Rostov (3-4 per day, 12hr., 113,900R).

Buses: Avtovokzal, ul. Gorkovo (tel. 99 65 69), next to the trains. Express buses #Jbə and 8Jbə leave every 10-15min. for Adler (45min., 4000R) daily from 7am-7pm, and buses #4 and 45c to Dagomys (26 per day, 35min., 2000R) and other coastal resorts. Buy tickets for Adler and Dagomys outside the station. Buses have been scaled back and the *kassy* inside the station are cl∅sed. Ask around at whatever outdoor *kassa* happens to be open or at the buses themselves.

Ferries: At sea port (tel. 996 62 77). Open daily 8am-7pm. **Hydrofoils** to: Trabzon (1 per day, 5hr., 290,000R) and Samsoon, Turkey (Џамсун; Tues., Thurs., and Sun. at 8am; 7hr.; 300,000R). Buses connect Samsoon to Istanbul (10hr., US$14; buy tickets in Samsoon).

Public Transportation: Buses run frequently in Sochi (1000-3000R). Fares rise with distance out of town. Tourist maps include bus routes.

Luggage Storage: 24-hr. lockers (6400R) at the train station. Downstairs in the bus station (5000-8000R). Open daily 7am-1pm and 2-7pm. In the ferry station (6000R). Open daily 5:30am-7am, 7:30am-12:30pm, 1:30-7pm and 7:30-11pm.

Pharmacy: Apteka Teatralnaya, Kurortny pr. 61 (tel. 92 22 69). Open Mon.-Sat. 8am-7pm, Sun. 9am-5pm.

Weather: tel. 99 70 41.

Post Office: ul. Vorovskovo 1 (tel. 92 20 15), corner of Kurortny pr. **Poste Restante** and **EMS** (tel. 92 28 10) in window to the right of building. Open Mon.-Sat. 8am-8pm, Sun. 8am-6pm. Postal code: 354000.

Telephones: Public phones are both free and reliable. **Mezhdugorodny Telefon** (Международный Телефон), ul. Vorovskovo 6, opposite the post office, deals with **long-distance** calls, makes **photocopies,** sends **faxes,** and has a 24-hr. **currency exchange** (with a fair rate). Open 24hr. **Phone code:** 8622.

ACCOMMODATIONS

Passengers arriving in Sochi by train are accosted on the platform by elderly women and young entrepreneurs offering **private rooms** or apartments for 10,000-150,000R, depending on the size, location, and time of year. When listening to their verbal advertisements, believe exactly one-half. Brokers, distinguished by red arm-bands, might charge a commission. They will say that their price is outlandishly low (this is hardly ever true) and may be reluctant to show you a room before you agree to take it. Expect to pay up front on arrival at the apartment. Elderly landladies are often happy to prepare meals and do laundry at mutually agreeable rates. Keep in mind, though, that a nosy *babushka* is almost as bad as a parent.

Sochi's over 80 **sanatoria** and **pansionaty** offer varying degrees of luxury and service, ranging from over 500,000R at the Radisson Lazurnaya to affordable hotels aimed at Russians. Foreigners are usually charged extra. Down a notch from these, **turbazy** are cheaper but might be farther from a clean beach.

- **Gostinitsa Chaika** (Чайка), ul. Moskovskaya 3 (tel. 92 05 47), across from the train station. Sunny rooms, many with nice views, that might unfortunately include peeling paint and a broken mirror. Showers included, but don't count on hot water or a stall. Singles 138,000R. Doubles 193,000R. If you can convince them you're a foreign student studying in Russia, it's 54,000R and 95,000R.
- **Gostinitsa Moskva** (Москва), Kurortny pr. 18 (tel. 92 36 17), at the sea port. Same Russian rooms, a little nicer than Chaika's, and a short walk to the beach. Single with shower head, fridge, and TV 146,000R. Double with same 244,000R.
- **Gostinitsa Magnolia** (Магнолия), Kurortny pr. 58 (tel. 92 92 92). Two adjacent hotels under one manager. Basic but liveable singles with sink, fridge, phone, hall toilet, and hot shower (80,000R plus 13,700R for 1st night). Doubles 110,000R.
- **Gostinitsa Primorskaya** (Приморская), Sokoglova 1 (Соколова; tel. 92 57 43), between Kurortny pr. and Leningrad beach. A palatial, old, yellow-and-white building with basic salmon rooms. Singles 60,000R. Doubles 80,000R. 1st-floor shower is hot but costs 6000R. Fills up quickly; reservations recommended.

FOOD

A public market, at the corner of ul. Moskovskaya and ul. Konstitutsii (Конституции), presents a wealth of ready-to-eat Caucasian delicacies as well as excellent Georgian bread and fresh fruits. The density of cafés increases dramatically as you approach the beach; some serve more or less edible food. **Kafe Kaliforniya,** (Кафе Калифорния; tel. 92 32 67), takes one back to Vermont with Ben and Jerry's ice cream (3000R per scoop; open daily 9am-midnight). Each hotel complex contains several restaurants. In theory, spicy Caucasian food is the local specialty, but most restaurants serve Russian fare. **Shashlychnaya Akhun Café,** at the base of the tower on Gora Akhun (see Sights, below), prepares spicy Georgian vegetable salads and barbecue kebabs. A substantial meal goes for 20,000R.

SIGHTS AND ENTERTAINMENT

First and foremost is the **beach** and its human attractions. More and more unclothed youths mix with the traditional geriatric crowd to people Sochi's beaches, but then you didn't come here to walk alone along the Black Sea shore. If you did, head north along the coast, or try the emptier and cleaner private hotel beaches. Hotel and private beaches charge admission (10,000R). Rent a wooden *lezhak* (лежак; lounge chair; 3000R), **jet skis** (150,000R per 10min.; open daily 9am-8pm), and **paddleboats** (30,000R per hr.). For a real thrill, try the **ziplines** that run from towers on the piers into the water (5000R; open daily 8am-8pm). Near the ferry terminal is a **waterslide park** "Аква Парк Маяк" (open daily 9am-midnight; 80,000R).

The city's remarkable **arboretum,** (Дендарий; *Dendrarit*), Kurortny pr. 74 (tel. 92 36 02; take bus #11 to "Цирк" *(Tsirk)*), contains 1600 types of plants from around the world (open daily 9am-12:45pm and 1:45-4pm). A cable car takes visitors from Kurortny pr. to an observation post at the top of the park, from which you walk back down through the park. **Park Riviera,** ul. Yegorova 1 (Егорова), on the south side of the ferry terminal across the Sochi river, begins with a massive mosaic of Vlad's goat-eed mug in hellish reds. It's a pretty park full of evergreens, outdoor cafés, marble statues of deer, and the occasional war monument. Enterprising folks sell ice cream, toys, and semi-pornographic paintings to strolling vacationers. The **observation tower** at the peak of **Gora Akhun,** an 8-km walk or taxi ride from Sputnik International Tourist Center on the road to Adler, affords a panoramic view of Sochi, Khosta, Adler, the foothills of the Caucasus, and, of course, the Black Sea (open Wed.-Mon. 10am-5pm). Don't count on finding transportation back down.

The **tea plantations** of Dagomys—the northernmost in the world—display their samovar collection and offer tea-tasting feasts to tour groups at Tea Huts (Чайные домики; *Chainiye domiki*). The huts open only when groups are expected, so make arrangements through one of the hotel service bureaus. For rainy days, Sochi boasts a **Museum of the History of the Resort-City** (Музей истории города-курорта; *Muzey istorii goroda-kurorta*), ul. Ordzhonikidze 29 (Орджоникидзе; tel. 92 23 49); an unremarkable **art museum** (Художественный музей; *Khudozhestvenny muzey*), Kurortny pr. 51 (tel. 99 99 47; open Tues.-Sun. 10am-5:30pm; 5000R); and a squalid **terrarium-aquarium**, ul. Konstitutsii 26, with barely living snakes, turtles, toads and fish (open Tues.-Fri. noon-6pm, Sat.-Sun. noon-7pm).

The city has a flourishing cultural life, with a major annual **independent film festival** in June and an **art festival** in September. During the peak tourist season in July and August, theater troops, orchestras and rock bands come from all over Russia to play for the vacationing elite. The **Winter Theater** (Зимний театр; *Zimny teatr*), ul. Teatralnaya 2 (Театральная; tel. 99 77 06), up the steps from the Zhemchuzhina or down ul. Teatralnaya from Kurortny pr., holds frequent concerts and shows (usually 40,000-80,000R)—some featuring the philharmonic (tel. 99 77 51; tickets 20,000R). There are also several outdoor **summer theaters** (Летние театры; *Letniye teatry*), among them one in the Frunze Park at ul Chernomorskaya 2 (Черноморская; tel. 99 77 72). Dozens of youthful late-night **discos** and **bars** flank the main beach areas. The weekly *Sochi* newspaper, available at kiosks, lists some coming attractions, or call Deputy Head of the Department of Culture and Tourism, Galina Korneeva (tel. 92 43 17); her husband, Sasha Korneev, is a local impresario. Zhemchuzhina, the up-and-coming local **soccer** team, plays at the Central Stadium on Kurortny pr.

THE NORTHWEST (СЕВЕРО-ЗАПАД)

Lakes and monasteries shine like cool diamonds in the frigid forests of Russia's northwest territory. Once Russia's sole access to the open sea, the region acquired castles and palaces befitting its service to the empire. Many now decay in romantic abandon, but the northwest's greatest prize—the grad that Pete built—stands as a living monument to the love that the Tsar and his nation once felt for the far north.

■ St. Petersburg (Санкт-Петербург)

Founded by Peter I (the Great) in 1703, Russia's new capital—won from the Swedes during the Northern War—was built according to a strict plan. The tsar drove thousands of laborers to early deaths in his efforts to drain the swamp on the Gulf of Finland. He then forced friends to build their palaces on the still shifty land. It was to this young city that westward-looking tsars tried to drag Russia from Byzantium and in its cosmopolitan streets that Pushkin and Dostoyevsky wrote their great works. The year 1917 brought an end to an empire and its imperial city—Petrograd subsequently deferred to Moscow in affairs of state. After Lenin's death in 1924, the city which had been Petrograd (changed from the German-sounding "Sankt Peterburg" during WWI) became Leningrad. Stripped of its name and its title, Leningrad saw insult turn to injury as a 900-day Nazi siege killed a million of its residents. The population did not recover until the 1960s; even today, almost every family can claim victims. Despite such tragedy, enchanting St. Petersburg has persisted as Russia's cultural capital, home to a returning café culture, an internationally-renowned ballet company, and one of the most prestigious art museums in the world.

ORIENTATION AND PRACTICAL INFORMATION

St. Petersburg (often called just "Petersburg") is in northwest Russia, a six-hour train ride east of Helsinki and nine hours northwest of Moscow. It sits on a former swamp at the mouth of the **Neva** (Нева) on the **Gulf of Finland** (Финский Залив; *Finsky Zaliv*). Several canals run roughly parallel to the river, and the main thoroughfare is **Nevsky prospekt** (Невский проспект), which runs from the **Admiralty** (Адмиралейство; *Admiraleystvo*) on the river to **ploshchad Vosstaniya** (Площадь Восстания) and **Moscow train station** (Московский Вокзал; *Moskovsky Vokzal*) before veering south to Aleksandr Nevsky Cemetery. Across the river and to the north of the Admiralty is the **Fortress of Peter and Paul,** the historic heart of the city. The area including Nevsky pr. and the Winter Palace help constitute mainland St. Petersburg; the rest of the city consists of islands, the two largest being **Vassilievsky** and **Petrogradsko.** The Metro is a convenient way to get around the center; better are **trolleybuses #5** and **7,** which go up and down Nevsky pr. During rush hour and at certain stations finding a seat is hard, but the Metro is very efficient. Walking is easy, as most major sights are close to one another, and the city makes promenading a pleasure. The *St. Petersburg Press* is available at hostels. Travelers should pick up a copy of the info-stuffed *Traveler's Yellow Pages for St. Petersburg.*

Tourist Offices: Sindbad Travel, 3rd Sovetskaya ul. 28 (3-я Советская; tel. 327 83 84; fax 329 80 19), in International Hostel. Geared to students and budget travelers. Arranges plane, train, bus, and ferry tickets, as well as escorted package tours and homestays. Big discounts on Helsinki tickets. Open Mon.-Fri. 9am-5pm. **Peter T.i.P.S.,** Nevsky pr. 86 (tel. 279 00 37 or 275 07 84; fax 275 08 06). The 1st door on the right. Very professional; as a result, it is not well liked by Intourist. Free info on practically everything, from clubs to train schedules to pharmacies. Extremely friendly and knowledgeable staff arranges visas, homestays, and boat and bus tours. English spoken. Open Mon.-Fri. 10am-8pm, Sat. noon-6pm.

Consulates: South Africa, nab. Reki Moyki 11 (Р. Мойки; tel. 325 63 63; fax 325 63 62). Open Mon.-Fri. 9am-5:30pm. **U.K.,** pl. Proletarskoy Diktatury 5 (Пролетарской Диктатуры; tel. 325 60 36; fax 325 60 37). Open Mon.-Fri. 9:30am-5:30pm. **U.S.,** ul. Furshtadtskaya 15 (Фурштадтская, formerly Petra Lavrova; tel. 275 17 01, 24-hr. emergency tel. 274 86 92; fax 213 69 62). M1: Chernyshevskaya. Open Mon.-Fri. 9:15am-1pm and 2-5:30pm. **Aussies, Canadians,** and **Kiwis** should contact their embassies in Moscow but can use the U.K. consulate in an emergency.

Currency Exchange: Look for the Обмен Валюты *(Obmen Valyuty)* signs everywhere. Changing money is easy now, since there is no more illegal on-the-street exchanging. **Central Exchange Office,** ul. Mikhailovskaya 4 (Михаиловская) off Nevsky Pr. and across from Grand Hotel Europe. M3: Gostiny Dvor. Decent rates for your dollars and traveler's checks. Credit cards accepted at 5% commission. Traveler's checks at 3%. Expect a long wait. If you can risk it, cash is more convenient here, or AmEx traveler's checks, for which the wait is shorter. Open 10:30am-7:30pm. Exchanges also at the **AmEx and post offices.** Keep your exchange receipts if you plan to change rubles back into dollars.

American Express: ul. Mikhailovskaya 1/7 (tel. 119 60 09; fax 119 60 11), in Grand Hotel Europe. Provides travel services including domestic and international flights, replaces lost and stolen AmEx cards, refunds and sells traveler's checks. For cardholders: arranges cash withdrawals from cards and holds mail—no packages. Send mail to: c/o American Express, P.O. Box 87, SF-53501, Lappeenranta, Finland. **Bank** and **currency exchange** inside. Open Mon.-Fri. 9am-5pm, Sat. 9am-1pm. Bank exchange open Mon.-Fri. 9am-12:30pm, 1:30-5pm, Sat. 9am-1pm.

Express Mail: DHL, Izmailovsky pr. 4 (Измайловский; tel. 326 64 00; fax 326 64 10). Packages and letters to the U.S. in 2 working days. Holds mail and packages, and provides courier pickup service. A 15-page document to the U.S. costs US$48. Open Mon.-Fri. 9am-6pm, Sat. 10am-4pm. A **branch office** in the Nevsky Palace Hotel, Nevsky pr. 57 (tel. 119 61 00; fax 119 61 16), is open Mon.-Fri. 9am-6pm. **Westpost,** Nevsky pr. 86 (tel. 275 07 84; fax 275 08 06), in Peter T.i.P.S. (see above). Cheaper service than most courier services by transporting mail to and sending it from the superior Finnish Postal Services. Sends and receives letters and packages to and from any country. A letter up to 20g to the U.S. costs 10,300R; a package up to 2kg costs 200,000R. Also rents postal boxes.

Photocopies: Xerox, ul. Sablinskaya 7 (Саблинская). M: Vasileostrovskaya (tel. 233 30 08). One page 500R, double-sided copy 800R. **Maska** (Маска), Bolshaya Morskaya ul., on the corner of Nevsky pr. "Ксерокс" written in the window. One page 700R. Open daily 11am-8pm.

Morskoy Prospekt
Primorski Park Pobedy
Kamennoostrovski Pr.
PETRO
PETROG
ST
Malaya Nevka
PETERHOF 25 km.
KRONSTADT 20 km.
Bolshaya Zelenina ul.
Malaya Neva
Bolshoy Prospekt
Kronver
Uralskaya ul.
Korablestroiteley ul.
Lyuteranskoe Cemetery
PRIMORSKAYA
Tuchkov most
Malaya Neva
Birzhevoy most
Novosmolenskaya nab.
Smolenka canal
VASILEVSKI OSTROV
Smolenskoe Cemetery
Maly Prospekt
VASILEOSTROVSKAYA
St. Petersburg State University
Universitetskaya nab.
Nakhimova ul.
Sredni Prospekt
Bolshoy Prospekt
Most Lytenata Shmidta
Nalichnaya ul.
Bolshaya Neva
Moyka canal
Glinki ul.
Dekabristov. ul.
OKTYABRSKI RAYON
Lermontovski Pr.
St. Nicholas Cathedral
Passenger Sea Terminal
Pryazhka canal
Sadovaya ul.
N
TEK
Staro-Petergofski Pr.
LENINSKI RAYON
Obvodnyy canal
Obvodnovo Canala Naberezhnaya
BALTIYSKAYA
Baltic Station

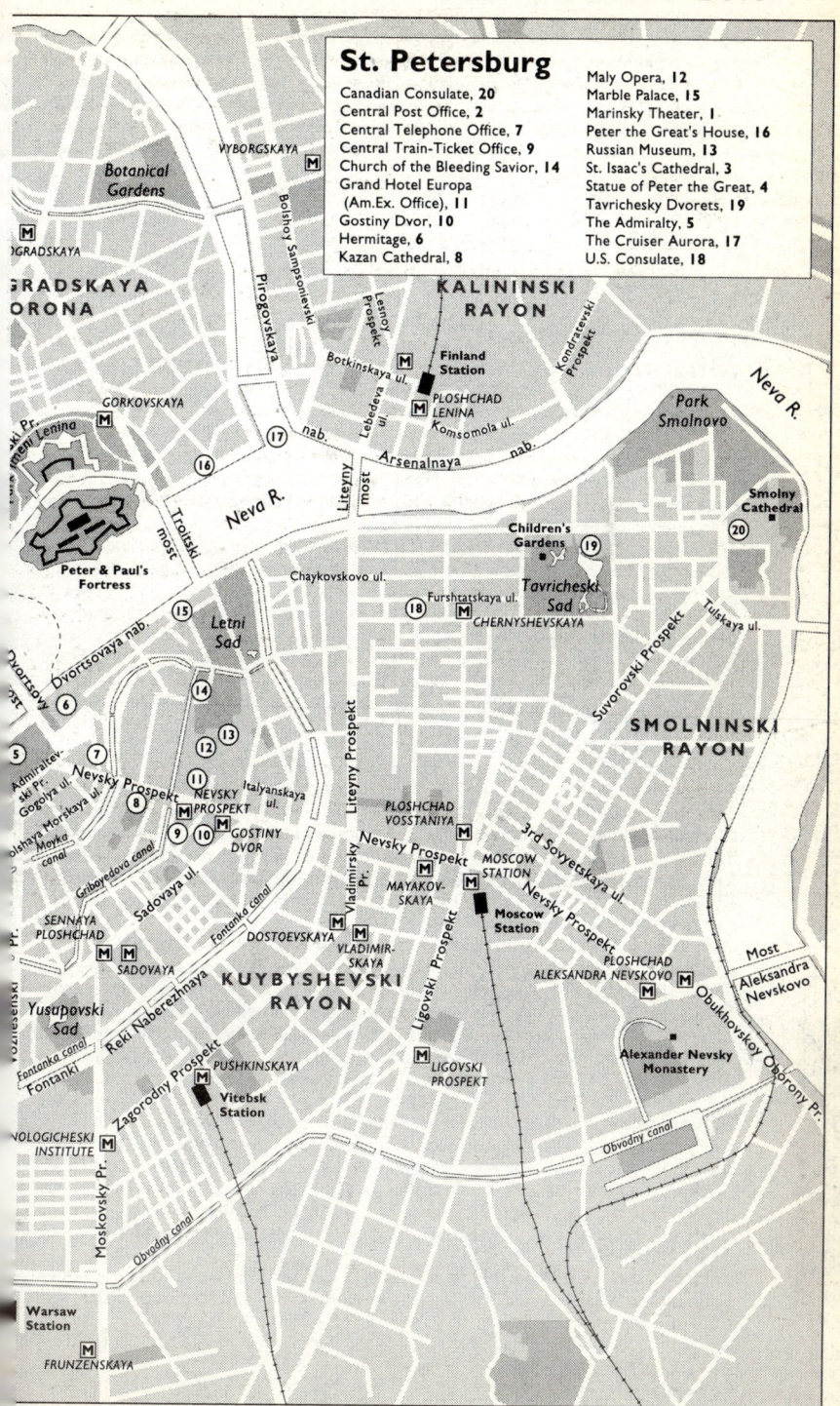

St. Petersburg

Canadian Consulate, 20
Central Post Office, 2
Central Telephone Office, 7
Central Train-Ticket Office, 9
Church of the Bleeding Savior, 14
Grand Hotel Europa (Am.Ex. Office), 11
Gostiny Dvor, 10
Hermitage, 6
Kazan Cathedral, 8
Maly Opera, 12
Marble Palace, 15
Marinsky Theater, 1
Peter the Great's House, 16
Russian Museum, 13
St. Isaac's Cathedral, 3
Statue of Peter the Great, 4
Tavrichesky Dvorets, 19
The Admiralty, 5
The Cruiser Aurora, 17
U.S. Consulate, 18

Flights: The main airport is Pulkovo (Пулково) with 2 terminals: Pulkovo-1 for domestic flights and Pulkovo-2 for international flights. For Pulkovo-2, take bus #13 from M2: Moskovskaya (Московская), or the youth hostels can usually arrange for you to be taken (or met) by taxi for a variable fee. A bus leaves from the Aeroflot (Аэрофлот) building at Nevsky pr. and Bolshaya Morskaya ul. and takes about 45min; buy tickets on the bus. **Air France** (daily direct flights to Paris), Bolshaya Morskaya 35 (tel. 325 82 52). Open Mon.-Fri. 9am-5pm. **British Airways,** Nevsky Pr. 57 (tel. 325 62 22). Open Mon.-Fri. 9am-5:30pm. **Delta Airlines,** Bolshaya Morskaya ul. 36 (tel. 311 58 19 or 311 58 20). Open Mon.-Fri. 9am-5:30pm. **Finnair** (daily flights to Helsinki; roundtrip youth fare US$160), Malaya Morskaya 19 (Малая Морская; tel. 315 97 36 or 314 36 45). Open Mon.-Fri. 9am-5pm. **Lufthansa** (6 direct flights per week to Frankfurt), Voznesensky pr. 7 (Вознесенский; tel. 314 59 17). **SAS/Swissair,** Nevsky pr. 57 (tel. 314 50 86).

Trains: St. Petersburg has 4 main railway stations that service both daytrips and overnight coaches. Carefully check from which station your train leaves.

Warsaw Station (Варшавский Вокзал; *Varshavsky Vokzal*), M1: Baltiskaya (Балтийская). To: Rīga (20hr., 157,000R); Tallinn (9hr, 76,000R); Vilnius (15hr.).

Vitebsk Station (Витебский Вокзал; *Vitebsky Vokzal*). M1: Pushkinskaya. To: Kiev (27hr., 259,000R); Odesa (36½hr., 216,000R); Novgorod (4-5½hr.).

Moscow Station (Московский Вокзал; *Moskovsky Vokzal*). M1: Pl. Vosstaniya. To: Moscow (15 per day, 6-8½hr., 200,000R), the Crimea, and Central Asia.

Finland Station (Финляндский Вокзал; *Finlyansky Vokzal*), M1: Pl. Lenina (Ленина), sends trains to Helsinki and Vyborg.

The **Central Ticket Offices** for rail travel (Централны Железнодорожные Кассы; *Tsentralny Zheleznodorozhny Kassy*) are at Canal Griboedova 24. Open Mon.-Sat. 8am-8pm, Sun. 8am-4pm. Foreign tourists must purchase tickets at the special **Intourist** windows #100-104 on the 2nd floor. Intourist also handles international tickets (windows #90-99; if you simply want information on prices, go to ticket window #89, inside the station to the left). Open daily 8am-noon and 1-7pm. There are also Intourist offices at each train station. If you miss your train, go to the *Dezhurnaya Kassa* (Дежурная Касса) within 3hr. to pay only a 6% surcharge for a new ticket; open 24hr.; otherwise, you will pay full price. Open 24hr. **schedule and fare information,** call 168 01 11 or 162 33 44.

Buses: Canal Obvodnovo (Канал Обводного); take tram #19, 25, 44, or 49 from the Moscow train station 10-15min. until just across the canal. Facing the canal, go right along it for 2 long blocks. The station is on your right; enter through the back. Often cheaper and more comfortable than trains if you are traveling during the day. Buy tickets on the day you leave. You can only buy one-way tickets. Station open daily 6am-1pm and 2-11pm. Advance ticket booth open 8am-2pm and 3-8pm. To: Tallinn (2 per day, 6½hr., 55,500R); Tartu (1 per day, 53,700R). Baggage costs extra, depending on destination (900-2100R).

Public Transportation: Buses, trams, and **trolleys** run fairly frequently, depending on the time of day, and are useful for in-city travel. Read the list of stops posted on the outside of the bus. Trolleys #1, 5, and 22 go from pl. Vosstaniya to the bottom of Nevsky pr., near the Hermitage. The buses are often so packed that you might have to jump off and on again at every stop to let people out. The **Metro** (Метро) tends to be comprehensible, efficient, and safe method of exploring the city (open daily 5:30am-12:30am). Four lines run from the outskirts of the city through points in the center. The driver announces the station at which you are arriving *as well* as the next station and the possible line change as you arrive. A Metro *zheton* (жетон; token), which costs 1200R, also works in phone booths for local calls. Bus, tram, and trolley *talony* (талоны; tickets) cost 1000R; you can buy them from the driver. Be sure to punch your ticket, as the fine for not doing so is 20,000R (not to mention great humiliation), and they do check. A 100,000R **monthly transportation card** pays for unlimited public transportation; purchase one at any Metro station during the first days of the month.

Laundromat: Russian Youth Hostel (see Accommodations below) has a washing machine but no dryer, and will wash your clothes for US$4. **Holiday Hostel** will wash and iron your clothes for US$2 per kg and return it the next day.

ST. PETERSBURG ■ 597

St. Petersburg Metro

- ❶ ---- Kirovsko-Vyborgskaya line
- ❷ —— Moskovo-Petrogradska line
- ❸ —— Nevsko-Vasileostrovskaya line
- ❹ – – – Pravobereshnaya line
- ┼┼┼┼ Rail lines
- Waterways
- Transfer stations
- ● End stops

❶ Devyatkino
- Grazhdanski Pr.
- Akademicheskaya
- Politekhnicheskaya
- Ploshchad Muzhestva
- Lesnaya
- Vyborgskaya
- Ploshchad Lenina
- Finland RR

❷ Prospekt Prosveshcheniya
- Ozerki
- Udelnaya
- Pionerskaya
- Chernaya Rechka
- Petrogradskaya
- Gorkovskaya

Neva River

❸ Primorskaya
- Vasileostrovskaya
- Passenger Ship Terminal
- Gulf of Finland
- Nevsky Prospekt
- Gostiny Dvor
- Chernyshevskaya
- Mayakovskaya
- Sennaya Ploshchad
- Sadovaya ❹
- Ploshchad Vosstaniya
- Moskow RR
- Dostoevskaya
- Vladimirskaya
- Pushkinskaya
- Vitebskiy RR
- Tekhnologicheski Institute
- Tekhnologicheski Institute
- Ligovski Prospekt
- Ploshchad Aleksandra Nevskovo
- Novocherkasskaya
- Baltiskaya
- Baltic RR
- Warsaw RR
- Frunzenskaya
- Narvskaya
- Moskovskie Vorta
- Elektrosila
- Elizarovskaya
- Ladozhskaya
- Kirovski Zavod
- Park Pobedy
- Prospekt Bolshevikov
- Avtovo
- Lomonosovskaya
- Moskovskaya
- Proletarskaya
- Leninski Prospekt
- Zvezdnaya
- Obukhovo
- Ulitsa Dybenko ❹
- ❶ Prospekt Veteranov
- ❷ Kupchino
- ❸ Rybatskoe

N

RUSSIA

Film and Photo Developing: Kodak Express, Bolshaya Morskaya ul. 30, does 1-hr. photo developing, takes passport photos, and sells film (1 roll of Kodak 24,000R). Open daily 9am-8pm.

Pharmacies: The 24-hr. **supermarket** at pl. Vosstaniya (see Food below) sells shampoo, Kleenex, and toothpaste, as well as tampons and pads. On the south side of Nevsky pr., just before the Admiralty (left as you face the Admiralty) is a pharmacy selling high-priced German lotions, cosmetics, and tampons. Open Mon.-Fri. 9am-8pm, Sat.-Sun. 10am-5pm.

Gay Information Line: Tchaikovksy Fund (tel. 395 02 96). The city's principal gay rights' organization. English speaker "usually generally" available.

Medical Assistance: American Medical Center, Reki Fontanka nab. 77 (Реки Фонтанка; tel. 119 61 01), **Polyclinic #2,** Moskovsky pr. 22 (tel. 316 38 77), and **Hospital #20,** Gastello ul. 21 (Гастелло; tel. 108 48 08), treat foreigners.

Emergencies: Police and ambulance drivers do not speak English. If you are a victim of a crime, report it immediately to the local police station—bring a Russian-speaker—and to your consulate.

Post Office: ul. Pochtamskaya 9 (Почтамская). From Nevsky pr., go west on ul. Gogolya (Гоголя), which becomes ul. Pochtamskaya. It's about 2 blocks past St. Isaac's Cathedral on the right, just before an overhanging arch. Come here to change money or make intercity or international calls. Mailing services are not reliable for international letters and parcels, but can be used fairly confidently for mail sent within the former Soviet Union. Letters sent within Russia 1100R, within CIS 1750R, international airmail 3250R. Express mail services offered: **EMS** open Mon.-Fri. 9am-5pm. Open Mon.-Sat. 9am-8pm, Sun. 10am-6pm.

Telephones: Central Telephone and Telegraph, Bolshaya Morskaya ul. 3/5 (Большая Морская). Face the Admiralty, and it's right off Nevsky pr. near Palace Square. For the phones in the front room, buy a phone card (25,000R) from the *kassa* in the 3rd hall. International calling, **faxing, e-mailing, xeroxing,** telegram, and P.O. Box services also offered. **DHL** branch office open Mon.-Fri. 9am-9pm. **AT&T Direct** is now offered directly from St. Petersburg (tel. (812) 325 50 42); you can also use this service to call collect. When your party answers, push the little round button bearing an arrow for a few seconds; it's the all-important volume control (there are good pictograms on the phones). **Local calls** can be made from any phone booth on the street; use Metro tokens. For **intercity calls,** use one of the *mezhdugorodny* (междугородный) phone booths at the Central Telephone office; they take special grooved *zhetony* (жетоны; tokens) sold across from the booths (2400R). When making long-distance calls, dial 8 and wait for the tone before proceeding. Open 24hr., except 12:30-1pm. **Phone code:** 812.

> The pipes and drainage system in St. Petersburg have not changed since the city was founded, so there is no effective water purification system, making contact with *giardia* unavoidable. For more info, see Essentials: Health, p. 22.

ACCOMMODATIONS

Nowhere is Russia's constantly changing political and economic situation more visible to the tourist than in the accommodations scene. Where once travelers were assigned a hotel by Intourist, now they can choose among deluxe new joint ventures, old Intourist dinosaurs, **hostels,** and **private apartments.** If you are planning to stay in Petersburg for longer than a few days, check out other options. *St. Petersburg Press* lists apartments for rent, both long- and short-term; pick up a free copy in the Grand Hotel Europe or at one of the hostels. The International Hostel's *The Traveler's Yellow Pages* has current listings of accommodation options.

Russian-speakers may want to consider a **homestay,** which can be arranged by the **Host Families Association** (HOFA; tel./fax 275 19 92 or 395 13 38), based at the St. Petersburg Technical University. They provide B&B in apartments less than 1km from a metro station, with a family guaranteed to have one English-speaking member. But be warned—what may seem like basic Russian hospitality on the part of the hosts (meeting you at the station, serving dinner, etc.) will show up as additional charges on your bill. HOFA can also provide tours and theater tickets. Given two to three weeks notice, the association will find you a bed in any city in the CIS. (Singles US$30, students US$25. Doubles US$50, students US$40. Discounts for non-central locations and families with poor English.)

There are two members of the national **Russian Youth Hostels Association (HI)**. Both hostels in St. Petersburg accept reservations by phone and offer services such as providing and registering visas, booking train tickets, and providing rides to the airport. They also sell maps and bottled water.

International Youth Hostel (HI), 3rd Sovetskaya ul. 28 (tel. 329 80 18; fax 329 80 19; e-mail ryh@ryh.spb.su; http://www.spb.su/ryh). Housed in a restored 5-story building in the city center near M1: Pl. Vosstaniya. The neighborhood is quiet and pleasant; the hostel itself is clean with basic Soviet furnishings. Rooms have 2-5 beds (50 beds total). Kitchen on the 3rd floor. Laundry service, cybercafé (e-mail US$2 per message; receiving e-mail free), TV, and VCR. Can get tickets for ballet, theater, trains, etc. Check-in by 9:30pm. Check-out 11am. US$17, students US$16, HI members US$15 includes sheets and breakfast. Reservations can be made from all over the world; from the U.S. and Canada, contact the California office (tel. (310) 379-4316; fax 379-8420; e-mail 71573.2010@compuserve.com). MC and Visa accepted. The hostel is a member of IBN, so you can book all other IBN hostels from here or vice versa.

Hostel "Holiday," ul. Mikhailova 1 (ул. Михайлова; tel. 542 73 64; fax 277 51 02). M1: Pl. Lenina. Exit at the Finland train station and turn left on ul. Komsomola (Комсомола), then right on ul. Mikhailova. Just before the river, turn left into a courtyard, then right. A "YH" adorns the wall ahead of you. The door stays locked (there's a code for guests); ring the bell. The entrance is on the 3rd floor; the hostel itself occupies 3 stories. Has the same services as the International Youth Hostel. A bar on site with an incredible view of the Neva and Peter and Paul's Cathedral. Open 24hr. Check-out 11am. US$16. Breakfast and sheets included. Dinner US$7. They'll celebrate your birthday for you if you're there for it. Reservations accepted.

FOOD

On the surface, Russian menus vary about as much as Stalinist architecture, but many restaurants guard top-secret methods of preparing old favorites, and some boast their own specialties. Even in highly touristed regions, menus are often exclusively in Cyrillic. Because of the small number of really good restaurants and the small size of most of these establishments, the top restaurants fill up fast. Make reservations (usually on the same day) by phone or in person; be aware that the telephone will not be convenient unless you speak Russian and are patient. Getting to restaurants often requires a good walk; make sure you know how to get there before you set off or you may arrive very hungry. A number of "ethnic" restaurants, which go beyond Chinese and Indian, offer cuisines from around the former Soviet empire. Breakfast and late-night snacks are difficult to find—most places are open 11am-11pm; hotels, supermarkets, and bakeries are off-hours options.

Fast Food

Carrol's (Карролс), ul. Vosstaniya and Nevsky pr. 45. A Finnish-owned chain that serves tasty hamburgers, french fries, and ice cream (double burger 14,200R, cheeseburger 8600R, fries 5700R). Open daily 9am-11pm.

Café Diasto (Кафе Диасто), Nevsky pr. 42., across from Gostiny Dvor. Dark, informal café with standing room in the front and tables toward the back. Russian fast food and pastries. Hamburger equivalent 5000R. *Pirok* (stuffed dough) with cabbage 1100R. Try the "Dessert Diasto." Open Mon.-Sat. 9am-9pm, Sun. 9am-7pm.

Minutka (Минутка), Nevsky pr. 24. A light and clean fast-food sandwich shop, offering large sandwiches for not-so-large prices. Sandwiches: tuna 26,000R, ham 25,500R. Salads 33,500R. Grab a cookie for 2500R. Open daily 10am-10pm.

Russian Cuisine

Bistro (Бистро), ul. Malaya Morskaya 14. A little café on the way to St. Issac's from Nevsky. Good Russian food at good Russian prices with an eye-pleasing display that works better than any menu. *Bliny* (блины) with meat 12,500R, salad 800R, pastries 1000R. Open Mon.-Fri. 10am-8pm, Sat. 10am-7pm.

Pelmennaya (Пелменная), Suvorovsky pr. 3 (Суворовский), about a block from the Russian Youth Hostel. This stand-up café serves the cheapest food in the city. Borscht 3000R, salad 4300R, *pelmeny* with butter 5300R. Open daily 10am-9pm.

Vetal (Веталь), Admiralteysky pr. 8. Left 1 block at the bottom of Nevsky. The western music does not detract from the decor of this traditional Russian restaurant—the St. Petersburg fireplace of blue and white tile is exquisite. Hearty food in a location ideal for a after-dinner stroll down Nevsky or through the Hermitage when you're done. Six kinds of *pelmenny* for 13,500R each. Borsht 13,000R.

Admiralteysky (Адмиралтейский), Bolshaya Morskaya ul. This new, up-scale restaurant impresses with its well prepared food and attractive interior. Popular with "new Russian" families who don't mind the slightly higher prices. *Shashlik* 47,000R, pork with mushrooms 49,600R, vegetarian tomatoes stuffed with mushrooms 21,840R. Open daily noon-11pm.

Restaurant Metropol (Ресторан Метрополь), ul. Sadovaya 22 (Садовая; tel. 310 18 45), off Nevsky pr. near Gostiny Dvor. Don't be intimidated by the grand staircase and huge dining hall. Opened in 1864, it became a restaurant for Party officials; now, it has waiters in tuxes longing for business. Tasty Russian food for reasonable prices in a hall that will make you feel like a king. Orchestra in the evenings and a floor for dancing, under an out-of-place disco ball. Caviar 60,000R, *solyanka* (солянка; meat stew) 29,000R. Open daily noon-midnight.

Ethnic Cuisine

Tbilisi (Тбилиси), ul. Sytninskaya 10 (Сытнинская; tel. 232 93 91). M2: Gorkovskaya. Follow the iron-wrought fence that wraps around the park until you see the Sytny (Сытный) market. Tbilisi is just around the corner. Or, take a left off Kronverkskaya ul. (Кронверкская). A cooperative that has maintained its atmosphere. A wide selection of sumptuous Georgian appetizers (*satsivi*—chicken in walnut sauce 15,000R) and hot dishes (*tolma*—meat wrapped in grape leaves 14,000R). A haven for vegetarians. Excellent but pricey Georgian wine; if you do splurge, order by the glass (7500R versus a bottle for 50,000R). Ask the staff which wine they recommend. English menu. Open daily noon-11pm.

Korea House (Корейский Домик; Koreysky Domik), Izmailovsky pr. 2 (Измайловский; tel./fax 259 93 33). M1: Tekhnologychesky Institute (Технологический Институт). From the Metro, cross Moskovsky pr., walk straight down 1st Krasnoarmeyskaya ul. (Красноармейская) to Izmailovsky pr., and go right. Traditionally decorated Korean restaurant specializes in delicious and reasonably priced Korean and Central Asian cuisine. Korean meat dish 32,000R. *Plov* (плов; fried rice with meat and carrots) 15,000R, *monty* (монты; large dumplings eaten in Kazakhstan) 30,000R. Open daily 1-10pm.

Tandoor (Тандур), 2 Voznesensky pr. (tel. 312 38 86), on the corner of Admiraleysky Pr., two blocks left from the bottom of Nevsky Pr. For a treat, head here, if only to see adorable Russian boys in Indian costume, complete with gold shoes. This tidy, tasteful restaurant with red carpeting and mournful music presents well prepared, fairly authentic cuisine thanks to an Indian chef and manager. The unfamiliar odor of good food wafting onto the street will entice you in if this description doesn't. Many vegetarian options US$6-8, lassi US$2, *naan* bread US$1. Entrées US$8-25. Open daily noon-11pm.

Kroonk (Крунк), Solyanoy per. 14 (Соляной; tel. 273 16 91). M1: Chernyshevskaya. Exiting the Metro, go right on Chernishevskaya ul., left on Furstadtskaya ul., right onto Liteyney pr., left onto ul. Tchaikovskoho, and then 3 blocks down take a left on Solyanoy. Frequented by well dressed Russians in the know, this cozy restaurant downstairs from the street serves a mix of mostly Armenian cuisine with some Russian fare for variety. Marinated mushrooms 12,000R, *tolma* "Erevanskaya" 17,000R. Entrées 30,000-35,000R. Open daily noon-10pm.

Cafés

Cafés have traditionally played a large role in St. Petersburg culture, where the likes of Dostoyevsky and Lenin met to discuss revolutions over coffee and cakes. Possibly to hush such dissent, the Soviets turned cafés into cold, uncomfortable places. Fortunately, many cafés survived the Soviet era and today evoke the spirit of intellectual debate that once wafted throughout the city. Ranging from dirty little holes in the wall to stylish coffee-and-chat houses, cafés in St. Petersburg often cater to smaller budgets, so you can eat cheap and mingle with natives.

- **Surprise** (Сурприз), Nevsky pr. 113 (tel. 277 00 97). New ice cream shop/café, airy and modern. Top off cool Italian ice cream (5500R per scoop) with a steaming cup of cappy (5000R). Or try one of the luscious pastries (10,000-19,000R).
- **Perstov Dom Bistro** (Перцов Дом Бистро), Ligovsky pr. 44. In a well lit alley, left off of Ligovsky, facing away from Nevsky Pr. This small, light café is exactly where you were not looking. No one will bother you in the modern interior. *Shashlik* 21,300R, sandwiches 5000R, *salyanka* 15,000R. Open daily 11am-11pm.

Supermarkets

St. Petersburg supermarkets offer quality imported products, but they charge for the convenience. All list prices in rubles, and even if not, the stores are required by law to take the local currency at the exchange rate they state. Most open at 11am, take a 1 to 2pm break for lunch, and close at 8 or 9pm, but a few 24-hour stores exist.

- **Babylon Super,** Maly pr. 54/56 (Малый; tel. 230 80 96), off Bolshoy pr. M2: Petrogradskaya (Петроградская). Open Mon.-Sat. 10am-9pm, Sun. noon-8pm.
- **Stockmann,** Finlandsky pr. 1 (Финляндский). M1: Pl. Lenina. Open daily 10am-9pm. AmEx, MC, and Visa accepted.
- **Spar Market,** Stachek pr. 1 (Стачек; tel. 186 51 77). Opposite M1: Narvskaya. Open daily 10am-8pm.
- **Antenta Supermarket,** Tuchkov per. 1115. M3: Vasileostrovskaya. Open daily noon-10pm.
- **Express Market,** Nevsky pr. 113 and ul. Kharkovskaya 1 (Харьковская). Imported Finnish goods. Open daily 10am-10pm.
- **Euromarket,** Suvorovsky pr. 12. A clean market with cheap prices near the Russian Youth Hostel. Open daily 10am-8pm.

Markets

Markets stock fresh produce, meat, cheese, honey, and, occasionally, a prepared dish or two, but are more expensive than state-owned stores. They are a Russian experience and require energy on the part of all involved. Sellers easily spot foreigners, and many will try to cheat you; watch out for fingers on the scales or money behind the table. If you are not satisfied, simply walk away; indeed a simple *nyet* will do wonders to bring the price down. Bargaining is what these places are all about; these are bazaars, not Safeways, after all. Don't forget to bring bags and jars. The **covered market,** Kuznechni per. 3 (Кузнечный), just around the corner from M1: Vladimirskaya (Владимирская), and the **Maltsevski Rynok,** ul. Nekrasova 52 (Некрасова), at the top of Ligovsky pr. (Лиговский), M1: Pl. Vosstaniya, are the biggest and most exciting. **Krondratevsky Rynok,** Polyustrovsky pr. 45 (Полюстровский), M1: Pl. Lenina, bus #138, is a pet market on weekends. (All markets are open Mon.-Sat. 8am-7pm, Sun. 8am-4pm; closed one day a month for cleaning.)

SIGHTS

St. Petersburg is a city obsessed with glory days. Citizens speak of "before the Revolution" as though it were the 1970s and of dear old Peter and Catherine as though they were first cousins. As a result, the museums scattered throughout the city are rich in history, and visiting them reveals as much about the city's present as its past.

There are essentially four kinds of museums in St. Petersburg: big, famous ones; fast-disappearing Soviet shrines; re-created homes of cultural figures; and churches, monasteries, and cemeteries. The first are a must, despite high foreigner rates and large tour groups. The second appeal largely to lovers of the absurd. The third are pilgrimage sights where you can see (and say you saw) this or that famous author's pen and toothbrush, but are less revealing if you don't read Russian. The fourth are monuments and memorials to the World War II dead.

> ### A Yank in a Museum
> Like most museums in Eastern Europe, those in Russia charge foreigners higher rates than natives. Expect to pay big time—sometimes 1000% more than the Russian rate—to peek at the artfully displayed false teeth of the mayor and a stuffed bunny or two. In desperation, some travelers don a fluffy fur hat, push the exact number of rubles for a Russian ticket toward the *babushka* at the *kassa*, and remain stoically mute. Once inside, pigs start to fly. Random wings close for "security" reasons. Totalitarian *babushki* stalk the halls making sure everyone sees *everything*. Rather than cover the floors, often made of precious inlaid wood, many museums ask visitors to don *tapachki,* giant slippers that go over your shoes and transform the polished gallery floor into a veritable ice rink. There are no guardrails—only irreplaceable imperial china—to slow your slide. Make sure your slippers fit well, especially if you have small feet, or you'll drag yourself around the museum only to slide to an unfortunate end on the stairs.

Hermitage (Эрмитаж)
Originally a collection of 225 paintings bought by Catherine the Great in 1763, the Hermitage now rivals both the Louvre and the Prado in architectural, historical, and artistic magnificence. Housed at Dvortsovaya nab. 34 (Дворцовая), the State Hermitage Museum (tel. 110 96 57) is the world's largest art collection.

In one day or even a week, a tourist cannot absorb the whole museum—indeed, only 15-20% of the collection is on display at any one time. Rather than attempting a survey of the world's artistic achievements, pick a building, or a time period and focus on it. There are no great "must-sees" like the *Mona Lisa;* you're free to pick your own. One Austrian writer was led through the Hermitage with his eyes closed until he reached the Rembrandts, so as not to be distracted by the rest of the glitter.

Lines can be long, so come early or on a weekday. Allow three to four hours to see the museum. It's easy to latch onto a tour group, especially if you understand Russian. (Open Tues.-Sun. 10:30am-6pm; cashier and the upper floors until 5pm. 40,000R, students 25,000R, Russians 10,000R; cameras 15,000R.)

The museum consists of five buildings: the **Winter Palace**, the **Little Hermitage**, the **Large Hermitage**, the **Hermitage Theater** (often closed), and the **New Hermitage**. Buy a English floor plan near the ticket booth for 500R, or consult those found on each level. The rooms are numbered, and the museum is organized chronologically by floor, starting with **Egyptian, Greek,** and **Roman** art on the ground floor of the Little and Large Hermitages, and **prehistoric artifacts** in the Winter Palace. On the second floors of the Hermitages are collections of 17th and 18th century **French, Italian,** and **Dutch** art. In rooms 226-27 an exact copy of **Raphael's Loggia,** commissioned by Catherine the Great, hangs just as in the Vatican.

Room 189 on the Winter Palace's second floor, the famous **Malachite Hall,** contains six tons of malachite columns, boxes, and urns. If you wondered why the revolution occurred, the decadence of this home might explain. On the third floor of the Winter Palace (the only building with three floors) are **Impressionism, Post-Impressionism,** and **20th-century** European and American art. If you're running late, visit them first—the museum closes starting at the top.

After commissioning the building of the Hermitage in 1769 and filling it with works of art, Catherine II (the Great) wrote of the treasures, "The only ones to admire all this are the mice and me." This, to the public's great fortune is no longer true, since the collection was made public in 1852. The Winter Palace, commissioned in 1762, reflects the extravagant tastes of the Empress Elizabeth, Peter the Great's daughter, and the architect Rastrelli. The collection began with the 225 canvases that Catherine bought in 1763. She then ordered Russian diplomats in Europe to start acquiring entire art collections for her. By the end of the 1760s, the collection had become too large for the Winter Palace, and Catherine appointed Vallin de La Mothe to build the Small Hermitage—a place in which she could get away by herself or with one of her lovers. The Big (or Old) Hermitage and the Hermitage Theater were completed in the 1780s. Stasov, a famous imperial Russian architect, built the fifth building, the New

Hermitage, in 1851. The tsars lived with their collection in the Winter Palace and Hermitage complex until 1917. Throughout this period, the rules that Catherine laid out for her guests at the Hermitage remained:

> —*One shall speak with moderation and quietly so that others do not get a headache.*
> —*One shall be joyful, but shall not try to damage, break, or gnaw at anything.*
> —*One shall eat with pleasure, but drink with moderation, so that each can leave the room unassisted.*

Try to do the same while you are here.

Russian Museum and Summer Palace

Residing in a grand yellow palace next to Pushkin's monument, **Russky Muzey** (Русский Музей; tel. 219 16 15; fax 314 41 53) boasts the largest collection of Russian art outside Moscow's Tretyakov Gallery (see Art Museums, p. 542). Nicholas II also made this the first public museum of Russian art by opening its doors to the masses in 1898. Although most of the 20th-century collection is either in storage or out of the country on tour, the museum is an excellent introduction to the breadth of Russian art history, and a reminder of how much has been going on here culturally for the past few centuries. The museum is reachable by M3: Gostiny Dvor; go down ul. Mikhailova (Михайлова) past the Grand Hotel Europe. While the building is being restored, enter through the basement in the right corner of the courtyard; go downstairs and turn left.

Inlaid wood floors and gorgeously gaudy ceilings make the museum itself a work of art. The chronologically arranged collection starts on the first floor. If you are at the top of the main staircase, head left to begin with the 14th- to 17th-century icons in the first two rooms. Then continue to 18th-century paintings and sculpture; downstairs are paintings and sculptures from the 19th century. Don't miss Repin's painting of the Ceremonial Meeting of the State Council (May 7, 1901), showing Tsar Nicholas II and his councilors at work. An exhibit of Russian folk art, including delicate ivory carvings and a set of ceramic teapots, resides on floor one. From here up the staircase by the giant bronze soldier, the Benois Wing devotes itself to modern art. Currently under repair, the wing only keeps its third floor galleries open. (Open Wed.-Mon. 10am-6pm; *Kassa* closes 1hr. early; 35,000R, students 17,500R.)

To the right of the Russian museum, the **Muzey Etnografy** (Музей Этнографий), Inzhenernaya ul. 4, bldg. 1 (tel. 219 11 74), offers hands-on exhibitions of the traditions, crafts, arts, and cultures of the 15 former Soviet Republics. Highly educational, the exhibit tactfully lends a greater understanding and appreciation of the cultural diversity that exists in this part of the world. (Open Tues.-Sun. 10am-6pm. *Kassa* closes at 5pm. 15,000R, students 7000R; Russians 3000R, students 1500R.)

The **Summer Gardens and Palace,** a lovely place to rest and cool off, lie behind the Russian Museum and directly across the river from Peter and Paul's Fortress. Two entrances at the north and south lead to long paths lined with the busts of famous Russians. The park's caretakers have adopted a philosophy of benign neglect—you be the judge. In the northeast corner of the gardens, Peter once kept his small **Summer Palace** (tel. 314 03 74). Peter lived downstairs, surrounded by heavy German furniture and lots of clocks, while upstairs resided his kids and wife Cathy, who upon his death became Russia's first tsarina. Individuals must join a tour (and it'll in Russian). Buy your ticket, and wait outside until they invite you in. (Gardens open summer daily 8am-10pm; off-season 8am-7pm. Palace open Wed.-Mon. 11am-6pm. Closed the last Mon. of the month. 15,000R, students 7000R.)

Mars Field (Марсого Поле; *Marsovo Pole*), so named because of military parades held here in the 19th century, extends right next to the Summer Gardens. The broad, open park is now a memorial to the hundreds of thousands of people who died in Leningrad in WWII. There is a monument in the center with an eternal flame. Don't walk on the grass; you'd be treading on a massive common grave.

St. Isaac's Cathedral and Environs

An awe-inspiring view of the city's rooftops waits from the dome of **St. Isaac's Cathedral** (Исаакиевский Собор; *Isaakievski Sobor;* tel. 315 97 32), a massive example of 19th-century civic-religious architecture designed by Frenchie Auguste de Montferrand. On a sunny day, the 100kg of pure gold that coats the dome shines for miles. Not a cheap thrill considering that the cost of building this opulent cathedral was well over five times that of building the Winter Palace, and that 60 laborers died from inhaling mercury fumes during the gilding process. The job took 40 years, in part due to a superstition that the Romanov dynasty would fall with the cathedral's completion. The cathedral stood finished in 1858, the Romanovs fell in 1917, and while we're about it, Rasputin was probably a charlatan, but that's all water under the mystic bridge.

Although the interior flabbergasts visitors for the first few minutes, once one gets used to the grandeur of the place, the details merit a look. Some of Russia's greatest artists have worked on the murals and mosaics inside. The chips in the marble columns appear courtesy of German artillery fire during the siege of then-Leningrad. Because the cathedral is technically a museum, the paintings have their titles explained in English. Still, the cathedral holds religious services and is packed with *babushki* at Easter. It's dedicated to St. Isaac, the saint with the great fortune to have his birthday fall on Peter the Great's, May 30th. (Museum open Thurs.-Tues. 10am-6pm; Colonnade—the climb to the top—open 10am-5pm. The *kassa* is to the right of the cathedral. 32,000R, Russians 5000R; colonnade 2500R.)

Despite the fact that the Nazi air force chose the cathedral as "reference point #1" during WWII, the starving citizens of Leningrad planted cabbages in the square directly in front; once these ran out they ate the square's rats. Photographs of the cabbage-field hang at the **State Museum of the History of St. Petersburg** (Государственный Музей Истории Санкт Петербурга; *Gosudarstvenny Muzey Istorii Sankt Peterburga*), Angliskaya nab. 44 (Английская; tel. 275 72 08), along the embankment, five minutes from the Admiralty heading away from the Hermitage. Every St. Petersburg inhabitant will tell you to go here; this museum makes the devastating effects of WWII clear. (Open Mon. and Thurs.-Sun. 11am-6pm, Tues. 11am-4pm; 15,000R, Russians 1000R.)

Nevsky Prospekt and Environs

The Prospekt begins at the **Admiralty,** whose golden spire, painted black during WWII to disguise it from German artillery bombers, towers over the Admiralty gardens and Palace Square. One of the first buildings in the young St. Petersburg of 1705, the tower's height supposedly allowed Peter to supervise the continued construction of his city. He also directed Russia's new shipyard and navy from its offices. The gardens, initially designed to allow for a wider firing range when defending the shipyard, hold the statues of important Russian literary figures.

On the river side of *Admiraleystvo* stands Etienne Falconet's **Bronze Horseman**—symbol of the city and its founder's massive will. Catherine the Great commissioned the meaning-laden statue as a "gift" to her father-in-law in 1782. It shows the famous Peter mounted on a rearing horse crushing a snake—symbol of both Sweden, which Peter I defeated in the Northern War, and the "evils" of Russia over which he triumphed. The horse stands on a rock from the site outside of St. Petersburg where Peter first surveyed the city, and the wave behind him represents the sea, as St. Petersburg was Russia's first seaport to the west.

Palace Square (Дворцовая Площадь; *Dvortsovaya Ploschad*), the huge windswept expanse in front of the Winter Palace, has witnessed many turning points in Russia's history. Here, Catherine took the tsar's crown after she overthrew her husband, Tsar Peter III. Here Nicholas II's guards fired into a crowd of peaceful demonstrators on "Bloody Sunday" in 1905. And here, Lenin's Bolsheviks seized power from Kerensky's provisional government during the quasi-mythical storming of the Winter Palace in the Revolution of 1917. Today vendors peddle ice cream and carry-out portraits, as the angel at the top of the **Aleksandr "Danimal" Column** waits for another riot. The column commemorates Russia's defeat of Napoleon in 1812. The inscription on the Hermitage side reads "To Aleksandr I from grateful Russia"; the angel is said to have the tsar's face. The column itself weighs 700 tons, took two years to cut from a cliff in Karelia, and required another year to bring to St. Petersburg. With the help of 2000 war veterans and a complex pulley system, it was raised in just 40 minute and now sits on a pedestal, held there only by its massive weight.

Muzey Pushkina (Музей Пушкина), nab. Reki Moiki 12 (наб. Реки Мойки), is just off Palace Square on the canal, the yellow building on the right. Aleksandr Pushkin holds a place in the hearts of Russians unequaled by any other native son. They worship and fear Papa Tolstoy; they *adore* Pushkin. Most Russians consider him as good as or greater than Shakespeare, and any Russian with more than a year of schooling can recite some of his verses. Pushkin's romantic exoticism may be due, in part, to his great-grandfather, an Ethiopian who served and studied with Peter I. Pushkin's early and tragic death gave him martyr status. This museum is not only the apartment where he lived, but the place in which he died. Pushkin died defending his beautiful, unfaithful wife's honor in a duel with a Frenchman who had begun to court her (some believe that the affair was contrived by Tsar Nicholas I, who did not approve of Pushkin's poetics). The poet was fatally wounded and died here several days later, in his beloved library. The clock there is stopped at 2:45, the time of his death.

Most of the museum is now empty, containing only prints from the early 19th century and items such as Natalya Pushkin's ballet slippers and many examples of the poet's drafts and sketches (Pushkin loved to sketch profiles of funny-looking people; he was said to be rather ugly himself, actually, perhaps indicating why his wife slept around). Downstairs is the apartment's original front door, with "Pushkin" scrawled across the upper panel, as well as the original notices posted by Pushkin's doctor about the poet's condition (an enormous crowd gathered outside the house when they heard the news). The books in the library are exact replicas; the furniture is original. Whether you are a Pushkin lover, or just hope to gain a little more insight into the nation's greatest obsession, this small and elegant museum is an hour well spent. There is a souvenir shop. Enter through the courtyard; the *kassa* and museum entrance are on the left (tel. 311 38 01; open Wed.-Mon. 10:30am-6pm, closed last Fri. of the month; 7000R includes a tour in English).

The Art Deco landmark bookstore, **Dom Knigi,** Nevsky pr. 28 (tel. 219 94 43), was the Russian headquarters of the Singer Sewing Machine company before the revolution. The globe at the top is that company's emblem. The store has lost most of its former glory—only the first two floors are open—but it's worth investigating. It is still organized the way it was during Soviet times—annoy the clerk at the fiction desk by asking if they have *Dr. Zhivago*. Capitalism has invaded the ground floor, where you can buy Microsoft Word and expensive office supplies. Farther down Nevsky towards the Admiralty, at #14, a blue and white sign has been kept up for 50 years beyond its time. It reads, in translation, "Citizens! During artillery bombardments this side of the street is more dangerous."

The colossal edifice across the street from Dom Knigi, modeled after St. Peter's in Rome but designed and built by Russian architects (and left to decay by the Soviets) is the **Kazan Cathedral** (Казанский Собор; *Kazansky Sobor*). Formerly the **Museum of the History of Religion and Atheism,** but now the **Museum of the History of the Russian Orthodox Church,** its gold cross was restored in 1994. The cathedral was originally created for the purpose of housing **Our Lady of Kazan,** a sacred icon now lost. While the Museum of Atheism used to show pictures of monks and nuns fornicating, today's mother-of-pearl carvings are comparatively tame. The few icons, robes, and bibles are displayed in glass cases, dwarfed by the interior of the cathedral—the real reason to pay the museum entrance fee. As one last attraction, Marshal Kutuzov, a famous Russian officer who fought Napoleon's forces in 1812, is buried here. As entering through the front or the main side door would be contrary to the "Russian Rule of Appearances" (the more dilapidated the outside, the more you appreciate the inside), a small door around to the left is actually the museum entrance. (Open Mon.-Tues. and Thurs.-Fri. 11am-6pm, Sat.-Sun. 12:30pm-6pm; *kassa* closes at 5pm. 15,000R, students 8000R; Russians 3000R, students 1500R.)

The plaza between the cathedral's wings has been the center of St. Petersburg's political and religious activity since Plekhanov, an early revolutionary, spoke out here in 1876. New political parties deliver speeches from the east wing. Stop to admire the monarchists, anarchists, fascists, hypnotists, Christian fundamentalist missionaries, and Hare Krishnas. Once an open square, the plaza was allegedly covered with lawn and turned into a garden to hinder large demonstrations—as if there weren't other large, open spaces for revolutionaries to congregate in this city. Do not wander around this area alone in the evening; the wings of the cathedral are reportedly a favorite meeting spot for prostitutes and their customers.

The colorful **Church of the Bleeding Savior** (Спас На Крови; *Spas Na Krovi*, a.k.a. the Church on the Spilled Blood), on the Griboyedov canal, sits on the site of Tsar Aleksandr II's bloody 1881 assassination. Though the temple has been under repair for the past 20 years and remains closed to the public, the minutely detailed mosaics on the exterior merit a close look. Farther down, at Nevsky pr. 35, stands the pale yellow **Gostiny Dvor** (Гостиный Двор; guest yard). Built in the 18th century as St. Petersburg's main marketplace, the fine building, undergoing restoration, is now the city's largest department store (open Mon.-Sat. 9am-9pm, Sun. 11am-8pm).

The **Sheremetev Mansion** (Дворец Шереметевых; *Dvorets Sheremetevykh*), nab. Reki Fontanki 34, lies a block from Nevsky pr. After the renovations have finished, it should be a beautiful tribute to the pre-revolutionary St. Petersburg nobility (Sheremetev was one of Peter the Great's marshals). For now, just look...

The **Theater and Music Museum** (Музей Театрального и Музыкального Искусства; *Muzey Teatralnovo i Muzykalnovo Iskusstva*), pl. Ostrovskovo 6, 3rd floor, is just off Nevsky Pr., a minute from M3: Gostiny Dvor. It's next to the formerly named **Aleksandr Rinsky Theater** (tel. 311 21 95), Russia's oldest; the first production of Nikolai Gogol's *The Government Inspector* was staged here in 1836. This museum's many posters, programs, set designs, and elaborate costumes make for a colorful visit (open Mon.-Sun. 11am-6pm, Wed. 1-7pm; 2000R, students free you say you're a student of the arts). Tickets to concerts and lectures (2000-20,000R) in the small concert room may also be bought at the entrance. In this same square stands the **Vaganova School of Choreography**, which graduated such greats as Vasily Nyzhinsky, Anna Pavlova, Rudolf Nureyev, and Mikhail Baryshnikov.

Muzey Anny Akhmatovy (Музей Анны Ахматовы), Fontanka 34 (Фонтанка; tel. 272 22 11), looking over a poetic park, exhibits the famous poet's personal possessions. Enter at Liteyny Pr. 51 (Линтейный) through an archway into a large, green courtyard and keep to the left, following the signs to the museum. Akhmatova, whose poetry spoke for many who suffered through the Soviet years, has become a national heroine. Her most famous poem, *Requiem*, was not written down for 25 years but existed only because it was passed on orally. (Open Tues.-Sun. 10:30am-6:30pm; *kassa* closes at 5:30pm; 10,000R, students 800R, Russians 2000R.)

Dostoyevsky Museum (Дом Достоевского; *Dom Dostoyevskovo*) occupies the writer's apartment at Kuznechny per. 5/2 (Кузнечный; tel. 164 69 50), around the corner to the right from M1: Vladimirskaya (Владимирская). The area resembles Dostoyevsky's St. Petersburg, though die-hard *Crime and Punishment* fans should check out Sennaya pl. (Сенная)—the actual setting where Dostoyevsky set the book's grizzly murder. The museum, well labeled in English, organizes expensive tours of the neighborhood. The apartment that witnessed the creation of *The Brothers Karamazov* displays the writer's notes and bills, all in perfect order, as the guide will explain, thanks to Anna, his secretary and wife. Indeed, little has changed here since Dostoyevsky's death. Even the clock on the table points to the hour of his demise—8:38pm, January 28, 1881. Film versions of Dostoyevsky's novels screen once a week. (Open Tues.-Sun. 10:30am-6:30pm; *kassa* closes at 5:30pm. Closed last Wed. of month. 12,000R, students 6000R; Russians 2000R, Russian students 1000R.)

The **Myzey Arktiki i Antarktiki** (Мьшей Арктики и Антарктики; tel. 113 19 98), on the corner of Kuznechny per. and ul. Marata (Марата), is one block from Muzey Dostoyevskovo. M3: Mayakovskaya. The museum dome houses an exhaustive collection of model ships, nautical instruments, and anything else Arctic expeditions could possibly have used. Meanwhile, rows of fox-furs and stuffed wolves snarl menacingly, glorifying humankind's invasion of the wild. Environmental disasters in the region are not on display (open Wed.-Sun. 10am-6pm, closed last Sat. of the month; 5000R).

Uprising Square (Площадь Восстания; *Ploshad Vosstantiya*) is the halfway point of Nevsky pr., marked by the Moscow train station. Some of the bloodiest confrontations of the February Revolution took place here, and it is here the Cossacks turned on the police during a demonstration. The obelisk in the center was erected only in 1985, replacing the statue of Tsar Aleksandr III removed in 1937. Across from the train station, a pale green building bears the words "Город-герой Ленинград" (Leningrad, the Hero City), in reference to and in remembrance of the crippling losses suffered during the German siege.

Aleksandr Nevsky Monastery

At the far end of Nevsky pr., directly opposite M3, 4: Ploschad Aleksandra Nevskovo, **Aleksandr Nevsky Monastery** (Лавра Александра Невского; *Lavra Aleksandra Nevskovo*), is a major pilgrimage spot and a peaceful place to stroll. The monastery got its name and fame from Prince Aleksandr of Novgorod, whose body was moved here by Peter the Great in 1724. In 1797, it received the highest monastic title of "lavra," bestowed on only four Orthodox monasteries. Placement of the dead has always been a concern of Russian Orthodoxy; not only are cemeteries of major importance and gravestones carefully sculpted, but the most desired place to be buried is under the entrance to the church (for it is considered that the more people who walk over your grave, the less your soul will suffer in purgatory). This belief was apparently not in vogue when Peter established Aleksandr Nevsky Monastery, for many of the tombs in the monastery's two cemeteries are way too massive to walk over. A cobblestone path lined with souvenir-sellers and beggars connects the monastery's cathedral and two cemeteries. The graveyard on the left is the 1716 **Lazarus Cemetery,** the oldest in the city. Going around the edge of the cemetery to the left, leads to the plain black tomb of **Natalya Lanskaya,** the wife of Aleksandr Pushkin. Smack in the tiny cemetery's middle lie the graves of two famous St. Petersburg architects: **Andrei Voronokhin,** who designed the Kazan Cathedral, and **Adrian Zakharov,** architect of the Admiralty. In a surprising concession to non-Russian speaking tourists, most of the graves have plaques in English.

Across the way, on the right side as you walk in, the **Tikhuin Cemetery** is not as old, but is larger, and its ground holds more famous names. The most important is **Fyodor Dostoyevsky** (who could only afford to be buried here thanks to the Russian Orthodox Church). The grave can be found around to the right, fairly near the entrance, strewn with flowers. Continuing along the cemetery's right edge, you arrive at the cluster of famous musicians: **Mikhail Glinka,** composer of the first Russian opera and a contemporary of Pushkin's; **Mikhail Balakurev,** left of Glinka, was a teacher of **Rimsky-Korsakov** and instrumental in gathering this group of musicians together in life. Balakurev's famous pupil's grave is easily recognized by its unfriendly angels and white marble Orthodox cross; many are drawn to **Borodin's** grave by the gold mosaic of a composition sheet from his famous *Prince Igor;* **Mussorgsky, Rubinstein,** and **Tchaikovsky** are in magnificent tombs next to Borodin. Tchaikovsky was buried here, despite the scandal associated with his death. Once Tchaikovsky's homosexuality was discovered and publicized, the conservative Conservatory deemed it more appropriate that the unfortunate musician commit suicide and end his brilliant career than disgrace its hallowed halls. Whether the composer truly complied or was murdered is, like most of Russian history, still unclear, but black angels watch over his tomb. However, it would have been easy for Tchaikovsky to kill himself; drinking a glass of St. Petersburg water would have done it—there was a deadly plague loose at the time. The tomb to the left of the entrance is that of **Stravinsky.**

The **Church of Annunciation** farther along the stone path on the left was the original burial place of the Romanovs, which were then moved to St. Peter and Paul Cathedral (exhumation is possibly the only Russian government activity as popular as rewriting history). The church, currently under renovation, used to house the

Museum of Urban Sculpture, but again belongs to the monastery. The **Trinity Cathedral,** at the end of the path is still functioning and teems with priests in black robes and workmen crossing themselves. The large interior contains many altars and select paintings by artists such as Rubens and Van Dyck. It is often possible to join English tours at the monastery. while the herd mentality may annoy you, the guides are often very knowledgable. Pay at the entrance to *each* of the cemeteries. (Cathedral open 9am-noon and 5-7pm—a board lists service times. Cemeteries open Fri.-Wed. 11am-5pm. 6000R, students 3000R.)

Smolny Institute and Cathedral

Bus #136 or 46 from the stop across the street from M1: Chernyshevskaya chugs to the **Smolny** (Смольный) complex. Once a prestigious school for aristocratic girls, the **Smolny Institute** earned its place in history when Trotsky and Lenin set up the headquarters of the **Bolshevik Central Committee** here in 1917 and planned the Revolution from behind its yellow walls. Now it is the municipal office of St. Petersburg and closed to the public. The gate buildings at the end of the drive read, from left to right, "First Soviet of the dictatorship of the proletariat," and "Proletarians of all nations, unite!" Farther down, again from left to right, are busts of Engels and Marx. Next door rises the blue-and-white **Smolny Cathedral,** notable for combining Baroque and Orthodox Russian architectural styles. The church, now a concert hall, is only open during performances (Sept.-May; 2 per week), but you can climb to the top and survey Lenin's—er, Peter's—city (open Fri.-Tues. 11am-6pm, Wed. 11am-5pm; *kassa* closes 45min. early; US$3).

Peter and Paul Fortress

Across the river from the Hermitage, the walls and golden spire of **Peter and Paul Fortress's** (Петропавловская Крепость; *Petropavlovskaya Krepost*) beckon. Turn right exiting M2: Gorkovskaya on Kamennostrovsky pr. (Каменностровский), the street in front of you (there is no sign). Follow the street to the river, and cross the wooden bridge to the island fortress. Here in summer, locals sunbathe standing up, and in winter, walruses, masochists in speedos, swim in holes cut through the ice.

Construction of the fortress began in May 1703, a date now considered the birthday of St. Petersburg. Originally intended as a defense against the Swedes, it never saw battle because Peter I defeated the northern invaders before the bulwarks were finished. With the Swedish threat gone, Peter turned the fortress into a prison for political dissidents, and sardonic inmate etchings now cover the citadel's stone walls. The fortress currently houses a gold-spired cathedral that gives the complex and several other museums its name. Purchase a single ticket at the *kassa* on the right just as you enter. (Open Thurs.-Mon. 11am-5pm, Tues. 11am-4pm; closed Wednesdays and the last Tues. of the month. Russians and convincing Russian speakers 3000R, students 2000R, children 1500R; otherwise, it's US$3.)

Inside, the **Peter and Paul Cathedral's** icons are currently under restoration, but you can see the graves of almost every tsar since Peter the Great, whose coffin still bears fresh flowers (open Thurs.-Mon. 10am-5:40pm, Tues. 10am-4:40pm). Just outside the church, Mikhail Shemyakin's controversial bronze statue of Peter the Great at once fascinates and offends Russian visitors with its scrawny head and elongated body. **The State Museum of the History of St. Petersburg,** just to the left of Shemyakin's statue, houses paintings and clothing from the late 19th century, as well as posters, sewing machines, and phonographs from the same era. It gives a nice feel for the grand old place this town once was (open Thurs.-Mon. 11am-6pm, Tues. 11am-5pm; closed last Tues. of the month).

Nevsky Gate (Невские Ворота; *Nevskye Vorota*) stands beyond the museum to the left. Here prisoners were sent to their executions. Plaques on the wall mark the water level of the city's worst floods. **Trubetskoy Bastyon** (Трубетской Бастион), in the fortress's southwest corner, is a reconstruction of the prison where Peter the Great imprisoned and tortured his first son, Aleksei. Dostoyevsky, Gorky, Trotsky, and Lenin's older brother also spent time here (same hours as museum).

Petrograd's Side (Петроградская Сторона; *Petrogradskaya Storona*)
Peter's Cabin (Домик Петра Первого; *Domik Petra Pervovo*), Petrovskaya nab. 6 (Петровская; tel. 232 45 76), as you exit the fortress, sits right along the river. From M2: Gorkovskaya, walk to the river, turn right and go two blocks down the road. The small brick house, set back in a park on the left, contains a log cabin—the first building constructed in St. Petersburg. It was the home of Peter I while he supervised the construction of the city; it is now a shrine, with all the furniture as it was and Peter's compass on his desk. (Open daily 10am-6pm, closed last Mon. of the month. 10,000R, students 5000R; cameras 5000R, videocameras 10,000R.)

Continue along the river past Peter's Cabin to the cruiser **Avrora** (Аврора). Initially deployed in the Russo-Japanese war, the ship later played a critical role in the 1917 Revolution when it fired a blank by the Winter Palace, scaring the pants off Kerensky and his Provisional Government. Inside are exhibits on revolutionary and military history (open Tues.-Thurs. and Sat.-Sun. 10:30am-6pm). The **Artillery Museum** (Артиллерпейский Музей), M2: Gorkovskaya, is directly across from the Fortress of Peter and Paul. This is one of the oldest museums in the city—opened in 1756 and moved to its present site in 1868. The building was initially a fortress built to protect the Peter and Paul Fortress (hmm...) from the Swedes, and as a result the walls are almost 1m thick. The museum's collection is heavily oriented towards cannons; there is even the toy cannon little Peter the Great played with. The 28,000 sq. m courtyard is full of tanks you can climb on—this museum provides a great break if you have had enough art and architecture of the 18th century. (Open Wed.-Sun. 11am-6pm, *kassa* closes at 5pm. 10,000R, students 5000R, cameras 10,000R.)

Muzey Politicheskoy Istory Rossy (Музей Политической Истории Россий), Bolshaya Dvoryanskaya ul. 4 (Б. Дворянская; tel. 233 70 48; M2: Gorkovskaya), is right down Kronverksky Pr. toward the mosque, then a left turn onto ul. Kuybysheva. It's housed in the mansion of Matilda Kshesinskaya, once the Marinsky Theatre's prima-ballerina and Nicholas II's lover (he built the beautiful palace for her). Soviet propaganda still pervades the museum, which focuses primarily on the 1905 and 1917 revolutions and then rushes past Stalin to end with a menacing photo of everybody's favorite nationalist, Vladimir Zhirinovsky. Even if you don't read Russian, the photos and relics are more interesting than most Petersburg museums. The printing press, revolutionary uniforms, and all other artifacts are carefully displayed. On the entrance's left side (use the same ticket), a couple of rooms contain the ballerina's possessions—portraits, programs, costumes—but little evidence of her tryst with the last tsar. In the same building, the few rooms of the **Wax Museum** (tel. 233 71 89) downstairs depict illustrious Soviets in wax. Lenin and Papa Stalin look as benevolent as ever, but Khrushchev looks deathly and Gorbachev nothing like himself (both museums open Fri.-Wed. 10am-6pm; 10,000R each, students 5000R).

Muzey Kirova (Музей Кирова), Kamennostrovsky pr. 26/28, 5th floor (tel. 233 38 22), M: Petrogradskaya (Петроградская), is 10 minutes to the right of the exit. A Bolshevik hero and probable Stalin victim, Kirov liked to hunt and it shows (he didn't just like to "hunt" animals, so who knows when the next historians will decide to close this museum). Two huge bear rugs and other stuffed unfortunates populate his re-created home. A major stop on the tourist route, this is probably the most magnificent apartment-museum in St. Petersburg; after all, Kirov was a politician, not a writer. The lower floor is full of Stalins—Stalin in dyed wool, on a carved wooden plate, on a porcelain vase, embroidered, etc., most donated by the executioner himself (open Thurs.-Tues. 11am-4pm; 8000R, students 6000R).

Vasilievsky Island (Василевский Остров; *Vasilevsky Ostrov*)
Facing the Admiralty from across the river, **Muzey Antropologhii i Etnografii—Kunst Kamera** (Музей Антропологии и Этнографии—Кунст Камера; tel. 218 14 12), is a natural history museum with a ghoulish twist. Most of the galleries depict the "lives and habits" of the world's indigenous peoples—Native Americans, Inuits, African tribes, Pacific Islanders, etc. In a central gallery, though, Peter's anatomical collection, bought from a professor at a surgical school in Amsterdam, welcomes only those strong of stomach. Two severed heads and deformed fetuses, including Siamese

twins, grace this exhibit to the then-modern art of organ preservation (by sticking them in jars of formaldehyde). On the top floor, another gallery, the **Lomonosov Museum,** defies explanation. Lomonosov was the founder of Moscow University and a well known scientist, but you'd hardly know it from this gallery. It contains, among other things, Peter I's dining room table, busts of Benjamin Franklin and Voltaire, and portraits of Catherine and Peter the Great—the latter done in mosaic. You must exit the museum the way you came, so if you missed the Navajo sand paintings the first time, you can catch 'em on the rebound (open Sat.-Wed. 11am-6pm; 10,000R, Russians 2500R; cloakroom 500R).

Menshikov Palace, Universitetskaya nab. 15 (Университетская; tel. 213 11 12), is reachable by M3: Vasileostrovskaya (Василеостровская), but it's better to cross the bridge north of the Admiralty and walk left; the palace is a yellow building with a small courtyard. Aleksandr Menshikov was a good friend of Peter I and governor of Petersburg. There was even a rumor floating around that Menshikov and the tsar were lovers. Peter entertained guests here before he built the Summer Palace, and then gave it to the Menshikovs, who employed Catherine I as a serving-girl before she became Peter's second wife. (Open Tues.-Sun. 10:30am-4:30pm. 4000R, students 2000R—in groups of 15 or so with a Russian-speaking guide.)

October Region (Октябрьский Район; *Oktyabrski Rayon*) Petersburg's romantic quarter sees canal Griboyedova meander through quiet neighborhoods with leafy parks. On the outer borders of the *rayon*, the large park **Yusupovsky Sad** (Юсуповский Сад), named after the prince who succeeded in killing Rasputin only after poisoning, shooting, and ultimately drowning the resilient monk, provides an island for peaceful picnics. In the district's center is the Nikolsky Cathedral and, visible from there, **Teatralnaya Ploschad's** Marinsky Theater.

Muzey Bloka (Музей Блока), ul. Dekabristov 57 (tel. 113 86 16), is accessible by M4: Sadovaya, but only because there is *nothing* closer; it can be a nightmare to get to. Trams #31 and 33 will take you to the corner of Pr. Makina. Or, if you're visiting the nearby synagogue, it's only a three-block walk. Of interest mainly to poetry lovers, Blok wrote during the late 19th and early 20th centuries. Married to the daughter of the famous scientist Mendeleev, the poet lived, wrote, and got depressed here. As any good museum *babushka* will tell you, he loved his mother too. Reason enough to give him a museum. The house, with many of Blok's paintings and personal possessions, is mostly intact. The weirdest room, the one where he died, contains only his death mask. (Open Thurs.-Tues. 11am-6pm. 3000R, students 1500R.)

The **Large Choral Synagogue of St. Petersburg,** Lermontovsky pr. 2 (tel. 114 11 53), is St. Petersburg's only functioning synagogue and Europe's second-largest (morning and evening services daily—call for times). Although the grounds are not well kept, once you enter (not through the original main door, but to the left) you may find an English-speaking guide. The synagogue celebrated its 100th anniversary

---

A Russian in a Museum

Most citizens of St. Petersburg enthusiastically assert that of Moscow and St. Petersburg, the latter is far more cultured. Most of the country's great writers, poets, and intellectuals lived here, and some contend that the Russian spoken in St. Petersburg is a purer, more beautiful form of the language. The lovely city was not always so cultured, though. In the 18th century, Peter the Great established the "Kunst Kamera," Russia's first museum, in order to make Russia seem more Western. Much to Peter's chagrin, however, no one came to visit his creation. Deciding to play to his subjects' base love of the macabre, the tsar sent henchmen throughout the eastern hemisphere in search of freakish curios. His scouts returned bearing two-headed fetuses, a skeleton of the world's tallest man, and other oddities to lure the Russian people. Still the subjects showed no interest, so Peter tried one last-ditch strategy: he offered a shot of vodka to anyone who came to the museum. After that, he had to start chargin' admission.

Someone back home *really* misses you. Please call.

With **AT&T Direct**℠ Service it's easy to call back to the States from virtually anywhere your travels take you. Just dial the **AT&T Direct** Access Number for the country *you are in* from the chart below. You'll have English-language voice prompts or an AT&T Operator to guide your call. And our clearest,* fastest connections** will help you reach whoever it is that misses you most back home.

AUSTRIA●◇ 022-903-011	GREECE● 00-800-1311	NETHERLANDS●...06-022-9111
BELGIUM● 0-800-100-10	INDIA✖...........................000-117	RUSSIA●▲▶ (Moscow).755-5042
CZECH REP▲ 00-42-000-101	IRELAND.............1-800-550-000	SPAIN◇.................900-99-00-11
DENMARK.................8001-0010	ISRAEL................177-100-2727	SWEDEN................020-795-611
FRANCE................0 800 99 0011	ITALY● 172-1011	SWITZERLAND●..0-800-550011
GERMANY.................0130-0010	MEXICO▽........95-800-462-4240	U.K.▲....................0800-89-0011

*Non-operator assisted calls to the U.S. only. **Based on customer preference testing. ●Public phones require coin or card deposit. ◇Public phones require local coin payment through call duration. ◌From this country, AT&T Direct calls terminate to designated countries only. ▲May not be available from every phone/pay phone. ✖Not available from public phones. ▽When calling from public phones, use phones marked "Ladatel." ▶Additional charges apply when calling outside of Moscow.

AT&T

Can't find the Access Number for the country you're calling from?
Just ask any operator for AT&T Direct Service.

Photo: R. Olken

Greetings from LET'S GO

With pen and notebook in hand, a change of clothes in our backpack, and the tightest of budgets, we've spent our summer roaming the globe in search of travel bargains.

We've put the best of our research into the book that you're now holding. Our intrepid researcher-writers went on the road for months of exploration, from Anchorage to Angkor, Estonia to Ecuador, Iceland to India. Editors worked from spring to fall, massaging copy into witty and informative prose. A brand-new edition of each guide hits the shelves every fall, just months after it is researched, so you know you're getting the most reliable, up-to-date, and comprehensive information available.

We try to make this book an indispensable companion, but sometimes the best discoveries are the ones you make on your own. If you've got something to share, please drop us a line. We're Let's Go Publications, 67 Mount Auburn Street, Cambridge, MA 02138 USA (e-mail: fanmail@letsgo.com). Good luck and happy travels!

on December 8, 1993 and has only around 70 regular members. In 1893 it had 5000; the decline is a sign of the persecution and emigration of Russian Jews. Make sure that the knowledgeable guides show you the wedding hall (open daily 9am-9pm).

It's easy to spot **Nikolsky Cathedral**, a magnificent blue-and-gold structure in striking 18th-century Baroque style. Turn right off ul. Sadovaya across the canal onto ul. Rimskovo-Korsakovo (Римского-Корсакого), near the Marinsky Theater and Conservatory. The entrance is directly across from the spectacular bell tower, whose bells are supposed to have special mystic powers. Inside, the smell of burning wax is particularly potent due to low ceilings (services daily at 10am and 6pm).

The **Central Museum for Railway Transport** (Центральный Музей Железнодорожного Транспорта; *Tsentralny Muzey Zheleznodorozhnovo Transporta*), ul. Sadovaya 50 (tel. 315 14 76; M4: Sadovaya), is a few blocks down toward Nikolsky Cathedral, next to Yusupovsky Sad. This is persuasive socialist propaganda at its best and a perfect place to take children. The first few rooms show the development of trains in the Soviet era, with plenty of pictures of joyous rail workers; of interest to those who delight in old paperwork are their diplomas and posters. The last rooms are by far the most exciting—model trains curve around the entire room; you must wait for the guide to press all the fantabulous buttons. The final room lets you walk through a section of an old "soft class" sleeper with plush upholstery and beautiful fixtures (open Sun.-Thurs. 11am-5:30pm; 1000R, students 500R).

Lenin Region (Ленинский Район; *Leninski Rayon*)

Near M1: Pushkinskaya (Пушкинская), **Vitebsk Station** (Витебск Вокзал; *Vitebski Vokzal*), Russia's oldest train station contains a replica of a 19th-century steam engine in a glass case. Nearby, Gorokhovaya ul. 64 (Гороховая) was home to Russia's infamous spiritual sex-machine, **Gregory Rasputin**. Although today the site is nothing of interest, Rasputin reputedly hosted fabulous orgies here until his untimely demise. In the long and noble tradition of bloodshed that so marks the Russian past, the **Semyonovsky Barracks** witnessed Dostoyevsky's aborted execution in 1849. It wasn't a great neighborhood back then either.

Kalinin Region (Калининский Район; *Kalininski Rayon*)

To truly understand St. Petersburg's obsession with WWII, come to the remote and chilling **Piskarovskoye Memorial Cemetery** (Пискаровское Мемориальное Кладбище; *Pisarkovskoe Memorialnoe Kladbische*). Close to a million people died during the 900 days that German's laid seige to the city. This cemetery is their grave. An eternal flame and grassy mounds marked with the year are all that mark the dead. The place is nearly empty, yet the emotion is palpable—this is the grave of a Hero City. The monument reads: "No one is forgotten; nothing is forgotten." Stop at M1: Ploschad Muzhestva (Площадь Мужества) and go left to the street. Walk left to the corner, cross Nepokorennykh pr. (Непокоренных) in front and catch bus #123 from the shelter. Ride about six stops (7-10min.). On the right will be a large flower shop and on the left the cemetery, recognizable by a low granite wall and two square stone gate buildings, each with four columns.

ENTERTAINMENT

St. Petersburg's famed White Nights lend the night sky a pale glow from mid-June to early July. In summer, couples stroll under the illuminated night sky and watch the bridges over the Neva go up at 1:30am. Remember to walk on the same side of the river as your hotel—the bridges don't go back down until 3 or 4am. For those more familiar dark nights, St. Petersburg offers ample activities, generally at little cost.

Classical Music, Opera, and Ballet

The city of Tchaikovsky, Prokofiev, and Stravinsky continues to live up to its reputation for classical performing arts, and it is easy to get US$0.50 tickets to world-class performances. The Marinsky Ballet, one of the world's best companies and the place where Russian ballet won its fame, often has inexpensive tickets available at the *kassa*. Sprinkled across the city are a few large concert halls. During the third week in June, when the sun barely touches the horizon, the city holds a series of outdoor evening concerts as part of the **White Nights Festival**. Check kiosks and posters for more info. Theater season ends around the time of this festival and begins again in early September, but check for summer performances at ticket offices at Nevsky pr. 42, across from Gostiny Dvor, or from kiosks and tables near St. Isaac's Cathedral and along Nevsky pr. It may well be more fruitful to go to the *kassa* of the theatre where your desired performance will be held. A monthly program in Russian is usually posted on kiosks throughout the city.

In general, theaters start selling tickets 20 days in advance; good seats sell out fast, but there are frequently cheap seats left the day of the performance. A model of the seating arrangement is always displayed. *Yarus* (ярус) are the cheapest seats, and if you come in close to the start of a performance, a *babushka* who works there might let you sneak into this section free. Intourist keeps many of the better seats, but charges exorbitant prices. Getting to the performance more than 15 minutes early is usually unnecessary; performances often start a few minutes late. Russians dress up for the theater and consider the straggly foreigner who arrives for a performance of *Uncle Vanya* in street clothes an insult to their culture.

For the most part, Russian singers, dancers, and orchestras are at their best when they perform Russian pieces. While the Maly Opera's rendition of *La Traviata* may be the worst Italian opera you've seen, Tchaikovsky's *Queen of Spades* (Пиковая Дама; *Picovaya Dama*) may well be the best staging and performance of Russian opera you will ever experience. Likewise, choose Prokofiev over Strauss when seeking a powerful and emotional orchestral event.

Marinsky Teatr (Марийнский Театр) Teatralnaya pl. 1 (tel. 114 12 11). M4: Sadovaya. 10min. along canal Griboyedova, then right onto the square. This imposing aqua building is one of the most famous theaters for ballet in the world. Pavlova, Nureyev, Nizhinsky, and Baryshnikov, all started here and it was here that Tchaikovsky's *Nutcracker* and *Sleeping Beauty* premiered. Although the ballet goes on tour for two months in the summer, and good seats are mostly sold out, it's worth a try. For two weeks in June, the theater hosts the **White Nights Festival,** for which tickets are easier to get. Tickets start selling 10 days in advance from 2000R on up. *Kassa* open Wed.-Sun. 11am-3pm and 4pm-7pm.

Maly Teatr (Малый Театр), pl. Iskusstv 1 (Искусств; tel. 314 37 58), near the Russian Museum. Second to the Marinsky for opera and ballet, but opens July-Aug. when the Marinsky is closed. Similarly impressive concert hall, and excellent performances of Russian ballet and opera. Tickets sold 20 days in advance. Ticket for foreigners up to 125,000R, Russians up to 20,000R. *Kassa* open daily 11am-3pm and 4pm-8pm. They check your documents at the *kassa* and the door.

Shostakovich Philharmonic Hall, Mikhailovskaya ul. 2 (tel. 311 73 33), opposite the Grand Hotel Europe. M3: Gostiny Dvor. Large concert hall with both classical and modern concerts. Acoustics are not perfect, due to its former use as a hall for Boyar Council meetings, which had no need for such subtleties. Tickets from 4000R, depending upon the concert and day.

Akademicheskaya Kapella (Академическая Капелла), nab. Reki Moiki 20 (tel. 233 02 43). M2: Nevsky Prospekt. Small hall for choirs, solos, and small orchestras. Concerts at 7pm. Prices from 900R. *Kassa* open daily noon-3pm and 4-7pm.

Glinka Maly Zal, Nevsky Pr. 30 (tel. 312 45 85). Part of the Shostakovich Philharmonic Hall, but the acoustics are better than in the main hall. Tickets from 18,000R, depending upon the concert and day. *Kassa* open daily 9am-7pm.

Conservatoriya (Консерватория), Teatralnaya pl. 3 (tel. 312 25 19), across from Marinsky Teatr. M4: Sadovaya. Student ballets and operas performed here; often excellent. Tickets from 2000R. *Kassa* open daily noon-6pm.

Yubileyni Sports Palace, Pr. Dobrolyubova 18 (Добролюбова; tel. 238 40 49), equally far from M3: Vasileostrovskaya and M2: Gorkovskaya.

Theater, Puppets, Circus, and Cabaret

Russian plays in Russian are generally better than Shakespeare in Russian. The Russian circus, while justly famous, is not for animal rights activists. In fact, even those who come garbed in fur coats and hats may want to run home and throw red paint on themselves after seeing a bear whipped into walking a tightrope. Nonetheless, the circus can be amusing and, of course, you don't need Russian to enjoy it.

Akademichesky Teatr Dramy Pushkina (Академический Театр Драмы им. Пушкина), pl. Ostrovskovo 2 (Островского; tel. 311 12 12). M3: Gostiny Dvor. Right on Nevsky pr., then right at a small park. Ballet and theater—mostly classics like *Hamlet* and *Cyrano de Bergerac*. The theater attracts some of Russia's most famous actors and acting companies. St. Petersburg citizens wait in line for hours for certain Moscow troupes performing Chekhov in the building built by Rossi in 1832. Summer ballet season starts July 25. Performances at 11am and 7pm. Tickets from 5000R, available 20 days in advance. *Kassa* open daily 11am-7pm.

Bolshoy Dramatichesky Teatr (Большой Драматический Театр), nab. Reki Fontanki 65 (tel. 310 04 01). M3: Gostiny Dvor. Conservative productions of Russian classics. Tickets from 1000R. *Kassa* open daily 11am-3pm and 4-6pm.

Teatr Marionetok (Театр Марионеток), Nevsky Pr. 52 (tel. 311 19 00). Puppet and marionette shows on irregular days. Closed July-Aug. Tickets from 3000R. *Kassa* open Tues.-Wed. and Fri-Sun. 10:30am-4pm.

Circus (Цирк; *Tsirk*), pl. Belinskovo (tel. 210 44 11), near the Russian Museum. M3: Gostiny Dvor. Russia's oldest circus. With the exception of a cool live orchestra, it has the requisite exploited animals and other trappings of a good Russian circus. Tickets from 7000R. Closed July-Sept. *Kassa* open daily 11am-4pm.

Music Hall (tel. 233 02 43), in Park Lenina. M2: Gorkovskaya. A fully decked-out (plumes and all) Russian cabaret. A very cheesy experience (our researcher stresses the "very"). Tickets from 9000R. *Kassa* open daily noon-7pm.

Shopping

The best place to go for souvenirs is Nevsky pr., just beyond Gostiny Dvor towards the Admiralty. If you speak Russian, use it—you're less likely to get ripped off. Comparative shopping is a good idea, too. Even the black market has fixed prices. Or try actual stores, where posted price tags can't sucker foreigners. Some of the most common items found as traditional Russian crafts are woolen flower-print scarves, *matryoshka* dolls (dolls within a doll), samovars, blue-and-white china from Gzhel (make sure it says Гжел on the bottom), semi-precious stones from the Urals. The factory where Russian tsars stocked their shelves, **Leningradsky Farforsky Zavod**, still fashions affordable teacups.

Souvenirs: The outdoor markets on either side of Nevsky pr. just beyond Gostiny Dvor have the widest selection of both classical and tacky Russian souvenirs (for example, *matryoshka* dolls painted with characters from *Aladdin* and *The Little Mermaid*). Prices are reasonable, and Russian-speakers can often bargain them down. The stands usually open at 11am to 8pm. Watch your moneybelt and keep an eye out for thieves. There are also a few **souvenir shops** where more interesting items can be found, often for better prices—though books tend to cost more than in the U.S. **Museum gift shops** are a good place to find things, too—often they stock a small selection of lacquer boxes and amber jewelry.

Crafts and Antiques: Antikvariat Rus (Антиквариат Русь), Kamennostrovsky pr. 17 (Каменностровский), sells silver candlesticks, samovars, old books, paintings, and silver tea-glass holders for reasonable prices. Walk 4 blocks north of Kamennostrovsky pr. out of M2: Gorkovskaya. Open Mon.-Sat. 11am-2pm and 3-7pm.

Bookstores: Dom Knigi (Дом Книги; open daily 9am-8pm) and **Dom Voyennoy Knigi** (Дом Военной Книги; open Sun.-Fri. 10am-7pm, Sat. 10am-6pm), Nevsky pr. 22 sell books, office supplies, and souvenirs, as well as maps and dictionaries. **Isskustvo** (Исскуство), ul. Gertsena at Nevsky pr. also offers art books, jewelry, and an eclectic assortment of CDs (US$8-15). Open daily 10am-2pm and 3-7pm.

Nightlife

During the pre-Gorbachev era, Petersburg was always the heart of the underground music scene, and this is still evident in the quantity of interesting clubs. There are plenty of dance clubs for Russian "businesspeople," too, but better evening fare can be found. Be careful going home late at night, especially if you've been drinking—loud, drunk foreigners might as well be carrying neon signs saying "rob me!" Clubs last no longer than the fleeting life of a college relationship; both hostels can recommend the newest places. Or check the *St. Petersburg Press* for ads.

The Shamrock, ul. Dekrabristov 27 (ул. Декабристов), directly across from the Mariinsky in Theater Square (Театральная Площадь). A shining example of Ireland's second largest export, this authentic Irish bar is a fun place to down a beer or two (or three). Cool music and a young, but not seedy, crowd. *Guinness* and *Kilkenny* 25,000R per pint. MC accepted. Open daily noon-2am.

St. Petersburg Rock Club (Рок Клуб), ul. Rubinsteina 13 (Рубинштайна; tel. 312 34 83). M4: Dostoyevskaya, in the courtyard and through the right door on the far wall. Soviet rock superstars like Kino and Igry got their starts in this dingy old building. Tickets are hard to get. Open Mon.-Sat. noon-8pm. Cover 10,000R.

Tunnel, in an old bomb shelter. Techno and dancing? This is the place. No address—it's a bomb shelter after all. Located on Lyubyansky per. (Любянский) between ul. Blokina (Блокина) and Zverinskaya (Зверинская). M2: Gorkovskaya.

Art Café, ul. Bolshaya Morskaya 58 (tel. 510 46 52), not far from Marinsky Theater. A small, informal jazz club in a back room. Also, features avant-garde poetry readings (whatever that means). Cover 5000R. Open Fri.-Sat. 7-11pm.

Rock around the Clock, in the "Saturn" movie theater, Sadovaya ul. 27 (tel. 310 02 37). M2: Sennaya Pl. (Сенная). Fairly high cover and expensive drinks, but the music is good and live bands play. Says "members only," but it's rumored that foreigners can get in. Open daily 9pm-6am.

Jazz Philharmonic Hall, Zagorodny Pr. 27 (Загородный; tel. 164 85 65 or 113 53 31). M1: Vladimirskaya. Nightly concerts at 8pm; jam sessions every Fri. and Sat. night until midnight. Tickets from 3000R, depending on the program (sold 2-8pm). Open nightly 8pm-until people leave.

Joy, Canal Griboyedova 28 (tel. 311 35 40), 2 blocks south off Nevsky Pr. Your basic nightclub, catering to tourists and businesspeople. Fairly good, recent music from the U.S. Cover is rather high, depending upon the evening and theme—usually around 60,000R, including 1 drink. Open daily 10pm-5am.

■ Near St. Petersburg

Ride the suburban *electrichka* trains any spring or summer weekend day and you will witness Russians' love of the countryside. Most Russians own or share a *dacha* outside the city and go there every weekend; families crowd out-going trains loaded down with fresh milk, potatoes, live chickens, new puppies, and perhaps lumber for a new construction project. The tsars were no different; they, too, built country houses, and several of these palaces have been restored for tourists. They make particularly good daytrips from St. Petersburg when one more stroll along Nevsky makes your butt itch. Although Petrodvorets and the Catherine Palace have small cafés nearby, they are grossly over-priced, so do as the Russians do and bring a picnic lunch to eat in the idyllic parks. And wear a jacket if your destination is Peterhof—the grounds abut the Gulf of Finland and the garden can get quite windy.

The three palaces stand on what was German territory during the siege of Leningrad in 1942-44. All were burned to the ground during the Nazi retreat, but Stalin provided the staggering sums of money necessary to rebuild these symbols of the tsars during the postwar reconstruction of the Soviet Union.

PETERHOF (ПЕТЕРГОФ)

Also known as Petrodvorets (Петродворец), it is the most thoroughly restored of the palaces. The entire complex at Peterhof is 300 years old, and many of the tsars added to it or expanded existing palaces. For years, scaffolding buried the most breathtaking fountains. However, they are supposed to be running as of June 1997.

Orientation and Practical Information Peterhof is an easy trip by **elec-trichka** (every 15min., 40min., one-way 1600R) from the Baltic Station, M1: Baltiskaya (Балтийская). Buy roundtrip tickets from the ticket office (Биллетные Кассы) in the courtyard—ask for "NO-vyi Peter-GOFF, too-DAH ee oh-BRAHT-nah." Find Novy Peterburg (Новый Петербург) on the map in the center of the courtyard, pick a train going beyond it, then find the rights track—keep your ticket for the ride home. Get off at Novy Peterburg, and either walk left down the road for about 15 minutes or take any bus from the station to the stop after the cathedral (1000R). Alternately, from St. Petersburg, take tram #36 from M1: Avtovo (Автово) and get off after 20 minutes at the circular bus station. Walk across the street and take the Express bus #343 (2000R). The crowds are heaviest on the weekend.

Parks open daily 9am to 9:30pm. Fountains flow May to September 11am to 8pm (9pm on Sun.). Museums open 10:30am to 6pm. The Grand Palace is closed Mondays and the last Tuesday of the month. Monplaisir and the Hermitage are closed Wednesdays and the last Thursday of the month. The Catherine building is closed Thursdays and the last Friday of the month. If you are not with a tour group, you can visit the Grand Palace individually noon to 12:30pm, 1 to 2:30pm, or 4:15 to 5pm.

Sights The **Grand Palace** (Большой Дворец; *Bolshoy Dvorets*; tel. 427 95 27) was Peter's first residence here, but his daughter, Empress Elizabeth, and then Catherine the Great greatly expanded and remodeled it. The rooms have been completely returned to their previous gaudy glory and a palace tour is worthwhile.

Golden cherubs guard the ceremonial stairs to the palace. Just before the throne room, a chamber larger than most one-family homes, the bizarre **Chesma Gallery** depicts the Russian victory over the Turks at Chesma Bay in 1770. Aleksandr Orlov supposedly arranged for a frigate to be exploded in front of the painter to ensure the authenticity of the images. Farther along, two Chinese studies flank a picture gallery that contains 360 portraits of the same eight women, all by the Italian Pietro Rotari. Apparently his widow, strapped for cash, sold the whole lot to Catherine the Great.

The last room on the tour—**Peter's study** lined with elegantly carved wood panels—is a rest for the eyes after all the glittering *frou-frou*. Much of the room inexplicably survived the Nazi invasion—the lighter panels are reconstructions, some of which took 1½ years to complete. (Palace 35,000R, students 17,500R; cameras 10,000R, videocameras 30,000R. You must check all handbags (400R).)

Below the Grand Palace, the **Lower Gardens** sit less well kept but more extensive than the Upper Gardens. To the right, a **Wax Museum** contains figures of the residents of Peterhof (open daily 9am-5pm). With the Grand Palace as a backdrop, the view up the cascade from the Gulf of Finland stuns (15,000R, students 7500R). Follow the sound of children's shrieks and giggles to the **"joke fountains,"** which, activated by one misstep, suddenly splash their unwitting victims.

On the other side of the garden stands **Monplaisir,** the house Peter actually lived in (the big palace was only for special occasions). Smaller and less ostentatious than its neighbors (he was the tsar with good taste), it is graceful and elegant. Long, marble-floored galleries flank the main wing, and the place is peaceful even on the busiest Saturdays (25,000R, students 12,500R). Next door is the **Catherine Building,** where Catherine the Great lay low while her husband was (on her orders) being overthrown (15,000R, students 7500R; cameras 5000R, videocameras 15,000R).

TSARSKOYE SELO (ЦАРСКОЕ СЕЛО)

About 25km south of the city, Tsarskoye Selo ("Tsar's Village") surrounds Catherine the Great's summer residence, a gorgeous azure, white, and gold Baroque palace overlooking sprawling, English-style parks. The area was renamed "Pushkin" during the Soviet era—most Russians and train conductors still use that name.

Orientation and Practical Information Although Pushkin and Pavlovsk can be combined in one day, a leisurely visit is more enjoyable. Take any **electrichka** from the Vitebsk Station (M1: Pushkinskaya), leaving from a sign-designated platform.

To buy your ticket, go to the right of the station to a gray bunker-like building. Ask for "Detskoe Selo" or "Pushkin" (one-way 1200R). Ask for "too-DAH ee oh-BRAHT-nah" if you want a ticket for the way home, too. Don't be worried that none of the signs say Pushkin; take the next *electrichka* that leaves. It's the sixth stop, recognizable both by the number of people who get off and because it is the first platform that looks like a station (½hr.). The conductor should mumble "Pushkin" at some point before you arrive. Once at the station, it's a 15-minute walk or 10-minute ride on bus #37 or 382 almost to the end (you're less likely to get lost with the bus). There will be a yellow building on the left and the palace barely visible through the trees on the right. Ask someone for the *dvorets* if you get confused.

Sights Built in 1756 by the architect Rastrelli before he went to work on the Winter Palace, the opulent palace was remodeled by Charles Cameron under the orders of Catherine the Great; she had the good taste to remove the gilding from the façade, desiring a modest, little *dvorets* (cottage) where she could relax. The Baroque Palace, named **Ekaterinsky Dvorets** (after Elizabeth's mom, Catherine I) was largely destroyed by the Nazis; each room exhibits a photograph of it in a war-torn condition. The **Amber room** suffered the most; its walls were stripped and probably lost forever (one rumor places the hidden furnishings somewhere in Paraguay). A sign in the room reads: "Ruin of the amber room is loss of all of mankind. You sacrifice us—we atone for our common duty to the world culture." While the English leaves much to be desired, the idea is clear—even the exorbitant entrance fees can't pay to completely repair these mansions. Despite this, many of the salons, especially the huge, glittering **Grand Hall** ballroom, have been magnificently restored. Elizabeth used to hold costume parties here. Today there is ample space for you to waltz around—even in *tapichki*. North of the main staircase the other stark rooms wait, one displaying a number of exquisite artifacts from East Asia. Tag along with one of the many English-speaking tours (open Wed.-Mon. 11am-5pm; 30,000R, students 15,000R, Russians 9000R; cameras 12,000R).

Although Catherine's Palace alone is worth the trip, many bring a picnic, taking the time to wander through the nearby parks (open 9am-8pm; 4000R, students 2000R). Aleksandr I's palace, though closed to the public, stands guard over a wild forest, and the rest of the 1400-acre **Catherine Park** is a gardener's paradise—a melange of English, French, and Italian styles. The **Great Pond** is the centerpiece of the English park; it is possible to rent **rowboats** here in summer. To the east lies the Italian-landscaped park where Catherine would ramble with her dogs. Some believe Catherine loved Muffy and Fido (or the Russian equivalent) more than her children, and they now rest in dog peace under the **Pyramid.** Numerous other architectural curiosities pepper the park. The **Ruined Tower** was built pre-ruined (saving later invaders the trouble). Next to Catherine's Palace, the **lycée** schooled the likes of Pushkin (open Wed.-Mon. 10:30am-4:30pm; 3000R, students 2000R). Pushkin, then 12, was one of the lycée's first students, and his cubbyhole can still be seen, along with the classrooms, laboratory, and music rooms.

PAVLOVSK (ПАВЛОВСК)

Nearly 29km south of St. Petersburg and an easy bus ride from Tsarskoye Selo, Pavlovsk is a modest and classical contrast to both Pushkin or Peterhof. Given to Paul I by his frightening mother, Catherine the Great, upon the birth of her grandson (the future Tsar Aleksandr I), Pavlovsk was one of the last imperial palaces to be built. Paul's German wife, Maria Fyodorovna, expanded the original three-story domed square to its current size and decorated it extravagantly, having little else to do while her husband played toy soldiers with his live regiments. Stalin would have been proud of her portraits' prevalence in the palace. Paul I and his imperious mother did not get along; as soon as she died, he moved back in.

From Petersburg, take an **electrichka** from Vitesbsk Station (M1: Pushkinskaya) to Pavlovsk (one-way 1600R). Any of the trains on platforms 1, 2, and 3 are fine; the longest wait is less than two hours. Get off at one stop past Pushkin (7 stops from

Petersburg). The conductor will say "Pavlovsk." Take bus #370 or 383 to the palace; it is the fifth stop and the palace stands on the left. These also go all the way to Pushkin. There is no place to eat at Pavlovsk; bring a picnic lunch. (Park open 10am-5pm. 5000R. Closed first Mon. of month. Palace open Sat.-Thurs., state rooms only on Thurs. 11am-5pm. US$6; Russians 5000R, students 3500R.)

Maria Fyodorovna's taste was perhaps more restrained than his mother's (it wasn't hard). Quite taken with the French ideas of decor, she filled Pavlovsk with old clocks and other decorative pieces of a Far Eastern feel. Thank architect Vincenzo Brena. The palace's biggest draw is its landscaped **park**—one of the largest in the world. During WWII, everyone worked around the clock as German forces approached to bury the palace's many treasures several meters underground—the Nazis were in the habit of destroying Slavic palaces. Although the Nazis did manage to loot and destroy much of Pavlovsk, it has been meticulously restored. In the garden a grave for the soldiers who died clearing Pavlovsk of mines guarantees that you can stroll the beautiful landscape without fear. Pavilions dot the parks. The circular **Temple of Friendship** represents a partial reconciliation between Maria and her fierce mother-in-law. Maria got along well with others though; she befriended Marie Antoinette, who gave her the toilet that is on display in the palace. While the palace was being built, Paul and Maria took a European tour worthy of your own itinerary—although they weren't exactly on a budget—they sat in a carriage for 190 of the days they traveled.

SHLISSELBURG (ШЛИССЕЛЬБУРГ)

About 35km east of St. Petersburg, Shlisselburg receives less travel guide coverage than other medieval Russian fortresses. With that in mind, one might assume that the most entertaining part of the trip is trying to say "Shlisselburg" five times—fast. However, the ruins of Shlisselburg hide a rich history that spans centuries, so we thought we'd remedy the paucity of coverage and give the fortress its due.

Orientation and Practical Information Shlisselburg, alternatively known as the Oreshek Fortress (Орешек Крепость; "nut" or "peanut" fortress), is located on a small island where Lake Ladoga feeds into the Neva river. To reach the fortress, catch **bus #440** across the street from M3: Prolitarskaya (Пролитарская); buy the 16,000R ticket from the conductor (1½hr.). Ride past the "Shlisselburg" stop to the last stop—"Петро Крепость" (Petro Krepost). From the bus station, walk across the bridge and make a left, heading toward the river. Then turn right at the statue of Peter the Great that stands in a shady little cove. On your left awaits the island **ferry** (6 per day, 3min., roundtrip 6000R). The fortress opens in summer—i.e., when the water isn't frozen (daily 9am-5pm; 5000R). No **food** is sold on the island or in town, so bring your own—the quiet leafy spaces beg for a picnic.

Sights The merchants of Novgorod built the original fortress in 1323, calling it "Oreshek"—perhaps due to the island's peanut-like shape—and used it as a trading outpost. When the pier burned down in 1352, the clever Novgorodians replaced it with a stone structure. Oreshek became a strategic military point in the 15th century, was rebuilt from scratch as a fortress, and would ultimately spend most of the 17th century under Swedish control. October of 1702 saw the forces of Peter the Great retake the fortress and rename it Shlisselburg. From this point on, it was the central base for Peter I's war expeditions against Sweden.

As with many fortresses, later in the century "the peanut" became a prison for political undesirables—intellectuals, writers, and revolutionaries. Continuing around to the left through an archway leads to a small courtyard and the **Old Prison**, built in 1789. Between 1826 and 1834, the Old Prison held members of the Decembrist group that, in 1825, attempted to overthrow the tsarist regime. From 1884 to 1906, it held death-row revolutionaries—perhaps most significant was **Aleksandr Iliyich Ulyanov**, elder brother of Vladimir Iliyich Ulyanov, a.k.a. **Lenin**. Aleksandr was a member of the terrorist political faction that led the assassination of Tsar Aleksandr III; he was executed at Shisselborg on May 8, 1887, and his death marked the beginning of his younger brother's deep resentment toward the tsarist government. Inside the Old Prison is a **museum,** explaining the building's history. The **3rd Cell** shows the fine amenities each Decembrist received, while the even grimmer **4th Cell** shows what later revolutionaries endured. Photos of some famous political prisoners hang in the courtyard.

Re-enter the main yard, and ahead to the left the **New Prison** stands darker and danker than even the Old Prison. It too houses a **museum,** displaying photographs and living conditions of inmates. Outside, an Orthodox Cross marks the **communal grave** shared by soldiers of the Northern War and WWII. Toward the left around the perimeter stands the **overseer's building,** built in 1911 and bombed completely by the Nazis during WWII. Beyond that, the 1911-vintage **Fourth Prison** building held revolutionaries until the revolution of 1917, at which point all the prisoners of Shlisselburg were freed. An **exhibition and monument** to the battle at Shlisselburg during WWII marks the middle of the yard. The Nazis attempted to obliterate the fortress, leaving only the sad remains of the day—including the 14th-century, free-standing, bombed-out **Novgorod Fortress Wall.**

■ Novgorod (Новгород)

Founded in the 9th century by Prince Rurik, Novgorod blossomed in the Middle Ages, at one time almost doubling its current population. One legend tells of how the town saved itself from the Suzdal army (in those days, warring princes were as common and pesky as mosquitoes in summer) by hanging an icon on the town's gates. When the Virgin's likeness began to cry, the besieging army fled in terror. And although the fierce Novgorodians also managed to fend off the Mongols that Moscow could not, Moscow won in the end when Ivan III and Ivan the Terrible subjugated the city. Novgorod's kremlin, Russia's oldest, was the first architectural landmark to be renovated after World War II. Many of the 230 churches built between 1100 and 1500 have survived to this day. Bigger and more thoroughly restored than Pskov, Novgorod makes a good introduction to early Russia.

ORIENTATION AND PRACTICAL INFORMATION

Novgorod has two centers—the **kremlin** on the west side of the river, and **Yaroslav's Court** on the east. There are some hotels on the east side, notably the Rossiya and the Sadko, but the **train station, bus station, telephone office,** and **hostel** rest on the west side. The west is laid out like a spiderweb, with the kremlin in the center. **Pr. Karla Marxa** (Карла Маркса) runs from the train station to the earth walls that surround old Novgorod; turn left here for the hostel. There are usually good fruit stands on this corner. From the halls, **ul. Oktyabrskaya** (Октябрьская, previously ul. Sovetskaya) runs to pl. Pobedy (Победы) and the kremlin. Purchase **maps** at **Gostinitsa Intourist,** from the kiosk at the kremlin's east side, or in the St. Petersburg youth hostel. Be warned; the latest revolution has not yet hit street signs.

- **Tourist Offices:** ul. Nikolskaya (Никольская; tel. 353 32), south of Yaroslavl's Court east of the river. Pass through an archway into a courtyard; there is a plaque reading "Новгородское Бюро." English tours of Novgorod priced according to group size. No maps, no brochures. Open daily 9am-5pm.
- **Currency Exchange:** ul. Velikaya 16 (Великая), inside the Hotel Intourist. Changes money from "any" hard currency.
- **Trains:** Straight ahead at the end of pr. Karla Marxa. To: St. Petersburg (2 per day; 5hr., 15,200R); Moscow (1 per day, 8hr.). More expensive than the bus, but a lot more comfortable. For regular tickets more than 24hrs. in advance go to *kassa* #5 or 6. Open daily 9am-noon and 1-8pm. For *lux* (люкс) or same-day tickets, go to the *sutochnaya* (суточная) *kassa* #3.
- **Buses:** End of pr. Karla Marxa, to the right as you face the train station. It's a small white building labeled "Автостанция." Daily buses run to Moscow (51,000R), St. Petersburg (3½hr.—when the driver is in a good mood, 29,300R), and Pskov (21,500R; one leaves in the early morning and arrives at midday). The departure

Novgorod

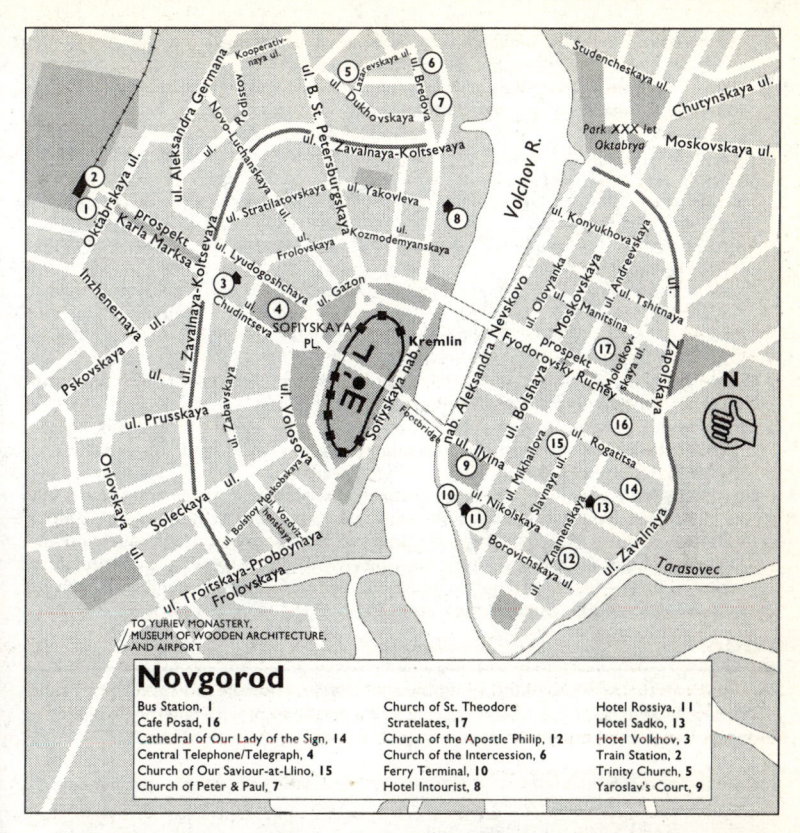

Bus Station, 1	Church of St. Theodore	Hotel Rossiya, 11
Cafe Posad, 16	Stratelates, 17	Hotel Sadko, 13
Cathedral of Our Lady of the Sign, 14	Church of the Apostle Philip, 12	Hotel Volkhov, 3
Central Telephone/Telegraph, 4	Church of the Intercession, 6	Train Station, 2
Church of Our Saviour-at-Llino, 15	Ferry Terminal, 10	Trinity Church, 5
Church of Peter & Paul, 7	Hotel Intourist, 8	Yaroslav's Court, 9

listings are somewhat confusing. To the right of destination listings are departure times (отправление из Новгорода). To the left, arrival times (прибытие в Новгород). **Luggage storage** to the left of the entrance. 1000R.

Pharmacy: Pharmacy #45, ul. Novo-Peterburgskaya 14 (Ново-Петербургская, former Leningradskaya). Sells basic foreign medications and toiletries. Naked woman car freshener 3300R. Open Mon.-Fri. 8am-7pm, Sat. 10am-5pm.

Post Office: ul. B. Sankt Peterburgskaya 9 (Б. Санкт Петербургская; old Leningradskaya). Open Mon.-Fri. 9am-2pm and 3-8pm, Sat. 9am-7pm. **Postal code:** 173001.

Telephone and Telegraph Office: pl. Pobedy, corner of ul. Gorkovo (Горького) and ul. Oktyabrskaya. Several phones on the left dial direct to Moscow. Otherwise, book your call in one of the other booths at the same *kassa*—pay in advance per min. (an annoying beep tells you time's up). Book international calls in advance at the *kassa* in the room on the left; your best bet is to call AT&T Direct in Moscow or a similar service as the wait for international calls can be several hours. Open 24hr. **Phone code:** 8160.

ACCOMMODATIONS

Novgorod's accommodations provide a wide variety of comforts and prices. The hostel, a Russian dorm-turned-cheap hotel, is the most viable option for budget travelers, but a few other old hotels offer reasonable rates. The Hotel Intourist is under construction and no one knows when this four-star complex will open.

Gostinitsa Roza Vetrov (Гостиница Роза Ветров), ul. Novo-Luchanskaya 27 (Ново-Лучанская; former Komslmolskaya; tel. 720 33). A Russian youth hostel. From the station, take a left onto Oktyabrskaya (Октябрская). Continue around left where the road turns into ul. Aleksandra Germana. Then take a right onto ul. Novo-Lyuanskaya. The hostel is on the right, the entrance on the small street before it. Tired of musty, old hotels? This converted dorm has shabby but clean, bright, and airy rooms with firm beds. The staff doesn't speak English, but is helpful and friendly. Kitchen with 2 stoves and 4 sinks. Private or semi-private baths with working shower, sink, and toilet. Single in double with shared bath 180,000R. Doubles with private bath 300,000R. Triple with 3 people 52,000R each. Reserve through the St. Petersburg International Youth Hostel or the Russian Youth Hostel Association. Small cafeteria downstairs sells soups, salads, and entrées for about 2500R (open daily 11:30am-3:30pm).

Gostinitsa Sadko (Садко), ul. Fyodorovsky Ruchei 16 (Фёдоровский Ручей; former Gagarina; tel. 753 66). The corridors are well lit, and the rooms include a proper shower as well as TV and phone. Singles 100,000R. Doubles 160,000R. Triples 200,000R. Reservations recommended.

Gostinitsa Rossiya (Россия), nab. Aleksandra Nevskovo (Александра Невского) at ul. Bolshaya Moskovskaya (Большая Московская, previously Lenina; tel. 341 85). The hallways are dark with a nest-colored decor. Rooms are clean and spacious, but the beds a little soft. Each room has a toilet and "shower" (a spray fixture attached to the wall). Doubles 160,000R. Baggage check available.

Gostinitsa Akron, ul. Frolovskaya 24 (Фроловская; previously ul. Nekrasova; tel. 780 84). From the train station walk along pr. Karla Marxa and Oktyabrskaya ul. 1 block and turn right on ul. Frolovskaya. Centrally located between the train station and kremlin. It has the basics—long dark hallways, dim rooms, and institutional wooden beds—for slightly more due to its prime location. Singles with private bathroom 210,000R. Doubles with same 150,000-180,000R per person.

FOOD

The few eateries with any kind of ambience cater to tourists and raise their prices accordingly. *Shashliks* and *sloiki* (слойки, a delicious pastry with jam) are available at a stand outside the kremlin; if it's sunny, picnic on a bench or by a lake.

Café Express (Кафе Экспресс), ul. Gorkovo 5/2. This little café with an upstairs standing table and a musty dining room downstairs serves delicious *pelmeni* (5600R) and salads (1500-2300R). Open daily 11am-11pm.

Café Posad (Кафе Посад), ul. Rogatitsa 14 (Рогатица; former Bolshevikov; tel. 948 49). Below street level, this warmly lit café serves up Russian standards for less than the hotel restaurants. Salads 5000R, *schi* (cabbage soup) 4000R, sandwiches 2300R, juice 2000R. Popular with young locals. Open Mon.-Sat. noon-midnight.

Detinets (Детинец; tel. 746 24), in a stone tower of the kremlin; follow the signs. Tables set into the walls of the bar are designed to appeal to the tour groups who fill the place. Reservations recommended. A double-sided wooden staircase leads to the restaurant on the 2nd floor of this old church. Mushrooms and *smetana* (16,035R) and *schi* (6516R). Open daily 11am-11pm.

Restoran Sadko (Ресторан Садко), Fyodorovsky Ruchei 16 (tel. 753 66), in Gostinitsa Sadko. Finally, a cheerful Russian restaurant—a funky marine mural complements red plush Star Trek chairs, and the room is light and airy. Well prepared Russian cuisine. And cloth napkins to boot! Salads 3000-6000R. Beef with mushrooms 18,000R. Open daily 11am-5pm and 6-11pm.

Pri Dvore (При Дворе), ul. Oktyabrskaya 3. Within 5min. of the kremlin and the hostel. Wide umbrellas shelter the large outdoor courtyard. Yummy *shashliks* (10,000R) grilled outside, extensive Russian menu indoors. Courtyard bar open daily noon-11pm. Restaurant open noon-4pm and 6-11pm.

Baskin Robbins, ul. Gorkovo 5/2. For the desperate in search of almost 31 flavors. 2-scoop cone 10,000R. Open daily 10am-11pm.

SIGHTS AND ENTERTAINMENT

Entering the **kremlin** from the lakeside affords a panoramic view of the fortress's massive brick walls, the **Novgorod horseman** (a statue commemorating the city's survival through the ages), and the sandy lakeshore spotted in summer with sunbathers.

The kremlin walls, punctuated by towers, were first built in the 11th century, when according to legend it was still custom to lay the first stone on the body of a live child. Wandering through the oldest kremlin in Russia is free, as are most of the interesting sights. To the immediate right of the lakeside entrance an array of bells stand at the base of the **belfry**. Continuing to the right past the sounds of a music school, walk straight to the **St. Sophia Cathedral** (Софийский Собор; *Sofisky Sobor*), the religious pinnacle of any trip to Novgorod. The oldest stone building in Russia, this 11th-century Byzantine cathedral is most imposing from the outside, where the Swedish west doors depict intricately carved scenes from the Bible. The dark interior obscures the few icons which remain (most are in the museum) and, with the exception of the inside of the dome, all the frescos were painted fresh in the 19th century (open daily 8am-8pm; services 10am and 6pm; free). The **Concert Hall** in the kremlin hosts recitals (*kassa* open Mon.-Fri. 2-7pm, Sat. noon-5pm).

Behind the cathedral are the **clock tower** (часозвоня; *chasozvonya*) and the **Chamber of Facets** (Грановитая Палата; *Granovitaya Palata*). The tower's bell used to call citizens to meetings of the *veche* (city council)—a partially democratic government. The Ivans quickly did away with both the bell and the *veche*. The Chamber, next door, contains many precious religious artifacts; but you require a guide to enter—buy your ticket at the museum and wait for a group to gather or arrive (open Wed.-Mon. 10am-6pm, closed last Fri. of the month). In the park's center, the **Millennium of Russia Monument** (Тысячилетие России; *Tysyachiletye Rossii*), is one of three identical ball-shaped monuments. The second stands in St. Peterburg in a park off Nevsky pr., the third in Kiev. Taking one minute to encircle this bronze depiction of all Russian history is bound to be less painful than it was to go through it—as shown by the numbers of fallen men holding daggers. The old favorites, Rurik, Prince Vladimir of Kiev, and Peter the Great are all here—as well as the hordes of others being smushed by a gleeful Dmitry Donskoy.

Directly behind the monument, the town's large **museum** conveys the full duration of Novgorod's history. Starting on the ground floor with thin arrowheads and birchbark inscriptions from the 12th century, move on through delicately carved combs and amulets from the 14th century. The rubles from the period were long and heavy metal rods—serious-looking things that look like they could improve the Russian economy today. Also on the ground floor are recreations of Novgorodian life through the centuries—with the requisite red rooms on the Soviet period. The second floor holds famous icons, including the one which saved the town from the Suzdal army. Go slowly through the first rooms, admiring the craftsmanship; the 20th-century art is not much to look at (open Wed.-Mon. 10am-6pm).

Across the footbridge from the kremlin and to the right, **Yaroslav's Court** is the old market center and the original site of the palace of Novgorod princes. There are the remains of the 17th-century waterfront arcade, several churches from the 13th-16th centuries, and the market gatehouse which is now a museum. The Court was being renovated in summer 1996, but the grounds are still open for exploration.

The **Yuriev Monastery** is the last of over 20 that once surrounded Novgorod. It is striking for its location, in the middle of broad and windy marshes, but little else. Take bus #7 from pl. Pobedy until the airport. Go left at the fork around a small church to see the monastery in front. The church has been heavily reconstructed, and most buildings are closed to the public (open Wed.-Mon. 10am-4pm). About 1km west, the **Museum of Wooden Architecture** is a collection of houses and churches from the surrounding towns, some dating from the 16th century (open Thurs.-Tues. 10am-6pm; 10,000R, students 5000R; cameras 6000R).

KARELIA (КАРЕЛИЯ)

Karelia, a sovereign republic of the Russian Federation, spreads between St. Petersburg and the Arctic Circle. Consisting of forest and lakes—60,000 lakes, the region boasts lakes Ladoga and Onega, which are the largest in Europe and second in Russia only to the great Baikal. Karelians are descendants of the Finns and consider themselves autonomous from and more cultured than the Russians. Signs, often in Russian and Finnish, give the capital, Petrozavodsk, a distinctly Scandinavian feel.

■ Petrozavodsk (Петрозаводск)

Easily accessible by night train from St. Petersburg, and with clean(er) air, small, quiet, streets, and (relatively) well kept buildings, Petrozavodsk is Russia's answer to a New England town—down to the Ben & Jerry's store in the center. Founded in 1703, the same year as St. Petersburg, Petrozavodsk (Peter's Factory) was originally a foundry and armaments plant. Later, tsars exiled misbehaving intellectuals and disfavored politicians here. Now, it is mostly a stopping point for an ice-cream cone, some rest, and a quiet stroll on Kizhi Island.

Orientation and Practical Information As of June 1996, Petrozavodsk had not undergone the wide-spread, street-name changing that makes Moscow and St. Petersburg lessons in Russian pre-revolutionary history. However, some streets are different from the maps, so be alert. **Pr. Lenina** (Ленина), the main road down the center of town, runs from the train station to **Lake Onega**. Everything necessary is within two blocks of this main road. The **train station** stands at the head of pr. Lenina, which runs into pl. Lenina. From there, take pr. Marxa (Маркса) to the **ferry dock** to reach Kizhi. **Trains** chug to Moscow and St. Petersburg (2-3 per day; 140,000R, Russian price from St. Petersburg *platzkartny* 40,000R, *koupé* 60,400R). Your best chance to paying the Russian prices is to buy a roundtrip ticket in St. Petersburg. Try to buy tickets for the train that starts or ends in Petrozavodsk to or from St. Petersburg, or you run the risk of riding with drunken sailors from Minsk. The train from St. Petersburg leaves from the Moscow Station (Московский Вокзал). The **tourist office Intourist**, pl. Lenina (tel. 763 06), in Gostinitsa Severnaya, triples as a **currency exchange** and source for train tickets for a *koupé* wagon if the *kassy* by the station are out. Intourist also offers guides to the city (40,000R) and **tours** (min. 15 people) to **Martsialyne Vody**, Russia's first mineral spa, and a nature reserve at **Kivach** (office open daily 10am-6pm). On pr. Lenina, pass Gostinitsa Severnaya, take a right on ul. Andropova, and a left on Sverdlova (Свердлова) to reach the **post office**, ul. Sverdlova 29. **Telephones** reside next door at ul. Sverdlova 31 (open daily 6am-2am). Make international call from Gostinitsa Severnaya—Intourist sells cards. Street phones are free. **Postal code:** 185035. **Phone code:** 814.

Accommodations As Karelia considers itself an independent territory, anyone not holding a Karelian passport (i.e., a Soviet passport that indicates one's ethnicity is Karelian) will pay higher prices. The prices quoted below are for non-Karelians and non-Russians, and, as always, are subject to value of the ever-fluctuating ruble. A pretty, old, red building outside, **Gostinitsa Severnaya** (Гостиница Северная), pl. Lenina (tel. 749 67), offers the Russian standard-issue, hospital-green corridors and old women cleaning everything with wet rags inside. The lean, airy rooms have TV and phone. (No English. Singles 105,000R, with bath and toilet 150,000R. Doubles 210,000R, with bath and toilet 250,000R. Reserve ahead.) Pink, 10-story **Gostinitsa Karelia** (Карелия), nab. Gyullinga 2 (Гюллинга; tel. 588 97), has small rooms with TV, telephone, primitive but functioning bathrooms. Walk five minutes from the ferry dock, head down pr. Marxa from pl. Lenina, and turn right on ul. Lunacharskovo (Луначарского). Pass the fountain, and take the first left directly overlooking the water (singles 158,850R, doubles 211,800R, triples 285,930R; breakfast 12,000R). **Gostinitsa Respublika Karely** (Республика Карелии), ul. Sverdlova 10 (tel. 727 71; fax 75 682), lets 23 tastefully decorated rooms with modern TV, phone, and spotless white bathrooms. From pr. Lenina, take a right on ul. Andropova (Андропова) and the first left onto Sverdlova. The name of this Finnish hotel evolves constantly, so the pink and white building lacks a sign (singles 185,000R, 15 doubles 308,000R, 4 suites 463,000R; breakfast 10,000R; sauna for guests).

Food Petrozavodsk has the usual collection of grimly basic (and basically grim) Russian restaurants—the glorious exception being **Ben & Jerry's,** Krasnaya ul. (Красная) corner of ul. Andropova, where you can get Vermont's finest for rubles. From the train station, walk down pr. Lenina, then go left on ul. Antikaynena (Антикайнена), and take the first right past the market onto Krasnaya ul. The ice cream and cones are made on the premises (small cone 2000R, large cone 3000R; open Tues.-Sun. 11am-8pm). Take a left as you face the ferry dock. to reach **Restoran Petrovsky** (Ресторан Петровский), ul. Andropova (tel. 709 92), just off pr. Marxa. The music from the dance floor gets loud, but the locals seem to like it. Wise shoppers opt for the salads over the *myasa po-petrovsky* (мясо по-петровский; entrées 5000-20,000R; open daily noon-5pm and 7pm-2am). **Restaurant Fregat** (Фрегат), Onezhskaya nab., 1 (Онежская; tel. 614 98), next to the port and the ferry ticket *kassa,* is a large room decked out in a colorful astronomical motif. The English menu features salads from 5000R and entrées from 8000R (open daily noon-1am; bar upstairs). The **Central Market** (Центральный рынок; *Tsentralny rynok*), ul. Antikaynena (Антикайнена), is a left off pr. Lenina two blocks from the train station (open daily 8am-6pm; closed 2nd Mon. of the month). *Produkty* (продукты; grocers) down pr. Lenina sell a wide range of breads, cheeses, fruits and vegetables, packaged goods, meat, and yogurt.

Sights Ask the people in Petrozavodsk what there is to see, and they will smile and laugh. The **waterfront** on the lake between pl. Lenina and the ferry dock has been beautified for strolling. Admire the statues and views while strolling to the dock to catch a hydrofoil to Kizhi. There is one church in Petrozavodsk, the **Bogosluzhena Tserkov,** ul. Pravdy 24 (Правды). Head to the west end of ul. Kirova, cross the bridge by pl. Kirova, turn left, and go right at the fork. The pretty green-and-white church with an elaborate *iconostasis* and dark, peaceful, extremely wooded cemetery are on the left. Worth the long walk only if you love churches.

■ Near Petrozavodsk: Kizhi (Кижи)

Kizhi, a undisturbed island serving as an outdoor museum of 18th-century wooden architecture, is the main reason to go to Petrozavodsk. An ancient pagan ritual site which drew Russian Orthodox colonizers in the 12th century, the 5km-long island still shimmers with mysticism. Covered in tall grass and Queen Anne's lace, Kizhi is essentially a nature reserve. Only the occasional wooden hut, church, or windmill—all part of the museum's display—dot the green hills and banks of the placid lake.

Wooden buildings, most of them moved from the Medvezhye region around Lake Onega, dot the south part of this hushed island; you must pay to enter this "muscum," but once on the premises, you are free to explore both the architecture and the natural beauty of what the Karelians call "our Greece." The striking **Cathedral of the Transfiguration** (Преображенский Собор; *Preobrazhensky Sobor*) and its 22 domes, all in unpainted wood, are visible from afar. Unfortunately, entry is prohibited; the cathedral must be left in peace so it will (unfortunately) decay slowly. Despite UNESCO protection, not one expert has figured out how to restore the church, built in 1714 without nails. Another church, the child-size 14th-century **Church of the Resurrection of Lazarus,** was moved here from the former Murom monastery and may be the oldest wooden building in Russia. Although most of the other buildings—a windmill, sauna, barn, etc.—are closed to inspection, three **peasant houses,** directly out of a Yiddish fairy-tale, are filled with peasant possessions.

The house of **"Wealthy Peasant Osheuner"** is a traditional *koshel* home. Beware: don't smack your head on the doorways of the small dark interior. The houses of **"Average Peasant Yelizarov"** and **"Poor Peasant Shchepin"** look strikingly similar to Osheuner's. A leisurely walk, including a relaxing picnic in the grass or on a dock should take about three hours—exactly the amount of time between when a ferry arrives and departs (open daily noon-5pm and 7pm-2am; 65,000R, Russians 1000R).

To catch the **ferry** from Petrozavodsk, follow ul. Lenina from the train station. Then walk down the hill to the waterfront path, which you take around to the right.

Buy tickets in the white building on the right through the second door. Walk through to the back of the building to get to the ferry *kassa*. The boat leaves at 1pm, returning at either 3:30pm or 8pm (mid-May to mid-Nov. or whenever hell, we mean, the lake freezes overt; 1¾hr.; roundtrip 40,000R).

THE KALININGRAD REGION (КАЛИНИНГРАДСКАЯ ОБЛАСТЬ)

Fate and a naval base have conspired to leave the Kaliningrad region *(Kaliningradskaya oblast)* a part of Russia, estranged from the rest of the country by 150km of Lithuania. A sandy area surrounded by forests and lakes, its separation anxiety dates back to a history as the German province of East Prussia. Though still a part of Germany during the interwar period, it was thrust into isolation by Poland's acquired corridor to the sea, and has been floating amid foreign nations ever since.

■ Kaliningrad (Калининград)

Sovietization was accomplished so completely after the Red Army's 1945 occupation that a contemporary observer would hardly suspect Kaliningrad had been a German city for 700 years. Home to 18th-century philosopher Immanuel Kant, former Königsberg (King's City), appropriately named for its importance in Prussia, was virtually razed by World War II. The erstwhile German inhabitants have disappeared: killed in the conflict, deported to Germany, or exiled to Siberia. For security reasons the city, named after Stalin's henchman, Kalinin, was only opened to tourists in 1991; before that it held 500,000 Russian troops and the Baltic Fleet. Today, amid the westernization in other Baltic States, Kaliningrad remains a desolate island of the old system.

ORIENTATION AND PRACTICAL INFORMATION

Obtainable at numerous bookstores and kiosks, the **map** "План города для туристов" *(Plan goroda dlya touristov)* provides information about museums and sights. From the bus and south train stations, **Leninsky prospekt** (Ленинский) runs north over the river, across an island with an old cathedral, continues through **Tsentralnaya ploschad** (Центральна) past the hideous House of Soviets, and ends at **ploschad Pobedy** (Победы), the central square. From this terminus, **prospekt Mira** (Мира) points west past the zoo, while **ul. Chernyakhovskovo** (Черняховского) travels east towards the central market and the amber museum.

Tourist Office: Gostinitsa Kaliningrad (Гостиница Калининград), Leninsky pr. 81 on the north end of Tsentralnaya pl., contains the bare-bones tourist service **Noktyurn** (Ноктюрн; tel./fax 46 95 78), to the lobby's left. Open Mon.-Sat. 8am-6pm.

Currency Exchange: Baltinvestor Bank, in Gostinitsa Kaliningrad (see above), accepts AmEx traveler's checks, and gives Visa and MC cash advances. Open Mon.-Fri. 9:30am-4pm. For changing money, spot an "Обмен Валюты" sign.

Flights: Aeroflot planes leave for Moscow (2 per day, depending on fuel, and such; US$50) from the airport, 25km north of the city; take the "Аэропорт" *(Aeroport)* bus from the main bus station (4000R).

Trains: Severny Vokzal (Северный Вокзал; North Station), north of pl. Pobedy behind a big pink building, sends trains to the Baltic coast. **Yuzhny Vokzal** (Южный Вокзал; South Station; tel. 49 37 00; info tel. 005), on the south side of pl. Kalinina, handles international connections. Open 3:30am-12:40am. To: Riga (2 per week, 10hr., 87,700R), Moscow (1 per day, 24hr., 176,700R), St. Petersburg (1 per day, 20½hr., 159,700R), Vilnius (1 per day, 7hr., 50,300R), and Warsaw (Mon. at 12:25, 10hr., 132,000R). International cashier open 8am-1pm and 2-8pm.

Buses: pl. Kalinina, east of Yuzhny Vokzal (tel. 44 36 35). To: Gdańsk (1-2 per day, 4½hr., 38,000R), Grodno (1 per day, 10½hr., 40,000R), Klaipéda (4 per day via the Spit, 4hr., 26,000R), Minsk (1 per day, 13hr., 70,000R), and Vilnius (1 per day, 8hr., 42,000R). *Kassa* open 6am-11:30pm. Some Polish buses are at the *Kyonigafto* desk (Кёнигавто; tel. 46 03 16; open Mon.-Sat. 6am-10pm, Sun. 6am-6pm).

Public Transportation: Trams and **buses** travel the streets in obscure, arcane patterns, charging 500R per ride (buy blocks of ten tickets on the bus or at some kiosks). Tram #10 traverses most of the city from the bus station past the central market, while tram #1 runs east-west from beyond the zoo towards the market.

Taxi: Taxis sit in every major square, especially at the train stations, zoo, and pl. Pobedy. The tourist office (tel. 46 95 78) also stands in as a taxi service.

Pharmacy: Apteka (Аптека), Leninsky pr. 63/67 (tel. 43 27 83). Fairly current compared to other stores in Kaliningrad, which isn't saying much. Open Mon.-Fri. 8am-8pm, Sat. 10am-6pm.

Express Mail: DHL, at the Hotel Kaliningrad Communication Center.

E-mail: Gostinitsa Kaliningrad communication center, Leninsky pr. 81 (tel. 22 13 74); e-mail kenig@sovam.com). 500R per 20Kb-page. Open daily 9am-6pm.

Post Office: Out of the way at ul. Leonova 22 (Леонова; tel. 27 30 89), a right off pr. Mira, way past G. Moskva (open Mon.-Fri. 9am-7pm, Sat. 10am-6pm). **Poste Restante** window #21. **EMS** window #8 (tel. 27 34 95). **Postal code:** 236 000.

Telephones: ul. Leonova 20, through the back entrance to the post office. **Faxes.** Open 7am-10pm. **Phone code:** 0112, or 8-007 on the old Soviet network.

ACCOMMODATIONS

Hotels (Гостиница; *Gostinitsa*) in K-grad play a simple zero-sum game: the owner will always win and you'll always lose. Foreigners (read: suckers) will spend US$100 per night for (sub)standard Soviet rooms. If the options below don't appeal to you, take a train to Svetlogorsk, a sea-side holiday town just a half-hour north of the city. There, hotels and sanatoria abound, and some are even eager to accept foreigners.

Gostinitsa Kyonigavto (Кёнигавто), Moskovsky pr. 184 (Московский.; tel. 46 76 52). Clean rooms, cold showers. 120,000R single, 200,000R double.

Gostinitsa Moskva (Москва), pr. Mira 19 (tel. 27 20 89). One of the precious few Russian hotels extending equal treatment to foreigners. Communication center on the 1st floor is more convenient than that nearby post office. Somewhat musty rooms. Singles 110,000R, doubles 150,000R, triples 135,000R (hey—they're still learning. With shower, singles 125,000R, doubles 200,000R, but hot water is iffy.

FOOD

Presumably forced to subsist for weeks on nothing but hardtack and limes, Kaliningrad's sailors seem to enjoy its few restaurants. Unless you've been similarly deprived, you probably won't feel the same. Luckily, there's the **central market** (Центральный Рынок; *Tsentralny Rynok*) at ul. Chernyakhovskovo's intersection with ul. Gorkovo (open daily 9am-6pm). The market was built for a 1930s trade exhibition, but currently merchants from Baku and their fruits cram its huge halls. **Universam,** Moskovsky pr. 83 (Универсам; tel. 43 26 77), does a reasonable impersonation of a supermarket (open daily 9am-10pm). A number of small *produkty* (продукты) have cropped up; they don't stock much, but they'll do in a pinch.

Restoran Belarus (Ресторан Беларусь), ul. Zhitomirskaya 14 (Житомирская; tel. 43 22 31). A throwback to the Evil Empire, Belarus serves some of the meanest beef stroganoff around. Try the *solyanka,* flavored with olives, lemons, peppers, and Georgian spices. Entrées 20,000R, soups and salads 15,000R. Live music most nights, otherwise MTV or its Russian equivalent. Open daily noon-11pm.

Italy Bar, Leninsky pr. 27/31 (tel. 43 07 53), south of the Mother Russia statue. Meager entrées around 30,000R and up. Brilliantly innovative garnishes—like a scoop of plain rice with some butter—for 12,000R. Pizza 18,000R. Popular with Baltic Fleet officers who come here daily to pinch the waitresses. Open daily 10am-2am.

Restoran Moskva (Ресторан Москва), in Gostinitsa Moskva (tel. 27 27 07). Breathtakingly Soviet, deep-red interior with weird stained glass is the main attraction besides low prices. They carry only a few of the items on the menu, so ask first. Beef stroganoff 8700R; beefsteaks 9200R. Open daily noon-5pm and 6-11pm.

The Three Candles (Три Свечах), on the terrace of the Drama theater (tel. 21 77 71). The most pleasant outdoor café in the city. People simply relax and watch the city rush past over a cold *EKU Pils* (10,000R) and sandwiches (5900-6600R).

The Smak (Смак). Mouths water and lips smack for the tasty, cheap burgers (6700R) spewing from these fast-food stands that litter the city (look for a yellow awning). Large fries for 4300R. Usually open daily 9am-8pm.

Stary Gorod (Старый Город), Leninsky pr. 21, entrance on the side. Packed with noisy sailors, and other hungry folks who come for the big portions rather than the atmosphere. Salad 2000-5000R, entrées around 10,000R. Not for those in search of a delicate dining experience. Open daily 9am-11pm.

SIGHTS

Kaliningrad's once-pretty *prima donna*, the old **cathedral** (director tel. 21 25 83) ages on the large island in the Pregolya River. Limited funds allowed for the restoration of only one of the cathedral's towers after a fire in the 1540s. Its scarred, burnt-out shell stands as both a reminder of Königsberg's German heritage, and a monument to the Russian conquest of the city. Plans to perform plastic surgery (currently in progress) may supply the old church with a third symbolic role, reflecting the heavy flow of German tourist money into the city. Inside, tombs line the cathedral's walls, but many have been vandalized or eroded over time (open daily 9am-4pm). One grave that has been immaculately kept is that of **Immanuel Kant,** the 18th-century German philosopher who lived his entire life in Königsberg and taught at the local university. Kant's burial ground originally looked less gaudy, but since WWII, pink marble colonnades have sprung up around it, eerily evoking Lenin's Tomb in Moscow. Walk around (outside) to the back of the cathedral to find it.

North of the cathedral, Leninsky pr. expands into **Tsentralnaya pl.,** another spot endowed with Soviet significance. Since 1255, when Teutonic knights first arrived in the area, a castle had guarded the hill east of the square. As part of the concerted effort made to turn Königsberg into a truly Soviet city, the 700-year-old Königsberg Castle was blown up in 1962 and replaced by Kaliningrad's **House of Soviets,** an H-shaped monstrosity that, after 35 years, has yet to be completed. Save some film for this poured-concrete paean to soulless Soviet architecture. The **Museum of Art,** Moskovsky pr. 60 (tel. 46 72 49), has rotating exhibits (open Tues.-Sun. 11am-7pm).

Ul. Shevchenko (Шевченко), which runs on the north side of the House of Soviets, rapidly changes into ul. Klinicheskaya (Клиническая) and begins to snake around the east edge of **Prud Nizhny** (Пруд Нижний), the smaller of the city's two lakes. Halfway up its length is the **Museum of History and Art** (Историко-Художественный Музей; *Istoriko-Khudozhestvenny Muzey*), Klinicheskaya 21 (tel. 45 39 02). The second floor is devoted to the heroic Soviet army and its conquest of the depraved German city of Königsberg in 1945. There is also a newer, less bombastic display on the Afghanistan War. Rotating exhibits of modern artists from the former Soviet Union make up the third floor (open Tues.-Sun. 11am-7pm, ticket office open 11am-6pm; 5000R, Russians 1000R). Further north, ul. Klinicheskaya ends across from the **Amber Museum** (Музей Янтаря; *Muzey Yantarya*), pl. Vasilevskovo (Василевского; tel. 46 12 40). These are not the crude yellow carvings one finds at local fleamarkets. Nearly 90% of the world's amber comes from the mines in nearby Yanar, and these are the best specimens of the lot. Tons of pieces in three amber shops downstairs, where prices are reasonable but not as low as you'd think—it *is* tree sap, after all (open Tues.-Sun. 10am-5:30pm; 5000R, students 1000R). The museum is housed in one of Königsberg's seven remaining **City Gates**; the other six, all in different styles, are worth seeing only if you appreciate Gothic brick monuments in need of repair.

Off Leninsky pr., on ul. Universitetskaya (Университетская), the University of Kaliningrad's garden confronts the **Bunker Museum** (Музей Блиндаж; *Muzey Blindazh*;

tel. 43 05 93), a network of rooms from which Nazis directed their defense of Königsberg. The museum presents the capture of the city in great detail; unlucky Room 13 has been left exactly as it was when the city's commander signed it over to the Red Army (open daily 10am-5:30pm; 5000R, Russians 1000R).

Wrestling baby bears welcome you to the **zoo**, pr. Mira, across from Gostinitsa Moskva (tel. 21 89 24); their grown-up relatives have learned to do tricks for tourists offering food (against the rules, of course). A lot of empty cages, but some animals and a pleasant, if labyrinthine park (open 9am-9pm; 4000R).

ENTERTAINMENT

The **Puppet Theater** (Театр Кукол; *Teatr Kukol*) in the **Kalinin Park of Culture and Rest** (ПКиО; *PKiO*) is two stops past the zoo on tram #1 or 4. The turn-of-the-century **Luise Church**, so designated for the eponymous Prussian queen, caters to the kindergarten crowd (box office open Mon.-Fri. 10am-5pm). You can find frequent **organ concerts** in the large brick church at ul. B. Khmelnitskovo 63a (Б. Хмельницкого), several blocks east and north of Yuzhny Vokzal. Prices and times fluctuate; check posters for more information. There's also the **Russian Drama Theater**, pr. Mira 4 (Драматический Театр; *Dramatichesky Teatr*, tel. 21 24 22), housed in a Weimar-era residence east of the zoo. Ask the friendly director Anatoly Kravtsov for a tour of the remarkable building. Tickets to performances run 8000-15,000R. Open daily 9am-9pm.

Nightlife in good ol' Königsberg was once a lot livelier (it was depraved, remember?). At **Diskoteka Vagonstra** (Дискотека Вагонстра), ul. Radischeva (Радищева), in a cavernous, unmarked grey building, presumed mafiosi rub shoulders with students and soldiers, and shimmy til dawn. Take tram #1 or 4 five stops past the zoo, and follow ul. Vagonstroitelnaya (Вагонстроительная), the street immediately behind the tram as you get off. The first street on the right is ul. Radischeva. At **Penta Club** (Пента Клуб), in the old stock exchange near Leninsky pr. bridge, foreigners make popular dance partners for the under-20 set (open Fri.-Sun. 7:30-10pm).

■ Near Kaliningrad: The Baltic Coast

ZELENOGRADSK (ЗЕЛЕНОГРАДСК)

High hills run north to the edge of the Baltic, and evergreen trees and salt air emanate a scent like that of pine-fresh *Glade*. Zelenogradsk, 30km from Kaliningrad, decorates the base of the Curonian Spit (Куршская Коса; *Kurshskaya Kosa*), a 2km by 100km peninsula that stretches up into Lithuania. The town became an incredibly popular Soviet holiday destination in the mid-1960s. It can still be tough to find a weekend spot on the wide, soft sand, but now the surf-side population is mostly from Kaliningrad. The Soviet Union's break up struck the tourist industry hard, and a backdrop of half-completed buildings along the boardwalk somewhat mars the beautiful beach.

Trains run from Kaliningrad's Severny Vokzal to the Zelenogradsk station (15 per day, 40min., 4000R; the last returns to Kaliningrad at 9:30pm), where you can **store luggage** in 6400R lockers. Just north of the train station, you can catch a **bus** to lovely Kaliningrad (5 per day, 40min. to Severny Vokzal) and other local destinations. The Zelenogradsk **market** (open daily 9am-6pm) is behind the station; stroll through, and pick up supplies before heading to the beach. **Exchange currency** at bad rates and cash Thomas Cook traveler's checks with 4% commission in Sberbank (Сбербанк; tel. 319 05, open Mon.-Fri. 8am-1pm and 2-6pm) on the second floor of ul. Lenina 8 (Ленина). Enter from the rear of the building. Beyond the market, the **post office**, Turgeneva 4a (Тургенева; tel. 319 67), licks 'em and sticks 'em in an odd honeycombed blue-grey building (open Mon.-Fri. 9am-2pm and 3-5pm, Sat. 9am-1pm). **Postal code:** 238530. The **telephone office** is housed in a wild pre-war brick construction at ul. Lenina 29, a right off of Turgeneva (tel. 323 07). It's fairly modern and open 24 hours. **Phone code:** 8250 from Kaliningrad, 01150 from elsewhere.

Further along ul. Lenina, **Café Vstrecha** (Кафе Встреча), Lenina 15, offers full meals for 20,000R, and shots of vodka for 3000R (open noon-midnight). Turn left at the post office and follow the street north through a small square, to reach the beach at the central part of the **boardwalk**. The beach to the right of the boardwalk is better; if you go far enough past the end, you'll arrive at the **nude bathing** area.

SVETLOGORSK (СВЕТЛОГОРСК)

The premier resort for fashionable Königsbergers, Svetlogorsk escaped the heavy hand of Soviet architecture and still retains much of its old German flavor, with tree-lined streets and turn-of-the-century villas set on high, coast-hugging dunes. Seemingly lined with more bars and eateries than in all of Kalingrad itself, ul. Oktyabrskaya (Октябрская) leads down to the center, and eventually, the beach. **Hotel Troika** (Гостиница Тройка), Kaliningradskaya 77a (tel. 330 63 or 330 81) has bright rooms with tall ceilings, big windows, a toilet, and even a lukewarm shower for DM23 per person. To the right of Svetlogorsk II, **Restoran Yantar** (Ресторан Янтарь), ul. Lenina 4 (Ленина; tel. 60 79), feeds its clients excellent *shashliks* (11,000R) on an outdoor terrace (open daily noon-11pm, Fri. and Sat. until 2am). Cafeteria-style Russian cuisine (you know what that means) is as cheap as it comes at **"Bar"** Oktyabrskaya 20, where a full meal runs under 15,000R (open noon-6am).

Buses from Kaliningrad are rare, but **trains** arrive hourly from Severny Vokzal (1hr., 4000R). There are two train stations, but they are only a kilometer apart. The first, Svetlogorsk I, has **luggage storage** (6400R); the second (get this—Svetlogorsk II), is closer to the beach, and there is even a chairlift to the sand (2000R, open Wed.-Sun. 10am-6pm). Not all trains stop at #2 though. Trains arrive from Kaliningrad (17 per day, 1hr., 4000-4800R), the last returning to the city at 7:56pm. Behind Svetlogorsk I, go left, then right onto the long, broad, paved path leading to the city; take a left off this path. Down the hill and over the river is Kaliningradsky pr. (Калининградский; around #35). Continue straight up the hill to tree-covered, steep ul. Gagarina (Гагарина). Left off Gagarina is the **post office,** ul. Ostrovskovo 3 (Островского; tel. 32 17; open Mon.-Fri. 8:30am-5pm, Sat. 8:30am-2pm). **Postal code:** 238 8550. Next to it you can **exchange currency** (open Mon.-Fri. 9am-1pm and 2-4pm). The **telephone office** is in the same building (tel. 3210; fax 46 32 74; open 24hr.). **Phone code:** 82533.

SLOVAKIA (SLOVENSKO)

US$1 = 30.41Sk (Koruny)	10Sk = US$0.33
CDN$1 = 22.21Sk	10Sk = CDN$0.45
UK£1 = 47.53Sk	10Sk = UK£0.21
IR£1 = 49.40Sk	10Sk = IR£0.20
AUS$1 = 24.04Sk	10Sk = AUS$0.42
NZ$1 = 21.20Sk	10Sk = NZ$0.47
SAR1 = 6.85Sk	10Sk = SAR1.15
DM1 = 20.60Sk	10Sk = DM0.49
Country Phone Code: 42	**International Dialing Prefix: 00**

Survivor of centuries of nomadic invasions, Hungarian domination, and Soviet industrialization, Slovakia has recently emerged triumphant as an independent country. With rocky mountains to the north and forested hills in the center, Slovakia is covered with natural wonders. It's no surprise that hiking and skiing have become national pastimes. Relics of the defenses against Tartars and Turks, castle ruins dot the countryside, and in smaller towns, even suburban factories have not compromised the old-time atmosphere. So for a lesson in isolated rurality, take a deep draught of Slovak wine, put on some hiking boots, and enjoy the freedom.

SLOVAKIA ESSENTIALS

Americans can visit Slovakia visa-free for up to 30 days; Britons, 180 days; and Irish, 90 days. Citizens of Australia, Canada, New Zealand and South Africa need a 30-day, single-entry visa (US$23, Canadians US$48; US$34 for double-entry, Canadians US$48; US$85 for 180-day multiple-entry, Canadians US$96) or a US$23 transit visa

(Canadians US$46). The processing takes two days. Apply at an embassy or consulate, or at the border (at an additional fee). Submit your passport, fee by cash or money order, as many visa applications as planned entries, and two passport photos for every application. See Essentials: Embassies and Consulates, p. 8. For a visa extension of up to 6 months, go to the local office of Alien and Border Police.

GETTING THERE AND GETTING AROUND

International bus and rail links connect Slovakia to all of its neighbors. Larger train stations operate **BIJ-Wasteels** offices, which offer 20-50% off tickets to European cities (but not Prague) for those under 26. **EastRail** is valid in Slovakia; **Eurail** is not. A *miestenka* (reservation, 6-7Sk) is required for international voyages (including the Czech Republic); buy international tickets at windows marked with a boxed "R".

Larger towns on the **railway** possess many *stanice* (train stations), *hlavná stanica* being the main one. Smaller towns have only one, and teensy-weensy villages usually own a decaying hut that posts an illegible schedule and shelters drunks. Tickets must be bought before boarding the train, except in the tiniest towns. **ŽSR** is the national train company; every information desk has a copy of **Cestovný poriadok** (58Sk), the master schedule. *Odchody* (departures) and *príchody* (arrivals) are on the left and right of schedules, respectively, but be sure to check revolving timetables, as the *nástupište* (train platform) often changes from the one listed. A reservation is needed for *expresný* trains and first-class seats, but not for *rychlík* (fast), *spešný* (semi-fast), or *osobný* (local) trains. Trains arrive and leave with abnormal promptness, except when coming from the Czech Republic. Train station **lockers** function only half the time, and then after you've figured out how to work them. Instructions for using the tangles of knobs and wires are in Russian, German, and Slovak, but even native speakers don't necessarily understand them. Insert a 5Sk coin, choose your own personal code on the *inside,* insert your bag, and try to shut it. If it does not lock, cry, and try another locker. Attempt ten times. If you fail, go to the luggage window. Otherwise, to reclaim your bag, arrange outer knobs to fit your own personal code. Sometimes, the aging circuit takes a few seconds to register and open.

In many hilly regions, **ČSAD** or **SAD buses** are the best and sometimes the only way to get from A to B. Except for very long trips, buy the ticket on the bus. Schedules seem designed to drive foreigners batty with their many footnotes; the most important are as follows: **X,** weekdays only; **a,** Saturdays and Sundays only; **r** and **k,** exclude holidays; **numbers** refer to days of the week on which the bus travels a given route—1 is Monday, 2 is Tuesday, and so forth. *Bremava* means including; *nepremava* is except; following those words are often lists of dates, day first, and then month. In the summer watch out for St. Cyril and Methodius Day, July 5.

The rambling wilds and ruined castles of Slovakia inspire great **bike** tours. The Slovaks love to tramp on two wheels, especially in the Tatras, the foothills of West Slovakia, and Šariš. **VKÚ** publishes accurate maps of all Slovak regions (59Sk, in German 80Sk), with color-coded trails.

TOURIST SERVICES AND MONEY

Access has opened up tourist services in major towns. They generally sell good maps and book inexpensive rooms.

After the 1993 Czech-Slovak split, Slovakia hastily designed its own currency which is now the country's only legal tender (no matter how ugly). One hundred **halier** make up one **koruna** (Sk). Keep your exchange receipts to change Slovak korunas back into hard currency. **Všeobecná Úverová Banka (VÚB)** operates offices in even the smallest towns and cashes **AmEx traveler's checks** for a 1% fee. Most offices give **MasterCard** cash advances and have Cirrus, Eurocard, MC, and Visa **ATMs,** referred to as **bankomats.** Many **Slovenská Sporiteľňa** bureaus handle **Visa** cash advances.

COMMUNICATION

The **mail** service in the Slovak Republic is efficient and modern. Almost every *pošta* (post office) provides **Express Mail Services,** but a trip to a *colnice* (customs office) is in order to send a package abroad. **Poste Restante** mail with a "1" after the city name will arrive at the main post office. Local **telephone** calls cost 2Sk; drop the coin in after you've been connected. Phone cards are beginning to flourish throughout Slovakia, but in smaller towns, change comes in handy. For: **AT&T Direct,** dial 00 42 000 101; **MCI WorldPhone,** dial 00 42 000 112; **Canada Direct,** dial 00 42 000 151; **British Telecom Direct,** dial 00 42 004 401. International calling cards are eerily limited to either two minutes or a half-hour. Slovakia's only **English-language newspaper,** the weekly **Slovak Spectator** (25Sk), is published in Bratislava and features propaganda on country politics and tourism. The entertainment section provides listings of eateries, nightlife, and theater in the capital.

LANGUAGE

Slovak resembles **Czech** more than independent-minded Slovaks like to admit (see the Czech glossary, p. 775). The official line is that the older generation speaks **German,** while the young learn **English.** Herds of German-speaking tourists assure that German will remain the country's second language for a long time, with the possible exception of the eastern region near Košice and Prešov. The *"r"* is rolled on the tip of the tongue. **Russian** is understood, but even ancient Greek is more welcome.

HEALTH AND SAFETY

> **Emergency Numbers: Fire:** tel. 150. **Ambulance:** tel. 155. **Police:** tel. 158.

Visitors are advised not to drink tap **water,** which is heavily chlorinated and may cause abdominal discomfort. Bottled water is available in grocery stores, but is almost invariably carbonated. A reciprocal Health Agreement between Slovakia and the U.K. entitles Brits to free medical care here. The sometimes putrid **restrooms** (15-25Sk) at train stations always have soap and toilet paper. K-marts carry American brands of **cold** and **headache medicine, tampons,** and **condoms.**

ACCOMMODATIONS AND CAMPING

Foreigners will shell out twice as much as natives. The best way to find a room is by asking at the local tourist office. You run the risk of all the inexpensive places being booked, but with the exception of holidays and resort areas (i.e., the High Tatras), this is rarely the case, and given the rate at which phone numbers change anyway, it's difficult to call ahead. **Juniorhotels (HI),** though uncommon, are a step above the usual brand of hostel. In the mountains, **chaty** (mountain huts/chalets) range from plush quarters for 400Sk per night to a friendly bunk and outhouse for 100Sk. **Hotels** in the boonies provide comparable service to those in cities but are much cheaper. **Penzións** are generally less expensive then hotels and, especially when family-run, often nicer. Two forms of *ubytovanie* (lodging) cater mainly to Slovaks and offer super prices for bare-bones rooms: **stadiums** and sport centers often run sport hotels on the lot for teams and fans (the requisite pubs on the ground floor are always hoppin'); **workers' hostels** generally offer hospital-like rooms and no pub downstairs. **Campgrounds** lurk on the outskirts of most towns, and for travelers without tents, many offer bungalows. They range from yucks to deluxe, and give good value for the money. Camping in national parks is illegal.

FOOD AND DRINK

Slovakia rose out of its thousand-year Hungarian captivity with a taste for paprika, spicy *gulaš,* and fine wines. The national dish, *bryndzove halušky,* knocks stomachs out with heavy dumplings smothered in a thick sauce of goat cheese. In fact, dumplings (*knedlíky* or *halušky*) come with everything—fruit, gravy, and fried pork steak (10-50Sk). Those who don't order them get strange looks from the waiter, who might bring them anyway. If dumplings are not for you, most restaurants also serve potatoes (*zemiaky*) and french fries (*hranolky*). Slovakia's second favorite dish is *piroby*, a pasta-pocket, usually filled with potato or *bryndzou* cheese, with bits of bacon on top. Also popular is *pstruh* (trout). *Kolačy* (pastry) is often baked with cheese, jam, or a black paste made from ground poppy seeds and honey.

Fine white wines are produced in the Small Carpathians northeast of Bratislava, especially around the town of Pezinok. *Riesling* and *Müller-Thurgau* grapes are typically used; quality varies greatly. *Tokaj* wines are produced south of Košice. You can enjoy any of these at a *vináreň* (wine hall). *Pivo* (beer) is served at a *pivnica* or *piváreň* (beerhall). Lovers of brandies will not be disappointed in Slovakia, home to the apricot *marhulovica*, the juniper-berry *borovička*, and the plum *slivovica*.

CUSTOMS AND ETIQUETTE

Tipping is common in restaurants, but in small amounts; most people round up to a convenient number, and 8-10% is generous. Tip by refusing change as you pay. Most **museums** close Mondays, and **theaters** take a break July to August. Stuck in the backwaters of Hungary for a millennium, Slovaks have guarded a fiercely conservative bent. Although **homosexuality** is legal, a couple walking down the street might receive stares or insults; usually everyone is so shocked, however, that no one interferes. The national gay organization, **Ganymedes**, arranges hotlines around the country, but few employees speak English. **Grocery store attendants** will accost you if you don't grab a basket by the store's entrance. **Westerners** are treated with respect, and, in small towns, surprise. Slovak women, especially the forty and over set, are not afraid to experiment with hair color and shocking variations on scarlet result.

LIFE AND TIMES

HISTORY

The Slovaks have never been very powerful, but they do have a distinct history. Settled by **Slavs** in the 6th and 7th centuries, Slovakia was incorporated into the Greater Moravian Empire in the 870s, along with Bohemia, South Poland, and what is now West Hungary. The empire converted to Catholicism in 880, but fell to invading Magyars in 906. Slovakia was soon assimilated by the **Kingdom of Hungary.** In the 12th century, a Hungarian king invited German **Saxons** from the Rhineland to help develop the area of the kingdom inhabited by the Slovaks. The Saxons founded several *Spiš* towns, including Poprad and Levoča. Though the Hungarians were defeated by the Mongols in 1241, and local rulers (the Csáks) came to rule Slovakia, the Hungarian monarchy regained control in 1308 and ruled Slovakia for two more centuries.

After the Ottomans defeated Hungary in the 1526 **Battle of Mohács,** Slovakia became a bulwark of the West against the Turks. The **Habsburg** emperors, who ruled Hungarian Slovakia between 1526 and 1918, eventually freed all of Hungary from Turkish occupation and by 1700 began to redevelop the region. **Lutheranism** and **Calvinism** had become popular among the German, Slovak, and Magyar communities of Slovakia, particularly in the East. The Habsburgs proceeded to restore **Roman Catholicism** in the lands, leading to religious wars in 1603 and 1669-71.

In the 19th century, various national movements emerged in the Kingdom of Hungary. Led by **L'udovít Štúr** and Jozef Šafárik, the Slovak movement voiced its concerns at **Liptovský Svätý Mikuláš** during the tumultuous **Revolution of 1848,** which brought little change to Slovakia but disaster to their Hungarian overlords. After the Austro-Hungarian *Ausgleich* (Compromise) of 1867, Hungary regained control over Slovakia. Slovakia remained one of the most submerged nationalities in the polyglot Austro-Hungarian Empire; without even their own province, they lived under direct

Hungarian rule. Ignoring the wise advice of Hungarian intellectuals, the Hungarian government, particularly under Tisza from 1875-90, launched the process of Magyarization, forcing many Slovaks to leave their homeland and alienating those who remained. The Slovak national movement blossomed in this period, but the "Czecho-Slovak National Committee," which had been meeting in Pittsburgh during the war, opted for a joint Czecho-Slovak state. On **October 28, 1918,** six days before Austria-Hungary sued for peace, Czechoslovakia was proclaimed an independent state, giving Slovakia the greatest degree of self-rule it had ever known. At the end of WWI, Slovakia was attached to Bohemia, Moravia, and Sub-Carpathian Ruthenia to form **Czechoslovakia,** a new state in the heart of Europe, with a federal capital at Prague and regional capital at Bratislava. The state made a good start, repelling an invasion of Slovakia by the Hungarian communist Bela Kun in 1919 and securing the withdrawal of Romanian troops from Ruthenia. It became a **liberal democracy** on an American model and one of the world's wealthier nations. Czechoslovakia was the sole state in Central or Eastern Europe that did not descend into fascist, authoritarian, or communist rule. Though the policies of the Czechs toward the German and Slovak minorities were relatively liberal, they were often not liberal enough for Slovak nationalist parties, who resented what they regarded as Czech domination.

Czechoslovakia was, after Germany, the strongest country in the area, and Hitler made it an early target. Abandoned by the British and French at Munich, and with Poland and Romania unwilling to permit Soviet assistance, the democratic state could not fight and buckled under German pressure in March 1938. By October 1938, Slovakia was proclaimed an autonomous unit within a federal Czecho-Slovak state. After German troops invaded Bohemia and Moravia in March 1939, Slovakia emerged as a collaborative Nazi puppet "independent state" under **Monseignor Tiso.** Authoritarian Hungary took advantage of the difficult position of the formerly prosperous, democratic state; in 1938, Hungary helped itself to a third of Slovakia. Resentment against the Nazis caused a two-month **uprising** in the summer of 1944.

After World War II, Slovakia joined the reconstituted democratic Czechoslovakia, which the **Communists** were only barely able to subvert, with massive Soviet support in February 1948. In theory, the 1960 constitution guaranteed Slovakia equal rights, but since the Communists gained power, Slovaks felt oppressed by a Czech-dominated government. Post-war Czechoslovakia expelled members of Slovakia's Hungarian and Saxon communities and was forced to cede Ruthenia to the Soviet Union. The Stalinist regime that emerged in Czechoslovakia remained subservient to Moscow until Slovak **Alexander Dubček** introduced his **"Prague Spring"** reforms in 1968. Soviet tanks crushed Dubček's allegedly disloyal government and the country returned to totalitarianism in 1969. With the defeat of the reformist regime, Slovakia acquired increased autonomy and Bratislava was made a "capital city" in 1969. Rural Slovakia underwent heavy industrial development. After the Soviet invasion, the Communists remained in power in Czechoslovakia until the **Velvet Revolution of 1989. Václav Havel** was appointed President and set about introducing a pluralistic political system and a market economy. In this atmosphere of increased freedom, and encouraged by Czechs eager to shed their poorer half, Slovak nationalism began to gain ground and ultimately triumphed in the **1993 Declaration of Independence.** Less than four years after Czechoslovakia had played a crucial role in burying the Soviet empire, the state ceased to exist, making an independent Slovakia a reality for the first time.

LITERATURE

If the dissolution of Czechoslovakia has been likened to a divorce, then Slovakia's literary accomplishments may finally escape the shadow of its more highly acclaimed spouse. Slovak as a literary language only began to emerge in the 18th century, and even then only because a temporary decline in literary Czech left room for Slovakia to produce its own locally colored devotional texts. Early examples of the Slovak novel, such as **Ignác Bajza's** *Rene* (1785) represented a Slovak version of Czech rather than a truly distinct language.

Slovak literature has often attempted to define itself through overtly nationalist themes. **Ján Holly's** lyrics and idylls of the late 18th century celebrate the Slovak land and people, and, like many subsequent Slovak works, owe a tremendous debt to indigenous folk poetry. Yet the work of Holly and his contemporaries still relied on a Czech-influenced version of West Slovak dialects.

Literary Slovak as an independent tradition began with the work of the 19th-century linguist, patriot, and nationalist **Ľudovít Štur.** Štur's "new" language—based on the Central Slovak dialects and accepted more widely than any previous attempt at standardization—inspired a string of nationalist poets. Foremost among these was **Andrej Sládkovič**, author of the national epic *Marína* (1846). Slovak writers' nationalist passions may only be surpassed by their amorous ones. Sládkovič's contemporary, the poet and revolutionary **Janko Kráľ,** launched an enduring tradition of Slovak Romanticism with his ballads, epics, and lyrics, a tradition followed by the rustic Slavophile poets **Vajansky** and **Hviezdoslav.**

As the Slovak nation came of age in the wake of WWI, gaining the greatest measure of independence it had yet enjoyed, so too did Slovak literature reach maturity. Besides the established nationalist and romantic themes, more cosmopolitan influences began to appear in Slovak writing: **E. B. Lukáč** introduced Symbolism to the Slovak tradition, Surrealism found a champion in **Rudolf Fabry,** and **Laco Novomeský** complemented his career as a Communist journalist with early poetic endeavors at so-called **Socialist Realism.**

The long-established primacy of poetic forms also began to give way to novels and short stories. As in poetry, though, rustic themes and the life of the village took center stage, often as an object of praise and celebration, but increasingly as the butt of scorn and ridicule. Although the latter attitude is less typical, its adherents have produced incomparably more creative work. **Janko Jesenký** savaged the tin-pot regional poo-bahs of the new Slovak administration after WWI in his two-part satirical novel *Demokrati (The Democrats).* He deromanticizes the small-town experience, portraying villagers as shallow, petty, Magyarized hypocrites.

The succession of the nominally independent, Nazi-puppet Slovakia and its reabsorption into a Communist Czechoslovakia did little for the country's literature. If the thought of reading a self-styled Slavic Zola who makes his model's political overtones seem subtle doesn't appeal to you, be sure to avoid the ham-handed novels of **Peter Jilemnický.** *The Untilled Field* succumbs to all the predictable excesses of the leftist political novel, with its set full of exploited peasants and greedy capitalists straight out of a Leninist version of Central Casting. Jilemnický's creative field would have been better left untilled, too. You'll fare no better with the stiff anti-fascist, anti-Clerical cant of **František Hečko.**

With its new-found independence, Slovakia may well experience a fresh literary renaissance. The creative and stylistic development that began almost two and a half centuries ago may finally, after a 50-year hibernation, begin again.

SLOVAKIA TODAY

Coming out of the 1993 velvet revolution with only 25% of former Czechoslovakia's industrial capacity and even less of its international reputation, Slovakia has had more trouble adjusting to the post-East-Bloc world than its former partner. Premier Vladimir Mečiar is accumulating power by returning to the political patterns of the past, ignoring the parliament and free market reforms and retaining industry under state control. Opposition leaders are hampered by the lack of a strong parliament. There are also problems with the Hungarian minority, and some Slovaks are having second thoughts about independence, particularly as the Slovak standard of living continues to lag behind that of the Czech Republic. Prime Minister Mečiar is virtually at war with the president and is rumored to have kidnapped his son. Meanwhile, despite Mečiar's promises that his nation is approaching stability, potential investors and allies are wary of dealing with the country until it emerges from its current political and economic funk.

Bratislava

Bratislava
Bratislava Castle, 6
Franciscan Church, 2
Michael Tower, 1
Old City Hall, 4
Primate's Palace, 3
Slovak National Gallery, 7
Slovak National Museum, 8
St. Martin's Cathedral, 5

Bratislava

After 80 years of playing second fiddle to starlet Prague, the burgeoning city of half a million has been thrust into a new role as the capital of Slovakia and the largest city in the country. Bratislava has a rich history of Celtic kings and diverse populations, but much of its past fell to plans of grand functionalism in the 1900s. At least it's succeeded at cleaning up the air, as witnessed by the giant digital box outside of K-mart displaying current dust levels. Young teens try out unfamiliar rollerblades in the tightly packed city center, which is hemmed in by chaotic roads and overseen by Bratislava's emblem, the four-towered castle (*hrad*). Though many travelers choose to see nothing but Bratislava's train station, those who want a glimpse of a thriving new capital and to enjoy an Old Town where the squares are filled with skate boarders, instead of tourists, will find a few days in Bratislava well spent.

ORIENTATION AND PRACTICAL INFORMATION

Bratislava lies on the banks of the Danube, a proverbial stone's throw from the Austrian and Hungarian borders. Avoid debarking at the **Nové Mesto train station,** which is much farther from the city center than **Hlavná stanica** (main station). From Hlavná, take tram #1 to **nám. SNP,** the administrative center. From the bus station, take bus #107 to **nám. J. Štúra** by the river. The **Dunaj** (Danube) runs east-west across Bratislava. In the city's south half, there is little more than a convention center, a roller-coaster Lunapark, and miles of post-war high-rises. **Most (Bridge) SNP,** which connects the two sections, becomes the highway **Staromestská** to the north. The road separates the king from his subjects. On a hill to the west towers Bratislava's castle, while the Old Town dwells to the east.

Tourist Offices: Bratislavská Informačná Služba (BIS), Klobučnicka 2 (tel. 533 3715 or 533 4370). Sells oodles of maps, gives city tours, and books rooms, private accommodations, hotels, and some summer hostels (250-300Sk). Open Mon.-Fri. 8am-7pm, Sat. 8am-2pm. Train station **annex** open daily 8am-6pm.

Consulates: Canada, Kolárska 4 (tel. 361 277; fax 361 220). **South Africa,** Jančova 8 (tel. 531 1582 or 531 5643). Open Mon.-Fri. 8:30am-5pm, Fri. 8:30-3pm. **U.K.,** Grösslingová 35 (tel. 364 420; fax 364 396). Open Mon.-Fri. 8:30am-12:30pm, 1:30-5pm. **U.S.,** Hviezdoslavovo nám. 4 (tel. 533 0861). Open Mon.-Fri. 8:30am-noon and 2-4pm.

Currency Exchange: Všeobecná Úverová Banka (VÚB), Gorkého 9 (tel. 515 7976; fax 515 8090), cashes AmEx traveler's checks and handles MC and Visa cash advances. A machine at Mostová 6 changes US$, DM, UK£ and Czech kč into sk at 1% commission. Open Mon.-Thurs. 8am-noon and 1:30-5pm, Fri. 8am-noon. **Train station branch** (tel. 204 5062) open daily 7:30am-6pm.

ATMs: Cirrus, Eurocard, MC, Primaciálne nám., train and bus stations. **Plus,** outside Slovenská Sporiteľňa in Hlavné nám. **Visa,** in the Old Town.

American Express: Tatratour, Františkánske nám. 3 (tel. 533 5536; fax 533 5538). Takes care of lost checks, cashes AmEx traveler's checks at 2% commission, sells traveler's checks at 1% commission, and holds mail. Open Mon.-Fri. 9am-4pm.

Trains: Bratislava Hlavná stanica (tel. 469 45), north of town at the end of Štefánikova. To: Budapest (11 per day, 3hr., 378Sk); Kiev (1 per day; 26hr., 1287Sk); Kraków (1 per day, 8hr., 879Sk); Lviv (1 per day, 14½hr., 913Sk); Prague (9 per day, 5hr., 229Sk); Vienna (4 per day, 1hr., 200Sk); Warsaw (2 per day, 8½hr., 1183Sk). International tickets at counters #9, 10, 11, 12, 15, 16. Reservations for *IC* and *Eurocity* trains costs an additional 100-220Sk. **Wasteels** at counter #15 or go to the office on the left as you enter Hlavná stanica. **Luggage storage:** 5Sk.

Buses: Mlynské nivy 31 (tel. 526 1312; fax 566 2887), east of the Old Town. To: Budapest (4 per day, 5hr., 300Sk); Prague (8 per day, 4½hr., 220Sk); Vienna (9 per day, 1½hr., 270Sk). Check ticket for bus number *(č. aut.)*; several different buses may depart simultaneously. **Lockers:** 5Sk.

Hydrofoils: Lodná osobná doprava, Fajnorovo nábr. 2 (tel. 363 518; fax 363 516), along the river. A scenic alternative to trains for Danube destinations. To: Devin Castle (1 per day; 1hr.; 60Sk, students 40Sk); Vienna (2 per day; 1hr.; 330Sk, students 210Sk); Budapest (1-2 per day; 3½-4hr.; 1000Sk, students 680Sk).

Public Transportation: All daytime trips on **trams** or **buses** require a 7Sk ticket bought at kiosks or the dusty orange automats found at most, but not all, bus stations. Night buses marked with black and orange numbers in the 500s require 14Sk. Most trams pass by nám. SNP, and a majority of buses stop at the SNP bridge's north base. The fine for joyriding is 500Sk, and the authorities do check. Tourist passes sold at some larger kiosks (1-day 35Sk, 2-day 65Sk, 7-day 105Sk).

Taxis: Hviezdoslavovo nám. (tel. 31 13 11). 24-hr. service.

Hitchhiking: Those hitching to Vienna cross the SNP bridge and walk down Viedenská cesta. This road also travels to Hungary via Győr, though fewer cars head that direction. Hitchers to Prague take bus #104 from the center to the Patronka stop. Hitching is legal and common, but not recommended by *Let's Go.*

English Bookstore: Big Ben Bookshop, Michalská 1 (tel. 533 3632; fax 533 3692). Open Mon.-Fri. 9am-6pm, Sat. 9am-noon.

Laundry: Improkom, Laurinská 18 (tel. 363 210). Same-day express service. Open Mon.-Fri. 8am-6pm, Sat. 8am-noon.

24-hr. Pharmacy: About 5 in town. Most central is at nám. SNP 20 (tel. 363 731).

Post Office: Main office at nám. SNP 5. **Poste restante** counter #6. Open Mon.-Fri. 7am-8pm, Sat. 7am-6pm, Sun. 9am-2pm. **Postal code:** 81000 Bratislava 1.

Telephones: On the second floor from the "Telefón Telegram" entrance of the post office. Open Mon.-Fri. 7am-9pm. Office at Kolárska 12 open 24hr. **Phone code:** 7.

ACCOMMODATIONS AND CAMPING

Bratislava's tourist agencies seem to requisition everything but retirement homes and orphanages to accommodate the summer rush of Vienna-bound crowds. July to August, a dozen dorms open up at hostels for backpackers who are "just passing through." But until the avaricious **ubytovanie** (accommodation) companies start kicking out grade-schoolers before the end of classes, cheap rooms and beds will be hard to come by in June. Most inexpensive lodging lies out in the Styx, but an efficient system of trams and night buses puts Charon to shame. The **BIS offices** (see above) find rooms on a moment's notice; they make reservations for a 20Sk fee.

Pension Gremium, Gorkého 11 (tel. 321 818; fax 330 653). Sterling showers and stuffed chairs in the heart of the Old Town. The single goes for 640Sk, the few doubles run 990Sk (deluxe double, 1300Sk). Shower and breakfast included. Only a few rooms, so call ahead. A popular café will feed you downstairs.

Youth Hostel Bernolak, Bernolákova 1 (tel. 397 723). From the train station, take bus #22, 23, or 210 or tram #3. Friendliest hostel in town with the best English; spacious singles (350Sk), doubles (420Sk), and triples (540Sk) with showers and toilets. 10% discount with Euro26, ISIC. Disco downstairs. Open July to mid-Sept.

Študentský domov Mirka Nešpora, Svoradova 13 (tel. 531 1908), up on the hill near the castle. Take bus #43 or 47 from the train station to Zochova, continue up the hill and turn right onto Svoradova. Nearly all singles, tidy, and not too far from town. Singles 180Sk, triples 120Sk per person. Open July and Aug.

YMCA na Slovenska, Karpatská 2 (tel. 498 005), 500m from the train station. A common overnight stop for those catching the next train out. Walk the long lane out of the train station and turn left on Šancová. Old terraced building. Sterile, spacious rooms with less sterile showers. The joint is hopping with a student bar and movie theater. Doubles, triples, and quints 200Sk per person.

Camping: Autocamping Zlaté Piesky, ul. Vajnorská (tel. 257 373), in suburban Trnávka. Take tram #2 or 4 to the last stop or bus #110 from Trnavské mýto to last stop. Campground and bungalows down by the lakeside, miles out of town. 80Sk per tent, 80Sk per person. 4-person bungalow 600Sk.

FOOD

Besides burgers, Bratislava's restaurants serve the region's spicy meat mixtures with West Slovakia's celebrated **Modra** wine. Offering escape from both cost and confusion is **K-mart's Potraviny** (grocery store), Kamenné nám. (open Mon.-Wed. 8am-7pm, Thurs. 8am-8pm, Fri. 8am-9pm, Sat. 8am-5pm, Sun. 9am-5pm). A **market** at Žilinská 5, near the train station, vends flowers and vegetables (open Mon.-Sat. 6am-4pm). A **non-stop deli** operates at Špitalská 45.

Piváreň U Eda, Biela 5 (tel. 533 28 44). A crowded central pub with generous portions and some of the best food in Bratislava. The *kuracia pečen vyprážaná* is not chicken, but chicken liver (64Sk). Real chicken costs 67Sk. German menu, but waiters speak English. Open daily 9am-10pm.

Café London, Panskà 17 (tel. 331 793), in the British Council's courtyard. Known for its mixed salad (42Sk), the café serves up Anglophile nostalgia with chicken salad, tuna, and roast beef sandwiches (39-72Sk). Mostly Italian-espresso-sipping, New-Yorkese-chatting, or *The-Times*-glossing Czechs. Open Mon.-Fri. 9am-9pm.

You Want Fries with That?

The only thing more incomprehensible than a Slovak menu is a Bratislavan menu at one of the city's ubiquitous burger stands. A cheeseburger costs less than a *hamburger so syrom* (hamburger with cheese) because, as the stand owner will explain with humiliating logic, a cheeseburger is made of cheese—and only cheese. A *pressburger,* named after Bratislava's old ancestor Pressburg, consists of bologna on a bun, and hamburgers are actually ham. Everything comes boiled (except the cheese) and stuck on a roll with diced cabbage, onions, and sauce.

Veľkí Františkáni, Františkánske nám. 10 (tel. 333 073), deep in the Old Town. Dishes range from bean soup (25Sk) to plates of roast duck that fly off into Sk infinity. The candle-lit wine cellar (where *Rizling Rýnsky* goes for 90Sk) is the focus of the restaurant; during the day it's reserved for tour groups, but after 5pm you too can partake of wine, folk music, and a 25Sk cover. Open daily 10am-1am.

Reštaurant Michaela, Michaská 11 (tel. 332 389), a sit down deli with a confusing menu. Fortunately, all the food's on display, so if you want, just point. Meat is 14-20Sk per 100g. Deli open Mon.-Fri. 8am-7pm, Sat. 8am-1pm; café-restaurant open Mon.-Fri. 9am-7:30pm, Sat. 9am-4pm.

SIGHTS

Medieval churches, aristocratic palaces, and burghers' houses line the stone streets and squares of the Old Town. Recently restored and refurbished, the quarter is a pleasure to wander through during the day and crackles with life at night. Outside the intimate confines of *Stará Bratislava* (Old Bratislava), things start to get rougher. To the west, a four-lane freeway now runs over what was once **Schlossberg,** the old Jewish suburb. To the east, a quarter of crumbling buildings begins, and from the castle spreads a view of the high-rises that taint the Danube's south shore. Fortunately, even Bratislava's hamburger stands are outnumbered by exhibits on arms, municipal fortifications, wine, feudal justice, pharmaceuticals, folk art, clocks, music, literature, police, Jewish culture, and "fellow compatriots".

Stará Bratislava (Old Bratislava)

Hlavné nám. is the Old Town's main square and center of tourist attractions. **Stará radnica** (Old City Hall) houses a complex of several buildings, the oldest of which harks back to Gothic times. Its distinctive yellow tower functions as one of Bratislava's trademarks, and on warm summer evenings brass bands play popular tunes on its balcony. The courtyard has survived as an elegant oasis; from here you can enter the **Bratislava Historical Museum,** Primaciálne nám. 1 (tel. 533 4690), with its fascinating collections of Gothic sculpture, aristocratic furniture, bourgeois mugs, Slovak books, and 19th-century pub signs. Downstairs, guards explain 13th-century torture in fervent Slovak, with the aid of graphic drawings and gruesome equipment (open Tues.-Sun. 10am-5pm; 10Sk, students 5Sk).

On the other side of the Old Town Hall, several restored buildings surround **Primaciálne nám.** The impressive Neoclassical **Primaciálny palác** (Primate's Palace, from the days when politicians were properly referred to as primates) witnessed the signing of the Peace of Pressburg (1805) by the victorious Napoleon and the temporarily vanquished Austrian Emperor Franz I in its **Zrkadlová Sieň,** or mirror hall. It is now a conference room, but tourists can peek in at the hall or the museum of tapestries in the palace's ornate rooms (open Tues.-Sun. 10am-5pm; 20Sk, students free). Adjacent to the square, the **Múzeum Johanna Nepomuka Hummela,** Klobučnicka 2, occupies the house where Hummel was born in 1778. Hungarian-Swabian by birth, the composer left his native Bratislava for the excitement of Stuttgart and Weimar, and is best known for his piano concertos. The museum displays Hummel memorabilia that illustrates life in 19th-century Bratislava (open Tues.-Sun. noon-5pm; 10Sk).

South of Hlavné nám. along Rybárska brána spreads long, wooded **Hviezdoslavovo nám.** The square is really a park surrounded by 19th-century architecture. Particularly striking is the **Slovenské národné divadlo** (National Theater), a restored neo-Renaissance building that has hosted performances for over a century. Mostová ends at **nám. Štúra,** with its clumsy monument to the much-loved namesake of the square. To the east of nám. Štúra, **Slovenské národné múzeum** (National Museum) houses the region's archaeological finds including casts of local Neanderthal skeletons (open Tues.-Sun. 9am-5pm; 10Sk, students 5Sk). On Rázusovo nábr., a sculpture garden leads to the four-story **Slovak National Gallery** at #2 (tel. 533 4276), which displays excellently preserved examples of Slovak Gothic and Baroque sculpture, frescoes, and paintings (open Tues.-Sun. 10am-6pm; 20Sk, students 10Sk).

A walk down Panská from Hlavné nám. leads to **Dóm svätého Martina** (St. Martin's Cathedral), a Gothic church and the site of the Hungarian kings' coronations for three centuries (open daily). Across Panská, **Lekáreň Gyógyszertár Apotheke Salvator** (Salvator Pharmacy), decorated with 19th-century cupids and lobsters, resembles a shrine more than a drugstore. Next to St. Martin's, the freeway travels south to the SNP suspension bridge, its reins held by a giant flying saucer, which one may enter for 10Sk. (For those reading this before arriving in Bratislava, never fear—it'll all make sense once you see the Mother Ship).

Adjacent to Hlavné nám., the **Franciscan Church,** with a Gothic tower and a more recent interior shelters a powerful organ that is sometimes heard from the square. From the church, Zámočnícka leads to **Michalská,** the busiest pedestrian street in *Stará Bratislava*. At the street's north end stands the Baroque **Michalská brána** (Michael Tower), a tall structure that once served as a watchtower, and now shelters the **Exhibition of Arms and Municipal Fortification,** with a rooftop view (open daily except Tues. 10am-5pm; 10Sk, students 5Sk).

North of the Michael Tower stretches **Hodžovo nám.,** a noisy nightmare of traffic and congestion. Up Staromestská at Konventná 13/15, the former **Evangelical Lyceum** has played a significant role in Bratislava's intellectual life and produced several renowned historical figures. Among its students were Slovak leaders Štúr, Kollár, and Šafárik, Swabian writers Eduard Glatz and T. G. Schröer, Hungarian poets Petöfi and Jókai, and Czech historian František Palacký. On the north side of Hodžovo nám., **Grassalkovičov palác** (Grassalkovich Palace), Hodžovo nám. 1, is the grandest of the city's grandest Hungarian aristocratic residences. Street lamps and a modern fountain disturb the white Baroque façade's composition, now being restored to serve as the seat of the President of the Slovak Republic. Behind the castle, the **Grassalkovich Gardens** offer escape from the noisy chaos of the square.

Bratislavský Hrad (Castle)

From the banks of the Danube to the Old Town's historic squares, the four-towered *Bratislavský hrad* remains a visible landmark. Of strategic importance for over a millennium, the castle burned down in 1811, and for many years was nothing more than a romantic ruin. Between 1953 and 1968, it was restored to its 15th-century appearance and now serves as the meeting place of the Slovak National Assembly and home to several collections of the **Mestské múzeum** (Municipal Museum), whose rich displays chronicle Slovak history, art, and culture. Be careful not to skip the basement, which houses a torture chamber with all the salient details in English. (Open Tues.-Thurs. and Sat.-Sun. 9am-5pm; 10Sk, students 5Sk).

ENTERTAINMENT AND NIGHTLIFE

For concert and theater schedules, pick up a copy of *Kám* at BIS. Although not in English, the info is easy to decipher. **Slovenská Filharmonia** plays regularly at Palackého ul. 2; buy tickets (600-700Sk) at the Reduta office beside the concert hall up to one hour before performances (tel. 533 3351). The Filharmonia and most theaters take their vacations in July and August. **National Theater** tickets (50Sk) are sold in the box office across the parking lot from the back of the Hviezdoslavoro nám. theater. Tickets for opera run 450-750Sk, and 150-600Sk for ballet (tel. 533 0069; box office open Mon.-Fri. 8am-6pm, Sat. 9am-1pm). Tickets for the internationally-known **Bohdan Warchal Quartet** are also available here. **Film Club Nostalgia,** Starohorská 2 (tel. 36 1713), hides among the ranks of Schwarzenegger purveyors. It plays oldies in Czech, English, and Woody-Allenease. Dance clubs are hard to find until a pub pushes its chairs and tables away and starts playing music.

Stará Sladovňa, Cintorínska 32 (tel. 32 1151). Known as Mamut, the mammoth-old malthouse serves up 20Sk *Budvar* to over a thousand patrons every night in one of Europe's largest beerhall complexes. It's hard to believe that country bands actually overpower the rumble of a thousand drunks. Garden open daily 10am-11pm. Hall open daily until midnight.

Charlie's Pub, Špitálska 4 (tel. 36 34 30). Charlie's patented leather chairs have been known to swallow weary souls into stuffed oblivion. If you want to dance, and can stand a few Bryan Adams ballads, a popular pub downstairs feeds on loud music 'til 4am. Cover 30Sk on most weekend nights. Open daily 9am-9pm.

Danglár, Hviezdoslavovo nám. 18. Salvador Dalí posters, cadres from Fritz Lang's *Metropolis,* and M.C. Escher prints adorn this basement pub's walls, where all they play is "good music"—70s rock, slow heavy, and easy punk. Slightly sketchy, cigarette-toting hip-and-grunge youth preside at the tables. Pool table in the back. Open Mon.-Fri. 4pm-2am, Sat. 6pm-2am, Sun. 5pm-1am.

Smíchovský Dvor, Mariánska 6 (tel. 363 590). They'll tell you Slovak beer is just as good, but here they serve Czech *Smíchov* (20Sk). Open Mon.-Sat. 11am-10:30pm.

■ Near Bratislava: Devín Castle

One of Danube's most enchanting and Slovakia's best-loved castle ruins perch on a promontory 9km west of Bratislava. Slavs first fortified the rock in the 800s under the Great Moravian Empire's King Ratislav, but the Magyars soon dismantled his state and claimed the hills. Devín remained a Hungarian stronghold guarding the Danube until Napoleon's troops sacked it and left the castle's winding walls to crumble. Decades later, the noble stones became a romantic symbol of Slovakia's past glory and its future independence. Under the Communists, the castle grew to symbolize totalitarianism. It sheltered sharpshooters, ordered to fire at anyone walking along the beach. Although the militiamen have left, vultures have made Devín's watchtower into a hunting lodge, and carry away unwary tourists in their deadly talons. Renovations to be completed by 1997 will better relate the Slovak saga. A **museum** exhibits archeological tidbits. From the Danube just below Bratislava Castle, take bus #29 to the village Devín. The parking lot at the end of Brigádnická leads to the castle (open May-Oct. daily 10am-5pm; 15Sk, students 5Sk).

CENTRAL SLOVAKIA

Northeast of Bratislava and south of the Tatras spreads a land of gentle, forested hills overlooked by Baroque-hungry Vienna-fans and muscle-flexing Tatra-climbers. Thus, the area of old mining and trading towns keeps to itself, somewhat unhappy for being slighted—blissfully unaware of what the average tourist boom entails.

■ Banská Bystrica

Banská Bystrica's wide town square is lined with cafés and graced by a rock fountain dating from the town's boom in the 13th-17th centuries. Another boom after World War II fortunately failed to destroy the core of town, and even Communism couldn't tarnish it. The factories remained outside the center hidden behind forested hills. Despite an engaging central square and numerous museums, the town remains virtually unknown to English-speakers and even the German tourists who drift through Eastern Europe seem to have forgotten Banská Bystrica.

Orientation and Practical Information Although the administrative capital of Central Slovakia has secluded itself in railway limbo, **buses** (tel. 745 479) leave for Bratislava (25 per day, 4 hr., 130Sk). **Trains** (tel. 742 132), next to the bus terminal, travel less frequently to Košice (1 per day, 4½hr., 158Sk) and Bratislava (1 per day, 4hr., 128Sk). **24-hr. luggage storage** costs 3Sk. To get to the town center, follow the underpass under the highway on the far side of the bus station from the train station. Walking up **Kukučinova** and then left onto **Horná** at the large pyramid, brings you to **nám. SNP.** The 20-minute walk can be avoided with the 5Sk **city bus** which leaves from the bus station and stops at the post office, just off nám SNP. This leads to the central square, nám. SNP. **Kultúrne a Informačné Stredisko (KIS),** nám.

SNP 1 (tel. 543 69), in the town hall, advertises the town's cultural events on its bulletin board. The staff provides free maps and info on Banská Bystrica's scant accommodations (open June-Sept. Mon.-Fri. 7:30am-6pm; Oct.-May Mon.-Fri. 7:30am-4:45pm). **VÚB**, nám. Slobody 1 (tel. 720 1111), **exchanges currency,** cashes AmEx traveler's checks, and offers a **Cirrus/MC ATM** outside. From nám. SNP, follow Horná to the east, and turn right on Kukučinova (open June-Sept. Mon.-Fri. 8am-noon and 1:30-5pm, Sat. 8am-noon; Oct.-May Mon.-Thurs. 8am-noon and 1:30-5pm, Fri. 8am-noon). A **24-hr. pharmacy** operates at Partizánska 12 (tel. 741 971). Follow Horná away from nám. SNP; after Kukučinova, Horná flows into Partizánska. The **post office**, Horná 1 (tel. 725 637), lies off nám. SNP (open Mon.-Fri. 8am-8pm, Sat. 8am-noon, Sun. 8-10am). **Postal code:** 97400. **Phone code:** 88.

Accommodations and Camping Large Banská Bystrica suffers from a surprising lack of rooms, and only one small budget hotel sits on the town's outskirts. **KIS** (see above) can arrange for hostels in July and August, but they fill up quickly. Call ahead. A few attractive options near Národná save the day with rooms that aren't so pricey. At **Hotel Passage Urpín,** Jána Cikkera 5 (tel. 724 556; fax 723 831). The essentials are all here—clean, pressed, and scrubbed. From nám. SNP, duck under the large arch on the left leading onto Národná. Turn left at the next block onto Jána Cikkera (singles 420Sk, with shower and toilet 460Sk; doubles 600Sk, with shower and toilet 680Sk; triples 900Sk; à la carte breakfast included). With a theater and a casino wrapped around it, **Národný dom,** Národná 11 (tel. 723 737; fax 249 74), off nám. SNP, is an entertainment package. The wide halls lead into wider rooms, each with radio and shoe horn. Hall bathrooms do not include showers (singles 360Sk, with shower 500Sk; doubles 600Sk, with shower 720Sk). **Hotel Turist,** Tajovského 68 (tel. 335 90), runs a **campsite** for those who really like roughing it. Take bus #31 from the train station. (70Sk per person; open May-Aug).

Food On a sunny summer day, nám. SNP blossoms with a bouquet of table umbrellas as cafés and restaurants vie for their share of the shuffling crowd. As nám. SNP narrows into Dolná and Horná, the crowd thins and so do the outdoor restaurants, but a few joints on the less-traveled paths offer lower prices and curious interiors. French baked goods have found *l'amour* at **Copaline Baguette,** Dolná 1 (tel. 725 868). Lines for the shop's legendary bread and sandwiches stretch into the street, but the crusty 30-75Sk creations, stuffed with tomatoes, cheese, lettuce, and the pickings of your choice, are worth the wait (open Mon.-Fri. 6:30am-midnight, Sat.-Sun. 8am-midnight). **Zemianska Reštaurácia,** Dolná (tel. 723 967), is worth visiting if only for the "English" menu, with "trout on the Hungarian art" and "fright potatoes." Their food (entrées 53-160Sk) is much better than their spelling (open daily 10am-10pm). For more greens, the **supermarket** on Kapitulská, off nám. SNP, stays open Monday-Friday 8am-6pm, Saturday 8am-1pm.

Sights and Entertainment Štátna gáleria, which occupies a few buildings in the Old Town, pleases every visitor, from grandpas to Lennon-spectacled revolutionaries. Originally a town hall, **Pretórium,** nám. Š. Moyzesa 25 (tel. 724 864), and the next-door **Barbakan** presents a taste of Slovakian abstract art. The gallery's "exhibition coffee," advertised as if it were a part of the tour, costs an extra 10Sk in the ground-floor parlor (open Tues.-Fri. 9am-5pm, Sat.-Sun. 10am-4pm). Outside the buildings, billboards advertise the town's cultural events. The Romanesque **Kostol Panny Márie** (Church of the Virgin Mary) guards an altar crafted by Master Pavel of Levoča's workshop. Farther up the hill, **Kostol sv. Kríža** (Church of the Holy Cross) hides a classic Gothic interior. Both churches are often closed. Graffitoed Renaissance houses surround nám. SNP. Near the castle area, the 16th-century **hodinová veža** (clocktower) battles with those who would correct its tilt.

Facing the nám. SNP fountain, the **Stredoslovenské Múzeum** (Museum of Central Slovakia) presents a decent slice of local history. Medieval trade-union insignias, folk costumes, and musical instruments document the region's development (open July-

Aug. Tues.-Sun. 9am-5pm; Sept.-June Tues.-Sun. 8am-4pm; 9Sk, students 6Sk). Above the entrance to the 14th-century **Bethlenov dom**, Dolná 8 (tel. 72 41 67), the Latin phrase *Bendictio Domini Divites Facit* ("the blessing of the Lord makes people rich") drives home the town's merchant philosophy. Inside hang the works of starving artists who probably still haven't acquired that blessing (open Tues.-Fri. 10am-6pm, Sat.-Sun. 10am-5pm; admission to each 20Sk, students 5Sk). Built according to the artist's own designs, **skuteckého dom**, Horná 55 (tel. 425 450), celebrates Dominik skutecký's (1849-1921) artistry. His depictions of daily life in the mining region merit a look (open Tues.-Sun. 10am-5pm; 20Sk, students 4Sk).

Most of Banská Bystrica's population chooses a sedate approach to recreation. Perhaps the most entertaining is the least expensive—endless walks around the town center and curious gawking on the benches of nám. SNP. In mid-June, the town hosts **Pivinex**, a celebration of beer, wine, and folklore. At **Piváreň Perla**, Horná 52, the copper vats of *Perla* stand bubbling right behind the bar. Both barflies and businessfolk enjoy the quality microbrew (12Sk) on communal tables and benches. Don't be shy about scooting in (open Mon.-Sat. 8am-10pm). The town's well known **Rázcesti puppet theater** at Kollárova 18 (tel. 245 67) sells tickets from 7am to 3pm on weekdays (30-50Sk; closed July-Aug.). Many young people spend evening hours in the park surrounding the Museum of Slovak National Uprising by Kapitalská ulica, where small children idly handle machines of war.

■ Near Banská Bystrica: Banská Štiavnica

Wedged into the highlands of Štiavnica, this medieval town of collieries runs like a thin vein of crude ore through the heart of Slovakia's mining country. Banská Štiavnica's immense 1764 **"Holy Trinity Column,"** commemorating the plague of 1710, dominates the slowly regenerating town square, **Trojičné námestie**. A collection of rocks and minerals sits behind glass cases at **Mineralogická expozícia**, Trojičné nám. 6 (tel. 225 44; open daily 8am-6pm, Sat.-Sun. 9:30am-6pm). Two doors up, **Galéria Jozefa Kollára** displays quality artifacts that span centuries. The permanent Edmund Gwerk and Jaroslav Augusta exhibits paint sincere portraits of the region's populace before the onset of modernization (open May-Sept. daily 8am-4pm; Oct.-April Mon.-Fri. 8am-4pm). Up the hill at Starozámocká 11 (tel. 321 13), reconstruction continued on the **Starý zámok** (Old Castle) in the summer of 1996. A stroll along Sládkovičova leads to the town's 17th-century **Klopačka** (knock-tower), which houses a resonant board that was once used to call the miners to work. An annex that served as a prison for "delinquent miners" now holds the exhibit "Developments of Mining Techniques in Slovakia". A detailed written description in English is available (open Mon.-Fri. 9am-5pm; 10SK, students 5SK). Sládkovičova ends by the prim white **Nový zámok** (New Castle), built in 1571 as a watchtower against Turkish invasions. Following the Turkish wars, it survived two centuries as a gunpowder storehouse for the mines and now houses the exhibit "Anti-Turkish Wars in Slovakia". Statues of Turks, a Turkish living room, weapons, and unobstructed views of the countryside from the top floor are perfect for a pleasant hour of musing. A bugler plays from the tower every quarter-hour. Tours in Slovak every 45 minutes are accompanied by a written translation in English (open in summer Mon.-Fri. 8am-6pm, Sat.-Sun. 9:30am-6pm; off-season Mon.-Fri. 8am-3pm; 20SK, students 10SK). Hella leads to the mining museum **Banské Múzeum v Prírode** at Hella 12 (tel. 229 71). The free open-air exhibit and the 30SK (students 15SK) descent into the old mine are worth the walk. Those with heart problems go "at their own risk" (open July-Aug. Tues.-Sun. 8am-6pm; Sept.-June Tues.-Sun. 8am-4pm; tours start when 15 people have arrived).

Buses drive six times a day (4 per day on weekends) between Banská Bystrica and Banská Štiavnica (2hr., 35SK), ending their trip a 20-minute walk away from the sights along **Dolná**. The new **MTIR tourist office**, Radničné nám. 1 (tel./fax 218 59), in the Old Town hall gives away and sells maps of the city (15SK), books rooms, and plans tours of the area (open Mon.-Fri. 8am-6pm). If the last weekend bus (at 1:45pm) leaves without you, a few pensions offer rooms. The luxurious **Penzión Matej**, Akademická 4 (tel. 239 60), spares no expense, with light, airy rooms, huge frame beds, lush towels, and plenty of hardwood (doubles 500SK, with private bath 700SK). The pension also hosts a popular **pub** downstairs. **Phone code:** 859

■ Liptovský Mikuláš

Lying in a wide valley near both the Low Tatras Mountains *(Nízke Tatry)* and the large man-made Liptovská Mara (lake), Liptovský Mikuláš is ideally situated as a base from which to explore the Slovak wilderness. Once notorious as the site of the execution of the Slovak Robin Hood Juraj Janošik, today the town simply provides cheap lodging and access to the hiking, skiing, fishing, and biking in the area.

Orientation and Practical Information Although the town's **bus station** bears the brunt of regional traffic, Liptovský Mikuláš is best approached by train. The **train station** (tel. 228 42) lies on Stefanikova, and the bus station (tel. 236 38) is the asphalt lot directly outside. Liptovsky Mikuláš is on the main **train** line from Košice (2 hr., 100Sk) through Poprad (40 min., 44Sk) to Bratislava (12-15 per day, 4hr., 158Sk). Five local trains also run daily to Poprad (1hr., 28Sk). **Buses** run to Poprad (5 per day, 1hr., 60Sk). The **town center** is an easy 10-minute walk from the bus and train terminals. Follow Stefanikova towards the gas station at the bus station's far end, then turn right onto Hodžova. The town's main square, **nám. Mieru,** lies just past the post office with the tourist office occupying a large chunk of the central Dom Služieb. **Informačné Centrum,** Nám Mieru 1 (tel. 224 18), sells maps, arranges bike rentals, and helps find accommodations (open mid-June to mid-Sept. Mon.-Fri. 8am-7pm, Sat. 8am-2pm, Sun. noon-7pm; mid-Sept. to mid-June Mon.-Fri. 9am-6pm). **VÚB,** Štúrova 19 (tel. 223 57), exchanges currency and has a **24-hour ATM** for Cirrus, Eurocard, and MC (open Mon.-Thurs. 8am-noon and 1:30-5pm, Fri. 8am-noon). An automatic machine **exchanges currency** at Štúrova 1. **Store luggage** at the train station (5Sk). The **post office,** Hodžova 1, is off nám. Mieru (open Mon.-Fri. 8am-8pm, Sat. 8am-noon). **Postal code:** 031 01. **Phone code:** 0849.

Accommodations and Food Blessed with an inordinate number of hotels and old school residences, this town is a boon for the budget traveler. **Informačné Centrum** (see above) provides info on accommodations. **Hotel Kriváň,** Štúrova 5 (tel. 522 414; fax 242 43), has location, location, location (singles 220Sk, with bath 300Sk; doubles 440Sk, with bath 600Sk; and triples 590Sk, with bath 800Sk).

Outdoor-oriented Liptovský Mikuláš has many **supermarkets,** but relatively few restaurants. Stock up on pre-hiking grub at a grocery in nám. Miera (tel. 248 41; open Mon.-Fri. 8am-7pm, Sat. 7:30am-12:30pm, Sun. 8-11am). **Liptovská Izba,** nám. Osloboditeľv 21, offers specialties of the Liptov region. Climb past the other patron's backpacks to get to the one-room interior where even the plates are made of wood. The menu is in Slovak, but waiters explain in German.

Sights The main one, **Múzeum Janka Kráľa,** nám. Osloboditeľov 31 (tel. 225 54), presents an excellent survey of the town's history. Don't be put off by the skull as you enter the museum. A written guide in English accompanies the exhibits (open Tues.-Fri. 9am-4pm, Sat.-Sun. 10am-5pm;15Sk, students 8Sk). Also on nám. Osloboditeľov, the **Kostol sv. Mikuláš** (Church of St. Nicolas) has stood since 1280. Statues of 19th-century nationalists and the saint himself surround the church (open Mon.-Sat. 9am-6pm, Sun. 8am-6pm). The **Old Evangelical Parsonage** (Stará evengeliká fara), Tranovskéno 8 (tel. 225 46), tries to convince visitors that Woodrow Wilson's 14 points in fact date back to the 1848 petition "Requirements of the Slovak Nation" (open Tues.-Fri. 8am-2pm, Sat.-Sun. by request in Múzeum Janka Kráľa; 10Sk, students 5Sk). **Židovská synagogá,** Hollého ulica, has by its door a wrenching bronze memorial to a community ripped from the town by the events of the 1930s and 40s. Across the Váh river in Palúdzka, Liptovský Mikuláš's left bank, **Kaštieľ Vranova,** Vranovského 1 (tel. 250 55), was once the prison of folk hero Juraj Jánošík. Jánošík fought with Rákóczi against the Habsburg rulers and then became self-employed, robbing from the rich to give to the poor. Captured by Liptov soldiers, he was tortured, tried, and gruesomely executed in 1713. The museum alone is perhaps not worth the 15-minute walk, but continuing another 15 minutes down the road (bear right when the road splits) you'll see Liptovská Mara, an immense lake which, when dammed, damned eleven towns to a watery grave.

Early July brings the world to **Východna** for its **Folklore Festival,** a drunken celebration of music, dance, and story-telling which lasts four days, just 20km east of Liptovský Mikuláš. If you're planning to stay in Liptovský Mikuláš, book rooms in advance, the festival coincides with the Feast of Cyril and Methodius, and all of Slovakia goes on vacation. For information, contact Regionálne Kultúrne Stredisko, Tranovského 2, 03180 Liptovský Mikuláš (tel. 229 80; fax 229 81).

■ Near Liptovský Mikuláš: Nízke Tatry

Liptovský Mikuláš is frequently used as a base for hiking in the **Nízke Tatry,** or Lower Tatras. Despite their name, they are not to be underestimated: the peaks of the mountains reach well above the tree line. See Essentials: Wilderness and Safety Concerns, p. 48, for some general tips on keeping healthy and happy while hiking. **Mount Ďumbier** is the highest in the area at 2043m. A good day-hike begins at Liptovský Ján (15min. by bus from Liptovský Mikuláš), continues along the river Štiavnica to Ďumbier's base (about 4hr.), and then leads up the steep trail from Chata generála M. R. Štefánika to the peak (1-2hr.). Trails from the top lead to **Prašivá** and **Tanečnica** peaks, down to Sedlo Javorie, and back to Liptovský Ján, or down into the **Demänovská Dolina** (valley) from which buses return hourly to Liptovský Mikuláš. A third option is to hike along a ridge to **Chopok** mountain (2-2½hr.) and then hike down to Jasná or catch a lift from the summit of Chopok to Záhradky (just outside Jasná), to return by bus to L. Mikuláš. The last lift returns at 4:45pm.

Less ambitious hikers may prefer to limit themselves to Chopok—**buses** go from Liptovský Mikuláš (17 per day, 30min., 12Sk) to the "Jasná" stop at Hotel ski, 1km before Jasná, where signs point toward a chairlift to Chopok. 45Sk gets you to the top of the chairlift (90Sk roundtrip), and a 20-minute hike beyond that is the peak and **Espresso Rotunda,** where tea (13Sk) accompanies a view that varies from magnificent to non-existent. The chair-lifted have a head-start on the hike to Ďumbier, 2½ hours away along an exposed ridge.

Demänovská madová jaskyňa, an **ice cave** midway between Liptovský Mikuláš and Jasná (15min. by bus from Liptovský Mikuláš, direction Jasná; 6Sk), is yet another treasure. Get off the bus at Hotel Kamenná Chata, and follow signs 15 minutes up the hill to a valley view. The ice cave features bones from Ice Age bears and signatures of more recent 18th- and 19th-century visitors. The last part of the tour brings visitors to a frozen waterfall draped beneath bleached stone. (July and August tours leave hourly 9am-4pm; mid-May to June and early Sept. Tues.-Sun. 9, 11am, 12:30, and 2pm; 50Sk, students 40Sk for Slovak tours; with sufficient demand, tours in German and English 100Sk, students 80Sk).

Ask at **Informačné Centrum** in Liptovský Mikuláš (see p.643) for info about **watersports;** they can also provide info on paragliding, horseback-riding, hunting, and climbing, and can arrange for bike rental (250-300Sk per day) in Demänovská valley. Guidebooks with cycling tours (Slovak 39Sk, German 49Sk) include maps that are easily understood. Windsurfing, boating, canoeing, and swimming—often with instruction—are available at **Autocamping Liptovský Trnovec,** 6km from Liptovský Mikuláš on Liptovský Mara.

VYSOKÉ TATRY (THE HIGH TATRAS)

Slovaks take great pride in Vysoké Tatry, a mountainous mecca for hikers, skiers, and nature-lovers alike. Only 26km long, the High Tatras are one of the most compact mountain ranges in the world. Sky-scraping peaks and a plethora of *plesos* (glacial lakes) make for eye-blasting panoramas, and, when the two high seasons arrive, kids, families, and toters of hot neon ski-pants come to check out the views. Find a *penzión* in a smaller town such as Horný Smokovec or Tatranská Lesná—buses and trains connect all areas—and enjoy the spectacular hikes.

▓ Poprad

Poprad was born when Czechoslovakia glued together four sleepy mountain villages with drab apartment blocks. A super-efficient tourist office and proletarian accommodations make this polluted conglomeration "the gateway to the Tatras." Most pass through quickly, abandoning the limited allure of Poprad for their real sight: the high Tatras rising sternly on the far side of the railroad station.

ORIENTATION AND PRACTICAL INFORMATION

Waves of wheeled wonders weave through Poprad, leaving for the Tatras and Spiš. **Trains** (tel. 312 44) leave from the north edge of town to Košice (every 1-2hr., 70min., 17Sk). **Buses** (tel. 233 90; information open Mon.-Fri. 7am-6pm) near the train station at the corner of Wolkerova and Alžbetina leave to Zakopane in the Polish Tatras (3 per week, more in season, 2hr., 70Sk), Banská Bystrica (16 per day, 2½hr., 99Sk), Košice (7-8 daily, 2hr., 76Sk), and surrounding resorts. *Tatranská Električká Železnica* (TEŽ) connects Poprad with the Tatran resorts (about 1 per hour, up to 18Sk depending on the destination), but buses are generally quicker and more frequent. To get from the bus station to the tourist office in **nám. sv. Egídia,** walk behind the station on **Wolkerova,** pass through the lower floor of the train station, and follow the green "Centrum" signs through the park and then down **Mnoheľova. Popradská Informačná Agentúra,** nám. sv. Egídia 2905 (tel. 186 or 721 700; fax 721 394) sells maps of Poprad and Eastern Slovakia, arranges for outdoor recreation in the High Tatras, and can handle almost any inquiry. They also assist in booking Poprad hotels, mountain *chatas*, and private rooms (open in high season Mon.-Fri. 8am-7pm, Sat. 9am-1pm, Sun. 2-6pm; off-season Mon.-Fri. 9am-5pm, Sat. 9am-1pm). **Tatratour,** nám. sv. Egídia 19 (tel. 637 12; fax 638 89) books private rooms (200-250Sk per person) and are the local **American Express** representatives, accepting traveler's checks at a 2% commission (open Mon.-Fri. 8:30am-5:30pm). **VÚB,** Mnoheľova 9 (tel. 605 1111), cashes AmEx and Visa traveler's checks at a 1% commission (open Mon.-Fri. 8am-noon and 1:30-5pm, Sat. 8am-noon). Cirrus/MC **ATMs** are around the corner. **Storage luggage** in the train station (5Sk). **Pharmacy: Lekáreň Altea,** nám. sv. Egídia 29 (tel. 724 222 or 724 223; open Mon.-Fri. 7:15am-5:30pm, Sat. 8am-noon). The **post office** is at Mnoheľova 11 (tel. 640 02; open Mon.-Fri. 7am-5pm, Sat. 8am-11am). **Postal code:** 05801. **Phone code:** 92.

ACCOMMODATIONS

Poprad eagerly accommodates the annual tourist hordes with **booking agencies** on every block and **pensions** around every corner. Most places are decent—it's really just a matter of the carpet's age and the softness of the toilet paper. **Hotel Európa,** Wolkerova 3 (tel. 327 44) rents old but well groomed rooms, which open upon a collage of the Tatras and the train station. Rooms facing the tracks are a bit loud (communal toilets and baths; singles 260Sk, doubles 400Sk, triples 460Sk). **Hotel Gerlach,** Hviezdoslavova 2 (tel. 721 945; fax 636 63), off Mnoheľova, is similar to Hotel Európa, but quieter. The wallpaper wilts, but plants puff out oxygen, and the sheets are as white as the day they were born. Keys to the bath are at reception. Shoot pool in the bar (singles 350Sk; doubles 450Sk, with bath 650Sk). The former workers' hotel, **Domov Stavbárov,** Karpatská 11 (tel. 638 77), west of Hviezdoslavova, now accommodates tourists. The austere rooms lack dirt or decoration, and the elevators have minds of their own. In any case, its a super deal at 120Sk. Ping-Pong tables amuse the masses on the ground floor. Free showers.

FOOD

Eateries range from sit-down establishments to stand-up sausage kitchens, from expensive ethnic restaurants to cheap bistros. Try a pint of a local brew, with *Spiš* this or *Tatranské* that. If local specialties have gotten confusing, **grocery stores** (*potraviny*) line the west part of the main square; one of the bigger ones is at nám. sv. Egídia 53 (open Mon.-Fri. 6:30am-7pm; Sat. 6:30am-noon). In **Slovenská Reštaurácia,** 1. maja 9 (tel. 722 870), off Štefánikova, plows and sickles make creative wall ornaments. Delicious *halušky* (small dumplings) with *bryndza* (cheese-filled pockets) go for 34-36Sk, bottled *Tatran* beer for 17Sk (open daily 11am-11pm; live Gypsy music nightly 5:30-10pm). Eat indoors on folk-art tables or imbibe a *pivo* in the intimate garden of **Egídius,** Mnoheľova (tel. 722 898). The restaurant is so popular you might find yourself sharing a table. *Tatranský pstruh* (trout) at 5Sk per 10g may be what brings the crowds (open daily 11am-midnight). **Balkan Espresso,** nám. sv. Egídia near Zdravotnícka (tel. 636 86), produces chocolate and cream-flavored joy for 6-10Sk (open daily 7:30am-7:30pm).

SIGHTS

Nám. sv. Egídia boasts a few medieval buildings; the most eye-catching is the fortified **St. Egídius Church,** erected by Saxons in the late 13th century. Closed intermittently for restoration since 1976, it was open in the summer of '96. Inside, the wall frescoes faintly echo a once vibrant interior (open Mon.-Sat. 10am-6pm).

Suburban **Spišská Sobota** can be reached by following Štefánikova east for 15 minutes, then taking a left by the ice hockey stadium on unmarked Kežmarská. A three-minute ride on **bus #2 or 3** in the same direction will also get you there. All major sights, including the medieval Saxon **Kostol sv. Juraja** (St. George's Church) that gave the village its original name of **Georgensberg,** lie on the tiny, central **Sobotské nám.** After 45 years of neglect, the whole district has been declared historic and is currently the site of ongoing restoration. Many already renovated houses boast spiffy wooden roofs and pastel wall paintings. The Renaissance **watchtower** was recently restored but still shows its age. **Podtatranské Múzeum** (Tatra Museum), Sobotské nám. 33 (tel. 721 323), features collections on Spiš folklore, and on the history of the village and its Hungarian and Saxon inhabitants until their expulsion in 1945—impressive blacksmithing and batik (open Mon.-Sat. 9am-4pm; 10Sk).

At **Vináreň sv. Juraj,** Sobotské nám. 29 (tel. 721 411), two brothers with big plans serve 12Sk beer—20Sk on weekends—and provide disco and live music on weekends. The winecellar cave refreshes on late summer afternoons (open Tues.-Thurs. 3pm-2am, Fri.-Sat. 5pm-4am, Sun. 4pm-midnight; cover 30Sk Fri.-Sat.).

For an old-fashioned *piváreň,* Poprad's central square closes early, but **Limba Bar,** Podtatranská (tel. 648 33), sticks around nightly until midnight. Take nám. sv. Egídia east into Vajanského, and then to a large roundabout; follow Partizanská to Podtatran-

---

Tatran Karaoke

Koliba is to Tatranská Lomnica as Karaoke is to Tokyo. Most restaurants in and around town have added a folk band and roasting spit to their dining room, hoping to attract locals and tourists in search of the latest Slovak hope for the Eurovision contest. You may not find ABBA-quality bands, but the ploy is working, and on a good night the *kolibas* bubble with Gypsy violin, drunken song, flaming *tatranský čaj,* and salmon broiling on the spit. By the end of the night, the beer in your veins might even start you singing in a tongue you never wanted to learn.

ská and turn right. Many hotels have ground-floor bars for friendly fun, and when you're through, all you need to do is struggle up the stairs. If the accordions don't play late enough, **Surprise City Club**, Štefánikova 4 (tel. 634 45), offers billiards and disco under black lights (open Sun.-Thurs. 2pm-4am, Fri.-Sat. 2pm-5am). The city and its environs host **folklore festivals** at least once a month, with something going on virtually every weekend in summer; get a free schedule of events from the tourist office.

▊ Tatranská Lomnica

With snow like Štrbské Pleso's, and sleeps as cheap as Smokovec's, Tatranská Lomnica is becoming increasingly popular as the High Tatras's budget ski resort. During summer, however, few hiking trails lead directly from this town, and the ear-popping lift to Lomnický štít is Tatranská Lomnica's only attraction.

Orientation and Practical Information Buses are the best way to get here from Poprad (every ½-1hr., ½hr., 12Sk). **TEŽ trains** (tel. 967 884) run from Starý Smokovec and Štrbské Pleso. The town's main street passes in front of the bus terminal and shoots off to the left, taking tourists past all the necessities of daily life; there are no street names. **Tatratour** (tel. 967 204; fax 967 992), in a small corner on the second floor of Obchodný Dom Javor, by the tracks, has skeletal information on the town's hotels (open Mon.-Fri. 9am-noon and 12:30-5:45pm, Sat. 8-11:45am). An **information board** about halfway between the train stop and Hotel Lomnica, away from the tracks, shows the location of hotels, **penziónes,** and restaurants and has a phone to call for reservations. If you know a little German, **Tatra-turist** (tel./fax 967 694), in Hotel Slovan helps planning hiking routes (open Mon.-Fri. 8am-4pm). **Currency exchanges** pop up around town, including **Slovenská Sporiteľňa** (tel. 967 259; fax 967 667), in the woods behind the train station, which cashes traveler's checks and gives cash advances (open Mon. and Thurs.-Fri. 7:45am-3pm, Tues. 7:45am-1pm, Wed. 8am-5pm). **Polhobank**, right on the track across from the railroad station, has a Cirrus/ec/Eurocard/MC **ATM.** In Slalom Restaurant, on the main road near the train stop, **WR Šport** (tel. 967 216) rents **bikes** (220Sk per day), rollerblades (120Sk per day), skateboards (100Sk per day), and **skis** (open daily 8am-8pm). The **post office** (tel. 96 72 00) lies behind the train station (open Mon.-Fri. 7:30-11:30am and noon-3:30pm, Sat. 8-9am). **Postal code:** 05960. **Phone code:** 969.

Accommodations and Food Campsites with bungalows wait minutes outside of Tatranská Lomnica, and a few surprises hide near the center. **Penzión Karpátia,** a few minutes towards Tatranska Lomnica from the "Tatranská Lesná" stop on the TEŽ, offers spacious institutional rooms with hall bathrooms for 250Sk per person. The large **Eurocamp FICC** (tel. 967 741; fax 967 346), 5km from town, is easily accessible, thanks to its own train stop (1 per hour, 4Sk). FICC offers sterile doubles with communal bathrooms (450Sk), a hundred spacious bungalows with spotless showers (quads 1300Sk), and tent sites (90Sk per person; campsite open June-Sept.). A sports store on the grounds rents bikes (220Sk per day) and roller blades (40Sk per day), and in winter, skis (150Sk per day; open daily 8am-8pm). A grocery store, disco club, bar, and movie theater make this a small town. A 10-minute walk away from the mountains from the Eurocamp FICC stop, **Športcamp** (tel. 967 288) offers tiny, shiny lacquered-wood rooms with shared showers (120Sk per person), and tent sites (65Sk per person; reception open daily 6am-10pm).

A few restaurants impress without all the revelry of *koliba*. **Reštaurácia Júlia** (tel. 967 947) serves up plates of old-fashioned Slovak goodness on placemats that grandma might have woven. Most entrées are 90-150Sk, but a huge dish of *halušky* or *pirohy* costs only 50Sk (open daily noon-9pm). **Slovenská Reštaurácia** (tel. 967 902), on the first floor of Hotel Renomal, sports a roasting spit but no band. Waiters preside sternly over a German crowd, serving 117Sk sirloin steak to the rich and 49Sk *pirohy* to the poor (open daily 11:30am-10pm). For the truly poor, a **supermarket** behind the railroad station stays open all week (open Mon.-Fri. 7:45am-8pm, Sat. 7:30am-2pm, Sun. 7:30am-noon).

Sights and Hiking The town houses **Múzeum TANAP-u** (*Tatranského národného parku;* Tatra National Park Museum), but the stuffed eagles sing a faint song compared to their sisters a few hundred meters up. The museum's highlight, the "terrifying stuffed bear," stands erect and bears her teeth for photographers (open Mon.-Fri. 8:30am-noon, 1pm-5pm, Sat.-Sun. 8am-noon; 10Sk, students 2Sk).

The **lift** to the top of the Tatras' second peak, **Lomnický štít** (2633.9m), begins with a leisurely cabin ride to **Skalnaté pleso** (1751.1m), a crystal-clear glacial lake (300Sk roundtrip). Another lift (*lanova draha*), five minutes from the town center, also hauls adventure-seekers to Skalnaté pleso; follow the blue trail or the signs to "*visutá lanovka*" (open June 15-Sept. 15 and Dec.-Feb. 7am-7:30pm; 150Sk one-way), and a third leaves from near Hotel Slovan. Skalnata chata welcomes tired hikers near the *pleso*. Even if you don't hike and use the lift, you might need a rest after the second, vertiginous ride from the lake to the peak. Bring tea and crumpets as Lomnický štít's crags and cliffs suit picnics, while vistas spread almost to the Alps.

Hiking is generally better from Starý Smokovec or Strbské Pleso, but a few full day hikes are accessible from Tatranský Lomnica's lift—from **Skalneté pleso** toward Lomnická vyhliadka and then to **Zamkovské chata** (1hr.) brings hikers within reach of **Malá Studená dolina** (valley) and **Téryho chata** (2hr.). Beyond, the yellow trail branches left toward Priečne sedlo and Zbonjnícka chata at the head of **Velká Studená dolina** (2hr.). This leads back toward civilization in the form of Hrebienok (3hr.) and its funicular down to Starý Smokovec. This is an ambitious hike—bring water, warm clothes, and a VKÚ map; start early and pay attention to weather. The blue trail from Tatranská Lomnica to **Vodopády Studeného potoka** (waterfalls) and back to Tatranská Lesná is gentler.

Starý Smokovec

Simply by walking through Starý Smokovec you scale the Tatras. Founded in the late 18th century, the oldest resort town in the region is also the most international. Many businesses are bilingual, and the tree- and flower-lined streets buzz with Hochdeutsch, Polish, Québécois, and Ohio English.

Orientation and Practical Information The resort is easily reached from Poprad by TEŽ **trains,** which arrive from Poprad (every ½-1hr., ½hr., 10Sk) and Tatranská Lomnica (15min., 6Sk) at the town's lowest point, south of Hotel Grand. **Buses** (tel. 29 84) to many Tatra resorts stop in a parking lot east of the main train station along the road to Horný Smokovec. Signs at street corners ease orientation in a town of nameless streets, and the map available at the tourist office helps even more. The mall **Dom Služieb,** near the west end of the town's artery, houses the tourist office, a bank, and a **pharmacy.** The friendly staff of **Tatranská Informačná Kancelária** (tel. 34 40; fax 31 27), in Dom Služieb, provides weather info, **maps,** and a full list of accommodations (open Mon.-Fri. 8-11:30am and noon-6pm, Sat.-Sun. 9-11:30am and noon-4pm). **Slovenská Sporiteľňa** (tel. 24 70), also in Dom Služieb, cashes AmEx and Visa traveler's checks at good rates with low commission (open Mon., Thurs., and Fri. 7:45am-3pm, Tues. 7:45am-1pm, Wed. 8am-5pm). **VÚB** (tel. 25 94), in the sports center close to the bus stop, cashes AmEx traveler's checks and gives MasterCard cash advances (open July-Aug. Mon.-Tues. and Thurs. 8am-noon and 1:30-4pm, Wed. and Fri. 8am-noon and 1:30-5pm, Sat. 8am-noon; Sept.-June closed Fri. afternoon and Sat.). A Cirrus/MC **ATM** waits outside. A **funicular** runs to Hrebienok (every ½hr., 30Sk). For equipment and guides, contact **T-ski** (tel. 32 00) in the lift station, which offers everything from ski classes to river-rafting trips, rents **bikes** (250Sk per day, afternoon 180Sk), **skis** (190-390Sk), and mountain **guides** (1000-3000Sk per day). For a runny nose, all sorts of drugs line the shelves of **Lekáreň U Zlatej Sovy** (tel. 21 64), on the second floor of Dom Služieb (open Mon.-Fri. 7:30am-noon and 12:30-4pm, Sat. 8am-noon). A **post office** (tel. 24 71) lies near the train station (open Mon.-Fri. 8am-noon and 1-4:30pm, Sat. 8-10am). **Postal code:** 6201. **Phone code:** 969.

Accommodations and Food Horný Smokovec, 1km east along Starý's main street, offers budget-friendly rooms and is home to **Slovakoturist** (tel. 28 27; fax 24 82), whose English-speaking staff books **mountain chatas** (350-450Sk), **private rooms** (200-250Sk), and cottages for six to eight people (about 2200Sk). **T-ski** (see above) arranges **private rooms** for 300Sk per person. The not-so-young **Hotel Plesnivec** (tel. 25 35; fax 29 93), near the lift station, even higher than Hotel Grand, rents aging rooms with communal bathrooms, but at a good price for a hotel in Smokovec (360Sk per person). **CKM Juniorhotel Vysoké Tatry** (tel. 26 61), in Horný Smokovec, two TEŽ stops towards Tatranská Lomnica, has clean if bare rooms, and a disco club (singles 275Sk, doubles 525Sk, triples 655Sk, and quads 760Sk; ISIC 200Sk per person). Reservations are recommended. **Hotel Šport** (tel. 23 61), also in Horný Smokovec but almost within sight of St. Smokovec, displays its best vinyl and linoleum in clean but aging singles (510Sk) and doubles (890Sk; prices include breakfast and are lower off-season; reception open 24hr.).

Most people eat "on the go." A first-rate **grocery store** across from Hotel Grand counterbalances the town's mediocre restaurants with a great selection and a terrace for pleasant outdoor munching (open Mon.-Sat. 7am-7pm, Sat. noon-7pm).

Hiking The funicular to **Hrebienok** (1285m), takes you to the heart of hiking country. An easy 20-minute green trail from Hrebienok leads to the foaming **Studenovodské vodopády** (Cold Waterfall). The eastward blue trail descends from the waterfall through the towering pines to **Tatranská Lomnica** (1½hr.). The long, red *"Tatranská magistrála"* trail travels west from Hrebienok through the chalet **Sliezsky dom** (1670m), to **Chata kapitána Moravku** on the shore of **Popradské pleso**. From here, descend the blue trail to **Štrbské Pleso**. The truly ambitious turn north off the *magistrála* onto the blue trail which climbs one of the highest Tatran peaks, the stony **Slavkovský štít** (2450m; about 8hr. from Hrebienok for advanced hikers only).

The *magistrála* also heads north from Hrebienok to **Skalnaté pleso** with a nearby *chata* (see Tatranská Lomnica: Sights and Hiking, p. 647). The leisurely climb (2hr.) leads along view-packed ridges. Take the green trail to the Cold Waterfall, change to the blue, and at the old cabin foundantion, head up on the red. The hike to **Malá Studená dolina** (Little Cold Valley) is also fairly relaxed; take the green trail from Hrebienok through barren landscape to **Téryho chata** (2015m; 4hr.; 200Sk, obligatory meals in season 170Sk).

An intense, six-hour hike leads through the immense **Veľká Studená dolina** (Big Cold Valley) to **Zbojnícka chata** (1960m; 250Sk per night; in season, guests must purchase a 175Sk per night meal plan). From Sliezsky dom, take the green trail to **Zamrznuté pleso** (Cold Lake; 2047m), change to the blue towards the *chata*, and follow the crashing **Veľký Studený potok** (Big Cold Stream), which will drop you off at the Cold Waterfall. From here, the green trail returns to Hrebienok. For tips on staying healthy and happy while hiking see Essentials: Wilderness and Safety Concerns, p. 49.

■ Near Starý Smokovec: Štrbské Pleso

Having hosted the "Interski" Championship in 1975, Štrbské Pleso has joined Poprad in a bid for the 2006 Winter Olympics. For the moment, the hotels and ski-jump towers that rose in the 70s clutter the placid **Štrbské pleso** (Lake Štrbské), while gaggles of schoolkids add screams and whistles to the mess. Then again, one can't hope to enjoy the Tatras' most-beloved ski resort alone. The town is the range's highest settlement and a great starting point for hikes.

For those who enjoy *les montagnes à la couch potato,* the **lift** (mid-June to mid-Sept. 8am-3:30pm; 80Sk roundtrip) takes visitors to **Chata pod Soliskom** (1840m), in a rocky loft overlooking the lake and the expansive plains behind Štrbské Pleso. A small restaurant under the lift station at the top, **Bivak Club**, offers tea (15Sk), shots of liquor (30-40Sk), and Tatran fast food: soup (30Sk), sausage with bread and mustard (35Sk), and of course, beer (25Sk). From July through October, a strenuous six-hour hike leaves here to visit five secluded mountain lakes (tarns, for you geo-freaks), the

VYSOKÉ TATRY (THE HIGH TATRAS)

Polish and Slovak Tatras

Ciemniak 2090m, **2**
Cold Waterfall, **22**
Furkotský štít 2405m, **14**
Gerlachovský štít 2655m, **19**
Giewont 1909m, **1**
Goryczkowa 1912m, **7**
Hladký štít 2066m, **11**
Kasprowy Wierch 1985m, **8**
Kopa Kondratowa 2004m, **5**
Kôprovský štít 2367m, **15**
Kriváň 2494m, **13**
Krížna 2038m, **12**
Krzesanica 2122m, **3**
Lomnický štít 2632m, **21**
Małołączniak 2104m, **4**
Mnich 2068m, **16**
Ostrva 1984m, **24**
Rysy 2499m, **18**
Slavkovský štít 2452m, **20**
Štrbské Solisko 2301m, **23**
Suchy Kondracki 1890m, **6**
Świnica 2300m, **9**
Mięguszowiecki Szczyt 2438m, **17**
Zawrat 2159m, **10**

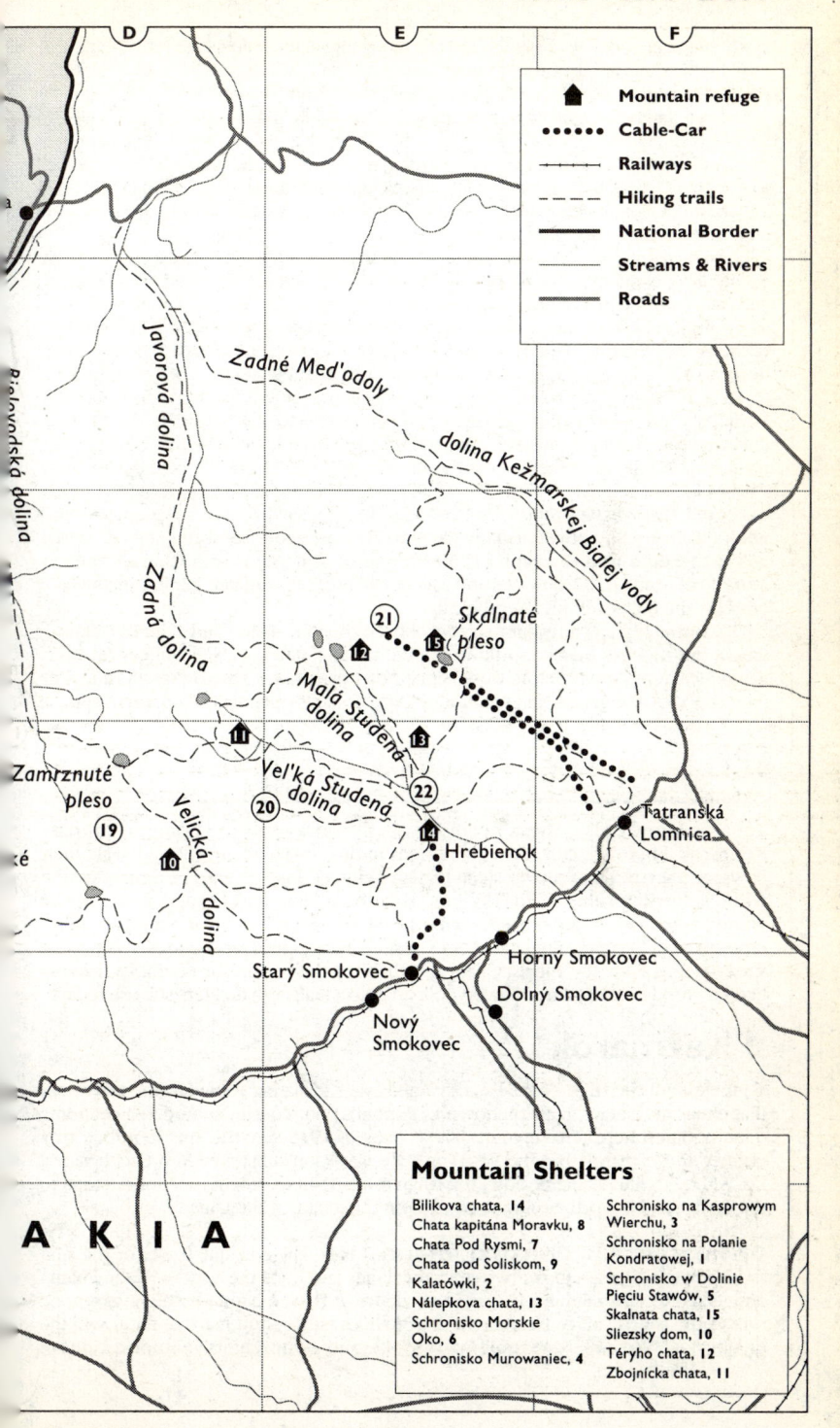

ŠTRBSKÉ PLESO ■ 651

Legend:
- 🏠 Mountain refuge
- ●●●●● Cable-Car
- ┼┼┼┼ Railways
- ---- Hiking trails
- ━━ National Border
- ── Streams & Rivers
- ═══ Roads

Mountain Shelters

- Bilikova chata, 14
- Chata kapitána Moravku, 8
- Chata Pod Rysmi, 7
- Chata pod Soliskom, 9
- Kalatówki, 2
- Nálepkova chata, 13
- Schronisko Morskie Oko, 6
- Schronisko Murowaniec, 4
- Schronisko na Kasprowym Wierchu, 3
- Schronisko na Polanie Kondratowej, 1
- Schronisko w Dolinie Pięciu Stawów, 5
- Skalnata chata, 15
- Sliezsky dom, 10
- Téryho chata, 12
- Zbojnícka chata, 11

sky-high **Furkotský štít** (2428m), and the valley **Mlynická dolina.** From the *chata*, follow the blue trail and turn right when you reach the yellow one. The path circles the mountain **Štrbské Solisko** (2301m), and leads back to the town.

The red path leading from Štrbské Pleso to **Popradské pleso** (1¼hr.) attracts all levels of hikers. Before reaching the lake, it branches into two trails: the green runs to the *pleso* along the rambling **Hincov potok** (stream), while the red continues parallel to it with a view of the stream's valley. **Chata kapitána Moravku** (1500m; tel. 921 77, 250Sk per person, reserve in advance) at the top, offers lakeside grogs—tea and rum, and their specialty, *popradské pleso.*

From the *chata*, the easy 15-minute yellow trail (open July-Oct.) takes you south to **Symbolický cintorín** (1525m). Built 1936-40 by the painter Otakar Štafl, the cemetery serves as "a memorial to the dead, and a warning for the living." Painted crosses, metal plaques, and broken propeller blades find a serene home on the side of mountain **Ostrva** (1984m). The trail ultimately ends at a paved blue path. The tired can descend the lacking-in-views blue trail down to a TEŽ stop (45min.), but backtracking to Štrbské Pleso is far more interesting. Another blue and then green trail from Popradské pleso provides a grueling three-hour trip to the Polish border at **Rysy** (2499m). The highest *tatranská chata,* **Chata pod Rysmi,** 250m below the peak, has rooms for 170Sk, and free hot tea for anyone who brings up 5kg of supplies from Chata Kapitána Moravku (both the trail and the shelter are open July-Oct.). The much easier red *"Tatranská magistrála"* trail leads for hours along scenic ridges to **Hrebienok** (see Starý Smokovec: Hiking, p. 648). Tortured tourists ascending the initial 459m to **Sedlo pod Ostrvou** (1959m), can be ridiculed from Chata Kapitána Moravku's terrace. But don't let the ascent discourage you from joining the sweaty crowd—the trail levels off after the ridge.

TEŽ **trains** leave hourly for Starý Smokovec (40min., 14Sk) and Poprad (70min., 24Sk), but the rare **buses** shuttle to Poprad faster (50min., 32Sk). Budget travelers should leave the town before dusk, since hotel prices beat the town's altitude. For food supplies, the **grocer's** in Obchodny Dom Toliar is open daily 7:45am-6:45pm.

SPIŠ

Tourists know Spiš only as neighbor of the Tatras and the home of touristy Kežmarok. But to the east, flatter land leads to tiny towns where villagers walk their cows, and scythes haven't yet faced the lawnmower. In the minds of romantics, the white sprawling ruins of Spišský hrad rule the region, and Levoča, home of the world's tallest Gothic altar, bustles with the wealthy merchants that put it there. Lederhosen and German-language menus plague West Spiš, but the locals don't just speak *Deutsch* for the tourists. Saxons inhabited the region for centuries, leaving behind wood-frame houses, flowery folk art, and a dialect that elders still use today.

■ Kežmarok

To the east of the High Tatras lies tidy, medieval Kežmarok. Although the slow train that chugs to the city treats the town as Poprad's poor cousin, culture and economy once boomed here. The revolutionary chaos of 1918 saw the Spiš Republic proclaimed in Kežmarok, but the fledgling state was soon subsumed into Czechoslovakia. Although life is quieter now, the town remains an excellent base for daytrips to the Tatras, and is worth seeing even without the mighty mountains.

Orientation and Practical Information The Baroque tower of the *radnica* (town hall) rises above two-story dwellings and leads the way to Hradné nám., connected to **Hlavné nám.** Hiding in an alcove at Hlavné nám. 46, the Anglophone staff of the **tourist office** (tel./fax 40 47) provides hard-to-find maps of the town, the quality *VKÚ Vysoké Tatry* trail map (59Sk), and comprehensive information on

Kežmarok's accommodations (open Mon.-Fri. 8:30am-5pm, Sat. 9am-2pm). **Slovenská Sporiteľňa,** MUDr. Alexandra 41 (tel. 30 41), **exchanges currency,** charges no commission, and gives Visa cash advances (open Mon. and Thurs.-Fri. 7:15am-3:30pm, Tues. 7:15am-1pm, Wed. 7:30am-4:30pm). A Cirrus/MC **ATM** waits outside the **VÚB bank** on Hviezdoslavova, off Hlavné nám. **Trains** depart for Poprad (13 daily, ½hr., 7Sk) from the stately, bright yellow station (tel. 32 89) northwest of the Old Town, at the end of MUDr. Alexandra. The **post office,** Mučeníkov 2 (tel. 25 55), lies farther past the VÚB, where the street changes to Mučeníkov (open Mon.-Fri. 8am-4pm, Sat. 8-10am). **Postal code:** 06001. **Phone code:** 968.

Accommodations and Food Kežmarok has few hotels, but they're all affordable. The tourist office (see above) helps find accommodations. The ski-lodge **Hotel Štart** (tel. 29 15; fax 29 16) off Pod lesom behind the castle has its own ski lift. Its wood-paneled singles cost 160Sk, and doubles with bath run 440Sk. **Penzión No. 1,** Michalska 1 (tel. 46 00), is family run and couldn't be friendlier. Doubles 176-246Sk, quads 352-493Sk. **Campsites** lie outside of town. Antler bedecked **Hotel Club,** MUDr. Alexandra 24 (tel. 24 01), earns local kudos. *Halušky s bryndzou* costs only 39Sk, although the prices rise steeply from there. A **grocery store** at MUDr. Alexandra 44 is kinder to your wallet (open Mon.-Fri. 7:30am-6pm, Sat. 7am-noon).

Sights and Entertainment Although only a few hundred meters of Kežmarok's city wall remain, the Old Town has succeeded in protecting itself from the encroaching forces of modernization. Renaissance houses line cobblestone streets, and curious arches peek into cat-filled alleys. Hlavná and Nová culminate at the impressive **Kežmarský hrad** (castle), Hradné nám. 42 (tel. 41 53). Owned in turn by the powerful Habsburgs, Thurzos, and Thökölys, and often at war with the town, the 15th-century fortification fashionably confounds styles by wearing a fine Renaissance decor on its stocky Gothic body. Its large empty tower was the 16th century prison of Beata Laska, the owner of the castle whose trip to the High Tatras—the first ever recorded—angered the husband she left behind. The castle's **Kežmarok Museum** presents a fascinating picture of the city's history. Medieval weapons and portraits of Austrian emperors merit a bite of your time, but the 19th-century newspaper clippings, posters, and books that convey the town's former importance are the museum's icing. The Baroque **Chapel of St. Elizabeth,** inside, is a product of local artistic talent (open June-Sept. Tues.-Sun. 9am-5pm; Oct.-May Tues.-Fri. 8am-5pm; obligatory, but painless, tours in German or Slovak start every ½hr. on weekends, off-season every hr.; 18Sk). Near the castle's rear, well preserved one-story wooden houses curve along **Starý Trh,** the old market.

In the middle of the Old Town, **Kostol sv. Kríža** (Church of the Holy Cross), dominates nám. Požiarnikov. Open by request at the priest's office opposite the back entrance to the church, the interior boasts several 15th-century Gothic altars, two organs, and the tomb of the Thököly family. The church, built to be a Catholic bastion against Protestantism, turned Protestant, and then Catholic again. Next to the church is the 1591 **zvonica** (watchtower), the most famous landmark in Kežmarok (closed to the public). The attractive **Hlavné nám.** lies in the shadow of the radnica's tower, visible from the countryside around Kežmarok. The original town hall burned down in 1922, and its modern replacement combines Gothic, Baroque, Renaissance, and Neoclassical elements. North of the *radnica* on MUDr. Alexandra rises the huge, arcaded **reduta,** the center of 19th-century Kežmarok's social life.

Down Hviezdoslavova, the two Evangelical temples—**Nový Evanjelický Kostol** (New Evangelical Church) and **Drevený Atikulárny Kostol** (Wooden Articulated Church)—have been transported to Kežmarok from two different planets. The old Baroque structure, with an entirely wooden interior, sits squat and sinking because of a medieval law stipulating that Protestant churches could have no foundation. Another anti-Protestant law restricted funds, and so it stands without any metal, nary a nail. The assistance of Swedish sailors explains the porthole-shaped windows. Next door, the pink and lime youngster rebels against the laws with an immense vaulted interior and intricate designs in glass and brass; the geometric patterns resemble those of Moorish mosques. The Kežmarok-born Imre Thököly, once exiled to Turkey for fighting the Habsburgs, now rests in peace in his own private vault. (Old church open for tours in English June-Sept. Mon.-Sat. 9am-noon, in German and Slovak 2-5pm; Oct.-May Tues.-Thurs. 10am-noon; 10Sk, 5Sk. New church open June-Sept. Mon.-Sat. 9am-noon and 2-5pm; Oct.-May Tues.-Thurs. 10am-noon.)

The *hrad* hosts a party every night at the **Castellan Club,** Bardejovská 5 (tel. 27 80), underneath the castle. Shake down under disco lights, shoot some pool, or just watch the fish behind the bar (open Sun.-Thurs. 8:30am-3pm, Fri.-Sat. 8:30pm-5am; weekdays free for women, 20Sk cover for men; weekends 30Sk cover for all).

Levoča

With practically everything in town named after him, Master Pavel of Levoča seems to have become quite an idol. In the early 16th century, the great Master set up his workshop here, developing an expressive style of woodcarving and creating the tallest Gothic altar in the world—the landmark that first put Levoča on the map. By the 17th century, the town's other major distinction as a center of trade had faded, and, bypassed by the new rail lines, Levoča missed the industrial revolution almost entirely. The town is now quiet, but echoes of the Middle Ages can still be felt in the beautifully preserved town square and museums.

Orientation and Practical Information Relegated to a sidetrack on Slovakia's railway system, Levoča is best approached by bus. The **bus station** rarely opens its info booth, but fares are paid on the bus, and departure times are listed on a large billboard. **Buses** for Košice (2hr., 62Sk), Poprad (½hr., 18Sk), and Prešov (2hr., 128Sk) leave hourly. To reach the walled center from the bus station, follow **Novoveská cesta** to the northwest, then walk northeast along **Probstnerova cesta.** For those with a pack and a half, the town's only **local bus** makes its serpentine rounds every 20 minutes to one hour (5Sk). It arrives eventually at **nám. Majstra Pavla,** the town's central square. The helpful **tourist office,** nám. Majstra Pavla 58 (tel. 37 63), has lots of information about both Master Pavel and the town. They'll also call around for hotel and *penzión* vacancies (open Mon.-Fri. 7:30am-5pm, Sat.-Sun. 9am-5pm). The small **VÚB,** nám. Majstra Pavla, changes both AmEx and Visa traveler's checks at 1% commission and gives MC and Visa cash advances (open Mon.-Tues. and Thurs. 8am-noon and 1-4pm, Wed. 8am-noon and 1-5pm, Fri. 8am-noon). Their MC/Cirrus **ATM** is across the square in the corner by Uholná ul. The **post office** is at nám. Majstra Pavla 42 (tel. 24 89; open Mon.-Fri. 8am-noon and 1-4:30pm, Sat. 8-10:30am). **Postal code:** 05401. **Phone code:** 966.

Accommodations and Camping The first weekend in July attracts 500,000 pilgrims to Levoča, so finding accommodations in and around the town may be difficult. The three hotels on Levoča's main square charge an exorbitant 1000Sk for rooms, but a couple of lodges nearby ease the crunch. Take the local bus from the bus station; **Hotel Texon,** Franciscího 45 (tel. 514 493), appears on the left like a white knight ready to save the luggage-laden in distress. The three-year-old hotel offers spanking-new rooms with Persian carpets and classy wall photos of Master Pavel's masterpieces (180Sk per person). Every two rooms share a bathroom. Reception is open "approximately" 8am-4pm, and prices are negotiable, so calling ahead may be advantageous. **Hotel Faix,** Probstnerova cesta 22 (tel. 452 235; fax 543 554), lies an easy five-minute walk from the bus station by the wall of the Old Town. Aging doubles (680Sk with toilet and shower, 440Sk without) come with a menu of toppings: shower 20Sk, ironing 20Sk. Two floors share one bathroom.

Food The tummy-tapping-good meals at some of Levoča's restaurants make a trip to the grocer's almost unnecessary. **U 3 Apoštolov,** nám. Majstra Pavla 11 (tel. 514 352), can satisfy 12 with its house specialties. The Apostles' Specialty (meat stew wrapped in a potato pancake with veggies) costs 98Sk. The courteous, tuxedoed waitstaff serves *levočské* and *spišské* specialties (60-170Sk) to tunes of the 90s. An extensive English menu provides days of interesting eats (open Mon.-Sat. 9am-10pm, Sun. 10am-10pm). With a photo of the restaurant's spiritual leader above the door, **Vegetarian,** Uholná 3 (tel. 45 76), has become popular among the traditionally meat-and-cabbage-oriented inhabitants. No wonder—the staff cooks up exciting new vegetable dishes daily (30-50Sk). The cafeteria-style service makes deciphering a Slovak menu unnecessary (open Mon.-Fri. 10am-3pm). The truly austere go to a **grocery store** at nám. Majstra Pavla 53 (open Mon.-Fri. 6am-6pm, Sat. 6am-noon, and Sun. 8am-11am).

Sights Levoča is a little giant when it comes to historical attractions, and it has made every attempt to accommodate the interested tourist. The 14th-century **Chrám sv. Jakuba** (St. Jacob's, despite the usual translation as St. James), which dominates the town's tiny square, proudly possesses the world's tallest Gothic altar. Master Pavel took ten years to carve this 18.62m masterpiece and didn't use a single nail. Although any good citizen of Levoča will deny it, legend has it that after the altar was finished, the town's merchants, concerned about seeing another such masterpiece built for a neighboring town, had the master killed. To the left of the altar, a medieval mural depicts the seven deeds of bodily mercy as well as the seven deadly sins. Another mural presents the sad tale of St. Dorothy. Thrust into a pagan land, she was given the choice of heathenry with a rich husband or chaste Christianity with a torturous death. What could she do? She was a saint, after all. Unfortunately, she never found the ruby slippers, and the mural shows her terrible fate. The church contains many more such legends, and the helpful, English-speaking tour staff is eager to elaborate. A 20Sk donation (10Sk for students) goes to restoring the church (open Sun.-Mon. 1-6pm, Tues.-Sat. 9am-6pm).

Nám. Majstra Pavla contains several museums—individually, delicious, but seen together, repetitious. The main **Spišské Múzeum,** at #40 (tel. 27 86; fax 28 24), carries a collection of intricate regional woodwork. A rotating exhibit by local artists waits upstairs. The architecture of the Gothic town hall (tel. 24 49) is more exciting than its exhibit of swords and armor. Nonetheless, there are some items of interest. According to legend, the seductive white lady now painted on one of the halls' doors betrayed the town by giving the city's keys to her lover—an officer in the invading Hungarian army. The sculpture of Siamese twins born here in 1554 also raises eyebrows. The last city museum resides in Master Pavel's workshop, **Dom Majstra Pavla,** at nám. the-man-himself 20 (tel. 34 96). His house now contains an impressive collection of the master's works and tools. (All city museums open Tues.-Sun. 9am-5pm; 10Sk, students 5Sk.)

On a hill 3km from Levoča, **Bazilika Panny Márie** (Our Lady's Chapel) hosts a pilgrimage of over 500,000 devotees the first weekend in July for St. Jacob's feast day.

■ Spišské Podhradie and Žehra

Tiny Spišské Podhradie lies in a valley between what were once the two most powerful forces in Spiš—the castle and the bishopric. The king is gone and so is the bishop, but a day in Spišské Podhradie is possibly the closest you'll ever get to living in a medieval hamlet. The 17th-century bishopric, **Spišská Kapitula,** sits atop a hill next to Spišské Podhradie. Despite their eviction by the Communist regime in 1948, the clerics have returned, and during the day are out *en masse.* Central Europe's largest castle, **Spišský hrad** sprawls in magnificent white over the mountain opposite. Although native Celts fortified their settlement here in the first century BCE, it was not until the 12th century that Hungarian kings began the *hrad's* construction. The castle, which first served as a regional center and later as home of the Thurzov and Czáky families, was abandoned when a 1780 fire destroyed the complex. Many paths lead to the castle, but perhaps the most satisfying is the little-worn, grassy, 2km trek from the left side of the town's cemetery. Watch out for cow patties. Once there, hike around the expansive ruins and visit the museum (inner castle including museum open May-Oct.

Tues.-Sun. 9am-6pm; 30Sk, students 10Sk). August 1996 saw a medieval festival in Spišský hrad—it may become an annual tradition. For more info, contact Spišské Múzeum v Levoči, nám. Majstra Pavla 40 (tel. 27 86).

Traveling 3km farther leads to the even tinier **Žehra.** One of Spiš's oldest settlements, the town boasts the white-washed, onion-domed **Church of the Holy Spirit,** whose interior frescoes date back to the 14th century. The church is officially open only for services, but the priest, who lives next door, is willing to let visitors peek.

Buses arrive in sp. Podhradie from Prešov (every 1-3hr., 1½hr., 24Sk) and Levoča (hourly, 20min., 10Sk), and the last ones leave for Prešov around 7pm and Levoča around 10pm. Missing the bus isn't so bad if private rooms are available: **Area Tour,** Marianské nám. 22 (tel. 811 154 or 811 209), arranges accommodations for 220-350Sk per person (plus 50Sk with breakfast), and sells maps (28Sk) and pamphlets on the town and surroundings (open Mon.-Fri. 7am-7pm). The town's only hotel, **Alfa,** sidl. Hrad 1 (tel. 811 619), offers white-washed doubles with less clean bathrooms, views of the castle, and a free wake-up call à la rooster (360Sk). Marianské nám. has little to offer in the way of restaurants, so try the **potraviny** (grocery) at #4 (open Mon.-Fri. 5:30am-7pm, Sat. 5:30am-2pm, and Sun. 7:30am-4pm). **VÚB,** Marianské nám. 34 (tel. 811 149), exchanges Visa and AmEx traveler's checks (open Mon.-Tues. and Thurs. 8am-noon and 1-4pm, Wed. 9am-noon and 1-5pm, Fri. 8am-noon). The **post office** at Marianské nám. 1 is also on the square (open Mon.-Fri. 6am-7pm, and Sat. 6am-10am). **Postal code:** 5304. **Phone Code:** 966.

■ Slovenský Raj

To the south of Poprad and on the other side of the Low Tatras lies the Slovenský Raj (Slovak Paradise) National Park, a true paradise of stately pines and untamed wilderness. The park is famed for its twisted rock formations, extensive cave systems, and excellent hiking and skiing.

Orientation and Practical Information Nestled in a gorge on the shores of the man-made lake Palcmanská Maša, Dedinky (pop. 400) is the largest of the towns on the Slovenský Raj's southern border. Infrequent **trains** link Dedinky to neighboring towns (7 per day, fewer on weekends) along the Margecany (1½hr., 34Sk) to Červená skala (40min., 155Sk) line; trains from Č. skala go to Banská Bystrica (another 2½hr.). A few brave **buses** venture into Dedinky from Dobšinská Ladová Jakyňa (1 per day), Dobšina (6 per day on weekdays, 2 per day on Sat., none on Sun.). More buses stop on the road to Dedinky 2km from town: to Poprad (10 per day, 70min., 45Sk). It is also one of the few towns with a **post office** (behind the wooden tower near the bus stop; open Mon.-Fri. 7:30am-3:30pm, Sat. 7:30-8:30am, except when it isn't). **Postal code:** 4973. **Phone code:** 942.

An old **map** of Slovenský Raj can be anywhere from an annoyance to a danger, so pick up the 1997 *VKÚ Slovenský Raj* from Dedinky's Hotel Priehrada (Slovak 59Sk, German 80Sk). The relief map lists trails, lodges, mountain springs, campsites, and much more. **Park admission tickets** are sold at entrances for a meager 10Sk that goes to conservation of the park and your own accident insurance. To start hikers on their way, a **chair lift** runs from behind the hotel to Chata Geravy (hourly, in summer Mon. 9am-3pm, Tues.-Sun. 9am-4pm; off-season daily 9am-2pm; one-way 40Sk, roundtrip 60Sk). Boating is a popular pastime on Dedinky's man-made lake. **Geret Tours** (tel. (92) 731 016, open daily in summer 9am-6pm), along the town's only road, rents four-person **rowboats** and two-person **paddle boats** for 30Sk an hour. Street **bikes** are 20Sk an hour; mountain bike tours will cost more. The park does not allow mountain bike rentals without a guide, but the enthusiastic, experienced owner/guide has created a photo-catalogue of stellar tours for about DM20 or 500Sk, including bike rental.

Accommodations and Food Accommodations are often booked a month in advance for July, August, and January. In Dedinky, **Hotel Priehrada** (tel. 982 12; fax 982 21) deals out dated rooms with a view of the lake for 200Sk a person (shared bath and toilets), and books 21 *chatas* behind the hotel, just as clean for 100Sk. **Penzión Pastierňa**, Dedinky 42 (tel. 981 75), above the church, may have fine rooms on shorter notice (300Sk per person), but the real gem is the restaurant downstairs; it's one of the few in town where relatively light *halušky* (40Sk) can be washed down with a shot of *Becherovka*. The chair lift from Dedinky will take you to **Chata Geravy** (tel. 982 41), which, while not excessively clean, is a great point for starting hikes. Small rooms with huge pillows go for 120Sk (communal bathrooms; half-pension 120Sk more; full-pension 160Sk extra; reception open 7am-10pm). In addition, almost every home in Dedinky doubles as a **pension** for 100-200Sk per person. Solo travelers be warned: owners may be reluctant to take just one, so keep looking. Nearby **Stratená**, a one-road town surrounded by jagged cliffs, may be a better bet. As many signs as there are houses advertise "Zimmerfrei" and "Free Room"; they'll cost around 100-200Sk. **Chata Stratenká**, Stratená 51, Stratená (tel. (942) 981 67), also offers rooms (330Sk per person). The rooms shine in the sun and bask in awe of the cliffs (shared bathrooms). Free TV on request, but half-pension (breakfast and dinner) costs an additional 120Sk.

Stock up on those necessary carbs at the **grocery** in Dedinky (open Mon.-Fri. 7am-6pm, Sat. 7am-5pm, Sun. 9am-5pm), or at the one at base of the ice cave trail (see below) which also operates a **buffet** with soup and bread (12Sk) to warm you up after the icy cave (open Tues.-Sun. 8:30-6pm).

Sights and Hiking Before setting off for the wilderness, there are a couple things you might want to know. First of all, camping or lighting fires is illegal within the park grounds. Secondly, some trails, mostly along cascades, are one-way—the VKÚ map marks them with arrows. Thirdly, in winter, when some of the park's waterfalls are most beautiful, certified guides must accompany hikers. Finally, don't worry about red marks on trails as long as you don't want to cut down any trees. They signal special reserved areas. See Essentials: Wilderness and Safety Concerns, p. 48 for general tips on keeping healthy and happy while hiking.

Biele Vody (White Waters, 1½hr.): This is the trail in all the pictures. The hike, heading up to one of the park's many rapids, involves ladders and is one-way, so there's no turning back even for bad cases of vertigo. From Hotel Priehrada in Dedinky, take the red trail to Biele Vody. The blue cascade trail will be on the left. Chata Geravy (see Dedinky) waits at the top and the green trail leads back down, or for 20Sk ride the roller-coaster lift.

Havrania skala (Crow's Cliff, 4hr.): The route to one of Slovenský Raj's most scenic cliffs follows the ridge overlooking Stratená. From Stratená's train station, take the green path to **Občasný prameň** (fountain). The first part leads through the town's alleys and past a few barking dogs but eventually ascends to a graveyard, quietly tucked into a gorge. The steep climb ends at the *prameň*. Before the fountain the trail changes color to yellow. Don't let this confuse you—head left on the yellow trail, which reaches the Crow's Cliff, then descends to the ice caves.

Malé-Zajfy (3hr.): The path from Stratená to Chata Geravy offers a leisurely pass through a golden meadow. Follow the Havrania skala trail until the *prameň*, then head right on the yellow trail, through wildflower fields and along a tiny creek.

Almost 150,000 cubic meters of frozen water survive from the last Ice Age in the 19-km stretch of **Dobšinská ľadová jaskyňa** (ice cave). The 30-minute tour covers only 475m of the cave, but that's enough to inspire awe at the ice monster lurking below, with hall after hall of frozen columns, gigantic ice wells, and hardened waterfalls. The well trodden 20-minute blue trail leads to the cave from the Stratená. (Open mid-May-June Tues.-Sun. 9:30am-2pm; July-Aug. 9am-4pm, Sept. 9:30am-2pm. Hourly Slovak tours 60Sk, with ISIC 55Sk; English 120Sk, with ISIC 110Sk.)

ŠARIŠ

Tucked in East Slovakia, Šariš has remained untouched by many of the political events of the last 80 years. The deeply religious majority never really liked the Communists, and to them, the current wave of fierce capitalism seems a little too gung-ho. Nonetheless, Košice did rule all of Czechoslovakia for three months in 1945, and long before the revolution, Šariš boiled as a hot-bed of anti-Habsburg revolt. For many years a borderland against Turkish invasions, the region and its sleepy towns still stand behind bastions built to repel the Saracens. Even Košice, Slovakia's second city, seems turned down to a one. German-speaking tourists are fewer here, with English in the running for second language; mostly, though, it's you and the locals.

■ Košice

Though the city's ancestors, medieval gold merchants, would wince at the blast furnaces and steel foundries that have replaced their fine metal shops, Košice's Gothic and Renaissance center has managed to survive fires, revolutions, an Ottoman invasion, and the city's intense industrial development. Eastern Slovakia's cultural and political heart now pulses with the lively conversations of theater-goers and the ribald jokes of wine-lovers.

ORIENTATION AND PRACTICAL INFORMATION

An **airport** sits outside the city. Košice's Old Town lies close to the train station. To get to the central **Hlavná** and the tourist office, exit the station and follow the "Centrum" signs across the park to **Mlynská**, which intersects Hlavná at Dóm sv. Alžbety.

- **Tourist Offices:** Hlavná 8 (tel. 186; fax 622 69 38). The staff provides maps of the city (26Sk) and nearly anywhere else in Slovakia, books rooms, and advertises Košice's numerous cultural events in a monthly pamphlet (4Sk). Open June-Sept. Mon.-Fri. 8am-6pm, Sat. 9am-1pm; Oct.-May Mon.-Fri. 9am-5pm, Sat 9am-1pm.
  Tatratour, Alžbetina 6 (tel. 622 48 72), situated near the cathedral. This local **American Express** representative will arrange a night's stay at an affiliated pension for 200Sk per person. Open Mon.-Fri. 8am-4:30pm.
- **Currency Exchange: VÚB** has branches liberally sprinkled throughout the city; the one at Hlavná 8 (tel. 622 62 50), right next to the tourist office, cashes traveler's checks and exchanges currency, both at a 1% commission.
- **ATMs:** In front of many VÚB branches, including Hlavná 8—MC/Cirrus linked.
- **Trains:** Predstaničné nám. Trains run west to Bratislava (13 per day, 5hr., 212Sk) and Prague (5 per day, 9hr., 403Sk). Eastbound trains to Kiev (2 per day, 17hr., 818Sk) and Lviv (2 per day, 8hr., 440Sk) often continue all the way to Moscow. Northbound trains pass through to Kraków (6 per day, 7hr., 547Sk) and Nowy Sącz, Poland (3 per day, 348Sk). Trains from Poland head to Budapest (6 per day, 4hr., 790Sk). Non-stop **luggage storage** and pesky **lockers**, both at 5Sk per bag.
- **Buses:** Next to the train station. Buses are bumpier and more expensive, but for trips in the region they are sometimes faster, and their routes are always more scenic. To: Brno (2 per day, 10½hr., 325Sk). If you're into long bus rides, Košice has a far-flung system with buses to destinations in Poland, Germany, and even Italy.
- **Public Transportation: Trams** and **buses** cover the city and its suburbs. Tickets cost 6Sk at kiosks and little orange boxes at bus stops (exact change required).
- **Taxis: Rádio Taxi** (tel.1833), or another private taxi firm (tel. 424 242).
- **24-Hour Pharmacy:** Toryská 1 (tel. 42 94 91).
- **Post Office:** Poštová 20 (tel. 617 13 88). Open Mon.-Fri. 7am-7pm, Sat. 7am-2pm. **Postal code:** 4001. **Phone code:** 95.

ACCOMMODATIONS

Although the cost of accommodations is generally higher in Košice than in smaller towns, a few hotels and *penziónsy* are manageable. Tourist offices have lists of accommodations, but prices may be old or have a minimum stay of one month.

Pension Rozália, Oravská 14 (tel. 633 97 14). From the station, take tram #6 to "Amfiteáter" and walk up Stará spišská cesta. Ten minutes of trekking will lead through a gentler suburb gushing with greenery and birdsong. Oravská appears on the right; there is no indication that #14 is a pension, but just ring. Small rooms with windows overlooking a garden for 150Sk per person. Call before making the trek. Be aware that "free" chauffeuring to the city center actually costs 100Sk.

Hotel Európa, Protifašistických Bojovníkov 1 (tel. 622 38 97), across the park in front of the train station. A posh 19th-century hotel whose bathroom tiles have been around since the Hungarian occupation. Communal toilets and one shower room for both women and men. Singles 330Sk. Doubles 570Sk. Triples 770Sk. For a private bath and fridge-equipped living room, apartments run 1200Sk.

Hotel Strojár, Južná Trieda 93 (tel. 54 406; fax 54 407). Tram #3 heads directly from the train station to "Hotel Strojár". This renovated hotel boasts nearly spotless rooms, firm beds, and a congenial manager. Every 2 rooms share a bathroom. Well worth the tram ride. Doubles 420Sk. Triples 570Sk. Apartments 700-900Sk.

Hotel Kosmalt, Kysucká 16 (tel. 423 511). By tram #6's "Kino Družba" stop. Rooms feature tired old bathrooms, industrial rugs, and a concrete view, but the sheets are clean, and the price is right (240Sk per person). Check-in after 2pm, but morning arrivers can leave bags with the friendly reception. Check-out 10am.

FOOD

Eateries flood the city center, but it quickly becomes apparent that most restaurant-goers live on a liquid diet of coffee, beer, and wine. A restaurant where people are actually eating merits a second look. For complete self-service, try the **K-mart** at Hlavná 109 (open Mon.-Wed. 8am-7pm, Thurs.-Fri. 8am-8pm, Sat.-Sun. 8am-1pm).

Ajvega, Orlia 10 (tel. 622 04 52), off Mlynská. Veggie pasta, pizza, soups, and salads. The *Maxi Zelo* (50Sk) defies the Slovak notion of "one salad, one vegetable" with tomatoes, peppers, cucumbers, and carrots all in one bowl. If there are no free tables on the ground floor, go up two flights. Open daily 11am-11pm.

Country Club Diera, Poštová 14 (tel. 622 05 51). If American flags, Confederate banners, and spaghetti Westerns on TV don't conjure up images of the Wild West, maybe a stuffed buffalo head or some grilled beef (60Sk) will. Open Mon.-Thurs. 11am-3am, Fri. 11am-4am, Sat. 3pm-3am, Sun. 3pm-1am.

Šomoši Grill Veverička, Hlavná 95 (tel. 622 33 60). The short-order cooks are superfast and the food is fried right at the bar. Plastic flowers decorate the white dining room, but its interior has escaped the plague of cigarette ads. Fried cheese and french fries for 51Sk. Open Mon.-Sat. 9am-9pm and Sun. 11am-8pm.

Aida, Poštova 4. Draws the crowds from the streets for sweets (6-10Sk) and ice cream (3Sk per scoop). Open daily 10am-10pm.

SIGHTS AND ENTERTAINMENT

The streets of Košice's Old Town provide a few full days of good walking tours. The town's six museums each costs 20Sk, with the ISIC 10Sk (open May-Sept. Mon.-Fri. 9am-5pm and Sun. 1-5pm; Oct.-April Tues.-Fri. 9am-5pm and Sun. 9am-1pm). Extensive drainage work in 1996 turned much of the Old Town into a muddy maze; this should be completed by 1997, but bring your boots just in case.

Bulbous **Hlavná** marks the heart of historical Košice. At the street's widest point, **Dom sv. Alžbety** (Cathedral of St. Elizabeth) towers above the Old Town. Originally designed as a high-Gothic monument, this confused cathedral has undergone repeated renovations and now stands as a cool conglomeration of almost every style known to Western architecture. In 1900, restorers built a crypt under the cathedral's north nave. Transported from Turkey in 1906 and entered into the vault, Košice's rebel son, **Francis Rakóczi II**, stirs up much less trouble in a sarcophagus. The cathedral's little brother, **Kaplnka sv. Michala** (Chapel of St. Michael), next door, serves as a mortuary and is closed to the public. Outside, a relief of St. Michael weighs the souls of the dead. On the cathedral's other side, **Urbanova veža** (Urban's Tower) is rumored to house the city's **metallurgical museum**, featuring cast-iron bells, pewter doorknockers, and golden candlesticks (closed in 1996). The tower's exterior arcade presents an array of tombstones, some dating back to Roman times.

Built of stones discarded from St. Elizabeth's Cathedral, the 19th-century **Jakabov Palác**, Mlynská 30, off Hlavná, served as the temporary home of Czechoslovakia's president in the spring of 1945. Off Mlynská, Puškinova leads to the closed **synagogue**. A strikingly graphic memorial to local Jews deported to concentration camps in 1944 hangs outside. North of the cathedral on Hlavná, on the other side of the fountain, which dances to music in the afternoons and evenings, stands the stately neo-Baroque **state theater**, built at the turn of the century.

Farther north, the 14m **Plague Column** commemorates the devastating plague of 1710. Running off Hlavná near the theater, Univerzitná leads to two museums, **Miklušova väznica** (prison) and **Rakóczi's House**, Hrnčiarska 7. The ticket office for both lies behind the gate at Hrnčiarska. All browsing is loosely guided, but not necessarily in English. Housed in the former city jail, **Miklušova väznica** reveals everything you ever wanted to know about life behind bars in the 17th- through 19th-centuries—prisoner graffiti, death verdicts, and torture instruments. The tour leads through reconstructed prison chambers, many with unflattering sketches of the executioner, and photo collections of actors demonstrating the various methods of torture and annihilation. So as not to torture the prison's delicate floors, visitors are asked to put on slippers (one size fits all...small feet). **Rakóczi's House** is a shrine to Rakóczi Ferenc II, Hungary's anti-Habsburg national hero. The museum contains furniture and an entire room from Rakóczi's home in Turkey, where he died in exile. Check out the guest book for the number of Hungarian visitors.

Hlavná eventually ends at Hviezdoslavova between the two main buildings of the **Východoslovenské Múzeum** (East Slovak Museum). Inside the one to the right, recent history shines with examples of the region's folk and religious art, such as dancing saints, gigantic Jewish wedding rings, and a life-size sculpture of a knight on horseback descending upon a peg-legged beggar. To the left, prehistoric remnants illuminate the saga of the Celts, Germans, and Slavs who settled the region. After the upper floors, the museum's pride awaits downstairs behind a two-ton door. In 1935, while laying foundations for a new finance headquarters at Hlavná 68, workers discovered a copper bowl filled with 2920 gold *tholars* and a Renaissance gold chain over two meters long. The vault displays this, as well as an additional 1992 discovery. The tour continues with an exhibit entitled "Money Through the Ages".

Information and tickets for Košice's four **theaters** and one **philharmonic** are available at the Hlavná 8 tourist office. Beer and wine halls are plentiful in the town center, so go explore. The intimate **Tokaj Vináreň**, Poštová 3, serves Slovak wine at 6-20Sk a glass among wine barrels and vines but focuses on selling by the bottle (open Mon.-Fri. 9am-6pm, Sat. 8am-noon). Satisfying a little known Slovak fetish for bluegrass, live music plays for line-dancers on weekend nights at **Country Club Diera**, 14 Poštová (tel. 622 05 51). Bartenders serve tequila shots (48Sk) and seven types of whiskey behind pictures of Annie Oakley and Davy Crockett. Luckily, the beer isn't American—a smooth, tall one of *Gemer* costs only 13Sk (open Mon.-Thurs. 11am-3am, Fri. 11am-4am, Sat. 3pm-3am, Sun. 3pm-1am). For unadulterated **disco** and 25Sk beers, head for **Hacienda**, Hlavná 65 (open daily 9pm-4am; cover 40Sk, weekdays 30Sk, women free Mon. and Wed.).

■ Prešov

In Prešov, cultural mish-mash is as common as good beer. Large contingents of Magyars, Gypsies, and Rusins maintain their diverse traditions, while clean-cut couples, black-clad widows, and Catholics flaunting their Sunday best underscore the town's uncitified intimacy. Beware, Prešov shuts down almost entirely on weekends.

Orientation and Practical Information Prešov's stem, **Košická**, sprouts straight out of the train station, blooming into **Masaryková**, then **Hlavná**. At the town square, Hlavná splits into two branches which re-merge after enveloping **St. Nicholas's Cathedral**. Northbound buses and trams (all except #19 and 31) travel between the station and the center; cross under Masaryková in the underpass and purchase a 5Sk ticket from the orange automats. Automats are at most bus or tram stops (exact change required). **Metské Informačna Centrum**, Hlavná 67 (tel. 186 or 731 113), provides town and hotel info (open Mon.-Sat. 7am-5pm, Sun. 7am-noon). **Exchange currency** at **VÚB**, Masaryková 13 (tel. 333 61), which accepts AmEx traveler's checks (1% commission) and gives MasterCard advances. Open Mon.-Thurs. 8am-noon and 1:30pm-5pm, Fri. 8am-noon. **Slovenská Sporitel'ňa**, Masaryková 10 (tel. 233 71), cashes AmEx and Visa traveler's checks at a 2% commission and provides Visa cash advances (open Mon. and Wed.-Fri. 7:30am-5pm, Tues. 7:30am-1pm, Sat. 8am-noon). An exchange machine at Hlavná 74 turns your home currency into crowns for poor rates. **Trains** (tel. 731 043) leave every 45min.-4hr. for Košice (50min., 18Sk). **Buses** (tel. 310 43), opposite the train station to Košice (1 or 2 per hour, 30-45min., 24Sk), Poprad (1-4 per hour, 1½hr., 17Sk), and all *šarišské* towns. The **post office**, Masaryková 2 (tel. 326 43), sits slightly south of the Old Town (open Mon.-Fri. 8am-7pm and Sat. 8am-1pm). **Postal code:** 08001. Coin and card **telephones** stand outside the post office. **Phone code:** 91.

Accommodations and Food A large number of inexpensive rooms hide in Prešov's southwest suburb, and, with the town's scarcity of tourists, vacancies are common. **Turistická Ubytovaňa Sen**, Vajanského 65 (tel. 331 70), offers a few rooms for 140Sk per person; call in advance. The well broomed doubles with cracking wallpaper at **Penzion Lineas**, Budovatelská 14 (tel. 723 325, ext. 28; fax 723 206), include toilets and baths (360Sk). From the station, walk towards the town center, take the first left on Škultétyho, and a left again at Budovatelská. The disco downstairs runs nightly until 6am, but doesn't disturb sleepers. **Hotel Hviezda**, 17. novembra 122 (tel. 318 92), was closed for renovation in the summer of '96, but it might be worth calling to see if their previously shining rooms are once again available.

Prešov boasts a well-spring of high-quality restaurants, but only a trickling have low prices. For the lowest, there is a **K-mart supermarket** at Legionarov 1, where Hlavná becomes Masarykova (open Mon.-Wed. 8am-7pm, Thurs.-Fri. 8am-8pm, Sat. 8am-4pm, Sun. 8am-1pm). Known locally as "Kramike", **Neptun**, Hlavná 62 (tel. 732 538), slightly off a side alley, serves as a restaurant and popular watering-hole. Enjoy 25-140Sk meals with wine (by the glass 9-12Sk, by the bottle 150-390Sk) under wrought-iron sculptures and candlelight flickers. The low rumble of conversation in this former dungeon is entirely in Slovak, as is the menu (open Mon.-Thurs. 10am-10pm). The restaurant transforms into a **disco** on Thursday, Friday, and Saturday nights, serving beers (18Sk) and "hangover soup" (*korbeľska kapustnica s klobásou;* 27Sk; disco open Thurs.-Sat. 8pm-3am; cover 20Sk). **Florianka**, Baštová 32 (tel. 734 083), sits next door to Slovakia's best hotel and restaurant management school, which has made this former firehouse its training ground. Sip *Šariš* beer near the old pushcart firetruck outside or enjoy hot meals (30-50Sk) in the restaurant's blazing red interior. Chefs are graded, and the food and the service score high marks (open Mon.-Fri. 11am-9:30pm). Saving the day on weekends, **Bagetèria**, Hlavná 36 (tel. 732 602), serves baguette sandwiches for 17-36Sk (open Mon.-Fri. 6am-10pm, Sat.-Sun. 7:30am-10pm). Down the street, **Veliovič Cukráreň** adds sweets (6-8Sk), heftier desserts (banana splits; 35Sk), and cappuccino (15Sk; open daily 8am-9pm).

Sights and Entertainment Hlavná's Renaissance houses stand back in deference to the town's old **Kostol sv. Mikuláša** (St. Nicholas's Cathedral). The Gothic cathedral's distinctive turrets physically attest to Saxon influence in Prešov during the late Middle Ages. The church opens its doors only irregularly outside of masses; long skirts and pants will spare you glares from a hundred eyes. Beside the Roman Catholic church at Hlavná 86, the 16th-century **Rákoczi Palace,** with its attic gable of plants and saints, houses the **Vlastivedné múzeum** (City museum; tel. 734 708). The lace work inside is impressive, and an exhibition on fire moves quickly from making it in the stone age to fighting it in more recent eras—it finishes up with several great old firetrucks parked behind the museum (open Tues.-Fri. 10am-5pm, Sat.-Sun. 11am-3pm; 20Sk, students 10Sk). Farther down the street, at #62, stands the 19th-century **Ruský Dom** (Rusins' Clubhouse). A second-floor office sells books on Russian history and culture, as well as the local Rusin newspaper. The column outside with its hammer and sickle seems even more anachronistic than the statue of Neptune near it. The latter was given to the town by a Jewish merchant in the 19th century as thanks for allowing him to settle in Prešov. Perambulate down to the Greek Orthodox **Katedrálny chrám sv. Jána Krstiteľa** (St. John's Cathedral) at the base of Hlavná to peek at the church's breathtaking altar.

On the west side of Hlavná, the restored Gothic building of **Šarišská galéria,** Hlavná 51 (tel. 725 423), features exhibits of Slovak art (open Tues., Wed., and Fri. 9am-5pm, Thurs. 9am-6pm, Sat. 9am-1pm, Sun 1:30-5:30pm; 6Sk, students 2Sk, Sun. free). Heading west from the town hall on Hlavná, the narrow **Floriánova** harks back to medieval times and leads to **Brána sv. Floriána** (St. Florian's Gate), a remnant of Prešov's early Renaissance fortifications. In the northwest of the Old Town, at Švermova 56, the ornate **synagogue's** exterior is undergoing repairs, but the well maintained interior is open to the public. Constructed in 1898, the synagogue was the religious center of Prešov's Jewish community until World War II. A **monument** erected in 1991 commemorates the six thousand Jews of Prešov who fell victim to the Nazis and the Tiso regime; the current community numbers only slightly over 100. The synagogue houses the **Múzeum Judaík** (Museum of Judaica; tel. 325 72; open Tues.-Wed. 11am-4pm, Thurs. 3-6pm, Fri. 10am-1pm, Sun. 1-5pm; tours in Slovak 10Sk, students 5Sk; in German 20Sk, students 10Sk).

Rumor has it that even Košice comes to Prešov for fun. See for yourself at any of Prešov's numerous pubs, *vinareňs,* and nightclubs. For a day of relaxation before the revelry, the town also has two theaters and a fine **Múzeum Vín,** Floriánova ul. (tel. 733 108). This demure drinking establishment in the basement of the Old Town hall serves a variety of Slovak, Moravian, and Hungarian wines (5-10Sk each) in the degustation room, and lets guests visit the museum's stocks. A 1763L wine barrel and 1.2m-tall, double-barrel-shotgun wine bottle wait at the end (open Mon.-Fri. 9am-6pm, Sat. 8am-noon; 10Sk). **Piváreň Smädný Mních,** Hlavná 41 (tel. 723 789), on a side passage, features the "Thirsty Monk" (13Sk) and many happy locals. Walk past the video game and descend to the cellar. Just don't try swinging on the wagon-wheel chandeliers (open Mon.-Thurs. 11am-11pm, Fri. 11am-1am, Sat.-Sun. 3pm-midnight). The town's best open-air beer garden, **Zahradný Dvor,** Hlavná 64 (tel. 723 538), upstairs from Neptun (see Accommodations, above), serves *Šariš* at a mere 11Sk. The tables are wood, and so are the gnarly branching sun shades (open Mon.-Sat. 8am-10pm).

■ Bardejov

For the last five centuries, Bardejov's monuments danced with disaster. The troubles began in 1494, when the vault of St. Aegidius's Church collapsed only months after its construction. Turkish armies, an earthquake, and three fires subsequently left the town in ruin, but the citizens have kept coming back with a vengeance. Bardejov's most recent restoration won a UNESCO heritage gold medal in 1986, and the strangely empty town now seems so perfectly medieval, that one would expect to hear the ghosts of Bardejov's medieval merchants milling about the quiet square.

Orientation and Practical Information The quickest way to enter and exit Bardejov is by **train;** to Košice (around 30 per day, 2hr., 40Sk) via Prešov (50min., 22Sk). The **bus station,** next to the train station, sends buses to Poprad (10

BARDEJOV ■ 663

per day, 2½hr., 68Sk) and local towns. From the **train station,** go left and take the path leading into the town's stone fortification. The straightest route leads to the center at **Radničné nám.** The **tourist office,** Radničné nám. 21 (tel./fax 726 072), beckons local crowds with its egocentric yellow "I," and sells over a dozen different guides about Bardejov and the region. The staff assists in finding rooms (open daily June-Oct. 15 8am-6pm; Oct. 16-May 8am-4pm). **Exchange currency** at **VÚB,** Kellerova 1 (tel. 722 671); they cash AmEx and Visa traveler's checks at a 1% commission and have a Cirrus/MC **ATM** (exchange open Mon.-Thurs. 8am-noon and 1:30-5pm, Fri. 8am-noon; ATM open daily 6am-10pm). **Polhobanka,** Dlhý rad 17 (tel. 67 45), supplies Visa cash advances (but only Mon.-Fri. 8am-2:30pm). The **post office** is at Dlhý rad 14 (tel. 726 610; open Mon.-Fri. 7:30-11:30am and 1-4pm, Sat. 7:30-9:30am). **Postal code:** 8501. Phone cards are sold in the outer foyer (open Mon.-Thurs. 7am-4:45pm, Fri. 7am-3pm), and **telephones** stand outside. **Phone code:** 935.

Accommodations and Food
Fearing the Old Town's fortifications or taxes, inexpensive hotels wait outside the city walls. Popular among teenage Slovaks, **Športhotel,** Katuzovovo 31 (tel.724 449), is ten minutes away from the train station. Turn right from the station and follow Slovenská; make a left on Kúpeľná, and after 200m, a right on Kellerova; take the first left after the bridge and the hotel will appear on the right. The last road is dirt, but the hotel is anything but. Airy rooms with toilet and shower glow with the handiwork of the hotel's maids (265Sk per person). **Hotel Toplá,** Fučíkova 25 (tel. 724 041), looks a bit grim from the outside, and the toilets and showers smell not of roses, but the rooms themselves are cheap and clean. From the train station, walk slightly left toward town and then take the first right onto Nový Sad which becomes Fučíkova (singles 254Sk, doubles 454Sk, triples 603Sk).

Restaurants in Bardejov are affordable, but few rise above the rabble of snack bars and drab beerhalls. **U Zlatej Koruny,** Radničné nám 41 (tel. 725 310), is one exception. This restaurant serves a wide variety of wines, as well as elegant entrées (35-120Sk), soups (10-20Sk), and—get them while you can—salads (10-30Sk). The question following an order of *halušky* is *"zakysanka?"* Answer yes if you'd like buttermilk, delicious with the heavy dumplings, but likely to make an afternoon nap a requirement (open Sun.-Thurs. 9am-10pm, Fri.-Sat. 9am-11pm). **Reštaurácia Na Bráne,** Nám SNP 50, at the end of Hviezdoslavova (tel. 722 348), tends a bit more toward drab beerhall-esque with its smoky interior, but the food (entrées 25-70Sk) is simple and good (open Mon.-Fri. 9am-9pm, Sat.-Sun. 9:30am-7:30pm). Serve yourself at **Supermarket Centrum,** Slovenská 11, across from the train station (open Mon.-Fri. 6am-6pm, Sat. 5:45-11:45am).

Sights
Bardejov may be the only town in Šariš where the square's centerpiece isn't a church. The maple tree at the south end is a gift from the USA, brought in 1991 by the illustrious former vice-prez Dann Kwuayle. The **radnica** (town hall) now serves as one of the town's museums. **Šarišske Múzeum,** Radničné nám. 48 (tel. 60 38), displays historic trinkets, including the key to the city, which the mayor's wife allegedly passed to her treacherous Turkish lover in 1697. Serenaded by harpsichord music, the tour leads past ancient steins and a slingshot that makes the story of David and Goliath believable. The **Ikony** exhibition, Radničné nám. 13 (tel. 722 009), houses a huge collection of Orthodox icons. The display "Nature of Northeastern Slovakia" in the **Prírodopisné Múzeum,** Rhodyho (tel. 722 630), will interest anyone who loves stuffed animals or loves to stuff 'em. (Museums open May-Sept. Tues.-Sun. 9am-noon and 12:30-5pm; Oct.-April Tues.-Sun. 8am-noon and 12:30-4pm; 10Sk, students 5Sk.)

Kostol sv. Egídia (Church of St. Aegidius), behind the town hall, contains eleven Gothic wing altars crafted between 1450 and 1510. In the 17th century, iconoclastic Calvinists took over the town and the church. Fortunately, they compromised with the town's merchants and let the altars stay as long as they remained shut. The most valuable is also the biggest: the 15th-century **Nativity Altar** (open Mon.-Fri. 9am-5:30pm, Sat. 9:30am-5pm, Sun. 11am-5:30pm; 20Sk, students 10Sk). Up a hill to the east of town, **Kostol sv. Kríža** (Church of the Holy Cross) stands watch over Bardejov's cemetery. A forest path leads past 14 stark Stations of the Cross before reaching the old graveyard overrun with weeds. A full panorama of Bardejov's valley stretches below, but watch out for the stinging nettles.

One of Bardejov's **bastions,** in the town's southeast corner, first served as a crossroads beacon and later as the local beheading stock. The tourist office has pamphlets on all the **walking tours** possible around Bardejov and its 14th-century towers.

About 4km from Bardejov, **Bardejovské Kúpele** works wonders with water cures and pure country air. Actual curing stations are off limits, but several free fountains run with the spa's acid water. The complex is an awkward collection of 18th- and 19th-century buildings in need of a paint job and more recent (and less ornate) hotels, all tied together by sidewalk and fountains. The spa's height was in the late 18th- and early 19th- centuries when Elizabeth, the wife of Austrian Emperor Franz Joseph; Alexander I of Russia; Emperor Joseph II of Austria-Hungary; and Napoleon's second wife, Marcia Luisa, all came for cures. WWI and the end of the Empire cut off the spa from the Hungarian aristocrats who had come in search for the great outdoors with the comforts of home. On the resort's outskirts, Slovakia's oldest folklore exhibition sits in a hectare replica of Šariš village life. In summer, the **skansen** hosts regular folk festivals and craft days (tel. 20 72; same hours as Bardejov museums). To get to Bardejovské Kúpele, take bus #1, 2, 6, 7, 10, or 11 to the end of the line.

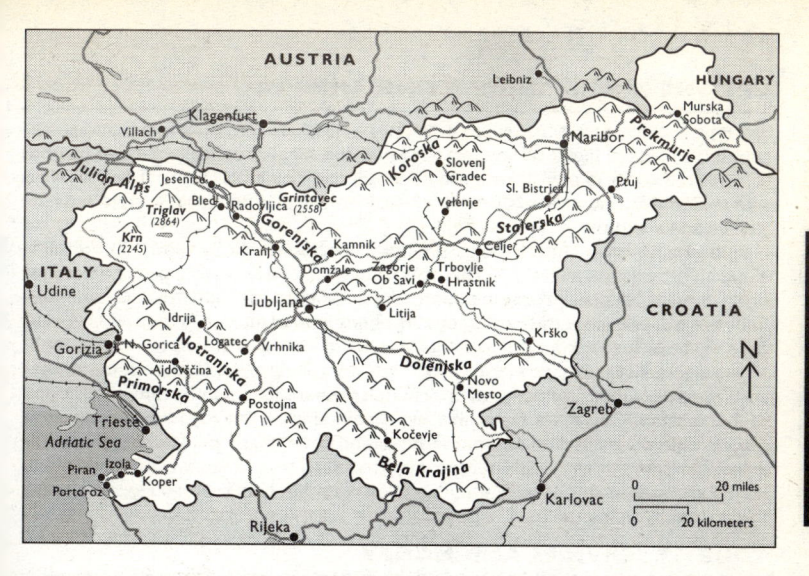

SLOVENIA (SLOVENIJA)

US$1 = 131Slt	100Slt = US$0.76
CDN$1 = 96Slt	100Slt = CAD$1.05
UK£1 = 205Slt	100Slt = UK£0.49
IR£1 = 213Slt	100Slt = IR£0.47
AUS$1 = 104Slt	100Slt = AUS$0.97
NZ$1 = 91Slt	100Slt = NZ$1.10
SAR1 = 30Slt	100Slt = SAR3.39
DM1 = 89Slt	100Slt = DM1.13
Country Phone Code: 386	**International Dialing Prefix: 00**

Worlds away from the conflict in Bosnia, Slovenia, the most prosperous of Yugoslavia's breakaway republics, has reveled in its independence, modernizing rapidly as it turns a hungry eye toward the West. For a country half Switzerland's size, Slovenia, on the "sunny side of the Alps," is extraordinarily diverse: in a day, you can breakfast on an Alpine peak, lunch under the Mediterranean sun, and dine in a vineyard.

SLOVENIA ESSENTIALS

Australian, Canadian, Ireland, New Zealand, U.K., and U.S. citizens can visit visa-free for up to 90 days, but South Africans need visas (US$35 for 3-month single-entry and transit; US$77 for 3-month multiple-entry). Apply by mail or in person in your home country, or at the border. See Essentials: Embassies and Consulates, p. 8. Processing takes a week, and requires your passport and the fee in cash, check, or money order. To prolong a stay, apply for temporary residency at an Office for Foreigners.

GETTING THERE AND GETTING AROUND

Slovenia is easily accessible by car, train, or plane. There are three international **airports:** commercial flights all arrive at the **Ljubljana Airport** in Brnik, with regular bus service to the city center 25km away. The reformed national carrier **Adria Airways** flies to European capitals and Tel Aviv. A regular **hydrofoil** service also runs between Venice and Portorož.

Ljubljana has many international rail links. **Trains** are cheap, clean, and reliable. You can usually find a seat on local trains, though it's best to avoid peak commuting hours around Ljubljana. For some international destinations (other than Croatia), discounts are available for travelers under 26; check at the Ljubljana station (look for the **BIJ-Wasteels** logo). Roundtrip tickets are 20% cheaper than two one-way tickets. Most stations have luggage storage. Say *"vlak"* for train, *"prihodi vlakov"* for arrivals, and *"odhodi vlakov"* for departures. Schedules usually list trains by direction.

Buses are 50-70% more expensive and usually slower, but run to some otherwise inaccessible places. Tickets are sold at the station or on board; put your luggage in the passenger compartment if it's not too crowded. *Let's Go* does not recommend **hitchhiking** as a safe means of transportation. However, hitchers report success although they advise avoiding the busy season.

TOURIST SERVICES AND MONEY

Tourist offices are located in most major cities and tourist spots. The staff are generally helpful, speak English, provide basic information, and assist in finding accommodations. Most businesses are open Mon.-Fri. 8am-7pm, and Sat. 8am-noon. Many restaurants remain open Sundays.

The national **currency** is the Slovenian **Tolar** (Slt), divided into 100 **stotins,** which you'll never need; shops round purchases up to the nearest tolar. Hard currency prices tend to be stable, but are usually set in Deutschmarks (DM) rather than US$, although most establishments accept both. **Exchange offices** abound. **Banks** are usually open Monday-Friday 8am-5pm and Saturday 8-11am. Rates vary (the ones for DM are slightly better than for US$), and some establishments charge no commission (a fact reflected in the rates). Major **credit cards** are accepted at banks, including AmEx and Diners Club, but the most widely endorsed is MasterCard/Eurocard, followed by Visa. There's a 20% **value-added tax,** but for purchases over 9000Slt, it is refunded at the border (ask the store salesperson for a tax-free check). **ATMs** don't exist outside the major cities.

COMMUNICATION

Postal facilities and services are reliable. **Post offices** are usually open Monday-Friday 8am-6pm and Saturday 8am-1pm, with night and Sunday service in larger cities. While there, stock up on one of the two types of **phone tokens** ("A" for local calls and "B" for long-distance), or purchase a **magnetic phone card** (750SltSlt per 50 impulses, which yields 50 local calls or 1½min. to America). **AT&T Direct** and similar services are not yet available, but will be sometime in 1997. Operators will assist in connecting calls if you dial 90 in Ljubljana, Kranj, Maribor, and Nova Gorica, and 900 in other Slovene cities. Calling the U.S. is expensive (over US$6 per min.).

English-language press is available in all larger cities. Slovenia receives **satellite programs** in English, and **Radio Ljubljana** releases English-language news, weather, and traffic updates. In summer, local TV stations produce nightly news in English.

LANGUAGE

Slovene employs the Latin alphabet and strongly resembles other Slavic languages. Most young people speak at least some **English,** but the older generation is more likely to understand **German** (in the north) or **Italian** (along the Adriatic). Many cities along the Italian border are officially bilingual, and the tourist industry is generally geared toward Germans, though most tourist office employees speak English.

When speaking Slovene, "č" is pronounced "ch", "š" is "sh", and "ž" is pronounced is "zh". "R" is at times a vowel (pronounced "er"), while the "v"s and "l"s turn silent at the strangest times. See the Slovenian glossary, p. 789.

HEALTH AND SAFETY

> **Emergency Numbers: Police:** tel. 92. **Fire:** tel. 93. **Ambulance:** tel. 94.

Slovenia's climate varies with the region: mediterranean near the Adriatic, alpine in the mountains, moderately continental on the eastern plains, and pleasant everywhere in summer, though snow may strew the Alps as late as June. A Slovene proverb says that if it *doesn't* rain on May 15, it *will* rain for 40 days afterwards, but don't use this as a reason to avoid spring visits—even the groundhog isn't always perfect.

Crime rates, especially for violent crime, are very low in Slovenia. Even in the largest cities, friendly drunks and poor drivers are the worst problems. Anti-gay acts are very rare, but the attitude towards **gays** and **lesbians** generally ranges from unsure to unfriendly. The occasional unwanted ogles and pick-up lines do occur.

ACCOMMODATIONS AND CAMPING

At the height of tourist season, prices are steep, services slow, sights crowded, and rooms scarce. The seaside, packed as early as June, causes claustrophobia in July and August. In the mountains, tourists tend to swarm in July and August, and student rooms are generally available late June to early September. **Hotels** fall into five categories (L (deluxe), A, B, C, and D) and tend to be expensive. **Youth hostels** and **student dormitories** are cheap, but are generally open only in summer. Usually, the best option is to rent **private rooms**—prices depend on location, but rarely exceed US$30, and most rooms are good. They're advertised on the street with *"sobe"* or *"Zimmer"* signs, or inquire at the tourist office. **Campgrounds** can also be crowded, but are generally in excellent condition. Bungalows are rare.

FOOD AND DRINK

Self-serve fast-food places have mushroomed in Slovenia, especially in the larger, more touristed cities. Traditional Slovene cuisine, however, is becoming increasingly hard to find; a *gostlina* or *gostišče* (interchangeable words for a restaurant with a country flavor) is the best bet for mouth-watering, homestyle cooking. A good national dish to start with is *jota*—a potato, bean, and sauerkraut soup. Salads, made with or without lettuce, are eaten alongside the main course, usually meat. *Svinjska pečenka* (roast pork) pleases the palate. **Vegetarians** should look for *štruklji,* large, slightly sweet dumplings that are eaten as a main dish. Slovenes also have good desserts; one of their favorites is *potica,* consisting of a sheet of pastry, spread with a rich filling, and rolled. The most popular filling is made from walnuts, though poppy seeds or fruit are both tasty. Should you find yourself in the northeast, *gibanica,* made from pastry, fruit, and cheese, should be a top choice for dessert. Potatoes are so popular that they've earned Slovenes the nickname of "spud-eaters". You're not in Idaho anymore, Dorothy. Or are you?

The country's **wine** tradition, preserved by monks and feudal lords in the Middle Ages, dates from antiquity. Look for familiar grape varieties on the label. *Renski Rizling* and *Šipon* are popular whites. Slovenia produces many unique red wines including the light *Cuiček* from the center of the country and the potent *Teran* bottled on the coast. The art of brewing is also centuries old in Slovenia. Not surprisingly, there are several good beers. For something stronger, try *Žganje,* a strong fruit brandy. The most enchanting is *Pleterska Hruška,* distilled by monks who know the secret of getting a full pear inside the bottle.

LIFE AND TIMES

HISTORY

The area now known as Slovenia was important as a **trade route** from the Baltic to the Adriatic as early as the 2nd millennium BCE. Settled by Bronze-Age **Celts** after 1300BCE, the territory was vanquished by the **Romans** in the early 2nd century BCE. The Romano-Celts enjoyed over 500 years of peace before the Empire fell, opening the area to Germanic and Slavic invaders. Modern **Slovenes** are descendants of the west Slavic tribes who migrated through Moravia to the Eastern Alps in the 6th century CE. It was in 623 that the Slovenes came under the Slavic rule of **Samo** (623-658)—artist Jean-Michel Basqiat later used this moniker as his graffiti tag, finally proving the long-suspected Slovene-American/Haitian creative link. The kingdom fell to the Franks after 748. Though the Slavs were assimilated into the Magyar and Bulgarian tribes, Carinthia—precursor of modern Slovenia—survived.

After the fall of the Frankish Empire in the 10th century, Slovene lands were given to the **German kingdom** and divided into Carinthia, Carniola, and Styria. The Slovenes were given a secondary place in the German kingdom, enserfed, and labeled "Wends". Clearly unaffected by the PC movement, the Germans didn't realize that "wends" is a verb, not a name for the Slovenes. The German kingdom could not hold on to these lands for long, and the territory occupied by Slovene speakers changed hands frequently. In the 9th century, Slav Prince **Kocely of Carniola** introduced Christian worship in the Slavic language and script. By the 980s, Carniola had been annexed by the Holy Roman Emperor Otto II and remained under imperial rule for the next millennium. The 1300s saw Carniola fall to the **Habsburgs,** who ruled the Slovenes until the 1900s.

During **WWI,** Slovene politicians pressed for the creation of an independent state of south Slavs, which was to consist of present-day Slovenia, Croatia, and Bosnia-Herzegovina. In 1918, **Yugoslavia** (Land of the South Slavs) was officially created, with the capital in Zagreb, and Slovenia ceased to be a part of the Austro-Hungarian empire. The new state was too weak, however, to withstand the attacks of Hitler's armed forces during **WWII.** When Yugoslavia fell in 1941, Slovenia was partitioned among Germany, Italy, and Hungary. The Germans took the region north of Ljubljana and the Sava, the Italians got Ljubljana and the areas south of the city, and the Hungarians received the plains in the west. After the German attack on the Soviet Union in summer 1941, Christian Socialists, and other left-wing groups joined the Yugoslav **partisan army** of **Josip Broz Tito.** Led by the Communist party, the army was eventually recognized by the British and Americans as an ally against Hitler, and as such, was supplied with arms to continue their fight.

In 1945, partisans occupied the territories that had been Yugoslavia's, and once again the state came into being, this time with Tito in command and with headquarters in Belgrade. Tito liquidated anti-Nazi Slovene politicians and leaders who failed to cooperate with the Communists. Tens of thousands of Slovene patriots were murdered at Kočevje. (The 50th anniversary of this mass murder was commemorated in 1995, thus ending five decades of silence.) Thus began the **Communist** era, which was to last until 1990. After the rift between Tito and Stalin opened in 1948, Yugoslavia introduced certain features of a market economy. Slovenia was soon acknowledged as its most Western and economically viable republic. Upon Tito's death in 1980, confusion invaded the scene of a seemingly peaceful and stable country. Long-suppressed **ethnic conflicts** re-emerged and threatened to shake the foundations of the entire state. Yugoslavia comprised several large ethnic groups with little in common, other than the fact that they were all descendants of Slavic tribes and happened to occupy neighboring territories. The efforts of the Communist party to find a leader to replace Tito failed. Without the fear of a strong hand in Belgrade, opposition speedily emerged in Slovenia, as well as in the other republics.

In December 1990, the plebiscite on the creation of a sovereign Slovene state resulted in over 80% of the voters opting for independence. Six months later, in **June 1991,** the Assembly proclaimed Slovene **independence** and sovereignty and the annulment of the Yugoslav constitution. The Yugoslav army responded with force, but after 10 days of violent clashes, it gave up the fight (July 7); Serbia, the driving force behind Yugoslavia and the conflict, had no border claims against the Slovenes, and no large Serbian minority lives in Slovenia (as opposed to Bosnia). The final step to independence was the new Slovene **constitution** of December 1991.

LITERATURE

Not surprisingly, the first book printed in Slovene was of an ecclesiastical nature: **Trubar**—considered the "father" of literary Slovene—published a catechism during the 16th-century Reformation in the Latin alphabet—a script Irish missionaries had imported in the 8th century. During the Enlightenment and Revival period (1768-1848), **Marko Pohlin,** an Augustinian monk, rose as a leading literary figure, authoring many works in Slovene: a grammar, a Latin, German and Slovene dictionary, and a bibliography of Slovene literature. At the same time a Slovene literary circle formed with Baron Žiga Zois, a wealthy landowner, at the center. Members included **Anton Tomaž,** the first Slovene historian and dramatist, **Vodnik,** the first Slovene poet and journalist, and **Jernej Kopitar,** the first modern grammarian and comparative philologist of Slovene. The Romantic period followed and witnessed the **War of the Alphabets**; it pitted the Latin alphabet against **Franc Metelko's** newly invented combination of Latin, Cyrillic, and brand-new letters. Fortunately for English-speakers, the Latin alphabet triumphed. During this time and throughout the later Realist period (1848-1899), writers such as **Fran Eriavec** focused on folkloric themes with a patriotic flavor.

Despite the Romantic themes of nationalism and freedom from foreign influence, Western European ideas seeped in during the first half of the 20th century, and shaped the Slovene Modernist and Expressionist movements; especially influential poets during this period included **Kebbe, Murn, Pobevšek, Seliškar,** and **Kosovel.** The advent of Soviet **Socialist Realism** after the Second World War crushed many of the modern and avant-garde trends that had diversified the Slovene literary movement. Slovene writers, as elsewhere in the East Bloc, lost a great deal of freedom, and were restricted to Communist allegories guised in the themes of war, patriotism, and peasant life. The rein loosened as the 50s approached and Symbolism and Existentialism hailed from neighboring non-Communist countries—post-war writers like **Cene Vipotnik, Jože Udovič, Zajc, Gregor Strniša,** and **Tomaž Šalamun** all contributed to Slovene literature's continued growth. At the end of the 70s, a number of Slovenian writers, including **Vitomis Zupan, Igor Torkar,** and **Jože Snoj,** came out with books that dealt with Stalinism in Slovenia. The post-modern trend of the 80s didn't pass by the Slovenian writers and the so-called **"Young Slovenian Prose"** movement, which had its strongest representation in short prose pieces. Today, Slovenian literature is widely translated, especially in neighboring German-speaking countries, and enjoys a level of activity rivaling the past.

SLOVENIA TODAY

On July 12, 1995, the European Commission approved Slovenian associate membership in the EU. The terms were favorable, but problems may arise because of the stipulation that Slovenia revise the 1975 Osimo Agreements with Italy. The required change could lead to the reacquisition of Slovene lands by Italians forced out of modern-day Slovenia after WWII and could result in Slovene rejection of EU membership. Parliamentary elections were scheduled for December 1996. Currently the Liberal Democratic Party (made up of former Communists) is in power, with Janez Drnovesek as president. Like many of the reformed Communist parties in the region, they have continued the reform process and have extended Slovene membership into international organizations such as the Council of Europe, the IMF, the World Bank, and, in January 1996, the Central Europe Free Trade Area.

Though the process of economic reform is far from over, the pains of transition have so far been easier to bear here than in many parts of Eastern Europe. In the early 1990s, the per capita GNP fell from US$8000 to US$6000, but is still far ahead of most Eastern European countries. Today, Slovenia attracts around three million tourists per year—mainly Austrian, German, and Italian—outnumbering by one million its own population, and prices are comparable to those in neighboring Austria. In prices and in politics, Slovenia seems to be pulling away from the other former East Bloc countries and staking a claim on a role in Western Europe.

Ljubljana

Though only the size of a provincial center, Ljubljana acts like the most confident of European capitals. Its Baroque monuments, Art Nouveau façades, and modern highrises, may be best viewed from the castle, but the city is best felt in the streets which see more restoration and rejuvenation everyday. Businesspeople, politicians, and professors mingle in the Old Town and along the banks of the green Ljubljanica, part of a new, modern economy. Above all, the city is what is has always been—the cultural capital of the proud, vivacious, and now independent Slovenia.

ORIENTATION AND PRACTICAL INFORMATION

The **train** and **bus stations** are on **Trg Osvobodilne Tronte (Trg of)**, north of the Old Town. Walking south on **Slovenska cesta** leads to the tourist office. To reach the central square, proceed perpendicular to Trg of along **Resljeva cesta,** bear right on **Komenskego,** then turn left on **Dalmatinova.** Another left on **Miklošičeva cesta** leads to **Prešernov Trg**. After crossing the **Triple Bridge**, the Old Town emerges at the castle hill's base.

- **Tourist Office: Tourist Information Center (TIC),** Slovenska 35 (tel. 215 412; fax 222 115). The friendly staff offers free maps and excellent brochures. Open Mon.-Fri. 8am-7pm, Sat.-Sun. 8am-noon and 4-7pm.
- **Budget Travel: Erazen,** Trubarjeva Cesta 7 (tel. 133 1076), in the Old Town. Geared toward students. ISICs (550Slt), tickets, info, and some gear.
- **Embassies: Australia,** Dunajska 22 (tel. 132 7341). Open Mon.-Fri. 9am-1pm. **U.K.,** Trg Republike 3 (tel. 125 7191; fax 125 0174). Open Mon.-Fri. 8am-4pm. **U.S.,** Pražakova 4 (tel. 301 427; fax 301 401). Open Mon., Wed., and Fri. 9am-noon.
- **Currency Exchange: Ljubljanska Bank,** Beethovnova 7, at the corner of Čankarjeva, has good, commission-free rates and cashes AmEx and other traveler's checks. Open Mon.-Fri. 8:30am-noon and 2-4pm, Sat. 9am-noon. The private *menjalnična* (currency exchange) **Publikun,** Miklošičeva 34, may be able to do even better. Open Mon.-Fri. 7am-8:30pm, Sat. 7am-1pm.
- **American Express: Atlas** (tel. 222 711), on Old Town's Mestni trg, a block from the river, holds mail, but doesn't cash traveler's checks or wire money. Open Mon.-Fri. 9am-5pm, Sat. 9am-noon; AmEx services available Mon.-Fri. 9am-3pm.
- **Flights:** Buses shuttle from the central station to the **airport** (tel. (064) 222 700), 26km away in Brnik 6-8 times per day (400Slt). **Adria Airways,** Gosposvetsta 6 (tel. 313 312); **Austrian Airlines,** Dunajska 107 (tel. 371 747); **Lufthansa,** Slovenska 54 (tel. 326 662); **Swissair** in Hotel Lev, Vošnjakova 1 (tel. 317 647).
- **Trains:** Trg of (tel. 131 5167). To: Budapest (2 per day, 10hr., 5370Slt); Munich (2 per day, 6hr., 8468Slt); Trieste (4 per day, 3hr., 1350Slt); Venice (3 per day, 6hr.); Vienna (1 per day, 6hr., 6300Slt); Zagreb (10 per day, 2½hr., 1220Slt).
- **Buses:** (tel. 133 6136) next to the trains. To: Budapest (1 per day, 8hr., 4350Slt); Munich (3 per day, 6hr., 5250Slt); Zagreb (5 per day, 3hr., 1510Slt).
- **Public Transportation: Buses** exact an 80Slt charge and run until midnight. Drop change in the box beside the driver or buy 60Slt tokens at post offices and newsstands. One-day, weekly, and monthly passes are sold at **Ljubljanski Potniški Promet,** Celovška 160 (tel. 159 4114).

ORIENTATION AND PRACTICAL INFORMATION ■ 671

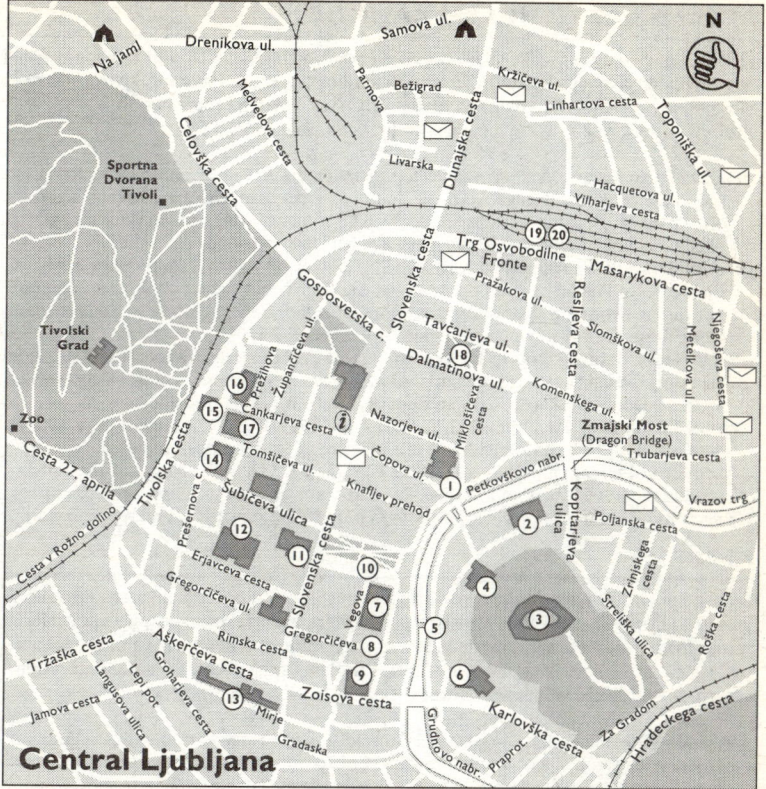

Central Ljubljana

- Bus Station, **19**
- Kongresni Trg (Congress Square), **10**
- Levstikov Trg (Levstik Square), **6**
- Ljubljanski Grad (Castle), **3**
- Mestni Trg and Stari Trg (Town Square and Old Square), **5**
- Miklošič Park, **18**
- Moderna Galerija (Museum of Modern Art), **15**
- Narodna Galerija (National Gallery), **6**
- Narodni Muzej (National Museum), **14**
- NUK- National and University Library, **8**
- Opera, **17**
- Prešernov Trg (Prešeren Square), **1**
- Roman Wall, **13**
- Rotovž (Town Hall), **4**
- SAZU (Slovene Academy of Arts and Sciences), **7**
- Stolnica (Cathedral), Škofijski Dvorec (Bishop's Palace)
- Semenišče (Seminary), **2**
- Train Station, **20**
- Trg Francoske Revolucije (French Revolution Square), **9**
- Trg Republike (Republic Square and Parliament Building), **12**
- Uršulinska Cerkev (Ursuline Church), **11**

Hitchhiking: Hitchers to Bled take bus #1 (Vižmarje) to its terminus. Those headed for the coast go to the end of bus-line #6 (Črnuće) or leave town via Tržaška cesta.
Taxis: call 97 00, 97 01, 97 02, 97 03, 97 04, 97 05, or 97 06.
Laundromat: Kam, Kardeljeva ploščad 14 (tel. 340 049), in bldg. C of the university campus. Open Mon.-Fri. 8am-noon and 2-6pm, Sat. 8am-3pm. **Tič,** Cesta 27, aprila 31, bldg. 9 (tel. 126 3233). Open Mon.-Fri. 9am-7pm, Sat. 8am-2pm.
Pharmacies: Prešernov trg 5 (tel. 133 5044). Open daily 24hr.; ring bell after 8pm.
Medical Assistance: In case of emergency, call **Bohoričeva Medical Centre** (tel. 323 060), or **Klinični center,** Zaloška 2 (tel. 131 4344).
Post Office, Pražakova 3 (tel. 314 573), 3 blocks south of the train in a tall yellow building; enter in back. Open 24hr. **Poste Restante** received at the Slovenska 32 (tel. 210 740) branch by the tourist office (50Slt per item); open Mon.-Fri. 7am-8pm, Sat. 7am-1pm. **Postal code:** 1000. **Phone code:** 061.

ACCOMMODATIONS AND CAMPING

The accommodations seeker has several choices in Ljubljana. Don't expect any Eastern European bargains though. On top of higher prices, there is a nightly **tourist tax.** Most prices are quoted in German marks. **TIC** (see Practical Information, above) will attempt to seek out a private single (DM20) or double (DM30-50).

Dijaški Dom Tabor, Vidovdanska 7 (tel. 316 069; fax 321 060), south along Resljeva, then east on Komenskega from the stations. The clean, private showers are only one of many pleasant features in this well kept hostel. 180 beds in doubles and triples. Checkout 11am. DM17 per person, breakfast included.

Dijaški Dom Ivana Cankarja, Poljanska 260-28 (tel. 133 5274), south along Resljeva, then east on Poljanska from the stations. Another youth hostel close to civilization, but further from transportation. Less popular but of only slightly lesser quality than Dom Tabor. DM18 per person. Open June 25-Aug. 25.

Park Hotel, Tabor 9 (tel. 133 1306; fax 321 352), near Dom Tabor. Socialist inside and out, but fairly well maintained. Most rooms have showers and toilets. Singles 4530Slt. Doubles 6260Slt. 20% student discount. Breakfast included.

Hotel Tivoli, Tivolska 30 (tel. 131 4359; fax 302 671). Well kept but not new. Singles 4400Slt, with an extra bed 5700Slt. Doubles 6900Slt. Breakfast included.

Autocamp Ježica, Dunajska 270 (tel. 372 901; fax 313 649). North of the railway tracks, Slovenska becomes Dunajska. Tall trees and green grass greet campers. Swimming and tennis. 900Slt per person plus 180Slt per night. Open year-round.

FOOD

Facing the Old Town and the three bridges, turn right to find bargain, river-front restaurants. Popular cafés line Mestni trg and Stari trg. **Maximarket,** a supermarket across from the Parliament building, stores everything you need—for a price, payable by MasterCard (open Mon.-Fri. 9am-8pm, Sat. 8am-7pm). Near the cathedral, Vodnikov trg hosts a huge **outdoor market** (open Mon.-Sat. until 2pm).

Vodnikov hram, Vodnikov trg 2, serves traditional, hearty fare in surroundings suffused with stained wood and antiques. Cheap entrées include *golaž* (400Slt) and *vampi* (tripe; 420Slt). Open Mon.-Fri. 5:30am-9pm, Sat. 5:30am-2pm.

Gostilna Pri Pavli, Stari trg at Levstikov trg. Serves *zrezek* (schnitzel, 980Slt), and *golaž* (440Slt). An even better deal, the daily *menü kosilo* (660Slt) includes soup, a luscious salad, and a meat entrée (often stuffed pepper). *Union* beer 200Slt. Open Mon.-Fri. 9am-10pm, Sat. 9am-3pm.

Šestica, Slovenska 38 (tel. 219 575). Wonderful outdoor feel, and a good choice for excellent Slovene food at slightly higher prices (entrées 800-1460Slt).

Daj dam, Cankarjeva 4. Cheap food, cafeteria-style. *Menü*—soup, salad, and entrée (650-800Slt). Vegetarian *menüs*. Open Mon.-Fri. 6am-9pm, Sat. 7:30am-4pm.

Pizzeria Romeo, on the south tip of Stari trg. Pleasant and popular, in the heart of the Old Town (pizza 680-880Slt). Open daily 11am-1am.

SIGHTS

The best way to learn about the city may be to meet in front of the **rotovž** (city hall), Mestni trg 1, for the free two-hour long walking **tour,** in English and Slovene (June-Sept. daily at 5pm; Oct.-May Sun. at 11am). Christened in honor of the great Slav poet France Prešeren, the main square, **Prešernov trg,** contains a Neoclassical **Franciscan Church** built in the 17th century. Native sculptor Francesco Robba crafted the impressive altar inside in 1736. Another easily identifiable attraction is the **Tromostovje** (Triple Bridge). In the 1930s, revered architect Jože Plečnik modernized the old **Špitalski Bridge,** supplementing the stone construction with two footbridges; his handiwork transformed it into one of Ljubljana's most admired architectural jewels. Plečnik also planned many of the city's parks and squares, and designed the open market, the Žale cemetery, and St. Michael's Church.

To the left of the Triple Bridge is the **Zmajski Most** (Dragon Bridge), built in 1901 to replace the old wooden "Butcher's Bridge". Originally named after the Emperor Franz Joseph, the locals never accepted it as such; since it was bedecked with dragons (Ljubljana's coat of arms), they naturally called it by its current name. Across the bridges, the **stolnica** (cathedral) occupies the site of an old Romanesque church dedicated by the boatmen and fishermen of Ljubljana to their patron St. Nicholas. Today's cathedral dates from the early 18th century; little original artwork remains, but visitors can still admire the 15th-century Gothic *Pietà*, the impressive triple organ, and the gold trim suffusing every shadow in the church with a mellow light.

From the cathedral, follow Ciril-Metodov trg to the Baroque **Mestni trg** (Town Square). Here you'll find the *rotovž*, near the Triple Bridge. In front spurts a fantastic fountain (1751) embellished with allegorical sculptures of three rivers—the Ljubljanica, Sava, and Krka—and wrought by the great local master Francesco Robba. From here, or anywhere in Old Town, **Ljubljanski Grad** (Ljubljana Castle) is a short hike up the hill. The castle dates from at least 1144, and though it may not impress, the views of Ljubljana surely will. To see the whole city at once, climb the tower for 200Slt (tower open daily 10am-dusk).

Trg Francoske Revolucije (French Revolution Square) and its environs were once occupied by the Teutonic Knights; the neighborhood named **Križanke,** the Slovene translation of their title, still remembers them. In the square, the Knights set up a monastery, which was demolished in the 18th century, then restored under Plečnik's guidance. It now hosts music, theater, and dance performances for the **Ljubljana International Summer Festival** (mid-July to late Sept.).

North of the library, Baroque **Kongresni trg** is named after the Congress of the Holy Alliance, signed in 1821 by the Austrian emperor, the Russian tsar, and the Neapolitan king. South of the square stands **Ljubljana University.** Westward, across Slovenska cesta, **Uršulinska Cerkev** (Ursuline Church) is nicknamed Holy Trinity Church because of the icons outside; the original wooden ones, placed there in 1693 when the plague spared Ljubljana, were later installed in the City Museum, and stone replicas were substituted.

Ljubljana's plentiful **museums** (each open Tues.-Sat. 10am-6pm, Sun. 10am-1pm; 400Slt, students 200Slt) cluster around the Slovene **Parliament** buildings, near Trg Republike. While there's everything you'd expect in a capital city—the National Museum and National Gallery, and the progressive Museum of Modern Art—in evidence, a graphic arts thread runs decoratively throughout. **Narodni Muzej** (National Museum), Muzejska 1 (tel. 21 88 86), exhibits collections on archaeology, ethnography, culture, and history. The nearby **Moderna Galerija** displays the works of 20th-century Slovene artists. Every odd year, it also hosts the **International Biennial of Graphic Art,** the largest such exhibition in the world. To the left of Moderna Galerija stands **Narodna Galerija,** Cankarjeva 20 (tel. 21 97 16), with the creations of Slovene artists from the Middle Ages to the present. Near the museums, across from Tivolska cesta, **Tivoli park** possesses some of Ljubljana's prettiest strolling grounds and excellent jogging paths. There's also **Tivolski Grad** (Tivoli Castle), built by Jesuits in the 17th century, and the **International Center of Graphic Art.**

ENTERTAINMENT

Cankarjev Dom hosts the **Slovene Symphony Orchestra** and well known jazz musicians from around the world, while **Tivoli Hall** is the venue for rock concerts, hockey, and basketball. Information on these events as well as ballet, opera, theater, and special museum exhibitions can be found in the *Where To?* brochure, published monthly and available at tourist offices. If nothing suits your fancy, join Ljubljana's large student population at the excellent cafés or bars lining the streets of Old Town, or in the dance clubs near the modern highrises.

K-4, Kersnikova 4 (tel. 131 3282). A different program every night from folk to heavy metal. Remodeled every year and always hip. Sunday is gay night. Open nightly 10pm-4am. Cover 300-400Slt. Ask for an ISIC discount.

Eldorado, Nazorjeva 6. The hippest club in town—it's even flashy in its daily disguise as a Mexican restaurant. Open daily 11pm-4am. Cover Fri.-Sat. 500Slt.

Babilon, Kongresni trg 2 (tel. 214 336). Once one of the most popular, still draws twentysomethings to its standard dance floor for standard dance music. Open Tues.-Sat. 10pm-4am. Cover 500Slt, women free.

Jazz Club Gayo, Beethovnova 8. Alternates live music with nights of classic jazz and cheap(er) drinks. Open Mon.-Fri. 10am-2am, Sat.-Sun. 6pm-2am. No cover.

Holiday's Pub, Slovenska 36. This American bar cross-dressing as a European pub is not to be missed. Slovenian yuppies come flashing cash to drink the bouquet of beers on tap—or perhaps to strike up a conversation with the hip young English-speaking bartender. Open daily until 3am.

Many of the city's events are organized under the auspices of several long festivals; the **Slovene Days of Music** take place at the end of April. From the middle of May to the end of June is the 45-day long **European Cultural Month,** while July and August bring many international stars to the **International Summer Festival. Festive December** rings out the year.

■ Near Ljubljana: Postojna Caves

Though the city itself has nothing exciting to see, Postojna has become famous throughout Europe for its two-million year old caves. Follow the signs from the center of town or ask anyone. The **jama** (cave), Jamska cesta 30 (tel. 25 041; fax 24 870), is 20 minutes northwest of the town (open daily 9am-6pm). Tours of the cave leave on the hour and last an hour and a half; part is on foot and part by train. English, German, and Italian tours cost 1600Slt (Oct.-April they leave on even hours, i.e., 10am, noon, 2pm). Bring a jacket or rent a cloak for 100Slt. The tour passes through only 20% of the caves 27km, but that's more than enough to wow most visitors with plant-like columns, curtains of stone, gorges, rivers, and multi-colored stalactites. The final "hall" you enter hosts frequent musical performances by Slovene groups.

Reach the town of Postojna via **bus** (1hr., 520Slt) or **train** (1hr., 476Slt) from Ljubljana, or come up from the coast at about the same price. The caves will probably only be a daytrip, but if you choose to stay, drop by **Kompas Postojve,** Titov trg 2a (tel. 212 64) in the city's center, which should be able to find a room for about 2000Slt (open Mon.-Fri. 8am-8pm, Sat. 8am-1pm).

If you're still not satisfied, there are numerous caves in the area (inquire at the tourist office). Natives claim that the **Škocjanske Jame** (Skocjan Caves) are much more impressive than the Postojne caves, but they are 11km from any public transportation. Call the cave's office (tel. (067) 601 22) for information (open Mon.-Sat. 10am-3:30pm). About 9km from Postojna is **Predjama Castle,** carved into the face of a huge cliff (open Mon.-Sat. 10am-5pm; 400Slt, students 200Slt). Just keep walking past the Postojna caves on the main road to find it.

JULIJSKE ALPE (THE JULIAN ALPS)

The Southern Alps are not as high as their Austrian or Swiss counterparts, but they are no less beautiful. The mountains cover the northwest of Slovenia, peaking at 2864m on Mt. Triglav in the heart of the Triglav National Park. This mountain range is also the source of one of the region's largest rivers, the Sava. The Sava Dolinka originates north of Triglav, and the Sava Bohinjka flows from the Bohinj Lake, south of Triglav; the two rivers meet not far from Bled to form the wider Sava.

■ Bled

This place is so beautiful, I couldn't help but win.
—Bobby Fischer, chess prodigy

Imagine Bled as a postcard: Green alpine hills, snow-covered peaks in the distance, a crystal clear lake, with a stately castle surveying it all. It's no wonder that people have been coming to Lake Bled for centuries to test their athletic skills or lose themselves in the romance of a warm summer evening. The 20th century has seen this community grow into a resort of international renown, but whether one is staying in the finest hotels or pitching a tent, the peace of the lake overpowers the crowds and urges each visitor to stay another day.

Orientation and Practical Information Trains stop in **Lesce**, 5km from Bled on the Ljubljana-Salzburg-Munich line (1hr., 420Slt). From there, take one of the frequent **commuter buses** (200Slt) to Bled. These stop on **Ljubljanska**, the main street, and at the main **bus station** (closer to youth hostels and the castle). Or, arrive here directly by bus from Ljubljana (1 per hr., 1½hr., 590Slt). Bled is spread around Lake Bled, with most buildings clustered along the east shore and Ljubljanska, which leads straight to the water. For tourist info, visit **Kompas Bled,** Ljubljanska cesta 4 (tel. 741 515; fax 741 518), and pick up a copy of the *Bled Tourist News* for the latest on hiking and skiing (open Mon.-Sat. 8am-8pm, Sun. 9:30am-6:30pm). **Currency exchanges** have bad rates and extract large commissions, so discard dollars in Ljubljana. In an emergency, try **General Turist** near the lake (open Mon.-Fri. 9am-4pm, Sat. 9am-2pm, Sun. 1-6pm). The **post office** stamps letters at Ljubljanska 10 (tel. 741 601; open Mon.-Sat. 7am-9pm). **Postal code:** 4260. **Phone code:** 064.

Accommodations and Food All accommodations prices are quoted in DM, but you can pay in Slt. **Private room** prices vary according to season. **Kompas Bled,** (see above), seeks out singles for 1650-2800Slt and doubles for 2340-4800Slt per person (tourist tax 130Slt per night). **Globtour,** Ljubljanska cesta 7 (tel. 741 515; fax 647 8185), rents singles (DM20-31) and doubles (DM34-52 per person), with a DM2 tourist tax. Both agencies charge 30% more for stays of less than three nights. Finding a private room yourself may save money; look for *"sobe"* signs, particularly on Prešernova cesta. The ever-popular **youth hostel,** Grajska cesta 17, was undergoing renovation in 1996. To see if it's all fixed up, walk five minutes northwest of the bus station or ask at a tourist office. **Camping Zaka-Bled,** cesta Svobode 13 (tel. 741 117; fax 742 288), sits in a beautiful valley on the opposite side of the lake. Refrigerators and electrical connections, sand volleyball, tennis and basketball courts, a store, a restaurant, and a beach, are all available. But, alas, no bungalows (checkout 3pm; DM12 per person; tourist tax DM1; open April-Oct.).

As long as you don't require a lakeside restaurant, prices aren't much higher than in the rest of Slovenia. **P-hram,** Cesta Svobode 19a, serves Slovene entrées for 650-800Slt—including delicious *kranjska klobasa* (Carniola sausage; 650Slt; open daily 9am-9pm). Locals justly recommend **Gostilna pri Planincu,** Grajska cesta 8 (tel. 741 613), visible from the bus station. This 1904 restaurant serves entrées (800-1100Slt) til 10pm, and pizzas (520-790Slt) til 10:30. The bar stays open until midnight. If all else fails, **minimarket Špecerija,** Ljubljanska 4, provides rolls, ham, beer (120Slt) and more (open Mon.-Sat. 7am-8pm, Sun. 9am-noon).

Sights The lake made the town famous, not vice versa. A stroll around the lake's 6km perimeter should take one-and-a half to two hours. The **island** in the center has **church** which has stood there since the 9th century. Though today's structure actually dates from the 17th century, a unique pre-Romanesque apse remains. There are a multitude of ways to approach the heart of the lake. Renting boats costs only 800Slt per hour and you can even play Gilligan's Island if you avoid the tourists near the castle. You can also travel via **gondola,** from the shore near the town (roundtrip 1½hr., 900Slt). You can even swim, although entering the church in a Speedo is hardly kosher. Dive in from a beach without a "No Swimming" sign; look for other swimmers, who tend to hang out on the west shores. The water is warm in summer, and in winter, it becomes a huge ice-skating rink.

Over 100m above the water perches the perfect medieval **castle.** Just start walking toward it; you can't miss the signs leading up. Castle admission also lets you into an excellent **museum** with art, furniture, weapons, and armor. You may, however, be content just to sit on the terrace and admire the superb view (open Feb.-Nov. daily 8am-7pm; Dec.-Jan. daily 9am-4pm; 300Slt).

You don't have to be surrounded by turrets and tourists to see the lake from far above. Numerous **paths** snake from the lake into the neighboring hills. The best one can be found by walking around the lake until the castle and the island are aligned—the path across the street takes about 45 minutes to climb. Otherwise, as you approach the castle, signs indicate trails leading up, should you not prefer the main road. Also, **mountain bikes** of assorted quality can be rented at either tourist agency (see above; 800Slt per ½-day, 1300Slt per day). The agencies can help make any of your sporting dreams come true…for a price.

All summer, **concerts** and traditional cultural activities take place on the island, on the promenade, and in the hotels. The tourist agencies (see above) carry a free monthly brochure of events. For such an enchanting place, the nightlife is, surprisingly, not. The **casino** near the waterfront is a sure bet (open nightly 6pm-2am). Across the hall are a late-night **restaurant** (open nightly 6pm-1am) and a **dance floor** which has seen better days, but still has a regular band to crank out slow-dancing favorites—bring a date. The younger crowd tends to find itself at the **Royal Club,** on the ground floor of the huge shopping complex on Ljubljanska ceska. A café by day, it's less-than-exciting by night, but at least the 500Slt cover charge can be redeemed in alcohol (open daily 10pm-4am).

■ Near Bled: Iški Vintgar

Make the rewarding trip to **Iški Vintgar** (Vintgar Gorge). Entrance to the gorge costs 200Slt, which is followed by a 1.5km-long walk along the edge of a raging green current slowly cutting its path through solid rock. The water rises highest in early June, but the white spray will splash you year-round. After crossing back and forth over the water, you'll end up at the **Šum Waterfall.** Afterward, you can take your soggy self to the **snack bar** in town, or climb to the bottom if you brought your own tasty treats. You can walk the 5km northeast of Bled—just follow the signs out of town. A special **bus** (tel. 741 114) makes the trip twice a day from the bus station June-Sept. (one-way 200Slt; leaves at 9:30 and 10:20am, returns at noon). If you miss it, take one of the frequent buses to Podham (80Slt), then follow the signs westward 1.5km.

▨ Lake Bohinj

Though only 30km southwest, Lake Bohinj is worlds away from its sophisticated cousin Bled. Protected by virtue of its position within the borders of Triglav National Park, this glacial lake, together with its surrounding wildflowers, waterfalls, and windy peaks, stands at the center of Slovenia's alpine tourism universe. Some come for the (unmotorized) water sports, but most people are here to ascend the heights and experience warm mountain hospitality on their return.

Orientation and Practical Information Six trains per day arrive in **Bohinjska Bistrica** from Ljubljana (2hr.). Then take the **bus** from the Bohinjska Bistrica's post office. Or just take the bus directly from Bled (1 per hr., 1½hr., 300Slt) or Ljubljana (1 per hr., 3hr., 700Slt). Buses to "Bohinjsko Jezero" generally finish their routes in Ribčev Laž; the stop after the sign is more central. Buses marked "Bohinj Zlatorog" take you through Ribčev Laž to the village on the west end of the lake, and occasional buses climb all the way to the trailhead for the Savica waterfall (see Sights and Hiking, below). The largest of the small towns east of the lake is Bohinjska Bistrica, 6km from the water, but you should find everything you need in **Ribčev Laž,** on the water's edge. The **tourist office,** Ribčev Laž 48 (tel. 723 370; fax 723 330), will help you with any info you need (open July-August daily 7am-9pm; Sept.-June Mon.-

Sat. 8am-8pm, Sun. 8am-6pm. Drop by the **Šport Klub Alpinum,** Ribčev Laž 50 (tel. 723 441; fax 723 446), near the church, to rent a high quality **bike** (DM5 per hr.; DM12 per ½-day; DM21 per day), or get the gear for **rafting, kayaking,** and **canoeing,** find a guides for land or water, or get a **fishing license** (lake DM35 per day, DM165 per week; river DM50 per day, DM225 per week; open daily 9am-7pm). The **post office,** Ribčev Laž 47, also **exchanges money** (open Mon.-Fri. 8am-7pm, Sat. 8am-noon). **Postal code:** 64265. **Phone code:** 064.

Accommodations and Food The tourist office (see above) has singles for DM13-19 and doubles for DM22-32 (prices are 25% higher from the 2nd Saturday in July to the 4th Sat. in Aug.; tourist tax DM2; 30% mark-up for stays under 3 days). **Avtokamp Zlatorog,** on the west side of the lake, has spaces for DM11-16 (July-Aug.) and DM7-10 (May-June and Aug.-Sept.).

The smell of fresh fish sizzling entices visitors into expensive, but worthy, local restaurants. **Restaurant Triglav,** Stara Fužina 23, brings in enough tourists to offer an affordable daily *menü,* with soup and salad (1100Slt). To find it, cross the bridge next to the church on Lake Bohinj, and walk 10 minutes to the next village—the view of the lake from the terrace beats even the prices (open daily 11am-11pm). If you need to prepare for your next hike, the **Mercator supermarket,** Ribčev Laž 49, by the tourist office, is open Monday-Saturday 7am-9pm, Sunday 7am-1pm.

Sights and Hiking Hiking is plentiful around Lake Bohinj, but there are a few rules o' the road of which you should be aware. Trails throughout Slovenia are well marked with a white circle inside a red circle; look for the blaze on trees and rocks. A bend in the trail may be marked by a bent red line. Where trails separate, a sign *usually* indicates which one is headed where. In Slovenia, hikers always greet each other on the path. As old-timers will remind you, the person ascending the path should speak up first; respect belongs to those who have already conquered the hill, not to those who are simply trying to. **Mountain bikes** are not allowed on the trails, but they can be fun on the "forest roads" and specially marked "carriage roads" (increasingly rough dirt roads). See Essentials: Wilderness and Safety Concerns, p. 49, for general info about hiking and safety.

Any number of trips can be made from the shores of Bohinj, from the casual to the nearly impossible. For a little guidance, free copies of *An Alpine Guide*—listing the region's best hikes of every difficulty—are for the taking at the tourist office (see above). Several good maps (around 1000Slt) are also available, but the ones that cover the most area without losing detail (1:50,000) are *Triglavski Narodni Park* and *Gorenjska,* which includes the area around Lake Bled.

The most popular and accessible destination is **Slap Savica** (Savica Waterfall). If you begin at the trailhead (a bus stops here), the hike is only 20 minutes. Just follow the signs—and the people. From Ribčev Laž, it's a 2-hour hike. You can follow the scenic road, or a more peaceful trail through the woods. After the road curves around the lake's southeastern promontory, the trail cuts off to the left, and rejoins the main road. Travelers report some success hitchhiking to the trailhead as well. Once there, it's a 200Slt fee to continue on to the powerful 60m-high waterfall. After you've seen it, you can return the way you came, or along a trail that skirts the north side of Lake

---

Coming to a Head...or Three

Topping off at 2864m, Mt. Triglav is more than just Slovenia's highest peak. Originally worshiped by pre-Christian Slovenes, it is now a symbol of Slovene identity. Since 1778, Slovenes have been climbing to the top of "Three Heads". The three-peaked contour was the symbol of the Liberation Front when Slovenia was occupied during WWII, and today can be seen on the national flag and coat-of-arms. Politicians make the hike to show off their national spirit, and if you make the hike, you will be treated like a returning hero: it's the one way of truly becoming a Slovene. Just don't forget to leave your name in the book at the top.

Bohinj. Look for its entrance across the street from the lower of Savica's two mountain huts, and keep to the westbound trail.

If, instead of turning west here, you follow the signs north toward the **Črno Jezero** (Black Lake), you will come to a more graceful waterfall (½hr.). The hiking is very steep here and becomes harder after the waterfall; be extremely cautious. Shortly after reaching the ridge line, a trail to the right *(dolina pod stadorjem)* leads northwest to **Planina Viševnik**. Turn south from this peak to **Pršivec** (1761m; 2½hr.), where the view of the lake is breathtaking. Return the way you came, or follow the trail east to return along the ridge to **Stara Fužina** and **Ribčev Laž** (2½hr.).

The more traditional way to reach Pršivec is from Stara Fužina. Leave Ribčev Laž along the road to the north, then follow signs to the natural **Hudičev Most** (Devil's Bridge). You'll have to pass through a closed gate, which is perfectly legal as long as you're not behind a steering wheel. Continue following the road to the left (not the trail along the river), and then the marked carriage road that turns into the woods on the left. **Vogar** peak is now about an hour away. Keep walking west from here. The path veers off of the plateau twice, so the views are breathtaking for most of the hike. Just keep to the left at the junctions to reach Pršivec (4hr.).

An easier hike from Hudičev Most is along the **Voje Valley**. Shortly after passing the bridge a sign describes the gorge and another directs you to the trail that descends along the riverbank. This is a popular hike, so you'll have to pay a 200Slt passage fee, just before a 20m gorge. Hike as far as you want; the gradual ascent along the **Mostnica River** leads to a waterfall called either **Slap Šum** or **Mostniški Slapovi** (1½hr.). The only real choice is to return the way you came.

While resting between hikes, you can take in a bit of culture. The key to the 15th-century **Church of John the Baptist** on Lake Bohinj can be found at the tourist office. Treat the church like the cultural monument that it is. The **Alpine Farming Museum** (tel. 723 095), 1.5km north in Stara Fužinz, exhibits materials from the life of a 19th-century dairy farmer. You may even be able to get a taste of local food (open Tues.-Sun. 10am-noon and 5-7pm; 150Slt; if no one's around, the curator is Mrs. Renata Mlakar at Stara Fužina 179). A few kilometers to the east, in **Studor**, is a century-old peasant house at #16; contact Grega Resman, Studor 14a (tel. 753 522).

Triglav (see below), the highest point in Slovenia, can be climbed from here. Some have done it in one day, but two days provide for a safer and more enjoyable journey. For 1000Slt, *How to Climb Triglav* details all the options. Triglav's 2864 meters may not seem like much of an ascent until you realize that, on a clear day, the sea is visible from the summit.

■ Bovec

Though surrounded by towering peaks, the small town of Bovec receives its temperate air from the Adriatic Sea. Don't think for a minute, though, that the crowds of Austrians and Italians are here to relax. In the winter, Bovec is one of Slovenia's premier ski resorts, and in the summer, the wild rapids of the aquamarine Soča river draw people here to kayak. If you don't have your own equipment, this can be an expensive venture: **Soča Rafting**, in the centrally located **Hotel Alp** (tel. 86 040; fax 32 221), charges DM49 for a rafting trip, including lunch and all the necessary clothing and transportation (1½hr.). For one day, a complete kayak kit costs only DM37, but you'll have to get yourself (and the boat) to the river and back (open Mon.-Fri. 10am-noon and 1-3pm, Sat.-Sun. 9am-6pm). Other agencies with similar prices abound, and many also offer **mountain bikes, bungee jumping, hydrospeeding** (a sort of jet-powered bodyboard), and the like.

Those with tight budgets need not despair. **Hiking** is wonderfully uncrowded here, as few people see the mountains for the river. Pick up a copy of *Bovec z Okolico* (Bovec and Surroundings), a well marked **map** available at Avrigo Tours (see below). Walk downstream about 5km, or take any of the buses headed in direction "Pod Čela," then walk downstream a few minutes more. Here, you can admire the spectacular **Slap Boka** (Boka Falls); at 106m high, and a third as wide, they're the largest in

Slovenia. You can hike to the falls in about an hour. Signs point the way, but if you take the trail to **Pri Boki,** farther down the road, you'll end up farther away. Other popular hikes head up the gorge of the **Koritnica river,** to the northeast. The total ascent is over 1500m.

You can reach Bovec by **bus** from Ljubljana (4 per day, 4½hr., 1460Slt). There are two routes; if possible, arrive by the **Vršič Pass.** After winding between some of Slovenia's highest peaks, the bus stops on the 1600m-high pass for a half-hour to allow travelers—and the bus—a rest. While here, ponder how bikers could make it up the steep roads, or just wish for a bike for the way down. The bus stops in Bovec's main square. **Avrigo Tours** (tel. 86 123; fax 86 064), across the street, serves as the nearest thing to a tourist office. Besides giving info, they can find **private rooms** (singles 1800Slt, doubles 2400Slt; tourist tax 200Slt; 30% charge for stays under 3 nights; open daily 8am-8:30pm, Sun. 9am-noon). To find a room on your own, head down the main street, then check on the small sidestreets. On your way, you'll pass **Alpkomerc,** the city's main grocery store (open Mon.-Sat. 7am-8pm, Sun. 8-11am). If you want your food cooked for you, go to **Letni Vrt,** by the bus stop. The prices are right: pizzas 400-600Slt, large salads 400Slt, and items from the grill 600-100Slt. It might have the most multilingual menu this side of the Danube. Downstairs, the **Elvis Club** is surprisingly lively; everyone from ages 14 to 40 ends up here to drink, dance, or simply stand around—you can't help falling in love with it, and besides, Bovec has nowhere else to go at night (beer 250Slt; open nightly 10pm-4am; no cover). The **post office,** complete with **telephones,** is just up the street from The King (open Mon.-Fri. 8am-6pm, Sat. 8-11am). **Postal code:** 5230. **Phone code:** 065.

THE SLOVENIAN COAST

Though Slovenia has only 40km of the Adriatic coast, this stretch of green bays, little seaside resorts, and recreational beaches has developed a personality all its own. Koper, by far the largest of the coastal towns, serves as the center for local governmental and industrial activities. For this reason, tourists with cash to spare head straight for the smaller towns where palm trees or fishing boats dot the shore. In the biggest resort town—Portorož, casinos, souvenir shops, and hordes of tourists crowd the expensive commercialized waterfront, but nearby Piran offers a slightly less hectic chance to glimpse this red-roofed-and-terraced edge of the Adriatic Sea.

■ Piran

Only 3km from Portorož, tiny Piran is just as touristed, but wears its hangers-on more charmingly. The peninsula, filled with narrow stone streets and gaily shuttered houses, still feels like medieval Venice, under whose rule Piran flourished. Follow the wharf to the central square, dominated by a **statue** of the famous violinist and composer Giuseppe Tartini, born in Piran. The narrow streets near the center merit a look. A short walk uphill, the Baroque-Renaissance **Church of San Giorgio** (built ca. 600CE and rebuilt in the 14th century), is Piran's most prominent church. Take a break from the midday sun to admire its cool, quiet interior. The tower is closed, but the terraces afford an amazing view of the sea. Walk along the quay to the odd old **church-cum-lighthouse** at the end of the peninsula.

To book a room or for more info on Piran, visit **Turistburo,** Tomažičev trg 3 (tel. 746 382; fax 746 047). Expect to pay DM26-29 for a single and DM44-49 for a double in **private accommodations,** plus a DM2 nightly tourist tax. Stays under four nights incur a 50% surcharge, but prices are 30% less in months other than July and August (breakfast DM6). **Penzion-Val,** Gregorčičeva 38a (tel. 75 499; fax 746 911), near the lighthouse, is clean and has hallway bathrooms. The prices are worth it, especially if you're alone, staying only a few days, and eating your meals in the restaurant downstairs (2900Slt per person, including breakfast, half pension 3640Slt, full pension

4200Slt; 10% more for less than 4 nights; 10% student discount). They prepare vegetarian meals on request. There is no beach, but you can enjoy a meal in one of the waterfront restaurants. **Pavel's** (tel. 747 101) entrées range from spaghetti to schnitzel (800-1500Slt; open Mon.-Sat. 11am-10pm). To get to Piran, you have to go through Portorož. Twelve **buses** per day head to Ljubljana through Postojna to Portorož (2½hr., 1470Slt). The nearest **train station** is on the outskirts of Koper. **Trains** arrive from Ljubljana (8 per day, 2½hr., 1270Slt), and a bus will take you to Portorož (2 per hr., ½hr., 220Slt). Once there, you can catch a bus (2 per hr., 100Slt) or the casino minivan (every 15min., 140Slt) to Piran.

UKRAINE
(УКРАЇНА)

US$1 = 1.83hv (hryvny)	1hv = US$0.55
CDN$1 = 1.33hv	1hv = CDN$0.75
UK£1 = 2.85hv	1hv = UK£0.35
IR£1 = 2.96hv	1hv = IR£0.34
AUS$1 = 1.44hv	1hv = AUS$0.69
NZ$1 = 1.27hv	1hv = NZ$0.79
SAR1 = 0.41hv	1hv = SAR2.43
DM1 = 1.23hv	1hv = DM0.81
Country Phone Code: 380	**International Dialing Prefix: 810**

Even by the standards of a newly crazed Eastern Europe, Ukraine is anarchic and dour. Foreign tourism is practically non-existent in this huge and diverse land—one need not depart from any beaten path because (aside from an ugly and expensive Intourist trail) there is none; the closest thing to a developed tourist industry are the *babushkas* selling meat pies at the train station for 20 cents instead of 15. Blame it on strict visa requirements, but the results are wonderful: as prices remain low, Ukraine will have you thinking not just in hryvny but in pennies. More importantly, the lack of established tourist trails, itineraries, and (yes) comforts means that traveling in Ukraine, you will see people, not just their touristy roads and souvenir shops. Museums cost nothing and are empty, medieval castles are still huge, dark, and unsupervised, while cobbled roads remain unpaved. Sometimes the most obnoxious discos lurk in opulent buildings, conjuring ancient visions of barbarians in Rome. If you want to bump into the girl you took to the 8th-grade dance, hit Poland or Prague, because Ukraine, with enough problems of its own, isn't expecting you.

UKRAINE ESSENTIALS

Foreign travelers arriving in Ukraine must have a **visa**, which requires an **invitation** from a citizen, official organization, or a tourist voucher from a travel agency. Regular, single-entry visa processing at an embassy or consulate—with invitation in hand—takes up to nine days (mailing time not included; enclose pre-paid FedEx or UPS envelope to speed the return) and costs US$30 (double-entry US$60; 72-hr. transit US$15). Three-day priority processing is US$60 (double-entry US$120), while same-day express costs US$100 (double-entry US$200; transit US$30). Your application should include a completed visa application, an private invitation or confirmation from a hotel in Ukraine, your passport, one passport-size photo, and the payment (plus a US$20 processing fee)—payable only by money order or company check. See Essentials: Embassies and Consulates, p. 8. Transit visas are available at airports and major border crossings; prices vary, but are still exorbitant.

The following organizations arrange visas and supply other services:

- **Home & Host International,** in the U.S. give them a ring at tel. (800) SOVIET-U or (612) 871-0596; fax (612) 871-8853.
- **Russia House,** in U.S. 1800 Connecticut Ave. NW, Washington, D.C. 20009, attn: Chris Poor (tel. (202) 986-6010; fax 667-4244). In **Russia,** 17 Leningradsky Prospekt, Moscow, Russia 125040 (tel. (095) 250 01 43; fax 250 25 03). Provides invitations and visas for all countries of the former USSR—visas are business visas, so your travels should be less restricted. No train tickets or hotel reservations.
- **Host Families International, HOFA,** will get HOFA guests invitations. See Russia Essentials, p. 521.
- **IBV Bed & Breakfast Systems,** 13113 Ideal Dr., Silver Spring, MD 20906 (tel. (301) 942-3770; fax 933-0024), will get you a visa if you'll stay at their expensive B&Bs.

If you arrive in the **Kiev airport** without a visa, you can get a tourist voucher-cum-invitation, which will allow you to then buy a visa. This will allow you to proceed through **customs**: declare all valuables and foreign currency above US$1000 (including traveler's checks) in order to settle your tab when leaving the country. The process takes several hours. Anyone planning to work in Ukraine must have an additional letter stating purpose of the work; the letter has to come from an official Ukrainian agency, even if you will be working for a foreign company. A copy of your invitation and letters of introduction should be carried on your person at all times, lest you be harassed by bored police officers.

Upon arrival in Ukraine you should check into a hotel or register with the hall of nightmares that is the **Office of Visas and Registration** (OVIR), in Kiev at bulv. Tarasa Shevchenka 34 (Тараса Шевченка), or in police stations in smaller cities, within your first three days in the country (US$10); visas may also be extended here. Your visa not only lets you into the country but also allows you to leave; DO NOT LOSE IT. Once you leave Ukraine, your visa becomes invalid. If you have a double-entry visa you will be given a re-entry slip (въезд; *vyezd*) upon your first arrival. Keep this with you—it is your ticket back into the country.

GETTING THERE

One of the easiest ways to get to Ukraine is by air. **Air Ukraine International** (tel. (312) 337-0004) flies from a number of European capitals (as well as Chicago, New York, and Washington, D.C.) to Kiev, Lviv, and Odesa. Air France, ČSA, Lufthansa, LOT, Malév, SAS, and Swiss Air also fly to Kiev, generally one to two times per week. Offices are located in Kiev.

Trains get you there much cheaper, however, and run frequently from all the neighbor states. When coming from a non-ex-Soviet country, prepare for a two-hour stop at the border when the wagons get a change of wheels.

Buses are a pain, unless you're traveling short distances. Taking a autocar from Przemyśl (Poland) to Lviv saves money and time (no 2-hr. wheel changes) and allows you to do a lot of shopping on board; the frequent connection is mobbed by Ukrainians running small-scale trade trips to and from Poland's east border.

Ferries across the Black Sea have now been reduced to a few routes from Odesa and Yalta to Istanbul. However, several companies run **ships** from Istanbul for US$97; you can be pretty sure of getting a place if you reserve a week in advance.

GETTING AROUND

For long distance travel, try to buy tickets two to three days in advance. However, if you're leaving from a town that's not the origin of the route, you'll only be able to obtain the tickets the day of. **Trains** go everywhere, and offer dirt cheap comfort. Unfortunately, getting **tickets** can drive people batty. Often a sales clerk will declare that there are no more places when in fact only the two upper classes are full—try the other classes as well. Otherwise, try again later at the Intourist office or at the ticket window at 8am, 2pm, or 8pm, when tickets are "re-distributed." As one Intourist agent put it, "All the tickets are trapped in a bag—once in a while, someone opens it and lets them out." Those confident of their Russian or Ukrainian try asking the conductor to seat them: "Мне нужно место; мы можем договориться?" (Mnye NOOZH-no ME-stoh; myh MOH-zhem doh-goh-REET-sah?—I need a place; can we work something out?). Generally, the conductor will charge the cost of the ticket, pocket the money him- or herself, and find them a place. Otherwise, those who positively need a ticket that day turn to the **scalpers** in the main ticket hall who ask: "Вам нужен билет?" (Vahm NOO-zhen bee-LYET?—Do you need a ticket?). They charge US$10-20 for overnight trips and might bargain. The tickets they offer are usually valid—check by showing one to a cashier and asking "Когда поезд приходит?" (Koh-GDAH POH-ezd pree-KHO-det?—When does the train arrive?). Most towns also have a **central ticket bureau** with an Intourist window. The lines are long and the cashiers unpredictable, but they are usually closer to the center.

Your **ticket** is labeled across the top with the train number, the date and time of departure, the car number, and type ("л" for "люкс"—*lyuks*, "к" for "купейний"—*koupeyny*, etc.). A few lines down you can find your place (место; *myesto*). If you've planned far enough ahead to have a choice of **class**, there are four to choose from. At the top is *lyux* (люкс), or *2-myagky* (мягкий; 2-person soft)—a place in a two-bunk cabin in the same car as 2nd-class *koupéyny* (купейний) which has four bunks. Both classes have the same type of beds: sort of cushioned, almost comfortable, with a roll-up mattress and pillow. The next class down is *platskartny* (плацкартний), an open car with 52 bunks. The bunks are shorter (less than 2m long) and harder. Places 1-37 are most stable. Places 34-37 are next to the unnaturally foul bathroom. Places 38-52 are on the side of the car—during the summer, the upper-side bunks get hotter than any place in Ukraine. Women traveling alone can try to buy out a *lyuks* compartment to avoid nasty drunks, or can travel *platskartny* with the regular folk and depend on the crowds to shame would-be harassers into silence. Avoid the *obshchy* class, where chickens taken to market might lay an egg on your seat when you get up to use the loo. In the upper classes, the car monitor will rent out **sheets** for US$2; in *platskartny*, most car monitors do not care if you bring your own sheets and use the roll-up mattress, but some grumpy ones will not let you use it unless you've paid for sheets.

Except in Kiev, where **platform** numbers are posted on the electronic board, the only way to figure out which platform your train is on is by the distorted announcement. In large cities, trains arrive some time before they are scheduled to depart, so you'll have a few minutes to show your ticket to fellow passengers, look helpless, and say "платформа?" (plaht-FORM-ah?). When tripping between Lviv and Kiev, choose trains #92 (to Kiev) and 91 (to Lviv). They have the reputation of lulling you to sleep in more comfort than the other trains. Moreover, both have special cars "Grand-Tour" (Гранд-Тур), that offer still greater coziness.

Buses are a bit more expensive but the best way to travel short distances. In large cities, buy tickets at least the night before at the regular ticket-windows with everyone else. In smaller cities, the *kasa* will start selling tickets only an hour before the bus's departure. Sometimes, they'll direct you to buy the ticket from the driver, but always try the *kasa* first. Each platform has its buses posted.

Relying on water transport is risky. **River transport** is also infrequent, but some routes do exist. Kiev hydrofoils go only as far as Chernihiv. The port agents know more than the Intourist offices, which feign ignorance of the existence of boats.

Taxis overcharge everyone, especially foreigners; agree on a price before getting in. State taxis (recognizable by their checkered signs) wait for passengers at taxi stands throughout cities. Unregulated "private transport" or "gypsy cabs" can be hailed by holding the hand at a downward salute. This is probably the most convenient and cheapest way to travel short distances within a city. If the driver doesn't take off, the potential passenger asks "Сколько?" (SKOL-koh?—How much?); the driver will say, "SKOL-koh dahsh?" (How much will you give?), etc. Figure out how many kilometers away your destination lies. In summer '96, the accepted price of a ride was 0.50hv per kilometer, but this change with the petrol prices. *Let's Go* does not recommend such private transport as a safe means of travel.

TOURIST SERVICES

The breakup of the Soviet Union technically brought about the demise of the official state travel agency, **Intourist,** which was responsible for foreigners traveling to Ukraine, but they still have an office in every city, sometimes under another name. They offer maps and hard-to-find train tickets but are used to dealing with groups, not individual travelers, so be sure to smile a lot, speak slowly, and be persistent.

MONEY

> *Oohh, they are nice. And they feel like real money, not just plain paper.*
> —Olha Paziak, retired Ukrainian teacher

On September 2, 1996, the Ukraine decided to wipe the extraneous zeros off most prices (back in the old days, an espresso cost 100,000Krb) by replacing the **karbovanets** (Krb; a.k.a kupon) with a new currency, **hryvna** (hv; гривна). Each hryvna (pl. hryvny) is worth 100,000 karbovantsi, so take 5 zeros off the price above and a shot of caffeine hopefully costs only 1hv. Whoo! Now *that* feels like budget travel. The currency change means that for the first time in five years, Ukrainians can use coins. One *babushka,* before trading karbovanets for the new metal **kopeks** (100kp=1hv), was quoted, "This is a special request from my grandson, who doesn't remember coins." The change occurred quickly in September 1996, so beware individuals who might try to hand over karbovanets as change; US$10 worth of change might quickly become US¢0.01. Hotels usually request hryvny, and only occasionally ask for dollars. International train tickets are usually sold partly in hryvny, partly in dollars. **Exchanging** dollars and Deutschmarks is fairly simple, and can be done at Обмін Валют (*Obmin Valyut*) kiosks. Exchange of other currencies is difficult; **traveler's checks** are not accepted, but can be changed to dollars at small commissions in almost every city in Ukraine. **X-Change Points** is another Renaissance thinker in the dark ages of Ukrainian finance—they have **Western Union** and can give Visa cash advances (currently available in Kiev, Odesa, Yalta, Uzhhorod, Dnipropetrovsk, and Lviv). You can also try the lobbies of fancy hotels, who will exchange dollars at lousy rates. **Private money changers** lurk near legitimate kiosks, and devise brilliant plans for taking your money. DO NOT exchange money with them. They offer rates no better than kiosks, and they might slip you a wad of useless karbovanets.

COMMUNICATION

Mail is cheap but slow; allow a minimum of two to three weeks from Kiev to any foreign destination. From other cities, it may never arrive, or even be picked up. In principle, you can drop pre-stamped mail in any "почта" (*pochta*) box, with twice-daily pick-ups, but post offices are usually a better bet. The easiest way to mail letters is to buy pre-stamped envelopes at the post office. The international courier service **DHL** is available in Kiev, Odesa, and Lviv.

Telephones are struggling out of the stone age. Order international calls at the post office for the cheapest rate by writing down the number and country you're calling; there is usually a minimum of three minutes per call, but you're not charged for the three minutes if they're not home; when the call is ready, 5-25 minutes later, you'll be pointed to the right booth. In Kiev, Utel (Ukraine telephone) has begun producing electronic **phonecards** available in US$10 and US$20 denominations (payable in hryvny). A minute to the U.S. costs US$3.30, 80 cents more than the average post office minute, but significantly less of a hassle. You can take advantage of Utel's new technology to make **collect calls** from some phones. Dial 27 10 36, and ask for an "ITNT" (a.k.a AT&T) operator. **AT&T Direct** is available from Utel or private phones; Utel charges US$1 for the connection; the number is (8) 101 11—wait for another tone after the 8. **MCI Direct** is (8) 100 13. From private or Utel phones, the international dialing prefix is 810. for intercity calls, order at the post office and pay up front; in some cities, payphones marked "міжміський" (*mizhmisky*) work with tokens. At some post offices you will be handed a **plug** when you pay for the first three minutes; insert it into the upper left corner of the front of the phone to get a dial tone, then dial (city code plus number). **Local calls** are free in most cities from any gray payphone. In Lviv, buy **tokens** at the post office or at kiosks. When calling abroad from a hotel, ask the operator to connect you to Utel who will connect you to an Anglophonic operator.

LANGUAGE

Your trip will go more smoothly if you can throw around a few words of **Ukrainian** or **Russian** (see Glossaries: Ukrainian, p. 789, and Russian, p. 787). In Crimea and most of Eastern Ukraine, accented Russian is more common than Ukrainian; even in Kiev most people speak Russian on the streets (although all official signs and announcements—such as on the Metro—are in Ukrainian). In west Ukraine, Ukrainian is preferred, and **Polish** more warmly accepted than Russian.

The Ukrainian alphabet resembles Russian (see the Cyrillic alphabet, p. 771); however, there are character and pronunciation differences. The most notable addition is

Just for the Taste

When the sun is high and the steppe is hotter than Chicago '95, Aussies thirst for a Foster, Czechs for a Pilsner, Dakotans for a Bud, but a true Ukrainian won't have anything other than a ladle of KVAS (КВАС). In Kiev you'll see it served from siphons and in the provinces from rusty cisterns. KVAS taste varies depending on the container, but it all comes down to acidic bread bubbles—like beer without the hops, based on a sour-dough solution that rushes tingling into your bloodstream. It's so addictive that Kiev drinks its KVAS all summer, even in rain, when groups of young tots, middle-aged shoppers, and teenagers in love huddle around toothless tap-masters, all trying to fit under a leeking umbrella.

the "і" (*ee* sound) and the "ї" (*yee* sound)—the "и" is closest to "s*i*t." The rarely used "є" sounds like "ye" in "yep!". The "ґ" (hard "g") has been reintroduced since independence but is not yet widely used, and the "г", pronounced "g" in Russian, comes out like an "h". Note: the "r" is rolled, though not flamboyantly. Useful phrases include "зачинено" (zah-chi-ne-no—closed) and "нема" (nyee-mah—there isn't any).

HEALTH AND SAFETY

> **Emergency Numbers: Fire:** tel. 01. **Police:** tel. 02. **Ambulance:** tel. 03.

In every interaction with a Ukrainian who's not after your green bills, you'll be told to keep your foreign profile low, watch your belongings, and not make easy acquaintances. Although **crime** is a widely advertised problem, the risk isn't much greater than in the rest of Eastern Europe. Try to blend into the local look (see Customs and Etiquette, p. 688), and you'll be able to give that extra unstolen dollar to a beggar upon leaving. Travelers who have been harassed by the police, say it's possible to get back on the law's good side with the aid of a US$20 bill.

Although Ukraine might seem somewhat like Pat Buchanan's dreamworld, there's probably more **racial diversity** here than in many other East European states. The openness of the university system to African and Arab students has brought, if not a sizable non-Caucasian population, than at least one that has accustomed the post-Tatar tribes of the steppe to complexions other than their own. Outside university cities such as Kiev and Lviv, discrimination might be more prevalent, although even the stereotypical Ukrainian face changes the further south you go.

Women traveling alone are often harassed. Women never go to restaurants alone and may feel frightened if they do, even at midday. Small cafés and cafeterias are safer options; even hotel restaurants may be dangerous. If need be, turn to an older woman for help in an uncomfortable situation; her stern rebukes will usually be enough to embarrass the most persistent jerks.

Authorities recommend boiling it for ten minutes before drinking. Fruits and vegetables from open **markets** are generally safe, although storage conditions and pesticides render thorough washing absolutely necessary. Any meats purchased at public markets should be checked very carefully and cooked quite thoroughly; refrigeration is a foreign concept and insect life thrives. Embassy officials declare that Chernobyl-related **radiation** poses only a minimal risk to short-term travelers, but the region should be given a wide berth.

Pharmacies are quite common, and medications prescribed by local doctors are usually available. Aspirin is the only available painkiller, and Tampax the sole brand of sanitary supplies, but plenty of cold remedies and bandages are at hand. In large hotels, imported medications may be available for hard currency. For sanitary napkins (гігієнічні пакети; ghee-ghee-eh-NEE-chnee pak-YET-ih) or condoms (презервативи; prey-zer-vah-TIV-ih), consult everyday kiosks; they are intermittently available.

It's a wise idea to **register** with your embassy once you arrive in Ukraine. Besides making the process of recovering lost passports much quicker, the embassy staff may be able to offer important information on travel or the situation in Ukraine.

Public restrooms range from yucky to scary. The pay (платный; *platny*) are cleaner and might provide toilet paper, but never go outside without **toilet paper** or something that could serve as such. Public restrooms are normally porcelain holes in the ground; due to weak flushing power, there is usually a waste basket for toilet paper.

ACCOMMODATIONS AND CAMPING

Some hotels accept foreigners even without a specific invitation but charge many times what a citizen would pay. Hotels fall into two categories, **"hotels"** and **"tourist bases"**—called "Турбаза" (TOOR-bah-zah), which usually form part of a complex targeted at motoring tourists, but are otherwise nearly indistinguishable from hotels. Though room prices in Kiev are astronomical, singles run US$2-25 throughout the rest of Ukraine. The phrase "самое дешёвое место" (SAHM-ah-yih dih-SHOHV-ah-yih ME-stoh) means "the cheapest place." Approaching cautiously, looking innocent, and not interrupting the receptionists' conversation can also lower your price.

Tourism is slow, so hotels usually have room. Make inquiries and hand your passport over to the **administrator** (администратор), who will ask for your фамилия (fah-MEEL-ee-yah—last name), where you arrived in the country, and how long you are staying. They may keep your passport during your stay. You will be given a **hotel card** (визитка; *veezeetka*) to show to the hall-monitor (дежурная; *deezhoornaya*; or чергова; *cherhova*) to get a key; surrender your key on leaving the building.

Conditions are usually adequate, although you will need your own **toilet paper** (buy it at kiosks or markets). Hot water is a godsend when you find it. Valuables (hot water, toilet paper, etc.) should never be left in the room unattended; the administrator usually has a **safe** where you can store them if absolutely necessary.

Private rooms are available through overseas agencies and bargaining at the train station. Prices run US$1-2 per person but conditions are quite variable, and the room always sounds better at the station. During the summer months, **university dorms** might put you up for a couple of nights, depending on whether the *kommandant* likes you. Come during business hours to see this powerful bureaucrat. A bed usually costs US$1-2. Most cities have a **campground** on the edge of town. The old Soviet complexes can be quite posh, with saunas and restaurants. Space in an electrified bungalow runs US$7-10 per night; tent space and use of facilities runs US$3-8. Free camping is illegal, and enforcement can be merciless.

FOOD AND DRINK

You can lose big eating at an overpriced restaurant, with the meal entering into a pitched battle with your stomach; or you can emerge triumphant, getting fresh beef-and-vegetable borscht, *kotleti* (cousin of the hamburger), and *kartoshka* (mashed potatoes) for under US$1 at a *stolovaya*. Look around you when you enter restaurants—if people are eating, you should, too. If not, they know something you don't. Move on. The more liquor a café serves, the worse its food is. The famed **stolovaya** (столовая), **yidalnya** (їдальня), and **cafeteria** (кафе), are dying bastions of cheap, hot food. There is usually a choice of two soups, two main dishes, and some *kompot* (a homemade fruit drink); pick up your tray, point to what you want (try to avoid picking up dishes that have already been doled), and pay your bill (usually about US$1) at the cashier. The busier it is, the fresher the food. Non-fresh *stolovaya* food can knock you out of commission for hours, while a delicious stolovaya meal is a triumph of the human spirit. **Vegetarians** can fill up here, although cucumbers, tomatoes, and carrots can begin to grate. Most restaurateurs' reactions to vegetarians are hostile, and the meat-free menu rarely has more than 'shrooms (гриби; *hribi*).

Produce is sold by the kilogram in jam-packed **markets** that fill enormous warehouses. Bring your own bags or buy them at nearby kiosks. Markets are open daily, usually by 7am, and close no earlier than 5pm.

State food stores are classified by content. Гастроном (*Gastronom*) sells everything but concentrates on packaged goods. Молоко (*Moloko*) offers milk-products. Овочі-Фрукти (*Ovochi-Frukti*) sells fruits and vegetables, often preserved in large jars. Мясо (*Myaso*) provides meat, Хліб (*Khlib*) bread, Ковбаси (*Kovbasi*) sausage, and Риба (*Riba*) fish. You must usually pay the cashier for the item you want (just tell her the price), point out the counter where you're about to obtain the merchandise, retrieve a receipt, and only then trade the receipt for the item (this also goes for the state department stores; Універмаг; *Univermag*). In the suburbs, there is one store per designated region, labeled simply "Магазин" (mah-ah-ZIN—store).

Liquor is available everywhere and is very cheap. A half-liter bottle of *Stolichnaya* costs about US$1.50—these are generally reliable and tastier than the moonshine (*samogonka*) Ukrainians might offer you in their homes. The quality of **beer** depends on the hardships it went through on the way here. The most popular is the *Obolon* (оболонь), but Lviv's *Zoloty kolos* (Золотий колос) and *Lvivske* (Львівське) outdo it quality-wise. Don't miss out on *Kvas* (Квас), poured for pennies from huge barrels in the street. It is an unholy and delicious mix of fermented bread and water. For more information on exactly *vas ist Kvas,* see p. 685. At mealtime, don't count on free water. Few eateries carry water even at cost; those that do, charge more for it than for juices.

CUSTOMS AND ETIQUETTE

A variety of attitudes has arrived in the land. Smiling was positively out before, but now being "nice" to each other is riding a high wave, though maybe not as high as in America. Even parties to which a foreigner might be invited assume a serious air from the start. Arrive bearing flowers and vodka for the hosts, and a grin for the other guests, but expect chit chat to soon evolve into political discussions. Unless you know the situation in Ukraine well, confine your comments to the beauty of the countryside and the weather. Don't defend your liberal views even it kills you to do so. Topics such as abortion, **homosexuality,** and cannibalism, although not taboo, usually provoke a negative reaction throughout the Ukrainian populace.

Although most locals never leave **tips,** most expats give the waitron 10% of the meal's price for a beer or two. Often, the server will collect the tip himself simply by giving no change after he takes your money.

LIFE AND TIMES

HISTORY

Ukraine has developed at the confluence of four major cultures: **Byzantine** to the south, **Muslim** nomadic horsemen to the east, **Russian** to the north, and **Polish** to the west. No one empire managed to control the fertile and developed Ukraine for long without being dispossessed by another warring empire. In this manner, west Ukraine developed a heavily Polish culture, and east Ukraine a Russian one.

The **Scythians** plied the steppe during the 8th to the 1st centuries BCE, replacing the battle-axe-wielding proto-Indo-Europeans before them. The Scythians terrorized their neighbors with brilliant archery and horsemanship. These semi-nomadic raiders, who only occasionally penetrated Ukraine proper, were in turn replaced by invaders from Central Asia. While the Crimea and the Black Sea coast were settled by **Greeks** and **Romans,** the Scythians of the steppe were succeeded by Sarmatians, Heruls, and **Ostrogoths,** the latter occupying the entire area from 250CE. The **Huns** rode out of Mongolia in the 370s, settling in the south for 300 years.

Recorded Ukrainian history, however, did not begin until the **Kievan Rus** dynasty sprang from the infiltrations of Viking and Baltic fur traders into the Dnipro River region in 882. They grew wealthy from the newly opened north-south fur trade among Constantinople, Novgorod, and the Baltic trading organizations, superseding the Judaic Khazars operating on the Volga. Though the Kievan aristocracy were Varangian Swedes, they created the first Slavic state and, more importantly, the first Slavic culture. They adopted and modernized Cyril's and Methodius's alphabet and searched for a religion suitable for a young, aspiring dynasty. Prince Vladimir chose **Christianity,** welcoming missionaries from Constantinople, and was baptized in 988. With the conversion came an influx of Byzantine ideas and culture, so enrapturing the Kievan Rus that they attempted to conquer their southern neighbors three times. After a few centuries of prosperity, the empire splintered as succession problems, meddling Byzantines, and slowing trade depleted its coffers.

Following Kievan Rus's collapse, Ukraine was divided between nomadic Cumans and Patzinaks and leftover Varangian parcels. The "Golden Horde," a fictitious term for Genghis Khan's **Mongol** army, moved in the 1230s, establishing khanates—the power bases in the area. **Batu,** Genghis Khan's grandson, conquered Kiev in 1240 and extended his rule into Europe until his death, which halted the seemingly inevitable penetration of the continent and allowed the khanates to splinter.

Ukraine soon became the center of numerous power plays. The **Cossacks,** armed bands on horseback, became the indigenous power structure. They supported themselves by renting their services to the Polish and Lithuanian kings, who occupied parts of Ukraine and had the native Cossacks ward off excursions from Constantinople and **Muscovite Russia.** The fiercely independent Cossacks revolted, however, in response to Polish expansion into their territory, rejecting their newly acquired place in the Polish nobility. The famous rebellion led by the *hetman* **Bohdan Khmelnitsky** defeated a Polish force and reclaimed Kiev and Lviv. An agreement with Moscow helped ward off Polish domination, and the Cossacks led the Muscovite expansion into Siberia. A treaty of 1667, however, divided Ukraine between Russia and Poland—indigenous culture was suppressed by both powers.

Ukrainian nationalism resurfaced in the 19th century, led by the poet **Taras Shevchenko,** who sought to revitalize the Ukrainian language and safeguard it from Polish and Russian cultural imperialism. The movement culminated in a *rada* (council) in Kiev declaring Ukrainian independence in 1917, taking advantage of the tsar's political weakness. The **Bolsheviks** set up a rival government in Kharkiv and seized complete power during the Russian Civil War in 1920. They solidified power after repulsing a Polish invasion, thus "defending" the Ukrainian State.

Under Communist rule, Ukraine was fully incorporated into the **Soviet Union,** answerable in all realms to Moscow. However, the nationalist movement endured, drawing strength from Soviet mismanagement and collectivization, Stalin's forced famine of 1932 (which claimed 7 million lives), hatred of Nazi invaders and Russian settlers, the long-standing ban on the teaching of Ukrainian in Soviet schools, and the Chernobyl disaster of 1986.

Ukraine finally pulled out of the Soviet Union on December 1, 1991, following an overwhelming vote by 93% of its population for complete **independence.** Ironically, Ukraine was a member of the United Nations for 46 years before it truly gained its sovereignty. Ukraine has also become the beneficiary of a sizeable nuclear arsenal, a still-disputed portion of the Soviet Black Sea fleet, and Europe's second largest army. Another legacy of Soviet rule are the foreign conquests, which until recently threatened Ukraine's existence; in the **1994 presidential elections,** 90% of the Crimean voters supported Kuchma and his promises to cooperate with Russia, while 94% of Lviv's population opted for Kravchuk's more nationalist agenda (even though he was once Ukraine's head Communist ideologue). Kiev sided with Kravchuk 60-35%. Kuchma won, and has essentially followed in Kravchuk's footsteps. There were riots in Crimea at the end of June, 1995, and the issue of police and non-Tartar mafia cooperation is increasingly contentious.

LITERATURE

Not limited to Greek, Roman, or French antecedents, Ukrainian literature has traditionally looked to diverse sources, finding inspiration in canonical classics and lesser known Polish, Czech, and Slovak texts. Some Ukrainian writers have even gone so far as to emigrate from country to country, making it tricky to sort out exactly who can claim them. Needless to say, Russia tends to assert its prerogative when it comes to authors of international repute, e.g. Mikhail Bulgakov and Aleksandr Pushkin.

The first "Ukrainian" literature was the outpourings of the Kievan Rus dynasty. Written in the Old Church Slavonic, translations initially constituted the mainstay of the textual supply. Among the genres exploited for this transfer of verbal wealth were various types of church literature, histories, didactic tales, and romances. Original texts soon sprung up in the "Monumental Style" of the 11th to 13th centuries—works embellished only by epithets and alliteration. The documents, infused with an attitude that Communists later attempted to impress upon unwilling Ukrainian comrades, concentrated upon exalting the unified Russian state. One of the most important works of the period, a chronicle attributed to **Nestor,** discusses the development of distinct nations and the coming of Christianity, while another tale combines myth and history into the conversion story of **Vladimir the Great.** He appears also in the *bylinas* (heroic ballads), that still exist—remnants of epics sung in Kievan Rus.

Although the adventures of the later **Prince Vladimir Monomakh** (1053-1125) are recounted in these, he maintains an independent literary claim to fame with his own works, synthesizing folklore and other exogenous sources.

In the 12th century a new "Ornamental Style," replete with symbolism and hyperbole was added to the mix. As the empire was losing strength, the tone of Ukrainian literature became disillusioned with the reality of the world and despairing of a harmonious kingdom on earth. The most important endeavors of this era were the *Paterikon* of the **Kiev-Pechersk Monastery,** and *The Song of Igor's Campaign.* The *Paterikon* compiles the correspondence of Simeon, a former monk at the monastery, and his friend Polycarp, who still inhabits it. Taken together, these letters constitute an epistolary novel that even the most expert 18th-century English practitioners would be proud of. The church did not retain exclusive control in this period, however, *The Song of Igor's Campaign* corresponded to the courtly tradition. Describing a campaign Prince Igor of Novgorod-Siversky undertook against the Cumans in 1185, the epic veils its intent under so many layers of symbolism that it is almost impossible to extract a single meaning. Artistically engineered, the piece is still famous today, and Vladimir Nabokov rendered it in English in 1960. The promise of new literary terrain that these texts displayed was squashed, however, when the Lithuanian-Polish alliance subsumed the territory Ukraine already possessed.

After a long stretch of semi-dormancy, Ukrainian literature re-emerged in the 17th and 18th centuries. Since the country was still politically disparate, these works were sometimes written in Polish or Latin, without any consciousness of belonging to the Ukrainian tradition. Emblematic and figured verses, with their ingenious visual suggestions, a well as parodic poetry, appeared in print everywhere. One of the most significant exponent of these pieces was **Ivan Velychkovsky** (d. 1726). Stories were simultaneously revitalized, and a new genre emerged—drama, which blossomed into a vital form with historical and morality plays. While some plays were comic, the *intermedia* performed alongside and supplied by authors like **M. Dovhalevsky** and **George Konysky** provided repositories for most of the humor.

In 1704, **Theofanes Prokopovych** composed a treatise entitled *Poetics* and tried out his own hypotheses in the play *Vladymyr.* The most accomplished contemporary author, who almost independently created the language of the Ukrainian vernacular, was **Ivan Kotliarevsky** (1769-1838). In his comic travesty of Virgil's *Aeneid,* called the *Eneïda,* Kotliarevsky not only incorporated all sorts of common Ukrainian idioms, but even transformed the heroes into Cossacks! Imagine Aeneas's horror.

Focusing on ethnography and the creation of scholarly histories of Ukraine, the Romantic movement rediscovered folk tales and added a national content to the newly developed Ukrainian style. Kharkiv, home to **Izmail Sreznevsky** (1812-80), **Levko Borovykovsky** (1806-89), **Ambrose Metlynsky** (1814-70), and **Nicholas Kostomarov** (1817-85), was an important literary center. Soon the center of Romanticism shifted to Kiev, where Kostomarov, **Panteleimon Kulish** (1819-97), and **Taras Shevchenko** (1814-61), probably the most famous individual in Ukrainian literature, joined the Slavophile Brotherhood of Sts. Cyril and Methodius, and created plans for the furtherance of their country; Kostomarov's *The Book of the Genesis of the Ukrainian People* opines that his society, though temporarily incapacitated, will once again rise as part of a pan-Slavic union featuring liberty and brotherhood for all.

Shevchenko supplied the higher level of language missing in previous works. While his poems sometimes resemble folksongs, his skill as a craftsman shines through. His poems spoke of Ukrainian autonomy and history, idealizing the Cossack period. Among his most well known works are a lengthy poem *Haidamaky* (1841), *Son* (*The Dream*)—formally akin to a mystery play—*Kavkaz* (*The Caucasus*), and *Poslaniie* (*The Epistle*). Kulish, on the other hand, was a novelist who painted a picture of the Ukrainian nation as containing disparate groups. Hiis historicizing novels include *Mykhailo Charnyshenko* and *Chorna Rada* (*The Black Council*). The sense of a national purpose Ukrainian authors evinced in the poems and stories of this period penetrated far beyond the confines of its country.

The subsequent Realism was related to Romanticism by their mutual dependence on folk sources. Ethnographism infiltrated into realistic novels and stories, where conflicts occur between various specifically Ukrainian classes, like the Cossacks, and the chumaks—or exalted wagoners. **Marko Vovchok** (the pseudonym of **Maria Vilinska-Markovych;** 1833-1907) treated the serfs' plight and the oppression foisted on her country by the Russians. Composed in a vernacular style, her tales were recommended by Shevchenko as a way to learn Ukrainian and its idioms. Many tales, like *Instytutka*, dedicated to Shevchenko, allow the reader to see the hollowness of the upper classes by giving the narrator the perspective of a serf. Contemporary poets include **Stepan Rudansky** and **Leonid Hlibov,** and among the novelists ranked **Ivan Nechuy-Levytsky** and **Panas Myrny.** The greatest realist of the late 1800s was **Ivan Franko** (1856-1916), a poet and novelist who drew from the thematic stash of other European writers, and experimented with psychological portraits.

Employing modernist techniques as well, Franko constituted one element of the transitional generation, which blossomed into the full-fledged Modernism of the early 20th-century Ukraine. In prose, **Mikhail Kotsiubinsky** (1864-1913) began the experimentation, which was expressed in *Fata Morgana*, a study of village life from a subjective and personal vantage point. **Lesya Ukrainka** (1871-1913) proved Ukraine's foremost figure in this period, however. Having begun with exotic lyrics, she passed into universal and psychological themes, including that of the poet's role, and eventually developed the verse drama, in which she adapted subjects from various periods and cultures to tear the country away from cultural self-absorption.

After WWII, experimental schools were suppressed by Russian forces. The Symbolist movement is best embodied by poet **Paul Tychyna,** Futurism was founded by **Michael Semenko,** and Neoclassicism represented by **Maksym Rylsky.** These authors, as well as numerous other, founded several organizations known popularly by their acronyms, which perhaps were more widely promulgated than the literature they represented. The fate of all these movements is exemplified by that of **Mykola Khylovy.** First praising the stated goals of the Russian Revolution, he gradually realized that the aims of the USSR could never be commensurate with those of a Ukrainian state, and rescinded his approval in later unsanctioned pamphlets. All the significant writers of the century, if they survived, followed his fate, censored into the point of oblivion. Now, as Ukraine feel its way out of a what was a dire economic situation, it simultaneously endeavors to acquire a new literary life.

UKRAINE TODAY

Though some people still promise a civil war, the nation's more serious problem is its shattered economy. Some estimates put unemployment at 40%, as factories stand still, agriculture tries to rid itself of Communist collectivization and psychology, and technological industries attempt to cope with the "brain drain." Perhaps most devastating, however, is the Communist work ethic—the old joke that "they pretend to pay us, and we pretend to work," is still valid as salaries remain unpaid, and workers at hotels, train stations, and stores act like it. But there appears to be light at the end of the ex-Soviet tunnel, with the economy actually expected to pull slowly out of its massive recession. By September 1996, the previously run-away inflation had consistently been held to 1-2% per month. Anew currency, the hryvna, was introduced to slash five zeros off the previous karbovanets.

Democracy has yet to arrive in any real sense. With a dominating left-bloc opposition in parliament, it is difficult for President Leonid Kuchma to implement radical reforms. On June 28, 1996, however, the parliament did approve a new constitution, calling for the introduction of a Senate in March 1998 elections. Ukraine's relations with Russia are still touchy in some areas—the status of the Sevastopol naval base is still up in the air. While the country plans to resist greater CIS integration and to seek EU membership, it is also trying to conclude a friendship and cooperation treaty with Russia. All this makes for a near anarchy, and in many ways, it is the most apt. For the budget traveler, although it does not make for a smooth trip, it means the freedom to see a nation in crisis as it attempts to find a place in a world that has left it behind.

Kiev (Київ)

> ...Most often of all I soothe my aged imagination with pictures of gold-domed, garden-cloaked and poplar-crowned Kiev.
> —Taras Shevchenko (from exile)

Laboring under Moscow's shadow, Kiev is not only having a hard time trying to divert tourists south but is also struggling to arrest its Ukrainian character after a long period as Russia's third city. With an economic crisis raging around the country and many regions' eyes turned to the capital for help, Kiev cannot find the time to care for itself. Artfully sculpted houses need more than a touch-up to regain their past glory—many are already gutted and abandoned. Mothers begging money for their sick children in metro stations cannot afford the threepenny rolls that bundled-up country women sell beside them. Meanwhile, a gaudy rich caste glories in its opulent couture and German cars. Kiev needs years to return to the magnificence of which Shevchenko spoke, although tourists will find sights worth a prolonged stop.

ORIENTATION AND PRACTICAL INFORMATION

Although the city straddles the Dnipro River (Дніпро), almost all the attractions and services lie within right-bank (western) Kiev. The **Metro's** three intersecting lines—blue (MB), green (MG), and red (MR)—cover the city center but leave most of the outskirts to trolleys and trams. The **train station** is at MR: Vokzalna (Вокзальна). Two stops away is the **Khreshchatik** (Хрещатик) stop and street, a broad and busy post-war boulevard that handles necessities, though not housing. Parallel and up from vul. Khreshchatik runs **Volodimirska vul.** (Володимирська), brimming with history. **Bulv. Shevchenka** (Шевченка) and **vul. Khmelnitskoho** (Хмельницького) run perpendicular to these. The center of Kiev is vul. Kreshchatik's **Maidan Nezalezhnosti** (Майдан Незалежності), a fountain-filled fun-spot next to the post office. You can buy **maps** here or in any kiosk.

Tourist Office: Intercity Travel, Hospitalna vul., 4 (Госпітальна; tel. 294 31 11; fax 220 54 46), on the 3rd floor, room 304 inside Hotel Rus (Готел Рус). As close to a tourist office as you get in Kiev. They give out lists of travel agencies across Ukraine, as well as *Kiev in Your Pocket* guides. Open Mon.-Fri. 9am-6pm, Sat.-Sun. 10am-4pm. **Hotel Intourist's lobby,** behind Hotel Rus at vul. Hospitalna, 12, stocks *Kiev Post*—a newspaper with the latest info on the city and where to have fun. Both hotels are at M: Respublikansky stadion (Республіканський стадіон). Upon emerging from underground, cross the plaza bearing left around the stadium fence, then ascend right past the garbage bins. Rus is before Intourist.

Embassies: Australia, vul. Kominternu, 18 (Комінтерну; tel. 225 75 86). **Belarus,** vul. Sichnevoho Povstaniya, 6 (Січневого Повстанія; tel. 290 02 01). **Canada,** vul. Yaroslaviv Val, 31 (Ярославів Вал; tel. 224 53 60 or 225 43 89). **European Community Office,** vul. Lipska, 5 (Ліпська; tel. 291 89 67). **Latvia,** vul. Desyatinna, 4/6 (Десятинна; tel. 229 23 60). **Russia,** pr. Kutuzova, 8 (Кутузова; tel. 294 79 36 or 294 63 89). Open Mon., Wed., and Fri. 9am-noon. **South Africa,** Chervonoarmiska vul., 9/2 (Червоноармійська; tel. 227 71 72), in Makulon. **U.K.,** vul. Desyatinna, 9 (tel. 229 12 87 or 228 05 04), also serves the **Irish,** open Mon.-Fri. 9am-1pm and 2-5:30pm. **U.S.,** vul. Y. Kotsyubinskoho, 10 (Ю. Коцюбинського; tel. 244 73 49, emergency tel. 244 73 45, 24-hr. voice-mail tel. 244 73 44). From Maidan Nezalezhnosti, get on trolley #16 or 18 at the top of the square. Get off at the 4th stop, and walk down between the NIKA and the fruit stands. Entrance at right for American citizens. Don't be intimidated by the line for visas—simply wave your passport about and the security guards will point you to the proper metal detector. When calling, don't be shocked by the Ukrainian who initially answers the phone; if you have a passport or visa problem, ask for the *konsulstvo* and get the loving American service you deserve. Open Mon.-Fri. 2-6pm.

ORIENTATION AND PRACTICAL INFORMATION ■ 693

Currency Exchange: *Obmin-Valyut* (ОБМІН-ВАЛЮТ) windows on every street and side-alley, and even in every dingy café-bar. They usually take only US$ and DM. These exchange counters don't deal in traveler's checks or credit card advances—those are accepted by most banks which offer slightly worse rates. **Legbank** (ЛЕГ-БАНК), vul. Shota Rustaveli (Шота Руставелі). From M: Palats sportu (Палац спорту), go northwest on vul. Rognidinska (Рогнидінська) and turn right on Rustaveli. If you've come bearing traveler's checks, they'll send you to the next-door entrance with a code for the lock (in 1996, the code was 003). Punch it in, climb a flight of stairs, and give your name and passport number to the doorman. He'll then take you to a representative who'll take the checks and give you a receipt that you must take back to the main office where koupons are stocked in heaps (2% commission). Visa cash advances. Open Mon.-Fri. 9am-6pm. **NIKA** (НІКА), bulv. Shevchenka, 2 (M: Khreshchatik), also changes AmEx checks and gives cash advances. Open daily 9am-9pm.

Western Union: vul. Priorizna, 17 (Прорізна; tel. 229 52 36), off Khreshchatik. Open Mon.-Fri. 9am-7pm, Sat.-Sun. 11am-4pm.

Flights: Kiev-Boryspil Airport (Київ-Бориспіль) welcomes foreigners ½hr. (by car) east of the capital. Cash-only exchange office. US$10-per-person **buses** leave from the front of the terminal at 2:20 and 3pm and drop passengers off at Hotels Dnipro or Rus. Cheaper is the city bus or a *marshrutne taksi* (маршрутне таксі)—both dump the newly arrived at MR: Livoberezhna (Лівобережна) for a mere 1.30hv (every 20min.). Buy your ticket on the bus. If you must take a **taxi**, a US$70 should be haggled down to US$35, though natives barter to US$10.

Airline Offices: Air Ukraine, pr. Peremohy, 14 (Перемогу; tel. 216 70 40 or 276 70 59). **Austrian Airlines, SAS,** and **Swissair,** Chervonoarmiska vul., 9/2 (tel. 244 35 40; fax 244 35 45), inside the blue-fence Makulon, corner of vul. Khreshchatik and bulv. Shevchenka. **Bulgarian Airlines Balkan,** vul. Khmelnitskoho, 12. Open Mon.-Fri. 10am-1pm and 2-5pm. **Hungarian Airlines Malév,** Volodimirska vul., 20 (tel. 229 36 61). Open Mon.-Fri. 10am-5pm. Inside Hotel Khreshchatik at vul. Khreshchatik, 14-16 are: **Air France** (tel. 229 13 95; open Mon.-Fri. 9am-5pm), **Czech Airlines CSA** (tel. 228 02 96; open Mon.-Fri. 9am-5pm), **LOT** (tel. 228 71 50; open Mon.-Fri. 9am-5pm, Sat. 10am-2pm), and **Lufthansa** (tel. 229 62 97; open Mon.-Fri. 9am-5:30pm).

Trains: Kiev-Passazhirski (Київ-Пассажирський), Vokzalna pl. MR: Vokzalna or tram #2. **Tickets** can be purchased at Intourist window #42 on the 2nd floor. Open daily 8am-1pm, 2-7pm, and 8pm-7am. Beware any clerk who demands payment in US dollars at an unreasonable price. There are also potential ticket-buying intermediaries on the main floor. **Advance-Ticket Kasas,** bulv. Schevchenka, 38. MR: Universitet (Універсітет), cross and go left down the Big Man's street. Your passport will not be demanded, but the long lines and many lunch breaks lead to an easy hour's wait. Open Mon.-Fri. 8am-7pm, Sat.-Sun. 9am-6pm. Kiev is one of the few places in Ukraine where there's no shame in going through **Intourist** (see Tourist Offices, above). Scalpers toss US$2-3 on top of the ticket's real price, but they may have tickets that no one else has. Locals ask a clerk to check if the ticket is valid before handing over the money. *"Pro-VER-teh, po-ZHA-lus-tah, EH-tot bee-LYET VAZH-ny."* means "Please, check if this ticket is valid." If Intourist or the *kasas* claim not to have tickets, don't despair—check again the day of, 6 and 2 hours ahead (you're right, it does *not* make sense). To: Kamyanets-Podilsky (1 per day, 11hr., US$7); Lviv (5 per day, 12hr., US$9); Odesa (6 per day, 11hr., US$7); Simferopol (3 per day, 20hr., US$13); Uzhhorod (3 per day, 19hr., US$12). For **international tickets,** you will need to present your passports to let them charge you a higher price. Witness: Bratislava (daily, 26hr., US$100); Budapest (daily, 24hr., US$115); Bucharest (Mon., Thurs., Fri.; 27hr.; subject to change); Minsk (daily, 12-13hr., US$20); Moscow (6 per day, 15-17hr., US$30); Prague (daily, 30hr., US$115); Warsaw (1-2 per day, 20hr., US$55).

Buses: Tsentralny Avtovokzal (Центральний Автовокзал), Moskovska pl., 3 (Московська), services long-distance destinations. To: Minsk (2 per day, 20.15hv); Moscow (2 per day, 42.02hv); Kharkiv (2 per day, 16.19hv). **Darnitsa** (Дарниця), pr. Gagarina (Гагаріна), sends buses to Dnipropetrovsk. **Pivdenna,** pr. Akademika Hlushkova, 3 (Академика Глушкова), and **Podil,** vul. Nizhni Val, 15a (Нижній Вал),

Central Kiev

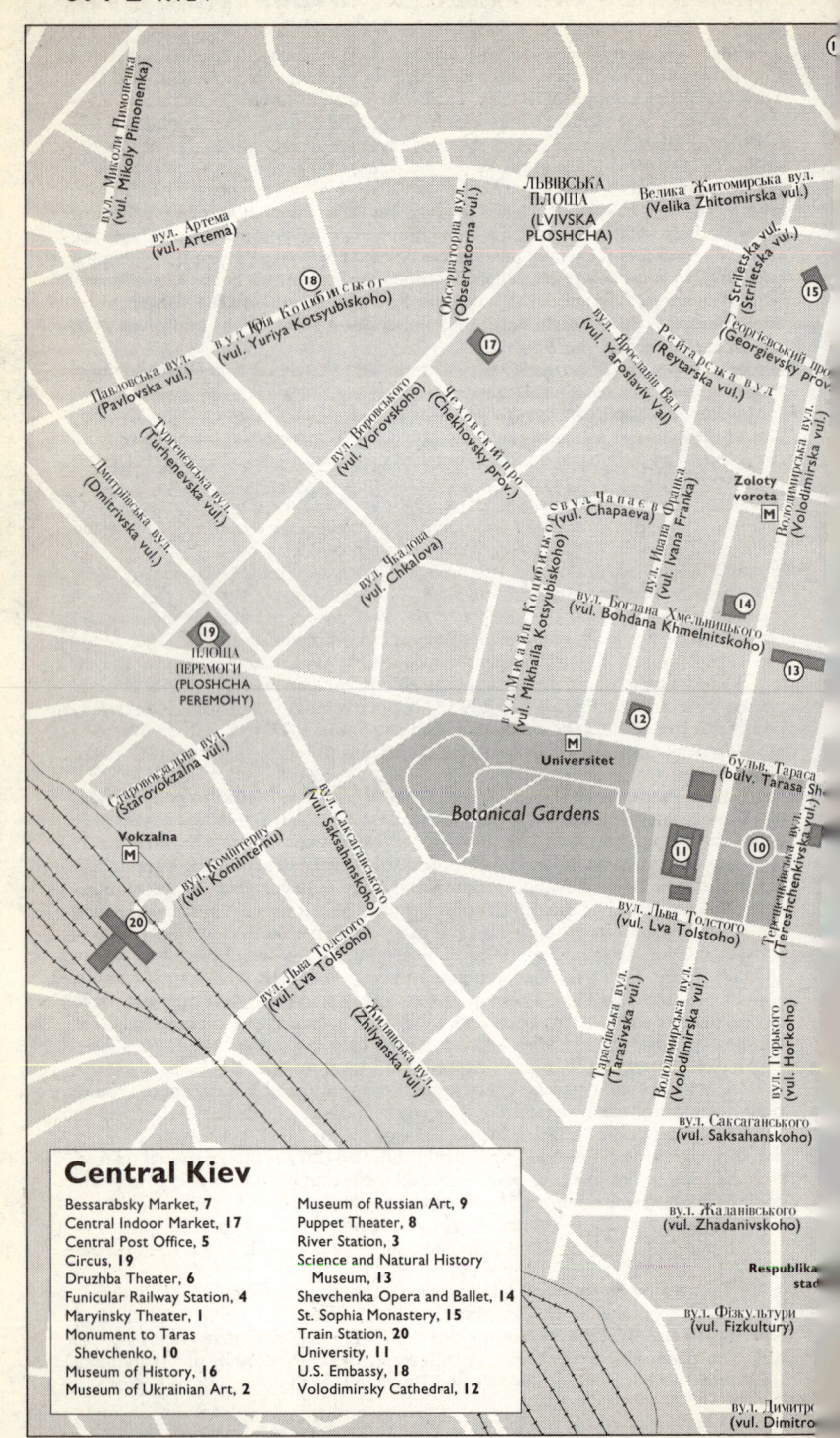

Bessarabsky Market, 7
Central Indoor Market, 17
Central Post Office, 5
Circus, 19
Druzhba Theater, 6
Funicular Railway Station, 4
Maryinsky Theater, 1
Monument to Taras
  Shevchenko, 10
Museum of History, 16
Museum of Ukrainian Art, 2
Museum of Russian Art, 9
Puppet Theater, 8
River Station, 3
Science and Natural History
  Museum, 13
Shevchenko Opera and Ballet, 14
St. Sophia Monastery, 15
Train Station, 20
University, 11
U.S. Embassy, 18
Volodimirsky Cathedral, 12

ORIENTATION AND PRACTICAL INFORMATION ■ 695

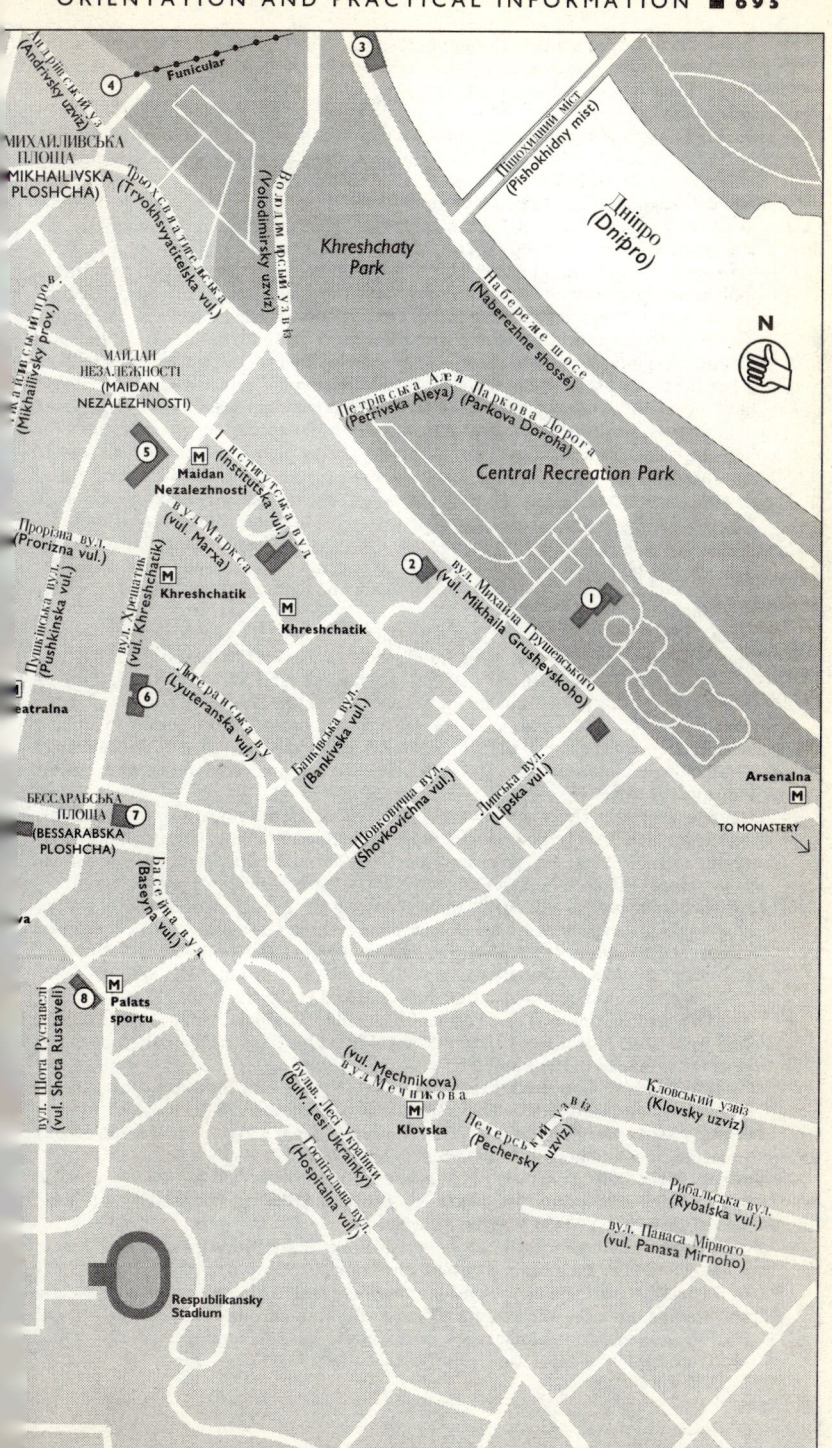

МИХАЙЛІВСЬКА ПЛОЩА (MIKHAILIVSKA PLOSHCHA)

Андріївський узвіз (Andriyivsky uzviz)

Funicular

Трьохсвятительська (Tryokhsvyatytelska vul.)

Володимирський узвіз (Volodimirsky uzviz)

Михайлівський пров. (Mikhailivsky prov.)

МАЙДАН НЕЗАЛЕЖНОСТІ (MAIDAN NEZALEZHNOSTI)

Пішохідний міст (Pishokhidny mist)

Дніпро (Dnipro)

Khreshchaty Park

Набережне шосе (Naberezhne shosse)

Петрівська Алея (Petrivska Aleya) Паркова Дорога (Parkova Doroha)

Central Recreation Park

(5) M Maidan Nezalezhnosti

Інститутська вул. (Instytutska vul.)

вул. Маркса (vul. Marxa)

Прорізна вул. (Prorizna vul.)

Пушкінська вул. (Pushkinska vul.)

M Khreshchatik
вул. Хрещатик (vul. Khreshchatik)

M Khreshchatik

(2) вул. Михайла Грушевського (vul. Mikhaila Grusheyskoho)

(1)

(6) Лютеранська вул. (Lyuteranska vul.)

Банківська вул. (Bankivska vul.)

Шовковична вул. (Shovkovichna vul.)

Липська вул. (Lipska vul.)

Arsenalna M

TO MONASTERY

БЕССАРАБСЬКА ПЛОЩА (BESSARABSKA PLOSHCHA) (7)

Басейна вул. (Baseyna vul.)

(8) M Palats sportu

вул. Шота Руставелі (vul. Shota Rustaveli)

(vul. Mechnikova) вул. Мечникова

M Klovska

Печерський узвіз (Pechersky uzviz)

Кловський узвіз (Klovsky uzviz)

бульв. Лесі Українки (bulv. Lesi Ukrainky)

Госпітальна вул. (Hospitalna vul.)

Рибальська вул. (Rybalska vul.)

вул. Панаса Мірного (vul. Panasa Mirnoho)

Respublikansky Stadium

N

connects to points south including Pereyaslav-Khmelnitsky. From M: Kontraktova pl. (Контрактова площа), take a short walk northwest along vul. Konstyantynivska (Констянтинівська) and hang a left onto vul. Nizhny Val.

Hydrofoils: Richkovy Port (Річковий Порт), on Poshtova pl. (Поштова; tel. 416 12 68). M: Poshtova pl. Boats brave the Dnipro's waves only as far as Cherkassy (2 per day, 3 on Sat.; 5½hr.; 8.14hv). Only the 7:30am boat stops in Pereyaslav-Khmelnitsky, offering to take you back to Kiev at 4:50pm (2¼hr., 5.21hv).

Public Transportation: Kiev's **Metropoliten** is clean and efficient, but it does not reach the university dorms. Local maps color-code the metro lines, though the cars and stations are all gray. Buy tokens at the "Каса" *(Kasa)* for 0.20hv or a monthly pass from a numbered kiosk for US$2.70. Monthly passes are good on all forms of public transportation. If you buy a pass, slide it through the slot on top of the turnstile to enter. You might get hit by the jaws of doom, but ignore them and go on. Guards watch all the time—you won't get away with anything. Check the map before you go down the escalator. At the bottom, the order of stations is posted on each side. In a place where some Latin subtitles would actually be useful (unlike near a bar), the stations are all in Cyrillic. Consult your handy *Let's Go* subway map. People may seem in a rude and unnecessary hurry to get on the train until the unforgiving doors slam on you. "Перехід" *(perekhid)* indicates a walkway to another station, "вихід у місто" *(vikhid u misto)* an exit onto the street, "вхід" *(vkhid)* an entrance to the Metro, "нема входу" *(nema vkhidu)* no entrance. Tickets for **trams, trolleys,** and **buses** are sold at numbered kiosks and must be punched on board. Autobus tickets cost 0.10hv, trolleybus/tram ones 0.20hv. The fine for not punching is a hefty US$0.70. Transport runs 6am-midnight, but some buses travel later. Beware trolleys and buses with identical numbers; they may have very different routes.

Taxis: A trip for a foreigner will cost a bundle; avoid taxis if you can. Otherwise, give the driver an address *near* your hotel; the driver won't assume so quickly that you're a foreign businessperson on an expense account. **State taxis** (tel. 058) are more consistently priced and are identifiable by the checkered sign on top. **Private cars** that function like taxis are cheaper; agree on a price before getting in and use your judgement. To signal that you need a ride, stand by the edge of the pavement and hold your arm down at a 45° angle. *Let's Go* does not recommend such private transport as safe.

Luggage Storage: There are several chambers at the train station, so remember where you left your bags. US$0.40. Open daily 8am-midnight, 1-7:30pm, 8pm-midnight, and 1-7:30am. Hotels charge more but are safer; you don't have to stay to store. **Hotel Rus** (see Tourist Offices, p. 692) charges US$2 per bag per night.

English Bookstore: Inside NIKA, bulv. Shevchenka, 2. MBR: Khreshchatik or Teatralna (Театральна). Books, papers, magazines. Carries the guide *Kiev City Guide*. AmEx, MC accepted. Open Mon.-Sat. 9am-9pm, Sun. 9am-8pm.

Pharmacy: Apteka #7 vnochi (Аптека #7 вночі), vul. Artema, 10 (Артема). Open 24hr. **Apteka,** corner of vul. Khmelnitskoho and vul. Ivana Franka (Івана Франка), sparkles with cleanliness and carries high-quality products. Open 24hr.; ring the bell 8pm-8am. **Hotel Intourist** and **Hotel Rus** also have well stocked hard-currency pharmacies in their lobbies.

Gay Information: Ganimed (Ганимед; tel. 419 17 82). Call for info in Russian and Ukrainian. Send mail to P.O. Box 833/5, Kyiv-211, Ukraine 254211.

Medical Assistance: Polyklinik #1, vul. Verkhna 5, room 336 (Верхна; tel. 296 66 68), treats foreign patients for hard currency. English spoken.

Express Mail: DHL, Sportivna pl., 1, room 101 (Спортивна; tel. 221 50 95), at Palats sportu. MG: Palats sportu. Open Mon.-Fri. 9am-6pm. **UPS,** vul. Ulianovikh, 11 (Ульяновіх; tel. 269 72 47). Open Mon.-Fri. 9am-6pm.

Post Office: vul. Khreshchatik, 22, next to Maidan Nezalezhnosti. **Poste Restante** at counters #24-28. Pre-stamped airmail envelopes (0.50hv) bought at counters #10 or 14 are the easiest way to send international mail. Otherwise, the staff weighs and stamps letters at the entrance behind the fountain. Info at counter #10 (no English spoken). To mail packages, enter on the Maidan Nezalezhnosti side. Open Mon.-Sat. 8am-9pm, Sun. 9am-7pm. **Postal code:** 252 001.

Kiev Metro

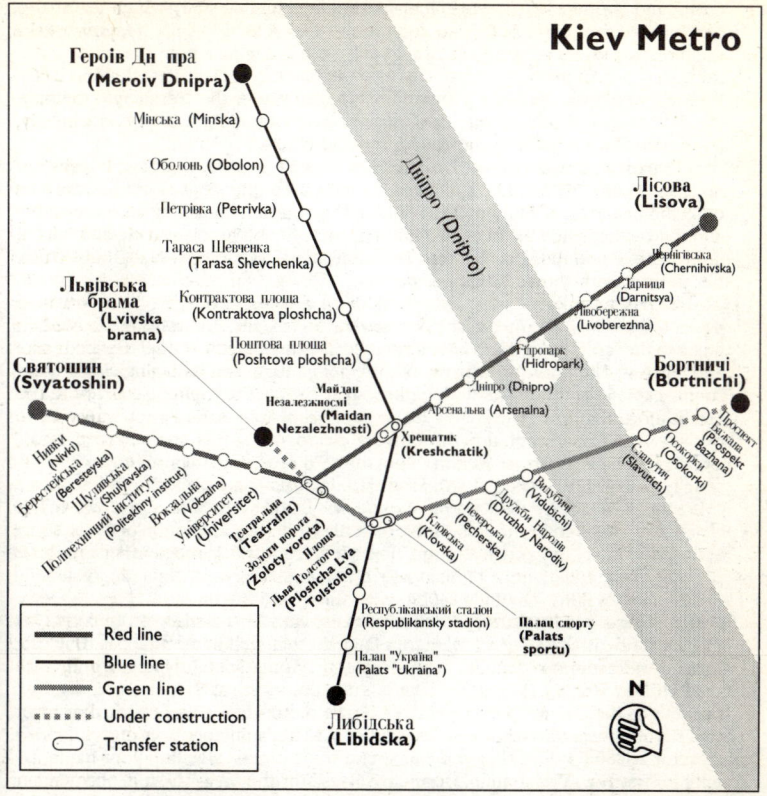

Stations (Red line):
- Героїв Дніпра (Meroiv Dnipra)
- Мінська (Minska)
- Оболонь (Obolon)
- Петрівка (Petrivka)
- Тараса Шевченка (Tarasa Shevchenka)
- Контрактова площа (Kontraktova ploshcha)
- Поштова площа (Poshtova ploshcha)
- Майдан Незалежності (Maidan Nezalezhnosti)
- Хрещатик (Kreshchatik)
- Театральна (Teatralna)
- Золоті ворота (Zoloty vorota)
- Льва Толстого (Ploshcha Lva Tolstoho)
- Республіканський стадіон (Respublikansky stadion)
- Палац "Україна" (Palats "Ukraina")
- Либідська (Libidska)

Stations (Blue line):
- Львівська брама (Lvivska brama)
- Святошин (Svyatoshin)
- Нивки (Nivki)
- Берестейська (Berezteiska)
- Шулявська (Shulyavska)
- Політехнічний інститут (Politekhny institut)
- Вокзальна (Vokzalna)
- Університет (Universitet)

Stations (Green line):
- Лісова (Lisova)
- Чернігівська (Chernihivska)
- Дарниця (Darnitsya)
- Лівобережна (Livoberezhna)
- Гідропарк (Hidropark)
- Дніпро (Dnipro)
- Арсенальна (Arsenalna)
- Печерська (Pecherska)
- Кловська (Klovska)
- Дружби Народів (Druzhby Narodiv)
- Видубичі (Vidubichi)
- Славутич (Slavutich)
- Осокорки (Osokorki)
- Проспект Бажана (prospekt Bazhana)
- Бортничі (Bortnichi)
- Палац спорту (Palats sportu)

Legend: Red line, Blue line, Green line, Under construction, Transfer station

Telephones: Mizhmisky Perehovorny Punkt (Міжміський Переговорний Пункт), at the post office or **Telefon-Telefaks** (Телефон-Телефакс) around the corner (entry on Khreshchatik). Some phones require an initial "8." To: Moscow US$0.60 per min.; U.K. and Ireland US$1.50; U.S. US$2.50. Tell how many minutes you want and pay up front. When making an international call from a private phone, dial 8, wait for a new tone, then dial 10, the country code, city code, and number. Both offices open 24hr. Calls within Kiev are free. **Utel phonecards** are available in denominations of US$10 and US$20 at the post office and upscale hotels. Utel phones are located in the post office, hotels, fancy restaurants, and Dim Ukrainski (Дім Український) across from Hotel Dnipro. **Phone code:** 044.

ACCOMMODATIONS AND CAMPING

Hotel prices in Kiev will seem rude at best. However, Kiev's large student population has to live somewhere. The setbacks are that "somewhere" ranges from somewhat distant to very distant, you never know who your roommate might be, and the *kommandant* may refuse to house a foreign tourist. **Diane Duval**—a former missionary living and working here—arranges accommodations from her home-based office (tel./fax 559 25 75, 9am-5pm Kiev time—that's GMT+2). If that fails, try her Russian- and Ukrainian-speaking colleagues (tel. 516 84 07; fax 516 84 86). She can arrange US$10-30 per person per night lodging. It's best to fax her a month in advance but two-day-notice emergencies are no stranger to Diane.

Grazhdanski Aviatski Institut Student Hotel, vul. Nizhinska, 29E (Нижінська; tel. 484 90 59). From MR: Vokzalna, go straight for 100m, take a left on vul. Kominternu, and another left on vul. Zhadanivskoho (Жаданівського) which leads to pl. Peremohy. From here, ride 5 stops on tram #1 or 3 to "Граматна" *(Hramatna)* in the direction you were walking. Walk back a block, swing a right onto vul. Nizhinska; cross the intersection diagonally into the block complex. Pass the first house, turn left, and walk until "Гостиница ФПК" appears above the entrance to the building 29E. Student hotel, not a dorm. Singles with shower 9.96hv. Doubles 8.92hv per person. Often full; call ahead. Cafeteria nearby (see p. 699).

Hotel Druzhba (Дружба), bulv. Druzhby Narodiv, 5 (Дружби Народів; tel. 268 33 87; fax 268 33 00). MB: Libidska (Либідська), take a couple steps south and turn left onto the major road. The hotel is 100m up on your left. Small, clean rooms. Short and narrow beds. It's the cheapest hotel in Kiev, the bathrooms work, and it's on a metro line. Often full, so call ahead and confirm reservations by fax. Doubles 50hv per person, with shower 70hv per person.

Hotel Bratislava (Братислава), vul. Malyshka, 1 (Малишка; tel. 551 76 44). M: Darnitsya (Дарниця). Take the west exit from the Metro, and Bratislava is the concrete beast to the left. The inside is not as Socio-Real as the outside though the beds short and narrow. The floors are hardwood, the colors dark, and with singles with bathroom at US$54 and doubles with bathroom at US$75, the rooms aspire to the high life in more than one way. They claim to sterilize toilets after each guest moves out—we can't confirm, but bathrooms are clean. AmEx, JCB, and Visa accepted.

Hotel Myr (Мир), prosp. 40-richcha Zhovtnya, 70 (40-річча Жовтня; tel. 264 96 46), near Holosivska pl. (Голосіївська). From MB: Libidska, take trolleybus #4 3 stops to "Магазин 'Ювілейний'" *(Mahazyn "Yuvileyny")*, and walk 500m. The still-Cyrillic "Гостиница Мир" tops the tall concrete wall, while the awning proclaims "Hotel Sputnik." This is the place, though. The view from the 15th floor isn't bad. The plunger in the toilets must be manually lifted. Exchange counter, café, restaurant, casino. Singles 80hv. Doubles 130hv, with shower 150hv.

Foreign Languages Institute, Chervonoarmiska vul., 73 (tel. 269 93 08; fax 227 67 88). Dorm beds US$3-7. Call Margarita Dvorzhetska well in advance, as they cater to groups. Reception Mon.-Fri. 10am-1pm and 2-5pm. Open July-Aug. 25 only.

Hotel Universitetsky (Університетський), vul. Lomonosova, 81 (Ломоносова). Take bus #38 to the end at "Ковалевської" *(Kovalevskoy)*, then go a little farther to the two 9-story buildings. ½hr. from the center. Call ahead before 5pm and ask for the director at 266 55 09. Ask if you can spend some nights, give him your name, and tell him when you're coming. Upon arrival, ask for the *"dee-REK-tor"* and insist on speaking with him, not the secretary. Refer to your phone call. 30hv per person in a double with shower.

Taras Shevchenko University, vul. Lomonosova. MB: Libidska, then bus #38 to "Гуртожиток" *(Hurtozhitok)*. Go to dorm #2, where the director's office is located. Same headache as with the Universitevsky (see above), but you're dealing with a different institution. The director's telephone number is 266 47 64; the dean's *(prorektor)* is 266 20 96.

Motel-Camping "Prolisok," pr. Peremohy, 179 (tel. 444 12 93). From MR: Svyatoshin (Святошин), take trolley #7 west to "Автостанція Дачна" *(Avtostantsiya Dachna)*, and go 2km down the highway. Dim, comfy motel doubles US$32.50 per person. Bungalows with kitchen and shower US$16 per person. Tent space US$7. A restaurant, sauna, and casino attract foreign tractor-trailer drivers.

FOOD

The number of people in Kiev's restaurant equals the number of coins in locals' pockets—very few. In fact, anticipate undisturbed solitude as you visit the capital's eating dens. Locals choose Kiev's speciality drinks over munchies: *Stolichnaya* vodka, *kava no skhidnomu* (кава по-східному; eastern-style coffee), and good-old *kvas* (квас). Vendors sell *kvas* (0.30hv per 0.5L) in the most-touristed areas—i.e. Khreshchatik and Podil, where most restaurants are found. Meals cost about US$7. Mini-Menu fast-food bars and markets sell cheaper food but the former are Western junk and the latter sell provisions requiring a kitchen for consumption. *Hastronom* (гастроном; supermarkets) abound, usually closing around 7pm.

FOOD

Restaurants

Stary Podil (Старий Поділь), vul. Sahaydochnoho, 6 (Сагайдочного). M: Poshtova ploshcha, walk right as you face the funicular. Hungry tourists dine in a white-washed room at lunchtime and a dusky boudoir at dinner. Stained glass provides the boudoir's only light. Cheap! The filling *kievskie bitki s garnirom* (cutlets with french fries and veggies) cost only 6hv. Open daily noon-midnight.

Pizzeria Lola (Пицца Лола), vul. Lva Tolstoho, 3 (Лва Толстого; tel. 224 74 23). MB: Ploshcha Lva Tolstoho, and follow the street west 100m. Lola's is in the basement on the left. So full of molten cheese, these Ukrainian pizzas put Italy to shame. Four wooden tables inside to support your personal circle of joy (additional seating outside). One-person cheese pizza 7.50hv, with 2 toppings 9hv. 0.5L of beer 3hv. Soda water 0.40hv. Open daily 11am-9pm.

Montanya Snack, vul. Volodimirska, 68 (tel. 221 70 45). MB: Ploshcha Lva Tolstoho, go west on Tolstoho, take the 2nd left on Volodimirska. Mostly Lebanese, with fast-food choices. Dishes come in "sandwich" or "meal" format—the first in pita and paper, the second on plate with veggies. Chicken shwarma sandwich 3.50hv. Open Mon.-Fri. noon-11pm, Sat.-Sun. noon-midnight.

Vesuvio Pizza (Везувіо Піцца), vul. Reytarska, 25 (Рейтарська; tel. 228 30 28). M: Poshtova, cross the square and bear right onto vul. Velika Zhitomirska (Велика Житомирська), hustle down the 2nd street to the left (vul. Striletska—Стрілецька) until its crosses Reytarska. This quiet, clean joint is a fave of refined French expats. If Mt. Vesuvius could taste its namesake's concoctions, it would orgasm, covering Italy in seeds of embarrassment. Less cheesy and more crispy than Lola's. Pizza from 9hv, real juice 1.30hv per glass. Open daily 10am-9pm.

Café Breeze (Кафе Бриз), vul. Igorivska, 5 (Іґорівська). MB: Poshtova. With back to the funicular, go left on vul. Sahaydochnoho, and hang the first right. Breeze blows down the stairs. Small niches with 4-person tables line the narrow yacht-like passage. Clients nibble seafood appetizers (3.50-7.00hv) and veggie-and-egg salads (1.40-3.15hv). Open daily 11am-11pm.

Yidalnya Kmutsya (Їдальня Кмуця), prosp. Kosmonavta Komarova (Космонавта Комарова), at vul. Hramatna. Close to the Student Hotel (see p. 697 for directions). The *yidalnya* occupies the 2nd floor of the tile-and-dirty-glass building. Fill a tray with *kasha* (buckwheat), rolls, eggs, and chicken. Then join the students and blue-collar workers stuffing themselves for a buck. Open daily 8am-7pm.

Kentucky Beirut Chicken, bulv. Shevchenka, 5 (tel. 229 02 94). Yup! A KFC imitation with Lebanese ownership. The higher prices are due to the Middle Eastern cabbage and sour cream salad. A small portion of chicken with fries costs US$6. English menu. Call for take-out or delivery (pay for the inflated price of the taxi).

Café Retro, vul. Rustaveli, 4 (tel. 225 23 55). MG: Palats sportu. The many mirrors allow the lonely diner to ponder his/her alter ego while reflecting the red carpeting and ornate ceilings. Late 80s American divas keep begging you to take a chance as you pick at a veggie salad (4hv) and a steak or variations entrée (9hv), and bolt down an espresso (1hv). Un-order the stale bread sitting on the table to avoid paying for it. Open daily 11am-10pm.

The Studio, Muzeyny provulok, 4 (Музейний пров.; tel. 228 72 08; fax 228 00 50). MBR: Maidan Nezalezhnosti. A right branch off vul. Mikhaila Hrushevskoho (Михайла Грушевського) as you walk southeast. Classy way to blow your budget while drooling over the British yuppies. Nightly jazz (11pm-2am) accompanies that 18hv veggie-and-meat salad, entrée, sandwich, or burger. Well stocked bar. English menu. AmEx, MC, and Thomas Cook traveler's checks and Eurocard, MC, and Visa accepted. Restaurant open daily 11:30am-11:30pm, bar til 2am.

Cafés

Kavyarnya Svitoch (Кав'ярня Світоч), vul. Velika Zhitomirksa, 8a (tel. 228 33 82). On the right as you follow the street from Mikhailivska ploshcha. *The* place to come for black coffee (1hv), accompanied by a toothsome chocolate (0.50hv). Svitoch—a famous Lviv confectioners'—opened its Kiev outlet in 1995, with this café next door. Popular with students. Open daily 9am-9pm.

Kalyna Kondyterska—Caffé Mokador (Калина Кондитерська), vul. Moskovska 29a (tel. 290 53 96). Out of MR: Arsenalna (Арсенальна), veer left, and walk 500m. Marble-tiled floors, large wood-framed windows, and 6 black-and-gray tables make the café a snug corner in which to dine on divine pastries. Sweet treasures for only 1.30hv apiece. Try the delectable pyramid (пірамід)—layers of cream and rich chocolate. Cappuccino (3.50hv), tea (1.50hv). Open daily 10am-10pm.

Kafe U Gheorga (Кафе У Георга), vul. Khreshchatik, 10. MBR: Maidan Nezalezhnosti. The main street's best grotto for a lunchtime shot of *Stolichnaya*. A semicircular counter, no tables, loud music about love and San Francisco, and sober, vodka-loving regulars. If vodka sounds too scary, order an eastern coffee (0.66lv), and chat with the barperson about your low tolerance. Open daily 10am-10pm.

Markets

Ukraine is all-European with its continental love of buying food that's fresh-no-preservatives, even though swarms of flies hover over it. The French have their *marchés*, the Kievans their *rynki*. Same continent, same difference.

Bessarabsky Rynok (Бессарабський Ринок; tel. 224 89 34), vul. Khreshchatik and bulv. Shevchenka, but technically at Bessarabska ploshcha, 2. The best of the Ukrainian bazaar-chic sprawl out their goodies here. Anything sells—soap, knitting needles, plum preserves. Consider coming here just for the Ukrainian countryside spirit in the middle of Kiev. Open Mon. 7am-5pm, Tues.-Sun. 7am-7pm.

Volodymyrsky-Kolhospny Rynok (Володимирський-Колгосний Ринок), vul. Chervonoarmiska, between vul. Telmana (Гельмана) and vul. V.-Libidska. MBG: Palats Ukraina (Палац України). Even larger than the Bessarabsky. Same deals: flowers, provisions, clothes, tapes, and unhappy furry animals. Open daily 10am-7pm.

Kolhospny Rynok (Колгоспний Ринок), vul. Vorovskoho (Воровського) and vul. Observatorna (Обсерваторна). 80s Europop stars on tape. Food, shoes, and Asian remakes of a most American symbol: the t-shirt. Bargains and bizarre items can be found at the row of kiosks upstairs. Open daily 10am-7pm.

SIGHTS

A millennium as the capital has left Kiev with a store of historical sights. Many of these mementos are crumbling only to give the downtown districts a deep-down decadent aura. Come now because renovations are underway, and in five years, the naturally weathered beauty may get a facelift and lose itself in thick polish.

Vul. Khreshchatik and Environs

The center of downtown Kiev lies on vul. Khreshchatik, a broad commercial avenue largely built after WWII—a monument to Soviet-style bigness. The street begins at the intersection with bulv. Shevchenka, where **Lenin** gazes serenely into the future surrounded by inspirational sayings—one of the rare Communist monuments in Kiev that has not been desecrated. Across the street, the blue-fenced **Makulon** complex, Chervonoarmiska vul., 9/2, was once the residence of top party officials; now it's the place to live for foreign businesspeople and ambassadors. On the opposite corner, **Bessarabsky Rynok** (see "Markets" above) is one of the most ornate of its kind. Walking along vul. Khreshchatik, you can check out the **central department store TSUM** (ЦУМ), where everything is sold in a terrifically confusing jumble of counters (open Mon.-Sat. 9am-8pm).

A few more steps lead to the corner of vul. Khmelnitskoho. Stroll up this street to the recently built and highly nationalistic **Muzey Literatury Ukrainy** (Музей Літератури України) on the left at #11 (open Thurs.-Tues. 9am-5pm; 0.20hv, students 0.05hv), and the **Opera House** on the right. The museum traces Ukrainian literature from its inception to the present, quoting Ivan Franko and Taras Shevchenko the entire way. English-speaking guides are available only through Intourist for an exorbitant rate, but the museum staff will happily explain everything in Ukrainian. Next door, the **Dramatichny Teatr** shows Ukrainian productions nightly.

Back on vul. Khreshchatik, you can spot the **archway** to vul. Lyuteranska (Лютеранська), which leads to a quiet, residential neighborhood along a street lined with pretty stone façades. The next archway leads to Kiev's most cosmopolitan area, *pasazh* with fancy, high-priced cafés and bars. Suddenly, you arrive at **Maidan Nezalezhnosti,** or "Independence Plaza" (formerly October Revolution Sq.). This is the very center of town; book vendors, occasional musicians, Tolkienists, angel-headed hipsters, and others taking a breather fill the terrace around the large fountains. It was the site of the 1905 uprising and of the execution of Nazi war criminals; the **statue of the little guy with a halo and crooked sword** was unveiled in 1996.

Veer to the right past the square onto vul. Institutska (Інститутська)—another fancy-façade-filled promenade. Just to the left as Institutska starts its ascent glows the bright-yellow **October Palace of Culture** (Жовтневий Палац Культури; Zhovtnevy Palats Kultury)—a Neoclassical rival to the equally eye-catching Rococo **Natsyonalny Bank Ukrainy** (Націоналный Банк України), also on the left. Tracing back from the bank and rocking your way to the left down vul. Baikova (Байкова) brings you to an architectural landmark of Kiev—the **Horodetsky Building** (Будинок Городецького; Budinok Horodetskoho). Its sadistic gargoyles make Gotham's Penguin and friends look like Barbies. Men and women gather to debate away the evening over tankards of beer or *kvas*. Right-wing, left-wing, and tourist propaganda is sold along the fountain walls, and the occasional street performer pleases crowds. At night, the metro stop underneath shelters **Kiev's best street musicians.**

Continuing along vul. Khreshchatik leads to the **Ukrainian House** (Український Дім; Ukrainsky Dim) on the left, across from Hotel Dnipro. Formerly the Lenin Museum, this stepchild of Communist architecture now houses commercial and cultural exhibitions and a carnival of kiosks. Up the stairs is **Khreshchaty Park.**

Khreshchaty Park

Referred to by locals as the "Yoke", the silver croquet wicket that towers over the park is the **Arch of Brotherhood,** a monument to Russian-Ukrainian union. The park is actually a series of parks, with many excellent views. To the left as you go through the Yoke you can see Prince Vladimir holding up a cross, overlooking the river where he had the whole city baptized in 988 despite freezing temperatures. Go right at the arch and into the park for the monument to brave football players. As the story goes, invading Nazis discovered that one of their prisoners was a member of the Dynamo Kiev soccer team; they rounded up the other players and arranged a "death match" against the German army's Luftwaffe team. Despite their weakened condition and a referee dressed in a Gestapo uniform, the Dynamo team won the match 3-0. They were immediately thrown into a concentration camp, where most of them perished in front of a firing squad. Farther still stands the **Maryinsky Palace,** built by Bartolomeo Rastrelli, the same guy who designed Kiev's St. Andrew's Church and much of St. Petersburg. The palace was built just for Tsaritsa Elizabeth's visit in the 1750s. It's closed to the public. Across from the lovely garden, where you are not allowed, stands the Ukrainian poet and revolutionary **Lesya Ukrainka,** gazing sensitively at the splendor of aristocrats and pondering the plight of Ukrainian workers. The park then moves towards Arsenalna metro stop, but if you resist its rigid paths, you might find the **Grave of Prince Askoldel,** who was murdered by the usurping Prince Oleg in 882. The most distinguished citizens of Kiev used to be buried here with Askoldel, but they've since moved.

Bulv. Tarasa Shevchenka

A walk past Lenin's metal figure takes you up a pleasant and shady, albeit broad and busy, street. The boulevard is dedicated to the poet Taras Shevchenko, whose paintings and poetry re-invented the Ukrainian tongue in the mid-19th century. Banished in 1847, he never returned to Kiev. At #12 stands the **Taras Shevchenko Museum,** one of the largest and most beautiful literary museums in the former USSR; the museum is well kept for good reason. It contains a huge collection of Shevchenko's sketches, paintings, and prints, as well as his correspondence and poetry. Exhibits are labeled in Ukrainian and Russian; an English tour is under 0.50hv (tel. 224 25 56; open Tues.-Sun. 10am-5pm; closed last Fri. of the month). On the street's left side, inside one of Kiev's many parks, a famous **monument** to the hero stands at least 1½ times taller than Lenin's paltry form. His namesake **university,** on the park's other side, still leads independent thought in Ukraine. Farther up stands the many-domed ochre **Volodimirsky Cathedral,** bulv. Tarasa Shevchenka, 20, built to commemorate 900 years of Christianity in Kiev. The interior blends Byzantine styles with Art Nouveau.

Mikhailivska Ploshcha and Environs

A funicular ascends the steep hill west of M: Poshtova, landing next to the recently up-graded **Mikhailivska ploshcha** (Михайлівська). The sprucing up has come with a new (May 1996) statue of snow-white Princess Olga surrounded by death-white St. Cyril, Methodius, and virtuous St. Andrew the (Orthodox) Apostle. The 10th-century Kievan Rus's overlady posed here petrified as early as 1911; she has since had many ups and downs, but hopes to hang onto her current upright elegance.

A left on vul. Tryokhsvyatitelska (Трьохсвятительська) as you're walking from the funicular leads to several interesting churches. First on the left sits the petite, white-washed and onion-domed **Church of the Holy Apostle Ioan Bohoslav** (Храм святого апостала Іоана Богослава; *Khram svyatoho Apostola Ioana Bohoslava*). Entrance is gratis, but most visitors buy a small candle (0.20hv) from the priests at the door. The dark niche shelters richly colored, gilded icons (open daily 8am-8pm).

Continuing down the street on the right, the stolid, Roman Catholic **Church of St. Aleksandr** (Костьол св. Олександра; *Kostyol svyatoho Oleksandra*) mixes serenity with multilingual holy chatter, offering masses in seven languages (open daily 7am-8pm; English mass Sun. 8pm).

Dandy back to Olga through **Volodmirska Hirka** park, full of tiny pavilions, panoramic viewposts over the Dnipro, and sculptures by folk artists who had one shot too many. This is a favorite gay cruising spot. Behind Olga to the right, the small Desatynna takes off to the beginning of **Volodimirska vulitsya.** Hang a left onto said street at #2 to find **Istorichny Muzey Ukrainy** (Історичний Музей України; tel. 228 48 64), which contains exhibits from the Stone Age to the present. Out front lie the very foundations of the Old City, preserved under glass. Tours are available in Ukrainian and German (open Thurs.-Tues. 10am-6pm). The museum sits near **ploshcha Khmelnitskoho,** a square of gorgeous 18th- and 19th-century buildings surrounding the monument to **Bohdan Khmelnitsky,** another national hero, frozen while checking his horse in mid-gallop. Across the *ploshcha* towers the enormous, elaborate **St. Sophia Monastery Complex,** Volodimirska vul., 24 (currently closed to the public). This is what tourists come to Kiev to see: golden onion domes, decorated façades, and exquisite Byzantine icons from the 11th century. The monastery was Kievan Rus's cultural center and the site of its first library. It is still the focal point in the increasingly complex question of Ukrainian nationalism. In July 1995, the Uniate Church wanted to bury its patriarch here, a request the government turned down. When the funeral procession led by the Ukrainian nationalist militia attempted entry into the complex, they were violently denied by the police. If it re-opens, act Ukrainian when you buy the US$0.30 entrance ticket; otherwise you may be charged US$3. Down Volodimirska vul. 300m stand the **Golden Gates** (Золоты Ворота; Zoloty vorota), which are actually made of wood and stone. They have stood here since 1037, marking the entrance to the city and separating it from the wilds outside. A museum devoted to the gates is now housed inside them (open Fri.-Tues. 10am-5:30pm, Wed. 10am-4:30pm; 10hv, students 0.50hv).

Andrivsky Uzviz and the Podil District

The easiest way to see the cobblestone **Andrivsky uzviz**—a winding road lined with cafés, souvenir vendors, and galleries—is to ride up and walk down. A funicular carries couch *kartoshki* up Andrivsky uzviz from MB: Poshtova every five minutes (daily 6:30am-11pm; 0.20hv). Look for signs saying "Виставка" (exhibition). Next to the entrepreneurs selling real Ukrainian pipes and Soviet Army hats, some independent galleries show the newest and boldest work Ukrainian visual artists have to offer, but most just sell touristy paintings of the street's looming, beautiful **St. Andrew's Cathedral** (closed for renovations in summer 1996; should be open by 1997). The edifice in question gazes proudly down on its street; you can learn about it and the avenue below at the **Andrivsky Uzviz Museum** at #22 (tel. 416 03 98; open Wed.-Sun. 11am-7pm; 0.50hv), but before starting the climb down, ascend the **Castle Hill Steps,** at the crossroads of Desatynna, Andrivsky, and Volodimirska, from where the best photos of the cathedral are taken. Once atop the steps, wander around the grounds on which the **Tithe Church** (Десатунна Церква; Desatynna Tserkva) used to convert pagan Kievans to Christianity in the 10th century. This, the oldest stone church of Kievan Rus (ca. 989-96), survived history only to be purposefully destroyed in 1937. Now only the stone foundations trace the architectural plan. Next to them, the gray **Ethnographic Museum** (Національний Музей Історії України; Natsyonalny Muzey Istorii Ukrainy) is worth a stroll through (open Thurs.-Tues. 10am-6pm; last admission 5:30pm; closed last Thurs. of every month). Back on Andrivsky uzviz, past the museum, **Bulgakov's House** at #13 (tel. 416 31 88) tells you all you need to know about the *White Guard*—but is only worthwhile if you've read the book (open Thurs.-Tues. 10am-6pm; 45-min. tour US$0.50).

Andrivsky uzviz spills out onto **Kontraktova ploshcha**—the center of **Podil,** Kiev's oldest district. Its collection of beautiful—and disintegrating—façades is colored by small **churches** of all faiths. In the *ploshcha's* north corner lies the **Kiev-Mohyla Academy,** the oldest university in this part of the world. Closed by the Communists, in 1996 it graduated its first class after reopening in 1992. Ramble around and chances are you'll bump into an American exchange student or at least fluent English-speaking Ukrainians.

Babyn Yar and St. Cyril's

The moving WWII monument at **Babyn Yar** (Бабин Яр) consists of a large group of carved figures and commemorates the place where victims of the Nazis were buried starting in September 1941. Although the plaques state that 100,000 Kievans died here, current estimates double that figure. Many of the victims, most of them Jews, were buried alive. Take trolley #27 eight stops from MB: Petrivka or trolley #16 from Maidan Nezalezhnosti (about 10 stops, depending on the optional stops). The monument stands in the park near the TV tower, at the intersection of vul. Oleny Telihy (Олени Телігн) and vul. Melnikova (Мельникова).

From Babyn Yar, four stops on trolley #27 northeast (catch it on the same side of vul. Telihy as Babyn Yar) towards MB: Petrivka take you to **St. Cyril's Church** (Кирилівська Церква; Kyrylivska Tserkva), the multi-domed shelter of Kiev's best frescos. From the trolley stop, ascend the stairs to you right. You can read the English version of the church's history inside. Many art students practice their drawing skills here. (Open Sat.-Wed. 10am-6pm, Thurs. 10am-5pm. 3.50lv; Ukrainians 1hv, students 0.20hv.)

Lavra and Environs

Kiev's oldest and holiest religious site is the mysterious **Kievo-Pecherska Lavra Monastery** (Києво-Печерська Лавра), which deserves a full day of exploration. Once the center of Orthodox Christianity, it housed monks, who lived and were subsequently mummified and entombed in its **caves**—the most interesting part of the complex. Buy a candle for 0.20hv as you enter in order to see. Don't wear anything too casual or the monks will get sore at you; they don't like people—when in the caves, you're only allowed to look at the monks whose palms are facing up (open Wed.-Mon. 9-11:30am and 12:30-4pm). Random people offer tours of the underground as you enter the complex, but the rotting remains are self-explanatory: these people were holy, so they get to be covered with gold-threaded fabrics after death. There are several churches, gardens, and museums on the grounds, as well as the Italian embassy. Most noteworthy are: the 18th-century **Great Cave Bell Tower,** from which you can get a fantastic view of the river and apartment blocks on the horizon mingling with golden domes (open Wed.-Mon. 10am-6pm; 1hv, students 0.50hv); the 12th-century **Holy Trinity Church,** which serves as the entrance to the monastery and whose interior (take a left upon entering) contains some beautiful frescos, a 600-kg censer, and the ruins of the 1073-78 **Assumption Cathedral,** destroyed many times, most recently by the Nazis. The monastery, which was a fortress and has 2m-thick walls to prove it, is also just a nice place to perambulate. The 2hv (students 1hv) paid at a *kasa* near the entrance gives you admission to all the churches and exhibitions but not the museums. The large ticket shows a map of the complex, though the labels are in Russian only. From MR: Arsenalna, turn left as you exit and walk 20 minutes down vul. Sichnevoho Povstaniya. Bus #20 can also take you here (2 stops southeast).

Farther along the same road is the hideously static metal **Motherland,** or huge lady with a little sword. The sword used to be bigger but was shortened when the monks raised a stink about it being higher than the bell tower. The statue celebrates the WWII victory and was designed by the wife of the sculptor of the Volgograd statue. Plans to tear down the tin lady and replace her with a monument to the victims of Chernobyl have not yet come to fruition, but the statue might fall of her own accord due to poor construction.

ENTERTAINMENT AND NIGHTLIFE

Sports and the Outdoors

During the soccer season (late spring until autumn), don't miss **Dynamo Kiev,** one of the top teams in Europe, even if soccer bores you. Check with the *kasa* at the Respublikansky Stadium, vul. Chervonoarmiska. MB: Respublikansky stadion.

On hot summer days, locals hang out at **Hidropark** (Гідропарк; MR: Hidropark), where you'll find an **amusement park** and **beach** on an island in the Dnipro. Tucked in a corner near the bridge, **Venice Beach of Ukraine** is where young buffs lift spare automobile parts to keep in shape. The beach has showers, toilets, and changing booths, yet no one seems to charge admission. **Rent boats** at Otdykh na vode—Fregat (Отдых на воде—Фрегат), on the east shore of Hidropark, near the metro bridge (boat or waterbike 2hv per hour; open daily 9am-8pm; last rental 6pm). The beach is also a hot pick-up spot for the college-age crowd (no charge).

The daily and weekend **bazaars** in the summer at Respublikansky Stadion are an experience in themselves, even if you don't buy any of the myriad sodas and cigarettes hauled here from all over the former Soviet Union. Everything is wholesale—buy in bulk and start your own kiosk. Try to come to Kiev on July 16, **Ukrainian Sovereignty Day,** when the city becomes a moveable feast, or on the last weekend in May, **Kiev Days,** when Andrivsky uzviz is jam-packed with smiling faces, *shashlyk* stands, orchestras, and souvenir stands.

Performances

Some of the most interesting theaters are on Andrivsky uzviz; most close in summer. For **tickets,** check with any **teatralna kasa** (театральна каса; open Tues.-Sun. 9am-5pm; tickets US$2-3). Most shows are in Ukrainian or Russian. Every March, however, international troupes come for a two-week **theater festival,** where you can hear *Macbeth* performed in Austrian or *Master and Margharita* in Australian.

- **Philharmonic,** Volodimirsky uzviz, 2 (tel. 229 62 51). Classic and classical. Undergoing renovations in 1996.
- **Shevchenka Opera and Ballet Theater,** Volodimirska vul., 50 (tel. 224 71 65 or 229 11 69). MRG: Teatralna. Huge and imposing. Several shows each week at noon and 7pm. Ticket office open Tues.-Sat. noon-2pm and 4-7:30pm, Sun. 11am-1:30pm.
- **Opereta** (Оперета), vul. Chervonoarmiska, corner of vul. Zhilyanska (Жилянська). MB: Respublikansky stadion. Favorites by Kalman, Lehar, and Strauss.
- **Kiev Youth Theater** (Київский Молодий Театр; Kyivsky Molody Teatr), vul. Prorizna, 17 (tel. 224 62 51). Possibly Kiev's best. In 1996, tickets for the opening night of Hašek's *Švejk* went for US$150 each. Irregular performances.
- **Lesya Ukrainka Russian-Drama Theater** (Театр Русской Драмы им. Леси Украинки; Teatr Russkoy Dramy imeni Lesi Ukrainki), vul. Khmelnitskoho, 5 (tel. 224 90 63). Classic and experimental Russian repertoires. Tickets sold Thurs.-Tues. noon-3pm and 4-7pm, Wed. noon-3pm and 4-6pm.
- **Puppet Theater,** vul. Shot Rustaveli, 13 (tel. 220 90 65) in an active synagogue (the Soviets were not without their wacky ironic flair). For adults and children.

Koleso, Andriyivsky uzviz, 8 (tel. 416 05 27). MB: Kontraktova Ploshcha. Theater and café. Ticket office open show days 5:30-7pm. Schedule posted outside.

Ivan Franko Ukrainian Drama Theater, pl. Ivana Franka, 3 (tel. 229 59 91). Serious, popular, and cheap.

Nightlife

Perhaps it is the foreboding presence of St. Sophia Cathedral or the fact that by midnight many people are too drunk to walk, but the capital simply doesn't live up to its big-city billing when it comes to nightlife. Although the scene is improving, young residents still take their bottles of *Stolichnaya* to the beautiful dark parks or **Maidan Nezalezhnosti,** where the fountains and spontaneous jazz are lit up.

The Cowboy Bar, vul. Khreshchatik, 15 (manager's tel. 244 34 64), in the *passazh.* A piece of Ukraine-imagined America on Kiev's Euro-chi-chi street that gathers all of Kiev's grunge. Raw, unpainted wood filled with cigarette smoke and live music nightly after 9pm. Behind the bar, where *Obolon* flows at 3hv per 0.33L, a "Wanted" poster promises a reward for the capture of "Robber boss Wild Bill." Cactus-land favorites like chili con carne (3-5hv). Open daily 6pm-2am.

Arizona BBQ, vul. Naberezhno-Khreshchatitska, 25 (Набережно-Хрещатицька; tel. 416 24 38). MB: Poshtova, then follow the river upstream for 5min. The bar/restaurant is on the left. Expats among the served and the servers. Thronged with multilingual empty chatter and overflowing with expensive beer (0.5L Obolon 5.70hv). Appetizers US$5, entrées US$8-12. Ironically, it's the unpretentious atmosphere for which you pay. The place last year's Cosmo crowd was schmoozing in 1996. AmEx, Eurocard, MC, Visa accepted. Open daily 11am-3am.

Rock Café (Рок Кафе), vul. Karla Marxa, 10. M: Maidan Nezalezhnosti, walk 300m along the street to the right of the giant steps. The café is on your right. Unpretentious expats hang with their local acquaintances. An easy going coffeeshop evolves into a busy cocktail bar at night. Plum coffee or ½-glass of sparkling water for 2hv, but you should know by now that in Kiev, hipness equals money. Outdoor seating. Open daily noon-midnight.

Vechirny Kyiv (Вечірній Київ), vul. Khreshchatik, 15, in the *passazh.* Some call its ice cream the best in Kiev. Walnuts and apricots in their creamy'n'frozen state do wonders for the palate. All natural. 100g scoop 1.20hv. Outdoor patio for seeing and being seen. Open daily 11am-4pm and 5-11pm.

Kiev's most popular discos pale next to the shining stars of Moscow, but keep you ears open for occasional **raves.** Discos **2000, Flamingo, Club Hollywood,** and **River Palace** are the primary rave breeding grounds. Covers run a steep US$10-15.

Gay and Lesbian Entertainment

After a local gay organization caused a scandal with a disastrously disorganized conference on gay activism in Central-Eastern Europe, the gay scene in Ukraine has failed to take off, unlike the one in Moscow. Because of the inability (so far) to organize, gay **nightlife** is limited to private parties and slightly irregular discos. The safest **cruising area** runs along the M: Khreshchatik-Bessarabska ploshcha promenade.

In the summer, the scene is revived substantially thanks to Hidropark; follow the mob to *Molodizhny Plyazh* (Youth Beach). There, buy a 0.50hv boat ride across a channel to the **beach** opposite, where the crowd is mixed and clothes optional. There's also a fully gay beach nearby, but it's muddy. Also, **Videosalon** (Видеосалон) of the Zelyony Teatr (Зелений Театр) projects gay films daily around 10pm.

For new-in-town **lesbians,** the Ganimed meetings and phoneline (see Gay Information, p. 696) and the mixed beach are the only options.

■ Near Kiev: Pereyaslav-Khmelnitsky
(Переяслав-Хмельницький)

Once the Cossacks' favorite military base, Pereyaslav witnessed the signing of both the Russian-Ukrainian 1654 agreement, which allied Ukraine with Russia and, five years later, a treaty which gave the Russian tsar control over the country. Perhaps in anger over the town's role in their subordination, Ukrainians neglected Pereyaslav over the next three hundred years. Pereyaslav, unsurprisingly, has been trying to hang on to its past glory—its noble heritage proven by ornate cupolas rising above parks' greenery. The town's most obvious attempt at historic preservation is its "Museum of Folk Architecture", an outdoor museum dedicated to the evolution of Ukrainian villages, from thatched roofs and ornate houses to Social-Realist monuments dedicated to the peasant spirit. Blind-ended paths that go off from the loop in different directions lead to the most grandiose sights: icon-filled churches, windmills, and kulak homes. Many houses keep collections of old instruments, ceramic art, or vehicles, each house guarded by a stately or scythe-bearing watchperson. Although not every old domicile and still-weeded vegetable garden is worth a stop, two sights are a must. Just to the left of the entrance extends a **Socialist-Realist park**, with sculptures, mosaics, and bas-reliefs, spiked with pre-WWII airplanes, trucks, and tractors. The second sight sits on an island set in the *skansen's* pond. A pagan temple stands watch over a meadow which seems made for that brown-bag lunch you brought from Kiev (*skansen* open Thurs. and Sat.-Tues. 10am-5pm, Fri. noon-5pm; 0.40hv, guided tour 2hv).

The bright cupola rising above Pereyaslav proper belongs to **Voznesensky Monaster** (Вознесенський Монастерь). Since 1975, it has functioned as the **Diorama-Museum of the Struggle for the Dnipro in the Region of Pereyaslav-Khmelnitsky** (Діорама-Музей Боï за Дніпро в Районі Переяслава-Хмельницького). The 0.20hv entry is a small price to pay for the thrill you get inside, as the diorama (a three-dimensional semi-panorama) almost makes you almost feel as if you're in the trenches (open Thurs.-Tues. 10am-5pm). A stride further down vul. Khmelnitskoho, on the left, **Muzey Kobzarstva** (Музей Кобзарства) displays more *kobzas* than you're ever seen in your life. What is a *kobza?* you might ask. Well, it's like a mandolin but with 50 or so strings. When the musician makes a mistake, he or she may blame it on the instrument. (Museum open Thurs.-Tues. 10am-1pm and 2-5pm. 0.20hv.) From the *muzey*, go back up vul. Khmelnitskoho, turning left on vul. Moskovska (Московська), the other sight-studded street in town. At the end of the street **Mykhaylivska tserkva** (Михайлівська церква) exhibits a **Museum of Costume** (Музей одягу; Muzey odyahu). The costumes are many and varied, but it's still the blue interior walls, ceiling frescos, and the tiny monastery garden that are most worth the walk and 0.20hv (open Thurs.-Tues. 10am-5pm).

The **hydrofoil** from Kiev (2 per day, 3 on Sat.; 2¼hr.; 5.21hv—it's the 3rd stop) drops you off 1km south of the *skansen*. From the river station, go left, then right onto the main road, and left onto the tree-lined alley that leads to a cupola-studded horizon. The avenue leads to the *skansen's* gates. You must go through this village-life museum to reach Pereyaslav-Khmelnitsky proper. Stay on the main dust road and bear right onto its descending branch. Exit through the museum gates, bear right towards the little river, and walk along it to the bridge on the left. Take the overpass and turn right on **vul. Lenina** (Леніна), whose second major intersection is with **vul. Khmelnitskoho** (Хмельницького)—the slowly pulsating aorta of Pereyaslav. **Ploshcha Vozzyednannya** (Возз'єднання), the heart, somewhat dead, is to the left.

To reach the **bus station,** walk left on vul. Khmelnitskoho and continue as the street bends first left then right (20min.). There are many buses to Kiev's Podil station, since most travelers coming south stop here (1½hr., 2.50hv). Buy the ticket at the "Міжміська каса" window #2. If the clerk refuses to take the money and blurts out something in Ukrainian, don't despair—she or he is telling you to pay the driver.

EASTERN UKRAINE (СХІД УКРАЇНИ)

Stalin continues to haunt Eastern Ukraine. The dream- or ghost-towns of Zaporozhe, Donetsk, and such were surely built with the combined efforts of the USSR's leading

RUSSIA
Let's Go East!
Your One-Stop Travel Center

St Petersburg International Hostel

Clean, Cheap, Central, Safe and Friendly
Visa Support, Nightly Movies, Cybercafe
Hostels in Moscow and Elsewhere

Sindbad **Budget Travel EXPERTS**

Cheapest Air & Train Tickets
InterRail & Eurobus Passes, Trans Siberian Express
Student, Youth & Hostel Identity Cards

We Service All Student & Youth Air Tickets

3rd Sovetskaya ul. 28, 193036, St Petersburg
tel +7 (812) 329-8018, 327-8384 fax 329-8019
ryh@ryh.spb.su http://www.spb.su/ryh

HOSTELLING INTERNATIONAL ACCREDITED AGENT

IBN INTERNATIONAL BOOKING NETWORK

HOSTELLING RUSSIA

North America Reservations
tel +1 (310) 379-4316 fax 379-8420 71573.2010@compuserve.com

LET'S GO® TRAVEL

We give you the world at a discount

Eurail Passes
Discounted Student Airfares

- International Student, Teacher & Youth ID Cards
- Best-Selling Let's Go Travel Guides
- Hostelling Essentials
- Extensive Line of Travel Gear

CALL TODAY FOR RESERVATIONS OR A FREE CATALOG:
1-800-5LETS GO
OR WRITE TO US AT
67 Mount Auburn St • Cambridge, MA 02138 • USA
travel@hsa.net

RUSSIA
Let's Go East!
Your One-Stop Travel Center

St Petersburg International Hostel

Clean, Cheap, Central, Safe and Friendly
Visa Support, Nightly Movies, Cybercafe
Hostels in Moscow and Elsewhere

Sindbad Budget Travel EXPERTS

Cheapest Air & Train Tickets
InterRail & Eurobus Passes, Trans Siberian Express
Student, Youth & Hostel Identity Cards

We Service All Student & Youth Air Tickets

3rd Sovetskaya ul. 28, 193036, St Petersburg
tel +7 (812) 329-8018, 327-8384 fax 329-8019
ryh@ryh.spb.su   http://www.spb.su/ryh

HOSTELLING INTERNATIONAL ACCREDITED AGENT

IBN INTERNATIONAL BOOKING NETWORK

HOSTELLING RUSSIA

North America Reservations
tel +1 (310) 379-4316 fax 379-8420 71573.2010@compuserve.com

LET'S GO® TRAVEL

We give you the world a discoun[t]

Eurail Passes
Discounted Student Airfares

- International Student, Teacher & Youth ID Cards
- Best-Selling Let's Go Travel Guides
- Hostelling Essentials
- Extensive Line of Travel Gear

CALL TODAY FOR RESERVATIONS OR A FREE CATALOG:

1-800-5LETS GO

OR WRITE TO US AT
67 Mount Auburn St • Cambridge, MA 02138 • USA
travel@hsa.net

workers. The country's largest cities lie here, and the region boasts the world's most polluted city—Kharkiv—whose rivers are the prime holiday spot for colonies of cholera. Still, you're likely to pass through one of these nightmares on the way to the Crimea. If so, a stop in Dnipropetrovsk will be least likely to endanger your health, and will allow you a glance of the ex-USSR's Five-Year-Plan heritage.

■ Dnipropetrovsk (Дніпропетровськ)

A city of currency exchanges, over a million inhabitants, and major river and rail shipping junctures, Dnipropetrovsk has an eclectic charm that keeps it from becoming a gloomy metropolis. Originally Katerinoslav, for its 1784 founder Catherine II, Dnipro has been open to individual foreign travelers only since 1990. They weren't missing much, although the city can be a fine stop on the way...elsewhere.

Orientation and Practical Information About 600km southeast of Kiev and equally north of Simferopol, Dnipropetrovsk sits on both sides of the **Dnipro** River as it turns right. Most essentials are on **prospekt Karla Marxa** (Карла Маркса), which begins as you bear right from the train station and continues to the top of a hill at **Oktyabrska pl.** (Октябрська). Take a left onto **vul. Lenina** (Леніна), heading toward a frighteningly confused theater building for the **tourist office** at #8 (tel. 45 15 09; open Mon.-Fri. 8:30am-noon and 1-5:30pm, Sat. 10am-3pm). Yogi Berra once said: "If you can't find a **currency exchange** in Dnipropetrovsk, you ought to have your head examined." **Privatbank,** vul. Serova-Naberezhna, 5b (Серова-Набережна), office #33 (tel. 78 11 35), sucks cash from your Visa at 3% commission; and at 5a, office #12 (tel. 41 32 31), exchanges traveler's checks (2% commission; open Mon.-Fri. 9am-noon and 1-5pm). **Trains** run to Moscow (3 per day, 45hr., US$25); Odesa (2 per day, 15hr.); Rostov-na-Donu, Russia (5 per day, 12-13hr., US$16); Simferopol (1 per day, 10hr., US$7). **Luggage storage** is available here. The **river station** is reached by taking a left out of the train station, another left past the bridge down vul. Pastera (Пастера), and then a right. In summer '96, **ferries** served only local destinations. **Faxes** and fun await at the **post office,** prosp. Karla Marxa, 62 (open Mon.-Sat. 8am-8pm, Sun. 8am-7pm; fax daily 8am-11pm). **Telephones** are next door to the post office. Open 7:30am-10:30pm. **Postal code:** 320 000. **Phone code:** 0562.

Accommodations and Food Accustomed to hosting dangerous CIA agents trying to get a look at the latest in Soviet missile systems, Dnipro's hotel technology doesn't yet have a place in its heart for tight-budget travelers. Offering rooms in the center of things at pr. Karla Marxa, 50, is **Tsentralny** (Центральний; tel. 45 03 47). The ceilings are high, the beds short (single US$15, doubles US$18; communal showers with occasional hot water US$0.60). **Astoria** (Асторія), pr. Karla Marxa, 66 (tel. 44 23 04), can give you a similar double with sink for US$23, but lacks a communal shower (with shower US$55). For a room with a view, head up to the park on tram #1, then walk down to the Dnipro to **Rassvet** (Рассвет), vul. Fuchika, 30 (Фучика; tel. 46 00 37). They will give you a double with shower, TV, and phone for US$20 per person, or a single for US$27.

The **central market,** at the intersection of pr. Karla Marxa and vul. Horkoho (Горького), on tram-line #1, opens daily 6am-5pm. Bread and drinks are also sold at the market next to the Tsentralny. **Cafeteria,** Schmidta, 7 (Шмідта), is, well, cheap (open Tues.-Sun. 8am-1pm and 2pm-6pm). Take bus А or Б from the train station.

Sights and Entertainment Tram #1 takes you up the hill to Oktyabrska pl. The second building on Lomonosov's right is the **Historical Museum** (Історичний музей; *Istorichny muzey*), with displays on the history of the city, lots of Cossack revolutionary items, a real *knort,* and some pictures of Cossacks you wouldn't want to see in your *koupé* (open Tues.-Sun. 10am-5pm; 0.60hv, students 0.30hv). Through the museum and past some displayed artillery is the **Transfiguration Monastery** (Преображенский собор; *Preobrazhensky sobor*), a slim structure only one-sixth of its intended size—Catherine II didn't cough up quite enough hryvni). The interior is simply designed, with stellar artistry in light hues (open daily 7am-noon and 3-6pm). This is also one of the few buildings in town without a currency exchange. Farther down the road begins the large **Park Shevchenka** (Парк Шевченка). The beautiful building used to be **Prince Potomkin's Palace** (Палац Потьомкіна; *Palats Potomkina*), but is now a center of student cultural life. In the distance, note mount Shevchenko towering above **Komsomolsky Island,** a favorite relaxation spot for kids who like to swim and throw rocks at trains. Boat rentals are available, and a **cable car** will carry those who cannot find the bridge.

Obscured by a large concrete building, an impressive **Holy Trinity Cathedral** rises from behind a statue of **Lenin**. At the end of trolley line #4 at pr. Kalinina, 66 (Калініна), a large church is now a **House of Organ Music** (tel. 52 30 05), with several shows a month (*kassa* open daily 2-5:30pm). At night, cruise the center of town—it might not be "hip" or "cool," but it is the center of town.

For the slickest café in Dnipro, head to Park Shevchenka. At vul. Fuchika, 9, **Café Pelican** (Пелікан) serves a beer that looks like *Guinness* and tastes distantly related to it (draft 4.50hv; it may contain the local water). The **theater**, ul. Lenina, 5 (tel. 44 52 35), has shows nearly every night (*kassa* open daily 10:30am-6:30pm; tickets 0.50hv and up). The city's well maintained parks have begun experimenting with lawnmowers, and the result is the smell of freshly cut grass on summer days.

THE CRIMEA (КРИМ)

Turn your watch forward one hour from Kiev time for the Crimea (GMT+3)

The Crimean peninsula has been inhabited since antiquity—most recently by Russians. Tsars' palaces stand alongside the sanatoria and resorts that in the past half-century have served the ailing proletariat of colder climes. The peninsula has drawn people to its shores for a simple reason—it is beautiful.

■ Simferopol (Сімферополь)

God made Crimea, and all Simferopol got was a lousy train station. Originally the site of the Scythian city of Neapolis and subsequently a Tartar town, Simferopol is still the hub where all Crimean roads meet. Outside of the train and bus bazaar, the peninsula's capital is calm and lazy. Nineteenth-century buildings and broad parks lie beyond the 100m walk from the trains to the trolleys heading for the coast.

ORIENTATION AND PRACTICAL INFORMATION

Aleya Lenina (Леніна) runs on both sides of a park leading away from the train station. **Trolley #2,** useful for accommodations, stops 20m down al. Lenina; it travels to the **city center,** where al. Lenina crosses **vul. Lyuksemburg** (Люксембург).

- **Tourist Office:** In Hotel Ukraina (Україна) at vul. Lyuksemburg, 9. Kiosks marked "Экскурсия" organize guided excursions; kiosks are also a source of maps.
- **Currency Exchange:** Plenty of "Обмен-Валют" from the train station onward. **Thomas Cook,** vul. Lyuksemburg, 17 (tel. 290 021), cashes traveler's checks (3%).
- **Trains:** vul. Gagarina (Гагаріна), reachable by trolleys #1, 2, 5, and 6. To: Kiev (2 per day, 16hr., US$7); Lviv (1 per day, 26hr.); Minsk (1 per day, 29hr.); Moscow (4 per day, 24hr., US$25); Odesa (1 per day, 12hr., US$7). Trains are often crowded during the summer, so buy your ticket early.
- **Buses:** The station is reachable by trolley #1, 2, or 6, 20min. from the train station. Buy tickets at least a day ahead, or ask the driver for standing-room. To: Bakhchisarai (4 per day, 45min., 1.20hv); Feodosia (6 per day, 2½hr., 4hv). Closer destinations via the regional station next to the train station.

Public Transportation: Trolley is the best way to **Yalta** (#52, 2½hr., 3.50hv), departing next to the train station (several per hr. 5:30am-11pm). Ticket windows are 50m to the left exiting the train station's main courtyard—look for the long lines: windows #1 and 2 for Yalta. Before noon it's usually possible to get a ticket for the next hour or two; after that spots fill quickly. There's no standing room, but "extra" tickets may be sold for high prices by people standing nearby.

Taxis: Stands are all over town, and private drivers hawk rides to Feodosia, Kerch, and Yalta. Fares multiply like rabbits if they learn you're a Brit or a Yank.

Luggage Storage: Downstairs between the train and trolley stations. Small bag 0.50hv, large bag 1.50hv. Open daily 8am-9pm.

Post Office: Next to Hotel Ukraina. Open Mon.-Fri. 7am-7pm, Sat.-Sun. 9am-4pm. A second one is at the train station. Open 24hr. **Postal code:** 333 000.

Telephones: At the post offices. Open 24hr. **Phone code:** 0652.

ACCOMMODATIONS

Turbaza "Tavraya" (Турбаза "Таврая"), vul. Bespalova, 21 (Беспалова; tel. 23 20 24), 2 stops on trolley #2 after the bus station or a 25-min. ride from the trains to "Таврая"—walk up. Recently furnished rooms, older bathrooms. Late-night bar. Single with shower, TV, and fridge US$15. Doubles US$20. Breakfast included.

Ukraina (Україна), vul. Lyuksemburg, 9 (tel. 27 55 73); take trolley #2 from the train station. This aging but central hotel has high ceilings and a nice courtyard, but no showers in the rooms. Singles with sink, TV, and phone US$18. Equally well outfitted doubles US$30. The aging communal showers may cost you extra.

Moskva (Москва), Kievska vul., 2 (Київська.; tel. 23 20 12), at the "Hotel Moskva" stop on trolley #2. Simferopol's largest hotel. Decent rooms, peeling paint. Singles with bath, TV, and telephone US$35. Similar doubles US$42.

FOOD

The **central market** at the intersection of pr. Kirova (Кірова) and vul. Kozlova (Козлова) is the place to stock up on groceries and a good way to see the city at work. A more accessible **market** outside the train station also sells the local specialties,

---

Who Owns Crimea?

In the 5th century BCE, Herodotus first recorded that Scythians and Greeks dwelled in Crimea, but invaders have continuously made their way across the isthmus to join the sun-bathing population. The Sarmatians followed the Scythians in the 4th century, and were subsequently supplanted by the Romans, Ostrogoths, Huns, Slavs, Khazars, and Varangians. The peninsula fell under Byzantium until the great Batu Khan (grandson of Genghis) took the region and opened Crimea to trade. Pleased with the land, many Mongols settled and became the indigenous Crimean Tartars.

The Crimea remained autonomous, until Russia annexed it in 1783 and refurbished it as beach resort extraordinaire. The Crimean War, in 1854, saw France and Britain clash with Russia over the city of Sevastopol. The Russians evacuated, leaving the Tartars to revive their national heritage, language, and culture. In 1917, the Tartars put together a *Kurultay*—Tartar National Constituent Assembly—which declared their autonomy against the will of the Bolsheviks. Russia soon regained control and paid its citizens to settle. The new settlers eradicated the reigning elite, and on the night of May 18, 1944, Stalin had the entire Crimean Tartar population, largely collaborating with the Germans, loaded into train cars and shipped to Uzbekistan.

Crimea was officially made part of Ukraine in 1954 as a "gift" from Khrushchev; now it seems a costly gesture. Russians continue to flood the resorts; they don't want to give up Crimea, but neither does Ukraine, who now reaps the financial rewards. The Tartars have also returned *en masse*, in the past five years demanding their land. Despite such turmoil, Crimea's beauty remains: tall mountains frame a view of lush forests and the light blue sea.

including small shrimp eaten from a piece of newspaper rolled into a cone. These should be eaten only when fresh—and can be sold only with a permit to prove it. Otherwise, **bars** serving food abound in the central pedestrian zone around vul. Karla Marksa (Карла Маркса), vul. Pushkina (Пушкіна), and vul. Gorkoho (Горького). Restaurants in **Hotel Ukraina** and **Moskva** cook up meals for the unadventurous, but then, if you were truly unadventurous, you wouldn't be in Ukraine.

SIGHTS AND ENTERTAINMENT

The city's major historical landmark is the **Neapolis archaeological site** (Неаполь Скіфський; *Neapol Skifsky*), a vast excavation of the former Crimean capital reachable by bus #4 from the train station. Most of Neapolis's loot, however, is contained in the **Regional History Museum** (Крімский Краєзнавчій Музей; *Krimsky Kraeznavchy Muzey*), at the intersection of vul. Pushkina and vul. Hoholya (Голголья; open Wed.-Mon. 9am-5pm; 1hv). The **Gorky theater** on vul. Gorkoho (Ukrainian for Gorky) at #10 presents frequent shows (*kasa* open daily 10am-8pm). The church-crazy and mosque-mad should take a stroll past pl. Radyanska (Радянська) onto vul. Lenina. Take a right onto vul. Proletarska (Пролетарська). The first religious building will appear on your right, the **Church of Sts. Peter and Paul** (Петронавлівська церква; *Petronavlivska tserkva*), complete with the requisite bell tower. Church #2, also on your right, is the recently renovated **Holy Trinity Cathedral** (Святотройька катедра; *Cvyatotroitska katedra*). The **mosque** sits off vul. Proletarska on vul. Kurchatova (Курчатова), in a small neighborhood of Tatars.

For something a little less reverent, kiosks in the vicinity vend **vodka. Café Raduga** (Радуга), right behind Hotel Ukraina, is hip and overpriced (open 24hr.). The city's **parks** are a joy, well maintained and full of people. Try the central parks near vul. Pushkina or the Children's Park (Детский Парк; *Detsky Park*), on vul. Shmidta (Шмідта) via trolley #2 or 4, with its mammoth concrete jungle gyms.

■ Near Simferopol

BAKHCHISARAI (БАХЧИСАРАЙ)

Among the dry, solemn cliffs of the Central Crimean steppe, the ancient town of Bakhchisarai quietly guards its secrets. An outpost of the Byzantine Empire at the end of the 6th century CE and subsequently the seat of Crimean Tartar power, the town is currently occupied primarily by blackberry-sellers. Bakhchisarai's **Khansky Palats** (Ханський Палац) was first built in the early 16th century by the second Crimean khan. It has been razed, re-created, and refined many times since then, and the additions are its true attraction. The palace encompasses numerous small rooms and a **courtyard** where the khan's harem hung out. Bought on the free (though black) market, these wives came cheaper than an official wife; since they were illegal, their movement was restricted. You'll also find the **Fountain Courtyard,** which contains the **Golden Fountain** and the famous **Fountain of Tears.** According to legend, the fount was built by a khan who had fallen in love with a fatally ill slave, and who desired company in his weeping. Pushkin made the fountain famous in his poem *The Bakhchisarai Fountain*. Two roses are retained in perpetuum for the fountain to shed tears on. (Museum open Wed.-Mon. 9am-5pm; 4hv.)

A right from the palace leads to the **Assumption Monastery** (Успеньский Печерний Монастырь; *Uspensky Pecherny Monastyr*), currently undergoing reconstruction. Carved out of a cliff in the 15th century, it became the center of Orthodox Christian life in the Crimea, perhaps because of its incredible view of the valley.

Still farther along the road, 1km east and up to the left, lies the mysterious and ancient **cave town of Chufut-Kale** (Чуфут-Кале). Built toward the end of the 6th century by order of Byzantium, it subsequently became the first capital of the Crimean Khanate. From this almost impenetrable location, the khans could jeer at potential invaders and shower them with hot oil. After the capital was moved to Bakhchisarai in the early 16th century, the Muslim population left and only Karaite Jews and Arme-

NEAR SIMFEROPOL ■ 711

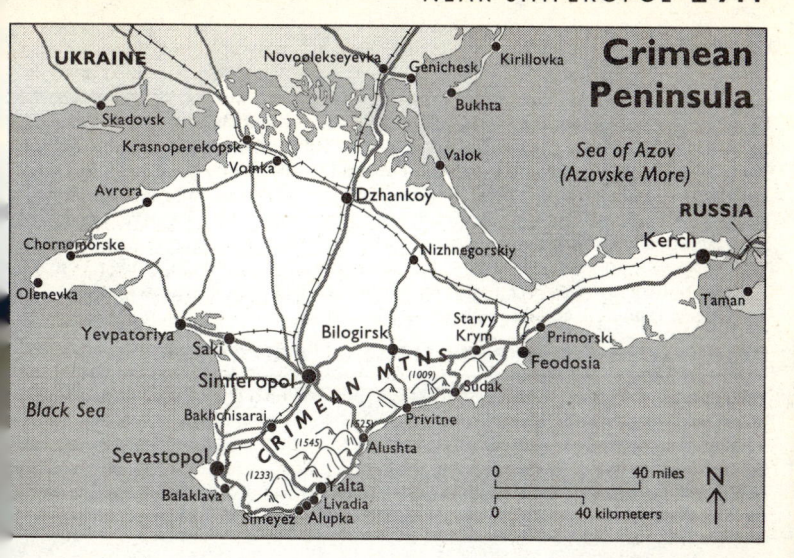

nians stayed. The fortress was renamed Chufut-Kale (Jews' Fortress). Try to see the cave complex near the South Gate—a Christian monastery. The architecture of nearby 15th-century **kenassas** (prayer houses) resembles that of synagogues.

Close and well connected to Simferopol, Bakhchisarai makes an ideal daytrip. Several daily **buses** make the trek to Bakhchisarai from Simferopol's main bus station (45min., final destination usually Sevastopol); or take the **electrichka** (more frequent and faster, destination also Sevastopol). From the back of Bakhchisarai's **bus station,** take a right, bear left, and then take the road into town. It's a half-hour to the *palats*. A town bus is supposed to run to the palace from the station, but takes a break (noon-4pm). Bus #4 connects the bus and **train stations.**

FEODOSIA (ФЕОДОСІЯ)

If you didn't think the smooth rocks of Yalta felt much like a beach, head east. Outside the ancient slave-trading town of Feodosia, a 16km stretch of bronzed sand speckled with tiny, smooth bits of seashell creates a shoreline that has attracted vacationers from Roman times to the present. The waters are slightly cooler than those in the south. Take a right at pr. Lenina (Леніна) to **ancient ruins.** But you don't have to leave the proximity of the bus station if you came for the **beach.** Cross the street, head right 50m, and cross the bridge over the tracks to get a gander at what you came for: the big, bad Black Sea. Going left will take you to a free beach, or pay 1hv for fewer crowds. From the bus station, **city buses** #2 and 4 head into town, where Russia's premier collection of **I. K. Aivazovsky's works** is on display. Not surprisingly, he mostly painted the sea—*Poseidon's Journey on the Sea* is particularly impressive for an artist who, toward the end of his life, grew sideburns that made Pushkin's look like a phase in junior high (open Thurs.-Mon. 10am-5pm, Tues. 10am-2pm; 3hv at the *kasa* across the street). Across the way stands the **Regional Museum** which displays the remnants of cultures that inhabited the Crimea, from Roman to Russian. To spend the night, inquire at **Astoriya** (Асторія; pr. Lenina, 9; tel. (06562) 323 51). Small, furnished singles are US$15, with bath US$30; doubles US$23, with bath US$34. Spaces fills up quickly, so call well in advance. **Café Assol** (Ассоль), at the intersection of vul. Libnekhta (Лібнехта) and Halereyna vul. (Галереїна), serves several semi-Russian dishes for US$1-2. **Buses** make the trip to Feodosia from Simferopol's main bus station (8 per day, 2½hr.) with Kerch (Керч) as their final destination. Getting back can be nightmarish; buy return tickets in advance when possible.

Yalta (Ялта)

Yalta is all about class—and we're not talking about the struggle of the proletariat here. The mountains form a semi-circle around the aged city before running into the most beautiful of seas; even the all-night discos blaring techno-pop merely dull the sheer physical grandeur. The tsars who created this resort may have been less-than-enlightened, but they knew how to relax. The city's old wooden houses sit on hills, and everything converges at the beach-front promenade, where buskers compete with America-worshipping post-Soviet consumerism for the hearts of vacationers. Still cheap by European standards, Yalta's prices are slipping out of the grasp of many Soviets, but the crowds, with all their gaudiness, will return. And when they do, Yalta, aged, dignified, and just plain cool, will endure.

ORIENTATION AND PRACTICAL INFORMATION

Yalta spreads along the coastline; pedestrian **nab. Lenina** (Леніна) runs from one end of town to the other. **Trolley #1** makes a circle around Yalta from the bus and trolley stations. Get off at **Sovetska pl.** (Советська), and walk 100m down **Moskovska vul.** (Московська) to get to the sea. The intersection of Moskovska vul. and nab. Lenina is **pl. Lenina,** featuring a statue of everyone's favorite revolutionary. A left here leads to the **Old Town,** whose main streets are **vul. Roosevelta** (Рузвельта) and **vul. Drazhinskoho** (Дражинського).

- **Tourist Office: Intourist,** vul. Drazhinskoho, 50, in the Hotel Yalta, arranges expensive, English-translated tours. Open daily 9am-6pm. For short tours, look for *Ekskursbyuro* (Экскурсбюро) kiosks along nab. Lenina, or just use the good book.
- **Currency Exchange: Import-Export Bank,** nab. Lenina, 3, takes traveler's checks at a 2% commission. Open Mon.-Fri. 9am-1:30pm and 2:30-5:45pm. **Bank Ukrainy,** nab. Lenina 3, exchanges traveler's checks. Open Mon.-Fri. 10am-5pm. **24-hr. exchange** at the corner of vul. Roosevelta and vul. Sverdlova (Свердлова).
- **Buses:** The **bus station,** Moskovska vul., 57, is connected to the **trolley** stop across the street. Trolleys leave every 20min. for Simferopol (2½hr.) and Simferopol airport. Slightly faster, but less convenient and more expensive, buses run to Simferopol and coastal points. Tickets for buses to nearby points can be purchased on board; tickets for trolleys should be purchased in advance to ensure a seat.
- **Ferries:** Ferries run to Istanbul (2 per week), and several **water shuttles** float daily to Alupka and Lastivchine Gnizdo. Buy tickets at the port at the *kassa* on the *naberezhna*, next to the pier. The water shuttles, only slightly slower and more expensive than buses, are infinitely more scenic and pleasant.
- **Public Transportation: Trolleys** run in the city. Buy tickets (0.20hv) at kiosks or from the driver and punch on board. Payment is strictly enforced.
- **Luggage Storage:** At the bus station. 0.40hv. Open daily 6am-10pm.
- **24-Hour Pharmacy:** Botkinska vul., 3 (Боткінська). Ring the bell from 8pm-8am.
- **Post Office:** pl. Lenina. Open daily 8am-8pm. **Postal code:** 334 200.
- **Telephones:** International calls are most easily made at the hotel **Oreanda,** vul. Lenina 35/2. To the U.S. US$2.50 per min. Open daily 9am-4pm. **Telefonna Stantsiya** (Телефонна Станція), Moskovska vul., 10, has cheaper rates but long lines. Open daily 8am-10pm. Intercity booths line nab. Lenina, but most of them are unreliable. Buy *zhetony* (tokens) at the post office (0.25hv). **Phone code:** 0654.

ACCOMMODATIONS AND CAMPING

The prices at Yalta's beachside hotels have increased dramatically and might continue to do so; the lone traveler will have difficulty getting a place in a double. Book ahead. Bus-station *babushki* often offer unbeatable deals.

- **Otdykh** (Отдых), vul. Drazhinskoho, 14 (Дражінського; tel. 35 30 79), in the Old Town. Small and often full. Some rooms have the views of the sea they write about in travel guides. No hall showers. Doubles with sink US$20; with bath, TV, and fridge US$37.

Central Yalta

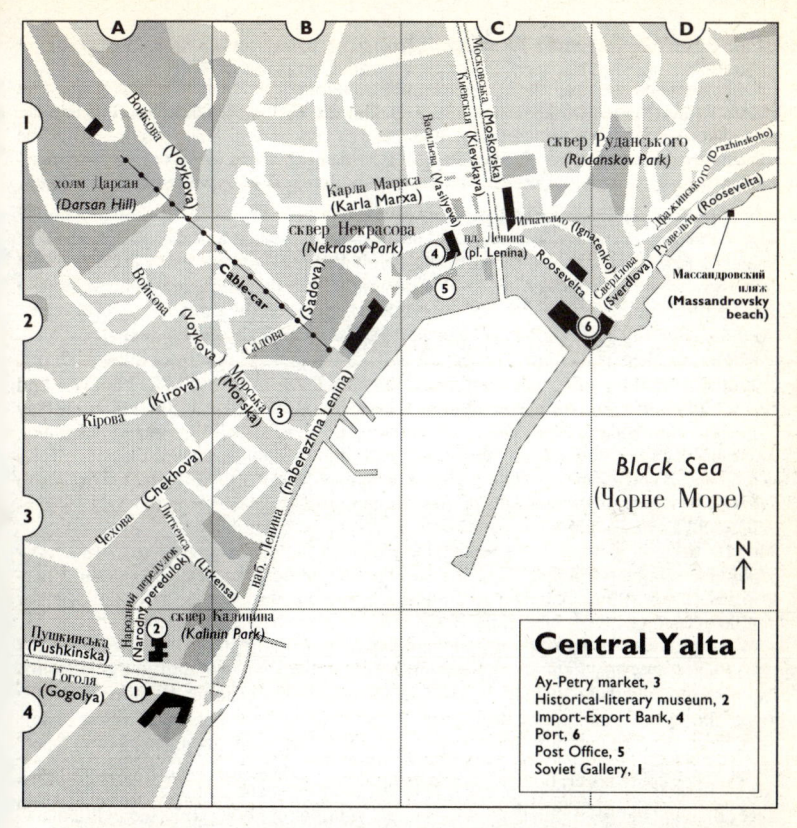

Ay-Petry market, **3**
Historical-literary museum, **2**
Import-Export Bank, **4**
Port, **6**
Post Office, **5**
Soviet Gallery, **1**

Volna (Волна), Sadova vul., 4 (Садова; tel. 32 39 40). Take trolley #1 from the trolley station or from Sovetska pl. to "Кинопрокат" *(Kinoprokat)*, backtrack 150m, and keep going up the stairs. Relaxed garden setting on a lovely hillside alleyway. Doubles with sink, TV, and fridge US$18.

Massandra (Массандра), vul. Drazhinskoho, 48 (tel. 35 25 91), edge of the Old Town. Recently renovated. Doubles with sink US$18; with shower, telephone, and fridge US$33.

Motel-Camping Polyana Skazok (Поляна Сказок), vul. Kirova, 167 (Кірова; tel. 39 52 19). Take bus #11, 26, or 27 from the bus station's upper platform to "Поляна Сказок" *(Polyana Skazok)*; it's about a 20-min. walk uphill from there through winding, wild-blackberry-lined roads. A real class-act campground in a charming high-altitude setting, with showers and kitchen facilities. Tents US$1 per person. Cozy bungalows for 2 in the supposed style of old Russian dachas US$7. Motel singles with bath US$15, with balcony US$20. Doubles with bath US$20, with balcony US$25. The newer, balconied rooms are much more comfortable.

FOOD

Many **restaurants** along nab. Lenina also serve food with their liquor. Some of them are even attractive and priced within reason. Have a look at **Restoran Gurman** with its English menu and vegetarian selections. A well stocked **Hastronom** (Гастроном), nab. Lenina, 4, sells bread for pennies, and there is a **general market** at the corner of Moskovska vul. and vul. Karla Marxa (daily 8am-6pm).

Café Siren (Сирень), vul. Roosevelta, 6. Freshly prepared Russian food, just like your grandmother used to make, if your grandmother was Russian. Borscht, *kasha*, *kak-det*, and some *kompot* US$1. Open daily 8am-8pm.

Café Krym (Крым), Moskovska vul., 1/2. Get in, eat, get out. Do not pass Go. Do not collect 1.50hv (US$1, full meal).

Pilmenna (Пильменна), vul. Sverdlova, 8 (Свердлова), at the base of vul. Drazhinskoho. Specializes in *pilmeny* (dumplings), go figure. *Plonty* with soup US$0.70.

SIGHTS AND ENTERTAINMENT

Yalta is a resort town, but the nightlife is sorely lacking—unless, that is, you're into endless hours of videopoker or strolling down the boardwalk in your tightest clothing. During the day, museums are everywhere and provide a much-needed break from the sun. The most prominent sight of all, of course, is the clear, green, sea.

Chekhov called Yalta home for the last five years of his life, and from the wealth of monuments and plaques, you can practically re-trace his every step. On nab. Lenina at the entrance of Gurman, you can see where he once slept, and on vul. Litkensa (Літкенса) stands the **school** where he taught. At vul. Kirova, 112, you can explore the **house** he built, the garden he planted, and the museum dedicated to him by his sister. Bus #8 takes you there every 40 minutes from "Кинотеатр Спартак" (*Kinoteatr Spartak*) on Pushkinska vul. This town is Disneyland for Chekhov fans.

The old **Soviet Gallery** lies at vul. Gogolya, 1, next to Hotel Oreanda (open Tues.-Sun. 10am-6pm; 3hv) and the **Art Gallery,** across the street at Pushkinska vul., 5 (open Tues.-Sun. 10am-6pm). Having sufficiently refined your taste, you can now stop at **Crimea Wines,** nab. Lenina underneath the "Marino" sign in the Casino Diana building (tastings hourly after 2pm).

By day, Yalta's parks are among the peninsula's most luxuriant; in **Primorsky (Seaside) Park Gagarina,** at the southwest end of nab. Lenina, you can find an **Exotic Fish Aquarium** (open daily 10am-8pm; 2hv). On Moskovska vul., about 10 minutes from town, the **circus** puts on a nightly show (May-Oct. Wed.-Sat 5pm, Sun. 4pm.; *kasa* open Tues.-Sun. 10am-6pm). If you aren't feeling childish enough yet, the **Fairy-Tale Meadow** (Поляна Сказок; *Polyana Skazok*) children's park, next to the campground, takes characters from Russian and Ukrainian fairy tales and immortalizes them in larger-than-life figures (open daily 8am-8pm). A number of **hiking trails** begin in Yalta, reaching the **Uchan-Su Waterfall** and other natural wonders. Consult the campground staff for advice. Lazier visitors use the **chairlift** to get to a high-altitude shrine to Zeus, where the jolly Greek stares out to sea. The lift lifts you from behind Casino Diana (June-Oct. daily 11am-9:30pm; 1.50hv).

Billboards posted everywhere announce upcoming acts, and everyone on nab. Lenina is doing something strange. Several upscale **bars** have also opened up here—the one at the beginning of Pushkinska vul. serves moderately expensive *Heineken* and *Amstel;* **Guinness Bar,** vul. Sverdlova, charges too much for the *Guinness* it serves, but shows its heart is in the right place by broadcasting the Rugby World Cup. The **Rock and Roll Store/Bar,** at the end of Pushkinska vul. near the "Кинотеатр Спартак" stop, might be playing good rock music, but then again it might not.

■ Near Yalta

HURZUF (ГУРЗУФ)

Eighteen kilometers from Yalta proper, Greater Yalta's streets are narrower and the houses older. Hurzuf is a quieter version of Yalta, replacing man-made tourist attractions with rocks jutting dramatically out of the sea and cliffs looking on the sea. **Chekhov** built his dacha where he could see it all, and it's now a museum. Young **Pushkin** spent two months here, making it worthy of a monument, too. Hurzuf's true charm, however, hides in the narrow streets winding among small old buildings, the cliffs, and the sea. Heading from the bus stop towards the sea, a right, then another right in Pushkino Sanitoria, and then the middle path, take visitors to the **Pushkin Museum** (open Wed.-Sun. 10am-5pm; 1hv). A left at the embankment, then a right down the narrow vul. Chekhova (Чехова), goes to the **Chekhov Museum** (open Tues.-Sun. 10am-5pm). Past vul. Chekhova on Leningradska vul. (Ленінградська), the Pionersky Camp contains a tunnel through a cliff, allowing a view of everything. Ask to see the *"tunel v skalé"* at the black fence on Leningradska vul. Farther still is a view of **Bear Mountain.** To get to the rocks rising from the sea, one of which houses a **bar,** rent a **paddle-boat** (5hv per hr.) on the embankment. Bus #31 goes from Yalta (every 40min., 50 min.).

LIVADIA (ЛІВАДІЯ)

An hour's hike or a 10-minute shuttle ride away, Livadia was the place where Yalta's renown began as a resort town, and where it reached history-book levels with the imprecisely named **Yalta Conference.** Churchill, Roosevelt, and Stalin met for a week in February 1945 at **Tsar Nicholas II's summer palace** (built in 1911) to finalize post-war territorial claims. Secretly, the Russians committed to enter the war against Japan after the German defeat (which Stalin did two months after the German surrender; although the bomb was dropped before Soviet troops could be engaged), and Roosevelt and Churchill apparently agreed to send back all captured Soviet troops (though they knew the men would be considered traitors). Some considered the conference a great cave-in on FDR's part, particularly regarding the Soviet presence in Eastern Europe; others, like one ideologically confused tour guide, think the conference guaranteed "fifty years of peace."

Shuttle #5 from "Кінотеатр Спартак" *(Kinoteatr Spartak)* in Yalta stops every 40-50 minutes across the park from the **Great Palace** (Великий Палац; *Veliky Palats*) where it all happened. The second floor has been converted into an exhibition hall and **Nicholas II museum,** but the rest has been preserved in memory of the conference. The exquisite marble and red-wood interior and the view from Nicholas's windows amply demonstrate that it was good to be tsar (open Thurs.-Tues. 10am-5pm; 5hv). The surrounding **park** is also nice—elevators take you down to an ordinary **beach,** if seeing the tsar's *"dacha"* has made you want to jump.

LASTIVCHINE GNIZDO (ЛАСТІВЧИНЕ ГНІЗДО)

Built in 1911 for a rich German who apparently wanted to get richer on postcards, the fragile Lastivchine Gnizdo (Swallow's Nest) **castle** perched upon a cliff looks like it might crumble into the sea at any moment. It won't be taking any tsars or counts with it, though, as it's now an expensive "Italian" restaurant with a view. Since the castle is itself largely a part of the spectacle, the best viewing site is on a nearby platform—that's where the true postcard photographers go. Some use the gaps in the fencing to sneak onto the **Sanatorium Zhemchuzhina's** beach and swim out to the rock, but stay safe; every now and then, a big wave smashes an unlucky swimmer against the rocks. To reach the castle, take one of the half-hour **ferries,** leaving hourly from Yalta's pier 7 (2hv), or **bus #27** from the bus station (0.60hv). The bus is only slightly faster and a lot less pleasant. Get off at the "Sanatorium Zhemchuzhina" or "Sanatorium Paris" stop. The path leading down is between the two. The last ferry back to Yalta departs at 6pm, the last bus at 8:30pm. Several cafés serve *shashliks* and chicken. From Lastivchine Gnizdo, both the ferry (½hr., 1hv) and the bus #27 continue to **Alupka.**

ALUPKA (АЛУПКА)

Alupka is home to the most extravagant *dacha* in Greater Yalta—**Palats Vorontsova** (Палац Воронцова), still an active compound, built by the wealthier-than-thou regional governor, Count Mikhail Vorontsov. The surrounding **park** is pleasant and has lots of big rocks for climbing. You can walk around the palace proper for free daily 10am-8pm, but to get inside and see how rich people once decorated their abodes (the museum part), you pay 4hv. Much of the palace has been closed for restoration; currently guests are allowed into four beautiful rooms and a statue garden (open Tues.-Thurs. and Sat.-Sun. 10am-5pm). The north of the palace faces **Mt. Ai-Petry,** and is correspondingly somber. The south, facing the sea, has a bizarre and magnificent façade. Six lions—a truly impressive marble one by the Italian master Leone Bonani, and five goofy-looking ones by his students—guard a marble portico with an Arabic invocation to Allah. What this is doing at the center of Vorontsov's palace is not exactly clear. Apparently, the English architect, who designed the palace from sketches of the surrounding views, thought the Black Sea here looked a lot like the Indian Ocean, and copied the design of an Indian mansion and its inscription. The story has it that when Tsar Nicholas I came to the palace, he was offended at the presumptuousness of its extravagance. Vorontsov merely pointed to the lettering, explaining to the tsar that, after all, all praise is due to Allah. In any case, it looks better than a Communist slogan.

ODESHCHINA (ОДЕЩИНА)

South of Kiev and west of the Crimea spreads the Ukrainian steppe and wooded half-steppe. Scythians, Slavs, and Sarmatians are the "S" nations that settled this part of the Black Sea Coast, later ruled successively by the Golden Horde, Lithuania, and Turkey. Never-sated Russia waited to bite into Odeshchina until 1791, after emerging successful from a three-year war with the Ottomans, and spat it out again after only a two-year mastication. Fortunately, the Empire's teeth took it easy on Odesa.

■ Odesa (Одеса)

Built by the Russians under French influence but located in the Jewish area of settlement, Odesa got its money from Catherine and Vorontsov and its attitude from the Jews, the Turks, and the Black Sea. During WWII, it was not the Germans who occupied most of Odesa, but the less-destructive Romanians, and the city survived with relatively little damage. The result: a conglomeration of huge French-style buildings with elaborate façades. Although Odesa lays some claim to Pushkin, the city's true literary son, Isaac Babel, earned the title with his colorful chronicles of the Jewish mob in Odesa's Moldavank region. Today, Ukraine's biggest port is a popular vacation spot, attracting sun-worshippers, café junkies, and drunken sailors alike. Here at the edge of the Black Sea—grim, stormy, gray—there's nothing left to do but drink vodka and listen to the sweet strains of *Macarena*.

ORIENTATION AND PRACTICAL INFORMATION

Odesa lies on a 50km strip along the Black Sea. Its central section is bounded by the **train station** to the south and the **port** to the north. All streets, recently renamed, are labeled in both Ukrainian and Russian. For verbal queries, you're still better off with the old names. The main **vul. Deribasivska** (Дерибасівська) is partially closed to traffic. From the train station, walk across the park to the Spartak stadium (Спартак), and take trolley #5 or 9 to the center. The terminus is **pl. Hretska** (Грецька), a block from vul. Deribasivska, also reachable by tram #2, 3, or 12 from the station. Heading toward the sea, it crosses **vul. Pushkinska** (Пушкінська). A right onto vul. Pushkinska from vul. Deribasivska leads to the train station, and a left ushers you onto the tree-lined **Primorsky bulvar** (Приморський), favored for its panoramic views of the sea. **Maps** are available at Hotel Krasnaya (Красная;1hv).

> **Tourist Office: Intourist,** vul. Pushkinska, 17 (tel. 25 85 20), in the lobby of Hotel Krasnaya. Trolleys #1 and 4 run here from the train station. Train, plane, and bus tickets. Open daily 9am-1pm and 2-5pm. The less hectic **service bureau** upstairs has plenty of advice on Odesa's sights. Some English spoken. Tours of the catacombs and other attractions are available (2.50hv). Same hours.
>
> **Passport Office (OVIR):** Krasny Pereulok, 5 (Красный Переулок; tel. 25 89 74).

Central Odesa

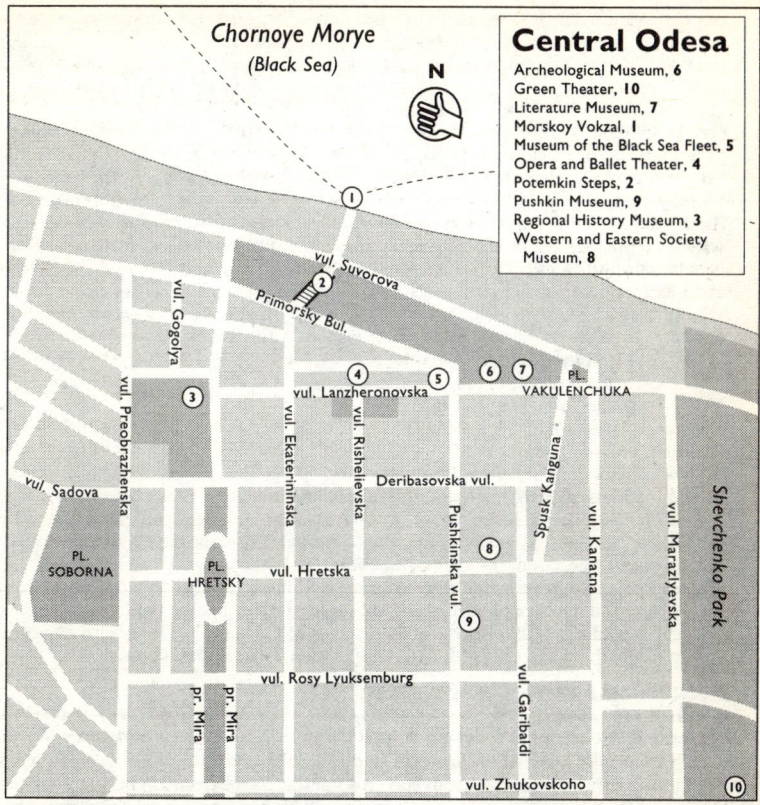

Archeological Museum, **6**
Green Theater, **10**
Literature Museum, **7**
Morskoy Vokzal, **1**
Museum of the Black Sea Fleet, **5**
Opera and Ballet Theater, **4**
Potemkin Steps, **2**
Pushkin Museum, **9**
Regional History Museum, **3**
Western and Eastern Society Museum, **8**

Tourist Police: Sped-Sluzhba (special service), vul. Zhukovskoho, 42 (Жуковського; tel. 28 22 66), at the intersection with vul. Preobrazhenska (Преображенська; old Sovetskoy Armii). 2nd floor to the left. Deals with crimes by and against foreigners. Much friendlier when it's the latter.

Currency Exchange: Obmin (Обмін) window at the Sea Port gives AmEx, MC, and Visa cash advances (5% commission) and cashes traveler's checks (3% commission). US$ and DM can be exchanged at any *Obmin Valyut* (Обмін Валют), all of which have similar rates. Those with more exotic currencies should head for **Hotel Londonska** (Лондонська), Primorsky bul., 11.

Flights: Airfare to Moscow depends on the plane. Russian and Ukrainian planes fly for US$140. Several airlines offer direct connections to European cities; check their offices in the airport for current prices. **Austrian Airlines** (tel. 25 33 78) goes to Vienna (6 per week), **Lufthansa** to Frankfurt (2 per week).

Trains: pl. Privokzalna (Привокзальна), at the south end of vul. Pushkinska. Tram #2, 3, or 12 takes you along vul. Preobrazhenska to the west end of vul. Deribasivska. Buy international or advance tickets in the International Room (Міжнародний Зал; *Mizhnarodny Zal*), to the left as you enter the building (open 8am-noon and 1-7pm), or at the **Central Ticket Bureau**, vul. Srednefontanska (Среднефонтанська). To find it, take bus #136 or 146 or cross the park and take the more frequent tram #17 or 18 to the *Sredni Fontan* (Central Fountain) and look for the large sign "Центральные Железнодорожные Кассы" *(Tsentralnye Zheleznodorozhnye Kassy)*. Also try the **Intourist office,** in Hotel Krasnaya, if their computer is working. If all else fails, **scalpers** hang out in the main hall to the right asking "*Vam nuzhny bilet?*" Check that the tickets are valid. To: Kiev (3 per day, 12hr., US$9); Lviv (one per day, 15hr., US$10); Simferopol (1 per day, 13hr., US$7). Connections to Moscow, Riga, and Warsaw. **Schedules** posted in the main hall.

Buses: vul. Dzerzhinskoho, 58 (Дзержинського). Take Tram #5 from the train station or 15 from downtown. Buy tickets at the station at least the night before, o purchase a standing-room ticket from the driver. To: Kiev (11hr., US$8).

Ferries: Schedules are unpredictable. **Black Sea Steamship Line booking office,** Potiomkintsiv pl., 1 (Потьомкінців), at the top of the Potemkin Stairs. Open Mon.-Sat. 9am-4pm. To: Istanbul (1 per week, US$90); Sochi (2 per month, US$100). **Morsky Vokzal** (Морський Вокзал), vul. Suvorova, 6 (Суворова), at the bottom of the Potemkin Stairs. Posh and empty. A window in the main terminal will tell you which companies are going where. To the left of the main dock, ferries head to beaches around Odesa. Tickets also sold on board.

Public Transportation: The train station and pl. Gretska are the main end points. Info in Russian available inside train station (1hv). **Trams** and **trolleys** are free, but can be very costly if, like those of other visitors, your wallet is lost in the crowd. Public transportation runs 7am-midnight.

Taxis: Marshrutne taxis, which take the same route as a trolley, are faster but cost 1hv. Private cars are cheap but risky.

Pharmacy: Apteka #1, vul. Sadova, 5. Open daily 8am-8pm. Ring the doorbell for late-night emergencies.

Medical Assistance: Polyklinik, Primorsky bul., 12 (tel. 22 43 87 or 22 42 67). Treats foreign patients for hard currency and other ailments.

Express Mail: DHL, vul. Rishelievska, 27 (Рішельєвська; tel. 24 42 69; fax 21 71 79).

Post Office: vul. Sadova, 10 (Садова). **Poste Restante** at counter #17; pre-stamped airmail envelopes, counter #19. **Postal code:** 270 000.

Telephones: At the post office. International and intercity calls to your left as you enter. State the number of min. you want (at least 3min.) and pay first (to the U.S. US$2.50 per min.). **Utel phone cards** at window #24. Local calls require *zhetony* (tokens) bought at the post office (0.35hv). Open 24hr. **Phone code:** 0482.

ACCOMMODATIONS AND CAMPING

There are a few choices in Odesa: you can **camp** or hole up in a **bungalow** at the campground on the edge of town; you can check into a **hotel;** a crumbling remnant of a glorious marble past; or you can stay in someone's **apartment.** The last is by far the cheapest (US$5 per person and up), but you'll be lucky to get anything near the center. Train-station hawkers are recognizable by their signs—some variation on "Сдаю комнату." Ask *"Skilko?"* (how much?). Fix a price beforehand and don't pay until you see the room. Collateral is often required for keys. Another, equally cheap and less restrictive, but slightly riskier option is to throw yourself at the mercy of the **dormitories.** They are generally cockroach-ridden, but you might get your own room and even meet some students. **Odesa State University,** Dept. of Foreign Students, vul. Mayakovska (Маяковська; 23 84 77), off vul. Preobrazhenska is in the center. Otherwise, the main dorms are at **Shampansky Pereulok,** the fifth stop of trolleys #5 and 9 from the train station. Ask to speak to the *kommandant.*

Prices are nebulous in the downtown **hotels** as well—make sure a ghost television or refrigerator isn't added to your bill. Truly budget-minded travelers request *"samoye deshovoye mesto"* (the cheapest place), which lands you in a triple or quad. Take tram #3 or 12 from the train station to the downtown hotels.

Tsentralny (Центральний), vul. Preobrazhenska, 40 (tel. 26 84 06). The tall marble staircase and elegant lobby complement the fine location. The rooms are spacious and bright but aging. Singles US$20, with bath US$30. Doubles US$35 per person, with bath US$50. Triples US$40. Showers US$0.50, on the first floor.

Pasazh (Пасаж), vul. Preobrazhenska, 34 (tel. 26 96 36). Skanky businesspeople aside, this hotel has a fair amount of charm and is next to the real Pasazh. Pleasant, boxy little rooms. Singles US$19, with shower US$31. Doubles US$25, with bath US$50. Triples US$36, with bath US$50.

Spartak (Спартак), vul. Deribasivska, 25 (tel. 26 89 24). Old and grand, trying to regain respectability. Large but sparse rooms. Bed in a big room US$8, with shower

US$15. Single with sink, TV, fridge US$20; with shower and telephone US$26. Doubles with sink US$28; with shower, TV, telephone, and fridge US$33.

Camping: Delphin (Кемпинг "Дельфін"), dor. Kotovskoho, 307 (Котовського; tel. 55 50 52). From train station, take trolley #4 or 10 to the terminus (a small loop in the road) and transfer to tram #7; get off 20min. later at "Лузанівка" (*Luzanivka*) and continue 500m. Far even for a campground, but the staff's friendly. No kitchen, but the cheap restaurant, sauna, bar, and private beach make up for it. Bungalows US$13 per person. Cottages US$7 per person. Tents US$4 per person.

FOOD

Odesa is blessed with good restaurants, a market, and cafés that go beyond "hip" into the realm of "meta-hip." *Odesky* eateries have a thing for the subterranean. Options line vul. Preobrazhenska south of vul. Deribasivska. The **Privoz market** (Привоз), vul. Privozna (Привозна), provides more food than the port can handle.

Café Reunion, vul. Tusegoho, 1 (Тусегого; tel. 23 89 46). A pleasant Tex-Mex restaurant in the heart of Odesa, with a straight-shootin' Texan owner. Enchiladas, barbecued ribs, gumbo, and super-hot chili—all with Russian ingredients and a view of the Black Sea. Entrées US$4-6. Open Tues.-Sun. noon-10pm.

Alye Paruca (Алые Паруса), vul. Deribasivska, 18 (tel. 25 34 38). An air-conditioned break for the vegetarian tired of cucumber and tomato salads—try the mushroom soup. Entrées start at US$4. Open daily 9am-midnight.

Kartoplyanki (Картоплянки), vul. Ekaterininska, 3 (Екатериниська). A busy, friendly Ukrainian eatery with excellent food; point to what you want. A potato-and-mushroom something is their specialty. Entrées US$1-2. Open daily 9am-9pm.

Café na Gretskoy (Кафе на Грецькой), vul. Gretska, 11 (Грецька), downstairs. Where the hyper-cool sip foreign liquor, discuss shopping, and look disdainfully at the regular folk enjoying juicy cutlets for US$2. Open daily noon-11pm.

Peking (Пекин), vul. Preobrazhenska, 21 (tel. 26 67 86), under the awning. The only place in town to get Chinese food. Mandarin spoken. Entrées start at US$6.

SIGHTS

Vul. Deribasivska is not just the center of town—it's a center of street culture, where jazz musicians play, mimes tailor their performance to the wishes of the most generous donor, open-air cafés attract young hipsters, and dozens of artists offer to draw your portrait (or caricature) for the price of a chocolate bar. At **Gorsad,** the center of vul. Deribasivska, artists display their achievements and sell elegant handiwork. Across the street is the famous **Gambrinus** (see Entertainment, p. 722). From vul. Deribasivska's west end, cross vul. Preobrazhenska to see the **statue of Mikhail Vorontsov,** the powerful governor of Odesa in the 1820s. Although the statue is ultra neat-o, it's a poor substitute for the cathedral that used to stand here, destroyed in 1936 in an effort to quell the ecclesiastico-political forces that threatened Soviet rule. The square is still called **Soborna ploshcha**—Cathedral Square; you can see pictures of the church in the **Regional History Museum** (Областний Історико-краєзнавчий Музей; *Oblastny Istoriko-kraeznavchy Muzey*), vul. Havanna, 4 (Гавана; tel. 25 52 02; open Sat.-Thurs. 10am-5pm; 0.40hv).

A block to the left on vul. Preobrazhenska grows the superbly aromatic **flower market,** where old women advise young men on the flowers they should bring to their sweethearts. At the other end of the Deribasivska pedestrian zone, turn left on vul. Rishelievska to find the **Opera and Ballet Theatre,** an imposing edifice that towers over the surrounding gardens. The nearby **Museum of the Black Sea Fleet** (Музей Морського Флоту; *Muzey Morskoho Flotu*), vul. Lanzhurinivska, 6 (Ланжыринивська; old Lastochkina; tel. 24 05 09), displays dozens of models of old ships in what was once a 19th-century aristocrats' club (open Fri.-Wed. 10am-5pm; 0.50hv; Russian tour 1hv). At #4, you can check out the **Arkheologichny Muzey** (Археологічний Музей) that houses artifacts found in the Black Sea region, dating back to ancient Greek and Roman times. Especially worth a look is the collection of gold coins stored in a basement vault (open Tues.-Sun. 10am-5pm; 1hv). The façade looks upon a small sculpture of classical figures and a garden. At #2, **Literaturny Muzey** (Літературний Музей; tel. 22 45 60), situated in an early 19th-century palace, offers a fascinating account of the city's rich intellectual and cultural history through its books, prints, and photographs; the collection includes the famous letter from Vorontsov asking that Pushkin be sent out of Odesa "for his own development" because he was, "getting the idea that he is a great writer." Consider hiring an English-speaking guide (10hv), as the museum's exhibits are labeled only in Russian (open Tues.-Sun. 10am-6pm; 0.30hv).

Retrace your steps and take a right at the Archeological Museum onto shady **Primorsky bul.**, the most popular spot in Odesa to stroll and people-watch. The statue of **Aleksandr Pushkin** has its back unceremoniously turned to the city hall, since the local government refused to help fund its construction. On either side of the city hall are the figures of **Fortuna,** goddess of fate, and **Mercury,** god of trade, the two symbols of Odesa. Strolling down Primorsky bul. you'll come upon the statue of the **Duc de Richelieu,** the city founder, whose concrete stare looks down toward the **Potemkin Stairs** (Потьомкінські сходи; *Potiomkinsky skhodi*) and **Morsky Vokzal,** renovated by the Italians and graced by a hideous golden baby in the parking lot. Director Sergei Eisenstein used these stairs in his epic 1925 film *Battleship Potemkin,* originating the oft-imitated visual cliché of a baby carriage loose on an incline, and the name has since stuck. The tired take the **escalator** back up.

Facing the sea, a left at this point will bring you to a **monument** commemorating the actual mutiny on that famous ship. At the end of Primorsky bul. to the un-restored **Palace of Vorontsov** (c. 1826), now a club for schoolchildren. To your left is the long white **Mother-in-Law Bridge,** built, they say, so an elderly lady could more easily visit her son-in-law, a high-ranking official in the local Communist party. For some **beautiful buildings,** head back down vul. Gogolska—farther along, the repressive **House of Scientists** houses a club for the intelligentsia.

At the end of Primorsky bul., take a right at vul. Pushkinska to head down one of Odesa's most beautiful streets. At vul. Pushkinska, 9, you can drop by the **Western and Eastern Society Museum,** more for the 1856 exterior than for the collection (open Thurs.-Tues. 10:30am-5pm; 1.50hv). Farther along, at #13, **Literaturno-memorialny Muzey Pushkina** (Літературно-меморіальний Музей Пушкіна) will commemorate the writer if its "three"-year renovations are ever finished. The 1821 building's noteworthy façade faces away from the sea to avoid salt-air damage. Finally, the **Regional Philharmonic,** built in 1894-99, looks out sternly from the corner of vul. Pushkinska and vul. Rozy Lyuksemburg (Розы Люксембург). A bit further down, the large, gray **Brodsky Synagogue** used to be the center of Odesa's large Jewish community, but today contains an archive. A left at the Philharmonic will take you toward **Park Shevchenka,** a vast stretch of greenery that separates the city from the sea; at the entrance stands a **monument** to the poet Taras Shevchenko.

When Odesa was being built, the closest rock was directly underground, which led to the creation of the world's longest series of **catacombs.** During the 2½-year Nazi occupation, the **Resistance** was based here, and the city has set up an excellent **museum** in their honor. Due to people getting lost and dying in the extensive network of caves, all but one entrance have been shut off, and to enter this one, 13km from the center, you have to be with a tour group. Intourist can get you a guide and car for US$20 per hour, or you can latch onto one of the Russian tours leaving intermittently from the train station. The subterranean museum re-creates the resistance camp—the well, bathrooms, dryer, and sitting room (with a picture of Stalin that tourists used to tear down constantly as *perestroika* progressed)—where 30 men and women held out for six months against German attacks. At Guard Point #1, soldiers had to sit in two-hour shifts in complete darkness to wait for German attackers. Graffitoed rocks have been transported from the original site—one declares "Blood for blood; death for death." This understated and haunting complex is one of the more moving WWII memorials in the former USSR.

Far from the busy commercial center of Odesa lies one of the more entertaining monuments, the **Memorial Complex of the 411th Battalion.** Spread out over a large park, all of the typical armaments of the Soviet forces are here in their colorful glory. You'll think the guns and torpedoes are impressive until you get to the other end of the park and see the tanks (even the turrets move), the bomber, and yes, the battleship, carried here in pieces by tractor-trailer. The best part is that they're all free for you to climb on, in, and around. The rocky **coast** is also a short walk away and worth a visit to see the cliffs which surround this area. At high tide, the sea provides its own brilliant, violent spectacle. The complex is on vul. Amundsena (Амундсена), reachable from the train station by bus #127 or tram #26, a half-hour trip.

ENTERTAINMENT

After some beers at Gambrinus, afternoon philosophizing is best done on Primorsky bul. or vul. Deribasivska, especially in Gorsad—the art hangout and bazaar; Saturdays afford a better catalogue of wedding-dresses than any fashion mag, as newlyweds have their pictures taken.

Performances
Teatr Opery ta Baleta (Театр Опери та Балета), at the end of vul. Rishelievska, has shows nightly; tickets go for 1-5hv unless a serious act comes to town, in which case they run from US$3-35. At these shows, Odesa's elite arrive in their most dashing attire. Saturday and Sunday matinees begin at noon, evening performances at 6pm. Buy tickets a day in advance, or at least that morning, from the ticket office to the right of the theater (open daily 8am-8pm). For **theater** tickets, consult the **Central Ticket Office,** vul. Preobrazhenska, 28 (open daily 10am-5pm). The **Green Theater** performs in Park Shevchenka on summer weekends at 6pm.

Shopping
Commerce is what port towns are all about—Odesa is no exception. First and foremost is the fabulous **Privoz market,** left of the train station on vul. Privozna. Several acres large, the market supplies just about everything you can imagine. Roughly speaking, fruit and vegetables are in the middle, milk products are in the northeast corner, and hardware and clothes around the edges. Keep your hands on your wallet. This is not a good place to change money—snatch-and-run theft is rampant (open daily 8am-6pm). Odesa's **Tsentralny Universalny Magazin TsUM** (ЦУМ), vul. Pushkinska, 21, is another shopping haven (open daily 9:30am-7:30pm). Along vul. Rishelievska, the **state department stores** sell everything from cloth to low-priced cassette tapes, and the city's fanciest **boutiques** cluster around vul. Sadova. Look for "Магазин" and an English word or woman's name—the best ones are below street level. Many require payment in dollars and most are closed on Sundays. Also try the **Pasazh** (Пасаж), next to Hotel Pasazh, a passageway leading from vul. Preobrazhenska to vul. Deribasivska; it's filled with expensive shops and fashion-conscious shoppers. **Gorsad** on vul. Deribasivska is the best place for classy souvenirs.

Beaches
The farther from the center, the cleaner the beaches, but they'll never challenge the Crimea. Most are reachable by public transportation. **Delphin** (Дельфін), on the edge of the park, and at **Arkadia** (Аркадія), the city's most popular with its wide stretches of sand, are also reachable by trolley #5 and bus #129. To the south, the **Golden Shore** (Золотий Беріг; *Zoloty Berig*) is farther away but boasts the most impressive sea and surf. Trams #17 and 18 stop here, as well as at **Chayka** (Чайка) and **Kurortny** (Курортний) beaches. The beach of the proletariat, **Chornomorka** (Чорноморка), lies just outside a high-rise monstrosity of a neighborhood. Take tram #29 to the terminus and keep going. Campground-dwellers can take advantage of their own beach as well as **Luzanivka** (Лузанівка), just down the street, where there is also an **amusement park.** Tram #7 goes right there. Tram #5 stops at **Lanzheron** (Ланжерон), the closest to central Odesa, at **Vidrada** (Видрада), with its pleasant sheltered **forest road** leading into town through Park Shevchenka.

Nightlife

Odesa has more bars than most people have brain cells, and most of them are tiny techno-pop-and-*Heineken* man-holes. However, Gambrinus shines like iced *Finlandia* in the classless drear of warm *Stolichnaya*.

- **Gambrinus** (Гамбринус), intersection of vul. Zhukovskoho and vul. Deribasivska. The dark, spacious interior resembles a Bavarian beer hall, and it's far too cool to be hip. Two gifted old guys provide the tunes, while you drink decent draft beer at 5hv per 0.5L and munch on the excellent *zakuski* (snacks). A historical landmark that used to be the center of Odesa's cultural scene before the Revolution, it is also an excellent place to party. Open daily 10am-11pm.
- **Bar Valday** (Бар Валдай), pl. Potiomkintsiv, 3. A younger scene. The average backpacker is rarely cool enough to enter; worth a shot only if you've packed enough black clothes. Serves food at US$5 and up. Open daily 9am-midnight.
- **Gulfstream**, at the yacht-club. An up-scale restaurant-cum-jazz club haunted by thirtysomethings. Entrées start at US$20, but you didn't come here to eat, did you? Open nightly 11pm-3am. Caution should be taken visiting here. It's in a poorly lit area with no taxis—go in a large group or arrange to have a car pick you up.
- **Kafé Bar** (Кафе Бар), at the Sports Palace (Дворец спорта) on pr. Shevchenko (Шевченко). A hip spot, packed even on weeknights. Dance the night away outside in the parking lot with club kids and mafiosi alike. Open nightly 10pm-4am.

WESTERN UKRAINE (ЗАХІД УКРАЇНИ)

Western Ukraine is trying to act cosmopolitan, tear Ukraine out of Moscow's grip, and move it closer to capitalist Europe. Among tiny, almost primitive villages, you'll find many castles—remnants of the border towns that over the centuries defended the interests of Poland, Turkey, and Russia.

■ Kamyanets-Podilsky (Кам'янець-Подільський)

Raised on a calcium rock some 500m above the Smotrich River canyon, Kamyanets has succumbed to invasion only twice during its near-millennium of existence. The town's two narrow bridges, which deny even lumbering tractors, have most recently protected Kamyanets' rich architecture from the concrete blocks of Soviet "progress." Currently, the city it stands as a tourist attraction without the tourists. As soon as Ukraine lifts its visa requirements, the stronghold will indubitably surrender to a third attack—that of tourists bound for a historical preserve that may rival Venice as an architectural *chef d'oeuvre* set amid natural wonder.

Orientation and Practical Information The small **Old Town** lies about a half-hour walk from the train station. **Trains** puff to Kiev (1 per day, 12hr., 14.40hv) and Chernivtsi (1 per day, leaves at 1:16am). **Chervonoarmiska vul.** (Червоноармійська, some remaining signs proclaim Красноармейская) runs straight from the train station toward town, where it crosses **vul. Hrushevska** (Грушевська; formerly ul. Lenina). Cross vul. Hrushevska at the end of Chervonoarmiska vul., and bus #5 will take you to the Old Town. On foot, head past the buses to the **market** (ринок; *rynok*, open daily 7am-6pm, except for selected Mon.). A right here, and you're on pedestrian **vul. Saborna** (Саборна)—a typical small-town boulevard lined with *stolovayas*, **currency exchange** booths, and people selling cigarettes and Pepsi. At its midway spreads **pl. Saborna**. At its far end in Hotel Ukraina (Україна), the second-floor **Avitsenna Transit tourist office** (Авіценна-Транзит) sells a useful set of brochures about the town for 5hv and throws postcards of the Khotyn castle into the bargain. The couple who run the place also organize tours of the Old Town (2-3hrs.

for 12hv, higher in English. Open Mon.-Fri. 9am-1pm and 2-6pm, and Sat. 9am-1pm). A left on vul. Lesi Ukrainki (Українки) at Hotel Ukraina, then a right onto vul. Knyaziv Koriatovichiv (Князів Коріатовичів) leads to the scenic bridge across the **Smotrich** (Смотрич) River and finally to the Old Town. Before the bridge on vul. Koriatorichiv, **Ukrsotsbank** (Укрсоцбанк) gives good rates for cash U.S. dollars (open Mon.-Fri. 8:45am-1pm and 2-6pm). At the other end of the same street, a 25-minute walk from the Old Town, the **bus station** sends travelers to Chernivtsi (1 per hour 7am-8pm), Khotyn (4 per day), and other local towns. Nearby sits the **post office** (open Mon.-Fri. 8am-7pm, Sat. 8am-5pm) and the **telephone** bureau (open 24hr.). **Postal code:** 281 900. **Phone code:** 03849).

Accommodations and Food Hotel Ukraina, vul. Lesi Ukrainki, 32 (tel. 391 48), directs the tourist from its trippily be-muraled lobby to small rooms with huge baths and (usually) hot water. (Doubles with sink 12hv, with bath 23hv, with bath and sitting room 35hv.) The Intourist **Hotel Smotrich**, vul. Saborna, 4 (tel. 387 00), was closed in 1996—who knows what might develop by 1997. If you can't bear the thought of being away from trains, an anonymous **hotel** (tel. 612 86) upstairs at the station rents triples for 5.40hv per bed.

Leading from the train, vul. Chervonoarmiska features the snooty **U Sashi** (У Саши) while vul. Saborna is gagged up by buck-a-meal **stolovayas**. **Stara fortetsya** (Стара фортеця), bulv. Skhidny, 1 (Східний), next to a rotund defense tower, dwells in the grandiose interior of an old home—winding wooden staircase, balcony, and ceiling-high wall paintings included. After crossing the bridge swerve left onto vul. Zarvanska (Зарванська), then corner another left, a right, and a left to descend straight down to the *fortetsya*. The smiling waitron offers advice on putting together a more-than-filling meal (5.40-7.20hv), if you can't decipher the hand-written Russian menu. The terrace seats afford an imposing vista over the Smotrich canyon (open daily 11am-11pm). En route to the castle, **Pid Vezheyu** (Під Вежею), at the bridge, comes in handy for a quick coffee and sandwich. Stop by at least to peak into the vaulted stone interior decorated with wrought-iron chandeliers and say "wow." (Open daily 9am-9pm; the cook takes a 2-3pm lunch break.)

Sights Kamyanets-Podilsky's small and quiet Old Town contains several bona-fide "monuments to architecture" (which is what those plaques the Soviets pasted buildings of any age say). Crossing the bridge to the Old Town, bear slightly right into a narrow cobblestone alley, vul. Petropavlivska (Петропавлівська). A right at the end onto vul. Tatarska (Татарська) leads to the 16th-century **Kushnirska Tower** (Кушнірська Башта; *Kushnirska Bashta*), whose stone **Windy Gate** (Вітряна брама; Vitryana brama) is famous for knocking off Peter the Great's hat. Backtrack along vul. Tatarska to get to the beautiful, 15th-century, Roman Catholic **St. Peter and Paul Church** (Кафедральний Петропавлівська костьол; *Kafedralny Petropavlivsky kostyol*), vul. Tatarska, 20, flanked by an 18th-century tower. Its elegantly understated (or looted) interior contains several delicately carved marble figures, including a shrine to the Blessed Mother on the right as you enter. Outside, a **Muslim minaret,** from the Cathedral's stint as the center of worship during the Turkish occupation, is topped with a golden Madonna that overlooks the entire town—the Poles placed it there on Vatican's order in 1756, as though to say to the Turks "Ha, ha!" The partition of Poland began shortly thereafter.

Coming Soon to a Videostore Near You

Pan Wołodyjowski: the true story of a sensitive young Polish general who boldly resisted the strictures of convention and the oppression of the Turks by blowing himself up in the gunpowder store of Kamyanets castle, which he had sworn to defend to the death. The film is in videostores; the tree stump which honors his heroic deed sits proudly in the garden of St. Peter and Paul Church.

Past the cathedral, a large square on the left contains a 16-18th-century **Ukrainian-Polish magistrate's house** (Будинок українсько-польського магістрату; *Budinok ukrainsko-polskoho magistratu*), the large building with the clock tower. Next door stands the 16th-century **Dominican monastery** (Домініканський костьол; *Dominikansky kostyol*), complete with fortified walls to keep out the infidels. A fire gutted the complex after it had almost been renovated, but its burned shell still merits a look. Beyond this is a large cobblestone square with some old houses—most notably, at the opposite end of the square, a 16th-century **Armenian merchant's house.** A right at the square is the Roman Catholic **Trinity Church** (Трінітарський Костьол; *Trinitarsky Kostyol*), with an inscription which boldly and honestly proclaims "Всё так не будет" ("Everything will not be like this"). Beyond this, another pleasant bridge takes you to the multi-towered **fortress**, the most famous of the town's aged structures. It was originally built of wood in the 11th century. The 16th-century residents finally realized that this was pretty silly, and rebuilt it with stone. The exterior is impressive as you cross the bridge, the interior wonderfully unsupervised. Some stroll about what's left of the walls; others pick apples from the trees in the courtyard. It's all quite medieval. (Open Sat.-Thurs. 8:30am-5pm, Fri. 8:30am-4pm; the ethnographic museum in the castle walls closes one hour early; 1hr, students 0.50.)

If your legs can still carry you, a number of curious defense bastions await by the Smotrich. At vul. Tatarska's north end, past the Petrpavlivska cathedral, *Staropochtovy uzviz* (Старопоштовий узвіз) drops down on the left to lead past the **Stefan Batory Tower** (Башта Стефана Баторія; *Bashta Stefana Batoriya*)—named after a victorious Polish king—and **Turkish walls** to the **Polish Gate** (Польська брама; *Polska brama*) complex. Together with the **Ruthenian Gate** (Руська брама; *Ruska brama*), the Polish Gate was an inventive form of defense, providing for the flooding of the canyon in case of attack. Vul. Ruska (Руська), offering a view of the town from the position of an invader, winds along the river. Wander east then north (away from the castle) to bend a sharp left after crossing under the bridge onto vul. Lyuksemburg (Люксембург) that continues south as **vul. Dobha** (Добга)—the center of the peaceful Armenian quarter. A 345° right onto vul. Virmenska (Вірменська) at Dobhas's end runs back to the center past a couple of churches: the **Church of the Annunciation** (Благовіщенська церква; *Blahovishchenska tserkva*) and the **Armenian Church of St. Nicholas** (Миколаївська вірменська церква; *Mikolaivaivska Virmenska tserkva*).

■ Near Kamyanets-Podilsky: Khotyn (Хотин)

The history of the **Khotyn castle** is tied closely to that of Kamyanets. The Turkish invasion of Central Europe, given impetus by their seizure of the Kamyanets castle, suffered a setback with the Turks' loss at Khotyn. The Polish-Lithuanian army led by Hetman Jan Sobieski defeated the Turks so orgiastically, that the *hetman* went on to be elected the next bearer of the Polish-Lithuanian Crown. The Khotyn castle thus stands indestructible despite the 1944 Communist invasion of Romanian Bukovina and its transfer into the Ukrainian SSR. Pack a picnic lunch, jump onto a **bus** from Kamyanets or Chernivtsi (4-6 per day, 1½-2hr.) and head for this romantic riverbank hideaway. From Khotyn's bus station, walk right onto vul. Shevchenka (Шевченка), corner a right, head past the statue, and the fortress will be in sight.

■ Chernivtsi (Чернівці)

From the late 1700s this city was part of the Austro-Hungarian Empire, but since 1940 it's been as red as Yeltsin's nose. Now, its cobbled streets are smoothly driven over by slick BMWs, and the glorious façades must maintain beauty among gaudy print shirts. Come here for a pleasant stroll in Habsburg brilliance, or for a view of cultural dissonance at the bizarre confluence of two crumbled empires. Wide unshaded avenues rush among turn-of-the-century façades, making Bukovina's capital seem like it received a major cash injection from some imperial patron of art.

ORIENTATION AND PRACTICAL INFORMATION

The Bukovina region's capital, Chernivtsi, is just 40km north of Romania, and the Romanians have yet to renounce their territorial claims. What they'd get is a city that climbs immediately up from the **train station.** Across the street, trolleys #3 or 5 shuffle their way to the center of town (2 stops). By foot, turn left and take a right onto **vul. Holovna** (Головна; formerly Lenina), which heads straight and then gently to the right into the **Old Town,** located at **Tsentralna pl.** (Центральна) at vul. Holovna's intersection with Ruska vul. (Руська). Vul. Holovna continues and bears left toward the Bukovina Stadium, **Park Shevchenka,** and the **bus station.**

Tourist Offices: Intourist, vul. Komarova, 13a (Комарова; tel. 487 77), in Hotel Cheremosh (Черемош) down the street intersecting Holovna at the bus station.
Currency Exchange: At numerous Обмін Валют *(Obmin Valyut)*. For traveler's checks, try **Aval Bank** (Аваль) in Hotel Tourist at vul. Chervonaoarmiska 184 (Червонаоармька; tel. 789 24). Open Mon.-Fri. 9:30am-1pm. **Export-Import Bank** is setting up shop at Holovna, 183 (tel. 373 13). Open Mon.-Fri. 9:30am-12:30pm. You can also try **Hotel Cheremosh,** vul. Komarova, 13a.
Trains: vul. Gagarina, 38 (Гагаріна). **Advance tickets** (more than 24hr. in advance) must be bought at vul. Holovna, 128. To: Lviv (2 per day, 5hr., 8.50hv); Kiev (daily, 14hr., 16hv); Uzhhorod (daily, 14hr., 12.60hv). Good luck getting information at tel. 424 10, or reserving (yeah) your tickets at tel. 055.
Buses: vul. Holovna, 219 (tel. 416 35). To: Kamyanets-Podilsky (hourly 8am-8pm, 2½hr., 3.70hv); Khotyn (6 per day, 1½hr., 2.50hv); Suceava in Romania (13 per day); Bucharest (3 per week); Chişinău (3 per day, 9hr.).
Public Transportation: The trolley conductor charges 0.10hv. From the train station, trolleys #3 and 5 go to the center along vul. Holovna and then continue to Park Shevchenka, Hotel Bukovina, and, 2 stops later, the advance train ticket office. A **taxi** from the bus or train station to Tsentralna pl. shouldn't cost more than 1.80hv, though the drivers will start haggling from 4hv.
Post Office: vul. Khudyakova, 6 (Худякова; tel. 235 63), 50m from Hotel Verkhovina. **Poste Restante** at window #5. Open Mon.-Sat. 8am-2pm and 3-8pm, Sun. 8am-2pm and 3-6pm. **Postal code:** 274 000.
Telephones: Mizhmisky telefon (Міжміський телефон), vul. Ryazanska, 5 (Рязанска), near the Hotel Verkhovina. Pay at the counter, announce the city you're calling, and get a booth assignment. Open daily 10am-10pm. **Phone code:** 03722.

ACCOMMODATIONS AND FOOD

Chernivtsi's boastful nicknames, which proclaim it a little Paris, Vienna, or Lviv, have apparently gone directly to the hotel industry's head; they have raised prices across the board. There is a **hotel** on the second floor of the train station, as well as the occasional people who wish to let a **private room.** Since Chernivtsi lies close to a state border, hotels request all guests to register with the public administration before letting a room. **VVIR** (ВВІР) is on vul. Suchavska (Сучавська), at the corner of Shuptetskoho (Шуптецького). From pl. Tsentralna, head along vul. Holovna towards the train and hang the first right onto vul. Sheptutskoho. The VVIR is down the street on the left, in a blue building; enter from the perpendicular vul. Suchavska. (Open Mon.-Fri. 9am-6pm but if you arrive on the weekend someone might still be around to stamp your hotel card—get it from the establishment where you want to stay before coming here.)

Hotel Kyiv (Київ; tel. 224 83 or 208 48), vul. Holovna, 46. Central, well furnished, livable rooms. Rather small, with interesting smells. Singles with TV and fridge 54hv, with shower 63hv; doubles with shower 90hv.
Hotel Verkhovina (Верховіна; tel. 227 23), Tsentralna pl., 7. Looks older, and couldn't be more central if it moved into the theater. The staff will be the first to send your rich foreign self up to the Kyiv—for once, they might be right; the Kyiv is both cheaper and more amenable to the comfort of its guests. Doubles 90hv, with shower 117hv.

There are **cafés** and **pizzerias** up and down vul. Holovna and the streets leading away from Tsentralna pl., especially vul. Kobilyanskoy (Кобилячської). None, however, are really worth mentioning. On vul. Ukrainska, by the Armenian Church, clean **Café Maestro** (Кафе Маестро) boils up rich soups for under a buck (try the *shchi*; щи; 1.35hv) and fries up meat at 3.60hv a cutlet. Like-priced vegetarian entrées (mostly mushroom) are available (open daily noon-11pm).

SIGHTS AND ENTERTAINMENT

The principle sights of Chernivtsi are the aged cobbled streets and the elaborate, well maintained 18th- and 19th-century façades that overhang them. Stroll about at your leisure, but don't forget to have a gander at the **university** at the end of vul. Universitetska (Університетська; take a right at Tsentralna pl. from the train station, vul. Ruska becomes vul. Ryazanska which becomes vul. Universitetska). The **theater** is another of Ukraine's beautiful houses of drama, with busts of Pushkin, Goethe, and the gang. Go barely past Tsentralna pl. from the train station and then head right. The *kassa* is to the right as you face Shakespeare (open daily 11am-2pm and 5-7pm). The cute, wooden 1607 **St. Nicholas's Church** (Миколаївська Церква; *Mikolaivska Tserkva*), vul. Sahaidachnoho (Сагайгачного), may still be under reconstruction, after a fire partially consumed it during disputes over whether it should be Russian Orthodox or Uniate. The **Orthodox Cathedral** (Православний собор; *Pravoslavny sobor*) at **vul. Kobylyanskoy**, the main ivy-colored promenade off pl. Tsentralna, has recently been restored. Inside frescos await avid eyes (open daily 7am-8pm). Farther down on the left, the **Armenian Church** (Вірменська Церква; *Virmenska Tserkva*), serves as the Hall of Organ and Chamber Music.

As the sun starts to set, locals move out of pl. Tsentralna's beaches and go hang out at pl. Teatralna (Театральна), near the theater. **Bar Teatralny** (Бар Театральний), on the south side of the square, gathers a mix of the rich and artful who refresh themselves with gallons of juice and soda. To assert your independent personality, get a cup of caffeine for 0.42hv (open daily noon-11pm).

■ Lviv (Львів)

Dear Abby,
Divorced from Poland in 1945 after 600 years of ups and downs, I just went through another split, from the USSR for whom I had cooked and slaved for over 45 years. I'm living with my mother now, old Kiev, but we don't even speak the same language! In spite of my age, I feel ready to be conquered by the world—I deserve to be admired, loved, and remembered. My Polish half-sister, Kraków, tells me that living with tourists creates come all sorts of ills, but I just want to be loved. Why won't someone enter my gates?
Worthy and waiting, Lviv.

ORIENTATION AND PRACTICAL INFORMATION

The center of the Old Town is **pl. Rynok** (Ринок), the old market square. Around it a grid of streets forms the Old Town, and along the west side, **pr. Svobody** (Свободи) runs from the Opera House to **pl. Mitskievicha** (Мішкевича). The hotels are all on this strip. Tram #1 (tram #9 in reverse) runs from the northwest train station to the Old Town's center, tram #6 to the north end of pr. Svobody.

Tourist Offices: The **Hotel George service bureau** (see Accommodations, p. 728) plans guided **tours** and possesses a lot of info about the city. Open Mon.-Fri. 9am-5pm. The **travel office** across the hall is the definitive place to get train tickets or schedule flights. Open daily 9am-6pm. New **maps** of Lviv for 1hv. For other questions, the friendly service desk of the **Grand Hotel** speaks English and will think you're staying in their hotel if you do too. Grand's city **tours** cost US$10 per hour; they **rent cars** with drivers at US$15 per hour.

Central Lviv

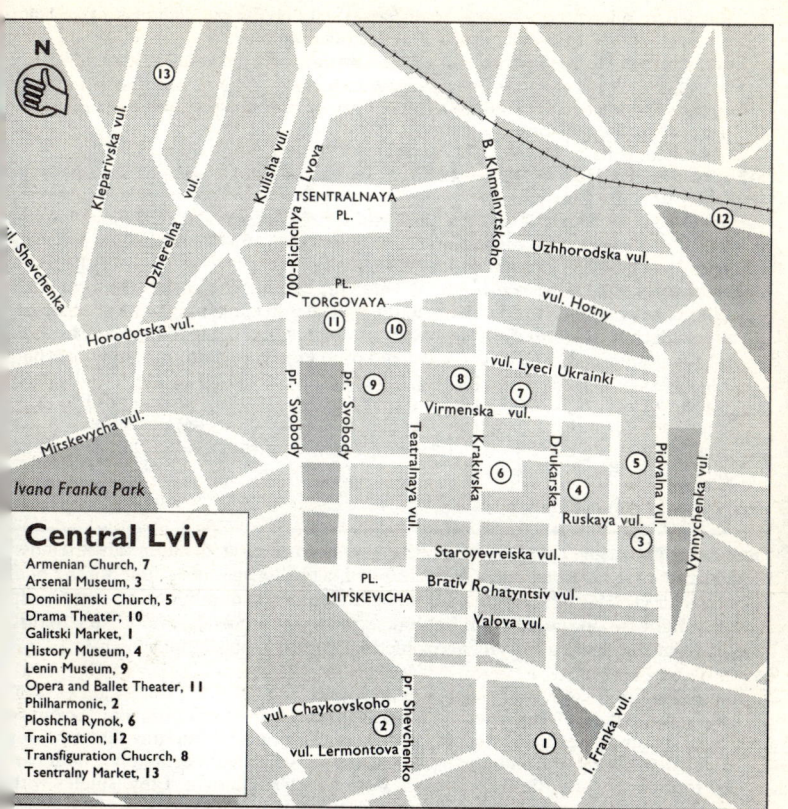

- Armenian Church, 7
- Arsenal Museum, 3
- Dominikanski Church, 5
- Drama Theater, 10
- Galitski Market, 1
- History Museum, 4
- Lenin Museum, 9
- Opera and Ballet Theater, 11
- Philharmonic, 2
- Ploshcha Rynok, 6
- Train Station, 12
- Transfiguration Chucrch, 8
- Tsentralny Market, 13

Currency Exchange: The **Hotel George exchange** cashes traveler's checks at 2%. Open Mon.-Sat. 9am-5pm, Sun. 9am-3pm. **Avalbank** (Авальбанк), vul. Slovatskoho, 1 (Словацького), in the post office, cashes AmEx and Thomas Cook traveler's checks and provides MC and Visa cash advances. Open Tues.-Fri. 10am-4pm.

Western Union: X-Change Points, in the post office. Open Mon.-Fri. 8:30am-1pm and 2-7pm, Sat. 8:30am-1pm and 2-6pm, Sun. 8:30am-1pm.

Trains: pl. Vokzalna (Вокзальна) at the end of Vokzalna vul. Bus #18 takes you to the bus station. **Tickets** available at windows #23-25 on the 2nd floor and at the Hotel George travel bureau. Buy tickets well in advance; international tickets should be reserved in the morning and bought 2hr. before scheduled departure. The travel bureau might be a much bigger help than the train station. To: Bratislava (1 per day, 13hr., US$40), Budapest (daily, 12hr., US$50), Kiev (7 per day, 11-16hr., US$8), Kraków (10hr., US$20), Moscow (4 per day, 22hr., US$20), Prague (daily from Moscow, 19hr., US$57), Warsaw (odd dates only, 12hr., US$25).

Buses: vul. Striska (Стрийська), on the outskirts of town. From the town, take trolley #5. From the station, bus #18 goes to the train station where trams into town are frequent. Extensive regional service. For long-distance destinations, buy tickets a day in advance. To: Brest (4 per day); Kraków (2 per day, 11hr., 20hv); Lublin (daily, 6hr., 14.50hv); Przemyśl (almost every hr., 4hr, 11hv); Warsaw (4 per day, 12 hr., 20hv). Buy tickets for Polish destinations at window #1 in advance, or take a same-day risk at window #2. You can also buy tickets at vul. Voronovo (Вороново, tel. 72 19 91) behind Hotel George next to Kashtan.

Public Transportation: Buy tickets (0.20hv) for **trams, trolleys,** and **buses** at kiosks; punch on board. Controllers are vigilant and ready to slap you with that US$1 fine if you dare ride without paying. Some kiosks sell a recent public transit **map**. Tram lines are marked in brown, trolley in red, and bus in blue.

Laundromat: Hotel George will take in wash for its guests; US$1 for a week's worth of underwear and socks.

Luggage Storage: Hotel George's 1hv per bag per 24hr. is probably safer than similar deals at the train and bus stations.

24-Hour Pharmacy: Apteka #23 (Аптека), vul. Zelena, 33 (Зелена).

Express Mail: DHL, vul. Tarnovskoho, 2 (Тарновського; tel. 75 48 66). Free pick-up. Open Mon.-Fri. 9am-6pm.

Post Office: vul. Slovatskoho, 1, a block from Park Ivana Franka, to the right as you face the university. **fresco:** on the second floor. Open Mon.-Fri. 8am-8pm, Sat. 8am-6pm, Sun. 8am-2pm. **Postal code:** 290 000.

Telephones: vul. Doroshenka, 39 (Дорошенка), around the corner from the post office. Order your call at the booth to the right as you climb up. For local and intercity calls, buy *zhetony* (жетоны; tokens) at the telephone office or at kiosks. Pick up the phone, wait for the dial tone, and drop in your *zheton* only when the person answers, or risk losing it forever. Intercity calls can be made only from the telephone office or from telephones that say "Міжміськи" (meezh-MEES-kee—intercity). Open daily 7am-11pm. Sending **faxes** (fax 76 15 85) costs US$0.35 per page. **Utel** cards available at Hotel George, the Grand Hotel, Hotel Dnipro, and the post office. **Phone code:** 0322.

ACCOMMODATIONS

Reflecting increasing numbers of tourists, Lviv is renovating its old Intourist haunts. Last year the Grand Hotel opened its gleaming salons to the public, but not the budget traveler (US$80 per person). Come next summer, a number of new establishments might be operating from behind statue-topped portals, and if they follow George's example, they'll even have something for the cash-strapped.

Hotel George (Готель Жорж), pl. Mitskievicha, 1 (tel. 72 59 52). Take tram #1 from the train station to "Дорошенка" *(Doroshenka).* This beautiful turn-of-the-century hotel, recently restored, becomes a great value because of the tiny 90% tariff for foreigners (compared with the usual 300-600%). At the city's center, it is both part of the scenery and the perfect place from which to enjoy it. Large singles with desk, coffeetable, telephone, sink, and a clean communal shower cost US$16, with bath US$45. Equally spacious and luxurious doubles with sink and telephone US$21, with bath US$53. Payment in US$ only. A decent breakfast is included. If you don't mind walking down the hall for a shower, this is part of the Lviv experience—and remember what a place like this would cost in Kraków.

Hotel Lviv (Львів), vul. 700-richcha Lvova, 3 (700-річчя Львова; tel. 79 22 70), just behind the Opera and Ballet Theater. If Hotel George has blown up or brought its foreigners' tariff up to speed, take tram #6 from the train station to "Оперни Театр" *(Operny Teatr),* backtrack about 50m, and take a left; the hotel is on the right. The facilities are not as pretty as in the newer hotels, but the location is central. Beds in 3 to 5-person rooms 12hv per person; in 2-person rooms 21-30hv, with bath 45hv. Doubles 45hv, with bath 67hv. Asking for rooms without television or refrigerator may lower the price.

Hotel Sputnik (Спутник), vul. Knyahini Olgi, 116 (Княгині Ольги; tel. 64 58 22). A 15 min. ride from the city center (tram #3 to the last stop). You may suffer from culture shock shuttling between here and the old part of town, but the facilities are wonderfully modern. Plus, it's practically next door to the concrete Универма *(Univermag)* department store, an architectural wonder of its time. All rooms with bath. Singles 52hv, doubles 57hv. Breakfast included.

FOOD

Pl. Rynok is the center of restaurants and cafés; the most convenient **market** is on pl. Shevchenko (Шевченко), a block past Hotel George, though it's not as big as **Novy Rynok** (Новий Ринок), reachable by bus #18. **Galitski Rynok** (Галицький Ринок behind the flower stands across from St. Andrew's Church, has fresh berries, honey, and vegetables (open in summer daily 7am-6pm).

Restaurants

Lviv is full of quick eateries serving Ukrainian fast food (beef and potatoes, borscht, etc.). There are also several elegant restaurants whose cuisine is on a jarringly lower level than their atmosphere would suggest.

- **Lisova Pisnya** (Лісова Пісня), vul. Sichovikh Striltsiv, 29 (Січових Стрільців). Close to the university, the "Forest Song" is run by students, making it a trendy place for some potato *deruny* (деруни) with pork (3.30hv), a late-night cup o' borscht (борщ; 0.90hv), or a teatime cappuccino (1hv). Open daily 10am-11pm.
- **Pizza Pronto,** vul. Horodotska, 61 (Городоцька) down the street from the circus not far from pr. Svobody. Its six simple tables are often occupied. No wonder. The pizzas (10-13hv) come hot, may be ordered by the slice (around 1.60hv), and can be vegetarian. Menu has English translations. The juices and soda are served up well chilled (0.60hv). Yum! Open daily 10am-9pm.
- **The Press Club,** pl. Vozzyednannya (Возз'єднання). No sign on the building, but the open brown door lets the passersby see this is a restaurant. Despite being "in" with the journalist crowd, the eatery remains an unpretentious, central location for a light noontime salad (0.85hv), a late wake-up coffee (0.60hv), or something heftier but equally affordable. Open daily 10am-10pm.
- **Domashni Stravy** (Домашні Страви), vul. Lichakivska at vul Solodova (Солодова) beside the Lichakivsky market. A zero-ambiance *yidalnya* into its 4th year thanks to private ownership. Yummy *chakhany* (1hv)—big chunks of meat in a thick broth. Open daily 10am-10pm.
- **Hlinyanska Vezha** (Глинянська Вежа), vul Vinnichenka, 3 (Винниченка). Famous for its *deruny* (potato pancakes) across town, it limits its menu to that and *chakhany*—a bean soup with potatoes and meat. A first-rate *yidalnya*. *Deruny* 1.55hv, *chakhany* 0.80hv, *kompot* 0.20hv. Open daily 9am-8pm.
- **Pizzeria Castellari** (Кафе Кастелларі), vul. Vinnichenka, 6, at the start of vul. Lichakivska (tel. 76 58 32). Thin-crust pizzas for 6-7hv are each enough for two. Descend down below the people-watching spot into a black-and-white, scrubbed, popular lunch spot. Salads 0.2hv, juices 0.65hv. The dough lacks that Roman "crisp," but this might be the only spot on the Steppe whose pies don't come out of deep pans. They pack the leftovers and offer take-out and delivery. Open daily 10am-10pm.
- **Kafe Teatralne** (Кафе Театральне), pr. Svobody, 24. A small, popular food-and-drink haven. The figures on the murals appear to be singing country tunes, but the walls rebound the sounds of Ace of Base. *Pelmeni* (meat-filled tortellini), *myaso* (cutlet), or *kovbasa* (sausage) with bread and vodka, juice, or coffee for under US$2. Open daily 9am-3pm and 4-8pm.

Cafés

Reflecting its Polish and Austro-Hungarian heritage, Lviv is a city of coffee and cafés. Although few elegant coffeehouses remain, there are a couple of spots to sit down and have a cup with friends. If a cup of cappuccino costs more than 0.60hv, you're being charged Intourist prices.

- **Italisky Dvorik** (Італійський Дворик), pl. Rynok, 6. Step into the Italian courtyard, where Lviv's coolest citizens sip coffee or cold juice among Renaissance statues and their own personal arches. It's the courtyard of a 16th-century Italian merchant's house, and a museum upstairs contains his richy-rich stuff. Not Lviv's best coffee, but undoubtedly its best coffee setting. Open daily 10am-6pm.
- **Bernardinsky Dvorik** (Бернардинський Дворик), behind St. Andrew's Church. Bored into a defensive well, this new café hums with life all day. Leave Lviv's rushing streets and enjoy an unadulterated view of the church. The coffee fetches an appropriately higher price (0.80hv or US$.45). Sip it outside to sink fully into the medieval surroundings. Open Mon.-Fri. 11am-11pm, Sat.-Sun. noon-11pm.

Mandriki (Мандрікі), vul. Hnatyuka 4 (Гнатюка). Good coffee, folksy modern carvings, and oak tables, but no 16th-century walls. Open daily 10am-4pm and 5-9pm.

Café Edem (Едем), vul. Kopernika (Коперника), off pr. Svobody. Snow-white tables, chairs, and counters occupy 2 pastel-blue carpeted floors where the trendily dressed young crowd comes for a coffee or a slice of pizza (2hv). Good pastries (0.35-0.80hv) and an assortment of juices (0.60-0.70hv) for the sugar-starved, and the usual array of bar regalia for the swillers. Open daily 10am-10pm.

SIGHTS

Lviv is not a city for the goal-oriented tourist. A gander about the Old Town's cobblestone alleys will lead past towering spires, hunched over homes, and architectural styles spanning the centuries. The tour begins on pr. Svobody. The dazzlingly complex exterior of the Opera and Ballet Theater (Театр Опери та Балету) is surpassed only by its interior, complete with gilded sculpture. It opens onto a pedestrian mall that runs down the middle of pr. Svobody. Exiting the theater, a walk down the boulevard's right side leads past shops and hotels, lodged in the façades of old Polish apartments. On the left, the **Natsionalny muzey** (Національний музей) commands attention if only for its impressive fronts. Part of the town's original **city walls and gates** still stand next to the museum. The main gallery offers two permanent exhibits and a changing one (usually of modern foreign art). The collections include several rooms of 14th- to 19th-century icons and two wings of Ukrainian paintings. The latter is the more interesting, showing the evolution on national brushwork and testifying that Ukrainian art developed alongside its Flemish and French counterparts. (Open Sat.-Thurs. 10am-5:30pm. 0.40hv, students 0.20hv, on Mon. students free)

A third of the way up pr. Svobody, at #15 (corner of vul. Hnatyuka) the **Muzey Ethnographii** (Музей Етнографії) harbors an exhibit of Ukrainian dress, archeological artifacts, painted eggs, and embroidery; it's worth a look inside, if only just for the fabulous marble staircase and lofty decorated ceilings (open Wed.-Sun. 10am-6pm; 0.50hv, students 0.20hv). Turn off onto vul. Hnatyuka, and at a fork in the road head left to **Park Ivana Franka** (Парк ім. Івана Франка), fronting on **Lviv University.** Franka looks kindly down on the students; the ones who walk all the way uphill through the park will be rewarded by the beauteous, ochre-walled, gold-studded **St. Iura Cathedral** (Собор св. Юра; *Sobor sv. Iura*) to the right; this 18th-century wonder remains youthful, thanks to the hundreds of baptisms it sees yearly (open daily 7am-1pm and 3-8pm). Under renovation in 1996, by '97, its interior should match the beauty of its outer surface. Towards the train, the church you pass on the tram is **St. Elizabeth's Cathedral.** Constructed by Poles when they first settled in Lviv, its spires purposefully reach higher than St. Iura's domes to assert the dominance of Polish Catholicism over Ukrainian Orthodoxy.

Back on pr. Svobody, you eventually reach the **Mickiewicz column,** honoring the Polish poet, patriot, and frat-boy. This is the site of concerts, crowded political discussions, and the occasional Hare Krishna sing-along. Turn left at the Ukraine movie theater and head toward the stone-gray 17th-century Bernardine Monastery, now the Greek Catholic **Church of St. Andrew.** The church boasts a cavernous interior covered in frescos and a massive altar of rich gold and black granite. To reach the Old Town's heart, make a sharp left here and take one of the narrow streets leading up to **pl. Rynok,** the historic market square, presenting a collage of four-story, richly decorated merchant homes dating from the 16-18th centuries. The square gazes lovingly at the **town hall** (ратуша; *ratusha*), a 19th-century addition, whose corners are guarded by statues of Diana, Venus, Neptune, and patron of Greek love Cupid.

There are enough museums around the square to help you with cocktail party banter for the next year. The **Istorichny muzey** (Історичний музей), pl. Rynok, 4, recounts the history of Lviv during the World Wars (open Thurs.-Tues. 10am-6pm; 0.50hv, students 0.20hv). The adjoining **Italian Courtyard,** pl. Rynok, 6, presents the household objects of the Italian *mascalzone* who lived here in the 16th century. (Open Thurs.-Tues. 10am-6pm.) The **Pharmacy Museum** (Аптека-музей; *Apteka-muzey*) occupies Lviv's oldest drugstore and sells bottles of iron-fortified "wine" designed to cure all ills; ask for the *vino* (open Mon.-Sat. 9am-7pm, Sun. 10am-5pm). Before going out with the artsy crowd, prepare to stun them with knowledge gleaned at the **Museum of Furniture and Porcelain** at #24 (Музей Меблів і Порцеляни; *Muzey Mebliv i Portselyany*; open Thurs.-Tues. 10am-6pm; 0.50hv).

Lviv is jam-packed with beautiful examples of ecclesiastic art and architecture; if you're going to get churched-out anywhere, this is the town for it. The best time for a temple tour is 5 to 7pm when the oft-shut doors open up for the prayer-thirsty faithful. When casting a glance inside, remain respectful of those who came here for spiritual inspiration—don't walk around, don't talk, and don't take pictures, please. Just beyond trident-armed Neptune's gaze is pl. Katedralna (Катедральна), where the main attraction is the Polish **Roman Catholic Cathedral** (open Mon.-Sat. 6am-noon and 6-8pm, Sun. and holidays 6am-3pm and 5:30-8pm). The huge decorated columns and dark apocalyptic frescos make this pinnacle-of-delicate-art-on-a-grand-scale one of Ukraine's most awesome cathedrals, since Kiev's are still closed. The church contains four altars along each nave and a ninth one to the right of the main altar, each worth a lengthy tête-à-tête with the central icon. Next door stands a small Renaissance chapel, **Kaplitsa Boimiv** (Каплиця Боїмів), which is the only example of Lviv's religious architecture that's more a tourist attraction than a house of worship. The chapel was ordered by a rich Hungarian merchant, Boim, and contains the rotted skeletons of 14 members of his family. Gaze up at the ceiling for a head-spinning view of the dome's spiral decorations. In the upper-left corner hangs Mr. Boim's emblem. Lacking noble origins he bought himself the title of a consul that gave him the right to an "emblem" (open daily 10am-5pm; 0.20hv). From Diana's column on pl. Rynok, follow vul. Ruska (Руська) east to the massive **Assumption Church.** As in all Russian Orthodox churches, every icon was painted by a scholarly and saintly monk. Here more so than in Catholic temples cameras are a no-no. The out-of-place befriezed main altar is a reminder of the times when the Russian Orthodox church suffered a brief spell under Greek Catholic supervision. Less strict about the piety of their art, the latter allowed the semi-laic Baroque to stamp a foot in the saintly haven. Next to the church, **Kornyakt's Tower** (Башта Корнякта; *Bashta Kornyakta*) hoists a bell 60m above ground.

To the left and back as you leave the church gates, the Dominican Monastery has been converted into a **Museum of the History of Religion** (Музей Історії Релігії; *Muzey Istori Relighi*), whose masterfully carved wooden figures are worth a look (open Fri.-Wed. 10am-6pm). If you head right as you leave the Assumption Church, you'll find the **Arsenal Museum,** Arsenala vul., 3 (Арсенальна), at vul. Pidvalna (Підвальна). Its curators have preserved iron examples of the many implements humans have employed to kill each other (open Thurs.-Tues. 10am-5:45pm).

Back on pl. Rynok, prowling north past the pharmacy museum along vul. Krakivska (Краківска), then bearing right on vul. Virmenska (Вірменська), lands you at the barricaded **Armenian Cathedral.** It seems so out of place one would never guess it has stood here since the 14th century. A passage runs from vul. Virmenska to vul. Lyeci Ukrainky (Лесі Українки) between the church and the bishop's hearth, letting the wanderer peek into the ecclesiastic back alleys. On Lyeci Ukrainky, a left steers you to the **Transfiguration Church** (Преображенська церква; *Preobrazhenska 'serkva*), one block away at vul. Krakivska, 21, a more modern building popular for weddings. Turn left as you exit the church, walk a few blocks, and take a right up the stairs to the ochre **Church of Our Lady of the Snow** (Костьол Марії Сніжної; *Kostyol Marii Snizhnoy*). Catch an evening or morning service (Mon.-Sat. 7:15am and 7pm; Sun. 9am and 7pm) to glimpse the elaborate altar.

To the left of the Snow Lady runs a path to the old market square. Across and to the right stands **St. John the Baptist Church.** Carefully preserved since the 13th century, it's one of the best postcard scenes in the city. Because it serves as the **Museum of Old Lviv**, it's open Tuesdays through Sundays from noon to 6pm. Vul. Uzhhorodska (Ужгородська) climbs to the right around the miniature church all the way up to **High Castle Hill** (Высокий Замок; *Vysoky Zamok*) where the television tower now stands. A right at the restaurant guides the cameras to a panoramic viewpoint above the Old Town. Farther east, take tram #2 or bus #7 from Halitska pl. (Галицька) or walk along vul. Lichakivska to vul. Krupyarska (Крупярська). Walk up the street on the left to the outdoor **Museum of Architecture**, also known as **Shevchenkivsky Hai** (Шевченківський Гай). Lying on a vast park, the museum harbors a collection of wooden houses brought here from around West Ukraine (open Tues.- Sun. 10am-6pm; 0.50hv).

Back on vul. Lichakivska, head down vul. Mechnikova (Мечникова), to the whitewashed chapel and the **Lichakivsky Cemetery** (Личаківський Цвинтар; *Lichakivski Tsvintar*). Inside Lviv's most famous necropolis are the tombs of Polish nobles beside the simple graves of local residents from throughout the centuries. Hidden from the life giving sun by a heaven of trees, Lichakivsky's paths provide a pleasant, if unorthodox, strolling ground. For a most instructive visit, follow Mechnikova down past the large empty space to the main gate. Upon entering, follow the path that takes off to the right at a 135° angle. It visits the graves of Ukraine's most famous artists. On its left side, a hammer-armed Stakhanovite decorates the eternal bed of **Ivan Franko** (Іван Франко)—a nationalist (or patriotic, depending on how you look at it) poet. Across the path from Franko sleeps **Lyudchenko** (Людченко)—Melopmene's favorite composer. Up and to the left of the footway a statue of a gorgeous man playing a stone lyre attempts to revive the golden voice of **Solomiya Kruzhelnitska** (Соломия Кружельницька), in whose honor Lviv holds the November opera festivals. The last individual grave lies close by, the sepulcher of **Volodymyr Ivasyuk** (Івасюк), an all-around artist, is marked by the standing figure of a young hunk looking for inspiration. At his tomb, take a right branch off the alley to reach the rows of graves of Ukrainian, Polish, and foreign soldiers who died in the defense of Lviv in the years 1918-19. The central arch hails them with a stereotypical Latin motto: MORTI SVNT VT LIBERI VIVAMVS—"they died so we may life free". South of the center, tram #2 returns to town; from downtown, take #4. **Strisky Park** (Стрийський Парк) is splendidly manicured, with swans and a greenhouse. Vul. Ivana Franka courses south to vul. Striska, which borders the garden.

ENTERTAINMENT

Lviv goes to sleep by midnight only because it starts celebrating by 8pm. Or even earlier, since pr. Svobody fills up after lunch with the sexagenarians singing wartime and harvest tunes to the accompaniment of an accordion. By eight, sounds of light jazz start filling the avenue from a sidewalk café, coffeehouses cloud up with fag fumes and auditoriums echo with arias or tragic monologues. Only here can you taste all this for pennies, so don't let the contentment of a Hotel George room immerse you in inertia; go out and turn contentment into pleasure.

Performances

Renowned opera, experimental drama, cheap tickets, and an artful population make Lviv's performance halls the second most-frequented institution—after cafés. All theaters post their schedules by the front entrance, although many host only irregular performances in the summer. Tickets range from US$1 to US$2, so now is the time to get that front-row seat that Broadway's neoned playhouses put out of reach. Purchase tix at each theater's **kasa** or at the **ticket windows** (театральни каси; *teatralny kassy*) on pr. Svobody, 37 (open Mon.-Sat. 11am-2pm and 4-7pm).

Teatr Opery ta Baletu (Театр Опери та Балету), pr. Svobody, 1—by now you know exactly where it is. Catch a Verdi or a Rossini for US$1 on the first balcony. Great space, great voices, great sets—a paradise in gilded Eden.

Philarmoniya (Філармонія) vul. Tchaikovskoho (Чайковського), round the corner from the George. Less frequent performances than at the Opera but with many renowned guest performers, usually from Kiev or Russia.

Ukrainsky Teatr Marii Zankovetskoy (Український Театр ім. М. Заньковецької), pr. Svobody, 26. Famous throughout the land, this home of drama produces the compositions of Ukrainian dramaturges—classical and experimental alike.

Lvivsky dukhovny teatr "Voskresinnya" (Львівський духовний театр "Воскресіния"), pl. Peremohy (Перемоги), at the end of vul. Hnatyuka that heads from the Ethnographic museum on Svobody. Although in Ukrainian, Voskresinnya presents 20th-century works—from Chekhov to Beckett—that many might have seen already performed in English. This will be more than a repeat experience in Cyrillic, though, as the theater's fame rests on the innovation of its shows.

Nightlife

After singing all day in the streets and coffee-ing up in the java houses, at night Lviv sits down in its squares and patios for yet another sing-along or one final cup. For an evening free of partisan arias, stop for a shot of whatever at a club-café, or swig some steins at "Zoloty Kolos." The closest **gay** life comes to being "organized" is the cruising area on pr. Svobody—from the Opera to the Shevchenko statue.

Klub-Kafé Lyalka (Клуб-Кафе Лялька), vul. Halitskoho, 1 (Галицького), below the Puppet Theater *(Teatr Lyalok)*. The jovial doorman will ask for the cover (1hv per couple quite suffices) with a big smile and give you information (in Ukrainian or accented Polish) on the other cool hangouts in the city. Downstairs, artsiness fights artfulness for supremacy. Shabbily dressed artfuls choose shots while arguing with the artsy sophisticated black-clad wine-sippers. A rarely cleaned wall of posters advertises past and future café concerts. On nights without live music, speakers exude soft Italian rock or Australian pop, etc. Graffitoed bedsheets hang from the ceiling while colorful modern art bespatters the poster-free walls. There's even a tiny dance corner in this murky actors' evening spot. 200mL of wine 2.60hv. Coffee 0.60hv. Open daily noon-11pm.

Klub-Kafé "za Kulisami" (Клуб-Кафе за Кулісами), vul. Tchaikovshovo, 7 (tel. 75 21 01 or 76 74 20), on the second floor of the Philharmonic, entrance to the left. Finally a bastion of bearable background music. Sounds of practicing philharmonic artists fly in through the windows by day. Hard liquors and suds available, but they would somehow seem out of place. Java and Marlboro all the way. Even mellower than Lyalka, "Backstage" offers 0.70hv cover for the musically gifted and those in the know. Open daily noon-midnight.

Klub-Kafé Vavilon XX (Вавилон XX), pl. Mitskevicha, 7, inside the cinema, at the end of the hallway on the left. The doorman doesn't let those without a club card in, but when told that the *shveetzar* (doorman) from the Puppet's Theater's café sent you here, you might get in even without giving him vodka money. Yellow lights, tables separated by glass-tube curtains, flax sheets hung on windows to keep out the light, and on top of it all, enough room to dance. Teens and early 20s clientele but no age is out of place. Coffee 0.60hv. Open daily 10am-10pm.

Café Porokhova Vezha (Порохова Вежа) vul. Pidvalna in the (gun) powder tower. No doorman! The round, cold-stone room with a high ceiling somehow manages to ventilate the liters of cigarette smoke exhaled (but never inhaled) here. Some bar-staff get by in English and will eagerly speak it even to Ukrainian-speakers from abroad. It's not a club so it's not filled with artists and artistes like the other 3 cafés. Open daily 10am-10pm.

Zoloty Kolos (Золотий Колос), vul. Kleparivska, 18 (Клепарівська). The USSR's best brewery continues to bubble-up the ex-USSR's best beer. Bottles stand for an 0.80hv grab at the entry to the cellar, or you can enjoy your hops n' malt for 0.65hv in the cafe. When *Zoloty Kolos* is unavailable, the weaker but equally tasty *Lvivske Pivo* foams on the tables. Open daily 10am-11pm.

■ Near Lviv: Zhovkva (Жовква)

Reflecting Ukraine's lack of concern for developing tourism, life in the dome-topped Zhovkva flows uneventfully from one vodka shot to another. Although in 1994 the government in Kiev made a symbolic step towards the preservation of Zhovkva's historic center by declaring the town a museum, all this meant was evacuating chicken coops from the churches and barricading the temples. The chickens politely moved to the castle and the park, probably paying more attention than the local human animals to the ministerial decision.

Zhovkva centers on pl. Vicheva (Вічева) around which much of the original city walls still stand. As the road from the bus stop penetrates into the square, a large **plan** of the city explains the historic significance of every monument. The explanations are in Ukrainian, but Zhovkva's clear layout makes it simple.

With your face towards the map, the walls to the right encircle the 1653 **Dominican monastery.** Although its gates remain shut, the tall building and extensive grounds underscore the Dominicans' influence here during the town's golden age—the turn of the 17th and 18th centuries. Turn left after entering the square and plod down along pretty burgher houses to the 16-17th century fortification marked by the **Zvirinetska Gate** (Звіринецька брама; *Zvirinetska brama*), a witness to the passage of Bohdan Khmelnitsky after a victory over those nasty Poles (who built the town). The **castle** (замок; *zamok*), to the right of the gate, has proven a perfect place to dry laundry on sunny days. Although its original 1594 state might have withered over the past 400 years, the 16-th century feel is stronger here than in the Coke-umbrella-filled fortresses of Western Europe. Further to the right along the walls, an 18th- to 20th-century **town hall** guards the symbolic **grave-monument** to the victims of the 1941 Stalinist repressions.

On the other side of the **Hlinska Gate** (Глинська брама; *Hlinska brama*) that borders the town hall, the Roman-Catholic **Parish Church** (Парафіяльний костьол; *Parafialny kostyol*) will start tourists' cameras clicking. Also closed, its shell alone commands admiration, with well maintained domes and cupolas bordered by a band of haut-reliefs. Behind it towers the belfry, erected in the early 17th century.

At the corner of the square behind the parish, walk a block into the grid of streets and take a left to the Greek-Orthodox **St. Basil's Monastery** (Ансамбль Василянського монастиря; *Ansambl Vasilyanskoho monastyrya*), built 1612. Arrive between 7 and 9 o'clock in the morning or evening to enter the Church of Christ's Birth, just inside the monastery grounds. Frescos cover every square inch of the church. Gilded sculptures and icons blend into this shiny background, though the alter's four-columned dome deserves a separate moment of appreciation. The bread at the church's center is for the priests, so hold your hungry horses.

Coming out of the monastery, take a left; another left leads to the disemboweled **synagogue.** Like the other abandoned buildings' exteriors, this synagogue's befriezed and beflaunted skin still remembers 16th- and 17th-century good times.

Buses for Zhovkva leave from Lviv's bus station #4 (not the main bus station) on vul. Bazarna (Вазарна), a left off vul. Dzherelna (Джерельна). Yup, it's at Tsentralny Market, amid tomatoes, bras, and hens. Buses to many towns stop in Zhovkva (e.g. to Maidan and Mokrytyn), so ask at the **kasy** about the one that's leaving as you speak (pay the driver 1.45hv). Zhovkva is the first stop with a bus station (45min.). From the bus, head left onto the road and into town (10min.).

TRANSCARPATHIA (ЗАКАРПАТТЯ)

Traveling from Kiev or Lviv to anywhere in southeastern Europe, you will find yourself drifting through rolling pine-covered hills carved by cold crystal streams. Unlike the Caucasus' jagged peaks, the quiet Carpathian Mountains are all about grazing, slowly lumbering from one gentle peak to another, chewing grass. Beyond the soporific Carpathians lie the border towns of Uzhhorod, Mukacheve, and Chop, influenced more by the mountains and the nearby countries than by Marx and his fallout. During the summer months, vacationers fill the region picking buckets of raspberries, while avoiding Crimea's Russian crowds and unstable politics.

■ Uzhhorod (Ужгород)

A true border town, 4km from Slovakia and 25km from Hungary, Uzhhorod subsumes the ethnic mix into its small, pleasant, if not altogether memorable Old Town, a remnant of about 800 years of Austro-Hungarian rule. On the outskirts of the town, ugly industrialization is progressing and stagnating, a remnant of fifty years on the very edge of the Soviet Union. It's gotten too big to be quaint, and now locals from several countries sit along the banks of the barely flowing Uzh River and wonder what a Habsburg would do in their position.

Orientation and Practical Information Aptly named Uzhhorod lies on both banks of the **Uzh** (Уж) River. The **train** and **bus stations** are both on the south side, which was more recently developed. From the train station, cross the street and pass the bus station on your left and head down broad **pr. Svobody** (Свободи). At pl. Kirila i Mefodia (Кирила і Мефодія), Hotel Zakarpattya's **Intourist** (tel. 325 72) sells international train tickets to Budapest (daily, 7hr., US$25) and Prague (daily, 16hr., US$53). Other tickets can be purchased at the **train station** to: Kiev (2 per day, US$11); Lviv (3 per day, 5hr. or overnight, 9hv). Many buses (1hr., 3hv) and trains (2hr., 3.50hv) run daily to Mukacheve—bus tickets are harder to obtain than train tickets. Take a right at the big hotel to get to the river and the **Old Town.** Cross the street after the bridge to get to the **Ukraine Export-Import Bank** (tel. 335 41), pl. Petefi, 19 (Петефі), which cashes traveler's checks at 2% commission (open Mon.-Fri. 9am-noon and 1-3pm). Take a left after the bridge and head down nab. Nezalezhnosti (Незалежності) for the long-distance **telephones** at #4 (open daily 7:45am-11:30pm). Past this, around the corner, is the **post office** (open Mon.-Fri. 9am-6pm, Sat. 9am-5pm), and its pride and joy, the **X-Change Points** that has **Western Union** and cashes traveler's checks and Visa at 5% commission. **Postal code:** 294 000. **Phone code:** 0312.

Accommodations and Food It's a bit of a hike from the train, but **Turbaza Svitanok** (Турбаза Світанок), vul. Koshitska, 30 (Кошицька ; tel. 343 09), is undoubtedly the best place for the budget traveler in Uzhhorod—or in the region, for that matter. A place in a double with shower and two meals costs US$8, but hot water is sporadic. Head across the river from the train station and take a left onto the main street running parallel to the river. Signs should lead you there (the *turbaza* lies about seven minutes up the fourth street to the right). Not only will they lodge and feed you, but this is the main **tourist office** for treks into the Carpathians. They have a branch at the Kostrina settlement—**Turbaza Dubovy Hai** (Турбаза Дубовий Гай; tel. 372 35), 1½ hour by commuter rail. Nearby, Mt. Krasiva rises to 1036m above sea level. If affordable, well located lodging doesn't suit you, spend your money at the luxury **Hotel Korona** (tel. 360 62), pl. Teatralna, 5, smack-dab in the center of the Old Town. Spacious, well furnished doubles with TV and bath cost US$60, with sitting room and a tea-set US$98. The traveler who fears being too far away from the train station should head past Hotel Zakarpattya on pr. Svobody to **Hotel Uzhhorod,** vul. Khmelnitskoho, 2 (tel. 350 60), which offers small singles with shower US$21, doubles US$37, and triples US$48. All of Uzhhorod's *yidalnyas* offer the same uneventful meals. The more populated the café the fresher the *pelmeni*...or the cheaper the vodka.

Sights Uzhhorod's three main tourist attractions have congregated next to one another with unheard-of consideration. Head right and up just after Hotel Korona. The huge and majestic Neoclassical exterior of **Kafedralny Sobor** (Кафедральний Собор) is on your left. The interior is impressive, but open only during services. Farther along, an unremarkable **castle** contains some statues, a museum, and pretty views of surrounding foothills and stagnant industry. The castle joined the 1704 Transcarpathian revolt against the Habsburgs, which ended with predictable results (open Tues.-Sun. 9am-5pm). Across the way, the **Popular Architecture Museum,**

vul. Kapitulna 33 and 33a (Капітульна), contains a dozen wood and stone huts from around the region. It's a delightful place for a picnic with the Habsburg family (open Wed.-Mon. 9am-5pm). Admission to both the castle and the museum is 0.50hv.

GATEWAY CITIES

Berlin, Germany

US$1 = DM1.48 (Deutschmarks)	DM1 = US$0.68
CDN$1 = DM1.08	DM1 = CDN$0.92
UK£1 = DM2.31	DM1 = UK£0.43
IR£1 = DM2.40	DM1 = IR£ 0.42
AUS$1 = DM1.17	DM1 = AUS$0.86
NZ$1 = DM1.02	DM1 = NZ$0.97
SAR1 = DM0.33	DM1 = SAR3.00
Country Phone Code: 49	**International Dialing Prefix: 00**

Berlin's population is united by a common notion that a city isn't just a place where people live and conduct business, but a place where things happen, citizens congregate, and politics are played out *en masse*. This mentality is a result of Berlin's extraordinary role in world history during the last half-century, from the 1950s and 60s when the city embodied the Cold War, to the late 1980s and early 1990s when the fall of Communist governments found Berlin straddling two distinct but no longer separate worlds. Change has not come without problems; the city still suffers from massive unemployment and a disorganized police force, and economic troubles and alienation have encouraged some youths to embrace xenophobic and neo-Nazi movements. But Berlin's dark side pales in comparison to the energy and diversity that make it one of the most fascinating cities on earth.

GERMANY ESSENTIALS

Germany celebrates these **public holidays:** New Year's (Jan. 1), Good Friday (April 4, 1997), Easter Monday (April 7, 1997), May Day (May 1), Ascension Day (May 8, 1997), Whit Monday (May 19, 1997), Unification Day (Oct. 3), and Christmas (Dec. 25-26).

Poste Restante is known as *Postlagernde Briefe*. Local **calls** should be made with a *Telefonkarte*, sold in all **post offices** in DM12, DM20, and DM50 denominations. Local calls cost 30pf. Phones accept 10pf, DM1, and DM5 coins, but not 50pf or DM2. You can often pay by credit card. The **national info** number is 011 88. From anywhere in Germany, the number for **AT&T Direct** is (0130) 00 10; **MCI WorldPhone,** (0130) 00 12; **Sprint Express,** (0130) 00 13; **British Telecom Direct,** (0130) 80 00 44; **Ireland Direct,** (0130) 80 03 53; **Canada Direct,** (0130) 00 14; **Australia Direct,** (0130) 80 00 61; **New Zealand Direct,** (0130) 80 00 64; **South Africa Direct,** (0130) 80 00 27. Remember that you must pay for the local connection time to the operator; if you don't have a phone card, be sure to have 30pf in change. In case of an **emergency,** call the **police** at 110; **fire** 112; **ambulance** 115.

When your **tongue** fails, try: *Guten Morgen/Tag/Abend* (GOO-ten MOHR-gen/tahg/AH-bend; Good morning/day/evening), *Entschuldigung* (Ent-SHOOL-dee-gung; Excuse me), *Ja/Nein* (ya/nine; Yes/No), *Wieviel kostet?* (vee-feel KOHS-tet…?; How much does…cost?), *Wo ist?* (Vo ist?; Where is…?), *Ich verstehe nicht* (ikh fair-SHTAY-uh nikht; I don't understand). *"ß"* is equivalent to *"ss"*.

Deutsches Jugendherbergswerk (DJH; tel. (05231) 740 10; fax 74 01 67) oversees **hosteling** in Germany. Rates start at about DM20 per night.

ORIENTATION AND PRACTICAL INFORMATION

Berlin surveys the Prussian plain in the northeast corner of reunited Germany, about four hours southeast of Hamburg by rail and eight hours north of Munich. Berlin is

Berlin Overview

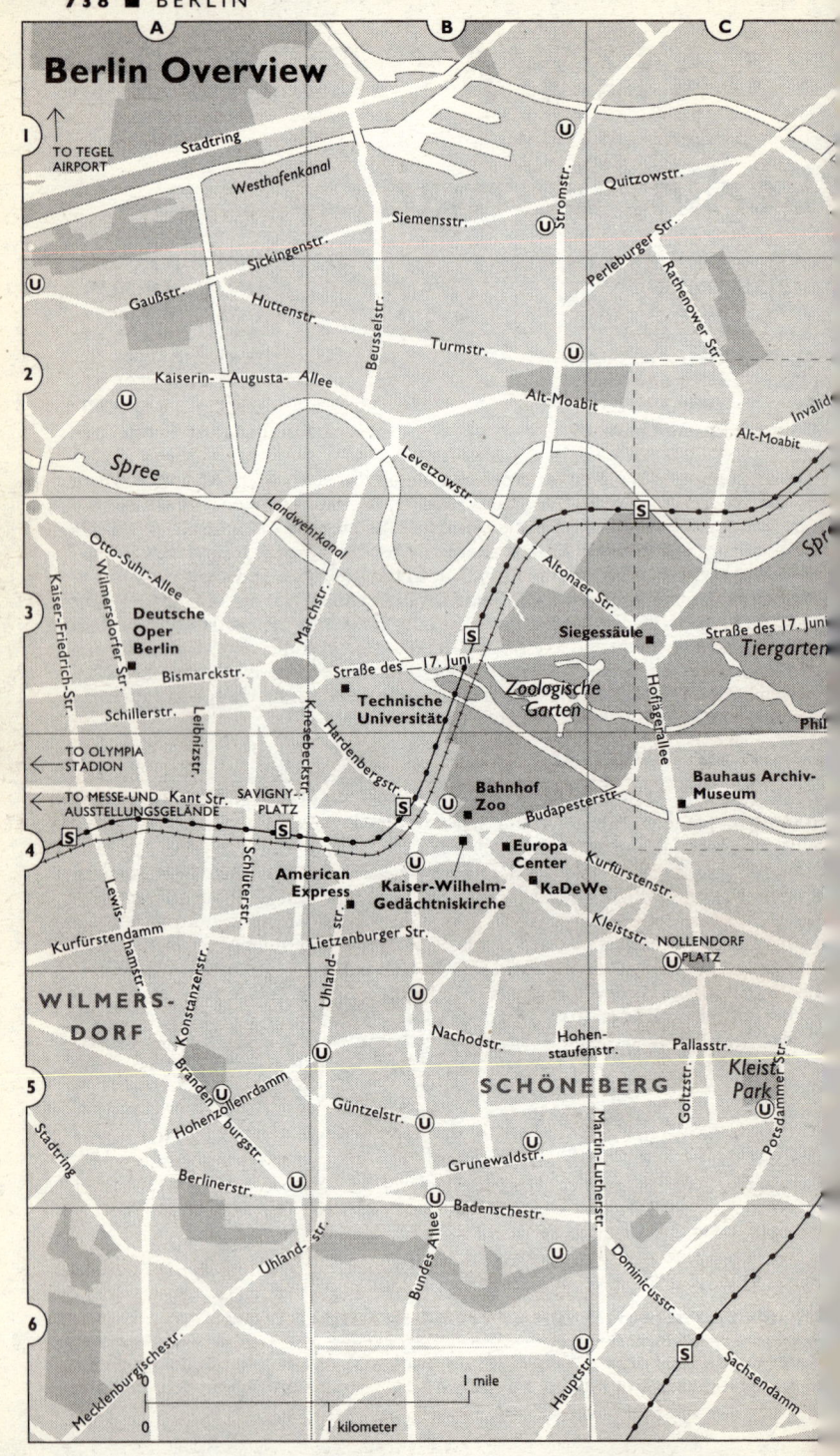

ORIENTATION AND PRACTICAL INFORMATION ■ 739

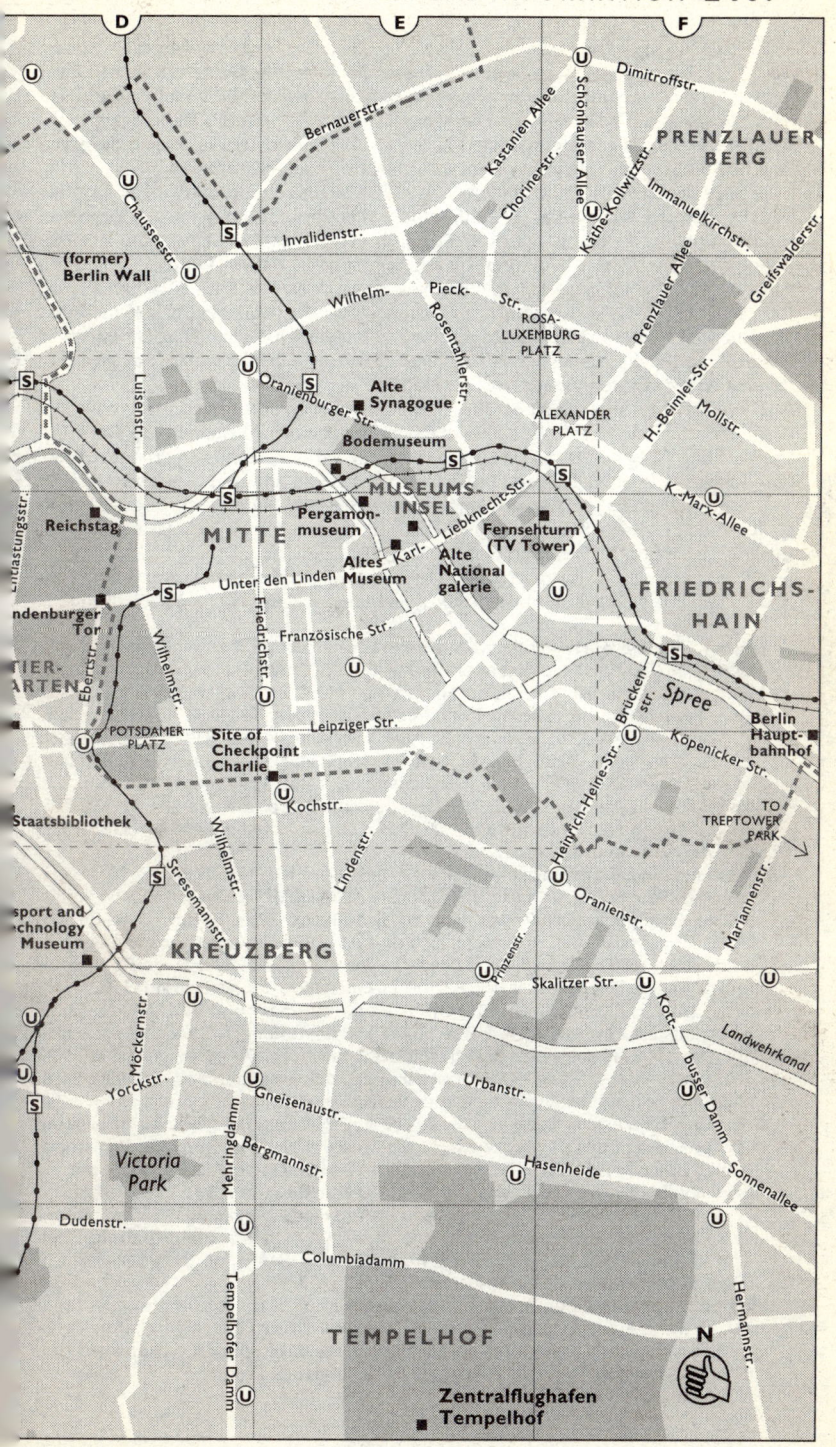

connected to other European cities as well: Prague is five hours away by rail, Warsaw six hours. For now, Western Berlin's **Bahnhof Zoologischer Gerten (Bahnhof Zoo)** remains the city's principal train station and a major focus of the its subway and surface rail systems. The situation is changing, though, as the eastern **Berlin Hauptbahnhof** surpasses the space-constricted Zoo Station. **Friedrichstraße, Alexanderplatz,** and **Lichtenberg** are other important eastern subway and rail stations.

Berlin's historic east and commercial west halves are connected by the grand tree-lined boulevard, **Straße des 17 Juni,** which runs through the massive **Tiergarten** park. The commercial district of West Berlin centers on Zoo Station and **Breitscheidplatz.** The district is marked by the bombed-out Kaiser-Wilhelm-Gedächtniskirche and the boxy tower of Europa Center. A star of streets radiates from Breitscheidpl. Toward the west run **Hardenbergstraße, Kantstraße,** and the great commercial boulevard **Kurfürstendamm,** or **Ku'damm.** Down Hardenbergstr. is Steinpl. and the enormous Berlin Technical University. Down Kantstr., **Savignyplatz** is lined with cafés, restaurants, and pensions.

The newly asphalted **Ebert Straße** runs along the path of the deconstructed Berlin Wall from the Reichstag to **Potsdamer Platz.** The landmark **Brandenburg Gate** and surrounding Pariser Platz, reconstructed with the aid of EU funds, open onto **Unter den Linden,** which leads to the historic heart of Berlin around **Lustgarten.** Farther east is the ugly but active **Alexanderplatz,** the East's growing business district. For 40 years, the alternative **Kreuzberg** and **Mitte** have been fringe back-against-the-wall neighborhoods of the West and East respectively.

If you're planning to stay more than a few hours in Berlin, the blue and yellow **Falk Plan** (DM9.80), available at most kiosks, is an immensely useful city map.

Tourist Offices: Berlin-Touristen-Information, Europa Center, Budapesterstr. 45 (tel. 262 60 31). From Bahnhof Zoo, walk along Budapesterstr. past the Kaiser-Wilhelm-Gedächtniskirche about 5min. Open Mon.-Sat. 8am-10:30pm, Sun. 9am-9pm. Branches in the main hall of **Tegel Airport** (tel. 41 01 31 45). Open daily 5:15am-10pm. Inside the **Brandenburger Tor,** south wing (tel. 25 00 25). Open daily 9:30am-6pm. All offices sell city maps (DM1) and book rooms for a DM5 fee.

Budget Travel: Kilroy Travels, Hardenbergstr. 9 (tel. 31 04 66). Open Mon.-Fri. 9am-6pm, Sat. 9am-1pm. **SRS,** Marienstr. 25 (tel. 281 67 61; fax 281 51 33). U-6: Friedrichstr. Books student flights and has a binder of last-minute specials. Open Mon.-Fri. 9am-6pm, Sat. 9am-2pm.

Embassies and Consulates: Australia, Uhlandstr. 181-3 (tel. 880 08 80). Open Mon.-Fri. 9am-noon. **Canada,** Friedrichstr. 95 (tel. 261 11 61). Open Mon.-Fri. 8:30am-12:30pm and 1:30-5pm. **Ireland,** Ernst-Reuter-Platz 10 (tel. 34 80 08 22). Open Mon.-Fri. 10am-1pm. **New Zealanders** should contact their embassy in Bonn: (tel. (0228) 22 80 70; fax 22 16 87). Open Mon.-Fri. 9am-1pm and 2-5:30pm. **South Africa,** Douglasstr. 9 (tel. 82 50 11). Open Mon.-Fri. 9am-noon. **U.K.,** Unter den Linden 32 (tel. 20 18 40). Open Mon.-Fri. 9am-noon and 2-4pm. **U.S.,** Neustädtische Kirchstr. 4-5 (tel. 238 51 74). U-Bahn: Unter den Linden. Supposed to open by 1997. If not, contact **U.S. Citizens Service,** 170 Clayallee (tel. 832 92 33). Open Mon.-Fri. 9am-noon. Telephone advice available Mon.-Fri. 9am-5pm; after hours a machine gives emergency instructions.

American Express: Uhlandstr. 173, 10719 (tel. 884 58 80). Mail held; all banking services. Long lines on weekends. Open Mon.-Fri. 9am-5:30pm, Sat. 9am-noon. Branch office at Bayreuther Str. 37 (tel. 21 49 83 63). Open Mon.-Fri. 9am-6pm.

Currency Exchange: Deutsche Verkehrs-Kredit Bank (tel. 881 71 17), Bahnhof Zoo on Hardenbergstr. 1% commission on traveler's checks (DM7.50 minimum fee). Open Mon.-Sat. 7:30am-10pm, Sun. 8am-7pm. Branch at **Hauptbahnhof** (tel. 426 70 29) is open Mon.-Fri. 7am-7:30pm, Sat.-Sun. 8am-4pm. **Berliner Bank** in Tegel Airport is open daily 8am-10pm.

Flights: Flughafen Tegel (tel. 410 11), West Berlin's main airport. From Bahnhof Zoo or Jakob-Kaiser-Platz U-Bahn station, take bus #109 to Tegel. **Flughafen Tempelhof** (tel. 690 91). Bus #119 to Kurfürstendamm. **Flughafen Schönefeld** (tel. 678 70), in Eastern Berlin, is connected by S-3 to the city center.

Trains: Bahnhof Zoo sends trains to the west, while **Hauptbahnhof** serves lines to the south and east. The stations are connected by S-Bahn. Trains from the east also arrive at **Berlin-Lichtenberg. Deutsche Bahn Information:** tel. 194 19. Be prepared for a long wait. Similarly long lines at offices in **Bahnhof Zoo** (open daily 5:30am-10:30pm) and **Hauptbahnhof.**

Buses: ZOB, the central bus station (tel. 301 80 28), is by the Funkturm. U-1: Kaiserdamm. Check *Zitty* and *Tip* for deals on long-distance buses.

Public Transportation: Construction and renovation will affect S- (commuter rail) and U-Bahn (subway) service for the next year; **Max, a bespectacled cartoon mole,** appears on posters and signs announcing disruptions in service. Information and tickets are available at the **BVG Pavillon,** Bahnhof Zoo (tel. 25 62 25 62). Open daily 8am-8pm. An *Einzelfahrschein Normaltarif* (single ticket) costs DM3.90 and is good for 2hr. after validation. An *Einzelfahrschein Kurzstreckentarif* (short-trip fare, DM2.50) allows travel through up to 6 bus stations (no transfers; not valid on airport bus lines) or 3 U- or S-Bahn stops (unlimited transfers). A 4-trip *Sammelkarte* (multiple ticket) costs DM13; each "click" is good for 2hr. A short-trip 4-ride *Kurzstreckensammelkarte* is also available for DM8.50. Buy tickets from machines, bus drivers, or ticket windows in the U- and S-Bahn stations. The **Berlin Tagesticket** (DM13) is a 24-hr. pass for the bus and U- and S-Bahn. A **7-Day Ticket** (DM40) is good for moderate-length stays. A monthly **Umweltkarte** costs DM93, a good value for longer stays. All tickets must be canceled in the red validation box before boarding to be valid. The U- and S-Bahn do not run 1-4am, except for the **U-12** and **U-9,** which run all night Fri.-Sat. An extensive system of **night buses,** centered on Bahnhof Zoo, runs every 15min. Pick up the free *Nachtliniennetz* map. All night bus numbers are preceded by **N.**

Luggage Storage: In the Bahnhof Zoo station. Lockers DM2, larger DM4; 72hr. max. At **Hauptbahnhof,** lockers DM2, larger DM4; 72hr. max. At Bahnhof **Lichtenberg** and S-Bahnhof **Alexanderplatz,** lockers DM2; 24hr. max.

Bookstores: British Bookshop, Mauerstr. 83-83 (tel. 238 46 80). English newspapers and magazines. Open Mon.-Fri. 9am-6pm, Sat. 10am-2pm.

Laundromat: Wasch Centers (tel. 852 37 96) are at Leibnizstr. 72 in Charlottenburg; Wexstr. 34 in Schöneberg; Bergmannstr. 61 in Kreuzberg; Behmstr. 12 in Mitte; and Jablonskistr. 21 in Prenzlauer Berg. All open daily 6am-10pm. Wash DM6 per 6kg, dry DM2 for 30min. Soap included.

Pharmacies: Europa-Apotheke, Tauentzienstr. 9-12 (tel. 261 41 42), by Europa Center (close to Bahnhof Zoo). Open daily 9am-9pm. Closed *Apotheken* post signs directing you to the nearest one open, or call 011 41.

Crisis Lines: Sexual Assault Hotline: tel. 251 28 28. Open Tues. and Thurs. 6-9pm, Sun. noon-2pm. **Schwüles Überfall** hotline and legal help for gays at tel. 216 33 36. Open daily 6-9pm. **Drug Crisis:** tel. 192 37.

Emergency: The American and British embassies have a list of English-speaking doctors. **Emergency Doctor:** tel. 31 00 31. **Emergency Dentist:** tel. 841 91 00.

Police: Platz der Luftbrücke 6 (tel. 110 or 69 90).

Post Offices: In the **Bahnhof Zoo** (tel. 313 97 99). Open Mon.-Fri. 6am-midnight, Sat.-Sun. 8am-midnight. **Poste Restante** at window #7. **Postal Code:** 10612. The branch office at **Tegel Airport** (tel. 430 85 23) is open daily 6:30am-9pm. In East Berlin, in the **Hauptbahnhof,** Postamt Berlin 17, Str. der Pariser Kommune 8-10. Open Mon.-Fri. 7am-9pm, Sat. 8am-8pm. **Postal Code:** 10243.

Telephones: At the post offices or Bahnhof Zoo. Public phones are rarer in the eastern part of the city. **Phone code:** 030.

ACCOMMODATIONS AND CAMPING

For a DM5 fee, **tourist offices** will find you a hotel room. There are also over 4000 **private rooms** *(Privatzimmer)* available in the city, the overwhelming majority controlled by the tourist offices. Expect to pay about DM80 for singles and DM100 for doubles, plus a single-night surcharge of DM5. Most tourist offices also carry the pamphlet *Accommodations, Youth Hostels, and Camping Places in Berlin*.

Hostels

Hostels fill quickly with German school groups (especially in summer and on weekends); call ahead. All HI-affiliated hostels are members-only, but for an extra DM4 some hostels will give nonmembers a stamp and let them spend the night. To buy an **HI card,** head to Tempelhofer Ufer 32, 10963 Berlin (tel. 264 95 20; open Mon., Wed., and Fri. 10am-4pm, Tues. and Thurs. 1-6pm); membership for non-Germans costs DM36. HI hostels often have strict curfews. Many accept written reservations.

The Backpacker, Köthener Str. 44, 10963 Berlin (tel. 262 51 40). U-Bahn 2: Potsdamer Platz, turn right on Stresemannstr., then right on Köthener Str. Well worn. One of the best budget options. Kitchen, free city map, and a staff that's all that. Anglophile atmosphere. Close to Mitte's action. No curfew. DM25, sheets DM3. Laundry facilities (DM5). Call or check in daily 9-11am. Re-opens May 1997.

Jugendgästehaus Feurigstraße, Feurigstr. 63, 10827 Berlin (tel. 781 52 11; fax 788 30 51). U-Bahn 7: Kleistpark, or bus #146 or 148. Dorms DM38. Singles DM55. Doubles with shower DM90. Breakfast included. Sheets DM5 if staying less than 3 nights. Call ahead from the station.

Die Fabrik, Schlesische Str. 18, 10997 Berlin (tel. 611 71 16; fax 618 29 74). U-Bahn 1: Schlesisches Tor. *Pension qua* hostel in a beautifully converted factory within walking distance of Kreuzberg's nightlife. *Mehrbettzimmer* DM30. Singles DM61. Doubles DM90. Triples DM115.

Jugendherberge Ernst Reuter (HI), Hermsdorfer Damm 48, 13467 Berlin (tel. 404 16 10; fax 404 59 72). U-Bahn 6: Tegel, then bus #125 (dir. "Frohnau/Invalidensiedlung") to "Jugendherberge". Distant from the center in a placid suburb, on the edge of the forest. 6-bed rooms DM26 per person, over 26 DM33 per person. Breakfast and sheets included. Key deposit DM10. Open Jan.-Sept.

Hotels, Pensions, and Camping

Many small pension and hotel owners cater to budget travelers. Most *Pensionen* and hotels listed in *Let's Go* are amenable to *Mehrbettzimmer,* where extra beds are moved into a large double or triple. The best place to find cheap hotel rooms is around Savignyplatz or along Wilmersdorfstr.

Hotel Transit, Hagelbergerstr. 53-54, 10965 Berlin (tel. 785 50 51; fax 785 96 19). U-Bahn 6,7: Mehringdamm, or bus #119 or night bus N19 (every 10-15min.). Party hard and crash gently in this supremely hip *Pension*. Big-screen (M)TV lounge open 24hr. Bar open until 2-3am. Singles DM85. Doubles DM102. Triples DM135. Quads DM170. Their "Sleep-In" deal allows you to share a *Mehrbettzimmer* with any other traveler (DM34). Breakfast included.

Pension Knesebeck, Knesebeckstr. 86, 10623 Berlin (tel. 312 72 55; fax 313 34 86), just north of the park. S-Bahn 3,5,7,9: Savignyplatz. Friendly, large *Alt-Berliner* rooms, with faux-Baroque stylings. Hearty buffet-style breakfast. Singles with shower DM95. Doubles DM120, with shower DM140. Big *Mehrbettzimmer* DM55-60 per person. Laundry machines DM2.

Hotelpension Cortina, Kantstr. 140, 10623 Berlin (tel. 313 90 59; fax 31 73 96). S-Bahn 3,5,7,9 or bus #149: Savignyplatz. Bright, convenient, and hospitable. Extra beds in rooms upon agreement. Dinky singles DM75. Doubles DM120-130. *Mehrbettzimmer* DM45-50. Breakfast included.

Hotel-Pension München, Güntzelstr. 62 (tel. 857 91 20; fax 853 27 44). U-Bahn 9: Güntzelstr. Small *Pension-cum*-gallery saturated with drawings and paintings by contemporary Berlin artists, exhibit posters from local museums, and sculptures by the owner. White-walled rooms with TV and telephone. Singles DM60-110. Doubles DM80-125. Write to reserve, or call before 2pm.

Hotel Sachsenhof, Motzstr. 7, 10777 Berlin (tel. 216 20 74; fax 215 82 20). Small and plainly decorated rooms that are clean and well furnished. Singles DM57-65. Doubles DM106-156. DM30 per extra bed.

FOOD

Berlin's restaurant scene is as international as its population; German food and drink shouldn't be foremost on your mind. One exception is the smooth, sweet *Berliner Weiße mit Schuß*, a concoction of local beer with a shot of syrup. A gloriously civilized tradition in Berlin cafés is *Frühstück*, breakfast served well into the afternoon, sometimes 24 hours. Budget eateries have traditionally been scarce in eastern Berlin, but this is rapidly changing. In addition, street vendors with all shapes, sizes, and flavors of cheap eats fill **Alexanderplatz** every day. Much typical Berlin food is Turkish: almost every street has its own Turkish *Imbiß* or restaurant. The *Imbiß* stands are a vital lifeline for the late-night partier; some are open 24 hours.

Aldi, Bolle, and **Penny Markt** are the cheapest supermarket chains, along with the many **Plus** stores in Wilmersdorf, Schönberg, and Kreuzberg. Supermarkets are usually open Monday to Friday 9am-6pm, and Saturday 9am-1pm.

- **Mensa der Freie Universität,** Habelschwerdter Allee 45. U-2: Thielplat or Dahlem-Dorf. Meals from DM2 (ISIC required). Open Mon.-Fri. 11:15am-2:30pm. The first floor **cafeteria** is more expensive. Open Mon.-Fri. 8:15am-4pm.
- **Café Hardenberg,** Hardenbergstr. 10. Big *Belle Époque* spot. Funky music, artsy interior, and lots of students. Breakfast served 9am-5pm (DM4-8). Most entrées well under DM13. Also good for a few drinks (grog DM4). Open daily 9am-1am.
- **Restaurant Marché,** Kurfürstendamm 15, just a couple of blocks down from Bahnhof Zoo and the *Gedächtniskirche.* Probably the most affordable lunch on the Ku'damm. The colorful cafeteria area is full of fresh produce, salads, grilled meats, pour-it-yourself wines, and hot pastries. Meals DM12-25. Open daily 8am-midnight.
- **Schwarzes Café,** Kantstr. 148 (tel. 313 80 38), near Savignyplatz. Dark walls, big-band music, and dapper waiters. A bit pricey, but they have breakfast at all hours (DM7-13). Open 24hr., except for Tues., when it closes early morning-6pm.
- **Baharat Falafel,** Winterfeldtstr. 37. U-1,4: Nollendorfplatz. Probably the best falafel in Berlin (DM5). Bright little shop with world music and custom watercolors. Open Mon.-Sat. noon-2am, Sun. 1pm-2am. Closed last week in July.
- **Kurdistan,** Uhlandstr. 161 (tel. 883 96 92). U-15: Uhlandstr. Exotic and most appetizing. Fabulous *Yekawe* (meat with rice, raisins, and cinnamon) DM15. Most entrées DM15-20. Open Mon.-Fri. noon-midnight, Sat.-Sun. 5pm-late.

SIGHTS

Between Eastern and Western Berlin

For decades a gateway to nowhere, **Brandenburger Tor** (Brandenburg Gate) is the structure that most commonly symbolizes united Germany. It is now the centerpiece of the city, opening east onto Unter den Linden (S-Bahn: Unter den Linden, or bus #100). Friedrich Wilhelm II built the gate in 1791 as an emblem of peace, but during the Cold War the gate came to represent East-West division as a locked door embedded in the Berlin Wall. The gate did not re-open until December 22, 1989, more than a month after the wall came down. The **Wall** itself is a dead dinosaur, with only fossil remains still visible. Raised overnight on August 13, 1961, the 160km-long barrier separated families, sometimes running through people's homes. Portions of it are preserved near the Hauptbahnhof and the Reichstag. The longest remaining bit, the brightly painted **East Side Gallery** (S-Bahn: Hauptbahnhof), is also world's largest open-air gallery. **Potsdamer Platz,** cut off by the Wall, was once one of Berlin's major transportation hubs, designed under Frederick Wilhelm I to approximate Parisian boulevards. Sony and Daimler-Benz recently purchased the land surrounding the Platz, with plans to convert it into a sprawling office complex. **Haus am Checkpoint Charlie,** Friedrichstr. 44 (U-Bahn: Kochstr. or bus #129), narrates the history of the Wall through film and photos. Upstairs there are exhibits on human rights, as well as artistic renderings of the Wall (open daily 9am-10pm; DM7.50, students DM4.50).

Western Berlin

Just north of the Brandenburger Tor sits the **Reichstag** building, former seat of the German Empire and Weimar Republic parliaments, and future home of the Federal Republic's governing body, the *Bundestag*. In August 1914, Karl Liebknecht's famous *"Nein!"* was one of a few votes in its halls against the impending First World War. In 1918, after Kaiser Wilhelm II had abdicated, the Social Democrat Philip Scheidemann proclaimed the German Republic from one of its windows. His move turned out to be wise, since two hours later Karl Liebknecht announced a German Socialist Republic down the street in **Palast der Republik.** Civil war conditions in Berlin and much of the rest of Germany resulted. In February 1933, just one month after Hitler became chancellor, the Reichstag mysteriously burned down. Hitler used the Reichstag fire to woo support for the infamous Enabling Act, managing to convince the "moderate" parties in parliament to help him become legal dictator of Germany. At the moment, the Reichstag is not a government building, although the major political parties have opened offices here. The lush **Tiergarten,** a vast landscaped park formerly used by the Prussian monarchs for hunting, spreads itself over the northeast corner of western Berlin. In the heart of the Tiergarten, the **Siegessäule** (Victory Column) celebrates Prussia's defeat of France in 1870. In 1938, the Nazis moved the monument from its spot in front of the Reichstag to increase its height and make it more impressive. Climb the 285 steps to the top for a panorama of the city. (Open April-Nov. Mon. 1-5:30pm, Tues.-Sun. 9am-5:30pm. DM1.50, students DM1.) The **Soviet Army Memorial** (yes, you're still in western Berlin) stands at the end of Str. des 17 Juni, flanked by a pair of giant toy tanks.

South of Nollendorfpl. is the **Rathaus Schöneberg,** where West Berlin's city government convened. On June 26, 1963, 1.5 million Berliners swarmed beneath the *Rathaus* to hear John F. Kennedy reassure them of the Allies' continued commitment to the city, 15 years after the 11-month Berlin Airlift. Kennedy's speech ended with the now-famous words, "All free men, wherever they may live, are citizens of Berlin. And therefore, as a free man, I take pride in the words *Ich bin ein Berliner."*

Schloß Charlottenburg (U-Bahn: Sophie-Charlotte-Pl. or bus #145 from Bahnhof Zoo), the vast Baroque palace built by Friedrich I for his second wife, presides over a exquisitely landscaped Baroque park. **Galerie der Romantik,** a state museum housing a first-rate collection of German Romantic paintings, is in a side wing (open Tues.-Fri. 9am-5pm, Sat.-Sun. 10am-5pm; individual sections of the castle DM1-4, students DM0.50-1.50; entire complex DM8, students DM3). The **Palace Gardens,** with their carefully laid rows of trees, footbridges, and fountains, surround the **Royal Mausoleum; Belvedere,** an 18th-century residence exhibiting porcelain; and the **Schinkel Pavilion,** with furniture designed by Schinkel (open Tues.-Sun. 6am-9pm; free).

Indispensable for a sense of Berlin's counterculture is a visit to **Kreuzberg,** an area laden with cafés and bars. For its more respectable face, get off at U-6,7: Mehringdamm and wander. Bergmannstr. features numerous old buildings and second-hand shops. At night, bohemian and punk clubs overflow onto Gneisenau Straße, which heads west from the intersection with Mehringdamm. The bars on Oranienstraße, U-Bahn: Kottbusser Tor, boast a more radical element. The May Day parades always start here. **Landwehrkanal,** a channel that runs from Tiergarten into Kreuzberg, is where Rosa Luxemburg's body was thrown after her murder in 1919; it was recovered only recently. The tree-dotted strip of the canal near Hallesches Tor, **Paul-Linke Ufer,** may be the most beautiful street in Berlin, with shady terraces and elaborate apartment façades. The east end of Kreuzberg, near the old Wall, is home to Turkish (half of western Berlin's foreign population) and Balkan neighborhoods. It boasts a correspondingly large number of ethnic cafés and restaurants, popular with radicals and students. From the Schlesisches Tor U-Bahn station, a short walk takes you to the recently re-opened **Oberbaumbrücke,** through a fragment of the wall, and into the Friedrichshain district of the former East Berlin.

Eastern Berlin

The Brandenburg Gate opens eastward onto **Unter den Linden,** once one of Europe's best-known boulevards and the spine of old Berlin. All but the most famous buildings have been destroyed, but farther down many 18th-century structures have been restored to their original Prussian splendor. Past Friedrichstraße, the first massive building on your left is the **Deutsche Staatsbibliothek** (library), with a pleasant café inside. Beyond the library is **Humboldt Universität,** once one of the finest in the world. Next door, the old **Neue Wache** (New Guard House), designed by the renowned Prussian architect Friedrich Schinkel, is today the somber **Monument to the Victims of Fascism and Militarism.** Buried inside are urns filled with earth from the Nazi concentration camps of Buchenwald and Mauthausen, and from the battlefields of Stalingrad, El Alamein, and Normandy. The honor guard in front changes on the hour, with a full ceremony Wednesdays at 2:30pm. Across the way is **Bebelplatz,** the site of Nazis' book-burning. The square houses a monument to the book burning, consisting of a hollowed-out chamber beneath the square. During the day, you can see a ghostly image of empty white bookshelves if you stand over the chamber; at night the chamber is illuminated. The impressive building with the curved façade is the **Alte Bibliothek.** The most striking of the monumental buildings is the **Zeughaus,** now the **Museum of German History.** From the museum you can enter the courtyard and see the tormented faces of Andreas Schlüter's *Dying Warriors.*

Berlin's most striking ensemble of 18th-century buildings is a few blocks south of Unter den Linden at **Gendarmenmarkt,** graced by the twin cathedrals of the **Deutscher Dom** and the **Französischer Dom.** Enclosing the far end of the square, the classical **Schauspielhaus,** designed by Schinkel, is Berlin's most elegant concert space and hosts many international orchestras and classical performers.

As it crosses the bridge, Unter den Linden opens out onto the **Museumsinsel** (Museum Island). To the left is the **Altes Museum,** with a big polished granite bowl in front, and the poly-domed **Berliner Dom** (Berlin Cathedral). Severely damaged by an air raid in 1944, the cathedral emerged from 20 years of restoration in 1993; the interior is ornately gaudy (open daily 9am-7:30pm; free). Behind the Altes Museum lie three other enormous museums and the reconstructed **Neues Museum.** At the center of this jungle of pediments, porticoes, and colonnades is the **Lustgarten** park, formerly Marx-Engels Platz, the parade ground of the Communist regime.

Across the Liebknecht Brücke, in the middle of a park stands a "conceptual memorial," consisting of steel tablets engraved with images of worker struggle and protest surrounding twin statues of Marx and Engels. The park and the street behind it used to be collectively known as the **Marx-Engels Forum;** the park has yet to be renamed, while the street is now called **Rathausstr.**

On the other side of the Museumsinsel, Unter den Linden leads to teeming, concrete **Alexanderplatz.** This atrociously ugly square was meant to be a showpiece for socialism. Friends often meet at the plaza's **Weltzeituhr,** the international clock, but the undisputed landmark is the **Fernsehturm** (television tower), the tallest structure in Berlin (open May-Oct. daily 9am-1am; Nov.-April 10am-midnight; DM8).

The graceful 15th-century church, **Marienkirche,** stands on the wide open plaza behind the *Fernsehturm.* Nearby is the gabled **Rotes Rathaus,** Old Berlin's famous red-brick town hall. Behind the *Rathaus,* the twin spires of the **Nikolaikirche** mark Berlin's oldest building. Inside the 13th-century structure, a small museum documents the early history of the city (open Tues.-Sun. 10am-6pm). The church gives the surrounding **Nikolaiviertel,** a carefully reconstructed *Altstadt,* its name.

Museums

Four major complexes—Charlottenburg, Dahlem, Museumsinsel, and Tiergarten—form the hub of the city's museum culture; smaller ones deal with every subject imaginable. Their prices are standardized: DM4, students DM2. A *Tageskarte* (good for all of the national museums, including the 4 above) is DM8; students DM4. The Charlottenburg complex is closed Fridays, the Museumsinsel, Dahlem, and Tiergarten Mondays. When museum-hopping, bring your student ID.

Pergamonmuseum, Kupfergraben, in Museumsinsel. One of the great ancient history museums. The scale is mind-boggling; gape at the Babylonian Ishtar Gate (575BCE), the Roman Market Gate of Miletus, and the majestic Pergamon Altar of Zeus (180BCE). Extensive collection of Greek, Islamic, and Far Eastern art. Open Tues.-Sun. 9am-5pm; Islamic art section open Wed.-Sun. 10am-6pm. Last entry 30min. before closing. On Tues., only the architectural exhibits are open.

Dahlem Museum, Arnimallee 23-27 and Lansstr. 8. U-Bahn: Dahlem-Dorf. Complex of 7 museums, each worth a half-day. Particularly superb is the **Gemäldegalerie** (Painting Gallery), a collection of Italian, German, Dutch, and Flemish Old Masters (including 26 Rembrandts). Open Tues.-Fri. 9am-5pm, Sat.-Sun. 10am-5pm.

Schloß Charlottenburg, Spandauer Damm (U-2: Sophie-Charlotte-Pl. or bus #145) contains several museums. The **Ägyptisches Museum,** across Spandauer Damm from the castle's main entrance, houses a fascinating collection of ancient Egyptian art, including the 3300-year-old bust of Queen Nefertiti. Also check out the **Sammlung Berggruen.** All open Mon.-Thurs. 9am-5pm, Sat.-Sun. 10am-5pm.

Neue Nationalgalerie, Potsdamerstr. 50. Bus #129 from the Ku'damm or S-1,2 or U-2: Potsdamer Platz. Part of the Tiergarten complex. A world-class collection of 20th-century paintings, many from the *Preußischer Kulturbesitz*. Brilliant works by Kokoschka, Kirchner, Beckmann, de Chirico, and more, plus a roomful of American abstractions. Open Tues.-Fri. 9am-5pm, Sat.-Sun. 10am-5pm.

ENTERTAINMENT

Berlin is *wild,* all night, every night. The best guides to theater, nightlife, and the extremely active music scene are the bi-weekly magazines *Tip* (DM4) and *Zitty* (DM 3.60). The monthly *Berlin Program* lists more events. The free magazine *Siegessäule* details gay events for the month and is available in gay bars and bookstores.

Nightlife

In western Berlin, the **Savignypl., Schöneberg, Wilmersdorf,** and **Kreuzberg** districts rock the house, but the *Szene* is shifting inexorably to the east. The east, in a word, is hot: low rents and a rising "alternative" population give the quarter's cafés and bars a grittier edge, which the slicker west side can't touch.

Quasimodo, Kantstr. 12a (tel. 312 80 86). S-3,5,7,9: Savignyplatz. This unassuming basement pub with attached *Biergarten* is one of Berlin's most crucial jazz venues, drawing in big names and lively crowds. Cover depends on performance, ranging from free to DM30. Concert tickets available from 5pm or at **Kant Kasse ticket service** (tel. 313 45 54; fax 312 64 40). Open daily from 8pm.

Big Eden, Kurfürstendamm 202 (tel. 882 61 20). U-15: Uhlandstr. It's no paradise, but the neon and mirrors will leave you dizzy. Funked-out post-Saturday Night Fever crowd shakes to disco, Haus, and techno. Open Sun.-Thurs. 8pm-4am, Fri.-Sat. 8pm-6am. Cover can run as much as DM15, but free before 10pm.

Metropol, Nollendorfplatz 5 (tel. 216 41 22). U-1,4: Nollendorfplatz, or night buses N19, N29, or N85. Fractile lights illuminate the dance floor in the loft, where lots of 16- to 25-year-olds groove. Sometimes big-time concerts take place in between dances. Cover DM15, before 10pm DM10. Open Fri. 9pm-6am, Sat. 9pm-8am. Call 216 27 87 for concert info (Mon.-Fri. 11am-3pm and 3:30-6pm).

SO 36, Oranienstr. 190 (tel. 615 65 81). U-1: Görlitzer Bahnhof. A mish-mash of wild *oeuvres:* Mon. serves up techno Electric Ballroom, Wed. is gay and lesbian disco night, Thurs. brings ska and hardcore, Fri. and Sat. get wild. Open Sun. after 7pm, Mon. after 11pm, Wed.-Thurs. after 10pm, Fri.-Sat. until late.

Schnabel Bar, Oranienstr. 31 (tel. 615 85 34). U-Bahn 1,8: Kottbuser Tor. Raucously upbeat swingers shake that booty non-stop to jungle music. Open 24hr., but the most heated dance scene runs midnight-6am.

KitKat Club, Glogauer Str. 2 (tel. 611 38 33). People with varying degrees of clothing, some copulating, some just digging the cool trance music in the jaw-dropping fluorescent interior, leave their inhibitions outside before entering this pit of sin. Open Tues.-Sun. after 11pm. Cover DM10. The Sunday after-hours party (8am

7pm) is popular, free, and more fully clothed. On Thursdays, the **Crisco Club** is for some serious homoerotics (men only!). Not for the faint of heart.

Tacheles, Oranienburgerstr. 53-56 (tel. 282 61 85). U-Bahn 6: Oranienburger Tor. Perhaps the greatest source of artistic pretense in all of Berlin. The art commune has decorated the interior with graffiti, collages, and exhibits. Bands, films, raves, and three bars serve up nightly entertainment. Open 24hr.

Concerts and Opera

Philharmonie, Matthäikirchstr. 1 (tel. 261 43 83). Bus #129 from Ku'damm to "Potsdamerstr." and walk 3 blocks north or S-2: Potsdamerpl. Check for tickets (around DM30) an hour before concerts or write far in advance. Closed in summer. Ticket office open Mon.-Fri. 3:30-6pm, Sat.-Sun. and holidays 11am-2pm.

Deutsche Oper Berlin, Bismarckstr. 34-37 (tel. 341 02 49). U-2,12: Deutsche Oper. Berlin's best opera. Main box office open Mon.-Sat. 11am-1hr. before performance. Ten minutes before performances, you can get student discounts of up to 50%. Tickets DM15-125.

Helsinki, Finland

US$1	= 4.50mk (markka, FIM)	1mk =	US$0.22
CDN$1	= 3.28mk	1mk =	CDN$0.30
UK£1	= 7.01mk	1mk =	UK£0.14
IR£1	= 7.29mk	1mk =	IR£0.14
AUS$1	= 3.54mk	1mk =	AUS$0.28
NZ$1	= 3.13mk	1mk =	NZ$0.32
SAR1	= 1.01mk	1mk =	SAR0.99

Country Phone Code: 358   **International Dialing Prefix: 990**

Less festive than Copenhagen but friendlier than Stockholm, peaceful Helsinki has long been a meeting point of West and East. Lutheran and Russian Orthodox cathedrals stand almost face to face, Red Army uniforms and medals are sold on the street, and St. Petersburg and Tallinn are but a short cruise across the Gulf of Finland. Cobblestone streets and well tended parks make Helsinki an ideal city for strolling; Mannerheimintie and the Esplanadi offer great people-watching. The southeast corner of the city is a nest of diplomats, elegant mansions, and aggressive traffic.

FINLAND ESSENTIALS

Citizens of the U.S., Canada, U.K., Ireland, Australia, and New Zealand can visit Finland visa-free for up to 90 days.

Most **shops** close at 5pm on weekdays (Sat. around 1pm), but urban **supermarkets** may stay open until 8pm (Sat. 4-6pm). **Kiosks,** especially those marked *elintarvikekioski,* sell basic food, snacks, and toiletries until 9 or 10pm. **Banks** are open weekdays 9:15am-4:15pm. Finns celebrate New Year's Day (Jan. 1), Epiphany (Jan. 6), May Eve and Day (April 30-May 1), Ascension Day (May 8, 1997), Midsummer (June 20-21, 1997), All Saint's Day (Nov. 1), and Independence Day (Dec. 6). Many stores and museums, as well as all banks and post offices, are also closed on Easter (April 30-May 1, 1997), and Christmas (Dec. 24-26).

Local calls and short long-distance calls within Finland usually cost 2mk; most **pay phones** take 1mk and 5mk coins. Phone cards (local calls 1mk) are available in 30mk, 50mk, and 100mk denominations. "Tele" or "Nonstop" cards work nationwide, but others only in the city where you purchase them. "Nonstop" phones are available at any post office. Call 118 for domestic **information,** 0800 941 09 for international information, 112 in **emergencies,** and 100 22 for the **police.** For **AT&T Direct,** call 980 01 0010; **MCI WorldPhone,** 1 980 01 0280; **SprintExpress,** 980 01 0284; **Canada**

Direct, 980 01 00 11; **British Telecom Direct,** 980 01 04 40; **Australia Direct,** 980 01 06 10. The **mail** service is fast and efficient.

The Finnish **language** is virtually impenetrable to foreigners. Watch out for town names that modify their form on train schedules because Finnish lacks prepositions. **Swedish,** often seen on signs, is the official second language; many Finns speak **English.** Useful words and phrases include *Missä on* (MEESS-ah OWN, "Where is?"), *Haluaisin* (HAH-loo-ay-seen; "I would like"), *Kiitos* (KEE-toss; "thank you"), *rautatieasema* (RAO-tah-tee-AH-sehma; "train station"), and *keskus* (KESS-kooss; "center"). Don't be surprised if a strange Finn asks you to throw away all inhibitions and partake in Finland's chief export, the *sauna.* "M" and "N" on bathroom and sauna doors designate men and women, respectively.

ORIENTATION AND PRACTICAL INFORMATION

Helsinki, "daughter of the Baltic" (personified in the Havis Amanda statue at the harbor), dangles on the southern edge of Finland. The central city's layout resembles a "V" with a large, bulbous point and several smaller peninsulas. The **train station** lies just north of the vertex, from which the **Mannerheimintie** and **Unioninkatu** thoroughfares radiate. The **harbor** and most sights are south of the train station. For candid and practical info, the free youthful paper *City* is unbeatable, while *Helsinki This Week* provides local news and a comprehensive list of current happenings. The recorded English message line (tel. 058) can help get you oriented as well.

Tourist Offices: City Tourist Office, Pohjoisesplanadi 19 (tel. 169 37 57). From the train station, walk 2 blocks south on Keskuskatu and turn left on Pohjoisesplanadi. Open late May to early Sept. Mon.-Fri. 8:30am-6pm, Sat.-Sun. 10am-3pm; mid-Sept. to mid-May Mon. 8am-4:30pm, Tues.-Fri. 8:30am-4pm. **Hotellikeskus** (Hotel Booking Center; tel. 17 11 33), in the train station, specializes in finding rooms (12mk booking fee), but also has city maps, youth hostel lists, and brochures. Open late May-Aug. Mon.-Sat. 9am-7pm, Sun. 10am-6pm; Sept. to mid-May Mon.-Fri. 9am-5pm. Both offices sell the **Helsinki Card,** offering unlimited local transportation, museum discounts, and other treats (1-day 105mk, 2-day 135mk, 3-day 165mk). The **Finnish Tourist Board,** Eteläesplanadi 4 (tel. 40 30 13 00), covers the whole country, including campgrounds. Open June-Aug. Mon.-Fri. 8:30am-5pm, Sat. 10am-2pm; Sept.-May Mon.-Fri. 8:30am-4pm. The **Finnish Youth Hostel Association,** Yrjönkatu 38 B (tel. 694 03 77), on the south side of the bus station, lists hostels and arranges Lapland lodgings. Open Mon.-Fri. 9am-4pm.

Travelers' Center: Lighthouse Café, in the Kallio Youth Hostel at Porthaninkatu 2 (tel. 70 99 25 91). Serves as a meeting point for travelers and offers some info about the city. Free luggage storage and ride board. Students welcome. Open June to mid-Aug. Mon.-Thurs. 8am-7pm.

Budget Travel: Kilroy Travels, Kaivokatu 100 (tel. 680 78 11). Sells Transalpino tickets, ISIC, and YIEE cards. Open Mon.-Fri. 10am-6pm, Sat. 10am-2pm.

Embassies: Canada, Pohjoisesplanadi 25 B (tel. 17 11 41). Open Mon.-Thurs. 8:30am-4:30pm, Fri. 8:30am-1:30pm. **Estonia,** Fabianinkatu 13 A (tel. 62 20 280). **Latvia,** Bulevardi 5 A 18 (tel. 47 64 72 22). **Lithuania,** Rauhankatu 13A (tel. 608 210). **Poland,** Armas Lindgrenintie 21 (tel. 684 80 77). **Russia,** Tehtaankatu 1 B (tel. 66 18 76). **U.K.,** Itäinen Puistotie 17 (tel. 66 12 93). In emergencies, **Australians** and **New Zealanders** should contact the British Embassy. **U.S.,** Itäinen Puistotie 14 A (tel. 17 19 31). Open Mon.-Fri. 9am-noon.

Currency Exchange: Rates are generally the same throughout the city, with a minimum 10mk commission on traveler's checks. **Forex,** in the train station, charges a 10mk fee for cash, 10mk per traveler's check, but no fee to change mk into foreign currency. Open daily 8am-9pm. Same rates at the handy **Poste Restante** office 50m west of the train station. Open Mon.-Fri. 7am-9pm, Sat. 9am-6pm, Sun. 11am-9pm. The **airport terminal** has money exchange (cash only); open daily 6:30am-11pm. **KOP** banks at the ferry terminals are open Mon.-Fri. 9am-6pm, Sat. 9-11:30am and 3:45-7:30pm, Sun. 9-11:30am and 3:45-6pm. Visa cash advances are available 24hr. from most bank machines.

ORIENTATION AND PRACTICAL INFORMATION ■ 749

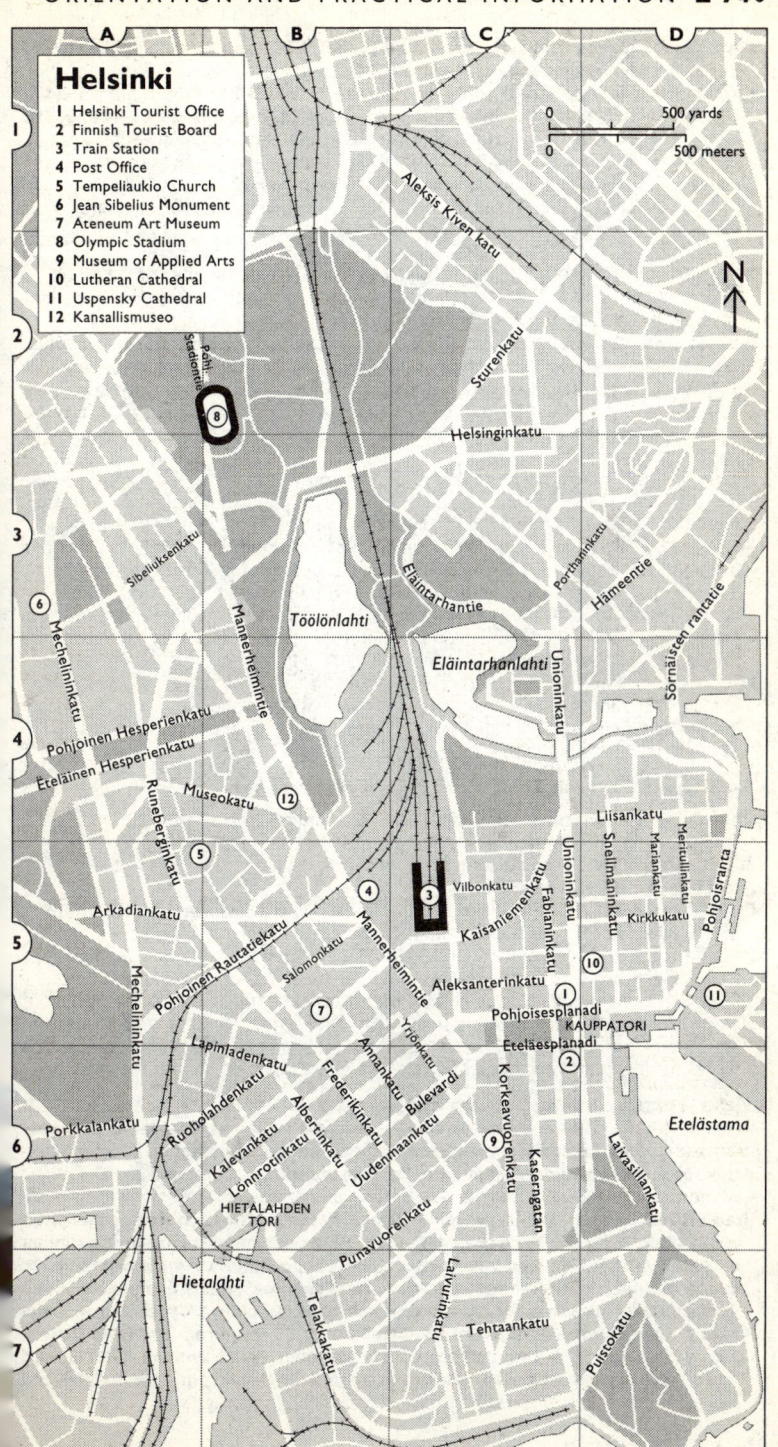

Helsinki

1. Helsinki Tourist Office
2. Finnish Tourist Board
3. Train Station
4. Post Office
5. Tempeliaukio Church
6. Jean Sibelius Monument
7. Ateneum Art Museum
8. Olympic Stadium
9. Museum of Applied Arts
10. Lutheran Cathedral
11. Uspensky Cathedral
12. Kansallismuseo

American Express: Full service at **Area Travel,** Mikonkatu 2D, 2nd floor (tel. 62 87 88). Open Mon.-Fri. 9am-1pm and 2:15-4:30pm.

Flights: For info, call 818 81 (Mon.-Fri.). Bus #615 runs 2-3 times per hour 5:20am-10:20pm between the **Helsinki-Vantaa** airport and the station square (15mk). The Finnair bus shuttles between the airport and the Finnair building at Asema-aukio 3, next to the train station (every 20min. 5am-midnight, 35min., 24mk).

Trains: Call 010 01 24 for info on trains to St. Petersburg (7½hr.; 265mk, Eurail and Scanrail 148mk) and Moscow (16hr.; 506mk, sleeper included). The station has **lockers** and **luggage service** (10mk each; service open daily 6:35am-10pm). Station open Mon.-Fri. 5:15am-1:30am, Sat.-Sun. 5:15am-midnight.

Buses: (tel. 96 00 40 00) The long-distance station lies near the post office, between Salomonkatu and Simonkatu. To: St. Petersburg via Lahti (3 per day, 8hr., 190-250mk). Buy tickets at the station or on the bus.

Ferries: Silja Line, Mannerheimintie 2 (tel. 180 41), is open Mon.-Fri. 8:30am-6pm, Sat. 9am-2pm. **Viking Line,** Mannerheimintie 14 (tel. 123 51), is open Mon.-Fri. 8:30am-6pm, Sat. 9am-3pm. The departure point for Silja Line, **Polferries** (tel. 9800 74 552), **Estonian Line** (tel. 669 944), and **Tallink** (tel. 2282 1277) ferries is south of Kauppatori (take tram #3T). For more info about touring the Baltic, call the **Baltic tourist info,** tel. 630 522.

Public Transportation: The **Metro** and most **trams** and **buses** run approximately 6am-11pm (certain bus and tram lines, including the indispensable tram #3T, continue until 1:30am). On weekends, **trains** run until 2:30am. Within Helsinki, rides cost 9mk; a 10-trip ticket goes for 75mk. All tickets are valid for one hour (transfers free) and are available at R-Kiosks and City Transport offices at Simonkatu 1, the Rautatientori metro station, and the Hakaniemi train station. Punch your ticket on board. The **Tourist Ticket** provides boundless transit in Helsinki, Espoo, and Vantaa (1-day 25mk, 3-day 50mk). You can purchase the tickets at City Transport and tourist offices. For transit information, call 010 01 11.

Laundromat: Your best bet is to check for facilities at youth hostels (5-15mk). Otherwise, look for the words *"Itsepalvelu Pesula"*. Wash at Suonionkatu 1. Wash and dry 51mk. Open Mon.-Fri. 8am-5pm, Sat. 8am-2pm. Or try Punavuorenkatu 3. Wash 25mk, dry 25mk. Open Mon.-Fri. 8am-8pm, Sat. 9am-2pm, Sun. noon-4pm.

Travelers With Disabilities: For information on facilities and transport, contact **Rullaten Ry,** Malminkatu 38 (tel./fax 805 73 93).

Pharmacy: Yliopiston Apteekki, Mannerheimintie 5 (tel. 17 90 92). Open daily 7am-midnight. The branch at Mannerheimintie 96 (tel. 41 57 78) is open 24hr.

Medical Assistance: The **Aleksin lääkäriasema,** Mannerheimintie 8 (tel. 601 911), receives and refers foreigners.

Emergencies: tel. 112. **Police:** tel. 100 22. Stations at Olavinkatu 1A, Kasarmikatu 25B, 2 Pikku Roobertinkatu 1-3, and the train station near platform 11.

Post Office: Mannerheimintie 11 (tel. 195 51 17). Open Mon.-Fri. 9:30am-5pm. The **Poste Restante** office sells stamps and exchanges money. Open Mon.-Fri. 7am-9pm, Sat. 9am-6pm, Sun. 11am-9pm. **Postal Code:** 00100.

Telephones: In the same building as the post office. Open Mon.-Fri. 9am-10pm, Sat.-Sun. 10am-4pm. Get the best rates by using a Tele or a Nonstop phone card, which works in all green Nonstop card phones. **Phone Code:** 90.

ACCOMMODATIONS AND CAMPING

During the summer, it's wise to make reservations, but just showing up is not extraordinarily risky. Most hostels offer laundry facilities, breakfast, and saunas.

Stadion Hostel (HI), Pohj. Stadiontie 3B (tel. 49 60 71; fax 49 64 66), in the Olympic Stadium complex. Take tram #3T or 7A, or walk 25min. from the train station. Enormous hostel (200 beds) has high ceilings, huge windows, a kitchen, and TV. Reception open June to early Sept. daily 8am-2am; mid-Sept. to May 8-10am and 4pm-2am. Bed in a dorm 55mk, nonmembers 70mk. Doubles 160mk. Sheets 20mk.

Kallio Youth Hostel, Porthaninkatu 2 (tel. 70 99 25 90). From the train station, walk 15min. north on Unioninkatu, or take the metro to Hakaniemi. Cozy 30-bed hostel. TV room and kitchen. Reception open daily 8am-11pm. Free lockers and storage room. 50mk, disposable sheets 10mk. Open June-Aug.

Hotel Satakuntatalo (HI), Lapinrinne 1 (tel. 69 58 51; fax 694 22 26). 500m southwest of the train station—turn right on Mannerheimintie, then left up Salomonkatu through the bus station; go down Lapinrinne. A dorm-*cum*-summer hotel. Clean and well run, with some great rooms. Kitchen and baggage storage. Restaurant serves lunch and dinner. Dorms 50mk. Singles 170 mk. Doubles 195mk. Nonmembers add 15mk. Sauna 20mk. Open June-Aug.

Eurohostel (HI), Linnankatu 9 (tel. 622 04 70; fax 65 50 44). Opposite the Viking Line terminal, 2km west of the train station. Take tram #4 (dir. "Katajanokka") past the port. Clean rooms. Kitchen. Singles 160mk. Doubles 200mk. Triples 300mk. Nonmembers add 15mk. Morning sauna included.

Academica (HI), Hietaniemenkatu 14 (tel. 402 02 06; fax 44 12 01). Just 700m from the train station; walk up Mannerheimintie and turn right, then left onto Arkadiankatu, left on Mechelininkatu, and right onto Hietaniemenkatu. Kitchen. Doubles 110mk per person. Triples 85mk per person. Quads 75mk per person. Nonmembers add 15mk. Open June-Aug.

Finnapartments Fenno, Franzéninkatu 26 (tel. 773 16 61; fax 701 68 89). From the train station, walk north on Unioninkatu (which turns into Siltasaarenkatu), turn right on Porthaninkatu, and left onto Fleminginkatu. Take a left at the intersection with Franzéninkatu. Home-style apartments in the center of the city. Singles 160-220mk. Doubles 320mk.

Camping: Rastila Camping (tel. 31 65 51), 14km east of the city. Take the Metro to Itäkeskus and then catch bus #90, 90A, or 96. Vast, cheap, municipal campground with washing and cooking facilities. 40mk per person. Cabins 210-320mk.

FOOD

Corporate monopolies make even groceries expensive; seek refuge with the **Alepa** chain (branch under the train station open Mon.-Sat. 10am-10pm, Sun. noon-10pm). Energetic epicureans can find a variety of wares at **Kauppatori** (Market Square), by the port (open June-Aug. Mon.-Sat. 7am-2pm and 4-8pm; Sept.-May Mon.-Fri. 7am-2pm), and nearby **Kauppahalli** (Market Hall; open Mon.-Sat. 8am-5pm, Sun. 8am-2pm). Or try one of Helsinki's many Russian restaurants.

University cafeterias. Humanists relate in the convivial main building, Fabianinkatu 33, while technocrats exchange impulses in outdoor-terraced Porthania, Hallituskatu 6, at Fabianinkatu. Both open June-Aug. Mon.-Fri. 10am-4pm; Sept.-May Mon.-Fri. 8am-6pm, Sat. 10:30am-2:30pm. Entrees 20mk. Students only.

Frutti Di Mare, 5 Yliopistonkatu, near the train station, has an all-you-can-eat pasta buffet for a low 29mk. Open Mon.-Sat. 11am-midnight, Sun. noon-10pm. Buffet kicks in only after 3pm weekdays, but is served all day on weekends.

Kasvis, Korkeavuorenkatu 3. Serves organically grown vegetable dishes (25-45mk) and homemade bread that they've been perfecting for 20 years. Enjoy your meal outside or inside. Open Mon.-Fri. 11am-10pm, Sat.-Sun. noon-10pm.

Kaspian, Albertinkatu 7. Popular Persian restaurant, but a bit of a hike from the city center. Try the chicken with apple and nut sauce. Lunch buffet on weekdays 36-38mk. Open Mon.-Sat. 10:30am-6pm, Sun. 1-6pm.

Namaskaar, Mannerheimintie 100. Voted the best ethnic restaurant by readers of a local magazine. Indian food extraordinaire, but a bit pricey. Daily lunch specials are the best bet at 35-55mk, served from 11am-3pm. Open Mon.-Fri. 11am-midnight, Sat. 2pm-midnight, Sun. 2-11pm.

Kappeli, Eteläesplanadi 1. Victorian Parisian fantasy that has catered to trendies since 1867 (Sibelius had a favorite table here). Warm pies 15mk per slice; mouth-watering entrees 38-55mk. Open daily 9am-4am.

SIGHTS

Tram #3T offers the city's cheapest tour (pick up a free itinerary on board). Or just walk—most sights are packed within 2km of the train station, and the tourist office stocks the booklet *See Helsinki on Foot*. The famed architect Aalto once said of Finland, "Architecture is our form of expression because our language is so impossible," and indeed, throughout the city boldly 20th-century creations blend with slick Neoclassical lines. Much of the layout and architecture of the inner city, however, is the brainchild of a German, Carl Engel. After Helsinki became the capital of the Grand Duchy of Finland in 1812, he was chosen to design an appropriate city. In **Senate Square,** on the corner of Unioninkato and Aleksanterinkatu, Engel's work is well represented by the **Tuomiokirkko.** After marveling at the Neoclassical exterior, though, you may be disappointed by the austere interior of the Lutheran cathedral. (Open May-Sept. Mon.-Fri. 9am-7pm, Sat. 9am-6pm, Sun. noon-6pm; Oct.-April Mon.-Sat. 9am-5pm, Sun. noon-5pm.) A few blocks to the east, on Katajanokka island, the contrasting Byzantine-Slavonic **Uspensky Orthodox Cathedral** defends the island with its red spikes (open May-Dec. Mon.-Sat. 9:30am-4pm; Jan.-April irregular hours). Behind the cathedral stretches **Esplanadi.** During the Swedish-Finnish cultural conflict in the 19th century, the boulevard became a vivid symbol of the dispute, with Finns walking on the south side and Swedes on the north. Today, cosmopolitan Esplanadi offers a wonderful melange of cafés, street entertainment, and people-watching.

Across from the train station sprawls Finland's largest art museum, the **Art Museum of the Ateneum,** Kaivokatu 2-4. (Open Tues. and Fri. 9am-6pm, Wed.-Thurs. 9am-9pm, Sat.-Sun. 11am-5pm. 10mk, students and seniors 5mk, under 18 free; special exhibits 25mk.) The **Kansallismuseo** (National Museum), 500m northwest of the train station at Mannerheimintie 34, sets out intriguing displays of Finnish culture, from Gypsy and Sami costumes to *ryijyt* (rugs), along with a splendid history exhibit. (Open June-Aug. Tues. 11am-8pm, Wed.-Sun. 11am-5pm; Sept.-May Tues. 11am-8pm, Wed.-Sun. 11am-4pm. 15mk, students 5mk.) **Temppeliaukio Church,** designed in the late 60s by Tuomo and Timo Suomalainen, is built into a hill of rock, with only its roof visible from the outside. From the train station, head west on Arkadiankatu and then right on Fredrikinkatu to the square where the church is buried (open Mon.-Fri. 10am-8pm, Sat. 10am-6pm, Sun. noon-8pm). The striking **Jean Sibelius Monument,** 750m north of the church in Sibelius Park, on Mechelininkatu, was dedicated to one of the 20th century's greatest composers by sculptor Eila Hiltunen. The monument looks like a cloud of organ pipes blasted into outer space (take bus #18 from the train station).

ENTERTAINMENT

Much of Helsinki nods off early, but only because the days are packed. Sway to afternoon street music on leafy **Esplanadi** or party on warm nights at **Hietaniemi beach.** Open-air concerts take place in **Kaivopuisto park** on Sundays in July, while **Hakaniementori** offers waterside beer gardens. Consult *Helsinki This Week* for current happenings, and the *City* or the weekly *Clubland* for bars and nightclubs. Finland is one of the few European countries where the drinking age—18 for beer and wine, 20 for hard alcohol—is usually enforced. Both bouncers and cover charges usually relax on weeknights; speaking English or German may help you get in. Tickets to some discos sell out before the evening begins; the super-cautious can buy in advance at **Tiketti,** in the Forum mall at the corner of Mannerheimintie and Simonkatu (3rd floor), or **Lippupalvelu,** Mannerheimintie 5. Starting in the last week in August, the two-week **Helsinki Festival** cobbles together a collage of arts events, from ballet to theater to rock concerts.

> **Cantina West,** Kasarmikatu 23 (tel. 63 98 60), south of the train station on Keskuskatu, then east on Eteläesplanadi. Fairly expensive Tex-Mex restaurant and bar with cacti on the tables. The happening place in Helsinki. 3 floors, live music nightly. Minimum age 22. Cover 35mk on weekends. Open Mon.-Thurs. 11am-3am, Fri. 11am-4am, Sat. noon-4am, Sun. noon-3am.
>
> **Manala** (Hell), Dagmarinkatu 2, just behind the Parliament building. Live bands, celebrity acts, and a maze-like, mysterious environment draw an international crowd. Cover depends on the act. Open nightly until 4am.

- **Old Students' House,** Mannerheimintie 3 (tel. 66 73 76). Pubs, dance floors, restaurant, beer patio, and sociable students. Beer 15-20mk. Cover 20-50mk for live bands. Open Mon.-Thurs. 11am-1am, Fri.-Sat. 11am-2am.
- **Storyville,** Museokatu 8 (tel. 40 80 07). Helsinki's choice jazz club. Diverse clientele. Nightly live tunes. Open Mon.-Sat. 8pm-4pm, Sun. 8pm-2am.
- **Corona,** Eerikinkatu 11. Smoky but respectable pool and beerhall. Shoot stick for 35mk per hour. Beers 18mk. Open Mon.-Sat. 11pm-2am, Sun. midnight-2am.
- **Kaark XII,** Kasarmikatu 40, down the street from Cantina West, is a lively pub and student hangout that becomes the most popular spot in town on Thursday nights. Open nightly until 2am.
- **H₂0,** Eerikinkatu 14. Helsinki's packed gay bar (mostly men). Open daily 4pm-2am.

Vienna (Wien), Austria

US$1 = 10.41AS (schilling, or ATS)	10AS = US$0.96
CDN$1 = 7.58AS	10AS = CDN$1.32
UK£1 = 16.22AS	10AS = UK£0.62
IR£ = 16.86AS	10AS = IR£0.59
AUS$1 = 8.20AS	10AS = AUS$1.22
NZ$1 = 7.23AS	10AS = NZ$1.38
SAR1 = 2.33AS	10AS = SAR4.27
Country Phone Code: 43	**International Dialing Prefix: 900**

The center of the Habsburg empire and a prime mover in the annals of European history, Vienna is undoubtedly a city of imperial tastes and proportions. Massive palaces and the shades of such luminaries as Haydn and Mozart keep watch over Vienna's busy streets, as a population of 1,760,000 ensures the city's status as the political and demographic center of Austria. It's important to recognize, however, that this idea of empire lies deep below the surface of this serene and softly-aged city. Smoke lingering in brooding coffeehouses, bronze palace roofs faded to a gentle green, and the hush that awaits the conductors baton temper the imposing urban landscape as the majestic city makes a quiet turn toward dusk.

AUSTRIA ESSENTIALS

Stores in Austria close Saturday afternoons and Sundays; many **museums** take Mondays off. The first Saturday of the month stores close at 5 or 6pm. Everything closes on New Year's (Jan. 1), Epiphany, Easter (March 30, 1997), Whit Monday (May 19, 1997), Corpus Christi, Assumption (Aug. 15, 1997), Flag Day (Oct. 26), All Saints' (Nov. 1), Immaculate Conception, and Christmas (Dec. 25-26).

English is the most common second **language** in Austria—**German** being the first, so communication shouldn't be a problem. Any effort to use the mother tongue, will win loads of fans; "*Grüss Gott*" (God bless) is the typical Austrian greeting.

You can make international **phone** calls from most phones. **Telephone cards** *(Wertkarten)*, available in post offices, train stations, and Tabak Trafik, come in 50AS, 100AS, and 200AS denominations. For **AT&T Direct,** dial 022 90 30 11; **MCI WorldPhone,** 022 90 30 12; **SprintExpress,** 022 90 30 14; **Canada Direct,** 022 90 30 13; **British Telecom Direct,** 022 90 30 44; **New Zealand Direct,** 022 90 30 64; and **South Africa Direct,** 155 85 35. Note that the use of any of these services is considered a local call, so you must have coins or a phone card.

> The Austrian telephone network is becoming digitized, and phone numbers may change without notice after this book goes to press. Emergency numbers will most likely remain as follows: **police,** tel. 133; **ambulance,** tel. 144; **fire,** tel. 122.

754 ■ VIENNA

Vienna

1. Bahnhof Wien-Nord
2. Franz-Josefs Bahnhof
3. Museum Moderner Kunst
4. U.S. Embassy
5. Allgemeines Krankenhaus
6. Sigmund Freud Haus
7. Universität
8. Rathaus
9. Burgtheater
10. Parliament
11. Naturhistorisches Museum
12. Alte Hofburg
13. Kunsthistorisches Museum
14. Neue Hofburg
15. Akademie der Bildenden Künste
16. Secession Building
17. Staatsoper
18. Künstlerhaus
19. Musikverein
20. Australian Consulate
21. American Express
22. Stephansdom
23. Museum of Applied Art
24. Bahnhof Wien-Mitte
25. Irish Consulate
26. U.K. Consulate
27. Unteres Belvedere
28. Oberes Belvedere
29. Südbahnhof
30. Westbahnhof

HOSTELS AND HOTELS

1. Porzellaneum
2. Pension Falstaff
3. Albertina Alsergrund
4. Zöhrer
5. Albertina Josefstaft
6. Albertina Auersperg
7. Pension Wild
8. Haus Pfeilheim
9. Believe-It-Or-Not
10. HI Myrthengasse
11. HI Neustiftgasse
12. Irmgard Lauria
13. Hospiz-Hotel CVJM
14. To HI Ruthensteiner
15. Pension Kraml
16. To HI Kolpingfamilie
17. Hochschule für Musik

AUSTRIA ESSENTIALS ■ **755**

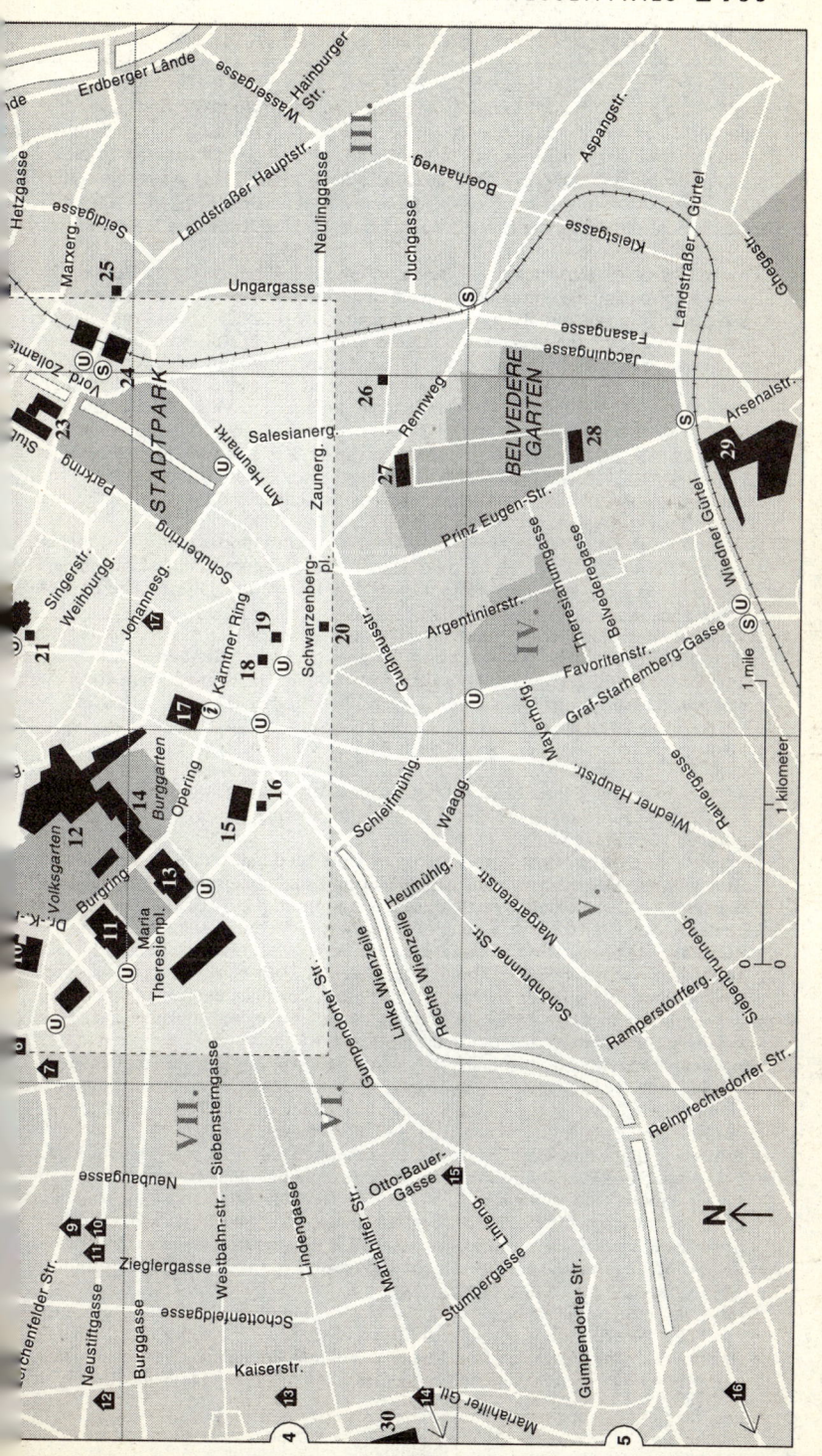

756 ■ VIENNA

ORIENTATION AND PRACTICAL INFORMATION

Vienna lies 40km from the Hungarian, Czech, and Slovak borders. The city is divided into 23 *Bezirke* (districts); the oldest area, *die Innere Stadt,* is the first. The **Ringstraße** separates the first district from the second through ninth districts, which spiral out in a clockwise manner. Street signs indicate the district number in either Roman or Arabic numerals (e.g. "XIII, Auhofstr. 26" is in the 13th). A good introduction to Vienna, the intersection of the **Opernring, Kärntner Ring,** and **Kärntner Straße,** is home to the Opera House, tourist office, and the **Karlsplatz** U-Bahn stop.

- **Tourist Offices:** I, Kärntnerstr. 38 (tel. 518 38 92), behind the Opera House. The small bureau dispenses brochures and a free decent city map. The brochure *Youth Scene* provides vital info for travelers of all ages. The office also books rooms (300-400AS) for a 40AS fee plus the first night's deposit. Open daily 9am-7pm. Branch offices at **Westbahnhof** (open daily 6:15am-11pm), **Südbahnhof** (open May-Oct. daily 6:30am-10pm; Nov.-April 6:30am-9pm), and the **airport** (open June-Sept. daily 8:30am-11pm; Oct.-May 8:30am-10pm). **Jugend-Info Wien** (Youth Information Service), Bellaria-Passage (tel. 526 46 37 or 526 17 99), in the underground passage at the Bellaria intersection. Enter at the Dr.-Karl-Renner-Ring/Bellaria tram stop (lines 1, 2, 46, 49, D, and J) or the Volkstheater U-Bahn station. The hip and knowledgeable staff has an accommodations list, cheap tickets to music events, and *Jugend in Wien.* Open Mon.-Fri. noon-7pm, Sat. 10am-7pm.
- **Budget Travel: ÖKISTA,** IX, Türkenstr. 6 (tel. 40 14 80). Books discounted flights; pop next door (Türkenstr. 8) for train tickets. The young staff understands budget travel and English. ISIC cards 60AS. Open Mon.-Fri. 9:30am-5:30pm. The **branch office** at IV, Karlsgasse 3 (tel. 505 01 28), keeps the same hours.
- **Embassies and Consulates: Australia,** IV, Mattiellistr. 2-4 (tel. 512 85 80), behind the Karlskirche. Open Mon.-Fri. 9am-12:30pm and 2-5pm. **Canada,** I, Laurenzerburg 2, 3rd fl. (tel. 531 38 (3000 or 0)). Open Mon.-Fri. 8:30am-12:30pm and 1:30-3:30pm. **Ireland,** III, Hilton Center, 16th fl., Landstraßer Hauptstr. 2 (tel. 715 42 47; fax 713 60 04). **New Zealand,** XIX, Springsiedlegasse 28 (tel. 318 85 05; fax 37 76 60). Open Mon.-Fri. 9am-5pm. **South Africa,** XIX, Sandgasse 33 (tel. 32 46 93). **U.K.,** III, Jauresgasse 10 (tel. 713 15 75), near Schloß Belvedere. Open Mon.-Fri. 9:15am-noon and 2-4pm. **U.S.,** IX, Boltzmangasse 16, off Währingerstr. Consulate at I, Gartenbaupromenade 2 (tel. 313 39), off Parkring. Open Mon.-Fri. 8:30am-noon and 1-3:30pm.
- **Currency Exchange:** Most **banks** are open Mon.-Wed. and Fri. 8am-3pm, Thurs. 8am-5:30pm, with a break from 12:30-1:30pm. Bank and airport exchanges have the same official exchange rates; expect a minimum 65AS commission for traveler's checks, 10AS for cash. Longer hours and smaller commissions are available at the **train stations.** The exchange counter at Westbahnhof is open daily 4am-10pm. The counter at Südbahnhof is open May-Oct. daily 6:30am-10pm; Nov.-April 6:30am-9pm. The **airport** arrivals hall also offers currency exchange. Open daily 6:30am-11:30pm. **Cash advances** with MC or Visa are offered at many banks. Most **ATMs** in the inner city accept Cirrus, Eurocard, MC, and Visa.
- **American Express:** I, Kärntnerstr. 21-23 (tel. 515 40), down from Stephansplatz. 15AS charge for exchanging cash. Holds mail for 4 weeks for members only—call about details. Open Mon.-Fri. 9am-5:30pm, Sat. 9am-noon. For 24-hr. refund service or lost traveler's checks, call toll-free (066) 68 40 or 935 121 152.
- **Flights:** For flight info, call 711 10 22 33; for other inquiries, dial 711 10. **Wien Schwechat** airport is 18km from Vienna, accessible by public transportation from the city center. One option is to take U-3 or U-4 to Wien Mitte/Landstraße, and then the S-7 from Wien Mitte to Flughafen/Wolfsthal (30AS, Eurail not valid). The train from Wien Nord to the airport does accept Eurail. **Austrian Airlines** (tel. 17 89) flies to Berlin (roundtrip 4870AS), London (roundtrip 3490AS), Paris (roundtrip 3333AS), and Rome (roundtrip 4290AS).
- **Trains:** For train info, call 17 17; line staffed 24hr. There are 3 main stations in the city. The **Westbahnhof,** XV, Mariahilferstr. 132, serves Salzburg (3hr., 396AS), Innsbruck (5-7hr., 690AS), and major western cities including Amsterdam, Paris, and Munich. To reach the city center, take U-3 "Erdberg" to Volkstheater or

ORIENTATION AND PRACTICAL INFORMATION ■ 757

Stephansplatz. The **Südbahnhof**, X, Wiedner Gürtel 1a, sends trains to Budapest (3-4hr., 326AS), Prague (5hr., 392AS), Rome (13½hr., 2160AS), and Venice (8hr., 670AS). If you arrive at this station, take tram D "Nußdorf" from the right side of the station or tram #18 "Westbahnhof" to Südtiroler Platz, and then take U-1 "Kagran" to Stephansplatz. The **Franz-Josefs Bahnhof**, IX, Althamstr. 10, handles mostly local trains. There are also two smaller stations: **Bahnhof Wien Mitte,** in the center of town, handles local commuter trains and the shuttle to the airport; **Bahnhof Wien-Nord,** by the Prater on the north side of the Danube Canal, is one of the main S-Bahn and U-Bahn links for trains heading north.

Buses: For bus information, call 711 01; line staffed daily 7am-7pm. Catch buses at the **City Bus Terminals** at Wien-Mitte/Landstraße, Hüttelsdorf, Heiligenstadt, Floridsdorf, Kagran, Erdberg, or Reumannplatz. BundesBuses run from these stations to local and international destinations. Ticket counters open Mon.-Fri. 6am-5:50pm, Sat.-Sun. 6am-3:50pm. International lines run agencies in the stations.

Public Transportation: Excellent **U-Bahn** (subway), **bus,** and **S-bahn** (tram) systems cover the city. Single fare is 20AS on board, or 17AS if purchased in advance at a ticket office or tobacco shop; a 24-hr. pass costs 50AS, and a 72-hr. pass 130AS. All passes allow unlimited travel on the system, except on special night buses. To validate a ticket, punch it immediately upon entering the bus, tram, etc. in the orange machine. If you ride with a ticket that is not stamped, you risk a 500AS fine. Tickets can be purchased from *Tabak* kiosks or *Automaten* in major U-Bahn stations. Most of the system closes around midnight, but special **night buses** run on reduced routes (25AS). Night bus stops are designated by "N" signs. Streetcar lines and U-Bahn stops are listed on a free city map, available at the tourist office; ticket counters sell comprehensive maps for 15AS. The public transportation **information** number (tel. 587 31 86; German-speaking) will give you directions to any point in the city. Staffed Mon.-Fri. 6:30am-6:30pm, Sat.-Sun. 8:30am-4pm. Information stands around the city will also help you out.

Ferries: Cruise with **DDSG Donaureisen** (tel. 727 50) to Budapest for 750AS, roundtrip 1100AS (daily April 8-Oct. 29). Buy tickets at tourist offices. Boats dock at the *Reichsbrücke* on the New Danube. U-1: Vorgartenstr.

Taxis: tel. 313 00, 401 00, 601 60, 814 00, or 910 11. Accredited taxis have yellow and black signs on the roof. Base charge 24AS plus mileage. Surcharges apply for night, Sun., and holiday service; luggage costs 12AS for 20-50kg.

Bike Rental: Best bargains at the **Wien Nord** and **Westbahnhof** train stations. 100AS per day (with train ticket from day of arrival 45AS). Elsewhere rental averages 30AS per hr. Grab the *Vienna By Bike* brochure at the tourist office.

Luggage Storage: Lockers at all train stations charge 40AS per 24hr.; they are adequate for sizeable backpacks. Checked luggage 30AS. Open daily 4am-1:15am.

Lost Property: Fundbüro, IX, Wasagasse 22 (tel. 313 44 92 11). Open Mon.-Fri. 8am-noon. For items lost on public transport, call 790 94 35 00 within 3 days.

English Bookstore: Shakespeare & Company, I, Sterngassse 2 (tel. 535 50 53). Open Mon.-Fri. 9am-7pm, Sat. 9am-1pm.

Gay and Lesbian Information: Rosa Lila Villa, VI, Linke Wienzeile 102 (tel. 586 81 50), in an unmistakable pink and purple building. Open Mon.-Fri. 5-8pm.

Laundromat: Münzwäscherei Kalksburger, III, Schlachthausgasse 19. Wash 90AS per 6kg, dry 10AS. Soap 10AS. Open Mon.-Fri. 7:30am-6:30pm, Sat. 7:30am-1pm. **Münzwäscherei Margaretenstraße,** IV, Margaretenstr. 52. Wash 95AS per 6kg, dry 25AS. Soap included. Open Aug. 7 to July 14 Mon.-Fri. 7am-6pm.

Crisis Lines: House for Threatened and Battered Women: tel. 545 48 00 or 408 38 80; line staffed 24hr. **Rape Crisis Hotline:** tel. 523 22 22; line staffed Mon. 11am-6pm, Tues. 2pm-6pm, Wed. 10am-2pm, Thurs. 5pm-11pm.

Medical Assistance: Allgemeines Krankenhaus, IX, Währinger Gürtel 18-20 (tel. 404 00). Your consulate can provide a list of English-speaking physicians.

Post Office: Hauptpostamt, I, Fleischmarkt 19. The vast office has telephones, faxes, and currency exchange counters (60AS charge per traveler's check, no charge for cash). Open 24hr. There are **branch offices** at the 3 main train stations and other spots throughout the city; look for yellow signs with trumpet logos.

Postal Code: A-1070 in 7th district, A-1230 in 23rd, etc.

Telephones: I, Börsepl. 1, near Schottenring. Open daily 6am-midnight. Buy **phone cards** at post offices and train stations for 48AS or 95AS per min. Local calls cost 1AS and u; long-distance 9AS per min. **Phone Code:** 0222 in Austria; 1 abroad.

ACCOMMODATIONS AND CAMPING

One of the few unpleasant aspects of Vienna is the hunt for cheap rooms in summer (June-Sept.). Write at least a few days ahead for reservations, and pick up lists of hostels and hotels from the tourist office. University dorms (actually singles and doubles) alleviate the problem slightly in July when they metamorphose into hostels. Those unable to find a hostel bed or dorm room should consider one-star *Pensions*, which are most common in the seventh, eighth, and ninth districts. Singles in these establishments start around 350AS, doubles around 500AS.

Hostels

Myrthengasse (HI), VII, Myrthengasse 7 (tel. 523 63 16 or 523 94 29; fax 523 58 49). From the Westbahnhof take U-6: Burggasse-Stadthalle, then bus #48A to Neubaugasse. Walk back on Burggasse one block, and take the 1st right (15min.). Comfortable, modern 2- to 6-bed rooms with washrooms, light pine furniture, and lockers. TV lounge and peaceful courtyard. Attracts an adolescent crowd. 160AS, nonmembers 200AS. Laundry 50AS. Wheelchair accessible.

Believe-It-Or-Not, VIII, Myrthengasse 10, Suite 14 (ring bell; tel. 526 10 88 or 526 46 58), across the street from the Myrthengasse (see above). Bohemian and social. Kitchen, living room, and 2 bedrooms with high ceilings. Zany caretaker's personal crash-course on Vienna is a must. Reception open daily from 8am. 160AS.

Schloßherberge am Wilhelminenberg (HI), XVI, Savoyenstr. 2 (tel. 48 58 50 37 00; fax 48 58 50 37 02). U-6: Thaliastr, then tram #46 from Joachimsthalerplatz to "Maroltingergasse", then bus #146B to "Schloß Wilhelminenberg". It's not as close to transportation centers as other hostels, but the trip is undoubtedly worth it. The building is to the left of a palatial castle; it offers fantastic views of Vienna. Quads with bathrooms 287AS per person.

Neustiftgasse (HI), VII, Neustiftgasse 85 (tel. 523 74 62; fax 523 58 49), around the corner from Myrthengasse (see above) and run by the same managers. Reception open daily 7:30-11am and 4pm-midnight. Lockout 9am-4pm. 2- to 6-bed rooms 155AS per person, nonmembers 195AS. Breakfast, showers, and sheets included. Laundry 50AS per load. Wheelchair accessible.

Gästehaus Ruthensteiner (HI), XV, Robert-Hamerlinggasse 24 (tel. 893 42 02; fax 893 27 96), 3min. from the Westbahnhof. Go right on Mariahilferstr., take the first left at Palmgasse, then the first right. Bright, clean rooms. Lockers and kitchen available for guests' use. Reception open 24hr. No lockout or curfew. Flexible 4-night max. stay. 10-bed rooms 139AS per person, 3- to 5-bed rooms 159AS. Singles 239AS. Doubles 450AS. **Bicycle rental** July-Sept. 89AS per day.

Hotels, Pensions, and Camping

Pension Kraml, VI, Brauergasse 5 (tel. 587 85 88; fax 586 75 73), off Gumpendorferstr. From the Westbahnhof, cross the Gürtel and go up Mariahilferstr. Take the 4th right onto Otto-Bauer-Gasse; make the first left on Königseggasse, then the first right (15min.). Clean, bright rooms. Singles 280AS. Doubles 570-590AS, with shower and toilet 780AS. Triples 750AS, with shower 875AS. Quad with shower and toilet 1160AS. Breakfast included.

Lauria, VII, Kaiserstr. 77, Suite 8 (tel. 522 25 55). From the Südbahnhof, take tram #18 to "Westbahnhof", then tram #5 to "Burggasse". Fun and eclectic place with a friendly staff. Kitchen and TV available. No curfew. Dorm beds 160AS. Doubles 480AS, with shower 700AS. Triples 700-800AS. Quad 850-940AS. Reservations recommended but require 2-day min. stay. Bring a lock for lockers.

Hospiz-Hotel CVJM, VII, Kenyongasse 15 (tel. 523 13 04; fax 523 13 04 13). From the Westbahnhof, cross the Gürtel, walk 1 block down Stallgasse, and turn left on Kenyongasse. This large, old building, now part of the Austrian YMCA, provides a quiet location close to the station. Reception open daily 8am-10pm. Singles 350AS, with shower 380AS. Doubles 640-680AS. Triples 900-990AS.

Wien-West I (tel. 914 14 49) and **II** (tel. 914 23 14), at Hüttelbergstr. 40 and 80, respectively, lie in the 14th district about 8km from the city center. For either, U-4: Hütteldorf, then bus #14B or 152 to "Camping pl. Wien West". Both offer laundry machines, grocery stores, and cooking facilities. 65AS per person, 61AS per tent and per car. Bungalows at Wien-West II (April-Oct.) 450AS. Wien-West I open July 15-Aug. 28; Wien-West II open March-Feb.

FOOD

Food and drink are inseparably linked in Vienna. Culinary offerings reflect the patchwork empire of the Habsburgs, but Vienna is perhaps most renowned for its sublime desserts and chocolates—unbelievably rich, and priced for patrons who are likewise blessed. Eateries in the touristy **Kärntnerstraße** area are generally overpriced. A better bet is the neighborhood around **Universitätsstraße** and **Währingerstraße**; reasonably-priced *Gaststätten, Kneipen,* and restaurants are easy to find. The delicacies at the open-air **Naschmarkt** are an especially filling option for vegetarian visitors to this carnivorous city (U-4: Kettenbrückengasse; open Mon.-Fri. 7am-6pm, Sat. 7am-1pm). For supermarket fare, try **Billa, Konsum,** or **Hoffer.**

Trześniewski, I, Dorotheergasse 1, 3 blocks down the Graben from the Stephansdom. One of Franz Kafka's old haunts. A famous stand-up restaurant, this unpronounceable establishment has been serving petite open-faced sandwiches for over 80 years. Open Mon.-Fri. 8:30am-7:30pm, Sat. 9am-1pm. Another **branch** with same hours at VII, Mariahilferstr. 26-30, in the Hermansky department store.

Levante, I, Wallnerstr. 2 (tel. 533 23 26). Walk down Graben away from Stephansdom; go left on Kohlmarkt, then right on Wallnerstr. Greek-Turkish dishes, many vegetarian. Entrees 78-130AS. **Branches** at I, Wollzeile 19; Mariahilferstr. 88a; and VIII, Josefstädterstr. 14. All open daily 11:30am-11:30pm.

Ma Pitom, I, Seitenstettengasse 5. In the "Triangle" area—walk down Potenturmstr., take a left on Fleischmarkt, right on Rabensteig, and right on Seitenstettengasse. Sophisticated and relaxed, with candles illuminating Mapplethorpe wall hangings. Brick-oven pizza 61-80AS. Open Mon.-Thurs. 11:30am-3pm and 5:30pm-1am, Fri.-Sat. 11:30am-3pm and 5:30pm-2am, Sun. 5:30pm-1am.

Tunnel, VIII, Florianigasse 39. U-2: Rathaus, and with your back to the Rathaus, head right on Landesgerichtstr., then left on Florianigasse. Dark and smoky, with the occasional divan instead of chairs. Italian, Austrian, and Middle-Eastern dishes with vegetarian options 40-120AS. Some of the cheapest beer in Vienna (24AS), the best pizza (50-80AS), and a breakfast menu (29AS) until 11:30am. Live music downstairs nightly. Open daily 9am-2am.

Blue Box, VII, Richtergasse 8. Take U-3 to Neubaugasse, turn off Mariahilferstr. into Neubaugasse, and take the first right. Interior looks like a funky nightclub, but the food is fresh, flamboyant, and original. You can't come to Vienna and miss this. Open Mon. 6pm-2am, Tues.-Thurs. and Sun. 10am-2am, Fri.-Sat. 10am-4am.

Café Hawelka, I, Dorotheergasse 6, 3 blocks down Graben from the Stephansdom. The award-winning Hawelka is dusty and glorious. *Buchteln* (sweet dumplings filled with preserves, served only at 10pm) 30AS. Coffee 25-40AS. Open Mon. and Wed.-Sat. 8am-2am, Sun. 4pm-2am.

Café Museum, I, Friedrichstr. 6. The café is near the Opera; head away from the *Innere Stadt* to the corner of Operngasse and Friedrichstr. Built in 1899 by Adolf Loos, with striking, curved red leather and lots of space, this comfortable meetingplace attracts artists, lawyers, and students. Open daily 7am-11pm.

SIGHTS

Tourist offices carry *Vienna from A to Z* (30AS), which lets you create your own tour. *Museums* (free) lists all opening hours and admission prices.

Start your odyssey at the **Innere Stadt's** Gothic **Stephansdom.** The smoothly tapering stone lace spire of this magnificent cathedral has become Vienna's emblem. (Tours in English Mon.-Sat. 10:30am and 3pm, Sun. 3pm; 30AS. Spectacular July-Sept.

evening tour Sat. 7pm; 100AS.) In the catacombs, the **vault** stores Habsburgs' entrails (tours every 30min. Mon.-Sat. 10am-noon and 2-5pm, Sun. 2-5pm; 50AS).

The **Hofburg** (Imperial Palace), rising from the southeast of the **Michaelerplatz**, was home to the Habsburg emperors until 1918, and now houses the president's office. Wander through the **Burggarten** (Gardens of the Imperial Palace), the **Burgkapelle** (where the Vienna Boys' Choir sings Mass on Sun. and religious holidays), and the **Schauräume** (state rooms open Mon.-Sat. 8:30am-noon and 12:30-4pm, Sun. 8:30am-12:30pm; tours 40AS, students 20AS). Also check out the **Neue Hofburg** (New Palace) and the **Nationalbibliothek** (National Library), which boasts an outstanding collection of papyrus scriptures and musical scores.

The Hofburg's Heldenplatz gate presides over the Burgring segment of the **Ringstraße**. In 1857, Emperor Franz Josef commissioned this 57m-wide and 4km-long boulevard to replace the city walls that separated Vienna's center from the suburban districts. Follow Burgring west through the **Volksgarten's** hundreds of rose varieties to reach the Neoclassical, sculpture-adorned **Parliament** building (tours July-Aug. Mon.-Fri. at 9, 10, 11am, 1, 2, and 3pm; Sept.-June Mon.-Fri. at 11am and 3pm). Up Dr.-Karl-Renner-Ring is the **Rathaus**, an intriguing remnant of late 19th-century neo-Gothic with Victorian mansard roofs and red geraniums in the windows. The **Burgtheater** opposite guards frescos by Klimt. To the north on Dr.-Karl-Lueger-Ring is the **Universität**. Nearby streets overflow with cafés and bookstores.

Across Albertinapl. from the Hofburg is the **Staatsoper** (State Opera House). If you miss the shows (standing-room tickets 20AS) at the Opera House, tour the glittering gold, crystal, and red velvet interior featured in the movie *Amadeus* and once home to Mahler's skilled conducting (tours July-Aug. 11am-3pm on the hour; Sept.-June on request; 40AS, students 25AS). Alfred Hrdlicka's poignant 1988 sculpture **Monument Gegen Krieg und Faschismus** (Memorial Against War and Fascism), behind the opera on Albertinapl., memorializes the suffering of Austria's people during WWII.

Music lovers trek out to the **Zentralfriedhof** (Central Cemetery), XI, Simmeringer Hauptstr. 234, where Beethoven, the Strausses, and Schönberg are buried. Take tram #71 (open June-Aug. 7am-7pm; May and Sept. 7am-6pm; April and Oct. 7am-5pm; Nov.-March 7am-dusk). If you need some cheering up after that, visit the **Hundertwasser Haus**, at the corner of Löwenstr. and Kegelgasse in the third district. A wild fantasia of pastel colors, ceramic mosaics, and tilted tile columns contribute to the rebellion in this blunt rejection of architectural orthodoxy.

Another must-see is the **Schloß Schönbrunn** and its gardens, which encompass 1.6 sq. km of glorious space. Tours of some of the palaces' 1500 rooms reveal the elaborate taste of Maria Theresa's era. Six-year-old Mozart played in the **Hall of Mirrors** at the empress's whim, and to the boy's father's profit. The **Great Gallery's** frescos are a highlight. However, the **Million Gulden Room** wins the prize for excessiveness; Indian miniatures cover the chamber's walls. (Open April-Oct. daily 8:30am-5pm; Nov.-March 8:30am-4:30pm; 80AS, English tours available.)

The **Prater**, extending southeast from the Wien-Nord Bahnhof, is a notoriously touristed amusement park that functioned as a private game reserve for the imperial family until 1766. The park is dotted with various rides, arcades, restaurants, and casinos. Rides range from garish thrill machines to merry-go-rounds to the stately 65m **Riesenrad** (Giant Ferris Wheel). The wheel, featured prominently in *The Third Man*, offers one of the prettiest views of Vienna (open Feb.-Nov. 10am-10pm, sometimes until 11pm). Beloved by children during the day, the Prater becomes less wholesome and more dangerous after sunset: peepshows and prostitution abound.

Museums

On the Burgring in what used to be the *Neue Hofburg* is the world-famous **Kunsthistorisches Museum**. The building is home to one of the world's best art collections, including entire rooms of prime Bruegels, Vermeer's *Allegory of Painting*, and numerous works by Rembrandt, Rubens, Titian, Dürer, and Velázquez. Don't miss the superb collection of ancient art and a transplanted Egyptian burial chamber. Gustav Klimt decorated the lobby (picture gallery open Tues.-Wed. and Fri.-Sun.

10am-6pm, Thurs. 10am-9pm; free). Fans of Klimt and his fellow radical Schiele should visit the **Austrian Gallery,** in the **Belvedere Palace,** entrance at Prinz-Eugenstr. 27 (open Tues.-Sun. 10am-5pm; 60AS, students 30AS).

The greatest monument of *fin-de-siècle* Vienna is the **Secession Building,** I, Friedrichstr. 12, built by Wagner's pupil Josef Maria Olbrich to accommodate the group of artists, led by Gustav Klimt, who scorned historical style and broke with the uptight Viennese art establishment. Works of contemporary artists adorn the walls, as does Klimt's 30m *Beethoven Frieze* (open Tues.-Fri. 10am-6pm, Sat.-Sun. 10am-4pm; 60AS, students 30AS).

Kunst Haus Wien, III, Untere Weißgerberstr. 13, built for the works of Hundertwasser, is one of his greatest works in and of itself. This crazily pastiched building also hosts international contemporary exhibits (open daily 10am-7pm; Hundertwasser exhibition 60AS, students 44AS). The **Historisches Museum der Stadt Vienna** (Historical Museum of the City of Vienna), IV, Karlspl. 5, to the left of the Karlskirche, houses collections of historical artifacts and paintings that document the city's evolution from the Roman Vindobona encampment through 640 years of Habsburg rule to the present (open Tues.-Sun. 9am-4:30pm; 30AS).

ENTERTAINMENT

You can enjoy Viennese opera in the imperial splendor of the **Staatsoper** (State Opera House; season runs Sept.-June) for a mere 20-50AS. Get in line on the west side about three hours before curtain for standing room (*Stehplätze*) tickets, sold only on the day of performance. Bring a scarf to tie on the rail to save your place during the show. Costlier advance tickets (100-850AS) are on sale at the **Bundestheaterkasse,** I, Hanuschgasse 3 (tel. 514 44 22 60), next to the opera along the Burggarten (open Mon.-Fri. 8am-6pm, Sun. 9am-noon; university ID—*not* ISIC—required). Get to the ticket office at 6-7am opening day for a good seat.

Heurigen (outside seating at picnic tables, with mugs of wine hung over the door) freckle the north, west, and south suburbs, where grapes are grown. **Grinzing** is the largest *Heurigen* area, but atmosphere and prices are better in **Sievering, Neustift am Wald,** and **Stammersdorf.** Hidden from tourists and therefore beloved by locals, **Buschenschank Heinrich Niersche,** XIX, Strehlgasse 21, overlooks the field of Grinzing. Take bus #41A from the U-6: Pötzleindorfer Höhe, walk a block uphill, and turn left on Strehlgasse (open Thurs.-Mon. 3pm-midnight; *Weiße G'spritzer*—white wine with tonic 18AS).

Pick up a copy of *Falter* for the best entertainment listings. Revelers tend to lose themselves in the infamous **Bermuda Dreieck (Triangle),** a collection of about 30 bars northwest of Stephanspl. bordered by Rotenturmstr. and Wipplingerstr. The action moves indoors from 11pm until 2-4am. The area around the U-3 "Stubentor station" is also a solid stomping ground of the hip. Other locals congregate in the cool ancient grottos of the **Bäckerstraße** area behind the Stephansdom. The **8th District** behind the university is also a target area for thirsty night-owls.

Benjamin, I, Salzgries 11-13, just outside of the Triangle. Go down the steps from Ruprecht's church, left onto Josefs Kai, and left on Salzgries. Persian rugs, velvet lounge, soul grooves, and airplane seats. *Budvar* and *Kapsreiter* 37AS and 43AS, respectively. Open Sun.-Thurs. 7pm-2am, Fri.-Sat. 7pm-4am.

Krah Krah, I, Rabensteig 8. From Stephanspl., head down Rotenturmstr., and continue slightly to your left on Rabensteig. 50 kinds of beer on tap. Outdoor seating until 10pm. Open Sun.-Wed. 11am-2am, Thurs.-Sat. 11am-3am.

Zwölf Apostellenkeller, I, Sonnenfelsgasse 3, behind the Stephansdom. To reach this underground tavern, walk into the archway, take a right, go down the long staircase, and discover grottoes that date back to 1561. Beer 37AS. *Viertel* of wine starts at 25AS. Open Aug.-June daily 4:30pm-midnight.

Mekka, VII, Mariahilferstr. 19-21. U-2: Babenbergerstr. Then walk up Mariahilferstr. It's on your left (3min.). This is the newest place in town. Candlelight, arabesque curves, chrome, and an oriental fringe along the bar. Three DJs mix house and techno. Some Sat. (or rather, Sun. mornings), Mekka holds "After Hours," where the bar and the dance floor stay open until noon-Sun. Cover 50-100AS. Open Tues.-Sat. 4pm-6am.

Appendices

■ Climate

Temp. (in °C) Rain (in cm)	January Temp. Rain	April Temp. Rain	July Temp. Rain	October Temp. Rain
Albania:				
Tirana	12/02 13.5	18/08 11.7	31/17 3.2	23/10 10.5
Belarus:				
Minsk	-4/-8 4.2	10/07 4.9	19/17 5.5	12/08 5.1
Bosnia:				
Sarajevo	03/-3 4.7	18/07 5.4	28/17 6.1	18/08 5.5
Bulgaria:				
Sofia	02/-3 3.6	16/05 6.1	27/16 6.8	17/08 6.5
Varna	06/-1 2.8	16/07 3.7	30/19 4.5	21/11 5.8
Croatia:				
Zagreb	02/-4 8.8	15/04 9.8	27/14 11.3	15/06 15.1
Czech Rep.:				
Prague	00/-5 1.8	12/03 2.7	23/13 6.8	12/05 3.3
Estonia:				
Tallinn	-4/-10 3.1	10/01 3.3	22/11 5.3	11/04 6.2
Hungary:				
Budapest	01/-4 3.7	17/07 4.5	28/16 5.6	16/7 5.7
Latvia:				
Rīga	-4/-10 3.1	10/01 3.3	22/11 5.3	11/04 6.2
Lithuania:				
Vilnius	-4/-10 3.1	10/01 3.3	22/11 5.3	11/04 6.2
Macedonia:				
Skopje	05/-3 3.9	19/05 3.8	31/15 2.9	19/06 6.1
Romania:				
Bucharest	01/-7 4.6	18/05 5.9	30/16 5.3	18/06 2.9
Constanța	03/-4 2.9	13/6 2.9	27/18 3.5	17/09 3.8
Poland:				
Warsaw	00/-6 2.7	12/03 3.7	24/15 9.6	13/05 3.8
Kraków	00/-5 2.8	13/03 4.6	24/15 11.1	14/05 4.9
Gdańsk	01/-3 3.3	09/02 3.6	21/14 8.4	21/14 6.1
Russia:				
Moscow	-9/-16 3.9	10/01 3.9	23/13 8.8	09/03 4.5
Petersburg	-7/-13 3.5	08/00 3.6	21/13 7.2	09/04 7.6
Irkutsk	-16/-26 1.3	06/-7 1.5	21/10 7.9	05/-6 1.8
Slovakia:				
Bratislava	01/-4 3.9	15/06 4.5	25/15 8.4	14/7 1.3
Slovenia:				
Ljubljana	02/-4 8.8	15/04 9.8	27/14 11.3	15/06 15.1
Ukraine:				
Kiev	-4/-10 5.8	14/05 4.5	25/15 9.1	13/06 3.3
Simferopol	03/-5 4.6	16/05 2.8	28/16 6.4	17/07 2.4
Gateways:				
Berlin	02/-3 4.6	13/04 4.2	24/14 7.3	13/06 4.9
Helsinki	-3/-9 5.6	06/-1 4.4	22/13 6.8	08/03 7.3
Vienna	01/-4 3.9	15/06 4.5	25/15 8.4	14/7 5.6

■ Train Travel Time (in hours)

	Budapest	Kiev	Prague	Moscow	Bucharest	Warsaw
Budapest	—	22	9	39	13	10
Kiev	22	—	30	13-17	17	20
Prague	9	30	—	39	22	12-14
Moscow	39	13-17	39	—	34	27-30
Bucharest	13	17	22	34	—	23
Warsaw	10	20	12-14	27-30	23	—

■ Country Codes

Albania	355
Belarus	7
Bosnia and Herzegovina	387
Bulgaria	359
Croatia	385
Czech Republic	42
Estonia	372

Hungary	36
Latvia	371
Lithuania	370
Macedonia	389
Moldova	373
Poland	48
Romania	40

Russia	7
Slovakia	42
Slovenia	386
Ukraine	7
Berlin, GER	49
Helsinki, FIN	358
Vienna, AUS	43

■ Weights, Measures, and Temperatures

Like the rest of the civilized world, Eastern Europe uses the metric system. The following are more precise metric equivalents of common English measurements.

1 millimeter (mm) = 0.04 inch
1 meter (m) = 1.09 yards
1 kilometer (km) = 0.62 mile
1 gram (g) = 0.04 ounce
1 kilogram (kg) = 2.2 pounds
1 liter = 1.06 quarts

1 inch = 25mm
1 yard = 0.92m
1 mile = 1.61km
1 ounce = 25g
1 pound = 0.55kg
1 quart = 0.94 liter

To convert from Fahrenheit degrees into Celsius, subtract 32 and multiply by 5/9. To from Celsius to Fahrenheit, multiply by 9/5 and add 32.

°C	-5	0	5	10	15	20	25	30	35	40
°F	23	32	41	50	59	68	77	86	95	104

Holidays and Festivals

ALBANIA

January 1	*National*	New Year's
March/April	*National*	Easter Monday
May 1	*National*	Labor Day
November 28	*National*	Independence Day
February/April	*National*	Ramadan
December 25	*National*	Catholic Christmas

BELARUS

January 1	*National*	New Year's
January 7	*National*	Orthodox Christmas
March 8	*National*	International Women's Day
March 15	*National*	Constitution Day (1994)
March/April	*National*	Catholic and Orthodox Easter Monday
May 1	*National*	International Labor Day
April/May	*National*	Rasounitsa (9th day after Easter)
May 9	*National*	Victory (1945) and Mothers' Day
July 27	*National*	Independence Day (1990)
November 2	*National*	Dzyady honors those who died in war
December 25	*National*	Catholic Christmas

BULGARIA

January 1-2	*National*	New Year's
January 7	*National*	Orthodox Christmas
March 3	*National*	1878 Liberation Day
March	*Ruse*	March Music Days
March/April	*National*	Orthodox Easter Monday
May 1	*National*	Labor Day
May 24	*National*	Cyrillic Alphabet Day
late May	*Sofia*	Music Weeks International Festival of Contemporary Music
early June	*Kazanluk*	Rose festival
June	*Madara*	Madara Music Days
June	*Burgas*	International Ballroom Dancing Contest
mid-June to July	*Varna*	Varna Summer
July	*Plovdiv*	International Chamber Music festival
August	*Varna*	International Jazz Festival
August	*Varna*	"Love is Folly" film festival
August	*Sunny Beach*	Golden Orpheus Festival of Pop Songs
August, Olympic years	*Koprivshtitsa*	Koprivshtitsa Folk festival
September	*Sozopol*	Arts Festival Apolonia
September	*Sunny Beach*	International child performer contest
Oct.-Nov.	*Pleven*	Katya Popova Laureate festival
November	*Sofia*	Sofia film festival

CROATIA

January 1	*National*	New Year's
January 6-7	*National*	Orthodox Christmas
March/April	*National*	Catholic and Orthodox Easter Monday
May 1	*National*	Labor Day
May 30	*National*	Statehood Day
mid-June	*Zagreb*	World Festival of Animated Films
June 22	*National*	Croatian National Uprising Day
late July	*Zagreb*	International Folklore Festival
July-August	*Zagreb*	Zagreb Summer Festival
July-August	*Split*	Summer Festival
August 15	*National*	Assumption Day
November 1	*National*	All Saints' Day
December 25-26	*National*	Christmas

CZECH REPUBLIC

January 1	*National*	New Year's
March/April	*National*	Catholic Easter Monday
May 1	*National*	Labor Day
May 8	*National*	Liberation Day
late May	*Prague*	Spring International Music Festival
late June	*Brno*	Strážnice Folk Festival
June 23	*Český Krumlov*	Midsummer's night medieval festival
1st week of July	*Karlovy Vary*	International Film Festival
July 5	*National*	Cyril and Methodius Day
July 6	*National*	Jan Hus Day
August	*Mariánské Lázně*	Frédéric Chopin Music Festival
September	*Karlovy Vary*	Dvořak Autumn Music Festival
October	*Prague*	International Jazz Festival
October	*Brno*	International Music Festival
October 28	*National*	Republic Day (1918)
December 24-26	*National*	Christmas

ESTONIA

January 1	*National*	New Year's
February 24	*National*	Independence Day (1918)
March/April	*National*	Good Friday, Easter Monday
May 1	*National*	May Day
June 3	*Tallinn*	Maikravi medieval fair
mid-June	*Tallinn*	Kantripäeväd (Country Music Days)
June 23	*National*	Victory Day (Battle of Võnnu, 1919)
June 24	*National*	Jaanipäev (St. John's Day)
late June	*Pärnu*	FiESTA music festival
early July	*Tallinn*	3-day Rocksummer rock festival
mid-July	*Tallinn*	Marine Days
mid-July	*Pärnu*	Anthropology film festival
late August	*Haapsalu*	White Lady festival
October	*Tallinn*	Jazzkaar jazz festival
November 16	*National*	Rebirth Day (1988)
December 25-26	*National*	Jõulud (Christmas) and Boxing Day

HOLIDAYS AND FESTIVALS ■ 767

HUNGARY

January 1	*National*	New Year's
late March	*Budapest*	Budapest Spring Festival
March	*Kecskemét*	Spring Festival
March/April	*National*	Catholic Easter Monday
May 1	*National*	Labor Day
May	*Siófok*	Balaton Festival
May/June	*National*	Whit Monday
late June	*Tata*	Tata's Water, Music, and Flowers Fest
late June	*Őrség villages*	Őrségi Vásár outdoor folk festival
late June, odd years	*Debrecen*	International Military Band Festival
June to July	*Sopron*	Sopron Early Music Days
June to July	*Győr*	Győri Nyár Arts Festival
June to July	*Pécs*	Summer Theater Festival
early July	*Visegrád*	International Palace Games
early July	*Debrecen*	Béla Bartók Choir Festivals
July	*Debrecen*	Jazz Days
July	*Eger*	Baroque music festival
mid-July to Aug.	*Szeged*	Open-Air Theater Festival
August 20	*National*	St. Stephen's Day
August 20	*Debrecen*	Floral Carnival
late Aug.-Sept.	*Kecskemét*	Hírös Festival of Food
early September	*Szilvásvárad*	Horse festival
September	*Eger*	Vintage Days
September	*Budapest*	Budapest Contemporary Music Festival
October 23	*National*	Republic Day (1956)
December 25-26	*National*	Christmas

LATVIA

January 1	*National*	New Year's
March/April	*National*	Catholic Easter Monday
April	*Rīga*	Baltic Theater Spring
May 1	*National*	Labor Day
2nd Sunday of May	*National*	Mothers' Day
late May	*Sigulda*	International Ballooning Festival
early June	*Rīga*	Gadatirgus arts and crafts fair
June 23-24	*National*	Līgo (Midsummer Night) and Jāni
July 6	*National*	Mindaugas Day
late July to Aug.	*Cēsis*	Cēsis Beer Festival
mid-August	*Liepāja*	Liepājas Dzintars rock festival
September 14-16	*National, Algona*	Ascension Day pilgrimage
September, even years	*Rīga*	Arsenāls international feilm festival
October	*Vilnius*	Vilnius Jazz festival
Oct./Nov.	*Rīga*	Bildes rock, folk, jazz, and art fest
November 1	*National*	All Saints' Day
November 2	*National*	All Souls' Day
November 11	*National*	Lāčplēsis Day honors war dead
November 18	*National*	National Day (1918)
December 25-26	*National*	Ziemsvētki (Christmas)

LITHUANIA

January 1	*National*	New Year's
February 16	*National*	Independence Day (1918)
March 4	*National, Vilnius*	St. Kazimieras' Day
March/April	*National*	Easter Monday
Mardi Gras	*Baltic Coast*	Užgavėnės
1st Sunday in May	*National*	Mothers' Day
last week of May	*Vilnius*	Folk music and dance festival
June 23	*National*	Rasos (Midsummer Night)
June 24	*National*	Joninės (St. John's Day)
July 6	*National*	Mindaugas Day
October	*Vilnius*	Vilnius Jazz festival
November 1	*National*	All Saints' Day
November 2	*National*	All Souls' Day
December 25-26	*National*	Kalédos

MACEDONIA

January 1-2	*National*	New Year's
January 7	*National*	Orthodox Christmas
January 13	*National*	Old New Year
March/April	*National*	Orthodox Easter Monday and Tuesday
April	*Skopje*	Cvetnici (Flower) Festival
May 1-2	*National*	Labor Days
May	*Skopje*	Opera Evenings
July	*Skopje*	Skopje Summer Festival
early July	*Ohrid*	Balkan Folklore Festival
late July	*Ohrid*	Ohrid Summer
early August	*Struga*	National Costume Festival
August 2	*Struga*	Struga Poetry Evenings
September 8	*National*	Republic Day
October 11	*National*	1941 Partizan Day
Oct./Nov.	*Skopje*	Skopje Jazz Festival

POLAND

In 1997, the biggest festival of all will be Gdansk's 1000th-year birthday party, with cultural events planned from April to November. In other years, the largest pilgrimages and crowds converge on the Częstochowa during the **Marian feasts and festivals.** For the dates of these festivals see Poland: Częstochowa, p. 448.

January 1	*National*	New Year's
March/April	*National*	Catholic Easter Monday
May	*Kraków*	International Short Feature Film Fest
May	*Zamość*	Jazz on the Borderlands
mid-May	*Łańcut*	Festiwal Muzyki Kameralnej
May 1	*National*	Labor Day
May 1	*Jelenia Góra*	Antiques and Oddities Market
May 3	*National*	Constitution Day
Thursday in June	*National*	Corpus Christi
June	*Kraków*	Lajkonik Carnival Parade
June	*Sandomierz*	Festival of Polish Folk Music
June	*Wrocław*	Jazz nad Odrą jam
July	*Zakopane*	Days of Karol Szymanowski's Music

HOLIDAYS AND FESTIVALS ■ 769

mid-July	*Jelenia Góra*	International Street Theater Festival
July-August	*Gdańsk*	Jantar Jazz Festival
July-August	*Mrągowo*	Country Picnic Festival
early August	*Gdańsk*	Jarmark Dominikański street fair
mid-August	*Sopot*	Opera Lesna's rock music festival
August 15	*Częstochowa*	pilgrimage
August 15	*National*	Ascension Day
late August	*Kraków*	International Street Theaters
late August	*Zakopane*	International Festival of Highlanders' Folk Music
September	*Gdańsk*	Polish Film Festival
September	*Kraków*	Jazz Festival
September	*Zamość*	Int'l Rendez-vous of Jazz Vocalists
September	*Jelenia Góra*	Knights' Crossbow Tournament
November 1	*National*	All Saints' Day
November 11	*National*	Independence Day (1918)
December 25-26	*National*	Christmas

ROMANIA

January 1-3	*National*	New Year's
4 days in April	*National*	Catholic Easter Monday
May 1	*National*	May Day
June 1	*Braşov*	folk Festivalul Junilor
June 24	*Suceava*	St. John the New festival
May-June	*Sibiu*	Jazz Festival
July 2	*Putna*	St. Stephen's Day
September	*Piaţa Sfatului*	International Golden Stag music festival
September	*Sibiu*	Cibinium music festival
December	*Oradea*	Bihor Culture Days
December 1	*National*	Union Day
December 25-31	*National*	Christmas

RUSSIA

January 1	*National*	New Year's
January 7	*National*	Russian Orthodox Christmas Day
February 23	*National*	Defender's of the Motherland Day
Feb. to March	*Near St. Petersburg*	"Goodbye Russian Winter" folk festivals
March 8	*National*	International Women's Day
March/April	*National*	Russian Orthodox Easter
April/May	*St. Petersburg*	Music Spring
May 1-2	*National*	International Labor Day
May 9	*National*	Victory Day (1945)
June 12	*National*	Independence Day
late June	*St. Petersburg*	White Nights
mid-November	*St. Petersburg*	Autumn Rhythms
November 7	*National*	Great October Socialist Revolution
late Dec. to Jan.	*St. Petersburg*	Russian Winter Festival

SLOVAKIA

January 1	*National*	New Year's and Independence Day
January 6	*National*	Epiphany, Three Kings Day
April	*National*	Good Friday and Easter Monday
May 1	*National*	May Day
May 8	*National*	Liberation Day
July 5	*National*	Cyril and Methodius Day
1st week in July	*Levoča*	pilgrimage
early July	*Liptovský Mukuláš*	Východna folklore festival
early July	*Banska Bystrica*	Pivinex beer and folklore fest
August	*Spišský hrad*	Medieval festival
August 15	*National*	Feast of the Assumption
August 29	*National*	Anniversary of Slovak National Uprising
September	*Bratislava*	Bratislava Jazz Days
September 1	*National*	Constitution Day
September 15	*National*	Our Lady of Seven Sorrows
November 1	*National*	All Saint's Day
December 24-26	*National*	Christmas

SLOVENIA

January 1-2	*National*	New Year's
February 8	*National*	Prešeren Day
April	*National*	Orthodox Easter Monday
April 27	*National*	Day of Uprising (WWII)
late April	*Ljubljana*	Slovene Days of Music
May 1-2	*National*	Labor Day
May 22	*National*	Whit Sunday
June 25	*National*	National Day
July and August	*Ljubljana*	International Summer Festival
August 15	*National*	Assumption Day
October 31	*National*	Reformation Day
November 1	*National*	All Saints' Day
December 25	*National*	Christmas
December 26	*National*	Independence Day

UKRAINE

January 1	*National.*	New Year's
January 7	*National*	Orthodox Christmas Day
March 8	*National*	International Women's Day
March/April	*National*	Orthodox Easter Monday
May	*Lviv*	National Virtuoso music fest
May 1-2	*National*	International Labor Day
May 9	*National*	Victory Day (1945)
late May	*Kiev*	Kiev Days
June 6	*Kiev*	Ivan Kupallo Day
July 16	*Kiev*	Ukrainian Sovereignty Days
August	*Yalta*	Crimean Stars folk celebration
August 24	*National*	Independence Day (1991)
1st week in Oct.	*Kiev*	International Kiev Film Festival
October 28	*National*	Liberation Day (1944)
November	*Lviv*	Kruzhelnitska opera days

Glossaries

THE CYRILLIC ALPHABET

Many non-Russian speakers who are traveling to Russia for the first time, find it bizarre that the chain restaurant, *PECTOPAH*, has formed such a monopoly in the Russian eatery division. Most chalk it up either to central planning or the "McDonald's effect", but there's a better reason for th "chain"'s success—*PECTOPAH* in Russian means "restaurant".

The source of all this misunderstanding is the Cyrillic alphabet—a script used in Bulgaria, Macedonia, Serbia, Russia, and many parts of the former Soviet Union. On mission in Great Moravia (part of modern-day Czech Republic and Slovakia), two 9th-century monks developed the alphabet's first form in order to translate the Bible into slavic. The monks, Cyril and Methodius, were Greek (which is why many Cyrillic letters look Greek) and Orthodox, so when Catholic powers gained control of the region that the monks were proselytizing, their disciples fled to the shores of Lake Ohrid (Macedonia) which, at the time, belonged to Bulgaria. There they founded the first slavic university, and the script spread swiftly to other slavic lands.

For many centuries, Cyrillic was a source of unity to the slavic nations who wrote in it, and its use (or non-use) still makes a political statement in some parts of the world. One of the major differences between the otherwise very similar Serb and Croat languages, is that Croatian is written in the Latin alphabet, while Serbian is written in Cyrillic. Furthermore, as Republics of the former Soviet Union are discovering their roots, they are learning their own scripts instead of Cyrillic, which for decades Moscow had made it the empire's the *scripta franca*.

The transliteration index given below is that of Russian cyrillic. Other languages include some additional letters and pronounce certain letters differently. Each country's language section outlines these disparities.

Cyrillic	English	Pronunciation	Cyrillic	English	Pronunciation
А, а	a	D*a*cha	Р, р	r	*R*ock 'n' *R*oll
Б, б	b	*B*ittersweet	С, с	s	*S*aucy
В, в	v	The *V*illage People	Т, т	t	*T*om
Г, г	g	*G*alina	У, у	u	Kit 'n' cab*oo*dle
Д, д	d	*D*an	Ф, ф	f	*F*at not *ph*at
Е, е	ye or e	*Ye*llow	Х, х	kh	C*h*utzpah (*hkh*)
Ё, ё	yo	*Ya*wn	Ц, ц	ts	Le*t's* Go
Ж, ж	zh	*Zh*irinovsky	Ч, ч	ch	*Ch*uck
З, з	z	*Z*any	Ш, ш	sh	*Ch*ampagne
И, и	i	Kathl*ee*n	Щ, щ	shch	Khru*shch*ev
Й, й	y	*Y*ak	Ъ, ъ	(hard)	(no sound)
К, к	k	*C*ure	Ы, ы	y	l*i*t
Л, л	l	*L*unch-lady	Ь, ь	(soft)	(no sound)
М, м	m	*M*egan	Э, э	eh	Al*e*xander
Н, н	n	*N*ancy	Ю, ю	yoo	*You*
О, о	o	L*a*w	Я, я	yah	*Ya*hoo!
П, п	p	*P*eter the Great			

ALBANIAN (SHQIP)

Phrases

English	Albanian	Pronunciation
Yes/no	Po/Jo	poh/yoh
Please	Ju lutem	yoo LOO-tehm
Thank you	Faleminderit	FAH-leh-meen-DEH-reet
Hello	Mirëdita	meer-DEE-tah
Good-bye	Mirupafshim	mee-roo-PAHFS-hihm
Good Morning	Mirëmëngjes	TEH-re ho-mih-KUHST
Good Evening	Mirëmbrëma	meer-mbreh-MAH
Excuse me	Më fal	muh-FAHL
When?	kur?	KOOR
Where is...?	Ku është..?	KOO uhsht
Help!	Ndihmë!	n-DEE-mih
How much does this cost?	Sa kushton/sa bën?	sah koosh-TOHN/sah bihn
Do you have...?	A keni ...?	ah KEH-nee
Do you speak English?	A flisni anglisht?	ah FLEES-nee ahn-GLEESHT
I don't understand	Unë nuk kuptoj.	oon nook KOOP-toy
Please write it down.	Të lutem m'a shkruaj.	ter LOO-tehm mah shkrooay
I'd like to order...	Dua...	doo-ah
Check, please.	Faturën ju lutem.	fah-TUR-en yuh LUH-tem
I'd like a room.	Dua një dhomë.	doo-ah njer DHOH-mer
Private shower	me dush?	meh doosh

Vocabulary

English	Albanian	Pronunc.	English	Albanian	Pronunc.
open	hapet	HAH-peht	meat	mish	mish
closed	mbyllet	MBU-leht	vegetables	perime	peh-ri-meh
arrival	mbritja	MBRIT-yah	water	ujë	ooy
departure	ndarjë	NDAR-yer	coffee	kafe	kah-FEH
station	stacion	STATS-ion	wine	verë	VEH-rer
roundtrip	vajtje-ardhje	VAY-te ARD-ye	juice	lëng	lerng
one-way	vajtje	VAY-tye	milk	qumësht	CHOO-mersht
bread	bukë	BOO-ker	beer	birrë	BEE-rrer
one	një	nyer	six	gjashtë	jy-asht
two	dy	duy	seven	shtatë	shtaht
three	tre	treh	eight	tetë	teht
four	katër	KAH-ter	nine	nëntë	nernt
five	pesë	PEH-ser	ten	dhjetë	dhyet
hundred	njëqind	ner-CHEEND	thousand	njëmijë	NER-meey

BULGARIAN (БЪЛГАРЦКИ)

Phrases

English	Bulgarian	Pronunciation
Yes/no	Да/Не	dah/neh
Please	Моля	MOE-lya
Thank you	Благодаря	blahg-oh-dahr-YAH
Hello	Добър ден	DOH-bur den
Good-bye	Добиждане	doh-VEEZH-dan-eh
Good Morning	Добро утро	doh-BRAW OO-troh
Good Night	Добър бечер	doh-BER VEH-cher
Excuse me	Извиниете	iz-ven-ete
When?	Кога?	ko-GA
Where is...?	Къде?	kuh-DEH
Help	Помош	Pomosht
How much does this cost?	Колко струва?	KOHL-ko STROO-va
Do you have...?	Имате ли...?	EE-mah-teh lee...?
Do you speak English?	Говорите ли английски?	govo-REE-TE li angl-EES-KEE
I don't understand	Не разбирам.	neh rahz-BEE-rahm
Please write it down.	Моля, напишете.	MO-lyah, nay-pee-SHESH-teh
I'd like to order...	Искам...	EES-kahm
Check, please.	Искам да платя.	EES-kahm dah plah-TYAH
I'd like a room.	Искам стая.	EES-kahm STAH-yah
Private shower?	с душ	s doosh

Vocabulary

English	Bulgarian	Pronunc.	English	Bulgarian	Pronunc.
open	отварят	ot-VAH-yaht	meat	месо	MEH-so
closed	затварят	zaht-VAH-yaht	vegetables	Зеленчуии	zelenchuyee
arrival	пристигащи	pristigashti	water	вода	vo-DAH
departure	заминаващи	zaminavashti	coffee	кафе	kah-FEH
station	гара	gara	wine	вино	VEE-no
roundtrip	отиване и връщане	o-TEE-van-e ee VRI-shtah-neh	juice	сок	sok
one-way	отиване	o-TEE-vahn-eh	milk	мляко	MLYAH-ko
grocery	бакалия	bah-kah-LEE-ya	beer	бира	BEE-rah
bread	хляб	khlyab	tea	чай	chahy
one	едно	ehd-NO	six	шест	shesht
two	две	dveh	seven	седем	SEH-dehm
three	три	tree	eight	осем	O-sehm
four	четири	CHEH-tee-ree	nine	девет	DEH-veht
five	пет	peht	ten	десет	DEH-seht
hundred	сто	stoh	thousand	хиляда	khee-LYA-da

CROATIAN

Phrases

English	Croatian	Pronunciation
Yes/no	Da/Ne	Da/Neh
Please/You're Welcome	Molim	MO-leem
Thank you	Hvala	FA-la
Hello/ Hi	Zdravo/Bok	ZDRAH-vo/bock
Good-bye	Dovidjenje	DO vidg-en-ya
Good Morning	Dobro jutro	DO-bro YOO-tro
Good Night	Laku noć	LA-koo noch
Excuse me	Molim vas	MO-leem vas
When?	Kada?	KA-da
Where is...?	Gdje je?	GDYE je
Help	U pomoć	OO pomoch
Leave me alone	Pusti me na miru.	PU-sti me na MI-ru
How much does this cost?	Koliko je košta?	KO-li-koh ye KOH-shta
Do you have...?	Imate li…?	EEM-a-teh lee
Do you speak English?	Govorite li engleski?	go-VOR-i-teh lee eng-LEH-ski
I don't understand.	Ne razumijem.	neh ra-ZOO-mi-yem
Please write it down?	Možete li napisati?	MOZH-e-te le na-PIH-sa-tee
I'd like to order...	Želio bih naručiti…	Jelim na-ROO-chiti
Check, please.	Račun, molim.	RACH-un, mo-leem
I'd like a room.	Želio bih imati sobo.	ZNEL-i-o bih EE-ma-tee so-bo

Vocabulary

English	Croatian	Pronunc.	English	Croatian	Pronunc.
open	otvoren	OT-vo-ren	meat	meso	MEH-so
closed	zatvoreno	zat-VOR-eno	vegetables	povrće	POH-ver-chay
arrival	dolazak	DOL-a-zak	water	voda	VO-dah
departure	odlazak	OD-la-zak	coffee	kava	KAH-vah
station	kolodvor	KOL-o-dvor	wine	vino	VEE-no
roundtrip	kružno putovanje	KRUH-zhno put-OH-van-ye	juice	sok	sok
one-way	jenosmjerna	JE-no SMI-er-na	milk	mlijeko	mil-YEH-koh
grocery	trgovina	terg-OH-vee-na	beer	pivo	PEE-voh
bread	kruh	krooh	tea	čaj	chi
one	jedan	ehd-NO	six	šest	shesht
two	dva	dveh	seven	sedam	SEH-dahm
three	tri	tree	eight	osam	O-sehm
four	četiri	CHEH-tee-ree	nine	devet	DEH-veht
five	pet	peht	ten	deset	DEH-seht
hundred	sto	sto	thousand	tisuća	TEE-soo-chah

CZECH (CESKY)

Phrases

English	Czech	Pronunciation

Basics

English	Czech	Pronunciation
Yes/no	ano/ne	ah-NOH/NEH
Please/You're Welcome	Prosím	PROH-seem
Thank you	Děkuji	DYEH-koo-yih
Hello	Dobrý den	doh-BREE den
Good-bye	Na shledanou	nah SLEH-dah-noh-oo
Good Morning	Dobré ráno	TEH-re ho-mih-KUHST
Good Night	Dobrou noc	doh-BROH NOTS
Excuse me	S dovolením	z-DOH-voh-leh-neem
Sorry	Promiňte	PROH-mihn-teh
My name is...	Jmenuji se ...	Y-mehn-oo-yee se
What is your name?	Jak se jmenujete?	yak se Y-mehn-oo-ye-teh
Help!	Pomoc!	pah-MOTS

Questions

English	Czech	Pronunciation
When?	Kdy?	k-DEE
Where is...?	Kde?	k-DEH
How do I get to...?	Jak se dostanu do...?	YAK seh dohs-TAH-noo doh
How much does this cost?	Kolik?	KOH-lihk
Do you have...?	Máte..?	MAH-teh

Understanding

English	Czech	Pronunciation
Do you speak English?	Mluvité anglicky?	MLOO-vit-eh ahng-GLIT-ski
I don't understand.	Nerozumím.	neh-rohz-OOM-eem
Please write it down?	Prosím napište.	PRO-seem nah-PEESH-tye
A little slower, please.	Prosím pomalu.	PRO-seem poh-MAH-lo

Dining out

English	Czech	Pronunciation
I'd like to order...	Chtel bych...	khtyel bikh
Check, please.	Prosím, ucet.	PRO-seem, OO-chet

Sleeping

English	Czech	Pronunciation
Have you a vacancy?	Máte volný pokoj?	MAH-te VOL-nee PO-koy
Private shower?	se sprchou?	SE-sprkh-oh

Vocabulary

English	Czech	Pron.	English	Czech	Pron.
Money			**Mail**		
bank	banka	BAN-ka	post office	pošta	POSH-ta
exchange	směnárna	smyeh-NAR-na	stamps	známka	ZNAHM-koo
Transportation					
arrival	prijezd	PREE-yezd	departure	odjezd	OD-yezd
one-way	jedním směrem	YED-nyeem SMNYE-rem	roundtrip	zpáteční	SPAH-tech-nyee
ticket	bych	bikh	reservation	místenka	mis-TYEN-kah
station	nádraží	nah-DRAH-zee	train	vlak	vlahk
bus	autobus	OUT-oh-boos	airport	letiště	LEH-tish-tyeh
Food					
bakery	pekařství	PE-karzh-stvee	grocery	potraviny	PO-tra-vee-nee
breakfast	snídaně	SNYEE-an-ye	lunch	oběd	OB-yed
dinner	večeře	VE-cher-zhe	menu	lístek	LIS-tek
water	voda	VO-dah	bread	chléb	khleb
pork	vepřové	VE-przhov-eh	vegetables	zelenina	ZE-le-nina
fish	ryba	REE-ba	beef	hovězí	HO-vye-zee
cheese	sýr	seer	chicken	kuře	KOO-rzheh
tea	čaj	tchai	coffee	káva	KAH-va
juice	sok	sok	milk	mléko	MLEH-koh
wine	víno	VEE-no	beer	pivo	PEE-voh
Days					
Monday	neděle	NEH-dyeh-leh	Sunday	pondělí	PON-dye-lee
Tuesday	úterý	OO-teh-ree	holiday	prazdniny	praz-DNI-ny
Wednesday	středa	stshreh-dah	today	dnes	dnes
Thursday	čtvrtek	CHTV'R-tek	tommorrow	zítra	ZEE-tra
Friday	pátek	PAH-tek	open	otveřen	OT-ve-zhen
Saturday	sobota	SO-boh-ta	closed	zatveřen	ZAT-ve-zhen
Numbers					
one	jedna	YEHD-nah	two	dvě	dv-YEH
three	tři	tr-ZHIH	four	čtyři	SHTEER-zhee
five	pět	p-YEHT	six	šest	SHEST
seven	sedm	SEH-duhm	eight	osm	OSS-uhm
nine	devět	dehv-YEHT	ten	deset	dess-SEHT
twenty	dvacet	dvah-TSEHT	thirty	třicet	tr-zhih-TSEHT
forty	čtyřicet	chteer-zhee-TSEHT	fifty	padesát	pah-des-AT
sixty	šedesát	sheh-des-AT	seventy	sedmdesát	SE-dum-des-AT
eighty	osmdesát	os-um-des-AT	ninety	devadesát	deh-vah-des-AT
hundred	sto	STOH	thousand	tisíc	TI-seets

ESTONIAN (ESTI KEEL)

Phrases

English	Estonian	Pronunciation
Yes/no	Jaa/Ei	yah/rhymes with "hay"
Please	Palun	PAH-luhn
Thank you	Aitäh	EYE-tah
Hello	Tere	TEH-re
Good-bye	Head aega	hehaht EYE-kah
Good Morning	Tere hommikust	TEH-re ho-mih-KUHST
Good Night	Head ööd	hehaht euht
Excuse me	Vabandage	vah-pan-TAGE-euh
When?	Millal?	mih-LAL?
Where is...?	Kus on...?	Kuhs on...
Help!	Appi!	APP-pi
How do I get to...?	Mina soovisin minna...?	MIH-nah soo-VIK-sin MIH-na
How much does this cost?	Kui palju?	Kwee PAL-you?
Do you have...?	Kas teil on ...?	kass tayl on ...?
Do you speak English?	Kas te räägite inglise keelt?	kass teh rah-KIHT-eh ihn-KLIS-eh keelt
I don't understand.	Ma ei saa aru.	mah ay saw AH-rooh
I'd like to order...	Ma sooviksin...	mah SOO-vik-sin
Check, please.	Arve, palun.	AR-vet, PAH-lu.
I'd like a room.	Ma sooviksin tuba.	mah SOO-vik-sin TUH-bah
Private shower?	duššiga?	DUSH-shi-ga

Vocabulary

English	Estonian	Pronunc.	English	Estonian	Pronunc.
arrival	saabub	SAA-boob	vegetables	kartul	KAR-tool
departure	väljub	VAL-yoob	water	vesi	VEH-si
roundtrip	edasi-tagasi piletit	E-dasi-TA-gasi PI-let-it	coffee	kohvi	KOH-fee
one-way	üheotsa piletit	EW-he-OHT-sah PI-le-tiht	wine	vein	VAY-een
station	jaam	yaam	juice	jamahl	ya-MAXL
grocery	toidupood	TOY-du-POOD	milk	piim	peem
bread	leib	LAY-eeb	beer	ôlu	elu
meat	liha	LI-ha	tea	tee	teee
one	üks	ewks	six	kuus	koose
two	kaks	kaks	seven	septiņi	SEHP-tih-nyih
three	kolm	kohlm	eight	astoņi	AHS-toh-nyih
four	neli	NEH-lih	nine	üheksa	EUW-eks-ah
five	viis	veese	ten	kümme	KEUW-meh
hundred	sada	SA-da	thousand	tuhat	TU-hat

HUNGARIAN (MAGYAR)

Phrases

English	Hungarian	Pronunciation
Basics		
Yes/no	Igen/nem	EE-gen/nem
Please	Kérem	KAY-rem
Thank you	Köszönöm	KUH-suh-num
Hello	Szervusz	SAIR-voose
Good-bye	Viszontlátásra	VI-sohn-tlah-tah-shraw
Good Morning	Jó reggelt	YOH reh-gehlt
Good Night	Jó éjszakát	YOH ay-sokat
Excuse me	Sajnálom	shoy-na-lawm
My name is...	...vagyok	vah-djawk
What is your name?	Hogy hívják	hawd HEE-vzaak
Questions		
When?	Mikor?	MI-kor
Where is...?	Hol van...?	hawl von
May I?	Kaphatok?	KO-phot-tok
How do you get to...?	Hogy jutok...?	hawd YOO-tawk
How much does this cost?	Mennyibe kerül?	MEN-hee-beh KEH-rewl
Do you have...?	Van...?	von
Understanding		
Do you speak English?	Beszél angolul?	BESS-el ON-goal-ool
I don't understand	Nem értem	nem AIR-tem
Please write it down?	Kérem, írja fel.	KAY-rem, EER-yuh fell.
A little slower, please.	Kérem, beszéljen lassan	KAY-rem, BESS-el-yen LUSH-shun
Dining out		
I'd like to order...	...kérek.	KAY-rek
Check, please.	A számlát, kérem.	uh SAHM-lot KAY-rem
Sleeping		
Have you a vacancy?	Van szabad szobájuk?	von SO-bbod
Private shower?	zuhanyzós?	ZOO-hon-yaw-yawsh

HUNGARIAN ■ 779

Vocabulary

English	Hungarian	Pronunc.	English	Hungarian	Pronunc.
Money			**Mail**		
bank	bank	bonk	post office	postán	pawsh-taan
exchange	valutabeválto	VO-loo-tob-be-vaal-taw	stamps	bélyeget	BAY-e-get
Transportation					
arrival	érkezés	ER-keh-zesh	departure	indulás	IN-dool-ahsh
one-way	csak oda	chok AW-do	roundtrip	oda-vissza	AW-do-VEES-so
ticket	jegyet	YED-et	train	vonat	VAW-not
station	pályaudvar	pa-yo-OOT-var	airport	repülőtér	rep-ewlu-TAIR
Food					
bakery	pékség	PAYK-shayg	grocery	élelmiszerbolt	A-lel-meser-balt
breakfast	reggeli	REG-gell-ee	lunch	ebéd	EB-ehd
dinner	vacsora	VOTCH-oh-rah	menu	a étlap	uh ATE-lop
water	víz	veez	bread	kenyér	KEN-yair
cheese	sajtot	SHOY-tawt	vegetables	zöldségek	ZULD-segek
fish	halételek	HA-le-te-lek	beef	marhahúst	MOR-ho-hosht
juice	gyümölcslé	DYEW-murl-chlay	pork	sertéshúst	SHER-taysh-shoost
coffee	kávé	KAA-vay	milk	tej	tay
wine	bor	bawr	beer	sör	shurr
Days					
Monday	hétf	ES-mah-spay-ev	Saturday	laupäev	LAU-pay-ev
Tuesday	teisipäev	TAY-si-pay-ev	Sunday	pühapäev	PEW-ha-pay-ev
Wednesday	kolmapäev	KOL-ma-pay-ev	holiday	ünnepnap	EWN-napnop
Thursday	neljapäev	NEL-yah-pay-ev	today	täna	TA-nuh
Friday	reede	REEE-de	tommorrow	homme	HOME-uh
Numbers					
one	üks	ewks	two	kaks	kaks
three	kolm	kohlm	four	neli	NEH-lih
five	viis	veese	six	kuus	koose
seven	seitse	SATE-seh	eight	kaheksa	KAH-eks-ah
nine	üheksa	EUW-eks-ah	ten	kümme	KEUW-meh
twenty	kakskümmend	kaks-KEUW-ment	thirty	kolmkümmend	kohlm-KEUW-ment
forty	nelikümmend	neh-lih-KEUW-ment	fifty	viiskümmend	veese-KEUW-ment
sixty	kuuskümmend	koose-KEUW-ment	seventy	seitsekümmend	sate-seh-KEUW-ment
eighty	kaheksaküm-mend	kah-eks-ah-KEUW-ment	ninety	üheksaküm-mend	euw-eks-ah-KEUW-ment
hundred	száz	saaz	thousand	ezer	E-zer

APPENDICES

LATVIAN (LATVISKA)

Phrases

English	Latvian	Pronunciation
Yes/no	Jā/Nē	yah/ney
Please	Lūdzu	LOOD-zuh
Thank you	Paldies	PAHL-dee-yes
Hello	Labdien	LAHB-dyen
Good-bye	Atā	ah-tah
Good Morning	Labrīt	LAHB-reet
Good Night	Labvakar	LAHB-vah-kahr
Excuse me	Atvainojiet	AHT-vye-no-yet
When?	Kad?	KAHD
Where is...?	Kur ir...?	kuhr ihr
Help!	Palīdzājiet!	PAH-leedz-ah-yee-eht
How do I get to...?	Es gribu iet uz...?	ehs GREE-boo EE-yet ooze
How much does this cost?	Cik maksā?	sikh MAHK-sah
Do you have...?	Vai jums ir...?	vai yoomss ir
Do you speak English?	Vai jūs runājiet angliski?	vye yoos RUH-nah-yee-eht AHN-glee-ski
I don't understand.	Es nesaprotu.	ehs NEH-sah-proh-too
I'd like to order...	Es vēlos...	ess VE-lwass
Check, please.	Rēķins, lūdzu.	RAY-kins, LOOD-zu
I'd like a *room*.	Vai jums ir brīvas *istabas*?	vai yums ir BREE-vas IS-tab-as

Vocabulary

English	Latvian	Pronunc.	English	Latvian	Pronunc.
arrival	pienāk	PEE-en-ak	vegetables	dārzeņi	DAR-ze-nyih
departure	atiet	AH-tee-it	water	ūdens	OH-dens
station	stacija	STAH-tsee-uh	coffee	kafija	KAH-fee-yah
roundtrip	turp un atpakaļ	toorp oon AT-pakal	wine	vīns	veens
one-way	vienā virzienā	VEEA-nah VIR-zee-an-ah	juice	sula	SOO-la
grocery	pārtikas veikals	PAHR-tih-kas VEY-kalss	milk	piens	PEE-ins
bread	maize	MAY-zuh	beer	alus	AH-lus
meat	gaļa	GA-la	tea	tēja	TAY-yah
one	viens	vee-YENZ	two	divi	DIH-vih
three	trīs	TREESE	four	četri	CHEH-trih
five	pieci	PYET-sih	six	seši	SEH-shih
seven	septiņi	SEHP-tih-nyih	eight	astoņi	AHS-toh-nyih
nine	deviņi	DEH-vih-nyih	ten	desmit	DEZ-miht

LITHUANIAN (LIETUVIŠKAI)

Phrases

English	Lithuanian	Pronunciation
Yes/no	Taip	TAYE-p
Please/You're Welcome	Prašau	prah-SHAU
Thank you	Ačiu	AH-chyoo
Hello	Laba diena	LAH-bah DEE-yen-ah
Good-bye	Viso gero	VEE-soh GEh-roh
Good Morning	Labas rytas	LAH-bass REE-tass
Good Night	Labanakt	lah-bah-NAKT
Excuse me	Atsiprašau	aHT-sih-prh-SHAU
When?	Kada?	KAH-da
Where is...?	Kur yra....?	Koor EE-rah..
Help!	Gelbėkite!	GYEL-behk-ite
How do I get to...?	Norėčiau nueiti h...?	nor-RAY-chee-yow new-ih-tih ee
How much does this cost?	Kiek kainuoja?	KEE-yek KYE-new-oh-yah
Do you have...?	Ar turite..?	ahr TU-ryite
Do you speak English?	Ar kalbate angliškai?	AHR AHN-gleesh-kye
I don't understand.	Aš nesuprantu	AHSH neh-soo-PRAHN-too
I'd like to order...	Norėčiau...	nor-RAY-cee-yow
Check, please.	Sąskaitą, prašau	SAHS-kai-ta, prah-SHAU
I'd like a room.	Ar turite laisvų kambarių	ahr TU-ryite lai-SVOO KAHM-bah-rio

Vocabulary

English	Lithuanian	Pronunc.	English	Lithuanian	Pronunc.
arrival	atvyksta	at-VEEK-stah	vegetables	daržovė	dar-ZHO-ve
departure	išvyksta	ish-VEEK-stah	water	vanduo	van-DAW
station	stotis	sto-TEES	coffee	kava	KAH-vah
roundtrip	grįžtamasio bilieto	GREEZH-tah-mah-sio BI-lieto	wine	vynas	VEE-nas
oneway	i vieną galą	ee VIE-naa GAH-laa	juice	sultys	SUL-tyees
grocery	bakalejos krautuvė	bah-kah-LYEH-yos KRA-tu-veh	milk	pienas	PEE-nas
bread	duona	DAW-na	beer	alus	AH-lus
one	vienas	vee-AYN-ahss	six	šeši	SHEH-shih
two	du	doo	seven	septyni	sehp-TEE-nih
three	trys	treese	eight	aštuoni	ahsh-too-OH-ni
four	keturi	keh-TUH-ree	nine	devyni	deh-VEE-nih
five	penki	PEHN-kee	ten	dešimt	deh-SHIMT
hundred	šimtas	SHIM-tahs	thousand	tukstantis	TOOK-stan-tis

MACEDONIAN

Phrases

English	Macedonian	Pronunciation
Yes/no	Да/Не	dah/neh
Please	Повелете	poh-VEL-et-ey
Thank you	Фала	FAH0lah
Hello	Добар ден	DAW-bahr-den
Good-bye	Довидување	DAW-ve-DOO-va-ne
Good Morning	Добро утро	DAW-broh OOT-raw
Good Night	Добро вечер	DAW-broh VYEH-cher
Excuse me	Дозволете	dohz-VOH-leh-teh
When?	Кога?	koh-GAG
Where is...?	Каде?	kah-DEY
Help!	Помош!	APP-pi
Leave me alone.	Оставете ме на мира.	Ohs-TA-ve-te mey na MEE-ra
How much does this cost?	Колку чини?	Kwee PAL-you?
Do you speak English?	Зборивате ли англиски?	ZVOR-oo-va-te li an-GLEE-ski
I don't understand.	Не разбирам.	neh rahz-BEE-rahm

Vocabulary

English	Macedon.	Pronunc.	English	Macedon.	Pronunc.
arrival	пристигнуване	pristignuvanye	vegetables	зеленчуии	zelenchuyee
departure	тругване	trugvanye	water	вода	vo-DAH
station	станица	stanitsa	coffee	кафе	kah-FEH
roundtrip	отиване и връшане	o-TEE-van-e ee VRI-shta-ne	wine	вино	VEE-no
one-way	отиване	o-TEE-vahn-eh	juice	сок	sok
grocery	бакалия	bah-kah-LEE-ya	milk	мляко	MLYAH-ko
bread	хляб	khlyab	beer	бира	BEE-rah
meat	месо	MEH-so	tea	чай	chahy
one	едно	ehd-NO	six	шест	shesht
two	две	dveh	seven	седем	DEH-veht
three	три	tree	eight	осем	O-sehm
four	четири	CHEH-tee-ree	nine	девет	DEH-veht
five	пет	peht	ten	десет	DEH-seht
hundred	сто	stoh	thousand	илјада	il-YAH-da

POLISH (POLSKI)

Phrases

English	Polish	Pronunciation
Basics		
Yes/no	tak/nie	tak/nyeh
Please/You're Welcome	Proszę	PROH-sheh
Thank you	Dziękuję	jeng-KOO-yeh
Hello	Cześć	tcheshch
Good-bye	Do widzenia	doh vee-DZEN-ya
Good Morning	Dzień dobry	jane DOH-brih
Good Night	Dobranoc	doh-BRAH-notz
Excuse me/Sorry	Przepraszam	psheh-PRAH-sham
My name is...	Nazywam się	nah-ZIH-vam sheh
What is your name?	Jak się pan(i) nazywa?	yak syeh PAN(ee) nah-ZI-va
Help!	Na pomoc!	nah POH-motz
Questions		
When?	Kiedy?	KYEH-dih
Where is...?	Gdzie jest?	g-jeh yehst
How do I get to...?	Którędy do...?	ktoo-REN-dih doh
How much does this cost?	Ile to kosztuje?	EE-leh toh kosh-TOO-yeh
Do you have...?	Czy są...?	chi sawng
Understanding		
Do you speak English?	Czy Pan(i) mówi po angielsku?	tcheh PAH(-nee) movie poh zn-GHEL-skoo
I don't understand.	Nie rozumiem.	nyeh roh-ZOO-myem
Please write it down.	Proszę napisać.	PROH-sheh nah-PEE-sahtch
A little slower, please.	Proszę mówić wolniej.	PROH-sheh MOO-veech VOHL-nyah
Dining out		
I'd like to order...	Poproszę...	po-PROH-sheh
Check, please.	Proszę rachunek.	PROH-sheh rah-KHOON-ehk
Sleeping		
Have you a vacancy?	Czy są jakieś wolne pokoje?	chi sawng YAK-yehs VOL-neh po-KO-yeh
Private shower?	z prysznicem	spri-SHNEET-sehm

POLISH

Vocabulary

English	Polish	Pronunc.	English	Polish	Pronunc.
Money			**Mail**		
bank	bank	bahnk	post office	pocztą	PO-schtawng
exchange	wymiany walut	vi-MYAH-ni VAH-loot	stamps	znaczek	ZNAH-chehk
Moving					
arrival	przyjazdy	pree-JAZ-dih	departure	odjazdy	od-JAZ-dih
ticket	bilet	BEE-leht	reservation	miejscówka	myey-SHOVKA
station	dworzec PKP	DVOR-zec PKP	train	pociąg	POH-chohnk
bus	autobus	OUT-oh-boos	airport	letiště	LEH-tish-tyeh
Food					
bakery	piekarnia	pye-KAHR-nya	grocery	spożywczy	spo-ZHI-vchi
breakfast	śnidanie	shnya-DAN-iye	lunch	obiad	OH-byat
dinner	kolacja	koh-LAH-tsyah	menu	menu	MEN-yoo
salt	sółł	soow	bread	chleb	khlyep
water	wodę	VOH-dah	vegetables	jarzyna	yar-ZHI-ny
vegetarian	wegetariań	ve-ge-tar-YAN	beef	wołowinę	vo-wo-VEE-neh
pork	wieprzowinę	vye-psho-VE-ne	chicken	roorczę	ROOR-cheh
fish	ryba	RI-bah	cheese	ser	sehr
coffee	kawa	KAH-vah	milk	mlekie	mlehk-yeh
wine	wina	VEE-nah	beer	piwo	PEE-voh
juice	sok	sok	tea	herbata	heh-RBAH-tah
Days of Week					
Monday	poniedziałek	pon-yeh-DZHEH-lah	Saturday	sobota	so-BO-tah
Tuesday	wtorek	FTO-rehk	Sunday	niedziela	nyeh-DZHEH-la
Wednesday	środa	SRO-dah	today	dzisiaj	DZHEE-sahy
Thursday	czwartek	CHFAHR-tek	tommorrow	jutro	YOO-tro
Friday	piątek	PYON-tehk	holiday	święto	sh-VION-to
Numbers					
one	jeden	YEH-den	two	dwa	dvah
three	trzy	tshih	four	cztery	cht-EHR-ih
five	pięć	pyench	six	sześć	sheshch
seven	siedem	SHEH-dem	eight	osiem	OH-shem
nine	dziewięć	JYEH-vyench	ten	dziesięć	JYEH-shench
twenty	dwadzieścia	dva-JYESH-cha	thirty	trzydzieści	tshi-JYESH-chi
forty	czterdzieści	chtehr-JYESH-chih	fifty	pięćdziesiąt	pyehn-JYESH-shont
sixty	sześćdziesiąt	shesh-JYESH-shont	seventy	siedem dziesiąt	sheh-dem-JYESH-shont
eighty	osiem dziesiąt	oh-shem-JYESH-shont	ninety	dziewięć dziesiąt	jyeh-vyen-JYESH-shont
hundred	sto	stoh	thousand	tysiąc	TI-sonts

ROMANIAN (ROMAN)

Phrases

English	Romanian	Pronunciation
Basics		
Yes/no	Da/Nu	dah/noo
Please/You're Welcome	Vă rog	vuh rohg
Thank you	Mulţumesc	mool-tsoo-MESK
Hello	Bună ziua	BOO-nuh zee wah
Good-bye	La revedere	lah reh-veh-DEH-reh
Good Morning	Bună dimineaţa	BOO-nuh dee-mee-tsa
Good Night	Noapte bună	NWAP-teh BOO-ner
Excuse me	Scuzaţi-mă	skoo-ZAH-tz muh
Sorry	Iertaţi-mă	ier-TAH-tzee muh
My name is...	Mă cheamă...	muh-KYAH-muh
What is your name?	Cum vă numiţi?	koom ver noo-MEETS
Help!	Ajutor!	AH-zhoot-or
Questions		
When?	Cînd?	kihnd
Where is...?	Unde?	OON-deh
How do I get to...?	Cum se ajunge la...?	koom seh-ZHOON-jeh-la
How much does this cost?	Cît costă?	kiht KOH-stuh
Do you have...?	Aveţi...?	a-VETS
Understanding		
Do you speak English?	Vorbiţi englezeş?	vor-BEE-tz ehng-leh-ZESH-te
I don't understand	Nu înţeleg.	noo-ihn-TZEH-lehg
Please write it down?	Vă rog scieţi aceasta.	ver rog SCREE-ets a-CHAS-ta
A little slower, please.	Vorbiţi rar.	VORE-bih-tsee rahr
Dining out		
I'd like to order...	Aş vrea nişte...	ash vreh-A NEESH-teh
Check, please.	Plata, vă rog.	PLAH-tah, VUH rahg
Sleeping		
Have you a vacancy?	Aveţi camere libere?	a-VETS CA-mer-eh LEE-ber-e
Private shower?	cu duş?	koo doosh

Vocabulary

English	Romanian	Pronunc.	English	Romanian	Pronunc.
Money			**Mail**		
bank	bancă	BAN-ser	post office	poșta	POH-shta
exchange	un birou de schimb	oon bee-RO deh skeemb	stamps	timbru	TEEM-broo
Transportation					
arrival	sosiri	SO-sir-ih	departure	plecări	PLAY-cuh-rih
one-way	dus	doos	roundtrip	dus-intors	doos-in-TORS
ticket	bilet	bee-LET	reservation	rezervarea	re-zer-VAR-eh-a
station	gara	GAH-ruh	train	trenul	TRAY-null
bus	autobuz	AHU-toh-bus	airport	aeroportul	air-oh-POR-tull
Food					
bakery	o brutărie	o bru-ter-REE-e	grocery	o băcănie	o ber-ker-NEE-e
breakfast	micul dejun	MIK-ul DAY-zhun	dinner	Masa de seară	MAH-sah day say-AH-ruh
lunch	dejun	DAY-zhun	menu	lista	LIS-tah
salt	sare	SAH-ray	bread	pîine	pih-YUNE-nay
water	Apă	AH-puh	vegetables	legume	LEH-goom
pork	carne de porc	CAR-neh deh pork	beef	carne de vacă	CAR-neh deh VA-cer
coffee	cafea	CAH-fay-ah	milk	lapte	LAHP-tay
wine	vin	VAY-een	beer	bere	BE-reh
juice	suc	sooc	tea	ceai	chay
Days					
Monday	luni	LUH-nih	Sunday	duminică	duh-MIH-ni-ku
Tuesday	marți	MAHR-tsih	today	azi	az
Wednesday	miercuri	MEER-kurih	tommorrow	mîine	MIY-neh
Thursday	joi	zhoy	open	deschis	DESS-kiss
Friday	vineri	VEE-ner	closed	închis	YUNE-kiss
Saturday	sîmbătă	SUIME-buh-tuh			
Numbers					
one	unu	OO-noo	two	doi	DOY
three	trei	TRAY	four	patru	PAH-tru
five	cinci	CHEEN-ch	six	șase	SHAH-seh
seven	șapte	SHAHP-teh	eight	opt	ohpt
nine	nouă	noah	ten	zece	ZEH-che
twenty	douăzecuci	doh-wah-ZECH	thirty	treizeci	tray-ZECH
forty	ptruzeci	pah-truh-ZECH	fifty	cincizeci	chin-ZECH
sixty	șaizeci	shay-ZECH	seventy	șaptezeci	shap-teh-ZECH
eighty	optzeci	ohpt-ZECH	ninety	nouăzeci	noah-ZECH
hundred	o sută	uh SOO-tuh	thousand	o mie	uh MIH-ay

RUSSIAN (РУССКИЙ)

Phrases

English	Russian	Pronunciation
Basics		
Yes/no	Да/Нет	Dah/N-yet
Please/You're Welcome	Пожалуйста	pa-ZHOW-a-sta
Thank you	Спасибо	spa-SEE-bah
Hello	Добрый день	DOH-breh DEN
Good-bye	До свидания	dus-vee-DAHN-ya
Good Morning	Доброе утра	DOH-breh OO-tra
Excuse me	Извините	eez-vee-NEET-yeh
My name is...	Меня зовут...	men-YA-za-VOOT...
What is your name?	Как вас зовут?	kak vac zah-VOOT
Help!	Помогите!	pah-mah-ZHEE-te
Questions		
When?	Когда?	kahg-DAH
Where is...?	Где?	g-dyeh
How much does this cost?	Сколько стоит?	SKOHL-ka STOW-eet
Do you have...?	У вас есть...?	oo vas YEST
Understanding		
Do you speak English?	Вы говорите по-английски?	vee go-vo-REE-te po an-GLEE-skee
I don't understand	Я не понимаю.	ya nee pa-nee-MAH-yoo
Please write it down?	Напишите, пожалуйста?	nah-pee-SHIT-yeh, pah-ZHAHL-stah
A little slower, please.	Медленее, пожалуйста.	MYED-lee-nyay-eh
Dining out		
I'd like to order...	Я хотел(а) бы...	ya khah-TYEL(ah) bi
Check, please.	Чч ёт, пожалуйста.	shchyot, pah-ZHAHL-stah
Sleeping		
Have you a vacancy?	У вас есть свободный номер?	oo vahss yehst svah-BOD-niy NO-mmeer
Private shower?	с душом?	s dushom

Vocabulary

English	Russian	Pronunc.	English	Russian	Pronunc.
Money			**Mail**		
bank	банка	BANK-a	post office	почта	POSH-tah
exchange	обмен валут	ob-MEN va-lut	stamps	марка	MAHR-doo
Transportation					
arrival	приезд	pree-JEZD	departure	отъезд	ot-JEZD
one-way	бодин конец	v ah-DEEN kah-NYEHTS	roundtrip	туда и обратно	too-DAH ee ah0BRAHT-nah
ticket	билет	beel-YET	reservation	заповедник	za-po-VED-nik
station	вокзал	vok-ZAL	train	поезд	POY-ezd
bus	автобус	av-toh-BOOS	airport	аэропорт	ayro-PORT
Food					
bakery	булочная	BOO-lahch-nah-yah	grocery	продукты	prah-DOOK-ti
breakfast	завтрак	zav-TRAK	lunch	обед	ob-YED
dinner	ужин	OO-zhin	menu	меню	menu
water	вода	vod-DAH	bread	хлеб	khlyeb
vegetarian	вегетариан	vegh-e-tah-rian	vegetables	обощи	ob-ah-shchee
pork	свиниу	svee-NEE-noo	beef	говядину	ga-VA-dee-noo
fish	рыба	REE-ba	chicken	курицу	KOO-ree-tsoo
coffee	кофе	KO-fee	cheese	шыру	SEE-roo
juice	сок	sok	milk	молоко	mah-lah-KOH
wine	вино	vee-NO	beer	пиво	PEE-vah
Days					
Monday	понедельник	pa-nee-DEH-lek	Sunday	воскреценье	va-skree-SE-ne
Tuesday	вторник	FTOR-neek	holiday	день отдыха	dyen OT-di-kha
Wednesday	среда	sree-DAH	today	севодня	se-VOHD-nya
Thursday	четверг	cheet-VERK	tommorrow	завтра	ZAHV-trah
Friday	пятница	PAHT-neet-sah	closed	закрыте	za-KRI-te
Saturday	суббота	soo-BOT-tah	open	открыте	ot-KRI-te
Numbers					
one	один	ah-DEEN	two	два	d-VAH
three	три	tree	four	четыре	che-TIH-rih
five	пять	p-YAHT	six	шесть	SHAY-st
seven	семь	s-YIM	eight	восемь	VOH-sem
nine	девять	DEV-yat	ten	десять	DES-yat
twenty	двадцать	d-VAHD-tset	thirty	тридцать	TREE-dset
forty	сорок	SOR-ok	fifty	пятьдесят	pya-de-SAHT
sixty	шестьдесят	shays-de-SAHT	seventy	семьдесят	SIM-de-set
eighty	восемьдесят	VO-sim-de-set	ninety	девяносто	de-vya-NO-sta
hundred	сто	stoh	thousand	тысяча	TIS-see-cha

SLOVENIAN ■ 789

SLOVENIAN (SLOVENSKO)

Phrases

English	Slovenian	Pronunciation
Yes/no	Ja/Ne	yah/neh
Please	Prosim	PROH-seem
Thank you	Hvala	HVAA-lah
Hello	Idravo	ee-drah-voh
Good-bye	Na svidenje	nah SVEE-den-yeh
Excuse me	Oprostite	oh-proh-stee-teh
Where is...?	Kje?	k-yeh
Help!	Na pomoč!	nah poh-MOHCH
How much does this cost?	Koliko to stane?	koh-lee-koh toh stah-neh
Do you have...?	Ali imate...?	AA-li i-MAA-te
Do you speak English?	Govorite angleško?	go-vo-REE-teh ang-LEH-shko
I don't understand	Ne razumem	neh rah-ZOO-mehm
open	odprto	od-prto
closed	zaprto	za-prto
one	ena	ena
two	dva	dva
three	tri	tree

UKRAINIAN

Phrases

English	Ukrainian	Pronunciation
Yes/no	Так/Ні	tak/nee
Please	Прошу	PRO-shoo
Thank you	Дякую	DYA-kou-yoo
Hello	Добрий день	doh-bree-DEN
Good-bye	До побачення	doh poh-BAH-chen-nya
Excuse me	Вибачте	VIH-bach-te
Where is...?	Де?	deh?
Help!	Поможіт!	pah-mah-ZHEET
How much does this cost?	Скільки коштує?	SKEL-kih kahsh-TOO-ye
Do you have...?	чи є у вас...?	chih yeh oo vahs...
Do you speak English?	Ви говорите по-англиськи?	Vih-ho-VOR-ihte poh-anh-lih-skih
I don't understand	Я не позумію	Ya ne roh-zoo-meee-yu
open	отчиненно	ot-chi-ne-no
closed	зачиненно	zah-chi-ne-no
one	одін	ah-DEEN
two	два	dvah
three	три	tREE

APPENDICES

Index

Numerics
2 Mai, ROM 516
5 Flavored Chicken 437

A
abortion 23
accommodations 45–48
  campgrounds 48
  convents 48
  dormitories 48
  hostels 46
  hotels 48
  monasteries 48
  private rooms 45
adaptors 33
Advance Purchase Excursion Fare 36
Afghanistan War 528, 626
Agapia, ROM 513
Aggtelek, HUN 280
Aglona, LAT 332
ailments
  cholera 22
  diarrhea 21
  diphtheria 23
  food-induced 21
  giardia 23
  heatstroke 20
  hepatitis A 22
  hepatitis B 23
  HIV and AIDS 23
  hypothermia 20
  insect-induced 21
  Lyme disease 21
  parasitic 22
  plague 642
  rabies 23
  sexually transmitted 23
  water-induced 21
Airhitch 38
Air-Tech, Ltd. 38
Aladzha Manastir, BUL 142
ALBANIA 55–72
  Butrint 70
  Durrës 67
  Gjirokastër 68
  Krujë 66
  Pogradec 71
  Sarandë 69
  Tirana 62–66
alcohol
  Albena champagne 140
  Becherovka 199, 200
  Egri Bikavér 278
  is poison 104
  krupnik 388
  kvas 76, 685
  loza 90
  Melnik wine 119
  Miód 388
  pálinka 253
  pleterska hruška 667
  raki 58, 65, 67
  rakija 90
  rakiya 105, 366
  slijivoca 90
  Unicum 253
  żganje 667
  żubrówka 388
Alupka, UKR 715
American Council of Teachers of Russian 521
American Express
  Bucharest, ROM 482
  Budapest, HUN 257
  cash advance 17
  credit cards 17
  Dubrovnik, CRO 165
  essentials 16
  holding mail 50
  insurance 25
  Kraków, POL 440
  Ljubljana, SLN 670
  Moscow, RUS 531
  Prague, CZE 175
  Rīga, LAT 320
  Sofia, BUL 109
  Split, CRO 162
  Tallinn, EST 228
  Tartu, EST 235
  Tirana, ALB 62
  traveler's checks 16
  traveler's services 17
  Varna, BUL 138
  Warsaw, POL 393
  Zagreb, CRO 154
anarchy 681
Anna Peartree 124
Anonymous 272
APEX 36
Apuseni Mts., ROM 492
Āraiši, LAT 336
Arbanasi, BUL 131
Arbore, ROM 511
Athopol, BUL 146
ATMs 17
attar 124
Augustów, POL 425
Auschwitz-Birkenau, POL 447

B
Bach, Johann Sebastian 199
Bachkovo Monastery, BUL 123
backpacks 32
Bahnhof Zoo, GER 741
Bakhchisarai, UKR 710
Balatonfüred, HUN 312
Balchik, BUL 141
Banská Bystrica, SLK 640
Banská Štiavnica, SLK 642
Bansko, BUL 117–119
Bardejov, SLK 662
Bardejovské Kúpele, SLK 664
Barons, Krišjānis 319, 334
Baryshnikov, Mikhail 326
baths
  Budapest 270, 274
  Moscow 552
Battle of Koydanovo, BEL 77
Batu Khan 688, 709
Becherovka 199, 200
beer
  -barrel bungalows 183
  Budvar, CZE 208, 209
  Budweiser, CZE 208
  controversy 220
  Eggenberg, CZE 211
  festival, LAT 336
  free 182
  is poison 300
  Kalnapilis, LIT 362
  museum 207
  Pilsner Urquell, CZE 199
  Pivinex 642
  Porteris, LAT 317
  Purkmistr, CZE 206
  Řezané, CZE 206
  Saku, EST 224
  Saris, SLK 662
  Spiš, POL 468
  Tatran, SLK 646
  Utenos, LIT 361
  żywiec, POL 388
BELARUS 73–86
  Brest 84–86
  Hrodna 83
  Minsk 78–82
Beliş Făntânele, ROM 492
Belushi, James 72
Ben and Jerry's 622
Beneš, Edvard 171
Berlin, Germany 737
bespectacled moles 741
Bessarabia 379
Białowieski Park Narodowy, POL 429
Białystok, POL 427–429
bicycles 44
Bielsko-Biała, POL 463–465
Bieszczady Park Narodowy, POL 459
BIJ (Billets Internationales de Jeunesse) 43
Birkenau, POL 447
birth control 23
bisexual travelers 30
  Also see gay information.
Biskupin, POL 435
Bitola, MAC 375
Black Madonna of Hájek 207
Black Sea Coast, ROM 514–517
Bled, SLN 674
boats 44
Bogamils 91
Bogdan the One-Eyed 379
Bolesław Chrobry of Poland 389, 433, 434, 445
Bolesław Śmiały of Poland 449

boots 33
border crossings
  POL to GER 409
Boris Godunov 527
BOSNIA 87–100
  Sarajevo 93–100
Bovec, SLN 678
Bran, ROM 504
Braşov, ROM 502
Bratislava, SLK 635–640
Brest, BEL 84–86
breweries
  Budvar, CZE 209
  HBH Beer House, HUN 288
  Pegas, CZE 216
  Perla, SLK 642
  Plzeň, CZE 207
  Shoumen, BUL 135
Brno, CZE 212–216
Brothers of the Sword 237, 318, 324, 334, 356
Bruegel 194
Brzezinka, POL 447
Bucegi Mts., ROM 504
Bucharest, ROM 480–488
Bucovina Monasteries, ROM 511
  Agapia 513
  Arbore 511
  Dragomirna 511
  Humor 511
  Moldoviţa 512
  Neamţ 513
  Putna 513
  Secu 513
  Suceviţa 512
  Vărateç 513
  Voroneţ 511
Buda Castle, HUN 272
Budapest, HUN 256–275
Budenz, József 298
budget travel agencies 35
Bug River, BEL 84
Bugac, HUN 291
Bühren, Baron Ernst Johann von 329
Bulduri, LAT 327
Bulgakov, Mikhail 529, 536, 545, 547
  his house, UKR 703
BULGARIA 101–146
  Aladzha Manastir 142
  Arbanasi 131

Athopol 146
Bachkovo Monastery 123
Balchik 141
Bansko 117–119
Burgas 142–144
Dobrinishte 119
Etura 126
Golden Sands 141
Kazanluk 125
Koprivshtitsa 123
Madara 136
Melnik 119
Nesebur 144
Pleven 127
Pliska 135
Plovdiv 120–123
Primorsko 145
Rila Monastery 117
Ruse 132–134
Shipka 127
Shoumen 134
Sofia 108–116
Sozopol 145
Trynavna 131
Valley of Roses 123–127
Varna 136–141
Veliki Preslav 135
Veliko Turnovo 129–131
Burgas, BUL 142–144
buses 43
Buşteni, ROM 505
Butrint, ALB 70

C

callback phone services 52
calling cards 52
camping 48
  equipment 48
  safety 49
Canute, King of Denmark 225
Căpriana, MOL 383
Carol I, King of Romania 478, 502, 505, 508, 515
Carol II, King of Romania 493, 508
Carpathian Mts.
  Poland 458
  Romania 473, 489, 498, 502, 506, 509
cars 43
cash cards 17
Catherine the Great 330, 527, 540, 583, 601, 603, 604, 610, 615, 616, 707, 708, 716
caves

Baradla, HUN 280
Cheile Peşterii, ROM 505
Dobšinská ice cave, SLK 657
Fertőrákos Quarry, HUN 307
Istálóskő cave, HUN 282
Scărişoara, ROM 492
Ceauşescu, Nicolae 478
cemeteries
  Jolly Cemetery, ROM 498
  Lichakivsky, UKR 732
  New Jewish, CZE 193
  Novodevichy Monastir, RUS 545
  Old Jewish, CZE 189
  Remuh, POL 446
  symbolický cintorín, SLK 652
  Tikhuin, RUS 607
  Vyšehrad Cemetery, CZE 193
Cēsis, LAT 335
České Budějovice, CZE 208
Český Krumlov, CZE 210
champagne, ringtoss for, LIT 357
Charles IV, King of Bohemia and Holy Roman Emperor 170, 171, 173, 187, 192, 194, 199, 206
Charles Robert of Hungary 501
Charousková, Marie 190
charter flights 37
Cheb, CZE 203
Chekhov, Anton 529, 545, 588, 714
  museum 715
Chernivtsi, UKR 724–726
Chernobyl, UKR 75, 77, 78, 704
Chişinău (Kishinev), MOL 380–383
Chochołowska, Dolina 462
Chopin, Fryderyk 400, 401, 405
Churchill, Winston 715

CIA World Factbook 5
Cindrel Mts., ROM 500
Citicorp 17
City phone codes are listed in Practical Information of large cities and at the end of small ones.
Čiurlionio, M.K. 353, 355
clothing 33
Cluj-Napoca, ROM 489–492
collect calls 52
Collegium Maius 444
consolidators, ticket 37
Constanţa, ROM 514
Constantine 272
consulates 5–8
Costineşti, ROM 517
converters 33
Copernicus 389, 418, 436, 438
Corfu 69
Cossacks 77, 586, 587, 607, 689, 707
Council 1, 25, 29, 35
Council Charter 35
Council on Int'l Educational Exchange 1
Country phone codes are listed in the Appendices.
courier flights 38
cow patties 655
credit cards 17
Crişan, ROM 518
CROATIA 147–166
  Dubrovnik 165
  Hvar 164
  Poreč 157
  Pula 159
  Rab 161
  Rovinj 158
  Split 162–164
  Zagreb 152–157
Cromwell, Oliver 415
Cucuteni, ROM 509
Curonian Spit
  Lithuania 361
  Russia 627
currency exchange 16
Curtea De Argeş, ROM 501
customs restrictions 11–13
  Australia 13
  Canada 12

Ireland 13
New Zealand 13
South Africa 13
U.K. 12
U.S. 12
Czartoryski family 444
CZECH REPUBLIC 167-220
  Brno 212-216
  České Budějovice 208
  Český Krumlov 210
  Cheb 203
  Františkovy Lázně 204
  Hluboká 210
  Karlovy Vary 199
  Karlštejn 199
  Konopiště 199
  Kutná Hora 198
  Mariánské Lázně 201
  Moravský Kras 217
  Olomouc 218-220
  Plzeň 204-208
  Prague 173-197
  Telč 217
  Terezín 198
Czerwone Wierchy 462
Częstochowa, POL 448-450

D

dainas 319
Danube Bend, HUN 275-278
Danube Delta, ROM 518
Dārziņi, LAT 327
Das Wampyr 488
Daugava River, LAT 320
Daugavpils, LAT 330-332
Debrecen, HUN 284
Defenestrations of Prague
  first 171
  second 171, 192
Devín Castle, SLK 640
Dientzenhopfer, Kilian Ignaz and Kristof 188, 190, 193
disabled travelers 31
diseases, see ailments
Dnipropetrovsk, UKR 707
Dobrinishte, BUL 119

Dobrogea, ROM 517
documents 5-15
  entrance requirements 11
  hostel cards 47
  IDs 13
  Int'l Driver's Permit 15
  invitations 11
Don River, RUS 572
dormitories 48
Dostoyevsky, Fyodor 529, 606, 607, 611
  Museum, Moscow 548
Dracula 488
Dracuuuula 493, 501, 504
Dragomirna, ROM 511
driver's permits 15
driving
  insurance 15
  permits 15
drugs
  hash 174
  love 141
  opium 536
  see alcohol, beer
Druskininkai, LIT 355
Dubček, Alexander 633, 172
Dubrovnik, CRO 165
Dubulti, LAT 327
Duccio di Buoninsegna 272
Dumbrava, ROM 500
Dunajec Gorge, POL 463
Dürer, Albrecht 194
Durrës, ALB 67
Dvořák, Antonin 193, 201
Dzerzhinski, Felix 78
Dzwon Zygmunta, POL 445

E

Eforie Nord, ROM 517
Eforie Sud, ROM 517
Eger, HUN 278
El Greco 272
electricity 33
Elizabeth, Queen of Hungary 270
Elizabeth, Queen of Romania 502
e-mail 53
Emajõgi River, EST 235
embassies 5-8
English, teaching 27

ESSENTIALS 1-54
  Accommodations 45-48
  Alternatives to Tourism 25-29
  Budget Travel Agencies 35
  Documents & Formalities 5-15
  Embassies and Consulates 5-8
  Gettin' It On-Line 4
  Getting There 34-39
  Health 19-25
  Insurance 25
  Keeping in Touch 50-53
  Money 15-18
  National Tourist Offices 1
  Packing 32
  Safety and Security 18
  Specific Concerns 29-32
  Travel in the Region 39-45
  Travel Organizations 1
  Useful Publications 4
ESTONIA 221-248
  Haapsalu 240
  Hiiumaa 245-247
  Kassari 248
  Kuressaare 242
  Lahemaa National Park 233
  Muhu 245
  Pärnu 238
  Saaremaa 244
  Tallinn 227-233
  Tartu 235-237
  Viljandi 237
Esztergom, HUN 277
Eszterházy Palace, HUN 308
Eternal Bloodsucker 488
Etura, BUL 126
exchanging currency 16
Express, HUN 250

F

Făgăraş Mountains, ROM 501
failed communist edifices
  House of Soviets, RUS 626
  Moscow swimming pool,

RUS 546
fare brokers 38
faxing 53
Federation of Int'l Youth Travel Organizations (FIYTO) 4
Feodosia, UKR 711
Ferdinand, King of Romania 502
Fertőd, HUN 308
Festetics Palace, HUN 311
festivals
  Baltoscandal, EST 240
  Country Picnic Festival, POL 425
  military band, HUN 286
  Prague Spring Festival, CZE 195
festivals, film
  Karlovy Vary, CZE 201
  Love is Folly, BUL 141
  Polish Film Festival, POL 417
  Sarajevo Film Festival, BOS 100
  World Festival of Animated Films, CRO 157
festivals, jazz
  FiESTa, EST 240
  Jantar Jazz Festival, POL 417
  Jazz Days, Debrecen, HUN 286
  Jazz na Kresach, POL 457
  Jazz nad Odrą, POL 468
  Sibiu, ROM 500
  Varna International Jazz Festival, BUL 141
festivals, music
  Cerbul de Aur, ROM 503
  Gdansk, POL 416
  Rock Summer, EST 233
  Slovene Days of Music 674
Festivalul Junilor, ROM 503
first-aid kit 19
FIYTO 4
flights 36-39
  Airhitch 38
  Air-Tech, Ltd. 38

charter 37
commercial 36
consolidators 37
courier companies 38
discount clubs 38
Eastern European 37
fare brokers 38
stand-by 38
Flughafen Tegel, GER 740
flying, see flights
folly 141
Font of Wisdom, LAT 335
footware 33
foreign version of American chain
 Hambo, ALB 66
 Hard Rák Café, HUN 295
 Hard Rock Caffé, CRO 156
 Kentucky Beirut Chicken, UKR 699
 Magic, MOL 383
Františkovy Lázně, CZE 204
freaks of nature
 Baikushevata Mura, BUL 119
 cave town of Chufut-Kale, UKR 710
 Chateau Bad Night, POL 461
 Contract Stones, EST 247
 Dobšinská ice cave, SLK 657
 Drifting Dunes of Parnidis, LIT 362
 Gauja National Park, LAT 334
 Hill of Crosses, LIT 356
 Iški Vintgar, CRO 676
 Käsma boulders, EST 234
 Lake Baikal, RUS 571
 Leaning Tower of Poland, POL 438
 Peștera Urșilor, ROM 497
 Scărișoara ice caves, ROM 492
 Slap Boka, SLN 678
 Sprudel Fountain, CZE 201
 Venice Beach of Ukraine, UKR 704
Frombork, POL 418

G

Gąsienicowa, Hala, POL 462
Gauja National Park, LAT 334
gay information
 Dohotourist, HUN 262
 essentials 30
 Ganimed, UKR 696
 Gay Information Center, CZE 180
 Gay Information Line, LIT 344
 Lambda Center, POL 396
 Latvian Association for Sexual Equality, LAT 322
Gdańsk, POL 412-417
Gdynia, POL 420-422
Genghis Khan 688
Gjiorkastër, ALB 68
glagolitsa script 106
Gniezno, POL 434
GO25 Card 15
Gogolya, Muzey, RUS 549
Golden Ring, RUS 557
Golden Sands, BUL 141
golf clubs, don't take them 13
Gorky Literary Museum, RUS 576
Gorky, Maxim 529
 Apartment, Moscow 548
Gorky, RUS, see Nizhny Novgorod
Grand Duchy of Lithuania 77, 349
Grand Dukes of Lithuania
 Kęstutis 349
 Jogaila 347
 Vytautas 340, 346, 349, 354
Great Northern War 225, 237, 318, 334
Great Plain, The, HUN 284
Gubałówka (1120m), POL 462
Győr, HUN 302
gypsies, Polish 448

H

Haapsalu, EST 240
Halstatt man 280
hangover cures
 breakfast for the hungover with spicy sauce 145
 hangover soup 661
Hauptbahnhof, GER 741
Havel, Václav 172, 187, 192
Haydn, Josef 308
health 19-25
 abortion 23
 advisories 24
 also see safety, ailments
 birth control 23
 first-aid kit 19
 HIV and AIDS 23
 immunizations 20
 on-the-road ailments 20-23
 women's 24
Hel, POL 422
Hell's Angels 122
Helsinki, FIN 747-753
Heltermaa, EST 245
Hero Cities
 Brest, BEL 85
 Leningrad, RUS 607
 Minsk, BEL 82
 Moscow, RUS 540
Hiiumaa, EST 245-247
hiking 45, 48-49
Hill of Crosses, LIT 356
Hill of Three Crosses, LIT 348
Histria, ROM 518
Hluboká, CZE 210
HOFA 521
Holy Mother of God! 586
Host Families Association (HOFA) 521
hosteling 46-47
 membership 47
 nat'l organizations 47
 reservations 47
Hostelling Int'l, HI 47
hotels 48
Hoxha, Enver 60, 67, 68, 69, 70, 72
Hrodna, BEL 83
Hruschka, Pleter 145, 667
Human 23
Humor, ROM 511
Hungarian National Museum, HUN 273
HUNGARY 249-314
 Aggtelek 280
 Balatonfüred 312
 Budapest 256-275
 Bugac 291
 Danube Bend 275-278
 Debrecen 284
 Eger 278
 Esztergom 277
 Fertőd 308
 Győr 302
 Jósvafő 280
 Kaposvár 296
 Kecskemét 289-291
 Keszthely 311
 Kőszeg 301
 Őriszentpeter 301
 Őrség, The 301
 Pannonholma Abbey 304
 Pécs 292-295
 Siófok 308
 Sopron 305
 Szeged 286-289
 Székesfehérvár 296
 Szentendre 276
 Szigetvár Castle 295
 Szilvásvárad 281
 Szombathely 298-301
 Tata 305
 Tihany 313
 Tokaj 282
 Visegrád 276
Hurricane Aldona 397
Hus, Jan 171, 188
Huzruf, UKR 714
Hvar, CRO 164

I

Iški Vintgar, SLN 676
Iași, ROM 506-509
IBUSZ, HUN 250
IBV Bed & Breakfast Systems 521
IDs
 GO25 Card 15
 ISIC 13
 ITIC 15
 student 13
 teacher 13
 youth 13
immunizations 20
infections, see ailments
insectivorous plants 302, 518
insurance

driving 15
homeowners' 25
ISIC 25
ITIC 25
medical 25
Travel Assistance
  International 19
Int'l Student Identity
  Card, ESS 13
Int'l Booking
  Network 47
Int'l Insurance
  Certificate 15
Int'l Reply Coupons
  52
Int'l Student Travel
  Confederation 4
Int'l Teacher Identity
  Card 15
Int'l Youth Discount
  Travel Card 15
Internet 4
  e-mail 53
Internet cafes
  Computer Club,
    ROM 495
  Cyberia Café, POL
    399
  Internet Café
    'Baza', POL 469
  Internet Café,
    Sarajevo, BOS 99
  U Louisa, POL 446
Irish pubs 196, 233,
  240, 326, 403, 416,
  420, 434, 446, 539,
  553, 614
Irkutsk, RUS 570
Iron Log House 304
ISIC 13, 25
ITIC card 15, 25
Ivan III the Great
  225, 318, 527, 530,
  540, 618, 621
Ivan IV the Terrible
  330, 332, 336, 527,
  530, 539, 540, 541,
  562, 577, 578, 618,
  621

J

Jaanipäev, EST 240
János Xanthus
  Memorial Museum,
  HUN 303
Järve, EST 244
Jelenia Góra, POL
  469
Jogānu rituāls, LAT
  319
John Paul II, Pope
  445
Jókai Mór Villa, HUN
  313

Jones, Indiana 70
Josefov, CZE 189
Jósvafő, HUN 280
Jūrmala, LAT 327

K

Kadarë, Ismail 56,
  61, 66, 68, 69
Kafka, Franz 174,
  188, 192, 194, 759
Käina, EST 245
Kaliningrad, RUS
  624-627
Kamyanets-Podilsky,
  UKR 722
Kant, Immanuel 624,
  626
Käo, EST 245
Kapelke, Wang 472
Kaposvár, HUN 296
Karaites 349
Kärdla, EST 245
Karel IV, King of
  Bohemia and Holy
  Roman Emperor
  170, 171, 173, 187,
  192, 194, 199, 206
Karkonoski Park
  Narodowy, POL 472
Karkonosze
  Mountains, POL 471
Karlovy Vary, CZE
  199
Karlštejn, CZE 199
Karlův most, CZE
  188
Karpacz, POL 471-
  472
Kasimir the Great,
  see Kazimierz
  Wielki
Käsmu, EST 234
Kasprowy Wierch,
  POL 462
Kassari, EST 248
Kaugatuma, EST 244
Kaunas, LIT 350-355
Kazan, RUS 577-579
Kazanluk, BUL 125
Kazimierz Dolny,
  POL 452
Kazimierz III Wielki
  389, 451, 452, 455,
  457
Kazimierz IV
  Jagiełłończyk 417,
  445
Kazimierz, Kraków's
  Jewish quarter, POL
  445
Kecskemét, HUN
  289-291
Ķemeri, LAT 327
Keszthely, HUN 311

Kežmarok, SLK 652
Khotyn, UKR 724
Khrushchev, Nikita
  528
Kiev, UKR 692-705
Kilometer Zero,
  ROM 485
King Stephen, see St.
  Stephen
Kirilla-Belozersky
  Monastery, RUS 565
Kizhi, RUS 623
Klaipėda, LIT 358-
  361
Koguva, EST 245
Konopiště, CZE 199
Koós-Hutás, Gergely
  313
Koprivshtitsa, BUL
  123
Kõrgessaare, EST 247
Körmend, HUN 301
Kościeliska, Dolina,
  POL 462
kosher 32
Košice, SLK 658-660
Kőszeg, HUN 301
Kotovski 383
Kraków, POL 439-
  446
Krasnoslobodsk, RUS
  583
kremlin, Moscow,
  RUS 539
Krujë, ALB 66
Kryžių Kalnas, LIT
  356
Krzyszu 446
Kuldīga, LAT 329
Kuressaare, EST 242
Kurshskaya Kosa,
  RUS 627
Kuršių Nerija, LIT
  361
Kurtenhof, LAT 327
Kutná Hora, CZE 198
Kuźnice, POL 462
kvas 76, 685

L

Lady with Ermine
  444
Lahemaa National
  Park, EST 233
lakes
  4000 of them 424
  Avrig, ROM 501
  Baikal, RUS 571
  Balaton, HUN 308
  Bled, SLN 675
  Bohinj, SLN 676
  Galvė, LIT 349
  Kovšy, LAT 333
  Ladoga, RUS 621

Ohrid, MAC 372
Onega, RUS 621
Łańcut, POL 457
Lastivishine Gnizdo,
  UKR 715
LATVIA 315-336
  Aglona 332
  Āraiši 336
  Cēsis 335
  Daugavpils 330-
    332
  Kuldīga 329
  Pilsrundāle 329
  Rēzenke 332
  Rīga 320-327
  Sigulda 334
  Ventspils 328
**laundromat, self-
  serve**
  Kraków, POL 440
  Rīga, LAT 322
  Prague, CZE 180
Lenin's Mausoleum,
  RUS 542
Leningrad, RUS 592
Lennon, John 189
Lermontov House-
  Museum, RUS 549
Lermontov, Mikhail
  588
lesbian travelers 30
  Also see gay
    information
Let's Go Picks 54
Let's Go Travel 35
Levoča, SLK 654
Levski, Vasil 106
  the bones of 114
Linnuse, EST 245
Lipizzaner horses
  281
Liptovský Mikuláš,
  SLK 643
LITHUANIA 337-
  362
  Druskininai 355
  Kaunas 350-355
  Klaipėda 358-361
  Kuršių Nerija 361
  Nida 361
  Palanga 356
  Paneriai 349
  Šiauliai 356
  Trakai 349
  Vilnius 342-349
Livadia, UKR 715
Ljubljana, SLN 670-
  674
long names
  Diorama-Museum
    of the Struggle for
    the Dnipro in the
    Region of
    Pereyaslav-

INDEX ■ 795

Khmelnitsky 706
museum of the
  First Congress of
  the Russian Social-
  Democratic Labor
  Party, BEL 82
October
  Revolution
  Tractor Plant no. 9
Tool-Makers'
  Association Hostel
  of Comrades 80
Scientific Research
  Institute of the
  Rose, Essential Oil-
  Yielding, and
  Medicinal Plants
  126
love 641
Lublin, POL 454
luggage 32
Lviv, UKR 726–733
Lysa Polana, POL 462

M
macabre
  1535 whipping
    post, POL 433
  bone church, CZE
    198
  Capucin church,
    CZE 215
  disattached arm
    188
  Dracula 501
  Kievo-Pecherska
    Lavra Monastery,
    UKR 703
  Macocha Abyss,
    CZE 217
  Špilberk Castle,
    CZE 216
MACEDONIA
  363–376
  Bitola 375
  Ohrid 372
  Skopje 368–372
  Struga 374
  Sveta Bogoroditsa
    375
Madara, BUL 136
Madonna of Pilsen,
  CZE 206
Majdanek, POL 455
Majori, LAT 327
make-out spots
  Aquarium, LIT 360
  Charles Bridge,
    CZE 188
  Jogānu rituāls 319
  Kissing Hill, EST
    237
  Lenin Stadium, RUS
    547

Malá Strana, CZE 190
Malbork, POL 417
Mamaev Kurgan, RUS
  582
Mändjala, EST 244
Mangalia, ROM 516
Maria Skłodowska-
  Curie 400
Mariacki, Kosciól,
  POL 444
Mariánské Lázně,
  CZE 201
Marie, Queen of
  Romania 502
marzipan 276
MasterCard 17
May Day parades,
  RUS 542
Medic Alert 20
medieval fairs
  Knights' Crossbow
    Tournament, POL
    470
  Spisský hrad, SLK
    655
Melnik, BUL 119
Mickiewicz, Adam
  347, 391, 444, 445
  monument to 400
Mihai Viteazul 478,
  485, 496
Mindaugas 340
Mindaugas's Day, LIT
  355
Minsk, BEL 78–82
minority travelers 32
miraculous icons
  Czarna Madonna,
    POL 450
  Weeping Madonna
    of Győr 303
Mlynická dolina, SLK
  652
Model Mugging 19,
  29
MOLDOVA 377–
  384
  Căpriana 383
  Chişinău
    (Kishinev) 380–
    383
  Orhei 384
  Vadul Lui Vodă 384
Moldoviţa, ROM 512
money 15–18
  AmEx 16
  ATMs 17
  by wire 18
  cash cards 17
  credit cards 17
  exchange 16
  from home 17
  transaction
    receipts 16

traveler's checks
  16
Mongols 77, 106,
  150, 253, 271, 526,
  688
Mõntu, EST 244
monument to brave
  football players 701
Moon, Temple of 537
Moravský Kras, CZE
  217
more __ than people
  cafes 70
  sheep 368
Morrison, Jim, not
  buried here 275
Moscow, RUS 530–
  554
  Arbat 546
  Assumption
    Cathedral 540
  Bolshoy Teatr 550
  Chekhov's House
    Museum 548
  Circus 550
  Dom Knigi 546
  Dostoyevsky
    Museum 548
  Gorky's
    Apartment 548
  GUM 539, 540
  Kazan Cathedral
    542
  kremlin 539
  Lenin's Mausoleum
    542
  Maly Teatr 550
  Manege 543
  Mayakovskovo
    Museum 547
  Metro 533, 543
  Moscow State
    University 547
  Moscow
    Synagogue 545
  Moskovskaya
    Galereya 549
  Novodevichy
    Monastir 544
  Novy Arbat 546
  Pushkin Museum
    of Fine Arts 542
  Red Square 539
  St. Basil's Cathedral
    539, 541
  St. Nicholas of the
    Weavers 546
  Tolstoy Estate 547
  Tretyakovskaya
    Galereya 542, 543
mountain peaks
  Cindrel (2444m),
    ROM 500
  Dumbier (2043m),

  SLK 644
  Furkotský štít
    (2428m), SLK 652
  Giewont (1090m),
    POL 462
  Lomnický štít
    (2634m), SLK 648
  Omul (2505m),
    ROM 505
  Rysy (2499m),
    POL, SLK 462,
    652
  Skrzyczne
    (1257m), POL 465
  Śnieżka (1602m),
    POL 472
  Štrbské Solisko
    (2301m), SLK 652
  Szyndzielnia
    (1026m), POL 465
  Tarnicza (1346m),
    POL 459
  Todorin, BUL 119
  Triglav (2864m),
    SLN 677
  Vf. Bbtrâna
    (1911m), ROM
    500
  Vihren (2914m),
    BUL 119
  Vitosha, BUL 116
Mozart, Wolfgang
  Amadeus 194
Mrągowo, POL 424
mud baths
  Kemeri, LAT 327
  Pärnu, EST 239,
    240
Muhu, EST 245
Mukhavets River, BEL
  84
Murfatlar, ROM 517
Murowaniec, POL
  462
museums of
  19th-Century Tartu
    Citizen, EST 237
  amber, LIT 357
  amber, RUS 626
  Arrested Thought,
    ROM 497
  baking, HUN 307
  beer-making, CZE
    207
  Czóbel, HUN 276
  devils, LIT 353
  fishing, POL 423
  goldsmithery, POL
    453
  Great Patriotic
    War, BEL 82
  Holocaust, LIT 347
  KGB, LIT 348
  Latvian

Occupation, LAT 324
Margit, HUN 276, 304
marzipan 276
musical instruments, POL 433
naive artists, HUN 291
Panorama, BUL 128
pharmacy, HUN 298, 307
posters, POL 402
Sanok history, POL 459
Schiele, CZE 211
Skansen, POL 459
time 560
Tryavna School of Icon Painting, BUL 132
underwater archaeology, CRO 165
Vas County Village, HUN 300

N
Nance-bo 145
Nasferatu 488
national tourist offices 1
Neamţ, ROM 513
Neptun, ROM 517
Nesebur, BUL 144
Nevsky, Aleksandr 557, 562, 563
Nicholas I, Tsar 716
Nicholas II, Tsar 527, 604, 609, 715
Nida as a state of mind 362
Nida, LIT 361
Nizhny Novgorod, RUS 572-577
Nízke Tatry, SLK 644
Noica, Constantin 500
Novgorod, RUS 618-621
Novocherkassk, RUS 587
Novosibirsk, RUS 568
nude mini-golf 159

O
Odesa, UKR 716-722
Ohessaare, EST 244
Ohrid, MAC 372
Oka River, RUS 572
old prisons

Dobó Istvan Castle, HUN 280
Miklušova väznica, SLK 660
Penzion Unitas, CZE 182
Shlisselburg, RUS 617
older travelers 30
oldest document bearing Hungarian words 304
Olimp, ROM 517
Oliwa, POL 416
Olomouc, CZE 218-220
Olsztyn castle, POL 451
OMRI 5
on-line info 4
Open Media Research Institute 5
Oradea, ROM 496
organ-based cuisine 69, 105, 114, 122, 348, 371
orgasmic pizza
Pizzeria Cosa Nostra, MAC 373
Pizzeria Kmotra, CZE 184
Vesuvio Pizza, UKR 699
Orhei, MOL 384
Orissaare, EST 245
Őriszentpeter, HUN 301
Őrség, The, HUN 301
Oświęcin, POL 447
Outhouse Hall of Shame, MOL 384

P
packing 32
Palanga, LIT 356
Palmse, EST 234
Păltiniş, ROM 500
Paneriai, LIT 349
Panga, EST 244
Pannonhalma Abbey, HUN 304
Pärnu, EST 238
Partitions of Poland 77, 340, 390
passports 8-11
Australia 11
Canada 9
Ireland 9
New Zealand 11
South Africa 11
U.K. 9
U.S. 9
Pavlovsk, RUS 616
Pear, Daniel 175

Pécs, HUN 292-295
Peredelkino, RUS 554
Pereyaslav-Khmelnitsky, UKR 705
Peter the Great 199, 225, 232, 318, 330, 332, 527, 528, 540, 551, 562, 564, 578, 588, 592, 601, 604, 608, 615, 621, 723
Peterhof, RUS 614
Petrograd, RUS 592
Petrozavodsk, RUS 621
Pięciu Stawów Polskich, Dolina, POL 462
Picasso, Pablo 194
Picks, Let's Go 54
Pilsrundāle, LAT 329
Piran, SLN 679
Pishev, Javor 119
plane
getting around by 39
getting there by 36-39
Pleven, BUL 127
Pliska, BUL 135
Plovdiv, BUL 120-123
Plzeň, CZE 204-208
Podlasie, POL 426
Pograbec, ALB 71
Poiana Braşov, ROM 503
Pöide, EST 245
poisoned umbrella tips 107
POLAND 385-472
Augustów 425
Białowieski Park Narodowy 429
Białystok 427-429
Bielsko-Biała 463-465
Biskupin 435
Częstochowa 448-450
Frombork 418
Gdańsk 412-417
Gdynia 420-422
Gniezno 434
Hel 422
Jelenia Góra 469
Karpacz 471-472
Kazimierz Dolny 452
Kraków 439-446
Łańcut 457
Lublin 454
Majdanek 455

Malbork 417
Mrągowo 424
Oświęcim 447
Poznań 430-434
Przełom Dunajca 463
Sandomierz 451
Sanok 458
Sopot 418-420
Święta Lipka 425
Świnoujście 409
Szczecin 406-409
Szczyrk 465
Tarnów 448
Toruń 436-439
Trail of Eagles' Nests 451
Tykocin 429
Warsaw (Warsawa) 392-405
Wieliczka 448
Woliński Park Narodowy 410
Wrocław 466-469
Zakopane 459-462
Zamość 456
Żelazowa Wola 405
Poprad, SLK 645-647
Popradské pleso, SLK 652
Poreč, CRO 157
postal services 50
Poste Restante 50
Postojna Caves, SLN 674
potato
Dan Quayle 663
fright 641
spud-eaters 667
Poznań, POL 430-434
Prague, CZE 173-197
Prahova valley, ROM 504
Pregolya River, RUS 626
Přemysl Dynasty 171
Prešov, SLK 660
Primorsko, BUL 145
Princip, Gavrilo 91, 99
Prostratic gland juice 368
Przełom Dunajca, POL 463
Pula, CRO 159
Pushkin 528, 616, 710, 714
    museum 714, 720
Pushkin Museum of Fine Arts, RUS 542

INDEX ■ 797

Pushkina, Literaturny Muzey, RUS 549
Puszcza Białowieska, POL 429
Putna, ROM 513

R

Rab, CRO 161
Rail Europe Inc. 35
rakija 90
rakiya 105
Rathaus Schöneberg, GER 744
rebel w/ or w/o cause
   Botev, Hristo 106
   Copernicus 418
   Dean, James 438
   Havel, Václav 172
   Hus, Jan 188
   magnio, pablo
   Palach, Jan 188
   Princip, Gavrilo 99
   Rakóczi II, Francis 660
   Rakovski, Georgi 106
   Skanderbeg 60
   Vaptsarov, Nikola 118
Red Bear Tours/ Russian Passport 520
Red Square, RUS 539
Rembrandt van Rijn 444
Remuh Cemetery, POL 446
reverse charge calls 52
Rēzenke, LAT 332
Rīga, LAT 320-327
Rila Monastery, BUL 117
ringtoss-for-champagne, LIT 357
rock stars
   ABBA 646
   Bach, J.S. 199
   Dead, Grateful 337
   Jackson, Michael 276, 487
   Lennon John 189
   Presley, Elvis 679
   Tsoi, Victor 546
   Zamfir live 495
   Zappa, Frank 337, 347
Rohuküla, EST 241, 245
ROMANIA 473-518
   Agapia 513
   Arbore 511
   Beliş Fântănele 492
   Black Sea Coast 514-517
   Bran 504
   Braşov 502
   Bucharest 480-488
   Bucovina Monasteries 511
   Buşteni 505
   Cluj-Napoca 489-492
   Constanţa 514
   Contineşti 517
   Cucuteni 509
   Curtea De Argeş 501
   Danube Delta 518
   Dragomirna 511
   Eforie Nord 517
   Eforie Sud 517
   Făgăraş Mountains 501
   Histria 518
   Humor 511
   Iaşi 506-509
   Magnalia 516
   Moldoviţa 512
   Neamţ 513
   Neptun 517
   Olimp 517
   Oradea 496
   Pălliniş 500
   Poiana Braşov 503
   Putna 513
   Săpânţa 497
   Saturn 516
   Scărişoara Ice Cave 492
   Secu 513
   Sibiu 498-500
   Sighetu-Marmaţiei 497
   Sighişoara 493
   Sinaia 504
   Snagov 488
   Suceava 509
   Suceviţa 512
   Timişoara 494-496
   Transylvania 489-498
   2 Mai 516
   Vama Veche 516
   Văratec 513
   Venus 516
   Voroneţ 511
rose oil 124
Rostov-na-Donu, RUS 583-586
Rovinj, CRO 158
Rubens, Peter Paul 190, 194
Rundāles Pils, LAT 329
Ruse, BUL 132-134
RUSSIA 519-628
   Irkutsk 570
   Kaliningrad 624-627
   Kazan 577-579
   Kirilla-Belozersky Monastery 565
   Kizhi 623
   Lake Baikal 571
   Moscow 530-554
   Nizhny Novgorod 572-577
   Novgorod 618-621
   Novocherkassk 587
   Novosibirsk 568
   Pavlovsk 616
   Peredelkino 554
   Peterhof 614
   Petrozavodsk 622
   Rostov-na-Donu 584-587
   Sergievsky Posad 554
   Shlisselburg 617
   Simbirsk 579
   Smolensk 555-557
   Sochi 589-592
   St. Petersburg 592-614
   Starocherkassk 587
   Suzdal 562
   Svetlogorsk 628
   Taganrog 588
   Tanais 588
   Trans-Siberian Railroad 565-572
   Tsarskoye Selo 615
   Vladimir 561
   Volgograd 580-584
   Vologda 563-565
   Yaroslavl 557-561
   Yekaterinburg 570
   Zelenogradsk 627
Russia House 520, 682
Russian Revolution of 1905 77, 225
Russian Revolution of 1917 225
Russian Youth Hostels 520
Russia-Rail Internet Travel Service 520

S

Saaremaa, EST 244
Sääretirp, EST 248
safety 18
   also see health
   Travel Assistance International 19
   wilderness 49
Sąjūdis movement 341
Sakharov Museum, RUS 576
Salaspils Memorial, LAT 327
Salme, EST 244
Sandomierz, POL 451
Sankt Peterburg, RUS 592
Sanok, POL 458
Săpânţa, ROM 497
Sarajevo, BOS 93-100
Sarandë, ALB 69
Sariš 658
Saturn, ROM 516
Saulkrasti, LAT 327
Scărişoara Ice Cave, ROM 492
Schiele, Egon 211
Schindler's List 446
Schwarzenbergs 210
Secu, ROM 513
senior citizens 30
Sergievsky Posad, RUS 554
shamans
   Olkhon island 572
Shevchenko, Taras 689, 690, 691, 700
   monument 720
   museum 701
Shipka, BUL 127
Shlisselburg, RUS 617
shoes 33
Shoumen, BUL 134
Šiauliai, LIT 356
Sibiu, ROM 498-500
Sienkiewicz, Henryk 391, 400
Sighetu-Marmaţiei, ROM 497
Sighişoara, ROM 493
Sigulda, LAT 334
Simbirsk, RUS 579
Simferopol, UKR 708-710
Sinaia, ROM 504
Siófok, HUN 308
Siske, HUN 313
Skanderbeg 59, 61, 66, 67
   Kastrioti, Gjergj 60
   roots of name 67
   sister of 67
Skopje, MAC 368-372
Skupi, MAC 366
sleepsacks 47
slijivova 90
Slovak Robin Hood

643
SLOVAKIA 629–664
  Banksá Bystrica 640
  Banská Štiavnica 642
  Bardejov 662
  Bratislava 635–640
  Devín Castle 640
  Kežmarok 652
  Košice 658–660
  Levoča 654
  Liptovský Mikuláy 643
  Nízke Tatry 644
  Poprad 645–647
  Prešov 660
  Slovenský Raj 656
  Spišské Podhradie 655
  Starý Smokovec 648
  Štrbské Pleso 649
  Tatranská Lomnica 647
  Žehra 655
SLOVENIA 665–680
  Bled 674
  Bovec 678
  Iški Vintgar 676
  Lake Bohinj 676
  Ljubljana 670–674
  Piran 679
  Postojna Caves 674
Slovenský Raj, SLK 656
Slowacki, Juliusz 445
Smolensk, RUS 555–557
Snagov, ROM 488
SocBloc architecture
  Brezhnev Flats, RUS 556
  Casa Poporului, ROM 486
  Cultural Center, Tirana, ALB 66
  House of Soviets, RUS 626
  Moscow swimming pool, RUS 546
  Prior, CZE 220
  SNP Bridge, SLK 639
  Socialist-Realist park, UKR 706
  Stalin's Palace, POL 401
  Viesnīca Latvija, LAT 331

war memorial, Minsk, BEL 82
Sochi, RUS 589–591
Sofia, BUL 108–116
Solidarity, POL 390, 391, 412, 416, 445, 455, 466
Sopot, POL 418–420
Sopron, HUN 305
Sörve Peninsula, EST 244
Soviet premiers
  Andropov, Yuri 528, 542
  Brezhnev, Leonid 528, 542
  Chernenko, Konstantin 528
  Gorbachev, Mikhail 528
  Khrushchev, Nikita 528
  Lenin, Vladimir 527
  Stalin, Joseph 527
Sozopol, BUL 145
Špilberk Castle, CZE 216
Spišské Podhradie, SLK 655
Split, CRO 162–164
St. Adalbert 193, 434
St. Basil's Cathedral, RUS 539, 541
St. Gellért 270
St. István, see St. Stephen
St. János of Nepomuk 297
St. Kinga 448
St. Ludmila 192
St. Petersburg, RUS 592–614
St. Stephen 271, 297
St. Stephen's Day 513
St. Vintír 193
St. Wenceslas 187
STA 25, 35
stand-by flights 38
  Airhitch 38
  Air-Tech, Ltd. 38
Starocherkasskk, RUS 586
Staroměstské náměstí, Prague, CZE 188
Starý Smokovec, SLK 648
Ștefan cel Mare 379, 383, 510
Ștefan cel Mare, tomb of 513
Stephen, King, see St. Stephen

stone age people 220
  6kč beers 174
  M. K. Čiurlionio Museum 353
  Pod lampou, CZE 208
  Scythians 688
  Taz Pub, CZE 196
strange sleeps
  Na Vlachovce, CZE 183
  Penzion U Výstaviště, CZE 209
  Penzion Unitas, CZE 182
Štrbské Pleso, SLK 649
Street Theater Festival, POl 470
Struga Poetry Evenings, MAC 374
Struga, MAC 374
student dormitories 48
study abroad 25
Štúr, L'udovít 632
Suceava, ROM 509
Sucevița, ROM 512
Sulina, ROM 518
Suzdal, RUS 562
Sveta Atanasie, MAC 375
Sveta Bogoroditsa, MAC 375
Svetlogorsk, RUS 628
Swedish Cookie 202, 239, 243, 555
Święta Lipka, POL 425
Świnoujście, POL 409
Szalafő, HUN 302
Szczecin, POL 406–409
Szczyrk, POL 465
Szeged, HUN 286–289
Székesfehérvár, HUN 296
Szentendre, HUN 276
Szépművészti múzeum, HUN 272
Szigetvár Castle, HUN 295
Szilvásvárad, HUN 281
Szombathely, HUN 298–301

T

Taganrog, RUS 588

Tallinn, EST 227–233
Tanais, RUS 587
Tarnów, POL 448
Tartu, EST 235–237
Tata, HUN 305
Tatran National Park, POL 462
Tatranská Lomnica, SLK 647
Tatras, High 462
teaching English 27
Tehumardi, EST 244
Telč, CZE 217
telephones 52
  calling cards 52
  codes 52
  collect calls 52
  reverse charge calls 52
Terezín, CZE 198
terrifying stuffed bear 648
Teutonic Knights 225, 243, 245, 318, 340, 389, 400, 417, 425, 438
The General of the Dead Army 56, 69
the world's
  best vodka 525
  cheapest place 687
  deepest lake 571
  largest bell 540
  largest floor mosaic 515
  longest series of catacombs 720
Thirty Years War 171, 190, 193, 215
Thomas Cook 17
Thracians 106, 115, 126, 136, 144, 372, 509
ticket consolidators 37
ticks 21
Tihany, HUN 313
time zones 52
Timișoara, ROM 494–496
Tirana, ALB 62–66
Tisza River, HUN 286
Tito, Josip Broz 92, 151, 367, 668
toilets from the Hungarian occupation 659
Tokaj, HUN 282
Tökes, Biserica, ROM 495
Tolstoy, Lev 529
  Estate 547
Tomáš Masaryk 171
Toomas 231

Tornimäe, EST 245
Toruń, POL 436-439
tourist offices 1
Trail of Eagles' Nests, POL 451
trains 39-43
 BIJ (Billets Internationales de Jeunesse) 43
 timetables 43
Trakai, LIT 349
Transitions Abroad 4
Trans-Siberian Railroad, RUS 565-572
Transylvania, ROM 489-498
travel
 advisories, U.S. Dept. of State 19
 getting around 39-45
 getting there 34-39
 literature 4
 organizations 1
travel agencies budget 35
Travel CUTS 36
traveler's checks 16
 American Express 16
 Citicorp 17
 MasterCard 17
 Thomas Cook 17
 Visa 17
Traveller's Guest House 520
Treaty of Brest-Litovsk 85
Tretyakovskaya Galereya, RUS 542
Trynavna, BUL 131
Tsarskoye Selo, RUS 615
Tulcea, ROM 518
Tykocin, POL 429

U

UKRAINE 681-736
 Alupka 715
 Bakhchisarai 710
 Chernivtsi 724-726
 Dnipropetrovsk 707
 Feodosia 711
 Huzruf 714
 Kamyanets-Podilsky 722
 Khotyn 724
 Kiev 692-705
 Lastivichine Gnizdo 715

Livadia 715
Lviv 726-733
Odesa 716-722
Pereyaslav-Khmelnitsky 705
Simferopol 708-710
Uzhhorod 735
Yalta 712-714
Zhovkva 733
Ulyanovsk, RUS 579
unique fish
 "trout on the Hungarian art" 641
 Crab of Kamchatka 360
 Exotic Fish, UKR 714
 koran 72
 Letnitsa trout 366
 omul 572
 salmon that adds brain cells 423
 sea lion kissing Helmut Kohl 360
 used as candles 571
 Velryba 184
USIT 36
Uzhhorod, UKR 735

V

Václav I 171
Václavské náměstí, CZE 187
Vadul Lui Vodă, MOL 384
valdude 124, 209, 448, 450, 495, 511, 514, 545
Valley of Roses, BUL 123-127
Valley of the Beautiful Women, HUN 279
Vama Veche, ROM 516
Văratec, ROM 513
Varna, BUL 136-141
Vazov, Ivan 108, 127
VDNKh, RUS 552
vegetarian hits
 Ajvega, SLK 659
 Alye Paruca, UKR 719
 Country Life, CZE 185
 Marquis de Salade, HUN 267
 Nove Miasto, POL 398
 stolovoyas, UKR 687
 travel guides 32

Vegetarian, CZE 200
Vegetarian, SLK 655
Vegetárium, HUN 267
Vegetka, CZE 219
Veliki Preslav, BUL 135
Veliko Turnovo, BUL 129-131
Ventspils, LAT 328
Venus, ROM 516
Vidzeme, LAT 318
Viitna, EST 234
Vilijampolė, LIT 354
Viljandi, EST 237
Vilnius, LIT 342-349
Visa 17
visas 11
 Albanian 56
 Belarusian 74
 Bulgarian 102
 Croatian 148
 Czech 167
 Estonian 221
 Hungarian 249
 Latvian 315
 Lithuanian 338
 Macedonian 364
 Moldovan 378
 Polish 386
 Romanian 474
 Russian 520
 Slovakian 629
 Slovenian 665
 Ukrainian 682
Visegrád, HUN 276
Viskoosa, see Kõrgessaare
Vladimir, RUS 561
Vladislav II 171
Volga River, RUS 572
Volga-Don Canal, RUS 580
Volgograd, RUS 580-584
Vologda, RUS 563-565
voltage 33
volunteering abroad 27
Volunteers For Peace 521
Voroneț, ROM 511
Vörös-tó, HUN 280

W

Wałęsa, Lech 390
Wallenstein, General Albert 190, 203
walls
 John Lennon, CZE 189

of Tears, BUL 115
Victor Tsoi, RUS 546
Warsaw (Warsawa), POL 392-405
Wasteels 43
Wawel, POL 445
Wenceslas I 171
Wenceslas IV 189
Wenceslas Sq., CZE 187
Western Union 18
Westerplatte, POL 416
what jello should have been 426
Wieliczka, POL 448
wiring money 18
Władysław Jagiełło, King 340, 459
Wodogrzmoty Mickiewicza, POL 462
Wojtyła, Karol 445
Woliński National Park, POL 410
women
 health 24
 travel 29
work abroad 27
World Wide Web 4
Wrocław, POL 466-469

Y

Yalta, UKR 712-714
Yaroslavl, RUS 557-561
Yekaterinburg, RUS 566

Z

Zagreb, CRO 152-157
Zakopane, POL 459-462
Zalalövö, HUN 302
Zamość, POL 456
Zawrat, POL 462
Žehra, SLK 655
Żelazowa Wola, POL 405
Zelenogradsk, RUS 627
Zhivkov, Todor 107, 131
Zhovkva, UKR 733
Zog, King Ahmet 60, 68
Zograf, Zahari 117, 123, 125, 129, 132

ALSO AVAILABLE FROM ST. MARTIN'S PRESS

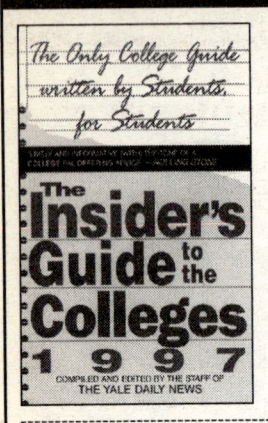

The Only College Guide written by Students, for Students

The Insider's Guide to the Colleges 1997

COMPILED AND EDITED BY THE STAFF OF THE YALE DAILY NEWS

FEATURES INCLUDE:

- Profiles of more than 300 schools in the U.S. and Canada, focusing on academics, housing and food, social life, student activities, and the campus and vicinity
- Insider tips on the application and admissions process
- Up-to-date statistics on tuition, acceptance rates, average test scores and more
- Plus: a College Finder, which picks the right schools in dozens of categories

---

Please send me ___ copies of **THE INSIDER'S GUIDE TO THE COLLEGES** (0-312-14627-2) at $14.99 each. I have enclosed $3.00 for postage and handling for the first book, and $1.00 for each additional copy.

Name _____

Address _____

City _____ State _____ Zip _____

Send check or money order with this coupon to:
St. Martin's Press • 175 Fifth Avenue • New York, NY 10010 • Att: Nancy/Promotion

---

"A crash course that could lead to a summer job— or a terrific party." —*Boston Globe*

THE OFFICIAL HARVARD STUDENT AGENCIES BARTENDING COURSE

With **THE OFFICIAL HARVARD STUDENT AGENCIES BARTENDING COURSE**, you could find yourself mixing drinks professionally and earning great money, or at least, giving fabulous cocktail parties!

- Over 300 recipes for the most asked-for drinks—including a section on popular nonalcoholic beverages
- Tips on finding top-paying bartending jobs
- How to remember hundreds of recipes
- How to serve drinks and handle customers with aplomb

Please send me ___ copies of **THE OFFICIAL HARVARD STUDENT AGENCIES BARTENDING COURSE** (0-312-11370-6) at $9.95 each. I have enclosed $3.00 for postage and handling for the first book, and $1.00 for each additional copy.

Name _____

Address _____

City _____ State _____ Zip _____

Send check or money order with this coupon to:
St. Martin's Press • 175 Fifth Avenue • New York, NY 10010 • Att: Nancy/Promotion

LET'S GO MAP GUIDE SERIES

This unique combination of pocket guide and street finder will be an essential tool for tourists, new residents, and natives alike.

Available Now:
- **New York City**
- **Washington, D.C.**
- **Boston**
- **San Francisco**
- **London**
- **Paris**

Coming in 1997:
- **Los Angeles** (March)
- **New Orleans** (March)
- **Rome** (March)
- **Chicago** (June)
- **Madrid** (June)
- **Berlin** (June)

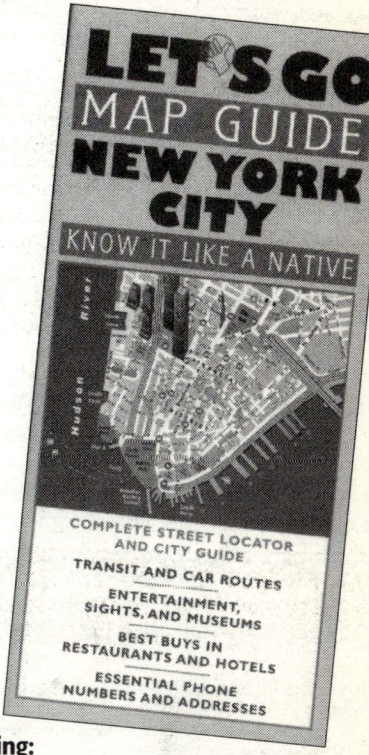

COMPLETE STREET LOCATOR AND CITY GUIDE

TRANSIT AND CAR ROUTES

ENTERTAINMENT, SIGHTS, AND MUSEUMS

BEST BUYS IN RESTAURANTS AND HOTELS

ESSENTIAL PHONE NUMBERS AND ADDRESSES

Featuring:
- Detailed maps of the downtown area, neighborhoods, city overview, and transportation routes.
- Complete descriptions, addresses, phone numbers, and prices for restaurants, entertainment, sights, museums, and hotels.

Please send me the following copies in THE LET'S GO MAP GUIDE SERIES at $7.95 each. I have enclosed $3.00 for postage and handling for the first book, and $1.00 for each additional copy.

Name_____

Address_____

_____

City_____ State____ Zip_____

No. of copies
- _____ New York (0-312-13764-8)
- _____ Boston (0-312-13765-6)
- _____ London (0-312-13766-4)
- _____ Paris (0-312-13767-2)
- _____ San Francisco (0-312-13768-0)
- _____ Washington, D.C. (0-312-13769-9)

Send check or money order with this coupon to:
St. Martin's Press • 175 Fifth Avenue • New York, NY 10010 • Att: Nancy/Promotion

★ Let's Go 1997 Reader Questionnaire ★

Please fill this out and return it to **Let's Go, St. Martin's Press,** 175 5th Ave. NY, NY 10010

Name: _____ **What book did you use?** _____
Address: _____
City: _____ **State:** _____ **Zip Code:** _____
How old are you? under 19   19-24   25-34   35-44   45-54   55 or over
Are you (circle one)   in high school   in college   in grad school
   employed   retired   between jobs
Have you used Let's Go before? yes   no
Would you use Let's Go again? yes   no
How did you first hear about Let's Go? friend   store clerk   CNN
   bookstore display   advertisement/promotion   review   other
Why did you choose Let's Go (circle up to two)? annual updating
   reputation   budget focus   price   writing style
   other: _____
Which other guides have you used, if any? Frommer's $-a-day   Fodor's
   Rough Guides   Lonely Planet   Berkeley   Rick Steves
   other: _____
Is Let's Go the best guidebook? yes   no
If not, which do you prefer? _____
**Which part of Let's Go do you feel needs most to be improved, if any
   (circle up to two)?** packaging/cover   practical information
   accommodations   food   cultural introduction   sights
   practical introduction ("Essentials")   directions   entertainment
   gay/lesbian information   maps   other: _____
How would you like to see these things improved?
_____
_____

How long was your trip?   one week   two weeks   three weeks
   one month   two months or more
Have you traveled extensively before? yes   no
Do you buy a separate map when you visit a foreign city? yes   no
Have you seen the Let's Go Map Guides? yes   no
Have you used a Let's Go Map Guide? yes   no
If you have, would you recommend them to others? yes   no
Did you use the internet to plan your trip? yes   no
Would you buy a Let's Go phrasebook   adventure/trekking guide
   gay/lesbian guide
**Which of the following destinations do you hope to visit in the next three
   to five years (circle one)?** Australia   China   South America   Russia
   other: _____
Where did you buy your guidebook?   internet   chain bookstore
   independent bookstore   college bookstore   travel store
   other: _____

Московский Метро

Московский Метро

Планерная
- Сходненская
- Тушинская
- Щукинская
- Октябрьское Поле
- Полежаевская
- Беговая
- Улица 1905 года
- Белорусская
- Баррикадная
- Краснопресненская
- Маяковская
- Пушкинская
- Чеховская
- Тверская
- Смоленская
- Арбатская
- Охотный Ряд
- Театральная
- Площадь Революции
- Боровицкая
- Арбатская
- Кропоткинская
- Парк Культуры
- Фрунзенская
- Спортивная
- Ленинские Горы
- Университет
- Проспект Вернадского
- **Юго-Западная**

Речной Вокзал
- Водный Стадион
- Войковская
- Сокол
- Аэропорт
- Динамо

Алтуфьевская
- Бибирево
- Отрадное
- Владыкино
- Петровско-Разумовская
- Тимирязевская
- Дмитровская
- Савеловская
- Менделеевская
- Новослободская
- Цветной Бульвар
- Тургеневская
- Чистые Пруды
- Лубянка
- Кузнецкий Мост
- Третьяковская
- Новокузнецкая
- Полянка
- Октябрьская
- Добрынинская
- Серпуховская
- Тульская
- Нагатинская
- Нагорная
- Нахимовский Проспект
- Каховская
- Севастопольская
- Чертановская
- Южная
- **Пражская**

Медведково
- Бабушкинская
- Свиблово
- Ботанический Сад
- ВДНХ
- Алексеевская
- Рижская
- Проспект Мира
- Сухаревская
- Комсомольская
- Красные Ворота
- Китай-Город
- Павелецкая
- Пролетарская
- Автозаводская
- Коломенская
- Каширская
- Варшавская
- Кантемировская
- Царицыно
- Орехово
- Домодедовская
- **Красногвардейская**

Улица Подбельского
- Черкизовская
- Преображенская Площадь
- Сокольники
- Красносельская
- **Щелковская**
- Первомайская
- Измайловская
- Измайловский Парк
- Семеновская
- Электрозаводская
- Бауманская
- Курская
- Чкаловская
- Марксистская
- Таганская
- Крестьянская Застава
- Волгоградский Проспект
- Текстильщики
- Кузьминки
- Рязанский Проспект
- **Выхино**

Крылатское
- Молодежная
- Кунцевская
- Пионерская
- Филевский Парк
- Багратионовская
- Фили
- Кутузовская
- Студенческая
- **Киевская**
- Смоленская
- Александровский Сад
- Библиотека имени Ленина

Новогиреево
- Перово
- Шоссе Энтузиастов
- Авиамоторная
- Площадь Ильича
- Серп и Молот

Дубровка
Печатники
Волжская
Люблино

Битцевский Парк

LEGEND
- ① Сокольническая
- ② Замоскворецкая
- ③ Арбатско-Покровская
- ③ Филевская
- ④ Кольцевая
- ⑤ Калужско-Рижская
- ⑥ Таганско-Краснопресненская
- ⑦ Калининская
- ⑧ Серпуховско-Тимирязевская
- ⑨ Люблинская
- Станции
- Станции Пересадок

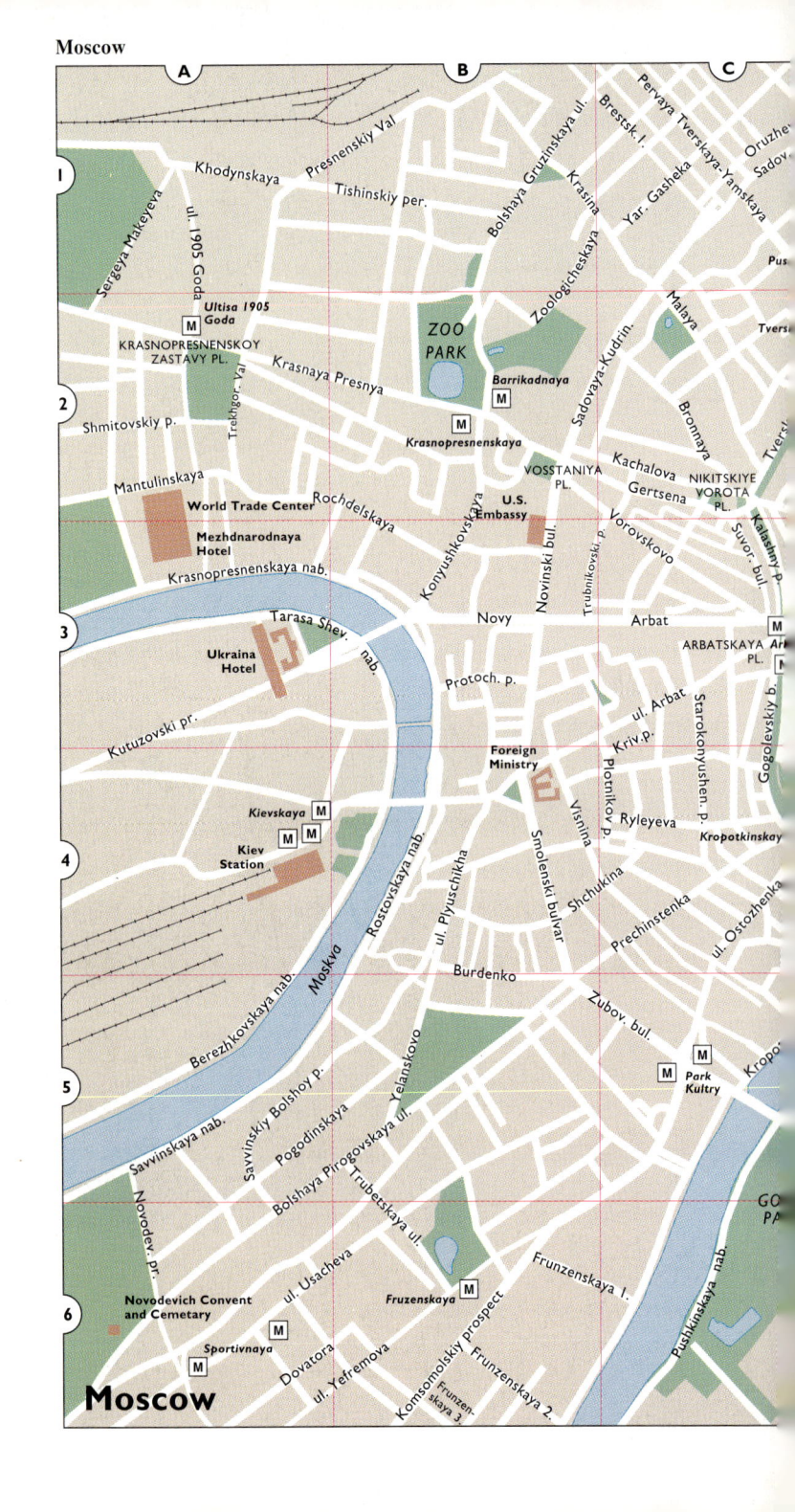

Moscow

A, **B**, **C** / 1–6

- Khodynskaya
- Presnenskiy Val
- Tishinskiy per.
- Bolshaya Gruzinskaya ul.
- Krasina
- Brestsk. l.
- Pervaya Tverskaya-Yamskaya
- Oruzhe Sadov
- Sergeya Makeyeva
- ul. 1905 Goda
- Ultisa 1905 Goda
- M (metro)
- KRASNOPRESNENSKOY ZASTAVY PL.
- Krasnaya Presnya
- Zoologicheskaya
- ZOO PARK
- Yar. Gasheka
- Malaya
- Pus
- Tvers
- Shmitovskiy p.
- Trekhgor. Val
- Barrikadnaya M
- Sadovaya-Kudrin.
- Bromnaya
- Krasnopresnenskaya M
- Kachalova
- NIKITSKIYE VOROTA PL.
- Tver
- Mantulinskaya
- Rochdelskaya
- VOSSTANIYA PL.
- Gertsena
- World Trade Center
- Konyushkovskaya
- U.S. Embassy
- Novinski bul.
- Vorovskovo
- Suvor. bul.
- Kalashny p.
- Mezhdnarodnaya Hotel
- Krasnopresnenskaya nab.
- Trubnikovski p.
- Tarasa Shev. nab.
- Novy Arbat
- ARBATSKAYA PL. M
- Ar
- Ukraina Hotel
- Protoch. p.
- ul. Arbat
- Starokonyushen. p.
- Gogolevskiy b.
- Kutuzovski pr.
- Foreign Ministry
- Kriv. p.
- Plotnikov p.
- Ryleyeva
- Kropotkinskay
- Kievskaya M
- Visnina
- M Kiev Station M
- Rostovskaya nab.
- Smolenski bulvar
- Shchukina
- Prechistenka
- ul. Ostozhenka
- ul. Plyuschikha
- Moskva
- Burdenko
- Berezhkovskaya nab.
- Zubov. bul.
- M Park Kultry M
- Kropo
- Savvinskaya nab.
- Savvinskiy Bolshoy p.
- Pogodinskaya
- Yelanskovo
- GO PA
- Novodev. pr.
- Bolshaya Pirogovskaya ul.
- Trubetskaya ul.
- Frunzenskaya l.
- Pushkinskaya nab.
- Novodevich Convent and Cemetary
- ul. Usacheva
- Fruzenskaya M
- Sportivnaya M
- Dovatora
- ul. Yefremova
- Komsomolskiy prospect
- Frunzenskaya 2
- Frunzenskaya 3.

Moscow

Moscow

Moscow Metro

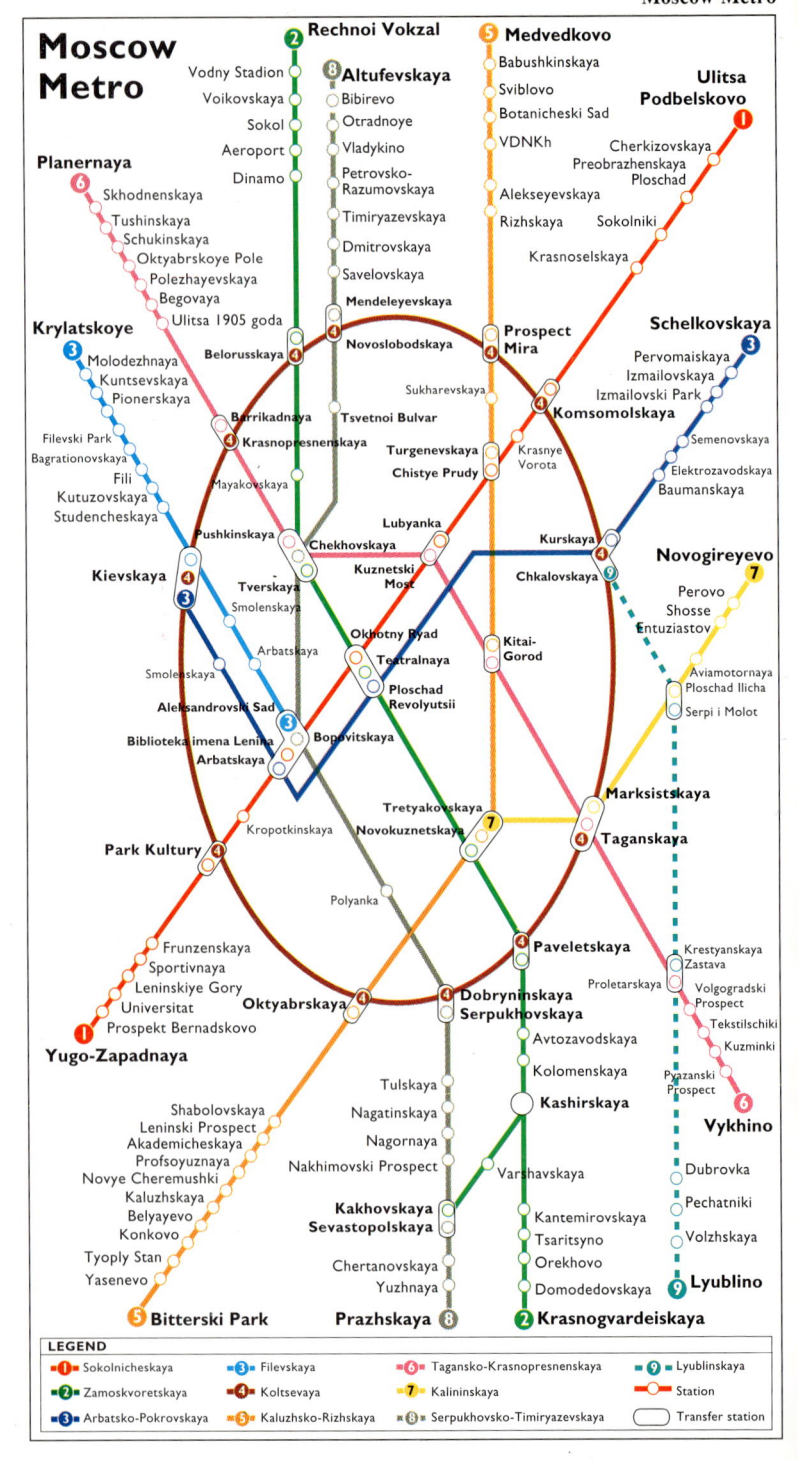